Honor, Humiliation, and Terror

Honor, Humiliation, and Terror

An Explosive Mix –
And How We Can Defuse It with Dignity

Evelin Lindner
MD, Psychologist, Dr. med., Dr. psychol.
2017

Other books by Evelin Lindner

Making Enemies: Humiliation and International Conflict

Foreword by Morton Deutsch
Westport, CT: Praeger Security International, Greenwood, 2006
This is the first book on dignity and humiliation and how we may envision a more dignified world, and it has been characterized as a path-breaking book and been honored as "Outstanding Academic Title" by the journal *Choice* for 2007 in the U.S.A.
More on www.humiliationstudies.org/whoweare/evelin/book/01.php

Emotion and Conflict: How Human Rights Can Dignify Emotion and Help Us Wage Good Conflict

Foreword by Morton Deutsch
Westport, CT: Praeger, 2009
More on www.humiliationstudies.org/whoweare/evelin/book/02.php

Gender, Humiliation, and Global Security: Dignifying Relationships from Love, Sex, and Parenthood to World Affairs

Foreword by Archbishop Desmond Tutu
Afterword by Linda Hartling in honor of Jean Baker Miller and Don Klein
Santa Barbara, CA: Praeger, ABC-CLIO, 2010
Review by social psychologist and Kurt Lewin expert David Bargal
"Highly recommended" by *Choice*
More on www.humiliationstudies.org/whoweare/evelin/book/03.php

A Dignity Economy: Creating an Economy that Serves Human Dignity and Preserves Our Planet.

Foreword by Linda Hartling, director of Human Dignity and Humiliation Studies, and Ulrich Spalthoff, Director of Dignity Press
Lake Oswego, OR: World Dignity University Press, 2012
More on www.dignitypress.org/wdu-press-books/dignity-economy and www.humiliationstudies.org/whoweare/evelin/book/04.php

For more chapters and papers by Evelin Lindner in full text on
www.humiliationstudies.org/whoweare/evelin02.php

Published by World Dignity University Press, an imprint of
Dignity Press
16 Northview Court
Lake Oswego, OR 97035
USA
www.dignitypress.org

Cover photo: We thank Jennifer Govan from Gottesman Libraries at Teachers College, Columbia University, New York City, for finding the image *Fire* by Awesomoman (own work) [Public domain], via Wikimedia Commons, https://commons.wikimedia.org/wiki/File%3AFire.JPG.
Back cover photo: © Stefan Buckmakowski, Hamelin, Germany, 2017 (www.blesius.de).

This book received financial support from the Norwegian Non-Fiction Literature Fund.

Printed on paper from environmentally managed forestry. See www.lightningsource.com/chainofcustody for certifications.

2nd revised edition
Print ISBN: 978-1-937570-97-2
eISBN: Apple 978-1-937570-98-9 and Kindle 978-1-937570-99-6

REVIEWS

See more on www.humiliationstudies.org/whoweare/evelin/book/05.php

At last, a book that dares to delve into all forms of terror that hold humanity hostage, including toxic corporate conduct, escalating violence, and ecocide practices and policies. Evelin Lindner offers us a globally informed, panoramic analysis of the risks humankind is facing. Her call for universal dignity will affirm, strengthen, and energize efforts that could save the world.

– Linda Hartling, Director, Human Dignity and Humiliation Studies and World Dignity University initiative.

Evelin Lindner is one of the most important present-day actors for peace, international solidarity and conflict resolution, human rights and democracy building, and in this book she addresses the most burning issues of our time – terrorism and the quest for a dignified world. In this book she further develops her theories on humiliation and thus deepens the understanding of the many unrestrained conflicts that threaten the world today.

– Inga Bostad, Professor of Philosophy, Director, Norwegian Centre for Human Rights, University of Oslo, Norway.

The feeling of humiliation is among the strongest of all human emotions. Evelin Lindner brilliantly explains how it contributes to terror and wars.

– Erik Solheim, Head, United Nations Environment Programme (UNEP), Nairobi, Kenya.

Evelin Lindner's new book is a different, and most welcome, exploration of the origins of terror. It convincingly argues that most current efforts to prevent terror are futile, and that what is at stake is a fundamental overhaul of global governance and resource distribution. Lindner's personal inquiry into the role of dignity and humiliation takes another giant step with this book, which is a must read that will force many of us to reexamine our own basic schemes of understanding.

– Kristian Berg Harpviken, Director, Peace Research Institute Oslo (PRIO), Norway.

In a time of increasing nationalism and populism, Evelin Lindner's global call for dignity and her fight against humiliation in all its forms are not only refreshing but deeply needed. The reader will find herself challenged and awakened by Lindner's personal journey and story. Indeed, Lindner forces us to ask what each and every one of us can do to create a more dignified, peaceful, and unified world – and one that is better governed, not just locally, but globally. Combining personal engagement with insight, experience, and a willingness to ask uncomfortable questions, Evelin Lindner confronts many of the challenges of our times head-on.

– Henrik Syse, Philosopher and Author, Peace Research Institute Oslo (PRIO), and Bjørknes University College, Norway, and Member of the Norwegian Nobel Committee.

Our sick and sorry world has too long been trapped in world views and modes of thinking that see hierarchy and domination, and separation of group from group as the necessary conditions of social order. Human beings accordingly live within a framework of values which denigrates those without the power to dominate and ridicules those who seek to transcend dominance in a quest for universal human dignity. Evelin Linder has not only instructed us in the dangers to the future of humanity inherent in this world view and these modes of thinking, she has given us the means to spring the trap in her explorations of the cycles of humiliation that comprise the trap and the lever to the spring that is the realization of human dignity. Now she offers us the possibility of liberation from the recent, most bitter fruit of systemic humiliation as inflicted by those who hold the power of dominance and those who aspire to seize that power, terrorism. Clearly, all that has been done by violence and war in the name of eradication of terror, has brought about new cycles of humiliation and escalation of violent retribution. In an exercise of informed and courageous imagination, Linder provides insights into paths of reconciliation and the healing of the wounds of separation, leading toward human unity in a global order in which human dignity is the norm. She provides a source of hope that can enable us to continue the quest for peace, and inspire us to learn the ways to achieve it.

– Betty A. Reardon, Founding Director Emeritus, International Institute on Peace Education

Lindner's book represents a clarion call to the global community to recognize the reality and power of our connectedness. Grounded in the wisdom of her lived experiences and informed by science, she illustrates how our greatest hope in the face of global terror and violence lies in our ability to recognize the ways we are all inextricably in relationship with one another. Lindner's book could not be more timely. In the face of the growing specter of terrorism worldwide, she calls upon the global community to recognize the power of context, and the way these threats are rooted in fundamental human needs we hold the power to honor and transform.

– Peter T. Coleman, Director, Morton Deutsch International Center for Cooperation and Conflict Resolution (MD-ICCCR), Professor of Psychology and Education, Social-Psychology Program, Department of Organization and Leadership, Teachers College, Columbia University, New York City.

Complex societal-systems are particularly vulnerable to disaffection, disruption, and disintegration; dignity and respect are the glue that binds and sustains our ever more complex and expanding relationships. By examining the connections between the emotional impact of humiliation and the behavioral expression of terror, Evelin Lindner explores the essence of the tension between community and exclusivity and how we learn to live together in order to avoid dying alone. Terror always has two faces and each is equally terrifying to the other; this is the source of its power. Terror is born in ignorance and thrives in prejudice and will only be defeated when we take our stance on common ground in mutual admiration and respect.

– Monty G. Marshall, Director, Center for Systemic Peace, Virginia, U.S.A.

This book calls for new forms of globalization informed by a new conception of global dignity that would transform both private and public sector action, individual and community responses and many global disciplines, be they humanitarian, development, environmental or conflict-related. The world needs this ingathering to unite the global human family toward one-world consciousness more than ever before.

– Gay Rosenblum-Kumar, former Head of the United Nations Interagency Framework Team for Preventive Action, and peacebuilding consultant

Lindner illustrates what strengthens families and ends war: Everyone has a story that needs, even cries out, to be listened to. Unheard and disregarded, very good, loving women, men, and youth can become hopeless, desperate, even violent, even terrorists. This is preventable and curable if we choose to become great listeners, especially to adversaries and those who have been invisible to us. Surprisingly to some and paradoxically, the first step to life beyond war is not to harm or humiliate, but to dignify your enemy.

– Libby and Len Traubman, Co-founders, Jewish-Palestinian Living Room Dialogue, California, U.S.A.

Dedicated to
all the victims of terror
–
past, present, and future.

Contents

Foreword by Linda Hartling

Are you prepared? Are you ready for the intellectual ride of your life? If you have this book in your hand you are well on your way to a global voyage of groundbreaking conceptualizations, a literary compass to a new world. Evelin Lindner is a modern day Magellan of thought, a Galileo of contemporary social science, a Michelangelo of human relations, and a Mandela of social transformation. This book is a realization of her lifelong expedition cultivating unbounded knowledge informed by global scholarship and direct connection to the lived experience of peoples of the world.

If you are ready to join in this journey, be prepared to think big. Lindner challenges us to look beyond the limits of conventional academic-institutional-corporate-nationalistic borders. This book is not written for those who restrict their studies to the silos of political think tanks or academic ivory towers. Rather, this is a book of deep transdisciplinary insight inspired by a visionary global community: world-renown philosophers, such as Arne Næss; conflict resolution scholars, such as Morton Deutsch; trailblazing pioneers in the study of humiliation, such as Donald Klein; revolutionary relational theorists in psychology, such as Jean Baker Miller; sociologists and economists of equality, such as S. Mike Miller; indigenous leaders and oral historians, such as Carmen Hetaraka; artists and poets, such as William Stafford and Francisco Gomes de Matos; and Nobel Peace Prize laureates, such as Berta von Suttner. Further, this book reflects Lindner's constant gardening of wisdom from countless quiet contributors who share their stories of struggle and resilience in the face of daily indignities and devastating disasters. Evelin Lindner organizes her whole life as a citizen of the world to bring us this globally informed treatise, a panoramic understanding of the risks humankind is facing in today's world.

At first glance, one might presume that it is a text about terrorism. Without question, Lindner offers indispensable insights to dismantle cycles of humiliation that can lead to terrorist acts. Yet this book is about something much bigger. It dares to delve into *all forms of terror* that hold humanity hostage to poisonous social practices, toxic corporate conduct, paralyzing political conflict, devastating aggression, and ecocidal practices and policies. Lindner doesn't rely on the timeworn tactics of polarizing people or vilifying individuals to draw attention to the urgency of her message. Instead, she empowers readers to understand the complex systemic conditions that have blinded us from creating new possibilities and solutions. She describes a promising future of mutually beneficial engagement and social arrangements that would help us save ourselves while saving others and the world.

Evelin Lindner and I began our lifelong conversation in 1999, after we both broke ground studying the impact of humiliation, a profoundly degrading experience that has largely been neglected in the literature until recently. Both of us, like others who join with us, have traveled to hell and back to learn the necessary lessons that compel our efforts to bring the benefits of equal dignity into every aspect of our life work. Both of us are firm in our belief in the basic goodness of human beings, a goodness that can get lost in the relentless fog of industrialized and institutionalized forms of modern-day humiliation and destructive conflict.

More than anything else, our research has taught us that there is no time to lose. We never stop talking about the urgency of preventing and repairing the pain of humiliation, what Lindner calls "a nuclear bomb of emotions." We never ought to step stop talking about dignity as the path to local and global change for the better. We never should stop talking how all of us can work together to create the dignifying conditions that provide for the growth and participation of all people while we protect and replenish our planet.

Evelin Lindner's book serves as a universal affirmation for those who courageously strive to build bridges of equal dignity in their own lives and around the world. In addition, this book is a universal invitation to all who wish to do their part to replace cycles of humiliation and terror with dignifying dialogue. The world needs you now. Are you prepared?

Linda M. Hartling, Ph.D.
Director
Human Dignity and Humiliation Studies
November 3, 2016, Portland, Oregon, U.S.A.

Preface

This book has been written for all readers interested in reflecting on humanity's future. It speaks to scholars and students in the field of public policy planning. It also speaks to those who wish to reduce terror around the world, in whatever form it might appear. And it speaks to those who use terror tactics or support them, including those who feel justified in fighting terror with terror.

The book aims at radicalizing its readers. Radicalizing toward dignity rather than terror, radicalizing in the sense of waking up to the *conscientization* that Paulo Freire called for, which means turning conscience into action for dignity.

The book is like a painting, a painting of the world as it stands in the twenty-first century. It is painted by an author who has lived globally, on all continents, for the past forty years. The book therefore uses a very personal brush, in the hope that its readers will be inspired to do the same.

The book embeds the topic of terrorism into practices of domination in general, domination over people and nature, and how they give rise to terror, both directly and as side-effects. The book argues that the terror that arises from competition for domination needs more attention from us, and that we overlook it at our own peril when we allow here-and-now incidents of terrorism to consume all our energy. If we focus on here-and-now terrorist acts too much, the big picture escapes us.[1] The author speaks from the perspective of a concerned global citizen who fears that the beginning of the twenty-first century will once be described as a dark age, dark not because of terrorism, but because of unsustainable social and ecological arrangements that first seed terror and then perilously both under-estimate and over-instrumentalize terrorism.[2]

This is the line of reasoning in this book in a nutshell: Violence, hatred, and terror are deeply intertwined with honor, heroism, glory, and love. The past five percent of modern human history on planet Earth, roughly the past ten millennia, were characterized by competition for domination, where "might" became "right." In this context, a culture of honor spawned, in which destruction merged with love: "It is my duty, if I love my people, to heroically destroy our enemies and secure all resources for us. It is my duty to make sure that we will never be humiliated." The guiding motto was *If you want peace, prepare for war.*[3]

We, as humankind, have constructed an entire world-system on top of this merger. The consequence, today, is the ubiquitous destruction of our social and ecological relationships. Terror and terrorism are intricate parts of the legacy of the past millennia, and only if we overcome this legacy, together, and in mutual respect, can we address the social and environmental crises of our time and the terror they bring us.

The script of honor and heroism that characterized the past millennia has created a world of victors and vanquished, of dominators triumphing over what they dominate, be it other people or nature. Global interconnectedness, however, is a radical game changer. In the new context, the old script no longer leads to victory. It now leads to the suicidal shredding of our entire sociosphere and ecosphere.[4] Global interconnectedness forces other mottos to the forefront, such as the African adage, *It takes a village to raise a child.* Or Mahatma Gandhi's *There is no path to peace. Peace is the path.*

Sadly, however, as for now, the global village fails its task. This is the most significant source of terror the world experiences. It is a dangerous illusion to believe that finite natural resources can be plundered without side effects. And it is an equally dangerous illusion to believe that global social challenges can be responded to with violence and war as if the world were still compartmentalized into unconnected sovereign regions. On a sinking ship, when all hands are needed on deck to change the course, in-fighting is a deadly strategy.

This line of reasoning is supported by the authors particular personal life path, which is neither Western nor non-Western. More than "traveling the world," she has lived globally, with all continents as her home, and she has done so for the past forty years. This global experience forces her eyes wide open to the fact that we, as humankind, have dug ourselves into a multitude of perilous crises, both despite and because of what we call progress.

Yet, the author also sees an immense window of opportunity waiting to be used. Unfortunately, so far, instead of recognizing the depth of the crises at hand and grasping the historic opportunity to exit, most of us choose to stay myopic. We tend to exaggerate negligible dangers, overlook gigantic dangers, and scorn the exit opportunity that history offers us entirely undeservedly. Meanwhile, terror contributes to, and is instrumentalized for masking or even closing this window of opportunity.

Domination and humiliation are intimately interlinked, and we live at a point in history where dynamics of humiliation are fueled ever more forcefully, not least through the breaking of the promise of equal dignity as it is enshrined in human rights ideals, and this in a shrinking world. This, in turn, engenders an atmosphere of terror, and inspires acts of terror that foreclose our most important task: global cooperation to save our ship from sinking, cooperation for a large-scale *dignity transition* toward a *decent* global village for all people and our planet.[5]

Apart from its main message, this book has several intermediate objectives and features. As we live in a historical situation where *sociocide*[6] and *ecocide*[7] combine, in the worst case, the world will turn into many small-scale off-limits zones of war and terror. As ecological and social climate degradation feed each other, this will spawn ever more terror if not halted.[8] It has been predicted that land degradation alone will force 135 million people to migrate in the next thirty years.[9] Climate change will lead to widespread social disconnection and terror.[10] We will find ourselves in a situation, where "the conflict entrepreneurs, the gang leaders, the under bosses," will recruit foot soldiers "from among those young men who see little other (or, at least, no better) way of avoiding being losers," warns, for example, Dan Smith, director of the Stockholm International Peace Research Institute.[11] In other words, if business-as-usual continues, humiliation entrepreneurs will find ever more fertile ground to spread terror.

To say it differently, the number of disaffected "children" in the global village will rise, and if they are manipulated by humiliation entrepreneurs, they will further weaken this village. They will make another African saying come true: "If a child is not initiated into the village, it will burn it down just to feel its warmth."[12] General Mark Milley, the United States Army chief of staff, predicted in 2016, that future wars will be a truly terrorizing mix: they could have "conventional forces, Special Forces, guerrillas, terrorists, criminals all mixed together in a highly complex terrain environment, with potentially high densities of civilians."[13] Most of the world's population will be caught in between.

In 2006, I wrote a book titled *Making Enemies: Humiliation and International Conflict*.[14] There I predicted: "It is likely that we may, in the future, experience – not *clashes of civilizations* – but *clashes of humiliation*."[15] The cover of that book showed the infamous Abu Ghraib prison in Iraq. My prediction was that more humiliation will create more enemies. By now, this prediction seems to fulfill itself in the worst imaginable ways. An American soldier who fought in Iraq in 2003 laments in 2015: "I helped create ISIS."[16] Prisoners who survived places like Abu Ghraib now lead Da'esh (or IS, ISIL, or ISIS[17]). Guantanamo-style orange prisoner's overalls are used by Da'esh fighters for those they behead.[18]

Allow me now to explain the adventurous path of this book. When I began working on it in 2010, only a few experts were interested in terrorism. The attention that had been given to this topic after the attacks on the Twin Towers in New York on September 11, 2001, had abated by 2010. The publisher who initially wanted me to write this book, ultimately found that not enough copies would sell. I was relieved, since I was working on another book, one addressing the interplay of humiliation and our economic systems.[19] Yet, then the Norwegian author's association encouraged me to write this book,[20] and first I thought of preparing a "quick book," a collection of what I had written before.[21] As it turned out, I could not bring myself to do so. The situation was simply changing too much after 2010.

First, in 2011, the terror attacks by Anders Behring Breivik in Norway brought new attention to the topic of terrorism.[22] Then, names such as Al-Qaeda and Da'esh began to dominate the news on a global scale.[23] By now, ever more aspects of terror have emerged, kinds of terror that I wrote about in my 2012 book on economic systems. In that book I warned that there will be no dignified future if we leave our contemporary economic structures in place, as they give primacy to the profit motive in ways that no regulations can stop it from ravaging our world. The ideals of human dignity that were adopted by the world community in 1948 after two horrific world wars represented a call for a *globalization of care*. Yet, this call was betrayed, and what we got was a *globalization of exploitation*.[24] By now, we see a *great regression*, with the ghosts from a formerly divided belligerent world returning from a world where people used to yearn for glorious retribution for humiliation. In today's interconnected world, such yearnings can easily end in all-out war.[25]

A smoldering atmosphere of hatred and authoritarian repression with fascist features now polarizes and terrorizes societies around the globe. Anders Behring Breivik's ideological anchorings shine through the rhetoric of newly elected leaders in places never expected before – from the Philippines to Hungary to the United States. Populists feed on frustration, the frustration among the victims of the globalization of exploitation. Populists stoke hatred, and then they channel it toward scapegoats. Scapegoats are those victims who are even less fortunate, those who only have their feet to vote, who only have the choice between fleeing or perishing on the spot: the poor scapegoat the poorest. Populists use terrorist acts as springboard to power, increasing the likelihood that terror regimes – state and/or corporate terror – will rise and be strengthened. Increasingly, we need to ask: Where does liberation from humiliation end and terrorism start? Where does national security end and state terror start? Where does business secrecy end and corporate terror start?

The emergence of a global trend toward authoritarian polarization has motivated me to change the initial book project's title from *Humiliation and Terrorism* to *Humiliation and Terror*. It became clear to me that I could only write a book on Terror with a capital "T," as terrorist acts are only indications of greater Terror. This is also the reason for why I am relieved that Dignity Press is a nonprofit publisher and that this book does not have to "make a profit." A juicy book on terrorism would most likely sell much better than this deeply reflective and complex book on Terror.

This book is a stand-alone book, while it is also part of the larger book project titled *Humiliation and Terror*. The larger book project has three main volumes that mirror the chronology of human history. This book is the first volume and describes the normality of terror in the past and how terror was an accepted path to honor, definitorial for most societies, how it permeated every detail of psychological and social life, and how this is still relevant today.[26] The second volume is planned to show how honor and dignity are irreconcilable at their core, and how this represents a dilemma that further complicates the situation today: in the context of dignity, terror transmutes from an acceptable path to honor to an unacceptable path to dignity.[27] The third volume is envisioned to show that the concept of dignity offers a path to a future with less terror, be it less structural terror or less local terror attacks.[28] Since I began working on this project, I have collected several tens of thousands of pages of material for all three volumes. However, as time and resources might not allow me to finalize volume I and II, this first volume has been expanded to comprise elements of all three.

Apart from the three volumes, several other sub-themes became so salient that they will need to be taken out into separate books. One is the concept of human nature and how the lens of honor has distorted it. Another is the great danger that flows from what I call *cross over*, namely, when feelings of dignity humiliation are responded to with tools of honor humiliation. The third separate book will have to be on my personal global life design as a research methodology, honoring the spirit of people like Alexander von Humboldt.[29]

As I see it, we, the global community on planet Earth, need a clear long-term strategy.[30] This is what motivates me to engage in this piece of *intellectual activism*.[31] I do that even though I have also been warned against writing this book. On one side, I am told that terror in general is too wide a field and that I should rather focus on terrorism. On the other side, I am also being warned against writing about terrorism. I am told that wishing to understand terrorism is to serve terrorists as their lackey and do their bidding, that wanting to understand the un-understandable condones evil.[32] I am told that evil can only be fought, not understood. Da'esh and other extremists "hate freedom" and are purveyors of a "hateful ideology,"[33] simply because they are evil, nothing more. This is what I hear: "How can people be so cruel! These terrorists are evil monsters, no humans! Don't write about them as if they were humans!"[34]

Also the humiliation argument makes some of my friends angry. The reason is that the humiliation argument itself can humiliate. Humiliation is being felt on all sides and instrumentalized in multiple ways, and the humiliation argument can be used and abused, causing ever new rounds of humiliation at ever higher meta-levels.[35] In the past, for instance, slave owners were convinced that "our slaves" live good lives with us, and that slaves would not even know how to live free lives. Also apartheid elites felt humiliated when they were accused of being humiliators. They saw "their blacks" living such good lives compared with other African countries, so how can they claim to feel humiliated, they simply are unthankful, lazy, or worse! Nowadays, some so-called foreign fighters have had a high education and good career prospects in the West. Some of my Western friends get angry at me for acknowledging that even some of those privileged guests in our midst might at times feel disrespected. I am told that a person who has received a benevolent treatment in "our society" ought not feel humiliated. Such a person ought to be thankful to us that we offer them the best of all worlds. I am told that it must be "their fault" alone, never "our fault," and that by granting "them" my understanding I betray and humiliate "us." My response usually is that my mission is to understand and invite all involved into critical self-reflection, rather than distribute blame. I call for self-reflection on all sides. Since I live in the West and in the non-West since forty years, I have ample experience with understanding all sides and call all sides to engage in self-reflection.

Peace activist and psychoanalyst Horst-Eberhard Richter (1923 – 2011) faced similar criticisms in his time. He gained deep insights into the psychology of terrorism, among others, by engaging in conversations with Birgit Hogefeld (born 1956), a former member of the West German Red Army Faction (RAF). Like me, also Richter was told that the inhumanity of terror requires its absolute ostracism and makes anyone who attempts to better understand it suspect of secret complicity. Richter's response was always that terrorism, in order to thrive, needs a political breeding ground. Scholars need to research the fertile ground of terrorism and endure being discriminated for doing so, as otherwise the threat would increase that one wants to prevent. He asserted that talking to RAF members did not mean approving of their deeds.[36] I assume that also Richter was impressed by what Mahatma Gandhi once formulated: "Hate the sin, love the sinner," or as philosopher Arne Næss put it: "There are no murderers, only people who have murdered."[37] We could follow up by saying: "There are no terrorists, only people who have committed acts of terror."[38]

In my 2006 book on humiliation and international conflict, I asked: "Children," "madmen," "criminals," "enemies," or "subhumans"? Which label fits terrorists best?[39] In this book, I would like to invite the reader to think even deeper. It may be the other way round: simply branding terrorists as "evil" may actually serve terrorist aims more than looking deeper. Humiliation awareness can liberate from the fear of seemingly "unexplainable" and thus unpreventable evil. Humiliation awareness can also turn the pain that is caused by terror into a motivation to embark on paradigm-shifting steps. In this way it can help bring about the very steps the global community has to take in any case if we wish to build a dignified future for our children, a socially and ecologically sound future.[40]

Through the experience of collecting material for the book, I understood that terrorism is the proverbial canary in the coal mine.[41] It is a warning sign for Terror with a capital "T." It warns that when the world is as interconnected as it is at the present point in history, organizing social life on Earth as in the past is no longer feasible. While terrorists are few, their activities hold the entire world hostage, not only through the immediate destruction they bring about, but also through the responses of affected societies. Examples are an excessive militarization, the undermining of civil liberties,[42] and an overall drift toward authoritarian regimes. Yet, while terrorism may be an over-exaggerated problem on one side, it also is being under-estimated. Examples include infrastructure, including vulnerable installations such as nuclear power plants that are insufficiently protected against terrorist attacks.

Global cycles of humiliation have the potential to trigger Terror on a scale that can set back all human rights milestones achieved so far. They can throw us back into a world of extremist empires on a path to annihilate each other.[43] Cycles of humiliation can be triggered advertently and inadvertently, for instance, through double standards, through failing the promise of equal dignity for all.[44] Therefore, only large-scale change both globally and locally can help us build a more dignified future. Small-scale efforts, as well-intentioned and partially successful as they may be, are like wanting to keep the walls of the proverbial coal mine from collapsing by simply patching the cracks.

Terror attacks share many characteristics with environmental catastrophes. Both occur suddenly and some may be due to causes that cannot be prevented – earthquakes and tsunamis for example, or, in the case of terrorism, psychologically challenged people will always be around. Yet, catastrophes often also entail elements of human error or systemic neglect of due preparation – the Fukushima Daiichi nuclear disaster may serve as an illustration. I use the phrase *structural disaster* for situations where appropriate long-term preparation is lacking.[45] Not just ecological disasters are to be expected in the future. As alluded to earlier, global ecological-institutional-social-psychological conditions will spawn more "social disasters," of which terrorism is a part. Global structural disasters, be they brought about by ecological overshoot or social overshoot, are likely to increasingly affect every world community in the coming decades, and it is therefore in every citizen's interest to learn about and plan for appropriate prevention and post-disaster intervention.[46]

Attempts to rebuild communities in the wake of environmental or social disasters can perpetuate old structural disasters or even introduce new ones. On the other side, disasters can also open novel pathways to more dignity. The global community is called on to create global conditions for *structural dignity* to flourish globally and locally, so that true global common-unity (community) can emerge. On our interconnected and finite planet we will otherwise see ever more environmental and social disasters happen. New international standards and protocols are needed for responding to environmental catastrophes or terror attacks. They will, however, create new catastrophes if they stay within the existing frames of structural disaster.

Dynamics of humiliation entail the potential to foment terror, and this unfolds in an almost prototypical manner now. This trend is sped up by the fact that we fail to adapt suitably to the historically new times of interconnectedness. In the past, tactics of humiliation and terror could indeed "succeed" insofar as they could push the defeated into submissive resignation to the point that they felt too powerless to rise up again. In an interconnected world, in contrast, when cycles of humiliation and counter-humiliation rush through the Internet at breakneck speed, humiliation has much more serious consequences. Teaching people "lessons" by way of humiliation no longer represents as feasible a path to "victory" as before. If not obsolete for ethical-psychological reasons, such lessons are simply unfeasible for practical reasons now, as they risk ending in collective suicide.[47]

Whoever believes that lessons in peace education would be a sufficient alternative, will be in for a disappointment. Peace education is useful and important, yet, not enough. Research in social psychology shows that particularly youths of thirteen to fifteen years of age, those in need to listen most, are the most difficult to reach. Especially adolescent males are the most vulnerable to be recruited by terror entrepreneurs. Most people do not reach their full brain capacity until the age of twenty-five. Many youths may therefore not be able to contain themselves, and their environment must shoulder this responsibility. Their communities have to hold and contain those young people in their vulnerability. "It takes a village to raise a child," is one African saying, "All kids are our kids" is another. For a world free of terrorism, it is the global village who is responsible for all of the world's children and youth. And not only young people need to be held. Mutual connection is a life-giving necessity for all. To realize this, the global community has to re-design the foundational constitutive rules of our currently existing world-system, away from competition for domination toward a *partnership model* of society.[48]

Adherents of the strategies of the past will want to misunderstand and discredit the message of this book so as to maintain a bygone world. I posit that they will do so at their own peril and at humankind's peril. We live in times of shifting paradigms, and if we wish them to shift toward more dignity, they will need a lot of intentional nurturing and courageous visionary thinking. Thomas Kuhn's work on how paradigms change is more relevant now than ever.[49]

Since I began to work on this book project in 2010, the inflation of types of terrorism has amazed – regime terrorism, vigilante terrorism, insurgent terrorism, left-wing terrorism, right-wing terrorism, ethno-nationalist terrorism, "jihadist" terrorism, lone wolf terrorism, single issue terrorism, or cyberterrorism.[50] Social media have an outreach that is more global than ever, a single radicalized lone wolf individual can now cause greater damage than ever before. At the same time, also the fear of terrorism can be instrumentalized more efficiently than ever. In a way, the newly elected leader of the United States, Donald J. Trump, could be regarded as a lone wolf who came to power on the promise of single-handedly standing up against all the new terror of the world and bring back a more familiar past.

A global *Blitzkrieg* of terror appears to be unfolding, fashioned on attacks such as the November 2015 attack in Paris.[51] The "dual usability" of everyday technology is being "democratized" – civil airplanes destroyed the Twin Towers in 2001, and now cargo trucks became weapons in Nice and Berlin in 2016. Traditional military equipment becomes increasingly useless, also in the face of cyberwarfare and bioterrorism.[52] And this happens while a rampant monetization of nature,[53] aiming to rescue shareholder primacy, aggravates the situation ever further.[54]

The Global Terrorism Index 2015 shows that, despite being highly concentrated in five countries, terrorism is spreading, with more countries recording attacks and deaths.[55] Over 32,000 people were killed in terrorist attacks in 2014 constituting an eighty percent increase from the previous year,[56] whereby the vast majority of victims of extreme violent extremism are Muslims.[57] If one were to include also state terrorism in these statistics – indeed, historically, the term terrorism was first used in the context of state terrorism[58] – the numbers would rise considerably: in the twentieth century, states are calculated to have killed about 170 million civilians.[59]

Da'esh is similar to Al-Qaeda but it goes further. Like Al-Qaeda, Da'esh regards itself as a group of holy warriors, crafting a new world order. Unlike Al-Qaeda, however, it does not come along as a secret organization; it presents itself as a holy state. With its unprecedented use of social media, it attracts recruits from all around the world who feel they can escape their daily frustrations and anonymity and enter a world of glorious recognition, honor, and fairness.[60] Da'esh presents itself as a shining global movement led by an international moral elite that will take historical revenge for past humiliations.[61] It is seen by its followers as a place free from corruption, a place where the dishonor of poverty and inequality is being bravely reversed.[62] Many of their enthusiastic supporters even actively disbelieve stories of beheadings and deem them to be Western propaganda.[63] They even overlook that male "jihadists" are committing horrific sexual violence.[64]

All this is more than a problem for a few experts in the Secret Services or for military strategists. The canary in the coal mine metaphor illustrates this. Mining workers took caged canary birds with them into mine tunnels because the birds would die if dangerous gases such as methane or carbon monoxide leaked into the mine. Thus, the workers were warned so that they could leave the tunnels in time.[65] Present-day terror, both as sense of terror and tactics of terror, may be more than a momentary imperfection in an otherwise healthy environment; it may signal that the core ways of how we as humankind arrange our affairs on planet Earth are increasingly incompatible with the reality of a shrinking and interconnected finite world.

It is therefore that this book is different from other books on terrorism. First, it looks from a bird's eye perspective on the human condition, including terrorism. It is a psycho-geo-historical bird's eye view[66] that embeds the phenomenon of terrorism into a transdisciplinary context that stretches from the origins of *Homo sapiens* to the predictable distant future. To better understand the alternative options open for the future, and to create appropriate routes for restructuring, all of humankind's history is looked at in this book: How did we, as humans, frame the human condition throughout our past, how did this lead us to where we are now, and where should we go from here? Indeed, "we still have work to do to understand what is it, within and among us, that must change, why, and how soon."[67] The most concealed and at the same time most dangerous trap would be believing we engage in "new," "bold," and "radical" change, while remaining within the old frame.[68]

Second, the book is provocative. It speaks not only *about* terrorism but also *to* those who see terror and counterterror as legitimate tools. Third, this book avoids blame – both "hawks" and "doves" of all sides are treated with radical empathy and radical respect.[69] Respect is accorded also to those who say that this book should not be written since "terrorists are evil per definition and reflecting on humiliation would mean naïvely doing the bidding of terrorists."

I am not an expert in terrorism studies. I do not wish to duplicate the immensely valuable expertise that has accumulated in the field. Yet, I have heard calls from scholars of critical terrorism studies, a sub-discipline of terrorism studies, for opening the field to insights from other perspectives.[70] This is, incidentally, also what I attempt to do in my work in general, not just in the case of terrorism. I always try to understand a field to the degree that enables me to reconstruct its core aspects from the perspective of dignity and humiliation. So far, I have done this with war and genocide (2000),[71] international conflict (2006 and 2009),[72] gender and security (2010),[73] and economics (2012).[74]

As noted before, my vantage point, my "plane of projection" or "mental position," resembles that of a bird, or even that of an astronaut.[75] Patterns often become visible from afar that would be difficult to discern from closer range, and small details can acquire new meaning from afar. I have yet to meet another person with a similar life design or path, a path that led me from the pain of my family's forced displacement toward global citizenship and transdisciplinary scholarship. I regard my life experience as a responsibility, as a duty to share the unique vantage point that emerges from this experience. My life has been a research project and an experiment. I am not a middle-class student from a Western society who makes brief excursions to *study* the world "out there," I *am in* the world.[76] The standpoint of a thinker does not present itself to the thinker: the thinker *is* that standpoint, and I agree that if one were to attempt to abstract away from the subjective perspective on the world, one would leave out precisely what one seeks to explain.[77]

I have invested forty years into living globally and developing an embodied connection with the entirety of humankind, an experience that serves as my path to understanding, a path from which also a holistic concept for a decent future for humankind has emerged. I do not follow any particular theory, it is rather that a model of the world has emerged in me from immersing myself into all continents and looking at theories and definitions of terms/ notions/ concepts as being parts of this world. I have learned how each era interprets the texts and concepts of the past in its peculiar contemporary way and that there is no guarantee for "truth,"[78] there is only the experience of "I understand."[79] With this caveat in mind, I allow myself to be drawn into "truth events" all around the world, humbly acknowledging that I will always be too late if I want to know what to believe. In this way, I live a life of *interbeing*.[80] I attempt to search for and nurture what physicists call "coherence domains," which means that I search for areas where hearts and minds can align, not just locally, but at a global level.[81] By engaging in "living translation,"[82] I follow my teacher philosopher Dagfinn Føllesdal, who advised me, back in 1996, that the phenomenon of humiliation can only be illuminated by rich descriptive studies.[83]

As a result, I accept all criticisms that accuse me of being too much of a generalist who lacks specific local expertise, because I do. I only highlight what works from my point of view.[84] The German phrase for term/concept/notion is *Begriff*, and it means that something has been grasped or gripped (*gegriffen*). I observe how all historical contexts "grip" reality in different ways, and what I do is attempt to trace the journey of humankind's grip on the human condition on our planet up to our present times, and to extend what I see into the future, so as to be able to describe future paths that appear to be preferable. Since I am aware that the world cannot be accessed as it is, I myself try not to grasp, but to "assemble."[85] My work is therefore the assemblage of what I have seen during the past forty years around the globe, and this assemblage is always painfully inadequate. It is but a humble attempt of meaning making while heeding "the responsibility to choose among potential meanings and to test and otherwise evaluate candidate interpretations."[86]

I am not driven by any quasi-religious dystopic desire to "save the world." It is rather joy that motivates me, joy when I see humankind's potential to shape informed strategies. At the same time, I am not driven by optimism or hope. I am willing to accept if humankind is unable to successfully address the myriad global challenges it has created for itself – indeed, we may cause our own extinction, as we watch life on Earth dying around us already now.[87] My work for our survival with dignity gives me a strong personal sense of inner coherence, yet, I am also willing to work for a dignified non-survival if need be.[88]

Many have read psychologist Steven Pinker's book *Better Angels*.[89] I go further back into the past than Pinker does – back to before twelve millennia ago – and, as a medical doctor and psychologist, I also venture into the future more, from diagnosis and prognosis to therapy. My life experience is also more global than what a Harvard professor can possibly achieve – he has to stay put much of the time except for occasional travels. The scope of my transdisciplinarity is therefore wider than Pinker's. With my colleagues worldwide, through lived experience, I can therefore work on building a theory of dignity and humiliation – or a model, or a portrait – that is transcultural and transdisciplinary. It entails elements from such diverse fields as history, social philosophy, political science, sociology, criminology, anthropology, psychology (clinical, cultural, community, social psychology), or neuroscience.[90]

In other words, my experience resonates with those who warn that one-dimensional approaches of "siloization" in academia and in life ought to be avoided.[91] To use an image from development aid, it is not a good strategy to build wells to provide clean water to African villages, while forgetting that the women, while going to the well, may be raped, kidnapped, or killed.[92] I wish to heed this warning, and from there this book got its breadth and depth. If we go through a list of some of the main problems that have a global and long-term impact that is definitorial for the new century, "such as water, forced migrations, poverty, environmental crises, violence, terrorism, neo-imperialism, destruction of social fabric," we must conclude "that none of them can be adequately tackled from the sphere of specific individual disciplines. They clearly represent transdisciplinary challenges."[93] "Any response to the human/ planetary condition in the early 21st Century that is at all adequate must be grounded in a longer, wider, deeper and more integrated grasp of the civilizational 'game' we are in."[94]

Also scholars from within the field of terrorism studies warn against silo mentalities. Peter Neumann is professor of security studies at the Department of War Studies at King's College London, and the director of the International Centre for the Study of Radicalisation, which he founded in 2008. Also he warns that people do not exist in a vacuum; they are affected and shaped by their social, economic, cultural, and political environments.[95] Therefore, both the study of terrorism and of humiliation has to be designed as a multi- and transdisciplinary approach. More even, a historical lens needs to be adopted to avoid myopic ahistoricity and *chronocentrism*. It has been warned, for instance, that within British criminological studies, there is a propensity to ignore writings that are over fifteen years old.[96]

If it is true that during the past five percent of modern human history, the past ten millennia or so, a culture of honor has spawned, in which destruction and bravery merged and violence and terror became intertwined with heroism and glory, then present-day's social and ecological degradation is a byproduct of this merger. None of these challenges can be adequately understood and addressed from one discipline alone, nor with myopic ahistoricity.

With its breadth, this book responds also to terrorism expert Alex Peter Schmid's admonition that a fuller exploration of the "milieus" that surround terrorist violence is needed. Schmid is the editor-in-chief of the journal *Perspectives on Terrorism*, and director of the Terrorism Research Initiative, an international network of scholars who seek to enhance human security through collaborative research. He notices "a certain fixation of much of the current research on the micro-level," on "vulnerable individuals, indoctrinated over the Internet or in physical locations and/or recruited by terrorist organizations," and calls for "more analyses on the meso- and macro-levels."[97]

Many experts on terrorism are men. Yet, also many women apply the "cool male" intellectual style that is now favored in many walks of academia. Its hallmark is a "hard" warrior-like style of critiquing, and a disdain for "soft" interpersonal kindness and Buberian I-Thou connection.[98] I was never able to go down this path. I could never turn people into "samples."[99] To me, this smacks of "the banality" of evil that Hannah Arendt has pinpointed.[100] I cannot write about counterterror in a style that furthers it. This book is therefore created with love,[101] with solidarity, with care for the Other, and a passion for enabling justice.[102] It is more like a painting than a scholarly presentation of a theory, and it is a painting that paints itself, with the painter's humble and loving involvement.[103] It is like a kaleidoscope or panorama painting,[104] an associative report of a life journey in its loving embeddedness into a global network of the relationships with people.

The associative approach goes back to my years of reading French thinkers – the notion of *différance*, for example, or the human embeddedness into ever-shifting webs of language, has impressed me early on.[105] It was later affirmed during my years in Japan by the "analogue" culture that I found there, which approaches reality organically, precisely like a painting, in contrast to Western styles, which are more abstract, more "digital," and mechanistic.[106] I am as inspired by philosopher John Dewey (1859 – 1952), whose bronze bust I greet every year when I am at Teachers College at Columbia University in New York City. Dewey ridiculed "the dogma of the immaculate conception of philosophical systems."[107] With my approach I also honor philosopher Arne Næss and his call for deeper questioning, for continuing to ask questions at the point at which others stop asking.[108]

A painting is not so much about "wrong" or "right." It is a manifestation of a painter's way of seeing, the painter's journey in search of new levels of meaning. And this manifestation is meant to inspire, more than to be judged and agreed or disagreed with – judgement can even be "an enemy of change."[109]

Therefore, not only do I write with love, I also ask the reader to read with love. To read in the spirit of *connected knowing*.[110] Readers will find a language of *unity in diversity*, of *listening others into voice*.[111] They will find conjunctions such as *and*, rather than posturing and putting others into place with *but* and *not*. By doing so, the book attempts to manifest a new culture, not just in theory but in its own praxis. It aims to show that a *post-terror* culture is a factual possibility, a culture of trust and cooperation, a culture, where the "buts" and "nots" of our world are respected as important identity markers, while, at the same time, connecting them through the creative insertion of "ands."

This book is thus not simply a variation or repetition of the approach of my other books, which were more stringent. This book is longer, in resonance with the slow living movement, intended for interested readers who would like to enjoy, together with me, both delving deeper into detail and moving higher up into a bird's-eye perspective so as to discern crucial patterns. Also, since times of crisis always call for more eyes to see and more voices to be heard, this book lets the world speak its own voice, not least through the global dignity fellowship of people that I am part of: as the initiator and nurturer of the Human Dignity and Humiliation Studies fellowship, I include many voices in this book.[112] In this concert of voices, my own is only one among many. It is important for me to make clear that this book is not meant to define what others in our fellowship should think. I wear two hats, in the spirit of unity in diversity – one hat in service of convening our global dignity family, and the other in my capacity of being part of the wide-ranging diversity of our global fellowship.

Hopefully, my readers will feel encouraged by this book, encouraged to more thoroughly explore and formulate their own personal perceptions of the world, to take more seriously what they see with their own eyes, rather than wait for experts to define the situation. The proverbial child saw something the experts overlooked, namely, that the emperor was naked.

Another aspect of walking the talk of dignity, of preventing and healing terror through dignity, is to avoid jargon and employ simple language. History shows that beliefs can be harmful – they can feed cycles of humiliation and violence – and this can become all the more dangerous when these beliefs are delivered in an expert jargon that aims to awe people into submission. Not only that, as social psychologist Michael Billig warns, technical terminology in general is regularly less precise than simpler language; in short, the attempt to appear scientific can undermine its very aim and become unscientific.[113] I therefore attempt to use a style that is more fluid and personal than the formalistic coded language that is standard in academia and that creates fortifications around academic disciplines, often insulating their insights from mainstream readers.

This book speaks to many audiences, to human rights advocates as much as to human rights critics, to those who condone terror tactics as much as to those who do not. It invites all those readers who resonate with human rights ideals to hone their humiliation awareness by understanding the fundamental difference between *dignity humiliation* and *honor humiliation*. In an interconnected world, this awareness is crucial. It also invites those who resonate with the moral universe of ranked honor, on the other side, to better understand how scripts of honor that worked in the past have very different effects now. In the name of honorable victory, "truth" had little weight in the past when each side perceived the other as evil in a context where "you are either for me or against me." In an interconnected world, in contrast, such scripts no longer lead to victory; they lead to all-out defeat.

This book is thus a perspective-training book. All sides are invited to put in use the human brain's plasticity for better perspective-taking, for stepping into the shoes of others.[114] The training this book aims at is to lead away from preconceived views, be they too rosy or too dark, and away from panic entrepreneurship. When we imagine that humankind is in a lifeboat, the boat will sink if global finger-pointing and infighting is all that happens. What is needed is an awareness of "we either all swim together or all sink together," an awareness that it is better to stop demonizing each other, and start reflecting on our shared weaknesses and strengths and find a better way forward together.

This book, in its attempt to do more than just speak *about* terrorism to readers who wish to understand and prevent it, also speaks directly *to* those readers who sympathize not just with the concept of honor, but also with practices of terror. And it does so with a unique message, a message that goes beyond "de-radicalization" or "counter-radicalization." It offers an alternative narrative to those who feel that spreading terror is a viable strategy to express grievances, and also to those who think that terror ought to be responded to with terror. At the core of this narrative is an effort to exit from the tunnel vision that hinders seeing complexity, a tunnel vision which, understandably, often accompanies the emotional pressure that surrounds terror.[115] To exit from this tunnel vision means heeding crucial differentiations: *description*, for instance, is different from *prescription*, *understanding* is different from *condoning*, and *respecting* is different from *accepting*. *Multi-partiality*, a term used in mediation, is needed when the aim is to move a situation from being destructive to being constructive, or, as pioneer in women's psychology Jean Baker Miller formulated it, when we want to move from "waging bad conflict" to "waging good conflict."[116]

This book takes it very seriously that *respecting* is different from *condoning*. Therefore, all sides are approached with radical respect, including those who regard terror as a legitimate tool, be it as first strike or as terror-for-terror response. Respect is necessary for terror to diminish, not least because it builds bridges between all actors, be they hawks or doves – "hawks" are understood in this book as those who believe that terror is purposeful and that spreading terror or reacting to it in an eye-for-an-eye manner is the right thing to do, while "doves" think that spreading terror is wrong and counterproductive no matter what. With radical respect, dichotomies can be transcended without anybody having to lose face. Learning together from past mistakes can be a proud endeavor; it does not have to be humiliating.[117] There is no shame in having been socialized into acting in ways that are more adapted to the past, for example, only because these ways become unfeasible in a changing present.[118] The large-scale psycho-geo-historical lens used in this book makes visible that it is a scientific inevitability rather than naïve charitable goodwill, at least if we wish to survive as a species, that we learn to bridge seemingly irreconcilable positions by extending respect to all sides, by refraining from demonizing any side.

As mentioned before, I have been reluctant to write this book, not least because there are very knowledgeable experts on terrorism around and my contribution may be too broad. Yet, the preparations for this book of about six years that spanned the entire globe have always pushed me to continue. On February 4, 2011, for instance, the Norwegian Police Security Service allowed me in for an interview. I asked my conversation partners: What would you need most from us, the academic community? They responded by saying that their most pressing questions are the following: Please explain how it is possible that one single individual can transmute into a lone wolf terrorist and traumatize whole societies? How does radicalization work? How can it be detected? How can it be prevented? Tragically, it was only a few months after I had this conversation, that lone Anders Behring Breivik, on July 22, 2011, brought precisely the trauma to Norway we had discussed.

Indeed, the term *radicalization* has been widely used in the past decade. In the rest of the book, I will follow terrorism expert Alex Schmid's preference and use the term *extremism* in the sense of *violent extremism* rather than the term radicalization.[119] The phrase *radical* stems from the Latin word *radix* or root. It suggests getting at the root of problems. My reason for preferring the terminology of extremism is that also people like Nelson Mandela can be placed into the category of radicals. Indeed, I myself am a radical, radical in my commitment to dignity.

If we take "religious fundamentalism" as something that is grounded in religious scriptures taken literally rather than "interpreted," and combine this with "extremism" defined as action that is verbally or physically violent, then we arrive at "religious extremism" as violent action justified and legitimized by religious scriptures, with divine forces being seen as direct support, or failure to be violent feared to incur divine wrath. As for secular fundamentalists and extremists, they are those who fight for secular goals, such as statism and nationalism.[120]

I am radical with respect to dignity, which, to me, also includes ideals of academic freedom.[121] In my opinion, research should be conducted to gain insights for the benefit of all of humankind in a context of academic freedom, rather than academic freedom being sold out for ulterior aims. Social sciences suffer in this respect, and psychology is perhaps most affected. Its history could be recounted as a story of trying to gain respect and avoid humiliation by appearing to be just as "scientific" as the natural sciences – a condition also known as "physics envy." This may explain why the natural sciences's number-crunching calculus-based style is being imitated in the field of psychology even where it is not necessary or even misleading. Philosopher Michel Foucault warned already in 1957 that psychology has inherited from the Enlightenment the desire to align itself with the natural sciences and to find in human beings the prolongation of the laws that govern natural phenomena.[122] Psychology is caught in the contradiction between its own purpose, which is understanding human beings, and postulates of anti-historical positivism.[123] Only in the formal sciences of mathematics, geometry and logic, can certainty and replication be achieved, while the fallibility inherent in the social sciences renders it fundamentally different.[124] The field of psychology is therefore always at risk to succumb to the very problems it is meant to elucidate and solve.[125] It is not surprising that research findings in the field of psychology are much "weaker" than claimed: only thirty-four percent of original studies published in top-tier psychology journals, for instance, can be replicated.[126]

In my work, I attempt to heed the insight that it is more honest, more connective, more respectful, and ultimately more scientific, to refrain from the façade polishing of wanting to "appear scientific."[127] As mentioned above, I greet John Dewey's bronze bust at Columbia University every November and December, when we organize our annual "Workshop on Transforming Humiliation and Violent Conflict."[128] Also molecular biologist Robert Pollack is based at Columbia University.[129] He warns that even present-day brain research shows that "the direction of scientific research is driven by private demons, not public needs."[130] He advises "scientists and others to abandon the notion that there is any such thing as the disinterested pursuit of truth. Instead, he calls us all to strive for a therapeutic self-awareness of our unconscious agendas and work for larger goals than personal immortality."[131] I am a radical follower of Pollack's guidance, and I do so by investing every second of my life into striving for the degree of selfless humility that is necessary for maintaining due self-criticism. I attempt to walk my talk by experimenting with my own life design to the very limit of what is practically and psychologically possible. I am painfully aware that it is perilous to overlook and push aside the darker parts of our soul, society, and history.[132]

At present, all around the world, I observe academia as a whole being pulled ever more forcefully into a government/corporate nexus.[133] Not least the funds for research increasingly depend on this nexus. Terrorist acts are political acts and therefore research on terrorism is being drawn into political spheres even more forcefully than other fields of inquiry. Research on terrorism thus represents a particularly visible manifestation of the larger trend of coopting academia for ulterior goals. After "the gloves came off" on the so-called war on terror, we hear that people flocked to Washington who claimed they knew something about counterterrorism, and they got "very rich."[134]

It is therefore of crucial importance that I clarify at this point that this book project is free of any funding connected with national or corporate interests, or, as peace researcher Jan Øberg would formulate it, free of MIMAC, the Military-Industrial-Media-Academic Complex.[135] I go to extreme lengths to protect my independence, which includes making severe personal financial sacrifices.[136] I opt out of the existing paradigm, so as to opt into a vision of a better future.[137] As founding president of a global movement for dignity, I am not employed anywhere, nor part of any national interest context, and I do not work for any anti-terrorist project or institution, which, per definition, would be embedded in particular national interests. I have no salary and I am not paid for lobbying against or for anything, even not for human rights. For me, human rights ideals of equal dignity are a very personal calling that defines every minute of my life, it is not a "job" nor a "hobby" for me.[138] My global life is a gift that I give to humankind out of love, and it helps me draw on all knowledges of all continents in support of this mission.[139]

Also "soft" bias can skew, of course, not just "hard" funding. I am not surprised that projects like mine have become more difficult after the attacks on the United States on September 11, 2001. A person under attack will be tempted to seek "root causes" solely on the attacker's side and denounce anybody as disloyal who dares to suggest that self-criticism may also be needed. Social psychology describes many human biases, for instance, the *attribution error* or *reactive devaluation*.[140] Such biases typically intensify under the emotional stress of conflict situations. Entire communities can fall prey to this trap, which can polarize the public opinion and party politics of entire societies.[141] At the national level, refusal to abide by such biases might be branded as treason, and "unpatriotic" researchers may risk being accused of not being scientific. Searching for "the root causes of terrorism" may be misunderstood as an effort to excuse and justify the killing of innocent civilians. In such situations, researchers will choose their words very carefully, particularly when also their financial base depends on what they say.

As reported above, I have indeed met all these criticisms myself. The reader of this book can be assured that I write with a bias toward the interest of all of humankind. My radical commitment to academic freedom, as it is grounded in my global life and global identity, compels me to serve the interests of all humankind rather than merely seeking my own advantage or that of certain subgroups. I define the entire human family as my family, including the "poisoned poor" of this world.[142] The reader will therefore search in vain for terms such as "abroad" or "overseas" in this book, or other formulations that betray a person's view on the world from a particular in-group perspective vis-à-vis out-groups. What the reader will find are concepts such as, for instance, *human security*, rather than *military security* for "us" from "the enemy." If I did otherwise, I would contribute to creating the very insecurity I profess wanting to avoid.

Born into Western society, privileged with an advanced education, I could choose to protect myself against the "poisoned poor." I could even avoid becoming aware that the well-off of this planet thrive because those at the bottom toil. Instead, I choose to open my eyes also to the poison. Mine is more than a theoretical position, it is my thoroughly lived reality. And it is informed, not least, by my family's harsh and traumatizing life experiences from war and displacement.

This book has the thrust of counter-radicalization[143] insofar as it heeds that extremism is a real-world phenomenon that calls for comprehensive explanations and cannot be solved by facile solutions. Simply removing or blocking radicalizing material from the Internet, for instance, would be insufficient.[144] Yet, as mentioned before, this book does not oppose radicalization as such. The reason is that radical opinions do not necessarily lead to political violence or terrorism.[145] People like Mahatma Gandhi, Martin Luther King, Nelson Mandela, Desmond Tutu, or Paulo Freire can be called radical in their dedication to building a common critical consciousness to nurture political transformation toward more dignity. Therefore, this book aims at radicalizing its readers toward the *conscientization* that not only Freire called for, also Freire's colleague Clodomir de Morais,[146] or people like Frantz Fanon.[147] They all asked us to turn conscience into action for dignity.[148]

To conclude this Preface, I hope to alert my readers to what the psycho-geo-historical lens that I use lets me see. It shows me that what we call terrorism today may altogether be a harbinger of much greater terror, Terror with capital "T" that looms if we, as humankind, continue to stay at the surface with our attention. As for now, we feel terrorized by here-and-now isolated emergency threats to the status quo, while we fail to feel terrorized by the fact that this status quo is unsustainable, at least in the longer term, and that it breeds terror rather than diminishing it. When incidents of terrorism happen, my hope is always that the shock will awaken people's attention to those deeper layers of terror-in-waiting. I hope that people will be propelled into more thorough reflection on long-term preventive action. However, usually my hopes are dashed. Like with climate change, inaction is fed both by denying the threat as much as by its opposite, namely, exaggeration to the point of defeatism – "there is nothing we can do; we're already doomed."

The image of the Blue Planet from the astronaut's perspective summarizes, publicizes, and symbolizes an immense window of opportunity for us to create a dignified world, including a terror-free world, at least free of systemic terror.[149] Having escaped nuclear annihilation during the Cold War, the nuclear threat now also flows from terrorism,[150] and even the "safest" installations, such as German nuclear plants, are highly vulnerable.[151] Hitherto unseen threats are just as global, human-made, and potentially lethal, and many go unseen – the recent genome-editing breakthrough is only one example.[152] What befits humankind now is a sense of emergency so as to truly see and use this historically unmatched window of opportunity that may not remain open for long.[153]

The Blue Planet image provides a powerful frame for collaboration. None of our forefathers was able to see anything comparable. None of our predecessors was able to fathom in the same way as present-day *Homo sapiens* that we are *one single* family living on *one tiny* and *finite* planet. None of our founders of religions, philosophies, or empires had access to the vast amount of knowledge that we possess today about the universe and our place in it. Anthropologist William Ury is among the few I have met on my global path who understands the extent to which our present historical times are unparalleled with respect to any other earlier period in human history: "For the first time since the origin of our species, humanity is in touch with itself."[154] "Having constructed a civilization capable of observing our still paradisiacal world from objectivity-inducing distances, we need to set aside our squabbles, recognize that we face a species-wide threat, and use our scientific-technical genius to protect the only known home of life in the universe."[155]

Why do we, as humankind, overlook the historic opportunity that is open to us to engage in deeper global cooperation, an opportunity greater than ever imaginable before? Why is our global government/ corporate nexus stuck in out-of-date games of competition for domination, games that also fuel terrorism? One reason may be the negative aspects of the recent rounds of globalization that we have witnessed, aspects that systematically hide its promises.[156] Its promises lie in what anthropologists call the *ingathering* of the human tribes. This ingathering entails a unique opportunity, the opportunity, namely, to unite the global human community, invite it into one-world consciousness and cooperation, not just as lofty rhetoric, but as hands-on lived global solidarity.

Many wonder, including the author, why even thinkers and activists who work for a better future for humanity seem rather disinterested in global governance. "Engagement with governance at a global scale is largely absent from the discussions within the degrowth movement. This is curious given the centrality of issues like climate change, free trade, and relentless global competition."[157] Perhaps the promise entailed in the ingathering of humankind goes also unseen and unused because it is such a novel phenomenon. And perhaps the toxic aspects of globalization are too complicated, causing people to recoil from focusing on the global level. In the author's view, even though this oversight is understandable, it is not excusable. Mechanisms of global plunder admittedly are so complex that only a minority of people is in a position to understand them, let alone do something about them. For most people, globalization simply dissolves the floor under their feet without any clear explanation, the more so in communities that were sheltered before. The world becomes confusing, fear-inducing, and frightfully "liquid," as Zygmunt Bauman formulated it.[158] The sense of insecurity that in former times was experienced only by displaced people, refugees, diasporas, exiles, or indigenous peoples, is now brought to the rest through globalization.

The result of this oversight is that the global space that waits to be humanized is left to forces of dehumanization. Even those among my friends stay timid who would have all the necessary resources to give a significant push to planetary solidarity. They leave it to social media, for instance, where the potential for planetary solidarity is being instrumentalized for profit, and this is still one of the more harmless abuses. Or, they leave it to a global nexus of finance, criminality, and terrorism, including the instrumentalization of the fear of terrorism. Others are more courageous, yet, also they make globalization only more toxic when they enact the "frequent traveler" version of global citizenship, viewing the world as a leisure park for the rich, at best, or targeting the commons of our globe as market opportunities yet to be exploited. Then there are those who are both daring and caring, those who wish to help, those who feel called to work for development, humanitarian aid, conflict transformation, and environmental protection. Yet, sadly, also they, only too often slide into the charitable-industrial complex that is part of the dark side of globalization.[159] Not enough, even the most well-intended global human rights advocates create conflict rather than prevent it when they hold the illusion that "bringing people together" and "raising human rights awareness" alone will translate into peaceful global cooperation. What human rights advocacy may do instead is throw inequality and disrespect into starker contrast than before, oblivious that this, in turn, can create expectation gaps that lead to feelings of humiliation that were not felt before. If these feelings of humiliation are magnified by globalization, together with means for violent backlashes, this mix can heat up and boil over. Terrorism is an intricate part of this mix.

This Preface and also this book will end with a call for action. As peace psychologist Michael Britton wrote in a personal communication: "In this time of re-organizing globally, can this human species that has so traumatized itself on a historical scale find within itself the capacity to heal and make a better experience of life, a happier overall experience of life, than what we've been used to? Can we venerate something better?"[160]

We can. During the past forty years, while researching these questions, I came to the conclusion that we, as humankind, have to, and can dramatically change the underlying structures, or *generative mechanisms*,[161] or *constitutive rules*[162] of our *world-system*.[163] We can co-create a decent global village for all people and our planet. Otherwise, I predict that hostility will increase, not least since one of its drivers, humiliation, becomes much more salient in an interconnected world than it was in previous historical times. It is therefore that I advise to take humiliation into account in radically new ways. When dignity is promised, but violated, it is not just any expectation gap that opens, it is a dignity gap, and this is extremely dangerous. The reason is that what I call *dignity humiliation* is more intense than the *honor humiliation* that has reigned while the world was not yet as interconnected as now. Having one's dignity humiliated excludes one from humanity and is therefore much more hurtful than having one's honor humiliated. If dignity humiliation were to stay internally coherent, it would lead to the conscientization of a Paulo Freire and to responses in the spirit of a Mahatma Gandhi and Nelson Mandela. Most often, however, it rather leads to what the author calls *cross over*, namely, to acts of revenge that are informed by the script of honor humiliation. If this cross over becomes our future, the resulting hostility will constitute a far greater danger than climate change or the exhaustion of raw materials, or any other disaster scenario, warn even optimistic economic commentators such as Samuel Brittan.[164]

My personal path of global living represents a radical hands-on experiment in global "family building."[165] I suggest that many readers of this book will find it worth investigating how also they can contribute more to creating a world of unity in diversity, rather than enduring a world of division without unity. Global solidarity and trust is tantamount to solving our global problems, which, if successful, will also diminish terror and fear.

These are my concluding words: Terror and terrorism will decrease when we, as humankind at large, stop overlooking the long-term and global challenges of our journey on planet Earth, when we cease waging artificial conflicts and instead dare to attend to our necessary conflicts. Necessary conflicts need to be addressed rather than neglected, and this has to be done in dignified and dignifying ways, without humiliating the humiliators. We need to use the presently available historic window of opportunity to become the global family we are, and to solve our family problems in ways good families do. Both terrorism and out-of-proportion counterterrorism hinders this overdue transition.

I have coined the term *egalization* to signify the true realization of human rights ideals of equal dignity for all. I call for globalization to be humanized by egalization – for *globegalization* – instead of accepting that globalization dehumanizes humanity through global domination and terror. I call for dignity-ism, or *dignism* to inform new global institutions that benefit from the promise that is entailed in interconnectedness. These institutions will need to manifest the principle of unity in diversity, meaning that we unite in respect for the dignity of our diversity, while at the same time guarding against global uniformity and global division. Such global institutions will enable the global community to overcome bygone cultural scripts and learn to practice the Freire-Mandela-Gandhi way of healing humiliation, overcoming terror, and creating a dignified future for our children.

In our times of global crises it is not only crucially important, it is also hugely enriching to invest in the nurturing of global solidarity in mutual respect. If we do, the nature of what we call terrorism will change and space will open for dignity to flourish. Today, terrorism is overemphasized for ulterior motives where it should be seen as a social problem, and on the other side, where it would require more attention and efforts to prevent it, it is neglected. Where terrorism does receive attention, it may be for the wrong reasons and with counterproductive consequences. In short, terrorism needs to be taken less seriously on one side and more seriously on the other side. Having escaped nuclear annihilation during the Cold War, similarly deadly threats, including nuclear threats, now also flows from terrorism. In a situation where opportunities for catastrophic terrorist acts increase, even from single individuals, it is hazardous and foolish to concurrently increase the breeding ground for terrorism.

Respectful global family building is more than feasible, it is also hugely inspirational and even fun. In our Human Dignity and Humiliation Studies community, as part of our global family building efforts, we encourage all our members to open their homes as Human Dignity Dialogue Homes or *Dignihomes*.[166] I meet many young people, all around the world, also outside of our community, who confirm to me that connecting with other people, connecting with "strangers," if done respectfully, can be exhilaratingly exciting, enjoyable, meaningful, and deeply satisfying.

"Only connect ...," wrote novelist Edward Morgan Forster (1879 – 1970) in the epigraph of his famous 1910 novel *Howards End*.[167] If his advice had been heeded in 1914, already the two world wars of the twentieth century could have been avoided. Respectful connection, respectful solidarity, considering the others' perspectives in addition to one's own, could have saved millions of lives. This book is another attempt at connecting, globally and locally.

Attempt

Between
What I think
What I want to say
What I think I say
What I say
What you want to hear
What you think you hear
What you hear
What you want to understand
What you think you understand
What you understand
We have ten potential barriers to communication.
But let's try anyway ...

Bernard Werber[168]

Acknowledgments

May I begin by extending my deepest gratitude to the core leadership team of the Human Dignity and Humiliation Studies (HumanDHS) fellowship, Linda Hartling and her husband Rick, together with Michael Britton, and Uli Spalthoff. Without their loving support, my life path and work would be impossible to even imagine. This fellowship, of which I am the founding president, with Linda as its director, has close to 1,000 invited members, more than 6,000 people on its address list, and 40,000 people from more than 180 countries who read the website humiliationstudies.org. Please meet the members of our Global Advisory Board, Global Core Team, Global Research Team, and Global Education Team on www.humiliationstudies.org. You will hear the voices of many of them in this book. You will see how this book is constituted of many gifts, gifts of insights given to me by this vast global network of friends. Because of that, this is not a book *about* a topic, it is a journey co-created *with* people, and I wish to express my deepest gratitude to the hundreds of people who extended their loving support. The reader will notice that many endnotes represent little love letters, and these letters are meant for all, not just for those mentioned by name. Expressions of appreciation are central to this book, to my life path, and to my work in general, as I aim to dignify our relationships in this world.

Genocide and terrorism are part of my work on humiliation since its inception in 1996. I was asked to write this book on humiliation and terrorism in 2010 and it took me a while to get used to the thought. I was in doubt as to whether I would be able to produce anything that could be useful. This book has therefore had a very difficult birth, and I have no words to thank all those who did not give up on me, who continued giving me courage to stay on this very difficult journey.

I began studying humiliation and dignity in 1996, when I was preparing a four-year doctoral research project at the University of Oslo on *The Feeling of Being Humiliated: A Central Theme in Armed Conflicts* (1997 – 2001). The project was designed to study the role of humiliation in the genocidal mass killings in Somalia in 1988 and in Rwanda in 1994, with Nazi Germany as a background. I am deeply grateful to the Psychology Department at the University of Oslo, to the Royal Norwegian Ministry of Foreign Affairs, and the Norwegian Research Council, for their commitment to this critical issue. Without their support, nothing of what followed in the subsequent years would have been possible. And without the support of the Norwegian Non-Fiction Literature Fund in 2011, this book would not have come into being either.

I owe profound gratitude also to my friends outside of Norway. In the United States, I wish to convey my deep-felt thanks to Morton Deutsch of Columbia University for his untiring support. He authored the Forewords for my first two books and organized our first Workshop on Transforming Humiliation and Violent Conflict at Teachers College in 2003. Also in this case, without his support, and the support of his wonderful colleagues, the work that followed is unthinkable. Please see www.humiliation studies.org for our conferences.

It is also a great privilege for me to be associated with the Maison des Sciences de l'Homme in Paris since 2001, initially through social psychologist Serge Moscovici. The first two conferences of Human Dignity and Humiliation Studies were inspired and hosted by Hinnerk Bruhns, and supported by Michel Wieviorka, at the Maison des Sciences in 2003 and 2004. By now, we have organized almost 30 conferences, all around the world, and they are unconceivable without the initial support from the Maison des Sciences de l'Homme.

On my path since 1996, I have received most generous support from hundreds of academicians and practitioners in anthropology, history, philosophy, political science, psychology, and sociology, and if I were to list them all here, this would fill many pages. I am simply without words, filled with infinite gratitude. Please see www.humiliation studies.org for our global dignity fellowship.

I also owe my insights into psychological dynamics to the clients who came to me in my capacity as a clinical psychologist, from 1980 to 1984 in Hamburg, Germany, and from 1984 to 1991 in Cairo, Egypt, before I moved on to social psychology and macro levels in general as my main focus. I am deeply indebted to all of them for being my "co-searchers for health." I extend equally warm thanks to all of my interlocutors and hosts all around the world, many of whom have to struggle daily to carry on with their work of dignity, often under the most difficult circumstances, not seldom threatened for life. Perhaps you would like to read more about my global life path on our website.[1]

I would like to end by conveying my profound love and gratitude to my parents Gerda and Paul Lindner, whose personal courage gave my work and life its direction and motivation. Also many others have become family to me throughout the past decades. Linda Hartling, for instance, is one of those who is more than a sister to me. In the spirit of *ubuntu, I am because of all of them*. Their voices can be heard throughout this book, and in their appraisals. Here are a few voices, representative for many (for more see the book's website):

Terrorism is a problem that needs to be reframed before it can be resolved. Evelin Lindner proposes a way to reframe it: as a clash of tradition with modernity. She proposes general principles for resolving it, and she spells them out drawing on her vast wealth of on-the-ground experience: Keep modernity´s promises by making human rights real, especially social rights like the right to livelihood. Extend traditional norms of caring for those who belong to your family or your community, to all your sisters and brothers who live with you on this blue planet that Martin Luther King Jr. called our "world house." Doing what is necessary to cure today's epidemics of terrorism is not easy or simple or fast, but it is possible. Reading this book is a good way to begin.

– Howard Richards, Research Professor of Philosophy, Earlham College, U.S.A., and Chile.

Breathtaking in its vision, meticulously researched and powerfully written, this book brings our world's struggles over dominance into sharp focus as the force driving terror in a century when global interconnectedness marked by the dignity of all parties is within reach. If you are looking for a realistic path forward, you'll find it here. This book's take on terror is so surprising, so unexpected, so profoundly compassionate and understanding of our common humanness and our needs for dignity and pulling together, it is extraordinarily insightful, promising and helpful.

– Michael Britton, Peace Psychologist, New Jersey, U.S.A.

Evelin Lindner insists in her new book *Honor, Humiliation, and Terror* on an holistic approach to terrorism. By encouraging us all to keep the image of the Blue Planet as seen from the astronaut's perspective upfront in our heads, she convincingly talks about the needs of this beautiful, unique and fragile planet of ours. The overreaction or counterproductive reaction to terrorism takes away focus from the real challenges to the survival of humanity and to the planet. It also entails a misuse for military purposes of the natural and human resources that are needed in order to reach the 17 Sustainable Development Goals of the UN. To obtain a life in dignity for all would entail a new way of thinking and acting, new production and consumption patterns based both on sustainability and solidarity. The UNESCO and UN vision of culture of peace, may, if enacted, help guide our path.

– Ingeborg Breines, former Co-President of the International Peace Bureau (IPB), former Director of Women and a Culture of Peace at UNESCO, and Special Adviser to the Director-General on Women, Gender and Development.

Introduction

To understand is to perceive patterns.

– Isaiah Berlin, social and political theorist, philosopher, and historian (1909 – 1997)[1]

For the first time since the origin of our species, humanity is in touch with itself.

– William Ury, anthropologist[2]

For the first time in history, humankind has the capacity of destroying its own future within a few generations. Ecological collapse has joined weapons of mass destruction as one of the two greatest perils of the Anthropocene. Irreversible disruption of the biosphere has shifted from the unimaginable to the plausible, with little sign that the necessary political will and institutional transformation will materialize in time to avert the possible demise of life-sustaining ecosystems.

– Allen White, expert on sustainability strategy, policy, tools, and standards, July 13, 2015[3]

The discourses of both, Islam and the West, have their internal theoretical consistency, yet, in their practice, both betray their own ideals. The West is unfaithful to its own values, which disqualifies it in the eyes of the people it claims to acculturate to democracy. The Arab-Muslim world no longer has neither the legitimacy of the family nor the patriotic legitimacy around which it was historically structured.

– Amin Maalouf, Lebanese-born French author[4]

First they ignore you, then they ridicule you, then they fight you, then you win.

– Mahatma Gandhi

Sometimes, I use the image of the sinking Titanic. The wealthy have their cabins on the upper luxury deck, where they dance and feast, while trying to hinder the poor from the lower decks to come up. They overlook that the poor may possess wisdom that could save Titanic from sinking. The poor have one dream: getting to the first floor. They try migration, or, in the worst case, some of them express their anger in terrorist attacks. All the while nobody notices that the entire ship goes down. And this, while those on the luxury upper floor are the primary holders of the material resources necessary to turn around the ship to avert the iceberg, even if only in the last minute. Those on the luxury upper floor do not notice the holes in the hull and the fire in the basement, and they are oblivious of the collision with the iceberg that is imminent. They feel safe behind the iron gates that separate the luxury floor from the rest. They have the illusion that simply blocking these gates harder will guarantee their safety. They paint their cabins pink and divert themselves by accumulating possessions and seeking entertainment thrills. Then they accuse the messengers, the scientists, of delivering over-dramatizing calls to wake up. It is therefore that scientists no longer dare to speak.

This scenario describes the proverbial "ship of fools."[5] The peak of foolishness is reached when fighting over access to the first floor makes the ship go down ever faster. There are not enough voices who call out that nobody is exempted from drowning: No money, no sense of entitlement, no resolve to be victorious can save only "me," while the rest goes down. Self-interest converges with common interest in a situation where either all drown or none. In a first step the ship would need to be reconfigured so all are included, have a voice, and can contribute to solution-seeking dialogue conducted in respect for each other's equality in dignity, rather than being caught in relational illiteracy or, even worse, mutual mistrust and violent cycles of humiliation.

Among climate scientists "gloom has set in": things are much worse than we think. But since people refuse to listen, the scientists "can't really talk about it."[6] Messengers of bad news are often accused of having psychological problems, of suffering from hysterical fear, or of lack of enthusiasm for progress. And for making "strange choices." In my case, I was born into the luxury floor, I am not one of those who live in the lower floors and try to crawl up. Why do I then not stay up and shut up? Why do I not at least limit myself to some charity and collect some money from the rich to give to the poor? Why do I tell the rich that they need to come out of their cabins and take responsibility? Because I would humiliate myself if I enjoyed myself on the first floor oblivious of the imminent catastrophe. I wish to go out, find my way to the bridge, face cold water and storm and the horror of the looming iceberg.

In this dire situation, are terrorism and humiliation important topics to write books about? Indeed, books on terrorism should better not be written if they were to abuse the topic for ulterior goals. The topic of terrorism is wide open to being overplayed and underplayed for ulterior goals. For instance, it can be overplayed to create fear in society, so as to prepare the ground for the curtailment of civil rights. The humiliation argument is as open to being instrumentalized. This book is being written in full awareness of the many possible pitfalls. It starts from the assumption that the topic of terror and terrorism, and of humiliation, is important when it is framed as "canary in the coal mine" (see Preface), a canary that wakes up Titanic's passengers and helps them rescue the ship from sinking, in other words, as "canary on the Titanic."

The link with humiliation is a crucial connection to be explored. Just to give one example: When there is no credible defense against nuclear terrorism,[7] and humiliation can drive terrorism, then sincere attention to the link between terrorism and humiliation is needed. I am writing these sentences in a house that is fifteen kilometers away from a nuclear power plant where local residents just went to court to have it closed down, not least because it is not protected against terrorist attacks.[8] In other words, I am fifteen kilometers away from possible extinction through humiliation, from a humiliation bomb.

Much is known about terrorism, considerable funds have been extended to combat it. Less is known about the motives behind the use of terror, particularly behind what is called "radicalization." As to the phenomenon of humiliation, it is known to everybody as a lived experience. The connection between terror and humiliation is perhaps the least explored. This book attempts to begin to shed light on this connection. And it does so in a very broad manner, starting far back in human history, based on the author's preference for transdisciplinary analysis, a preference motivated by forty years of global living.

This book is the first volume of a larger book project titled *Humiliation and Terror*, however, it is also a stand-alone book. As briefly mentioned in the Preface, the book project has been designed in three volumes, each consisting of three sections. This is the first volume, which describes how, throughout the past millennia, spreading terror was accepted as a legitimate tool for dominating others and gaining honor and glory, and how this mindset is still prevalent in large parts of the world today. The second volume is envisioned to trace how, over time, terror came to be seen as the very opposite, namely, as an unacceptable tool to gain dignity, as part of an unacceptable culture of domination. The dignity message is presently on the rise, despite continuous serious setbacks, setbacks at times so significant that the dignity gained risk being lost again entirely. The third volume is planned to look at the future. It will address how only a global citizens movement can be strong enough to create a culture of dignity.[9] The future will be characterized by care for our human family and its habitat, a family where all members are respected as equals in dignity and rights, a family united in diversity and respect for the limits of its ecological basis of livelihood. The third volume carries the uplifting message, based on forty years of the author's global experience, that a world citizens movement is possible, and that it can gather the strength to overcome present-day arrangements, arrangements that lead to our planet's resources being depleted, inequality to rise, and unity be pushed into uniformity and diversity degraded into division.

This is Volume I that looks at the past, and how it is still relevant today. As time and resources might not allow me to finalize volume I and II, this volume has been expanded to comprise elements of all three. It speaks of the *security dilemma*, and how horrific a dilemma this is, with terror as its essence. Its motto is: *If you want peace, prepare for war.*[10] Terror became part and parcel of human culture on all continents throughout the past millennia, part of the emotional fabric of culture. Men were trained to stay alert for defense, while women were sent into the house to ensure a next generation would grow up.[11] This book shows how this mindset still characterizes the world, even in Western societies that profess the opposite. "Seapeople" ended the Bronze Age. Rome was attacked from all sides. The Huns, the Mongols the Vikings suddenly appeared on the horizon like thunder storms. The Spanish destroyed the Inca Empire. Civilizations were brutally destroyed. Now, physicist Stephen Hawking advises to stop all SETI activities, all Search for Extraterrestrial Intelligence, because he fears that, if these efforts were to work, how can we be sure that not similar hordes of raiders and conquerors find their way to planet Earth from outer space?[12]

Volume II and II acknowledge, that today, for the first time, there is a window of opportunity to change both the reality and culture of terror. However, we need to understand that we have to proactively and intentionally create this new situation.[13] If not, cultural inertia will close the window of opportunity again.[14] We have to quickly overcome any "future shock" even though "too much change in too short a period of time" will be necessary to bring about.[15] We have to constructively address the fact that "the human mind changes much slower than material circumstances. It limps at least three or four generations behind, clinging to outdated ideas and ideals, while political, economic and military realities race ahead."[16] Particularly men will have to learn to live without the danger that their honor traditionally depended on, and refrain from creating artificial danger in order to recreate a familiar arena for their sense of honor. This is relevant for men in power and for men without power. Men without power would need to discontinue engaging in violence and terrorism to create terror, and men with power would need to discontinue waging "war against terror" to create counterterror. Men would also need to learn to accept that women who come out from their homes into the public sphere are not representing a danger, they do not have to be intimidated back into the house.

The entire book project acknowledges that considerable difficulties will have to be overcome on the journey away from humiliation and terror toward more dignity. Also, clearly, no culture of dignity will ever eradicate all terror. Psychological damage from trauma, for instance, will always lead some people to wanting to terrorize others, not to mention that terror can also emerge as an unintended side effect of otherwise well-intentioned actions.[17] Yet, what a new culture of dignity can do, is remove system-inherent humiliation and terror.

The structure of this book project follows anthropologist William Ury's a "simplified depiction of history," where he pulls together elements from anthropology, game theory, and conflict studies to describe three major types of society in chronological order: simple hunter-gatherers, complex agriculturists, and the current knowledge society.[18] I use Ury's historical periods to insert pride, honor, and dignity. I do that in the spirit of sociologist Max Weber's *ideal-type* approach, which allows for analysis and action to proceed at different levels of abstraction.[19] I label the first 95 per cent of human history, when foraging dominated and circumscription did not yet set limits for migration, as the *era of pride*, or, more precisely, the *era of pristine untouched pride*. I call the past five per cent of human history, the period of complex agriculturalism, the *era of honor*, or, more precisely, the *era of collectivist ranked honor*. I work for a future of dignity, a vision for the future of humankind that is inspired by human rights ideals, and I call this the *era of dignity*, or, more accurately, a *future of equality in dignity for all, as individuals, in solidarity*.

I have coined the word *egalization* to match the word *globalization* and differentiate it from phrases such as equality or equity.[20] The term egalization is short for equal dignity for all and avoids claiming that everybody should become equal and that there should be no differences between people. Equal dignity can perfectly well coexist with a hierarchy that regards all participants as possessing equal dignity; it cannot coexist with a hierarchy that defines some people as lesser beings and others as higher beings. The pilots in a plane, for instance, are masters over their passengers when in the sky, and clear hierarchy and stark inequality characterize this situation. This does not mean, however, that the pilot team now has to look down on their passengers as lesser beings.[21]

If we imagine the human world as a container with a height and a width, globalization addresses the horizontal dimension, the shrinking width. Egalization concerns the vertical dimension. Egalization is a process away from a very high container of masters at the top and underlings at the bottom, toward a flat container with everybody enjoying equal dignity in solidarity.

The horizontal line in Figure 1 represents the line of equal dignity in shared humility. This line does not signify that all human beings are equal, or should be equal, or ever were or will be equal, or identical, or all the same. The horizontal line illustrates a worldview that resists *rankism*, meaning that secondary differences are not essentialized and not ranked into differences at the core of human worthiness.[22]

Egalization means inviting masters to step down from arrogating superior worth, and encouraging subordinates to rise up from humiliation, up from being held down and given lesser value. Masters are being humbled and underlings elevated, and all are entrusted to co-create, together, a new future of equality in dignity for all.

Clearly, masters, those in privileged positions in society, if they wish to save their privileges, will resist the call to adopt a new humility. They can do so openly, or by hijacking the discourse of equal dignity as a cover for inequality in praxis. Masters who openly suppress such calls will argue that they are entitled to their privileges and that they cannot accept the humiliation of humility; supremacists will defend their arrogation of supremacy against attempts to humble them by crying out "humiliation!" Covert resistors have many covers to hide behind, for instance, they can make ideals independent from reality or distort ideals into strawmen to make them appear aversive. Even the most benevolent idea, such as that of equal dignity, may be used to maintain inequality. The oppressed underling may be told, for example, that he is equal in dignity with the master, that he should therefore "coexist peacefully" with the master and refrain from demanding systemic humiliation to be abolished.[23] The strawman approach was used, for instance, when slavery was about to be abolished and it was forecast that this would lead to the breakdown of society and that slaves would be psychologically unable to handle freedom anyway. Even such well-intentioned ideas as a basic income for all may serve as a cover for inequality.[24]

Equal dignity means equal chances to unfold diversity, and this presupposes a certain amount and a certain kind of equality on the ground, whereby equality is not to be confused with uniformity. The confusion of equality with uniformity is a popular strawman. Dignity is not truly equal in a context of unequal chances. Equal chances make diversity possible, which is the opposite of uniformity. "Equal dignity should not be misconstrued as a strategy to equalize individuals through social conformity."[25]

This book project follows the timeline of the transition to egalization: Volume I attends to the era of honor, Volume II shall focus on the presently unfolding transition toward dignity, including the dilemma that arises when dignity slides into irreconcilable opposition to honor, and Volume III will explore strategies for creating dignified futures.

Peace linguist Francisco Gomes de Matos admonishes: "Academic books tend to end their chapters too conventionally."[26] In response to his call, this book includes "thought-provoking questions" for in-depth reflection and research. This is to inspire dialogue that is both dignified and dignifying – or *dignilogue*, a term coined by Gomes de Matos.

The book presents vignettes and examples from my global life experience and when I do so, I usually protect the identity of people by paraphrasing and summarizing, except where I obtained consent. My global life is embedded into many linguistic contexts, and I translate examples into English sometimes without indicating what the original language was (I think, speak, and write in four languages continuously, and are familiar with many more).

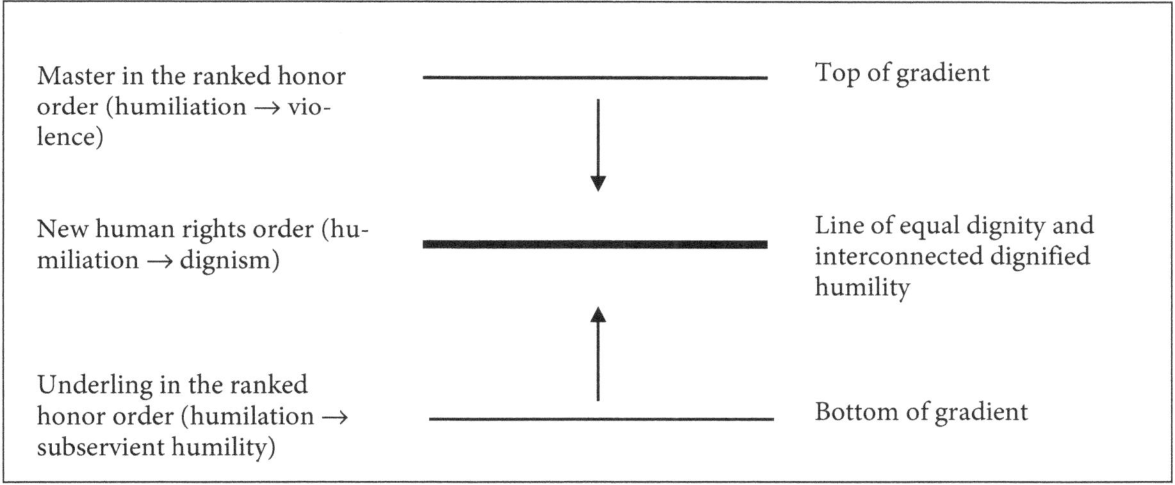

Figure 1: The historical transition to egalization

This book project is intended for an audience interested in reflecting on humanity's future. It also speaks to interested scholars and students in the field of public policy planning. It is written for those who wish to reduce terror around the world, in whatever form it might appear. It is also written for those who use and support terror tactics, including those who feel justified in fighting terror with terror. After reading, hopefully, all will see that we live in historical times so novel that terror tactics are no longer only unethical, the new situation turns terror into an impractical and ineffective tool even for those who believe in its legitimacy. In an interconnected world, the path of a Mahatma Gandhi or Nelson Mandela achieves more than the Hitler path; in a world where interdependence overrides the traditional dichotomy of dependence versus independence, the Freire-Mandela-Gandhi path addresses grievances and humiliation more effectively than retaliation with humiliation for humiliation could ever achieve. Domination as a strategy was part and parcel of the world as long as the choice was only between independence and dependence; in an interconnected world, methods of domination, including that of terror, lose the feasibility they once had.[27] This book invites all parties dealing with terror to recognize that times have changed and that more effective pathways are available. With respect to responding to humiliation and expressing feelings of humiliation, the better paths are those that aim at inclusive dignity. This book ends with a "letter to America," reminding the United States, as a superpower, that they carry a particular responsibility for the entire world.

This book project is undertaken with the kind of "tough love" that I call for in my 2010 book on gender, humiliation, and global security.[28] Desmond Tutu wrote in the Foreword to that book:

> My dear friend Nelson Mandela could have followed the example of Rwanda's Hutu leadership· He would certainly have had the power to unleash genocide on the white elite in South Africa. He did not. He chose inclusiveness rather than humiliating domination and he chose humility rather than arrogant revenge. I once said in an interview: "I think this is what we've got to say to white people of this country: You don't know how lucky you are."[29]

This book project also follows the call of peace psychologist Michael Britton, who admonished me on February 7, 2015:

> I think this book cannot be written by the mind. It must be written by the heart. The heart must hold the pen, use the hand to do write its message, with the mind standing by to be of assistance, but only that, not in charge. This is what speaks to people, I think, the heart communicating to their hearts ... with only enough mind data and ideas to help their minds be of assistance to their hearts. It is a calling out of the heart within the heart, the heart within the perimeter parts of the heart that have become a wall, frozen, hardened or on fire with hate and the like. It is the message that helps melt and dissolve all that, and that reaches to the heart within, the heart that grasps equal dignity, that feels only equality, that has compassion for ourselves and therefore also deeply for others and their journeys, that's what I think makes a book eloquent and touching, moving with the possibility that people may move into action in new ways – or into the stillness that ends old ways of acting and makes space for new ways to emerge.[30]

Tough love requires radical understanding, which necessitates radical empathy, which, in turn, cannot be achieved without radical respect. Hannah Arendt, in her discussion of the moral dilemmas presented by the Jewish Holocaust, suggested an extreme category of evil, more extreme than the Kantian definition of evil.[31] The Kantian moral imperative defines it as evil if one treats others as means to achieve some end, rather than treating them as ends in themselves. Arendt felt that *radical evil* goes further. The victims of Auschwitz were neither means to some end, nor an end in themselves; the victims were regarded as valueless and useless objects that were superfluous and expandable.

If this is so, can radical evil ever be forgiven, and if yes, under which conditions?[32] My experience as a therapist indicates that the dehumanization of the Jews that Arendt alludes to, a dehumanization that was later also meted out against others, for instance the Tutsi in the Rwandan genocide, has intricate underlying psychological dynamics.[33] To my observation, people who dehumanize others struggle with a very counterintuitive problem: they do not succeed in convincing themselves of their own claim that those others are actually worthless. They obsessively attempt to believe it, because it would be a relief for them to be able to do so. Yet, do truly useless objects merit such attention and such hatred? Why was so much effort invested into eradicating useless objects? Because they were not really seen as useless. I observe something very unexpected underlying this dynamic, namely, admiration for the power of the enemy, and fear of this power. Declaring a powerful enemy to be useless is an instrument of ultimate humiliation out of overwhelming fear, based on admiration. In this sense, the victims indeed are means to some end, and also an end in themselves. Understanding this, to me, is applying radical empathy to radical evil. And there can be no forgiveness, not least because the notion of forgiveness entails the illusion of closure. Something much more difficult and radical than forgiveness is needed, in my view, namely, the shouldering of the radical collective responsibility that all of us are called on to carry together if we want to create the proverbial village that it takes to raise a child. This book is written with this radical sense of empathy and responsibility.

In my work, I do not claim that humiliation always leads to violence and terrorism, nor that violence and terrorism always originate in humiliation. I also acknowledge that the humiliation-terrorism argument is being used to legitimize or delegitimize, rightly or falsely, claims that terrorists are in fact heroic freedom fighters, or, inversely, that terror is a declaration of war that requires war-like responses.

All questions are taken seriously in this book: Are people who use terror tactics terrorists? Or heroic liberators and defenders of freedom? If terrorists, are they evil? If evil, is their evilness cold-blooded or hot-blooded, rational or irrational? Are terrorists cowards or brave? Is spreading terror their main aim that they enjoy, or collateral damage they regret? Or are they insane psychopaths incapable of rational thinking? Or do they simply lack the personal capacity to understand that less violent strategies would be more appropriate? Are terrorists to be "taken out," "flushed out," crushed and eradicated like pests? What about state terror? And is terrorism a credible danger? Or is war on terror, or "countering violent extremism,"[34] simply a cover-up to curtail civil and political freedoms and a pretext for an overblown military industry?[35] Or is terrorism an underestimated danger? Can terror be fomented unwittingly through thoughtless negligence?

This book project's main "answer" is to formulate such questions differently. Many books dealing with terrorism are very detailed. They "zoom in," so to speak, and this is very valuable. This book project "zooms out" and attempts to make large-scale patterns visible that may be lost when the focus is on familiar details. From a distance, unfamiliar details may become interesting and the book will then zoom in on them. As philosopher Isaiah Berlin said: "To understand is to perceive patterns."[36]

As mentioned in the Preface, I draw on a global transcultural experience of forty years. This enables me to apply large-scale psycho-geo-historical lenses to contextualize contemporary phenomena. What interests me is the punctuation of history. Only in hindsight do we use terms such as Nazi Germany, or apartheid, and only in hindsight are these terms clear enough so that no further explanation is needed. Today, these terms encapsulate the awareness that these were moments of historic failure, moments when humankind ought to have stood up rather than stood by.[37] While it went on, the majority of people concentrated on business-as-usual, few were aware that emergency was unfolding that required extraordinary resistance. Many simply wished to be left undisturbed by "undue" dramatization, hoping that the promises of those in power, those who pushed the agenda of the day, would turn out to be right with their promises of a brighter future and that all sacrifices toward that goal would be worth it.

What I see is that we live in similar times now. What has crystallized throughout my global life is a kind of *Leitmotiv* of present-day affairs that connects all continents. What I see manifesting everywhere is a gigantic struggle surrounding the transition from a divided world driven by the *dominator* model of society, to use the terminology of social scientist Riane Eisler,[38] to an interconnected world that understands that only the *partnership* model is feasible. Eisler is a social scientist and activist, who has developed a cultural transformation theory, through which she describes how during the past millennia otherwise widely divergent societies all over the globe followed what she calls the dominator model of society, rather than a partnership model.[39] In my terminology, it is the transition away from traditional ranked honor, to the equality in dignity that human rights ideals promise, away from higher-born beings presiding over lesser beings, toward a world where everybody is ranked as equal in worthiness.

At this particular historical point, what I see happening, is that one of those models seems to be winning, paradoxically, under the guise of the other. Wherever I go, on all continents, I see inequality on the rise, which means that the dominator paradigm succeeds in praxis, yet, ironically, often promoted by partnership rhetoric.[40] I witness human rights defenders working ever harder and achieving some progress, yet, in balance, the social fabric is being hollowed out and natural resources exploited more than ever.[41] I see human rights talk and partnership rhetoric being abused to provide an ideological façade for a reality that manifests the stark opposite. A glitzy party is thrown on credit, so to speak, a party for a few at the expense of the many and of future generations. Many are so dazzled by the glitz of the party, or at least by the promise of glitz, that they are successfully coopted. Understandably, those who benefit from the party praise it as if it were sustainable, they are victims of a *positivity bias*.[42] Yet, slowly, ever more people "know enough to prefer not to know."[43] As mentioned in the Preface, I predict that our time once will be called "the dark era of the 21st century," an era where the dominator model overstayed its *raison-d'être*, and social and ecological resources were sold out under the pretense of the partnership model.

Terror has its particular place in this situation. During the past millennia, almost everywhere on the globe, terror was widely used and accepted as a legitimate strategy to keep one's enemies out and one's own people down. Terror was employed to stay safe from neighboring enemies and to create and maintain traditional hierarchies within dominator societies of collectivist ranked honor. In times when the choice was only between independence and dependence, human rights ideals fitted badly. This has changed now; at least in rhetoric those ideals are increasingly being acknowledged, however, praxis has not yet adapted much.

In official parlance, tactics of terror are by now being widely condemned. Many see them as a violation rather than a solution, at least in the so-called democratic world. In reality, the use of schemes such as "waterboarding," or the kidnapping of foreigners in so-called renditions, have continued to violate international human rights standards, as much as does the ongoing plundering of the planet's resources. What still needs to be understood is that in an interconnected world those old strategies no longer work, and that keeping them alive artificially is not just shortsighted or unwise; it is dangerous. Terror transmutes not just from an acceptable path to honor into an unacceptable path to dignity, it also transmutes from a possible path to *military* security for a group or nation into an impossible path to *human* security for all of humanity.[44]

Rather than grasping the new reality of interconnectedness and interdependence, many still live as if the past were not bygone. This is understandable, since too many small-scale changes at the surface make it difficult to discern the significance and novelty of the new situation. A digitalized image flood masks the paradigm-changing importance of the one important revolutionary image, namely, the astronaut's view of the Blue Planet that invites us to see ourselves from outside for the first time.[45]

As part of this slowness, many maintain doubts that stem from a bygone past. For instance, around the globe, I meet people who doubt that global friendship is possible; they believe that it is naïve to expect that humans will ever be capable of global solidarity. I have invested forty years of global living into testing this question. My experience indicates that human nature indeed is open to global friendship. I like to offer doubters the following proverb: "The person who says 'it cannot be done' should not interrupt the person doing it."[46] Standing by in passivity is problematic. Even more problematic is it, when people actively and artificially maintain a past that ought to be left bygone. We know that relationships play a crucial role for the well-being of people,[47] and we know that humankind can only face its global challenges in global cooperation. Why should we give up, before even having tried, give up the golden opportunity we now have to invite a divided species of *Homo sapiens* into a global dignity family?

It seems to me that the so-called attribution error is being committed at a historical scale now, meaning that intrinsic and extrinsic factors are being misattributed.[48] Humankind did not embrace enmity and belligerence easily; it was forced into it by the so-called security dilemma, a dilemma that holds people in a brutal grip (I will explain more in Chapter 1). Yet, in a situation where the security dilemma is weaker, people are liberated from seeking military security and can embrace human security. Global interconnectedness has the potential to weaken the security dilemma; it is a radical game changer. Torturing the planet and each other no longer renders victory and success; it comes back in kind, like a boomerang. Human rights ideals encapsulate the adaptations that humankind is now called on to bring about, however, only if these ideals are being manifested in praxis, not just in empty rhetoric. In this situation, it is not simply negligent, it is dangerous to disparage human rights ideals, or to engage in empty human rights rhetoric, be it out of ignorance, hypocrisy, or cynicism.[49] Paying lip service to human rights ideals only to cover up for strategies of domination is not only inherently contradictory, unconscionable, and deceitful, it is dangerous.

The first paragraph of Article 1 of the Universal Declaration of Human Rights, which was adopted by the United Nations General Assembly on December 10, 1948, could also be read as a definition of what Riane Eisler calls the partnership model of society: "All human beings are born free and equal in dignity and rights. They are endowed with reason and conscience and should act towards one another in a spirit of brotherhood (and sisterhood)." The dominator model of society was built on a different version of this sentence, namely, "All human beings are born unequal in dignity and rights. Some are endowed with more reason and conscience and should act towards inferiors in a spirit of superiority." Or, another version: "All human beings are born unequal in worthiness and rights – all people are born into their rank and they are meant to stay there, only some might move up or down due to their own doing or undoing – and, as an unavoidable consequence, there will always be some who are more free than others, there will always be elites who preside over their subordinate collectives."

Riane Eisler's choice of words – dominator versus partnership – I find very suitable. Throughout the decades of my global living, my observations have resonated with her terminology. I have observed human worthiness and value be measured in two profoundly different ways, which, if applied rigorously, are mutually exclusive.[50] On one side, I see the worthiness of people be measured on a ranking scale from high to low – with divinity at the top and dirt at the bottom – this is the dominator model. On the other side, I see the ranking of human worthiness on this kind of scale being rejected, this is the partnership model.[51] As mentioned earlier, I have chosen to give the label of *honor* to the dominator model, or, more precisely, *collectivistic ranked honor*, while I assign the label *dignity* to the partnership model, or, more precisely, *respect for equal dignity for all, as individuals, in solidarity*. The process from the first to the second model I call *egalization*. To illustrate how honor and dignity can slide into mutually exclusive positions, I often use the example of honor killing: in one context the girl must die, in the other she can live (more later).[52]

By deciding on defining honor and dignity in such specific ways in my work, I draw on a basic insight in semiotics, namely, that meanings do not reside in words.[53] Philosopher Jacques Derrida spoke of *différance*.[54] Words are associated with meanings through socially constructed rules of correspondence between signifiers and meanings. "Culturally encoded meanings can be widely shared or widely contested among diverse people, and they can be relatively fixed or relatively fluid across time."[55] By assigning honor and dignity such precise places in my work, I exercise my linguistic right to label the cultural codes in the way I see them work in the world. I continue, however, to use the verb "to honor" in less conceptually circumscribed ways in other contexts, for instance, when I want to honor people with my respect.

In my work, I use the interpretive frame[56] of dignity and humiliation to reconstruct the core aspects of different fields, and so far, I have done this with war and genocide (2000),[57] international conflict (2006 and 2009),[58] gender and security (2010),[59] and economics (2012).[60] In using dignity and humiliation as interpretative frame, I follow anthropologist and social scientist Gregory Bateson (1904 – 1980) and his concept of interpretive frames in the social sciences.[61] Also sociologist Erving Goffman (1922 – 1982) described frames as cognitive schemata or mental frameworks that shape our perceptions, interpretations, and representations of reality, that mentally organize our experience, and that provide normative guides for our actions.[62] The concept of frames and framing has subsequently been used in different ways across the social and psychological sciences; yet, all assume that people rely on acquired structures of interpretation to make sense of an otherwise overwhelming amount of information and experience. Frames are the "conceptual scaffolding" that we rely on to construct our understanding of the world.[63]

The experience of humiliation is profoundly different in a dominator context as compared to a partnership context. Honor ranks people into "high-born" beings who preside over "lesser" beings in terms of submission/domination, in contrast to a partnership context, where people respect each other's equality in dignity and engage in respectful dialogue. Honor humiliation is part of a cultural script that entails the social pressure, or the "duty," to retaliate against violations of honor, whereas dignity humiliation rather awakes an inner urge to stand up in the face of violations of dignity. In honor contexts, the typical counterterrorism approach is eradication and repression – peace and security are defined in terms of enemies successfully being cleansed out and one's own people safely under control. In contrast, in social contexts that embrace the partnership of equality in dignity, peace is conceptualized as inclusive dialogue between equals, and countering terrorism focuses more on creating social conditions that prevent its emergence.

At present, the transition from honor codes to dignity norms affects almost all segments of society, locally as well as globally, and the humiliation-terrorism link is shaped according to the context in which it is embedded. Responses to terror in an honor context condone terror-for-terror, while this is irreconcilable with ideals of equal dignity. Responses grounded in human rights ideals, to be credible, have to be congruent with human rights values, which means that terror cannot be responded to with strategies that belong to the honor context.

This book project advocates a path to a terror-free world – at least free of the kind of terror that systems can prevent – through better *generative mechanisms*[64] and *constitutive rules*[65] for our *world-system*.[66] It calls on scholars to do their work, in particular sociologists, since "the proper object of study of sociology is not human actions. It is the social relations that pre-exist human actions and make them possible ... pre-existing social relations, concatenated in social structures."[67] It recommends to all parties to recognize that in an interconnected world an inclusive culture of dignity is not just superior to a culture of honor, it is the *only* option. And this means to strive for dignity in ways that are dignified and that have dignifying effects. Scholar Stephan Feuchtwang formulated succinctly how double standards cause double damage: "To recognize humanity hypocritically and betray the promise, humiliates in the most devastating way by denying the humanity professed."[68] The new reality of an interconnected world leaves only one feasible counterterror strategy on the table, namely, global efforts to manifest equal dignity for all, locally and globally, in rhetoric and in reality. Sympathizers of terror tactics will not be convinced to embrace a dignity culture if humiliated by double standards, on the contrary. Therefore I call for fully realizing human rights ideals and refraining from empty human rights rhetoric and double standards.

As explained in the Preface, I have coined the term *egalization* to signify the true realization of human rights ideals. I call for globalization to be humanized by egalization – in short, I call for a joint effort to reach *globegalization* – instead of accepting that globalization dehumanizes humanity through global domination and terror. I call for dignity-ism, or *dignism* to manifest unity in diversity in our world rather than division without unity. I call for new global institutions, for the globalization of care and solidarity to replace the current globalization of exploitation and oppressive uniformity, a globalization that allows for diversity, rather than divisive nationalisms.[69]

After WWII, the United Nations promised unity in diversity to heal a world fractured by war, it promised that "all human beings are born free and equal in dignity and rights." Unfortunately, this promise, and the expectations it created, was not taken seriously enough. Particularly during the past decades, a globalization of exploitation has increasingly undermined unity and replaced it with oppressive uniformity.[70] It may have begun with a corporate backlash against Rachel Carson and her message of the "silent spring,"[71] later being institutionalized by Ronald Reagan and Margaret Thatcher.[72] By now we see a new backlash, a populist backlash against the corporate backlash. Populists now lead an uprising against so-called elites. This would be a beneficial backlash if it meant saving global unity in diversity from global uniformity. Yet, it risks re-fracturing the world again, driving diversity toward hostile division.[73]

As my experience indicates, true unity in diversity can only be achieved through a globalization of care and solidarity, and through the insight that unity in diversity is a never-ending process, a balancing act that must be calibrated by continuous dialogue, rather than the outdated oscillation from one extreme to the other by way of violence and oppression. Letting unity degrade into rigid uniformity at first, only to turn it into violent division, and from there back to uniformity again, is foolish.

To benefit from the opportunities entailed in interconnectedness, new institutions of unity in diversity must unite in equal dignity for diversity and guard against global uniformity as much as against global division. Such global institutions will enable the global community to overcome bygone cultural scripts and learn to practice the Freire-Mandela-Gandhi way of healing humiliation and approaching terrorism through *understanding rather than condoning* and *respecting rather than appeasing* (Gandhi's term *satyāgraha* is assembled from *agraha* or firmness/force and *satya* or truth-love).[74]

Many questions guide my research on humiliation and dignity.[75] Here come some of the questions devised in 1996. I would like to ask these questions also now, ask those who sympathize with terrorism, as well as those who oppose it and who wish to prevent it:

- How do you define humiliation?
- Have you yourself ever felt humiliated, and if yes, how?
- How is humiliation felt and acted upon in different cultural contexts?
- How is humiliation felt and acted upon in different historical periods?
- How do meta-emotions influence experiences of humiliation?
- Do feelings of humiliation always lead to violence? Or only under certain circumstances? If yes, under which circumstances?
- Do feelings of humiliation always entail feelings of shame? Is there a difference between humiliation and shame?
- What is the difference between humiliation and humility?
- What about the role of anger?
- Is there a difference between the humiliation of honor and the humiliation of dignity?
- Is there a difference between humiliation at a group level and humiliation at the individual level?
- Which humiliation is more salient, that of one's reference group, or one's own personal humiliation?
- Does it make a difference if the humiliation is witnessed by others, and, if so, by whom?
- Is there a difference between humiliations experienced during childhood as compared to adult life?
- Is there a gender perspective to how humiliation is felt, perceived, experienced, judged, and acted on?
- How does a terrorist/violent freedom fighter feel about the killing and maiming of people who have nothing to do, at least not directly and immediately, with his/her humiliation and pain?
- Does humiliation play a role in terrorism/violent freedom fighting?
- Is there an element of vengeance in actions that inflict terror?
- Can terror create a better world, either here or in the hereafter?
- Does violence beget violence?
- Are there more effective ways than violence for achieving political goals, even against ruthless opponents?
- What is needed to defuse terrorism that emerged from humiliation?

In 1996, I began to prepare my doctoral research in Somalia and Rwanda, on the background of Nazi Germany.[76] Human Dignity and Humiliation Studies emerged from this work, starting in 2001. Psychologist Linda Hartling is the only scholar I am aware of who did her doctoral research on humiliation earlier than me.[77] She is now the director of Human Dignity and Humiliation Studies, while I am the founding president. On June 11, 2016, Linda Hartling devised the following tasks for our online doctoral course "Dignity Studies: An Introduction to the Dynamics of Dignity and Its Violation," at the Western Institute for Social Research in Berkeley, California, in cooperation with our World Dignity University initiative. Tasks for studying dignity and humiliation call for attention to:

- Analysis of the relationship between human dignity and humiliation
- Analysis of the relationship between globalization and humiliation/human dignity
- Differences and similarities of the concepts of shame, humiliation, and dignity
- Differences and similarities of the concepts of humility, humiliation, and dignity
- Differences and similarities of the concepts of equality, egalitarianism, equity, and equal dignity
- Analysis of the interaction between human dignity and human resilience

Also Alex Schmid, director of the Terrorism Research Initiative asks important questions that are relevant to this book project:

- Why do many share background characteristics of terrorists without becoming terrorist themselves?
- Why are well-educated, affluent, and apparently well-integrated individuals also susceptible to radicalization?
- Who is most vulnerable to radicalization?
- What is the role of the Internet in radicalization?
- Is Islamist radicalization different from other, more secular forms of radicalization?
- Are certain types of counterterrorism and repression causing (further) radicalization?
- Is radicalization taking place on both sides: among the defenders as well as the attackers?[78]

The author's background and approach

For decades, I have listened to my father's tales of history. He was born in 1926 and experienced Nazi Germany's rise and fall. Later, he studied its history to understand how the Nazi era ever could happen. He described to me in minute detail the step-wise take-over of state institutions by Adolf Hitler and his entourage.[79] Also after the war, trauma was not over for my father's family, as they lost their homeland, Schlesien (or Silesia) in Central Europe. They were forcibly displaced to Hamelin, near Hanover. He has said things such as: "I am a Silesian, Germany has destroyed my life, Hitler has raped me." While I write these sentences in my parents' house, I read about one such Nazi helper, Hartmann Lauterbacher, then Nazi Gauleiter of South Hanover-Braunschweig and fanatical SS Gruppenführer. Still on April 4, 1945, a few days before Allied troops reached Hanover, Lauterbacher went on radio and newspaper with the message "Better dead than slave" and he declared that "... those who hoist white flags and surrender without a fight, deserve death."[80]

Sometimes, I use traffic as a metaphor to illustrate how societies can be organized.[81] Traffic lights are meant to serve the common good by creating a level playing field. Equal dignity for all means that every driver has the same rights before traffic lights: the size of the vehicle, its color, and its price do not affect the driver's status or rights, neither whether the drivers like or dislike each other. All have to stop in front of a red light. What the German Nazi regime did, was hijacking the traffic lights so that a few big cars got through even at red traffic lights, and not just any big cars, but big cars whose drivers terrorized all others into joining them in perpetrating more terror, ultimately wreaking such havoc that it ended in suicidal mass homicide.

As many researchers point out, and as also my own global observations indicate, at the current point in history, humankind as a whole finds itself at a crossroad that is structurally similar – albeit in a more covert manner, since a clear leader figure is lacking: a "privatized monetary hegemony" is in the process of taking over institutions that ought to cater to the common good.[82] What I observe is a kind of "modern world terror" through de-solidarization.[83] Only those who live rather isolated in ghettos of wealth are not aware of it.[84] Sociologist Pierre Bourdieu coined the term *heteronomy* for situations where the autonomy of societal spheres is being hijacked by other spheres,[85] and it seems that this is happening now: the economic sphere is taking over the rest. With the election of Donald J. Trump as president of the United States, this trend might even increase, only in a different form, we might see a "turn from a neoliberal Wilsonian globalized system of trade and alliances to a Hobbesian nation-centered system organized by thug capital (oligarchs in Russia, hedge-fund and private-equity in the greater US)."[86] John Peter Berger, art critic, novelist, painter, and poet, formulated it as follows:

> What is distinct about today's global tyranny is that it's faceless. There's no Führer, no Stalin, no Cortés. Its workings vary according to each continent … but its overall pattern is the same, a circular pattern…. The division between the poor and the relatively rich becomes an abyss. Traditional restraints and recommendations are shattered. Consumerism consumes all questioning. The past becomes obsolete. Consequently people lose their selfhood, their sense of identity, and they then … find an enemy in order to define themselves. The enemy – whatever their ethnic or religious nomination – is always found among the poor.[87]

Born in 1954, I had the privilege of spending the first six years on a traditional farm in Europe, where I experienced a very high degree of community solidarity. Every person on the farm and in the village was embedded in community relationships that gave sufficient psychological anchorings so that jointly, all together, could afford to face an uncertain future.[88] If one uses the river as a metaphor for life, then swimming together in the flux of life offers safety even if events at the macro level are out of one's reach of control. In contemporary Western societies, this kind of solidarity has largely been lost since I was a child. And there seems to be little opposition. Almost everywhere on the globe, wherever I go, I see people aspiring to the Western way of life. It promises that owning material possessions will provide more safety and satisfaction than relating to others.[89]

What is the result? When I think back, I remember seeing how women first became increasingly isolated as "housewives" in their suburban "dream houses," and by now, the Western world is filled with lonely people.[90] I spent seven years in Cairo in Egypt (1984 – 1991), working as a psychological counselor and clinical psychologist, and this experience threw this Western trend into stark contrast for me. Two main groups of clients came to me: foreigners working or studying in Egypt, and Egyptians from traditional backgrounds. After seven years of experience, I could distill differences between my clients from the West and the non-Western clients that related to my own past. At the core of the life experience and pain of almost all of my Western clients was a sense of existential loneliness and *anomie*.[91] Indeed, loneliness now affects over forty percent of older adults in the U.S.[92] In contrast, this loneliness was unconceivable even as a concept for those of my Egyptian clients who had a traditional extended family and neighborhood around them. Those clients came to me with very different problems; they suffered from the fact that what is called "collectivism" can entail very detrimental aspects for mental health. I learned to appreciate, from inside, how the caring aspects of collectivism can offer a great sense of protected belonging, yet, how it can also become chokingly oppressive.[93] The latter happens when powerful family members abuse their influence for personal advantages, rather than working for the common good of all family members. To use the river metaphor again, those powerful abusers promise guaranteed safety to those who submissively align themselves behind them, and they inflict pain on those who do not.

Many of my Western clients, on their part, had given up swimming altogether and were attempting to cling to fixities, to the abstract rules of the market and its promises of status, safety, and happiness. Their psychological faring showed what every psychologist would predict, namely, that this kind of experiment is bound to fail. Market rules and material possessions are not only fickle and easily lost, they are also unable, even when at their best, to provide the same level of psychological anchoring and nurturing that community relationships can provide.

By now, also in Egypt, family networks and neighborhoods are increasingly being dissolved by Western culture's influx, often below awareness, despite of local culture, or in combination with it, or hidden behind its cover. Often this happens in ways that at first glance are not identifiable as such; my Egyptian friends report, for instance, that "modern" architecture now separates people and systemically destroys communal life.

As has dawned on me over time, throughout the sixty years of my life, humankind needs to progress from collective fatalistic swimming to a new kind of intentional and informed collective swimming. What is bound to fail is illusionary clinging, be it to power through traditional status or through money. Over time, I began to understand that even my own personal life path had passed through a similar learning curve. My personal journey went from being born into a displaced family who yearned for safety, first by looking for permanent safety, and only later following the Freire-Mandela-Gandhi path of intentionally daring to embark on the fluidity of co-creating social change.

I have met only very few people who were exposed to the sort of experiences – many of them painful – that now provide me with a global and transdisciplinary bird's eye perspective. Being born into a family that was forcibly displaced, a family deeply traumatized by war and displacement, I was not as smoothly socialized into the larger environment I was born into as the children of native inhabitants of that region. The resulting inner distance turned me into the proverbial child who sees the emperor without clothes.[94] Yet, unlike the child in the legend, for me, it took years to speak out loud. Children often assume that others are right and they are wrong, and for children born into a alienating identity like me, this effect is compounded. I was always unsure of what I saw. I was so aware of my own failings and shortcomings, that I initially would blame myself for not seeing what so many others seemed to see. Only over time, over the past decades, have I learned that my family's background of displacement may have provided me with a perspective that also has its advantages.[95] Surprisingly often, my observation that "the emperor has no clothes" turned out to be correct. At some point, I also found other "children" like me. In other words, I combine extreme caution, humility, and even fear, with a gaze that has proven to be worth sharing with others, despite of my hesitation.

I always saw myself as "emergent from a dynamic field of possibilities," rather than as a unified "subject," and was very happy to come across the work of Karen Barad on physicist Niels Bohr's insights.[96] Another physicist, Michio Kaku, uses lovely metaphors for those fields of possibilities.[97] Unsurprisingly, creative experimentation is what I engage in, rather than critique.[98] I resonate with equal dignity also in the ways philosophy and science are conducted,[99] and *nondualism* is my metaphysical orientation (I will explain more further down).

Displacement has provided me with caution and an inner distance, yet, over time, also with the courage to face both myself and the world at closer hold. It has given me a desire to promote "never again" – never again war, genocide, and displacement – a desire that made me live globally because I needed to develop a gut feeling for how people in different cultures define life and death, conflict and peace, love and hatred, and how they look at others.

Displacement provided me also with a deep comprehension of all expressions of rigidification and polarization, of why people become vulnerable, vulnerable to preferring uniformity in division over unity in diversity, what makes them wish to belong inside an "inverted refrigerator" – inside warm and outside cold[100] - in defiance of "them" who reject "me."[101] I have no problems comprehending how gangs can terrorize for honor, how sects can offer certitude of salvation, and why some Silicon Valley futurists look like missionaries.[102] I have a deep comprehension for young disaffected men who create meaning for themselves by combining the aesthetization of violence in Western films or computer games with religious and ideological legitimization and use the internet as recruiter and weapon for regaining what they perceive as their lost honor.

I have continued the displacement of my family until I reached the limits of the globe. At some point my initial identity of "I belong nowhere" transmuted into "I belong everywhere." Global living creates unique experiences not easily sharable with people who have more local perspectives, be it geographical locality or the locality of the global ghetto of the rich. Standpoint theory captures aspects of this experience.[103]

Since I feel increasingly compelled to concede that my observations turned out to be valid only too often, I force myself to describe what I see, even though it is not easily communicable.[104] Therefore, I need the reader to use *connected knowing*, rather than *separate knowing* when reading this book.[105] I need the reader to be aware that I am speaking from a place few people share and that it is very easy to misunderstand me. I often have difficulties to "translate" my perspective so that it can be understood by others. Sometimes people feel personally attacked, for instance, when I critically review the path of humankind as a whole and say "we" have done this and "we" may need to find new ways. Clearly, no single person can be personally responsible for all of past human history, yet, it is possible to feel personally responsible for co-reflecting on the past so as to jointly draw lessons for the future.

From where I stand, I often feel that I am "in the wrong film," and I often do so in ways that are different from others who also feel that something is "wrong." I see that the human beings inhabiting this planet share more than they wish to admit and that they are thoroughly able to manifest the fact that *Homo sapiens* is one single family, able to apply the script of "good family relationships" to all humans, even to all living creatures. I have used much effort to understand how it ever could happen that this script could be sidelined. I wonder: Is it terror – of whatever kind – that hinders people to leave their chains behind and unfold their human potential to connect as equals?[106] How could politics ever become a "fake-progressive, populace-bamboozling game,"[107] or the "manipulation of populism by elitism"[108]?

As mentioned above, what emerged from my traumatic family background was *Geschichtsbewusstsein*[109] (awareness of history) and the wish to stand up for "never again." My life became a project, a project with the aim of learning about the world so I might be better equipped to help make it more humane. I am an intercultural *voyager*, a label coined by psychologist David Matsumoto.[110] Unlike a *vindicator*, a voyager uses the challenges of cultural diversity and intercultural conflicts as a stage for forging new relationships and new ideas. I cherish meeting strangers and encountering strangeness with the entire range of my vulnerabilities.[111]

I have now lived as a global voyager for several decades, doing more than merely "traveling" to, or "visiting" "other cultures": I have become part of many cultures and have acquired a gut feeling for the major language families. My personal experiential cultural realm is now trans- and metacultural, rather than monocultural, bicultural, or multicultural. My background from a displaced family has enabled me to empathize with the suffering of the marginalized and excluded around the world. Being born into a female body has given me access to more spheres in segregated societies than a man would have. The fact that my family accidentally was displaced into a privileged societal context has given me a higher education without incurring insurmountable debts, and a passport that allows for easy global mobility. In sum, I have being enabled to invest my life into "never again" both by suffering and by privilege.

My educational background is broad – I hold two PhDs and define myself as a transdisciplinary social scientist and humanist with an ongoing interest in natural sciences (initially, I planned to study physics). Usually, academic careers become more specialized over time, with the first semester providing a general introduction, only to narrow down into specialized fields later. My path is the inverse. With my education, I could live the privileged life of a professor at a university in a wealthy part of the world, yet, rather than consuming my privileges for myself, I choose to invest them into serving the greater common good, and I do so by always attempting to further widen my horizon.[112] I believe that peace scholar Johan Galtung is correct in his observation that peace researchers are so few because the mobility that is necessary to know the entire world (beyond traveling to vacation destinations, conferences, or doing field work) is prohibitive, not least because also scholars depend on attaining financial stability, if only to pay their mortgages.[113]

As a result of this need for financial stability, as I see it, not just peace research, also academia as a whole fails to live up to its ideal of academic freedom, a freedom that ought to be used to serve the common good for all, rather than serving existing societal structures, or personal self-interest.[114] I have sacrificed all privileges that others take for granted to heed the call of international relations scholar Richard Falk for a "widespread reorientation of individual identities toward a new model of citizen," and have become what Falk calls "a citizen pilgrim," a citizen "whose principal affinities are with the species and its natural surroundings rather than to any specific state, ethnicity, nationality, civilization, or religion."[115] Psychologist Jan Smedslund calls this path being a critical visitor in this world.[116]

Let me conclude by honoring my doctoral advisors Reidar Ommundsen and Jan Smedslund by sharing the following letter I wrote to Jan Smedslund on October 23, 2013, after reading Smedslund's autobiographical book, a book in which he looks back on his sixty years as a psychologist, a book that deeply touched me[117]:

> Dear Jan, when I read your thoughts about rationality and understanding, I am reminded that I never, to my memory at least, have encountered a situation where I could say: "I do not understand." In other words, even the most murderous genocidal acts in Rwanda I do "understand" in the sense you refer to: I understand the "rationality" behind it. (Understanding, clearly, does not mean condoning.) Initially, I often felt that something must be wrong with me, for why do I see no "irrationality," for why do I see cruelty be inflicted so "rationally"? Why do I fail to see "evil" as a "rational" motive on its own, on a par with wanting to do "good"? I only see the rationality of a fundamentally social human nature, who, to quote you on Piaget's terminology "can only accommodate to (learn about) what is already assimilated (incorporated in one's conceptual system)," which, as I understand you, is a tenet you would also accept as basis for your psycho-logic?[118] I see, for instance, the rationality of wanting to do good for one's in-group, something that the targeted out-group may perceive to be evil or irrational (terrorism, genocide). Or, I see limited rationality, such as in children who still grow up, or in adults who never grow up, or in people who are traumatized und thus unable to unfold their potential, or in people living in social bubbles which limit their views on how those who live outside of these bubbles may experience the world.
>
> Being born into a displaced family, followed by a global life, could be the reason for why I seem to "understand" even the worst of "evil" (again, this has nothing to do with condoning it). Global living emerged from my roots in a displaced family, perhaps comparable to your background of having had a mother who exposed you to different cultural contexts already as a child and youth. As you mention in your book, this was one of the factors for the ensuing mobility in your life. This is valid also for me. Perhaps it is the personal experience from these displacements that gives you (and me?) a deeper and more comprehensive understanding of the range of unity in diversity in humankind? I mean the human potential for connection on one side, for unity (including your conceptualization of psycho-logic, which could be said to be a wonderful expression of this unity), and on the other side the range of possible diversity (where a not-knowing approach is required). From my point of view, your approach is self-evident (independent of the fact that I still need to study the details of your psycho-logic better), and it does take an effort for me to artificially narrow down my horizon to understand the rationality of why your approach also meets criticism. I sense a category error at the bottom of this criticism, at least in some cases, a profound misunderstanding of

> your position, while in other cases, your position might be understood too well, its subversiveness noticed, and then resisted.
>
> In the year 2001, I wrote an article "The Concept of Humiliation: Its Universal Core and Culture-Dependent Periphery," where I feel that it is in line with your thinking, as it ranges from the unity of psycho-logic to the diversity of not-knowing.[119] The article has the following abstract: "This article argues that the concept of humiliation may be deconstructed into seven layers, including a) a core that expresses the universal idea of "putting down," b) a middle layer that contains two opposed orientations towards "putting down," treating it as, respectively, legitimate and routine, or illegitimate and traumatizing, and c) a periphery whose distinctive layers include one pertaining to cultural differences between groups and another four peripheral layers that relate to differences in individual personalities and variations in patterns of individual experience of humiliation."

Let me end my overview over my background and approach here. I plan to write a book on my global life design, and why it also is a valid research method. What I see is that we, as humankind, need to be much more ambitious than simply wanting to succeed as a "modern/industrial culture," we need a radically new, a truly "post-industrial and co-creative form of civilization."[120] The reader may enjoy the little video on dignity, where Ragnhild Nilsen interviews me about the World Dignity University initiative.[121]

The significance of dignity and humiliation in our time

What is dignity?[122] Dignity is extremely difficult to conceptualize. It might need to remain without content altogether.[123] Some deem it to be a useless concept. Ruth Macklin is a philosopher and professor of bioethics. In her opinion, dignity indeed is a useless concept. She writes that dignity "seems to have no meaning beyond what is implied by the principle of medical ethics, namely, respect for persons: the need to obtain voluntary, informed consent; the requirement to protect confidentiality."[124] Psychologist Steven Pinker concurs; he suggests that autonomy is a more practical and specific term than dignity.[125]

The notion of humiliation, as well, elicits uneasiness. As Linda Hartling observes: "It is often felt to be humiliating to talk about humiliation. People do not like to talk about their feelings of humiliation because there is a sense of powerlessness involved with not being able to prevent these types of experiences."[126] The humiliation argument is even met with hostility. It is not unusual to be accused of using "unreasonable humiliation" as hideous tool to turn perpetrators into victims and blame victims of being perpetrators.[127]

The notion of humiliation meets skepticism also in certain segments of academia, this has been my experience since I began with my research on humiliation in 1996.[128] Some scholars in the peace and conflict area, for instance, prefer more "sterile" concepts, such as "cultural relative deprivation," without reflecting on why such deprivation may sometimes be accepted as God-given and sometimes rejected as humiliating. Humiliation appears to be lacking academic neutrality, detachment, and objectivity – it seems to be too "soft," despite the fact that it has the potential to create the "hardest" of outcomes. The latter has been demonstrated not least very recently by American President Donald J. Trump when he showed the power of the "politics of emotions." Many of his followers hail from the humiliated "forgotten people." Not only in the United States, authoritarianism is on the rise around the world,[129] ringing in "the end of a cycle."[130] It started in neglected backyards, unbeknownst to urban intelligentsia; now it challenges the boundaries of what is thinkable and unthinkable, the boundaries of what is accepted as rational or irrational.[131]

Humiliation is an act, an emotional state, a social mechanism, that is relevant for anthropology, sociology, philosophy, social and clinical psychology, or political science. Its multidisciplinarity may be another reason for why the notion of humiliation has almost not been studied on its own account. The phenomenon of humiliation is very complex. Broadly speaking, humiliation can be studied as (1) an internal experience, as a feeling, an emotion, (2) as an external event, in cases of degrading interpersonal interactions, bullying, abuse, violent conflict and extremism, terrorism and genocide, or (3) as a systemic condition, with apartheid as illustrative example.[132]

Humiliation-attrition can have the effect of wearing down people to the point of apathy, depression,[133] and inertia.[134] Research shows, that the combination of loss and humiliation is the strongest predictor of major depression.[135] Research also shows that humiliation is the most intense human emotion – it leads to the mobilization of more processing power and a greater consumption of mental resources than other emotions: "humiliation is a particularly intense and cognitively demanding negative emotional experience that has far-reaching consequences for individuals and groups alike."[136] Protracted cycles of humiliation can lead to the very paralysis and apathy that also *learned helplessness* engenders.[137] A seemingly "peaceful" society can be the result, peaceful because the price for keeping structural violence covert[138] is paid for by its members' pain.[139] While feelings of humiliation can result in apathy and depression, they can also lead to "going black," to *humiliated fury*, as psychologist Helen Lewis called it,[140] representing what I call the *nuclear bomb of the emotions*. This fury might find its way into domestic violence, or it can express itself in large-scale atrocities, such as genocide or terrorism, when extremist humiliation entrepreneurs instigate cycles of humiliation. This is the Hitler path. Yet, there is also the Freire-Gandhi-Mandela path. Feelings of humiliation can awaken what Paulo Freire called *conscientization* and motivate people to work for constructive social change.[141] This is the path of moderation, the path of those whose aim is to change humiliating systems without using humiliation as a tool. This is also my path.

On my global path, I have observed that human rights ideals have by now influenced the *Zeitgeist* even where they are being opposed, which means that humiliation is increasingly conceptualized as antisocial, as independent from shame, and as antipode to prosocial and dignified humility. Human rights ideals separate *humiliation* from *shame*.[142] In "The Journey of Humiliation and Dignity," I have attempted to describe the historical path that the discourse of humiliation has taken.[143] I analyze the historical path of words such as *humiliation, humility*, and *shame*, and how *humiliation* became antisocial, while *humility* stayed prosocial, or, more precisely, how meek humility transmuted into dignified humility.

Through my work on humiliation and dignity, since 1996, I have been in many ways ahead of time in contributing to the "emotional turn" that is now slowly unfolding in several fields of inquiry, for instance, in international relations theory,[144] including in the field of psychology itself. In my 2009 book on emotion and conflict, I have tried to lay out how recent conceptualizations of emotions have moved away from rigid categorizations toward viewing emotions as nonlinear, dynamic, and relational, and how definitions of affect, feeling, and emotion vary from author to author.[145] What is increasingly being acknowledged, though, is that no discourse can be "purely" based on rationality; it always depends on what the participants feel constitutes rationality.[146]

In my work, I go even further than a mere "emotional turn," I follow pioneer Jean Baker Miller in her relational-cultural theory, which signals an emotional-relational turn, not just an emotional turn that would still be stuck in Western lone-hero individualism.[147] Miller was early out in emphasizing the role of relationships and community, building on Lev Vygotsky and cultural-historical activity theory.[148] I resonate with "relational realism," with the "relational subject" approach more than with a "plural subject" approach, and tend to regard "the relation" itself as having causal effects.[149]

While emphasizing the significance of the relation, I do not mean to advocate any "us versus them" tribalism, nationalism, or fascism. The Darwinian forces of natural selection once acted on tribes, tribes among neighboring tribes; by now, the shrinking of the world invites those forces to act on one *single* human tribe as a whole.[150] If *Homo sapiens* wishes to avoid being selected out as a species,[151] a new kind of tribal patriotism is needed, one of globally interconnected "we" *ubuntu* individuality, of a "we" unity that nurtures and celebrates the diversity of individual and group identities worldwide.[152] I dedicate my entire life to the "relational recovery" of a world community. I am inspired by the fact that human activities are culturally bounded, as this means that it is possible to nurture a culture where humans understand that they are "multi-beings" who can trust each other, rather than bounded selfs doomed to stay divided by mistrust.[153]

Wherever I go on my global path, I see how dangerous it is to leave emotions to populists, and how this opens space for terror. As the new United Nations Secretary-General António Guterres, also I see racism, colorism, xenophobia, anti-Muslim hatred, anti-Semitism, and other forms of intolerance gaining ground in public discourse, stoked by populism.[154] Holocaust survivor Harry Linser said the same about the rise of Nazism in Germany, when I had the privilege of staying with him in 2003 and listening deeply to his analysis.[155] When I lived in Sarajevo in 2016, people would tell me, with tears, that the uneducated rural population in their *Hinterland* was susceptible to propaganda of nationalist hatred and that it was this rural population that brought polarization upon the region and ultimately mayhem upon the city. The lessons they advised other cities to learn was to give much more attention to their *Hinterland*, rather than neglecting and looking down on it, expecting it to merely serve as a source of food or as a leisure opportunity. Examples abound. Populists are surfing the sense of humiliation that accumulates in the *Hinterland*.[156] In India, a skewed balance of power favors rural issues and interests "to get the votes in the village and use that power to rule and plunder the cities."[157]

Militant extremists of all ideological orientations all around the world establish strongholds in isolated rural regions. It is easy to erect relatively secret training camps in remote places, since the villagers, even if they do oppose such activities, are usually quickly silenced. Remote regions in countries such as Germany are as vulnerable as those in other countries.[158] Bosnia has a mostly moderate and secular Muslim population, with radical Muslims being a minority, yet, Da'esh (or IS, ISIL, or ISIS[159]) was able to set up a stronghold by secretly buying land near an isolated village surrounded by deep woodlands, a location that makes it an ideal launching pad for terrorist campaigns in Europe.[160]

Already Adolf Hitler was a master of seduction of *die kleinen Leute*, as they were called in Germany, or "the little people," "the powerless." In the United States, they have become known as the "forgotten people." Already my grandmother sighed: "we are powerless against those 'up there.'" Hitler offered a grand narrative of national humiliation and invited "the little people" to join in and invest all their personal grievances, everything they suffered from due to personal or general political and economic misery. Prior to that time, few leaders had ever deemed "the little people" worthy of any particular attention. Hitler provided them with an unprecedented sense of importance. They greeted him as a savior, a new kind of leader who promised love and unparalleled significance instead of subordination and insignificance. Hitler evoked feelings of heroic resistance against national humiliation, convincing the German people that the true destiny of the Aryan race was to lead and save the world. In this way, Hitler earned himself such loyalty that he could do nothing wrong; a whole country followed him into suicidal mayhem. Hitler wrote: "The people in their overwhelming majority are so feminine by nature and attitude that sober reasoning determines their thoughts and actions far less than emotion and feeling. And this sentiment is not complicated, but very simple and all of a piece. It does not have multiple shadings; it has a positive and a negative; love or hate, right or wrong, truth or lie, never half this way and half that way, never partially...."[161]

Hitler was not alone, evidently; Lenin, Mao, many have discovered the soul of the masses as a resource to exploit, in particular people's fear of humiliation as the strongest motivator, fear of humiliation now and in the future.[162] Not without reason was genocide called "solution" in Germany, even "final solution" (*Endlösung*), as a promise to salvage people once and for all from the fear of being humiliated in the future. In Germany Hitler singled out "the Jews" as alleged humiliators, Lenin pointed at "capitalist conspirators," in Rwanda "the Tutsis" played the role of humiliators to be exterminated.[163] Fear of future humiliation can be very strong, so strong that even manifest wealth and security fail to insulate against it: In February 2017, Liechtenstein, one of the places in the world with the highest per-capita income, voted populists into parliament, out of fear of losing its cultural identity to immigrants, in absence of any immigrants.[164]

Bioethics philosopher Richard Ashcroft offers a fourfold classification of the prevalent viewpoints on human dignity.[165] The first position is to deplore dignity talk as straight forward incoherent and *misleading* talk, as Macklin does.[166] Then, there is dignity strictly reducible to *autonomy*.[167] Third, thinkers such as Amartya Sen and Martha Nussbaum focus on *capabilities*, functionings, and social interactions.[168] Fourth, dignity is seen as a *metaphysical property* possessed by all and only human beings, a position mainly to be found in European bioethics and in theological writings.[169]

Discourse analysist Michael Karlberg sees three contrasting interpretive frames for human dignity: the *social command* frame, the *social contest* frame, and the *social body* frame.[170] The social command frame is a legacy of patriarchal and authoritarian modes of thought, where an "alpha male" dominates and leads the pack. In other words, it fits into what Riane Eisler calls the dominator model of society. It also fits into the pedagogical framework of a *strict father* model that cognitive linguists George Lakoff and Mark Johnson describe.[171]

The social contest frame emerged, in part, in response to the acute injustice and oppression flowing from the social command frame, Karlberg explains. It draws on the social Darwinist metaphor of the "survival of the fittest," misunderstood as "might is right." It draws on metaphors of war, sports, fighting, and market competition. The underlying normative assumption is that society only needs to harness everyone's self-interested and competitive energy into contests, to produce winners and losers, and, in the long run, the (surviving) populations will be better off."[172] It is hoped that collective well-being will flow from structuring all social institution as a contest of power, no longer as rigidly oppressive power hierarchies.

The social body frame has roots in diverse cultures that have been "reemerging in a modern form over the past century, in response to the ever-increasing social and ecological interdependence humanity is now experiencing on a global scale."[173] At the core of this frame is an understanding of society as an integrated organic body, where the well-being of every individual or group depends upon the well-being of the entire body and is achieved by maximizing the possibilities for every individual to realize their latent potential to contribute to the common good, within social relationships and institutional structures that foster and canalize human capacities accordingly.

Human beings are capable of competition and cooperation, egoism and altruism, and it is our cultural environment, our education and training, our opportunities for moral development, and the institutional structures we act within that guide the direction.[174] Viewed from a social body frame perspective, as Karlberg makes clear, it is imperative for humankind now to learn how to cultivate every individual's latent capacity for cooperation and altruism, and to do so widely, systematically, and effectively, not least by fostering the individual's consciousness of the oneness of humanity.[175] "Such a consciousness entails a radical reconception of the relationship between the individual and society, the implications of which are conveyed in a compelling manner by the social body metaphor."[176]

The founder of the health and human rights movement, epidemiologist Jonathan Mann, explains why our concepts of dignity are so fuzzy: We are all explorers in the larger world of human suffering and well-being, yet, our mappings of this world is not always equally well detailed. He writes:

> And our current maps of this universe, like world maps from sixteenth century Europe, have some very well-defined, familiar coastlines and territories and also contain large blank spaces, which beckon the explorer. … The definition of dignity itself is complex and thus far elusive and unsatisfying. While the Universal Declaration of Human Rights starts by placing dignity first, "all people are born equal in dignity and rights," we do not yet have a vocabulary, or taxonomy, let alone an epidemiology of dignity violations. Yet it seems we all know when our dignity is violated or impugned.[177]

For theologian Paul Tillich – his ideas were further developed by Martin Luther King Jr. in his doctoral dissertation – *love* is the fundamental ethical commandment. For Tillich, love has "being," while justice has no separate being apart from being a way to put love into practice.[178] Love is also what Howard Richards, philosopher of social science and scholar of peace and global studies, speaks of when he explains that "natural" human rights were not created by nature or by a social contract, they were created by history.[179] Human rights are historically constructed social realities, with two long key historical periods of gestation culminating in the declarations of rights, first at the time of the French Revolution and then after the Second World War. The first period engendered the *Déclaration des Droits de l' Homme et du Citoyen* (1789), while the second brought the Universal Declaration of Human Rights (1948):

> Human rights, then, are a gift of history that help us to put into practice the fundamental ethic of love, also known as solidarity. Rights give love the force of law. For those who are not religious, Mahatma Gandhi offered a secular argument for a love ethic: if love were not the law of our species, our species would never have survived and we would not be here today.[180]

Also Donald Klein, a pioneer in the field of community psychology, speaks about the human ability to feel "awe and wonderment" in the face of this world and its living creatures.[181] In my book on *big love* as antidote against "big hate," I explain that my personal "religion" indeed, is "love, humility, and awe for a universe too large for us to fathom."[182]

In my work, I conceptualize honor and dignity as a movement of the Zeitgeist in a historical context from *collectivist inequality in honor* to *individual equality in dignity*. I have formed the term *egalization* for the latter. This movement itself is a collective process, where honor firmly locks the individual in a group hierarchy, while equal dignity ideals aim to free the individual from the group and make everyone equally worthy. Article 1 of the Universal Declaration of Human Rights begins with the phrase, "All human beings are born free and equal in dignity and rights."

On the path of my global life, I found only very few world regions where equality in dignity is part of the cultural heritage. Norway is one of them, perhaps due to its remote geopolitical location.[183] When I come to Norway, I do not need to explain what equality in dignity – *likeverd* – means, a deep understanding is embodied. In most other world regions cultural heritages champion hierarchical inequality and the sentence, "All men and women are born with unequal honor and rights, and some are freer than others." In most world regions, even people who advocate human rights often cannot escape the deep sense of inequality they carry in their body and soul, their bodymind.[184]

Throughout my life, I have "tested" the hypothesis of whether it is possible to approach all human beings on this planet as *one* family, and I can attest that there is a profound human eagerness to connect.[185] These are thick attractors, to use the language of Peter Coleman's dynamical systems theory. Peter Coleman is professor of psychology and education director at the Morton Deutsch International Center for Cooperation and Conflict Resolution in New York. He and his colleagues use a *dynamical systems* approach to conceptualize the intransigence entailed in intractable conflict.[186] Coleman identifies *attractors*, or dominant mental and behavioral patterns that offer a coherent map of the world to people, and a stable platform for action.

To turn the human eagerness to connect into true connection, respect for equality in dignity for all is needed. When respect and recognition fail, those who feel slighted are prone to highlight differences so as to "justify" rifts, rifts that could easily be bridged were it not for the barriers of humiliation. In that way, *clashes of humiliation* are dangerous, while *clashes of civilizations* can turn out to be enriching. The very aim of the Human Dignity and Humiliation Studies fellowship that I dedicate my life to, is precisely to contribute to convening a global dignity community that is enriched by its diversity.

The above mentioned criticism of the notion of dignity has not hindered dignity's rise to fame: "Why are philosophers invoking the notion of human dignity to revitalize theories of political ethics?"[187] The recent so-called Arab Spring was often described as "dignity revolution." Shibley Telhami, Anwar Sadat Professor for Peace and Development of the University of Maryland, wrote to me in a personal communication on May 16, 2013:

> Considerable evidence through public opinion research over a period of two decades confirms what ordinary citizens across the Arab world chanted during their revolts: One of the central driving forces behind the Arab uprising is the pursuit of dignity and overcoming a pervasive sense of humiliation not only in the relationship between rulers and ruled but also between Arabs and the rest of the world.

Nayef Al-Rodhan, a philosopher, neuroscientist, and expert of the geopolitics of globalization and transnational security, adds, "what drives history is not primarily the search for freedom, but rather the profound human quest for dignity."[188] I had the privilege of being invited by Nayef Al-Rodhan to the 9th International Security Forum, May 30 – June 1, 2011, in Zürich, Switzerland. He writes:

> Dignity, more than the absence of humiliation, is a holistic set of criteria indispensable for good governance: reason, security, human rights, accountability, transparency, justice, opportunity, innovation, and inclusiveness. Indeed, the call for dignity has been the theme of the Arab Spring. The revolutions were prompted by leaders' failure to respect and ensure the dignity of their citizens. The protesters were driven by underlying discontent and frustration with arbitrary and disrespectful security forces, lack of economic opportunities, malfunctioning public services, and the arrogance as well as corruption of an affluent ruling class. The numerous failings in governance of incumbent regimes thus culminated in collective dignity deficits that made a critical turning point for the region inevitable. The question was not if, but when. Therefore, both the Arab Spring and its aftermath need to be dissociated from the overly repeated dictum of liberal democracy, as it was not rooted in freedom but rather in a search for dignity.[189]

Al-Rodhan continues explaining that "the lack of collective dignity felt by so many in the Arab world is the result of a combination of internal autocratic and corrupt regimes, with predictable ineffective and unaccountable governance, supported by external actors with short-term geopolitical interests."[190] Al-Rodhan observes a sense of collective cultural siege and hopelessness about the future in the Arab world. Furthermore, the West is perceived as disrespectful and dismissive of the people of the Arab-Islamic world, its culture, and its pivotal historical contributions to world civilization. This sense is reinforced by "the persistence of inhuman conditions for the stateless Palestinians, despite clear violations of human rights and international law, endless UN resolutions and concrete Arab peace plans." Al-Rodhan concludes that these factors together have produced "a number of fatalistic perceptions and dignity deficits that are plaguing a region and limiting its tremendous potential," and he continues:

> On the domestic front in these countries, it is possible to gather all these deficiencies in public governance under a parsimonious, yet comprehensive list – a dignity index. I define dignity in its wholesome sense as much more complex and inclusive than just the absence of humiliation. Its absence reflects in a number of collective dignity deficits: lack of reason, lack of security, human rights abuses, lack of accountability, lack of transparency, absence of justice, lack of opportunity, lack of innovation and lack of inclusiveness. Together, these collective dignity deficits have created mounting frustration due to limited institutionalized channels through which citizens could effect meaningful political change.[191]

Al-Rodhan calls on the West to put significantly more effort into building trust with the Arab world. Deep mistrust flowing from memories of betrayal by Western arrogance has to be overcome. Remember, for instance, the 1916 Sykes-Picot Agreement, concluded in secrecy, through which the French and British established control over the Arab provinces of the Ottoman Empire while pretending to help Arabs escape Ottoman hegemony.[192] This is not forgotten in the Arab world, Al-Rodhan attests.

The examples from the Arab world are meant to give the reader a feel for the topic of humiliation. Academia carries a particular responsibility to protect society from destructive cycles of humiliation. I am among those who fear that academia is failing this responsibility. Higher education presently maximizes its training functions and certification processes, while failing its most important *raison d'être*, namely, "the liberation of the human mind to think about the needs of society and engage the capacities of the individual to address those needs."[193]

According to what I observe, the failure to take feelings such as humiliation seriously, and the need to heal them, has to do with the culture that the security dilemma engendered. In my books *Emotion and Conflict* (2009), and *Gender, Humiliation, and Global Security* (2010), I discuss the reasons for why emotions have long been overlooked in academic inquiry.[194] The background is a tradition that gives significance to everything that is "hard," worthy of "male" rationality, while emotions smack of "softness" and "female" irrationality. This is also why emotions become more prominent as a field of research not always for the best of reasons. "Hard" functional Magnetic Resonance Imaging technology can now make brain areas visible which are involved in emotion, and this means that emotion can now be studied "hard." And this, while brain scan data do not solve the problem of inference, but simply remove it from one site of-speculation to another.[195] In other words, the striving for "hardness" often seems to be more of an obsession with "pseudo-hardness."

The root for this obsession is a rather "soft" psychological problem with the "physics envy" that I have mentioned before and that I observe in social sciences, particularly in psychology, all around the world. In my view, it undermines academia's relevance for real life and the very scientificity of science. Indeed, scientist and novelist C. P. Snow might be right in saying that it was a mistake to split the intellectual life of Western society into the sciences and the humanities.[196] This split may have served what Michel Foucault called *governmentality*, namely, the manipulation of populations.[197] Philosopher and sociologist Jürgen Habermas denounces "scientism" as "science's belief in itself: that is, the conviction that we can no longer understand science as one form of possible knowledge, but rather must identify knowledge with science."[198] There is a German saying, "Die herrschende Meinung ist die Meinung der Herrschenden, und die öffentliche Meinung ist die veröffentlichte Meinung" (The ruling opinion is the opinion of the ruling, and public opinion is the published opinion).[199]

Also in terrorism research, funding agencies place great hopes in social sciences to provide them with explanatory models fashioned on natural sciences.[200] Renowned scholar Michael Billig's most recent book has a telling title, *Learn to Write Badly: How to Succeed in the Social Sciences.*[201] Billig laments the present trend toward mediocre technocratic thinking and writing in academia, driven by an increased push toward competition that forces scholars to build self-importance, even if only achieved through overly technical terminology.

I call it *voluntary self-humiliation* when experts are complicit in keeping societies in a collective "Stockholm syndrome."[202] *Stockholm syndrome* is a name for capture-bonding, a psychological phenomenon in which hostages express empathy and sympathy and have positive feelings toward their captors. The present "captor" of society, and this includes academia, is the raising pressure from a nexus of corporate and national interests, which brought a new wave of "hardness" worship, this time cloaked in the language of modernization and efficiency. As a result, what is sold out, literally, is academic freedom and integrity, what is sacrificed is an invaluable academic tradition of cooperation for the sake of gaining relevant insights for the sake of the common good, together, in cooperation, rather than merely competing for funding.

This trend of hollowing out quality for the sake of quantity in the academic world is made possible by the fact that scientists, as most others, depend on their "job" for financial stability, but more, perhaps also by a certain lack of courage. I often hear entrepreneurs look down on academicians, saying:

"Academics are cowards and clever rationalizers: they present cowardice as a virtue necessary for 'objective detachment.'" I must admit that I sometimes feel compelled to agree with these harsh judgments, even though I am an academic myself. While humility is a virtue that is indispensable for true integrity, including scientific integrity, humility turns into a violation if it serves as a hideout for cowardice in the face of abusive power.

What many academicians tend to overlook, is the immense influence they do have, even if they do not aim for it and simply wish to secure a career. Their influence is being instrumentalized precisely because of its potency. Where would fascism have been without its philosophers?[203] "Murderous professors" stood behind the Rwandan genocide in 1994.[204] Cambodia's Pol Pot studied with Nicos Poulantzas (1936 – 1979), a Greco-French political sociologist in Paris. Pol Pot turned Poulantzas' academic reflections into rigid ideology and implemented it in his homeland. Seeing what he had set in motion, Poulantzas later committed suicide.[205] Also the recent documentary film *Inside Job* exposes the degree to which academic influence contributed to preparing the ground for what later turned out to be devastating economic crises.[206]

On my part, I would like to do my utmost to use the potential that academia has to influence society; yet, I want to use this influence responsibly, for the benefit of the dignity of all. In my view, not shying away from terms such as "humiliation" is part of this endeavor. As Michael Billig reminded us, technical terminology is often less precise than simpler language. I would add, often also less scientific and less relevant for "real life."

If we look back, we observe that subsequent to the 1948 Human Rights Declaration, at first, political rights were emphasized, then came economic, social, and cultural rights, signed 1966 and in force starting from 1976.[207] Now, I sense the time has come for dignity to be taken seriously. It is not by accident that the word dignity comes first, before rights, in this foundational sentence: "All human beings are born free and equal in dignity and rights."

Many, however, are still taken aback by the fact that dignity cannot really be defined, that it resides, not so much in academia, but in the bodies and souls of people. I meet many doubters around the world. Ruth Mackins and Steven Pinker have been quoted earlier. While Pinker suggests that autonomy would be a better concept than dignity, others have suggested to me that focusing on the notion of *pride*, or that of *respect* would be preferable.

Legal philosopher and international law scholar Oscar Schachter reflects:

> We do not find an explicit definition of the expression – dignity of the human person in international instruments or (as far as I know) in national law. Its intrinsic meaning has been left to intuitive understanding, conditioned in large measure by cultural factors. When it has been invoked in concrete situations, it has been generally assumed that a violation of human dignity can be recognized even if the abstract term cannot be defined.[208]

Whenever I am urged to foreground respect, I ask the following question: Respect for what? Respect can also be connected with ranked honor: A man who beats his wife, for instance, may do so to force her to respect his supremacy. Apartheid was a context where citizens were requested to pay respect to systemic humiliation. The problem would also not be solved by making the phrase longer, by saying, for example: We need "respect for dignity." Also this phrase would be incomplete. The reason is that also the notion of dignity has a history similar to that of ranked honor – the notions of *decorum* or *dignitary* betray this.[209] The concept of a *dignitary* points at a person who is "higher" in rank than others. The only formulation that expresses the entirety of human rights ideals, would be a formulation such as this: "respect for equal dignity for all, together, as individuals in solidarity," or, "the respect, in solidarity, for equality in dignity for all individuals."

What we encounter when we hear about dignity revolutions unfolding around the world, or when human rights defenders use the phrase dignity, is an *enthymeme* (Greek: ἐνθύμημα, *enthumēma*). This means that a speaker spells out only certain aspects of an argument and leaves other parts out because she assumes that the audience holds those parts in their minds (*en thymo*). In a narrow sense, an enthymeme is an informally stated three-part deductive argument, with an unstated assumption that must be true for the premises to lead to the conclusion. In a broader usage, the term describes all incomplete less than hundred percent arguments.

Philosopher Hubert Schleichert wrote a book on "how to discuss with fundamentalists without losing your mind – instructions for subversive thinking."[210] In this book he explains the *enthymeme* phenomenon with the following example:

> Meier says: I think X should be prime minister again; times are difficult, and X has ruled for ten years. But Müller replies: I think X should not be prime minister again; times are difficult, and X has ruled for ten years. These two enthymematic arguments look alike, but lead to opposite theses. The reason is clear: The two arguments use two different, unspoken arguments. For the analysis, it is necessary to make the unspoken arguments explicit; often it is here that the real bone of contention lies. Meier goes by the sentence: When times are difficult, a veteran leader should not be replaced. Müller, on the other hand, takes the exact opposite position.

In other words, people who call for respect and dignity do not necessarily talk about the same thing. The case of terror can illustrate this. Those who engage in terror tactics often justify them by saying that there is no other way to gain respect and dignity. The victims of such tactics will have a very different view and feel that it is precisely everybody's dignity that is being violated.

Freedom is another example. People who call for freedom may call for freedom for all, or they may call for freedom for might to become right. In the first case, the end-result will be equality in dignity, in the second case, inequality will ensue.[211] A culture that defines freedom as absence of restraints, including freedom for dominators to turn might into right, tends to keep those dominators in power, dooming the broader masses to the role of exploited victims. Collective bondage is the result of liberty without solidarity, of liberty without equality and fraternity. Freedom in disharmony with the natural environment is wishful thinking and not freedom.[212] Wherever freedom is just another word for "the market," invaluable traditions of community care are lost. To say it with the motto of the French revolution: Liberty must be made compatible with a duty to share, only then can also equality and fraternity be expressed. When solidarity (*fraternité*) is sold out for a misguided definition of *liberté*, when solidarity is seen as nemesis for individual freedom, *égalité* likely is lost as well.[213] Only a culture that defines liberty as a *level playing field protected by appropriate constitutive rules, nurtured in the spirit of servant leadership* can protect liberty as a common good for all.[214] Community is a word that suggests defining freedom as Martin Luther King Jr. defined it, namely, as a call to moral responsibility, or as Martha Nussbaum and Amartya Sen define it, as capability to do things.[215]

It is thus not respect, nor pride, nor honor, nor simply dignity alone that describes the core of the moral universe that human rights ideals constitute, it is respect for equal dignity for all. And this equal dignity is an embodied sense, the sense of being able to stand straight, upright, and carry one's head high, rather than bow down in submissive meekness or stick one's nose up in hostile arrogance.[216] In contrast to either arrogant upmanship or meek "downmanship," equal dignity expresses itself in a posture of proud and dignified humility, looking into the eyes of others as equals with calm confidence. Philosopher Franz Josef Wetz describes dignity and self-respect as an "orthopedic challenge": it is the art to walk upright.[217] Human dignity is thus not merely a philosophical abstraction or a legal construct, "it is a phenomenological reality that has its basis in human consciousness."[218] Human dignity, rather than a justification for norms, is a *Haltung* (posture, demeanor, attitude), a good that must be attained, preserved or regained.[219] Dignity is a sense of self-worth, "which we have a duty to develop and respect in ourselves and a duty to protect in others," while acknowledging that there are diverse interpretations of dignity.[220] Human rights can thus not be justified by simply mentioning the word dignity.[221] "For meaningful dialogue on the subject, it is therefore necessary to listen carefully and ascertain whether conversation partners are using the same or at least a similar concept of dignity. If not, fundamental disagreements can remain hidden to the detriment of constructive consensus."[222]

All around the world, I observe human worthiness and value be measured in those two fundamentally different ways: on one side looking up and down, and on the other side looking straight. Those two ways, if applied rigorously, are mutually exclusive.[223] If we think of a ranking order that ranges from high to low – with divinity at the top and dirt at the bottom – then people can either be ranked somewhere on this ladder into higher and lesser beings, or the practice of ranking humans can be rejected.[224] I have chosen to give the first practice the label *honor*, or, more precisely *collectivistic ranked honor*, which corresponds to Eisler's dominator model of society. Honor is a normative paradigm rather than a code of law, it is a set of informal values that contain intellectual and affective elements that keep those who subscribe to it engaged in it.[225] Honor is a collective phenomenon that shapes everything from the micro to the meso and macro level, from emotions to institutions. People are born into it, socialized into a group pressure that affects the whole range of meta-emotions – how people manifest feelings[226] – to norms and institutions in a society.

The second approach is that of refusing to rank human worthiness, that of meeting everybody in the middle in shared proud humility, where nobody is expected to look up at others in meek humility or look down on others in arrogance. I use the label *dignity*, or, more precisely *respect for equal dignity for all, together, as individuals in solidarity* for this approach. This corresponds to Eisler's partnership model. The word *egalization* describes the process.

Both approaches are being promoted collectively, yet, in the first case, the individual is fixed in "her place" in the ranked collective to which she belongs, in a world where her collective has a certain rank among other ranked collectives, and each individual is given more or less worth according to her place in this order. In the second case, the collective is all of humanity with all of its members being accorded the same worthiness. By assigning honor and dignity such a precise place in my conceptualizations, I exercise my linguistic right to label cultural codes as I see them work in the world.

The partnership model is more in line with human nature than the dominator model. This is what I observe all around the world. Sociobiologist Edward O. Wilson has studied *eusociality* (Greek *eu*, good/ real and social), the highest level of organization of animal sociality. The highest level includes, among others, cooperative care for the young.[227] Edward Wilson makes the argument that among humans, there is no such thing as a "naturally" isolated selfish individual who violently defends her self-interest and needs religious or moral pressure or intellectual or abstracts ideas to behave prosocially.[228] Human prosocial behavior such as solidarity, altruism, care, and compassion, evolved through evolution. Prosocial virtues developed during human natural and cultural evolution, and are therefore part of human nature. There is no "primitive" human nature that needs to be civilized.

Humans need recognition. The evolutionary universal of the struggle for recognition was already described by philosophers Kant and Hegel. Philosopher Georg Wilhelm Friedrich Hegel (1770 – 1831) made the concept of recognition fundamental to his philosophy, and taught that a good life is dependent on being held in regard by others. Human self-consciousness, he argued, depends on being recognized by others as a person who possesses worth. Hegel's discussion of the "struggle for recognition" has inspired extensive literature in contemporary political theory, see, among many others, philosopher Axel Honneth,[229] or sociologist Zygmunt Bauman.[230]

Political scientist Neera Chandhoke from the University of Delhi in India explains: "If, for Kant, the idea of *Achtung* or respect contains the nucleus of his 'Categorical Imperative,' for the Scottish moralists, recognition or disapproval motivates individuals towards the attainment of desirable virtues."[231]

Philosopher Max Scheler set out related issues in his classic book *Ressentiment*.[232] Scheler stated that a person at her core is a loving being, *ens amans*, who may feel ressentiment (comparable to resentment) when not recognized.[233] The philosophy on the politics of recognition, building on

Scheler, supposes that it may lead to violence when people suffer humiliation as a result of non-recognition. In "The Politics of Recognition," philosopher Charles Taylor argues that identity politics is motivated by a deep human need for recognition, with injurious effects of various forms of misrecognition.[234] Taylor links the Romantic idea of authenticity and the authentic self with Enlightenment thinkers, such as Kant, for the modern notions of equality and dignity.[235]

Political scientist, sociologist, and social anthropologist Liah Greenfeld used the example of Ethiopia and Eritrea to suggest that ressentiment plays a central role also in nation building.[236] North American struggles for recognition and "need for positive self-regard,"[237] so political scientist Alexander Wendt, may actually "explain much of the *Realpolitik* behavior, including war, which Neorealists have attributed to the struggle for security."[238]

Also political scientist Reinhard Wolf uses the terminology of resentment for the long-lasting simmering sense of humiliation. Wolf focuses on hierarchical social settings where a resenting person or group is in a weak position and feels that others enjoy undeserved power and/or prestige. Such a person or group will not necessarily express resentful feelings with open anger. Evidence for their experience can only be found indirectly in their discourse. The desire to bring a more powerful actor down from a weak position can only be achieved through the help of allies. Those allies, however, must first be mobilized, they have to be convinced, grievances must be explained, and the alleged offenders' high status delegitimized. Wolf recommends researchers who wish to detect this phenomenon to watch out for accusations of unfair status shifts, for the invocation of normative principles that call for rectifying "unfair" policies, for justifications for retributive measures, for insinuations that tarnish the social or moral status of the alleged wrongdoer, for signs of *Schadenfreude* when the other experiences setbacks, and, at last, for the presence of revenge fantasies.[239]

As I will explain in more depth later, I observe that the violation of dignity, or what I call *dignity humiliation*, is more hurtful than *honor humiliation*. I observe that the promise of 1948, namely, that everybody deserves to be respected as equal in dignity, represents a revolutionary promise, and that it is therefore that its violation smarts so much more than the violation of honor. Within a ranked system of honor, a person's own assessment, along with that of her peers, determines whether she thinks that her rank is being degraded unduly or not. Human rights ideals offer much more, they offer the right to everybody to be respected as equal in dignity. When this promise is broken, it humiliates more intensely, as it immediately exiles the victim from the human family altogether. Therefore, ironically, human rights ideals often increase feelings of humiliation, precisely because human rights raise higher hopes. It is devastating when empty human rights rhetoric and double standards betray them.

The damage would be smaller if no promise had been given in the first place. Yet, the promise, now that it has been unleashed, as much as it is being betrayed, cannot be put back into the bottle. I see it having force all around the world. The desire to rise from being pushed down is increasingly felt, deeply, and this is experienced beyond language. It is the desire to be respected as an equal fellow human being among fellow human beings.

The sentence that "all human beings are born free and equal in dignity and rights" speaks of dignity and of rights. Initially, after 1948, the concept of equal rights was in the focus, while equal dignity goes far beyond mere legal concepts. Since equality in dignity is what carries human rights ideals, human dignity has to guide human rights. Neglecting human rights violates human dignity, and vice versa. When the focus on rights becomes too narrow, dignity can be undermined. Nurturing dignity must therefore not be left to the legal field and its professionals alone. Every single citizen who subscribes to human rights ideals, and society as a whole, is called on.

An entire society can advance or violate human dignity. Impunity, for instance, is a violation perpetrated by society. Many consider it to be an ongoing form of systemic torture. This is what psychologists and doctors say, for instance, in Chile, Argentina, Uruguay, and Peru, those who work with torture survivors and families of disappeared persons. I had the privilege of learning about their work in 2012.[240] My colleague Nora Sveaass is one of their messengers.[241] Sveaass is the chair of the board of Health and Human Rights Info platform that works to bridge the gap between health care professionals and human rights activists, including legal professionals in the field.[242] "Justice, Truth, Dignity" is the motto of the International Center for Transitional Justice, and this is their vision: "We strive for societies to regain humanity in the wake of mass atrocity. For societies in which impunity is rejected, dignity of victims is upheld, and trust is restored; where truth is the basis of history. We believe that this is an ethical, legal, and political imperative and the cornerstone of lasting peace."[243] The renowned "Joinet/Orentlicher" principles stipulate the right to *know*, the right to *justice*, the right to *reparation*, and, fourth, the guarantee of *non-recurrence*.[244]

As the discussion of humiliation has shown, one way to approach a deeper understanding of equality in dignity is through exploring its violations. Philosopher Avishai Margalit does this with his notion of *non-humiliation*,[245] philosopher of criminal justice John Kleinig with *non-degradation*,[246] philosopher and political theorist Philip Pettit with *non-domination*,[247] and physicist and educational reformer Robert Fuller with his rejection of *supremacism* and *rankism*.[248]

Some have linked terrorism to poverty, while others reject this argument and highlight humiliation: "... our emphasis must be on subjective perceptions of national, religious, and ethnic humiliation, rather than on the humiliation, genuine as it may be, which is associated with poverty."[249] Political scientist Robert Pape found that communal humiliation inspires suicide bombers to make an occupying power suffer the same level of humiliation they have felt.[250] Political scientist Dominique Moïsi observes that a culture of humiliation "helps unite the Muslim world around its most radical forces and has led to a culture of hatred."[251] Moïsi describes a worldwide clash of emotions between a *culture of humiliation* in the Middle East, a *culture of hope* in central Asia, and a *culture of fear* in the West, fear of loss of identity and control, fear of economic instability, immigration, and terrorism.

Yet, also the humiliation argument has been passionately rejected, together with the poverty argument, as "reductionist master explanations," and, instead, the rise of political Islam has been pinpointed.[252]

This book resonates with all explanations in certain ways, through contextualizing them as expressions of mindsets that are embedded into historically evolved worldviews of honor and dignity.[253]

Also I came to explore dignity through research on humiliation. My conclusion after I had carried out my doctoral research in Somalia and Rwanda, on the background of Nazi Germany, was that *clashes of civilizations* are not the problem,[254] but *clashes of humiliation* are.[255] The reason is that feelings of humiliation potentially have the force of a *nuclear bomb of the emotions*.[256] This is an adaptation of my summary from 2006:

> Based on many years of research on humiliation, I would suggest that feelings of humiliation come about when deprivation is perceived as an illegitimate imposition of lowering or degradation, a degradation that cannot be explained in constructive terms. All human beings basically yearn for recognition and respect. When they perceive that recognition and respect are withdrawn or denied they may feel humiliated. For that to happen, it does not matter whether this withdrawal of recognition is real or misread. Both the violation of ranked honor and of equal dignity can elicit feelings of humiliation, yet, diametrically opposed metascripts for how humiliation should be felt and acted on will be activated in response. The strongest force for creating rifts and destroying relationships is dignity humiliation, or, more precisely, the violation of the promise entailed in the human rights ideals that all people are part of *one* family with all members having the right to enjoy equal dignity.[257]

I conclude by saying that I find it promising that the desire for recognition unites us human beings and thereby provides us with a platform for contact and cooperation. Ethnic, religious, or cultural differences, or conflicts of interests, all carry the potential to engender creative cooperation and problem solving, and diversity can be a source of mutual enrichment. Yet, and this is my warning, this can only succeed within relationships characterized by respect for equality in dignity for all. When respect and recognition fail, dangerous clashes of humiliation will ensue, where those who feel victimized turn potentially enriching diversity into hostile division. Clashes of civilizations, to be a source of inspiration, need a context of respect for equal dignity.

Inviting the reader into this book project

> *I'm envious of people who can open their mouths and have perfectly formed sentences and paragraphs come out. When I'm speaking in public – even right now, frankly – I'm inwardly wincing at every word that pops out of my mouth. I want to retract them all immediately, and re-phrase. Like so many people who write, I started because I wanted to gain possession of the things in my head that, when I opened my mouth, came out all wrong. Words are like little kids; you don't want to send them out of the house until they're dressed and have brushed their teeth. At a lectern I'm a fumbler, the most inarticulate buffalo in the world.*
>
> – Dwight Garner, book critic[258]

Terrorism expert Alex Schmid warns of a major gap in current counter-radicalization (CT) efforts: "… a goal which has not been reached despite more than ten years of CT efforts, is the formulation of an effective counter-narrative to the single narrative of Al-Qaeda and its affiliates which claim that Islam is under attack and defensive Jihad against the West is the obligation of every Muslim."[259] This book project aims at offering such a counter-narrative.

In other words, this book is very ambitious. Because of that, it is written in fear. Dwight Garner's words quoted above describe very well how this manuscript came about: in fear, fear overridden by pain, every day since its start in 2010, overridden by the pain flowing from a sense of responsibility that weighs too heavy.[260] It is the responsibility of wanting to include "excluded knowledges" and wanting to "be in the world" also of the excluded.[261] It is the responsibility of wishing to express how my life is about *being*,[262] rather than *having* – be it having material possession or knowledge – that my life is about expressing the "truths," however tentatively, about what I have been seeing during the past forty years of my life all around the globe.

As mentioned earlier, I am not employed anywhere, I do not wish to make my work "useful" for any monetary or career purposes of my own, or for national or any other particular interests; I live in service of the interest of humankind, of sentient beings in general. My laptop is the globally mobile "headquarters" and home of the members of our dignity fellowship worldwide. My wish is to transform the world toward more dignity. Therefore my work speaks, and should speak, not only to experts – in the case of this book experts in the field of terror tactics – it needs to speak to all people. The aim is not just to address terrorism or any other particular challenge, but to engender much deeper and more comprehensive understanding and change.

Rowan Williams was the 104th Archbishop of Canterbury. He pairs novelist George Orwell with poet, social activist, and Trappist monk Thomas Merton when he writes about the responsibility to write honestly:

> Destructive politics is inevitably bound up with forgetfulness of our humanity, in one way or another – the organized inhumanity of tyranny, the messianic aspirations of communism, the passion for control on the part of managerial modernity, the naked and brutal murderousness of terrorism. But Merton explicitly, and Orwell implicitly, remind us that this is not just about bad governance or oppression. If we talk and write badly, dishonestly, unanswerably, what we are actually doing is getting ready for war. The habits of mind that make war inevitable are the habits of bad language – that is to say, the habits that grow from uncritical attitudes to power and privilege: contempt towards the powerless, towards minorities, towards the stranger, the longing for an end to human complexity and difference.[263]

We live in times where unprecedented dangers loom. The 2017 Doomsday clock is at two and a half minutes to midnight, back to where it was when I was born six decades ago at the height of the nuclear confrontation between Eastern and Western Bloc.[264] Perilous climate shifts will happen within decades, not just centuries.[265] And all this will drive resource pressure and mass migrations, which in turn, will breed crime and terror.[266] In this situation, we, as humankind, have to come together.

The Donner Party was a group of American pioneers who set out for California in a wagon train in May 1846. They had to spend the winter of 1846 to 1847 snowbound in the Sierra Nevada. Those, who were alone, without family, died in the snowstorms. Family members survived.[267]

We, as humankind, can, and need to, manifest that we are *one* family, now that we are in such a perilous situation. In my work, I therefore wish to do two things, first, I look "deeper," and, second, I wish to "stand in solidarity." These are the words of Rabbi Lynn Gottlieb, one of the first ten women to become a rabbi:

> I've had to look at all of the elements that bind us in relationship and try to look at what is maintaining a violent status quo and what actually promotes peace. It's not always obvious and it's not always intuitive. And many people think that they're doing a good thing when in fact they may actually be sustaining a very negative status quo. Without addressing the roots of the violence, you may actually be just putting a bandage on a bleeding wound. You have to look at the wound itself and listen to the voices of those who receive the brunt of the violence. I think there's a lack of understanding about what nonviolence is in some quarters because people who have never been on the front lines don't really understand what's at stake. Life and death is at stake. And nonviolence means that you are standing in solidarity – and when you do that you stand in solidarity with *both sides*.[268]

I wish to contribute to creating what philosopher John Dewey has called a *great community*.[269] I work so that the public spheres within world society will become more educated and develop *civic intelligence*.[270] I work so that we can arrive at sensible judgments and sustainable solutions for the problems we all face. On this path many things are important, among others, to "avoid pathologizing human suffering," to avoid "psychologizing sociopolitical dimensions," and to avoid "moralizing the psychological or psychologizing the moral."[271] For me, the modern hero is the *nurturer*, the *gardener*, the skillful and wise *navigator* of a ship in distress – not the *warrior*,[272] not even the "warrior for peace." Author Ursula Le Guin has observed this:

> Americans are given to naming enemies and declaring righteous war against them. Indians are the enemy, socialism is the enemy, cancer is the enemy, Jews are the enemy, Muslims are the enemy, sugar is the enemy. We don't support education, we declare a war on illiteracy. We make war on drugs, war on Viet Nam, war on Iraq, war on obesity, war on terror, war on poverty. We see death, the terms on which we have life, as an enemy that must be defeated at all costs. Defeat for the enemy, victory for us, aggression as the means to that end: this obsessive metaphor is used even by those who know that aggressive war offers no solution, and has no end but desolation.[273]

I so much resonate with Le Guin when she promises: "I will try never to use the metaphor of war where it doesn't belong, because I think it has come to shape our thinking and dominate our minds so that we tend to see the destructive force of aggression as the only way to meet any challenge. I want to find a better way."[274] Like Le Guin, I wish to refrain from reducing positive action to "fighting against." As much as I can, I try to avoid using words such as *non*violence or any other *anti*-terminology. I refrain from talking of "waging peace" – I believe one cannot be aggressively peaceful. One can be firmly peaceful.

The task of a nurturer and navigator is to help monitor reality aptly and forge strategies that are adaptive. Global interconnectedness is a new reality for humankind, and it requires new strategies. The new *Realpolitik* has to be more inclusive and more preventive than the old one. Concepts such as "enemies and friends" are no longer feasible.[275] The only viable concept left is a world of *neighbors*, who, while "good" or "bad," always need to coexist without mayhem. Couples, when they divorce, can move away from each other, yet, there is no empty continent available today to which human communities could move when they dislike each other, no other planet to escape to. Huge prisons cannot be the solution either. We are stuck together on this planet. We need to learn to be inclusive. Humankind needs to learn, at a minimum, what divorced couples with joint custody for their children learn, namely, cooperation even if they hate each other. Loving each other is the maximum ambition; yet, this is not necessary for the success of humankind's shared custody for our joint home planet. And we need to become aware of the significance of prevention. In medicine, there is prevention and treatment. When prevention was neglected and treatment fails, the patient might die. Humankind will turn out to be that "dead patient" unless preventing deadly conflict takes priority over post-hoc "treatment" of terror and mayhem. And prevention means getting out of short-term re-actionism toward the long-term construction of a better world. Tactics of terror are powerful and efficient to attain domination; they are uselessness to attain partnership.

Why is this book so long, even after having been shortened by more than half? I often hear the argument that we live in times where people only read executive summaries. That might be true. I have written several papers on terrorism that can serve as such summaries. For those who wish for a rather quick summary, my chapter on terrorism that I wrote for Latha Nrugham might be suitable and it is online.[276] Then I recommend the paper on the journey of humiliation and dignity,[277] and my 2006 book on humiliation and international conflict.[278]

Yet, we do not ask a painter only to paint small pictures. Some people want large pictures. This book is written for them, even if only very few. I could have gathered the essays I wrote on terrorism in the past into a normal-size book. Yet, I wanted to go deeper here, also for my own sake. I join sociologist Hartmut Rosa in his search of forms of un-alienated life, I am aware of the relationship between acceleration and alienation, and I wish to escape this "feverish stagnation" of acceleration.[279] This is therefore a "slow book." Like slow food, and slow living.[280] The length of this book also responds to philosopher Dagfinn Føllesdal's urge to me, already in 1996, to map out "in rich descriptive studies" how feelings of humiliation emerge.[281]

This book is part of a larger book project with the title *Humiliation and Terror: Defusing and Preventing an Explosive Mixture*. Initially it was titled *Humiliation and Terrorism*, and later renamed to *Humiliation and Terror*. Tens of thousands of pages of notes of interviews and conversations, and other material, have been collected for this project since 2010. The larger project proceeds from Volume I, which focuses on the *past* (and how it still is with us), on the *present* (Volume II), and from there to the *future* (Volume III). These were the original titles of the three volumes of this book project:

Volume I	The Past: Terrorism in the Name of Honor – Terror as Accepted Path to More Honor
Volume II	The Present: Terrorism in the Context of Dignity – Terror as Unacceptable Path to More Dignity
Volume III	The Future: Toward a Terror-Free World

This book is the first volume of the overall book project and it is also a stand-alone book. As time and resources might not allow me to finalize Volume I and II, the first volume has been expanded to comprise elements of all three.

Each volume has the following sections that build on each other throughout the three volumes. These are the originally envisioned titles:

Volume I – The Past: Terrorism in the Name of Honor – Terror as Accepted Path to Honor (see Abstracts for each section[282])
Section 1: The Security Dilemma – Too Far Apart and Too Close Together
Section 2: Honor Humiliation – Pressure from Outside, the Duty to Retaliate
Section 3: Peace the Traditional Way – "Balance of Terror" – Keeping One's Enemies Out and One's Own People in Line

Volume II – The Present: Terrorism in the Name of Dignity – Terror as Unacceptable Path to Dignity (see Abstracts for each section283)
Section 1: The Dignity Dilemma – Too Close Together
Section 2: Dignity Humiliation – Urge from Inside to Retaliate
Section 3: Peace the New Way – Inclusive Dialogue between Equals

Volume III – The Future: Toward a Terror-Free World (see Abstracts for each section284)
Section 1: Globalization Through Egalization
Section 2: Walking the Gandhi and Mandela Path – Understanding without Condoning, Respecting without Appeasing
Section 3: Practicing the Human Dignity Way – Toward a Future of Careholdership for Global Equality in Dignity

Several other books concepts have spawned in the process. All over the planet, I give talks and lectures. Usually, lively conversations ensue afterwards. Most topics are talked about in a relaxed manner – explorations and reflections are shared in a friendly atmosphere. There are two exceptions. Two issues heat up feelings more than others and make people upset or even outraged at me. One or two people in the audience usually speak up in public or approach me in private after my lecture, and it can happen that they are outright furious at me. It is as if I had personally hurt them, betrayed them, either that they feel I tried to willfully mislead them, or, at best, that, in their eyes, I am guilty of dangerously negligent ignorance.

One of those two hot topics is the notion of equal dignity for all. Many seem to believe that equal dignity means equality, and that equality indicates that there are no differences, that all are forced into identicalness, forced to become indistinguishable copies of the same, as, for instance, in present-day North Korea. I have coined the word *egalization* to differentiate the notion of equal dignity from phrases such as equality, equity, egalitarianism, or identicalness. The term egalization avoids claiming that there should be no differences among people. Egality can coexist with hierarchy that regards all participants as possessing equal dignity, such as the hierarchy between parents and children or between the pilots of a plane and its passengers; egality cannot coexist, however, with hierarchy that defines some people as more worthy than others.[285]

The other topic is human nature and whether it is fundamentally "evil or good." Whether humans are a fundamentally peaceful or warlike species. It is often the same person who questions both equal dignity and human nature, which initially surprised me and made me wonder how these two themes are connected. I got my first taste of this dynamic when anthropologist William Ury gave a keynote lecture whose message was similar to mine, and this was in 1999 in Belfast, Northern Ireland.[286] I was flabbergasted at the level of wrath Ury encountered after his talk. It took me years to get used to similarly heated attacks after my talks. In the beginning, I was simply startled. Then I was shocked. Until I began to expect this criticism.

In the eyes of the people who get angry at me, I fail to sufficiently acknowledge the evilness at the core of human nature. They see a "desire to dominate,"[287] an *animus dominandi*,[288] or an "inherent will to power"[289] that will always keep human nature in its grip.[290] Others answer the question "is our species an antisocial or a prosocial animal?[291] by confirming that humans are part of the eat-or-be-eaten world of living creatures, and that therefore human nature is imbued with an aggressive territorial sense and thus is predominantly antisocial in its essence. In the Anglophone world, some refer to the work of Napoléon Chagnon.[292] Others take out Steven Pinker's book *The Blank Slate*,[293] and are angry at me because they think I am promoting a "blank state" hypothesis of human nature, or, alternatively, that I reject it for the wrong reasons. Jean-Jacques Rousseau's name is often associated with the view on human nature as "good," while for Thomas Hobbes, human nature was "bad" and untrustworthy. Those, who adhere to the latter conceptualization, the "pessimistic, hard-nosed conservatives" so to speak, tend to label all disbelievers as appeasers, who, with their "naïve optimism," increase the risk of war rather than decreasing it.

In my view, the very dichotomy is misleading and dangerous. It creates a world that is more dangerous than it otherwise could be, since it precludes solutions that build on the insight that humans are social beings who carry the potential for both, war and peace. To address this question, I have set out to write a separate book with the working title *Human Nature, Honor, and Dignity: If We Continue to Believe in the Evilness of Human Nature, We May Be Doomed.*

Then there is a third misunderstanding that is related to the second. It is the expectation that more effective global governance must be avoided because it would inevitably mean global dictatorship and loss of local identities. This view I meet in North America among those who define freedom as absence of constraints,[294] and in the east and south of Europe, where trust in government is lower than in the west and north of Europe.[295] In my view, the argument of small government versus big government is another false choice. When I studied Somalia, I saw how its government is too small, while North Korea's is too big, one may say, an observation that acknowledges that the solution is *good* governance, rather than *too much* or *too little* government. The same is valid for global governance. Leaving a global power vacuum, as happens now, invites global terror into all segments of life; it creates precisely the global tyranny that is feared.[296] To use the traffic metaphor, the absence of traffic lights does not mean freedom; it means that strongmen gleefully set up their own lights, worse than anybody would wish for.

Then there is a fourth misunderstanding, or, better, a fourth unexpectedly strong reaction. When working on Volume II of this book project, I became more aware of why the study of humiliation elicits skepticism in certain circles. To formulate is provocatively, avenging honor humiliation is "for men," while crying about dignity humiliation is "for sissies." Let me explain. Honor is like an armor, and this armor must be defended in duel-like responses among equal men, particularly in aristocratic elites.[297] Honor humiliation has a tradition of requiring aristocratic elites to go for duel-like revenge, while underlings have to succumb to it in meek and subservient humility. Almost all women belong to the latter category. A man unable to keep up his armor is expected to feel shame and anger over his weakness. As explained earlier, dignity humiliation is more intense than honor humiliation as a feeling, yet, it calls for a less violent response. It is more intense insofar as it exiles the victim from humanity altogether, rather than merely lowering him on a ranked ladder; since human rights ideals of equal dignity represent a higher promise than ranked honor, also their violation is more salient, and, in addition, this promise applies to everybody, not just to power elites.[298] As the advent of human rights ideals on the world stage makes the phenomenon of humiliation more relevant, this is also why the academic field of humiliation studies is a rather new field. This is also why it is being nurtured by a person like me, who draws on a very particular life experience that includes the peripheral regions of the world, where the disappointment over broken promises of dignity is more palpable than in power centers.

While dignity humiliation is more intense as a feeling, dignity humiliation at the same time calls for less violent responses. In contrast to going to duel, the ideal path for healing dignity humiliation is dialogue among equals in dignity, dialogue that leads to peaceful social change, in short, the Freire-Mandela-Gandhi path. Unsurprisingly, this is anathema to those who are accustomed to believing that only losers whine, while real men fight back. They will want to respond to dignity humiliation and its heightened intensity not like a Nelson Mandela; they will want to respond with the traditional script for defending honor.[299] This is why many misunderstand my work as too "soft" and therefore irrelevant: killing enemies rather than healing humiliation is their formula. They identify with the differentiation of "hard" (male) science versus "soft" (female) feelings. All this increases the impact of the phenomenon of humiliation in the contemporary world, and it increases the need for academia to explore it and society to prevent and heal it.

A fifth case refers to those who think that I claim that all humiliation leads to violence or that all violence is caused by humiliation. Clearly, humiliation often leads to apathy, depression, and inertia; specific circumstances are required for humiliation to lead to violence. It may be "going black" into hot rage, or acquiring the necessary resources to rise from depression, or one may be recruited by humiliation entrepreneurs.[300] And then we had a Nelson Mandela who showed that humiliation can lead to constructive social change: he transformed humiliation in ways similar to what Paulo Freire and Mahatma Gandhi would have commended; he avoided the path toward genocide that fellow African country Rwanda saw.

Dynamics of humiliation can start with simple misunderstandings. Psychologists have identified at least four layers of communication where it can falter: the layer of facts or "matter," the layer of "self-disclosure," of "relationship," and of "appeal."[301] To give a commonplace example, imagine a wife having prepared a meal and eating it with her husband. He says: "There is something green in the soup." On the layer of facts, he points at something being green, on the self-revealing layer he discloses that he does not know what it is, on the relationship layer he indicates that she may know what it might be, and on the appeal layer he asks her to enlighten him. His wife may understand something very different: On the layer of facts, she hears that there is something green, on the self-revealing layer she may infer that this makes her husband feel uncomfortable, on the relationship layer she may hear him saying that, in his eyes, she is a bad cook, and, at last, on the appeal layer, she might hear that she should leave the green stuff out next time. Ultimately, the wife may reply, irritated: "My God, if you do not like it here, you can eat somewhere else![302]

A simmering sense of humiliation, presumably, if it is not already the backdrop of such a scene, will be the consequence of such misunderstandings. As mentioned previously, some scholars use the terminology of resentment, or ressentiment, for such smoldering emotional states.[303] As soon as resentment is manifest, it dissolves willingness to cooperate in good faith, it removes trust, it pits "me" against "the other," and this is as disruptive for a marriage as it is for society at large. It may express itself in myriad ways, along the entire gamut of possible polarizations, be it sexism or colorism or any other similar "-ism." Clinical psychologist Narendra Keval calls it a "perversion of thinking."[304] Keval describes racism as a "bewildering mix of anxieties, feelings and fantasies" expressed in a "nostalgic gaze that is infused with a toxic interplay of grievance, murderous rage, and vengeful feelings and fantasies that have resulted from a real or imagined narcissistic injury to the self, group, or nation."[305] As populist movements are on the rise on all continents,[306] Keval's description, apt not just for the "racist state of mind," shall round up this fifth case:

> In a racist state of mind grief and mourning for such losses are replaced by manic omnipotent states which aim to triumph over feelings of powerlessness through an inflated sense of self that claims superiority over others who are made to become the bearers of inadequacy or inferiority. The compensatory excitements of hatred, cruelty, and violence can lead to a collapse of a triangular mental space that damages the capacity for curiosity and concern for others. The tragic consequences of this psychic assault is a rupture at the very core of identity and the self which aims to thwart the desires and emotional freedom of others.[307]

There are many more misunderstandings that I frequently come across. I am used to think in complementary terms, for example, yet, support for one direction is often misunderstood as rejection of another. Wanting more dignity for women, for instance, does not mean hating men; it means wanting more dignity for all. For me, dignity is best manifested as unity in diversity, thus transcending the traditional dichotomic thinking of either/or. I like to say "yes and ..." rather than "but no ..." in the spirit of nondualism. Usually, therefore, when I emphasize one argument, this does not mean that I deny another; I often add it and contextualize it. In general, as a nondualist, I appreciate all approaches and all angles, be they theoretical and practical. I value novel insights and like to benefit from them by connecting them to other ideas, rather than discrediting and "criticizing" them for what they lack, or suppressing those ideas which can be misunderstood and misused. For instance, when I talk about humiliation as cause for enmity and violence, I do not deny other causes, and I do not deny that the humiliation argument can be misunderstood and misused. Or, only because I have developed a global life design, this does not mean that I criticize those who do not live like me. I only wish to inspire. With our dignity organization, we do not aim at building an empire. We wish to nurture relationships. Initially, our aim was to offer platforms for unlimited public dialogue in our network, yet, we had to abandon this initiative, not because we like to exert control, but because the need to moderate such platforms and protect their integrity was too overwhelming. We support the ideals on which the United Nations are built and we highly appreciate all idealistic and dedicated people who work within it.[308] Our work is meant to be complementary, in support of these ideals, rather than in opposition. Gay Rosenblum-Kumar, for example, is one of our dignity heroes; with her global work for preventive action, she has manifested the UN's highest ideals.[309]

While collecting material for this book, I have watched with surprise how different "boxes" filled up and called for being addressed in separate articles and books. First, it became clear that a book is needed on my global life design, with the working title *Bringing Dignity to Globalization: Living Globally as Research Method and Practice*. Second, it would overload this book to include the research on the significance of the concept of humiliation and dignity and I wrote a separate paper.[310] Third, the already mentioned book on human nature emerged as a concept. Fourth, describing the intriguing inconsistency of dignity humiliation leading to honor responses may become too long for Volume II.

This book grew out from lived experience, from immersing myself into the daily life on all continents over many years. By striving to never be a "visitor," "guest," or "field researcher," who "travels" and stays in hotels to "study a "case," but by living in families, by being part of communities on all continents as fellow human being, for the past forty years, I have developed a deep sense of what moves people of all walks.[311] Also my seven years of working as a psychotherapist and counselor in Cairo, Egypt, from 1984 to 1991, with clients of many backgrounds and cultures, was deeply formative for me. The theme of terrorism was prominent already then. I am filled with deep gratitude toward all people who have opened up to me.

As founding president of the Human Dignity and Humiliation Studies fellowship, and co-founder of the World Dignity University initiative, I am co-responsible for our annual conferences, and I usually spend several months at their respective locations. We gather for one global conference at a different location each year, and this has led us since 2003 to Europe (Paris, Berlin, Oslo), Costa Rica, China, Hawai'i, Turkey, New Zealand, South Africa, Rwanda, and Chiang Mai in Northern Thailand. In 2012, I spent several months in six countries in South America, and we plan to have our Dignity Conference in the Brazilian Amazon in 2019.[312] We also come together for a second conference each year in December, that is our Workshop on Transforming Humiliation and Violent Conflict at Columbia University in New York City, with Morton Deutsch as honorary convener (he passed away on March 13, 2017, ninety-seven years old, and we will celebrate his memory by continuing this workshop series). By fall 2017, we will have held thirty conferences all around the world.[313] All our efforts are a labor of love, we have an almost zero budget, no monetary incentives are involved.

This book grew also out from more formalized efforts. For instance, during the time I lived in Japan, I met with Ramesh Thakur of the United Nations University, UNU, in Tokyo. It was on July 21, 2004. He invited us to develop two large research projects, and in 2005, together with Paul Stokes,[314] I worked on those projects for one year. One was titled *Terrorism and Humiliation: Why People Choose Terrorism*, to be carried out with nine research teams of young scholars and their academic advisors in cooperation with UNU.[315] The aim was to shed more light on the choices made by people who turn to terrorism, so as to help prevent it more effectively. The other project had the title *Refugees and Humiliation: How Dignity is Degraded When You Are a Refugee, or a Displaced or Stateless Person*, and was envisioned to be carried out with twenty-one research teams. Unfortunately, due to the support from UNU not materializing as expected, both projects could not be realized. However, several researchers are still interested to continue. "Terrorism and Humiliation: The Case of

Pakistan," for instance, is the project proposed by Zahid Shahab Ahmed now.[316]

I am in continuous conversation with many hundreds of scholars, thinkers, practitioners and activists all around the world, many of them members in our Human Dignity and Humiliation Studies fellowship, either in its global advisory board, or core team, research team, or education team. On different occasions, I have been in contact with scholars who work with terrorism in particular, and who have shared valuable insights with me. I highly appreciate the expertise developed in Norway, as it is inspired by the Norwegian cultural heritage of respect for *likeverd* (equality in dignity), *dugnad* (solidarity), and global responsibility (see the Nansen passport). The Norwegian cultural heritage resonates deeply with the human rights ideals. It supports Riane Eisler's partnership model of society and my notions of *globegalization* and *dignism*.[317] I therefore value very highly the work of scholars such as Tore Bjørgo, Lars Gule, Brynjar Lia, Thomas Hegghammer, Laila Bokhari, Petter Nesser, Morten Bøås, among others,[318] and, of course, the work of the Peace Research Institute Oslo (PRIO).[319] The prediction from Norway is that "jihadi attack plot frequency" in Europe may see progressively higher peaks in the coming years.[320]

Furthermore, I highly value knowing Monty Marshall and having learned about his work with Ted Gurr. We met for the first time at the expert group meeting on "Structural Threats to Social Integrity: Social Roots of Violent Conflict and Indicators for Prevention," organized by the Social Integration Branch of the Division for Social Policy and Development of the United Nations' Department of Economic and Social Affairs, in New York City, December 18-20, 2001.[321] Then, Clark McCauley, a social psychologist and editor of the journal *Dynamics of Asymmetric Conflict: Pathways Toward Terrorism and Genocide*, has enriched several of our annual Workshops on Transforming Humiliation and Violent Conflict at Columbia University through his presence.[322] Alex Schmid is the director of the Terrorism Research Initiative, and I very much value his reflections, for instance, on radicalization versus extremism.[323] I also met Robert Lambert, lecturer in Terrorism Studies in London, at the NATO advanced research workshop titled "Indigenous Terrorism: Understanding and Addressing the Root Causes of Radicalisation Among Groups with an Immigrant Heritage in Europe," in Budapest, Hungary, in March 7–9, 2008.[324]

I have gathered large amounts of informal material for this book since 2010, in South America in 2012,[325] in South East Asia in 2014,[326] and in Africa in 2013 and 2015,[327] apart from my annual periods, each year for several months, in Europe and the U.S.[328] The full list of encounters, contacts, and material covers thousands of pages. Allow me to share a few snapshots of some more formal conversations in the Appendix to this section of the book. Let me include one snapshot here:

> Erik Solheim was Minister of International Development in Norway, when our conversation on humiliation and terrorism took place in the Ministry of Foreign Affairs in Oslo, Norway, on January 10, 2011. Until being appointed minister, he was as a diplomat and a participant in the Norwegian delegation that worked to resolve the Sri Lankan Civil War before the outbreak of the Eelam War IV. On May 3, 2016, United Nations Secretary-General Ban Ki-Moon announced that Solheim takes over the post of executive director of UNEP, the United Nations' Environment Programme. In our conversation in 2011, Solheim offered important examples of the role of humiliation, for instance, how it can trump material wealth. I have summarized and translated his reflections from Norwegian.[329]

What more do I wish to attain with this book project? What more can you expect? I wish to help us look through the *legitimizing myths* that maintain a situation even where it is detrimental to everybody's interest.[330] Particularly, when a *chosen trauma* is part of such myths, it is dangerous.[331] When a chosen trauma that is experienced as humiliation is not mourned, this may lead to the feeling of entitlement to revenge, and, under the pressure of fear and anxiety, to collective regression and ultimately to violence.

I wish to help us, all of humankind, to leave behind what I call *voluntary self-humiliation*.[332] No longer do we live in a disconnected world, but an interconnected world, and I wish to help us leave behind outdated mental and behavioral patterns that are bound to lead to ruinous results in the new context we live in. As mentioned above, psychologist Peter Coleman and his colleagues developed the dynamical systems theory, where they identify attractors, dominant mental and behavioral patterns that offer people a coherent map of the world, and a stable platform for action.[333] Like others before him,[334] Coleman observes the counterintuitive effect that many people justify the status quo even if it damages their interests,[335] a process that has also been called *penetration*, or "implanting the top dog inside the underdog."[336] This book project wishes to contribute to undoing this self-inflicted humiliation.

Even scientific paradigms resist change, despite the fact that it is the very essence of the scientific methodology to be open to new evidence.[337] Philosopher of science Thomas Kuhn observed that before paradigms shift, they rigidify, due to those who identify with them, benefit from them, and therefore stand up for them.[338] Paradigms are thus sustained even as "stubborn facts" cast them in doubt: "I know, but I can't believe it." This situation persists until a tipping point lets the dam break and a path opens for a new paradigm. "First they ignore you, then they ridicule you, then they fight you, then you win," this is a quote associated with Mahatma Gandhi. It may only be a new generation of people who are able to ask radically enough new questions that undermine the edifice.

This book project aims at hastening the tipping point, and it does so in a dignifying way, by pointing out, for instance, that human beings are social and cultural beings, and that they wish to belong. Beliefs guide our relationship both with our ecosphere and sociosphere, which means that we need to live with the world, and with others and ourselves.[339] This makes us vulnerable to being manipulated and this is one reason for why manipulation works with such great success. To belong, people are willing to internalize ideologies into their psychological structures, including ideologies that are detrimental to their own and common interest.[340]

Coopting people not only to accept and maintain their own bondage voluntarily, but to misrecognize it as "honor" and "heroism," or as "freedom," is the ultimate refinement of what I call the art of domination, or voluntary self-humiliation. Societies can be held in collective capture-bonding, a collective Stockholm syndrome where hostages identify with their captors.[341]

This book project is also written with the aim of radical global reconciliation, which goes much further than forgiveness; it requires radical understanding, which, in turn, necessitates radical empathy, and this cannot be achieved without radical respect.[342] It is not sufficient to engage in tolerance, compassion, or charity, it is not enough to be "against war and for peace." A much deeper paradigm shift is needed. Bertha von Suttner calls for *active disgust*. Von Suttner wrote the book *Die Waffen nieder*, or *Lay Down Your Arms!*, which brought her the Nobel Peace Prize in 1905.[343]

In the spirit of Bertha von Suttner, this book project aims at radicalizing its readers, in the sense of waking them up to the *conscientization* that a Paulo Freire called for, together with Freire's colleague Clodomir de Morais,[344] and Frantz Fanon,[345] Mahatma Gandhi, Martin Luther King, Nelson Mandela, and Desmond Tutu. They all were radical in their dedication to building a common critical consciousness to enable political transformation. In my language, this means acknowledging humiliation, it means embracing feelings of humiliation to turn their energy into constructive action.[346] This, to me, is true resilience. Resilience that simply means callousness is not the answer.[347] Callousness isolates and dehumanizes. Remember those Vietnam veterans who could open up to their spouses only after they had joined a therapy group and shared the atrocities they had witnessed and committed.[348]

Conscientization requires courage. What if Nelson Mandela had decided that apartheid is acceptable and everybody should live with it? Wherever I turn on our planet these days, I notice, with horror, people who fail to feel active disgust, who fail to stand up and rather stand by.[349] There are too few "Mandelas" around, Mandelas who have the courage to identify humiliation, particularly systemic humiliation, and stand up rather than stand by.

Standing up is different from entertaining phobic fear, and it is also different from its opposite, neurotic avoidance of fear. The human mind seems to have a cognitive *eudaimonic* blind spot, meaning that we tend to either grossly overestimate how tragic a situation is, or we grossly underestimate it.[350] What is needed is a proper level of concern and worry. Crisis psychiatrists inform us that only one thousandth of one percent of people in society are severely psychologically disturbed, while twenty percent suffer from either neurotic lack of fear, or from "neurotic fear" such as phobias.[351] In the face of crisis, including terrorism, what is needed is avoiding neurotic responses of any kind, instead getting appropriately fearful, duly alert, and constructively angry.

Due caution is needed in the face of risks, be it risks flowing from detrimental reverberations of economic arrangements, nuclear power, or terrorism. When appropriate caution is denigrated as personal weakness or "sissiness," then the lifesaving human capacity to use fear for protection remains unused. Unfortunately, the cultural training within the dominator societies of the past millennia has brought a masculine culture to the fore that idolizes fearlessness.

The book therefore wishes to make the reader constructively fearful and angry. We need to muster the courage to use fear as due warning signal. I am worried when I see global challenges increasing the need to be fearful, while its legitimacy decreases and its lifesaving utility goes unused. The case of terrorism is particularly complex. On one side, I see people being denigrated as cowards when they take the risk of terrorism seriously, for example, when nuclear power plants are not sufficiently protected against terrorist attacks. On the other side, the risk of terrorism is amplified when it serves the aim to underpin, for example, the curtailing of civil liberties or as a pretext for re-invigorating the security dilemma and increasing military expenditure. It is reckless to be oblivious of the fact that large-scale military responses to terrorism may even increase terrorist activity[352] – when counterterrorism efforts go too far, this helps terror organizations to mobilize new supporters for terrorism.[353]

In this way, the risks flowing from terrorism are both dangerously played down, and dangerously played up. If reasonable balance were the outcome, it would be acceptable. However, it is not. The result is that what is being done, is easily misguided, and what should be done, fails to be done. What should not be done is being done, namely, instrumentalizing terrorism for ulterior goals. What should be done is the weaving of global social cohesion, yet, this is neglected.

This book also aims to help build safe spaces. To avoid panic backlashes into outdated solutions, calmness and balance are needed when new paradigms must be manifested. There is a "tension between the necessity to build safe spaces for learning and trust building on the one hand, and the need to de-stabilize habitual notions of the self and the other."[354] Doubts and questions must be allowed, dissonance addressed and not suppressed. "… it is crucial to create and maintain a learning climate which avoids threat of identities, humiliation and the rise of resentments."[355]

How can we know when the "village" is safe enough to raise its children? If we look at predictors of a society's peacefulness, it is not its level of wealth, democracy, or ethno-religious identity. The best predictor is how well its women are treated.[356] Clearly, there is still a long way to go to make the world a safe space. Violence affects seventy percent of girls and women around the world.[357]

To round up, the peacefulness of world society is under threat from tactics of terror, both by states and non-state actors. In the twentieth century states killed about 170 million civilians; the ratio would be 340 to one, if the death from non-state terrorist groups over the same period of time were calculated at around 500,000.[358] In other words, so far, states have killed many more than non-state terrorists.

While world wars afflicted the twentieth century, which had a start and an end, by now, I observe a continuous atmosphere of terror permeating all continents. This atmosphere stems from the systemic degradation of social and ecological resources promoted by economic arrangements. The world is organized around investor return and "wealth protection" for a few. This, to me, is the most hideous source of terror. I work for a world society that represents a safe space for all its members, free of hideous terror.

Let me conclude with a poem by Judy Wicks, who works for a more compassionate, environmentally sustainable and locally based economy:

Good Morning, Beautiful Business

maximization of relationships, not of profits;
growth of consciousness and creativity, not brands and market share;
democracy and decentralized ownership, not concentrated wealth;
a living return, not the highest return;
a living wage, not the minimum wage;
a fair price, not the lowest price;
sharing, not hoarding;
simplicity, not luxury;
life-serving, not self-serving;
partnership, not domination;
cooperation, not competition;
win-win exchange, not win-lose exploitation;
family farms, not factory farms;
biodiversity, not monocrops;
cultural diversity, not monoculture;
creativity, not conformity;
slow food, not fast food;
our bucks, not Starbucks;
our mart, not Wal-Mart;
a love of life, not a love of money.

Judy Wicks[359]

What about terrorism and radicalization?

What does this book project aim at with respect to terrorism and radicalization? Much has been said in the Preface. For instance, that I wish to radicalize the reader, toward dignity, toward the path of a Bertha von Suttner, Paulo Freire, Mahatma Gandhi, or Nelson Mandela.

Arie Kruglanski is a social psychologist who studies violent extremism, and he explains: "There are strong correlations between humiliation and the search for an extremist ideology. Organizations like ISIS take advantage of people who, because of racism or religious or political discrimination, have been pushed to the margins of society."[360]

On June 12, 2016, Omar Mateen, a 29-year-old security guard, killed 49 people and wounded 53 others in a terrorist attack inside Pulse, a gay nightclub in Orlando, Florida, United States. This shooting was considered the "deadliest mass shooting by one person in United States history."[361] Who was this shooter? Why did he commit such a hate crime? Was he a self-radicalized terrorist, a religious extremist caught in a "clash of cultures" as a child of first generation immigrants, a bullied adolescent who should have been attended to by mental health services, a youth in a sexual identity crisis, a security guard who wanted to avenge his failure to become a police officer, a young homophobic man, a misogynist suffering from "toxic masculinity," or all of the above?"[362]

Counterterrorism is difficult to conceptualize and address. There are short-term and small-step interventions to be considered, as well as long-term and large-scale change. This book focuses on the latter. Long-term change aims at preventing tactics of terror, and at creating a global society in which tactics of terror no longer find fertile ground to grow. The reader of this book is most probably at the cusp of such long-term change efforts, otherwise she would not have chosen to look at this book.

Yet, also long-term prevention has to begin with small-steps. Mahatma Gandhi reminded us to *be* the change we want to see in the world. In Gandhi's spirit, the reader is called on to read this book in ways that manifest this ambition.

Terror leads to fear. Fear can hamper constructive conflict transformation when it creates "tunnel vision" and blind *fight or flight or freeze* responses. However, as mentioned earlier, there is also sensible fear, appropriate caution, which can enhance solutions when it sharpens our senses and alerts our thoughts. Interestingly, research shows that women often react with *tend and befriend* reactions to stress.[363] I would be happy if the reader could read this book with a tend-and-befriend attitude, with dukes down rather than dukes up,[364] with a lovingly critical sense of *satyāgraha*.

The book is an invitation to you, the reader, an invitation into a journey of mutually enriching co-reflection, rather than a rigid statement of alleged truths for you to conform or oppose. This book is inscribed into a culture of *deliberate discourse*, in Aristotle's terminology, rather than a culture of debate.[365] We know of the Socratic dialogue, and that constructive controversy is often more beneficial than confrontation. When Aristotle spoke of deliberate discourse, he thought of joint discussion of the advantages and disadvantages of proposed actions aiming at synthesizing novel solutions embedded in creative problem solving.[366] Psychologist Carl Rogers has developed a client-centered therapy and student-centered learning, where a person does not judge or teach another person but facilitates another's learning.[367] Researcher Mary Belenky calls for *connected knowing* rather than *separate knowing.*[368] In connected knowing "one attempts to enter another person's frame of reference to discover the premises for the person's point of view."[369]

A reader of this book who takes a connected approach will read it with an empathic, receptive eye, instead of only inspecting the text for flaws. And she will suspend judgments of right and wrong until later in the book. The quality of judgments falls short if based on quick reflexes of uninformed bias. The urge to shortcut to biased judgments I beg you therefore to keep on hold. "First understand, then judge," this is the motto of this book project and my dignity work in general.

Connected knowing, incidentally, can also be called "women's ways of knowing."[370] Philosopher Agnes Heller, in her theory of the consciousness of everyday life, describes how masculinity, on an ordinary, everyday level, reproduces itself through the interplay of individual consciousness and social structures, and how the masculinist models of consciousness objectify world order, obfuscating how fluid and continuously malleable it is in reality.[371]

Jürgen Habermas advocates *public deliberation*.[372] We should *grapple* with issues.[373] The concept of *nudging*, at least as long as it also teaches resistance to paternalistic manipulation, can be important.[374] Social psychologist Morton Deutsch has suggested persuasion strategies and nonviolent power strategies.[375] *Listening into voice* is how psychologist Linda Hartling calls it, and social scientist Andrew Dobson agrees that listening is "the new democratic deficit."[376] Linda Hartling explains:

> The expression "listening into voice" draws our attention to the fact that human communication is a bi-directional experience. It is a phrase that encourages us to attune to the fundamental relational nature of speaking. It reminds us to look beyond the individualist myth that speaking is a one-way experience in which the speaker is solely responsible for communicating effectively. Speaking is interactive. It is a two-way experience in which both (or all) people participating in the relationship can chose to listen and engage in a way that will help others to effectively express and clarify their ideas.[377]

Sociologist Seymour M. Miller recommends *let-it-flow thinking* to prevail over *verdict thinking*.[378] The Buberian *I-Thou* orientation,[379] the terminology of *capabilities* and human *flourishing* by Martha Nussbaum and Amartya Sen,[380] or the teachings of *dialogue* by Paulo Freire point into the same direction.[381] David Bohm,[382] Otto Scharmer,[383] Leonard Swidler,[384] and, finally, Inga Bostad,[385] are other like-minded thinkers.

Understanding in the sense of comprehending (not necessarily condoning!) is hard work. It requires time and effort. It involves looking at the world and learning to see the landscapes in which people act. It is helpful to imagine being a traveler from another galaxy who visits planet Earth and writes reports back home. *The Hitch-hiker's Guide to the Galaxy* was a novel that gained cult status. Imagine you are a galactic traveler. I believe that the galactic perspective of "big history" is not only fascinating, but also highly useful.[386]

I am aware that any "explanation" of why cruelties such as terrorism or genocide happen, can be misconstrued as "excusing" them. Philosopher Hannah Arendt paid a very high price for her concept of the "banality of evil."[387] She was accused of being a cold person, lacking love for the Shoah victims, or being a self-hating Jew. The painful result was that she, after having had to flee Nazi Germany, was excluded also for a second time, this time from her new home community in the United States. I have personally experienced this dilemma not least in Rwanda, where I carried out my doctoral research in 1999, and where we held our Annual Dignity Conference in 2015.[388] Scientist Jared Diamond wrote this about the genocide in Rwanda and the misunderstandings that can arise:

> However, regardless of whether we arrive at an oversimplified one-factor explanation or an excessively complex 73-factor explanation for a genocide doesn't alter the personal responsibility of the perpetrators of the Rwandan genocide, as of other evil deeds, for their actions. This is a misunderstanding that arises regularly in discussions of the origins of evil: people recoil at any explanation, because they confuse explanations with excuses. But it is important that we understand the origins of the Rwandan genocide -not so that we can exonerate the killers, but so that we can use that knowledge to decrease the risk of such things happening again in Rwanda or elsewhere.[389]

Why can connected knowing be the change we want to see in the world? As will become clearer throughout this book, terror tactics are embedded into a complex confluence of two very different cultural mindsets and their conflict-laden transitions, namely, that of ranked honor on one side, and of unranked dignity on the other. As will be discussed later in this book, in a world of global interdependence, social and ecological sustainability is best served by the latter mindset.[390] Also the long-term prevention of terror is best achieved by a transition toward a world united in equal dignity.

The ranked world model is a male-dominated model, where opponents fight for victory and domination.[391] Explaining this mindset is the focus of Volume I of this book project. The unranked world, in contrast, aims to be a world where cohesion is being co-created. This will be discussed in Volume II and III of this book project. Cohesion is best created by drawing on the traditional "female" script of tend-and-befriend, the script of listening-into-voice and bridge-building, rather than on the "male" script of fighting for victory and domination.[392]

I therefore recommend using the female script for long-term prevention more in the future, and invite the male fight response to be used only in well-defined situations of emergency. I call on the reader to use connected knowing to jointly journey through this book, so that we can draw on the best from both, the traditional female and male role scripts, and choose mindfully when and where elements of either fit best. Let this book be an invitation to create psychological safety for the entire global community, to create a sense of confidence that nobody will be embarrassed, rejected, or punished for speaking up, a "climate characterized by interpersonal trust and mutual respect in which people are comfortable being themselves."[393]

I said that I wish to radicalize the reader toward dignity. I explained that polarization into extremism is different from radicalization. For Alex Schmid it is an "unfortunate tendency to equate radicalism with extremism and both with terrorism while at the same time using the term 'terrorism' as shorthand label for political violence in general."[394] Social psychology research sheds light on the psychological factors that increase extremism and the polarization of attitudes, not just with respect to terrorism, but also in society at large, and it shows how they flow together to make it self-enforcing.[395] It begins with people overestimating their awareness of factual evidences and being unaware of their own ignorance.[396] Then they seek out information that resonates with their existing preferences.[397] When they encounter new information, they will incorporate it in biased ways so that it strengthens their current preferences,[398] they will associate with likeminded people,[399] and expect that other people's views are as extreme as their own.[400] In sum, extremism and attitude polarization is hard to avoid, once such reinforcing loops are set in motion.[401] Moderation becomes ever more difficult. Extremism therefore harms and destroys what is beneficial about democracy.[402]

Polarization has even damaged terrorism research itself. Alex Schmid observes that most of the literature "sees radicalization as a one-sided phenomenon, not realizing that it can take place in a polarized conflict relationship on both sides of a conflict dyad."[403]

This book project aims to attenuate and heal extremism, to de-radicalize from violence, and, instead, to radicalize toward constructive dignifying paths. I concur with those who say that current deradicalization programs would better be named "terrorism risk reduction initiatives."[404] I concur with Alex Schmid that the label Countering Violent Extremism (CVE) is more useful than the Global War on Terror (GWOT) label of the Bush Jr. administration.[405] Even though the exact contours of CVE are not clear, it is a "soft power," noncoercive approach to countering terrorism. Its professed goal is prevention, prevention by trying to "eliminate or minimize those factors that lead individuals to join violent extremist organizations or to support such groups."[406]

This book project takes a large-scale approach, also here concurring with Alex Schmid's view, namely, that the study of individual and small group radicalization, unfortunately, has become a substitute for a fuller exploration of the causes of terrorist violence in the "radical milieu."[407] Also another terrorism expert, Clark McCauley, warns that current research suffers from a certain fixation on the micro-level, on "vulnerable individuals, indoctrinated over the Internet or in physical locations and/or recruited by terrorist organizations," while "more analyses on the meso- and macro-levels is needed."[408]

Counter-radicalization has been defined by the United Nations Counter-Terrorism Implementation Task Force as "Policies and programmes aimed at addressing some of the conditions that may propel some individuals down the path to terrorism."[409] Elaine Pressman, an international expert in the risk assessment of violent political extremism, made a comprehensive list of de-radicalization, disengagement, and protection factors.[410] Alex Schmid summarizes the objectives of national de-radicalization programs, among others, as reducing the number of active terrorists, reducing violence and victimization, and increasing the legitimacy of the government or state agency.[411] Schmid calls on counter-radicalization efforts to put their main focus "not the terrorists themselves but rather the strengthening and empowering of the community from which they might emerge and which might, if neglected, be deemed potentially supportive of them."[412]

This book project heeds all of Schmid's admonitions. It also follows him when he says, "researchers should be aware that it is not only rational choices that are involved here but also individual arousal or collective waves of emotions triggered by traumatic experiences and major events."[413]

Alex Schmid acknowledges that, while his recommendations are in line with the UN Global Counter-Terrorism Strategy of 2006, 261,[414] this does not mean that they are being implemented: "... the implementation of the Global Strategy in all the UN Member States has been an altogether different matter: it is a costly, time-consuming process and limited by the absence of capacity and political will in many states as well as handicapped by the lack of a universally accepted legal definition of terrorism."[415]

Médecins Sans Frontières, or Doctors Without Borders, is a highly respected international humanitarian-aid non-governmental organization working in war-torn regions and developing countries facing endemic diseases. In order to be able to speak and act freely, MSF remains independent of all political, religious, or economic powers. I was impressed by Jason Cone from MSF, when he spoke on "Human Rights and Humanitarianism: Contradictory or Co-dependent?" and reported on the discussions within the organization on how the MSF mission can best be manifested: through *realism*, *confrontation*, and *abstention*.[416]

I ask myself: What is the best way forward for a terror-free world community? This book speaks to all of humankind, while resisting being coopted as "ancillary" to efforts of war and combat, including efforts aimed at "the elimination of terrorists."[417]

These are some of the obstacles on this journey in a nutshell: The powerful, those with privileges, will always feel humiliated when their supremacy, to which they feel entitled, is doubted – *loss aversion* is a well-known psychological dynamic.[418] By disparaging doubters as "terrorists," cycles of humiliation are set in motion. Also those at the bottom, those who see terror tactics as legitimate tools in asymmetrical situations, create cycles of humiliation. Cycles of humiliation engender stress, which, in turn, hinders sound reality testing. It can even create *addiction to humiliation*, where enmity is artificially fabricated.[419]

At the same time, "problems without a face" are overlooked, such as systemic ecological and social risks, precisely, because they are faceless. Other risks are augmented and instrumentalized to maintain privileges. Terrorism is part of this mix. The risks flowing from terrorism are being underplayed and overplayed in the service of power, be it power through traditional tyranny or power in the name of profit maximization. The danger for us, as humankind, is to get obsessed about the wrong risks, and fail to watch out for the real risks. The danger is to forget that present-day interconnectedness requires new strategies. Humanity has joint custody of its habitat, planet Earth. Terror tactics, including those employed to counter terrorism, play on submission and domination. To attain the very partnership that we need, such tactics are useless.

Margaret Mead said: "Never doubt that a small group of thoughtful, committed citizens can change the world. Indeed, it is the only thing that ever has." This book is part of a growing movement of thoughtful, committed citizens, and you, the reader, you are included. Plato (circa 428 – 348 before the Common Era[420]) recommended justice, wisdom, courage, and moderation (or *sophrosyne*, a sense of limit, moral sanity, self-control, and moderation guided by true self-knowledge). Faith, hope, and love were added later, together constituting the seven cardinal virtues. Aristotle highlighted *phronesis* (Latin *prudentia*), or "practical wisdom."[421] A more recent list entails eight core values: love, truthfulness, fairness, freedom, unity, tolerance, responsibility and respect for life.[422] Today, the world is well advised to follow Norway's example: it asked its philosopher Henrik Syse to teach its banks *sophrosyne*.[423]

In my *Gender, Humiliation, and Global Security* book, I called on everybody to join hands in redefining love, to make it visible, to give it a preeminent place, not just as an inconsequential feeling, but as a principle around which we live and organize our lives and the world. This love can never be too strong in securing the *sophrosyne* and *phronesis* that are necessary to create a world of balance. Let us make use of the extraordinary force that love can project. Let us make use of it for creating a better world, a world without systems of humiliation, a world of dignity. Let us employ firm, forceful, consequential, resolving, resolute, unyielding, potent, authoritative, powerful, courageous, undaunted, fearless love.

Satyāgraha is what is needed to wage good conflict. This is also the message of my *Emotion and Conflict* book (2009). And waging good conflict is what can heal and prevent terrorism. Jean Baker Miller, a pioneer in women's psychology, taught that conflict is a necessary part of growth and change. Conflict is not the problem – the way we engage in conflict is. Miller encourages us to learn how to "wage good conflict."[424]

Overcoming Terrorism

For Terrorism, there are no simple explanations
For it may involve persons, groups and even nations
As a result of premeditated or provoked evil acts
The loss of precious lives becomes painful, shameful historical facts
Terrorism: an outcome of uncontrolled emotions?
Combined with the escalation of political commotions?
In the way of Global Citizenship, Terrorism stands
that's a tough challenge every global change agent understands
Terrorism is a global adversary
To overcome it, establishment of global citizenship is necessary
To overcome Terrorism, safe, sustainable, life-dignifying cooperation is needed
As Evelin Lindner farsightedly advocates: legislation on Global Citizenship should be heeded

Composed by peace linguist Francisco Gomes de Matos for this book
Recife, Brazil
January 9, 2013[425]

Section One

The Security Dilemma – Too Far Apart and Too Close Together

Dulce et decorum est pro patria mori.
It is sweet and proper to die for one's country.

– Horace (65 – 8 BCE[1])
Roman lyrical poet, *Odes* (III.2.13)

Si vis pacem, para bellum.
If you want peace, prepare for war.

– Publius Flavius Vegetius Renatus,
writer of the late fourth century Roman Empire[2]

Not by speeches and votes of the majority are the great questions of the time decided … but by iron and blood.

– Otto von Bismarck (1815 – 1898),
first Chancellor of Germany, in 1862[3]

– the faith is true and adorable which leads a soldier to throw away his life in obedience to a blindly accepted duty, in a cause which he little understands, in a plan of campaign of which he has little notion, under tactics of which he does not see the use.

– Oliver Wendell Holmes
"The Soldier's Faith," 1895[4]

Adolf Hitler's view of the world's "primeval, correct state": "Races struggle against each other, kill each other, starve each other to death, and try and take land."

– Timothy Snyder, historian[5]

War for peace.

– Svetozar Marović,
political leader in Montenegro, 1991[6]

My neighbor, my enemy.

– Stover and Weinstein,
investigators of war crimes and human rights abuses, 2004[7]

Fear thy neighbor as thyself.

– Slavoj Žižek, philosopher and cultural critic, 2007[8]

Introduction to Section One

Global change is the name of a role-play that researchers use in psychological research on authoritarianism.[1] When people with a strong sense of authoritarianism played the game, the outcome was dramatic: The simulated future of the world became highly militarized and eventually entered the stage of nuclear war until the entire population of the Earth was declared dead. In contrast, when people of less authoritarianism played the same game, the result was world peace and global cooperation.[2]

On my global path throughout the past forty years, on all continents, I have lived with people from all walks of life, from indigenous communities in the rainforests to city dwellers in the world's slums and palaces. Underneath many layers of complexity and diversity,[3] I have learned to distinguish those two core ways of being-in-the-world that the game story depicts. The reader guesses rightly that I count myself into the second group of people.

Here is an imaginary story. Imagine you are a victim of a tsunami, lying injured on a beach. Someone stands above you, looking at you, assessing you. What he tries to determine is whether you are worth saving or not. You will be left to die if no profit is to be gained from saving you, be it profit in terms of prestige or money. Suddenly somebody else appears, lifts you up, and drags you into safety. It is a person who acts spontaneously, without delay, and does what is needed, just like a caring parent or sibling would do. The first person angrily shouts at the second: "But we are a business, not a charity! And, by the way, this one is not 'one of us'! Why do you help?!" The second person shouts back: "But we are all human beings!"

These are the two groups of people I meet. Recent social psychology experiments have confirmed what I see: People bound in authoritarian collectivism tend to blame victims rather than aid them, while those who regard all people as equally worthy, tend to come to help.[4]

In this book, Volume I of the overall book project, I will primarily focus on the first approach, the "profiteering" approach, and try to shed light on how it came into being. I will make clear that I see it becoming ever more dysfunctional at the historical juncture that humankind finds itself just now and that my experience indicates that the second way is better suited for a dignified future for humankind. Later, I will reveal that I observe two blind spots also in the second group, one blind spot pertaining to global governance, and the other concerning communication skills. The topic of global governance will be touched upon at the end of this book project.[5] As to dignifying communication, I attempt to model it by using a writing style that inspires reflection and exploration rather than debate and discussion.

The tsunami story depicts two main ways of being-in-the-world. The first approach is based on the view that worthiness is ranked, while for the second, worthiness is un-ranked. Terror is defined, felt, enacted, and reacted to in profoundly different ways in each of these contexts. The first approach, to say it simplified, has the potential, in the worst case, to lead to an Adolf Hitler, a terror entrepreneur, or a Mafia leader, while the second represents the Freire-Mandela-Gandhi path.[6]

The first approach carries the belief that everything on this planet is ordered in a way that some things and some beings are worth more and others less, that some are "we" and others are "them," that a calculus of gain and loss, of up and down, of in and out, is the backbone of the naturally or divinely ordained order of the world,[7] and that civilization would be lost if this order were not respected, protected, and reproduced. The unwilling helper in the tsunami story is committed to maintaining a world of domination and submission, of inclusion and exclusion. In order to achieve that, he has to stay continuously alert to remain *above* the world rather than *in* the world. He has to interrupt any uncensored flow of being-in-the-world, always keeping an inner distance from his own self and that of others, so as to be able to incessantly gauge, before acting, the "correct" friend-enemy calculus, the correct worthy-unworthy domination-submission ratio.

Particularly men, whose male identity is anchored in wanting to avoid "descending" into femaleness, have almost no pause from this inner toil. They learn to continuously stay detached, particularly from women and femaleness, so as to avoid falling prey to "sissiness." At the societal level, this manifests in sentences such as the one uttered by the reluctant helper, a sentence that often also goes as follows: "Don't cry like a woman! We are a business and not a charity!" I observe this calculus of gain or loss in terms of material resources, or in terms of honorable "masculine" status – be it now or later, maybe even after death – being inserted before action all around the world. It happens overtly and covertly; it can even be found wrapped in human rights rhetoric that at the surface carries the opposite message.[8]

The damage that this inner disconnection work brings to the world has been formulated well by Ta-Nehisi Coates, an African-American author. He brings to his readers the experience of the black body in the face of the "Dreamers," Dreamers being those "people who believe themselves to be white." Here Coates explains this to his black brothers:

> We are captured, brother, surrounded by the majoritarian bandits of America. And this has happened here, in our only home, and the terrible truth is that we cannot will ourselves to an escape on our own. Perhaps that was, is, the hope of the movement: to awaken the Dreamers, to rouse them to the facts of what their need to be white, to talk like they are white, to think that they are white, which is to think that they are beyond the design flaws of humanity, has done to the world.[9]

The second approach stands for the human rights tenet of "all human beings are born free and equal in dignity and rights,"[10] and, ideally, this includes the entire biotic and abiotic world. This is the motivation of the helper who saves your life. The profit-oriented helper would formulate this tenet completely differently, he would say: "All human beings are born unequal in worthiness and rights – or at least over time they end up being superior or inferior due to their own doing or undoing – and, as an unavoidable consequence, there will always be some who are more free than others."

I meet people walking the second path, the path of global inclusivity and equal dignity, independently of whether they have ever heard about human rights ideals or not. Often, indigenous or poor people have an unmediated understanding of it. According to what I have seen, this is also the human default way of being.[11] In Buddhism, *ariyapariyesena*, or the "noble search," means directing one's *tanha* (thirst) toward a desire for deep, long-lasting internal transformation, rather than toward *anariyapariye- sena*, or "ignoble search," which is the fruitless race for external acquisition and ascent on the status ladder. In Western societies, by now, the fruitlessness of this race is increasingly being felt. A widespread sense of alienation rises, attributed to the "deadly impact" of acceleration in modern life.[12]

I am aware that adherents of the ranked worldview believe that theirs is the human default approach; yet, as I said, my experience over four decades, on all continents of this planet, is that it is not. My experience suggests that ranking the world into layered worthiness is the result of a cultural-social-psychological learning process that took place in the course of the past millennia of human history. This observation has a hopeful implication, namely, that this worldview can also be un-learned, and, as I see it, also needs to be un-learned, not least if we wish to decrease terror in the world and create a decent future for coming generations.[13]

In my work, I use the terminology of *honor* – or, more precisely, *collectivistic ranked honor* – for the first path's notion of ranked worthiness. I use the terminology of *dignity* – or, more precisely, *equal dignity for all, together, as individuals in solidarity* – for the second concept of un-ranked worthiness. The second path follows the motto of *unity in diversity*, diversity uniting through respect for equal dignity, and it contrasts the profiteering helper's worldview of uniformity in division. I also find the image of the river useful, the river of life. I compare the first path with clinging to objects that protrude from the river, wanting to climb ever higher, seeking safety in overtowering others, while the second approach aims at finding safety in learning how to swim in the flux of life in mutual support of each other.

Other scholars have found other labels for those two basic worldviews. Political theorist Philip Pettit differentiates domination from *non-domination*,[14] while scholar Riane Eisler employs the terminology of a *dominator* model of society versus a *partnership* model.[15] In a dominator society *rankism* rigidifies rank.[16] Also in polls these two clusters have been found, one cluster has been labeled "on the right," the other the "human rights" cluster.[17] Cognitive linguists George Lakoff and Mark Johnson describe the *strict father* model, a pedagogical framework that produces obedient inferiors, in contrast to the *nurturant parent* model that nurtures responsible and aware citizens.[18] Cross-cultural psychologist Michael Harris Bond describes an *other-directedness and practicability* dimensions characterized by obedience and religious observance, versus *self-directedness and civility*, "a socialization agenda for agency, self-enhancement and initiative."[19]

When I speak of collectivist ranked honor versus equality in dignity for all human beings (including dignified relationships with nature), I apply the *ideal-type* approach conceptualized by sociologist Max Weber's, which differentiates various levels of abstraction.[20] The two approaches to life that I describe here are at the core of the concept, at the highest level of abstraction. At that level, these two approaches are so different that they cannot be reconciled: it is either being removed or not removed from the world, either above or in the world, either separated from or with oneself and others. It is domination or non-domination, either the manifestation of the dominator model of society or the partnership model.

The practice of so-called honor killing offers a stark illustration: In the honor context, a girl who has been raped may be killed by her family, while in a partnership context she will live and receive trauma therapy. In other words, at the core, it is either life or death, nothing in between. To use traffic as a metaphor, a country has to decide whether it wants right-hand driving and left-hand driving: It is not possible to realize both versions at the same time or allow for a slow transition from one to the other, where everyone has the freedom to do what they prefer.

In sum, the dominator model cannot be reconciled with a dignified future for humankind. The findings of the global change game experiment points into this direction. The first outcome, all-out death and destruction, was also Adolf Hitler's path, one of mass homicide, including suicide for himself and the destruction of the very country he had pledged to make great.[21] History offers myriad examples, more or less stark, of the script of total war, including total self-destruction. The first reaction of American President George W. Bush when he began to grasp what happened on September 11, 2001, seems to have been informed by this mindset, as he immediately spoke from within the script of war: "We are at war ... somebody's going to pay."[22]

I write this book to alert us to the degree to which this model suffuses our feelings, our thinking, and our actions, even though many of us may not be aware of it. The global peace outcome of the global change game can be illustrated by the message that came out of Norway in 2011, after it had experienced its equivalent to 9/11: "If one man can show so much hate, imagine how much love we all can show together."[23]

Philosopher Theodor Adorno and his colleagues studied authoritarianism.[24] They thought it was an aspect of personality. Yet, new insights emphasize the role of the context: authoritarianism emerges under circumstances of social threat.[25] This is also my observation on my global path, namely, that a context of threat, when it lacks easily accessible pathways for solutions, tends to create and maintain a world of terror and terrorism even in its attempts to fight it.

Consequently, the conclusion is unavoidable that only a large-scale transition to the second approach can solve, not only the problem of terrorism, but the challenge altogether of how humankind can survive on planet Earth in decency. As long as the dominator mindset prevails – in whatever segment of global and local society and in whatever overt or covert manifestation – terror will remain an "institution" at the core of society. Terror tactics will remain a useful tool for domination and for competition for domination. A large-scale transition presents itself as the only realistic way out, despite the fact that it seems unrealistic to expect it to happen, given the fact that the traditional dominator culture is so ingrained. Yet, as everybody will agree, big challenges do not become smaller through denial or faintheartedness.

To bring about such a large-scale transition, deep historical exploration is indispensable, and therefore this book uses such a broad approach. As mentioned earlier, some may misunderstand the message of this book as "apologism," others might refuse to separate understanding from condoning. Unfortunately, I fear, such misunderstanding will only contribute to worsening present-day's situation. I dedicate my entire life to inviting all people into the partnership way of being-in-the-world, and I applaud those who identify with it. I warn, however, that manifesting this path requires much more work and effort than even its staunchest sympathizers may realize – the problem of the blind spots alluded to earlier, for instance, stands in the way.

This leads back to the question of human nature's default state. Where does the dominator mindset come from, including terror as a useful tool? Has it always been part of the human condition? Is it human nature to be *Homo dominator* and *Homo terroris*? If not, when and where and why did this mindset emerge? If the dominator mindset stems from social threat, from where did that threat originate?

Chapter 1

The Dominator Mindset – Where Does It Come From?

From where did the dominator mindset emerge? According to renowned geographer Jared Diamond, agriculture is to blame. The invention of agriculture was "the worst mistake in the history of the human race," as it brought "starvation, warfare, and tyranny."[1] The winner of the 2006 essay competition of the journal *The Ecologist* openly lamented:

> Agriculture has disinherited us from our hunter-gatherer heritage and made it impossible for us to live in the egalitarian, consensus-based societies of our ancestors.[2] Instead, it forces on us a new set of social structures; structures of alienation and dominance which both support, and are supported by, the continuation and spread of agriculture. Our utopian visions of the future, freed from present problems by human ingenuity and technical competence, might be possible on paper, but they are unlikely in reality. We have already made the biggest mistake, and spent 10,000 years perfecting a disastrous invention, then making ourselves ever more reliant on it. However, the archaeologists who give us glimpses of our ancestors, and the anthropologists who introduce us to our cousins, have been able to show us why we dream what we do. What we yearn for is not just our imagined future; it is our very real past.[3]

Advocates of a Paleolithic diet would add that agriculture brought unprecedented health problems.[4] Before writing these lines, I took a little bicycle tour in the countryside where I stayed at the time, and I cringed when I saw the word "dominator" written in huge letters across the land machine that I saw standing by the road.[5]

Is Jared Diamond right? Is agriculture the "original sin"? Or is there a deeper problem, of which agriculture is only one expression, and the amalgam of warfare and tyranny, including terror, is just another manifestation? Perhaps the problem lies in the inner logic of domination, in the fact that strategies of domination range all the way from solution to tragedy?

The Ozone depletion was detected not too long after Freon was triumphantly introduced in the 1930s.[6] Is war and terror the equivalent of the Ozone hole, in this case for the strategy of domination? Only that it took millennia for the full range of its destructiveness to show?

Most terrorist experts have presumably never thought about the invention of agriculture and its possible link to terror. It may be too distant a connection, reaching too far back into history. And to understand it, one has to study all of humankind's history and learn about the ways humans have organized their affairs on Earth throughout history: much too much effort.

And terrorism experts will not be alone in their skepticism. Funding agencies will not wish to pay salaries for historical speculations. Many researchers will therefore conclude that rather than losing one's focus in grandiose historical guessing, it is better to study the factual expressions of terror as they occur here and now, and devise concrete counter-measures.

Yet, if there is a problem that continuously escapes solutions, those who really wish to work for change need to dig deeper, even if it is difficult. If more thorough solutions are required, they remain required also if it is difficult to attain them; simply declaring to be insignificant what one fails to embark on is self-betrayal. The question of the why and what of domination, and how its strategies came to dominate, may be the most significant topic to consider. Ducking it may be at the core of perpetuating terror. As long as domination is seen as a legitimate way to shape the human condition, those who instill it, will see terror as legitimate tool as well.

No challenge, including terrorism, war, and genocide, may be "solvable" on its own as long as the paradigm of domination is accepted. It will cause both *sociocide*[7] and *ecocide*[8] systemically: "In prevailing legal and economic systems, the human relationship with the natural world has been one of exploitation and domination, and environmental destruction has been accepted as collateral damage in the pursuit of profit."[9] This wrote lawyer Femke Wijdekop, who calls for the introduction of the *legal duty of care* toward the natural world, for *ecocide law* to challenge the view of nature as a lifeless "object" for human use. She calls for enshrining in law that the presently unfolding massive anthropogenic damage to ecosystems is a crime.[10] Linda Sheehan of the Earth Law Center in Redwood City in California, adds: "We have taken great strides in the last century to recognize the inherent rights and dignity of people. The next step is to expand our recognized community further, to embrace the inherent rights and dignity of the natural world."[11]

Ruben Nelson, executive director of Foresight Canada, wrote in his contribution to the Great Transition Network Discussion titled "The Degrowth Alternative," on January 30, 2015:

> Some focus on consumption, others on the lack of humanity, others on the environment, others on governance, others on the financial system, others on (fill in your favorite here) ... And, as is characteristic of a Modern mindset which does pieces better than wholes, we tend to neglect the development of an integral enough view to have some reasonable confidence that we understand not only that we are on a path to destruction, but why we are on this path, how we got here and what it will take to nurture a fundamentally different trajectory and form of civilization.

I wish to invite the reader into understanding the landscape of the dilemmas within which tactics of terror are inscribed. For this analysis, phenomena are central such as *circumscription*, a term used in anthropology, and *security dilemma*, a term used in political science. At first glance, again, this may seem far-fetched for the topic of terrorism. Please bear with me, as this conceptualization helps our understanding, and it does so by opening space for novel and constructive interpretations of present-day realities, including terror.

Most importantly, this conceptualization opens space for respect. Respect is at the core of terror-free interventions. This conceptualization opens space to defuse and prevent hostile confrontations. With this conceptualization, bitter mutual enmity can be foregone, hostility can be unmasked as lack of historical understanding and scope, and energy that is now invested into hatred and counter-hatred can be freed for constructive syntheses at higher levels of understanding. This, in turn, can stimulate forward-looking mutually respectful cooperation for change, and this is precisely the *raison-d'être* of this book: it attempts to shed light on commonalities, hoping to increase space for cooperation through lowering existing barriers, be it barriers between "cultures," "ideologies," "nations," "religions," "races," or "sexes."[12] Such barriers, though *imagined*, as historian Benedict Anderson would say,[13] are often experienced as real, and are frequently intentionally hardened for the sake of maintaining domination. When this happens, biases intensify, causing situations to spiral out of control through perilous miscalculations of internal and external attributions of causation (see more later in the book).[14]

Many new world models wait to be envisioned and alternative world histories wait to be narrated. Human existence on Earth can be shaped in radically new and more sustainable ways in the future. This book's argument is that the move from terror to decency[15] can only succeed as part of a large-scale transformation of the entire *world-system*.[16]

Planet Earth is finite and circumscription makes it palpable

"Terrorism is taking an innocent stranger and treating him as an enemy whom you kill to create fear," said anthropologist William Ury in a talk in 2010.[17] The opposite of terrorism would be: "Taking an innocent stranger and treating him as a friend whom you welcome into your home." Ury is one of the initiators of the Abraham Path, an initiative that promotes a paradigm change "from hostility to hospitality, from terrorism to tourism."

In his talk and in his books, Ury speaks of his experiences with the San Bushmen in South Africa, and how conflict between opponents is contained by what Ury calls the third side system. When conflicts arise, the first action the Bushmen take is to hide their poisonous arrows that they use for hunting. Then, they sit and talk, for two or more days, until they achieve reconciliation. If this cannot be accomplished, they send one of the opponents away to neighbors for a period of cooling off.

This has been the default script for conflict resolution all around the world in early history, prior to the emergence of entities like states, says anthropologist Robert Carneiro, father of circumscription theory.[18] Quarrelling opponents separated, and sometimes they moved permanently away from each other. As long as the human population on planet Earth was small, there was always untouched land available to move to. This is how planet Earth was populated.[19]

However, now comes the question: What is the solution if no other valleys are available to go to? When all valleys are taken, so to speak? To say it simplified, this is when war makes sense, with terror as cause, as tool, and as outcome.

Let us take a step back at this point. To unshackle imagination and creativity, so that alternative pathways for arranging human affairs on planet Earth become imaginable, I usually recommend to begin with a gaze from afar. Barbara Rowen Sivertsen wrote a fascinating book titled *Shianshenka: The Rise and Fall of the Perfect Creation*, where she describes imaginary civilizations of sentient creatures in ecological environments that either own or lack certain characteristics of the present humanly inhabited world.[20] Sivertsen then goes on to simulate possible alternative trajectories that various evolutions and histories could take. Educated as a biochemist and having been a science teacher for many years, she is uniquely equipped to broaden our understanding of imaginary multiverses.

After having awed the mind's eye by reading Sivertsen's book and having simulated possible worlds and narratives, the next step could be to ask what we, the human species, actually know about our presently existing world. Indeed, recent news are dramatic.[21] In 2012, the Higgs boson was discovered; its mass is unsettling. The comforting supersymmetry hypothesis might be wrong; the multiverse theory has been strengthened.[22] This means that Einstein's dream of "naturalness," or the dream of the laws of nature being sublimely beautiful, inevitable, and self-contained, might have to go. Humankind faces the harsh prospect that the laws of nature in our present world may represent an arbitrary and messy outcome of random fluctuations in the fabric of space and time.[23] Physicist Werner Heisenberg might have been right in his prediction that the philosophical consequences of quantum physics will eventually be more significant for humanity than its technical possibilities.[24]

Human lives have unfolded in a unique context of one sun, one moon, and a thin atmosphere that entails oxygen.[25] At some point in evolution, human infants have developed heads so large that they must exit from the female uterus prematurely, and much of their early development occurs outside of the womb.[26] As a consequence, the human body has evolved to make human's much more susceptible to cultural influences than any other animal – humans are uniquely *naturally cultural*. I will address this topic in more depth in my forthcoming book on human nature. Also terror is part of culture. Terror is a manifestation of the potential of humans to carry out a very wide range of acts.

Modern *Homo sapiens* seems to have emerged roughly 200,000 years ago – perhaps even 300,000 years ago[27] – and we populated planet Earth beginning from Africa. Throughout the first ninety-five percent of human history, very roughly, our forebears wandered the planet as migratory foragers. Then, at some point, starting around 12,000 years ago, the situation began to change dramatically. The reasons are hotly discussed.[28] One reason is that planet Earth has a limited surface. Humankind began to be affected by what anthropologists call *circumscription* (from Latin *circum*, around, *scribere*, to write). Anthropologist Robert Carneiro has been introduced above. Circumscription means limitation, enclosure, or confinement.[29] At some point, the human population campaign was bound to feel the impact of the limited size of the planet. This experience marked the end of what I call humankind's "first round of globalization": around ten thousand years ago, *Homo sapiens* had populated the entire globe, or at least those parts that were known and easily habitable.[30] If planet Earth were larger, it would have taken more time to reach this point, if smaller, it would have occurred faster. If larger, most of us would still be mobile wanderers.

Evidently, our forebears did not understand this. The experience of circumscription "informed" them only indirectly of the fact that planet Earth is finite in size; it is only in hindsight that we know about this fact.[31] What we can conclude is that the recent five percent of human history were different from the first ninety-five percent. The past five percent unfolded under the shadow of circumscription.

Modern day environmentalists point at the same predicament, circumscription, when they speak, of resource scarcity, or "peak" everything (for example, oil). Thomas Robert Malthus (1766 – 1834) is seen by some as the distant founder of modern day environmentalism.[32] He taught that suffering was inherent in nature and was caused by the inevitable and irreducible population pressure on the means of subsistence.[33] Many environmentalists may be unaware of his explanation of the cause, namely, that the ensuing suffering was willed by God to "rouse man from his natural sloth and achieve a higher purpose."[34] Indeed, "man" was roused, however, in horrific ways. Not least Adolf Hitler sought *Lebensraum* (literally life-space) for his people out of "ecological panic," a panic that led to war and genocide, and this can happen today as much as in the past, warns historian Timothy Snyder.[35]

Back to historical times when planet Earth was inhabited by fewer *Homo sapiens* than today and pristine land still was to be found. As long as land was abundantly available, opponents could start their own little communities slightly apart. Not only Robert Carneiro,[36] also world-systems scholar Christopher Chase-Dunn explains that throughout human history, as long as there was sufficient space, migration was the preferred strategy to solve conflicts or ease the consequences of population pressure.[37] Humankind's default choice to solve conflicts, accommodate newcomers, and maintain peace, is to preserve inclusiveness by widening the inhabited space. This is the kind of peace that includes diversity, rather than the kind of peace-and-quiet that is achieved when opponents are forced into submission. It is the peace of the African philosophy of *ubuntu* which says, "I am because you are: I am human because I belong, I participate, I share."[38] It is the peace of the spider web, as in the African proverb: "When spider webs unite, they can halt even a lion." Spider webs can be enlarged and this strengthens them, cutting them apart weakens them.

At the end of his talk about the Bushmen's lessons to us, anthropologist William Ury advised that we, as humankind, should recover some of the wisdom of the ancient past that existed prior to circumscription. Also archaeologists share his views. Archaeologist Ingrid Fuglestvedt wrote to me: "At the bottom of my Stone Age interest is my political view that the egalitarian hunter-gatherers, especially the animists, are the best societies this world has ever witnessed. This is not a reference to the Garden of Eden; it is to acknowledge that some systems are better than others in taking care of everybody's integrity, both human and animal."[39]

Many people shake their heads in disbelief when they listen to the Urys or Fuglestvedts of this world. They accuse them of wishful naïvité. In my upcoming book on human nature – on the question of whether human nature is "good or evil" and whether we humans are natural dignifiers or natural humiliators – I plan to address my suspicion that even our very concept of human nature has fallen prey to the consequences of circumscription. In that book, I will thematize why everybody who speaks like Fuglestvedt feels compelled to guard themselves by inserting little caveats, like, "this is not a reference to the garden of Eden." In my opinion, the very future of humankind depends on overcoming views on human nature that are distorted by the experience of circumscription.

Circumscription is painful. I am convinced that it is of crucial importance – if we want to understand today's world and find solutions – to deeply grasp that the bulk of human evolution unfolded during the first ninety-five percent of human history without circumscription, in a context that was much more benign than now. It was during the recent five percent of history that the finite size of planet Earth made itself felt in all its painfulness.

In 2013, I had the great privilege of being invited as a visiting scholar by Catherine Odora Hoppers, then the holder of the South African Research Chair in Development Education at the University of South Africa in Pretoria.[40] Odora Hoppers made me deeply understand the pain of circumscription. She grew up in Uganda and described the many forms of livelihood of her Acholi family, from gathering to hunting to cultivating. "The historical conditions of the possibility of unemployment did not exist until Africa was conquered by Europeans."[41] A traditional Sub-Saharan saying goes as follows: "When you have a visitor, give him food for the first three days, on the third day give him a hoe." Such a saying, evidently, can only come into being in an environment where circumscription is not yet salient. Otherwise, there would be no land available to give away to a visitor to cultivate food. This illustrates that circumscription, while it became relevant for the first time in regions like the Fertile Crescent 12,000 years ago, did not make itself felt evenly throughout the world. Odora Hoppers' sharing gave touching insights into the ripping pain that circumscription causes when it emerges. In the case of Uganda, it was introduced through colonization – it was through Sir Harry Johnstone's 1900 Agreement between the British and Baganda that the general population lost access to their *unappropriated lands*[42] – and this brought fear, insecurity, and a deep sense of terror to the entire population.

In Europe, circumscription was intensified when the commons in England were enclosed, starting during the sixteenth century. It had two consequences: first, those who managed to get land under their control could intensify production,[43] second, those without control of land had nowhere to go. In England, those put off their land first faced idleness, and then they faced the outlawing of idleness, which pushed them into early capitalist manufacturing – "bloody legislation" forced people from serfdom into wage-labor, so goes the interpretation.[44] Sociologist Eric Mielants speaks of "terroristic" laws.[45]

In the mid-seventeenth century, in France, the *grand renfermement* was enacted, or the grand locking-up of surplus populations. Philosopher Michel Foucault wrote about this in his book on madness and civilization.[46] It was about 1650 when King Louis XIV ordered hospitals to be created where misfits and troublemakers should be locked up, people who refused to go to mass, blasphemers, invalids, indigents, mentally retarded people, people who walked the streets talking to themselves, troublemakers, old people with no family to support them, dangerous people given to rages, people who denied Christ or thought they were Christ, and so on. Howard Richards, philosopher of social science and scholar of peace and global studies, presented a deep analysis of Foucault's descriptions to Catherine Odora Hoppers and me in Pretoria in 2013[47]:

> The result was similar whether they were deranged and impoverished because they were socially rejected, or whether they were socially rejected because they were deranged and impoverished. In either case, France had a surplus population. A royal decree of April 27, 1656, founded a General Hospital charged with preventing "… begging and laziness as the sources of all disorders.[48]

After Richards' lectures, Catherine and I would always engage in dialogue with him. He explained how "the terrible truth" of that past also afflicts modern society: Many people are connected with other people only through fragile contracts now – no longer through trust and mutual communal sharing. Which means, if there happens to be no contract, people are without support altogether.[49]

On July 4, 2013, I gave a talk in Cape Town, South Africa,[50] where I attempted to extend my narrative of human history by including modern-day occurrences of circumscription. By now, all Africa is affected. "The cultures and very survival of indigenous peoples in Africa are seriously threatened. They are ignored, neglected and fall victims of land grabbing and land dispossession caused by extractive industries, agribusiness and other forms of business operations."[51] Land grabbing increases not only in Africa, also in other parts of the world, and this heightens the experience of terror. I witnessed it personally also in Brazilian Amazonia in 2012.[52] By now, the process of "accumulation by dispossession" does not stop at water and land grabbing, it goes on to the enclosing also of the intellectual and digital commons, or the privatization of public education and social security.[53] The most recent tightening of circumscription was introduced through certain aspects in trade agreements, such as the "T-treaty trinity" agreements,[54] which would make massive corporate resource grabs possible by overruling national efforts to protect commons. "It is through transnational state (TNS) apparatuses that global elites attempt to convert the structural power of the global economy into supranational political authority," wrote sociologist William Robinson.[55] Three mechanisms now make the continuation of financial accumulation possible despite of natural resources becoming ever more scarce: financial speculation, raiding public budgets, and militarized accumulation, which includes the "war on terror" as a source for profit-making. What is needed, namely, better strategies of joint stewardship in the face of finiteness, is made ever more difficult.[56] William Robinson:

> Globalization has brought a vast new round of global enclosures as hundreds of millions of people have been uprooted from the Third World countryside and turned into internal and transnational migrants. Some of the uprooted millions are super-exploited through incorporation into the global factories, farms, and offices as precarious labor, while others are marginalized and converted into surplus humanity, relegated to a "planet of slums." Surplus humanity is of no direct use to capital. However, in the larger picture, surplus labor is crucial to global capitalism insofar as it places downward pressure on wages everywhere and allows transnational capital to impose discipline over those who remain active in the labor market.[57]

The security dilemma creates conquerors and raiders, and vice versa

Physicist Stephen Hawking advises to stop all SETI activities, all Search for Extraterrestrial Intelligence, because he fears that, if these efforts were to work, they may simply attract raiders and conquerors from outer space.[58] Hawking reminds us of an important lesson: If one is too far apart and does not know about each other's existence, there is no danger to be conquered or raided. It is wiser to keep it that way, rather than risking contact. This was the situation once also on planet Earth. The Inca leader Atahualpa was unprepared when white men arrived on his shores. Who were they? Were they *runa quicachac*, "destroyers of peoples," or were they *viracocha cuna runa allichac*, "gods who are benefactors of the people"?[59] The outcome was terrible for the Inca, and Hawking fears similar outcomes for humankind. Terror is the right word.

Wherever circumscription became palpable, the solution of simply moving on to new land with untouched abundance was blocked. When "the next valley" began to be taken by other people roughly 12,000 years ago, to say it simplified,[60] the human condition transmuted from the win-win situation that early foragers enjoyed who migrated freely surrounded by untouched abundance, into the win-lose of "either we have the resources or they have the resources."[61]

Complex agriculture can be interpreted as one form of human adaptation to the changing conditions, as it meant using technological innovation to intensify the yield of resources so as to produce more food from the same land area.[62] Agriculture represents a strategy of domination, of taking control of resources rather than letting resources take the lead and following them, as our mobile foraging forebears used to do. As a result, those who had intensified the yield from land through agriculture became rivals for land.

A much more brutal strategy of exploitation emerged alongside agriculture. Raiders became rivals for the harvest of farmers. Raiding cultures – and in my doctoral research I studied the Somali warrior culture – instill pride in their children, pride for standing up straight and roving freely. They teach their children disdain for farmers and farmers' willingness to "humiliate themselves" by bowing down to work the soil.[63] Cutting a tree is more "successful" in the short term than growing a tree. After spending time in Somaliland, I am no longer surprised why Somalis are so competent pirates and raiders. Also guerilla tactics in war and terrorism are raiders' tactics: attack and run or die.

Land needs to be mine if I am to harvest the plants in autumn that grew from the seeds I sowed in spring. Hobbesian fear of sudden attacks from other people from outside one's area was bound to become an inescapable all-defining state of emotion when the risk of such attacks increased. And, indeed, this emotion has since become part of the cultural core staple of human communities all around the globe to the degree that it informs also today's terrorism. As mentioned before, also nowadays, even people with non-authoritarian inclinations, when they are sufficiently frightened, for instance by terrorism, can be scared into acting like authoritarians.[64]

Dialogue with nature, and dialogue with each other, became replaced by domination over nature and each other. And this, in turn, inspired the myth that is virulent until today – which also inspires terrorism and counterterrorism – namely, that Hobbesian competition for domination is the only possible "state of nature" – and that partnership and dialogue are "unrealistic."

In conclusion, circumscription, as it blocks expansion, has the potential to spawn belligerence and create an atmosphere of terror and violence. Examples abound, also from recent times. Stephen Corry is the director of Survival International.[65] In the 1970s, he stayed in a settlement of the Aguaruna, an indigenous people of the northern Peru. Corry observed deadly raids continuously going on with another community a couple of miles away. Missionary and petroleum company activity had drawn most Aguaruna into settlements along the riverbanks, and this newly enforced proximity exacerbated enmities that were very much less salient before. Belligerence was thus caused by circumscription, rather than by "primordial" human aggressiveness.[66]

The security dilemma is another word for a new cause for worry, a worry that pre-Neolithic foragers were spared. The security dilemma introduced a new factor that had to be included into the calculus of "what is and what can be done": At any moment, not just some wild animal or natural catastrophe could hit, or the occasional deranged fellow human could create trouble, now some human out-groups could organize and turn up as conquerors or raiders of one's newly stored wealth. No longer could one simply move on to the next valley to find abundant wild food as easily as before. A new and historically unprecedented reason for fear and for war was born. Whatever sense of ontological security was there before, flowing from embeddedness into community and nature, faced a new systemic threat.[67]

Beginning circa 12,000 years ago, until recently, the security dilemma was overwhelmingly definitorial as a frame for every detail of human life almost everywhere on the globe. The term *security dilemma* is used in political science to describe how mutual mistrust can bring groups of people who have no intention of harming one another into bloody war.[68] The security dilemma is tragic because its logic of mistrust, fear, and paranoia is inescapable: "I have to amass weapons, because I am scared. When I amass weapons, you get scared. You amass weapons, I get more scared." The realism theory was and still is the dominant view in the field of international affairs today and it mostly focuses its attention on external factors such as the geopolitical balance of power. The enemy's exact motivation is not necessarily understood; it is simply assumed that those enemies want more power, more land, and more resources. Empathy for the enemy is not welcome,[69] mutual trust is difficult to imagine.

Pearl Harbor is a good illustration of the problems that arise when distance is too far for trust. Wherever I live, I attempt to acquire a deep understanding of the cultural sensitivities and inclinations of a society, and I have lived both in Japan and the United States.[70] And we had our Annual Dignity Conference of 2009 near Pearl Harbor.[71] Pearl Harbor might not have happened, had not erroneous translations and misunderstandings characterized the relationship between Japan and the United States. Shigenori Togo was Japan's Foreign Minister at the time, one of the few doves in the Japanese Cabinet, opposed to war: "Japanese historians often claim that the U.S. misinterpreted some of the country's telegrams – for instance, that Togo's 'Five Points Plan' was translated as a 'final offer' when Togo never said that."[72] Young political scientist and legal scholar Toshihiro Minohara has recently unearthed formerly unknown material and he says that the Japanese "were doing the same thing. Even though there was no error in the translations, they were still misinterpreting the U.S.' intentions."[73] As to Japan's "sneak attack" on

Pearl Harbor, the Foreign Ministry in Japan seems to have wanted to deliver an official war declaration in time, yet, the Japanese army caused the "delay in the transmission of a telegram containing the concluding and crucial part of the memorandum in order to protect the secrecy of the Pearl Harbor attack."[74]

The Vietnam War can serve as another example. In 2001, Robert McNamara, Secretary of Defense at the time, together with international relations expert James Blight, invited to a Critical Oral History project. They invited American and North Vietnamese leaders who were prominent in the run-up to the Vietnam War. What emerged was that the war may have been fought for a misunderstanding.[75] Each side feared the other side's imperialistic aims. Americans saw North Vietnam as a pawn of the Chinese, intent on spreading communism throughout Southeast Asia and beyond, and Vietnam thought that U.S. intended to occupy Vietnam. Both views, however, were incomplete and false. North Vietnam only wanted to re-unite the north and the south, as it was prior to colonial interventions, and Americans only wanted to prevent the imperialist aims they imagined being fomented in North Vietnam and China.

The book *Die Waffen nieder*, or *Lay Down Your Arms!* brought its author, Bertha von Suttner, the Nobel Peace Prize in 1905. She describes the logic of armament prevalent in Europe in the decades prior to the First World War:

- Meine Rüstung ist die defensive (my efforts to arm are defensive)
- Deine Rüstung ist die offensive (your efforts are offensive)
- Ich muß rüsten, weil du rüstest (I have to arm myself because you arm yourself)
- Weil du rüstest, rüste ich (because you arm yourself, I arm myself)
- Also rüsten wir (so we arm ourselves)
- Rüsten wir nur immer zu (so we arm ourselves ever more).[76]

To recapitulate, the security dilemma emerged, historically, when what I call human history's first round of globalization ended as it "hit" the fact that planet Earth's surface is limited.[77] The transition from migratory foraging lifestyles to sedentary complex agriculturalism ensued. As Jared Diamond points out, with the so-called Neolithic revolution the atmosphere of terror was seeded. Also sociologist Zygmunt Bauman concurs that nature – the entire unprocessed, pristine world – became our "enemy" since the time we began to practice agriculture.[78] Not only nature became the object of domination, though. Als humans were turned into underlings by other humans, in the same way wood was turned into timber.[79]

Since it first emerged, the atmosphere of terror has made itself ever more visible. The Bronze Age came, and then the Iron Age, and they brought ever more deadly weapons. By now, with the nuclear era, this terror has turned into an overwhelming threat, first in the Cold War, and now through being "democratized" globally, with the risk that nuclear weapons fall into the hands of terrorists.[80]

Terror and fear of terror are at the core of the security dilemma, in myriad manifestations. It is only now, at the current historical juncture, for the first time, that opportunities open up for humankind to radically intervene in this state of affairs and intentionally nurture something thoroughly new, namely, true global cooperation. Until very recently, due to the security dilemma's cultural consequences and expressions, such a venture was virtually impossible. Bertha von Suttner was far ahead of her time when she called upon the world to lay down arms. Instead, two world wars ensued. Margaret Thorp,[81] or Jeannette Rankin,[82] or Sonja Lid,[83] all these women were ahead of their time. As mentioned before, also I am ahead of our time, one might say, by wishing to help advance the "emotional turn" in international relations theory, and in hoping that international relations theory may transmute into *global internal relations theory*.[84]

The security dilemma plays out when states (or social units) are both too close and too far apart – too close to each other to forget that the other exists and may represent a threat, but too far apart to be able to safely gauge the other's true objectives and intentions so as to develop trust. The essence of the security dilemma is "too much distance for trust, therefore obligatory mistrust, with trust being devalued as naïvité and weakness."

Again, this is more than just ancient history. The term *Thucydides trap* is still being used by present-day strategists and political scientists. It describes how the very structure of the international system is driven by the fear that a rising power instills in an already established powerful empire. Conflict and war can arise between those two powers, irrespective of diplomatic efforts to avert it.[85] Thucydides was an Athenian historian (born circa 460 before the Common Era[86]), and he famously wrote: "It was the rise of Athens and the fear that this inspired in Lacedaemon (Sparta) that made war inevitable."[87] We are reminded of Thucydides when we think of China's rise to power, or when we read: "At its core, the Iranian nuclear conflict is about trust. The U.S. does not believe that Iran's intentions are purely peaceful, while Iran believes the nuclear issue is simply a pretext for regime change."[88] Even though Iranians had showed deep collective commiseration after the 9/11 attack on the Twin Towers in New York,[89] still, U.S. President George W. Bush included Iran into the "axis of evil" in his State of the Union Address on January 29, 2002, saying, "Some of these regimes have been pretty quiet since September the 11th. But we know their true nature."[90] All those who reject the recently reached agreement with Iran, do so because they feel that distrust is still the only reasonable option.[91]

The security dilemma forces bloody competition to the fore even where nobody is interested in going to war. War can simply emerge out of mutual distrust. The security dilemma is tragic because its logic of mistrust and fear is inescapable: *igitur qui desiderat pacem, praeparet bellum* is the advice given by Publius Flavius Vegetius Renatus, a writer of the Later Roman Empire. It means in English: "therefore, who desires peace, prepare for war."[92] Indeed, this is the very motto of the security dilemma as it evolved throughout the past millennia. It leads to another motto: "the best defense is a good offense." Even the most peaceable leader could not withstand this logic.

Terror, together with its counterterror responses, is inscribed into this very culture. Terror is the very name of the security dilemma and the brutality of its iron grip. Everybody was caught in this iron grip, nobody could escape it. It would be wrong to ascribe evilness to individuals who are caught in such an iron grip. It would mean committing the *correspondence bias*. The correspondence bias is the human tendency to believe that others act in the way they do because they believe in it; our mind has a tendency to overlook that others might have been forced by external circumstances to act against their will.[93]

Bertha von Suttner described the mood that characterized Europe in the decades before World War I:

> "To arms! To arms!" was now the general cry. For defensive purposes it was necessary that we should arm ourselves. Prussia maintained that we were secretly arming; therefore she proceeded to arm herself. What is the use of all this clash of arms if neither intends to attack? Whereupon my father quoted the old proverb, Si vis pacem, para bellum. Each keeps an eye upon the other; each accuses the other of malice aforethought.[94]

In a world characterized by what philosopher Thomas Hobbes called anarchy,[95] in a world where the security dilemma is strong, it is unsurprising that fear defines everything and overrules everything else. Political theorist Carl Schmitt, in his 1922 work on political theology, referred to *the sovereign* as the one "who decides on the state of emergency."[96] Later, Hans Joachim Morgenthau, one of the founding fathers of the realist school of international relations theory, discussed the existence of a *dual state*.[97] Ola Tunander, research professor at the Peace Research Institute Oslo in Norway,[98] follows Morgenthau when he describes how the U.S. state has at the surface a "regular state hierarchy" that acts according to the rule of law and appears democratic, yet, that there is another, more or less hidden "security hierarchy," which Tunander calls *security state*, also known as *deep state*. This deep state is the one that decides, for instance, whether and in which situation a "state of emergency" should be declared, and it will veto the decisions of the regular state, limit the range of democratic politics, and override the democratic state's political alternatives and "securitize" them.[99]

If we now take a step back and try to locate war and terror within the context of a strong security dilemma, then we could begin by making a list ranging from (1) *no war* to (2) *unavoidable war* to (3) *war as livelihood.*[100]

The earliest so far known conclusive archaeological evidence for attacks on settlements is a Nubian cemetery in Sudan dated at 12,000 – 14,000 years before the Common Era.[101] Systematic war seems to have been absent (1) until it originated independently in different parts of the world at dates around 4,000 years before the Present.[102] As soon as war had emerged as a strategy, it forced people into preparedness for defense (2), yet, it also became a form of livelihood (3). The latter unfolded both as crude raiding and as sophisticated military strategy, such as the strategy of feeding and funding armies with the resources of occupied territories under the motto of *bellum se ipsum alet* (war feeds itself).

Only as long as people are too far apart and not aware of each other, the danger of being attacked from outside is absent (1). As mentioned above, not without reason does physicist Stephen Hawking advise to switch off any Search for Extraterrestrial Intelligence, because he fears that, if it were to work, it may simply attract raiders and conquerors from outer space.[103]

As world population increased, circumscription set in, and for the people who were invaded by others for the first time, this was presumably as terrorizing as it is for unsuspecting indigenous populations today when they are removed from their territories and resources. We are justified in saying that circumscription can produce terror.

War in defense (2) and war as livelihood (3), these are the two faces of war that are fed by the security dilemma and in turn feed it. As mentioned earlier, I have studied the belligerent raiding culture of tribal peoples in Somalia. Indeed, from Vikings to Mongols, throughout history, mobile raiders brought terror. When I lived in Cairo, the knees of many of my Egyptian friends trembled when I took them to the desert: too strong was their fear of evil spirits lurking in the desert, spirits fashioned on the nomads (*Arab* means "nomad" in Arabic), who, throughout history, would attack *fedayeen* farmers in the Nile Delta from nowhere.

If we think of terror, then the sedentary civilizations that emerged within the context of circumscription, those based on agriculture, created an additional reason for terror for themselves. Sedentary civilizations are usually more rigidly hierarchical than mobile raiding cultures[104] – rigid hierarchy is the essence of the dominator model of society – and, as a result, they face double terror. First, there is the terror from conquerors and raiders who threaten from outside, second, hierarchy is something that always risks being resisted from within by rebellions and revolutions. Those who spread terror within may consider themselves to be revolutionaries or freedom fighters, yet, they will be regarded as terrorists by those in power, and the response will be an oppressive terror regime. Nelson Mandela was initially seen as a terrorist, and, due to "fear of communism," he ended up on the U.S. terrorism watch list, from where he was removed only as late as on January 1, 2008.[105] The Dalai Lama is seen as a terrorist in China now, while revered as a bearer of wisdom in the West.[106]

If we think of the best options that people had in a divided world in which the security dilemma was strong, then raiders and conquerors approaching from outside could only be stopped with classical diplomatic and military strategies. The *just war* literature has its place here.[107] If one wanted to avoid violent rebellions from within, and also wanted to refrain from suppressing them with a terror regime, the best way was through functioning social and legal systems that offered pathways for social change without violence.

A globally interconnected world leaves only the latter solution on the table. Since no "outside" sphere exists anymore, activities such as raiding, free-riding, exploitation, rebellion, and revolution merge. The only remedy left to stem them is the "inside" solution, namely, binding legal instruments, in this case globally enshrined, that prevent the raids of exploiters and free-riders, and enable peaceful pathways for change. In short, from the viewpoint of sedentary societies, and since planetary society is confined within the boundaries of planet Earth, we now find ourselves in a global sedentary society. In that context, terrorists can be seen as raiders or exploiters from within who need to be contained. In today's parlance, those raiders might be anything from Al-Qaeda to vulture funds. Freedom fighters, on their part, would need to follow Mahatma Gandhi's path of fostering social change rather than turning to violence.

In a divided world, *bimodal alienation* reigns, a term that Thomas Scheff uses. He researches the sociology of emotions and describes a double type of alienation between contending groups, that is, isolation between groups – too far – and engulfment within them – too close.[108] Scheff proposes that bimodal alienation is the pre-condition for wars of aggression.[109] Scheff draws on sociologist Norbert Elias's conceptualization of *I-self*, *we-self*, and *I-we balance*, whereby the I-self suffers from too much distance and isolation in independence, the we-self suffers from too little distance and engulfment in dependence, and only an I-we balance represents true solidarity in interdependence.[110]

The third case of conquering and plundering, the case of using it as livelihood, or *bellum se ipsum alet*, represents, one may say, the "perfection" of a culture of terror. The plunder of colonies, for instance, was built on elaborate strategies of terror. It often started with a small-scale outreach with gifts and trade, which later transmuted into the terror of exploitation. The East India Company, for instance, was an English stock company, which eventually came to rule large areas of India and exercised military power with its own private armies. It has been dubbed "the first multinational."[111] British politician and prime minister William Gladstone (1809 – 1898) labeled the colonial wars as "criminal assaults on innocent people."[112] Therefore, the present-day Occupy Movement warns of a culture of terror when it decries the plunder of the ninety-nine percent by the one percent.[113]

China first reached out to the world in the fifteenth century, from 1405 to 1433, when Admiral Zheng He traveled with large fleets to the Indian Ocean. They contented themselves with only dispensing and receiving gifts and goods along the way.[114] Also in North America, early settlers were initially respectful of the native people of their land, and only later-arriving settlers increased exploitation and abuse. Today, two countries exist in North America that do not even include their native people's history into their own history, thus finally legalizing the terror of decimation.[115] Also the identity of a freedom-loving out-door country that Australia stands for, seems almost untainted by doubt or remorse, until today, remorse for the systemic terror that was inflicted and still is being inflicted. I was a keen observer when I spent time in Brisbane in 2007.[116] In Australia, the first major Aboriginal missions and protectorates were established during the 1830s and 1840s, and this brought an expansion of pastoralism, destruction of native habitat, and dispossession of indigenous people.[117]

Legalization of the spoils of terror is often the last step. This is valid not just for states and not just for bygone history. Just recently, Russian "gangsters," for instance, attempted to evolve from illegal activities to becoming legal business people.[118]

Slave trade is somewhat of a counter-example, as its terror went from legitimacy to illegitimacy, even though it persists under different labels until the day today.[119] In other cases, definitions of legitimacy or illegitimacy remained undecided. Sea captain Francis Drake (circa 1540 – 1596), for instance, was a hero to the English, yet, to Spaniards he was known as *El Draque*, the Dragon.[120] In the early sixteenth century, the Spanish Conquistador Hernán Cortés caused the fall of the Aztec Empire, opening large portions of mainland Mexico to the exploitation of the King of Castile. Today, European hegemonism is officially despised in South America, yet, particularly in former Spanish colonies, many power elites still look down on their countries' first people. I was a witness during my time in South America in 2012.[121]

Wherever I go on this planet, I meet members of privileged elites who are confident of their entitlement today as much as in the past. Many of those who grew up in a Brahmin caste family, for instance, broadcast an elite confidence. This elite confidence presents itself as primordial, a priori, without any doubt, very sure of itself, a confidence directly drawn from a sense that this superiority is divinely ordained or nature-given. Apparently, British domination has not made a significant dent on Brahmin supremacy. Then there is the Han Chinese sense of superiority, which might have been similar to the Brahmin expression until the West humiliated China. Now it appears to be more of a defensive elite sense. I came to China in 1983 for the first time and this was what I sensed: "You, the West, abused us even though we are the most evolved people on Earth, how could you do that! Now we will get back at you!" Whenever I spend time in China since, I intuit an urge for revenge, if ever so polite. The delight with which everything from the West is being copied, for example, while this is lamented by the West as stealing, is seen by many in China as legitimate retrieval. Most recently, China felt humiliated by Norway, as the Nobel Peace Prize was awarded to dissident Liu Xiaobo.[122] Then there is the United States' sense of superiority, which may, at least partly, derive from the Puritan belief in might being right, might representing divine approval and thus supremacy being earned. Also here I observe a smoldering, yet deeply buried urge to take revenge, an urge that flows from transgenerational pain in white families, pain from humiliation inflicted by "Old Europe" when it sent its very own people packing to America, from where they now feel duty-bound to manifest moral exceptionalism to the world.[123]

The dominator model streamlines everything into up and down

The security dilemma emerged from one division and created a second division: it is predicated on a horizontal division of *inside versus outside* – in-group friends became differentiated from out-group allies or enemies – and it pushes for vertical divisions of *up* and *down* that underpin the stratified strongman dominator model[124] of collectivistic and ranked honor societies.[125] The early cooperative spirit of foragers transmuted into the collaboration of "us" against "them,"[126] and this led to "us" above "them."

I have written a book about the effects of the security dilemma on gender roles, and how it first brings women inside, into the private sphere, while men are sent into the public sphere, an arrangement that subsequently brings women also down.[127] The past ten thousand years' systemic push for male aggressiveness and female subservience may even have become hardwired, at least to a certain extent[128]: women display a propensity to react with a *tend and befriend* reaction to stress, rather than *fight or flight*, as their male counterparts.[129] Perhaps this is an adaptation to the practice that men were often killed when communities were invaded and conquered, while women were captured alive.[130]

Over time, the overall dominator system was refined ever more, by what I call the "art of domination."[131] Social psychology has contributed with several theoretical models, among others, social dominance theory,[132] system justification theory,[133] and dynamical systems theory.[134] (See more further down.) As a result, the domination/submission structure became ever more sophisticated over time and concealed in Orwellian language, until it had reached its most recent expression, which may be found in the imperative of profit maximization under the banner of "freedom."[135]

One way of building ranked hierarchies was through incorporating vanquished enemies at the bottom. Indian jurist, economist, politician, and social reformer Bhimrao Ramji Ambedkar explains the origins of the untouchables in India as being descendants of the defeated, "broken" tribes of ancient India.[136] Similar outcast minorities exist in Somalia. Whenever I found the opportunity during my doctoral research in 1998 and 1999, I would ask people how they thought this cleavage came about. Former Somali Ambassador Hussein Ali Dualeh explained to me in an interview on January 9, 1999, in Nairobi, that "professional groups" (like barbers, or metal workers), "are being looked down upon by the nomads not because they are of lesser quality."[137] He continued, "On the contrary, they are very intelligent. But the story is that they were powerful clans, then, at the center part of history they became oppressors. And so all the other clans ganged against them and defeated them. This is part of our mythology."[138] Another member of a majority clan explained to me about one of the minority groups: "When you look at them you see that they are extremely intelligent and could be very dangerous, they have, after all, the tradition of making secret poison,[139] perhaps it is therefore that we [the free-born and 'noble' Somalis] keep them dispersed so that they cannot unite and hit back at us. I believe we are actually very afraid of them!"[140]

All around the world, in Western and non-Western world regions, I have heard narratives that follow the same line as explanation for why women are, and ought to remain, subjugated: It is suspected that women once were oppressors of men and that men have succeeded in liberating themselves.

Not only vanquished enemies are the ones at the bottom of dominator societies. Throughout history, ruling elites have attempted to reshape societal structures so as to achieve ever-higher levels of subjugation of their underlings. Also today, a first step is the reconstruction of societal structures under seemingly unobjectionable pretexts such as "adjustment" or "reform," while obfuscating the true aim, namely, to bind societal structures tighter into a larger machinery. As soon as all structures are turned into pliable cogwheels, it is easier to command the machinery from the top and pool everybody's resources according to the needs of the power elite.

Also here, examples from recent history abound. Hitler spoke of *Gleichschaltung*, or the successive streamlining of all aspects of society into a system of totalitarian control and coordination. China offers a more sophisticated example. In her 2015 doctoral dissertation, educational sociologist and China expert Jingyi Dong describes how it began with an "institution and discipline adjustment," *yuanxi tiaozheng* 院系调整, in 1952, and ended with the Anti-Rightist Campaign in 1957, which marginalized academic authorities and expelled a great number of the top teachers and students from the campus.[141] A form of Chinese *governmentality* emerged, in which inner life became subject to government regulated moral demands.[142] South African writer Prince Mashele offers an impressive description of how South Africa succumbs to such a dynamic just now.[143] The presently increasing trend to streamline societies all around the world into profit-maximizing machineries, under pretexts such as "effectivization" and "optimization," may be interpreted as most recent example.

The security dilemma aggravates the commons dilemma

Back to the question: Is agriculture the "original sin"? Is Jared Diamond correct in suggesting that agriculture brought starvation, warfare, and tyranny? And, in extension, did agriculture therefore also bring terror into the world?

Undoubtedly, the shift that began to emerge about twelve millennia ago was the most significant turning point in human history, except for the present historical juncture. And, indeed, Jared Diamond might be right that we need to rethink how we evaluate the first turning point in order to better address the second, the present one.

The topic of terrorism is deeply embedded into the culture that came into being after that first turning point. It brought an atmosphere of simmering terror that has terrorized the world since. This atmosphere has desensitized people to the feeling of being terrorized, and to the application of practices of terror. Over time, we, as humankind, got so used to this state of being that it became part of our "normality." We mistake it for a natural phenomenon and fail to appreciate that it is a response, a human adaptation, which is in our hands to influence and change. Only our pre-Neolithic ancestors, if they could visit our times, would perhaps tell us to what degree the recent five percent of human history are an exception. Five percent is only a glimpse compared with the entirety of human history.

The historically most recent expression of this situation is the modern world-system, with "a vast periphery of poverty organized around several successive imperial centers,"[144] with the superpower United States as the last imperial center since World War II, followed by what has been called the Global North, and even more recently, the global government/corporate nexus of a *transnational state*.[145]

Philosopher Glen Martin reasons that Hobbes, Kant, and other thinkers do not go far enough. Indeed, "absolute fragmentation under the concept of sovereign territories," places "nations in 'a state of nature,' a condition in which there is no law but only the rule of the most powerful and a perpetual competition for power."[146] What Hobbes, Kant, and other thinkers overlook is that nations are not truly sovereign in this state of nature and system of war, argues Martin: "The primary competition among sovereign nations involves struggles over wealth," and the "political and financial elite of nations and their multinational corporations vie for control of the wealth-producing process in relation to weaker countries (including control of production, services, natural resources, trade relations, and financial interactions)."[147]

The frequency of war during the past millennia created a situation similar to the laboratory of psychologist Martin Seligman, who, in the 1960s, discovered the phenomenon of *learned helplessness*. He carried out experiments with dogs that were exposed to small electric shocks while they could do nothing to avoid them. In a second round of the experiment, the dogs were given a chance to escape, yet, to everybody's surprise, they did not: they had adapted to their helplessness and they simply endured those new shocks.[148] The insights from Seligman's research later became the basis for the torture methods called "enhanced interrogation techniques" used by the American Central Intelligence Agency, which aimed to induce helplessness in suspected terrorists.[149]

Many people remain helplessly caught in the past when asked to escape from the maelstrom of war and terror, when asked to grasp the fact that, given present-day global interconnectedness, a world without war and terror is more feasible than ever. When people remain caught in the past, they re-create it in a self-fulfilling prophecy, and thus effectively close the very window of opportunity that otherwise stands open.

The ongoing emasculation of African American males through their slave experience could be seen as an example of this dynamic.[150] As the Jewish male who was forced into meekness in the Eastern European Shtetl,[151] also black men were looked down upon and ridiculed, as if meekness were their nature – the correspondence error was committed – thus turning learned helplessness into humiliation.[152]

Scholar Robert Burrowes describes the combination of fear and helplessness as a state of "unconscious terror."[153] Twenty-two years old Elliot Rodger murdered six people in Santa Barbara, California, on May 23, 2014.[154] It was a crime that emanated from a sense of helplessness, of being caught in cycles of humiliation, projecting them onto the Other. In such cycles of humiliation and projection, all sides tend to misperceive the Other as intentionally hurtful: "Rodger blames women. Women blame misogyny. Misogynists blame feminists."[155]

Rodger was one of the many angry males who can be found in the *manosphere* (man plus blogosphere), or *androsphere*, or *mandrosphere*.[156] Also Christopher Harper-Mercer, the Oregon shooter, who killed nine people of October 1, 2015, seems to have been part of this sub-culture that is permeated by humiliation.[157] Anders Behring Breivik blamed feminism. He killed young social democrats in Norway in 2011, because he believed that their party partook in a Cultural Marxist plot to undermine traditional European values.[158] Nearly fifty percent of lone-actor terrorist attacks in the United States are abortion-related and share more demographic similarities with locations where violent hate crime is committed, as compared to the seventeen percent of group-based terrorist attacks.[159]

As alluded to in the Introduction, in my work, I often compare humankind's situation with that of the steam-ship Titanic, at a point when there still is a chance to avoid sinking. Also Robert Burrowes uses Titanic as an example. For more than four billion years, until 1790, the Earth had offered life-support systems for billions of species. But then, coal, oil, and gas fueled the industrial revolution, and now it is "game over for the climate" – and there is little time left to act. Burrowes asks: But will we act? His answer: "Many people won't act, particularly those people whose fear works in the same way as most of those involved in the 'Titanic' disaster.... Or, more accurately, unconscious terror."[160] Burrowes adds, "... what I see when I observe elite and most other responses to our current epidemic of violence whether in the form of war, exploitation of countries in the global 'South,' environmental destruction, domestic violence or otherwise, I see their (unconscious) fear lead them away from insightful analyses and visionary solutions because they are compelled by their fear to live in delusion (which requires no action)."

Are there alternatives? Yes. The joint protection of the world as our commons waits to be realized now. Many indigenous peoples have practiced this way of life, those who respected the famous seven-generation sustainability rule.[161]

It is true that circumscription introduces zero-sum circumstances and a win-lose situation and that this increases the likelihood of divisions among people. Only an environment that rests on a win-win situation lends itself to easy cooperation.[162] Yet, also a win-lose situation can be tackled by cooperation rather than competition for domination; it only requires more effort. When our Human Dignity and Humiliation Studies network held its annual conferences in Hawai'i and New Zealand in 2009 and 2011,[163] Princess Lehuanani from Hawai'i, and Carmen Hetaraka of Maori background, both taught us this: destroying is easy; much greater efforts are required to weave webs of harmony. These efforts are those of respect, patience, acceptance, compassion, and love.

Why is so much more effort required to make a win-lose situation constructive as compared to a win-win situation? There is the so-called *commons dilemma*, or, as ecologist Garrett James Hardin has named it, the "tragedy of the commons."[164] Commons face two threats: first, there are conquerors and raiders who may invade one's commons from outside, second, free-riders may hollow out one's commons from inside. In 2007, Hardin wrote: "An unmanaged commons in a world of limited material wealth and unlimited desires inevitably ends in ruin. Inevitability justifies the epithet 'tragedy,' which I introduced in 1968."[165] In other words, what Hardin describes, is the long-term problem that occurs when the seven-generation rule is violated, when short-term competition for domination trumps long-term all-inclusive cooperation.

Cooperating to jointly protect everybody's commons is more difficult than out-competing rivals and privatizing the commons for one's own advantage. This difficulty is compounded in a divided world where the security dilemma engenders fear. When enemy attack looms, people are terrorized into seeking safety in submitting themselves to perceived protectors. From the protectors' point of view, this sense of terror might at some point become an asset. Protectors might even create or maintain the security dilemma artificially so as to hold on to the privileges connected with their protector role. The more a protector transmutes into an oppressor and exploiter, the more fear will be needed as a tool to prolong this situation. In this way, fear will beget more fear, and no degree of protection will truly prevent and heal this. In this way, throughout the past millennia, power elites ceased to protect their people and their commons, and rather used the opportunity to become free-riders on these commons. A very tangible example were kings reserving forests for their own luxurious hunting exploits, while their hungry subordinates were forbidden to use the forest as their commons.[166]

Yet, for the creation and maintenance of systems of submission and domination the detour via an enemy image stoked by the security dilemma might not even be necessary. The fearsome stress from being helplessly exposed to difficult times might suffice, just as with Seligman's dogs. Joseph McCarthy's right-wing populist movement shed stark light on the role of fear. In 1958, public policy scholar Martin Trow wrote one of the earliest articles on the so-called McCarthy era and its social basis.[167] Trow found that self-employed entrepreneurs and small businessmen were those most susceptible to McCarthy's demagogy. Trow identified continuous fear underlying their lives as reason, a severe lack of stability and predictability, which, in turn, fostered a readiness in them to find scapegoats. Since then, small business owners have supported similar protest politicians, including George Wallace, Ross Perot, or David Duke.[168] As it seems, insecurity creates fear, and fear is stressful, and this makes people vulnerable to falling in line behind dominators who promise to fight an "enemy." Sociologist Wilhelm Heitmeyer puts forward a related theory of social disintegration, known as the "Bielefeld disintegration approach," to explain the syndrome of group-focused enmity.[169]

Throughout the past decades, the sense of uncertainty has increased in many segments of

Western society. Researchers speak of a "stress epidemic."[170] As the Western world has become wealthier, instances of clinical or major depression have grown.[171] Stressed people might get depressed or seek scapegoats, both paths entail the potential to strengthen dominator structures. Squeezing people into life situations that are ever more stressful will therefore be a welcome tool that may be used, openly or concealed, by power elites.

Evidently, also the threat of terrorism creates fear and stress, which, in turn, can be instrumentalized to maintain the dominator model of society. Scholar Robert Burrowes might have a point when he warns:

> By harping on the "threat of terrorism" to scare domestic populations, Western elites and their allies are able to maintain their perpetual war in pursuit of control of essential diminishing natural resources – particularly fossil fuels, strategic minerals and water – while increasing their social control of domestic populations through increasingly repressive domestic legislation that guts human rights and civil liberties, including those in relation to dissent, while increasing the powers of "intelligence" services and the police as they consolidate the surveillance state.[172]

The presidential race in the United States that unfolded while I wrote these lines, and the rise of populism in Europe, all may serve as ultimate illustration. By now, far-right forces pursue "militarism, a racist mobilization against scapegoats," they shift away from social welfare to social control states, "bolstered by mystifying ideologies rooted in race/culture supremacy and an idealized past."[173]

Chapter 2

How Spirituality Fell Prey to the Security Dilemma

The dominator model of society reigned throughout the past millennia almost everywhere on the globe. Yet, it seems that pushing people into hierarchy was not always an easy task. A lingering memory seems to have prevailed, a memory from historical times prior to the onset of the security dilemma. Many founders of religions and philosophies criticized power, they were "renouncers," from Brahmins in late Vedic India, to Socrates and Plato in ancient Greece.[1] Christianity, Islam, or the Sikh religion, many religious uprisings initially asked questions such as: "Are not all people equally worthy?"[2] "Is it not illegitimate to oppress people in the name of God?" Is not also the degradation of our environment a violation?[3] Theologian Martin Luther (1483 – 1546), for instance, opposed the humiliation of "papal tyranny."[4] Founders of many religions had followers precisely because they rekindled the revolutionary message of equality in dignity – no longer wanting only higher-placed "dignitaries" to have access to divinity.

The first chiefdoms emerged in West Asia roughly 7,500 years ago, and the first archaic states appeared circa 5,000 years ago. At some point, a "legitimation crisis of the early state" occurred, explains philosopher and sociologist Jürgen Habermas.[5] "Prophet-like" figures emerged, who risked their lives to hold existing power structures accountable to a universally egalitarian ethic.[6] The so-called axial age is a term coined by philosopher Karl Jaspers for philosophical, religious, and technical developments that arose in relatively independent cultural regions in the world in a relatively short period of time, from eight to two hundred years before the Common Era.[7] The results are still relevant today.[8]

However, wherever egalitarian messages rose their head, they did not find much space to remain and flourish, at least not during the past ten millennia.[9] Power- and control-oriented hierarchies "swallowed up" this message very swiftly each time it emerged, and this usually happened when those awakenings became institutionalized.[10] There is a German saying, "Sagt der König zum Bischof: Halt Du sie dumm, ich halte sie arm," translated, "Says the king to the bishop: You keep them dumb, I keep them poor."

One illustration is to be found in ancient Greece and Rome prior to Abrahamic monotheisms. The world was experienced as a place of terror, explains scholar Raymond Helmick.[11] People were at the mercy of forces of love and hate, fire and storm, drought and flood, war and peace. It became the stuff of religion to personify these forces:

> It meant that the world was a place of terror. The disparate forces, hypostatized as gods and goddesses, might have a king of the gods, but no true unity. All had their own agendas. So far as we were concerned, they were at best indifferent, at worst actively hostile. The work of religion was to hold these dangers at bay by the bribery of sacrifice, always risky as too much deference to one might incur the jealousy of others, and hubris was sure to incur punishment. By bribery we could strive for the safety of ourselves, our families and those others who were dear to us – a tribe, a community, a nation – but it was hard to get beyond that. And we knew that in the end we would lose, that these dangerous forces would ultimately defeat us. We could only be doomed. It is a religion of terror.[12]

Then the Abrahamic monotheisms told people that they "must not fear, but should take courage, because the Lord is with us." Yet, as already Sigmund Freud has noted, also monotheisms became imperial, demanding submission.[13]

Religion always was a welcome tool to maintain systems of submission and domination by invoking divine legitimization. Evolutionary biologist David Sloan Wilson explains how domination and submission were portrayed as "natural" or "God-given" and how subordinates began to accept such models of social behavior and refrained from even thinking of contesting. Domination and submission became the template of social behavior at each layer of the unfolding hierarchy.[14]

Psychologists Jim Sidanius and Felicia Pratto speak of *legitimizing myths*, or compelling cultural ideologies that are taken as self-apparently true in society and that disguise any use of force or discrimination and make it acceptable.[15] Political scientist Stuart Kaufman speaks of myth-symbol complexes.[16] Psychologist and systems theorist Norbert Bischof related the development of myths to the psychological development of individuals, and how this underpins their credibility and power.[17] Albert Morris is a grandson of the last Jewish caretaker of the Tomb of Ezra in Mesopotamia, and in his book *Civilisation Hijacked*, he decries the (ab)use of religion throughout the centuries.[18]

Absolute rulers all over the world have claimed that their power was God-given. Scandinavia offers one of many examples of this strategy. Gro Steinsland is a scholar of medieval studies and the history of religion, and she has studied the power of rulers and the ideology of rulership in the Nordic societies from Vikings through the medieval age, from about 800 until 1200. She describes how the myth of *hieros gamos*, or "sacred marriage," gave the ruler and his lineage a unique position above other people.[19]

Legitimizing myths change over time. Felicia Pratto and Andrew Stewart describe how they morph. For instance, the United States' expansion of its territory through the 1800s was underpinned by the doctrine of manifest destiny, indicating that Native Americans were "savages."[20] Twentieth-century and twenty-first-century occupations of other nations are no longer seen as "colonization" by the United States, but as "democratization," with many in the U.S. feeling proudly superior to the old colonial powers of Europe, viewing themselves as the world's premier egalitarian democracy. Pratto and Stewart enumerate the list of justifications that are being used now: national security, national interest, national liberation, religious purity, combined with stereotypic images of the enemy as "barbaric, especially in contrast to images of one's own nation and allies as virtuous," and all this "can justify war, pre-emptive strikes, arms build-ups, violations of national sovereignty, terrorism, and violations of the International Humanitarian Law." Pratto and Stewart make clear that even "liberal" legitimizing myths can be used to justify the use of force or warfare, for example, when the invasion of Afghanistan was to liberate its women from the oppression by the Taliban. Massive and brutal violence was employed also by Marxist and "egalitarian" revolutionary movements, from the Russian revolution to Peru's *Sendero Luminoso* (Shining Path).

Legitimizing myths may entail and be reinforced by a *chosen trauma*. Psychiatrist Vamik Volkan's theory of collective violence explains that when a chosen trauma that is experienced as humiliation is not mourned, this may lead to a sense of entitlement to revenge, and, under the pressure of fear and anxiety, to collective regression and ultimately violence.[21] One of his books is titled *Blind Trust*.[22]

Chosen traumas can become encoded into culture. The annual Orange Walk held in Northern Ireland each July, for instance, celebrates the Protestant victory of Prince William of Orange over King James II in 1690, and thus "evokes past grievances and losses associated with the protracted conflict over Ireland," thus activating latent psychosocial triggers for "more hostile Catholic-Protestant relations."[23]

Psychologist John Jost and his colleagues have developed system justification theory, which draws on social identity and social dominance theories, as well as notions such as self-interest, intergroup conflict, ethnocentrism, homophily, ingroup bias, out-group antipathy, dominance, and resistance.[24] They find that there is a general ideological motive to justify the existing social order, and that this motive is partially responsible for the astonishing fact that subordinates internalize their own lowliness. When subordinates internalize their own inferiority, they often do so at an implicit nonconscious level of awareness, which, paradoxically, is sometimes strongest among those who are most harmed by the status quo.[25]

Psychologist Peter Coleman and his colleagues developed the dynamical systems theory, where they draw on, among others, social dominance theory,[26] and system justification theory.[27]

Yet, then they go further. They acknowledge that systems are dynamic, not static. Coleman identifies *attractors*, or dominant mental and behavioral patterns that offer a coherent map of the world to people, and a stable platform for action.[28] If we look at legitimizing myths, reinforced by a chosen trauma, will can conclude that they constitute strong attractors.

As for the kings of the past, it is not unusual also for today's wealthy to view their prosperity in religious terms, as a sign of their god's approval. In the course of my international life, I have witnessed the almost divine status of money – in each world region and cultural realm differently expressed – money being welcomed as a quick path to fame, in contrast to the much more arduous traditional paths to hard-earned status. I see it being very pronounced in certain segments of the American society, for instance, sometimes with a New Age underpinning, sometimes without, all culminating in a quasi-religious adoration of money as something holy.[29] And I see the adoration of money also very pronounced in China, in the Chinese tradition of wishing for "wealth and a long life," visibilized, among others, in the burning of money as religious sacrifice.

Sociologist Max Weber (1864 – 1920) saw a connection between the religious teachings of John Calvin and the rise of capitalism.[30] Also Adam Smith, in his 1759 book *The Theory of the Moral Sentiments*, taught that divine providence has decreed that humans should follow their natural inclination to pursue self-interest, since "what is natural" is also "what God intended," meaning that if people fail to pursue their self-interest, they are not only unnatural, but also disobedient to God's will. Moreover, providence had also arranged, "as if by an invisible hand," that the work of individuals would be harmonized so that the good of all would result from each pursuing his own good.[31] Later, Russell Herman Conwell, Baptist minister and Temple University founder, gave the famous speech *Acres of Diamonds*, first in 1913, where he fused Christianity and capitalism: "To make money honestly is to preach the Gospel," and to get rich "is our Christian and godly duty."[32]

In earlier times it was common sense that kings derived the right to rule directly from the will of a god and that only gods could judge unjust kings, making it a sacrilegious act to depose a king.[33] Now, it seems that so-called neoliberalism is the new "common sense" that cannot be criticized, lest it be seen as sacrilegious.[34] Political scientist Susan George concurs: "No matter how many disasters of all kinds the neoliberal system has visibly created, no matter what financial crises it may engender, no matter how many losers and outcasts it may create, it is still made to seem inevitable, like a divine act, the only possible economic and social order available to us."[35]

By now, worldly riches are being interpreted as proof for divine blessings all around the world, which means that divine proof has been brought down from heaven to Earth. Canonizing a saint requires a long process of verification, while money as proof for the gods' recognition is easily quantifiable.

Capitalism was promoted by thinkers such as Montesquieu, Sir James Steuart, and Adam Smith, initially with the moral aim to attenuate sinful passions by way of more "harmless" commercial activities. The three primary passions intended to be curbed were love of power, lust, and avarice, all thought to produce wicked behavior. One available solution to repress them would be by pure reason, however, to change avarice from a vice to a virtue, to rename avarice into "advantage" or "interest," and in this way repress the first two, was seen as a much more innovative solution. This is how economist Albert Hirschman (1915 – 2012) reconstructs the intellectual climate of the seventeenth and eighteenth centuries. The pursuit of material interests was no longer condemned as the deadly sin of avarice, but elevated to be a savior from the other destructive "passions of man."[36]

The differences between the hierarchical societies of the past millennia and present-day arrangements may thus be much less dramatic than present-day rhetoric indicates. In the past, individuals were only more "frozen" into fixed institutions – such as feudalism and the divine right of kings – while today slightly more room is given to the majority of people to choose in which category of subjugation they wish to partake. Clearly, also much of this new space for choice is only an illusion: Still today, across countries and eras, birth predicts more than fifty percent of one's income or education status, and eighteenth-century wealth still impacts income distribution today.[37]

Evolutionary economist Ulrich Witt focuses on *motivation* and *coordination*. He reasons that leaders in the past often had no choice but to employ draconian and even abhorrently cruel measures, since "the higher the productivity, however realized, the more resources could be controlled and instrumentalized for political and military competition."[38] In this way, those leaders sacrificed motivation for coordination. Openly draconian measures have subsided by now, at least in most contemporary Western societies that espouse egalitarian values, yet, coordination and motivation are still foundational mechanisms. Witt observes that motivation is still being sacrificed, albeit now obscured in *contracts*: "it is not difficult to recognize the features associated with the dominance-based mechanism relying on the template of superior and subordinate with its long cultural tradition – the fact not withstanding that it now comes in the civilized version based on voluntary contractual arrangements."[39]

Also terror and counterterror can be seen as expressions of a divine mission. Martyrdom has been regarded as a divine duty in many religions, and present-day suicide bombers draw on this legitimization. Among early Christians, some even actively provoked their martyr death at Roman hands. In 185 CE, the proconsul of Asia, Arrius Antoninus, felt so beleaguered by Christians clamoring for martyrdom, something which he was expected to enact, that he called out that if they wanted to kill themselves "there was plenty of rope available or cliffs they could jump off."[40]

Neil Whitehead is a scholar of the anthropology of violence, and he has dissected the cultural conceptions of martyrdom in Palestine.[41] He warns that a scholarly discourse on "suicide terrorism" that focuses merely on the political strategies behind acts of violence, "fails to consider their cultural dimensions, which are key to understanding how these acts gain popular support and become potential individual motivations."[42] Mona Eltahawy, an Egyptian-American journalist, takes the entire globe as her cultural context when she speaks about the Muslim Brotherhood in Egypt and the "Christian Brotherhood" in the United States of America, both divinely inspired.[43]

Divine legitimization and fear can be combined in both, terror and efforts to counter terror. Reza Aslan, a scholar of religious studies, differentiates cosmic war from holy war. In a cosmic war, the participants act out a battle on Earth, which they believe is taking place in the heavens. This is more than rival religious groups fighting an earthly battle for material goals.[44] Aslan also differentiates "islamists" from "jihadists," and argues that islamists have legitimate goals and can be negotiated with, in contrast to jihadists, who wish to return to an idealized past of pan-Islamic, borderless communalism. Also on the American side, Aslan argues, there is a feeling of taking part in a sacred and cosmic war, for which one must be prepared to sacrifice the so-called smaller things of life. The rhetoric of "war on terrorism," Aslan argues, sets itself up in "cosmic dualism" to Al-Qaeda's jihad. American psychotherapist Carol Smaldino supports that view and adds: "In our case [that of the United States], our fighting terrorism, our setting ourselves up as the alleged moral leaders of the world, involves having fear as the most important value of any."[45]

Peace researcher Johan Galtung offers an overview over the world's religions messages.[46] He identifies Judaic religious extremism as territorial (the Promised Holy Land), Christian extremism as missionary, and Islamic extremism as punitive, all entailing a push for war: *ex occidente bellum* (Latin: from the west, war). Unfortunately, Galtung points out, Eastern religions' messages are not strong enough to declare *ex oriente pax* (from the east, peace): Hinduism has the caste system, which means internal structural violence, Buddhism prescribes nonviolence, yet, some Buddhists, as in Sri Lanka, Myanmar, or Thailand, use violence to defend their state with Buddhism. Daoism is undecided, yet, a rising yin or yang may be promising, while Confucianism, even though it disapproves of "bad emperor" violence, is built on feudal structural violence. Japanese state Shinto, in turn, was fashioned on Christian state religions when it justified external violence.

How about the secular counterparts to religions, the ideologies, the -isms, this is the next question

Galtung asks.[47] First, he points at an important difference, namely, the global fault lines regarding nature, gender, generation, race, class, nation, and territory, which are seen by many religions as immovable Manichaean dualisms and part and parcel of the divine order. Secularism, in contrast, sees them as moveable, either for worse or for better: for worse, such as in slavery, colonialism, or war, or for better, such as in human rights ideals. In other aspects they are similar. Religions speak of God versus Satan, and of Paradise versus Hell in afterlife; political parties of enlightened nationalism and statism as well promise paradise, this time on Earth and defined as upper class rewards from capitalist growth, versus hell or poverty and misery. Incidentally, the latter definition also entails that inequality is an incentive that must be maintained rather than overcome. Secular fundamentalism means strong attachment to one side of the fault lines dividing gender, race, class, nation, or state, while secular extremism (which may be fundamentalist or not), uses violence against the Other across those very fault lines.

In my work, I conclude that the significance of the Neolithic transition that commenced around twelve millennia ago is matched only by the significance of present times. A similarly important transition waits to be manifested at the present juncture in human history. I see two main rounds of globalization, the first ending with the Neolithic revolution when all continents of planet Earth had been populated by *Homo sapiens*. Now the second round is ending, as all-out circumscription loudly signals a final "stop."

My personal choice in this situation is to live as a global citizen, by now with forty years of global experience. I concur with discourse analyst Michael Karlberg when he speaks of the social body frame of dignity with its roots in diverse cultures, and that "it has been reemerging in a modern form over the past century, in response to the ever-increasing social and ecological interdependence humanity is now experiencing on a global scale."[48] It is in this globally interconnected context that the social body frame of dignity receives space to come to the fore, and, this is my view, needs intentional support to come to the fore more. Another major shift is now materializing and must materialize, similarly profound as the Neolithic revolution, namely a shift away from domination toward partnership. If not, the state of terror that the security dilemma brought with it, will multiply in its manifestations and become suicidal for humankind. The "necrophilic, phantasmagoric systems of domination and war," as philosopher Walter Benjamin called it, now endanger the very survival of *Homo sapiens* as a species.[49]

How could first steps toward this new transition look like? Perhaps de-glorifying the transition toward agriculture is a first step to help the new concept of dignity to flourish. Many people I meet around the world believe that agriculture was the greatest historic innovation of human genius, because it meant that "we took control." I ask: Is it true that it is always a good thing "to take control"? Or was it simply the best that we, as humankind, could do at the time, in a situation where shifting conditions compelled us to adapt? Maybe it was a sub-optimal adaptation? Perhaps this adaptation no longer works today? Perhaps its inner logic will prove to be self-destructive for us if we continue to intensify it? Perhaps it has outlived its usefulness? Perhaps we can forge better adaptations now? After all, we have knowledge now that we did not have 12,000 years ago!

Most people are unaware that prehistoric foragers were better nourished than most subsequent populations, so-called primitive and civilized alike.[50] Richard Manning is an environmental author with a particular interest in the history and future of agriculture and poverty. He wrote a book titled *How Agriculture Has Hijacked Civilization*.[51] Journalist and author Jeffrey Warner chimes in. Warner has for many years lived with indigenous peoples and has documented their lives. He decries the loss of deep knowledge about humanity's relationship with nature:

> ... cultures have been shredded ... fragmented ... burned by global economics and greed – development, this supposed progress! At least we still can witness facets of traditional culture, in its ongoing stages of disintegration. This questions the direction of humanity overall. Fundamentally different ways of life, these paradigms that nowadays define the existence

> of the indigenous peoples, interact with each other as humanity overall relentlessly continues with this attempt to stitch together the natural with the synthetic. People do still have their voices, and some good may even be forthcoming with modernity, but there's malice amidst this grace. Pain and scars remain from nails hammered into the coffins that contain precious cultural jewels, that proven mastery of how to survive on Planet Earth.[52]

The concept of *oneness* connects traditions that may have existed prior to the emergence of the security dilemma and that managed to persist despite of it.[53] Many believe that oneness also resonates with the latest in quantum physics.[54] Theologians from many traditions, mystical writers, scientists, humanists, holistic philosophers, they all form a burgeoning global movement of religious and "inter-spiritual" people.[55] They speak of *post-individual consciousness*,[56] *unity consciousness*,[57] *planetary consciousness*,[58] and *organic oneness* of humanity.[59] The distinction between "us" and "nature" becomes meaningless, it is no longer a question of "us" needing to protect "nature" when we are all part of the same system and "looking after ourselves and seeking to balance our activities with the interests of 'others' becomes 'natural.'"[60]

Chapter 3

Also Human Nature and Cultural Diversity Fell Prey to the Security Dilemma

We are left believing that while many people have impulses that are generous, kind, and responsive to other human beings, at bottom, they are selfish, self-seeking, and out for themselves. Self-interest, we say, is basic. But it is not the basic element. It is just one possibility.

– Jean Baker Miller,
pioneer in women's psychology[1]

Throughout the past millennia, the security dilemma, the confrontation on the battlefield, the male dominator culture that is predicated on it, all that had an all-out definitorial impact on all spheres of life.[2] The concept of *Homo dominator* that evolved in this context may have been the most prominent casualty, at least viewed from a more recent historical perspective. We know now that this concept is dangerously misguided. Humans are social creatures who draw more psychological satisfaction from connecting than from dominating.[3] In societies that value all people as fellow humans first and foremost, and insist on the dignity of everyone, all are happier, be they rich or poor.[4] With this chapter, I wish to invite the reader to do two things: first, embrace a new definition of human nature, and, second, at the same time refrain from arrogant indignation over the shortsightedness of our ancestors or those who still hold *Homo dominator* views today.

Brain research teaches that "the adult brain is far from being fixed. A number of factors, such as stress, adrenal and gonadal hormones, neurotransmitters, growth factors, certain drugs, environmental stimulation, learning, and aging, change neuronal structures and functions."[5] Not least chronically increased levels of fear have a structural impact, and if entire communities are exposed to stressful fear, over long time, the alterations will be widespread and may be regarded, falsely, as part of default human nature.

Allow me now to gather some facts of what happened in *Homo sapiens*' pre-Neolithic history. Human life was once characterized by a level of mobility that was unthinkable in later epochs. The globe became peopled by modern humans from Africa because our ancestors were able to cover vast distances. The pioneering Paleolithic lifestyle involved both high mobility and a high degree of egalitarianism.[6]

Furthermore, humans are social animals who are able to be super-cooperators. Cooperation is central to the four-billion-year-old puzzle of life, says, for instance, evolutionary biologist Martin Nowak. Indeed, it is cooperation, not competition, that is the defining human trait.[7] This is also what social psychologists have found,[8] and we learn it from evolution theory, from developmental research, and child language acquisition.[9]

As has been mentioned in the Introduction, sociobiologist Edward O. Wilson has studied *eusociality* (Greek *eu*, good/real and social), the highest level of organization of animal sociality, which includes cooperative care for the young.[10] Humans are no "naturally" isolated selfish individuals, who violently defend their self-interest and therefore need to be pressured to behave prosocially, be it by religious or moral pressure or by intellectual or abstracts ideas imposed on them.[11] There is no "primitive-brutal" human nature that needs to be civilized. Humans' prosocial behavior, such as solidarity, altruism, care, and compassion, has evolved through evolution. Prosocial virtues have developed during human natural and cultural evolution, and are therefore part of human nature. Evolutionary theorists have recently reminded us of *between-group selection* in addition to *within-group selection*, and they inform us that "altruistic groups beat selfish groups."[12]

Indeed, my doctoral research in Somalia provided me with deep insights into what solidarity means.[13] Many in Somalia survive only due to the willingness of their diaspora family members dispersed in the rest of the world to provide them with financial support: "Somalia's tight clan bonds have helped to set up worldwide banking networks."[14] Someone in America or Europe, for example, "can give dollars to his local clan banker, and the equivalent will be collected by his family from the remittance bank in Galkayo within 24 hours. There are no receipts and no disputes. These remittances, hundreds of millions of dollars a year, keep Somalia going."[15]

Already historian Ibn Khaldun (1332 – 1406) spoke of solidarity, *asabia*, meaning the solidarity that makes people trust and support each other.[16] He observed how easily empires can fall at the hands of nomadic warriors who suddenly emerge from outside, and, in the blink of an eye, destroy cultural complexity that grew over centuries. He theorized that nomads draw their strength precisely from *asabia*.

Evolutionary theory has looked also at other phenomena, such as at *coordination* and *motivation*. Motivation thrives best when coordination is achieved in an egalitarian context, rather than in an authoritarian top-down context. The reason is that an egalitarian context furthers intrinsic motivation, not just extrinsic motivation.[17] Evolutionary economist Ulrich Witt observes the same two basic human "phylogenetic footprints" that also I describe in my work: first, the inclination toward hierarchy in early hominids; second, the rise of egalitarianism thereafter, during the majority of *Homo sapiens*' history. Only more recently, following the Neolithic Revolution, the older hierarchical script has returned,[18] due to circumscription and its consequences.[19]

Early on, people were much less divided than later. Late-Pleistocene foragers were able to roam and connect over vast areas.[20] Just to give an example, settlement patterns and rock art demonstrate that all of Northern Europe, up to the high north of Scandinavia, was once one single mutually connected social territory without boundaries, and this lasted until roughly 9,000 years before the Common Era.[21]

Then the security dilemma began to interfere. As it was definitorial during the past five percent of human history, everything prior to it, understandably, now risks being looked at through a lens that is biased and skewed by the effects of the security dilemma. Famously, for instance, the Neanderthals have been demonized thoroughly undeservedly.[22] This bias is not conscious, it became embedded into the ecology of mind, as cyberneticist Gregory Bateson would call it. What is also overlooked is that the pace of genetic evolution is slow, and that the radical changes over the last ten to fifteen thousand years in the dominant production technology from foraging to complex agriculture were the result of cultural evolution, in other words, of collective learning, collective formation of habits and customs, within changing constraints on social interactions. At the same time, underlying the cultural changes, the innate social behavior traits that had been shaped by natural selection during the long epoch of early human evolution, remained part of "the genetic endowment."[23]

Long-term species-wide nonconscious effects have been studied, among others, by psychologist Julian Jaynes[24] and psychiatrist Iain McGilchrist. Both have researched, each in his particular way, the "divided brain and the making of the Western world."[25] They both build on the idea of the unconscious and its power that has been widely proven by research. Basically, research shows that we live in something that could be called an illusion. Our brains begin to unconsciously prepare our decisions several seconds before they reach our awareness.[26] The left hemisphere creates the illusion of meaningful scripts and a coherent self and offers explanations for our behavior post-hoc – and these explanations may or may not be trustworthy.[27] Conscious attitudes inform behavior only when they are focused on; when not, unconscious attitudes guide behavior.[28] This automatism is often very appropriate for a given situation, yet, sometimes it is not.

A strong security dilemma increases fear and stress; and since the security dilemma impacts all details of life in all of society, its influence is all-definitorial and thorough.[29] When Alexander the Great burned Persepolis, when the Mongols destroyed Baghdad, when the Visigoths sacked

Rome, when the Crusaders captured Jerusalem, nobody could opt out. And these events were only the most extreme ones, serving as stark reminders to everyone, even the most peace-loving person, that such catastrophes could happen at any time, suddenly, to everybody. Not without reason is Europe filled with historical fortresses and city walls, and the Chinese built the Great Wall. Fear of attacks from outside was compounded when rulers transmuted from protectors to oppressors; then even one's own superiors had to be feared.

If we look at causes of aggression, we find them at biological, environmental, and psychological levels.[30] When we consider the psychological level, we know that feelings of fear can lead to sadness and depression,[31] but also to violent behavior.[32] Fear manifested in the face of attackers from outside and in the face of one's own superiors, and over time this fear seems to have become so ingrained that many people cave in even to the mildest form of authority today. The famous Milgram experiments have shown that it was enough for the organizers to wear a white "expert" coat.[33] "War makes murderers out of otherwise decent people. All wars, and all decent people," these are the words of the last Nuremberg prosecutor alive, Ben Ferencz, at the age of 97.[34] Sociologist Zygmunt Bauman has explained how the lessons-learned from this experiment are of concern for us all.[35]

Causes of aggression can also be found in dynamics of humiliation, as they are often associated with feelings of powerlessness. This may lead to apathy, but also to violence, be it physical, verbal, or psychological. Examples abound, in history, as much as today. Whenever formerly privileged segments of society resent equality – for instance, when men oppose calls for gender equality – because they misunderstand those calls as oppression, violence can become a way of regaining the sense of the control they feel entitled to.[36] Violence can feel like a liberation from involuntary passivity caused by humiliation. This sense of liberation can remain, or even be heightened – even if it leads to martyrdom – in contexts where humiliation is virulent in societal structures over long time.[37]

Groups tend to be more competitive and aggressive than individuals alone, not least because responsibility for own actions is diluted and barriers for aggressive behavior reduced.[38] The renowned Robbers' Cave experiment showed how fast and almost automatically inter-group hostility can evolve.[39] More even, the minimal group paradigm suggests that even the most irrelevant group differences can lead to heated in-group/out-group dichotomies.[40] Not enough, also within groups, aggression can occur, for instance, when resources become scarce or rank is contested.[41] Only common superordinate goals that are attainable, and that are determined by common consent among equals, can overcome these strong splitting tendencies.[42]

Any increase of fear and stress is a double-edged sword. Admittedly, "the acute stress response enables us to rapidly detect threats, respond adequately, restore homeostasis when threats are no longer present, and better prepare the organism for future challenges" yet, "it causes us to have difficulty focusing our attention, retrieving information from memory, and making decisions that require complex thought. Extreme and prolonged stress can furthermore have pathological sequelae such as post-traumatic stress disorder and depression."[43]

Stress thus creates tunnel vision. Therefore, the experience of threat increases ideological responses,[44] and it also increases the probability for biases to intensify. Among those biases is the so-called correspondence error, meaning that we tend to overlook external circumstances that force others to behave as they do against their will and against their nature.[45] As a result, when others hurt us, we may attribute to their "nature" or their ill will what in reality is caused by their circumstances. When the security dilemma is strong it is precisely this bias that intensifies and leads to narrating reality as follows: "When others hurt us, they intend to do so, because they are evil. And a man's duty and pride is to be a hero in the face of evil."[46] Alternative narratives lose out, such as "When others hurt us, it might be beyond their control. Perhaps they were duty-bound to act as heroes in combating us. Perhaps we can repair the damage together."

Human nature is neither "evil" nor "good." It entails the potential for a very wide range of acts. The perpetration of terror is one, and this might be done out of a sense of heroic duty rather than evilness. Few are born with sadistic tendencies. Indeed, brain damage to the prefrontal cortex impairs moral judgments.[47] Trauma suffered during childhood or adulthood can produce sadistic tendencies later in life.[48] Mental illnesses are caused by a combination of genetic and epigenetic preload, a weakening of the brain's stress axis, early childhood trauma, and negative experiences also in later childhood and adolescence.[49] The outcome of harmful childhood experiences may be, for instance, that a false or "alien self" develops, which then hinders healthy "mentalizing," as those researchers hypothesize who attempt to integrate empirical research with psychoanalytic theory.[50]

Yet, all this is perhaps the least problem that humankind faces, since a functioning society can contain a few individuals with antisocial tendencies. The most significant problem lies not in human nature, but in the influence of the security dilemma: to say it provocatively, if love for one's own in-group calls for terrorizing enemies, it is love and cooperation that drive terror, rather than evil sadism.

Massacres perpetrated out of loyalty and devotion, out of unselfish love for one's tribe, one's nation, dynasty, church or ideology, far outnumber individual crimes committed for selfish motives, explains critic Arthur Koestler.[51] As long as the notion of "we" is built on a "non-we," as long as our "we" does not comprise all of humanity, out-group hostility is to be expected. This problem has been pinpointed by researchers on group selection in evolution as far back as in the 1930s.[52] A tribe whose members show altruism toward each other and cooperate is more likely to survive than a less cooperative tribe, with out-group aggression being the "other side of the coin."[53]

Yet, a strong security dilemma makes it difficult to acknowledge that the enemy may act out of love when he attacks "us." The security dilemma pushes for a biased view of the enemy's motives, and, in extension, for a biased view of human nature as a whole. As soon as human nature is seen as essentially evil, no other explanation than this "nature" is necessary to justify harsh retaliations. As soon as the default motivation ascribed to people is that they intend to inflict harm "naturally," only fear of punishment and counterforce remain as options to hinder them, and this view then gives authoritarian leaders the right to rule with an iron fist over their own people. It is then the duty of strongmen to protect themselves and their own against evil, to heroically stand tall. In this situation, heroism becomes more heroic when it faces more extreme and unmitigated evil. The purer the evil, the more heroic the resistance. Heroism and evil depend on each other. Without evil, there is less opportunity for heroism. A man who identifies manliness with heroism in the face of evil, therefore needs evil. In that way, the existence of evil becomes an asset. The dominator model's definition of civilization is an institutional staging of this narrative. Civilization is seen as a bulwark that keeps evil people from devouring others like blood-hungry monsters.

Indeed, until recently, the prevailing anthropological theories of evolution were male-oriented, based on the image of a monogamous, nuclear family with males subordinating females; these theories disregarded or degraded the contributions of females to human evolution.[54] The invention of language, (male) cooperation, and the large human brain, for instance, have been attributed to hunting behavior, war, and eating meat.

Male bias slowly changes now, as more women enter the social sciences.[55] These women have taught me, over time, to expect this bias and ask questions that I would not have asked before. I ask Jean-Louis Dessalles, for example, who researches the evolution of language and hypothesizes that language is a means to create social security when the invention of weapons made it more probable to be killed by surprise. Indeed, when chimpanzees kill an intruder, five killers are needed to accomplish this deed, and still they get hurt in the process. Weapons make killing much easier. This is Dessalles' narrative and I appreciate it. Yet, I ask: What about poisoning? Long before the invention of weaponry that is associated with men, humans knew about poisoning unsuspecting victims. Perhaps Dessalles, since he is a man, did not consider this?

Or, to come back to my favorite question: Is it true, as many claim, that agriculture "frees" people from "having to be" mobile, making them "independent" from the seasons, "enabling" them to settle down, which then leads to such great things as villages, kingdoms, and empires? Conservative prehistorian Hermann Parzinger indeed describes the transition from foraging to sedentary farming as an entirely positive process, toward ever higher levels of human progress and achievement. He explains that early humans learned cultivating plants and breeding animals, and as their experience grew, it was "inevitable" for sedentary life to emerge. As agriculture made life more predictable, women somehow "had" more children, populations grew, and differentiations between larger and smaller settlements emerged, finally culminating in potent complex cultures with priests, scripture, and so forth.[56]

What about Jared Diamond's verdict that was mentioned earlier, namely, that the invention of agriculture was "the worst mistake in the history of the human race," as it brought "starvation, warfare, and tyranny"?[57] Let me suggest another possible narrative: Foragers, since they use land extensively, depend on the availability of uncontested land with "a sufficiently large biomass that can periodically be visited."[58] Given that planet Earth is limited in size, circumscription was bound to kick in at a certain point, even with a small increase in human population over time, combined with ongoing migration. As a result, at some point, people got stuck (sedentary), and were forced into agriculture, even though it was an inferior technology.[59] Agriculture is in many ways less predictable than abundant wild food. Initially agriculture delivered a lower supply of calories than foraging,[60] with longer and harder work and deteriorating health standards.[61] More even, life became more dangerous, since raiders arrived on the horizon, the security dilemma arose, together with the dominator mindset: social relationship became vertical, unequal, with dominators presiding over subordinates. All this was made possible by new technology.[62] Today, in an interconnected world, all this is a tragically dangerous legacy, because it devalues the moderation and dialogue that is so needed now.

In my own life, it took me decades to overcome the bias that "nomadism" is primitive, and "settling down" is more "mature," and only now do I proudly stand by my experimentation with modern forms of foraging. I have learned first-hand, not least by witnessing bitter struggles between pastoralists and agriculturalists in Somalia, how unhelpful the mainstream belief in the supremacy of agriculture can be.

Philosopher Agnes Heller and her theory of the consciousness of everyday life have been mentioned before. She describes how masculinist models of consciousness objectify world order, obfuscating how fluid and continuously malleable it is in reality.[63] The security dilemma may be the very force behind this model of consciousness. It fosters a culture characterized by tunnel vision, black-versus-white thinking and evilness-versus-goodness frames, while reality is much more nuanced.[64]

And it is this tunnel vision that also creates a false view on human nature, a view that amplifies, elevates, reifies, and essentializes into "evilness" whatever appears evil.[65] The security dilemma pits "my beloved in-group members" against "those evil out-group enemies."

This misleading view of human nature may be conceptualized as one of the most insidious conspiracy theories humankind has ever thought up, a conspiracy theory that is fired up by the security dilemma and serves power elites. Research shows that lack of control increases illusory pattern perception,[66] and that particularly people with low education are vulnerable to adhere to conspiracy theories.[67] Vulnerable are also those who are inclined to embrace faith and extremism, all of which applies more to women than to men wherever the status of women is inferior in society.[68]

Indeed, the security dilemma strongly undermines any sense of control, its potential for brutal surprises leaves everybody in its outreach per definition unprepared and "uneducated," facilitating the preference of faith and extremism over levelheadedness. Instead of shouldering the responsibility of manifesting the humanity that humans are capable of, it is easier to exorcize evil demons from others, to "bribe" satanic, angry, or disappointed gods, to buckle under the biblical doctrine of "original sin," and to kill evil enemies, all of which externalizes evil as something unexplainable "natural" inflicted on us from outside.

The fact that the security dilemma can be attenuated now as the world shrinks, is being denied by those who hold on to this "sectarian" Manichaean mindset, and whoever wants to leave a sect must expect to be ostracized from family, friends, and community. This has also happened to me.

What's more, the security dilemma also facilitates the rise of power elites whose privileges depend on keeping their followers in fear of the evilness of human nature. As author and satirist Mark Twain (1835 – 1910) formulated it: "The statesmen will invent cheap lies, putting the blame upon the nation that is attacked, and every man will be glad of those conscience-soothing falsities, and will diligently study them, and refuse to examine any refutations of them; and thus he will by and by convince himself that the war is just, and will thank God for the better sleep he enjoys after this process of grotesque self-deception."[69]

Bertha von Suttner, in her 1889 novel *Die Waffen nieder*, enumerated the arguments brought to the table in defense of war, arguments she encountered in her social environment in Europe at the time:

1. Wars are the decree of God; the Lord of Hosts has himself ordained them (see Holy Writ).
2. Wars have always existed; therefore they will always continue to exist.
3. The Earth, without this destructive agency, would suffer too great an increase of population.
4. Perpetual peace would relax and enervate the race, and a consequent demoralization would ensue.
5. War is the best means for the development of self-sacrifice, of heroism, in short, for the strengthening of character.
6. Mankind will always differ. Complete harmony in all respects is not possible; different interests must be antagonistic; consequently, to expect perpetual peace is an absurdity.[70]

Von Suttner concluded that belligerence is always proven right, as it is based on circular reasoning. It starts with, "admittedly, war is a terrible evil, yet, like with all laws of nature, there is no choice, we have to live with them." The circle continues with its own inversion: "admittedly, war is not a law of nature, it is human-made, yet, it must be waged, because, far from a terrible evil, it is of highest value, as it brings the best out in us and ennobles human nature." Again, what becomes clear is that heroism needs evilness: what is more heroic than standing tall in the face of evil?

The widespread belief in the evilness of human nature is therefore perhaps the prime casualty of the security dilemma. This dilemma is tragic precisely because it spawns strategies of domination and a culture of war despite of human nature, rather than because of it. Even the worst "enemies" do not necessarily hate each other, even if they ascribe hatred to each other. Throughout history, people often ended up in enemy camps only through arbitrary political coincidences. Also killing is not part of human nature, and this applies to killing people as much as to killing animals (see Chapter 15). It would be much easier for humans to kill if this were more hardwired. Not without reason are soldiers trained to avoid looking their victims in the eyes. The youths who make up militia groups all over the world are often perpetually drugged.[71] Societies as a whole fail their responsibility to care when they close their eyes to avoid facing the "unheroic" fact that many war veterans commit suicide.[72] It is not "in the blood" of a soldier to be abler to kill than civilians are.[73]

(Male) anthropologists with a military background go as far as to look at cooperation from the angle of war and claim that war was the origin of cooperation.[74] Undoubtedly, cooperation within an army helps overcome the enemy, but is war therefore the evolutionary source of cooperation? Did men learn to cooperate through war? It is a view that seems to inspire men engaged in the earlier mentioned *manosphere* (man plus blogosphere), or *androsphere*, or *mandrosphere*, a blogosphere that congregates around an agreement that the main problem of modern time is "the extensive tearing of the social contract by decades of feminist tinkering."[75] In this blogosphere we read: "Contrary to men who were selected for selflessness, women were selected for selfishness. The woman who tried to get as much as she could (even at the expense of others) was more likely to survive and reproduce. Men who had to work together to protect and provide for the tribe had every incentive to be loyal."[76]

Facts discount this attempt to protect male superiority. The United States Agency for International Development asks: "Why invest in women?" and explains: "A woman multiplies the impact of an investment made in her future by extending benefits to the world around her, creating a better life for her family and building a strong community," or, "when women have the same amount of land as men, there is over a 10 percent increase in crop yields."[77]

The security dilemma also forces short-termism to the fore, since victory in war is like cutting trees, while the long-term growing of the forest brings no glory. The security dilemma thus gives aggressive behavior an important advantage, and its potential for short-term "successes" invites gullible people to seek this opportunity. The result, by now, is that "humans function as unsustainable 'super predators.'"[78] No other animal has managed to cause the extinction of so many other species.[79]

The promise of quick and easy heroism might also be at the core of the very attraction that holy war exerts on so-called foreign fighters who travel far for the fast "success" of martyrdom.[80] Younger people, still in their formation stage, appear to be particularly vulnerable to this trap, as most people do not reach their full brain capacity until the age of twenty-five.[81]

What can be done now to stop falling into the trap of unsustainable short-term "success"? What can be done to regain long-term wisdom? We know that the famous indigenous seven-generations horizon is enshrined in human nature, be it in men or women. It had a chance to flourish before the security dilemma became salient. Thereafter, the security dilemma and its effects overruled it.

Emotional-relational literacy and intelligence is needed now, it seems, more than rational capabilities. Sociologist Donald Carveth, director of the Toronto Institute of Psychoanalysis, contrasts two forms of conscience, one born of identification with aggressors, the other born of identification with nurturing.[82] Carveth points at the ideologies of domination, such as sexism, racism, heterosexism, classism, or childism, as something that is internalized from "unconscionable societies into the unconscionable superego."[83] It is a mistake, Carveth warns, to think that the way to "goodness" can be found in overcoming "beastly evil" with "good rationality." He finds the roots of morality not in reason, but in feeling, in sympathetic identification or "pity."

A number of other therapeutic efforts to liberate and heal the "inner child" resonate with Carveth's message.[84] Still, Carveth faces an uphill struggle to be heard. The reason, to my observation, may be that also emotion and feeling has fallen victim to the security dilemma.[85] In a dominator context, superiors wish for obedient underlings. They ask their underlings to invest their "passions" only into elite agendas. "Post-truth" was named word of the year 2016 by *Oxford Dictionaries*, as an adjective "relating to or denoting circumstances in which objective facts are less influential in shaping public opinion than appeals to emotion and personal belief."[86] As I observe it, since 2016, one set of "elite" passion-controlling post-truth is in the process of being replaced by another set of post-truth by a rival sub-set of the elite: the promise that deregulated markets would rise all boats was a post-truth promise that was labeled "fact," and now, as the failing of that promise causes uproar, post-truth transits toward a new version of the same futile promise, and it is being propelled by the manipulation of passion just as much as the first one.

In classical Chinese literature, self-cultivation uses the metaphor of "polishing jade," or "to bring out the beauty and luster of a precious gem."[87] The polishing has as its aim to smooth out all strong emotions, be they negative or positive, as both are seen to cause illness and social disharmony. The aim is equanimity, which, in turn, is expected to lead to harmonious relationships and a harmonious society. Throughout my years in Asia, I have observed how effective this cultivation of "emptiness" of the heart-mind can be. I would welcome and applaud it, if it only had channeled feeling and desire into a harmonious experience. Yet, I sense that it has done more, and it has done damage: it left many people as almost empty shells. At the current point in time, I see this trend increase, for instance, in China, where a moral vacuum emerges with the rapid unleashing of market forces. Individuals are more socially isolated and morally confused now, desperate to find more fulfilling models of selfhood and relationships, observes political theorist Daniel Bell.[88] The current psycho-boom in China lives on importing Western concepts, which do bring healing, sometimes, however, more often they worsen the situation. Some people benefit when they become more aware of their emotions, yet, others simply become more "efficient" in effacing themselves to fit into a market economy.[89] In this way a new type of "enslavement" is created in Asia now,[90] masking "the government's inability to provide for its people with structural remedies."[91] As already reported earlier, a form of Chinese *governmentality* has emerged, in which inner life is subjected to government-regulated moral demands.[92]

A "true self" cannot develop in a vacuum as an abstract idea. It must be lived in a social context, it emerges in encounters with others, as Martin Buber has always insisted.[93] My observations in Asia, but also in other traditionally hierarchical societies such as Germany or Rwanda, dovetail with psychologist Alice Miller's warnings that Donald Winnicott might have been too optimistic in expecting a fully developed true self hiding behind a false self.[94]

In Japan, the ultimate result of utter self-effacement in the presence of authority was massive defeat in war. Historian John Dower, in his book *Embracing Defeat: Japan in the Wake of World War II*, introduces Japanese philosophers who decry this effacement and call for a turn-around, for genuine *shutaisei* – true subjectivity or autonomy at the individual level – to enable people to resist the indoctrinating power of the state.[95] Dower presents Natsume Soseki (1867 – 1916), one of the premier philosophers and novelists of modern Japan, who called for a spirit of individualism vis-à-vis the state. Also novelist and essayist Sakaguchi Ango (1906 – 1955) affirmed the need for genuine *shutaisei*. For Sakaguchi, each individual needs to create his or her own "samurai ethic," his or her own "emperor system."[96]

Traditional authoritarian group pressure can lead to a "false self" without a "true self." Yet, so does modern-day individualism. The social isolation of people in individualistic societies brings about the same sad outcome. If people accept to function like machines in a treadmill race – be they seduced by consumerism, or by the prospect of being "winners" in such a race – they cannot develop a true self. When the notion of freedom is being abused to create individualism without solidarity, this prevents the flourishing of a fully developed personality. The baby is thrown out with the bath water, so to speak, when the liberation from authoritarian domination that Sakaguchi Ango calls for, is misunderstood as "liberation" also from compassion and from respect for each other and nature. Influential author Ayn Rand, unfortunately, has seduced many to throw the baby out with the bath water; this is what she has confessed: "If a life can have a theme song, and I believe every worthwhile one has, mine is a religion, an obsession, or a mania or all of these expressed in one word: individualism."[97]

What is needed, instead, are people anchoring *shutaisei* in mutual solidarity. In my book on gender and humiliation, I therefore warn against getting rid of feelings altogether, and advocate the *satyāgraha* approach of a Mahatma Gandhi, an approach of all-encompassing *big love* as antidote against "big hate."[98]

Another emotional capability that is needed is the ability to approach all challenges of life with a *psychological growth* mindset, or a *task-oriented learning-mastery* orientation, rather than with a *fixed* mindset, or *ego-oriented performance* orientation.[99] Research shows that those with an ego orientation entertain an implicit entity theory of intelligence, they regard intelligence as rigid and try to look smart and avoid mistakes. It is preferable to think that intelligence is malleable, to adhere to an incremental theory of intelligence, and to nurture an intrinsic motivation to achieve mastery in a task, a desire to learn new things so as to grow, even if this might get confusing, lead to making mistakes and not look smart. Students with mastery goals are more successful in their studies,[100] and they will later be more successful in adapting to the malleability of life in general. They will refrain, to remind of recent stark examples, from destroying ancient statues to purify the land from idolatry.[101]

At the current point in time, in an interconnected world, global society is in dire need to assume its responsibility of acknowledging that human nature is open to be shaped by its environment. Molecular biologist Robert Pollack is based at Columbia University, where I had the privilege of meeting him, for the first time, in 2004. He warns that DNA ancestry tests are vastly overrated. He asserts that we have good science to document "how governments, corporations, oligarchies, syndicates or other formations can propagate – or not – the fate of millions: whether by maintenance of civil society or by acts of outright war; whether by comprehensive education or by refusing to fund reparative safety nets of food and shelter for all young children; whether by ethics of fairness and respect or by the perpetuation of racial hatred or gendered indignity."[102] Regardless of epigenetic burden, Pollack asserts, we now understand that social structure has a significant role in the remediation of even organic trauma.

To conclude, the concept of human nature became a casualty of the security dilemma. The security dilemma caused the insight to falter that human nature is social and cooperative, and instead brought to the fore a belief in the evilness of human nature. It created the idea that war is an asset, and it fostered the unfortunate dichotomy of "soft" feelings versus "hard" facts.[103] Ultimately, the idea of *clashes of civilizations* emerged.[104] The correspondence error led to an overly static view of the world as divided into "cultures" or "civilizations" that resemble "containers" with more or less opaque walls. Excessive attention was given to those cultural differences that have a firm basis in "real" differences, such as, for example, the fact that one culture may be more adapted to the mountains while others live along the seashore or are traders. Usually, only a few "holes" are considered connecting those containers – this is called "diffusion" – meaning that cultures are seen to influence each other to some degree, yet, never to the point that they would lose their appetite for clashing.

Unfortunately, this view can work as a self-fulfilling prophecy: it warrants fear and prepares for hostility. Rather than creating peace and stability, it tends to create the opposite. Just now, in preparation for precisely such clashes of civilizations, world military powers develop ever more sophisticated technologies and methods for destroying populations.[105] Futuristic manifestations such as neuro-warfare will make the situation ever more dangerous, thus decreasing security rather than increasing it.[106]

The view that cultures are closed containers is also part of post-modern thought when it highlights cultural separateness rather than connection.[107] In the case of post-modern thought, this is done with the desire to respond to difference with respect rather than fearful hostility. "Respect for other cultures" might indeed help to maintain peace, even if only, again, in a self-fulfilling fashion. Yet, such respect can go too far. Postulating that different cultures are fundamentally impenetrable, unknowable, and enigmatic to one another, carries the risk of overlooking possible common ground on which reconciliation can be built when open violence breaks out.

As I have lived globally for so many decades, I am part of a global human culture that we all share. Later I will explain my "sunflower" identity, which thrives on unity in diversity. I cherish *hybridity*: Ideologies and practices are "thoroughly wrapped up in complex personal and social trajectories,"[108] and hybridity means to engage in moment-to-moment strategic blending. Many fear hybridity, yet, it has been common throughout history and it is not harmful. What is harmful are "boundaries and the social proclivity to boundary fetishism," writes sociologist Jan Nederveen Pieterse.[109] Hybridity is seen as a problem only by those who essentialize boundaries: "The importance of hybridity is that it problematizes boundaries."[110]

Anthony Marsella has spent a lifetime collecting cultural typologies in his capacity as a cross-cultural psychopathologist, psychotherapist, clinical cultural psychologist, and multicultural psychologist.[111] As he reports, the making of cultural typologies has a long history in the social sciences, done by cultural anthropologist, psychologist, psychiatrists, and sociologists on the basis of cultural, psychological, psychiatric, and sociological dimensions. Here is Marsella's list (cited in no order) of attempts to place culture into dichotomous mental maps:

- Normal versus Abnormal Cultures (Ruth Benedict)
- Integrated versus Disintegrated Cultures (Alexander Leighton[112])
- Tough versus Easy Cultures (Arsenian and Arsenian)
- Continuous versus Discontinuous Cultures (Ruth Benedict/Margaret Mead)
- Gemeinschaft versus Gesellschaft (Ferdinand Tönnies[113])
- Apollonian versus Dionysian (Ruth Benedict)
- Oppressive versus Suppressive (Francis L. K. Hsu[114])
- Traditional versus Modern (Many)
- Western versus Non-Western (Many)
- Shame versus Guilt (Cultural Anthropology)
- Collectivistic versus Individualistic
- Indigenous versus Non-Indigenous
- Urban versus Rural (Sociology)
- First World versus Third World
- Post Modern Versus Non-Post Modern (Critical Psychologists)

Marsella warns that, today, we live in new times. No longer is it a question of "us" and "them." There is no "other" anymore, "as human beings with the capacity for reason, conscience, and compassion, we must stop humancide, earthcide, lifecide."[115]

Anthropologist and philosopher Benjamin Lee speaks of *critical internationalism.*[116] The field of indigenous psychology is on a similar path.[117] It asks mainstream psychologists to muster the self-reflexivity of competent multiculturalists who are able to see themselves and their field in a new light, namely, as an indigenous psychology rooted in the historical and cultural context of Europe and North America.[118] The view from *nowhere* that natural sciences claim[119] must transmute into local views from *somewhere.* A synergy of multiculturalism and internationalism can create a shift from "one somewhere" to "another somewhere." Together, the local constructions of meaning and global consciousness can use multiple "somewheres" to arrive at shared visions and goals.[120] In my work, I call for "harvesting" from all world cultures.[121]

Indigenous psychologists see current Western concepts of the field of psychology as decontextualized visions with an extreme focus on individualism, mechanism, and objectivity:

> This peculiarly Western mode of thinking is fabricated, projected, and institutionalized through representation technologies and scientific rituals and transported on a large scale to the non-Western societies under political-economic domination. As a result, Western psychology tends to maintain an independent stance at cost of ignoring other substantive possibilities from disparate cultural traditions. Mapping reality through Western constructs has offered a pseudo-understanding of the people of alien cultures and has had debilitating effects in terms of misconstruing the special realities of other people and exoticizing or disregarding psychologies that are non-Western. Consequently, when people from other cultures are exposed to Western psychology, they find their identities placed in question and their conceptual repertoires rendered obsolete.[122]

The message of this chapter is clear. As a result of new global interconnectedness, maintaining isolation is more difficult now than before. It is no longer as easy to uphold the correspondence bias. One may be confronted with explanations on social media written by "the enemy," who insist that they are not acting out of free-floating unmotivated hatred, or out of lust to unfold any evil nature. On the contrary, they may feel duty-bound to re-act to certain conditions, and this might include a sense of hurt and humiliation. This is why authoritarian regimes block free access to global social media, precisely to hinder people from realizing that other people's desire for revenge may *not* stem from any evil human nature, but from a sense of victimization, be it through disrespect and humiliation they themselves experienced and feel, or from their love for fellow victims.[123]

Throughout the past millennia of human history, we lived in a divided world, in fear. We learned to believe that human nature is evil. If we wish to decrease terror in the world and create a decent future for coming generations, now we can and we must build a new context that allows us to learn a new lesson, namely, that it is possible to rekindle our more ancient heritage of loving mutuality and sociality.[124]

Whenever cultural divides are emphasized – be it out of fear of difference or out of the wish to respect difference – what is overlooked is that people on this planet were astonishingly connected and mobile prior to the Neolithic Revolution. Today, the world is even more interconnected, thus linking back to our pre-Neolithic body-mind. The rise of interconnectedness opens space for the insight that human nature is primarily social, that "cultures" are *not* closed containers, that they are *not* mutually incommensurate "silos." In an interconnected world, relationships define the overall situation, rather than the trope of separation and isolation. Relationships can lead to friendship. Yet, they can also lead to humiliation. When this happens, clashes of humiliation may occur. They can and must be healed and prevented. When this succeeds, clashes of civilizations can turn into *dances of civilizations.*[125]

Chapter 4

The Rise of the "Art of Domination"

In the context of a strong security dilemma, even the most peaceable leaders cannot withstand the pressure to invest in domination. If they did, they would be toppled, either by their own people or by their enemies. Two kings of the sixth and seventh centuries in France were ridiculed as *lazy* "do-nothing" kings (*rois fainéants*), because they neglected their "duty" to subdue their underlings. As a result, one of their immediate subordinates, a *maire du palais*, a manager of the palace, took over the throne.[1]

Over time, domination has been taken to ever higher levels of sophistication. Masters have various options to keep followers in line who are not flocking to them voluntarily, options ranging from the use of brute force to more subtle and covert approaches. The highest level of sophistication is the "soft power" of cooption.[2] Coopted underlings not only accept and maintain their own bondage voluntarily, they *misrecognize* it, for instance, as "honor" and "heroism," or even as "freedom." This is the ultimate refinement of the art of domination.[3] Total cultural hegemony is achieved when "a governing power wins consent to its rule from those it subjugates,"[4] in other words, when a majority has been successfully trapped in a collective *Stockholm syndrome*, a predicament where hostages identify with their captors.[5]

Human beings are social and cultural beings. They yearn for connection. This yearning to belong, to avoid disconnection, is central to human survival. Sadly, those who are skilled in the art of domination manipulate this yearning. When no other relational option for authentic connection is open, people become vulnerable to internalizing ideologies into their psychological structures that are not necessarily beneficial for them, including ideologies of submission and domination.[6] This process has also been called *penetration*, or "implanting the top dog inside the underdog."[7]

An "artful" strongman leader will know his "social psychology" and aptly use it in more or less sophisticated ways to turn his underlings into a homogenous group of obedient followers. He will suppress conflicts that might divide them,[8] except for those conflicts that help him rule better – the famous divide-and-rule strategy. He will use the contact hypothesis to make underlings accept their lowliness,[9] he will engage in the de-categorization and re-categorization of identities to form his subordinates' identities according to his needs,[10] and he will frame history in ways that make it appear as if his version of reality always existed and will always exist.[11]

The engineering of false consciousness through divide-and-rule strategies, in combination with coopting victims to become perpetrators, is perhaps the most advanced art of domination. An "artful" strongman leader will use the human willingness to admire elites and will engineer status differentials, for instance racism, as a way to save his classist supremacy: when underlings are busy humiliating lower echelons on the ladder of honor, on the grounds of imagined race, for instance, the strongman can protect his domination. What happened in the United States after white men had been freed from bondage is this:

> Many slave owners in both the North and South were also political leaders. Soon, they began to pass laws that stipulated different treatment of white indentured servants, newly freed white men, and African slaves. No white indentured servant could be beaten while naked, but an African slave could. Any free white man could whip a Black slave, and most important, poor whites could "police" Black slaves. These new laws gave poor whites another elevation in status over their Black peers. It was a slow but effective process, and with the passing of a few generations, any bond that indentured servants shared with African slaves was permanently severed.[12]

The divide-and-conquer strategy that was used works through splitting social relations vertically, offering some people a step higher on the ladder of rank with the illusionary promise that they can reach the top. Martinique born Afro-Caribbean philosopher Frantz Fanon tasted this illusion when he tried to be more French than French, only to find out that he would always be "black."[13] Many women share this disappointment when they deem their own views to be equally valid as those of men, only to find out that many men prefer other men as their reference group rather than women. In all cases, people who have good reason to build solidarity among each other waste their time on humiliating those they deem their inferiors. Only too late do they detect that they are caught in an illusion, that they are victims of what sociologist Pierre Bourdieu calls *deferred elimination*, when people exhaust themselves for a future that ultimately is closed to them, thus eventually eliminating themselves[14]:

> Not surprisingly, however, poor whites never became the economic equals of the elite. Though both groups' economic status rose, the gap between the wealthy and poor widened as a result of slave productivity. Thus, poor whites' belief that they now shared status and dignity with their social betters was largely illusory.
>
> …
>
> For more than four hundred years, wealthy elites have depended on the white underclass to "help keep America great." But who are we keeping it great for? When will we realize we have more in common with all poor people than with rich capitalists and corrupt politicians who manipulate the system to increase their own wealth, power, and control? Instead of wondering which billionaire will finally reach out a hand to raise us up, we should stop waiting and start acting.[15]

When disappointment has sufficiently accumulated, as has happened in the United States in the past years, elite populists such as Donald J. Trump can feed on it. American citizens in the so-called Rust Belt voted him in on the impossible promise to make good on a previous impossible promise. *Trumpismo*, as it is called in Italy, emerged, with a highly sophisticated instrumentalization of popular anger at elites. Populist leaders such as Trump, on their part, may have a very different, very personal agenda. Perhaps they simply want to use popular disappointment to out-humiliate their own fellow elite rivals. A particular elite member can ride popular support to leave behind his elite rivals to himself climb to an even higher top.[16]

In my doctoral research, I have studied cases where leaders used entire populations to enact large-scale humiliation campaigns.[17] I have looked at dictators such as Germany's Adolf Hitler and Somalia's Siad Barre, among others, and searched for their personal experiences of humiliation as possible explanations for their will to power.[18] Both experienced personal humiliation on many levels. The case of Hitler has attracted enormous interest among scholar and a range of possible sources for humiliation has been examined, from plausible to hypothetical.[19] Also Trump's choice to run for president in 2016 in the United States may have been motivated by a personal sense of humiliation.[20] And he sees world affairs through the lens of humiliation when he exits from the Paris climate agreement so that "the world won't laugh any more."[21]

History has known rulers with sadistic pleasure in dominance, and perhaps they were bullied as children and later in life bullied back.[22] History has known cruel leaders who, rather than hiding their cruelty, used it to keep the rest in fearful submission.[23] In a context, however, "where violence is morally condemned, or met with attempts to stop it, such actors will try to hide their acts, divert public attention, or interpret/explain their actions as legitimate."[24] This is what I call the *art of domination*.

Both subordinates and superiors wish to belong. Once an elite group and an elite culture has emerged, also in that case, its members will wish to belong to it. If this elite culture sees exploitative strategies as legitimate, its members may maintain them even where regard for the common good would be more beneficial even for the elite members themselves. Beyond their *heterotelic* usefulness to maintain hierarchy, such strategies may become *autotelic*, meaning that they are committed for their own sake.

Elite theory may be interesting in this context. Elmer Eric Schattschneider (1892 – 1971) was a political scientist who argued that contemporary democratic systems are far from being true to their own definition and are rather "skewed, loaded and unbalanced in favor of a fraction of a minority."[25] Franz Leopold Neumann's book *Behemoth: The Structure and Practice of National Socialism, 1933 – 1944*, retraced how Nazism came to power in the German democratic state and how this may happen again in any modern capitalistic democracy.[26] Political scientist Ernst Fraenkel built on sociologist Emil Lederer who argues that the *Machtstaat*, or "power state," is distinct from the "regular" legal state or *Rechtsstaat*, and that the power state "has its historical origins in the European aristocratic elite, which still plays an important role within European society even after the triumph of democracy.[27] The "elite acted behind the scene in the 1920s, but considered it necessary to intervene in support of the Nazi Party in the 1930s to prevent a possible socialist takeover."[28] Earlier the notion of the *dual state* or *deep state* was introduced. The notion of *state capture* is related: while "corruption" focuses more on the moral failings of individuals at the micro level, state capture is failure at systemic levels.

Causing people to misrecognize their own interest through penetration and *naturalization*[29] has a long tradition. One of the capstones of the art of domination is the concept of honor. The power elites of traditional authoritarian regimes – and this is being practiced increasingly again nowadays – use the fear entailed in the security dilemma to invite their underlings into the *méconnaissance* or misrecognition of what honor truly means.[30] Overlords ask their underlings to do their bidding under the banner of heroic honorable sacrifice, they ask them to regard it as a blessing to offer their own demise and perhaps even the common good for the benefit and honor of their masters.[31] The so-called Communist Bloc achieved elite supremacy and mass submission by coercing the masses into learning to be enthusiastic and "highly motivated" for "altruistic sacrifice."[32] Western lone-hero culture uses a rhetoric of individual freedom, the freedom to choose one's own place in a large machinery that ultimately renders similar outcomes, only more covertly. To say it differently, Western culture's art of domination is carried out under the banner of individual freedom, whereby everybody is encouraged to leave behind traditional ways of maintaining social cohesion, solidarity, and communal sharing – altruism is now suspicious. Instead, everybody is called on to learn to be enthusiastic and "highly motivated" for possessive individualism and consumerism.[33] The end result is similar in all cases, only more or less covertly achieved. As so-called inequality increases, at the present point in history all over the world, it becomes ever more visible how a small glocal power elite accumulates ever more influence.[34] Sociologist William Robinson speaks of a *transnational capitalist class*, "made up of the owners and managers of transnational corporations, and transnational state apparatuses" that now attempts "to exercise global political authority."[35]

Michel Foucault uses the word *governmentality* for the kind of governing that emerged in Europe during the sixteenth century, when an earlier form of governmentality, namely, feudalism, was disappearing. Governmentality was realized through the creation of specific "expert" or "professional" "knowledges," as well as the construction of expert institutions and disciplines, as, for example, medicine, psychology, and psychiatry.[36] Economist William Russell Easterly speaks of a "tyranny of experts," be it experts of divine or secular manipulation.[37] Sociologist Amitai Etzioni points at a present-day example, when he refers to major food marketing corporations spending millions of dollars to study human urges, only to proceed to designing, packaging, and advertising foods that are beneficial for corporate profits rather than for health.[38]

People "learned" many things through the art of domination throughout the past millennia. For instance, they learned to abhor "laziness" – which included throwing out such invaluable assets as the creativity that flows from contemplation and the sense of embeddedness into the rhythms of nature.[39] Instead, people learned to obey the much more mechanistic laws of what is called modern work ethics. Historical sociologist Karl Polanyi is one of those who has described very well how state intervention created markets, together with the *Homo economicus* way of feeling and acting.[40]

Sociologist Max Weber linked the protestant work ethic, particularly the Calvinist branch, with the spirit of capitalism. Others turn this thesis on its head: It might have been the earlier mentioned "bloody legislation" against those who had been put off their land by the enclosure of the commons, which gave legitimacy to Protestant work ethics.[41] (A supportive factor seems to have been literacy.[42])

Economic historian Deirdre McCloskey calls the Industrial Revolution "the Great Fact," and sees dignity at its core. She disputes explanations such as the exploitation of wageworkers, slavery, colonialism, Protestantism, Catholicism, science, temperate climates, temperate citizens, political revolutions, or lower transportation cost and its resulting expansion in trade. She explains the rise of the Industrial Revolution by the increase of dignity for people engaging in business, insofar as the rhetoric surrounding the dignity of business and markets changed, first in The Netherlands, then in the United Kingdom."[43]

Whatever the reason, the willing worker emerged, through a combination of direct coercion and indirect religious, philosophical, and cultural legitimization, facilitated by technical and cultural innovations. The willing worker volunteers to be proud of becoming a cogwheel in a large machinery. This machinery has turned out to function in many ways "successfully," yet, at the price of a "mission creep" that transformed the concept of work ethics and dignity from something potentially promising into something limited and narrow. McCloskey describes in her trilogy the mission creep of dignity in the context of industrialization: how markets and innovation first became virtuous and then suspect.

A forager or traditional farmer-gardener still had "a life" and did not "go to work." Theirs was the most comprehensive anchoring of a person's being-on-this-planet, or what anthropologist Alan Page Fiske calls communal sharing. Fiske found that people, most of the time and in all cultures, use just four elementary and universal forms or models for organizing most aspects of sociality, models that mirror the mathematical scales of measurement of *nominal*, *ordinal*, *interval*, and *ratio*: Interaction can be structured (1) according to what people have *in common*, (2) according to *ordered differences*, (3) according to *additive imbalances*, or (4) according to *ratios*.[44] When people emphasize what they have in common, they embrace the motto of "one for all and all for one," or "every family member gives what she can and gets what she needs." Fiske calls this model *communal sharing* (1). Family life is often informed by communal sharing. Trust, love, care, and intimacy can prosper in this context. This is the arena for the dignity of a *Homo amans*, the loving being (*amans* is the present participle of Latin *amare* or to love).[45] This overlaps with the term *Gemeinschaft* (community) that sociologist Ferdinand Tönnies coined, in contrast to *Gesellschaft* (society).[46] The African philosophy of *ubuntu* has its place here. "Communal Sharing relationships are formed among people who are considered and who consider themselves equal (in one or more aspects). The participants in this relationship feel togetherness; they are bounded; they have something in common (interest, origin, blood, etc.), and refer to themselves as 'we.'"[47]

When people, however, set out to create ordered differences, it is the model of *authority ranking* (2) they use. Authority ranking involves asymmetry among people who are ordered along vertical hierarchical social dimensions – it can be a good parent, or it can be a brutal dictator who follows a *Homo dominans* path. *Equality matching* (3) is the model for arranging interactions in terms of additive imbalances and implies a model of balance such as taking turns, for instance, in car pools or babysitting cooperatives. The *market pricing* model (4) views relationships as defined by proportions or rates, and this is the arena of *Homo economicus*.

Indigenous psychologist Louise Sundararajan recommends studying Fiske's insights carefully, not least because many indigenous communities give primacy to communal sharing as guiding principles for their social and societal life, combined with the caring version of authority ranking, rather than allowing life and society be defined and thus impoverished by less comprehensive frameworks, such as equality matching or market pricing.[48] As anthropologists have found, market pricing has not evolved as a more clever way to engage in *exchange*, as many believe; it is rather *reciprocity* and mutuality that is practiced in indigenous communities.[49]

At the present point in history, every aspect of life at all corners of the planet, is moving toward what Fiske calls market pricing. On the surface, in official rhetoric, this is done to benefit all, yet, statistics of rising inequality show that its underlying *raison-d'être* might be to benefit a few, and this at the prize of wearing down the social and ecological fabric of the entire world.[50] The Internet is perhaps the most recent victim, as it is being nudged from an arena for liberation to being tweaked into a tool of economic exploitation.[51] Sundarajan reminds us that "neoliberal governmentality" operates not through the domination and oppression of citizens, but "by making their subjectivity a target of influence."[52]

In this context, also the notion of "work" traverses a mission creep. In former times, slaves were beaten into work. At some point, slavery was abolished. However, this did not mean that workers no longer had to live in fear; now they had to fear "no job, no food." Over time, in Western countries, labor movements fought for improved conditions. Workers could go to well-deserved retirement in old age. Now fear of humiliation became salient: When a job is the path to "earn" the respect of society, then losing the job means losing respect. In many contexts it is seen as a virtue to self-humiliate oneself into "wage slavery," so as to "earn" not just one's livelihood, but one's respect. By now, this path to respect has become more stony again, with precarious working conditions increasing even in Western countries.[53] "If meaning has since chattel slavery and factory servitude disappeared from many people's work, then it is only as a result of vocations transforming into jobs – the declension of life's purpose into drudgery, the replacement of realizing one's potential into the slave-like consignation to what Gorgio Agamben calls 'bare life.'"[54]

A problem arises when employers and investors are blindly regarded as unequivocally "good" people, who "create" jobs and thus "gift" an arena to people where they can "earn" their living and respect. Philosopher Howard Richards describes this *Zeigeist* in this way: "The proposition that more investor-friendly reforms will serve the common good is treated as a given needing no proof; as if it were a joke that had already been told; as if those who did not understand the joke and did not know when to laugh, or did not know whether to laugh or cry, were not so much mistaken as left out of the conversation, deprived of voice," writes Richards, and adds: "The historical conditions of the possibility of unemployment did not exist until Africa was conquered by Europeans."[55]

By now, inequality has increased dramatically,[56] and the "leisure class" who lives in luxury – rather than "working hard" – accuses its critics of suffering from envy. The blaming of the victims of systemic inequality has reached even Scandinavia by now, a former haven of equality.[57] To be entrepreneurial is now being idolized, and the self-mutilation into wage slavery, while still lingering on as a virtue, is now also seen as a sign of weakness, crowded out by an ever-cruder call for "liberty." Cruder at least as long as the system is configured in a way that even the most zealous entrepreneurship risks ending in ever more sophisticated forms of self-exploitation and self-humiliation. In this way, also the benefits of formerly more equal societies, such as in Scandinavia, are now being lost.[58]

Adherents to the traditional order of honor who regard the application of humiliation as prosocial are now coming back. This is how I was reprimanded by a celebrated Indian economy professor in 2002, and by a renowned Chinese organizational consultant in 2006: "Employees need to be humiliated, otherwise they do not work! Humiliation is an important tool in the workplace! It teaches people the right work ethics! Don't take this tool away from us!"[59] This argument is increasingly voiced in the corporate sector in many parts of the world now, and ever extremer forms of entrepreneurship are being advertised that call for the individual to be so "highly motivated" that she becomes her own humiliator.

Not only Deidre McCloskey describes a mission creep of the concept of dignity. Others have done so as well. Sociologist Mark Regnerus explains it as a transition from what he calls Dignity 1.0 to Dignity 2.0.[60] Dignity 1.0 held sway from times far back before Catholic Pope Leo, continuing until Immanuel Kant and the 1948 Universal Declaration of Human Rights, whereafter it was used less during the nineteenth and twentieth centuries. It re-emerged in the 1990s, argues Regnerus, however, as Dignity 2.0. Dignity 2.0 is similar to its predecessor insofar as it has to do with inherent worth, the reality of the good, and rights seen to be flowing from dignity. However, while Dignity 1.0 pointed at the ability to "flourish as the person one is and should become" and to help other persons to do the same, Dignity 2.0 seems to disregard flourishing in favor of freedom, autonomy, and independence.[61] Another sociologist, Christian Smith, warns, "flourishing personhood" needs to be nurtured by all social practices, institutions, and structures, otherwise it will be damaged.[62]

Also social theorist Margaret Archer thinks that dignity is of utmost importance.[63] Like the first two mentioned sociologists, also she has a Catholic background.[64] Archer emphasizes the four pillars of Catholic social teaching: human dignity, solidarity, subsidiarity, and the common good, and she calls for transforming late modernity into a "civilization of love."[65] All these authors stand for a progressive Catholicism, compatible with liberation theology.[66]

The notion of the common good, or *bonum commune* in Latin, has been expanded in international law since Augustine of Hippo and Thomas Aquinas to mean *bonum commune humanitatis*, the common good not just of one nation, but of all of humanity – in German this is *Weltgemeinwohl*.[67] Catholic development organizations, such as Misereor, now emphasize the *Weltgemeinwohl* as global social and ecological responsibility.[68]

Clearly, as I would add, as humanity's common good is intricately linked also with nature, international law needs to be even more inclusive and expand into *bonum commune humanitatis et naturae*, meaning the common good of humanity as part of nature.

Discourse analyst Michael Karlberg speaks of the *social command* frame of dignity, in contrast to the *social contest* frame, and the *social body* frame, whereby the social body frame corresponds to Regnerus' Dignity 1.0, and the social contest frame to Dignity 2.0.[69] Karlberg recommends looking at the religious tradition of the Baha'i community, "which has over a century of experience applying non-adversarial models … in an integrated and mutually reinforcing manner."[70]

The social body frame of dignity does not neglect autonomy; it only embeds it differently than Dignity 2.0. Karlberg explains:

> The social body frame thereby entails respect for individual agency and autonomy (within the bounds of moderation). This is because the development of an individual's latent potential, and the direction of that potential toward the common good, cannot be imposed on an individual against their will. Rather, it can only emerge as an expression of a will that is informed by a consciousness of the essential unity and interdependence of humanity. Therein lies the key to human dignity within the social body frame: it is achieved through the voluntary subordination of self-centered instincts and appetites to the well-being of the entire social body.[71]

Karlberg emphasizes the responsibility of all social institutions – families, schools, media, corporations, and the state – to foster and protect the development of the human potential, channeling it toward the common good. And this implies more than merely guaranteeing individual liberty: "It implies fostering the consciousness of the oneness of humanity and providing a framework for acting upon this consciousness in our private and public lives."[72]

All these scholars build the same bridges that also I attempt to build in my work, namely, between modernity and the two countermovements against modernity that often are hostile to each other. The two countermovements have been described as the *traditionals*, those who wish to turn back into an imagined past, and the *cultural creatives*, who turn their eyes toward a new future.[73] Also the cultural creatives branch is divided, at times even at loggerheads, as one group turns their attention *outward* to become activists, while others turn it *inward* to gain new levels of consciousness.[74] All those groups, movements, trends or branches have the potential to manifest a constructive path to dignity, a path that nourishes unity in diversity. Yet, all those groups also have the potential to abuse the terminology of dignity, and when this happens, in the worst case, it can lead to a definition of dignity that an inquisitor would dream of: oppression under the banner of good intentions, or the Colonia-Dignidad kind of dignity that destroys dignity rather than nurturing it.[75]

In my life, I weave all three orientations into my personal "religion," which is "love, humility, dignity, courage, and awe and wonderment."[76] I dedicate my entire life to nurturing an "intentional community," "a thriving ecology of change," where all branches feel included and find an "ecology of mutual support."[77]

Not only the notion of dignity has seen a mission creep. Other spheres of life have been affected as well. The Enlightenment represented and still represents a great promise. Philosopher Immanuel Kant put considerable hopes on the Enlightenment and its capacity to free humankind from domination. Kant wrote in 1784 that, hopefully, even governments might once find it advantageous to treat people as more than mere machines, rather in accordance with what is appropriate for their dignity.[78] Enlightenment "has always aimed at liberating human beings from fear and installing them as masters," affirm Frankfurt School theorists Max Horkheimer and Theodor Adorno.[79] Yet, what is the present-day outcome? Instead of freedom and thriving, Horkheimer and Adorno concluded in the aftermath of the rise of Nazism and the tyranny of Hitler's dictatorship: "the wholly enlightened earth is radiant with triumphant calamity."[80]

How did the modern project so brutally fail? Because we participate in our own oppression, say Horkheimer and Adorno, in unison with Michel Foucault, when they describe cultural and social "progress" as a process of coercion.[81]

Political scientist David Held explains how Adorno and Horkheimer tried to find an explanation for why domination did not cease when it should have done so according to ideology.[82] Traditional Marxist sociology saw the source of domination in the tension within capitalism, between the "relations of production" and the "material productive forces of society." Which means that domination should have disappeared when state intervention in economy abolished this tension. In other words, traditional Marxist sociology could not explain why new forms of social domination arose in forms such as National Socialism, state capitalism, and mass culture.[83]

The *Dialectic of Enlightenment* is one of the fundamental works of critical theory of the Frankfurt School, where Horkheimer and Adorno subject Enlightenment to a radical critique.[84] Sociologist and philosopher Jürgen Habermas does not follow Adorno and Horkheimer in all of their thoughts, yet, also he sees that in the era of modernity the liberation of the Enlightenment has turned into mass deception, into a new form of enslavement – a subtle "culture industry" seducing the masses to remain unaware of their own complicity with their own enslavement.[85]

To solve the puzzle, Horkheimer and Adorno hypothesized that already at the beginning of human history, *instrumental reason* was fostered when the subject asserted itself against a threatening nature. This instrumental reason then came to rule over internal and external nature. Horkheimer and Adorno see domination as threefold, (1) domination of nature by human beings, (2) domination of nature within human beings, and (3) the domination of some human beings by others. It is precisely due to that reason's inherent character of domination, that the Enlightenment movement ultimately regressed into mythology, and, as a result, into the "entanglement of myth and enlightenment," in the words of Jürgen Habermas, setting in motion a universal self-destructive process.[86]

All critical theories of whatever denomination emphasize a dialectic of emancipation and liberation from domination and oppression. All critical theorists engage in developing theory and praxis centered on emancipation, on theoretically reflective social action.[87] African-American sociologist Patricia Hill Collins is one of them and she conceptualizes people's experience of and resistance to oppression on three levels: (1) the level of personal biography, (2) the group or community level of the cultural context created by race, class, and gender, and (3) the systemic level of social institutions. Black feminist thought emphasizes all three levels as sites of domination and therefore also as potential sites of resistance.[88]

Also my own observations and analysis over the past forty years of global living led me to assume that domination started very early in human history. It began rather gently – with language and toolmaking – all of which represented rather prosocial applications of domination, short of unleashing domination's dark sides. If we reflect on language, we note that it may have been the first application of the idea that something can be put down; after all, we subject nature to our linguistic labels.[89] The Latin root of the word *sub-ject* reveals it: *ject* stems from *jacere*, to throw, and *sub* means under. Tool-making was another step. Chimpanzees know how to use tools, fashioning twigs to gather larvae out of tree holes. In other words, they are able to instrumentalize nature for their own advantage, albeit in a limited manner. Admittedly, early *Homo sapiens* were not very proficient in making tools either, at least compared to modern humans. Early attempts to subjugate nature were, therefore, remarkably modest. With time, however, humankind excelled at the "trade" of domination.

Then circumscription entered the arena, and the pressure of circumscription brought domination's dark sides to the fore. They ultimately "turned the entire unprocessed pristine world into our enemy," to use Zygmunt Bauman's words,[90] and they contributed to turning not just nature, but also fellow human beings into tools in the hands of their masters. I wrote in 2006:

> We can conclude that at the core of the notion of humiliation we find the theoretical possibility that something can be put, pushed, or held down. Once human beings conceived of this theoretical possibility, they transformed it into manifold practices. Initially, only abiotic nature was put and held down. Later the idea was expanded to include the domestication of animals and also human beings were held down.[91]

Here is another example of domination's dark side, in this case its destructive influence on the idea of cosmopolitanism. Physicist Paul Raskin is the author of the widely known essay titled "Great Transition."[92] He finds concise formulations for why the cosmopolitan idea was pushed aside: it could not thrive in a world dominated for millennia by "fractious states and fractured ideologies":

> Aristarchus of Samos posited a sun-centered solar system in the third century BCE,[93] way ahead of its time. The heliocentric perspective did not take root until Copernicus reintroduced it in the more resonant historical context of emergent modernity, eighteen hundred years later. Around the time of Aristarchus' precocious Copernicanism, the Stoics were advancing the equally revolutionary theme of universal citizenship· Socrates echoed the concept: "I am not an Athenian or a Corinthian, but a citizen of the world." Like heliocentrism, however, the cosmopolitan idea was premature, unable to thrive in a world dominated for millennia by fractious states and fractured ideologies.
>
> Now, well into the onset of the Planetary Phase of Civilization, at last the subjective ideal of global citizenship resonates with the objective imperative for identity and polity to embrace its new and proper sphere, Earth. This convergence of dream and need sets in motion the rise of a historic dynamic that can enable a movement for a Great Transition, if we can seize the moment. The possibility and the urgency are reasons enough to take courage and together quicken our steps.[94]

Knowledge itself has become a victim of the art of domination. As mentioned earlier, in 2013 in Pretoria, South Africa, Catherine Odora Hoppers, Howard Richards, and I engaged in a dialogue on Michel Foucault. Odora Hoppers made it emphatically clear how important it was for her, as an African, to learn from Foucault about the connection between knowledge and power – governmentality is another word for knowledge as power.[95]

Not only Africa, also India had to learn this lesson. Historian Deepak Tripathi explains how the British brought the concept of knowledge as power to India, side-lining the concept of knowledge for its own sake.[96] In his book *Imperial Designs: War, Humiliation and the Making of History*, Tripathi describes how the British East India Company first arrived on the Indian subcontinent to trade, then it ruled large parts of India for a century, until the 1857 rebellion,[97] only to take direct control of India in the following year: "The Great Game between the British and Russian Empires for supremacy in Central Asia had been going on since the early nineteenth century. With the advent of the twentieth century came the discovery of oil in modern day Iran, Iraq, Saudi Arabia and smaller Gulf states. A certain body of scholarship and thought evolved in the West. Philosophers, writers and colonial administrators associated with these ideas came to be known as orientalists."[98]

Tripathi describes how knowledge was commercialized and the ancient Indian concept of knowledge was pushed aside, knowledge as basis for ambitious and open-ended inquiry. Tripathi refers to literary theorist Edward Said and his distinction between pure and political knowledge[99]: "Inquiry in an area of pure knowledge has no predetermined goal for overtly political and economic ends, even though its broader significance for such purposes may not be in dispute. However, political knowledge, directed and financed by powerful entities, for economic gain at the cost of someone else is different. Its aims are narrow, often unjust and lead to conflict."[100]

The most globally impactful success of the art of domination in recent history is perhaps the belief in the necessity of unending economic growth. Stephen Purdey is an international relations specialist and here is his view on how economic growth remains a top policy priority around the world:[101]

> First, economic growth is politically expedient. Growth, as John Kenneth Galbraith once called it, is the ultimate social lubricant. It draws support and approbation from all sectors of society – rich and poor, employers and employees, public and private sectors alike, because they all stand to gain. The "rising tide lifts all boats" mantra is universally appealing and therefore politically compelling. It is also, of course, a utopian economic model which hints at an abrogation of governmental responsibility, even as it helps us understand the lure of growth. Second, and more to the point in this conversation, the growth paradigm is morally convenient. It serves as a surrogate for distributive justice, as an easy way to sidestep the difficult ethical choices which governments would otherwise have to make in an economic context circumscribed by physical limits.

Purdey explains how the growth paradigm serves as an "irresistible image of the future that is cornucopian, equitable, and ecologically benign" and how it promises that by integrating developing and transitional economies into the free global market, global issues such as North-South fault lines will be overcome. However, Purdey warns, this is an illusion. It is an illusion to believe that in the future constructed capital goods will be there to safely replace the resources depleted now, and that the beneficence flowing from prosperity will protect non-human species and their habitat. It is an illusion to hope that there will be no need to share with the poor, or with future generations, or with other species. He warns of an "economic surrogate spawned by the false belief that betterment follows necessarily from the unrestricted freedom to grow." Purdey concludes that as long as ethically robust socio-political oversight remains absent, ecological degradation and other pathologies will continue on a planetary scale. He calls on scholars of philosophy, ethics, and also religion, to assume their responsibility in bringing this oversight into being.

To conclude this chapter, as it seems, all those mission creeps here described result from the successfully applied art of domination. And this seems to have affected all aspects of human affairs throughout the past millennia, wherever dominator societies became strong. Liberation movements typically only had a short time span to thrive: as soon as they came out from "under the radar" and attempted to become institutionalized, they were incorporated into the dominator context, and their original mission was hijacked by art-of-domination strategies if they were not destroyed openly and directly. The cases presented here are only a few of many. Examples range from political revolutions to religious uprisings to philosophical and scientific revelations. Kurt Grimm is associate professor at the Department of Earth and Ocean Sciences at the University of British Columbia in Canada, and he writes:

> The common denominator between evils committed by religious institutions (colonialism, cultural genocide, institutionalized degradation …) is perhaps not religion, but the institutionalism of religion. As evidence, see all of these many evils (and more) also occurring in non-religious institutions. For prominent examples of secular-to-atheist institutionalism, consider Hitler, Stalin, Pol Pot, and Mao's cultural revolution. Note their secular and intelligent rationales.[102]

The art of domination is like a chameleon, it creatively adapts to new situations, and it is able to hijack and divert even the most sincere emancipation and liberation movement. The art of domination is like a parasite, eating its host from the inside. Terminology that carries well-intentioned connotations, can emerge over time with completely inverse meanings. Reconciliation, conflict resolution, peacemaking, coexistence, for instance, can be achieved through dialogue among equals, yet, the same terms can also be used to mean something very different, namely, the quiet submission of underlings under the dictate of superiors.[103]

If we look at the slogan of the French revolution, *liberté, égalité, fraternité* (solidarity), then we see that also these three terms are highly vulnerable to being subverted. As discussed earlier, liberté, or freedom, is highly susceptible to being defined in ways that ultimately undermine it.[104] As to égalité, also this has been touched upon earlier, many founders of religions had equal dignity at the core of their message at first, yet, power- and control-oriented hierarchical institutions "swallowed up" this message very swiftly. Since these ideals moved to the forefront of Western consciousness about 250 years ago to form the core of present-day human rights ideals, they are under constant "mission creep" onslaught, overtly and covertly. As to fraternité, or solidarity with our global human family, *Broken Treaties* is a 2017 documentary film that can serve as parade example.[105] It shows how native populations were cheated out of their homeland step by step. As to solidarity in protecting our shared habitat, planet Earth, sociologist Riley Dunlap's work refers to the same dynamic when he outlines the development of "organized denial" in response to climate change and environmental efforts.[106]

The use of terror tactics is intimately inscribed in the art of domination. Terror is the ideal utensil in the tool kit of the art of domination. Terror leads to shock and awe in its victims, be it oppressive superiors or insubordinate inferiors. Journalist Fareed Zakaria relates how the editors of Al-Qaeda's webzine *Inspire* explain the rationale behind micro-terrorism: "We do not need to strike big," they say. "Attacking the enemy … is to bleed the enemy to death," a tactic they dubbed "the strategy of a thousand cuts."[107] The strategy of a thousand cuts is efficient from down up as much as from up down. Osama bin Laden's target for terror was what he saw as oppressive superiors – the authoritarian regimes in the Arab world, supported by the world's superpower America. Superpowers, in turn, typically target with terror those they regard as their insubordinate inferiors.

As long as short-term shock and awe proves to be a successful strategy to humiliate others into humility – or is conceived or misconceived as successful strategy – it will last. Terror is a very cost-effective application of the art of domination, since very few resources are needed to create huge effects. The 7/7 bombings in London in 2005, for instance, "are estimated to have cost less than £8,000, including trips overseas in preparation."[108] Likewise, unmanned combat aerial vehicles (UCAV), also known as combat drones, bring terror and death at a fraction of the cost of soldiers on the ground.[109] Drones can easily also be used by non-state terrorists.[110]

The artfulness of domination expresses itself in the sophistication of setting in motion mission creeps, almost undetectable for the unsuspecting citizen. These mission creeps are very easy to overlook. If humankind continues to overlook them, it might do so at its own peril.

Chapter 5

How Pressure-Cooker Vents Explode

At the core of studies of war and security, of genocide and terrorism, we always find circumscription and the security dilemma and its reverberations. A culture and mindset of domination is one of these reverberations, it is the master reverberation.

Undoubtedly, domination has had its "successes." Europe would have become part of the Persian Empire of Xerxes I, had not the Spartans fought bravely at Thermopylae in the year 480 before the Common Era.[1] Japan would have been swallowed up in Kublai Khan's empire at the end of the thirteenth century, had it not been for its samurais' bravery.

A culture and mindset of domination, admittedly, can be useful, at least in the short-term. In the longer term, the price can be high. The highest price is paid when this culture lives on beyond its usefulness and becomes all-destructive.

Locusts are successful in what they do; they destroy the very substrate of their livelihood. Humans can do the same. Particularly when rewards are expected in afterlife, domination strategies risk being limitless, as damage on Earth is irrelevant. When salvation or honor are expected to be measured and celebrated in some kind of afterlife, earthly arguments count little and there is no counterargument against honorable martyrdom – be it martyrdom in form of individual terrorism or collective all-out nuclear annihilation.[2] Humans have learned to dominate nature, they learned to fly, and they can now transport passengers in the air, yet, they can also transport bombs that by now can annihilate all life on Earth.[3]

As soon as domination is in place, also potentially self-destructive forces are in place. Domination, as soon as it is established as a strategy, introduces tragic traps, traps that are caused, not least, by the fact that domination has no inherent endpoint, except for the total destruction of its substrate. Locusts only survive because they move on, they fly to the next pasture; could they ravage all surfaces of the planet at the same time, they would cause their own extinction. This is the very trajectory humankind is currently following. What is lacking, are built-in mechanisms that would hinder domination from being driven to the point of self-destruction.

Historian Gareth Porter speaks of the "perils of dominance."[4] Native American scholar Jack Forbes has denounced the Western compulsion to consume the Earth as "cannibalism": "Brutality knows no boundaries. Greed knows no limits. Perversion knows no borders."[5] Philosopher Eric Hoffer adds: "You can never get enough of what you don't really need." "Accumulation" is a linchpin of earlier forms of market exchange that produced a system driven by capital accumulation, says philosopher Howard Richards, pointing at Karl Marx's account of how one form of exchange leads to another.[6] As a result, it is now a physical necessity to keep the accumulation of capital going, explains Richards: "Life depends on production. Production depends on profit. Therefore, life depends on profit. Ergo, life depends on the accumulation of capital. The dependence of life on accumulation implies that every feature of society – education, religion, art, sports, media, family, taxes, wages, police, courts, music, architecture, agriculture and so on and on – must be compatible with accumulation."[7]

The 2016 science fiction film *Stille Reserve* shows the logical next level to be expected for the future.[8] An insurance company may create a system in which people do not have the right to their own death. In this film, the majority citizens, most of whom are in debt, are resuscitated after death and kept alive in an artificial twilight state. Their debts are paid off by exploiting their mental and physical resources; their bodies are used as human spare parts, as childbirth machines, and their brains as information storage. Only those few who were able to afford a "death insurance" can escape this fate and are allowed to die.

Already Aristotle (circa 350 BC) warned against the loss of moderation.[9] Also today, a psychologist such as Friedemann Schulz von Thun warns that every guiding principle can only remain constructive when it is balanced by a counter-value –

generosity without frugality, for instance, can become wastefulness, and frugality without generosity miserliness.[10] Domination is a principle that does not know when it is enough, worse even, when it is failing, it will try harder to dominate.

Adolf Hitler's obsession with might-is-right domination is a powerful example, as it brought not just mass homicide, it was also suicidal for Hitler himself and self-destructive for Germany. Germany offers other illustrations of self-destructive strife for domination as well. Not long after young Kaiser Wilhelm II was enthroned in 1888, he removed Otto von Bismarck. Bismarck was a conservative Prussian statesman who had shaped German and European affairs from the 1860s until 1890 with a kind of balance-of-power diplomacy.[11] The emperor, however, believed in cruder power-over politics and discarded Bismarck and his approach. Bismarck warned that "the crash will come twenty years after my departure if things go on like this."[12] Indeed, the Kaiser had to abdicate twenty years later, almost to the day of Bismarck's death, at the end of the First World War, when his hubris had been paid for with the death of millions and the defeat of Germany.

Then came Paul von Hindenburg, Chief of the German General Staff, who tried to protect Germany from learning the painful lesson of defeat and from becoming aware of how suicidal the concept of honor–through–domination is.

Hindenburg "rescued" the reputation of the German military after its defeat in World War I by employing an "honorable lie," a lie that turned out to have horrible consequences. He claimed that the army would have been victorious – "im Felde unbesiegt" – if it had not been for the civilians at the home front, especially the republicans who overthrew the monarchy.[13] This stab-in-the-back myth, or *Dolchstoßlegende*, stigmatized the politicians of the newly emerging Weimar Republic as "November Criminals," or *Novemberverbrecher*, since they had signed the Armistice on November 11, 1918. This lie undermined the future of Germany. The Weimarer Republic's first unsteady steps into democracy were curtailed and subsequently cut short altogether by Adolf Hitler, again with the support of Hindenburg.

The Dolchstoß story harked back to the famous *Nibelungenlied*, the *Song of the Nibelungs*, dating from about 1180 to 1210. Its hero, Siegfried, was betrayed and stabbed in the back. Adolf Hitler's Schutz- staffel (SS) held dear the motto *Meine Ehre heißt Treue* (My honor is called loyalty) drawing on the concept of Nibelung loyalty, or *Nibelungentreue*, a loyalty that is so absolute and unquestioning that it is potentially disastrous. Nazi potentate Hermann Göring, in his Stalingrad speech in 1943, at a point when total defeat was imminent, still spoke of this Nibelungentreue, the duty to fight to the last man, no matter what.[14]

In Japan, the samurai code of honor, *bushido*, entails a similar concept of loyalty. It is best illustrated by the tale of the *Forty-Seven Ronin* (leaderless samurai), who defied the Emperor of Japan and avenged the disgrace of their dead master, accepting certain death for themselves as a result.[15]

Through being born and raised in Germany, and having spent three years in Japan, I know of the larger than life sense of noble meaning that such loyalty can inspire. I feel deep respect for loyalty and bravery. When I point at the dark sides of blind loyalty here, I do so with profound respect.

Yet, the dark sides become overwhelmingly clear now, as the world shrinks. Yohan Shanmugaratnam is a young journalist with a Tamil-Japanese background, writing for *Klassekampen* (The Class Struggle), a Norwegian daily newspaper. He reminds of the once famous Third World project and its death, a death that now creates monsters such as Da'esh, which he calls "sect without borders."[16] He concludes that the Third World as a project, admittedly, collapsed partly due to their leaders incompetence and inability to handle their national elites, yet, also due to active undermining from the powerful countries. Fundamentalist forces have emerged from its ruins, and, as South Asian historian Vijay Prashad writes in "The Darker Nations," they have become monsters that nobody can tame anymore.[17]

Beware of stoking the security dilemma to protect domination

It is more reckless for elites to escalate domination in a shrinking world than it was in the past. Elites have many motives to escalate domination, perhaps because domination is the only strategy they know, or because they are convinced of the effectiveness or righteousness of their leadership mission, or because they wish to hold on to the privileges connected with supremacy, or as part of an addictive obsession with cycles of humiliation.[18]

It is reckless to tighten circumscription and artificially strengthen the security dilemma so as to bolster domination. It is reckless to invent outside enemies where there are none, as a path to protect and reinforce domination. History tells many stories of attempts to keep the security dilemma strong where it would have had a chance to weaken. In a globalizing world, wars on terror,[19] and new kinds of weapons such a drones, represent the historically most recent tools for this ultimately disastrous strategy.[20]

In 2012, I was invited to the Rio+20 United Nations Conference on Sustainable Development in Rio de Janeiro. Yet, I chose to follow the invitation of Dan Baron and Manoela Souza to create an "alternative Rio+20 week" at the very frontier of the industrialization of the Amazon, namely, in Marabá, Pará.[21] I chose Marabá instead of Rio+20 because, as I had learned, the voices of the people in the Amazon are not heard, even not in Rio, and I wanted to hear them and bring their voices to a larger audience. In hindsight, my decision was vindicated, as Nnimmo Bassey, chairman of Friends of the Earth International, summarized the Rio+20 event as follows: "Governmental positions have been hijacked by corporate interests linked to polluting industries."[22] By now, in 2017, "corruption has penetrated the Amazon rainforest like an illness that infects everything,"[23] said Ruben Siqueira, coordinator of the Pastoral Land Commission during the VIII Panamazonic Social Forum, which brought together in the Peruvian Amazon jungle representatives of civil society from eight Amazon basin countries.

I welcome contemporary efforts to enshrine *ecocide* as a crime in law, in the hope that this might help to mitigate abuse:

> If the massive damage and destruction to the environment is criminalized, environmental defenders will have the law at their side in their work to protect the environment. It would be much harder to brand them as "terrorists" or enemies of progress if the protection of the environment is recognized as a matter of the highest international concern. Instead of using the law against them – limiting the operational space of environmental NGOs or the freedom of expression of individual environmental defenders in the name of "national security" – environmental defenders would be recognized for performing a legitimate task of international concern – the protection of ecosystems – that in fact should be taken up by the government.[24]

I also welcome a shift from guilt to responsibility. Many criticize that the "rights" of one group of humans, namely, those who act as guardians for non-humans, are irreconcilable with the rights of others, at least within the adversarial nature of our legal system. Lawyer Femke Wijdekop answers this criticism as follows:

> I recently learned that the original meaning of the word "lawyer" is actually "healer of the woes of the community," pointing to a much more holistic understanding of doing justice. The adversarial character of our legal system is not set in stone. There is an emerging international movement called the Integrative Law Movement, which aims to create a legal system oriented towards values-based, creative, sustainable, and holistic solutions that build and strengthen relationships – instead of a legal victory of one party at the expense of another. Ecocide law can be seen as being a part of this Integrative Law Movement since it is meant to help build a sustainable relationship between humans and the natural world and is aimed at protecting the rights of all the inhabitants of an ecosystem, through prohibiting its destruction or loss to such an extent that peaceful enjoyment by the inhabitants of that territory has been or will be severely diminished (definition of Polly Higgins).[25]

My hosts in the city of Marabá were Dan Baron, Mano Souza, and their Rivers of Meeting community project (Rios de Encontro) in Cabelo Seco (dry hair[26]), which is the founding community of the city at the confluence of two rivers, Rio Tocantins and Rio Itacaiúnas, in Pará. Pará is a state in northern Brazil, double the size of Western Europe, with some land owners owning up to half a million cattle.[27] On June 21, 2012, I witnessed an action of the Landless Workers' Movement in Brazil (Movimento dos Trabalhadores Sem Terra, or MST) on Cedro Farm, near Marabá.

The Food and Agriculture Organization of the United Nations, FAO, wrote about Brazil in 2000:

> Few countries of the world have such a skewed land distribution pattern as in Brazil. The agricultural development favors the *latifundium* (large private agricultural estate operating with commercially exploited labor force). Only a small minority from the members of the land oligarchy who allied themselves to the industrial, financial and trade capital investments, have profited from this, while the majority of the population were driven out and excluded. During the last 25 years more than 30 million agricultural workers, men and women, have had to quit their land and a further 4.8 million farming families can only dream of having their own piece of land. One of the most shocking consequences of this injustice is hunger: of the 31.5 million people suffering from hunger in Brazil, half of them live in the countryside.[28]

During my months in South America in 2012, I got a deep sense of the interlinkages between circumscription, domination, and terrorism: activists who oppose land grabs, environmentalists who oppose resource grabs in general, risk being killed.[29] Power elites tighten circumscription, increase domination, and eliminate opposition, not seldom under the banner of counterterrorism. In Brazil, this is done either covertly, by bribing entire cities and their cultural lives as in the case of Marabá,[30] or, if this proves insufficient, gunmen are hired, with government authorities standing by. Other governments are more direct in their application of violence, under the guise of fighting terrorism. In Chile, for instance, anti-terrorism laws are used against Mapuche indigenous peoples struggling to recover their ancestral land.[31]

Similar dynamics can be observed on all continents, wherever resources wait to be exploited. "Ethiopia's use of terrorism laws to criminalize peaceful dissent is a disturbing trend," experts note. "The wanton labeling of peaceful activists as terrorists is not only a violation of international human rights law, it also contributes to an erosion of confidence in Ethiopia's ability to fight real terrorism. This ultimately makes our world a more dangerous place."[32]

Also more long-term systemic strategies can be observed. Those who intend to raid resources, can do so openly and crudely, or they can extract them with more sophisticated long-term tactics of oppression. Systematic colonization is such a strategy. This includes present-day's refined colonization of the future through the exploitation by market ideologies that proceed in so sophisticated ways that it can count on the consent of its victims, and its destructive outcomes are then labeled with rather harmless and bland sounding terms such as "inequality."[33]

Also the security dilemma can be stirred up in open ways or more covertly. What began to happen in 2014 in the Ukraine might have been such an attempt to keep the security dilemma strong. After the fall of the Berlin Wall, space opened for the rise of One World without the security dilemma. Many had high hopes. Yet, as it turned out, such hopes were built on the illusion that "victors" would be able to let go of the notion of victory and instead embrace the rise of global partnership. When the reunification of Germany happened twenty-five years ago, at the end of February 1990, German Chancellor Helmut Kohl visited American President George H. W. Bush. When presented with the idea that German membership in the North Atlantic Treaty Organization (NATO) might need to be negotiated and perhaps compromises would be unavoidable, Bush replied: "To hell with that ... We prevailed, they didn't!"[34]

Nikolaj Sergeevič Portugalov was a Russian politician who played a central role when the German reunification was negotiated. A documentary film shows him very calmly explaining how deeply he personally feels the national humiliation of Russia through American arrogance, and how this is almost too painful to tolerate. American foreign minister James Baker and German chancellor Helmut Kohl, who had promised to refrain from moving NATO's borders closer to Russia, subsequently broke that promise.[35] As historian Mary Sarotte's research shows, Western promises to refrain from NATO expansions were given only orally and never written down.[36] Mikhail Gorbachev (or Gorbačev), then the leader of the Soviet Union, allowed Germany to freely choose their membership, perhaps due to the dire financial situation of his country and secret German financial support.[37] On February 10, 2016, NATO agreed to expand its military presence in Europe even further,[38] which, on the Russian side, is interpreted as a NATO mission creep in Eastern Europe, fomenting Cold War II[39] or "Cool War."[40] Historian Andreas Rödder concludes that, indeed, the triumph of the West was the humiliation of the Soviet Union.[41]

Russia experts report that Vladimir Putin initially was much more open and sympathetic toward the West and that it was the West's disregard that subsequently alienated him and provoked him to turn into the "hardliner" he became.[42] Zbigniew Brzezinski, a former presidential national security advisor, explains that Russia now "is in the process of trying to regain its own national pride after the shattering of the USSR."[43]

November 9, 2014, marked the 25th Anniversary of the fall of the Wall. Mikhail Gorbachev, 83-year old, visited Berlin, bringing warnings that a new Cold War is immanent.[44] In the same year, also a number of Nobel Peace Prize winners expressed their fear of a "new, more dangerous Cold War."[45] Peace researcher Jan Øberg warned: "We find a totally new effort on both sides to use social and other media to tell how dangerous 'they' are to 'us.' There is a clear tendency to 'fearology' – to instill fear in the citizens on both sides about the capabilities and intentions of the other side."[46] Øberg continues: "Those of us old enough to have lived under the old Cold War feel pain at witnessing today's result of the post-1989 Western triumphalism and ignorance about all the alternatives to NATO and its expansion that the dissolution of the Soviet Union and the Warsaw Pact offered."[47] In 2016, Øberg adds that there could be true peace today "if NATO had drawn the logical conclusion at the demise of its *raison d'être*: the existence of the Soviet Union and the Warsaw Pact. But triumphalism coupled with humiliation of the Russians was the chosen path – and it has ended in a new Cold War – different but also the same."[48] Former American presidential candidate Dennis Kucinich comments: "There are some people trying to separate the U.S. and Russia so that the military industrial intel axis can cash in. There's a game going on inside the intelligence community where there are those who want to separate the U.S. from Russia in a way that would reignite the Cold War."[49] Indeed, "russophobia" does not need communism as justification, as it has long historical roots.[50]

Øberg reports that one of Gorbachev's closest associates expressed the following at the dissolution of the Soviet Union: "We are going to do a terrible thing to you in the West: We are going to deprive you of your enemy."[51] Øberg hypothesizes that Western leaders simply could not adapt to the new situation – a kind of "ideological lag" perhaps? In their need to legitimize the continued existing of NATO, Øberg observes, they were "saved" by September 11, 2001, and the war on terror.

Clearly, Western powers and Russia are not alone in wanting to maintain or regain national pride. A variation of the Cold War narrative is the religious narrative of Armageddon. Or, China is a rising power as well, casting off its "century of humiliation" in a bid to become a force in regional and world affairs.[52] Particularly after Donald J. Trump has been elected to become president of the United States in November 2016, it is not unthinkable that China and Iran will replace Russia as prime enemies for the United States.[53] And if it were true that Trump is "Russia's man in the White House," then this would represent the most creative revenge for NATO arrogance and expansion.[54]

In a shrinking world, however, it is hazardous to hold on to the belief that humiliating enemies is a safe path to making them humble, to ensuring their humility. The outgoing United Nations Secretary-General Ban Ki-Moon offered a clear warning: it is unforgivable that efforts to abolish nuclear weapons have ebbed, making any re-ignition of the Cold War ever more dangerous.[55]

Beware of creating "vents"

It is inherent in the strategy of victory through domination that blessings can transmute into curses very quickly, while the after-effects of the curses can last for centuries.

In the early eighth century CE (Common Era), the slow infantry of the Frankish Empire was unprepared when Muslim Arabs took Spain and the Pyrenees in a "jihad," a "holy campaign." In response to the lethal challenge, the legendary "way of life of the knight" was born that was to have a lasting influence on European culture, for good and for bad. The Frankish knight's armor protected effectively against the deadly arrows of the Arab attackers and led to victory; the Arab advance into Europe was halted in the Battle of Tours in today's Southern France in the year 732.

Then came the problem. At all times in history, whenever peace is achieved, warriors become jobless. This happened also to those knights after this battle. They turned into a marauding threat to their own people, triggering bloody feuds among competing aristocratic families. Knights were bound by allegiance to local feudal lords, and, as we hear, those lords indulged in unlimited lust for power and belligerence in the face of a weak central power. *Non militia, sed malitia* – not soldiers, but a disease – this was how the utter savagery of the Frankish warhorse riders was deplored in the tenth century. In short, those knights no longer generated security, but terror.

Their "rampant blood lust" was of concern to secular and religious leaders.[56] In search for solutions, clerics used their control over salvation as leverage "to begin developing a theological underpinning to ease Christian-on-Christian violence."[57] Beginning in the late-tenth century, they proposed the *Pax Dei* (Peace of God) and *Treuga Dei* (Truce of God), with the aim to limit places and times for war. They created a distinction between knights that fought for justice and order (*militia*) and those who did not (*malitia*). The *Pax Dei* drew on Roman law's rational principles regarding violence; after all, Roman law had been set up, among others, to resolve disputes between heads of households (*patres familias*).[58] *Pax Dei* survived in some form until the thirteenth century.

Similar efforts to put limits on people wanting to take the law into their own hands were laid down in the *Sachsenspiegel* (roughly, Survey of Saxon Law), the most important law book and custumal of the German Middle Ages, written around 1220, and by the Constitutions of Melfi, promulgated in 1231 by Emperor Frederick II. One of the copies of the *Sachsenspiegel* is kept in Wolfenbüttel, Lower Saxony, in the north of Germany, not far from where I write these lines just now.[59]

If we think of present times, then humankind's present task, clearly, is to engage in a globally driven creative process of formulating, implementing, and wisely recalibrating a *Pax Mundi* (World Peace).

What humankind should beware of on its path, however, is the strategy of creating "vents" for peace. The knights' reputation was "saved" by Pope Urban II on November 27, 1095. He gave the most influential speech of the Middle Ages, when he called all Christians in Europe to war against Muslims to reclaim the Holy Land. This he did, while there was no reason to attack Jerusalem, since Christian pilgrims had free access to travel there and were welcomed by the Mamelucks who ruled over the city. Yet, the Pope exclaimed *Deus vult!* or "God wills it!" The only reason he gave for war and terror was that "infidels" should not "own" what was seen as the navel of the world, namely, Jerusalem. In this way, the Pope created a "vent" that channeled internal pressure elsewhere.

What the Pope did was emulated also by Saudi Arabia and Egypt in more recent history. They sent their extremists to fight the Soviets in Afghanistan in support of the United States. The principle is like a pressure-cooker vent: "If you keep [the cooker] all sealed up, it will blow up in your face, so you have to design a vent, and this Afghan jihad was the vent," writes journalist Andrew Cockburn.[60] *Bitter Lake* is a 2015 BBC film by Adam Curtis that shows how Saudi Arabia sent their extremists to Afghanistan.[61]

Saudi Arabia still has reason to create vents today. It is an extremist, fundamentalist, missionary state, rich enough to expand their Wahhabi and Salafi doctrine worldwide,[62] while at the same time eager to hold safely outside of its own borders those "great tomb-destroyers, shrine-eradicators,

Bamyan Buddha-liquidators, the Salafists."[63] The head of Saudi intelligence reportedly shouted at Tony Blair, when he visited Riyadh soon after 9/11, saying that those attacks were a "mere pinprick" compared with the havoc those extremists planned to unleash in their very own region: "What these terrorists want is to destroy the House of Saud and to remake the Middle East!"[64]

Not just Saudi Arabia has been in need of vents, also the United States is. At the historical moment at which this book is being written, its population appears to turn on itself in self-destructive partisan hatred. Private and national traumas have accumulated over centuries,[65] feeding a warrior spirit that needs new arenas after the Cold War.[66] The United States has been described as another of those most fundamentalist countries in the world. Scholar and social critic Noam Chomsky, for instance, says provokingly: "It's very hard to find any country where over a third of the population thinks that the world was created a couple of thousand years ago, or where the majority of the population is expecting the Second Coming, and about half of them expect it in their own lifetime.

Things like that are just unknown in other countries except maybe Saudi Arabia or something. I'm not even sure there."[67]

The result of the creation of "vents" is not necessarily negative, at least not in the short term. The path of the knight can illustrate this. From brutal warriors emerged noble and selfless fighters, fighters for a culture of justice and faith, thus laying the foundation for the subsequent high regard for knightly culture. The Pope's call served as a common objective for the heavily armed warriors and channeled their fanatical enthusiasm into church politics. Through the fight against the infidels and the liberation of Christian Jerusalem, a unique knight culture developed, with a blend of wild combat readiness, Christian faith, and noble behavior standards. Militant courage, bravery, and self-sacrificing loyalty counted as much as sophistication, education, and sense of poetry and music.[68]

For the Knights Templar, this culminated in a call for a crusade to defend the Patrimony of Christ. The Templars were the product of a long evolution "beginning with the Pauline imagery of the Christian as a soldier battling his/her own spiritual demons," writes Reverend Father Thomas Bailey in his 2012 doctoral dissertation on the Templars.[69] Noticeably, their philosophy is reminiscent of jihad, as it is being conceptualized as struggle with one's own inner desires.[70] Bernard of Clairvaux (Bernardus Claraevallensis, 1090 – 1153) was the primary reformer of the Catholic Cistercian order. He praised the Templars: "It seems that a new knighthood has recently appeared on the earth.... It ceaselessly wages a twofold war both against flesh and blood and against a spiritual army of evil in the heavens" (written between 1120 and 1136).[71] Clairvaux was a deeply spiritual leader, opposed to the "luxurious" lifestyle that had become prevalent among some of the clergy of his time. At one point, Clairvaux's personal regime was so austere that he became ill, going too far in his wish to return to the Rule of Saint Benedict of Nursia (circa 480 – 547), of *pax* (peace) and *ora et labora* (pray and work). When I lived in Paris, I made an effort to learn about his historical time. In 2003, for instance, I visited the Abbey of Fontenay, the world's oldest preserved Cistercian site, located in the départment of Côte-d'Or in France, founded by Clairvaux in 1118.

Over time, however, the Knights Templar became rich, too rich for their rivals for power to tolerate. In 1307, they were arrested and their order was destroyed. They were vilified as "wolves in sheep's clothing," who, disguised "in the habit of a religious order" would vilely insult religious faith, thus again crucifying "our Lord."[72]

The crusades may have had a certain civilizing effect on marauding knights, at least for a while, and they have engendered a code of noble bravery. Yet, understandably, this did not turn their victims into friends, and this problem lasts until today. The crusades set in motion cycles of humiliation of historic scope, later followed by the hubris of Mark Sykes and François Georges-Picot, who singlehandedly created seven built-in conflicts in the region.[73] The results can be seen in present-day Da'esh's ability to attract supporters,[74] now returning the script of holy campaigns against infidels. The genie that Pope Urban and his successors let out of the bottle is ravaging the world now.

The famous *Nibelungenlied* was mentioned earlier, created between about 1180 and 1210 CE. Its historical background was the suffering of ordinary people under the autocratic nobility and their dysfunctional relationships at the time of *malitia*. The poem demonstrates the detrimental effects of *hochvart* and *übermuot* – haughtiness, arrogance, and hubris.[75] The hero Sivrit (Siegfried) was "the type of self-centered young man who fails to grow up."[76] The poem was intended as a warning against 0the sin of pride, showing "how this tendency to sin vitiates the human virtues ... a community which forgets God will destroy itself."[77] The story was narrated as a tragedy, "a tragedy of godless self-will, which is at the root of all human sin."[78]

Later, in Nazi-Germany, the poem's message was completely misinterpreted: "To regard it as a revival of the pagan Germanic spirit in an over-sophisticated age is absurd."[79] In Nazi-Germany, the poem was exploited as a vehicle of national pride, and it was abused, as mentioned earlier, among others, by Hermann Göring, leading member of the Nazi Party (NSDAP), when he compared the desperate situation of the German soldiers in Stalingrad with the situation of the Nibelungen in the burning hall of King Etzel's castle.[80] Nazism called for the return to alleged Germanic greatness and heroism, to hypothetical typical Germanic "virtues" such as the unconditional pledge of allegiance and male chivalry; a return to alleged superior Germanic creative forces, for which the Third Reich promised to provide space so that those virtues could thrive "again." By doing so, Nazi-Germany created the very tragedy that the Nibelungenlied decried. The type of self-centered young man who fails to grow up was intentionally created in the *Hitlerjugend* (Hitler Youth), and the shortsighted and ultimately self-destructive recklessness of Siegfried's actions was elevated to national politics.

Beware of neglecting replenishment

There are myriad ways in which the destructiveness of domination can make itself felt. As has been discussed before, humans are not just passive objects, they are also subjects with their own intentionality, and therefore domination can create violent cycles of humiliation rather than the wished-for calm and quiet of humble servants. The dominator culture's misguided views on human agency, and the mutilating manipulations it inflicts, easily set in motion such cycles of humiliation.

There are other malign effects as well, which have to do with carrying capacities. Locusts have been mentioned before. Locusts are not aware that they destroy their substrate. They have never developed strategies of replenishment and would simply die out if they had exhausted all there is for them to eat on planet Earth. Yet, even though humans know about the need for replenishment and maintenance, similar exhaustion processes can unfold also for humans, particularly when strategies of domination become chronic.

The negligence of maintenance and replenishment is a hideous killer. The human body can illustrate this.[81] When people are in danger, adrenaline rushes into their blood stream and the maintenance tasks of the body are put on wait. For a short while, this is tolerable. However, under conditions of continuous states of emergency, when essential maintenance is neglected for too long, the body breaks down. Heart attacks – the typical emergency troubleshooter disease – are the outcome.

The health of the planet is no exception. Also planetary boundaries can be overstretched.[82] Environmental problems – more greenhouse gases than ever before being released into the atmosphere, biological diversity rapidly declining, fish stocks in the oceans dwindling, and so on – indeed remind of the scorched earth that locusts leave behind. Sustainable development expert Gwendolyn Hallsmith decries "the systematic impoverishment of nature and humanity wrought by privatized monetary hegemony" and warns "without changing the dominant 'resource allocation system' by democratizing the monetary system, we will not be able to reverse the damage. It will continue, unabated, and will make the lives of future generations less and less tenable on a scorched Earth."[83]

Neuroscientist Peter Sterling reminds us that the current race to the bottom has neurological correlates insofar as core brain circuits drive animals and humans to feel good when they receive something better than expected, "a warm spot when we are cold, a berry or nut when we are hungry ..."[84] What happens, however, when all basic needs are satisfied, is that our innate neural circuits drive us to seek new satisfactions. This "need" cannot be controlled by legislation or social pressure, warns Sterling, and it is the reason for why four out of nine identified planetary boundaries are already behind us.[85] Liebig's Law indicates that "a chain is only as strong as its weakest link," meaning that "we don't have to wait for all nine boundaries to be transgressed before global calamity threatens; all it takes to shred the ecosystem web is for one boundary to be breached far enough, long enough.... The most extreme dooms-dayers insist that near-term human extinction is now assured. Forget trying to save civilization, they say; think planetary hospice instead."[86] By now, this "need" drives industrial-scale use of chemical pesticides, herbicides and fertilizers; food production as a branch of global industry; reliance on fossil fuels and accelerating climate change; the transformation of fresh water into a depleting resource and the mass extinction of other life forms.[87] The demand for natural resources is more than fifty percent larger than what the natural systems are able to regenerate.[88] Sixty years of analysis show by now that the levels of consumption in the rich world are grossly unsustainable, by a factor of 5 to 10, "yet just about all people and governments are still blindly obsessed with increasing consumption and GDP.[89]

In other words, the slogan "to each according to his need" has transmuted from an individually attractive slogan to a collectively suicidal one. Not only Peter Sterling wonders: How can "current addictions to sweet, greasy foods, mood-enhancing drugs, industrial-scale gambling, and pornography" and the yearning for high status symbols such as automobiles or jet travel" be replaced by a diversity of satisfying experience such as "contacts with nature, opportunities for exercise, making music, art, and writing"?[90]

A world of ever increasing competition for domination is bound to live in continuous danger of collapse, as replenishment is neglected. This applies to the physical carrying capacity of the planet as much as to the human communities' social fabric's carrying capacity. Pakistan is a contemporary example. UNDP's Human Development Report 2014 was titled "Sustaining Human Progress: Reducing Vulnerabilities and Building Resilience."[91] It provided a status of all countries using vital indicators of human development, with Pakistan ranking on place 146 out of 185 countries:

> Being a chronic security state, the country drains much of its resources on traditional security measures. Contemporary concepts of human security are alien to the policy makers. Paranoia of internal and external threats has fettered human development since inception. Even war-torn countries are earmarking better resources on human development.... The security mania has eclipsed the basic needs of citizens. It is an implausible idea to secure borders without securing basic human needs of citizens. According to a report of Social Policy and Development Centre "Social Impact of the Security Crisis," allocation for health and nutrition in federal government's public sector development program registered a marginal average annual increase of 0.4 percent over the last five years. Whereas the security related expenditure during last ten years registered an average growth of 20.6 percent. The figures speak volumes for our misplaced priorities.[92]

Naseer Memon is a development professional, who had been working with development sector and corporate sector organizations in Pakistan for the past twelve years.[93] He wrote in 2014:

> We have a distinction of hosting more than 80 percent polio cases in the world. More scandalous is the fact that polio virus with Pakistani provenance is now sneaking into polio-free countries prompting disconcerting travel embargoes. Dengue and malaria mosquitos deride our hubris of being a nuclear power. Terrorism, bad governance, corruption and failure on human development are some of the factors impinging on image of Pakistan. Characterized as a security state, the country has developed an image of a problem child in the region. Enigmatically, the decision-makers are hardly sensitive to the faltering image of the country.

> Their unremitting obduracy and addiction to a confrontational approach is ostracizing Pakistan in the world community.[94]

The neglect of sound education all around the world may serve as yet another example. Appropriate education is part and parcel of long-term maintenance for a society. Emancipatory education, in the sense of Wilhelm von Humboldt's ideal of *Bildung* – rather than simple *Ausbildung* or training – liberates hearts and minds and allows a person's potential to flourish. Yet, education can also be instrumentalized to intensify inequality. Chinese scholar Jingyi Dong has been introduced earlier, with her doctoral dissertation on the role of Chinese higher education institutions.[95] Dong applies Pierre Bourdieu's notions of the *field* and *heteronomy*, and describes what happens when one field is "invaded" by another and no longer autonomous. Dong observes that Chinese universities are dominated by heteronomous forces, meaning that its academic capital has been dramatically devalued in relation to political, social, and economic capital.[96]

Dong's analysis of the situation in China fits also the predicament of present-day higher education in other parts of the world. Dynamics in Western countries resemble that in China in their basic gist insofar as they fail emancipatory Bildung.[97] "If universities are society's higher training centers, and humanity is rampant with huge misconduct at its highest levels, it comes as no surprise that universities are largely training centers for misconduct," this is a critical voice that warns that only around five percent of academic efforts counter this trend with more holistically oriented, systems based, interdisciplinary efforts.[98] The question is: Will universities ever be "more than producers of trained destroyers," and will they ever "manage to get other people thinking?"[99] If producing "generalizable knowledge" is the only legitimate form of research, then humanity's most important reflections will qualify as invalid: "What are we, what are we not, what should we be, and what can we be, these are not hypothesis-forming questions … our consciousness is by definition generally not generalizable, and it is in our consciousness that the central issue lies."[100]

More Americans than ever enroll in college now, yet, instead of reducing inequality, the current American system of higher education reinforces it. For-profit colleges in the U.S. "enroll nearly a tenth of college students, use nearly a quarter of federal student aid dollars allocated through Title IV of the Higher Education Act of 1965, and they account for nearly half of all student loan defaults."[101]

Joni Odochaw offers a related case from Northern Thailand. He is a wisdom teacher in the field of natural resources and environmental management in the Karen village of Ban Nong Thao in Northern Thailand. He was brought to us by amazing Chayan Vaddhanaphuti, founding director of the Regional Center for Social Science and Sustainable Development at Chiang Mai University, which hosted our 23rd Annual Dignity Conference in 2014.[102] Together with three colleagues, I had the great privilege of spending three days in Joni Odochaw's village. We were able to learn from him and his family to better understand the dilemma of education, television, and the digital world, and how they can either be beneficial or destructive for sustainable ways of living. Odochaw and his son and nephew introduced us to their "Lazy School" concept, and eloquently explained how traditional community learning used to work: Everybody in a traditional Karen village had the skills to be student and teacher.[103] A young man, Peter Dering from the United States, was there as the first student of the Lazy School, and he gave this advice to the world: "Our vision must be to expand community learning to include modern knowledge through technology, rather than lose community learning!"[104] I am sure that Pasi Sahlberg from the Finnish Ministry of Education and Culture would have liked to be with us. After all, also Finland shows the world, how education can be dignified and succeed.[105] I highly admire the courage of Joni Odochaw and Chayan, since in Thailand, as in so many other parts of the world, people who speak up against authorities, might simply disappear. I highly admire Odochaw's ability to think creatively while living in an atmosphere of fear and potential terror, and I hope that people from Finland and all educators from around the world who wish to dignify education will support them and learn from them.

Systems theorist Alexander Laszlo decries how the institutionalization of life/work/learning in siloed social structures artificially separates the many aspects of productive life:

> We go to school to learn (but we are not meant to be productive in a way that earns us money, and we are generally not there for our pleasure or enjoyment), we go to work to productive and earn money (but we are not supposed to spend time learning new things for our professional development, and we are generally not there for our pleasure or enjoyment), and we go on vacations to relax and have fun (but we are not meant to be productive in a way that earns us money, nor are we are not supposed to spend time learning new things for our professional development). Why can we not create institutions where we are productive and earn a living at the same time as we learn new and interesting things that advance us in life and we have fun doing it?[106]

Beware of putting cooperation into the service of competition for domination

Domination-overdone causes collapse not only through neglect of long-term maintenance, it also undermines the benefits from otherwise beneficial practices. Cooperation, for instance, is a singularly successful strategy. Its advantages are useful even for winning competition for domination. Armies comprising soldiers that cooperate were always more successful than those who did not. Yet, when competition for domination becomes a self-replicating cultural script, rather than a response forced by the security dilemma, all gains risk getting lost.

Social psychologist Morton Deutsch is the late director emeritus of the Morton Deutsch International Center for Cooperation and Conflict Resolution at Teachers College, Columbia University, in New York City.[107] Deutsch is one of the founders of the study of cooperation, and emphasizes the advantages of cooperation, for instance, that cooperation is far superior to competition. Deutsch has also been a main supporter of the Human Dignity and Humiliation Studies project since its inception, and honorary host of the annual Workshop on Transforming Humiliation and Violent Conflict at Teachers College since 2003. Without his moral and intellectual support, I could not have written my books.

Another scholar who has understood cooperation's advantages, is evolutionary biologist Peter Turchin. Like geographer Jared Diamond in *Guns, Germs, and Steel*, also Turchin uses his particular expertise to think about the rise and fall of empires.[108] Turchin argues that a society's capacity for collective action is key to the formation of an empire, with examples being the formation of the Roman and Russian empires, as well as the United States. He theorizes that large-scale cooperation in complex societies gives societies significant advantages over competitors in war, and that war even was the driving force behind the formation of such complex stratified societies.[109] In other words, in the context of a strong security dilemma, steadfast in-group cooperation provides a competitive advantage over out-groups.

But, says Turchin, as the rich get richer in an empire, in-group cooperation degrades into in-group conflict, and dissolution follows. What Turchin describes, is nothing but what I call the dark side of a culture of domination, the scorched-earth side. When elites continue with competition for domination within their in-group after having out-competed outside enemies, cooperative complexity falters, and exploitative stratification arises. When divide-and-rule strategies in the interest of a few undermine unity in diversity for the common good, then leadership is no longer an act of benevolent mentorship like a good parent would apply; it becomes an act of oppressive exploitation by self-serving elites.

International business woman and writer Margaret Heffernan teaches this very lesson also to present-day corporations. She highlights the usefulness of cooperation and warns that competition regularly produces what we want to avoid: rising levels of fraud, cheating, stress, inequality and political stalemate.[110]

What we learn is that in a divided world in the grip of a strong security dilemma, cooperation against the "enemy," cooperation for the sake of out-competing out-groups, was a recipe for success when defending against outsiders, but only as long as competition could be kept outside one's in-group's borders. The dark side of this success was that particularly religious underpinnings of cooperation against enemies could motivate not just defense but also aggression against out-groups. Such underpinnings have legitimated terror against non-believers and turned religion into a weapon for belligerent state ideologies. Believing that "God is on our side" stirred people to cooperate in perpetrating the worst atrocities with pride.

The recipe for full success within an in-group is a culture of cooperation for the sake of in-group flourishing for and in itself, rather than for the sake of competing for domination, lest internal fragmentation will eventually ensue. Evidently, more than ever before, this is of crucial importance in today's historically unprecedented situation of global interconnectedness, with only one single world community in the making. Cooperation for the sake of global ecological and social flourishing is now called for. What is needed is the complete abandoning of any cultural script that misrepresents competition for domination as successful strategy, or, even worse, that seeks to legitimize in-group cooperation by out-group enmity. Global cooperation toward a Great Transition is called for.[111] And religion can help foster this; there are many examples of positive religious influences – from Dietrich Bonhoeffer to Mahatma Gandhi to Desmond Tutu – that speak to this point.[112]

What we see, however, is that present-day cooperation is still caught in the past. Cooperation is still enacted within the old paradigm. Corporations, for instance, encourage their employees to cooperate among themselves so as to out-compete competitors, an approach taught as "strategic warfare for managers."[113] In this environment, managers who apply extreme, even pathological power-over strategies, have an advantage to reach leadership positions.[114] "Wall Street today is like war – violence but without the guns," explains John Fullerton, founder and president of the Capital Institute, who worked at JPMorgan for nearly two decades until 2001.[115] He often begins his talks by quoting environmental activist Wendell Berry: "Over a long time, and by means of a set of handy prevarications, our economy has become an anti-economy, a financial system without a sound economic bases and without economic virtues."[116] Economist Joseph Stiglitz concurs. In 2014, Stiglitz concluded that during the past decades, politics have commodified and corrupted American democracy:

> As World War II faded into memory, so too did the solidarity it had engendered. As America triumphed in the Cold War, there didn't seem to be a viable competitor to our economic model. Without this international competition, we no longer had to show that our system could deliver for most of our citizens.... Economic and geographic segregation have immunized those at the top from the problems of those down below. Like the kings of yore, they have come to perceive their privileged positions essentially as a natural right.[117]

Business magnate, investor and philanthropist Warren Buffett chimes in, "It's class warfare. My class is winning, but they shouldn't be."[118] He warns that fighting over the debt ceiling "ought to be banned as a weapon" like "nuclear bombs, too horrible to use."[119] When managers wage warfare against competitors in a globalizing interconnected world, they contribute to the destruction not just of an empire, they hinder the emergence of a viable global common-unity (community) and foreclose a dignified future for their own children.

The security dilemma taught our species competition of domination, and empires and states have engaged in it throughout past millennia, with corporations having followed suit. Today, even the single individual goes down the same path. In contexts that promote extreme individualism, the boundaries of the security dilemma are being shrunk down to each individual's personal life. Through this shrinkage, every person is separated from her fellow beings. Everyone is her own state, so to speak. Everyone is forced into Machiavellian *hominus hominem lupus est* (man is a wolf to man, or, more colloquially, dog-eat-dog) relationships that in honor contexts are reserved only for the power elites.

Linda Hartling went to visit B Reactor at the Hanford Site, near Richland, Washington, on September 14, 2016. It was the first large-scale nuclear reactor ever built, as part of the Manhattan Project, the United States nuclear weapons development program during World War II. She found a poster in the reactor which says: "Security is an individual responsibility: be an individualist." She was reminded of my reflections on how the security dilemma has been "individualized." The security dilemma is a dilemma of mutual mistrust that states are caught in. Ruling elites of states are the ones to "manage" this dilemma, it defines *Realpolitik*, meaning that there can be no trust, since an ally may turn into foe overnight. This poster invites every citizen to partake in this mindset.

States cannot escape the security dilemma as long as the world is divided. Yet, the global citizenry can overcome it among themselves, they can learn how to nurture trust. If they, however, continue to foreground mistrust instead, the inner cohesion of local and global society is in danger.

Sociologist Ferdinand Tönnies was mentioned earlier, and his coinage of the term *Gemeinschaft* (community), in contrast to *Gesellschaft* (society).[120] He describes Gesellschaft as a place where individuals remain in isolation, living in mutual fear and veiled hostility toward each other, only refraining from attacking each other out of fear of retaliation. The state then protects this civilization through legislation and politics and glorifies it as progress toward perfection. *Anomie* is sociologist Emile Durkheim's terminology[121] for the sad result that ensues, which sociologist Max Weber would call *Entzauberung* (disenchantment)[122] in "modernity as iron cage." Or, in a more precise translation of the German term *stahlhartes Gehäuse*, it would be modernity's "steel-hard casing."[123] Sociologist Saskia Sassen calls it the twenty-first century's *systemic expulsions.*[124]

To round up, present-day Western culture seems to be fraught with risks, risks flowing from a blissful, even triumphant, overdoing of competition for domination in all forms. Despite of these risks, due to its promise of short-term success and victory, the script for competition for domination is rapidly globalizing.[125] Cooperation as a way of being together for all people is being weakened systemically. Instead, increasingly, every individual is being sent into competition against everybody else, with the arena of cooperation shrinking until there is no other space left except the inner psyche of a person: A person's various inner voices are now meant to "cooperate" with each other so as to serve the aim to turn the person into an ever more efficient participant in what is called the "rat race." Business seminars teach better time management and efficiency training to "improve" people's ability to align their various inner parts so as to function more smoothly in that race, a race that ultimately does not serve them, but increases inequality. Vulnerable individuals thus navigate the terror of "war zones" of insecurity, prevented from forming strong collectives of cooperation, collectives that otherwise would give them the power to set different agendas and create resilience both for individuals and for society at large.[126]

The so-called Washington Consensus had its roots in the U.S.-based Heritage Foundation in 1980, when it launched its agenda in the context of the election of Ronald Reagan, an agenda that still defines the world. Twenty project teams involving three hundred participants were brought together to develop policy recommendations for all government departments and published them in a thousand-page book.[127] Margaret Thatcher was Prime Minister of the United Kingdom during those years, and she knew something very important, namely, that economic design "has cross-cutting significance because it mediates our relationship to nature and to each other."[128] In 1981, she summarized her goal as follows: "economics is the method: the object is to change the soul."[129]

By now, the "soul" has successfully been changed. "Greed" has transmuted from a vice to a virtue, giving a new "modern" justification to traditional masculine role descriptions of domination and disdain for "female" nurturing. It has created a "generation me" of "excellent sheep." Those "sheep," in turn, create a psychologically and cognitively stunted next generation, unable to develop the relational wisdom that is needed.[130] Profiteering, now elevated to a virtue, fails to improve "human well-being at scale," and instead devastates our planet: even the business publication *Forbes* acknowledges this.[131] The spirit of profiteering is well illustrated by the DICE model that is widely used by economists and that calculates that even a disastrous four degrees centigrade temperature increase would only reduce GDP by four percent, and a six degrees centigrade increase would reduce GDP by less than ten percent, not counting the price that large parts of the planet would become uninhabitable: "In such models, Africa could be gone but global GDP may still increase."[132]

Is it surprising that so-called foreign fighters, those who leave the West to fight "holy war," feel as attracted by the promise of warmly inclusive collectivism and heroic victory as supporters of nationalist populists?[133] Unfortunately, the promise of victory is empty for all.

Beware of letting "purity" destroy diversity

"Pathological" power-over strategies were once the preserve of a few, who applied them ruthlessly. The security dilemma rewarded brutal leaders. Those who could destroy faster than others, those who could drive brutality to levels others could not even imagine, were sure to win victories.

Brutality is precisely one of Da'esh's hallmarks; with unprecedented ruthlessness, it destroys human life as well as cultural heritage, be it manifested in living communities, such as the Yezidi community, or built in stone, such as the 2,000-year-old temple of Baal Shamin in the historic Syrian city of Palmyra. Yet, Da'esh is not alone: "Just as authoritarian fundamentalist Muslims are determined to repulse American culture from Islamic societies, authoritarian nationalist Americans are determined to repulse Muslim culture from the United States. These ethnocentric forces are mirror images."[134] We fear when we hear from the United States of Donald J. Trump that "it's about creating a society where propaganda reigns and dissent is silenced."[135]

History offers many examples of the ruthlessness with which unity in diversity has been destroyed, how complexity has been streamlined and the high culture that complexity engenders was turned into "low culture." Many are aware of the Moorish Kingdom of Granada and how culture flourished there in a context of diversity, until the uniformity of "purity" was imposed by Christian backlash.[136] In 1492, the Spanish Golden Age ended, the *Andaluz convivencia*, where Jews, Christians, and Muslims engaged in dialogue; it ended at the hands of religious intolerance, massacre, and inquisition of Christian monarchs.

Historian Deepak Tripathi tells similar tales of destruction in his book *Imperial Designs: War, Humiliation and the Making of History.*[137] He recalls the cultural greatness of Mesopotamia as a cradle of civilization whose origins go back more than six thousand years. In the era of the Abbasid caliphate (750 – 1258), the terms "Arab" and "civilization" became synonymous and Mesopotamia experienced a period of great glory. Baghdad was a place of immense learning and culture – of the arts, literature, medicine, and mathematics. Yet, unfortunately, wealth made it a target for invasions. In 1258, the Mongols came, under Hulagu, the grandson of Genghis Khan, who attacked the land, killed the last Abbasid caliph and plundered Baghdad.[138]

A poet like Rūmī – with his full name Jalāl ad-Dīn Muhammad, also known as Mawlānā, "our master" – thrived in another such era of high culture. He lived from 1207 – 1273, most of his life under the Persianate Seljuq Sultanate of Rum. The sultanate prospered during the late twelfth and early thirteenth centuries. While the Seljuq sultans were able to successfully withstand the Crusades, in 1243, they succumbed to the advancing Mongols. By the first decade of the fourteenth century, the cultural richness of Rum had disappeared.

There is another great poet, Hāfez, who lived circa 1320 – 1389, with his full name Khwāja Shams-ud-Dīn Muhammad Hāfez-e Shīrāzī. His name indicates that he was connected with one of the oldest cities of ancient Persia, namely, Shiraz, also known as the city of poets, literature, wine, and flowers. As early as 2,000 BCE,[139] Elamite clay tablets refer to Tiraziš, and in the thirteenth century, encouraged by its ruler, Shiraz became a leading center of the arts and letters. In 1747, exposed to Afghan raids, the city was besieged and sacked, most of its historical buildings damaged or ruined, with its population falling to 50,000, one-quarter of what it was during the sixteenth century.

In all those cases, rich complexity, the true success story of humankind's achievements, was destroyed by the disastrous "success" of crude domination.

Also Europe was in danger of being annihilated by domination-overdone. "Not to appear weak" was the motto that led to "suicidal madness," a present-day description of American and Russian rearmament during the Cold War in the 1960s.[140] "Whoever bears in mind that Bundeswehr and U.S. Army were ready to level Germany to the ground, will never change his belief that delusion is an essential characteristic of the military."[141] Harald Kujat, from 2000 to 2002 Chief of Staff of the German armed forces, the Bundeswehr, and Chairman of the NATO Military Committee from 2002 to 2005, explains that during the sixties, nuclear weapons were regarded as "normal" weapons and that its risks were simply not seen. On the contrary, people were intoxicated by the possibilities of nuclear weapons, as was German minister of defense from 1956 – 1962, Franz Josef Strauss. Former German chancellor Helmuth Schmidt explains that the Soviet generals, in contrast, knew full well that whoever starts a nuclear war, starts a world war, and "they were scared, rightly so."[142]

The easier weapons can be accessed,[143] the more also terrorism can lead to mass destruction, particularly, when martyrdom is seen as "success" if only in afterlife, and "the path to victory is soaked with blood of the martyrs."[144] Life in heaven after death is desired by martyrs, and it means apocalypse without pity, lacking the prudent fear of the Soviet generals, so to speak. From a martyr's point of view, when honor is sacred and beyond profanity, it provides meaning that cannot be found on Earth. From their point of view, the neoliberal *Homo economicus* model of human nature is something for weaklings, something only for those who sell out their honor for money. A true aspirant to martyrdom cannot be bribed, at least not with earthly assets, he is beyond earthly deliberations and negotiations. When the reward comes after death, life on Earth is unimportant, and wanting to hold onto it is a sign of dishonorable cowardice.

Within the cultural universe of honor, the victims of a martyr attack will call the martyr "cold-blooded" and "coward," yet, his in-group will celebrate him for his passion and courage. Only those outside of the world of honor will be puzzled by such war-inspired language of "courage versus cowardice."

Precisely those religious terrorist groups who are hotly motivated, rather than simply being "cold-blooded" pragmatic dominators, will be the last to lay down arms. Pragmatic concerns or blood-letting will not impress them.[145] Political goals of religiously motivated groups are wide, amorphous, and non-negotiable and do not respond easily to political processes of inclusion.[146] Committing terror in the name of God, for them, means doing God's work.

Thomas Merton, poet, social activist, and Trappist monk, identified the following as a fundamental human problem: *Prometheanism*, or wanting to steal divinity from God rather than laboring at being human.[147]

As long as the world was not yet as interconnected as it is now, the dualistic mindset of "good in-group versus evil out-group" increased the chances for victory over one's enemies if maximized. Identity complexity was unwelcome. Power elites shaped social identity and it was supposed to be monolithic.[148] The West conquered the world as colonizers in this way, and it still draws on the accumulated power from colonial times in many ways, from unfair global trade rules to using up the world's resources.

Philosopher Michel Serres advocates "mixing and blending" and suggests that it is not by eliminating and isolating that we grasp *the real* fully; it is by combining, by putting things into play with each other, by letting things interact. In his book *The Troubadour of Knowledge*, he uses the metaphor of the "educated third," which, to Serres, is a "third place," where a mixture of culture, nature, sciences, arts, and humanities is constructed.[149] Philosopher Kwame Anthony Appiah makes a case for *contamination*.[150] He rejects visions of purity, tribalism, and cultural protectionism, and welcomes a new cosmopolitanism. Philosopher Emmanuel Lévinas highlights the Other, whose *face* forces us to be humane.[151] Terms such as *métissage*, or intermingling, mean that both "I" and the "other" are changed by our contact. Peace educator Werner Wintersteiner builds on Lévinas and on métissage in his *Pedagogy of the Other*, where he suggests that the basis for peace education must be "the stranger," and that we need to learn to live with permanent strangeness as a trait of our postmodern human condition and culture.[152]

Beware of sacrificing communal dignity

Robert Reilly, a senior fellow at the American Foreign Policy Council, speaks of a "spiritual disorder" suffered by men who feel a loss of meaning in a Western secular political order, and who respond with a willingness to commit terror in the name of God; these men are afflicted with a "perverted outcome of a search for meaning."[153]

The *Homo economicus* model of human nature could be regarded as a "perverted outcome of a search for meaning" as well. By now, it has gained much traction, not just in the West, all over the world. Present-day economic arrangements inspired by this model now risk becoming as destructive as war-raids and terror attacks in the past. My personal sense of humiliation from *Homo economicus* values has led also to my "radicalization," yet, unlike religiously motivated terrorists, I radicalize toward equal dignity, toward a future of dignity for all. I radicalize like a Bertha von Suttner, Mahatma Gandhi, Dietrich Bonhoeffer, Paulo Freire, or Nelson Mandela, while a young man who joins Da'esh, radicalizes back into the past's worldviews of ranked honor.

I am a prosocial radical, following those who once wished to abolish slavery, and who now wish to instill environmental awareness and campaign for equal human or animal rights.[154] I am a radical in the sense of the suffragettes of the second half of nineteenth century England, when the term *radical* was ascribed to political positions that were liberal, anti-clerical, pro-democratic, and progressive. The term radical was once used to describe a wing of the Liberal Party whose demands have become mainstream entitlements since then. I sense the need for radical change, yet, using coercion and violent revolution, in my view, would mean nothing but a counterproductive retrograde step rather than a step forward.[155] I am not a radical in the sense of any "anti-liberal, fundamentalist, anti-democratic and regressive agenda."[156] I resonate with terrorism expert Alex Peter Schmid's words: "While radicals might be violent or not, might be democrats or not, extremists are never democrats."[157] I am radical in not being extremist.

Even though research on attitudes shows that "radicalization of attitudes need not result in radicalization of behavior,"[158] in my case, I have brought my behavior into line with my attitudes to a very high degree, with the result that I gift every minute of my life to bringing more dignity into the world. My radicalization is inspired by the direct and systemic humiliation that I observe at all levels, micro, meso, and macro levels, all around the world.[159]

As alluded to earlier, I see the *Homo economicus* model of human nature seep into the world's fabric in ways that risk unleashing even more destructive effects than the *Homo dominans* model of human nature ever did.

If societies – India, for instance – want to modernize, they have to get rid of their extended families, this was, for instance, the opinion of thinkers such as Francis Fukuyama, Samuel Huntington, or Harvard's David McClelland.[160] Yet, the very opposite may be what is needed. South-African religious studies scholar Chirevo Kwenda explains that social cohesion in Africa does not flow from state sovereignty, liberal democracy, the advance of modernity, or the global economy, but depends on the millions of African people willing to sacrifice social connection and to bear the uncomfortable burden of speaking and acting in ways that are profoundly unfamiliar to them.[161] Catherine Odora Hoppers gave a speech at the UNESCO in Paris in 2008, where she made the point that whatever social cohesion is still to be found in Africa, it exists despite of, rather than because of modernity.[162]

Philosopher Thaddeus Metz, professor at the University of Johannesburg, South Africa, connects cooperation and dignity in ways that remind of Regnerus' Dignity 1.0.[163] He offers an alternative to the influential conception of dignity in the West, where dignity is seen to inhere in our rationality or autonomy. Metz invokes an Afro-communitarian conception of human dignity and develops the idea that human beings have dignity as part of their communal nature, in virtue of their capacity for what he calls "identity" and "solidarity."[164] Consensus is the foundation of this communal practice, rather than the will of a majority or a monarch. Even when retributive punishment is meted out after a violation, it still contains elements of reconciliation between the offender, his family, the immediate victim, and the broader community.

"The dignity of human beings emanates from the network of relationships, from being in community; in an African view, it cannot be reduced to a unique, competitive and free personal ego," this we learn from South African theologian and academic leader H. Russel Botman.[165]

Metz explains that sub-Saharan thought brings together two different sorts of relationship, that of identity and that of solidarity. Identity is the sharing of a way of life, identifying with each other, and conceiving of one another as a "we," which is not the same as solidarity as the caring for others' quality of life, or what English speakers would call love or friendship: "One could identify with others but not exhibit solidarity with them – probably workers in relation to management in a capitalist firm. One could also exhibit solidarity with others but not identify with them, e.g. by making anonymous donations to a charity."[166] African thought combines those two logically distinct kinds of relationship.[167] Metz lays out:

> To exhibit solidarity with one another is for people to care about each other's quality of life, in two senses. First, it means that they engage in mutual aid, acting in ways that are expected to benefit each other (ideally, repeatedly over time). Second, caring is a matter of people's attitudes such as emotions and motives being positively oriented toward others, say, by sympathizing with them and helping them for their sake. For people to fail to exhibit solidarity could be for them to be indifferent to each other's flourishing or to exhibit ill will in the form of hostility and cruelty.[168]

Metz lines up a number of sub-Saharan thinkers and their descriptions of their sense of community: "Every member is expected to consider him/herself an integral part of the whole and to play an appropriate role towards achieving the good of all";[169] "Harmony is achieved through close and sympathetic social relations within the group";[170] "The fundamental meaning of community is the sharing of an overall way of life, inspired by the notion of the common good";[171] "(T)he purpose of our life is community-service and community-belongingness."[172]

Metz argues that when our dignity is grounded in our capacity for communal or friendly relationships, then to degrade this capacity means violating human rights. The innocent have the right not to be killed, enslaved, or tortured because such actions disrespect the capacity for community of all involved, victims and perpetrators. If the project of the West is to destroy communal practice and the dignity connected with it, then, we may predict, it does so at its peril.

The toxic spiral of ever increasing domination is prone to play out like ancient Greek tragedy. Its hero typically has a "tragic flaw" called *hamartia*, writes Mimi Stokes-Katzenbach, expert on ecopsychology, environmental communication, and sustainability as an art.[173] *Hamartia* is another word for ignorant, mistaken, or accidental wrongdoing, for "fatal" mistakes in tragic situations. Tragedy flows from a "tragic flaw" of the human mind, a cognitive *eudaimonic* blind spot, which, in the service of happiness, makes us "fudge the data," insofar as we either grossly overestimate how tragic a situation is, or grossly underestimate it – we either deny that the climate deteriorates, for instance, or we lament that there is nothing we can do and we are already doomed.[174]

The tragedy of a strong security dilemma is that domination "pays" within its own framework. An overshoot of the domination strategy – as long as it does not lead to everybody's destruction – can bring "victory." The past "successes" that Western dominator culture achieved in colonizing the world and tapping its natural resources, has led to the belief in human "omnipotence, exceptionalism, and invincibility,"[175] to a degree that the ability to adapt to changing conditions is dangerously diminished now. As long as the only definition of success remains the scramble for the world's diminishing natural resources through the intensification of domination, for which even the security dilemma is artificially kept strong, ever more circumscription will be the result. And as soon as weapons threaten total world destruction, meeting the threat of preemption with preemption in the spirit of general Carl von Clausewitz's motto "the best defense is a good offense," the ultimate and seemingly inevitable endpoint will be a scorched planet Earth.

History tells the tale of the demise of the Classic Maya in Mexico,[176] and the decline of Angkor in Cambodia.[177] A similar dynamic appears to be unfolding when we consider present-day's destruction of natural and human resources through global warming and environmental disasters, combined with the shredding of the social fabric.[178] We live in times in which divide-and-rule strategies systemically weaken people's resilience, with the result that they are more vulnerable to succumbing to being dominated, that they even become complicit in their own domination. Global systemic frames keep divide-and-rule strategies in place – the most recent tightening is being introduced through certain aspects in trade agreements, such as the "T-treaty trinity."[179] A weakened world population, the longer they take part in that game, will forget about the power of social cohesion, and increasingly unlearn how to nurture the cooperation of collective solidarity. Social critic Vance Packard (1914 – 1996) has described these scenarios in his books already long time before I even began thinking about them.[180]

John Barry, of Queen's University Belfast, thinks that "undifferentiated economic growth as a permanent feature of the economy is an ideology, an ideology which serves elite interests in disciplining populations and in removing issue of socio-economic redistribution and inequality from the political agenda."[181] Given that money is a claim on resources/goods, he writes, "unless we can eat inflation, and unless we simply view monetary increases in the value of economic activity as the object of economic growth, this monetized conception of GDP is a form of double think. It presents the *phenomenal* (in Kantian terms) or throughput / resources / energy / pollution' (in Daly's terms) as *noumenal*."[182] In the philosophy of Kant, a *noumenon* is a thing-in-itself, an object as it is in itself independent of the mind, rather than a phenomenon known through perception. In other words, we live in a world caught in utopian illusionary double think that serves domination; we mistake what we perceive as real.

John Barry suggests the following three criteria or tests that any sound economic policy or strategy ought to fulfill: (1) Does it increase or decrease carbon intensity, resource use, and pollution? (2) Does it increase or decrease socio-economic inequalities? And (3) does it increase or decrease qualitative measures of human flourishing?[183]

Philosopher of social science Howard Richards, adds his insight: "A growth imperative is a commodification imperative and a financialization imperative. It dehumanizes life and hamstrings policy choices whatever the physical possibilities of doing more with less may turn out to be. It makes it unlikely that the physical possibilities will be realized with social justice, or even realized at all – and that is just the beginning."[184]

The topic of terrorism is intimately embedded into the problem of domination overshoot. In a divided world, as long as the security dilemma was strong, elites had to defend their privileges against two groups: their rivals inside their own group, and those threatening from outside. In a globally interconnected world, one single inside realm is left, with no outside. It is more difficult than before to narrate reality as a stand-off between mutually isolated empires who consider the other as "outside." The only enemy left is the inside rival, the inside enemy, the terrorist. To legitimate domination, either terrorism can be instrumentalized, or attempts can be undertaken to re-divide the world. The Ukraine conflict that simmers while I write these lines risks precisely that, to re-divide the world. The Syrian conflict follows suit. The so-called Islamic State uses globally interconnected technology for doing the same at a global scale by setting itself up against the infidel rest.

The individual terrorist, or the terrorist organization, however, is not the only source of terror. There is also the Orwellian structural terror that flows from a global government/corporate nexus,[185] terror that serves what investor Warren Buffett decried as "class warfare."[186]

The United States Task Force on Disorders and Terrorism drew up six categories: civil disorder, political terrorism, non-political terrorism, quasi-terrorism, limited political terrorism, and official or state terrorism.[187] Two categories, in particular, fit the predicament described in this sub-section: first, there is "political terrorism," or violent criminal behavior designed primarily to generate fear in a community for political purposes. Second, there is "limited political terrorism," which denotes genuine political terrorism that is characterized by a revolutionary approach, referring to "acts of terrorism which are committed for ideological or political motives but which are not part of a concerted campaign to capture control of the state."

Nelson Mandela was on the list of terrorists in the United States until 2008. He dedicated his life to his dream to liberate his black brothers and sisters, his entire country, and to bring it into a future world of freedom and wealth for all.[188] As his dream now falters, many of my South African friends wish that Mandela had stayed in power much longer, and that he had embarked on changing not just South Africa but the entire world-system. Those who brought the Arab Spring on its way had similar dreams. Facebook et al. gave the illusion of this dream being fulfillable. Yet, it is an Orwellian world, where liberation from local oppression merely represents a step into global oppression. Facebook, for instance, would not be able to accumulate as much wealth as it has by giving away everything for free. It accumulates its profits by turning its users into "sellable eyeballs," transforming people into currency, thus exploiting their desire for connection for ulterior ends in unprecedented ways.

Civil disorder[189] will increase in tact with the failure of present-day's definition of a perfect world as a "shopping mall paradise." This definition is bound to fail its promise in the longer run, not least due to infinite growth being an impossibility in a finite world.[190] Collective violence is likely to increase, and this might instigate ever more criminal terrorism and pathological terrorism,[191] including an increase in intimate terrorism, or intimate partner violence.[192]

To conclude, at the current historical juncture, humankind stands between domination and non-domination, halfway between unequal and equal dignity for all. This is a transition which is similarly significant as the Neolithic Revolution. The Neolithic Revolution represented a transition from one set of conditions to a drastically different set of conditions. Twelve millennia ago, this transition occurred unplanned; it simply unfolded. Today, we have much more knowledge about our situation and can and must intentionally and responsibly co-create this transition to make it constructive.[193] To help with this process is why I write this book.

What if we, as humankind, were to focus on cooperation now? What if we were to study anthropological research and re-invent, for instance, old practices of social taboos against violence as a frame for more peaceful societies?[194] Why not learn from indigenous peoples' seven-generations time horizon? In my work, I suggest to harvest all those cultural skills and traditions that can help create a dignified future, and to leave behind all those that hinder this.[195] Why not sit together today, as humankind, liberate ourselves from all limitations that flow from human-engineered domination, and lovingly accept and respect those limitations that indeed have the status of laws of nature, such as the finiteness of our planet?

It is laudable to be well-intentioned and honest; yet, nowadays, my global experience tells me that good intentions are not enough. Global challenges urge everybody who has good intentions to shoulder responsibilities that earlier generations did not have to shoulder, namely, reaching beyond one's immediate surroundings and envisioning and engaging in responsible global systemic change toward a dignified world, a world where dignity can flourish globally and locally.[196] Nelson Mandela shouldered the responsibility to promote deep paradigm change for a whole society.[197] The same profound systemic change is needed now globally.[198] Physicist Paul Raskin calls it a *Great Transition*.[199] It needs to be brought about by a *global citizens movement*,[200] and it can only succeed with "a systemic transformation from a market-centric to a commons-centric form," confirms also Michael Bauwens of the P2P Foundation.[201]

It pays to look for creative ideas outside of mainstream frames. Nomadic foragers, for instance, could teach those societies who overburden their women with continuous pregnancies to space child birth at four-year intervals (foragers must carry toddlers until they can keep up with the adults).[202] Those societies with sub-replacement fertility, on the other side, could learn how to place higher value on life-giving. Or, history could be told not as a succession of wars and victories, but as a succession of lessons learned from each other. Just to give one example, even though Greece and Persia were at war with each other for hundreds of years, still, they also learned from each other. Why not highlight the mutual learning more? Why highlight only victory and defeat?

At the present point in history, we, as humankind, voluntarily opt for producing a scorched Earth. We artificially re-ignite the security dilemma instead of grasping the opportunity that global interconnectedness offers to attenuate it. We hold on to Vegetius' motto *If you want peace, prepare for war* without necessity. And this while we are in a new situation, a situation where we can de-elect the scorched earth option. If we succeed in turning around, politically spinned hatred in the service of the security dilemma will become redundant, and space will open up for the Gandhi-inspired tenet that *peace is the path*. A world citizens movement has the potential to change our collective path, to reclaim the force of collective solidarity, because at a global level, systemic frames can be transformed from short-term profit-seeking to safeguarding the long-term survival of all of humankind in its vulnerable finite habitat.

Author Charles Eisenstein advises that, rather than "resist terrorism" within the Orwellian paradigm of maximizing domination, the Mandelas of today, the Gandhis, the Freires, the von Suttners, must build a dignified commons world. "The relationships, organization, and tactics of an activist movement must reflect the kind of society they want to create" in the spirit of Gandhi's "be the change you want to see."[203]

Beware of creating clashes of humiliation

The risks connected with letting domination be the measurement of success are manifold, irrespective of whether this is done wittingly or unwittingly, even if done with the best of intentions or with the conviction that "God wills it." It may lead, as mentioned earlier, not to Samuel Huntington's famous *clashes of civilizations*,[204] but to *clashes of humiliation*."[205] The latter are far more dangerous than the first, since they are fueled by a perception of having been slighted by violations of worthiness, rather than merely irritated by cultural difference.[206] As there are more weapons in circulation now than ever before, fueling clashes of humiliation becomes ever more dangerous, particularly when these weapons can fall into whoever's hands. Some 15,600 pieces of equipment – including "weapons, weapons systems, and sensitive items" – went missing, for instance, from United States Army facilities in Bagram and Kandahar alone, as was reported in 2014.[207]

Precisely clashes of humiliation might be the correct diagnosis for the rise of Da'esh in 2014.[208] It could be interpreted as an extreme backlash in response to the experience of humiliation by external and internal domination. It was not least the Prime Minister of Iraq from 2006 to 2014, Nouri al-Maliki, who enabled ISIS' rise by overdoing domination through using Iraq's counterterrorism laws to imprison Sunni dissenters: "Maliki has even resurrected a Saddam-era law that makes it a criminal offense to criticize the head of the government."[209]

Why did Samuel Huntington focus on clashes of civilizations and overlook humiliation? Domination-overdone might be the very reason. When the tightening of domination is carried too far, clashes of humiliation are easily misrecognized as clashes of civilizations. The above-mentioned correspondence error, when intensified by domination, doubly facilitates this misrecognition: what is situational is essentialized, what is caused by hurtful relational dynamics is mistaken to be the result of a priori cultural or religious differences, particularly from a mainstream American perspective that lacks millennia-old historical roots.[210]

Through my global experience of forty years, I can attest first-hand that cultural differences are often very relational, they are constructed, not seldom in response to the impact of dynamics of humiliation. As has been discussed earlier, to regard "cultures" as separate "containers" is such a social-psychological construction. Cultures have long been conceived of as "silos" with more-or-less opaque walls, with a small allowance for "diffusion," meaning that cultures are in contact with each other and may learn from each other, yet, without altering their basic nature as isolated containers. Postmodern thought uses this view as its very foundation, "postulating that different cultures are fundamentally impenetrable, unknowable, and enigmatic to one another."[211]

During my doctoral fieldwork in 1998 and 1999 in Somalia and Rwanda, I saw the creation of culture difference in action. In Somaliland, I was implored to urge the world to recognize Somaliland as an independent republic. The argument was that former dictator Siad Barre and his allies, Somali clans from the south, had humiliated the north to a degree that they could no longer be part of the dream of a united Somalia. Ethnic Somalis share the same language, culture, and religion, yet, the north now insists that the "cultural differences" between them and the other Somalis are too significant for a continuation of political unity.

In Rwanda, genocide was informed by a similar narrative. Those identifying as Hutu, feeling humiliated by having been servants (*Hutu* means servant) for many centuries, created a "culture" of their own, in contrast to Tutsi patron culture, as they did no longer want to be part of a culture defined by their former dominators. Removing their patrons from power in 1959 was not enough; in 1994, genocide against their former masters became a horrific "tool" to "prevent" future humiliation.

Many examples show how easily feelings of humiliation can foment divisions. Sociologist Liah Greenfeld uses the examples of Ethiopia and Eritrea to show the role resentment plays in nation building.[212] Humiliation generates resentment, and this creates rifts. As a result, differences are highlighted, cultural or national, while commonalities are neglected that could be built on.

While this book is being finalized in 2017, experiences humiliation drive an ever growing wedge between Turkey and Europe. Turkey as a nation feels humiliated by Europe,[213] and immigrants from Turkey feel humiliated within Europe:

> Turkish people living in Germany ... have long felt persecuted by German degradation and arrogance. They feel humiliated and betrayed. And they don't believe in the good intentions of German politicians when they talk about integration and leading culture.[214]

In conclusion, the security dilemma, through its tragic effect of creating confrontation, throws identities into sharper contrast, thus rigidifying existing fault lines between cultural realms and inviting tactics of domination. As soon as domination plays out in the form of dynamics of humiliation on top of the mistrust that characterizes the security dilemma, existing differences are further deepened in reaction to humiliation, and new fault lines are created artificially.[215] This is particularly salient in the presence of a dream of unity when unity is felt to be imposed through cruel domination rather than nurtured through dialogue, as in the case of Somaliland and Somalia. And also the 2003 Iraq war has illustrated how a dream of bringing democracy to all regions of the world can turn sour when it comes with bombs. Howard Richards, philosopher of social science and scholar of peace and global studies, has this to say about the threat of radical Islam:

> Race relations in the USA are equally relevant. Drug gangs in the favelas of Brazil and in the barrios of Mexico are equally relevant. So is ethnic violence in Africa and in Asia. On the surface the tense atmosphere around the world everywhere is like the tense atmosphere in a California jail: everything is about race. A bit below the surface everything is about justice, or rather injustice. It is about anger that begins as deep resentment against injustice experienced as humiliation, and develops as rage dreaming of revenge.[216]

The distinction between "us versus them" becomes ever more meaningless in a shrinking world, as we are all part of the same world. It is therefore of utmost importance to refrain from recklessly seeking salvation in tactics of domination that risk turning into cycles of humiliation. Instead, all sides need to refrain from domination, and this includes steering clear of re-igniting the security dilemma artificially. Not to forget, also the distinction between "us versus nature" is meaningless, meaningless as "us versus them."[217]

Clearly, these reflections are not only important for the topics of war, genocide, and terrorism, but for human survival on planet Earth in general. Humankind needs a dream of unity now – unity within the human family and with nature – to nurture the cooperation necessary to face its global challenges. This dream of unity can be destroyed when dynamics of humiliation manifest in ways that re-fracture the global village into "enemy villages."

Inspiring and Thought-Provoking Questions

for in-depth reflection and research

If you want peace, prepare for war.

– Publius Flavius Vegetius Renatus,
writer of the late fourth century Roman Empire[1]

There is no path to peace. Peace is the path.

– Mahatma Gandhi

The world is over-armed and peace is under-funded.

– Ban Ki-moon,
Secretary-General of the United Nations[2]

John Bolton, Former U.S. Ambassador to the United Nations, and dedicated American patriot, wrote this on February 21, 2014, in the midst of negotiations on the so-called Iran deal,[3] in a fund raising message to the subscribers to his emails:

> Dear X, … are you comfortable with the fact that Iran's power is growing and America's power is declining? I'm certainly not.
> I formed John Bolton PAC for one purpose – to see that our leaders remain committed to restoring American economic and national security.
> X, will you help me fight back against enemies like Iran and stop American decline with an immediate contribution of $25, $50, $100 or more right away?
> Barack Obama does not truly see America as exceptional; instead, he sees America as just another player in an increasingly multipolar world that includes an ascending Iran.
> Imagine this – if Iran completes its nuclear weapons program those ships in the Atlantic could be carrying nuclear tipped missiles. Its radical Islamic regime could park them off of New York, Boston or Washington and directly threaten American power and security.
> And why can they do this?
> Because Obama has made us weak.
> X, we need to act right now. Will you make an urgent contribution to my PAC and help me reverse American decline?
> We must be prepared to do what it takes to protect the idea of American exceptionalism and our basic Constitutional priorities – the preservation of which are essential not only to our security, but to our prosperity as well.
> I'm done accepting second rate leadership for the best nation in the history of mankind.

I wrote this book as an invitation to you, the reader, to transcend knee-jerk reactions of "I agree" or "I disagree" in the face of messages such as that sent out by John Bolton. I would like to invite you to rather take a step back, in deep respect for all players and all positions, in a radical effort to respectfully understand where we all come from. Then, I invite you to join me and my colleagues in imagining possible futures for humankind that are dignified and sustainable.

Let us begin with acknowledging that patriots are sincere people. John Bolton certainly is such a sincere person. My question to you: Are there different kinds of patriotism? If yes, which kind of patriotism, and for whom, will bring us closer to a dignified future for all humankind? And which patriotism will diminish our chances?

John Bolton wishes for the United States to project more power into the world. Noam Chomsky is another American patriot. He writes that the U.S. "has a brutal record of aggression and subversion":

> Its military spending virtually matches the rest of the world combined, and it is far more technologically advanced. No other country could dream of having a network of hundreds of military bases all over the world, nor of carrying out the world's most expansive campaign of terror – and that is exactly what (President Barack) Obama's drone assassination campaign is. And the U.S., of course, has a brutal record of aggression and subversion.[4]

We see two patriots here, and it seems that they stand for diametrically opposed positions of patriotism. What is too little for one is too much for the other. One is a patriot for "America on top of the rest," the other for "America with the rest."

How come? We find the same situation the world around, because patriots are everywhere, patriots who even give their lives for their ideals. In 2014, the world's governments together spent over $1,700 billion on their military forces, informs the International Peace Bureau in Geneva, Switzerland.[5]

The International Peace Bureau, IPB, is one of the world's oldest international peace federations. Ingeborg Breines is its former co-president and a pillar of our dignity work since its inception. The IPB held a congress on disarmament in Berlin in September 2016,[6] asking the following questions[7]: Should not these funds go into nurturing a culture of peace? Should they not go into climate change mitigation/adaptation, and preserving biodiversity? Into humanitarian programs to support the most vulnerable? Into peace, in form of disarmament, conflict prevention and resolution, and human security? Into public services/social justice, human rights, gender equality and green job-creation? Into sustainable development, new production and consumption patterns, anti-poverty programs, UN Sustainable Development Goals?[8]

Norwegian women now urge: Why is there no Department of Peace in all governments around the world, why is there only a Department of Defense?[9] In the United States, the Department of War was dissolved in 1947, and in 1949, the Department of Defense began its existence. Now it is time for yet another innovation.[10]

How come that we have two so different mottos in the world today: First, *If you want peace, prepare for war* and, second, *There is no path to peace. Peace is the path*? And why is the first motto winning out, if we believe Ban Ki-moon's words that the world is over-armed and peace is underfunded? Where do you stand? What do you intend to do?

Perhaps you would like to begin with putting yourself into the shoes of our historical forebears? Many early humans explored untouched wilderness and were unaware that others were living in other world regions, doing the same. They were blessed by ignorance. "What the eye does not see, the heart does not grieve over," is a proverb that describes their situation.

At a certain point, when the planet had filled up with people, one began to have neighbors. This altered the overall situation fundamentally, because my neighbor can easily also become my enemy. The title of this section of the book is "The Security Dilemma – Too Far and Too Close." It points at the problems brought about by what is called the security dilemma and how humanity adapted to it throughout its history. This dilemma is strong when out-groups are too close for being unaware of each other, but too far apart for mutual trust.

Compare these two sentences: "Did the lion eat Fred?" with "Did the lion eat, Fred?"[11] As you see, the words in these two sentences are the same, it is only the punctuation that is different, and, as a result, the meaning becomes entirely different.[12] As long as the security dilemma culture is strong, historical memories obsessively use punctuation marks as following: "*Your* leader cannot be trusted! You did *this* to us! Therefore *we* have no choice but to regard *you* and your people as a threat and prepare for action!"[13] The other side is as convinced of their moral righteousness, only that the chronology is punctuated in a slightly different way: "*You* forget that your leader did *that* first, which forced us to do *this*!"[14]

If we follow historical and political scientist Benedict Anderson in that communities are *imagined*, then all sides are convinced that their punctuation of events is the only correct one.[15] What we remember are not facts but historical constructions and reconstructions.[16]

My personal life project is to imagine *one single* planetary community, the community of *Earthland*,[17] where people work together toward a universal heightening of consciousness, a globally shared *noosphere*, so that we can find common punctuations for our memories.[18]

What makes this effort difficult? What facilitates it? Why is it so difficult to follow the words of Oregon poet laureate Edwin Markham (1852 – 1940)? He wrote:

> Outwitted:
> He drew a circle that shut me out –
> Heretic, rebel, a thing to flout.
> But Love and I had the wit to win:
> We drew a circle that took him in!

Why is it so difficult to draw a circle that takes everybody in? Why is it so tough to redefine *my enemy* into *my neighbor*, with whom I can build mutual trust? In my 2006 book on humiliation and international conflict, I wrote:

> In the global village, all concepts, ideas, and feelings formerly attached to out-group categorizations lose their validity. When there is only *one* in-group left, there can be no out-group. Out-group notions now "hang in thin air" without their former basis in reality. When a tree dies, it no longer bears fruit. People may need time to grasp this, but they cannot escape this new reality.
>
> Words such as *enemies, wars, victory,* and *soldiers* stem from times when the human population lived in many separate *villages*. Under the new circumstances *we* are citizens of *one* village, with no imperial enemies threatening from outside. There is, indeed, no *outside*. Likewise, there is no *they* anymore; there is only *us*.
>
> A village comprises good and bad neighbors, while enemies traditionally have their place outside of the village's boundaries, as have soldiers, wars, and victories.
>
> A village enjoys peace when all inhabitants get along without resorting to violence. Words such as *war, soldier,* or *victory* are anachronistic now. The only language that fits the new situation is the language of policing, because safeguarding social peace within a village calls for police to help sustain a cohesive social web, not soldiers seeking victory.
>
> The only sentence that fits the reality of any village, including the global village, is, "We are all neighbors; some of us are good neighbors, some are bad neighbors, and in order to safeguard social peace we need a responsible society, and police, no longer soldiers to defend against enemies in wars."[19]

At present, we witness many related transitions of language. The Cold War spawned the last truly convincing large-scale *enemies*. Now, we tend to have *asymmetries*. The traditional notion of the *soldier* is presently changing to entail *peace keepers* and *peace enforcers*.[20] The *warrior-soldier* who left home to reap national and personal glory, fame, and triumph, is becoming obsolete. The word *enemy* is replaced by the word *terrorist*, with terrorists being "inner enemies, very bad neighbors," the only subgroup of enmity that can exist inside an in-group.[21]

Why are those conceptual shifts going on, what do they mean, and what should we do about them?

On November 25, 2014, I saw Suzan-Lori Parks' play, "Father Comes Home from the Wars" (Parts 1, 2 and 3) at the Public Theatre in New York City.[22] A slave named Hero is the lead figure in this play. The play reflects on freedom in its various manifestations. Hero is a thoroughly well-intentioned honest man: for instance, he is opposed to stealing. Therefore he will not run away from his master, since a slave like him has a considerable monetary value and running away would be like stealing. At the same time, Hero is not without freedom, at least in certain ways. Freedom, for him, is whatever choices are placed in front of him within his slave-status. He cannot fathom freedom outside of that status; he cannot envision the freedom of "owning oneself." Slavery is an unescapable frame of life for Hero, like a law of nature, and he has difficulties grasping that this frame is made by humans – which means that it can also be undone by humans. Slavery, including living with a never-ending sense of fear and terror, is a "given" for Hero. In other words, Hero accepts and succumbs to a system of domination that is human-made, rather than forced upon him by nature's constraints.

To me, this play made palpable our widespread inability, also nowadays, as individuals, as local communities, and as global community, to fathom the possibility of wider definitions of freedom. Many mindsets and frames of contemporary life are human-made and can be changed, far from representing laws of nature. Clinging to the need to dominate, be it over nature or "enemies," is one of those outdated mindsets. The opportunity to let go of those cultural scripts is open now, global interconnectedness invites us all to engage in intentionally nurturing and dignifying our world's social and ecological spheres instead. There is no need any more to bow to sentences such as "we are a business and no charity," sentences that insinuate that profit maximization is a first-order frame with the status of a law of nature (see the Introduction to Part One of this book). Like Hero, we, as humankind, seem to fail to recognize that we humans are agents, that we are intentional subjects rather than passive objects. Particularly at the present juncture in history, a juncture of risk and possibility, we may need to radically reconsider what we should accept as givens. We might find that we accept totally unnecessary limitations to our freedom, limitations designed by us, humankind, limitations that can be un-designed.

George Lakoff wrote the book *Whose Freedom? The Battle over America's Most Important Idea.*[23] Can we, as humanity, learn to use our freedom to hold hands and shoulder our responsibility to engage in global solidarity for a dignified future for all?

On my journey throughout the world, I have never met a social context as loving as in the Nile Delta of Lower Egypt. Of course, there are also dark sides there, the dark sides of collectivist hierarchies, and I learned about them when I worked as a psychotherapist in Cairo from 1984 to 1991. Still, I had not seen a similarly high degree of psychological expertise and relational skill taught within families elsewhere. It did not surprise me to see so many Western women choosing to marry an Egyptian man, attracted by the warmth in their families. It did not surprise me that Anwar el-Sadat made peace with Israel in 1979. And I am also not astonished that UN Secretary-General Boutros-Boutros Ghali from Egypt is one of the fathers of the notion of *human* security (versus *national* security): As far back as in 1992, in his Agenda for Peace, he called for "an integrated approach to human security" to address root causes of conflict, spanning economic, social and political issues.[24]

The Nile Delta is a big "island" surrounded by desert, for many millennia, and perhaps it is this insularity that has inspired a culture of "talk first, avoid shooting," rather than "shoot first," a motto which seems to fit more in Upper Egypt? Sadly, also Lower Egypt is losing much of its psychological advantages now, no longer an island, but now becoming part of a globalizing world.

Among my many friends and adopted family members in Egypt was late Ambassador Aly Maher El Sayed, advisor to the Bibliotheca Alexandrina.[25] He wrote to me in 2014:

> Dear Evelin Lindner. Thank you for your multilingual wishes and accept my very best wishes to you for a happy and peaceful year 2014, with *right* stronger than *might*, with justice and respect for dignity of all human beings regardless of race, faith or nationality.... Moderation will prevail against the forces of darkness and extremism as the huge majority of the Egyptian people oppose these forces.... High regards, Ambassador Aly Maher El Sayed.[26]

Planet Earth is a little island surrounded by a vast universe. Can we all learn to lovingly hold hands in solidarity and moderation? Or not? Can we exit from the security dilemma? Can we bring about a global *dignity transition*? Can we then prevent and heal the *dignity dilemma* that we create when we fail to treat each other as equals in dignity?

Appendix: Selected Interviews

Large amounts of informal material were collected for this book since 2010, in South America in 2012,[1] in South East Asia in 2014,[2] in Africa in 2013 and 2015,[3] and each year for several months in Europe and the U.S.[4] The full list of encounters, contacts, and material covers thousands of pages. In the following, allow me to share a few snapshots of some more formal conversations.

• *Erik Solheim* was Minister of International Development in Norway, when our conversation on humiliation and terrorism took place in the Ministry of Foreign Affairs in Oslo, on January 10, 2011. Until being appointed minister, he was as a diplomat and a participant in the Norwegian delegation that worked to resolve the Sri Lankan Civil War before the outbreak of the Eelam War IV. On May 3, 2016, United Nations Secretary-General Ban Ki-moon announced that Solheim takes over the post of executive director of UNEP, the United Nations' Environment Programme. In our conversation in 2011, Solheim offered important examples of the role of humiliation, for instance, how it can be much more significant than material wealth. I have summarized and translated his reflections from Norwegian.[5]

• *Abid Qayyum Raja* is a Norwegian lawyer and politician born in Oslo in 1975 into a family of Pakistani descent. In 2010, he was awarded the Fritt Ord Honorary Award of Freedom of Speech. Our conversation on humiliation and terrorism took place in Oslo on January 10, 2011. I have summarized and translated his reflections from Norwegian.[6] We began our conversation on experiences of humiliation during childhood and adolescence and how they may lead to extremism. Then, we went on to the role of economic and religious factors. Raja ended our conversation with two warnings. The first warning went to Muslims who say that the number of radicalized people is small. Raja observes that, indeed, many Muslims expose others to hatred and that therefore four values need to be emphasized to them:

- tolerance (for example with respect to homosexuals)
- equality, and respect for it
- democracy (as opposed to divine laws)
- a society of open debate, with freedom of expression

Abid Raja's second warning went to those who stand for social democratic moral relativism, and to scientists who are too afraid. His message was that academics need to shoulder their responsibility much more sincerely, that disciplines such as sociology of law, criminology, psychology, and sociology of deviance need to become much more involved, and that the analysis of crime needs to be better linked with that of terrorism. Furthermore, just looking at social causes is much too simple: the individual has a role in this as well. Individuals who preach radicalization, who run a madrassah, or an equivalent on the Internet, they all know about humiliation as a potential resource. They instrumentalize humiliation experiences of young people for their purposes.

• Norwegian Police Security Service: *Trond Hugubakken* is communications director at the Norwegian Police Security Service (Politiets sikkerhetstjeneste, PST), the police security agency of Norway, comparable to the British MI5 Security Service. Josefine Aase was a senior advisor for PST at the time when our conversation on humiliation and terrorism took place in their Oslo headquarters on February 4, 2011. Our conversation was part of a series of meetings that I had with members of security police also in other countries, for instance, in Hamburg, Germany, on October 22, 2010, or in Hannover, Germany, on July 19, 2011.

Hugubakken and Aase opened our conversation by explaining the role and mandate of the security services in Norway. They then reflected on the "bunch of guys" explanation of radicalization (such as put forward by Marc Sageman[7]), in contradistinction to the "ideological conviction" explanation. They indicated that they see none of those explanations being more accurate than the other.

As to humiliation as a cause, they reflected on the difference between youths who were born in Europe or came to Europe as a child, and who have a much larger range of choices as compared to those in the Middle East and other parts of the world outside of Norway, who are likely to experience more humiliation. Western societies, on their part, may be guilty of under-challenging their children, a trend that can be observed in many Norwegian schools, for instance, when those who fail are indulged rather than encouraged to learn mastery. In such a context it is made easy to avoid effort and turn to victim identities instead.[8]

When asked which questions are most pressing for the security services, questions that researchers ought to focus on more, Hugubakken and Aase replied that radicalization needs to be studied more. They recommended the work of Petter Nesser, who has based his doctoral dissertation on in-depth, inductive analyses of case studies.[9] Research on de-radicalization and rehabilitation programs "is still in its infancy" was their message.[10] "In the end, de-radicalization remains a much more elusive concept than is generally assumed."[11]

A 2016 study by the Norwegian Police Security Service shows that young men of multiethnic backgrounds with low education, high crime rates, and insecure integration into the labor market are particularly vulnerable to being radicalized by extremist Islam.[12] In France, the label *banlieue* has emerged since the 1970s for low-income housing in urban suburbs with mainly foreign immigrants living in poverty traps, where disaffected youths are driven into the arms of terror entrepreneurs.[13] Gilles Kepel, a French political scientist and specialist on the Islamic and contemporary Arab world, for instance, connects the radicalization of young people in France's suburbs with the dysfunctional sociology of these banlieues, combined with the role of Islam.[14]

• *Laila Bokhari* is a political scientist with Norwegian and Pakistani background. She is part of a larger network of Norwegian researchers who work with militant Islam, also Brynjar Lia, Thomas Hegghammer, and Petter Nesser.[15] As mentioned earlier, I value their views in particular, not least because their perspectives are informed by the Norwegian cultural heritage of *likeverd*, *dugnad*, and global responsibility. I had the privilege of learning from Laila Bokhari on several occasions. Extremist networks comprise "the leader," "the adventurer," "the born again," and "the mother martyr."[16]

• *Petter Nesser* is a senior researcher with the Terrorism Research Group at the Norwegian Defence Research Establishment. I thank him for sharing his deep, nuanced, and differentiated insights in Oslo on June 17, 2011. I have summarized and translated his reflections from Norwegian.[17] It was very enriching for me to relate to with him my experiences with young clients during my years as psychological counselor in Cairo, Egypt, from 1984 to 1991. We began by speaking about the Muslim Brotherhood and how they sought inspiration from Nazi Germany. Nesser explained how diverse the Salafi movement is, and pointed at an interesting merger of two lines of influence, namely, Salafist purity of thought combined with anti-imperialist theory. He highlighted the story of Mohammed Bouyeri as an illustration of the intricate interplay of all factors. Nesser's particular interest is in discerning the patterns and processes that lead to the formation of movements. He differentiates "entrepreneurs" from "protégés," "misfits," and "drifters."

• *Tore Bjørgo* is the director of the Center for Research on Extremism: Right-Wing Extremism, Hate Crime and Political Violence at the University of Oslo, Norway. He is also adjunct professor at the Norwegian Police University College, where he has been professor of police science and research director. It was a privilege to be introduced to him in 1995, and to learn from him in more depth on February 13, 2012, when he summarized his views on extremism for me. I have summed up and translated his reflections from Norwegian.[18] Bjørgo described five main paths into extremism (be it right-wing, left-wing, religious, or otherwise sectarian). First, there are victims of mobbing, who suffer from being humiliated and feeling humiliated, and who are empowered when they wear the outfit of extremists and thus also signal that they are not alone. Victims of mobbing often are in need of protection on a very practical level, something they receive from their extremist peer-group. Joe Erling Jahr, for instance, is a young man who committed a racist motivated murder (*Holmlia-drapet*) in Norway and was sentenced to eighteen years of imprisonment. He himself had been a victim of violence. When he was fourteen years old, he was attacked in the train by a group of youth with Somali background who robbed children, and, as it seems, this event motivated him to seek out a right-wing milieu.[19] The second group are seekers of thrill. The case of Andrew Wenham in Australia can illustrate this. He was attracted by "adventure" and professed that he did not even know he was part of a group.[20] Third, there are people with a sense of injustice; for instance, they may react with right-wing radicalization when they see that asylum seekers receive privileges on the housing market or in the health services. Fourth, for people with a need for belonging and friendship who are excluded elsewhere, extremist peer-groups are attractive because they include them. Fifth, the people, who actually identify with the ideology, are the smallest group.

• *Hamed El-Said* is an expert on de-radicalization, and I had the privilege of speaking with him on January 5, 2012. I was introduced to him through Ariel Lublin and Francis Mead,[21] who made the 2011 documentary film *Second Chance in Saudi Arabia – Saudi's Rehab* for United Nations Television, as part of a series of films for the United Nations to look at how and why people leave terror groups.[22] The film documents a program for former extremists, featuring, for instance, Khalid Al-Jhani, a former explosives trainer for Osama Bin Laden in Afghanistan. He was later captured and held in Guantanamo for over four years and then returned to Saudi Arabia. There, he passed through a rehabilitation program, and, today, he lives as an integrated citizen in society. The film features also Hamed Al-Shaygi, a professor of sociology, who helps run the Saudi rehabilitation program for young men accused of involvement in extremist violence. Instead of further punishment, so Al-Shaygi's position, education is key to the new approach, "for them to have dignity."[23] In our conversation, Hamed El-Said highlighted that Islam has a tradition of forgiveness, and that the tribal tradition, as well, sees terrorists as misguided family member, as misled sons. I replied that this view very much resonates with the adage that "it takes a village to raise a child." Reflecting on this saying leads to the insight that the "global village" now carries this responsibility. Framed in this way, the view on young terror-perpetrators as *children*, indeed, is preferable to seeing them as *enemies*.[24]

• Tom Koenigs is a German politician and Member of the German Federal Parliament, in Berlin. He is chairman of his party in the Committee on Human Rights and Humanitarian Aid, and is a full member in the United Nations' subcommittee on International Organizations And Globalization. Our conversation on humiliation and terrorism took place in Berlin on April 12, 2011. I have summarized and translated his reflections from German. From February 2006 until 2007, Koenigs was the Special Representative of the UN Secretary-General for Afghanistan for the United Nations Assistance Mission in Afghanistan. His report on suicide attacks in Afghanistan 2001 – 2007 would merit an entire chapter in this book.[25] He explained that in Afghanistan, suicide attacks began appearing with regularity only in 2005 and 2006, and that "the community's initial response was to reject the possibility that Afghans themselves might be involved."[26] Even more, the notion that suicide might be combined with killing others was considered alien before the assassination of Ahmad Shah Massoud on September 9, 2001, two days before September 11, 2001, when two planes flew into New York City's World Trade Center Towers.[27]

• *Norbert Müller* is a member of the board of Schura, a merger of mosque associations in Hamburg, Germany. Our conversation on humiliation and terrorism took place in Hamburg, Germany, on October 22, 2010. Norbert Müller shared his views on the reasons of why highly educated young men from Hamburg ever could set out to commit terror in New York on November 9, 2001. I have summarized and translated his reflections from

German. He explained that the situations of American Muslims is different as compared to German Muslims, and he laid out in detail how the debate has evolved in Germany during the past forty years.[28]

• *Wolfgang Kaleck* is a civil rights attorney and the general secretary for the European Center for Constitutional and Human Rights. I had the privilege of learning from him in Berlin on May 17, 2011. I have summarized and translated his reflections from German.[29] Kaleck reported that a few years ago, there were few publications on the topic of transitional justice, however, this has changed since, and publications are now streaming in. Wolfgang Kaleck's first conclusion from his work is that "justice does heal." Legal action does have an effect on the individual and the community. Kaleck works with victims who are either suffering themselves, or their family members were affected. Kaleck recommended having a look at the International Center for Transitional Justice with their motto "Justice, Truth, Dignity."
There is no standard model for dealing with the past, he noted, but a number of precedents have been established through the work of special rapporteurs and experts of the United Nations on the issues of impunity, reparations, and best practices in transitional justice.

Of course, and Kaleck makes this very clear, legal tools are not the only path to healing, they cannot achieve everything, as they are too limited. What is needed is an interplay between political, cultural, legal means. When the overall goal is human dignity, then criminal law has a door-opening function on two levels: first, when impunity prevails due to political and economic upheavals on the national level, and, second, international law is often more evolved than law at the national level. In Uruguay and Brazil, for example, previous regimes have announced amnesties to make peace with the military. They are now prompted to rethink these decisions, as these amnesties violate international law.

Terrorism is a category that is rather discredited in the legal environment, because it is too open to political manipulation: there is the terrorist, then there is the freedom fighter, and there is state terrorism. It makes little sense to continue to expand the concept of terrorism. It is preferable to address relevant events with existing legal instruments. At the national level, this would be arson, homicide, or damage to property, and at the international level, we speak of war crimes and crimes against humanity. Such categories apply to all sides, be it the Taliban, for instance, or Western forces in Afghanistan: in all cases, civilians ought not be harmed.

A personal note: I was amazed to detect an unexpected relational connection between the Global Responsibility Festival "Hamburger Ideenkette" that I have organized in Hamburg, Germany, in 1993, and the painful history of Chile. German parliamentarian Freimut Duve supported this festival in Hamburg in 1993, and only through Kaleck's report did I understand that Duve had also given great courage to Beatriz Brinkmann when he visited her in prison in Chile in 1986. I regret that I did not know about this connection when I lived in Chile in 2012. Brinkmann works now with the International Rehabilitation Council for Torture Victims in Chile, a center for mental health and human rights, that aims to alleviate the physical and emotional suffering of persons affected by torture or other forms of political repression.

• *Aurangzaib Khan* is a journalist in North Pakistan.[30] He is intimately familiar with the situation there, among others, in the Swat valley, "the land of the terrorists."[31] He lives surrounded by families in distress, affected by terrorism and terrorism-related disappearances. On May 3, 2011, he shared with me his grief and indignation that some 30,000 people have died due to terrorism since 2001, leaving behind families with little or no support. Extremist groups enlist and indoctrinate youth, and this throws their entire families into misery, as they are shamed and blamed, and banished out of community. Khan's main message is the following: "Humiliation is grounded in helplessness and giving a voice and platform to victims of terrorism will empower them and help them overcome their humiliation. This in turn will help the victims define the importance of peace in the public sphere rather than a callous or quota driven media, which finds satisfaction in sensation."

• It was a privilege to meet also with another voice from Pakistan, *Shahid Kamal*. At the time of our conversation in Berlin on May 15, 2011, he was Pakistan's Ambassador to Germany. His main topic is global connectivity, and how all segments of society may best contribute to nurture it.[32]

• *Gary Page Jones* worked with Norwegian People's Aid in Somalia, when I did my doctoral research there, and I had the privilege of meeting him in Hargeisa, Somaliland, on November 29, 1998.[33] Since then, he has continuously supported Human Dignity and Humiliation Studies. He shared his international experiences with me in a Skype meeting between New York City and Nairobi on October 28, 2012. At that point, he was the head of the Somalia team of UNICEF's Global Fund HIV/AIDS.

Gary Page Jones is one of those bridge builders between theory and practice that I see as crucially important for the world. He holds enormous knowledge in the field, precisely the knowledge that researchers need but can never accumulate, regardless of ever so elaborate "field trips."[34] I am delighted that my encouragement has inspired Jones, and soon his doctoral dissertation will be finished. In our conversation in 2012, he pointed out that simply providing people with information about how to behave, for instance, in the context of the HIV and AIDS epidemic in Africa, does not lead to the behavioral change that is desired. He recommends Behavior Change Communication, a comprehensive process of intervention with individuals, communities and societies that passes through the following stages: from unaware, to aware, to concerned, to knowledgeable, to being motivated to change, to practicing trial behavior change, to, finally, sustained behavior change. This methodology combines several behavior change theories that have evolved during the past decades, including the diffusion of innovations model,[35] the stages of change model,[36] Albert Bandura's self-efficacy model,[37] and the behavior change continuum by the World Bank.[38]

When I met Gary Page Jones for the first time, I also had the privilege of learning from another bridge builder, Matt Bryden and his War-torn Societies Project Somalia. This project used a participatory action-research approach[39] that encouraged all external and internal actors in war-torn societies to collectively analyze their complex situation. The aim was to better integrate the different forms of international assistance – humanitarian, economic, political, military – and to better align "such assistance with local and national efforts."[40]

On the other side of the theory-praxis divide stands another bridge builder and supporter of Human Dignity and Humiliation Studies who practices participatory action-research in very particular ways. Sociologist Maggie O'Neill bases her work on the theoretical concept of *ethno-mimesis*, an inter-connection of sensitive ethnographic work and visual re-presentations. It is both a methodological tool and a process for exploring lived experience, for instance, that of displacement, exile, belonging, and humiliation. O'Neill particular research focus is on prostitution, women's experiences, routes into prostitution, affected communities, and forced migration.[41]

All these approaches have the potential to contribute to the task of making "the village" fit to "raise its children," and in these ways preventing those children, as much as possible, from turning to violent terror.

• *Joanna "Jo" Berry* is the daughter of Sir Anthony Berry who was killed by the Irish Republican Army (IRA) in the Brighton hotel bombing on October 12, 1984. The bomb was planted by Patrick Magee, whose aim was to kill Prime Minister Margaret Thatcher and her cabinet, as they stayed at the hotel for the Conservative Party conference. After the release of Patrick Magee in 1999, Jo went to meet him several times. These meetings, over ten months, formed the basis of a BBC documentary film first broadcast on December 13, 2001.[42] In November 2000, Jo met with Magee in public, in an effort to achieve reconciliation in the context of the Good Friday Agreement of April 10, 1999.

On May 5, 2011, when we had our conversation on humiliation and terrorism, I expressed my gratitude and admiration to Jo for her courage to step into the public realm with all of her vulnerability.[43] In my view, vulnerability is essential for dignity, and it is detrimental for the future of humankind that vulnerability is seen as a weakness in the context of honor.[44] Jo explained how she had listened to Patrick Magee and how her aim had been to give him his dignity, even if she disagreed. She reported how she would say to herself, "I can be vulnerable and open and allow him his dignity. I am not blaming him and making him responsible for my pain, even though there is, of course, a responsibility on his side."

When her father was killed, Jo was twenty-seven years old. Before that, she had lived in the Himalayas and had read Gandhi, in other words, she had been on an unusual spiritual path in life. However, the bomb changed everything. Before, she could meditate and feel inner peace, afterwards, meditation seemed no longer relevant, as in the real world people do get killed. For her to survive, she had to reinvent herself. She asked herself: Do I still wish to contribute to peace? If yes, how? She did not really know what she could do. At that time, little work had been done in the area of reconciliation. She trusted serendipity, that things would happen to help her, and, step-by-step, the journey started. She remembers it as a clear moment of decision, already two days after the killing, that something in her decided: "I am not going to blame 'them,' the killers!"

Mahatma Gandhi would have loved our conversation, as he once formulated: "Hate the sin, love the sinner," or as philosopher Arne Næss put it: "There are no murderers, only people who have murdered."[45] Also Dan Bar-On would have joined in with joy. He was born in Haifa in 1938, to German-Jewish parents from Hamburg, the very city where I later studied both psychology and medicine. For twenty-five years he lived in a Kibbutz, tending fruit trees and studying behavioral sciences. In 1987, he travelled to Germany, and in 1992, he initiated the discussion circle "To Reflect and Trust" between perpetrators and victims of the Holocaust.[46] Also he was a true gardener of peace. Annette Engler worked with him, and she is now part of the Global Appreciative Nurturing Team of our Human Dignity network.[47] I am sure that also Elizabeth Ford applauds Jo Berry. Elizabeth Ford is the Chief of Psychiatry for Correctional Health Services in New York City, and she calls on everyone to acknowledge the humanness in all prison inmates.[48]

I asked Jo what she would say to a young person who contemplates violence. Jo's reply: "What I have learned is that there is a cost to your own humanity, which is very hard to get back. Once you have crossed that line of violence, your humanity is profoundly affected. To make your point nonviolently is much more powerful!" She continued that she could understand why young men might decide to use violence. Yet, "I urge them to achieve their aims in nonviolent ways. This is much more radical! More rebellious, more subversive, more play in it!"

I told Jo about my experience in Egypt with my Palestinian clients from 1984 – 1991, and explained that these young people seemed to have no other script but violence into which to pour their deep moral hurt. Jo's recommendation: "Today, the situation has changed. Today, more nonviolent scripts are available. It is easier to demonize, but the problem is much bigger than that."

The killer of her father chose violence because he thought there was no other way. He talked of human rights, yet, he could not see her father as a human being. Today he does. He professes that Jo's willingness to listen "disarmed" him: she moved him from honorable invulnerability to the dignity of vulnerability.

Section Two

Honor Humiliation – The Duty to Retaliate

A man deserves to be killed and not to be humiliated!

– Somali proverb

Plutôt mourir debout que de vivre à genoux. (Rather die standing, than live on your knees.)

– Albert Camus (1913 – 1960), philosopher[1]

Those who kill for honor ...

– Suzanne Goldenberg on honor killing[2]

Humiliation is the root of all terrorism.

– Peter Gabel, editor, *Tikkun*[3]

If I've learned one thing covering world affairs, it's this: The single most underappreciated force in international relations is humiliation.

– Thomas Friedman, *New York Times* columnist[4]

"I became a jihadist because the Frenchman spat on my sister and called her 'You dirty Arab' ..."

– A young man of Arab background in France[5]

Everyone knows how the Muslim country bows down to pressure from west. Everyone knows the kind of humiliation we are faced with around the globe.

– Faisal Shahzad, confessed attempted bomber
of New York's Times Square, May 1, 2010[6]

The politics of humiliation is fluid, mobile and capacious as it increasingly spreads and infects almost every public and commercial sphere where ideas are produced and circulated. As an ideology, it is politically reactionary and morally despicable. As a strategy, it seeks to denigrate and silence others, often targeting those already disadvantaged, while promoting unthinking self-interest, arrogance and certitude at the expense of critical thought, dialogue and exchange.

– Henry Giroux, scholar and cultural critic[7]

Introduction to Section Two

Imagine you are a knight in medieval Europe. You are young, newly married, and busy building your life. Imagine another knight comes along and challenges you to duel by throwing one of his gauntlets on the ground in front of you and your peers. You have no choice. You must pick up the gauntlet, accept the challenge, and get "satisfaction" for the insult to your honor. You have the duty to restore your humiliated honor by demonstrating your willingness to risk death, yours or your opponent's death. This is your inescapable obligation to your own honor and your family's honor, even though this may be the very last thing your heart desires at this point in your life. You want to go home, love your wife, have children, and live long.

Readers with Western backgrounds may have difficulties in understanding this worldview and its inescapability for those caught in it. The reason is that honor humiliation is profoundly different from dignity humiliation. The phenomenon of humiliation is defined and lived fundamentally different in a context where the security dilemma has spawned the honorable dominator culture, as compared to a context of partnership and ideals of equal dignity. In the first context, the belief reigns that enemies choose to be enemies due to their evil human nature – their evil power lust, for instance – in the second, human nature is seen as social in essence, capable of "evil" and of "good."

The 2012 documentary film *Banaz* chronicles the honor killing of the girl Banaz.[1] This film illustrates not only the "duty to kill" that the victim's family felt to "heal humiliated family honor," it also shows to which degree the British police was unprepared to handle such cases. Banaz fled to the police to seek protection, but the police simply brought Banaz back to her parents, thinking she was drunk and had made up a story of her father wanting to kill her. By doing so, the police delivered her to her execution. Banaz was a loving young woman, and she died. She died because of honor humiliation and because honor humiliation was not understood in her Western environment. Death is also what a wider world risks, if honor humiliation is not respectfully understood and addressed, and this is one of the reasons for why I write this book.

Banaz' death would never have been mourned, if not for the loving understanding of one individual female police officer who brought the case to a proper follow-up and to public visibility, so that police action can become more appropriate in the future. I wish to follow this police officer's example of loving and respectful care in the midst of difficult dilemmas.

Terrorism and migration are inscribed into such dilemmas in many ways, as is fear of terrorists and migrants. Ahmad Mansour is a Muslim psychologist living in Berlin. This is what he observes: Right-wing German activists see immigrants from honor cultures as "wild animals," bent on raping and terrorizing, while left-wing "harmonizers'" treat them as pet animals to be "protected" by explaining away their cultural problems. Both are equally racist.[2]

This is the second section of the book, and it asks: In which context did the brutal script of honor and of honor humiliation come into being? After all, a young man who decides to become a "holy warrior" may act on this very script when seeking to kill or be killed. According to political scientist Mohammed Hafez, there are indeed three corresponding "jihadist" narratives that mobilize for martyrdom: "humiliation of Muslims at the hands of foreigners; impotence of official Muslim governments in the face of hegemonic powers; and redemption through faithful sacrifice."[3]

This is the answer: The script of honor and honor humiliation came into being in an atmosphere of terror that characterized the past millennia almost everywhere on the globe, an atmosphere in which a culture emerged for which terror is normal, terror in all forms, suffered and perpetrated.

Where did this atmosphere of terror originate from? During roughly the past five percent of the history of *Homo sapiens* on planet Earth, communities around the globe lived in constant fear of being raided or conquered by other humans. The Huns, the Vikings, the Mongols, these names instilled terror. Their raids were like devastating hurricanes – those raiders came, caused mayhem, and disappeared. Others went even further and came as conquerors. All empires, from the Persian Empire to the Roman Empire to the British Empire, came into being in this way. In the language of political science, the *security dilemma* was strong during the past millennia of human history.

When the security dilemma is strong, it acts as an inescapable iron grip that defines and shapes everything within its reach. Fear of attack becomes all-definitorial. Preparations for defense have top priority. This is the context within which honor came into being, expressing itself in all walks of life, with honor humiliation in tow. And religions were instrumentalized to serve this predicament.

The security dilemma is strong when people live too far apart to be able to trust each other. The security dilemma attenuates as mutual trust increases. This is precisely what growing global interconnectedness offers: it opens space for building trust, worldwide. Yet, there is a problem. Interconnectedness also increases the probability for people to feel humiliated when they sense that their honor or dignity is being disrespected. Humiliated people no longer feel motivated to do what people who trust each other gladly do, namely, cooperate to responsibly solve conflicts and share burdens together. Worse even, also violence can ensue. The fear that flows from a strong security dilemma can trigger violence. Unfortunately, feelings of humiliation can become an even stronger trigger for violence. And violence will increase even more when what I call a *cross over* happens, when feelings of dignity humiliation lead to responses from the tool kit that aristocrats traditionally use to respond to honor humiliation.

Bertha von Suttner had a great talent to describe how fear and honor combine to make war an all-consuming reality. She herself looked at it from the point of view of dignity humiliation, envisioning the Suttner-Freire-Gandhi-Mandela-path to address it, at a time – she died just a few days before the First World War began – when this perspective was utterly marginal in comparison to honor humiliation and its call for revenge:

> It was a trying time. War had broken out. One forgets that there are but two antagonistic forces, and people talk as if there were some mighty third party which set these two at each other's throats. Hence the whole responsibility is thrown upon this mysterious force which regulates the fate of peoples.... This conception of war was the general one. Nothing else was talked of on the streets or in the parlor; we read nothing else in the newspapers; we prayed for nothing in the churches save the success of our armies; wherever we went, earnest faces and excited voices showed that people had no thought for other matters. Business, amusement, art – all were but secondary affairs. It seemed at times as if we had scarce the right to think of anything else while this great struggle over the world's fate hung in the balance. The frequent proclamations, couched in the well-known phrases confident of victory and prophesying national renown; the glitter and clash of arms and waving of battle-flags as the troops marched through; the stirring public orations and newspaper articles glowing with patriotic ardor, this eternal appeal to virtue, honor, duty, courage, sacrifice; the recurring assurances of the unconquerable justice of our cause, defended by the noblest and best of nations; – all these established a sort of heroic atmosphere, which filled the whole people with enthusiasm and roused a general conviction of our being the noblest citizens of the noblest of times.[4]

To live in continuous fear of death, or, what many fear more, humiliating enslavement, is a terrifying experience that makes people vulnerable.[5] Awareness of mortality is difficult to bear for humans under any circumstances, and wherever the security dilemma is strong, it heightens this awareness. Terror management theory, first developed in the late 1980s,[6] analyzes how humans are terrorized by their awareness of their mortality, and how this impacts their attitudes and choices.[7] In 2008, I had the privilege of being invited, together with Tom Pyszczynski, one of the fathers of terror management theory, to a research workshop in Budapest in Hungary that focused on "indigenous terrorism" and "the root causes of radicalization among groups with an immigrant heritage in Europe."[8] Pyszczynski shared with us two studies he had carried out to explore how terror management theorists can become more aware of cultural contexts. He studied martyrdom and deadly military interventions and whether being reminded of death increased or decreased support for it. Iranian college students who participated in this study, when reminded of death, supported martyrdom more than peers who had been exposed to topics that were aversive but unrelated to death. Politically conservative American students reacted similarly; when reminded of death, they supported extreme military interventions by American forces that could kill thousands of civilians. Politically liberal American students, however, did not support such strategies.[9]

These findings support psychologist Fathali Moghaddam in his exploration of the actions of suicide bombers. Also he sees terror management theory failing in explaining certain types of terrorism: "Terror management theory and other similar explanations rest on the assumption that individuals consciously or unconsciously fear death and are first and foremost concerned to stay alive. This assumption makes sense from the perspective of Western liberal values, but it is misleading in the context of a culture that gives value to martyrdom and the sacrifice of one's life for the great cause."[10]

What we learn from this research is that being reminded of death has psychological effects. Clearly, a strong security dilemma per definition reminds of death: Whenever enemies appeared on the horizon throughout the past millennia, it often meant to kill or be killed. In this context, one's own personal life and death became subservient to the survival of one's own collective; enemies needed to be destroyed, even if I paid with my own personal life. Honor is the cultural mindset that prescribes that death is to be heroically embraced, not feared. Divine legitimization solidified this mindset.

Jonathan Shay, neuroscientist, medical doctor, and clinical psychiatrist, introduced the term *moral injury*.[11] Shay sees the brain, mind, social system, and culture as the "four avatars" of the human existence, with none having ontological priority. The brain is not prior to the other three realms, all co-evolved with each other, at the same ontological level – each is the others' environment.[12] The security dilemma profoundly impacted all four avatars of the human existence during the past millennia.

About twenty veterans a day take their own lives in the United States, according to official estimates.[13] Shay listened to veterans for years, and now he campaigns against the diagnostic jargon of Posttraumatic Stress Disorder (PTSD). There is no illness, he argues, no malady, disease, sickness, no disorder: what veterans suffer from is *war injury*, a psychological injury from war, and it should therefore be called Posttraumatic Stress *Injury*.[14] In 2010, Shay was honored for "building public awareness and acceptance of post-traumatic stress disorder as a serious and bona fide war injury."[15]

Moral injury happens when "what is right" in one's local culture is being betrayed, either by a person who holds legitimate authority, or by oneself,[16] in a situation where one is aware that the stakes are high.[17] Moral injury impairs the capacity for trust, increases despair, suicidality, and interpersonal violence.[18] The injured person expects every other person she encounters to be only interested in harming, exploiting, or humiliating her. As a result, the injured person may "run and hide" to avoid others, up to the point of suicide, or, she may create false fronts, feeling entitled to strike first. James Edward Jones, professor of world religions and African studies, uses the term *post-victim ethical exemption syndrome*.[19]

The very transition from the terminology of *disorder* to the terminology of *injury* in connection with war trauma that Shay stands for, shows how the *Zeigeist* is on the move. "What is right" is in the process of changing. As long as society expects men to bravely kill enemies, it is a *disorder* when those men cannot stomach the trauma connected with doing so. Only when society grows unsure about who is the enemy, and whether killing human beings can be justified altogether, it becomes an *injury* to be wounded by doubts such as: Those people I just killed, perhaps they were our fellow human beings? The shift in diagnoses makes palpable how the classical security dilemma is waning. It is attenuating through the current shrinking of the world, which makes it ever more difficult to keep enemies and friends apart.[20]

When the security dilemma first made itself felt, this must have been an immense shock for unsuspecting people not used to this level of brutality. The first experiences of war must have caused unprecedented moral injuries. Also today, so-called uncontacted tribes will react with horror if suddenly faced with a modern soldier in full gear.

During the past millennia, due to the security dilemma being strong, the right to strike first became enshrined in a culture of honorable heroism, particularly for young males. And these males were prone to create false fronts as a way to maleness, not necessarily only as a result of moral injury. As soon as their maleness was culturally linked to heroism, they were in need of arenas for war and would create them even where there was no need for war. In this way, injuries were inflicted and suffered, distrust and war were perpetuated even where they could have been overcome.

As mentioned earlier, I follow Alex Schmid's preference of the term *extremism* in the sense of *violent extremism* rather than radicalization.[21] The word radical stems from the Latin word *radix* or root. Its etymology suggests getting at the root of problems. People like Bertha von Suttner, Mahatma Gandhi, or Nelson Mandela can be placed into the category of radicals. As psychologist John Horgan has noted, not every radical becomes a terrorist and not every terrorist holds radical views.[22]

Radicalization is the signature of the world in the grip of the security dilemma. Terrorism expert Alex Schmid explains: "… we tend to assume that radicalization is something that occurs only on the other side, not noting that in responding to terrorism, the polarization process in society – and between societies – often radicalizes both sides."[23] Also social psychologists Clark McCauley and Sophia Moskalenko have pointed out that radicalization happens not just to "them," it also happens to "us."[24] Professor of media, culture, and communication, Arun Kundnani adds: "Western states themselves 'radicalized' following 9/11 as much as non-state actors, both becoming more willing to use violence in a wider range of contexts."[25] Eliza Manningham-Buller, director general of MI5 between 2002 and 2007, told a parliamentary enquiry in 2010: "Our involvement in Iraq radicalized, for want of a better word, a whole generation of young people – not a whole generation, a few among a generation – who saw our involvement in Iraq and Afghanistan as being an attack on Islam."[26]

In other words, radicalization is not a monologue, it emerges in relationships and heats up all sides. And the security dilemma works like a dynamo for this dynamic. It drives ever more radical cultural adaptations of collective mobilization that subjugate self-interest into a larger group cause, and it transforms terror and counterterror from merely representing desperate means of last resort into honorable cultural scripts. In my 2009 book on emotion and conflict, I analyzed how it is possible that honor can become a higher goal than survival and how this can become suicidal. Honor is a form of faithfulness, and terror and war can be an act of loyalty. Giving one's life in suicide terrorism can be seen as the purest form of faithfulness. It defies worldly rationalities, including the rationality of the Western *Homo economicus* model of human nature. The *Homo honoris* model of human nature indicates that divine rewards can be expected for heroic martyrdom after death. The slaughter in the many wars of the past could be described as mass terror suicide martyrdom.

Today's suicide terrorism proves that the security dilemma's culture has survived until now. It has survived into times where the call of the day is very different, namely, global solidarity, no longer playing the game of honor. As I have explained before, this is why I became a radical, radical in my commitment to dignity, to transcend the game of honor.

The security dilemma is characterized by two binary opposites, as structural anthropology would call it, namely, *inside* versus *outside*, and *up* versus *down*, or, to be more precise, the security dilemma is predicated on one fault line, and creates a second one:

1. The security dilemma arises when in-groups are caught in fear of potentially hostile out-groups, who, if not killed, may kill. The security dilemma is predicated on the horizontal differentiation of inside versus outside. In this context, it is an honorable duty to kill one's enemies.[27]

2. The security dilemma pushes for the vertical differentiation of up versus down. The result are stratified male-dominant "strongman" collectivist and ranked honor societies. In this context, power elites have the duty to defend their honor by killing enemies who attack from outside, they have the duty to engage their peers in duel-like combat in defense of their status, and the duty to hold their inferiors down.[28]

Honor is the term I use in my work to denote the cultural script of the duty to keep the dominator model of society in place. It is the duty to go to duel-like combat against equal peers or enemies in case they become a threat, and the duty to keep inferiors in their due lowly place by way of routine humiliation. To inflict humiliation on others so as to avert or avenge one's own humiliation is an intricate part of honor. Still today, this is a script that informs cultures in many parts of the world. Terrorism draws on this cultural script. It is therefore crucial to understand its inner logic.

Leo Tolstoy wrote in 1894:

> In order to obtain and hold power a man must love it. Thus the effort to get it is not likely to be coupled with goodness, but with the opposite qualities of pride, craft and cruelty. Without exalting self and abasing others, without hypocrisy, lying, prisons, fortresses, penalties, killing, no power can arise or hold its own.[29]

In my work, I use anthropologist William Ury's historical periods as starting point for my model. Ury goes from simple *hunter-gatherers* to complex *agriculturists*, and from there to a global *knowledge* society.[30] I go from *pride* to *honor*, and then to *dignity*. If we estimate that *Homo sapiens* appeared in the Middle Paleolithic about 200,000 years ago,[31] then the first ninety-five percent of human history were spent with populating the planet as if it had no limits, and I call this period the *era of pristine untouched pride*. Then followed a short period, representing the past five percent of human history, the *era of collectivist ranked honor*. The human rights vision for the future of humankind could be named a *future of equality in dignity for all as individuals, in solidarity*.

Humankind began with pristine pride, and then, pressed by the tragedy of the security dilemma, for a brief and rather malign and hurtful last five percent of our history, we went into ranked honor. Today, we have the unprecedented historical opportunity to attenuate the security dilemma, and thus return to pristine pride. Or, to be more precise, pride can no longer be pristine, since it has been touched and mutilated by the last millennia's experience of humiliation. Therefore, the hoped-for future of human dignity could be described more appropriately as a period of liberation from the traditional practice to rank human worthiness. It is a transition toward un-ranking human worthiness, a move toward the equality in dignity of *non-domination*, as political theorist Philip Pettit calls it,[32] the manifestation of the *partnership* model of the world instead of the dominator model, as described by social scientist Riane Eisler.[33]

This section of the book looks at the intricate and often hideous ways in which the ranking of human worth into supposedly "higher" beings who deserve more, and "lesser" beings who deserve less, was enforced throughout the past five percent of human history in most world regions. It illustrates how subordinates were kept in inferior positions not just by overt oppression, but also by being covertly coopted. It also shows how this is still ongoing nowadays, not just in explicit honor cultures, but also implicitly, in contemporary Western cultures that foreground individualism. Under the cover of the promise of equal dignity, present-day Western individualist culture amplifies inequality. *Power distance* is a term used by social psychologist Geert Hofstede in cultural dimensions theory, meaning the distance between the top and the bottom of a hierarchy within a society, and this power distance increases all around the world just now.[34]

Terror is inscribed into the conundrum of these overtly enforced and covertly achieved rankings, which all stand in opposition to the ideal of equality in dignity for all. This development makes people ever more vulnerable. Terror entrepreneurs find ever more willing followers, in all societies.

Whoever is socialized into a hierarchical context, and has learned to identify with descriptions of the world given by strongmen, is more than others vulnerable to voluntarily and passionately invest whatever personal sense of humiliation they may harbor into narratives offered by terror entrepreneurs. And those terror entrepreneurs may want to engage in terror for honor, or in terror in the name of war on terror.

Political scientist Mohammed Hafez reflected on the theme of humiliation and how it is seen from a certain Muslim perspective:

> The theme of humiliation relies on framing the war in Iraq as one in a series of aggressions and defeats by Muslims at the hands of "crusaders," "Zionists," and "apostates." Just as important, humiliation is as much about personal stories of suffering and indignity as it is about collective deprivations and grievances. The theme of impotence due to collusion resonates with the wider Muslim public who live under oppressive regimes that do not challenge U.S. hegemony and have failed Muslims time and again in Palestine, Chechnya, and Iraq. Not only are Muslim governments not fighting back, they are perceived as active collaborators in the humiliation and subjugation of Muslims. The theme of redemption through sacrifice is presented as the way out of the malaise. Groups frame martyrdom as an act of redemption, empowerment, and defiance against unjust authorities. Volunteers for suicide attacks are not brainwashed victims of opportunistic recruiters, nor are they manipulated individuals who are by calculating terrorists. Instead, groups portray suicide bombers as inspired individuals with heroic motivations seeking opportunities to fulfill their obligation to God, sacrifice for the nation, and avenge a grieving people.[35]

Chapter 6

Honor Is Like Armor, and Heroes Are Proud of Their Battle Wounds

Die Waffen nieder, or *Lay Down Your Arms!*, was the title of a novel in 1889. It brought its author, Baroness Bertha von Suttner, the Nobel Peace Prize in 1905. In that book she asks: "Don't ministers and diplomats have to avoid war?"[1] A diplomate explains this to her: "Do you think, Baroness, that it is always our duty to maintain peace? It would be a noble mission, but impracticable. We are charged to guard the interests of our respective States and dynasties, to watch against any threatened infringement of their powers, and to seize every opportunity for supremacy, jealously to maintain the honor of the land, and to avenge insult."

Bertha von Suttner describes how war is being portrayed to society:

> The supreme incentive to the noblest manly virtues, which are courage, endurance, and self-sacrifice; through it the greatest earthly glory can be attained; and, lastly, it is the most important factor in the progress of civilization. The mighty conquerors and founders of the so-called empires of the world, as Alexander, Caesar, Napoléon, were commended as the most notable examples of human greatness; the benefits and successes of war were set forth in most laudatory fashion, while the evils resulting therefrom were piously ignored – such as the moral and physical degeneration, the poverty, and the barbarism.[2]

Sociologist Max Weber, in his enthusiasm for war, wrote in 1916 during World War I that "death for the fatherland is the only death in which a man is sure to die for an earthly cause that is worth it," war represented to him "the dark majesty of this greatest of all trials."[3] In Weber's historical sociology, war was omnipresent, this is what historian Hinnerk Bruhns explains.[4] For Weber, war was a kind of natural phenomenon of political history, a form of unavoidable "eternal struggle of nations" (ewiges Ringen der Nationen), comparable to economic competition, only that economic war is conducted with "peaceful ammunition" (friedliche Kampfmittel).[5]

For Napoléon Bonaparte, Emperor of the French, honor meant to choose death over dishonorable peace.[6] The result was what could be called mass martyrdom. Many have suggested that Napoléon had a personal problem that drove him into suicidal homicide even more than others: He felt inferior compared to the ancient royal houses in Europe and this may have made "dishonorable peace" even more unpalatable to him than it might otherwise have been.[7] All ended in the Battle of Leipzig in 1813, when Napoléon's forces were defeated, then Paris captured, and in April 1814, Napoléon was forced to abdicate and was exiled to the island of Elba. By then, he had caused unprecedented and needless suffering. But the lesson was not learned. Also after defeat in the Franco-Prussian War of 1871, French popular literature and media still were filled with themes of honor and revenge. Paul Déroulède's 1872 *Songs of a Soldier* was sold in more than 100,000 copies. Here is an example:

> Revenge will come, perhaps slowly
> Perhaps with fragility, yet a strength that is sure
> For bitterness is already born and force will follow
> And cowards only the battle will ignore.[8]

The idea of humiliation and revenge also played a central role in the rise of Nazi-Germany after Germany's defeat in World War I in 1918. More than the defeat, what infuriated many Germans was the fact that, on June 28, 1919, the German government had signed the Treaty of Versailles. This treaty intentionally aimed to humiliate Germany so as to bring it down from aggressive arrogance and make it humble and less dangerous.[9] Yet, many Germans were not able to feel humbled; they felt dishonored and humiliated. Adolf Hitler later "surfed" on the accusation that this treaty was the *Schmach von Versailles* and a *Schanddiktat* (the "disgrace of Versailles" "dictated" on the country).

Clearly, humiliation was only one part in the overall quandary of Nazi Germany; the apocalyptic and cataclysmic politics that ensued "can come only from a mix of many other ideological and other factors, including eliminationist anti-Semitism, a profound racism that held the world to be composed of warring races in a struggle for dominance and survival, and a strategic vision and the opportunity to finally fulfill certain long-standing imperial aspirations."[10] When humiliation comes from "a sense of deep resentment at not being where one feels one belongs," from not being "on the throne of the world," this resentment may get harnessed into what historian Richard Landes calls an *active, cataclysmic apocalyptic movement* that kills millions of people.[11] The active agent of destruction in this movement is the "true believer" who thinks that "a massive cataclysm of destruction marks the imminent apocalyptic transition to the millennial world of perfection."[12]

When World War II was lost, and Hitler, in his bunker in Berlin, heard the Russian troops only a few meters away, and the entire city was in rubble, he still refused to capitulate. In 1932, he had laid out, in an open letter, that all problems of Germany had been caused by those German politicians who, with their signature in 1919 in Versailles, had consented to extortion, shame, and disgrace (*Schmach und Schande*).[13] He, Hitler was to set out to restore Germany's honor from the disgraceful signature in Versailles, not repeating it. The German refusal to surrender when the country was already hopelessly crushed, led to millions more unnecessary deaths.[14] Hitler delivered Germany to total destruction and himself to suicide.

Born in 1954, in a family displaced to what would become West Germany, I grew up in the midst of the aftermath of the "Hitlerzeit," witnessing how people around me lived with the memories and reverberations of this catastrophic time. From listening to them for decades, I sensed how the invocation of humiliation of honor indeed had served Hitler and his followers as a unifier, like a birth channel through which a great variety of other factors, from personal feelings to ideological constructs, could be brought into being: A monster was born through the birth channel of humiliation.

Peace researcher Johan Galtung speaks of the *deep culture* of a civilization, or the deep cosmology or deep code, and that this deep culture may contain codes and building blocks that dispose for, or legitimize violence.[15] Political scientist Stuart Kaufman speaks of *myth-symbol complexes*, which, given the opportunity to mobilize around them, may lead to violence.[16] Examples for such codes, blocks, or complexes are "militant, aggressive or violent customs and norms of action, connected to patriarchy and honor codes,"[17] connected also to the idea of being part of a cosmic Manichaean struggle between good and evil.[18] As it seems, there is a close relation between deep culture and violence.[19]

Maintaining honor, triumphing over humiliation, this is also the core narrative of much of present-day's terrorism. The designers of terror strategies perpetrate acts of terror to give humiliation back to whoever they point out as enemy. Books on terrorism typically touch upon humiliation, be it explicitly or implicitly. They describe feelings of humiliation and acts of humiliation – the sense of humiliation that brings its victims to wanting to triumph over humiliation by inflicting counter-humiliation through terror. Terminologies used are, for instance, grievance, disillusionment,[20] marginalization or alienation,[21] relative deprivation,[22] or horizontal inequalities.[23]

Whoever observes Da'esh, to give one example, notices that, indeed, they carefully emphasize the elements in the caliphate's history that symbolize the times when Islam had its honor intact and could triumph over humiliation. A person from the West might not immediately understand the symbolism of the black uniforms and flags that remind of the black robes of the Abbasids in the eighth century, Islam's Golden Age, when Iraq and the Levant were part of the great borderless Islamic caliphate.[24] Author Christopher Hitchens defends his use of the term "fascism with an Islamic face" by arguing that Islamism and fascism "both are bitterly nostalgic for past empires and lost glories. Both are obsessed with real and imagined 'humiliations' and thirsty for revenge."[25]

Stephen Holmes teaches at the New York University School of Law, and this is his view: "The mobilizing ideology behind 9/11 was not Islam, or even Islamic fundamentalism, but rather a specific narrative of blame."[26] Holmes points at Friedrich Nietzsche's classic study of resentment,[27] when he suggests that every sufferer seeks a "guilty" agent on whom feelings can be vented directly or in effigy: "If suffering is seen as natural or uncaused it will be coded as misfortune instead of injustice, and it will produce resignation rather than rebellion. The most efficient way to incite, therefore, is to indict."[28]

Honor is collective and ranked

Thomas Scheff, researcher on the sociology of emotions, once told a double joke in Yiddish and English that illustrates how the honor of masters is not the same as the honor of underlings:

> "Two Jews got into a fight. Neither managed to win the quarrel. Finally, they agreed to have a duel." This, explained Tom, is the first joke, because duels were something for aristocrats, not for insignificant Jewish underlings. "Next morning, before dawn, one of the opponents arrived at the little clearing in the forest where the duel was to take place. There he waited. And waited. And waited. His opponent did not come. He simply did not show up!" Now comes the second joke: "Finally, a messenger arrived with a note from the opponent. In the note, the opponent apologized for being late, and suggested that the other should already start with the duel without him!"[29]

Clearly, normally, honor was not funny. What we learn from Bertha von Suttner is that one hundred years ago, an individual's wish for peace – like her wish for peace – would be overruled by the honor of the collective, an honor that in her time was defined solely by its ruling elites, mostly men. There were the occasional female leaders, yet, a woman could only be a leader as long as she was imbued with the male ethos. If those elites believed that their honor was in need to be defended, they did not necessarily go to duel themselves, they sent out their people into duel-like wars, expecting them to sacrifice their lives. It was not important whether those who died were in agreement with their superiors decisions or not. Elites sent others into duel, they coopted inferiors into their personal affairs-of-honor by way of collective honor rhetoric.

In most societies with honor as organizing principle, two core aspects can be conceptualized: (1) honor is enforced by group pressure, and (2) honor is ranked insofar as higher-positioned individuals preside over subordinate ones, usually higher males over lesser males and females.

As to the first point, honor is played out as a collectively shaped universe of meaning, more so than pride and dignity (at least in the way I define those concepts in my work). Honor is a collective phenomenon that shapes everything from the micro to the meso and the macro level, from emotions to institutions. It is a learned response to group pressure, a pressure that affects the whole range of emotions and meta-emotions – or how people manifest feelings[30] – up to the norms and institutions in society at large. Sociologist Amitai Etzioni speaks of "normative paradigms," a set of informal values that contain both intellectual and affective elements which keep those who subscribe to them emotionally engaged in them.[31]

Second, in most cases, honor is linked to a vertical ranking of higher beings over lesser beings. In this ranking order, lesser beings are expected to go as far as die for the honor of their superiors. Inferiors are taught – and often successfully internalize – that this is their privilege and duty. From the point of view of "honorable men," peace-loving individuals like Bertha von Suttner are unpatriotic traitors. At best they are misguided and ignorant – due to "female weakness" in the case of women[32] – at worst they are peddling ill-intentioned malicious "love for the enemy."

On my journey around the world, I met only few cases where an oppressive hierarchy was somewhat cushioned and offset, namely, by the solidarity that a collective can also engender. One example I have already mentioned is the culture of the Nile Delta. I could observe at close hold how emotional warmth and empathy with peers could overrule respect for and fear of superiors. During my doctoral field work in Somalia, I learned about another variation. I learned that the humiliation of one clan member could be elevated to the collective level of clan humiliation from the bottom up, rather than imposed from the top down.[33] To use psychiatrist Vamik Volkan's theory of collective violence, individual trauma could be "elected" to be regarded as collective trauma in a bottom-up fashion.[34] Somalia's harsh semi-desert has spawned a culture of proud and independent warriors, where every man of a certain age is an elder.[35] An aggrieved clan member could attend a meeting of elders, present his personal case of grievance, and the council would decide as to whether to adopt this case as a collective responsibility to be avenged in the name of the clan, or not.

Viking culture, incidentally, had once developed in similar ways in its harsh Nordic region. Norwegians of today are still as proudly egalitarian as Somalis. Norwegians have, however, learned to leave behind violence, even though there is still an "alarming tendency to quarrel with their neighbors."[36]

In more hierarchically ranked societies, however, subordinates were not allowed to retain such an extent of personal pride. Instead, they learned the lesson of collective honor, often so well that they even ended their own lives when they failed honor. Many samurai took their own lives – and this was even ritualized – when they failed to defend their masters, or fell into dishonor in any other way, even if only by accident. And wherever female chastity was made to symbolize male honor, raped girls gave their lives "voluntarily" and committed suicide, rather than waiting for her family to resort to honor killing – even though the girl was the victim of aggression and not the perpetrator.

In Africa, Rwanda stands in stark contrast to Somalia. Genocidal killing was perpetrated in both countries, however, while in Somalia this was done by instrumentalizing its citizen's pride, in Rwanda, it was carried out by using their obedience.

I have lived in Japan for three years (combined). The work done by David Matsumoto and Sachiko Ide supports my view that politeness in Asia is not so much a question of individual volition and choice but rather a question of social structures and the fear enshrined in them.[37] Under the Tokugawa shogunate, the last feudal Japanese military government which existed from 1603 to 1867, the majority of the Japanese population lived in fear of their superiors, even in fear for their lives. Only a small minority of the ruling elite was spared this fear. A samurai had the right to kill commoners for perceived affronts, it was called *kiri-sute gomen*, or "authorization to cut and leave" the body of the victim. Japanese language encodes this fear at the very core of its expressions of politeness, as it employs specific personal pronouns for each person according to gender, age, rank, degree of acquaintance, and other cultural factors. Politeness is thus mostly based on the fear enshrined in what in Japan is called *wakimae*, or "finding one's place" within prescribed social norms.

I began learning Chinese when I was nineteen years old, it was in Germany in 1973, when few in the Western world were interested in Chinese. I learned that in Chinese social relations and everyday speech *face* refers to the social perceptions of a person's prestige and authority (*mianzi*, Chinese 面子), and to the confidence and trust in a person's moral character within a social network (*lian*, Traditional Chinese: 臉, Simplified Chinese 脸).[38] So-called polite lies are not just acceptable, they are expected.

Honor in Iraq can be described with three words: *sharaf, ithiram,* and *ird*. Victoria Fontan, scholar of conflict resolution and peace studies, reported from her fieldwork in Iraq that *sharaf* is honor bestowed on a man whose service or lineage are found deserving by his peers; *ithiram* is the honor he can gain by imposing himself on others by force; and *ird* is the honor measured according to his success in protecting his women from intruders.[39] *Sharaf* is something that is being given to a man – he can only invite it through benevolent actions – while *ithiram* and *ird* depend on him and his ability to impose his will on his environment. Together, these three elements describe the standing a man can claim to have in his social context.[40] Women are his substrate.

Also in other cultural realms, honor is regarded as either derived from a lineage or gained through personal achievement. In the Filipino language, humiliation means *pagkapahiya* or "being shamed" or "being hurt" and it connotes "losing one's face." For the Muslims living in the Philippines, since their religious, cultural, ethnic, and historical conditions are different, the concept of humiliation also includes "humiliation as an affront to their religion and culture."[41]

In Europe and the United States, "pistols at ten paces" and other forms of dueling were once common.[42] Two men whose portraits adorn contemporary American dollar bills were involved in duels.[43] The most famous political duels were fought in Missouri between Charles Lucas and Thomas Hart Benton, who killed Lucas in 1817. For Lucas, honor was part of his descendance from Norman nobility, while Benton rather sought honor through his own actions.[44] The practice faded in the north of the United States in the early nineteenth century, while staying strong in the south and west.

Dueling persists in rural areas in some developing nations until now, yet, more importantly, its spirit still informs the deep structure of modern-day cultural scripts in all world regions.[45] Historian Donald Kagan suggests that at the national level, honor reigns in today's world no less than it did earlier, only that "national honor" is now partly concealed by human rights rhetoric and no longer invoked as openly as in the past.[46]

Sociologist Erving Goffman (1922–1982) introduced the concept of *face* into social theory as a sociological universal. Face, according to him, is a mask that people strive to maintain in social situations.[47] Research in social psychology has since confirmed that the social humiliation of losing face can lead to retaliation even at the cost self-damage.[48] As mentioned above, also philosopher Emmanuel Lévinas speaks of the face. However, there is an interesting difference between both, in resonance with my differentiation between honor humiliation and dignity humiliation: while Goffman looks from within the *Zeitgeist* of honor on face as a *mask*, Lévinas gives voice to the new *Zeitgeist* of dignity when he highlights the face of the *Other*.[49]

The collectivist character of honor means that it is worn like a masklike armor. People may defend their group's honor against humiliators merely out of duty, without feeling any particular personal emotion. People may find themselves caught in games of honor beyond their control – *affaires d'honneur* important to their group – without themselves identifying with these affaires as individuals.

As noted before, I spent seven years in Cairo, Egypt (1984 – 1991), where I worked as a psychological counselor and clinical psychologist, first at the American University in Cairo, and then at my own private practice in Cairo from 1987 to 1991. I once counseled an Egyptian lawyer who had studied in Europe and had almost forgotten his roots in the Egyptian countryside where blood feuds were common. One day, to his great surprise and shock, he was visited by villagers who told him that he was next in line to be killed. He knew neither why nor by whom. He had done nothing to elicit other people's hatred. His place in the genealogy of his extended family was sufficient to give him a place in the honor game.

Albania could serve as another example for honor's nature as armor that is put onto an individual by the collective. Blood feuds were officially banned during the 40-year rule of Albania's communist-era Enver Hoxha, but in the chaos that accompanied the fall of communism in the early 1990s, the practice resurfaced. Under the ancient Albanian code called *kanun* (law), the victim's family invokes its right to take revenge on any male adult in the extended family who caused the loss of one of their members. As a result, hundreds of children across Albania are now living virtually imprisoned in their homes for fear of being killed, even though they themselves would wish for nothing more than being liberated from this collective yoke.[50]

The label *honor-shame culture* versus *guilt culture* was popularized by anthropologist Ruth Benedict.[51] During my years in Japan, I met many, who, like Japanese psychoanalyst Takeo Doi, found her analysis humiliating, because she ranked American (Christian) guilt culture higher than Japanese shame culture.[52] Benedict described American (Christian) culture as a guilt culture, where the individual's internal conscience counts most, and Japanese culture as a shame culture, where the emphasis is on how outsiders perceive a person's moral conduct.

During my time in Japan, I had the privilege to learn about *amae*, or "sweetness in interdependence."[53] Takeo Doi translates *amaeru* as "helplessness" and the desire to be loved. My sense is that in Japan, people have been caught in the harshest of hierarchies for centuries, and it is this frame that made them "helpless." In such a harsh context, the "helplessness" of *amae* is not a sign of weakness – as outsiders might misattribute – but of resilience. Resilience in the way Egyptians have learned to defy their occupiers for the past two thousand years by forging relationships of warmth among themselves, or in the way "slave culture" has carved out niches of livability for their members.[54] Natsume Soseki (1867 – 1916) was introduced earlier, one of the premier philosophers and novelists of modern Japan, who called on his compatriots to learn a spirit of individualism vis-à-vis the state. Also novelist and essayist Sakaguchi Ango (1906 – 1955) called for *shutaisei* – true subjectivity or autonomy at the individual level – meaning that each individual should create his or her own "samurai ethic," his or her own "emperor system" to resist the indoctrinating power of the state.[55]

In my work, I draw all lines of thought together and recommend a combination of *shutaisei* with *amae*: In Japan, many people may indeed benefit from acquiring more *shutaisei*, now that the shogunate is bygone history, while in the West, people would benefit from acquiring more *amae*. *Shutaisei* needs *amae*, and *amae* needs *shutaisei*: individual autonomy needs loving solidarity, none can be beneficial without the other.

While Ruth Benedict presumably did not intend to instrumentalize research to help maintain Western preeminence and humiliate others, others in academia might be less interested in serving all of humanity and more focused on furthering particular aims. Lately, also "Arab culture" has been subsumed into the honor-shame category, and as it seems, even torture methods have been shaped with the help of this categorization.[56] For Africa, a power-fear category has been added, used by Christian missionaries.[57]

As mentioned before, I use the Weberian *ideal-type* approach, which allows for different levels of abstraction, and I do find all abstract categorizations very interesting, yet, only as long as they are complemented by highlighting complexity and diversity at others levels.[58] Furthermore, I am not interested in simply "understanding other cultures," and certainly not in facilitating any missionary desire. I am interested in understanding how we – we as humankind, we as global human family – may unite enough so that our diversity does not transmute into hostile division. This is important particularly now, as we live in times when our global interconnectedness can quickly amplify hostility to the point where it spells the extinction of our species. I am fascinated and inspired by the diversity I encounter around the globe, both cultural and biological diversity, and I feel deeply enriched by the potential for love that I observe that all humans share, which, to my view, can serve as a starting point from which future global unity can emerge.

Honor predates religion. When I lived in Egypt, many of the Muslims and Christians I met shared more of the honor culture among them than I shared with either group. The differences between them were small compared with their distance from a dignity culture. Still, I had no problem understanding their honor approach, even understanding it deeply, and the reason was that I grew up in a displaced family in Europe, many of whose members had been recruited into fundamentalist Christian orientations that share the same mindset. In other words, I had learned already early in life that Christian faith does not necessarily contradict the honor code, on the contrary, it can even prop it up.

Anybody familiar with the Mafia in deeply catholic Italy will be able to discern the elements of honor there.[59] *Omertà* is a code of silence that speaks directly to the masklike nature of honor and its links to humiliation and humility. It is a code of honor that dictates non-cooperation with authorities, and non-interference in the illegal actions of others. In Corsican language: "Cu è surdu, orbu e taci, campa cent' anni 'mpaci" or "Who is deaf, blind and silent, lives 100 years in peace." The word *omertà* has been linked to Latin *humilitas*,[60] yet, it seems to rather stem from the archaic male concept of honor. The *Oxford English Dictionary* traces the word to the Spanish word *hombredad*, meaning manliness, modified after the Sicilian word *omu* for man. A man is manly when he is his own boss, when he does not bow to rulers (except to his own "Mafia" rulers). *Omertà* originated and remains common in Southern Italy, it is also rooted in rural Crete, Sardinia and Corsica, and it has since been "exported" into the rest of the world wherever Italian neighborhoods have established themselves.

It is not surprising that also terror groups use *omertà* as a tool. The so-called Hofstadgroup in The Netherlands, for instance, operates just like the Italian mafia: "Those who do not honor the oath of silence – the Islamist *Omertà* – will be liquidated."[61]

The code of secrecy is well suited for illegal activities in general, and drug trafficking is another apt example. Just in these days its influence increases, as the demand for drugs rises due to the social fabric of societies and the mental health of individuals being worn down, turning them into customers for drugs. The winners are Mafia-type enterprises that peddle illegal drugs, and the pharmaceutical industry that profits from selling legal drugs. Even strong states are now increasingly unable to maintain "law and order," risking to bring back times in which endemic, and sometimes epidemic, banditry reigned, all bound by honor codes.[62] The spectrum is wide and includes everything from "Robin Hood banditry" to Mafia, to secret orders.

To formulate it in terms of the security dilemma, what happens in such cases is that groups create artificial borders around themselves – walls of secrecy rather than walls of brick or steel. In this way, they create their own secret "state," be it in opposition to unwanted authority, or as a safe haven in the absence of authority, or as mediators between different authorities, or a combination of all.[63] The fact that these secret formations use the honor code so radically and uncompromisingly as the Mafia does, proves how effective the honor code is in forming a streamlined collective force, able to withstand domination and able to dominate. The security dilemma represents the very blueprint of a context that has brought to the fore such adaptations.

How come that in the West the honor code is less relevant now? "The earliest recorded use of 'to humiliate' meaning to mortify or to lower or to depress the dignity or self-respect of someone does not occur until 1757," this was a sentence that startled me when I first read it in 1997 in the book on humiliation and honor by legal scholar William Ian Miller.[64] What Miller observed was that the collectivist masklike nature of honor, the face as a mask, changed in the English language in 1757, and transmuted into less masklike and more individualistic dignity.[65] His observation resonates with my intuition that humankind is in the process of traversing a historical path, still with an uncertain outcome, from masklike collectivist and ranked honor to the equal dignity of each single individual, and that this process evolves gradually. The notions of *decorum* and *dignitary*, for instance, represent an intermediary stage, a bridge between ranked honor and equal dignity, as they already apply to individuals but still rank them: *dignitaries* are individuals of higher rank.[66]

When Miller looked into the *Oxford English Dictionary* (*OED*), he observed that the *OED* usually prefers the *state* to the *feeling* in its glosses for the various forms of *humiliate*, and that it does not define humiliation or related words as an emotion. Then he found a few incidences where emotion began to shine through and humiliation impliedly was understood as an emotion, namely, in cases where *mortification* and *mortify* were explained as meaning "the feeling of humiliation," and "to feel humiliated."[67]

Even though Miller cautions against making claims that are too grand, he intuits the effects of romanticism, industrialization, and capitalism on the articulation and conceptualization of the individual and the self. Miller reflects:

> One could hazard the claim that as late as the seventeenth century the self did not feel emotions at all; instead the emotions were borne almost as a quasi-juridical status or as allegorical personae that the subject put on masklike. When one was sad, one became the character Sadness in a moral and social drama, with its behavior thus constrained by the role. But when one could at last feel sad, sadness became a feeling, a perturbation of the nerves coupled with the effects of the thoughts one might have about that perturbation. The new self could thus be something more than its feelings; it

> could be more detached from them, more ironical, perhaps more restrained, and definitely more self-conscious. And this last characteristic – self-consciousness – might also tend to make this new self more likely to feel such emotions as humiliation and embarrassment than heretofore. This claim may seem a bit mystifying, but it is not without some reason. It is reasonably consistent with some of the drift of Norbert Elias's work.[68]

William Fulbecke (born 1559/60, died in or after 1602) was a lawyer, legal scholar, and historian, who did pioneering work in international law. In 1602, he laid out what a religious man may or may not do in the rite of *homage* or *hommage*, a rite whereby a noble man became the "man," "homme," or vassal of another man in the feudal system. The lord would give his vassal protection and a fief (land providing a means of subsistence), and in return, the vassal would promise annual military service to his lord. What Fulbecke criticized with this custom was that a religious man belongs to God, and, therefore, he should avoid formulating his allegiance to his lord in ways that compromise his relationship with God. In short, a religious man should not say *Ego deuenio homo vester* (I am going to be your man[69]) and thus "humiliate himselfe to execute the rite of homage." This is the counsel Fulbecke gave to a religious man in 1602:

> By our law he may do homage: but may not say to his Lord *Ego deuenio homo vester*, because he hath professed himselfe to be onely God his man, but he may say: I do vnto you homage, and to you shalbe faithfull and loyall.[70]

Indeed, when reading these lines, it becomes clear that it is not a personal emotion of humiliation that was at stake in Fulbecke's time; what we see is the description of a place in a collectivist ranking order, with a god at the top, whose primacy ought to be respected. Honor had the power to enclose and hide people behind a mask or an armor. And honor was both a yoke and a protection.

As mentioned earlier, I was able to understand the protective aspect of honor better during my doctoral research in Somalia. I learned how a personal grievance could be brought before a council of elders, who then decided whether to elevate it from the level of one member to the level of the entire group.[71] The aggrieved person would feel very gratified if the clan associated itself with her case of humiliated honor and promised to act on it as a group. This group cohesion, however, was not necessarily stable; the aggrieved person and the clan would need to skillfully and proactively maintain it after the initial decision; some clan members would always resent having to join in redressing a violation they did not suffer themselves. Yet, in practice, collective action to be taken in the face of honor humiliation could be created bottom-up. The founding father of Somali studies, anthropologist Ioan Lewis, praised the advantages of this *pastoral democracy*, and how it makes possible a bottom-up process of honor in an egalitarian pastoral context driven by individual clan members' personal sense of being slighted.[72]

In other societies, however, particularly in those depending on agriculture, and in the face of a strong security dilemma, the trope of honor humiliation turned into a culturally defined top-down script that functioned also in the absence of any bottom-up process. Honor humiliation turned into a core pillar of the dominator model of society, to use Riane Eisler's terminology, independent of anybody's individual inner urge to redress it. Even if nobody from above explicitly steered it, it was still top-down insofar as it was seen to be divinely-ordained.

The Islamic prophet Muhammad was born on the Arabian peninsula into a strong clan culture of honor and vengeance. Many might not know that he was a revolutionary who attempted to overcome this code. In his Farewell Sermon that he delivered toward the end of his life, he ascertained that "Abolished are also the blood-revenges of the Days of Ignorance."[73] Muhammad often broke all rules of honor, for instance, when he entered into the Treaty of Hudaybiyyah with the Quraish tribe of Mecca. Muhammad accepted utterly humiliating conditions, a behavior that was unheard of in his time. In other words, Muhammad did not necessarily act in alignment with the honor code of his time, on the contrary, in many ways and on many levels, he attempted to transform and overcome it.[74]

Clearly, his revolution failed, at least to a large extent. The honor culture proved to be very strong. The leaders of Da'esh, for instance, rather that aiming to manifest the revolutionary spirit of their prophet, follow the very honor rules he aimed to overcome.

The fact that honor in most cases is not just collective but also ranked, has myriad consequences. There is a basic human desire for connection and belonging, or what Thomas Scheff calls the need for a secure social bond.[75] Scheff focuses on the notion of shame and how shame signals a threat to this bond. In a system of domination and submission, the social bond that Scheff refers to entails two fundamentally different kinds of bonds, namely, bonds between equals, and bonds between unequals. One could also call them horizontal and vertical bonds, each very different from the other. While shame between equals is a signal that a bond of mutuality is threatened, shame between unequals signals that a bond of domination/submission is threatened. In a domination/ submission system, shame means dishonor, losing rank, or even life, thus a truly terrifying threat.

In a dominator society, only the bond between equals at the very top of society is comparably free and unrestrained, as it faces the pressure of the security dilemma unmediated. Since underlings usually form the majority of the population in such a context, all other bonds – also horizontal bonds among equals in lower strata – are defined by and restrained within the web of vertical bonds between masters and underlings. Underlings are bonded to their duty to self-efface and to submit to being tools in their masters' hands. They are in bondage to the masters' expectations, among them that underlings ought to show love and respect to their masters and share in their masters' hatred for whoever the masters had chosen to identify as enemy.[76]

In dominator societies, bonds often represent bondage more than connection, and it is only in the context of equality in dignity that connections can be liberated from bondage and be called connection. In our work, both psychologist Linda Hartling and I therefore prefer to replace the term *bond* with other expressions, such as, for instance, *connection*, because the term "bond" elicits too much of an association with "bondage."

Also sociologist Pierre Bourdieu gave a lot of thought to honor.[77] He describes honor as a game of challenge and counterchallenge:

- to challenge a person is to accord him a certain dignity, for it connotes a recognition of equality
- to challenge a person incapable of responding is to dishonor oneself
- only a challenge coming from an equal deserves to be taken up[78]

In traditional honor societies, elites are socialized into translating perceptions and feelings of humiliation into an urge to fight back, with the aim to win the competition for domination with rivals. They defend their honor against humiliation with the sword in duels, or in duel-like wars. Over time, ever more lethal weapons were developed to achieve ever more "competitive" forms of competition for domination. At the same time, underlings were given no choice but to put their lives on line for their masters. Inferiors had no right to invoke humiliation as a violation of their honor when superiors inflicted it. Inferiors were expected to engage in quiet obedience when they were used and abused by their superordinates. They had to accept humiliation as a conduit to humility. This is the system of emotions and meta-emotions that I call honor humiliation – with all their cultural, political, social, and psychological scripts for action and institutional structures.

In a ranked society, aristocrats have more honor than their subordinates. Honor humiliation for elites means a license to become enraged and seek redress, while for inferiors it is the opposite. Inferiors do not have the privilege to become enraged when humiliated, on the contrary, they have the duty to swallow all pain, deny rage, and, instead, force themselves to obediently feel loving respect for their superiors, however oppressive they may be. A beaten wife, a beaten child, for instance, is expected to thank her tormentor for his love: "For whom the Lord loveth he chasteneth, And scourgeth every son whom he receiveth," we learn from the Bible's New Testament.[79] A beaten wife cannot challenge her husband to duel.

In this context, it was an expression of equality, when also lower classes adopted dueling.[80] Thomas Scheff's joke told earlier illustrates how the honor of masters was not the same as the honor of underlings, and how, when inferiors tried it out, they did not necessarily understand its rules correctly.

Even in death, the difference between superiors and inferiors was upheld. Ruling men were eligible for privileged execution, in contrast to their underlings. The "blood eagle," for instance, was an exceptionally gruesome method of execution for particularly "worthy" enemies.[81] In other cases, execution methods were chosen that avoided the spilling of royal blood,[82] or the shedding of the blood of those with higher powers.[83]

In traditional honor based societies, each social stratum – be it called caste, class, group, or subgroup – cultivates indigenous idiosyncratic scripts of honor. The honor of a slave is different from the honor of a master, but both defend their honor, if they can, against attempts by equals or superiors to push them further down, or attempts from below to pull them down. The servant or slave – the words *servant* and *to serve* stem from the Latin word *servus*, meaning slave – who works in the emperor's private suite, for instance, would attach honor to this important rank and resist being degraded to the quarries. Every stratum in a hierarchical society has its own honor code, including the very lowest ranks. Everybody resists being debased into a rank that is lower than she feels entitled to. For a wife, this might mean that she even craves that her husband beats her as a sign that he sees her. For a religious person, this might mean to ask for debasement on earth when this translates into a higher rank in afterlife.

Social systems of ranked honor are always vulnerable. The master-slave dyad is continuously fragile, as already philosopher Georg Wilhelm Friedrich Hegel has observed.[84] It needs to be confirmed and defended continuously. If a ruler did not hold down his subordinates in their *sub* position, he was called "lazy." As mentioned earlier, the "lazy kings" (*les rois fainéants*) of the sixth and seventh centuries CE in France, for example, were ridiculed because they allowed their immediate subordinates, the *maires du palais*, the managers of the palace, to usurp power – one of these official functionaries indeed eventually took over the throne in the year 751.

This is where terror becomes relevant. Throughout history, those in power routinely employed terror tactics on their common people, so as to maintain their subjugation:

> The Argentine and Chilean military terrorized segments of their respective populations during the 1970s as a means of securing political control they had recently acquired.[85] Josef Stalin systematically terrorized through large-scale execution and incarceration during the 1930s to solidify his position as Premier in the USSR,[86] the Slobodan Milosevic regime promoted ethnic cleansing in an attempt to maintain Serbian control of Bosnia and Kosovo,[87] and Saddam Hussein terrorized the Kurdish and Shi'ite communities in Iraq that opposed his dictatorial regime. State terrorism can also take place indirectly. Such is the case when one nation supports a rebel group's terrorist activities in a rival nation it wants to weaken, such as current Pakistani support of Kashmiri rebels and clandestine U.S. support of Nicaraguan "freedom fighters" (Contras) in the 1980s.[88]

The Danish cartoon drawings and their effects may conclude this sub-section. Abid Raja is a Norwegian lawyer and politician for the Liberal Party (*Venstre*). He was born in Oslo into a family of Pakistani descent in 1975. In 2010, he was awarded the Fritt Ord Honorary Award of Freedom of Speech. I summarize some of Raja's thought-provoking reflections and translate them from Norwegian:

> The Danish cartoon drawings create hatred only because a common platform for conversational dialogue is lacking. The drawings were seen as a slap against Muslims, as warfare by way of the intellectual pen, with the strong reaction that it triggered being instrumentalized as "confirmation" of Islamic "barbarism." Those who made these drawings, knew about the consequences in Pakistan. If you think that

the drafters did not know this, then you're naive. They knew that in Pakistan, most people are illiterate, they cannot react with the pen, just with the sword. And respect for the Prophet is more important for them than even respect for God, since they have a more personal relationship with the Prophet. First, they experience personal and then social humiliation, and then come these drawings on top of this humiliation, as a sophisticated form of terror.[89]

Honor is linked to gender

> *"That foolish boy, what he knew? I carried him for nine months. I took care of him. I fed him when he was hungry. Then he will take people country and give it away?"*
>
> – Mother of a young man in Liberia, Africa, tired of the unimaginable brutality of male supremacy in her country[90]

On my global path, I have sometimes been a man and sometimes a woman, or, more precisely, I have been part of male spheres and female spheres in societies. In 1998, I witnessed something a woman was not supposed to participate in (and, indeed, I made a point to be an observing guest only).[91] In Somalia, *khat*-chewing sessions are a celebration of male glory, glory longingly yearned for while unattainable.[92] I understood first-hand how noble male warriors are proud of standing up straight and never bowing, and how they feel depressed when there is no arena for them to stand straight. They would rather die than do "lowly" work. They look down on farmers who bow down to work their fields. And they apply similar contempt to their toiling women, those who keep society together and feed their idly depressed men. "Women are oppressed and men depressed" was an evocative saying I often heard not only in Somalia. It fits many places as impeccably, both in Africa and beyond.

Males dream of glory in many places around the world. In the United States, in 2016, millions of unworking men in the prime of life are out of work and are *not* looking for work, rather sitting in front of screens, stoned, watching fictions of male glory.[93] There is an army of prime-age men out there, with an abundance of time, yet, they do not contribute to society. They could do charitable work, religious activities, volunteering, child care, or help in the home. They do not do so.[94] Zero status work would be worse than depressed idle dreaming.[95] "America's quiet catastrophe: millions of idle men," writes the *Washington Post*.[96]

How come that "women are oppressed and men depressed"? Why is it that men prey on women and girls? Why do societies shame the victims? Why do governments fail to punish deadly crimes? Why does the world deny itself the fruits of women's full participation? These were questions asked by former United Nations Secretary-General Ban Ki-moon on November 25, 2016.[97]

Not far away from the United Nations headquarters in New York City, you find the Metropolitan Opera. Opera offers vivid history lessons regarding those questions. It makes intensely palpable how honor, love, and war were profoundly intertwined during the past millennia. On October 29, 2016, I saw the opera *Guilleme Tell* by Gioachino Rossini that had its world premiere in Paris in 1829.[98] Mathilde is a Habsburg princess and she is in love with a man who is too low in rank for her. She encourages him to work for their love by going back to the battle field to gain glory and honor. She sings: "He is worthy of my love, yes. In the one who loves you, yes, it is honor itself that rules." Her lover replies, "In the one I love, yes, it is honor itself that rules."[99] In other words, Mathilde, by playing by the rules of honor, lets honor rule love. *Turandot*, brought to us by Giacomo Puccini, was a different woman.[100] Turandot was a feminist in her time – twelfth-century[101] – when feminism was unthinkable. In many ways her story foreshadows that of later pioneers, such as Bertha von Suttner (1843 – 1914), or Rosa Mayreder (1858 – 1938), or contemporary women such as Nilüfer Göle, who all build bridges between the past and the future.[102] Turandot's story is set in a time when opposing war and resisting the dictates of honor could only be expressed in the form of "crazy" behavior, and this was precisely what Turandot turned to. She was a princess who used the tools available to her in her time for denying her participation: First, she expressed her resistance to forced marriage by placing the hurdles for any suitor so high that it meant certain death for them. When finally one suitor succeeded to gain her hand, against all expectation, she implored her father to refrain from giving her away like a slave.

Today, the Nobel Peace Prize is given to people who work for ending war, and women are no longer to be treated like chattel. And what I conceptualize as *big love* is more than only a personal experience of love, as it is for Turandot at the end of the opera, when she eventually does fall in love with her suitor.[103]

Radames, the Egyptian military commander in the opera *Aida*, was a man capable of truly great love, yet, he was trapped between love for his country and love for the daughter of the enemy, Aida. He paid with his life for betraying the first for the latter.[104] Any *Homo honoris* culture, any *Homo dominans* culture forces people into brutal choices between different loves. At the present point in time, if humankind is to create a future worth living in, *big love* needs to be elevated to the level of a global *Homo amans* culture – a loving being culture – that brings together all of humankind into one united family.

As we see, honor ranking is profoundly linked to gender. The dominator model places men at the top and women down. Allow me to be personal. In my global life, I have experienced, very directly, how men can view women as sexual objects, and how men in power can regard access to "women" as their due reward. Men in high positions, men for whom I felt the highest of respect, whom I regarded as my esteemed grandfatherly mentors, suddenly arranged for our next meeting in a bedroom. I remember how I once backed out in shock, and, initially, was so ashamed on his behalf that I pretended, for his sake, that it never happened.

It took me years to understand that it was the exceptionality of my father that had provided me with false expectations. My father is an exception insofar as he went through war experiences that were so traumatic that he learned to renounce any form of male supremacy and became a profoundly humane and wise human being, deeply respectful of women. After I had grown up, I ventured out into the world and found myself in an unexpected reality, a reality that was profoundly humiliating to me. This experience repeated itself over the years in very different contexts and different ways: Here, I was, a human being just like all men, with an educational background matching few, wishing to learn from respected elders on my path to serve humanity, and some of these elders suddenly and unexpectedly degraded me into a sexual object. The idea of a sexual encounter with these men was so far outside of my ability to imagine, that I could not even think of it without nausea. Not enough, also my wish to find a truly equal life partner to create a family was fraught with the same problem, only that it took me more time to detect it. I had discounted the habit of many younger men to grope and molest as simply "immature" and had learned to keep safe distance in the streets of this world. Still, I kept my hopes up for more respectful inter-human encounters with men who would be more reflected. The experiences I went through all too often taught me otherwise; they taught me about the destructiveness of the dominator script, into which men have no choice but to be socialized. This script makes blind, and few reflect as deeply as my father, even men who profess their respect for women as equals in rhetoric. My father's support made me strong, yet, on the other side, it left me also very unprepared, so unprepared that the subsequent humiliation cost me years of tears. In my book *Gender, Humiliation, and Global Security*, I therefore call on fathers to embrace their responsibility to reflect deeply on themselves, and then to both support and prepare their daughters.

When I share my personal experiences here, my personal life is not what I wish to highlight. I rather see a learning path in front of me, a path out of the male dominator script toward the partnership script, a learning path that concerns all of society. It is not just a question of individual culpability. I myself am no exception on this learning path. Also I was caught in the masculine script when I was young. Also I initially failed to grasp and adequately formulate why concepts such as "warriors for peace" are inherently self-contradictory. It took me long to understand why war-like rhetoric such as "fighting," "combatting" or "battling" against the ills of this world, or for a better future, is counterproductive. I have therefore no problem putting myself into the shoes of young people who feel fired up by ideals of warriorhood.

Anthropologist Helen Fisher is known for her work on the biology of love and attraction, and she found four personality styles in her research on brain chemistry and romantic love. She found the "explorer," who expresses primarily the dopamine system, the "builder" (serotonin), the "director" (testosterone), and the "negotiator" (estrogen).[105] When I look at these categories, I would say that throughout the past millennia, males more often than women were allowed and expected to be explorers, directors, and builders, builders of empires, while women were given the task to build homes and create harmony. I myself started out as explorer-director when I was young, hoping to negotiate my way to building a family, unaware that I still lacked the skills of a negotiator and builder. It took me decades to express all four styles. Now I am an explorer who is curious and creative, who goes out into the world, I am a director who is analytical and firm rather than aggressive, and I am a compassionate negotiator who attempts to support all those who also engage in global family building. Considering traditional gender scripts, I first expressed the male explorer and director script, and complemented it later with the female script of lovingly building a home, in my case, a global home. My father has shown me the way, something I only understood very slowly. I still have to learn to reach out better to those who are afraid of being explorers and who lack negotiator skills – the dogmatic and dictatorial builders and directors so to speak – and give them the courage to allow the fullness of their potential to unfold. In the last chapter of my book on gender, I recommend women of my age, those who have had a chance to hone all of their capabilities, to shoulder their responsibility for the global family by heeding research results that indicate that society needs collectives of peacemaking women as main stewards of resources and containers of potential male aggressiveness.[106]

Philosopher Michel Foucault's views on power and domination seems to have traversed a similar learning journey like mine. In 1972, he still put strong emphasis on power as domination.[107] In 1976, he seems to have changed his mind when he stated that "one cannot make revolution through terror," because "we cannot create inspiration for the revolution by sowing terror among the people."[108] In 1982, he admitted that he had overemphasized domination and power,[109] and in 1984, he stated that power "should be given legal rules, techniques of management and also of morality, an ethos, a practice of self, so that the games of power can be played with a minimum of domination."[110]

The security dilemma pushes for gender segregation, which, in turn, slides into gender ranking, or what is called patriarchy. In my book on gender, I describe the differentiation between *inside* and *outside* realms and how I encountered it everywhere I went on this globe. I describe the traditional role description for females, namely, to stay *inside* to nurture the next generation and maintain everything that is inside, be it in the private sphere of the house, the space within city walls, or the internal administration of a state as we see in a country such as Norway. Males, in contrast, are expected to shape what is called the *outside* public sphere and to secure the border between both spheres. Originally, sending men out to protect women might not have translated into men being worth more than women. Yet, the female realm eventually moved into a subordinate position in relation to the male sphere. Eventually, maleness became associated with "activity," "productivity," "conscious and moral/logical strategizing," while the female aspect was regarded as, and made to be, passive, unproductive, unconscious and "amoral/alogical."[111]

Philosopher Friedrich Wilhelm Nietzsche (1844 – 1900) became famous for the quote, "You go to women, do not forget the whip!" – the man shall be brought up for war, he wants danger and diversion, while the woman shall reinvigorate the warrior and be his most dangerous toy, all else, to Nietzsche, "is folly."[112]

All major religions developed negative views on women, women as potential spoilers of male purity and honorable courage.[113] When World War I was lost, sociologist Max Weber wrote:

> Instead of looking for "the guilty one" after a war, as old women would do – whereas it is the structure of society that produces war – any male and somber attitude will say to the enemy: "We lost the war – you have won it. This is now behind us: Now let's talk about what consequences are to be drawn in accordance with the objective interests that were involved – the main thing – given the responsibility of the future, which primarily burdens the winner." Anything else is undignified and will avenge itself. A nation can forgive the violation of their interests, but not the violation of their honor….[114]

Even today, few women are included in the public spheres of the world. In 2015, fifteen years after the Security Council adopted the ground-breaking resolution 1325 on Women, Peace and Security, women's participation is still "symbolic or low," also in those peace initiatives where the UN plays a key role.[115]

All around the world, I have met highly aware, educated, enlightened, and self-reflective men, men asserting that they respected women as equals, who still saw wo-men as no-men. I observe that traditional socialization sits very deep, also today, leading young men to be constantly alert of the task to remain a man. This includes avoiding to listen to female perspectives on life and the world, lest he might become a no-man and lose his masculinity. A boy learns that it is his foremost task to remain on the right side, to keep only men as his reference group, with women suitable, at best, as no-man assistants. Gender identities are not conceived of as a continuum connected by shared humanity. Rather, men and women are seen as opposites, thus giving priority to gender over shared humanity. Even highly educated men have given me historical explanations and justifications for this worldview. I was told that men and women are enemies because in ancient times women once ruled, but men, with their superior capabilities, at some point managed to defeat women. Men thus accomplished to contain unruly and chaotic female irrationality by way of male rationality, and therefore, men now have the responsibility to prevent women from realizing their childish plans to get to the top again and bring chaos over the world once more.

Indeed, all this is not a story of the past. By now, in 2017, "the women's movement around the world is facing a backlash that hurts both men and women," informs the United Nations Human Rights Chief.[116] The *manosphere* (man plus blogosphere), or *androsphere*, or *mandrosphere*, has been mentioned earlier.[117] Conservative political commentator Rush Limbaugh is one of many voices who laments the "chickification" or the "sissying" of society by a trend toward being "soft and weak," an indication of the "emasculation or castration" of men in society.[118]

"Being the products of vertical gender structures many men know only verticality, fearing the alternative," observes Johan Galtung.[119] Some men cannot imagine that feminists might not hate men, might not wish to subjugate men, but rather wish to nurture something new, namely, equal dignity. "Political correctness!" has become another word for "humiliation!" cried out by those who cannot imagine shared humility.

Limbaugh and his colleagues seem to be unaware that, as the world becomes more interconnected and complex, it is not due to male cowardice or female vice when traditional "female" scripts of negotiation come to the fore. It is not male cowardice or female vice when gender categories soften up, it is the waning of the classical security dilemma in a shrinking world, and with it, the waning of a clear-cut enemy image.[120] The novel geopolitical situation is responsible. The war that is ongoing in Syria while I write these lines is a good example for how identifying distinct enemies becomes ever more difficult. It no longer makes sense to call on men to prove their maleness by "mustering the courage to hit hard."

Likewise, it is a perilous path to associate male dominance with sexual potency and the erected penis: "The most common cause of impotence is stress and tension, reinforced by the supposed ideal of male omnipotence."[121] Every fifth man in Germany, just to give one example, suffers from erectile dysfunctions.

Ebrahim B. is a young man from Wolfsburg in Germany, the city of Volkswagen, where young men like him were an integrated part of society without any apparent grievances. He is the first German IS-returnee who now talks openly in front of a camera.[122] By now, he distances himself from Da'esh. Ebrahim B. explains that he joined Da'esh, among others, because he was attracted by the promise of access to women.[123] Not only do some believe in the promise of 72 virgins in paradise for martyrdom, there is also the possibility to marry four wives in the here-and-now. Ebrahim smiles tellingly when he says: "Who does not want to have that...?" Having easy access to four sexual objects, to be free to use them whenever he may wish so, what an exciting promise! Ebrahim proves to be a true child of Western market ideology regarding access to the market of women: here he was an average boy from Wolfsburg who saw the chance to transform himself into a sexy sought-after holy warrior.

In an honor society, men are regarded as the principal actors, no matter how important female activities may be for the functioning of the family and society as a whole. He is the actor, she is his object and substrate. He is the defender of honor. He is regarded as responsible, self-reflexive, and rational. He is expected to protect *his* women, at least as long as he values them as a resource, as a prize, or a symbol of *his* honor, or as mother of *his* children. As sociologist Pierre Bourdieu has observed, a man can derive honor only from the recognition paid by another man (not from a woman), and, in addition, it must be a man of honor, an honorable rival.[124]

A woman who lives in an honor society learns that she either is not a human being, akin to domestic animals, or a lowly human being. In both cases, she is perceived as a passive recipient of male actions, as "substrate" to be used or thrown away by him, on the level of household items or domesticated animals, or on the level of children or slaves.

It is therefore that woman can move freely in blood feud societies, and why only men are "worthy" of being killed "honorably."[125] And this is why rape can be carried out as a "proud" manifestation of male control and dominance, both over women and over other men. This is why, in war, rape is a weapon that can be used against enemy men to demonstrate how weak they are, how unable to keep their women safe.[126] Only a proponent of the partnership model of society, like poet Stephen Gill, can call rape a "mindless" weapon, when he says: "... rape is a terror and terror is the extreme form of fear. Rapists should be treated like any other terrorist. Raping women is terrorism and terrorism is a mindless attack on humanism."[127] In an honor context, rape is not "mindless." Only within the context of the partnership model of society will the use of rape as weapon be condemned as a war crime.[128]

In war, while men were killed, women were often captured alive when communities were invaded and conquered. Women were seen as "resources" rather than as "people." Female bodies seem to have adapted to this situation by developing a specific reaction to stress – women tend to react with a *tend and befriend* reaction to stress, rather than *fight or flight*.[129]

Earlier, I told the story of Turandot, and how she attempted to escape from the lowly position of women in the world of honor. Boudica is another woman who tried to resist. Boudica was a queen of the British Celtic Iceni tribe. Her husband hoped that his daughters would be recognized as rightful heirs by the Roman occupiers of Britain after his death. Yet, his testament was ignored. When he died, the Romans annexed his kingdom, flogged Boudica, raped her daughters, and Roman financiers called in their loans. Boudica mobilized the Celts to take revenge and an estimated 70,000 to 80,000 people were killed in the three Rome-dominated cities that Boudica and her men destroyed. Ultimately, however, her fate was sealed. The Romans crushed her in the Battle of Watling Street in 60 or 61 CE.[130]

Honor cultures, not just in the Arab world and in Africa, regard the woman's hymen as a symbol of the family's honor. This is one justification for the practice of female genital cutting.[131] Through this practice, the family's honor is "protected." Only "unopened" girls can serve as proof that their males were able to protect them. This is more than simple mate guarding in animals.[132] In traditional honor societies, a female typically is a token, or representative, of the family or group to which she belongs. Daughters or sisters are valued "gifts" for marriage into other families her males want as allies. Only intact girls, "closed" girls, signifying that they are "unused," are suitable as honorable gifts. The intact hymen of an unmarried woman is thus a visible manifestation of the intactness and flawlessness of her men's armor of honor.

I myself grew up surrounded by a conservative Christian family who held similar views, albeit attenuated, yet, pointing into the same direction.[133] Therefore, I have no problem understanding the "logic" in such mindsets.

In my doctoral dissertation, I describe how shocked I was when my Somali interview partners suggested pathways to peace I would never be able to imagine participating in myself. After having shared with me the deep sense of humiliation that had alienated Somaliland from the rest of Somalia, to my dismay, I heard how peace and reconciliation usually is being reached when clans have fallen out with each other and want to reconcile: in order to stabilize the situation in the long term, "women should be exchanged between the groups for marriage. These women will embody the bridges between opposing groups, since they have their original family in one group and their children in the other."[134]

Throughout my global life, I witnessed many variations of what is called honor killing.[135] I witnessed what can unfold in traditional societies when a girl is seen to bring shame upon her family, when she has been, for instance, raped. I learned to deeply understand how a group, in this case the girl's family, can consider the family as the significant entity deserving love and protection, rather than the individual member of the family. Or, more precisely, I learned how a representative of the group (a leader, an elder, often the father, yet, also the mother), can decide for a collective as if the collective were a single person or a unified body. A family member who had been "spoiled" could be regarded as a diseased limb that must be amputated to avoid infecting the entire body of the family-person: loving one's family and holding its honor dear required healing through "surgery" – redeeming humiliation by cutting out the diseased part – or what is called honor killing.

In certain Muslim contexts, a raped woman may not dare to go to the police, because she might be accused of *zina*, unlawful sexual intercourse. She will be punished for a crime perpetrated on her, a crime of which she is the victim.[136] "In Iraq, a woman who suffered rape is considered to be dead to society, as she is held responsible for having enticed males to abduct, rape or molest her."[137]

The same unapologetic brutality toward women can manifest itself also in domestic violence. A Saudi religious scholar raped his five-year-old daughter Lamia and tortured her to death.[138] A social worker from the hospital where Lama was admitted said the girl's back was broken and she had been raped "everywhere." When the father brought her to the clinic, he said that he had doubts about his daughter's virginity and therefore wanted to have her checked by a medic. The father was sentenced to pay "blood money" to the mother of the girl after having served a short jail term. The ruling was based on national laws that a father cannot be executed for murdering his children. Nor can husbands be executed for murdering their wives.

What we see it that in such a context, the woman's body is the symbol of male honor, and it can either be intact or severed. If severed, it is her fault, not his. Her "owner" feels victimized, even though she is the victim, because he feels his honor slighted. The aforementioned correspondence bias is a welcome way to avoid culpability: since his honor is hurt by her, this violation must be her shameless intention and her fault, not his or any man's responsibility.[139] He reacts in the spirit of the post-victim ethical exemption syndrome that scholar James Edward Jones describes as response to humiliation.[140] This is also why, in war, women are often raped in front of their families, precisely to disallow her men to opt out and put the blame on her, to prove that it is the men who fail to protect their women, to force the men to feel the full force of the humiliation on them, to make sure to emasculate the men and leave them without excuse.[141]

One of Afghanistan's favorite sayings is "women are for children, boys are for pleasure."[142] The practice of *bacha baazi* (dancing boys) – which involves powerful or wealthy men sexually abusing young boys who are trained to dance in female clothes – is on the rise again, this we learn from the U.S. State Department in its 2013 human rights report.[143] The use of *bacha baazi* has grown since 2001, after the Taliban were ousted. The "Taliban had a deep aversion towards *bacha bazi*, outlawing the practice when they instituted strict nationwide sharia law," because "one of the original provocations for the Taliban's rise to power in the early 1990s was their outrage over pedophilia."[144] The 2009 U.S. Army Human Terrain Team report explains that heterosexual relationships are only allowable within the bounds of marriage, and that Pashtun honor requires a man who wishes to marry to be able to demonstrate his ability to support a wife and family, including abundant wedding-gifts for the bride and her parents: "Therefore, given the economic situation of most young Pashtun men and the current state of employment and agriculture within the Pashtun regions of Afghanistan, marriage becomes a nearly unattainable possibility for many."[145] In a situation where strict social control from Taliban rulers no longer enforces stricter rules, young boys are now sexually abused again. Many boys spend their formative years in Taliban Islamic religious school or madrassahs where their mothers are absent, in other words, where the female element is missing that could perhaps instill some respect for women: "Women are foreign, and categorized by religious teachers as, at best, unclean or undesirable," the report explains.[146]

The story of Malala Yousafzai vividly illustrates tribal honor in Pakistan's Swat valley, where women were ordered to cover their bodies and not allowed to go to school or do shopping.[147] Malala is a Pakistani activist for female education and the youngest-ever Nobel Prize laureate.

To understand the meaning of the female body-cover, it is useful to think of it as the protective walls of a house, or the walls of a tent, made mobile: she takes those walls with her while walking outside, and in this way, she stays inside, where she belongs. The body-cover is a concession, short of the ideal, as traditionally, a woman was to leave the house only twice: An old saying, not only in Egypt, prescribes that a "good" woman ought to leave the house only twice in her lifetime, first, when she gets married and moves from the house of her father to the house of her husband, and second, when her dead body is carried to the cemetery.[148]

An all-female moral police, the al-Khansaa Brigade, was established in Da'esh's main city of Raqqa soon after it took over the city. This brigade set out to beat and arrest women who were not complying with the required dress code.[149]

What such beating enacts, is the drama of two competing paths to honor, one via traditional status and the other via money. Both paths bring terror to women. The tribal male honor code attempts to "beat out" rapidly globalizing Western manifestations of another kind of male honor, namely, the one based on money. Provocatively formulated, tribal honor covers female skin to protect the status of her owners, while in Western market-oriented contexts, glossy magazines display naked female skin to fill the pockets of masters who gain honor through financial means rather than tribal status.

What we learn is that misogyny is not the reserve of "backward societies." It is pervasive on all continents, in all cultural realms.[150] No world region is exempted, Western cultural realms included.[151] Even in countries like Norway, hailed for their gender equality, this can be observed. A 59-years old well-known politician recently abused a thirteen years old girl and then declared that this was her fault, since her "persuasiveness" or *overtalelsesevne* was so strong.[152] Once more, we see the correspondence error at work: "since you attract me, it is your responsibility to protect me from you." This is why women's hair and body must be hidden in non-Western contexts, or exposed in Western contexts, in ways that leave no doubt that the female body has the status of an object.

In both cases, female attractiveness is feared to be so strong that it undermines and weakens male control and superiority. Many males feel compelled to "tame" their "dangerous" women, to oppress and disrespect them, so as to turn them into safe sources for a male sense of worth. And many women are coopted to the point that they feel guilty when they fail to serve their men subserviently enough. I met this attitude when I worked in Egypt. Eighty-six percent of Egyptian women surveyed in 1995 thought that husbands were justified in hitting their wives, for instance, when she failed to put the food on the table in time, or if she refused sex.[153]

Women remain being providers of male honor, and thus of the male sense of worth, rather than fellow human beings all over the world. Women and men are seen in a top-down relationship, rather than as dialogue partners on an equal footing. Traditional honor and modern market economy combine in intensifying this trend: "Violence against women and girls is a global pandemic that destroys lives, fractures communities and holds back development … but violence against women and girls does not emerge from nowhere. It is simply the most extreme example of the political, financial, social and economic oppression of women and girls worldwide," observed former United Nations Secretary-General Ban Ki-moon in 2014.[154] Maltreatment of women is the "most horrendous" human rights issue in the world today – there is a parallel between "the way black people were treated in some parts of the country when I was a child to the way women and girls are treated all over the world now," these were the words of Jimmy Carter, the 39th president of the United States and 2002 Nobel Peace Prize recipient.[155]

In my book on a dignity economy, I highlight the similarity of the situation in Somalia and the City of London.[156] Warlords in Somalia put militia boys on pickup trucks or pirate ships, provide them with weapons and drugs, and sometimes with young girls as sex slaves. In the City of London, young "city-boys,"[157] are put into the investment bank and the bar, their weapons are "financial weapons of mass destruction,"[158] and many thrive on cocaine or reward themselves with expensive sex parties.[159]

As we see, there are two "royal" paths to honor for a man, first via traditional rank, second, via new money. Those who cannot attain honor through money in Western contexts, therefore have a "fall back" option, namely, the pathway of tribal honor. "Yesterday, the guys still sold drugs, today they find to Allah, tomorrow they move to Syria," explained prison chaplain Martin Husamuddin Mayer who works in Wiesbaden, Germany.[160] He observes that "prisoners are the ideal clientele for religious-extremist recruiters because they have crossed the threshold of violence."[161] These boys have no idea of religion, the only thing that attracts them is the sense of superiority they can attain when following extremist preachers in their conviction of being the only true believers.[162]

I was born in Hamelin. It is a small town in Germany with a youth detention center that serves a larger region. Recently, in this center, Marco G. discovered Islam when he was nineteen. After his release, he moved with his wife and child into a center of the Islamist scene in Germany, the Rhineland. On September 8, 2014, he stood trial, together with three other Salafist converts, accused, among others, of having tried to carry out a bomb attack at Bonn's main railway station on December 10, 2012.

Thomas Mücke is a pedagogue and managing director of the Violence Prevention Networks in Berlin, working with vulnerable radicalized youth.[163] His conclusion is that extremists are not just a-religious, they are even anti-religious.[164] He explains that in the biographies of these young people the absence of a father always looms large, causing them to look for father figures, for a family substitute. They often come from educationally disadvantaged backgrounds, are isolated, rarely ever had a sense of achievement, and feel they have failed. They suffer from "precarious conditions of recognition," as sociologist Wilhelm Heitmeyer formulated it.[165] They are looking for belonging. Being part of a great cause, for them, is like a dream come true.[166]

What Heitmeyer talks about are the "misfits" and "drifters" as Norwegian terrorism expert Petter Nesser and his colleagues explained to me when we met in Oslo, and as reported in the Appendix to the first part of this book.

Ahmad Mansour is a Palestinian-Israeli psychologist and author who also lives in Berlin, since 2004. Mansour is an Islamism expert and engaged in initiatives against radicalization. He focuses on the culture of oppression in the name of honor in Muslim families and reckons that the increased religiosity among Muslim youth is a socio-cultural phenomenon comparable to any other youth culture.[167] His views resonate with those of Gary Barker, the coordinator of a multi-country survey on men titled IMAGES (the International Men and Gender Equality Survey), one of the largest ever surveys on men's attitudes and behaviors related to violence, fatherhood and gender equality.[168] His book has a telling titled that summarizes the dilemma: *Dying to be Men: Youth, Masculinity and Social Exclusion*.[169]

Symbolic empowerment is the term that Mark Juergensmeyer uses for terror that is justified by religion. Juergensmeyer's expertise is in the field of religious violence and global religion. Juergensmeyer found that terror provides empowerment particularly to men feeling humiliated in a modern secular world.[170] Michael Kimmel, expert of masculinities, explains how some see honor as the only true backbone of a meaningful life and healthy society, and how they perceive ideas such as freedom, democracy, peace, and equality as evil ideas.[171]

Current attempts to use violent means against violent religious terrorists risks helping charismatic leaders to recruit ever more supporters. The reason is that meaning is sought in a cosmic Manichean struggle for good and against evil, a worldview that is inherent in the honor mindset.[172] When all sides are convinced to fight for "good," fighting will beget more fighting, rather than ending it, and attacks from the other side will merely be seen as an affirmation of one's own goodness. For members of such groups, arguments from outsiders tend to have little impact, and violent attacks simply confirm their worldview.

Documentary maker Deeyah Khan, born in Norway with a Pakistani-Afghan background, looks back on profoundly painful personal experiences with honor, and she writes on "jihad masculinity":

> Our media provides a continuing message that for men, heroism is defined through association with control, independence and the ability to commit violence, from superheroes to crime dramas. Most world leaders are male, and many present exaggeratedly masculine personas, such as dressing up in military garb at any opportunity, in a show of strength and dominance. The message seems to be that if young men are not respected, some of them will settle for being feared. Extremism is a complicated issue, but without addressing how it appeals to men and boys, we may be missing an important motivation, and a way to address the problems in our towns and cities. Feelings of humiliation and emasculation are keenly felt, and can lead to extreme and violent behaviors in many contexts. Building a culture in which varied forms of "being a man" are accepted and respected may help all our boys and young men to feel more comfortable in their own skin, able to live according to their own desires than trying to fit themselves into a prewritten gender script … and less likely to assert their masculinity through violence and brutality.[173]

Pål Refsdal is a Norwegian freelance journalist, photographer, and filmmaker who has reported from many war zones.[174] In the summer of 2013, Refsdal lived for six weeks with Muslim rebel fighters in Syria who were part of the Al-Nusra Front, including fighters hailing from Syria, Saudi Arabia, and Britain.[175] His film sheds light on the various motivations behind wanting to become a martyr. A Syrian fighter he filmed, for instance, explained that he was motivated by his dismay at the brutality with which the Syrian dignity revolution had been suppressed by the Syrian government. The British fighter was appalled by Western double standards. Another young man, one from the Gulf States, aimed at martyrdom because he wished to care for his family by sparing them hell and facilitating their preferred access to paradise. His way of thinking is reminiscent of historical Europe, where one child was "given" to the church, as one son was selected to save the family.

The right combination of factors can turn anyone into an extremist, says neuroscientist Ian Robertson.[176] Robertson lists five factors: (1) savagery begets savagery, victim becoming victimizer, (2) submersion in the group, (3) the out-group as objects, (4) revenge, and (5) leaders. Robertson describes the toxic mix:

> You can see it in the faces of the young male Islamic State militants as they race by on their trucks, black flags waving, broad smiles on their faces, clenched fists aloft, fresh from the slaughter of infidels who would not convert to Islam. What you can see is a biochemical high from a combination of the bonding hormone oxytocin and the dominance hormone testosterone. Much more than cocaine or alcohol,

> these natural drugs lift mood, induce optimism and energies aggressive action on the part of the group. And because the individual identity has been submerged largely into the group identity, the individual will be much more willing to sacrifice himself in battle – or suicide bombing, for that matter. Why? – Because if I am submerged in the group, I live on in the group even if the individual "me," dies.[177]

What Robertson points at is the tragedy of the security dilemma. When people bond together, oxytocin levels rise in their blood, and this is experienced as thrill. The dark side of this thrill is a greater tendency to demonize and dehumanize the out-group. In that way, selfless immersion into one's in-group anaesthetizes compassionate empathy for the out-group.[178]

Cool Men and the Second Sex, is the title of a book by expert on gender issues Susan Fraiman. She analyzes the "cool male" intellectual style favored increasingly even in contemporary academia.[179] Fraiman identifies "a lingering, systematic masculinism among some of the best-known, left-leaning, evidently 'cool' cultural workers, many of whom explicitly ally themselves with women's concerns."[180] Also women in academia now use this style of "hip masculinity" to indicate their superiority over a "femininity" that they "maternalize" and associate with hopelessly backward stasis and rigidity, in contrast to fluid postmodernity.[181]

In other words, the world of masculine honor and female shame is not something of the past, it is well and alive even in arenas such as academia that profess to stand for the very opposite.

As mentioned earlier, when working on Volume II of this book project, I became more aware of why the study of humiliation elicits skepticism in certain circles. To formulate it simplified, honor is "for men," while dignity is "for sissies," or, more precisely, avenging honor humiliation is for men, while crying about dignity humiliation is for women. The problem with this view is that humiliation becomes ever more relevant in our contemporary historical times, precisely because of dignity humiliation. Dignity humiliation is more intense than honor humiliation since dignity humiliation removes the victim from humanity altogether, which is more hurtful than merely being lowered on a ranked ladder. Human rights ideals of equal dignity represent a higher promise than ranked honor and therefore also make its violation more salient.[182]

Many suggest that "hard facts" such as poverty would be better predictors of violence and terror than, for instance, humiliation. Others use terms such as "relative deprivation." Yet, also here is a problem: There is no automatic link between poverty and terror.[183] Many people interpret poverty as divinely ordained or nature's order and remain utterly peaceful. To elicit violence, poverty or relative deprivation must first be interpreted as a violation, as a humiliation, perpetrated by a humiliator. Even equal dignity can provoke violence when it is interpreted as humiliation. Traditional male supremacists of honor, for instance, may identify the ideal of equal dignity for women as a violation. They may feel their honor diminished and may open the master's toolbox for responding to honor humiliation by trying to beat and rape women back into subservience. Others may feel their dignity humiliated when equal opportunities are promised but not delivered. They might respond in the Suttner-Freire-Gandhi-Mandela way, yet, they may also respond with the traditional script for defending honor, namely, violence and terror.

More mass shootings must be expected from "toxic masculinity," particularly when there is a "national attachment to dominance models of manhood" as in the United States.[184] The Gandhi path is anathema to those who have been told that real men fight back and losers whine. The situation becomes particularly dangerous when dignity humiliation, with its heightened intensity, is responded to with the violence and terror of the traditional aristocrat's tool kit for avenging honor humiliation. This represents a *cross over* from feelings of dignity humiliation to acts of vengeance for honor humiliation. It gets even more dangerous in present-day's interconnected world, where access to such strategies is democratized. All this increases the relevance of the phenomenon of humiliation million fold. It is therefore that the phenomenon of humiliation presses itself to the fore of our attention now, this is why it was my global life that made me a pioneer in the field of humiliation studies, and it is why more research on humiliation is urgently needed. What stands in its way, is male honorable disdain for whatever appears to be "soft" or "weak," and male honorable disdain for attempts to treat "the enemy" as fellow human being.

Honor is both competitive and cooperative

In a divided world, honor means cooperating within one's own group so as to be more competitive for dominating other groups.[185] During my doctoral research in Somaliland, I learned firsthand about clan honor and how it once was honorable to continuously test the neighboring clan's competitive ability. Camel raids were regular "trainings."[186] As attractive as this strategy may seem for the winners of such competitions, the danger with this strategy is that it may eat its children.

Let me explain. History shows that groups can easily fragment and new alliances can emerge from former adversaries. Somalia, with its proud egalitarian warrior culture, is a prime laboratory to learn about the fickleness of fusion and fragmentation, and how it leads to never-ending mutual mistrust and drives a whole country into all-out failing. When enemies suddenly are to be allies, one would wish one had never treated them as enemies. In a globalizing world, this happens all the time, at every corner of the globe. Humankind needs to cooperate globally, given that it faces severe global challenges, and it would be better if cycles humiliation had never been unleashed.

Akbar Ahmed, the chair of Islamic Studies at American University and a former Pakistani ambassador to the United Kingdom and Ireland, warns that it might be a mistake to focus on religious extremism and overlook the values of tribal honor and revenge.[187] Also assassinations by drones follow a "tribal ideology," Ahmed suggests, namely, that the death of civilians is justified in pursuit of a larger cause; this strategy, rather than ending terrorism, may simply inspire tribal survivors to seek revenge in the future, rather than convince them to use peaceful means.[188]

The presently advancing ingathering of the human tribes on planet Earth is not the first time that new and larger groups coalesced from smaller ones. History offers innumerable examples. The story of Athens and Sparta is one of them. First, Athens and Sparta were enemies, competing for domination among themselves. Then Persia threatened to out-compete them from their outer borders, and suddenly those former adversaries had to foster cooperation, unity, and cohesion among themselves.[189] Hellas succeeded; Persia was kept out. Those who love science fiction fear that humankind may not unite as successfully if aliens were to attack planet Earth once from outer space. Already now, their fear is validated: climate degradation is a global threat, comparable to an alien attack, yet, when it is suspected to be a hoax thought up by hostile fellow earthlings, it fails to unite humanity.[190]

Another reason for why winning in competition can eat its children is backlash. A historical example is the Tennis Court Oath (*Serment du Jeu de Paume*), a pivotal event during the first days of the French Revolution, when a new cooperation emerged – rebels who had gathered at a tennis court swore loyalty to each other and to the revolution.[191] Those who had previously thought they had won the competition in society, lost their heads under the guillotine.

A more recent example is provided by Adolf Hitler. He managed to create unprecedented cohesion among formerly neglected segments of German society, the so-called *kleinen Leute* (little people), the "little" invisibilized people, by inviting them into a grand national narrative of humiliation and thus giving them a new sense of worth.[192] Hitler turned their lingering low spirit and sense of shame into a narrative of humiliation they were justified to resent and avenge. He preached that all were victims of acts of humiliation, and that rebellion and retribution was the call of the day, not shame; or, if shame, then shame over having shamefully succumbed to humiliation instead of having resisted.[193] Hitler taught his followers to reject the humiliators' intentions to shame them, to reject the *Schande von Versailles* (the disgrace of the Treaty of Versailles after WWI), and, instead, to rise from shame by fighting against humiliation.

Shame had its place only in shame over shame, shame for having failed to separate humiliation from shame, for having remained cowed in shame in front of one's humiliators. Hitler used the national political sphere as an arena for the orchestration of passionate feelings of humiliation to achieve the homogenization of the German nation.[194]

> Hitler's "Mein Kampf" makes obvious that the idea of fighting is crucial for his ideology: Fighting secures the continued existence and progress of mankind. Ideologies such as Marxism on the other hand, which try to abandon fighting, are the cause of the decline and fall of mankind. Hitler's own fight was directed against Marxism and its – alleged – Jewish originators. This required the melting of the people into a fighting community – this provided the basis for Hitler's program of "Gleichschaltung" and the inner homogenization of the German nation.[195]

As soon as a cohesive sense of national mission was in place among his followers, Hitler instrumentalized it to hijack state institutions and launch a world war. The phenomenon of mass shooting, spree killing, and rampage killing in Western societies follows the very same script of rejecting humiliating shame, instead displaying potency.[196] It is dangerous enough when such a script inspires lone individuals; if this script inspires entire groups, it can spell humanity's demise. While I write these lines, many Americans hope that U.S. President Donald J. Trump will stop short of hijacking state institutions and launching a world war. Yet, in both cases, the body language of the unfairly treated victim, the pouting and sulking expression of indignation on their faces, has heightened the emotional power of their performances, which, in turn, has created deeply emotional bonds with millions of followers.

Saudi Arabia pays a high price for having been the winner of competition in the past; the terrorist backlash now threatens not only their own country, also the rest of the world. In the early twentieth century, under charismatic Sufi scholar king Sayyed Muhammad al-Idrisi, the Yemeni tribes of the Asir Province in the al-Bahah region were proud of Asir's independence. Yet, after al-Isidri's death in 1922, forces of Abd al-Aziz ibn Saud overran the region and an estimated 400,000 people died. Yemeni-Asiri culture has remained under Saudi onslaught since. Humiliated, repressed, shunned, and marginalized, Asiris became international "jihadis": they went to Afghanistan to fight the Russians in the 1980s, and to Chechnya in the 1990s. After the 1991 Gulf War, when the Saudis allowed American troops to be based on the Arabian Peninsula, sacred land for the Asiris, also the United Sates was included on their list of enemies. Four of the thirteen 9/11 hijackers, those who stormed the cockpits and controlled the passengers, hailed from the regions of al-Bahah and Asir or from the Wadi Hadhramaut in southern Yemen, where also Osama bin Laden's own family has its roots. "Bin Laden demonized the United States, accusing it of genocide against Muslims and repeatedly contending that the presence of U.S. troops in Saudi Arabia ever since the first Gulf War in 1991 was a far graver offense than the Soviet invasion of Afghanistan, even though that had led to the death of one million Afghans and had sent five million more into exile."[197]

The honor ideology that motivates Asiris can be found also in other world regions. In 2013, peace psychologist Daniel Christie taught in Pakistan and observed that also Pakistan's students are steeped in that culture:

> - Many students and faculty believe it is naive to think problems can be solved nonviolently. Very often only violence works.
> - There is the belief that violence is inevitable in human affairs.
> - There is no clear separation between conflict (perception of incompatible goals) and violence (actual behavior intended to harm).
> - A related set of ideas is that violence (or force) is necessary and unavoidable.
> - It sometimes is necessary to kill others to defend your religion.[198]

John Bolton is a former U.S. Ambassador to the United Nations. He was introduced earlier. He has founded the John Bolton Political Action Committee that aims at rescuing America's honor. He wrote about U.S. President Barack Obama: "This is a president who does not believe in American exceptionalism, a president who is uninterested in national security and America's place in the world, who considers our strength part of the problem."[199] Bolton's world is defined by competition for domination over adversaries. Therefore, he wishes to bring together Americans into stronger inner cooperation so as to gather strength to remain victorious in this competition. Those who voted for Donald J. Trump to become the president of the United States in 2016, clearly were impressed by such a goal.

Honor is a "heroic" mutilation

Honor is like an armor. It means bracing oneself with a steel harness. Every surgeon in the world has to do that: to be a surgeon means overcoming one's fear of blood to be able to cut into the flesh of the patient. Honor entails the duty to be willing to be either the "surgeon" who inflicts pain, or the "patient" who suffers pain, so that the collective can survive. This requires placing the duty to kill or be killed for the sake of the collective above all personal desires – be it the desire for a comfortable life, or for the survival of oneself and one's immediate family and loved ones. At the core of honor we find the duty to defend the collective, even at the cost of one's own life. Feuds, honor killing, duels, they all draw on a script of painful but necessary redress and "healing."

As in the case of surgery, defending honor is regarded as highly virtuous and prosocial. Like surgery, it is not regarded as a cruel moral degeneration. A surgeon does not cut into a patient's flesh in sadistic "cold blood," but out of noble altruism. For honor, the collective is the body, the locus of control is anchored in the collective, more than in the individual.[200] Defending honor is seen as heroic courage precisely because it needs to be done in "cold blood." Heart and mind need to be so noble that they can save the body by sacrificing a limb, or save the collective by sacrificing an individual. Many tacticians of terror draw on this script and therefore, for them, killing in "cold blood" is noble and heroic.

Honor culture was often very successful in tackling threats, at least as long as the security dilemma was strong. It was successful surgery so to speak. Victory over attacking enemies meant life rather than death for the victors, freedom rather than slavery. It was more likely for a community with a strong honor culture of loyalty and bravery to achieve victory than for a community without it.

Yet, the honor culture has also damaging effects, effects that can prove to be more harmful than the original threat. This has always been the case but is even more true now as the security dilemma weakens and waits to get help to weaken more. The human family will not survive in a globally interconnected world full of weapons if the honor culture persists; it needs to be left behind, honorably, without humiliating its adherents, as this would trigger new cycles of humiliation.

The honor culture is harmful in many ways. Many mythologies, modern and ancient, carry knowledge of the damaging effects of the honor culture and thus reflect what happened in the course of history when circumscription and the security dilemma arose. This knowledge shines through mythical visions of life as once more fulfilling, more paradisiacal – a garden Eden – and that life subsequently got damaged and curtailed.[201] Indeed, the past five percent of human history were detrimental to the human psyche.

The honor culture is harmful even for those who benefit from it. To return to the image of the human body, in an honor culture, elites are allowed to use the right arm, the sword arm, to devise strategies and give orders, representing the sympathetic system of the body that prepares for flight or fight. Their left arm, the one that stands for maintenance and care, akin to the parasympathetic system, is bound behind their backs. Their subordinates suffer the inverse infliction. None can use both arms, none can reach an inner balance, none can unfold their full potential.

Honor culture has always been harmful in this way, yet, as long as the security dilemma was strong, this damage was regarded as a price that had to be paid. Only now, when the security dilemma attenuates, the opportunity opens to recalibrate culture in more benign ways.

The old custom of foot binding in China, now forbidden, is perhaps the most evocative example of the detrimental impact of honor and how it can be overcome. Bound feet were a prerequisite for marriage for one thousand years and this was especially hard on the poor who could not afford servants.[202] In other words, the pain of subjugation that once was institutionalized as "what is appropriate," is now outlawed.

"Korean honor" may serve as another example for the detrimental impact of honor. *Jeong* is an experience in Korean culture, and it is embedded into the emotional and psychological bonds that have their roots in the collective nature of Korean society which divides the world into different degrees of "us versus them."[203] When this bond is broken, *haan* and *hwabyung* may arise. *Haan* is intense chronically suppressed anger in response to the violation of *jeong*. *Hwa-byung* is its final explosion and translates into English as "fire disease." Its physical and psychological symptoms have been described as a Korean folk illness.[204] Two massive acts of killing in the United States may have their roots in this Korean fire disease. On April 2, 2012, a 43-year-old former nursing student named One L. Goh killed six people and wounded three others at the Oikos University in Oakland, California, with a .45-caliber handgun, before killing a former classmate in the school's parking lot. On April 16, 2007, another young man, Seung-Hui Cho, massacred 32 people at Virginia Tech University.[205]

> Both [*haan* and *hwabyung*] describe a state of hopeless, crippling sadness combined with anger at an unjust world. And both suggest entrapment by suppressed emotions. Both words have been a part of the Korean lexicon for as long as anyone can remember, their roots in the country's history of occupation, war and poverty. Perhaps the best way to distinguish between the two words would be to say that haan is the existential condition of immutable sadness, whereas hwabyung is its physical manifestation. Those afflicted with hwabyung describe a dense helplessness and despair that always feels on the verge of erupting into acts of self-destruction.[206]

As discussed before, the belief in the evilness of human nature seems to have its roots in the security dilemma's power to shape culture. The Korean example shows how human nature can get caged into rules to a degree that its carrying ability is overstretched and violence ensues, how violent behavior can occur not because of, but despite of "human nature." If a society wishes to avoid such outcomes, it would need to offer its people a more humane space to unfold themselves. Present-day psychotherapists, for instance, would perhaps prescribe counseling sessions to young Koreans with fire disease to avoid such violent escalations.

In the context of the security dilemma, to be a hero means to be able to kill the enemy. Yet, also killing is not part of human nature. It can only be done by overloading human nature. It is heroic precisely because killing is difficult. Rather than driven by any "evil" instinct in human nature, the basic fabric of human nature is vulnerably social. To be brave, soldiers have to train not to look their victims in the eyes, lest that would stop them from killing.

When the humaneness in human nature gets overloaded for a limited time span, the traumatized person can rebound. This is different when overload is chronic and structural. Children are often affected more fundamentally when exposed to abuse. Childhood injury to the brain combined with indifferent or cruel parenting can be found in the biographical backgrounds of serial killers.[207] Those with genetic alterations in monoamine oxidase A (MAOA) activity seem to tend to react more aggressively.[208] Also the neuromodulator nitric oxide seems to be related to aggression.[209] Serotonin, dopamine, or norepinephrine are all found to play a role in aggression; high testosterone levels combined with low serotonin levels seem to be particularly salient for violence.[210]

The twelve school shooters included in a study in the United States all sought revenge for having experienced humiliation.[211] When psychologist Peter Langman studied school shooters, he found as most prominent background factors dysfunctional or abusive home life, mental health problems, school discipline, as well as hurtful romantic rejection.[212]

Also stress plays a role. If mother and child are exposed to malnutrition and psychological stress, this can influence the child both prenatally, in early childhood, and later in life. The most vulnerable phase is during the growth and combination of dendrites in the brain, until the third and fourth year of life. Damage can be irreversible and affect the entire adult life of an affected child. If this happens, females seem to react more with depressive disorders, while borderline disorders may form in males: "For men, these could display an evolutive process of adaption to warrior personalities in conflict areas, while women are handicapped in their development, and, at the same time, social sorrow and misery are perpetuated."[213]

Several methods have been developed during the past millennia to make the heroism of killing possible despite of its "unnaturalness." One way is to work oneself into rage. The *Iliad* by Homer – the "Bible" of the Greek-speaking world – begins with the word *μῆνιν* (*mēnin*), or wrath, divine anger. The *Iliad* tells the stories of men who are "professionally violent." Violence was regarded as an entirely legitimate, indeed, the only honorable way to resolving disputes. The *Iliad's* principal theme is "The Wrath of Achilles." Achilles epitomizes the rage of men fighting for honor, vengeance and personal gain, victory, survival, and "the intoxicating adrenalin rush of licensed savagery."[214]

Furor Teutonicus (Teutonic fury) describes "mad rage" in battle of a Germanic tribe called the *Teutones*, and it means mercilessness toward enemy and oneself alike, brought about by alcohol consumption.[215] *Berserkers* (or *Berserks*) were Norse warriors in coats of wolf or bear skin fighting in fury brought about by beer, the fly agaric mushroom, and trance through frenzied rituals and dances. *Varzesh-e Pahlavani*, the "Sport of the Heroes," or the "Sport of the Ancients," a traditional discipline of gymnastics and wrestling in Iran, was originally an academy of physical training for military purposes. Also war propaganda is a method with the aim to bring people "out of their minds"[216] and into the furor necessary to be willing to kill. The humiliation narrative is particularly useful for such propaganda, due to its high potential to work like a drug.[217]

Bertha von Suttner describes how the situation began to change in her time, at least partly. War was at times already seen as "necessary evil," in other words, at least as evil, no longer as glorious aim in itself. Today, if we look at the world community, all approaches exist side by side – war as an arena for glory, war as necessary evil, war as unnecessary evil – sometimes all are mixed, sometimes they undermine each other, and usually each warring party misconstrues the other side's motives. Killing from a distance is in a way a compromise, a combination of honor and dignity tool kits. While honorable killing on close hold is difficult, learning to shoot over radio or with drones can be done with considerably more ease as it shields the killer from the death he inflicts.

Timothy Kudo, a Marine captain, was deployed to Iraq in 2009, and to Afghanistan from 2010 to 2011. He explains how he, already in his first week in Afghanistan, "learned" killing. A voice over radio asked him: "There are two people digging by the side of the road. Can we shoot them?" He was dismayed when he realized that there was nobody but him to decide.[218] "Take the shot," he responded. He explains:

> It was dialogue from the movies that I'd grown up with, but I spoke the words without irony. I summarily ordered the killing of two men. I wanted the Marine on the other end to give me a reason to change my decision, but the only sound I heard was the radio affirmative for an understood order: "Roger, out." Shots rang out across the narrow river. A part of me wanted the rounds to miss their target, but they struck flesh and the men fell dead.

James Elmer Mitchell was one of two psychologists involved in designing interrogation methods for the American secret service, as the 2014 U.S. Senate report on the torture program of the Central Intelligence Agency C.I.A. exposed.[219] In his work, Mitchell and his colleague built on psychologist Martin Seligman's research on "learned helplessness,"[220] and on the Chinese interrogation methods that were used on American soldiers during the Korean war.[221] The psychologists gave out the following recommendations for how to treat potential terrorists: "humiliation, painful stress positions, confinement, sleep deprivation – and waterboarding."[222] The aim was to give the captive a "sense of hopelessness."[223] The majority of Americans still thinks today that, indeed, torture was justified after the 9/11 attacks.[224] A minority believes that the designers of such interrogation strategies themselves ought to feel ashamed and humiliated by the fact that they meted out such inexcusable humiliation on others.[225]

Several contradictory terminologies and narratives surround what Mitchell and his colleague designed. The very presence of such contradictions shows that American society hoovers in the middle of its transition between the honor paradigm of competition for domination on one side, and the dignity paradigm of partnership on the other side. Authoritarians say: Torture is needed, not only is it what the enemy deserves, it also renders vitally important information that protects our security; and therefore, the C.I.A. report ought not to be released in the first place, as it helps the enemy. People on the opposite side of the political spectrum say that torture is never needed, even if it were to render results, and that the report must be released.[226] Incidentally, in 2001, the initial C.I.A. framework for its detention program had "envisioned a system in which detainees would be offered the same rights and protections as inmates held in federal or American military prisons."[227] As mentioned earlier, also in roleplaying situations authoritarians tend to seek dominance over others by being competitive and destructive instead of cooperative.[228] Politicians from the Republican Party in the United States have been shown to share a nationalistic and conservative economic philosophy, combined with an acceptance for social inequality, support for capital punishment, and opposition to abortion and gun control legislation.[229]

A kind of middle position would be the hope that patriotism and humanism could be combined through a sophisticated "mild" and "humane" design. "So long as there were medical professionals present in the interrogations, the government could claim the interrogations had been 'safe, legal and effective" – in short, not torture at all."[230] James Elmer Mitchell has professed that he is proud of having combined patriotism with humanism, and he therefore questions the report,[231] denying that he merely gave the C.I.A. and the White House cover.

The case of Pakistan may conclude this sub-section. For Pakistan, the defeat of the Pakistani army on December 16, 1971, after a vain attempt to hinder Bangladesh to become independent, was perhaps "the darkest moment in its history and the ultimate humiliation."[232] In the Indo-Pakistan war, Pakistani forces were accused of mass murder, torture and rape. Tens of thousands of Pakistani soldiers were taken prisoners of war. As a result, a dangerous nexus between the military and militant "jihadi" groups was created that now threatens Pakistan from within.

The practice of forming militia groups to do the government's bidding that was applied in East Pakistan is now also used in Afghanistan and Kashmir. Ikram Seghal, a defense analyst who lectures in Pakistani military colleges, warns that it is therefore that the biggest internal challenge to Pakistan today is terrorism.[233] The military has stifled the country's democratic development, undermining its very fabric: "I'm a soldier and proud of being a soldier. But all the ills of Pakistan are because of the armed forces intervention in the civilian affairs," says Lieutenant general Abdul Qadir Baloch.[234]

Pakistan has long supported militant Islamist groups in their opposition against India, not imagining that this violence would once turn against them on their own soil. Whenever Kashmir militant groups waged guerilla warfare against Indian forces, they could count on Pakistan's support; among them were those groups that carried out the 2001 attack on the Indian Parliament and the 2008 Mumbai attacks.[235] There was no Islamist opposition against Pakistan.

Dramatic change occurred in 2001. Pervez Musharaff, president of Pakistan, began to support the NATO-led intervention in Afghanistan and became a key player in the American-led war on terror.[236] Since then, Pakistan is afflicted with an anti-state conflict, and Musharaff himself was the target of numerous assassination attempts. On one side stood Al-Qaeda and the tribes in the tribal areas in the border region to Afghanistan, and on the other side the Pakistani regime and the NATO-led International Security Assistance Force (ISAF) in Afghanistan. A spiral of violence ensued and has not ended since.[237] Over the past decade, Pakistan has had the highest number of terrorism-related deaths in the world, exceeding the combined terrorism-related deaths for both Europe and North America.[238]

The story of the young man Omar Khyam, a computer student from Crawley in West Sussex, England, and a school cricket captain, shows how the extremist violence that was stoked in the conflict between Pakistan and India, far away from England, ultimately found its way also into the West.[239] Initially, Khyam connected his two cultures in very constructive ways – he supported England in football and Pakistan in cricket. The turning point came in 2007. Khyam recalls that it was the Afghan war and Britain's role in it, it was when he "first heard other British Muslims talk about committing acts of violence in the UK."[240] He trained with the Lashkar-e-Taiba group in Kashmir, the group that carried out the 2001 Indian Parliament attack. In 2004, he spearheaded a fertilizer bomb plot in the United Kingdom.

Honor is potentially suicidal

In Japan, the samurai code of honor is called *bushido*. It is best illustrated by the aforementioned tale of the *Forty-Seven Ronin* (*ronin* are leaderless samurai), a tale I learned about during my years in Japan. Those ronin were samurai who defied the Emperor of Japan and avenged the disgrace of their dead master, facing certain death as a result."[241]

Nazi potentate Hermann Göring, in his Stalingrad speech, spoke of *Nibelungentreue*, the duty to fight to the last man, no matter what.[242] The result were millions of dead bodies – suicidal mass homicide.

In Somalia, I learned how men can sit together during long nights and proudly plan for potentially deadly heroism, while looking down on their women who struggle to keep daily life going.[243] Dying for a higher cause of greatness and power can be seen by some as more heroic than allowing heroism be distracted by the banalities of daily life, let alone becoming the obedient servant of other powers: "A man deserves to be killed and not to be humiliated!" is a Somali proverb.

Deadly heroism is not a prerequisite of places like Somalia. Somalis always told me that they feel that American cowboy culture is very much like Somali culture. Stephen Homes, a law professor at New York University, wrote a book about "America's reckless response to terror," where he argues that America was very lucky: The response to the 9/11 attacks could have been far deadlier than the attacks themselves if Saddam Hussein actually had possessed the weapons of mass destruction he was suspected of having – the American forces would have faced consequences they were not equipped to control and "would have abetted the greatest proliferation disaster in world history."[244]

At the very core of the ethos of honor and resistance against honor humiliation stands the readiness for martyrdom, including mass martyrdom. Geoffroi de Charny (circa 1300 – 1356) was a French knight and Europe's most admired knight during his lifetime. He wrote that only facing great dangers that are motivated by pure honor would earn a knight true glory, with martyr-death as its culmination.[245] French nobles of the time therefore preferred to die in battle (at most be captured and pay ransom), rather than flee the field and thus dishonor themselves. Due to this ethos, almost the entire French nobility was wiped out in the first period of the Hundred Years' War (1337 – 1453), when they faced English attackers who surprised them with "dishonorable" terror tactics and "treacherous" weapons.[246]

When I lived in Cairo, Egypt (1984 – 1991), I had the privilege of being present during an interview that anthropologist Jan Brøgger conducted with Farag Foda (or Faraj Fawda, 1946 – 1992), a prominent Egyptian professor, writer, columnist, and human rights activist, who only a few years later, in 1992, was assassinated by Islamist militants.[247] Foda vividly explained how all -isms had failed Egyptians – everything from nationalism to socialism – and how all their great hopes had been dashed. One year after Foda, also Gamal Hamdan (1928 – 1993) died, most likely killed. I regret not having met Hamdan while I lived in Cairo, since I would have been able to learn immensely from him. He was known as one of the most distinguished nationalist thinkers after the Egyptian Revolution of July 1952, and author of *The Personality of Egypt* (*Shakhsiīya Misr*).[248] He chose to live a simple life in distance from both political and academic authorities, refusing to give in to the "allure of the petro-dollar" that other intellectuals fell for.[249] Hamdan was extremely critical of political Islam – or Islamism – and linked its re-emergence with the socio-economic changes caused by the oil money boom since the 1970's. We read in his posthumously published texts:

> The Islamic awakening, as referred to by radical groups, is nothing but the awakening of the dead or the dance of the slaughtered. It has not ceased for one or two centuries. In other words it is the "oily awakening" (*sahwa naftīya*) revived by the crazy power of petroleum.... Political Islam had emerged as a phenomenon in the past, in the nineteenth century in particular, as the result of political incapability; that is, the backwardness of civilization faced with the crisis of imperialism. Political Islam is a political reaction, a display of ignorance toward civilization and of religious *Jahiliya* (the pre-Islamic time of ignorance). In the twenty-first century, it will be a form of superstition inherited from backwardness and a terrible nightmare – not a pleasant dream.[250]

During my time in Egypt, I gained deep insight into what also political scientist and historian Reza Pankhurst describes, namely, the general disenchantment with the political systems under which most Muslims have been living.[251] As Pankhurst explains, this is why many look to the caliphate for a leader who is accountable, who could save them from present-day dictators, kings, and oppressive state-security type regimes.[252] Yet, as Foda's fate illustrates, honor culture is not the solution. Foda was assassinated in 1992 by members of the Islamist group al-Gama'a al-Islamiyya after having been accused of blasphemy by clerics at Al-Azhar University. In other words, here a thinker was eliminated who would have brought future-orientated innovative creativity to Egypt, who would have brought greater hope to the country than those past failed -isms. The subsequent path of the Arab Spring, Egypt's dignity revolution, retraced Foda's fate in its ultimate descent into a ruthless regime of honor, imposing it not just on one individual, but on an entire society. The Occupy Movement, as well, was initiated by dignifiers criticizing economic humiliation, yet, it ended in humiliation entrepreneurs promising honor.

The fate of Farag Foda and the Arab Spring illustrate also how the term radicalization could fall victim to the cultural adaptation that the security dilemma engendered. Foda was a radical, yet, as terrorism expert Alex Schmid reminds us, radical fringe movements have been constructive in the past, they were necessary for the renewal of political, economic and social systems throughout history.[253] Therefore, radicalism and extremism must be kept apart. As discussed earlier, I myself could be described as a radical, similar to von Suttner, Freire, Gandhi, or Mandela. As Schmid writes, "the relatively 'open' societies of Western democracies still leave plenty of room for radicalism as opposed to extremism."[254] It is extremism that is divisive and destructive in its supremacism, rather than radicalism, whether it is secular or religious extremism. Extremism threatens "the way of life of citizens and denizens in open societies."[255]

Schmid enumerates four elements that characterize extremism: first, the use of force/ violence over persuasion; second, uniformity over diversity; third, collective goals over individual freedoms; and fourth, giving orders over engaging in dialogue.[256]

What we understand is that "honorable" extremism is not just spawning terror for a few, it is not just deadly to critics like Foda, or countries like Egypt, it is deadly for a dignified future for world society altogether. Worldwide, corporate-political elites now regard it as their righteous honorable entitlement to maintain their superiority and privileges, and they are oblivious of the fact that this may lead to all-out suicide.[257] On April 6, 2016, twenty-one young plaintiffs – ranging in age from eight to nineteen – filed a landmark climate change lawsuit against the Federal U.S. government, claiming that the continued development and burning of fossil fuels violates their constitutional rights: "This lawsuit is made necessary by the at-best schizophrenic, if not suicidal, nature of U.S.

climate and energy policy," is the verdict of James Hansen, a climate researcher, who headed NASA's Goddard's Institute for Space Studies for more than thirty years.[258]

In 2012, historian Eric Hobsbawm died at the age of 95. The year before he died, he explained what is the greatest threat facing the world in the post-9/11 era, in his view:

> The greatest threat facing the world is not religious extremism per se but the conditions which have generated it; life in unjust societies transformed at uncontrollable speed, as rules and conventions that had regulated social and personal relations for most of their history are discarded. There is no doubt that in many parts of the world extremist versions of traditional faiths, themselves in rebellion against older established religious practice, have been major beneficiaries of this situation, particularly where they can be combined with xenophobia. These dangerous innovatory tendencies are usually confined to minorities, though these sometimes succeed in establishing strong political positions, as have Jewish extremism in Israel and ultra-evangelicalism in the USA, or even supremacy, as in Iran. No traditional religion is immune to infection. The democratization of non-European politics has brought more power to those open to the appeal of religious practice and weakened the relatively freethinking political elites which (like the Founding Fathers of the USA and most of the post-1945 secular reforming rulers of Islamic countries) recognized these dangers. How far will this be counteracted by the explosive rise in the proportion of human beings with higher secular education? Or dangerously reinforced by the insecurities of our century? We do not know.[259]

We do not know? As I observe, the problem of extremist responses to honor humiliation is now compounded by the fact that feelings of dignity humiliation are more intense than feelings of honor humiliation.

When those intensified feelings of humiliation spawn responses informed by scripts of honor humiliation, the situation is aggravated. "Honorable" terror is still the most familiar response as way out of humiliation; the path of a von Suttner, Freire, Gandhi, or Mandela is still not established deeply enough as a cultural code. Humiliation in honor societies – honor humiliation – can be categorized into four variants.[260] Elites use *conquest humiliation* to subjugate formerly equal neighbors into a position of inferiority. When a hierarchy is in place, elites use *reinforcement humiliation* to keep it in place – which includes techniques ranging from seating orders and kowtowing rules to brutal and customary beatings and killings. Pierre Bourdieu's "symbolic domination" has its place here, with acts of unconscious or pre-conscious intimidation, with "symbolic violence which is not aware of what it is (to the extent that it implies no act of intimidation)."[261] A third form of humiliation, *relegation humiliation*, is used to push an already low-ranking underling even further down. *Exclusion humiliation* means eliminating victims altogether, exiling, or even killing them.

Human rights conflate all four types of humiliation into the last category: all human rights violations exclude victims from humanity altogether. This situation produces intense pain and suffering because losing one's dignity means being denied one's status as part of the family of humanity. I call this type of humiliation *human rights humiliation* or *dignity humiliation*. It is a deeply destructive and devastating that hurts people at their core. It is in this context that practices of humiliation once considered normal, such as being beaten or tortured, acquire labels such as victimhood or trauma.[262] *Domestic chastisement* transmutes into *domestic violence*, and *genocide* is no longer a "solution" (*Endlösung*).

In today's world, dignity humiliation is on the increase. The experience of rising global interconnectedness confirms the fact that human nature is social. "Cultures" are not closed containers, not mutually incommensurate "silos." The coming-together of humankind in a shrinking world amplifies this connectedness. A global community of friends is now possible through globalization. Unfortunately, globalization also increases the range of people who can humiliate each other or feel humiliated, be it justified or not. And this dynamic is aggravated when the promise of equality in dignity is broken by double standards. I observe moral injury from dignity humiliation now increasing on a global scale.

In this situation, extremists on all sides uphold the correspondence bias: They keep inferring from their own pain that those who caused it must have wanted to inflict it out of purely evil intentions. They believe that others hurt "us" out of free-floating unmotivated hatred or mere lust to unfold their evil nature, while "we did nothing to them" that possibly could cause them to feel slighted. Those engaging in terror are caught in this bias as much as those engaging in counterterror. Taking dignity humiliation seriously and wanting to follow Bertha von Suttner is still seen as dishonorable weakness on all sides. The more the other is perceived as evil, the more terror tactics are deemed to be honorable and necessary.

	Honor Humiliation	Dignity Humiliation
(1) Conquest humiliation: A strong power reduces the relative autonomy of rivals who were previously regarded as equals, and forces them into a position of long-term subordination. A new hierarchy is created, or a new upper tier is forced upon an existing hierarchical order.	X	–
(2) Relegation humiliation: An individual or group is forcefully pushed downward within an existing status hierarchy.	X	–
(3) Reinforcement humiliation: Routine abuse of those less powerful in order to maintain their self-perception that they are, indeed, inferior.	X	–
(4) Exclusion humiliation: An individual or a group is forcefully ejected from society, for instance through banishment, exile, or physical extermination.	X	X

Table 1: Four variants of humiliation, thanking sociologist Dennis Smith, 2001, p. 543

In the past, it was easier than now to maintain this mindset. The situation becomes more complex in a shrinking world, where it gets ever harder to uphold the correspondence bias. This book is written to help it weaken further. I wish to confront all sides with the explanations given by the other side, explanations that may suggest that free-floating unmotivated hatred or lust to unfold evil nature might not necessarily be the best explanation. I wish to suggest that it might be worth considering that even acts of violence may emerge in response to feelings of humiliation, or out of love and solidarity with fellow humiliated victims.

In the midst of a standoff, it requires courage to step outside of the correspondence bias and paint a more nuanced picture: the person who does so risks being brandished as a traitor. Norwegian researcher Cecilie Hellestveit is such a courageous author. She points out, for instance, that it is not sufficient for Norwegian politician to say, "Oh, we had good intentions when we broke international law in Syria," and hope that others will honor their good intentions, while at the same time insisting that Russia proves its dangerous intentions when it does the very same thing, namely, break international law.[263] Indeed, I begin to wonder when I see my friends in Crimea be so genuinely overjoyed to be liberated and back home in Russia – they feel that they have suffered long enough from having their Russian identity suppressed and an Ukrainian identity forced upon – and unsurprisingly, they look at Norwegian politicians and their intentions in exactly the inverse way.[264]

Monty Marshall, director of the Center for Systemic Peace at the University of Maryland, is another courageous scholar. He describes how the very definitions of terrorism are marred by dilemmas: Conceptualizations of terrorism are all too often "politically motivated." Analysts attempt to rationalize distinctions between civil and uncivil applications of violence: there is (useless) terror and (useful) enforcement, (undisciplined) terrorism and (disciplined) war, and (dishonorable) terrorists and (honorable) "freedom fighters."[265] Conceptual confusion is further exacerbated, Marshall adds, by the often cavalier usage of the pejorative term "terrorist" to refer to any political opponent, much as "communist" was used for political effect in the West during the Cold War.[266]

Monty Marshall recommends a broad definition for terrorism, as given by Bruce Hoffman, director of the Center for Security Studies at Georgetown University: Terrorism is "the deliberate creation and exploitation of fear through violence or the threat of violence in the pursuit of political change."[267]

Wolfgang Kaleck is a civil rights attorney and the general secretary for the European Center for Constitutional and Human Rights. In our conversation in Berlin on May 17, 2011, he explained to me that terrorism is a category that is rather discredited in the legal environment, as it is too open to political manipulation: there is the terrorist, then there is the freedom fighter, and there is state terrorism.[268] It makes little sense to continue to expand the concept of terrorism, he told me. What should be done instead is to address relevant events with existing legal instruments. At the national level, legal instruments that are suitable are those that address, for instance, arson, homicide, or damage to property, and at the international level, we speak of war crimes and crimes against humanity. Such categories apply to all sides, he pointed out, be it the Taliban or Western forces in Afghanistan: in all cases, civilians ought not be harmed.

To conclude this chapter, we, all of humankind, can only address our global challenges constructively if we cooperate globally, if we become at least good neighbors, perhaps even friends. In this situation dignity humiliation can be seen as proof of the human desire to connect as equals, as a chance to heal it and nurture good neighborly relations. The world is thus confronted with the task to acknowledge, prevent, and heal both honor humiliation and dignity humiliation, and to refrain from responding to terror in ways that are informed by the honor code.

When I worked as a psychological counselor in Egypt from 1984 to 1991, also Palestinian clients came to me. I will tell their story later. For them, it was dishonorable to study in Cairo and live a good life, while their families in Palestine suffered. Due to the asymmetry of the situation, they deemed that terror tactics, including suicidal ones, were honorable. I attempted to convince them to change their conceptualization of the situation from honor humiliation perpetrated on "us by them," to dignity humiliation hurting "all of us." I encouraged them to refrain from responding with local terror tactics against "them," and rather join hands to develop global "dignity tactics" for all of us, humanity at large.

Chapter 7

The Rise of the "Art of Humiliation"

The beheadings carried out by Da'esh stand in a tradition of killing that once was much more common. Such practices appear barbaric to many in the twenty-first century only because, nowadays, domination is often wrapped in much more sophistication and less visible cruelty. While competition for domination was hidden in the proverbial *fog of war* in former times (a term coined by Prussian general Carl von Clausewitz, 1780 – 1831), now, it is rather Orwellian fog that is created when cruelty shall be obscured and secrecy protected. Access to potentially subversive technology is being curtailed, access to the Internet blocked, mobile phone cameras are unwelcome wherever abuse shall go unseen.

Two scripts can be discerned when we look at the influence of the security dilemma. Killing a worthy male enemy is honorable heroism, while killing women and children is dishonorable slaughter, more like "cleaning up dirt."[1] A cleaning job is a lowly task, part and parcel of the traditional role description for women wherever a realm is defined as "inside": It is the woman who traditionally cleans the house, not the man – and it is therefore humiliating for an honorable man to engage in such activities.[2] The differentiation of *inside* versus *outside* realms has been introduced earlier. The heroic script for males plays out wherever outside realms are defined – outside of the city walls or outside of the country's borders – or at the border between inside and outside realms – patrolling the country's borders. The traditional male script does not dehumanize the enemy, as this would mean that the second script would apply, the "female" task of having to clean up dirt. Simple slaughter is unheroic, only fighting a worthy enemy is heroic. The male script therefore ascribes honor to its adversaries, including, if needed, the honor of mighty Satanic evilness.

The script of male honor reflects that the security dilemma is not a personal psychological problem. The security dilemma is a brutal state of the world that pits people against each other even when they do not want it. The security dilemma is a tragedy into which people are forced whether they wish it or not. It leaves people only one path to pride, namely, to stand in this situation with honor and bravery. The security dilemma was a cruel teacher, and the lesson is deeply inscribed still today even in cultural realms such as Germany. While I write these lines in May 2017, a young Syrian sought asylum in Germany to avoid being drafted into Bashar al-Assad's army in Syria, an army that commits war crimes. A German court rejected his plea and treated him as a cowardly shirker by explaining to him the "soldier's duty" (*soldatische Pflicht*): "The soldier must overcome the human impulse of fear.... Fear of personal peril is no excuse when the soldier's duty demands to face the danger."[3]

To overcome his fear is one of the soldier's duties, yet, there is also another duty, namely, to treat his enemy with respect. It would be dishonorable to use the security dilemma as a pretext to satisfy personal desires to humiliate people. Let me give an example. The script of male honor manifested itself in many aspects of Nazi ideology, and a number of its military leaders acted on it. The war theatre in North Africa during World War II offers an example. Pierre Messmer, French officer in Bir Hacheim, explains that the war in North Africa was a "war without hatred," a "clean war," "une guerre propre," where enemies respected each other as equals.[4] On the German side, Field Marshal Erwin Rommel disobeyed orders from Hitler to simply "exterminate" (*erledigen*) supposedly "unworthy" enemies, for example, the 3,600 soldiers who were entrenched in the fortress of Bir Hacheim, among them Germans and Austrians who had joined the Foreign Legion.[5] Isaac Levy, Jewish Chaplain in Africa, reported that there was no sign of antisemitism in the German Africa Corps.[6] Rommel was a professional soldier (*Berufssoldat*), who had internalized the rule that soldiers should never involve themselves in politics, this is at least what his son Manfred Rommel later explained: "die Soldaten sind nicht für die Politik da" (soldiers are no politicians).[7]

Those German officers who attempted to assassinate Hitler on July 20, 1944, were imbued with the script of male honor when they acted,[8] yet, just like the young Syrian asylum seeker of today, they were regarded as cowardly shirkers by their peers and the majority of the German population. Even long after the war, the children of these officers were not hailed as children of heroes but ostracized as *Verräterkinder* (children of traitors).[9]

When the German delegation signed the armistice ending World War I on November 11, 1918, they expected to be treated as honorable enemies by the victors, yet, to their dismay, they were treated like *Abschaum* (scum).[10] After World War I, German nobility had difficulties in keeping up enthusiasm for monarchism in Germany, not least because the German emperor had failed honor. After the defeat in 1918, he had simply cowardly "deserted" into exile.[11]

While male honor was idolized in Nazi ideology, also the script of "cleaning up dirt" was enacted. These two scripts not only existed alongside in Nazi Germany, they were both driven to their extremes. Some of those who were involved tried to keep them apart by closing their eyes for the dishonorable "cleaning" activities perpetrated by Germany, while others attempted to combine them. Hermann Göring, Adolf Hitler's former heir, belonged to the first group. When the war was lost for Nazi Germany, he felt he was in a position to negotiate with the victors "from man to man" and was surprised to be indicted in Nuremberg. He declared that he had nothing to do with concentration camps – that Heinrich Himmler was the one who was responsible – as he himself would never do anything as dishonorable as killing women and children.[12] In other words, Göring closed his eyes for German dishonor. He was not alone. For many decades to come, the German Wehrmacht (the German army) followed him on this path.[13]

Heinrich Himmler, on his part, connected both scripts in the most unseeming ways. He defined it to be the highest form of bravery to preserve male honor while engaging in lowly female cleaning tasks. The message of the second speech that Himmler held to high ranking Nazi leaders, or *Gauleiter*, in Posen on October 6, 1943, was as follows: Admittedly, killing Jews is a horribly dishonorable job, yet, as it is necessary, future generations will be thankful.[14] In his first Posen speech on October 4, 1943, Himmler applauded his SS-men for managing to stay "honorable" – "anständig" – despite having carried out such dishonorable tasks as exterminating people like pests.[15]

Some may want to believe that Himmler was an exception. Yet, he spoke from within the *Zeitgeist* of his century. Sociologist Max Weber wrote in April November 1915, in the middle of World War I, to his mother:

> We have proven that we are a great civilized nation: people who live in the midst of a refined culture were able cope with the horrors of war (something that would be no difficulty for a Senegal-negro!), and then to come back, and, despite of this, remaining so fundamentally decent, as the great majority of our people is – that is real humanity.[16]

Japan, China, and the Koreas are now bound together in cycles of humiliation that are inscribed in similar conundrums. North Korean leaders are proud of the nuclear threat they can project precisely because this gives them the status of a respected enemy, worthy of being defeated in war rather than be cleaned away like dirt.

Then there is the controversial Yasukuni Shrine in Tokyo, another story of honorable enemy and dishonorable dirt. I spent altogether three years in Japan and it was very interesting for me to visit this shrine. For many Japanese, the dead military leaders who are buried there are patriots who deserve to be honored. For China and Korea, they are war criminals who perpetrated unspeakable atrocities. The Nanjing Massacre in 1937, when the Japanese captured Nanjing, was the epitome of those outrages. The Japanese desire to honor their "patriotic" war criminals is felt to be deeply humiliating in China and Korea, while Japanese nationalists, in turn, perceive their former enemies' protests to be humiliating.[17]

Terror can be staged like a reality show, which, on its part, has perfectionized the art of humiliation. In November 2008, in Mumbai, a series of twelve coordinated shooting and bombing attacks lasted for four days, carried out by ten members of Lashkar-e-Taiba, an Islamic militant organization based in Pakistan: " ...the raid on Mumbai was a brilliantly devised piece of horrific terrorist show business," is the evaluation of documentary maker Dan Reed.[18] "Violence is the realization of power, as both the staging and enactment, imaginary and practice of power."[19]

During the Mumbai attacks, the media that covered the mayhem, magnified terror by using the terminology of war (as also used in the phrase war on terror). State and non-state actors were depicted as warring parties: "The Mumbai attacks were scripted and staged in a conscious effort to obtain maximum media coverage, which also made the masterminds dependent on the media. The war story created by the media featured violence simply as a means of 'fighting a battle,' obscuring the significant role of violence as a display of force by both security forces and 'terrorists.'"[20] In other words, the trope of war was employed to amplify drama, providing the status of respected/evil enemy where it was not called for. As a result, when new anti-terror laws were enacted in India following the attacks, they were deemed by Amnesty International as "violating international human rights standards."[21]

Also the 2015 attacks in Beirut and Paris were masterpieces of staging.[22] An extra dramaturgical twist was added by carrying out the Paris attack directly following the Beirut attack, as this would demonstrate to Da'esh followers that Paris would be mourned with great Western media attention, while the suffering in Beirut would be neglected.[23] Also the 2016 attacks in Istanbul[24] emulated the Mumbai script by bringing terror to the doorsteps of the symbols of prosperity.[25]

Through its media support, staged terror could be called the pinnacle of the art of humiliation. Victims can do little to protect themselves in the usual chaos that reigns, and even efforts to respond to acts of terror may merely throw the victim's helplessness into starker contrast. This, in turn, will then provoke the desired overreactions on the other side. Seldom do efforts to respond render images of heroism: The hope held by some that a "a good guy with a gun" would be an effective protection against "a bad guy with a gun," is vain, as statistics show that the role of armed civilians in successfully confronting shooters is negligible.[26]

Terror can be staged like a reality show, which, on its part, has perfectionized the art of humiliation: "More than sex, more than violence, humiliation is the unifying principle behind a successful reality show," is what we read in *The New York Times*.[27]

Psychotherapist Carol Smaldino warns that also politics are increasingly being staged in this way and that the success of a candidate such as Donald J. Trump "surfs" on people's addiction to reality show.[28] War, terror, politics, all are inspiring the art of humiliation and are inspired by it.

The unspeakable art of humiliation: Cleansing shame over admiration

In my work, I have studied several cases where I wondered why the enemy was dehumanized. Why were the Jews dehumanized in Germany, the Tutsi in Rwanda, or the Isaaq in Somalia? If they were so worthless, why were they not simply marginalized a bit more than they already were? Or, if they were so threatening, why were they then not ennobled as worthy enemies? This would have provided them with a status that would have elevated fighting them to the level of heroic resistance, rather than having to turn to demeaning cleansing? The argument that dehumanization makes killing "easier" is not necessarily valid: for an honorable man, it should be the very opposite. In a paper on that topic, I ask:

> Is it not curious that minorities such as the Isaaq in Somalia, Tutsi in Rwanda, or Jews in Nazi Germany, even when they were objectively rather subdued and politically marginalized, still seemed so threatening to genocidal perpetrators that exterminating them seemed the only "solution"? Why was it not sufficient simply to marginalize them? Why did the perpetrators feel a need to go to elaborate lengths to "send messages" to the victims – messages, that is, of humiliation? Does a simple scapegoat explanation suffice?[29]

What is often called the inferiority complex may offer an explanation. The explanation may lie in the perpetrators' psyche, in their shame over their admiration for the enemy. Siad Barre was impressed, like all Somalis, by the cosmopolitan and educated Isaaq clan; Hutu servants once looked up to their Tutsi aristocracy; and Adolf Hitler, when he still lived in Austria, was bound to be impressed, perhaps initially even admire, the Jewish influence on Austrian intellectual life, as Hitler's book *Mein Kampf* betrays. My analysis is that when elite admiration becomes a reason for shame, the targets of this admiration can no longer be treated as worthy enemies – as this would acknowledge admiration – they are treated like the lowest of dirt.

How can admiration become shameful? In my paper "Genocide, Humiliation, and Inferiority," I try to explain this:

> The more societies are influenced by ideals of human rights, the more salient feelings of humiliation become – in a threefold fashion. First, subalterns feel more humiliated in a system where elites are no longer accepted as benevolent patrons, but come to be viewed as evil oppressors. Second, feelings of inferiority may provoke feelings of shame at such inferiority.
>
> Third, subalterns may feel retrospective shame – that is, shame that they ever admired elites and bowed before them. All three elements may be translated, in the absence of countervailing influences, into an urge to purge and "cleanse" shame and humiliation, along with the people who are seen as triggering these emotions.[30]

Elite admiration can become shameful, as happened in Rwanda, when formerly accepted norms of hierarchy are replaced by egalitarian ideals, or, as in the case of Siad Barre and Adolf Hitler, through personal experiences of humiliation. Through the extermination of the objects of admiration – the Jews, the Tutsi, the Isaaq, in these cases – it is not just the annihilation of their physical existence that is being achieved, perhaps more important for the perpetrators is to cleanse themselves from their own shame.[31] In that situation, applying the female cleaning-off-dirt script on victims means denying them the status of honor, an expression of the strongest humiliation possible and the surest way to free oneself from one's unwanted admiration for the victims.

This script is as relevant for genocidal cleansing as it is for terrorism. Also the label terrorist has joined the list of demeaning names by now, names such as pests or cockroaches that were used in Rwanda for the Tutsi. Nowadays, labeling rivals as terrorists is becoming increasingly popular as a way to deny them the status of honor. Iraq's dictator Saddam Hussein, for instance, labeled the people of the Marshlands in the south of his country – the "Garden of Eden" that is now a UNESCO World Heritage Site – as terrorists, after their Shiite ayatollah Muhammad Sadiq al-Sadr had defied Saddam Hussein's rule.[32] In a genocidal onslaught, Saddam Hussein destroyed their entire way of life and cohesion as a people.[33]

Admiration turned into shame and then turned into terror, this is now also a global predicament. My global experience indicates that the coming-into-being of an ever more interconnected world is a "love story" that carries the risk of all love stories – it can turn sour when betrayed. Disappointed lovers may shout and scream in an attempt to get the yearned-for love back, yet, shouting and screaming will most probably only lead to divorce.

Many a young man in the West who sympathizes with extremist activities, might do so because he at one point admired and loved the West:

> Elites are typically admired, loved, and envied, and the rich West is not excluded from this phenomenon. What the French court was to Europe, the West is to the global village. Copies of the castle of Versailles can be found everywhere in Europe and copies of the Western style of life over the entire earth's surface. Elites are often quite uninformed about the masses, but the masses always know what the elites are up to.[34]

What does a young man in the West do when he feels that his love story has turned sour? When equal dignity proves to be an unattainable promise, he feels betrayed. Just like lovers start shouting, he might opt for the old and well-established script of heroic honorable defense to earn the recognition he otherwise feels is denied. He might be oblivious of the fact that it is vain to hope that bomb attacks will elicit love, as little as shouting can produce love in marriage. To stay in the marriage image, such a young men would have to learn the lessons that marriage counsellors offer to quarrelling lovers.[35] Other young men might have moved away even further from their former love object and given up on the West's promise of dignity entirely. They may feel shame over ever having admired it. In that case, they may attempt to cleanse their own shame by treating their victims like dirt. Unlike the first group, the second will be beyond the reach of dialogue.

Society will have to learn to recognize the need of young men for dignity earlier in the process, before they slide away too far. Those who still clamber for recognition from the West through "shouting" are in need of "marriage counselling" before they disengage thus far that they only wish for divorce, or more, for the demise of their former love object.

Particularly those with an absent father will need preventive attention. A young man, when he listens to Islamic lecturer Anwar al-Awlaki's recordings, will find the father figure he yearns for. Al-Awlaki was killed by an American drone, and since then, he projects even greater authority than when he was living. Martyrdom gave him an iconic status as a "knight of Islam":

> The Tsarnaevs, Chechen-born brothers who set off two pressure-cooker bombs at the Boston Marathon in 2013, owed part of their ideological training and their bomb-making skills to Awlaki's online work. "Listen to Anwar al-Awlaki's ... here after series," Dzhokhar Tsarnaev, the younger brother, tweeted a few weeks before the attack, "you will gain an unbelievable amount of knowledge." Chérif Kouachi, one of the Algerian-French brothers who massacred the staff of the satirical newspaper Charlie Hebdo in Paris in January, told a TV station in his last public words before being shot by the police that "Sheikh Anwar al-Awlaki" had sponsored the attack. The list of plots and attacks influenced by Awlaki goes on and on.[36]

Anwar al-Awlaki was one of those who tried to "arouse the sleeping body of the Islamic Nation." Terrorism expert Alex Schmid recalls a statement of an analyst close to Al-Qaeda regarding the "Manhattan raid" of September 11, 2001:

> Al-Qaeda has, and always had, a specific aim: to arouse the sleeping body of the Islamic Nation – a billion Muslims worldwide – to fight against Western power and the contaminations of Western culture. In support of this aim, the 9/11 attacks were designed "to force the Western snake to bite the sleeping body, and wake it up."[37]

This quote shows that Al-Qaeda strategists are no mindless berserkers; they are highly intelligent adversaries and experts of humiliation to be taken extremely seriously. If we say that humiliation is "a nuclear bomb of emotions," and perhaps the most toxic social dynamic there is,[38] then this bomb can indeed be triggered by inflicting a steady stream of micro-humiliations. By applying terrorism, even micro-terrorism, adversaries can be driven to retaliate. This then opens the opportunity to target them as the true aggressors, as deserving "defensive" attack. It opens the opportunity to teach billions of Muslims to stop admiring superiors – be they their own or foreign – and instead learn to be ashamed of ever having admired them.

Also counterterrorism responses have driven what I call the art of humiliation to its most extreme modern forms of hazing, bullying, and torture. Psychologist Martin Seligman's research on "learned helplessness" has been mentioned before. In the original experiments, Seligman worked with dogs who "learned helplessness" by being trapped during traumatic experiences. Later, they would no longer attempt to flee, even when this became possible.[39] After the American Medical Association and the American Psychiatric Association had decided that it would violate their members' oaths to patients to participate in the interrogations, we hear that psychologists came to the C.I.A.'s rescue. As already discussed earlier, on the C.I.A.'s behalf, two contract psychologists, James Elmer Mitchell and John "Bruce" Jessen, who had previously been Air Force trainers in the Survival Evasion

Resistance Escape (SERE) program,[40] developed theories and practices of interrogation based on learned helplessness.[41] It has been said that those psychologists gave the C.I.A. and the White House the "cover" they needed; interrogations were deemed to be "safe, legal and effective" in the presence of medical personnel.

> In the "Salt Pit," a then-secret C.I.A. prison in Afghanistan, John "Bruce" Jessen watched carefully in late 2002 as five agency officers rushed into a darkened cell and grabbed an Afghan detainee named Gul Rahman. "It was thoroughly planned and rehearsed," Jessen later explained, according to a C.I.A. investigator's report. "They dragged him outside, cut off his clothes and secured him with Mylar tape," before beating him and forcing him to run wearing a hood. When he fell, they dragged him down dirt passageways, leaving abrasions up and down his body. Jessen added a critique. "After something like this is done, interrogators should speak to the prisoner to give [him] something to think about," he told the investigator. On November 20, 2002, Rahman was found dead in his unheated cell. He was naked from the waist down and had been chained to a concrete floor. An autopsy concluded that he probably froze to death....[42]

The subtle art of humiliation to keep underlings humble

Within the script of honor, honorable enemies deserve to be treated respectfully as equals, while subordinates are in a different category entirely. Under the laws of the *Twelve Tables*[43] – the ancient foundation of Roman law – the head of the family, *pater familias*, for instance, had *vitae necisque potestas*, or the "power of life and death," over his children and his slaves, often also over his wife. He had the power to kill or sell into slavery those he had "under his hand," or *sub manu* (*emancipation* is therefore the deliverance out of the hand of *pater familias*). *Droit de seigneur* is yet another term in this list, signifying the tradition wherein the lord of an estate was allowed to deflower any virgin who lived on his land.

In the context of the dominator model of society, honorable leaders had three responsibilities, first, to treat "peer" enemy leaders with respect and either fight them honorably or ally with them, second, to keep underlings in due humility through routine humiliation, and, third, to relegate the tasks of raising the next generation and maintaining daily life to the female sphere, be it its women or lowly men.

The first task, victory over one's opponents in competition for domination is the most important one in this context, the one that provides honor and meaning. The other two tasks are subservient to the first, they are there to be attended to so that the first can be successful. To fulfil the second task, that of keeping underlings in due humility, openly displayed brutality always had its place, and still has.[44] Many rulers throughout history have used brute force to hold inferiors down – from violence and terror, to torture to killing. Psychologist Steven Pinker has illustrated these practices:

> Many conventional histories reveal that mutilation and torture were routine forms of punishment for infractions that today would result in a fine. In Europe before the Enlightenment, crimes like shoplifting or blocking the king's driveway with your oxcart might have resulted in your tongue being cut out, your hands being chopped off, and so on. Many of these punishments were administered publicly, and cruelty was a popular form of entertainment.[45]

Even though direct and open brutality always had its place, over time, dominant groups often tried to replace brute force with more sophisticated approaches. In the course of the past millennia the art of domination became ever more refined, and it did so in different parts of the world in various ways and at various degrees. More sophisticated approaches have many advantages, among them that they can be more effective than open violence. It can be more cost-effective – in short, it can save money – to make overt applications of brute force redundant. Recently, the death penalty in the United States was put in question not for ethical considerations, but because it is very costly.[46]

There are many ways sophisticated domination can make use of humiliation, be it humiliation as direct effect, side effect, or main tool. Shame and humiliation can be used in "artful" ways. Keeping people in fear of humiliation is perhaps the most effective tool. The *art of domination* can become the *art of humiliation.*

History offers impressive examples for how, for instance killing was replaced by symbolic emasculation and humiliation. Saint Clotilde, or Chrodechildis (475 – 545) was part of the Merovingian dynasty that ruled the Franks in Europe for nearly three hundred years.[47] After the death of her son Chlodomer in 524, Chrodechildis took over the protection of her grandchildren, her dead son's three minor sons, to secure their inheritance in the kingdom. Yet, she was unable to protect the children and they were captured. She was put in front of a decision that few in contemporary France will be able to grasp: She had to decide whether the children should be shorn and thus rendered incapable of ruling – hair was the symbol of the Frankish royalty – or be killed. She decided that she rather wanted them dead than emasculated. Her other son Chlothar went ahead and killed his ten-year and seven-year old nephews, only the third boy escaped and later followed an ecclesiastical path. In other words, it was preferable for Merovingian rulers that rivals should die. This then changed with their successors, the Carolingians: they replaced killing with humiliation.

The Sultans of the Ottoman Empire offer another example. From Mehmed II until Ahmed I, they killed potential rival successors to the throne. Mehmed III (1595 – 1603) killed nineteen of his brothers and half-brothers.[48] Later sultans no longer murdered aspiring competitors but kept them under house arrest in the *kafes* (the cage), which was part of the Imperial Harem of the Ottoman Palace. Also here, killing was replaced with humiliation.

Also religion offers examples. Many ancient gods were seen as openly vengeful if not appeased, while divine agency became more indirect later, at least in some cases. I was born in Hamelin, Lower Saxony, in Central Europe. In the center of the city is a church, the "Marktkirche," featuring a remarkable relief from the fourteenth century, that of "Jesus the Judge." The relief depicts two swords emerging from Jesus' mouth. The two swords symbolize secular and spiritual power. Jesus is accompanied by angels with the instruments of torture with which he himself was tortured. Similar descriptions can be found in many churches of this time.[49] In later medieval representations, however, one sword was replaced by the lily of grace.[50] In other words, we see a gradual transformation of the Christian god from a mighty dead-bringer to a "graceful" humiliator.

This transformation, however, was not necessarily accepted by all Christians, and is not even today. Dalton Thomas is a preacher who, in the face of terrorist threats, scolds "Western church's spiritual bankruptcy" for forgetting about God's vengeance. He writes:

> The problem with the idea that New Testament grace supersedes Old Testament vengeance (false and hollow categories) is not only that the New Testament is brimming with sobering statements of the holy fury of God, but that His vengeance is (in a very real way) more terrifying now that the blood of the holy Son of God has been shed. The surety of God's vengeance is solidified in the New Testament, not abrogated.[51]

Also South America can serve as an example for the emergence of subtler forms of domination over underlings through the application of humiliation. During my time in South America in 2012, I met many who grappled with the question of why South America has been so violent, and what can be done about it.[52] Over timer, formerly unapologetic colonial brutality has become replaced by somewhat more whitewashed strategies, among them strategies labeled as antiterrorism. Political scientist and human rights expert Sonia Cardenas explains that even unarmed indigenous groups in the region are now viewed as terrorists, "especially in the context of the U.S.-sponsored 'global war on terror' and the 'war on drugs.'"[53] Relying on antiterrorist laws, governments detain indigenous activists who attempt to mobilize for greater rights and the return of their territory, and they meet them with systematic violence without due process and for extensive periods of time. Ricardo Diaz, an indigenous representative of the largest opposition party in Bolivia, describes what happens: "It's true that indigenous peoples are a threat, from the point of view of the political and economic powers-that-be. They see us as terrorists, but we aren't, because our struggle is open, legal and legitimate."[54]

Sonia Cardenas wonders why decision makers who wish to maintain stability and retain power violate human rights norms. She asks: "What remains unclear is why engaging in repression is deemed an appropriate response to domestic instability. The choice to violate human rights can be particularly perplexing since other viable responses often exist, and violations can elicit global opprobrium."[55] Cardenas concludes: "This is where the role of ideology enters the picture."[56] Cardenas points at exclusionary ideologies such as anticommunism, racism, bigotry, sexism, national security doctrine, neoliberal economic orthodoxy, impunity, and the war on terror. She explains that these ideologies serve to label certain categories of people as "legitimate outsiders" or enemies, and that, from there, "the slippery slope to de-humanization follows easily."[57]

I would suggest that what happens is perhaps not de-humanization – since this presupposes that there once was humanization – but rather an inability, or arefusal, to humanize in the first place. During colonial times indigenous people were ranked as creatures so far removed from "civilized" people that they did not even count as fellow human beings. Now, they demand to be recognized as fellow humans, in other words, they wish to rise up on the ladder of worthiness. Those who are steeped in past colonial cultural codes, however, find it difficult to widen their scope of who is equally worthy. Cardenas explains that Catholicism, which underpinned colonialism, promoted the notion of the health of an organic state: "In this context, it is not surprising that state leaders late in the twentieth century described political opponents as 'cancers' to be extirpated from the body politic."[58]

Animal rights traverse the same trajectory just now on a global scale: Animal rights are slowly coming into a wider consciousness, and many even in the West are still reluctant to consider animals as fellow creatures. The case of misogyny might have its place here, too, at least partly. Whoever feels that women are not to be taken seriously as fellow human beings may react in ways similar to those of authoritarian South American rulers, refusing to humanize women and resisting their empowerment. However, clearly, the case of women is more complicated, as it can also serve as an example for the above described dynamics of shame for admiration. A son might love and admire his mother when young, and later learn to feel ashamed over ever having done so. As a result, he might push women down actively, even with venom. The present trend of market-driven pornography in Western countries might speak to that point, as this pornography entails ever more brutal humiliation of women.[59] The staging of humiliation when girls are hanged after rape in countries such as India may flow from similar motives.[60]

Another application of the art of humiliation is to covertly set in motion cycles of humiliation, and thus keep awareness and fear of humiliation alive. False flag operations have always been a popular strategy. The Gleiwitz incident on August 31, 1939, was a false flag operation by Nazi forces who posed as Poles and attacked the German radio station Sender Gleiwitz in Upper Silesia, Germany (since 1945: Gliwice, Poland) as a pretext to invade Poland. This happened, while my parents lived in Lower Silesia.

Later, Jews who were transported away to be killed were told that they were going to work: *Arbeit macht frei* (Work Sets You Free) was the slogan appearing on the entrance of Auschwitz and other death camps. Many of the Germans I spoke with during the past decades told me – and I think many did not lie – that this was indeed what they believed when their Jewish neighbors were transported away: that they would be going to "work."[61]

After World War II, similar dynamics unfolded in the German Democratic Republic commonly known as East Germany. Victims of its *Stasi* (Ministry for State Security) did not dare to share even with close friends what they were suffering, because what happened to them was so unbelievable. The length to which the Stasi went, and the sophistication they invested in surveilling and damaging their victims, was beyond imagination.[62] In the lives of the victims, suddenly everything went wrong, in ways that were inexplicable to them: A job was terminated without explanation, application letters never got an answer, marriages broke due to alleged imaginary affairs. In 1976, the Stasi started a secret strategy with the telling code name *Operation Zersetzung* (Operation Disintegration) with the declared aim to inflict maximum damage on victims by way of covert methods. The Stasi thus meted out state-sanctioned psychological terror and frequently caused existential crises that resulted in depression and suicide. Many sufferers learned only after the fall of the iron curtain that it was not bad luck but the Stasi that had been behind all their mishaps. To date, thousands of former GDR citizens are considered permanently traumatized.[63]

What the Stasi did was skillfully applying philosopher Marshall McLuhan's insight: "Only puny secrets need protection. Big secrets are protected by public incredulity."[64] The application of "unimaginable" interventions could be counted as the eighth *master suppression technique*, this is what social psychologist and politician Berit Ås told me.[65] Berit Ås is famous for having coined the phrase *master techniques* and has described them in her work.[66]

Feelings of humiliation entail anger and shame over not being able to redress the degradation that is felt to be so undeserved. Just as the Somali proverb suggests: "A man deserves to be killed and not to be humiliated." A proud culture of noble warriors does not allow humiliation to prevail. Norway has an equally proud Viking past that may still shine through in Norwegians having an "alarming tendency to quarrel with their neighbors": "It's seen as a matter of honor not to give in to a neighbor's demands, and we expect or hope that the other side will take the initiative for some sort of reconciliation," explains Dag Are Børresen of the insurance company HELP Forsikring.[67]

Yet, most people do not live in proud warrior cultures. Many are worn down by humiliation-attrition to the point of apathy, depression, and inertia.[68] They turn their rage inward and become depressed.[69] The very paralysis and apathy that also learned helplessness engenders can be the result,[70] and a seemingly "peaceful" society, peaceful because the price for keeping structural violence covert[71] is paid for by its members' pain.[72]

Even my most peace-loving Palestinian friends, however, admitted to me that it is possible to drive even the most apathetic people to "madness" by subjecting them to continuous experiences of humiliation. While it is true that feelings of humiliation can result in apathy and depression, they can also bring people to "go black" in *humiliated fury*, as psychologist Helen Block Lewis has called it.[73] These feelings can transmute into what I call the *nuclear bomb of the emotions*. In that case rage turns outward and explodes into hot desperate and self- and other-destructive rage.[74] Violent retaliation, even if self-destructive, can be experienced as ultimate liberation from one's own shame over one's helplessness at the hands of one's humiliators. This may play out as passionate murder and/or suicide. A young man – call him Ahmed – told me that he felt triumphant humiliation, without any sense of shame, when he was beaten and almost killed by the military. This sensation, he reported, proved to him that he was able to heroically resist oppression.[75] As long as he meekly bowed to the humiliation of oppression, as long as he tried to hide from it out of fear of humiliation, he felt unbearable shame and guilt. Feeling shame-free triumphant humiliation liberated him, made him resilient and gave him new pride.[76] In a way, he reacted to humiliation the Somali-way, thus becoming a noble warrior, no longer a meek underling.

The phenomenon of mass shooting, spree killing, and rampage killing may follow similar scripts: the rejection of shame over humiliation, and the display of potency, including its suicidal consequences.[77] It is the separation of shame from humiliation, and then the liberation from this shame, in short, the experience of shame-free humiliation as victory and triumph.

Ahmed "went black," he simply could not endure his own shame anymore. Many years later, in my conversations with representatives of the Security Services in Norway, Josefine Aase highlighted the factor of choices, and how the lack of choices might contribute to "going black":

> Those born in Europe, or who came there as a child, do not belong to the economically deprived. Sociological models are therefore not well suited. They have many choices other than terrorism.... Taliban, or for those who live in Pakistan or the Middle East, however, show different dynamics, much more acute frustration. Palestinians were apparently the first Muslims in modern times, in the 1990s, who used suicide bombers (*Assassins* were using similar methods 1,000 years ago), and then, in 2006, the Taliban came. The LTTE or the Tamil Tigers were the first in modern times who used this as *modus operandi*.
> Islamists are concerned with pure doctrine. In Palestine the situation is different from Europe. In Gaza there are fewer choices. The humiliation experienced is much more significant. They can "go black," and then the usual assessment values dissolve: lost honor must be avenged at whatever cost.[78]

Experiences like that of Ahmed confirm that humiliation cannot necessarily be conceptualized as part of the shame continuum, particularly not in contexts where the human rights promise of equality in dignity has become salient. When this promise is being betrayed, feelings of humiliation may occur without any feelings of shame. Mandela, for instance, refused to feel ashamed when he was humiliated. Young Ahmed chose the path of violence to liberate himself from shame, while Nelson Mandela chose the path of constructive social change. In my work, evidently, I follow Mandela.

Ahmed was just one young man among many young men, and his violence was of little consequence for society at large. Yet, it is another story when leaders mobilize an entire movement to counteract humiliation. Nelson Mandela did so, as did Adolf Hitler. While Mandela engendered constructive social change, Hitler unleashed mayhem. Hitler attempted to redress humiliation by inflicting humiliation on the supposed humiliators, thus spinning the spiral of the cycle of humiliation. The Hitler-script seems to be the template also for present-time efforts to bring back a glorious caliphate.[79]

At the level of states, "diplomacy of humiliation" is another application of the art of humiliation over underlings, or those perceived as such. Bertrand Badie is a specialist on international relations and his 2014 book is titled *Le temps des humiliés*.[80] In December 2015, we met in Paris and he explained to me how humiliation has become common in international relations. The historical background is the rise of revanchism between the two world wars, a poorly managed decolonization, and now the inadequacy of the old powers and their diplomacy in an increasingly globalizing world. He warned that past uprisings against humiliation – from the Bandung conference in 1955 to the Arab Spring in 2011 – ought to be taken as wake up calls now. What is needed are other forms of governance, an international order in which the humiliated find a respected place. He warned against "diplomacy clubs," such as the Security Council and the G7, which exclude emerging states such as India, Brazil, Turkey, or Russia, who are therefore forced to adopt unproductive deviationist strategies.[81]

As discussed before, the fear that flows from a strong security dilemma is a painful burden. Yet, it can also be used as an asset, as an asset for the art of humiliation. Throughout history, this fear has served as a "fuel" that masters have used to keep their underlings docile. Masters attempted to keep this fear looming, so as to have it handy when needed. Fear was used to keep subalterns in subservience, away from disobedience, and to maintain their usefulness as tools in the hands of their masters. "Perhaps it is a universal truth that the loss of liberty at home is to be charged against provisions against danger, real or pretended, from abroad," wrote James Madison, Father of the U.S. Constitution and 4th American president, in 1798.[82]

The human desire for connection and belonging is used by some as an invitation to abuse. When elites systematically frustrate their underlings' desire for a secure connection, the leverage of this strategy is people's fear of psychological isolation, or what pioneer feminist Jean Baker Miller called *condemned isolation*.[83] The Christian concept of the original sin, for example, kept inferiors in a continuous state of being at fault, in never-ending fear of condemned isolation, before death, and even after death.

Over time, the scene of crime moved ever more into the victims' own psyche. At some point, masters no longer had to instill fear by keeping underlings in dread of physical isolation – of being imprisoned, or exiled, or killed. Underlings learned to feel ashamed already before failing their master's expectations. The "lesson" was successfully learnt when the oppressed had fully internalized the master's image and submitted to oppression "voluntarily." To use Sigmund Freud's terminology, a superego was created that was an unforgiving humiliator – not as an individual pathology but as a systemic cultural effect. Johan Galtung's phrase of *penetration*, or "implanting the top dog inside the underdog" is as descriptive.[84]

This is when domination is most "cost-effective." As soon as underlings are so "primed," continuous humbling, shaming, and humiliating is "sufficient" an investment to maintain domination. This is what is at the core of what I call honor humiliation – the expectation that humiliation will produce humility in underlings – a strategy that was seen as legitimate almost everywhere on the globe until the English language showed signs of change in 1757.

Underlings who had learned to feel ashamed at even contemplating disobedience were the most useful. While haughty inferiors needed brute force to be kept docile, shame-prone underlings did not; it was much easier to manipulate them into meek humility. The "best" subalterns were those who would keep from ever surpassing their role as tools in the hands of their masters, with shame marking the limits of transgression.

Sociologist Norbert Elias, in his seminal book *The Civilizing Process*, explained how the process of subjugation had a humbling effect on fierce and proud knights, lords, and commoners at the French royal court. Unruly and self-important local warlords were "civilized" by being taught the lessons of shame and social anxiety.[85]

In similar ways, during the past millennia, almost everywhere on the globe, underlings were humiliated into humility, into a permanent state of shame, into constant fear of more shame and dishonor, with dishonor being defined as lack of deference and usefulness to masters. Whoever forfeited their usefulness as a tool descended in rank, lost honor, was perhaps even punished by torture and death.

Not only shame and humiliation were instrumentalized, though. Also love and hatred were manipulated in ways that made domination easier. Underlings were expected to subserviently love their superiors and their superiors' friends, and dutifully and "enthusiastically" hate their superiors' enemies.

Not just in the past, also contemporary sects and terrorist groups use these strategies of domination and submission. Leaders of sects and terror groups are terror entrepreneurs who create a culture of blind obedience among their followers by way of the art of humiliation.

Contemporary politics use humiliation as a tool as well. In U.S. politics in 2016, a battle raged "between an inexperienced candidate who was an expert at personal humiliation, and an experienced candidate who proved to be a novice at political humiliation. The result was pure carnage."[86]

Ridicule and condescension is a popular tool in the toolbox of the art of humiliation. It has particularly virulent effects when male honor is being humiliated.[87] While writing these lines on August 13, 2014, I listen to two Norwegian politicians discussing the tragedy under way in Northern Iraq, where Da'esh persecutes Christians and other religious minorities.[88] The conservative camp had won the elections in Norway in 2013, and the representative of the conservative camp declares, "The Islamic State must be crushed once and for all!" He accuses the left-leaning politician's call for more humanitarian help as squeamish, as preferring "soft" interventions over "hard" ones out of cowardice. In other words, his parlance is "security dilemma talk." Under a conservative leadership, this mindset has become more acceptable in Norway throughout the past years in other realms as well, be it the economy or international relations.

An air of indignated righteousness and "honorable male" self-importance is sometimes used to denigrate alternative views. It has become normalized to overlook that in a globally interconnected world, what once might have been appropriate, now turns counterproductive. The insight is bypassed that isolated manifestations of ideas and their promoters can no longer be "crushed" in one quarantined locality, since ideas now go around the world and inspire movements that replenish after being "crushed" in one place. The conclusion is denied that the only remedy in this new situation is to do something about the breeding ground from which such ideas flow.

On September 14, 2015, a similar duel played out in the Norwegian media,[89] this time between a conservative political strategist, and a peace researcher. The conservative expert criticized the peace researcher for painting too "idealistic" a picture and lacking realism in a situation where ethnic Norwegians will become a minority in Norway in the future and immigration will become a security problem, given that mobilization for violence happens along ethnic and religious fault lines.[90] The peace researcher countered that violent conflict has been shown to be associated more with bad governance and lacking access to resources for mobilization, and with poverty,[91] rather than with multi-ethnicity.[92]

Not just in Norway, everywhere in the world, those who identify with dominator mindsets characterize as "hopelessly idealistic," or even cowardly "female," all those who point out that the world has changed and that new paradigms wait to be manifested. What is overlooked from the point of view of the dominator mindset is the insight that it is no longer adequate to continue pursuing isolationist "identities" of groups, religions, or nations, even not the identity of being humans. This is the argument of psychologist Anthony Marsella, who suggests that we have "to move beyond such all-too human dynamics, even beyond our identification and pre-occupation with humanity altogether (such as humanism, humanitarian, or humanistic) and to "move to an identity with life – *lifeism*."[93]

In the spirit of lifeism, the views of both Norwegian experts introduced above could be invited to join forces in this third-level synthesis of identity. My personal view is that Norway can be proud of being a carrier of an indigenous Scandinavian culture of equality in dignity (*likeverd*), and that it is worth protecting it for the sake of global unity in cultural diversity.

Keeping underlings in continuous fear of humiliation has been achieved in myriad ways throughout history, both in overt and covert ways.[94] As was discussed earlier, more effective than humiliating people openly, is to coopt people with the velvet-glove of "sweet persuasion." This can be done at the level of the individual, yet, it is even more effective at the systemic level, because in that way humiliation becomes so subliminal that it is difficult to detect its source.[95]

In his book *Discipline and Punish*, originally published in French in 1975 as *Surveiller et punir*, Michel Foucault offers a detailed analysis of how power found a very sophisticated systemic way of disciplining people, namely, by becoming "cellular." Throughout the eighteenth century, systematic discipline was established in the army, in schools, in churches and convents, in hospitals, in orphanages, and in factories and other workplaces. People were confined in limited spaces where they could be more closely observed and more efficiently controlled.[96] People's time and tasks were scheduled more narrowly, first in the monasteries with around-the-clock routines of *ora et labora*, and eventually in all institutions.[97] Examinations turned individuals into cases, and files turned them into documentary records.[98] Perpetual systematic small-scale punishments combined with systematic small-scale rewards penetrated these disciplinary institutions. Perpetual punishing was useful because it compared, differentiated, and established hierarchies, it homogenized and excluded, in one word, it *normalized*.[99]

Anthropologist Clifford Geertz called Foucault's *Discipline and Punish* "Whig history in reverse." Whig history depicts the story of the past as a story of continuous improvement, of steady implementations of human rights and human value, as gradual progress and triumph of freedom. Foucault, in contrast, tells the opposite story, the story of the rise of un-freedom and loss of liberty.[100]

Howard Richards, philosopher of social science and scholar of peace and global studies, concurs with Foucault when he points out that, while the open and direct wielding of power still plays an important role, the most significant problem for humanity now is not the power of particular actors.

The most pressing problem is that humanity is caught in structural traps.[101] Rules are *causes*, Richards warns, they are not just mere fiction. Richards reminds us of Sir Henry Maine, who, in 1861, characterized the transition from traditional to modern society as a transition from a society based on *status* to a society based on *contract*.[102] And contract presupposes rules. As alluded to earlier, Richards sees as main culprit the fact that successors of Roman law[103] now rule the entire *world-system*.[104] The art of humiliation in this system manifests itself in "that money buys truth, that the historically created lenses of method create the objects seen, and that ever-more-sophisticated mendacities are making truth ever-more-unrecognizable even for those who may have the good fortune to encounter it."[105] It is a "terroristic" world-system.[106]

Jan Josef Liefers is an actor and activist who grew up in communist East Germany (or GDR), and was part of the movement for freedom that eventually brought down the Berlin Wall.[107] The 25th anniversary of the fall of the wall was celebrated on November 9, 2014, among others, by a gathering of contemporary witnesses on German television.[108] In that show, Liefers shared that there had been three East Germanies: There was the less than perfect reality that you lived in every day (except for the ruling elite who lived in comparable luxury), then there was the official version you could read about in the newspapers, which was steered by the elite and had little to do with the first one, and then there was a third one, namely, how you ideally imagined reality to be if it actually manifested its own ideology's ideals. After the fall of the wall, many felt that "capitalism" had triumphed and proven to be the better system. Yet, twenty-five years after the first enthusiasm, many former East Germans describe the contemporary situation as very similar, only more obfuscated, now veiled in a rhetoric of freedom.

Financial journalist Michael Lewis appears to agree with Liefers when he explains that the practices in the world of finance are "as bad nowadays" as they were when his book *Liar's Poker* first came out twenty years ago – only that the actors now hide better what they do.[109] Also journalist Chris Hedges seems to resonate with Liefers' conclusion when he writes in 2013: "The seesaw of history has thrust the oligarchs once again into the sky. We sit humiliated and broken on the ground. It is an old battle. It has been fought over and over in human history. We never seem to learn. It is time to grab our pitchforks."[110] Hedges quotes novelist Willa Cather, who wrote in 1913: "There are only two or three human stories, and they go on repeating themselves as fiercely as if they had never happened before."[111]

The sophisticated wielding of power by way of rules and structures that Foucault described are thus not just a matter of the past, they are still at work. As a result, as the Western world has become wealthier, instances of clinical or major depression have grown.[112] The World Health Organization informs that America is the most anxious country on the globe by a wide margin, its citizens more likely to suffer from clinical symptoms of anxiety than anywhere else on the planet.[113]

Philosopher Charles Handy calls the fact that people cannot live fully productive lives, "the corporate sin."[114] Legendary management consultant William Edwards Deming (1900 – 1993) enumerated "seven deadly diseases" of management, among them "emphasis on short-term profits," and "evaluation by performance, merit rating, or annual review of performance."[115] Though richer countries tend to have happier citizens than poor ones, once people have a home, food, and clothes, extra money does not make them happier. What does creates happiness is mutual connection: only being connected in mutually respectful relationships produces genuine satisfaction. This insight can even be measured: A formula for the monetary equivalence of friendship indicates that 50,000 British Pounds would be needed to compensate for lacking social connections with friends.[116] A meta-analysis has shown that the lack of social integration and social relationships increases mortality risk similar to, or even more, than other risk factors such as smoking and alcohol consumption or lack of physical inactivity and obesity.[117] In the workplace, when dignity is missing,[118] people may even die earlier; investing effort in one's work is health-promoting only when it is being recognized and appreciated in one's social context, and if one has a relatively high sense of influence over the overall situation.[119]

While I write this book, Germany is a country envied by many – it is even called Europe's dynamo. Yet, it has also turned it into a thoroughly "exhausted society."[120] "Clinical depression costs economy up to 22 billion euros each year," is the message of a 2011 report from a large German insurer, Allianz Deutschland AG, together with the Rhineland-Westphalian Institute for Economic Research, titled, "Depression – How an Illness Weighs on our Souls."[121] In 2001, sixteen percent of the work force in Germany were "highly motivated," while ten years later, there are a mere thirteen percent left.[122] This means that a vast majority, almost ninety percent of German employees go to work without really enjoying it. *Innere Kündigung* is the German word for self-detachment from the job, resignation in all but name, demotivation syndrome, resigning in spirit, mentally giving up, inner resignation, inner or inward withdrawal.[123] It means that employees turn up at their workplace and leave their souls at the door.

Also in Norway, as in many other parts of the world, I observe that methods that once originated from the United States of America are being emulated, usually with a time lag, even when they are already going out of fashion in America. Competition-oriented goals and performance management ideologies are one example. In recent years, these ideologies have taken over Norwegian schools, hospitals, and other institutions. Employees must fill out long formulas and are given grades.[124] Only now, criticism is rising in Norway, including in the largest Norwegian corporation, Statoil.[125]

Clearly, wherever creativity is needed in a workplace, the old-fashioned methods of slavery, even if smartly wrapped in rules and regulations, cannot serve this need. Those methods only succeed, at least to a certain degree, where manual labor is at stake, where people toil in fields or factories. As soon as creativity is required, demeaning people into cogwheels is counterproductive. One is inclined to ask, just as Sonia Cardenas asked in South America: Why is not creativity fostered more? A world of cogwheels, it seems, is what is preferred over creative people who might think independently and develop resistance to insidious strategies of humiliation.

Young men from Western countries who join Da'esh flee the cogwheel universe – they might have liked to become part of it but failed, or they have seen through the hollowness of the promise. In no case does the conspicuous consumption that sweetens modern cogwheel culture match the meaning that honorable heroism can provide.

To keep inferiors inferior – be it in the context of old-fashioned honor or in that of contemporary rules and contracts – in all cases it helps to maintain their ignorance. Particularly girls have been kept out of school, as the famous example of Malala Yousafzai has made widely known, the Pakistani activist for female education and the youngest-ever Nobel Prize laureate. Yet, children can be kept ignorant also in school. I had the privilege of spending time in Bolivia in South America, and to get acquainted, if only superficially, with their Mennonite communities. Some of these communities provide extreme examples of how ignorance can be maintained by way of schooling. Every day, their children have to sit in "school" for hours and engage in rote learning in a language they do not understand.[126] The male leaders of the community openly admit that one of their prime goals is to keep women under the rule of men. Rape in families is seen as normal.[127]

Also schools and universities can be places of ignorance rather than enlightenment and preparation for critical thinking. Fundamentalist religious teachings are as widespread in schools as are nationalistic agendas, in the past and now. The most sophisticated application is the current trend in academia around the world to turn away from *Bildung* and emphasize *Ausbildung* or training. No longer is the aim of education to nurture responsible citizens, it is rather the creation of "excellent sheep."[128] Education has become an "industrial sorting machine," rather than an "educational supporting experience."[129]

On November 5, 2011, I listened to Juliet Schor, who was giving one of the Thirty-First Annual E. F. Schumacher Lectures in New York City.[130] Juliet Schor was part of the Harvard Business School faculty in 1984, when it was taken over by Martin

Feldstein, who had served in the Ronald Reagan administration. When she came to Harvard, she expected to teach the "radical economics" part of the introductory economics class "Social Analysis 10: Principles of Economics," commonly referred to by Harvard students as "Ec 10." But, as she reported, this part was abolished by Feldstein. From 1984 onward, young economy students no longer learned about the entire breadth of the spectrum of economic systems and thoughts.[131] Schor speaks of the *captured state*, which needs to be *re-captured*.[132] By now, some Harvard students have reacted and demand alternative economics to be taught again.[133]

In recent years, social media have received much attention. Anat Hochberg-Marom, an Israeli expert on global terrorism and marketing, has studied global business organizations such as Google and Facebook, and she compares them with global terrorist organizations. She found that "they use the same models and strategies as businesses to achieve political power and influence worldwide public opinion."[134]

Another tool for maintaining ignorance is secrecy, including government secrecy. When they are being unearthed, political scandals illustrate this.[135] During the Cold War years, for instance, the cooperation of the C.I.A. and the press was very close, and this was largely held covert and done in highly sophisticated ways.[136]

Evidently, secrecy can also fire back, for example, when it breeds conspiracy theories, including those that have the potential to instigate hatred and acts of terror. Then secrecy does not create humble populations but humiliated and angry ones.

A variation of secrecy is the execution of political agendas by proxy. Civil society originally has the mandate of autonomously forming institutions that manifest the interests and will of citizens, the mandate to advocate for human rights, free speech, and accountable government. This mandate, however, can be made to fail:

> Since at least the 1970s, authentic actors like unions and churches have folded under a sustained assault by free-market statism, transforming "civil society" into a buyer's market for political factions and corporate interests looking to exert influence at arm's length. The last forty years have seen a huge proliferation of think tanks and political NGOs whose purpose, beneath all the verbiage, is to execute political agendas by proxy....[137]

Last but not least, religious explanations are useful to justify humiliation. If those at the bottom of society are perceived as merely reaping the reward of their *karma*, then it is the gods' will to trample on them and humiliate them. On March 10, 1925, Mahatma Gandhi asked: "Is it fair to exclude a whole section of Hindus because of their supposed lower birth from public roads which can be used by non-Hindus, by criminals and bad characters, and even by dogs and cattle?" The orthodox Hindu reply was that, indeed, the untouchables were reaping the reward of their karma and that God is using the orthodox Hindus "as His instruments in order to impose on them the punishment that their karma has earned for them."[138] Orthodox Hindus warned Gandhi against depriving them of their "age-old privileges," and Gandhi's plea "to talk with some reason at least" produced the following reply: "Reason is out of place in matters religious."[139]

Russell Herman Conwell (1843 – 1925) was an American Baptist minister, orator, philanthropist, lawyer, and writer, who held similar views. This is what he said in his lecture *Acres of Diamonds*, first given in 1913:

> Some men say, "Don't you sympathize with the poor people?" of course I do, or else I would not have been lecturing these years. I won't give in but what I sympathize with the poor, but the number of poor who are to be with is very small. To sympathize with a man whom God has punished for his sins, thus to help him when God would still continue a just punishment, is to do wrong, no doubt about it, and we do that more than we help those who are deserving. While we should sympathize with God's poor-that is, those who cannot help themselves-let us remember that is not a poor person in the United States who was not made

> poor by his own shortcomings, or by the shortcomings of someone else. It is all wrong to be poor, anyhow. Let us give in to that argument and pass that to one side.[140]

Also the idea of racial supremacy has been celebrated in quasi-religious ways. Similar to the Aryan *Übermensch*, dominator societies are often ruled by supremacists who are convinced of the legitimacy and usefulness of their superiority. German SS officers under Hitler, for example, learned that humiliating *Untermenschen*, demeaning them and "reminding them of their worthlessness," was an honorable and noble duty. *Meine Ehre heißt Treue* (my honor is loyalty) was the German motto, loyalty to the "Führer's" vision of a world of Aryan *Übermenschen*. Young German soldiers, together with millions of Germans, were imbued with the ideology that demeaning and mistreating those who "belonged" down was their honorable duty. An officer who disobeyed this mandate would not only risk losing his life, he would risk the loss of his and his family's honor. Obedience to the Führer's will was his supreme honorable duty not merely for the sake of his immediate superordinates or political leaders, but for the sake of the entire German people, and, in his mind, even for the sake of the global order as a whole. The Aryan race was seen as the savior of the world and young German soldiers learned that it was their highest duty to safeguard Aryan supremacy and thus secure a bright future for the entire globe.

To conclude this chapter, let us look ahead. At the current point in history, a bright future for the entire globe is achievable, not through supremacism, but through globally uniting in mutual respect for everybody's equal dignity in diversity, in respect for the finiteness of planet Earth.

Political scientist Ted Gurr has worked on the social psychological concept of relative deprivation as root source of political violence.[141] His colleagues, political scientists Jack Goldstone and Jay Ulfelder, describe the way out of this violence. They explain that liberal democracy enhances a country's political stability. In their article "How to Construct Stable Democracies,"[142] they show that economic, ethnic, and regional effects have only modest impact on political stability within nations.[143] Stability is rather determined by a country's patterns of political competition and political authority. Goldstone and Ulfelder call for more research into "how some emerging democracies manage to foster free and open competition without descending into factionalism and why some leaders are more willing to accept meaningful constraints on their authority."[144] Goldstone and Ulfelder recommend that "the focus must be shifted from arguments over which societies are ready for democracy toward how to build the specific institutions that reduce the risk of violent instability in countries where democracy is being established."[145]

This advice gives important support to those who speak out for global systemic change, since also a global society will draw stability from having the right kinds of institutions.[146]

Chapter 8

Humility Remains Indispensable

A caveat: With my argument against honor, I do not wish to disparage all notions of honor. And when I describe humiliation as unsuitable path to humility, I do not wish to denigrate humility. Honor is not always a destructive concept. When I lived in Egypt, I was deeply touched by the almost spiritual pride and poise, the honorable dignity, with which my nomad friends in the desert behaved, how they greeted and moved, how it was possible that they did not see it as a problem to walk for half a day back to their camels through the middle of the desert after having rescued me from being stranded. And the poorest dweller in the unbelievably densely populated city of Cairo had the same calm air of honor and dignity, of worthiness, of selfless self-possession. They manifested the opposite of the hectic Western city person whose ostentatious self-possession at times appears to betray a rather futile search for a missing self. In my counselling practice in Cairo, I received clients from all backgrounds – Western and non-Western – and had the privilege of gaining deep insights into these differences. Not only people in Egypt impressed me. I know of no Western person who would be able to go through the tribulations of a young boy from Afghanistan or Eritrea who traverses continents in search for a better life in Europe to support his family back home. There is a strength in these people that should humble every person in the West who is arrogant enough to feel entitled to have access to all modern amenities. I cannot but think that only people like those who can walk the desert with their honor intact will survive when the next cyberwar has wiped out all the crutches of modern technology.

The word honor means integrity and trustworthiness. Around the world, men are proud that their honor makes it possible to confirm a deal with a hand-shake rather than a written contract. I know many who are contemptuous of contracts. *Hawala* (*Hewala*, also known as *hundi*), for instance, is a system based on the honor of large global networks of brokers through whom informal value transfers can be enacted outside of traditional banking. This system has its core in the Middle East, North Africa, the Horn of Africa, and the Indian subcontinent. When I was in Somaliland in 1998 for my doctoral research, I learned to appreciate to which degree this system keeps large families afloat through remittances from a few family members holding out far afield in other parts of the world. Even though a number of *Hawala* networks were closed down after September 11, 2001, accused of funding terrorism and money laundering, the system has proven to represent nothing but a functioning traditional system. Even international NGOs, donor organizations, and development aid agencies now use it.[1] Its foundation is trust bound by honor based on family relations and regional affiliations. In other words, when I speak about the detrimental effects of honor in ranked societies, I speak of a particular aspect of honor.

Also humility has several aspects. There is the meek, submissive, and helpless humility, and then there is the dignified and proud humility. Even the lowest level of poverty in a society is not necessarily a place of helpless humility. A *sādhu* is a religious Hindu ascetic, and even if he walks naked, in humility, he will be dressed in his honor and dignity. A monk choosing poverty to live closer to the higher powers he worships accepts lowliness to realize divine humility, and it is an honor for him to live in poverty. Humility can be an immense asset. Recent research in social psychology shows to what extent humility is prosocial and merits being called a virtue.[2]

It would be arrogant to frame everybody as a passive and weak victim who appears to hold a lowly position. Inversely, it would be wrong to attribute evil intentions to everyone in a place of power – truly benevolent patronage from above does exist. Good parents are nurturers from above.

The point I want to make in this book is different. During the past millennia, nobody could escape a world framed malignly by the security dilemma. Everybody was a victim of this large-scale tragedy, those with power as much as those without. Also dignified honor and proud humility fell victim to this systemic framing. The aim of this book is not to blame victims. It is to invite all of us to benefit from the window of opportunity that opens at the present juncture of history, the opportunity to get together and nurture a large-scale transformation that undoes the shackles of the past. It should be a transition from meek humility to dignified humility, rather than from meek humility to arrogant narcissism. A transition from rigidly regulated oppressive and exploitative honor to humble and honorable dignity, rather than simply making exploitative honor unregulated and "free."

Humility is at the core of the human rights movement and the emergence of a dignified individual.[3] We may ask: Why does the *Zeitgeist* "allow" for the idea of equal dignity to move to the forefront now, why not earlier? The emergence of the modern meaning of the verb *to humiliate* in 1757 co-occurred with a number of other transitions, which may all have to do with the humbling of humankind. The revolutionary scientific insights about the size and fragility of planet Earth may have had a humbling effect. In 1867, Charles Kingsley (1819 – 1875), professor of modern history at Cambridge, said this: "Inductive Physical Science, which helped more than all to break up the superstitions of the Ancien Regime ... set man face to face with the facts of the universe."[4] Nicolaus Copernicus (1473 – 1543) developed a heliocentric model, with the implication that planet Earth is not the center of the universe. At first, this view was not accepted as scientific standard, only much later, perhaps because its message was too humiliating? Perhaps it is humiliatingly humbling to realize that the species *Homo sapiens* may not be as *sapiens* (Latin wise, judicious) and not as mighty as once thought? Even supportive evidence produced by Galileo Galilei (1564 – 1642), Tycho Brahe (1546 – 1601), and Johannes Kepler (1571 – 1630) was, for a long time, not sufficient. Only on October 31, 1992, did Pope John Paul II express regret for how the Galileo affair had been handled, and officially conceded that the Earth was not stationary.[5] Charles Darwin (1809 – 1882) and Sigmund Freud (1856 – 1939) later added more humbling lessons, explaining that *Homo sapiens* is just another animal, one that is not even in control of herself: dreams and hypnosis make evident that the psyche of humans keeps most of its thoughts and feelings hidden. All those humiliating lessons in humility undermine what Stephen Purdey calls "the paradox of exceptionalism":

> We are at once Earthbound and transcendental beings, wonderfully alive to a morally charged universe yet grounded in a mortal physicality. These two features of our existence should be harmonious, but our sense of exceptionalism has made us arrogant, imperiously dismissing any dependence on our natural setting.[6]

Sociologist Michael Ott summarizes how modern enlighteners such as Nicolaus Copernicus, Galileo Galilei, Charles Darwin, Karl Marx, Friedrich Nietzsche, and Sigmund Freud, with their scientific discoveries, "inflicted the deepest wounds on the narcissism of the human species, and thus produced the inversion of theoretical focus from self-love to object-love":

> The earth is not the center of the universe; humanity is not high above the animals; human beings are not equal but organized into antagonistic social classes that have fought each other throughout history; moral values are not higher than values of vitality; Ego is not the master in its own psychic house.[7]

The same historical processes could also be narrated differently, namely, as the coming of humankind to itself, as a process of owning our own humanity, taking our own responsibility more seriously rather than offloading it onto divine forces.[8] As discussed before, the meaning of *to humiliate* changed in the English language in 1757. Prior to that, humiliation and humility were both regarded as prosocial, it was the duty of humans to humiliate/humble themselves before God.[9] In 1757, at first it was the individual that moved to the forefront, still remaining ranked, as expressed in the word *dignitary*, a word that indicates that here was an individual who had more dignity than other individuals. Only later came the idea that every individual has equal dignity.

If we try to narrate the historical process from the beginning, then humanity lived in dialogue with the spirits of nature throughout the first ninety-five percent of our history prior to the Neolithic Revolution. Then we began to feel at the mercy of unpredictable and vengeful gods who were fashioned on the template of the dominator society – we became fearful children of powerful and angry parents so to speak. This was followed by the idea of chosen people – some children became arrogant and believed that their servile humility in front of their powerful and angry parents had earned them to be elevated over other people and over nature. At the current point in history, humanity tries to reach adulthood. For arrogant children to become responsible adults, they have to leave behind both servile humility in front of their gods and arrogance in front of their peers and nature: they need to learn dignified humility in front of the world.

Not only dignified humility is a huge asset. Shame is similar. Shameless people pose a threat to mental health and social cohesion. The self-esteem movement in the United States failed due to the lack of humility: When empowerment leads to a shameless sense of entitlement, then the result is a "generation me," a generation of young Americans, who are more confident and assertive, yet, also "more miserable than ever before."[10] For a society to keep together, enough people must have the intrinsic motivation to embrace dignified humility and shame.

Even if humility is imposed from outside by force, even when it is extrinsically motivated, it is still valuable. The art of humiliation has proven to be able to generate some measure of "peace and quiet," or, more precisely, more quiet than peace, a quiet kept in place by fear. Peace researcher Johan Galtung calls the absence of direct violence negative peace, in contrast to positive peace, which is the absence of structural violence.[11] Nobody can doubt that the Iraq of Saddam Hussein, for instance, was quiet, even if only as a result of living in the grip of fear. The same is valid for the North Korea of Kim Il-sung, Kim Jong-il, and Kim Jong-un. Post-Saddam Iraq and post-Gaddafi Libya illustrate how peace through fear does not automatically transmute into peace through dialogue – rather, the situation can end in all-out violence when fear through oppression wanes and dialogue is not yet in place.

Masters striving to ease their burden of domination have developed the art of domination, and in that context, as more or less unintended side effect, highly beneficial varieties of humility and shame sometimes arose. Today, global interconnectedness opens space for humanity to nurture those beneficial varieties intentionally. We, as humankind, can turn the nurturing of humility from an unintended side effect into the intended main effect. We can exit from the past's way to peace through fear and guilt and create peace through dialogue in mutual respect and dignity. This includes rediscovering the humility our forefathers seem to have possessed prior to the Neolithic Revolution, the humility that is needed to live in dialogical relationship with nature, acknowledging that we are part of nature.

A spirit of service is what is needed now. Here spirituality can help, says, for instance, Christoph Bals from Germanwatch, when he observes that religion can motivate actors who will not be motivated by morality (the "why" of action) alone or by science (the "how" of action) alone.[12] Arthur Dahl, president of the International Environment Forum in Geneva, Switzerland, adds: "It is religion, not science, that speaks to the need to subjugate pride, ego, and selfish desires to the altruism, humility, trustworthiness, and spirit of service that humans are capable of."[13]

Arthur Dahl's claim may need to be qualified, though: Religiously motivated humility that is inscribed into the dominator culture may translate into arrogant enmity, enmity against infidels, for instance. Religion can be a powerful instrument to foster altruism and cooperation, cooperation among believers, yet, this cooperation may very well flow from hatred for non-believers. Humility within one's in-group can motivate terrorism against out-groups. To be truly beneficial, not just locally but globally, humility born out of servile subservience to superiors needs to be replaced by a different kind of humility, by the humility of wishing to serve all of humankind in our capacity of being part of nature.

Many distinguish between institutionalized religiosity and spiritual religiosity, between religiosity as religious tradition, as the institutionalized practice of religion, and on the other side the kind of spirituality that lies outside of institutions and was experienced long before the concept of religion was ever known. It is the latter concept that has the potential to unite globally, while the former carries the potential to divide.

Catherine Odora Hoppers is the former holder of the South African Research Chair in Development Education at the University of South Africa in Pretoria,[14] and she speaks of *transformation by enlargement*, by which she means that *modernity's other* needs to be included in the process of transformative human development. Modernity's other are those who are placed outside of modernity, those who are unable and/or unwilling to benefit from modernity and economic development.[15] Odora Hoppers' solution is to embrace Indigenous Knowledge Systems.[16] Transformation by enlargement is the best recipe for overcoming also faith-based divides and fanatism. It means transformation through overall inclusiveness. Together with philosopher of social science Howard Richards, Odora Hoppers works for the development of a common vision, one on which all people can agree, so that we, collectively, can overcome the crises of our times.

Pascal Boyer is an anthropologist who is known for his work in the field of cognitive science of religion. He sees the recurrent properties of religious concepts and norms in different cultures as by-products of our standard cognitive architecture.[17] Psychologist Justin Barrett explains the agenda for the Cognitive Science of Religion (CSR) as follows: "Primarily, CSR draws upon the cognitive sciences to explain how pan-cultural features of human minds, interacting with their natural and social environments, inform and constrain religious thought and action."[18]

So, what are those pan-cultural features of human minds? And how are religious thoughts and actions inscribed? And how are these features of minds formed in their specific natural and social environments? The answer lies in a trans- and multicultural analysis that encompasses the pan-cultural as much as the culturally particular, and how individual differences arise from this. Incidentally, this means also that the concept of religiousness shares the same layeredness that also characterizes the phenomenon of humiliation.[19]

Would it help to be cautious with the concept of God? Yes. Rwanda is a country that has learned this lesson through pain. Interestingly, only the (few) Muslims of Rwanda have not participated in the genocide. The Catholic Church in Rwanda, however, goes through difficult times now, and I have learned about this first-hand when I carried out my doctoral research there in 1999, and then again in 2015, when we organized our 25th Annual Dignity Conference in its capital Kigali in 2015.[20] During the 1994 genocide, when faithful Tutsi sought safety from Hutu butchers in churches, Catholic nuns and priests told them that their god had abandoned them and delivered them to death. One of the help-seekers asked: "Father, can't you pray for us?" Father Athanase Seromba, who led the Nyange parish massacre, shall have replied: "Is the God of the Tutsis still alive?" before ordering bulldozers to crush the church walls on those who huddled inside.[21] The Vatican has still to apologize for its support of the genocide, I was told in Rwanda, and this neglect weighs particularly heavily since the Vatican has apologized for other failings, such as the sexual assaults of priests. My friends in Rwanda ask: Is sexual abuse more important than genocide?

I had the privilege of being welcomed in a Catholic Convent during my two months in Rwanda in 2015, and the nuns who gave me the most loving home had decided to give *love* priority over religion. We spoke in French together, let me translate and paraphrase their position as best as I can: My beloved nuns shared with me that they no longer would say, as before, "We invite you, the people of this world, to accept the Christian god of the Catholic Church! Since our lord is love, you will realize that all people have to love each other!" Now they say: "Love comes first, and there is no need for religion to legitimize love, as it is the highest responsibility that we humans must shoulder, and people of all faiths, atheists included, can come together in this love."

This love can be so strong that it does not even shy away from death. To demonstrate this strength, my dear nuns are displaying a picture of Felicitas Niyitegeka in their dining room. Dignity Press, the publishing house of the Human Dignity and Humiliation Studies fellowship, published a book on Felicitas, written by Father Jean d'Amour, a young 29-years old priest, and launched the book at our conference.[22] Felicitas was a lay sister with Hutu background who oversaw a group of young Tutsi women. When the Hutu butchers came to kill them during the genocide of 1994, Felicitas' brother attempted to save her. Yet, she preferred to face death together with her protégés. She was able to write this letter to her brother before she met death:

> Dearest brother,
>
> Thank you for your willingness to save me. But instead of saving my life by abandoning the 43 people about to die, I prefer to die with them. Pray for us that we may arrive in heaven and say goodbye for me to our mother, brothers and sisters. Once in heaven I will pray for you to God. Thank you very much for thinking about me. And if God saves us as we hope, we'll see one another tomorrow.
>
> Your sister Felicitas

Felicitas' humility is exemplary and wherever this kind of humility characterizes a society, we could surely call it civilized.

Sociologist Norbert Elias has been introduced earlier. He explored in depth how civilized behavior emerges and is most known for his book titled *The Civilizing Process*. Elias founded figurational sociology, where he studied the relationships between power, behavior, emotion, and knowledge, and how they evolve over time.[23] Also Emile Durkheim, Karl Marx, Max Weber, and historians such as Marc Bloch have developed similar lines of reasoning.

Elias thematizes what I would call the underling's version of shame. He studied the French court and how feudal lords were seduced into bowing to the absolute ruler. Elias dissected how the process of subjugation had a humbling effect on fierce and proud knights, lords, and commoners. Unruly and self-important local warlords were "civilized" by being taught the lessons of shame and social anxiety. The *civilized habitus* that Elias describes could also be called the *successfully humiliated habitus*.[24]

Also certain forms of forgiveness evolved in this context. Psychologist Michael McCullough studied the evolution of forgiveness and found that people dampen their desire for revenge when the perpetrator is kin, when the relationship with the perpetrator is too valuable to sever it – for instance, when it would be too risky or even life-threatening to even contemplate revenge – or when the perpetrator has become harmless.[25]

The French court, the Indian caste system, the Chinese system of kowtowing, and the Japanese bow, all express and reinforce strong hierarchies that are constructed around obligatory forgiveness in the face of superiors, around practices of ritual humbling, in other words, around a successfully humiliated habitus.

Researcher Tony Webb has studied shame and he doubts that the past millennia can be called "civilized":

> Somewhere back in the past there were cultures with a more mature understanding of shame than today. In some today there are elements of this understanding still.... For most, we live in an immature guilt culture, one in which shame is fused with fear through social and cultural institutions that are based on blame, shaming, labels of guilty, punishment and, if you are lucky but don't count on it, forgiveness.[26]

Norbert Elias described how haughty subordinates were contained through the internalization of social anxiety. Also legal instruments have served similar goals. Roman law, as it has evolved over many centuries, had such effects.[27] As reported earlier, in the Middle Ages, the Catholic Church enshrined spiritual sanctions in a *Gottesfrieden* to limit the violence of feuding.[28] The *Song of the Nibelungs*, the epic poem in Middle

High German created at the beginning of the thirteenth century, is a protest against the destructive infighting of an arrogant nobility that made ordinary people suffer.[29] The *Sachsenspiegel* is the most important law book of the German Middle Ages, and it prohibited frontier justice. For contemporary examples of haughty citizens waiting to be reined in – waiting to be "civilized" – one may look at the United States and the widespread reluctance to let go of gun ownership. Or to Texas, where a 2009 poll found that forty-eight percent of the Texas Republicans who were surveyed supported secession from the United States.[30]

The world is full of cases where the humility that is needed for apology and atonement is still waiting to manifest. The 1965 – 1966 Indonesian genocide, in which up to one million people were killed because they were suspected of being communists, may serve as one of many examples. This mass killing not only fails to be acknowledged, it is even still being praised, and most surviving victims cow.[31] Also the West has so far failed to acknowledge their role in this killing.[32] When I look back on my time in Indonesia in 1981, then I remember how I was not yet ready to internalize "their" history as "my" history, as "our" history, the history of all of humankind. I still was in the frame of mind of "traveling to another country" and learning about "another culture." Today, I find myself looking at the world from a different standpoint. I feel global responsibility for all atrocities ever done by humans to humans on all continents. I feel responsible for preventing the repetition of atrocities in the future wherever on our globe. At the same time, I cherish all of humankind's cultural achievements ever as "mine," be it the pyramids in Egypt, the Buddhas of Bamyan, the poems of Rūmī, Japanese aesthetics, or Belgian chocolate.

If we look at terrorism, then societies may call themselves civilized that develop pathways for people who have perpetrated violence to redeem themselves,[33] possibilities for perpetrators of terrorist atrocities to give up terrorism.[34] The Danish Aarhus program may serve as an example, as it refrains from using force to stop people from going to Syria and instead attends to the roots of radicalization, namely, the link between humiliation and the search for an extremist ideology.[35]

Francis Mead is a former BBC journalist who currently makes documentaries for the United Nations. He made two documentaries on reintegration, *Algeria: The Terrorist Who Came Home*,[36] and *Second Chance in Saudi Arabia – Saudi's Rehab*.[37] These films are part of a series of films made for the UN, looking at how and why people leave terror groups. In his film on Algeria, Mead followed Djamel, a former terrorist, now father of ten children. The film also gives voice to Ahmed Adami, a former security officer, who explains that those who engaged in terrorism were young men without perspective and confidence, seduced by propaganda. The film traces the doubts that grew among the terror-fighters and how they looked for an Islamic scholar who could put an end to fighting in Algeria. They found a Saudi scholar, Muhammad Saalih Al-Munajjid, who sent a *fatwa* to the fighters in Algeria ordering them to stop fighting. Djamel explains:

> We started to doubt terrorism. At the beginning we had power. We had trucks, cars, groups and weapons, but after three and half years it all began to fall apart.... We realized religion was about good conduct, not violence. At this point, our doubts grew stronger and we thought we were probably sinful.... We got a fatwa on a tape from Mecca, from a scholar called El Sheikh Muhammed Salah El Woudhim. He said the following: "To my brothers-in-arms in the Algerian mountains: stop the killing."[38]

Richard Barrett of the UN's terrorism monitoring group that supports global de-radicalization efforts, explains how a sense of futility began to set in:

> There was a sort of complete exhaustion on both sides – an understanding that the horrific murders that were going on at that time were actually not leading to any future for anybody and that there had to be a real effort to bring society back together again.[39]

Francis Mead's film on Saudi Arabia documents an integration program for former extremists. At one time Khalid Al-Jhani was an explosives trainer for Osama Bin Laden in Afghanistan. He was later captured and held in Guantanamo Bay Detention Camp for over four years. He was then returned to Saudi Arabia, where he passed through the Saudi rehabilitation program for young men accused of involvement in extremist violence. This program is being supported by Hameed Al-Shaygi, professor of sociology.[40] In the film, he explains that instead of further punishment, education is key to the new approach of the a rehabilitation program. The aim of this program, he explains, is "for them to have dignity." Today Al-Jhani leads an almost normal life.

On January 5, 2012, I had the privilege of speaking with Hamed El-Said, another expert on de-radicalization who also participated in the film, through the introduction of Francis Mead.[41] See more about our conversation in the Appendix to the first part of this book. He highlighted that Islam has a tradition of forgiveness, and that also the tribal tradition sees terrorists as misguided family member, as misled sons.

By now, an increasing number of concepts and witness accounts is available on how extremism can be overcome. Young Zak Ebrahim wrote a book that offers intimate insights into how it felt to grow up as son of the man who planned the 1993 World Trade Center bombing in New York City.[42] He argues that people like him, who were conditioned to become terrorists during their early years, are better prepared than others to prevent terrorism later, because they can use parts of the extremist ideology to support peace rather than terror. Yet, he warns, the rest of society should not stand by in passivity. Everyone, he argues, independent of their background and knowledge of terror agendas, can use their inherent empathy to overcome hatred.

Here is another witness account. Anna Sundberg hails from a well-to-do background in Sweden. When she was a young student, searching for life's meaning, it took only two weeks for her to be drawn into a Salafist community, where she eventually spent sixteen years.[43] She got married and had three children with Algerian Al-Qaeda member Said Arif, who is by now assumed killed in Syria in 2015.[44] She followed her husband all around the world, covered in a *niqab*, sharing her fellow group members' belief of being closer to their god than others, belonging to a chosen few. Her little family lived in places like Berlin, as well as under the most basic circumstances in a secret Mujahedin training camp in Georgia, on the border with Chechnya.

Her message now, after she has emerged transformed from her past, is that people can always change, that one should never give up on a person, and that families and communities would need to be much more attentive to young people and their desire for meaning in life. She is the best example of how the most radical changes can happen extremely fast in the lives of young people – it took only a few weeks for her, when she was an adolescent, to decide to embrace Islam.

For six years, Dominic Schmitz from Mönchengladbach in Germany was a convinced Salafist. He evangelized in his city and on YouTube. He married a woman who was picked for him by his superiors. They had children. Then he quit. Now he explains why he became a Muslim, what fascinated him in the Salafist scene, and why he now distances itself from it: what for the young Schmitz represented stability, something to hold on to, later, when he became an adult, transformed into a prison.[45]

As has been reported before, in Aarhus, Denmark, young men who traveled to Syria, who trained with Da'esh, and who now return home, if they have not committed crimes, do not face arrest and prosecution.[46] "We don't look at young people as sick or monsters," says one of the mentors who tries to turn these young men around by making them feel welcome in society. The mentors in this project strive to replace both a missing father and the Da'esh family, thus helping the young men find their dignified place in society.[47]

Such a strategy is also what mothers in France desperately ask for, mothers of children who left for Syria.[48] Journalist Nicolas Hénin, who was kidnapped in Syria, now warns that the West needs to understand its own mistakes: what he calls for is *radical respect*.[49]

What is needed, it seems, is a journey for young people caught in meek humility to rise up to the dignified humility of responsible citizens. Servile humility is no sign of honor, it is a humiliation. When rising up from servile humility, however, the aim cannot be arrogant superiority. The aim must be dignified humility.

Chapter 9

Méconnaissance, or How One Can Damage One's Own Best Interest

Do you know the Stockholm syndrome? It describes a form of traumatic bonding.[1] In 1973, a group of hostages was held by robbers in a Stockholm bank for six days, while their captors negotiated with the police. During the standoff, the victims became emotionally attached to their captors, at one point even rejecting assistance from government officials, and defending their captors after they were freed. One woman fell in love with one of her captors. Many years later, she wrote a book about her experience, and she gave a rare interview, in which it became clear that she may indeed have fallen in love due to the dynamics of the Stockholm syndrome. Or, perhaps her genuine bridge-building humanity motivated it?[2]

The *art of humiliation* can create the Stockholm syndrome systemically, in entire societies. When this happens, psychological damage is driven to its peak – it is turned from involuntarily suffered damage to voluntarily inflicted damage. Victims are doubly victimized, they are coopted into becoming co-perpetrators, co-oppressors, not only of others, also of themselves. This has deeply mutilating effects, to the point of endangering life. *Méconnaissance* (misrecognition) and *naturalization* are related concepts, used by thinkers such as Roland Barthes, Pierre Bourdieu, and Michel Foucault.[3]

Entire populations can learn what philosopher Emmanuel Kant called *selbst verschuldete Unmündigkeit*.[4] This is often translated as "self-incurred immaturity." I would translate it as "the voluntary relinquishing of independent critical thinking." I sense that the security dilemma's most recent cultural product, Western individualism, has usurped the English translation. Maturity is a rather individualistic concept, it has something to do with growing up, with becoming an adult. Yet, as I see it, Kant's *Unmündigkeit* is not an individual psychological predicament, neither ordinary human imperfection in general. What he points at is large-scale social pressure, and it would be a category mistake to search at the wrong level of analysis and action when we seek solutions.

Here we might also find the explanation for the observation by philosopher of science Thomas Kuhn that even the most "scientific" paradigms often resist the most necessary revision, despite the fact that it is the very essence of the scientific methodology to be open to new evidence.[5] It is possible that also scientists are caught in the Stockholm syndrome.

It may also be the explanation for why we humans kill. As has been noted elsewhere in this book, humans are not "natural killers." If we are not natural killers, why then do we kill? Have we simply forgotten about our true human nature? Is it that we need to be reminded of our true human capabilities? The answer may lie in recognizing that in the context of a strong security dilemma, in a divided world, killing or being killed often was an unavoidable choice. The security dilemma may have been the most gruesome captor of human nature. If so, then it would be misguided to believe that simply reminding people of their peaceful capabilities would be enough. To transform a violent world into a peaceful world, it is insufficient to only call for nonviolence or nonkilling. More so, such wording is even counterproductive in itself. First, it draws attention to what it wishes to overcome through its own wording.[6] Second, "anti-" and "non-" negations replicate the culture of war, the culture of "fighting" "against" something by using the very tools of what they want to overcome.

Clearly, awareness of the human capacity for peace is important, yet, in order to flourish, this peaceful human nature needs space. This can only happen in a more united world without the "big captor," the security dilemma. Our *world-system*,[7] our global *generative mechanisms*,[8] our *constitutive rules*,[9] wait for a transition as significant as the Neolithic Revolution.

Propaganda inspired by the security dilemma has two main story lines. One goes as follows: "Our enemy is equally honorable as we are, he is a noble opponent in a duel-like stand-off that we both are compelled to partake in because honor dictates it. Nobody can escape it who wishes to stay honorable." The other story line is: "Enemies are evil natural killers, while 'we' are more civilized and have overcome this evil trait; and only because we are noble defenders of our honor, we sometimes have to kill, despite our noble nature." Thus, says this propaganda line, "we" are noble killers, while "they" are natural killers.

The first line is often that of elites who know each other. In the context of a strong security dilemma, all are equally caught in the security dilemma's tragedy. For elites, honor means to know that enemies can be potential allies. At the time when World War I began in 1914, the monarchs who fought each other could as easily have been allies. The German Kaiser Wilhelm II was a first cousin of the British Empire's King George V, as well as of Queens Marie of Romania, Maud of Norway, Victoria Eugenie of Spain, and the Empress Alexandra of Russia. As a result of the First World War, while the empires of first cousins Tsar Nicholas II of Russia and Kaiser Wilhelm II of Germany crumbled, the British Empire of King George V expanded to its largest extent.

The fact that enemies can also be allies is difficult to sell to underlings, particularly to those sent out into war to do the killing. Killing a potential ally is not easy, and therefore, throughout history, security dilemma propaganda often tried to "facilitate" the killing of enemies by telling the second story of enemies as evil natural killers, with whom, clearly, alliances are unimaginable. This is also why elites kept alliances secret. The so-called Molotov-Ribbentrop or Nazi-Soviet Pact of 1939 between arch enemies Nazi Germany and the Soviet Union remained in force until broken by Hitler's government by invading the Soviet Union on June 22, 1941. There was a secret protocol to the pact whose existence the Soviet Union denied until 1989. Equally covertly, it is being rumored that the Unites States may have cooperated with subgroups of their archenemy, Al-Qaeda, as recently as 2015 as part of a proxy war against Bashar al-Assad in Syria.[10] As I write these lines, collaboration with Russian President Vladimir Putin and Syrian President Bashar al-Assad against Da'esh is being discussed in Washington, yet, after having treated both as enemies more than as allies for so long, alliances are bound to be difficult to justify.[11]

Clearly, the two views are hard to combine, that of the enemy as noble rival and that of the enemy as natural killer. Secrecy is one way to bring both views together. Another is to openly face and acknowledge the role of the security dilemma.

Many people I meet around the world state that "it is unrealistic to feed illusions of peace on Earth, we need to be realistic and prepare for defense." These people have a point as long as the world is divided. Yet, the reason for having to prepare for defense is not that humans are natural evil killers. Killing is also not a consequence of psychological or moral aberration. If we think along such lines, we fall for security dilemma thinking and psychologize a situation that is set in motion by the security dilemma's unescapable grip. Psychology comes into play later, when a strong security dilemma is maintained where it could be attenuated. As long as we believe in the natural evilness of "enemies," we allow our adaptation to the security dilemma to become decoupled from its cause and stand alone, now misrecognizing it as human nature. It was our historical adaptation to circumscription that spawned the security dilemma, and this, in turn, brought us armament and war. Our new contemporary context of global interconnectedness offers us space to leave these adaptations behind. If we fail to understand this, we do so due to misrecognition.

In her book *Die Waffen nieder*, or *Lay Down Your Arms!*, author Bertha von Suttner offers an illustration of the dilemma of honor:

> "Aha, Martha! aha, Doctor!" cried my father, triumphantly. "Did you hear? Even Tilling, who is no friend of war, acknowledges to being an advocate of the duel."
>
> "An advocate? I have not said that. I only said that in certain cases I would of course resort to the duel, as I have several times been obliged to do, just as I have from loyal obligation entered every campaign. I conform to popular prejudice as to laws of honor, but I do not mean it to be understood that this same code of honor conforms to my ideal. By and by, when this ideal attains the mastery, the receiver of an unmerited injury will not be regarded as disgraced; only upon the boorish offender will the

> disgrace fall. It will then be considered as immoral to seek personal revenge, as in other respects, in cultivated society, it is intolerable to take the law into one's own hands."[12]

When I lived in Japan, I got acquainted with the work of anthropologist Emiko Ohnuki-Tierney. She has a deep understanding of Japanese ways of being-in-the-world. Méconnaissance is brilliantly illustrated in her book *Kamikaze, Cherry Blossoms, and Nationalisms.*[13] Ohnuki-Tierney dissects the hideous ways in which young, highly intelligent, and morally ambitious Japanese students were manipulated into becoming suicide bombers in World War II – their suicide missions were called *tokkotai* operations in Japan, only in the West they became known as *kamikaze* operations. Ohnuki-Tierney became motivated to write her book when she read the diaries of these young students. She was astonished and almost shocked, because she had expected something totally different – more, she was deeply touched. These diaries made clear to her that most of these highly educated young men did *not* want to die nor kill. They had been "persuaded" to "volunteer" by way of méconnaissance.[14]

This is how it worked. The aesthetics of Japan's cherry blossom symbolism originally signified life and birth. This symbolism was instrumentalized by the Japanese authorities to signify death. Aestheticization was employed to make horrifically ugly cultural practices appear beautiful, both visually and conceptually. Slowly, in a salami tactic fashion, the more militaristic the country became, the cherry blossom symbolism was transformed to aestheticize death on the battlefield. To die was as "beautiful" as the fleeting existence of the cherry blossom in its elegant falling from the tree.

Also the image of "a shattering crystal ball" (*gyokusai*) was used to aestheticize death. The term originated in *The Chronicle of Beiqi*, a chronicle completed in the year 636 CE during the Tang dynasty in China. The shattering crystal ball trope refers to the beautiful way in which a crystal ball shatters into hundreds of pieces. The Japanese military government adopted the term to encourage mass suicide in the face of a hopeless situation. The expression began to appear as early as 1891 in a school song that declared that Japanese soldiers would fight irrespective of how many enemies were there, and they would die like a shattering crystal ball. One dramatic incident occurred when the Japanese military headquarters decided to abandon their men on an island that was too heavily surrounded by American ships. There were only 550 American casualties, while 2,638 Japanese soldiers died, many through suicide.

Also the Nazi propaganda machine abused the trope of beauty, the beauty of pathos, and thus it succeeded in making evil seem desirable and "normal."[15] The *Reichserntedankfest* (the Reich Harvest Thanksgiving Festival), for example, was a monumental Nazi celebration between 1933 and 1937 on the Bückeberg, a small hill near the town of Hamelin. I was born many years later, in 1954, because my parents had been forcibly displaced to that region from their homeland in Silesia. This festival was part of a cycle of Nazi celebrations of grand pathos, ranging from the annual party rally at Nuremberg to Hitler's birthday festivities. Hamelin and the Weserbergland were very enthusiastic about trying to cast themselves as a national socialist core country. In addition to the Reichserntedankfest on the Bückeberg, the region prided itself of the fact that the party hero Horst Wessel was born there. When I visit my parents in Hamelin now, I sometimes pass in front of the Bückeberg, and I am amazed how forlorn it looks, lost in a forgotten corner in Central Europe where a nuclear power plant has been built precisely because it is such a remote region. It is almost unbelievable that as many as 1.2 million people attended the festival in 1937, feeling greatly elevated when Hitler, with the exalted grandiose pathos that Charlie Chaplin so well caricatured, walked through the *Führerweg* (Führer's parade route) to the harvest monument.[16]

The above described Japanese tactics of aestheticization were so sophisticated that they convinced highly educated students to see their suicide killing mission as noble. Yet, also cruder manipulations follow the same step-by-step script of warping hearts and minds. I was in Sierra Leone in 1976 and learned about the bright sides of its culture as well as its dark sides.[17] Later, I was not surprised when both government and rebel forces coerced children into fighting during the vicious ten-year civil war from 1991 to 2002. The story of Ishmael Beah shows the intricate methods that were used to create obedient death-bringing "robots" in the hands of masters. Beah is a former child soldier who killed more people than he can count. In his book *A Long Way Gone*, he explains how his commanders and co-killers became his "family."[18] When he was about to be freed, initially, he was unwilling: he was enraged at the prospect of being taken away from his "family." He had simply been too successfully made to love destruction for the sake of his masters' military victories, the destruction of others' lives and of his own psyche, and, as a result, he misrecognized his own best interest. It took him a long time, after liberation, to awake to the *Mündigkeit* he so much needed.

The same approach, clearly, is also employed by other terror entrepreneurs. Children are made to learn killing in their play: "now behead this doll."[19] As Amitai Etzioni remarks about Da'esh, it is precisely the "beheading of civilians; frying, burying, and crucifying people alive; using children to fight; and turning girls into sex slaves," which has "engendered an unusually worldwide shared moral understanding that they ought to be vanquished."[20]

The "fuel" that keeps obedience going, in the case of child soldiers, is the vulnerability of children, their dependence and thus openness to be manipulated into keeping their new "family's" favor. It is the abuse of the child's need to belong, the relational exploitation of the child's yearning to stay connected. Not only in Africa are children manipulated and drugged and find themselves capable of becoming truly terrible killers under the influence of mixtures of cocaine and gunpowder. Even though exact figures lack, hundreds of thousands of children under the age of eighteen, some as young as eight years old, serve in government forces or armed rebel groups all around the world.[21]

"Grooming" children is possible because it is in human nature to be open to cultural influences, particularly when young. The brain is only fully developed when a person is in her early twenties.[22] Child soldiers are not the only horrifying arena for such "grooming," however. In the Rochdale grooming gang case in Rochdale, Greater Manchester, England, twelve men were convicted of child sexual exploitation in 2012.[23] Since the market for sexual abuse of children is very profitable, babies are now being "groomed" from birth to develop a dissociative disorder so that they can be sexually abused for decades and will never be able to report it. They will simply cooperate and be "well-behaved." People who have no pedophile orientation themselves, who have no personal sexual interest in children, abuse them in front of cameras to create video material for sale. Germany is one of the production locations. Gaby Breitenbach, a specialist on dissociative disorders, admits that the expertise about dissociation (and how to create it) is now almost more advanced in this "business" than among therapists.[24]

Journalist Peter Taylor begins the third episode of his documentary film *Generation Jihad* with the words of Hamad Munshi: "Please pray for me that I get martyred in a state of true faith."[25] A friend of Munshi apologizes on his behalf: "He was groomed! He was a kid and radicalized!" Taylor asks: Can the government's national strategy prevent the next Munshi from being radicalized and groomed? In other words, can méconnaissance be prevented or undone? Since it is the collaboration of the oppressed themselves that contributes to their subordination,[26] only they can change the situation by discontinuing this collaboration. Abdelasiem Hassan El Difraoui, a political scientist of Egyptian-German descent, an economist, documentary director, and producer,[27] formulates the conclusion in his documentary film *The Language of Al-Qaeda* as follows: The solution is for critical voices to come out from within Islam, preferably the voices of former recruits to "jihad" warfare, those who can report on their experiences and explain why they regret their involvement.[28]

As much as the willingness to kill can be elicited by way of misrecognition, also the willingness to be humiliated and even accept death without protest can be created in this way. Mao Zedong visited rural areas in 1925 and 1926 and what he learned led him to see something that was contrary to Marxist orthodoxy, namely, the peasants' ability to create an atmosphere of terror as a model for revolution. He wrote about the peasants in Hunan Province in 1927: "They will smash all the trammels that bind them and rush forward along the road to liberation. They will sweep all the imperialists, warlords, corrupt officials, local tyrants and evil gentry into their graves."[29]

Interestingly, only a few years later, the Chinese peasants had successfully "unlearned" to rise up. In her 2015 doctoral dissertation, educational sociologist and China expert Jingyi Dong traces how peasants in China were brought to misrecognize their own interests to the point of mass dying: "... during the Great Famine between 1959 and 1961, the peasants just died silently in their villages, whereas in similar cases in history, starving peasants would form waves of refugees that might lead to peasant uprisings."[30] In the Great Famine between 1959 and 1961, more than thirty million people died of starvation despite the fact that there was no large scale natural disaster. Dong describes how the humiliation of the peasants of China was achieved through the exploitation of the education system and how peasants still today misrecognize that they are being humiliated.[31] She builds on sociologist Pierre Bourdieu's work, who defines the school system as an arena for misrecognition and a mechanism of social reproduction.[32]

How could it happen that millions of Chinese peasants died in silence? How come that they still misrecognize their true situation now? Dong describes how the First Emperor of China mainly depended on military forces, while the modern repertoire is much more sophisticated. Dong refers to peace researcher Johan Galtung's notion of *protective accompaniment*, a term that describes forms of domination that are much more sophisticated than open force: protective accompaniment means "penetration-segmentation preventing consciousness formation, and fragmentation-marginalization, preventing organization against exploitation and repression."[33] By using such strategies, a dominant group is capable of "implanting the topdog inside the underdog ... giving the underdog only a very partial view of what goes on ... keeping the underdogs on the outside ... keeping the underdogs away from each other."[34] Dong describes the various strategies that the Chinese repertoire of domination included: cultural violence served as breeding ground, other forms of violence were justified, structural violence helped internalize cultural violence, and direct violence was institutionalized. Fragmentation, penetration and segmentation, all strategies aimed at depriving peasants of their freedom and identity. Using Galtung's terminology, this was a "positive approach," in contrast to the use of direct violence as a "negative" approach."[35] Dong explains:

> Most of the monarch dynasties, even though lasting for centuries, invariably collapsed, and an important force that defined the comings and goings of dynasties was peasant uprisings. When asked for the countermeasure to prevent this historical periodicity, Mao gave the solution, "democracy."[36]

How was this "democracy" shaped after the Communist Party's victory in 1949? Dong describes "the destruction of the patriarchal system, the introduction of the People's Commune and urban-rural segregation that reconstructed the entire society and perpetuated the structure of violence."[37] And this is why the peasants died silently: "The party-state adopted both the positive and negative approaches to weave a systemic and imperceptible web of manipulation but always remained remote and impersonal. It was difficult for the peasants to identify the real culprit, and very hard for them to move from bewilderment and dissatisfaction to consciousness formation."[38]

How is it possible that entire populations can overlook their own best interest? This question is of concern also for research on terrorism. More even, it concerns the survival of humankind on our planet in general. How come, for instance, that some people regard terror as "the best strategy" to defeat enemies while overlooking that this risks to be utterly self-defeating and destructive, particularly in an interconnected world? How come that news of the degradation of the planet are regarded as propaganda, while the clear messages that the planet sends out go unheard? At present, it seems the entire world population overlooks the need for a "global trajectory toward a socially equitable, culturally enriched, and ecologically resilient planetary civilization."[39] It seems that the art of humiliation has been driven to the point that we, as humankind, now misrecognize the very basis of our humanity.

In my book *Emotion and Conflict* (2009), I grappled with these questions and studied many scholars' thoughts about what makes us see the world as we do, why do we have the worldviews we have, where a certain *Zeitgeist* comes from, and why we often succumb to it uncritically.[40]

Beliefs can be understood as feelings, as lived and embodied meaning,[41] and this includes meta-emotions, or how people feel about feelings.[42] Beliefs serve two goals, first, they help with reality testing and understanding of the world, and, second, they provide support for our psychological and social need to live with others and ourselves. According to self-determination theorists Edward Deci and Richard Ryan, three universal innate psychological needs motivate the self to initiate behavior, namely, the need for competence, for autonomy, and for psychological relatedness.[43] After birth, it is the culture of our family of origin that provides the meaning we attribute to our life, later come institutions such as school, followed by larger social contexts, such as the communities where we live out our lives.[44] "This lifelong socialization channels our temperamental predispositions, cognitive architecture, and competencies into a sense of what constitutes a worthy life and how to achieve it within our *Lebenswelt*."[45]

Many scholars operate with the notion of *field*. Gestalt psychologist Kurt Lewin, for instance, saw the field or life space of an individual or a collective as a *Gestalt* where motives, values, needs, moods, goals, anxieties, and ideals are interwoven.[46] *Doxa* is a term stemming from ancient Greek "to expect," "to seem," meaning common belief or popular opinion. Sociologist Pierre Bourdieu used this term to describe what is taken for granted and seen as self-evident in a given social space or field in society, and how it can come to represent the only "possible discourses" of what is thinkable and sayable.[47] *Doxa* tends to take the dominant for the universal, says Bourdieu, and this is reminiscent of Michel Foucault's view on discourse and discursive formation,[48] or how knowledge is intertwined with power to count as "truth."[49] For Bourdieu, our *habitus* is informed by doxa, with habitus meaning a system of dispositions or "socialized subjectivity," the entirety of conventions, beliefs, and attitudes that all share, the "orchestrated improvisation of common dispositions."[50] This, in turn, is reminiscent of political scientist Benedict Anderson and his explanations of how communities are ideated and *imagined*.[51] For Bourdieu, the dispositions of our habitus tend to reproduce the structures of the field and vice versa, thus resolving sociology's hotly discussed antinomy of objectivism and subjectivism. Sociologist Anthony Giddens, on his part, introduced the term *structuration* to overcome the structure-actor dualism in social sciences, to show that structure and agency stand in a dialectical relationship where none can exist independent from the other.[52] Recently, biologist David Sloan Wilson and anthropologists Robert Boyd and Peter Richerson have brought structural functionalism back, in the form of multilevel selection theory, after group selection had gone out of fashion for a while, in favor of individual selection theory.[53] In psychology, also Jean Baker Miller, in her relational-cultural theory,[54] emphasizes the role of relationships and community, as does cultural-historical activity theory inspired by Lev Vygotsky.[55]

In homogeneous societies, shared habitus can make rules redundant. Rules are not redundant, however, when a society is not homogenous. This is the case with world society. World society has never been homogenous, but now the situation is aggravated due to the crossfire of transitions: The honor-dominator model of society exists alongside the dignity-partnership model, both of which are irreconcilable at their core. As mentioned before, in my work, I sometimes use the example of so-called honor-killing to illustrate how irreconcilable they are: In an honor context, a girl who brought shame on her family's honor can lose her life in honor killing, while she is entitled to trauma therapy in a partnership context: in other words, it is an either-or situation, it is either life or death. What adherents of the dominator model misrecognize, is that their worldview – the girl must die – has evolved in a particular historical context, namely, in the grip of a strong security dilemma – and that this worldview is no longer fitting when global interconnectedness takes over. The same is valid for those who use terror as a strategy. They act on the "truth" of their field when they turn to what they see as freedom fighting, or, on the side of counterterror strategists, when they see themselves as heroic patriots. By doing so, they reproduce, on their adversary's side, the image of them as "cold-blooded," "cowardly," or "mad." In that way, terror reproduces itself as either heroic or cowardly. This worldview is outdated in an interconnected world, it becomes suicidal for all.

The partnership model is the only suitable adaption to interconnectedness. As this model is rather novel, historically, it is unfamiliar and untested. The millennia-old honor culture is anchored in much sturdier doxa. Therefore, honor culture still dominates the world – be it openly or through double standards – and most people still seek their meaning of life there. In addition come those elites who want to hold on to their privileges – who thus have an interest to keep the security dilemma strong – and who are thankful for the opportunity to legitimize inflicting terror tactics on whoever they define as enemy. And the majority of people, as they are still used to follow elites, will follow. The psychological phenomenon of *defensive avoidance* helps keep them blind.[56]

We have already heard about philosopher of science Thomas Kuhn who describes how *paradigms* shift.[57] Before they shift, they rigidify, because those people who identify with them, if ever so misrecognizedly, stand up for them. They are finally toppled by a new generation of people who ask new questions that undermine the paradigm's edifice.

The fields of philosophy, sociology, and psychology offer many related concepts. Philosopher Peter Frederick Strawson, for instance, speaks of *shared conceptual schemes* that form an interconnected web of our conceptions about the world, and how we, as humans, think about reality.[58] Sociologist Amitai Etzioni speaks of *normative paradigms* that are beyond any codified law, as they are sets of informal values that contain intellectual and affective elements that keep those who subscribe to them engaged in them.[59]

Many related concepts for how we believe in our own recognitions and misrecognitions are known, with varying terminologies. *Horizon* is a term used by philosophers Emmanuel Kant, Edmund Husserl, or William James. Philosopher John Searle's notion of *background* speaks to the same phenomena,[60] as does the *tacit knowledge* of historical sociologist Karl Polanyi.[61] Social psychologist Daryl Bem speaks of *zero-order beliefs*.[62] Social researcher Hugh Mackay introduced the *invisible cage* as a metaphor for the tacit effects of life experience, cultural background, and current context on an individual's view of the world.[63] We have *mental models*,[64] on which we base "preferences without inferences," says social psychologist Robert Zajonc,[65] and linguist George Lakoff speaks of *frames* "that allow human beings to understand reality – and sometimes to create what we take to be reality."[66] *Interpretive frames* have surface frames and deep frames, with deep frames shaping our deepest assumptions about human nature and the social order: "Without the deep frames, there is nothing for the surface message frames to hang on."[67] Not least conflict "is framed by the structure, and the conflict parties may limit their perspectives on the conflict, so that structural aspects of the conflict remain invisible," explains linguist Basil Bernstein.[68] As mentioned earlier, peace researcher Johan Galtung points at *deep culture* as something that contains codes and building blocks that may dispose for, or legitimize violence.[69]

We have cultural mindsets, or cultural *scripts*, which means that we have "structures within which we store scenes," or "sets of rules for the ordering of information about Stimulus-Affect-Response Sequences."[70] Psychiatrist Eric Berne illuminates script theory in his book titled *What Do You Say After You Say Hello?*[71] The "automaticity" of such processes is astounding[72] – we use rapid cognitions, in other words, we "think without thinking."[73] An impulsive system exists,[74] and attitudes, including stereotypes, are activated "automatically"[75] in a rapid interplay of implicit and explicit attitude changes.[76]

Common sense is an "organized body of considered thought,"[77] and according to social constructionism, all knowledge, including the most basic and taken-for-granted common sense knowledge of everyday reality, results from social interactions, which, over time, are regarded to be "natural."[78] Sociologist Talcott Parsons has used the concept of *gloss* to discuss the idea of how "reality" is constructed.[79] Then there is the term *truthiness*.[80] Social constructionism is often regarded as a sociological construct because it conceptualizes the development of social phenomena in relation to social contexts, while social constructivism is a more psychological construct, addressing how the meaning of knowledge is relative to social contexts.[81]

Cultural contexts, be they national, ethnic, organizational, team or family, may also be called *plausibility structures*, this is how cross-cultural psychologist Michael Harris Bond calls it, and he borrows the term from sociologist Peter Berger.[82] Plausibility structures are the sociocultural contexts for systems of meaning within which these meanings make sense, or are made plausible. Beliefs and meanings held by individuals and groups are supported by, and embedded in their sociocultural institutions and processes.

The most sophisticated present-day method of the art of humiliation through misrecognition is perhaps the use of double standards, the instrumentalization of partnership rhetoric to cover up for dominator strategies. Anthropologist Stephan Feuchtwang has studied grief, and he wrote to me: "I am intrigued by two of your contentions. One is that breeches of the promise of human rights create severe humiliation. Why not a sense of betrayal and hypocrisy, which is not the same as humiliation?"[83] I replied:

> Absolutely, as far as I can judge, there is a deep sense of betrayal and hypocrisy. But then emerges the next question that those who feel thus ask: "Why do these people preach empty human rights rhetoric to us? Is it in order to fool us about their wishes to stay at the top and continue exploiting us?"
> The motive sensed behind the betrayal is arrogance and the wish to stay at the top. This then is felt to be humiliating.[84]

Feuchtwang responded with an observation that touched me: "to recognize humanity hypocritically and betray the promise humiliates in the most devastating way by denying the humanity professed."[85] As civil rights attorney Clive Stafford Smith concurs, "Hypocrisy breeds hatred."[86]

My global experience indicates that double standards are brought into the world in many forms, from open betrayal to covert distraction. Covert distraction is carried out, for instance, by offering *false choices*. In my book on a dignity economy, I walk through some of the humiliating effects that flow systemically from present-day economic arrangements: (1) scarcity and environmental degradation, (2) ubiquitous mistrust, (3) abuse as a means, (4) debilitating fear, (5) false choices, and (6) psychological damage.[87] In the chapter on false choices, I refer to psychologist Jean Baker Miller's coinage of this phrase.[88] False choices can be created and kept alive, not least, through the dynamics of humiliation. The emotional intensity of humiliation undermines balanced moderation when hot feelings lead to tunnel vision.[89] Cycles of humiliation deepen fault lines and create dogmatic enmity. This facilitates the rise of false choices, obscuring that there might be important common ground, significant overlap and shared interest – negotiation theory teaches that *interest* may bring us together where *position* separates us.[90] In this way, past dynamics of humiliation can undermine the quality of today's deliberations, leading to very unhelpful outcomes, which, in turn, can have humiliating effects on everybody's future. Philosopher Kathleen Dean Moore recommends:

> Always be on the lookout for false dichotomies ... especially when a dilemma offers a choice between two nasty alternatives and forces you to do what you think is wrong to avoid a greater evil. Ask a few questions: Whose interest is served by presenting a problem as the choice between two stark alternatives? What caused our choices to become so limited? What is the third way?[91]

The notion of class struggle may serve as another example of how reality itself is not what drives us, but our recognitions, including our misrecognitions. Pierre Bourdieu always rejected the historical narrative that class conflict is the "motor of history."[92] His position is that a class is defined simultaneously by its "being" and its "being-perceived,"[93] and that class lies in the relationship between structure and agency,[94] just like objectivism and subjectivism are connected, or nominalism and universalism.[95]

Also philosopher of social science Howard Richards warns against one-sided explanations. He is an adherent of critical realism and ascribes causal powers to *cultural meanings*. He is critical of too much focus on notions such as power, or habitus, and rather emphasizes the significance of *norms* and *rules* as causes, not just as consequences or fictions. He criticizes social scientists who shy away from traditional causal analysis of phenomena, who recoil from using the word *norm*, and who instead use terminologies of practice, discursive and non-discursive practices, relations, performances, codes, frames, routines, symbolic structures, or (in the case of Pierre Bourdieu and his followers) habitus.[96] Richards warns that if we, as humanity, wish to get out of our structural traps, we have to analyze them with critical realism.[97]

Critical realism is a philosophical position that rejects the notion that everything is self-referencing text.[98] It connects Enlightenment with postmodernism: It regards Enlightenment as a moment in the history of culture and not as eternal truth, but it also appreciates that there is a world outside of the text. Howard Richards lives in Chile and is deeply familiar with the work of Brazilian educator Paulo Freire and his terminology of *themes* in a thematic universe of cultural meanings and how they guide, orient, and thus move behavior. Richards thus welcomes postmodernism's achievements, but warns of going too far. He invites into following critical realism in expanding causal analysis instead of giving in to contemporary linguistics too much, or to its analogues in structural and post-structural anthropology or Lacanian psychoanalysis.[99]

Howard Richards proposes *moral realism* as a worldview that cooperates with existing schools of ethical thought and existing moral codes and sentiments "such as utilitarianism, Aristotelian virtue ethics, Kantian dignity ethics, Gandhi's ethic of nonviolence, the social teachings of the world's religions, the philosophies of John Rawls and Phillipe van Parijis, the songs of John Lennon and Joan Baez, ancient Chinese and African wisdom, the several psychologies of moral development, and so on."[100]

Perhaps I can contribute to this discussion by sharing my own experiences. All over the world, I am asked whether my stance is pro-capitalist and anti-socialist, or anti-capitalist and pro-socialist. I always want to ask back: "Is this not like asking: Are you pro-paradise or anti-paradise?" What does this question entail? It seems to entail a category mistake. Is not here a belief in an ideology misrecognized as reality? Religion promises paradise in the afterlife by the grace of god, while capitalism and socialism promise paradise in this world, if not now then at least in the future, by way of acting on scientific laws. In all cases, power elites use and manipulate these ideologies in their favor – they convey the message that they serve the people's wish to enjoy paradise, while withholding that they may only seek their own paradise. There are, of course, also true believers among elites, who authentically believe in their promise's validity, and there are other people who are able to look through all rhetoric and forge their own experiences of reality, both with respect to divinity and human arrangements. Both "capitalism" and "socialism" offer a "scientific" promise of a paradisiac future in this world, with Adam Smith and David Ricardo seen as founders on one side, and Karl Marx, Friedrich Engels, and Vladimir Ilyich Lenin on the other side. In the case of "capitalism," the famous "invisible hand" is expected to create a paradisiac future by combining self-interest with the division of labor, while socialism is the "scientific" promise of a paradisiac future through everybody's altruism offered to the state as manifestation of victory in the class struggle. As it turned out, so far, both approaches produce rather similar lived realities: The Nomenklatura in the Soviet Union has been described as a "new class" that dominated the rest of society as a form of state capitalism.[101]

Ecological economist Herman Daly thinks that this is what happened:

> The exploitation of the proletariat by capitalists has been eased by economic growth – by

> shifting the exploitation on to nature. Class warfare between labor and capital has been softened by a truce between these classes to jointly exploit a third party – nature. The big difficulty we now face is that "vengeful nature" is revolting, and the truce is over.[102]

So, if there is no class struggle (Bourdieu and Daly), what is there? Perhaps misrecognition of domination brought about by structural traps (Richards), hidden behind false choices that obfuscate true responsibility (Miller)?

Peace researcher Vidar Vambheim has proposed network exchange theory to shed light on the obfuscation of responsibility. In his doctoral dissertation, Vambheim attempts to conceptualize both bullying and terrorism with the help of network theory. In the case of bullying, network bullying is different from bullying perpetrated by a single bully, and it is also different from the frenzy of a lynch mob:

> Different people in a network may take turns in "picking on" or humiliating an already stigmatized person or group from time to time. This will keep the order intact, and preserve the identity of the group: The aesthetic experience of participating in such acts (e.g. ridiculing the outsider = a feeling of belonging to the in-group) can keep a network of people together. Actions that reproduce the feeling of collective strength [we-ness + power] or prestige [attractiveness + power] tend to be reproduced and legitimized by rationalization after the fact.[103]

Herman Daly's words are warnings: What will happen if we, as humankind, do not wake up? Adolf Eichmann was the Nazi war criminal who organized the logistics of the Holocaust. His example shows that horrible things can happen when people do not wake up. Eichmann thought of himself as a mere tool in the hands of his superiors. On January 27, 2016, a letter was published that Eichmann wrote on May 29, 1962, in which he petitioned Israeli President Yitzhak Ben-Zvi for clemency: "There is a need to draw a line between the leaders responsible and the people like me forced to serve as mere instruments in the hands of the leaders."[104]

Where do we, as humanity, stand? Are we caught in our misrecognition of domination brought about by structural traps? Are we lost in networks, and their myriad false choices that crowd out the few important choices? And does all of this perhaps obfuscate our true responsibility? Where are then our true choices and where is our true responsibility? It might be that the only true choice is to recognize our own double standards, and to proceed into a joint global exploration of how we may achieve a truly dignified future for all of humankind, including a dignified relationship with our planet. Can we understand that there is no "us versus nature," that we are all part of the same system?[105] Can we understand that we are one single human species that is part of a tiny planet?

Chapter 10

How Voluntary Self-Humiliation Is Possible

Aristocratic French thinker Alexis de Tocqueville (1805 – 1859) wrote in his classic text *The Ancien Regime and the Revolution* (1856) that the danger of revolution is greatest not when poverty is so severe that it causes apathy and despair, but when conditions had been improving, and, in particular, when only a few had been benefiting and not the rest.[1] What Tocqueville alluded to is the *expectation gap* that arises when improved conditions create hopes, while at the same time also improving access to the means for revolt when those hopes are being betrayed.

Expectation gaps can set in motion a whole range of reactions. In India, for instance, female suicide rates are highest in parts of the country with the best education and economy, "probably because women grow up with greater aspirations only to find their social milieu limits them," explains psychiatrist and researcher Vikram Patel.[2] Or, another example, Erik Solheim was Minister of International Development in Norway when we talked in 2011. He reminded me of the colonial period and how it was perceived as humiliation only at the end of the colonial era, at a point when those who had been colonized were already much better off, particularly in Africa.[3]

Since the times of Alexis de Tocqueville, social mobilization theory has flourished. Social scientist Gustave Le Bon (1841 – 1931) wrote about the psychology of the *crowd* in 1895.[4] In 1950, sociologist David Riesman spoke about the *lonely crowd*.[5] Later, sociology developed a rich plethora of terminologies for related phenomena, such as *relative deprivation*,[6] or *framing*,[7] all built on a *rational choice* approach.[8]

Alexis de Tocqueville did not live to see the labor movements engage in class conflict. He did not live to see how those movements later waned, and how new "middle-class" identities came to the fore, inspiring anti-war campaigns and movements to protect the environment and civil rights. Names of scholars who followed Tocqueville are, among others, Alain Touraine,[9] Ronald Inglehart,[10] Jürgen Habermas,[11] or Charles Tilly.[12]

In former times, scholars usually did not regard emotions as important for social mobilization. Only very recently this has changed. Sociologist James Jasper, for instance, recognizes the role of emotions in his theorizing on *moral shock*. He writes this about social movements: "Especially after humiliations, revenge can become a primary goal."[13] Moral shock is a term that describes visceral unease and outrage, triggered by events that may be personal or public, and that bring together emotional, moral, and cognitive dynamics. Even a film can trigger this shock, a film with images of injustice and cruelty. Moral shock can bring a person to political action even "without the network of personal contacts" which are emphasized "in mobilization and process theories."[14]

Holocaust survivor Elie Wiesel passed away on the day I wrote this sentence, on July 2, 2016. He helped the term *Holocaust* solidify this word's associations with Nazi atrocities against the Jews. In 1986, he was awarded the Nobel Peace Prize for his role in speaking out against violence, repression, and racism. When accepting the prize, he said:

> I swore never to be silent whenever and wherever human beings endure suffering and humiliation. We must always take sides. Neutrality helps the oppressor, never the victim. Silence encourages the tormentor, never the tormented. Sometimes we must interfere. When human lives are endangered, when human dignity is in jeopardy, national borders and sensitivities become irrelevant. Wherever men or women are persecuted because of their race, religion, or political views, that place must – at that moment – become the center of the universe.[15]

As already Tocqueville observed, it is not easy to stand up rather than stand by, even when this is what the situation calls for. A new situation, new information, however important and pressing, does not mean that people necessarily take it in, let alone react on it. It seems that sometimes the need to maintain a coherent map of the world, a map one is familiar with and used to, is stronger. Even those who live in disadvantaged positions may choose familiarity over rebellion and prefer to continue living in pain.

Evidently, this does not mean that learning is impossible. As classical social psychology research suggests, ambiguous and conflicting information can engender new interpretations and attitudes at individual, interpersonal, and collective levels.[16] Intercultural research shows that when cultural assumptions are called into question, a "stress-adaptation-growth" process can unfold.[17] Creativity can be enhanced through interactions of "mutually contradictory but equally compelling forces."[18] "Disorienting dilemmas" can unsettle fundamental beliefs and call into question inflexibly held values, thus bringing about transformative learning.[19]

However, also the opposite can happen. There is also an inverse relation between information ambiguity and transformation. Uncertainty may be more difficult to bear than certainty, even if this certainty is painful and it would be better to opt for change. Uncertainty might even harden existing belief systems of the map of the world one is familiar with; *loss aversion* might override the most relevant new information.

"Unwittingly Manipulated into Self-Humiliation" is the title of a section in my book *Emotion and Conflict.*[20] There, I offer a list of concepts and words that capture the dynamic of what I call *voluntary self-humiliation*. Let me share a few here.

Learned helplessness is a term coined by Martin Seligman that has already been introduced earlier in this book. It describes helplessness as a learned state, produced by exposure to unpleasant situations in which there is no possibility of escape or avoidance.[21] It is disastrous when learned helplessness transforms into what may be called *learned perpetration*. The fate of the child soldiers throws this into stark light.

If we ask how learned perpetration is possible, on one side, it is due to the basic human need for coherence, familiarity, recognition, connection and belonging, and on the other side to millennia of cultural learning within the dominator model of society. Human beings are social and cultural beings, and they wish to belong.[22] This makes them vulnerable to internalize into their psychological structures ideologies that justify their own abdication.[23] The dominator model turns people into tools in the hands of their superiors and this has deeply mutilating effects, at macro and micro levels. The *art of humiliation*, as I call it, takes this mutilation furthest – it turns it from involuntary mutilation to voluntary mutilation. It victimizes its victims doubly insofar as it coopts them into becoming co-perpetrators, co-oppressors, not only of others, also of themselves. Indeed, it is the ultimate refinement of the *art of domination* to bring people into voluntary self-humiliation, coopting underlings to maintain their own bondage voluntarily and misrecognize it as "honor" and "heroism," or even "freedom."[24] Concepts such as *méconnaissance* (misrecognition) and *naturalization* have been introduced earlier.[25] It is the inculcation, into a population, of what philosopher Emmanuel Kant called *selbst verschuldete Unmündigkeit*,[26] as I would translate it, "the voluntary relinquishing of independent critical thinking."[27]

Theodor Adorno has studied how easily people can develop an authoritarian personality and slide into subservience to superiors.[28] Alice Miller documented the cruelty of childrearing methods, and how they facilitated the rise of Hitler's Nazism.[29] Cognitive linguists George Lakoff and Mark Johnson described the underlying pedagogical framework that produces obedient inferiors, which they call the *strict father* model, as opposed to the *nurturant parent* model.[30] The strict father model makes its adherents think in terms of direct causation rather than systemic causation: "the father expects the child or spouse to respond directly to an order and refusal should be punished as swiftly and directly as possible."[31]

Cognitive dissonance is another term relevant here because it highlights how, when a belief system is enforced by way of oppression, people may not just *adapt* to it pragmatically, to avoid dissonance they will even *adopt* the unwanted belief system.[32] Nanci Adler is a Russianist who studies Soviet terror and the fate of Gulag returnees. She has explored how Russian society comes to terms with the Communist past and how the institutional aftermath of mass victimization unfolds. Soviet terror was a system that enforced its ideology by executing, imprisoning, and exploiting dissenters, alleged dissenters, and alleged associates of dissenters. To her astonishment, Adler found a great paradox: Still today, many Gulag victims retain their allegiance with this system and continue to venerate its leaders.[33]

Jean Baker Miller and her colleagues call such adaptations *strategies of disconnection*,[34] meaning that people, while they yearn to participate in connections with others, will keep important parts of themselves out of connection – those parts that they believe are too threatening for a relationship.[35] Cognitive linguist George Lakoff explains how it is possible to hold mutually contradicting worldviews in one mind at the same time: each view has its own neural circuitry in the brain, and they can coexist without any problem when they are linked by a circuit that works through mutual inhibition: "When one is turned on, the other is turned off; when one is strengthened, the other is weakened."[36]

Strategies of disconnection and identification with the oppressor are not necessarily individual processes; they can also unfold as collective social processes. Critical discourse analysis shows how power dynamics produce and are reproduced by dominant discourses.[37] Elites, as they have disproportionate access to the means of cultural production, can shape such dominant discourses to serve their interests, be it wittingly or unwittingly. As a result, social realities are constructed and taken for granted that benefit "some participants at the expense of others."[38]

As has been discussed earlier, Johan Galtung forged the notion of *penetration*, or "implanting the topdog inside the underdog,"[39] illustrating the fact that acceptance of subjugation may become a culture of its own, a collective way of managing the cognitive dissonance between commands coming from above and feelings coming from one's heart. Michel Foucault's idea of *governmentality* has its place here; just like penetration, it can make governing so much easier if only widespread enough. Also the concepts of *méconnaissance* (misrecognition) and *naturalization* have their place here, as they describe social, cultural, and societal processes of penetration.

Ranajit Guha and Gayatri Chakravorty Spivak use the term *subaltern*.[40] Subaltern studies conceptualize history from "below."[41] Also the *colonization of the lifeworld*, a phrase coined by Jürgen Habermas,[42] describes the "seduction to accept domination." More recently, Patricia Hill Collins spoke of *controlling images* that are being imposed by a dominant culture, images that are voluntarily or involuntarily accepted by disempowered subordinate groups.[43] This resonates with the concept of the Stockholm syndrome mentioned earlier,[44] and how an emotional bond can emerge between hostages and their captors "when the hostages are held for long periods of time under emotionally straining circumstances."[45]

Philosopher of science Thomas Kuhn observed that scientific paradigms can be sustained even in the face of "stubborn facts" which cast them in doubt,[46] leading to utterances such as, "I know, but I can't believe it." This situation persists until a tipping point lets the dam break and space opens for a new paradigm: "First they ignore you, then they ridicule you, then they fight you, then you win," is a quote associated with Mahatma Gandhi. It may take a new generation of people to be able to ask radical enough new questions so that the old paradigm can be unlocked and dislodged.

Sociologist Amitai Etzioni has reflected on the reasons for such persistence. It requires great effort and investment to form a new normative paradigm and a legal code that underpins it:

> Decades of moral dialogue, consensus building, legislation, court cases, and public education slowly build such a paradigm. Millions of people come to believe in it, weave it into their worldview and political preferences, and even intertwine it with their personal identities. Hence the strain of dissonance between the paradigm and reality may be high before one can expect a paradigm to break down and it be replaced with a new one.[47]

Political scientist Stuart Kaufman refers to *myth-symbol complexes*, which, given the opportunity to mobilize around them, may lead to violence.[48] *Legitimizing myths* are at the core of such paradigms, and, as has been explained earlier, they may entail *chosen traumas*. This combination can be so compelling that it leads to "blind trust" overriding any critical inquiry.[49] When a chosen trauma is experienced as humiliation and not mourned, this may lead to feelings of entitlement to take revenge and, under the pressure of fear and anxiety, to collective regression and ultimately to violence.[50]

Psychologists Jim Sidanius and Felicia Pratto explain the role of legitimizing myths, or compelling cultural ideologies, that are taken as self-apparently true in society, and how they disguise the use of force and discrimination and make it acceptable.[51] They describe how such myths can maintain inequality among different groups in society, and how this materializes through three mechanisms. The first mechanism is exemplified by slavery's "official terror" of institutional discrimination. Second, there is the aggregated individual discrimination of one individual against another, an effect that only becomes palpable at a larger scale, when many people commit it, rather than just a few. With the third mechanism, behavioral asymmetry, Sidanius and Pratto refer to the "keeping in one's place," which is accepted and upheld by both, superiors and inferiors. The passive and active cooperation of subordinates with their own oppression is what "provides systems of group-based social hierarchy with their remarkable degrees of resiliency, robustness and stability."[52]

Psychologist John Jost and his colleagues have developed system justification theory, which includes social identity and social dominance theories, as well as notions such as self-interest, intergroup conflict, ethnocentrism, homophily, ingroup bias, out-group antipathy, dominance, and resistance.[53] They find that there is a general ideological motive to justify the existing social order, and that this motive is partially responsible for the astonishing fact that subordinates internalize their own inferiority, if only at an implicit nonconscious level of awareness, which, paradoxically, is sometimes strongest among those who are most harmed by the status quo.[54]

Already in the last chapters, the fields of inquiry that offer related concepts were mentioned, such as philosophy, sociology, and psychology. Psychologist Peter Coleman and his colleagues developed the dynamical systems theory, where they included, among others, social dominance theory,[55] and system justification theory.[56] Yet, they went further: they acknowledge that systems are dynamic, not just static. Coleman identifies *attractors*, or dominant mental and behavioral patterns that offer a coherent map of the world to people, and a stable platform for action.[57] Like Tocqueville and others after him,[58] also Coleman observes the counterintuitive effect that even members of disadvantaged groups often agree with their own oppression and discrimination and justify the status quo.[59]

Psychological phenomena such as *defensive avoidance* have been mentioned earlier.[60] Psychotherapist Carol Smaldino writes the following about mechanisms of denial and resistance: "When, however, people in general cannot change focus or perspective in the midst of seeing the facts of any matter, statistically, educationally and in the flesh, we have what you might call a serious resistance. And when there is a resistance that insists on denial at any cost, we have a clinical problem that is both pervasive and alarming."[61] Smaldino sees the health of contemporary world society as a whole in danger for the reason that important information lands on deaf ears: Scientists, because they meet resistance, are getting tired of explaining the dangers of "present ways of mining, and farming and fracking."[62] Smaldino calls on therapists like her, those who know that where there is resistance to information there are underlying reasons such as fear, greed, desperation, or panic: "When people are afraid to change, they have reasons, which also deserve respect, not pummeling with repetitions of the same information again and again. We know this: we know addicts don't change for the nagging, and that many of us in general have an allergy to being lectured." Smaldino hopes that society can heal and remember the positive lessons from the sciences, from history, and from our own imaginations, namely, "that the ways of studying and the ways of implementing information can be experimental, can be new, and can involve the energy of people who are witness to a difficulty they care about."[63]

In other words, leaving behind the status quo is not easy, even if ever so necessary, and only a few people will do so. People might fail to wake up even if the attractor loses its pull, as Coleman would formulate it, even if reinforcing feedback loops among elements within the dominant attractor become weakened and new information provides platforms for new kinds of action. Only those with a particular set of resources will act, the proverbial child who sees that the emperor has no clothes, and, in addition, who says this out loud.

Once people do rise up, however, there is another danger: from bowing too low they may rise up too far. Their former reluctance to carry their heads high may turn into its opposite, into turning their noses up too arrogantly, into what James Edward Jones calls the *post-victim ethical exemption syndrome*.[64] They may turn the golden rule on its head: "Do bad unto others because they (or someone else) did something bad to you." The Rwandan genocide is a striking example where subordinates overrode all inner barriers and meted out unspeakable cruelty on their former masters.

Incidentally, the academic discipline of psychology plays a significant role in the dynamics of humiliation and self-humiliation. Ignacio Martín-Baró was a social psychologist, philosopher, and liberation theologist who was murdered by the Salvadoran Army. He observed that North American psychology professionals had learned to attain social position and rank by finding ways to "contribute to the needs of the established power structure."[65]

This leads to the question of why psychologists agreed to support the C.I.A.'s plans for interrogation, while the American Medical Association and the American Psychiatric Association did not.[66] Maybe the answer lies in the history of the field of psychology itself. It could be narrated as a story of self-humiliation in the face of perceived humiliation. The field began its existence as an underdog (and still is, in many ways). In a Western world that is still characterized by a male culture of domination, listening to women does not afford prestige. Foregrounding "hard science" – be it through quantitative methodologies or the application of the latest technologies – is the accepted path to gaining respect, honor, and dignity. Emotions, relationships, and qualitative approaches look too "soft" and taste of the female sphere. Indigenous peoples share the lowly status of women, and therefore, also listening to indigenous peoples' voices provides little prestige. Psychologists, in their wish to avoid being humiliated as "touchy-feely quacks" (to formulate it provocatively), therefore overlook not just feelings, but also the wisdom of women and indigenous peoples. Only lately, indigenous psychologists have begun to stand up against this trend.[67] As to feelings, it has been mentioned before that it may be the arrival of new "hard" imaging technology that provides prestige (and funding) to the study of soft emotions, rather than an increase in intrinsic interest to explore emotions. The discipline of psychology may have become victim of an emotional trap – in this case clambering for respect out of fear of humiliation – that is part of their own field of inquiry.

During the Great Famine mentioned previously, Chinese peasants just died silently in their villages. Their silent acceptance of their fate demonstrates the power of what I call self-humiliation. People can become complicit in their own oppression and exploitation, a strategy that is successful in China as in the West. Educator Jingyi Dong explains that Mao Zedong admired the first Chinese Emperor Qin, who was known as a ruthless leader. Mao surpassed him. Even Qin did not succeed to silence his underlings to the degree Mao did.[68] Under the label of "democracy," Mao's rule put in place the most ruthless governance, the extreme opposite of what is usually associated with the concept of democracy.

A similar dynamic might unfold globally just now. If democracy is seen to equal consumerism, then democracy is built on misrecognition, and the presently observable widespread passivity of people all around the world in the face of the degradation of the social and ecological foundations of human livelihood may replicate the passivity of the dying Chinese peasants.

On April 4, 2011, I had the privilege of speaking with Tom Koenigs, Member of the German Federal Parliament in Berlin. Tom Koenigs was the Special Representative of the UN Secretary General for Afghanistan when he researched the suicide attacks in Afghanistan from 2001 to 2007.[69]

He explains that in Afghanistan, suicide attacks began to appear with regularity only in 2005 and 2006, and that "the community's initial response was to reject the possibility that Afghans themselves might be involved."[70] More even, the notion that suicide might be combined with killing others was considered alien before the assassination of Ahmad Shah Massoud on September 9, 2001, two days before September 11, 2001, when New York City's World Trade Center Towers were taken down.[71] Since then, the world has been "groomed" into taking suicide attacks to be the "Muslim norm."

The strategy of grooming people into voluntarily engaging in self-humiliation is a step-by-step desensitization tactic. In the second episode of his documentary film *Generation Jihad*, journalist Peter Taylor shows how the internet is being used to radicalize young Muslims and groom them for terrorism.[72] The internet is an ideal grooming arena, since it turns the world into a global community, making extremist forums and harmful information easily accessible from anywhere. Taylor shows how a young Muslim in Bradford became an Al-Qaeda predator at the center of a terrorist cell that reached out to Bosnia, Pakistan, America, and Canada. "It's a very dark world," says terrorism consultant Aaron Weisberg in the documentary. "They expose themselves to violence and to visual portrayals of violence ... and become desensitized and inclined to try and perpetrate violence on their own." And their parents are in denial. They are convinced that their child could never hurt a fly.

Propaganda, mass persuasion, or, how it is also called, "spin," are all variations of the art of domination. In her world-renowned book, *Eichmann in Jerusalem: A Report on the Banality of Evil*,[73] Hannah Arendt analyzed how evil actions may not necessarily be the result of evil intentions but rather of the perpetrators' banal lack of critical distance to what has become "normality." In Rwanda, officials employed Radio Mille Collines the same way Joseph Goebbels did in Nazi Germany, to groom the population into the normality of un-normality. Not only the South Africa of apartheid was "governed by illusion."[74]

Sigmund Freud's nephew Edward Louis Bernays (1891 – 1995) combined Freud's psychoanalytical concepts with the work of Gustave Le Bon on crowd psychology[75] and Wilfred Trotter's ideas on the instincts of the "herd."[76] Contemporary industrial mass production – including that of unhealthy and damaging products – is often promoted through precisely such covert manipulations. The market of cigarettes is an example: Women were lured into smoking by the manipulated image of women smokers as torches of freedom.[77]

To conclude, the duress of the security dilemma made people learn how to damage others and themselves. For centuries, dominators strove to hold their in-groups in line against enemy out-groups to keep themselves in power. Ultimately, the strategies of manipulation that they developed damaged everybody's integrity. The art of domination through routine humiliation, and through manipulation into self-humiliation, as it was honed and optimized during the past millennia, has mutilated the bodies and souls, the hearts and minds of all, both superiors and inferiors. This strategy is malign, not benign.

This is a conclusion, however, that is only possible to draw from a standpoint that knows about growing global interconnectedness, because in this context the security dilemma can weaken and space can open for insights to emerge that were impossible or taboo before. The new insight is this: in present historical times, involuntary self-humiliation no longer needs to continue. While it was relatively easy to manipulate people into self-humiliation in the past, space opens now to unmask and undo it. What may have been involuntary self-humiliation in the past should therefore now be labeled *voluntary self-humiliation* wherever it still continues.

Colonel Tilling is the father of Bertha von Suttner's heroine in her 1889 novel *Lay Down Your Arms!* He wishes for a "fresh, breezy war" and is disappointed that "there seems no prospect of one."[78] A cabinet minister replies: "Chance is always in your favor, Colonel Tilling ... not that there are any dark clouds on the horizon now, but it takes but a little, in the present condition of

European politics, to cause an outbreak. As Minister of the Interior, I am naturally anxious for peace, but I am willing to recognize the different standpoint from which military men regard it." Tilling feels obliged to make a caveat:

> Allow me to assure your Excellency that I am far from desiring war, and I protest against the idea that the military standpoint should be any different from the humane one. We are here to defend our country when attacked, just as the fire department stands in readiness to put out a fire. Both war and fire are misfortunes with which no humane man could wish to afflict his fellow-creatures. Peace is the highest good, or rather it is the absence of the greatest evil. It is the only condition which conduces to the welfare of the whole nation, and yet you would recognize the right of a portion of the people, the army, from motives of grossly personal ambition, to desire to precipitate the greatest misery and suffering upon all. To carry on war in order that the army may be kept busy and satisfied is like applying the torch to houses in order to employ the fire department.[79]

If activist and author Chris Hedges had been present in this conversation, he would have retorted that the myth about war is fabricated, and that the truth about war is that it leaves those who return from it alienated, angry, and often unable to communicate.[80] Hedges warns that war's reality, known only too well to those who have been in combat, has since Tilling's times been ever more hidden from public view. Ever more industrial ways of killing and slaughtering have been driven by amoral decisions of politicians and military leaders who direct and fund war. Hedges finds powerful words:

> War perverts and destroys you. It pushes you closer and closer to your own annihilation – spiritual, emotional and, finally, physical. It destroys the continuity of life, tearing apart all systems, economic, social, environmental and political, that sustain us as human beings. War is necrophilia. The essence of war is death. War is a state of almost pure sin with its goals of hatred and destruction. It is organized sadism. War fosters alienation and leads inevitably to nihilism. It is a turning away from the sanctity of life.[81]

Chapter 11

How Dominator Economics Terrorize

A beautiful tyranny misnamed partnership

The relationship
To which we are wedded is a beautiful tyranny Misnamed partnership.

Our partnership
Is a partnership of unequal partners
Of unequal powers and unequal opportunities
A partnership honeycombed
With labyrinths of genteel deception, division and exclusion.

In our partnership
One party represents
An imperial order of unprecedented sway and intrigue
Into whose hegemonic bosom
The other is conveniently entombed.

In our partnership
One party is the source, center and symbol
Of all knowledge, civilization and salvation
The other a mere consumer
Of high culture and QUIPs1.

We are stakeholders in a bizarre covenant
That folds enslavement
In intoxicating benevolence and grace
Our partnership is afflicted with saintly inhumanity.

In the cold mathematics of our partnership
Our partnership is our destiny.
Amen.

In a globalizing world, a new kind of security dilemma emerges.[1] The classical security dilemma's fault lines run between states or between identity groups.[2] For the past millennia, this has defined a multi-divided world. Now one single new global fault line settles on top of the many old ones. As military and financial power interlinks and a global village emerges, the new dividing line runs between the global village's elites and the village's majority. The result is an atmosphere of terror emanating from ubiquitous economic domination.[3] Globalizing neoliberalism is being denounced as a form of terror even by right-wing populists now,[4] no longer only by left-wing critics.[5] In the Global North, this domination was wrapped in "artfully" crafted covert systemic and structural forms, while it is much more directly and openly palpable in the Global South. Prior to recent financial crises, its front figures appeared on the covers of business magazines and were hailed as the new heroes of the world – it was hoped that their energy and visionary sense of mission would create economic growth that would trickle down to the "rest."[6] The global village's majority, on their part, particularly in the Global South, lacks the necessary resources, and is too exhausted from purely surviving, to even think of developing their own opinion. They are not able to stand up and create better ways to live together and with nature. Also in the Global North many remain passive, others elect populist leaders who abuse their simmering sense of humiliation to advertise as solution the removal of the new security dilemma and the triumphant resuscitation of the old one.

Not everybody in the Global North descends into apathy or feels desperate enough to elect populist leaders. There are those who write poems like the one above by Hassan Keynan from Somalia, now with UNESCO. Yet, they are few. Most of those who have the privilege of possessing enough resources to engender significant change do not use those privileges in that way. Instead, they invest them into making themselves pretty in the market place through "personal branding,"[7] they create attractive facades around their own little personal territories. Behind those facades, naiveté breeds freely, naiveté about what happens in the rest of the world, with the result that good conscience can remain undisturbed. Unscrupulous unwitting *strategic ignorance*,[8] or worse, aggressive cluelessness,[9] can safely be maintained.

While open and direct forms of colonialism as a path to domination now carry a negative connotation, economic competition and profit maximization do not. Globalization enthusiasts and anti-globalization populists are both believers of "monocapitalism," as Mark McElroy calls it, expert on sustainable organizations. Monocapitalism maintains and grows only one form of capital, namely, economic capital, at the expense of all others.[10] McElroy calls for "multicapitalism," meaning "capitalism designed to maintain all vital capitals, not just one of them: natural, human, social, constructed, and economic at required levels."[11] The real economy has at least eight dimensions, with human well-being depending more on the first seven dimensions than on private wealth: "ecological wealth, human agency, trust between humans, faith in the future, cultural wealth, community wealth, public wealth, and personal wealth."[12]

Terrorism, corruption, trafficking of drugs and people, bank crashes, tax evasion, industrial torture of animals, social and ecological dumping on a global scale, all are seen as unavoidable externalities to this monocapitalism, while they may be the truest children of its logic, sometimes even its pillars.[13] Already Eugen Kogon, a German opponent of the Nazi Party and concentration camp survivor, saw the concentration camps as the most effective expression of the system that surrounded them.[14] Philosopher Walter Benjamin did not survive the Nazi regime, and his warning is still important today: he warned against the "necrophilic, globalizing social system of neoliberal capitalist domination that is invading every corner of the globe."[15] Illustrative cases have multiplied since Benjamin found his tragic death. Drug cartels' hyper-capitalistic "narconomics," for instance, could be seen as a true manifestation of the overall system.[16] Corruption is as structurally anchored, and it is not surprising that it is on the rise, even in countries like Germany, otherwise proud of observing high ethical standards.[17] In Korea, the "gifts" of corruption that have become customary to offer are so expensive that the country's economy dependents on them: Curbing corruption therefore becomes equated with damaging the country's economy.[18] In a globalized and digitized world, also digital terrorist tactics transmute into one of the most effective weapons. When I wrote these sentences, on May 12, 2017, the WannaCry ransomware attack started, infecting more than 230,000 computers in 150 countries. Corporations and military forces around the world now understand the new danger and employ cyberwar specialists on a massive scale.[19]

Most of the mathematical modelling that mainstream economists engage in, is too limited and has even been considered bogus.[20] Life depends on investments and sales, which both are fragile and tend to fail – "the physical welfare and the sense of self-worth of the people depend on an unreliable economic motor with built-in tendencies toward social chaos and ecological disaster."[21] Fordist/Keynesian regimes of accumulation cannot be remedied with a neoliberal regime of accumulation, nor vice versa.[22] In 2017, philosopher Howard Richards predicts: "...believers in America First, and in 18th century French natural rights philosophy, and 20th century Austrian economics will soon suffer a precipitous decline."[23]

As I see it, terror will stay as a systemic feature as long as limitless maximization is aimed at in an overall context that is finite. Efforts to stem corruption, for example, may occasionally achieve small victories, yet, they will lose the overall struggle in the long run.[24] In my view, unless humankind musters the courage to look at the larger picture and treats the cause of the disease, the symptoms will stay. Bringing back the classical security dilemma and re-dividing the world is not the path to healing. It rather risks bringing back all-out suicidal world war.[25] The path to healing is *global citizenship of care*.[26] To come back to the image of the Titanic used earlier in this book, it is hazardous to focus all attention on the cracks on the luxury top floor while the ship starts colliding with the iceberg. It is much more important to change the course of the ship, and to reconstruct it entirely.

Boko Haram in Nigeria may serve as an illustration for how corruption and terrorism interlink, and how both of them act from the logic of competition for domination.[27] Boko Haram means "Western influence is sin," and it became known internationally for its kidnapping of 276 schoolgirls. Many see the story of Boko Haram simply as one of crazy radicalized religiousness. Perhaps it is not. It started with a population's legitimate frustration over corruption, frustration over elites exploiting their people increasingly shamelessly. People hoped that stricter rules might stem this rise in corruption, and that religion could provide those rules. A politician appeared on the stage who promised to implement precisely those rules if elected. But as soon as he was in power, he betrayed his promise. The leader of the movement of the frustrated who had helped the politician into power thus lost his credibility.[28] His followers got enraged. He should have been given the opportunity to lead his followers back into more moderation, yet, the government killed him. A more violent leader replaced him and started to use terrorism as a tool. The country's national army was called in to protect the population against those terrorists. But the army soldiers, as they hailed from other parts of the country, were ignorant of this region. Fearful and nervous, they overreacted. They committed atrocities against the very population they were sent to protect from terror. They alienated the population, driving them into the arms of the enemy, the formerly frustrated people now turned into terrorists. The terrorists sought refuge in neighboring countries. An international military coalition was created to counteract this. As a result, also the neighboring countries were drawn into violence. Since also Libya had been driven into disintegration by military intervention, a whole region is in danger now.[29] In 2016, "this is the largest crisis on the African continent."[30] And Da'esh is there to serve as inspirer and technical advisor. Finally, the internet is there to serve as technical platform for Da'esh. In conclusion: It started with corruption, then came protests against it, then it continued with terrorism, and it ended by throwing half a continent into mortal danger, even threatening security worldwide.

Fatima Akilu calls for a Nigeria that offers young people space to flourish and shine, as only this can discourage them to fall for the false promises of religious extremists.[31] Fatima Akilu is a psychologist who was schooled in Tunbridge Wells, south of London, and then became head of Nigeria's de-radicalization program.

My conclusion after forty years of global living is that the entire world community must follow Akilu's advice. And, to stay in the image of the Titanic, doing so requires a deep recalibration of Titanic's course and design. Making business-as-usual ever more "effective" is like aiming full speed at a crash with the iceberg. I concur with economist Kamran Mofid, who cries out, "Call me an idealist, a dreamer, whatever. But, believe me, unless we address and tackle the causes of injustice, inhumanity, poverty (spiritual and material), inequality, loneliness, anger, frustration, hopelessness..., resultant from neoliberal economic policies, then, the world falls deeper and deeper into the abyss."[32] Indeed, loneliness now affects over forty percent of older adults in the U.S.[33]

Mofid's global view on the predicament of humankind lies outside of the scope of awareness of most players. Yet, as long as we stay within too narrow a scope, I fear that we simply keep having the choice between several false promises. No "strong belief" will help, no belief in heroic winning over enemies, no belief in religion or ideology, no belief in the wisdom of the market, and no certitude of salvation à la Silicon valley. No well-meant conferences and laudable initiatives will suffice. Only the African insight will help that "it takes a village to raise a child." In other words, prevention is needed. And this prevention must be global and systemic. By now, even where such insights emerge, prevention efforts stay within a frame that is too limited. Efforts "tilt at windmills like Don Quixote," since the larger frame counteracts them.[34]

For a society that wishes to make the African adage work, that wishes to help adolescents to become supportive members of society, it is important to understand the role of risky adolescent behavior from the point of view of evolution. As much as such behavior often has pathological consequences for long-term individual and societal welfare, it was once well adapted for short-term survival and reproduction in the environments of our forebears.[35] Therefore, wise societal policies must make provisions for risky adolescent behavior and factor it in.

Many indigenous peoples define the entire ecosphere as "not for sale."[36] *Living Well* is an indigenous social system that focuses on reciprocity between people and Earth.[37] "When all the trees have been cut down, when all the animals have been hunted, when all the waters are polluted, when all the air is unsafe to breathe, only then will you discover you cannot eat money," is a Cree prophecy. Economist and political scientist Ernst Friedrich Schumacher (1883 – 1950) observed that, in contrast to indigenous philosophy, "modern man does not experience himself as a part of nature but as an outside force destined to dominate and conquer it."[38] It is in this context that terrorism has emerged, in all its forms, including as "terroristic" legislation, as has been mentioned earlier[39]: we live now in a "terroristic" apartheid *world-system*,[40] where humiliation is systemic.

Many such "terroristic" trends have emerged during the past years. One of them has been the replacement of the terminology of "indigenous" with the label "poor," in this way pulling also indigenous populations into a monetized world: "Basic needs for the poor is the usual justification for outsiders to extract resources…-"[41] Perhaps even the argument that poverty causes terrorism and that economic growth therefore will alleviate terrorism, may be brought forward, at least in some cases, to legitimize the monetization of the world.[42] The terminology of poverty thus risks supporting a trend that ultimately will impoverish and terrorize all.

The indigenous lifestyle is under siege, not least because there is the *tragedy of the commons*, or the commons dilemma. This is a dilemma that gets ever more tragic the more circumscription intensifies, the more population puts pressure on resources, the more people lose faith in burden sharing, and the more they lack skills and tools to contain free-riding.[43] *Mutual coercion mutually agreed upon* is the ideal way to protect commons, as it was already proposed by philosopher Jean-Jacques Rousseau in 1762 in his exposition of the general will and the social contract,[44] and this "is only now beginning to be understood by scientists of society facing practical problems in complex systems."[45]

Colonizers were free-riders; they stole the commons of the colonized. The English economist John Atkinson Hobson (1858 – 1940), after having observed the Second Boer War in South Africa (1899 – 1902), wrote his magnum opus titled *Imperialism* in 1902, where he concluded that colonial wars had the economic motive to facilitate investment of excess money of the rich and to create markets to sell excess manufactured goods, driven by an excessively unequal distribution of incomes in the industrialized countries.[46] To him, this was an altogether immoral set-up, as it led to immense suffering among colonial peoples and among the poor of the industrial nations.

More recently, particularly during the past thirty years, the exploitation of the commons has been re-defined as legitimate "business opportunity." In economist David Korten's words, "Today's borderless global economy pits every person, community, and firm in a relentless race to the bottom, as private economic power extends out and governments compete to attract jobs and investment by offering the biggest subsidies and the lowest regulatory standards."[47]

The outcome is social and ecological damage, it is *sociocide*[48] and *ecocide*.[49] While most people choose to remain "comfortably unaware," global depletion is running amok.[50] Trying to monetize nature is a "last-ditch attempt on the part of the shareholder primacy doctrine to stay relevant,"[51] and, as this is bound to fail, terror will increase.[52] As the sustainability problem is "defined out" of the economic paradigm, the economic system can freely destroy its own social and ecological host. Ecological economist, environmental scientist, and futurist Richard Sanders writes:

- The basic problem is that humanity is consuming way more than the planet can sustain and this level of consumption is growing exponentially.
- The messaging in our society and the dominant worldview are primarily about consuming and consuming more (and acquiring the purchasing power to do so).
- The financial system (fractional reserve) is essentially a pyramid scheme that will collapse if debt doesn't continue to grow exponentially (locking us into exponential growth).
- The sustainability problem is subsumed into the economic paradigm to ensure the economic system prevails (at least until it destroys it ecological host).[53]

Boko Haram started with popular frustration and ended in terrorism. Similarly, at the global level, a "democracy-free-trade-TPP-oligarchy-neoliberalism"[54] creates global risks, which then are responded to with solutions that are even more hazardous. In 2016, Chad's President Idriss Déby Itno bitterly complained about foreign powers following their own interests – as they did, for instance with Libya – at the peril of local peoples who are left with disastrous consequences that destabilize entire regions.[55] Or, director and founder of Global Trade Watch, Lori Wallach, called the Trans-Pacific Partnership (TTP) a corporate Trojan horse that handcuffs domestic governments, limits food safety, threatens environmental standards, financial regulation, energy and climate policy, and establishes new powers for corporations.[56] The financial industry, including multinational investment management corporations such as BlackRock, have been described as a global cartel.[57]

Solutions for the problems of this world are being advertised. One of them is building fences. The 2013 World Risk Report informs that India is building a 3,000 km long barbed fence against the expected environmental refugees from flatlands of Bangladesh.[58] Not to speak of the fences now in the planning in Europe and the United States.[59]

Dani Rodrik, former professor of international political economy at Harvard University, calls the inherent tension between democracy, national sovereignty, and radical economic globalization the *globalization paradox*.[60] He contends that it is impossible to uphold these three elements simultaneously – only two can co-exist at the same time. He argues that extreme economic liberalization and deregulation (what he calls hyper-globalization) must therefore be curbed in order to uphold democracy and sovereignty.

Giving primacy to profit maximization – letting it lead where it should serve – has often been described as an outgrowth of European raiding culture.[61] South African economist Sampie Terreblanche explains that globalization, with its origins from Europe – from Portugal, Spain, the Netherlands, England, and, today, the United States – has three of their institutions play global "hardball": Political institutions engage in nation-building, military institutions engage in warring, and capitalist institutions engage in amassing wealth.[62] By now, the result is this: "Much of the Western world has fallen into the hands of a plutocracy which has no long-term interests but only a demand for short-term profit, and has turned over management of policy to the military-industrial interests and the fear-mongers," this writes theologian Raymond Helmick.[63]

André Vltchek is a provocative philosopher, novelist, filmmaker, and investigative journalist, who has traveled the world and has witnessed incidents of suffering that most people who live in the West never see, neither on television at home nor in "ghetto-like" vacation locations if ever so "exotic." In the face of the 2015 refugee crisis in West Asia and Europe, Vltchek is angry:

> When one looted country after another begins to sink, when there is nothing left there, when children begin dying from hunger and when men commence fighting each other over tiny boulders and dirty pieces of turf, pathetic boats, or dinghies, begin crossing the waterways, bringing half starved, half-mad refugees to the European sea-fronts decorated with marble. What a horrifying sight! ... That is what you reduced the world to, Europe – you, and your huge, insatiable offspring – North America![64]

How economism terrorizes body and soul

"What if sociologists had as much influence as economists?" asks senior economics correspondent Neil Irwin in the *New York Times*.[65] Psychologists Maureen O'Hara and Anthony Marsella indict academia, not just the field of economics, also other fields, including the field of psychology, for failing their responsibility to be self-critical. All human activities, including scientific research, goes on within specific psycho-spheres, warns O'Hara, and citizens and policy makers who consume research "are mostly unaware of the tacit, culture-specific assumptions embedded in studies," and in this way, much research serves "the interests of corporatization and the interests of the established power elites."[66] In the field of psychology, there is a concealment of a heavy Western bias, and this is hazardous, warns Marsella, as there are far-reaching ideological and moral consequences inherent in every psychology:

> These consequences assume pernicious outcomes when the economic, political, social, and historical determinants of the psychology are accepted as the foundations for its "truth," and are used to justify its imposition upon others as universally applicable with no self-reflexive analysis of its ethno-centric and nation-centric biases. What occurs as one psychology is pushed as dogma, and this is a colonization of mind and behavior, even in the absence of military and other forms of conquest. It is still violence. It is still immoral! It is still nothing more than a hegemonic effort to homogenize the world.[67]

The homogenization of the world proceeds both through "other-colonization" and "self-colonization."[68] Clearly, it is not always a straightforward smooth process. Here is a case. After Japan's defeat in 1945, the American influence in the country became significant. From the late 1940s onward, Japan widely implemented American management approaches, until, through the 1950s, the Japanese workforce was becoming increasingly dissatisfied. In 1959, Japan came close to a communist revolution with strikes and management lockouts. American consultants failed to understand the situation. A Japanese professor, Kaoru Ishikawa, explained what happened: "... the reason for our problem is that we have copied the American system of management and it is alien to our culture! Before coming into the factories our workers came from the rice fields, they were part of family groups and a group culture. Being treated like robots where nobody asks them anything, nobody involves them in anything is demeaning to the individual and it denies the company the use of their brains."[69] Ishikawa acknowledged that going back to the traditional craft system was impossible, as it would be uneconomic. Yet, he wanted to restore the workers' sense of pride, self-respect, and team spirit, and therefore brought *craftsmanship* back into their lives. He called this approach *quality circles*, and published it in 1964 in a managerial textbook in the West.[70] The concept spread throughout Japan and by 1978, one million companies reported to have established such quality circles.

In the West's psycho-sphere, unsurprisingly, its own raiding culture meets less resistance.[71] It appears as part of a culture of individualism, a culture that drives misrecognition and is driven by it. The result is that systemic ills are overlooked and victims blamed.[72]

What is interesting about individualism is that it is enforced collectively, albeit stealthily. Examples from daily life illustrate this. The desire to "live in one's own house" is seen as the norm and those who admit that they yearn for community rather than property, may soon find themselves marginalized. Or, if offspring does not move out of their parents' home at a certain age and refuses to "stand on their own feet," the collective will see this as a problem. In this way, by pushing for the loss of collective cohesion, the collective brings about its own demise, thus causing the "anomie (de-culturation) and atomie (de-structuration)" now found in the West.[73] There seems to be little resistance. As humans primarily are social beings, and born into and embedded in social environments, they appear to stay within the cultural confines they were born into, even if those confines are deleterious.

Western culture of individualism can be conceptualized as an extension of the traditional ranked culture of the dominator model of society, only that human rights ideals of individual freedom are made to serve a covert and refined application of the art of domination: a misrecognized argument of "freedom" coopts people to accept and maintain their own bondage voluntarily. If we say that a new security dilemma now plays out between an economic elite and the rest, then extreme individualism could be seen as the application of the divide-and-rule strategy to keep underlings down. Extreme individualism means that each individual regards her own self's boundaries as if it were a country and the fault lines of the security dilemma were shrunk down around her personal territory. Through this shrinkage, every person is separated from her fellow beings. Everyone is forced into Machiavellian *hominus hominem lupus est* relationships, which in honor contexts are reserved to elites. Ruthless individualism systemically pushes for narcissism, the narcissism of packaging oneself into a competitive saleable "product" for the purpose of "personal branding."[74] Rather than care, what is idolized is entrepreneurship, entrepreneurs going to work like warriors. Business therefore resembles war. The website Clausewitz.org, for instance, professes that it is dedicated to putting the insights of historical war leaders into the modern workplace.[75] Also people's relationships outside of the workplace are affected by this war culture. Even in countries such as Germany, known for its caution with respect to private ownership of guns, more people now feel the need to protect their own personal borders and obtain weapons.[76]

The push toward all-out competition for domination has its price, a price that is paid for by nature and by people, particularly by women. As domination is a male cultural script, women are bound to lose out wherever this script intensifies.[77] A survey by the U.S. National Bureau of Economic Research shows that although many objective measures of the lives of women in the United States have improved over the past thirty-five years, measures of subjective well-being have declined both absolutely and relative to men.[78] This result is found across various datasets and measures of subjective well-being, and it is pervasive across demographic groups and industrialized countries. A new gender gap is emerging, with higher subjective well-being for men, thus turning around the gap of the 1970s, when women reported higher subjective well-being than men.

Further, a culture of extreme individualism and primacy of profit maximization systemically undermines ethical behavior and trust.[79] It erodes the very reason for trust. This is an extremely damaging effect, since social trust is directly linked to health,[80] and, if we think of terrorism, trust is crucial if terrorism is to decrease.

In the health sector it becomes particularly visible how systemic distrust can become a question of life and death. Director-general of the WHO, Dr. Margaret Chan warns:

> Today, many of the threats to health that contribute to non-communicable diseases come from corporations that are big, rich, and powerful, driven by commercial interests, and far less friendly to health … Here is a question I would like to ask the food and beverage industries. Does it really serve your interests to produce, market, globally distribute, and aggressively advertise, especially to children, products that damage the health of your customers?

> Does this make sense in any mission statement with a social purpose?[81]

Increasingly, people ask: How can I be sure that my physician does not put his profit before my health?[82] Why are baby bottles toxic?[83] Why are baby food advertisements so misleading?[84] Why is unhealthy food endorsed by celebrities, who get paid millions for this?[85] Why are psychiatrists on drug makers' payrolls and promote bipolar disorder even in young children, a condition that was once thought to affect only adults and adolescents?[86] Why does nobody question the "medical community's enthusiasm for pathologizing entirely natural emotional responses to (among others) humiliating experiences"?[87]

The list is much longer. Every third head physician in Germany believes that due to economic reasons patients are subjected to unnecessary surgery that is incompatible with health-related consideration, because surgery is lucrative and hospitals are in need of funds.[88] Aryeh Shander is an anesthesiologist who, despite encountering many obstacles, continues to raise his voice against certain intensive care practices in the United States.[89] One concrete example is the case of blood transfusions. Such transfusions can save lives in absolute emergencies, yet, increasingly, research shows that blood transfusions can also be very detrimental to health. They represent miniature transplantations and carry the same risks as other transplantations. Yet, neither physicians nor the managers of the blood donations system are interested in informing unsuspecting patients of those risks; some do not want to unnecessarily incite panic for lack of alternatives, while others worry about their business model.[90]

Who terrorizes whom here? Clearly, humanizing healthcare is what is needed.[91] Yet, would this be possible, and would it be enough? Only humanizing globalization would remove the systemic viruses that infect all segments of society, including healthcare.

What terrorizes more – capitalism or socialism?

The reader may wonder: But do we not hear proud announcements everywhere that throughout the past decades "millions of people have been lifted out of poverty"?

Yes, there are successes. On a series of health indicators, for instance, the world is improving and people live longer.[92]

By definition, however, throwing a party is a short-term activity, not a sustainable one. If "success" builds on an unsustainable overuse of resources, it cannot last. China is a good example; when people have no clean air to breathe, the price for wealth is too high. Journalist Roberto Savio warns that, instead of economic growth representing "a rising tide lifting all boats," and "capital trickling down to everybody," social and ecological resources are hollowed out and plundered, with consumption patterns rapidly depleting the world's non-renewable resources.[93] The insight that wealth and income extremes hurt all is now on the increase the world around,[94] and Oxfam informs us that the annual income of the richest one hundred people is enough to end global poverty four times over.[95] "We can no longer pretend that the creation of wealth for a few will inevitably benefit the many – too often the reverse is true," concludes Jeremy Hobbs, executive director of Oxfam International.[96]

Clearly, and this does not need to be expanded on here, also the academic discipline of economics has lost much of its credibility since the rolling global growth crisis began in 2007, broke in 2008, and has now entered a phase of uncertainty.[97] Increasing inequality divides society and endangers humanity's common future.[98] We hear ever louder calls for a radically new orientation.[99]

"We may have democracy, or we may have wealth concentrated in the hands of the few, but we cannot have both," this saying is being attributed to former Supreme Court Justice Louis Brandeis (1856 – 1941).[100] The Oxford Committee for Famine Relief, Oxfam, an international organization dedicated to poverty eradication, disaster relief, advocacy, and policy research warns that extreme economic inequality is harmful for many reasons: it is morally questionable; it can have negative impacts on economic growth and poverty reduction; and it can multiply social problems[101]:

> It compounds other inequalities, such as those between women and men. In many countries, extreme economic inequality is worrying because of the pernicious impact that wealth concentrations can have on equal political representation. When wealth captures government policymaking, the rules bend to favor the rich, often to the detriment of everyone else. The consequences include the erosion of democratic governance, the pulling apart of social cohesion, and the vanishing of equal opportunities for all. Unless bold political solutions are instituted to curb the influence of wealth on politics, governments will work for the interests of the rich, while economic and political inequalities continue to rise.[102]

The relatively new field of neuro-economics confirms that the *Homo economicus* model of human behavior needs to be revised; emotion plays a much greater role than earlier hypothesized. The belief held by many, particularly by many men, the belief in their competency in "hard" rationality, is profoundly flawed: it is "soft" emotionality that is at the core of supposed bulwarks of rationality such as the world of finance.[103] Financial bubbles are similar to drug experiences, involving the nucleus accumbens, a region in the basal forebrain that plays a significant role in addiction.[104]

As mentioned earlier, in Somalia, during my doctoral research, I learned how the "city-boys of London" resemble the Somali militia boys on pickup trucks or pirate ships. In the 2010 documentary film *Inside Job*, Jonathan Alpert, a New York therapist whose clients include many high-level Wall Street executives, reports: "These people are risk-takers; they're impulsive. It's part of their behavior; it's part of their personality. And that manifests outside of work as well. It's quite typical for the guys to go out, to go to strip bars, to use drugs. I see a lot of cocaine use, a lot of use of prostitution."[105] Indeed, research suggests that testosterone is linked to money trading,[106] and that people with a strong personality trait of greed tend to engage in particularly risky and reckless behavior.[107] In experimental research, greedy individuals are less aware of negative outcomes and have difficulties in learning from experience, especially from mistakes. Their investment banking can be expected to be risky and thus contribute to stock market bubbles.

The fact that money can be accumulated unlocks doors that would better stay shut. Not just can global and local economies be ruined, also ruining peace can generate profits. Producing weapons has always been lucrative,[108] but, and this is new, social media have now democratized the pathway to profitable enmity: each individual can make money for themselves and for social media platforms by spewing hatred.[109] The effect – the rise of polarization and extremism in society – can be maximized by investing in automated Internet bots that multiply hate-inducing messages, thus distorting public discourse and undermining the foundation of democratic processes.[110]

Is this the time to return to the old capitalism versus socialism debate? It seems, better not. Unsuitable dichotomies carry the risk of creating what Jean Baker Miller calls *false choices*.[111] What is needed, instead, are Miller's *alternative arrangements*, so that *The Real Wealth of Nations* can flourish.[112] Scholar Riane Eisler is the author of a book with this title, and she calls for entirely new social categories. She advises to go beyond conventional dichotomies such as capitalist versus communist, Eastern versus Western, industrial versus pre- or post-industrial, right versus left, religious versus secular. We could extend this list with realism versus idealism, hatred versus love, altruism versus egoism, self-interest versus common interest, collectivist versus individualist, big versus small government, visible hand versus invisible hand,[113] globalization versus localization, and so forth.

Clearly, to overcome false dichotomies and open up space for alternative arrangements, novel outlooks are needed. To avoid the capitalism versus socialism dichotomy, the term "monetary hegemony" is perhaps a suitable term, since it describes the dominator economics that characterize reality on the ground in both systems. Sustainable development expert Gwendolyn Hallsmith uses this phrase when she warns against "the systematic impoverishment of nature and humanity wrought by privatized monetary hegemony." She urges that, "without changing the dominant 'resource allocation system' by democratizing the monetary system, we will not be able to reverse the damage. It will continue, unabated, and will make the lives of future generations less and less tenable on a scorched Earth."[114] Journalist Antony Loewenstein spent years researching "the ways in which our world is being sold to the highest bidder without public consent."[115] Jørgen Randers is an expert in future studies and limits to growth, and he warns: "It is profitable to let the world go to hell."[116] In other words, monetary hegemony has been wielded in all contexts, "communist" and "capitalist," privatized and state, each time with the promise of well-being for all, while creating ill-being except for a few.

Culture scientist Christina von Braun asks: Why do we believe in the power of money, even though most people have no idea of how financial markets work? Sociologists, philosophers, and theologians point at money as the most significant global religion of present times. Von Braun puts forward the argument that money and religion are much closer connected than we usually recognize.[117] When she looked for explanations, the concept of sacrifice became a prime candidate. What if agriculture was once perceived as a violation of the earth, and out of guilt, sacrifices were offered in the spirit of "if I give God money, God lets nature flourish"? Von Braun describes how in early Greek antiquity a new form of currency was "certified" through rituals of sacrifice in the temple, and how Christian theology extended this concept and developed a money economy based on the concept of sacrifice.[118]

Indeed, agriculture has been felt to be a violation by many. I lived with Linda Hartling and her husband in Portland, Oregon, in 2009 and 2011, and saw the website of the Confederated Tribes of Grand Ronde in Oregon saying: "According to our ancestors, there were prophecies against cutting into the earth and planting crops."[119]

Philosopher of social science Howard Richards warns that the global religion of money may be more than just a matter of faith. Also Richards positions himself outside of any socialism versus capitalism debate when he suggests to go back to Roman times to understand the ground pillars of present-day's global economic institutions of whatever ideological wrappings, be they "scientific" capitalism or socialism, with Adam Smith and David Ricardo legitimizing the first, and Karl Marx, Friedrich Engels, and Vladimir Ilyich Lenin the second. Richards explains that all systems are built on the same basic principles of Roman law and that the solution therefore lies in changing those foundations.[120]

Roman law allows people to believe, for instance, that there is "no responsibility" where there is "no contract." The shredding of social cohesion in societies can thus be justified with the exclamation: "But this is not my responsibility!" In this way de-solidarization is legitimized and an impersonal way of relating to other people promoted, to people as mere abstract role-bearers in contracts. Personal social skills of solidarity are de-emphasized, and the traditional family spirit of communal sharing that indicates that everybody ought to receive according to need and give according to ability is weakened.[121] Worse even, the myth is fed that individual independence is the norm for the health of a person and a society, and that this is achievable only through an abstract societal system, a system to which everybody ought to turn for livelihood and social contacts. Solidarity should only be administrated through the system, such as through giving charity (in the Anglo-Saxon world), or paying taxes (in Continental Europe, for instance). People who still engage in direct solidarity are derogated as failing "independence," of breeding "losers," who "live off others" and fail to learn to "stand on their own feet." As such mindsets gather influence, even love and marriage can be replaced by the purchase of temporary closeness.[122] Young people are thus socialized into excluding the most fulfilling forms of interpersonal interdependence – the Buberian meeting of souls of I-Thou[123] – and are prevented from learning to combine dependence and independence into rich interdependence, into mutual interconnection. In sum, profound psychological damage is inflicted on individuals and society; the space that humans need to unfold their potential is curtailed and amputated.[124]

Richards gives a brief overview over how Roman law came to define the ethics of our time and now even rules the world.[125] Richards follows John Dewey's *naturalistic pragmatism*,[126] and the more recently developed philosophical position that connects Enlightenment with postmodernism, namely, *critical realism*.[127] He follows Charles Taylor and John Searle[128] in that *constitutive rules* govern our bargaining society, and Roy Bhaskar in that *generative mechanisms* produce the phenomena we observe.[129] He also follows Anthony Giddens in that today's postmodern condition is one of *radicalized modernity*.[130] And he follows Immanuel Wallerstein in pointing out that it is one single set of constitutive rules, namely, the successors of Roman law principles,[131] that now defines the modern *world-system*.[132] And these rules now act as a *systemic imperative*, as historian Ellen Meiksins Wood formulated it.[133] Richards calls for a new logic of cooperation and solidarity to become strong enough to limit this imperative running amok.

The same systemic imperative has already formed the backdrop for colonialism with its massive deconstruction of indigenous cultures,[134] and now it stands behind what is known as neoliberalism, which, Richards suggests, should be called *neo-Romanism*. It also drives the so-called war on terror with its thrust against people described as ideological fundamentalists and extremists, and, more even, altogether against traditional ways of life that resist the ethics of modernity.[135]

When the feudal *Gemeinschaften* of the Middle Ages disintegrated, capitalism dissolved personal bonds through arms-length transactions defined by Roman law.[136] The Roman contract law was revitalized as market relationships became dis-embedded from social relationships, a historical process well described by economic historian Karl Polanyi.[137] Richards explains that he personally feels that his own humanity is being terrorized, tortured, and humiliated just by watching this trend deepen everywhere around the world. After forty years of global life, I cannot but resonate with him.

In response, neither Richards nor I wish to return to some idealized past. I learned to value the social glue that traditional collectivist societies offer their members when I worked as a psychotherapist in Egypt. Yet, I have also seen how destructive it can be when collectivism turns into oppression. I therefore welcome the liberation from those oppressive aspects of traditional collectivist models. I do see the advantages of creating larger and more abstract networks of relationships, I am an admirer of Paulo Freire's colleague Clodomir de Morais who calls it the "artisan weakness" not to let go of control.[138] Yet, there is a "too little" and a "too much," and the ability of collectivist communities to create social glue should be valued, protected, and nurtured. What individualistic Western societies do is throw out the baby with the bath water.

Sociologist Mark Granovetter has studied whether strong or weak social ties are more useful, and he comes out on the side of weaker ties.[139] He builds on sociologist Ferdinand Tönnies (1855 – 1936) and his differentiation of *Gemeinschaft* versus *Gesellschaft*.[140] In a Gemeinschaft, people have strong ties and thoroughly share norms, a setting that is easily disrupted by even minimal dissent. Having many weak ties to a number of people, in contrast, provides more space for individual autonomy and diversity, argues Granovetter. My personal life path confirms this insight, at least in part.

However, together with author Frank Schirrmacher, I warn that the weakening of ties can go too far. He is critical of the shrinking of social relationships to a minimum, of the dissolution of the family in its capacity as "survival factory." In situations of emergency it becomes apparent how dangerous this is. Schirrmacher uses as illustration the tragedy of the settlers of the Donner Party, a group of American pioneers who set out for California in a wagon train in May 1846. They had to spend the winter of 1846 to1847 snowbound in the Sierra Nevada. Those who were alone, without family, died in the snowstorms, while those who were with family survived.[141]

In conclusion, as soon as people are dislodged from their relationships, they risk being "unfrozen" too far. Terrorism experts speak of *unfreezing* when young people become dislodged from their familiar social contexts and fall prey to terrorism entrepreneurs.[142] Similarly, whole societies can unfreeze their members, disconnect them, so that they become willing to partake in a rat race, which can be made ever more brutal once enough people are "hooked."

Richards' overall analysis is that "the dynamic of capital accumulation has been a major, perhaps the major, dynamic of modern history; as has social exclusion, which is another consequence of the same normative structure."[143] He concludes that if *disconnection* is our contemporary condition, and if *dominium* (ownership) and present-day's post-Roman law principles are the root problem, then *integration* is the answer of our time to solve the problems and to serve life. In that situation, local governments cannot be counted on for help, fears Richards, since their whole duty is to serve post-Roman law, enforce contracts, and protect the security of investments, as they are forbidden to interfere with the free mobility of factors across borders. Even improving global *regulatory* rules would not help create a level playing field for all, what is needed are better global constitutive rules.[144] The example of Scandinavian countries shows that even though they have a tradition of equality and have done better for a while, also their model is ultimately inherently unviable.[145]

Capitalism is the title of a complex interdisciplinary documentary series in six episodes by Ilan Ziv, offering a succinct summary of capitalism's timeline.[146] In the medieval cities of Venice and Bruges, trade developed to high levels of sophistication. Then, Spanish Conquistador Hernán Cortés appeared on the stage of history and caused the fall of the Aztec Empire. He was a gambler and hazardeur, who needed more than trade, namely, plunder. He maintained a lifestyle of owing money to investors expecting returns. And this is what capitalism is today. It is not free trade; it is the freedom to participate in plunder or else be marginalized and excluded, excluded to the point of starvation.

After the enclosure of the commons in England, which started during the sixteenth century, brutal "terroristic" laws, as sociologist Eric Mielants called them,[147] were enacted to punish poverty and idleness. Poverty was seen as a moral problem deserving punishment, rather than a societal problem.[148] Anthropologist David Graeber describes how the enclosure movements, together with the criminalization of debt, contributed to the destruction of English communities:

> The criminalization of debt, then, was the criminalization of the very basis of human society. It cannot be overemphasized that in a small community, everyone normally was both lender and borrower. One can only imagine the tensions and temptations that must have existed in a community – and communities, much though they are based on love, in fact, because they are based on love, will always also be full of hatred, rivalry and passion – when it became clear that with sufficiently clever scheming, manipulation, and perhaps a bit of strategic bribery, they could arrange to have almost anyone they hated imprisoned or even hanged.[149]

A planned, well-funded intervention to manipulate the framing of the cultural story of society began near the end of the nineteenth century. Adam Smith and David Ricardo are only post-hoc justifiers of what was already there, with slavery incidentally representing a glaringly blind spot in Smith's analysis. Adam Smith, in his 1759 book *The Theory of the Moral Sentiments*, taught that divine providence has decreed that humans do and should pursue self-interest, meaning that if people do not pursue their self-interest, they are not only unnatural, they also sin against God's providence, since "what is natural" is "what God intended."[150] Providence, in its wisdom, had it arranged that everybody pursuing their own self-interest would result in the general good of all "as if by an invisible hand." Interestingly, the phrase "invisible hand," appears only once in Adam Smith's book and, to make matters worse, even in a different context.[151] It seems that it was taken out of its context later, and suffered a fate similar to that of Darwin's "survival of the fittest" – misunderstood and spun to serve the general *Zeitgeist*. By the invisible hand, all-knowing providence would harmonize the work of individuals, so that the good of all would flow from all pursuing their own personal good. Preachers such as Russell Herman Conwell (1843 – 1925) supported this message.[152]

The documentary, while masterly tracing capitalism's manipulative path, does not omit that there is also reason for hope. Our economic arrangements are social constructions, rather than manifestations of scientific concepts that mirror immovable natural laws. Therefore, these arrangements are open to being changed through social construction. Slavery and child labor are examples that may inspire hope, as they are perfect expressions of a free market, yet, nowadays, they are regarded as illegitimate (even though still existing in practice, with almost 40 million slaves toiling for the global economy[153]).

If I am to summarize this story provocatively, then the present-day concept of the free market appears to be a misunderstanding. Systemic terror is perpetrated with the best intentions, out of the conviction that this is the best arrangement of all worlds and that it is worth paying any price to maintain it. The misunderstanding was amplified by individuals such as Ayn Rand, who combined her own psychological tribulations with a misinterpretation of Adam Smith and reified the result into a pseudo-scientific dogma.[154] Alan Greenspan, chairman of the Federal Reserve Board of the United States from 1987 to 2006, was one of many who had been influenced by Ayn Rand. He had the stature to admit that the dogma was flawed and that the whole intellectual edifice had collapsed. When the system broke in 2008, he was "in a state of shocked disbelief" and admitted that he had been wrong in thinking that relying on banks to act on self-interest would be enough to protect shareholders and their equity.[155] Scholar David Harvey formulated it as follows: "The internal contradictions within the flow of capital that have precipitated recent crises contain the seeds of systemic catastrophe."[156] In former times, colonies were drained of their resources, by now, the entire world is the colony.[157]

Like a big ship cannot be turned fast, also global economic structures cannot be changed fast, among others, because a mass consumer culture is now well embedded in the global psycho-sphere. The embedding process has been narrated by William Leach in *Land of Desire*,[158] or the *BBC* video series *Century of the Self*.[159] Unfortunately, systemic catastrophe looms larger in 2017 than only one year earlier, not least since admirers of Ayn Rand have become more influential after the ascent of Donald J. Trump to the American presidency.[160] Ayn Rand biographer Jennifer Burns explains: "For a long time, she has been beloved by disruptors, entrepreneurs, venture capitalists, people who see themselves as shaping the future, taking risky bets, moving out in front of everyone else, relying only on their own instincts, intuition and knowledge, and going against the grain."[161] Indeed, shaping a new future is urgently needed now, the question is: what kind of future?

Why are humans such willing victims and perpetrators of economic terror?

The measurement of GDP/GNP was invented to make society's economy more manageable. Yet, over time, it has proven to have rather dark sides, not least because it fails to show the destructive effects of consumerism.[162] The words of prominent politician Robert Kennedy in 1968 sum up its predicament:

> But even if we act to erase material poverty, there is another greater task, it is to confront the poverty of satisfaction – purpose and dignity – that afflicts us all. Too much and for too long, we seemed to have surrendered personal excellence and community values in the mere accumulation of material things. Our Gross National Product, now, is over $800 billion dollars a year, but that Gross National Product – if we judge the United States of America by that – that Gross National Product counts air pollution and cigarette advertising, and ambulances to clear our highways of carnage. It counts special locks for our doors and the jails for the people who break them. It counts the destruction of the redwood and the loss of our natural wonder in chaotic sprawl. It counts napalm and counts nuclear warheads and armored cars for the police to fight the riots in our cities. It counts Whitman's rifle and Speck's knife, and the television programs which glorify violence in order to sell toys to our children. Yet the gross national product does not allow for the health of our children, the quality of their education or the joy of their play. It does not

> include the beauty of our poetry or the strength of our marriages, the intelligence of our public debate or the integrity of our public officials. It measures neither our wit nor our courage, neither our wisdom nor our learning, neither our compassion nor our devotion to our country, it measures everything in short, except that which makes life worthwhile. And it can tell us everything about America except why we are proud that we are Americans. If this is true here at home, so it is true elsewhere in world....[163]

Myriad examples can illustrate the atmosphere that is brought about by dominator economics. In Greece, a university professor, Antonis Manitakis, was the minister of administrative reform and e-governance from 2012 to 2013. He reports of having been "blackmailed" by people who "spread fear and terror," he reports of having been humiliated into submission by officials of the so-called Troika, a committee led by the European Commission (Eurogroup), together with the European Central Bank and the International Monetary Fund.[164]

What is the result of such humiliation? Greek politicians fear that it risks bringing back the terror of Nazism, just as it raised its head in inter-war Germany, when Germans toiled under humiliating economic hardship. "If you humiliate a proud nation for too long and subject it to the worry of a debt deflation crisis, without light at the end of a tunnel then things come to the boil," predicts Greek economist Yanis Varoufakis.[165] "Calculated humiliation" is what he observes being used to keep an economic system in place that had crashed in 2008.[166] The result "is one of history's greatest ironies, namely, that Nazism is rearing its ugly head in Greece," a historical cradle of democracy.[167]

Takis Ioannides is a researcher of Greek philosophy and a poet who describes himself as "citizen of Planet Earth." In desperation, he wrote to me in April 2014: "The big economic crisis but mostly the civilization crisis terrorizes the citizens of my birth-country!"[168] In October he cried out:

> The crisis in Greece is awful, in my opinion we have a civilization crisis. The taxes terrorize all citizens. For example, we have very old aged retired farmers, with a small pension, who live with what they produce, living in their small villages. Now they have to pay taxes for their own little house and their garden and fields! They feel completely unsafe, being in panic. If they don't have money to pay the taxes, they will lose their house, fields garden.... According to officially figures, more than 2,500,000 Greeks live under the limits of poverty, 2,500,00 more are too close to poverty. The state is against the citizens. Life is unsafe, due to medical problems in hospitals, in social security, in pensions, in employment, in human values.... THIS IS REAL HUMILIATION OF HUMANS. Isn't it terrorism or not?[169]

The subprime crisis in America produced manifold expressions of humiliation. It started with the U.S. government's laudable intention to dignify poor people by enabling them to own their own house. Many were given loans they could not repay. The banks repackaged these loans and made sizable profits. When the bubble burst, many people lost their homes. They were worse off than before, not only had they lost their homes, now they had also to unlearn the link between dignity and owning a home. This was double humiliation. Legal expert Bernadette Atuahene speaks of "dignity taking" when people have not just their property but also their dignity removed; in those cases "dignity restoration" is needed, which is much more than mere material reparation.[170] The subprime crisis thus inflicted double humiliation by misusing the concept of dignity: for the victims, it started with the promise of more dignity and it ended in double humiliation.

Anthropologist Alan Page Fiske has been introduced earlier. He found that people, most of the time and in all cultures, use just four elementary and universal forms or models for organizing sociality. Interaction can be structured according to (1) what people have *in common*, according to (2) *ordered differences*, (3) *additive imbalances*, or (4) *ratios*.[171] The initial promise to the victims was framed within the spirit of authority ranking and communal sharing, but then market pricing kicked in, was given priority, and destroyed the promise. Those who went around to offer loans to people began their campaign by using a rhetoric of communal sharing, like good parents who wish to give their children a chance to rise up in society by earning more dignity. They made their victims believe that they enacted the benevolent and dignifying form of authority ranking by giving the victims the impression that here they were so lucky to meet a benefactor who helped them understand that their ability to repay a loan with interest would make them rise up on the scale of worthiness. Yet, as soon as the loan had been accepted, the game suddenly changed – the frame of market pricing replaced the frame of communal sharing. At that moment, it became painfully clear to the victims that, far from being treated caringly and fairly as family members, they were in fact abused. The end result was their rapid descent on the scale of status, and the difficult task of rescuing their sense of worthiness from the illusion that it could be increased through house ownership and earned by repaying loans.

Some of the micro-finance schemes around the world seem to follow the same script, as they leave people more impoverished than before.[172] The film *Caught in Micro Debt*, shown on Norwegian state television on November 30, 2010, sheds critical light on the practices of micro lending, once hailed as a way forward.[173] In 2015, I spent two months in Rwanda to organize our 25th Annual Dignity Conference there.[174] I got my earlier impressions confirmed that also in Africa the time period that is allowed to repay a loan is frequently too short, the interest too high, and too little help is given to succeed with the projects that were financed by these loans (compounding the systemic barriers that make success improbable, even if help were given). Micro-credit expert Warner Woodworth, who participated in our conference, tellingly affirmed the nature of the subprime crisis: "Yes, this was double humiliation!" Later, he mentioned that, indeed, micro-finance has been abused: He reported that some of his colleagues began as not-for-profit initiatives and then turned into for-profit companies. Woodwarth also agreed with my doubts about any model that is based on the production of ever more "stuff" for sales, as this is unsustainable on a planet with limited resources anyway. Howard Richards concludes that all attempts to bring people out of poverty by bringing them into the money market as it is defined today, are foredoomed.[175]

I resonate with Woodworth's argument that donations and charity can have humiliating effects, yet, to my view, it is not lending that solves this problem. In 2006, I wrote: "Even the most benevolent help can humiliate without the helper being aware of it. International aid is a prime example. Resentment and violent backlashes typically shock those who thought they were doing good."[176] The ideal of many helpers is "help to self-help," which means enabling people to "learn to fish" rather than simply "receive fish" and thus remain recipients of charity. However, when lending conditions are predatory, it is not help to self-help for the needy that is being achieved; rather, lending is of help to a few investors, achieved by hooking the needy to associate dignity with market pricing, thus weakening communal sharing, the true source of dignity.

In conclusion, the aim of present-day systems of market pricing is not necessarily benevolent community-oriented help toward sustainable self-sufficiency, all too often, those systems are rigged toward profit for a few. The rhetoric of poverty reduction is abused to hook people on definitions of dignity that later trap them as willing victims to be exploited in money-making systems whose *raison d'être* is far from serving those victims' interest. The "all boats are lifted up" narrative may work in certain cases in the short term, yet, not for all, and not in the long term. As Canadian international relations specialist Stephen Purdey warns: "The "rising tide lifts all boats" mantra is universally appealing and therefore politically compelling. It is also, of course, a utopian economic model which hints at an abrogation of governmental responsibility, even as it helps us understand the lure of growth."[177]

Increasingly, all around the world, I observe that even the very poorest in society become targets of very sophisticated exploitation. My recommendation is the following: Let us refrain from connecting dignity with owning stuff, with getting money, or with being able to pay money, including paying back loans, particularly, when they were given with false promises. Let us listen to Howard Richards' message of "the strategic value of acts of solidarity, and of separating the right to live from the duty to sell."[178] Let us go beyond the *double movement*, as political economist Karl Polanyi called the doomed project of first dis-embedding the economy from society to give market pricing priority – including "false commodities" such as land, labor, and money – and then trying to remedy the damage by re-embedding the economy into society through social interventions such as labor laws.[179] Let us go back to the indigenous seven-generations rule of "slow thinking,"[180] and a long time horizon.[181]

Many put their hopes on free trade agreements. Yet, also here, rhetoric and reality may only produce "false dawns,"[182] dawns for raiding rather than caring. Jeronim Capaldo, from the Global Development and Environment Institute at Tufts University, had this to say: "According to our study, TTIP will exacerbate, not solve, Europe's economic problems: increasing unemployment, worsening inequality, reducing workers' purchasing power, undermining the dynamism of intra-EU trade, and exposing European countries to asset bubbles and financial contagion from the United States.... At this fragile time in Europe's economic recovery, TTIP looks like a mistake."[183] Fairer global arrangements seem to be the solution, rather than returning into isolationism, as suggested on the right side of the political spectrum.

Recent research in neuroscience sheds light on the question of why humans so readily hook up to consumer culture. It suggests that it might not be pleasure that is served by core brain circuits, but learning, the kind of learning that was well-adapted for the lives of early foragers, yet, that no longer fits a consumer world.[184] Industrial relations expert Vaddhaka Linn points at the opportunity that is entailed in these findings, namely, that re-learning is possible and cravings for "ever more" can be tamed and changed.[185]

When we look at the links between war, terror, and money, we see that both terror and counter-terror strategies can be lucrative. For *New York Times* journalist James Risen, "the war on terror became this enormous search for power and status and cash... That's essentially what Dick Cheney meant when he said the gloves come off ... enormous money going into a deregulated industry, meaning the counterterrorism industry."[186] Some even speak of a "bogus war on terror" that has a very different aim, namely, to prepare for the repression of the social struggles that must be expected from so-called austerity reforms that produce rising inequality and social misery.[187] Cultural critic Henry Giroux warns: "Under this regime of widening inequality that imposes enormous constraints on the choices that people can make, austerity measures function as a set of hyper-punitive policies and practices that produce massive amounts of suffering, rob people of their dignity and then humiliate them by suggesting that they bear sole responsibility for their plight."[188]

After the U.S. occupation of Iraq, the poverty and inequality that was created by elites and multinational corporations in their plunder of Iraq's wealth, by now functions as a great recruiting tool for Da'esh, says Sabah Alnasseri, professor at York University's Department of Political Science.[189] The new liberal policies brought in by the American-led Coalition Provisional Authority did away with the social securities of the people, and replaced them with the institutionalization of systemic corruption by small elites and systematic plunder of the wealth of Iraq. Young people have no prospect, which means that if militias offer them 500 American dollars a month and a share of some of the plundered resources, they may simply join.

The devil's dynamo

The military-industrial complex is sometimes called "the devil's dynamo": Immensely rich corporate oligarchs are able to buy the votes of politicians and the propaganda of mainstream media, while propaganda-numbed citizens allow their politicians to vote for bloated military budgets, which further enrich corporate oligarchs, and make the circular flow continue.[190]

Terror finances itself, among others, through kidnapping and drug trafficking. Wildlife crime is now "one of largest global organized criminal activities, alongside drug, arms, and human trafficking; illegal trade in wildlife and timber products finances criminal and militia groups, threatening security and sustainable development."[191] Tobias Käufer is a foreign correspondent in Bogotá, Columbia, and he warns that terrorists, guerrillas, paramilitaries, traffickers, religious fanatics, all live off drug trafficking, and that the fight against drugs cannot be won under current conditions.[192]

Not only global terrorism is on the "winning side." Winning is also a global financial system that opportunistically looks the other way, to the point of self-denial, when it accumulates immense profits from laundering enormous cash flows. On the winning side, moreover, is an arms industry that supplies all sides, the drug cartels, and the states that desperately try to defend themselves against those cartels. On the losing side, says Käufer, is the rest of society; young people who slip into addiction and crime to pay absurdly high street retail prices of drugs; humiliated girls and women who give up their bodies and their dignity to organize the next kick. Democracy watches helplessly as entire cohorts of politicians are bought with drug money. Courageous civilians, human rights activists, priests, those who face the Mafia, are murdered like a piece of dirt to be disposed of in landfills.

To recapitulate this chapter, rankings of human worth and value evolved throughout the past five percent of human history. Such rankings and the debate about their legitimacy or illegitimacy have always formed important parts of cultural discourse, both diachronically throughout history, as well as synchronically in contemporary times. During long stretches of history, it was almost universally accepted as natural order of things that human beings were ranked along a vertical scale, with those of more worthiness at the top and those of lesser value at the bottom.

As noted earlier, in my work I label the past five percent of human history as *period of ranked honor*. I call societies that are structured this way *collectivistic societies of ranked honor*. The period of honor was preceded by the first ninety-five percent of human history, or the *period of pristine pride*. At the current point in history, humankind finds itself in transition, in a time of hope that the future may deserve the label of a *world society of equal dignity for all, as individuals, in solidarity*.

Just now, many would agree that the hope for a more dignified future is in trouble. Humanity seems to have taken one step ahead, only to take two steps back. The systemic imperative, as Ellen Meiksins Wood calls it,[193] is that the accumulation of capital has to be kept going, which means that life depends on accumulation, which, in turn, "implies that every feature of society – education, religion, art, sports, media, family, taxes, wages, police, courts, music, architecture, agriculture and so on and on – must be compatible with accumulation."[194] As a result, many societies now increasingly show totalitarian traits in their push for more control. Instruments of control, such as surveys and measurement, are now being introduced even in otherwise egalitarian societies such as Norway.[195]

In an honor society, each stratum has its own honor. To humiliate means maintaining this hierarchical order by "reminding" those further down of their "due" place. Typically, men are placed higher and women below them. In an honor society, humiliation is accepted as honorable tool to keep "peace and quiet" through maintaining stability, law, and order, the order of the vertical ranking of human value and essence. During the past ten millennia, many succumbed to the *art of domination* through *voluntary self-humiliation*, disguised in various definitions of honor.

The contemporary epoch is characterized by a hopeful transition to a new order of equal dignity for all that contradicts traditional norms of ranked worthiness. In this new context, humiliation is no longer seen as legitimate enforcement of honor but as illegitimate violation of dignity. However, this transition is patchy and traditional culture scripts stay alive, even under the cover of sophisticatedly adapted human rights rhetoric. Tactics of terror are inscribed in various ways into cultures of ranked honor and cultures of equal dignity, all on top of the complex and conflictual transitional relationships between both.

What needs to be done? Howard Richards suggests looking at the basic cultural structures that define the modern Western historical development and now the entire world-system. These structures are derived from Roman law, and these are therefore the basic structures that need to be corrected. The basic pillars of Roman law are *suum cuique* (to each his own), *pacta sunt servanda* (agreements must be kept), *honeste vivare* (to live honestly), and *alterum non laedere* (not hurting others by word or deed). Romans set up these rules, among others, to resolve disputes between heads of households (*patres familias*).[196] In other words, these rules were introduced to solve certain problems. Unfortunately, as Richards points out, this solution has invited new problems:

- *Suum cuique* (to each his own) needs now to be corrected, namely, by socially functional forms of land tenancy and socially functional forms of property in general, since otherwise it gives legitimacy to those who have monopolized economic capital in their own hands, and it allows them to maintain or even increase this inequality.[197]
- *Pacta sunt servanda* (agreements must be kept) needs to be corrected by mutual beneficial reciprocity and responsibility for one another's welfare regardless of whether there is a contract or not. Otherwise it legitimizes negative externalities, as there is no responsibility where there is no contract. Indeed, there is no written contract with the next generation and with nature. Human action should seek to promote positive externalities and avoid negative ones. As Linda Hartling formulates, healthy relationships are a "centrality" to survival of humankind, not an externality.[198]
- *Honeste vivare* (to live honestly) needs to be corrected by recognizing that our very identity is relational.
- *Alterum non laedere* (not hurting others by word or deed) needs to be corrected to promote an ideal of service to others, above, and beyond the obligation not to harm them. Honeste vivare and alterum non laedere risk entitling perpetrators of sociocide and ecocide to regard their deeds as legitimate as long as they do not violate the first two principles.

Richards posits that these corrections will liberate us from the present one-size-fits-all global regime of capital accumulation. They will generate new and multiple ways of integrating factors of production to provide goods and services that support life.

Inspiring and Thought-Provoking Questions

for in-depth reflection and research

"What is this: honor!
I am happy to be a coward!"

– Abu Muntasir, "Godfather of the British jihadi movement"[1]

Anybody who believes exponential growth can go on forever in a finite world is either a madman or an economist.

– Kenneth Boulding[2]

Imagine, there is a war. Would you be willing to die so that your loved ones can live? Yes? And you would feel noble? Yet, what do you say when your noble willingness means that all die and nobody is left to live?

Imagine you suffer. You suffer from being discriminated against, rejected, aggressed, hated, and oppressed. You yearn for liberation and respect, but you feel weak, discouraged, and downcast. Now you gather all your energy to convince yourself to once and for all claim your rights to be respected as a full human being. How far will you go? Will you turn the golden rule on its head and call on your people to "let us do bad unto them because they did bad to us"?[3] The Rwandan genocide is a striking example, where unspeakable cruelty was perpetrated on former masters.

Imagine a situation where you have to kill or be killed. What would you choose? To kill or be killed? Hutu were told to kill their Tutsi neighbors to show their allegiance with the Hutu cause. *Hutu* means servant. Hutu had learned to be obedient. Would you have obeyed and become a killer? Or would you have accepted being killed instead? Would you have been one of the moderate Hutu who were killed because they resisted? Or would you have killed even your own Tutsi family members? The International Panel of Eminent Personalities confirms: "Hutu women married to Tutsi men were sometimes compelled to murder their Tutsi children to demonstrate their commitment to Hutu Power. The effect on these mothers is also beyond imagining."[4]

Imagine a situation where you have to kill, or else be labeled as a coward, what would you choose? Would you be able to continue living and be stigmatized as unmanly and disloyal? Do you have the courage to be a coward? Deeyah Khan is a human rights activist and she made the documentary film *Jihad*, a film that expresses the message of this book in the profoundest ways.[5] Khan met with the "godfather of the British jihadi movement," Abu Muntasir.[6] He initially felt contempt for the "weakness" of democracy and advocated violent struggle to uphold honor, both his honor and his people's honor. Now, Muntasir sobs: "I rather live as slave and have my kids go to school ... what is this: honor! I am happy to be a coward!"

Like Muntasir, also another former Islamist extremist and now British politician, Maajid Nawaz, once despised democratic ideas.[7] Today, both regret their former extremism. Where do you stand?

Do you have the courage to be vulnerable? Patrick Magee of the Irish Republican Army killed Jo Berry's father in 1984. Jo went to meet him. She listened to him and said to herself, "I can be vulnerable and open and allow him his dignity. I am not blaming him and making him responsible for my pain, even though there is, of course, a responsibility on his side." I asked Jo what she would say to a young person who contemplates violence, and she said: "What I have learned is that there is a cost to your own humanity, which is very hard to get back; once you have crossed that line of violence, your humanity is profoundly affected. To make your point nonviolently is much more powerful! I urge you to achieve your aims in nonviolent ways. This is much more radical! More rebellious, more subversive, more play in it!"[8]

The killer of Jo's father chose violence because he thought there was no other way. He believed in human rights; yet, this did not make him see Jo's father as a human being. Today he does. He explains that it was Jo's listening to him that "disarmed" him. To say it differently, he moved from honorable invulnerability to the dignity of vulnerability.[9] Can you?

What would you do if you lived in Albania and your fate were to be killed in a blood feud by an avenging neighboring family the moment you left the confines of your home? And what would you do if you were the one in line to be the avenger and killer?

What would you do if your cultural values were being ridiculed and your people's honor soiled and humiliated? What would you do if you felt that your culture's rules demanded action from you, even though cowardice would be so much easier? Honor is not for the weak, is not that right?

Adolf Hitler engaged Germany in "preventive" extermination of the World Jewry he feared was intent on dominating and humiliating the world. Had you lived in Germany at the time, what would you have believed, or not believed? What would you have chosen to know or not to know? Also in Rwanda, in 1994, the justification for the genocide against the Tutsi was that it was necessary to undo past humiliation and prevent future humiliation. What do you say to a person, who profoundly believes in narratives of that kind today?

Carol Smaldino has worked as a social work psychotherapist for over twenty-five years in the United States and in Italy. She reminds us of psychotherapist Carl Jung, who said the Holocaust could happen anywhere, and that the United States might be a particularly vulnerable location. The reason he stated was that American culture highlights the positive and lacks a deeper appreciation of the darker parts of its own history. Slavery, for instance, was a big part of American history that was not only relevant in the past, it is also a contemporary legacy. Jung found America "particularly lacking in the capacity to admit wrong and to find ways of dealing with the healing effects of apology and reparations."[10] What about you? What do you say to Carol Smaldino, when she is afraid that society at large is afflicted with a mental problem, namely, that of denial, that of resistance in the face of reality?[11]

Among many climate scientists, today "gloom has set in," because things are much worse than we think, but, since people refuse to listen, the scientists "can't really talk about it."[12] Do you listen?

Perhaps the solution lies in empowering people? Perhaps this will inspire them to develop more responsible and critical ways of dealing with the world? In my work, I follow Linda Hartling and Jean Baker Miller in using the phrase *sense of worth*[13] in the place of the phrase *self-esteem*, due to the problems associated with the self-esteem movement.[14] I also follow Steve Kulich, professor of intercultural communications at Shanghai International Studies University, in his preference of the phrase *entrustment*. He said this: "First I have empowered my students. Then they became nasty people. Today, I no longer use the word empowerment. I use entrustment."[15]

Are you an empowered person? Empowered to the point of arrogance? Have you developed a sense of entitlement to look down on the weak and exploit them? Or are you empowered so that you can be entrusted with society's common welfare?

Indeed, unfettered self-esteem creates ruthless individualism, and it has created an epidemic of narcissism and bullying not just in the U.S.[16] Kristin Neff, scholar of human development, culture, and learning sciences, suggests that it would be better to develop self-*compassion* than self-*esteem*, as self-compassion is free of narcissism, selfishness, and self-defensive aggression.[17] Where do you stand? Are you a person of high self-esteem who enthusiastically participates in competition for domination wherever it is possible? Or are you capable of self-compassion?

Are you an enthusiast of Ayn Rand, as so many young American students are these days, particularly after the 2008 economic crisis?[18] In her public appearances, Ayn Rand praised the 1917 February

Revolution in Russia and the spirit of liberation from oppression that carried it.[19] Then came the October Revolution, which hijacked the situation and coopted people back into oppression. It did so, among others, by abusing the argument of altruism, asking people to offer themselves to the state. This is why Ayn Rand came to reject altruism and highlight the virtue of uninhibited self-interest.[20] Ayn Rand had a painfully oppressive mother, which may have made her defensive, hard, even arrogant, and opposed to and disdainful not just of oppression, but also of warmth and solidarity. She rejected oppression, she rejected bondage in a hierarchy, which is great. Yet, she went too far, she also rejected loving mutual connection among peers. Solipsistic arrogance was the result. By now, her arrogance seems to have been misperceived as mastery by her followers, and, as soon as this misperception was "mainstreamed," it helped lend legitimacy to coldness throughout society. Ayn Rand is quoted as saying, "We can evade reality, but we cannot evade the consequences of evading reality." This lesson is indeed now being inflicted on her followers and on the world as a whole by the economic crises that began to unfold in 2007 and 2008. Have you learned this lesson? Bondage must be distinguished from mutual connection, and mastery is when one succeeds in liberating mutual connection from bondage.

Yet, we cannot simply blame Ayn Rand. She only intensified the push of an already existing Zeitgeist. In recent years, particularly in Western societies, the notion of dignity itself has become a victim of this Zeitgeist, in two ways. On one side, the notion of dignity became reduced to autonomy, on the other side, it was used for the protection of certain minorities, while forgetting about other minorities. They now decry this preference as "political correctness" and have elected Donald J. Trump as the president of the United States. As a result, no longer is diversity being celebrated, what is indulged in, is division. Political scientist Mark Lilla has this analysis:

> The fixation on diversity in our schools and in the press has produced a generation of liberals and progressives narcissistically unaware of conditions outside their self-defined groups and indifferent to the task of reaching out to Americans in every walk of life.... At a very young age our children are being encouraged to talk about their individual identities, even before they have them. By the time they reach college many assume that diversity discourse exhausts political discourse, and have shockingly little to say about such perennial questions as class, war, the economy and the common good.[21]

The desire to dignify certain groups, as it appears, made other groups, among them the voters in Middle America, feel so humiliated that they now resonate with Trump's "juvenile viciousness," because for them, "the narcissism of prevailing closed-minded progressive ideology was no longer to be tolerated. In the end, the alternative was worse than Trump."[22] The rhetoric of diversity, with its focus on African-American, Latino, L.G.B.T. and women voters, seems to have elicited feelings of exclusion and humiliation in those left out. "If you are going to mention groups in America, you had better mention all of them. If you don't, those left out will notice and feel excluded."[23]

Worse, not only did some feel left out, some learned the *cult of victimhood*. The overuse of the notion of dignity made victimhood transmute into an entitlement: the culture of dignity became a culture of victimhood.[24] The self-esteem movement that psychologist Jean Twenge describes in her work, led to a narcissism of entitlement.[25] When progressives now lament the rise of fake news and "alternative facts," finger-pointing would be inappropriate, warns social psychologist Jonathan Haidt. What is needed is an acknowledgment that they introduced the elevation of emotion over reason, permitting feelings alone to guide reality.[26] Haidt argues that the cult of victimhood in law and process "causes a downward spiral of competitive victimhood" and generates a "vortex of grievance."[27]

No wonder that men accused of sexism now feel entitled to the position of victims of reverse sexism. No wonder that the "forgotten people" who have voted for Donald J. Trump, feel they are the victims of a "devil" (aka socialism, Obama, Hillary, and so forth).

The passion and obsession with which this victimhood is being maintained by the supporters of Donald J. Trump – I am on some of their email lists and have over the years acquired a deep sense of the burning intensity of their bitterness and wrath – reminds of Avishai Margalit. In his work on memory, he describes how a victim may hold on to memories of humiliation to be able to hang on to anger.[28] What is maintained is the *post-victim ethical exemption syndrome*.[29] Stories of humiliation may even be invented to maneuver others into the role of loathsome perpetrators. In my work, I speak of the *addiction to humiliation*.[30]

Mark Lilla calls for "a post-identity liberalism," which "should draw from the past successes of pre-identity liberalism. Such a liberalism would concentrate on widening its base by appealing to Americans as Americans and emphasizing those issues that affect a vast majority of them."[31] I would suggest to widen the base even more, namely, by appealing to all human beings as fellow human beings on a tiny planet.

Imagine you work for a mining company and you are tasked to protect its interests. You can't afford to lose this job as your family's livelihood depends on it. Would you hire gangs of killers and rapists if nothing else helps? Aleta Baun is an activist from Indonesia's Timor Island who has campaigned for the past decade against mining companies.[32] At one point she organized a multi-day campaign where indigenous women blocked the path to a marble mine by sitting on the site and weaving their traditional cloth. What happened? A group of over thirty men ambushed and surrounded her when she was alone:

> "At one point they were debating whether to kill me or rape me," she said, explaining that they decided murder was not viable because there were too many witnesses present. "They decided not to rape me because there were too many men waiting to take their turn," she said, adding that in the end they stabbed her in her legs and took all of her money. The authorities arrested and prosecuted the men responsible for the attack. However, Baun said, such legal action did not get to the heart of the issue as the orchestrators of the assault – those who paid the attackers – were never charged.[33]

On which side would you stand? Would you risk your livelihood by letting the women go on to protest? Or would you think that rape strategies are effective and necessary to protect your livelihood?

What would you do if you were the chief executive of a company and had to inflict damage on the ecological and social environment surrounding your company so as to serve your mandate to serve shareholder value? You cannot give in to the protests of nonprofit organizations, is not that right? Why? Because a business is not a charity, is not that right? And the "best and the brightest" will leave the company if they cannot maximize profit, is not that also right?

What would you do, if you no longer could speak openly and freely, when much more sophisticated methods than rape would be used, for instance, secretive *Stasi*-like methods, methods which you would be ashamed to report even to your closest friends? This has happened. As mentioned earlier, the secret police *Stasi* in former communist East Germany employed a secret strategy with the code name *Operation Zersetzung* (Operation Disintegration), for which state-sanctioned psychological terror was meted out that caused existential crises in the victims' lives, crises that resulted in depression and suicide.[34] Where would you stand? Would you help the Stasi to refine their methods? Or would you warp your soul to justify their methods and close your eyes to them? Or would you risk personal destruction by resisting?

Henry Giroux, theorist of critical pedagogy, wrote this on the politics of humiliation:

> The politics of humiliation is fluid, mobile and capacious as it increasingly spreads and infects almost every public and commercial sphere where ideas are produced and circulated. As an ideology, it is politically reactionary and morally despicable. As a strategy, it seeks to denigrate and silence others, often targeting those already disadvantaged, while promoting

unthinking self-interest, arrogance and certitude at the expense of critical thought, dialogue and exchange.[35]

Giroux warns that an anti-educational reform movement now shapes the United States, a movement that uses the politics of humiliation to create "stereotypes about public schooling, teachers, and marginalized youth." The "dominant media and corporate elite" that celebrates the "very market-driven values that plunged America into a financial catastrophe" supports this movement. Giroux identifies a grave lack of critical language, of civic courage, and of public values. He concludes that, "when a country institutionalizes a culture of cruelty that increasingly takes aim at public schools and their hard-working teachers, it is embarking on a form of self-sabotage and collective suicide whose victim will be not merely education, but democracy itself."[36] Where do you stand?

Are the "T-treaty trinity" agreements[37] a path to well-being for all? Or a path to the well-being of a few? Who benefits from investor protection at all cost, or from the privatization of the commons? Is there a way to transcend market-based democracy and arrive at democracy-compliant markets"?[38] Or not?

Howard Richards, philosopher of social science and scholar of peace and global studies, has been introduced before. He asks: "How can we 'grow' the economy to create livelihoods for everybody, and simultaneously 'de-grow' the economy to make the biosphere sustainable?"[39] What is your reply?

Neva Goodwin, co-director of the Global Development And Environment Institute at Tufts University, summarizes the challenges humankind faces in a nutshell. Her main point is that the essentials of life need to be de-commodified. When she reflects on future economic systems, she concludes that they have to connect the following requirements and satisfy them:

- income
- satisfaction of basic needs
- ensuring that the essential work of society gets done
- giving honor and recognition to those who do the essential work
- protection and restoration of natural resources[40]

What is your view? International banker Mayer Amschel Rothschild (1744 – 1812) is quoted as saying: "Permit me to issue and control the money of a nation, and I care not who makes its laws."[41] In 1935, Canadian Prime Minister William Lyon Mackenzie King said: "Until the control of the issue of currency and credit is restored to government and recognized as its most conspicuous and sacred responsibility, all talk of the sovereignty of Parliament and of democracy is idle and futile."[42] "We may have democracy, or we may have wealth concentrated in the hands of the few, but we cannot have both," is a saying attributed to former Supreme Court Justice Louis Brandeis (1856 – 1941).[43]

Perhaps we have to listen more to scientists and let experts decide? The essence of the scientific methodology is openness to new evidence, is not this true? Philosopher of science Thomas Kuhn has been introduced earlier, together with his observation that even scientific paradigms resist change. What then? Is there any hope? Sociologist Amitai Etzioni suggests that we need to factor in the fact that people have the tendency to sustain paradigms even in the face of "stubborn facts" which undermine them, and that transitions should therefore perhaps be carried out more gradual.[44]

We live in times of existential risk without historic precedent. We have no time for gradual transitions. We live in the *Planetary Phase* of human history, whose impact brought us the *Anthropocene*, a geological epoch of our human making (*anthropos* means human).[45] It could also be called the *Econocene*,[46] or *Capitalocene*,[47] or *Obscene Epoch*.[48] Obscene because the stable planetary state called *Holocene*[49] not only a stable planetary state, it is also the only state in which human life can flourish. Already tiny dislodgings of its basic parameters would make life impossible on planet Earth. Several tipping points have already been reached, irreversibly altering the state of the Earth system.[50]

So, we know what is wrong. And the future is unknown. When established strategies fail, there are two ways out. First, one can hope that strengthening them will help, assuming they fail because they are too weak. Or, second, one can abandon them, assuming they are altogether misguided. Where do you stand? Do you work for pushing through business-as-usual ever more effectively? Or do you try to envision entirely new forms of future "business"? Or, perhaps you work for returning into a golden past? Perhaps you have given up thinking for yourself and prefer to simply follow leaders who promise a better future? Perhaps you find consolation in the thought that if you only stay strong in your beliefs – belief in your leader, your faith or ideology – everything will end well? If so, remember how many large-scale historical experiments with ideology-based systems have ended in tyranny and massive bloodletting.

These are the dilemmas of our time in one paragraph: The Vikings, the Huns, the colonizers, the Hitlers, all were dominators who enslaved people and plundered resources. Today, the threat is systemic, and even many of those who would otherwise have the strength and resources to resist, are coopted into blindness. In this situation, anger is no option, as also the "oppressors" are blind themselves, living in their classist bubbles.[51] What blinds most is arrogant hubris, it makes blind to betrayal, it makes blind to how we are being betrayed,[52] and how we betray others.[53] The old template of revolution and rebellion, the script of standing up *against* the status quo does not work in this new and complex situation. The only script that does work is standing up *for* a new future. Yet, if you are a hotheaded young man, standing up *for* something does not impassion you – who yearn for glory in battling *against* something. Only old wise people can understand this, but by now they might no longer have the strength to stand up. Can you combine both, balanced wisdom with strength?

What about *nonreformist reform*, to use an expression of the French eco-socialist thinker André Gorz? It means conceiving and pursuing reforms that deliver practical results here and now, while keeping the path open for more radical change in the future.[54] Is this a good plan, or would it be too slow?

Johan Rockström is an environmental scientist, and he explains that we live in a historical situation that changes everything we ever knew, whether we like it or not:

> Our current economic logic no longer works, as we confront potentially infinite costs at the planetary scale, rendering concepts like "externalities" and "discounting" useless. The nation-state becomes questionable as a useful unit for wealth creation when policy at the local level depends on regional and global actions and feedbacks. Governance shifts upwards in scale, but still needs rooting and interaction across scales. Sharing finite planetary budgets will require fundamental value changes. Planetary regulation needs to spur innovation and technological breakthroughs. Ethical norms need to evolve to embrace a universal belief that all citizens in the world have the right not only to an equitable share of the available environmental space, but also to a stable and healthy environment. No facet of contemporary society will be unaffected by the Anthropocene.[55]

Rockström explains that the window for a turnaround to navigate the world back into a safe operating space remains open, yet, only barely. The planet has not yet completely tipped away from its *Holocene* equilibrium. The good thing is that humanity now is "in the driver's seat" and has everything needed to succeed. What will not help, though, is to pursue social, environmental, and economic goals separately. They need to be pursued concomitantly. The urgency of the challenges ahead demands a two-prong strategy with respect to timing: We have to act now to foreclose imminent disaster, and, at the same time, work on changing our consciousness and values in the long term, with the aim to create "institutions that equitably integrate people and planet."[56] Since piecemeal approaches will not be enough to reconnect human development with the biosphere, a new paradigm is needed, "in which the economy is seen as a means to achieving social goals and generating prosperity within the limits of the Earth – not as an end in itself."[57] This can only succeed with the collective effort of nations, businesses, institutions, and citizens.[58]

Have you ever heard about *subsidiarity*? What do you know about *unity in diversity*? Unity in diversity needs the subsidiarity principle to manifest a decent future for humankind. Did you notice that I speak of a world where globalization is humanized through *egalization* (short for equal dignity for all) and solidarity, thus allowing for *dignism* (dignity-ism) to flourish?

Unity in diversity is a principle that can help operationalize egalization. The African *ubuntu* philosophy manifests it: "we are two, and we are one, and this at the same time." Another word for this is *nondualism*. I learned much about nondualism during my years in Japan from 2004 to 2007.[59] Nondualism means separation *and* connection, agreement *and* disagreement, one *and* two. It needs competency in nondualist thinking to grasp the value of unity in diversity and how it can become a synergistic win-win game: Unity does not have to become oppressive uniformity, and diversity is not the same as unrestricted freedom for divisiveness. Unity and diversity can grow together if kept in mutual balance and nurtured and celebrated simultaneously.

Let me explain more about nondualism. Philosophy of mind is the ontology of the mind, of mental events, mental functions, mental properties, and of consciousness and its relationship to the physical body. The dominant Western metaphysical orientation that has underpinned its expansion during the past centuries was *dualism*. Dualism holds that ultimately there are two kinds of substance. René Descartes' dualistic view of a mind-body dichotomy is perhaps the most widely known expression of dualism. Dualism is to be distinguished from *pluralism*, which claims that ultimately there are many kinds of substances, as well as from monism, which is the metaphysical and theological view that all is *one*, either the mental (*idealism*) or the physical (*materialism* and *physicalism*).

Are you a dualist or a nondualist? When I lived in Japan, I was introduced to intercultural communication scholar Muneo Yoshikawa's work.[60] Yoshikawa brought together Western and Eastern thought into his nondualistic *double swing model*, where unity is created out of the realization of difference. Individuals, cultures, and intercultural concepts can all blend in constructive ways by applying this model, which can be graphically visualized as the infinity symbol, or Möbius strip ∞. Yoshikawa drew on Martin Buber's idea of *dialogical unity*, the act of two different beings meeting without eliminating the otherness or uniqueness of each. And he drew on *soku*, the Buddhist nondualistic logic of "not-one, not-two," that is described as the twofold movement between the self and the other that allows for both unity and uniqueness. Yoshikawa calls the unity that is created out of such a realization of difference also *identity in unity*: The dialogical unity does not eliminate the tension between basic potential unity and apparent duality.[61]

Nondualism is not a preserve of the East. Even though current political events now tarnish the realization of this ideal in the U.S.,[62] it remains present in the motto on the Great Seal of the United States which says, *E pluribus unum*, Latin for "out of many, one."[63] The Center for Multicultural Education at the University of Washington in Seattle has assembled recommendations for the United States and has titled them as *Diversity Within Unity: Essential Principles for Teaching and Learning in a Multicultural Society*. This is what they recommend: "*E pluribus unum* diversity within unity is the delicate goal toward which our nation and its schools should strive."[64]

I would like to invite you to become a *global citizen of care*.[65] This is because I sense that one way to create more unity and at the same time celebrate the diversity in our world is by inspecting all our human cultures and "harvest" from all cultural worldviews, from all practices, and all social-psychological skill sets those that have unifying and egalizing effects.[66] Rich harvest can be found on all continents.[67] *Living Well* has been mentioned before. It is an indigenous social system that focuses on reciprocity between people and Earth.[68] Catherine Odora Hoppers is the former South African Research Chair in Development Education at the University of South Africa, and she speaks of *transformation by enlargement* for the academy, whereby she means that also Indigenous Knowledge Systems needs to be included.[69] 2014 was the last year of the UN Decade for Indigenous Peoples, and global dignity advocate Kjell Skyllstad warns: "We cannot ignore what amounts to genocide in our continued contribution to the eradication of the peoples who contain the key to our own survival."[70]

We, as humankind, should not allow unity to degrade into uniformity, be it through oppressive "communism" or obsessive consumerism. And we should not allow diversity to degrade into the division of everybody-against-everybody, as it happens through extreme individualism in hyper-capitalist contexts.

What do you think? Are you with me on this path? If yes, what can help us? Have you thought about the traditional African philosophy *ubuntu* as a philosophy for living together and solving conflicts in an atmosphere of shared and dignified humility?[71] Ubuntu dovetails with Martin Buber's I-Thou approach and is in harmony with the ideal of equal dignity enshrined in human rights as much as in many religions around the world.

The subsidiarity principle makes unity in diversity operational. *Holarchy*,[72] or *regulatory pyramids*,[73] are related concepts. Even the human brain embeds subordinate *loops* into superordinate loops.[74] In legal thought notions such as "legal pluralism," "complementarity," and "qualified deference" are relevant.[75]

The European Union uses the subsidiarity principle, meaning that local decision-making and local identities are retained to the greatest extent possible, while allowing for national, regional, and also international decision-making when needed.[76] Also governance systems for large-scale environmental problems can only be effective through such nested layers.[77] Subsidiarity, per definition, is always in flux, always "in crisis," since a continuous recalibration of superordinate and subordinate layers is needed. Will you be able to bear this continuous crisis? Or will you want to short-circuit back into "good old" fixity?

The case of Rwanda can illustrate the delicacy of such calibration efforts and dynamics. After the 1994 genocide against the Tutsi, Rwanda now uses a *single* recategorization policy, which means that all of its citizens are defined as citizens of Rwanda and are no longer identified as Hutu or Tutsi. The single recategorization approach replaces the original group boundaries with a superordinate identity.[78] Scholars often recommend that *dual* recategorization should be used instead, so as to avoid "identity threat" and backlash,[79] as dual recategorization makes both superordinate and subordinate identities salient.[80] Yet, the case of Rwanda shows that there is no simple answer to this question, particularly not in a post-genocide context.[81]

Sunflower identity is the name I have coined for my personal global unity-in-diversity identity of fluid subsidiarity.[82] Through my global life, the core of my identity (the core of the sunflower, so to speak) is anchored in our shared humanity, not just in theory, but in practice, since I truly live globally since forty years. My identity is anchored more securely than any human identity ever before. An ethos of globalism, a patriotism for *Earthland*, offers a much stronger mooring than any we-against-them nationalism, simply because its territory is the entire planet, rather than imaginary state boundaries. All identifications are fickle, except for one, sociologist Norbert Elias said it already in 1939: "Only the highest level of integration, belonging to humanity, is permanent and inescapable."[83]

If you suffer from rootlessness and torn identities, you can find a safe home by one simply move: just accept all humans as family, or, even better, accept all sentient beings as family.[84] All uncertainty, and all divisive finger-pointing ceases when all the blame and all responsibilities for the world lie on the shoulders of us all together, on the shoulders of *one single Us*. All victim identities filled with trauma and humiliation[85] can heal. *Afropolitanism* is not enough, *Americopolitanism* is not enough – what is needed is global unity-in-diversity *cosmopolitanism*.[86]

Could you become a global citizen of care like me? Yes. First, the technological means to reach the limits of our globe are now more available than ever, in other words, it is possible to live on all continents (I am aware of the legal barriers, therefore I admire Garry Davis and his World passport[87]). Second, it is psychologically perfectly feasible to relate to all human beings as fellow family members as most people are able to respond in kind. My personal experience has shown me that. When asked, "Who are you?" I respond: "I am a human being," "I am a citizen of this planet, like you." I avoid saying, "I am of this or that nationality," or "I am of this or that profession," and so forth. I rather add, "I am a human being who is born with a certain passport," or, "I have studied medicine and psychology." I even avoid saying, "I am a woman." I am extremely careful with the little word *am*, as it connotes essence.

How do you present yourself when asked: "Who are you?" "Where are you from?"

At the periphery of my identity (the nested petals of the sunflower, so to speak), it is profoundly enriching to find safety in learning to "swim" in the flux of diversity rather than to "cling" to fixed positions. The mastery of being-in-movement provides a greater sense of security than fortress walls and fences. Rather than seeking safety in one particular local culture, what fulfills me is finding safety through the nurturing of loving relationships. It is a pleasure to continuously pendulate in the spirit of nondualism, to have a *protean self*,[88] and to be a *voyager*.[89] A voyager uses the challenges of cultural diversity and intercultural conflicts for forging new relationships and new ideas, while *vindicators* vindicate their pre-existing ethnocentrism and stereotypes.

Allow me to close with some thoughts on my personal experiences and choices. My personal global life design is the result of many years of deep reflection on the issues discussed here, and of profoundly principled choices drawn from these reflections: I wish to walk my talk, to *be* the change, not just to talk about change. This means more than nurturing a sunflower identity through fluid subsidiarity. It means also that I accept constant economical pressure and refrain from seeking relief in the present mainstream paradigm of market pricing. My mission is to nurture I-Thou *inter-human* solidarity, rather than *inter-cultural* tolerance.

How do you bring healing into a world where human relationships are increasingly being hollowed out by now?[90]

It would be incoherent with my life philosophy and would damage me severely psychologically, were I to define my purpose in life primarily in terms of being a supplier or a target of the sales of products and services. Allowing myself to feel deficient lest I buy or sell something, would humiliate my humanity to its core.[91] My dignity is independent of my ability to produce sellable products or services. If I were to reduce my creativity to serve "personal branding," so as to become a product of myself and for myself,[92] I would feel like I were in *Pleasantville*.[93] I am only too aware of the legacy of slavery informing modern forms of "scientific" management, and I do not wish to be part of the insidious language of "human resources."[94] I do not wish to partake in being fooled by the term "free" market when this means that public services are being "dismembered, outsourced, closed down, the source of profit for a few and an impoverished society for the many."[95]

I refuse to "have a price."[96] I wish to have a *life*, not a *job*.[97] I have studied economics enough to know that society would be better off if it organized itself without the concept of job.[98] How come that the same people who eschew marrying "for money" accept living for money and confuse livelihood with monetary income?[99] I react with disgust when I am called upon to buy something because it is "cheap" or discounted, or to pay a high price because "I am worth it." I am profoundly sickened by advertisement, as I am not a wallet on two legs. I profoundly resent being taken for a person of substandard intelligence by advertisement, since I am not that ignorant: I am aware that only human connection can create happiness.[100] Filling my life with momentous excitements over "owning" stuff, excitements to which one quickly adapts, is absurdly void of meaning to me. I connect my own good with everybody's good, and only this is truly fulfilling. I follow philosopher Immanuel Kant when he says that "everything has either a price or a dignity," and that "whatever has a price can be replaced by something else as its equivalent; on the other hand, whatever is above all price, and therefore admits of no equivalent, has dignity."[101] Only connection with humans and with nature can create fulfillment. I see myself as a gardener, a nurturer of our sociosphere and our ecosphere.[102] I once trained as a clinical psychologist and medical doctor, and now I attend to the health of all of humankind in its symbiosis with planet Earth.

What do you say? How should we, as humanity, build societal systems that do not plunder, humiliate, and terrorize? Would it help to measure happiness instead of the Gross Domestic Product (GDP), the monetary measure of the market value of all final goods and services produced in a period? Perhaps not.[103] What about other indices, for instance, the Happy Planet Index?[104]

Are you among those who call for less greed and more generosity? Would more charity be the solution? These days, even charities are being accused – some rightly, others not – of supporting militias, including terrorist activities.[105] Then there is what has been called "weaponized" conservative philanthropy, which hijacks the conservative agenda and cannibalizes and dominates it.[106] And even charities that do focus on the common good are often operating in such uncoordinated ways with each other that they create overall chaos rather than sensible overall improvement.

Imagine that you are rich and wish to build a ship. Now you approach your wealthy friends for donations. One friend loves sails, another motors, a third furniture: the result will never be a functioning ship, or functioning global and local economic systems for that matter.[107] Charity donations can therefore not be the path to global strategies. If a master plan is left to be drawn up by a few powerful wealthy individuals – as well-intentioned as they may be – who analyze the world's needs and place their investments according to their personal preferences, what will remain wanting is global systemic design creation, not to speak of the potentially disempowering impact of charity.[108] Think of the sinking Titanic: The wealthy might see cracks in their luxury cabin and repair them, while overlooking the holes in the bulk of the ship further down, where all the poor people live.

> Welcome to the age – and whimsy – of the new billionaire class and the precariousness of vanity projects. With so much money sloshing around, and more and more of the super-wealthy pushing into areas beyond their expertise, it is likely we will see more headlines about the failure of some of these fanciful investments and philanthropic experiments.[109]

So, you might say, if charity does not suffice, and since governments cannot be trusted, there is no way forward. If you live in the north of Europe, where trust within society is higher than elsewhere,[110] you will have no problem following me now: In my view, small government versus big government is a false choice. I studied Somalia, and its government is too small, while North Korea's is too big, one may say, an observation that acknowledges that the solution is *good* governance. And good governance means heeding the subsidiarity principle, and this is as valid for local as for global governance.[111] Citizens who respect themselves build respectable governance structures, rather than accepting abuse from oppressive elites, be it that those elites use big or small government.

Global governing systems are located at the highest macro-level frame. Global *generative mechanisms*,[112] and *constitutive rules*[113] shape all layers and spaces below them. Leaving a power vacuum at the highest global level invites global terror into all segments of life at all levels below, and it now creates precisely the global tyranny that is feared by those who aim to avoid big government. Only when *communal sharing* – Alan Page Fiske's concept of solidarity – guides the design of such rules, can unity in diversity and dignity flourish at all other levels. Only this can secure, qua system, that face-to-face inter-human solidarity can unfold also at local micro levels. Dignifying charity can find its deserved space here. In contrast, if market pricing is the definitorial guiding principle, and the social and ecological damage it inflicts is simply abetted through charity and regulatory rules, the result will be more social and ecological degradation. Buberian I-Thou relationships are crowded out when inter-human relationships are defined and dominated by abstract contracts based on monetary exchanges, and when this informs global constitutive rules. In such a context, the capacities of local movements and nation-states to effect change is too restricted.

There is no alternative to creating trans-national and trans-local capacities, which means interlinking, globally, the efforts of all local "civic and ethical entrepreneurial networks that are currently in development."[114] This is why I invest my lifetime into creating a dignity movement, not just locally, but globally.

My question to you: How will you contribute so that a worldview of unity in diversity can gain credibility and become a global trend? A forest grows in silence, only cutting trees appears to be "action." Honorable men who yearn for glory want "action." How can growing the forest become glorious? How can we nurture a culture, globally and locally, that values growing the forest of unity in diversity rather than seeking glory in cutting the trees of diversity to create dictatorial uniformity?

Section Three:

"Peace" the Traditional Way – A Balance of Terror

Keeping One's Enemies Out and One's Own People in Line

Terrorization has always been employed by revolutionaries no less than by kings, as a means of impressing their enemies, and as an example to those who were doubtful about submitting to them.

– Gustave Le Bon (1841 – 1931),
social scientist, 1916[1]

I swear by God this sacred oath that to the Leader of the German state and people, Adolf Hitler, supreme commander of the armed forces, I shall render unconditional obedience and that as a brave soldier I shall at all times be prepared to give my life for this oath.

– The Wehrmacht Oath of Loyalty to Adolf Hitler, 1934[2]

Religion pervades intensely the whole frame of society, and is according to the temper of the mind which it inhabits, a passion, a persuasion, an excuse, a refuge …

– Percy Bysshe Shelley (1792 – 1822),
Romantic poet, in *The Cenci*, 1819[3]

The seven blunders of the world that lead to violence: wealth without work, pleasure without conscience, knowledge without character, commerce without morality, science without humanity, worship without sacrifice, politics without principle.

– Mahatma Gandhi

We are living through a very dangerous time … in the attempt to correct so many generations of bad faith and cruelty, when it is operating not only in the classroom but in society, you will meet the most fantastic, the most brutal, and the most determined resistance. There is no point in pretending that this won't happen.

– James Baldwin (1924 – 1987),
essayist working for equitable integration not only of black people in America,
in *A Talk to Teachers*, 1963[4]

Only curiosity about the fate of others, the ability to put ourselves in their shoes, and the will to enter their world through the magic of imagination, creates this shock of recognition. Without this empathy there can be no genuine dialogue, and we as individuals and nations will remain isolated and alien, segregated and fragmented.

– Azar Nafisi,
Iranian-American writer[5]

Introduction to Section Three

When I was young, I lived with an unrelenting sense of terror. It was the very "balance of terror" of the Cold War that gave me a dread that was so strong that I could not imagine accomplishing my highest wish, which was to have a family and bring children into this world. I felt it would be utterly irresponsible to make plans for a "normal life" in times of imminent carnage. I was living at that point in the center of Europe, only a few kilometers west of the iron curtain. This was the battlefield that would be the first to be annihilated, within hours, when the apocalyptic showdown between the United States and the Soviet Union was to start. And it could be expected to happen any minute. Every day could be the last day. One wrong move, one little mistake by a soldier with the finger on a trigger, one little "glitch," and a deadly war machinery would be set in motion. Even without knowing, by then, how many dangerous glitches actually happened, the Cold War represented continuous hot terror to my inner emotional landscape and it poisoned my outlook on my own future and the choices I had in life.

When Morton Deutsch edited his book *Preventing World War III* in 1962, I was eight years old.[1] Had I known then how many "close calls" lay in waiting, I would perhaps not have dared to continue living. As previously classified material becomes accessible now, one very close call occurred in 1980 in Damascus, Arkansas, when a repairman did routine maintenance work on a Titan II missile, the United States' largest intercontinental ballistic missile with a nuclear warhead attached to it. A socket fell off his wrench and almost set off the missile.[2] In 1983, the world could have ended, and my life would have evaporated within minutes or hours, if not for a single person, Stanislav Petrov. He was a Soviet military, who, luckily, allowed his civilian training to override his military training in acceptance that he would be demoted: when a satellite signal came in that American missiles were in the air to attack the Soviet Union, he judged, in the few minutes that he had, that this was a false alarm.[3]

Today, the Cold War is over (hopefully). The level of fear and risk that once was accepted as necessary to deter the enemy and win the competition for domination, no longer needs to be accepted. Yet, the catastrophic nuclear accident at Chernobyl in 1986, and the Fukushima Daiichi nuclear disaster in 2011, make clear that the same culture of domination, in this case domination over nature, has continued even in the absence of any enemy. By now, the world engages in an altogether hazardous race for domination over social and ecological resources.[4]

Like the adrenalin junky who needs risks, it seems that humanity cannot do without domination and it only finds new ways and explanations. Like an adrenalin junky, we manipulate and ridicule those who worry, and brutal domination is still portrayed as progress. Manipulation and ridicule is employed to applaud freedom for unbridled competition, irrespective of how immense the environmental and social costs are: "The growing culture of humiliation in the United States suggests that anyone who does not believe in the pursuit of material self-interest, unbridled competition and market-driven values is a proper candidate to be humiliated," writes scholar and cultural critic Henry Giroux. My global life shows me that his verdict is valid not just in the United States, but globally, and increasingly so.[5]

Ironically, the risks created by such "progress" in the race for economic domination, produce new risks and new enemies: "Today, with growing prospects of nuclear terrorism, we see emerging among the public either paralyzing fear or irrational denial," writes a developer of civil defense solutions in the United States.[6] Indeed, paralyzing is the fear for those who know about the true extent of possible nuclear carnage, and irrational the denial of the fact that victory cannot be mistaken for safety.

In a self-fulfilling fashion, any war on terror risks creating *enemies* where there were none before. Re-animating the old security dilemma by re-dividing a world would close the window of opportunity to truly unite that opened after the end of the Cold War.[7] Instead of *war*, the language of *policing* is more suitable for an interconnected world; terrorism is an internal problem for the entire world community rather than a stand-off between enemies. If the world community wishes to contain terrorism, it is a maladaptation to draw on a culture of domination that emerged in a bygone era of a strong security dilemma. Indeed, some have understood that: In his book *Dirty Wars: The World Is a Battlefield*, investigative journalist Jeremy Scahill puts "a human face" on the "casualties of unaccountable violence that is now official policy: victims of night raids, secret prisons, cruise missile attacks and drone strikes, and whole classes of people branded as 'suspected militants.'"[8]

This section of the book explains how peace is defined and manifested in cultures shaped by a strong security dilemma, and how maintaining this definition of peace risks foreclosing a dignified future for humankind now. The security dilemma is a tragic quandary that keeps all players in a permanent state of terror, and it was strong until the end of the Cold War. Generation upon generation of people during the past millennia were socialized within its confines, and, unsurprisingly, this led them to overlook that it is a historical phenomenon that can be undone. It led them to believe that this sad state of affairs has an eternal and universal status, just like a natural law. People lived in unrelenting fear of neighboring tribes, kingdoms, or states, as even the best alliances could morph into enmity very fast. Philosopher Thomas Hobbes had a name for this state of the world: the anarchy of the "state of nature."[9] Out of fear, people would fall in line behind strong leaders, who only too often turned out to be ruthless oppressors of their own people more than wise and helpful protectors. If a protector wants to be truly wise and helpful in today's context of global interconnectedness, she has to build global trust and undo the security dilemma. The expertise that is needed to do so is amply available. The problem is cultural inertia and the disinclination of those profiting from the old set-up to lose their privileges.

What is particularly tragic with the security dilemma is that the competition for domination that it engendered has no endpoint. The following questions illuminate this: When is deterrence of enemies and oppression of followers strong enough? Where are the limits? If torture can save the lives of our people, is it not irresponsible to forego torture? These questions show that all safety valves get removed when moderation becomes immoral and maximization a virtue. What maximizing patriotism and maximizing profit have so far produced is "the nuclear arms race and global economic crisis by design."[10]

Under conditions of a strong security dilemma, peace is a word for the calm and quiet that reigns when power arrangements are successfully kept in place through firm control. It is called peace when rival out-groups keep each other in check by "horizontal or external control" – a tool that includes the threat of mutual destruction – and when master elites use "vertical or internal control" to keep their subordinate groups subordinate.

Realpolitik is the name for such peace efforts, and it is the most influential script also today. Carrots-and-sticks negotiations aim at creating allegiances against enemies, and the methods range from offering material and/or status rewards to threats with violence. Power and honor are the currency. Human rights ideals are welcome only when they serve power. Losing power is worse than losing peace or violating human rights. Honor is the highest ideal, worth dying for if necessary. Losing power is losing honor and losing honor is losing power. Sacrificing honor for peace is seen as equal to cowardly self-humiliation. Only honorable peace is worth having. Honor humiliation can be redressed by death and therefore warrants homicide and suicide.

Honor is for men to have and for women to submit to. For men, it is important to avoid appearing to be "wimps" or a "sissies," in other words, a man must avoid appearing "female." Honor thrives on contests of "strength" and "victory," on "keeping the upper hand," and on "teaching lessons and sending strong messages."

Tribal honor in Pakistan manifests this mindset, as does the *southern honor* in the United States of America that historian Bertram Wyatt-Brown describes in his book with the same title.[11] In 1898, the Spanish-American War was openly fought to restore national honor. Also the warriors who wish to reinstate a lost caliphate are fired up by the bloody and heroic script of honor.

Journalist Gregg Jones wrote a book titled *Honor in the Dust,* where he looks back on the Philippine-American War and concludes that what is fascinating "is not how much war has changed in more than a century, but how little."[12] The McKinley-versus-Roosevelt era eerily resembled the Bush-versus-Obama stand-off, and even the hardliners' torture methods are similar in both periods. Theodore Roosevelt utterly disliked any "unintelligent, cowardly chatter for 'peace at any price.'"[13] A vocal anti-imperialist movement in United States tried to attenuate the country's growing expansionist zeal, in particular Roosevelt's "bulldog ambition." Rather than moving Roosevelt's heart, however, the outcries of the peace faction strengthened his conviction that war was needed. When McKinley hesitated to send troops to Cuba, Roosevelt decided that McKinley had "no more backbone than a chocolate éclair."[14]

Conceptualizations such as "*the* enemy – *they* want to break *our* will, but *we* won't let it happen," are embedded in gut feelings that are imbued with the code of honor. In such a context, humiliating "*the* enemy" is felt to be legitimate. It is a weapon to call a brave enemy a coward, because it removes him from the ranks of equals in honor (see Chapter 7).

After the world wars of the twentieth century, at least in the Western world, human rights ideals moved to the forefront and ideas of honor, humiliation, and revenge were no longer used as openly as justifications for war as before. Yet, these ideas never disappeared, they were only more hidden from sight. Honor never stopped playing a strong role when powerful elites dealt with each other at national and international levels. Honor remained strong in foreign policy matters, in armed services, and in diplomatic staffs, more so than among the lower echelons of the average citizenry. As historian Donald Kagan observes, a passion to retain a state's "honorable" preeminence, reigns in today's world no less than it did earlier, only that "national honor" is now partly concealed by human rights rhetoric and no longer invoked as openly as in the past.[15] The 2016 presidential race in the United States brought the old spirit of honorable manliness back into a wider and more visible arena.[16]

In an honor society, worthiness is ranked. From the point of view of honor it is unavoidable, either divinely ordained or nature's order, that human worth is *not* equal and that "higher" beings preside over "lesser" beings, and that those lesser beings subject themselves to their masters' beliefs and decisions. The concept of ranked honor could be seen as the single largest "master manipulation" ever perpetrated, as it gives master elites the power to define what is and what ought to be.[17] It is the very fear entailed in the security dilemma that makes this possible. It gives elites the necessary leverage to convince subordinates that honor means giving their lives for their superiors.

Fear and paranoia are at the core of the security dilemma, fear of the enemy and fear of being humiliated. Fear of being humiliated even trumps fear of death: "Better dead than red." Fear also trumps pluralism and human rights. Political scientist and Middle East expert Shibley Telhami knows that "transitions are destabilizing," and usually this is not "a good thing for democracy, pluralism and human rights": "Deep insecurity and economic deprivation, often short-term results of a weakened central authority, provide fertile ground for those who want to rule with an iron fist – as fear trumps pluralism and human rights."[18]

Fear can debilitate. As Egyptian political satirist Bassem Youssef has rightly observed, fear makes humans go against their best judgment. This is also what Ahmed Akkari has learned, a Lebanese born hate preacher in Denmark, who stirred up the Muslim world against the Danish cartoons. Now he has turned around. After having read Søren Kierkegaard, he reports, "I realized more and more how I was manipulated. They did not listen to me, they did not want a dialogue, they had only one goal: to defend their opinion and to enforce it."[19] The First World War was perhaps the first moment that this very insight also dawned on the proudest of warriors, namely, when they began to understand the uselessness of being slaughtered as cannon fodder.[20]

Fear can be instrumentalized. Fear sells, fear works, fear intimidates, fear makes humans go against their best interest, fear is a winner, and still "fear has no future," this is what Bassem Youssef said in 2014 after he had to seek refuge in Germany. He had to cancel his popular weekly talk show "Al Bernameg" in Egypt because his message was so provocative that his safety was in jeopardy.[21] Bassem Youssef poignantly summarizes the security dilemma's inner logic of fear, a logic that rallies people under a joint identity and therefore lends itself to being instrumentalized to keep people under control.[22]

It will take time before Bassem Youssef's message will be heard, his message that it may seem convenient to instrumentalize fear, at least in the short term, yet, that it is counterproductive in the long run. As for now, the Arab Spring did not ring in summer. Instead, it turned back into the winter of yet another demonstration of the resilience of an all too familiar culture of domination.

Also present-day economic laissez-faire rules recreate the old-style competition for domination.[23] Production depends on capital accumulation and if there is no capital accumulation, there is no production, even if it would be needed, and, inversely, when it serves capital accumulation, production is maintained that is hazardous and not needed. Whenever investors lose confidence that their investments will be profitable, production and employment will decline: "This gives the capitalists a powerful indirect control over government policy: everything which may shake the state of confidence must be carefully avoided because it would cause an economic crisis," explained economist and Nobel Prize candidate Michal Kalecki already in 1943.[24]

In 2014, Howard Richards, philosopher of social science and scholar of peace and global studies, warned: "As long as democracy is held hostage by the overriding imperative to keep the state of investor confidence high come what may, society will be in important ways ungovernable with respect to any policy goal: environment, decreasing the exposure of children to violence on TV, raising wages, making society in general more egalitarian, etc."[25]

Chapter 12

The Security Dilemma Was Once Inescapable

If we wish to understand terrorism, it is of utmost importance to grasp that during the past millennia the security dilemma was inescapable. Many people in modern-day Western societies look down on our forebears from a position of moral righteousness, while, in my view, it is of utmost importance to respect the sincerity and "goodness" that stands behind the motivation to protect "one's own people." This is important if we wish to transcend the war paradigm and attain a more united and peaceful world. Lately, the security dilemma has been artificially and unnecessarily intensified,[1] and this book is written to halt this trend. Yet, this does not mean that this dilemma has always been merely socially constructed.

Whenever the security dilemma is strong, fear of being attacked and destroyed, or dominated and humiliated, is bound to push aside all other considerations except for patriotic self-defense. Solidarity, loving kindness, altruistic love of caritas, all this does not apply to enemies.

"Thou shalt love thy neighbor, and hate thine enemy," this is what we read in the fifth chapter of the Gospel of Matthew in the Bible's New Testament (King James Version). "Hate your enemy" was the duty of nations and its subjects visa-à-vis its enemies, while "love your enemies" (Matthew 5:44) was valid only in private.[2]

In 1927, the "crown jurist of the Third Reich," political theorist Carl Schmitt (1888 – 1985), wrote a famous book on "the concept of the political."[3] It was the twentieth century's answer to Machiavelli's *Prince* of 1532. Schmitt wanted to draw attention to the *factum brutum* (brute fact) of politics, to the reality behind liberalism's "demilitarized and depoliticized" concepts, namely, the struggle between friend and foe. For Schmitt, the distinction "friend versus enemy" is the essence of politics, parallel to morality's good versus evil, aesthetics' beautiful versus ugly, or economics' profitable versus unprofitable. The political enemy, or public enemy, is not to be confused with a private adversary toward whom one feels antipathy. *The political* shows up when a people is fused together against external enemies and against traitors in their own ranks; when it is fused in a struggle to conquer and retain political power, regardless of any normative ties, as it is facing the deadly possibility of physical annihilation. Schmitt was enthusiastic about Adolf Hitler's rise to power, because Hitler fulfilled Schmitt's ideal of the head of government being a strong and efficient power performer with distance to democratic control, a "Caesarian" regime that secures a unified state-will, a *Führertum* legitimized by popular acclamation. Schmitt's sovereign decides what is true, what is fact, and defines who is an enemies to be fought and who is not. Schmitt despised liberals, but had respect for "the atheist-anarchist socialists" as mortal enemies, who, he admitted, had "diabolical format." Many other leaders' mindsets mirrored Schmitt's message, among them was Mao Zedong, who is widely quoted as saying, "Politics is war without blood, while war is politics with blood."

Later, in 1963, Schmitt saw the era of sovereign nation states coming to an end, as they lost their belligerent monopoly.[4] As a result, he sees non-state actors, partisans (or terrorist, as we would say) being the last truly political actors of present times, as they do not shy away from the friend versus enemy dichotomy. Their primary objective is not territorial conquest but the eradication of decadent lifestyles, and "absolute enmity" makes civilian and military targets indistinguishable for them. From Mussolini to the leftist terrorists of the 1970s in Italy and West Germany, to Steve Bannon's "clash of civilizations" narrative as an apocalyptic mirror image of Da'esh's rhetoric, or Richard Spencer, the man behind America's "Alt-Right," all resonate with Carl Schmitt's dream of an autocratic strongman acclaimed by a popular movement.[5]

This book argues that *description* is not *prescription*, just as *understanding* is not *condoning*, or *ontology* is not *advocacy*.[6] As long as the security dilemma was inescapable, it was appropriate to describe it, and to call on men and women to adapt their cultural scripts to it. Indeed, in the middle of a fight against a brutal enemy, everything may go lost if soldiers no longer obey their generals but hesitate because they have doubts, or ask for democratic decision processes. Yet, there is no need to *prescribe* a security dilemma, no need to maintain this culture when there is an opening to exit from it. "Anarchy is what states make of it," is the telling title of an article.[7]

Why can't people leave behind a dilemma that is tragic, even when the doors stand glaringly wide open? There is *learned helplessness*, then there is the *Stockholm syndrome*, both were discussed earlier in this book. Humans also suffer from *loss aversion*: better heroism than peace. What some call the *hero syndrome* has been described as a phenomenon where people – including firefighters, nurses, police officers, or security guards – create an emergency so that they can step in as heroic saviors.[8] The *Munchausen syndrome by proxy* is a term used when caregivers fabricate or exaggerate health problems in those in their care to gain attention and sympathy.[9]

Is it wise for us, as humanity, to succumb to such dead ends? Let us think: When tuberculosis was still untreatable, hospitals were built in many mountainous regions. When the disease could be treated, not just one lone nurse lost her job, all personnel did, all of them lost their familiar path to recognition. Their mountain retreats had to close down. Should we now elect leaders who promise to make the disease untreatable again? Bringing back a strong security dilemma is as absurd.

The prisoner's dilemma game is a game that illustrates many of the implications of a strong security dilemma in a divided world. This game gives players the chance to cooperate or betray one another. The outcome is very different when the players will never meet again or if they have to live together also in the future. A strong security dilemma in a divided world is a frame that indicates that most enemies will never meet again. In contrast, in an interconnected world all have to live together also in the future. The new situation calls for new strategies, those that political scientist Robert Axelrod has explored in his computer models. He found that the evolutionary "tit-for-tat" strategy – also known as *reciprocal altruism* – is remarkably successful and defeats all other strategies; it increases the benefits of cooperation over time and protects participants from predators.[10] Even more successful is the *win-stay, lose-switch* (also win-stay, lose-shift) strategy, which is what real-world players often follow – it means playing the same strategy in the next round if the previous one was a success, while switching strategy if not.[11]

Much social science research has been invested lately in understanding how uncooperative free-riders can be being punished. When students played the prisoner's dilemma game and were told that this was a community game, they cooperated, while they cheated on one another when the game was framed as a Wall Street game.[12] When students tried to predict what other players would do in the next round, their predictions went wrong when they assumed that other people's moves represented their personal inclinations. What they overlooked was that the others' behavior depended on the overall framing: Wall Street or community.[13] In other words, it seems that social and societal frames are what counts and that individual propensities are less causative as driving forces for the punishment of free-riders, also "in the wild": "there is no evidence that cooperation in the small egalitarian societies studied by anthropologists is enforced by means of costly punishment. Moreover, studies by economic and social historians show that social dilemmas in the wild are typically solved by institutions that coordinate punishment, reduce its cost, and extend the horizon of cooperation."[14]

The security dilemma is a frame that enforces cooperation within in-groups and non-cooperation between hostile out-groups. The expectation is that the death of the enemy will end the game with that player. Within in-groups, trust and altruism are enforced, with inferiors expected to trust their superiors: after all, a tightly knit and disciplined military is better prepared to overcome the enemy. In the context of a strong security, this is the *conceptual scaffolding* or *interpretive frame* that everybody relies on to construct their understanding of the world.[15] Interpretive frames are part of every discourse and its systems of categorization, its metaphors, narratives, frames, and other interpretive devices that influence cognition, perception, and action within communities that share the same discourse.[16]

"Thou shalt love thy neighbor, and hate thine enemy" has many implications. One is the push for dominator societies with strongmen at the top and women down. In my book on gender and humiliation, I describe how in the context of a strong security dilemma and a dominator society, one way to achieve "peace and quiet" within a society is to keep only ruling elites informed and the rest ignorant.[17] Through this dynamic, women, in particular, descended into a position similar to that of children, together with lowly men. Most women were not regarded as adult persons. Few women were born into leadership positions and enjoyed an education similar to males. Most girls were systemically kept ignorant, "under the hand" (Latin *sub manu*) of a father or elder husband. It is therefore not surprising that women, caught within such frames, could not emancipate themselves (*emancipation* is the deliverance from the hand of pater familias). Their childlikeness was forced on them at all levels, micro, meso, and macro levels.

As mentioned earlier, in war, while men were killed, women were often captured alive when communities were invaded and conquered. Women were seen as "resources" rather than as "people." Female bodies seem to have adapted to this situation by developing a specific reaction to stress – women tend to react with a *tend and befriend* reaction to stress, rather than *fight or flight*.[18]

Males, if they were not killed, could transform from enemies to allies. Modern-day terrorism is no exception. Journalist Peter Taylor describes the following for Northern Ireland:

> Had anyone looked into a crystal ball at the time and told me that one day Martin McGuinness would become Northern Ireland's deputy first minister I would have thought they were joking. "Terrorists" can and do become statesmen. I remember meeting Gerry Adams in darkened rooms in the 1970s when he was on the run from the "Brits" and never imagined that one day he would be feted by presidents and prime ministers. Covering republican and loyalist political violence in Northern Ireland. I gradually realized that however abhorrent it might be, the violence was not "mindless."[19]

The East-German officer who was the first to open the Berlin Wall offers a similar illustration. His doctoral dissertation discussed how terrorists could best be kept out of communist Germany.[20] When thousands of East Germans gathered at the border in 1989, wanting to visit the West, he changed sides: He chose to open the gate to fellow human beings, rather than regarding them as "terrorist enemies" and causing a blood bath.

In a dominator context, childlikeness is systemically enforced on inferiors. As it seems, living in an individualistic and atomized context of profit-driven industries of mass culture can have similar effects. Sociologist James Côté asks: Why are so many people in the industrial West simply not "growing up" in the traditional sense, why do they remain more like adolescents and seem to avoid responsibilities?[21] Is it desirable to turn life into a vague and prolonged youth – into arrested adulthood – in the pursuit of personal, individual fulfillment? Côté calls for visions for a truly progressive society where such anomie could be avoided.

James Côté is not alone in decrying this new trend. Several other authors worry as well, yet, many offer solutions that stay within the same outdated paradigms they criticize. Conservative journalist Diana West, for instance, defines successful adulthood as going back to the culture of the security dilemma.[22] Right-wing fundamentalist Christians appear to choose this is solution as well,[23] as do young extremists, be they so-called neo-Nazis or foreign fighters who travel to fight for Da'esh.[24] What they do is flee an abstract system, a system where freedom and anomie are too closely knit together, and they seek solace in collectivist honor codes. Another author who decries the phenomenon of perpetual adolescence, is former record producer Andrew Calcutt, and he seems to use another rather unsuitable script, namely, the very adolescent protest culture that he criticizes.[25] Young extremists often combine both: They are young and, historically, it has often been part of adolescent identity search to be "protesting against authorities," while honor codes offer welcome "ammunition" for such protest.[26]

In my work with dignity, I recommend "growing up" and refraining from child-like defiant protesting[27] – be it against lack of freedom or overstretch of freedom. The "pleasure of protest" can go too far.[28] I suggest instead that we harvest the best from all worlds. This means liberation from the oppressive aspects of traditional hierarchies, while preserving whatever those hierarchies have to offer with regard to solidarity and social cohesion. Likewise, it means resisting the anomic aspects of Western individualism, while realizing its potential for freedom. I myself take the promise of freedom much more seriously than most of my peers, and I do so by working for a dignified future for all as responsible adults, rather than joining adolescent protesters who only re-manifest what they decry. I consider it feasible to take the best of all worlds, avoid all malign aspects, and build a global culture of interconnected individuality – rather than remaining stuck in the alienation of ruthless individualism or in the rigidity of oppressive collectivism.

All worldviews, be they religious or secular, can "grow up" from the impact the security dilemma had on them. Religious and secular worldviews have those two versions on offer, to say it simplified: one version that fits a strong security dilemma and another version that transcends it.

Vidar Vambheim is a sociologist of education in the north of Norway, the land where indigenous Sami have suffered from humiliation at the hands of majority Norwegians since they can remember. As I have already mentioned in the Introduction, I highly appreciate the Norwegian perspective on the world, since it draws on a cultural tradition of equality in dignity, solidarity, and global responsibility. In the past, in the north of Norway, unfortunately however, this cultural heritage did not include the Sami. This has changed recently and the Sami have now their own parliament. When I think of Vidar Vambheim, I appreciate Johan Galtung's view that new useful ideas often emerge not in the power centers of the world, but in the periphery.[29] Norway represents such a periphery, and the north of Norway is the periphery of the periphery. Their experience with humiliation, and how to deal with it, is profound.

Vambheim discusses dialogue as an alternative to war on terror, and he asks which kind of dialogue may be useful in the context of asymmetric conflict.[30] He describes how those who are attracted to terrorism "feel humiliated and disempowered by visible as well as invisible 'forces' that encroach upon their world," forces that are so multifaceted and complex that they come to represent the devil.[31]

The role of the devil, or the dimension of a hereafter is particularly salient with respect to the likelihood of dialogue to succeed or not. Journalist Adel Elias conducted an interview with Hassan Nasrallah, the third Secretary General of the Lebanese political and paramilitary organization Hezbollah, in Beirut in 1997.[32] In this interview, Nasrallah explains how happy and proud the martyr death of his eighteen-year-old son makes him, his wife, and the entire family, and how he is not opposed to his next son, fifteen years old, wishing to follow his elder brother. A martyr is holy and will have the privilege to speak up for his family in the face of god. This is not a banal death, this is not an ordinary loss – we are not engaged in dishonorable slaughter, Nasrallah assures the journalist – this is holy accomplishment in an honorable war.

Many religious terrorists feel like Nasrallah. They see themselves in a cosmic battle between two Manichean forces, those of good versus evil,[33] and they wish to save or restore what they believe is "god's order," "moral order," "purity,"[34] or a "spiritual world order as God once created it, which was meant to last just as it once was, forever."[35] Suicide bombers may "truly believe that they will achieve grace, redemption and reward for their deeds in the afterlife."[36] Peace researcher Johan Galtung calls the core path from conflict to war the Dualism-Manichaeism-Armageddon syndrome.[37]

As to the likelihood of dialogue to succeed and achieve "peace on Earth," to say it short: if too many people believe that peace on Earth means foregoing and betraying their eternal responsibilities in the heavens, there will be no peace on Earth. Those whose theism or atheism motivates them to sell out peace on Earth in favor of belief systems beyond this world, stand in opposition to those whose theism or atheism give them reason to prioritize peace on Earth.

For their World Values Survey, political scientists Ronald Inglehart and Christian Welzel have found two major dimensions of cross-cultural variation in the world, and they show them on a world map.[38] They call their first dimension "survival values versus self-expression values," and their second dimension "traditional values versus secular-rational values." My observations, after four decades of global life, resonate with these findings, only that I would call the first dimension "ranked collectivist values versus the ideal of equality in dignity for each individual," somewhat in line with "collectivism versus individualism," and I would call the second dimension "focus on responsibilities after death versus pragmatic life before death."

It is the "focus on responsibilities after death" that has most impact on whether dialogue will succeed or not. A focus on responsibilities after death can be both, the most helpful for dialogue to succeed, or the most unhelpful. Nelson Mandela had this focus, and this was immensely helpful. He saw his responsibility beyond his here-and-now life and well-being. He resisted being bribed into a comfortable life – after all, he was a privileged man within the black community and could certainly have chosen to stay out of prison and rather take care of his family within the system of apartheid. By standing up, by giving priority to his sense of responsibility beyond a comfortable life in the here and now, he brought a much-needed vision of peace to the world. Mandela was able to use the traumatic experiences of his life to walk his path to freedom, and in this way, he ultimately gave something priceless to the world: He liberated social healing from its reputation of being something for cowards only and connected it with heroism.[39]

Dogmatic orientations, in contrast, be they religious or secular, collectivist, or individualist, may literally allow the world to "go to hell" for their respective versions of "the truth." Dogmatic orientations can be fired up and intensified by fear and a sense of threat. A New York lawyer, Anika Rahman, captured the effect of the sudden polarization that happened in the days after 9/11 in an article in the *New York Times*: "I am so used to thinking about myself as a New Yorker that it took me a few days to begin to see myself as a stranger might: a Muslim woman, an outsider, perhaps an enemy of the city. Before last week, I had thought of myself as a lawyer, a feminist, a wife, a sister, a friend, a woman on the street."[40]

Some conservative Christian groups in the U.S. hold dogmatic views that support violence. Nearly fifty percent of lone-actor terrorist attacks are abortion-related.[41] And Christian Zionists think of Armageddon when they support the maximalist claims of Jewish political Zionism, including Israel's sovereignty over the entirety of historic Palestine, including Jerusalem. They view the modern state of Israel as a fulfillment of the prophetic scriptures and as necessary stage toward the second coming of Jesus.[42] They eagerly await and even welcome "the unfolding of a series of wars and tragedies pointing to the return of Jesus."[43] Sixty-two percent of Evangelical Republicans in the United States of America see Islamic traditions as being incompatible with those of the West, while only fifty-four percent of non-Evangelical Republicans hold this view. American partisanship on Israel policy is carried by the ten percent of Americans who are Evangelical Republicans and who listen to Christian radio or watch Christian television.[44]

When we think of terrorism that is inspired by Christian faith, this involves anti-abortion "single issue terrorism" against individuals and organizations that provide abortion, and this is regarded as a considerable domestic terrorist threat by the U.S. Department of Justice.[45] The United States National Abortion Federation has compiled statistics on incidents of violence and disruption against abortion providers for close to forty years by now, and their 2015 statistics show "a dramatic increase in hate speech and internet harassment, death threats, attempted murder, and murder."[46] In 2015, a heavily edited, misleading, and inflammatory video stoked unprecedented hatred.[47] "Since 1977, there have been 11 murders, 26 attempted murders, 42 bombings, 185 arsons, and thousands of incidents of criminal activities directed at abortion providers."[48]

Yet, not only religious extremism follows this grammar, also economic extremism, says peace researcher Johan Galtung. This grammar entails "the chosen people in the context of a Manichean struggle, the promise of a homeland, and the expectation of future glory."[49] Just like religious fundamentalists, also market fundamentalists feel they are the chosen people, the promised land is a market share, and there is the dream of conquering the whole market. The United States presidential election of 2016 illustrated Galtung's observation. Presidential candidates Ted Cruz and Donald Trump both seemed suited to lead a "Christian Caliphate," as they both are bent on dominion, Cruz more on Christian Dominionism and Trump more on the dominion of money.[50]

Faith in God and faith in money go together not only in the West. One of the starkest examples is Mecca, a dream destination for millions of faithful Muslim pilgrims: it is currently being changed into a commercial Disney-style hub that provides enormous profits to Saudi Arabia.[51] "Islam has been trafficked as though it were a bonded slave, dressed up in bells and baubles to be whipped and sold in the marketplace," writes social activist Maniza Naqvi.[52] Leading expert on contemporary Muslim thought, Ibrahim Abu-Rabi, explains:

> Globalization has often aided the political elite in the Muslim world to spread their version of "false consciousness" by means of the mass media and given them the technological means toexercise full hegemony over society. Capitalism in the Muslim world, although concentrated in few hands, is deeply entrenched. It is part of the global capitalist system. As such, it competes with other capitalist groups or formations in the pursuit of unlimited wealth and power, when possible. Domestically, Arab capitalism assumes a relentless pursuit of power in order to protect its economic interests while constantly pursuing greater wealth. Instead of working for the progress of its society, capitalism in the Arab world seeks only the preservation of its hegemony and the expansion of its control. This expansion takes the form of a meager investment in religious institutions in order to exploit the religious feelings of the masses for its materialist ends.[53]

Peace researcher Johan Galtung points at the traumatic experiences that form the background for Manichean dualism.[54] In my 2006 book on humiliation and international conflict, I included a section where I describe how I learned about the trauma carried at the heart of American society,[55] the cradle of market fundamentalism with its secular and religious underpinnings.[56] Trauma can drive the *post-victim ethical exemption syndrome* that scholar James Edward Jones describes as an outgrowth of humiliation.[57] The result of this syndrome is a "dukes up" attitude: "Don't tell us what is right, now, after having let us down in the past! We have learned that we can only trust ourselves and now we will triumph!"

What I observe is that mystics of all religions as well as from non-religious orientations often provide a Mandela-like thrust for peace. They celebrate a deep connection with their social and natural surroundings, independently of whether they are lone seekers of wisdom or draw inspiration from a collective vision.[58] A secular orientation is no guarantee for peace, nor is a religious one. A secular orientation may make one vulnerable to being bribed, bribed into war industry, for instance, in return for a handsome salary. A religious orientation may make one vulnerable to condoning supposedly divinely ordained cruelty – the Inquisition provided a stark example, as did Catholic nuns and priests who were complicit in the genocide against the Tutsi in Rwanda,[59] not to speak of the killing of "infidels" by members of Da'esh.Also traditional gender roles do not offer any guarantees. Both the female and male script can inspire the creation of dogmatic "fake worlds" that are dangerously insulated from reality. Male heroic courage, if interpreted as reckless fearlessness, might be invested into ruthless domination over nature and people and lead people to seek salvation in terror and war. Female submissiveness, on the other side, may feed the creation of Kafkaesque "cute" princess worlds, and, in their worst manifestation lead to the application of the trope of "cleaning" to ethnic cleansing and genocide.[60]

Through my work and in my personal life, I attempt to realize the best parts of both scripts: I gather heroic "male" courage so as to work for the "female" script of nurturing dignity.

Vidar Vambheim dissects how religious terrorists, driven by a sense of traumatic humiliation, draw people into their arena step-by-step who would otherwise be uninterested, thus creating new trauma in the society around them. It starts with myth-symbol complexes that are familiar to the population and that terrorists can invoke.[61] Then, terrorists will insist on total submission to their supposedly divinely guided will. Their religious zeal may be authentic, or, it may be manipulated by other actors who have ulterior motives, such as those of the "deep state."[62] The insistence on total submission will deepen fault lines among ordinary citizens. Vambheim observes:

> Terrorist actions force neutrals to become attentive, obedient, silent and cautious. They want to attract media attention, achieve symbolic empowerment through media reach, and recruit supporters and cadres to their organizations. Terrorist actions work as recruitment adverts for their organizations, and once the fear or expectation of violence is established, the rules of the game change in favor of violent actors on both sides of the conflict. This is common to all terrorism.[63]

Vambheim makes a distinction between "militants / belligerents" and "soft / moderates," where members of all camps can be individuals, organized political groups, communities, nations, or supra-state actors. Also in my research, I found that the significant fault lines do not run between Islam and the rest, or between Palestinians and Israelis, or between the West and the rest. The significant fault lines run between fundamentalists and moderates in each camp, even though important aspects of history, culture, language, nation, religion, and identity are shared in the same camp. In 2006, this was my conclusion: Fundamentalists, throughout the world and from all backgrounds, have much in common with each other, despite the cultural differences that appear to separate them. The same applies to moderates. Yet, also fundamentalists and moderates have much in common with each other: they all care for well-being. They differ, however, in whether this well-being is seen to be achievable before death or after death, and they differ in how to achieve it, by collectivistic or individualistic means.[64]

Under which circumstances can we expect dialogue to succeed? We can realistically expect symmetric dialogue to happen in good faith among actors who recognize each other as equals, observes Vambheim, in other words, between the moderates on both sides of the dividing line of a conflict. Good faith dialogue is unlikely, however, between hardliners, and also between hardliners and "softliners."

What can be done? Vambheim offers his Cold War experiences as inspiration. He explains how hawks on both sides "dug deeper trenches and built higher walls between the camps" with their belligerent propaganda of "freedom" on one side and a rhetoric of "equality" on the other side. Both sides believed in their ability to win a nuclear and even a star war, pouring huge investments into their respective military-industrial-scientific complexes. When Vambheim defended his doctorate in Trondheim on April 1, 2016, he was over sixty years old and reported on a long life filled with peace work experience. Living near Murmansk, a city not far away from the north of Norway, where the Soviet Union carried out nuclear explosions,[65] Vambheim had refused to remain a passive onlooker and had become an active participant in the political process. He did so by taking part in the actions of "softliners." He shared with the audience how he and his co-activists took a ship to Murmansk in the middle of the Cold War.[66] He remembers how the softliners insisted to be heard, how they insisted to be respected as political actors on a par with the hardliners:

> In the West, leaders of the peace movement were subject to surveillance and bullying by intelligence services, police and mass media. In the socialist camp the leaders of peace movements were treated even worse: Gagged, arrested, interrogated, put in house arrest or

> prison like enemies of the state. However, people on both sides resisted the pressure, visited and met with one another legally or illegally, supported and demonstrated for, and kept up the good dialogue with their peace partners on the other side. From this perspective, the peace movements came out of the Cold War as the winners over the Cold War.[67]

Clearly, to rein in hawks – rather than submitting to them or fighting them in kind – certain psychological skills are needed, among them that of equanimity. Pema Chödrön is the first American woman who became fully ordained as a Buddhist nun and teacher and thus bridges many worlds. She has become known for books that explain the Buddhist approach to inner balance, both for individuals, and, in extension, for societies.[68] In her *Guide to Fearlessness*, she writes about the advantages of equanimity, the advantages of avoiding judgementalism, of avoiding to cling to fixities and staying in flux instead.[69] In her chapter on "Meeting the Enemy," she explains what bravery means, namely, to steer clear of self-deception.[70]

In the beginning of this book, I mentioned that I observe two blind spots in the peace movement, one blind spot pertaining to communication skills, and the other relating to global governance. Pema Chödrön speaks to the first point and offers the solution, which resonates with what I call *dignicommunication*.[71]

Yet, the peace movement may need to become more ambitious than only resisting hawks and the security dilemma culture, as important as this is. In my view, the peace movement needs to become more proactive and attenuate the security dilemma more intentionally. At the present point in time, the United Nations represent the world's highest level organization. Yet, it is nothing more than a club of nations.[72] This means that global unity in diversity is not anchored in global institutions in ways that are strong enough.[73] These institutional anchorings need to be improved. The fear that characterizes the security dilemma cannot be confronted by individuals with Mandela-like wisdom and equanimity alone. It does not suffice to tamper with superficial reforms either. Deep *constitutive* rules need to be re-designed.[74] In South Africa, it did not suffice to change *regulatory* rules, something much more radical had to be done, namely, the laying of entirely new foundations and the erection of an entirely new edifice. South Africa is faltering by now, not least because this work is still waiting to be done at the global level.[75]

New global institutional structures need to be devised. Only globally inclusive human security arrangements can create a scenario where humankind is spared the scare of mighty outsiders unexpectedly turning into war enemies.[76] Only globally inclusive human security arrangements can define terrorism as internal threat to the "global village," a threat that must be contained rather than "crushed." Rather than focusing on local *military* security, a focus is needed on jointly created systems of global *human* security. Only then can humankind concentrate on jointly protecting and replenishing its social and ecological resources. Only then can South Africa flourish, together with all other world regions.

When this work has been done, true peace can emerge. Our bodies demonstrate this. Adrenaline pours into the blood stream in response to danger and pushes maintenance processes into the background. It is not the fault of adrenaline when the body collapses in cardiac failure. Continuous stressful fear and preparedness for emergency trumps long-term maintenance, and this is dangerous. Only in the absence of emergency can true long-term nurturing and replenishing happen in the body. After a heart attack – the proverbial *Managerkrankheit* (manager disease) that I learned about during my medical studies – a manager would be advised to radically change his lifestyle, lest the next heart attack will kill him.[77] In Japan, this is called *karōshi*, literally "overwork death." The next heart attack of the world body may kill it.

A culture of global human security, clearly, is still unfamiliar and untested, and it is easier to cling to the culture of military security, even if there is no need for emergency preparedness anymore. As it seems, however, the world's powerful may not be able to let go. And the masses allow themselves to being coopted, not least because also they find it difficult to muster the courage and imagination that is needed to dare envision radically different futures. To conceptualize all of humankind as one global interdependent system is unfamiliar for people who are used to look at the world from the point of view of local security.

A brief window of opportunity to create truly globally inclusive security arrangements stood open after World War II, the period when the United Nations were founded and the Universal Declaration of Human Rights was adopted. When German chancellor Konrad Adenauer called for German rearmament to anchor the Federal Republic in the West, this window already started to close. Critics accused Adenauer of buttressing the division of Germany, of losing sight of German reunification, and of foreclosing the recovery of the territories that were lost in 1945 when Poland and the Soviet Union shifted westward.[78] My parents hail from precisely these lost territories, so I know much about the emotional depth of the trauma that is connected with losing one's homeland and one's hope to ever regain it.

The biggest problem, however, was not national or regional. The biggest problem was that a significant window of opportunity was being wasted at the global level. Unsurprisingly, the Soviet Union responded to the establishment of NATO with the implementation of the Warsaw Pact. The Cold War came to terrorize the world for decades, including my personal life.

As it seems, the motto of *If you want peace, prepare for war*[79] can only be left behind in a globally inclusive context. While the founding of the United Nations was last century's attempt to achieve this, another window of opportunity stands open now, after the Cold War ended. This window may not stay open for much longer. The strategy of domination which is now driven by the profit motive may close it again.[80] And this, while the human family has unprecedented access, more than ever before in human history, to knowledge and to tools to intentionally create circumstances for peace and dignity to reign systemically on the entire globe. We can jointly exit from the security dilemma. This will create a new dilemma, however, namely, what I call a *dignity dilemma*. Yet, this dilemma is much easier to overcome than the security dilemma: by dismantling all systemic humiliation, by engaging in a large-scale *dignity transition*.

A future waits to be created where patriotism embraces not only one ethnic group, not only one nation, not only one continent, but all of planet Earth, and not just "us humans" vis-à-vis nature, but *all of us as integral part of nature*.

Chapter 13

Patriots Deserve Respect

Transitions must be nudged forward one step at a time, with respect, otherwise backlashes can throw them back ten steps in a moment. This is what happened twice in the twentieth century when two world wars brutally ended periods of awakening, and millions died. The sense of humiliation among conservatives in the United States fed a strong conservative backlash, from the John Birch Society to the promise keepers,[1] up to the recent triumph of authoritarian culture that now polarizes the United States.[2]

Radical respect has a huge advantage: it opens space for a dignified future. If we accept that we, as humankind, have learned to stoke enmity in the past – in a divided world in the grip of the security dilemma – then we can un-learn it together now. Collectively, we can make use of the shrinking of the world and refuse letting outdated cultural adaptations continue to divide us. For that, we need to patiently and lovingly nurture this journey, without indulging in fits of indignation against "the other side."

Let us begin. Nobel Peace Laureate Mairead Maguire believes that the dream of Irish freedom and self-determination in 1916 was legitimate, only the violent methods to achieve this freedom were ethically and morally wrong. She writes:

> Patrick Pearse, who took part in the 1916 Easter uprising, eulogized the redemptive nature of blood sacrifice. Pearse wrote, "We may make mistakes in the beginning and shoot the wrong people; but blood is a cleansing and a satisfying thing and the nation which regards it as the final horror has lost its manhood, and slavery is one of them, without the shedding of blood there is no redemption as the blood of the martyrs was the seed of the saints, so the blood of the patriot will be the sacred seed from which alone spring new forces and fresh life into a nation which is drifting into the putrescence of decay."[3]

I deeply resonate with Maguire's differentiation between "good" yearnings and "wrong" methods, or, perhaps better, methods that become wrong when the context changes. If we wish to create a world without terror, in my view, it is of utmost importance to understand why some people use terror tactics – be it in the name of terror or counterterror. To do that, it is vital to appreciate yearnings separate from methods and avoid letting the evaluation of one skew the evaluation of the other: good yearnings deserve to be fully acknowledged, even if the methods used to act on them are to be utterly condemned. For instance, the sincerity and "goodness" of the wish to protect one's own people deserves full respect, even if the methods need to be rejected. Even law enforcement literature informs us that there might be noble causes for ignoble deeds.[4]

This book is written to foster radical respect and this chapter warns against indignation entrepreneurship. It is written to discourage speaking about others with ridicule and contempt. Attributing evil intentions without deeper knowledge, demonizing the other, all this is part of the culture of a strong security dilemma, and it maintains it. In short, peace activists are no "warriors for peace," since working for a peaceful world by way of methods and rhetoric of war is inherently irreconcilable. And there are no terrorists, only people who have committed acts of terror.

If we look back on the past millennia, we see that it has always been costly to strive for peace by following the motto of *If you want peace, prepare for war*, but the price was usually deemed necessary to be paid. It is only in an increasingly interconnected world that this motto becomes counterproductive entirely. The same applies to terror tactics; they were once acceptable and become counterproductive now. Likewise, demonization was once acceptable and becomes counterproductive now, and this includes the demonization of people who commit acts of terror. Demonizing others fires up cycles of humiliation that may set in motion spirals of humiliation that bring back the old strong security dilemma, and this can be deadly for all of us.

Philosopher Friedrich Nietzsche advised to be close to one's friends, but never to walk over them, and, most importantly, to respect the enemy that is in our friend. Inversely, "contrary to a war, combat implies not the suppression of one's opponent, but always presupposes some respect for – and even love of – the enemy, because one shares in the strength and excellence of one's enemy."[5]

The radical respect advocated in this book goes further: it calls for respect also for the "enemy" within ourselves, or, better even, to abandon the terminology of enmity altogether and hold hands in our shared "brokenness" from the experience of being human.[6]

Admittedly, radical respect is difficult to muster. Readers from all ideological walks will cringe when reading this chapter. Also the reasons for why radical respect is needed now are not easy to grasp. The old worldview is too entrenched, and it needs courage to think independently enough to ponder why old dearly held worldviews should become counterproductive in a new interconnected world. In the previous chapters, I have already highlighted how those among us who have not yet grasped the novelty of global interconnectedness usually stand clueless in front of those of us who have, accusing us of being weak-minded blue-eyed "sissies," at best, or unpatriotic evil traitors at worst.

Bertha von Suttner suffered such accusations when she worked for peace before World War I, and it continued even after Germany lost also the second world war. Until 1945, refusing military service meant execution. In 1945, some mothers no longer wanted to lose their sons to horrific dishonorable atrocities and slaughter, and it was one woman in particular, Friederike Nadig, who helped bring the right to refuse military service into the German Constitution in 1948.[7] Nadig was one of the four "mothers" of the Constitution of Germany, and not least due to her influence Germany was the first country to include the right to refuse into its fundamental political principles. Yet, the overall *Zeitgeist* was not ripe for that. In 1956, despite strong opposition in the population, and despite mothers demonstrating against it, a new German army was formed and the first young Germans were conscripted again. In 1957, the first conscientious objectors exercised their constitutional right to refuse military service and albeit these young men should have been hailed, should have been welcomed as enlightened messengers of a better future, they were aggressed, declared insane, or suspected of having succumbed to evil brainwashing.[8] Even in 2017, a young Syrian man who had refused military service in Bashar al-Assad's army in Syria and who sought refuge in Germany, was rejected for failing his duty as a soldier.[9] Here, again, we see the two sides I alluded to earlier: On one side there are those mothers who, like good midwives, understand that a new historical time needs help to be born, and on the other side are those who are horrified at this "insanity."

This chapter wishes to deepen the message from the previous chapters, the message that all sides deserve radical respect and that nobody deserves to be branded as evil – not those who understand the historical novelty of the present situation, and also not those who fail to understand it. Attributing evilness to people on whatever side hinders the necessary birthing process of a more dignified world rather than helping it. A suggestion: those who love weapons need to be treated with the same respect as those who do not love weapons.[10]

Former American President Barack Obama entered office with the declared goal to heal a polarized society, and in 2016, after eight years, he left behind a much more fractured country. He was aware of the humiliating impact of "arrogance," of how dangerous it is to neglect what I call dignity-communication.[11] I highly respect Obama for having given up on trying to pretend to be white so as to climb the ladder of status; he avoided the very trap that Frantz Fanon described so well in his work.[12] Instead, Obama attempted to invite everybody into mutual enriching dialogue among equals. What he overlooked was that his skin color inscribed him into an already existing dynamic of humiliation, a situation that presented him with a dilemma that would have required extremely high levels of communicative skills to channel into dignifying outcomes. His dilemma was that he deepened the sense of humiliation among his black brothers and sisters whenever he failed to show sympathy with their suffering, yet, whenever he fulfilled their expectations, he risked unleashing the wrath of those on the other side, the privileged side, some of whom felt humiliated when called to embrace humility.[13] This book, too, runs the risk of making all sides angry, despite its author's desire to build bridges.

I call on those who get angry to understand, deeply, that their anger might not be the result of their personal inclinations, but the result of a millennia-old systemic push of a strong security dilemma that made it important to clearly differentiate between enemies and friends, between perpetrators and victims, between "good people like us" and "bad people like them." It was once important to maintain such clear-cut dichotomies since "bad people" needed to be kept outside. Dichotomies were reinforced, if necessary through pressure, persecution, torture, terror, and war. "Love your enemy," even when it was practiced, usually did not mean respect for the enemy in the capacity of being a fellow human being, it was either respect for the force of evil in the enemy or an expression of condescending charitability.[14] The insight that victims can be perpetrators, and vice versa, and that even "we, who believe to be the good people" might be perpetrators, wittingly or unwittingly, is avoided also today. Apologies for slavery, or for having exterminated indigenous populations around the world, or for the brutality of colonization, still need to get much clearer and be followed up with much more substantial consequences.

Angela Marquardt is a woman who had to pay a very high personal price for the socially maintained irreconcilability of good versus bad. Born into communist East Germany, she became a respected politician after the fall of the Wall, priding herself of being a "clean" politician, free of affiliations with the *Stasi* (East German Ministry for State Security). Yet, in 2002, her files were found in the Stasi archives, and they revealed that she indeed had committed herself to cooperating with the Stasi at the age of fifteen. When this was exposed, she was publically harassed and had to withdraw from political life. Years later, she accidentally ran into the very man who had been her Stasi "case officer." This incident shocked her into deciding to write a book to tell the story of her agonizing journey after falling from grace. It was a journey into her own memories while reading her files, a journey to reconstruct the abuse she had experienced as a child and adolescent, an abuse that had made her betray herself.[15] To survive psychologically after her fall from grace, she had to train herself to respect the enemy, the enemy in herself, and to do so deeply. She had to first learn radical empathy for her inner enemy, and then radical respect, otherwise she would not have been able to survive and write this book.

I believe that this "training" in radical respect is needed for all of us now, at least if we wish for a more dignified future for humankind. Part of this training is to grasp that within the confines of a strong security dilemma, throughout the past millennia, "to be a good person" meant to want to prevail over one's enemies, to want to crush them. It was not very feasible to want to create a globally inclusive world and transcend the very notion of enmity. This task is not only feasible now, it is obligatory.

True patriots

Let me now introduce a good person to you. It is former U.S. Ambassador to the United Nations John Bolton. Nobody will doubt that he is a sincere patriot. He wrote in an email to his supporters on March 12, 2014:

> Dear (name of the recipient) ...
> Our biggest national security threat is Barack Obama.
> This is a president who does not believe in American exceptionalism, a president who is uninterested in national security and America's place in the world, who considers our strength part of the problem, and who believes that America is the cause of international tension....
> Conservatives need to take this year to mobilize

> the vast majority of Americans who believe as we do – that America is the greatest nation on earth and that our leaders should start acting like it.[16]

Nobody will doubt that also Pamela Geller is a sincere patriot. As with John Bolton, I highly respect also the depth of her conviction. She is the president of the American Freedom Defense Initiative, and it is her passionate wish to guard against any possible threat from enemies. Since complexity and nuance undermine such efforts, to her, emphasizing complexity means betraying one's own people and helping the enemy. By doing so, she acts faithfully according to the lessons humankind learned in a divided world in the grip of a strong security dilemma where it was obligatory to differentiate in-groups from out-groups, us from them, moral inclusion from moral exclusion, "what my people deserve" from "what your people deserve."[17]

Geller attacks the Council on American-Islamic Relations (CAIR) that was established to promote a positive image of Islam and Muslims in America. In an email to subscribers, on December 23, 2015, she celebrates her victory in triumphing over CAIR's attempts to "rebrand the word 'jihad' as something peaceful and benign," and expresses satisfaction that her campaign had "succeeded in injecting jihad into the vernacular and the public discourse whenever news about Islamic horror and savagery is reported."

John Bolton and Pamela Geller invest all their passion and good intentions into protecting the honor of the United States. They and their followers probably agree with the necessity to protect their country through the use "enhanced interrogation" methods on suspected terrorist, methods that others call torture.[18] For them only an "inverted refrigerator" world is a safe world, a world that produces warmth inside, and coldness vis-à-vis outsiders, so that outsiders never are in doubt as to how unwelcome they are.[19]

Their sincerity, in my view, deserves everyone's respect. Their sincerity honors the security dilemma's logic that has ruled all over the world for millennia. I say so notwithstanding the fact that I know only too well that in the novel context of an interconnected world, this logic becomes self-defeating and counterproductive. In other words, when I show deep comprehension and respect, it does not mean that I condone when a cultural mindset is kept alive where it becomes self-destructive.

John Bolton and Pamela Geller are no fringe examples, precisely because the security dilemma's culture is so compelling. The 2016 presidential race in the United States threw this fact into stark contrast. Conservative presidential candidates such as Ted Cruz and Donald Trump on one side, and democratic candidate Bernie Sanders on the other side continued the 2012 stand-off between the "coalition of restoration" and the "coalition of transformation."[20] As with Bolton and Geller, nobody will doubt that many followers of Ted Cruz or Donald J. Trump were patriots when they applauded their recommendations to use carpet-bombing or torture methods like water-boarding.

Pamela Geller responded to the November 2015 Paris attacks[21] as follows:

> The idea that the United States of America cannot defeat the Islamic State or Al-Qaeda is absurd, and the whole world knows it. But we choose not to use our strength. We choose to be victims. It's shameful.
>
> And clearly, since everybody knows that we are not physically weak, where is the basic dignity that any nation should have, to stand up for its own values? If nothing else, when we find ourselves involved in a war, we should fight it and finish it. You either win or you will be defeated….
>
> When Muslims attack, the left attacks us. MSNBC, the Guardian, and Salon all ran pieces blaming the "right-wing" for the Paris attacks. Outrageous, but not surprising. The media is aligned with the jihad force. As the jihad heats up in the West, the media is becoming more clumsy and desperate in its attempts to deflect attention away from the jihad and back to its favorite bogeyman, "right-wing extremists." Now, even when the evidence of Islamic jihad responsibility is everywhere, as it is with the Paris attacks, "journalists" still find ways to put the blame on the "right-wing" that they hate far

> more than they do bloodthirsty jihadis, whom they don't dislike at all.
> If you have an ounce of self-esteem, when someone comes at you with a gun, you answer with force. If he is out to destroy you, you owe it to yourself to defend yourself. We need to understand that the left is as dangerous, if not more so, than the suicide bomber, for obscuring this basic fact – because leftists have the legitimacy of the mainstream, the imprimatur of respectability, and they wield this spurious legitimacy like a club to destroy all opposition to their totalitarianism.
> We need to go to war against the left. We have to get that into our heads. We have to accept that terrible reality. They want to destroy our freedom. They want to destroy our country. They want to steal our children. That's war. There is no one on the right who has the correct philosophy about this. The left demands the right to lie, and they are lying to the American people on a massive scale, even to the extent of making people think there is something wrong with loving and defending our nation.[22]

Bolton's and Geller's worldview, their gut feelings of what is right and what is wrong, is embedded in *southern honor*.[23] The administration of the United States of America of George W. Bush was implanted in that honor as well. According to historian Bertram Wyatt-Brown, southern affinity with the warrior ethic involves the following elements:

> That the world should recognize a state's high distinction; a dread of humiliation if that claim is not provided sufficient respect; a yearning for renown; and, finally, a compulsion for revenge when, in issues of both personal leadership calculations and in collective or national terms, repute for one or another virtue and self-justified power is repudiated.[24]

Social psychologists Richard Nisbett and Dov Cohen have studied the psychology of violence in the culture of honor in the southern parts of the United States.[25] This culture informs street gangs as much as the politics of nations. Historian David Hackett Fischer found that the American South "strongly supported every American war no matter what it was about or who it was against."[26] Southern honor was openly invoked by the 2016 Republican presidential candidates Cruz and Trump, yet, also prior to that it had never seized to guide the policies of the country even if less frankly.[27] The terminology of "unlawful combatants," for instance, betrays the spirit of southern honor in President George W. Bush's thinking. Terrorists are seen as unlawful within the honor code not only because they perpetrate mayhem, but because they commit "treason" against the rules of honor. Regardless of the fact whether their deeds require courage or not – as mis-invested as this courage may be – terrorists acquire the status of unlawfulness in the honor code, not least because "hiding behind civilians" means "cowardice." Their unlawfulness then makes them "free" to be treated unlawfully.

The culture of southern honor in America is no fringe example also in the rest of the world. Many people in Russia are happy with the Trump presidency. These are not people manipulated by their government, but people who truly believe that a Trump administration will bring peace.[28] They highlight the following sentence in Donald J. Trump's foreign policy speech: "Our goal is peace and prosperity, not war and destruction." This is the entire quote:

> I will not hesitate to deploy military force when there is no alternative. But if America fights, it must fight to win. I will never send our finest into battle unless necessary – and will only do so if we have a plan for victory. Our goal is peace and prosperity, not war and destruction.[29]

Others would be cautious in highlighting only the last sentence and putting all trust in it. Many would highlight the first sentences instead and predict war to increase at the hands of the Trump presidency rather than peace. I abstain from highlighting any of these sentences. What this chapter intends to draw attention to is the wish for peace that unites all sides, while the path to peace is conceptualized differently. All sides wish for peace, what they differ in, is the "punctuation" of the narrative, and the consequences they draw. I myself refrain from allying myself with either punctuation, and before introducing my own, I make sure that I fully acknowledge both sides, that I face the "messy truth" of the overall situation, as author and attorney Anthony Kapel "Van" Jones would formulate it.[30] Novelist Chimamanda Adichie warns of "the danger of a single story."[31]

Van Jones coined the word "whitelash," or white backlash, to describe why Americans may have elected Donald J. Trump as president, repeating the sequence of Reconstruction in the nineteenth century that was followed by a century of Jim Crow, as well as repeating the sequence of the civil rights movement of the 1950s and '60s that was followed by President Ronald Reagan and the rise of the religious right.[32] Also here, if we want to look for commonalities first rather than differences, "backlash" might be a formulation that is too polarizing. Perhaps it is rather *loss aversion* that is at work,[33] a bias that is common to all sides, namely, the fear of losing one's hoped-for future. In Europe, even in seemingly wealthy countries such as Germany politicians now win elections who promise to stem the tide of migrants from Europe's southern shores.[34]

Many of my readers will shudder when they see how I try to make a stance palatable that they find deeply repulsive. This is part of the perspective-taking training that this book is dedicated to. It means comprehending that the honor code has evolved in a divided world with a strong security dilemma, and that in that context it could very well be lifesaving to maximize division.[35] The all-out destruction of enemies by military interventions was often successful. The situation in Iraq and Syria in 2016 is a stark illustration of the fact that this is no longer that easy now. Victory could mean life over death in the past, regardless of the fact that some victories usually were Pyrrhus victories. It is only in an interconnected world that all victories become Pyrrhus victories.

Similarities form the foundation of divisions

Revenge for humiliation suffered is at the core of male honorable loyalty with nation, religion, tribe, gang, or family.[36] It is not the male-female dimension that is the driving force, it is the male-male dimension. Honorable male psychology that drives violence is infused with humiliation between males: "Humiliation is the social form of shame and is deeply rooted in the same-sex relations of childhood groups, rituals of passage, and problematic relationships with father figures."[37]

The male-male dimension is the driving force of the gang culture that Nisbett and Cohen studied in the south of the United States, and it also drives terrorist groups. It is therefore not surprising that the head of a Danish gang has traveled to Syria to fight.[38] This dimension is also stronger than religion. Experts observe that unlike with Al-Qaeda, religion becomes ever less relevant for Da'esh recruits now, with some "discovering" religion mere weeks before getting active.[39] Prisons are the ideal recruiting ground, since people with criminal records make for particularly able terrorists. They bring important skills that terror needs, such as, to name only one aspect, familiarity with generating funds illegally; and if religion can give them a sense of redemption, all the better.[40] What all have in common – gangs, criminal offenders, and terror entrepreneurs – is the salience of male-male honor and expertise in wrecking the world.

When I lived in Egypt (1984 – 1991), I observed that a deep honor culture connects all segments of its population, be they Christians or Muslims. All are embedded in a dominator culture where a strong hand is expected to enforce "true" values. I only had to think of the above-mentioned *traditionals* in the West to understand Egyptian culture of whatever religious orientation.

Recent research in the United States confirms my intuition. In their level of religious commitment, Muslim Americans resemble white Evangelicals and black Protestants most closely.[41] Muslims' conservatism matches that of white Evangelicals on social issues such as homosexuality, and Muslims are as likely, or more, than Evangelicals or any other group to support that government should have a role in protecting morality.[42] Also conservative Christians and conservative Jews are close to each other. Christian Zionists see a revived nation state Israel playing a central role in the rise of the Antichrist and the Battle of

Armageddon, and therefore eagerly await and even welcome "the unfolding of a series of wars and tragedies pointing to the return of Jesus."[43] Around 20 – 25 million fundamentalist Christians in the U.S., with evangelical Republicans as the strongest segment, hold views that bring them close to conservative forces in Israel.[44] In other words, conservatives of all camps share similarities.

Also the trope of war brings people's views into alignment. Rabbi Dov Lior, chief rabbi of the Kiryat Arba settlement in the West Bank, issued a religious ruling saying that Jewish law permits the destruction of Gaza to keep southern Israel safe: "At a time of war, the nation under attack is allowed to punish the enemy population with measures it finds suitable, such as blocking supplies or electricity, as well as shelling the entire area according to the army minister's judgment, and not to needlessly endanger soldiers but rather to take crushing deterring steps to exterminate the enemy."[45] Many progressives, for instance in Norway, criticize Israel's treatment of Gaza. Yet, also in Norway, people once felt compelled to adapt to war. Gunnar Fridtjof Thurmann Sønsteby (1918 – 2012) was one of the most highly decorated citizens in Norway, for his role in the Norwegian resistance movement during the German occupation of Norway in World War II. At the age of 80, he admitted that also the resistance movement sometimes made wrong decisions. He had this explanation: "But one must remember that war was going on. It did happen that we had to kill without being sure that the person concerned was an informant. But the decisions were right, there and then."[46]

Patriots and traitors

In war logic, the traitor is almost worse than the enemy, since traitors question the rigidity of fault lines. Traitors expose that it is possible to cross those fault lines. Executing those who have left Islam could be seen as an institutionalized practice informed by this logic. Many may expect that this practice is favored most in the Middle East-North Africa region where we hear about the cruelty of Da'esh, however, it is even more favored in South Asia, which is often associated with more moderate Islam.[47]

Lakhdar Brahimi was the United Nations Special Representative in Afghanistan from 2001 to 2004. He explains how war logic also informed American strategies.[48] It started with the shock of 9/11. Before 2001, the United States saw terrorism as something acceptable for the Arab world or for Europe, however, the moment America was hurt on its own territory, it could not accept it. Psychologist Clark McCauley, editor of the journal *Dynamics of Asymmetric Conflict: Pathways Toward Terrorism and Genocide*, explains why. He concludes from surveying research that humiliation is a toxic mix of anger and shame that is not always easy to acknowledge and admit to.[49] As an American citizen, he observed at close range the deep sense of humiliation that arose immediately after the 9/11 attacks and how it was quickly suppressed thereafter, as it was too difficult to admit to. The subsequent ten years saw a long feedback loop starting with anger at the attack, transmuting into shame at not having been able to do anything about it, ending in anger at feeling ashamed. These reactions were particularly intense because the attack came at a moment, McCauley reports, in which "the world was our oyster – the Soviet Union had fallen, and we had almost childish trust and confidence that we were in charge and that nothing could really go wrong anymore."[50] McCauley's journal focuses on asymmetric conflicts between state and non-state groups associated with extremes of violence, which cannot be understood only in terms of realist appraisals, or tit-for-tat models, or security dilemmas. McCauley explains:

> Emotion is an important contributor to asymmetric conflict, and humiliation is the prototypic emotional experience of asymmetric conflict because humiliation begins with asymmetric power. Disrespect and harm from the stronger group elicits anger in those who identify with the weaker group. Fear of the stronger suppresses expression of anger by the weaker. At the same time, the weaker experience shame for having let fear suppress anger. It is the concatenation of suppressed anger, fear, and shame that defines humiliation.[51]

This concatenation resulted in the dangerous sustainment of unnecessary fault lines and in accusing those who want to bridge them as traitors. Lakhdar Brahimi explains this in a 2013 documentary film that shows how Afghanistan's President Hamid Karzai unwittingly became such a traitor.[52] Arturo Muñoz, a former C.I.A. senior officer, describes in the documentary how Karzai went to Kandahar, to the Southern Pashtuns, to pacify the country by negotiating the town's surrender, following the old tradition that the defeated party accepts a deal and keeps its dignity. To save the life and honor of Mullah Omar, commander and spiritual leader of the Taliban, the Southern Pashtuns indeed promised to "stay in Kandahar" and not disturb the rest of the country.[53] Yet, U.S. Secretary of Defense Donald Rumsfeld, mistakenly conflating Taliban and Al-Qaeda, abrogated that agreement, declaring that no one who has supported terrorism was to live in peace and dignity.[54] Brahimi now concludes that, as a result, "une guerre contre des phantom" was waged, "a war against ghosts," not least since Osama Bin Laden had left Afghanistan already before 2001. To Brahimi, the first mistake was made under the Bush administration when Karzai's peace agreement with the Taliban in Kandahar was rejected. This was followed by a second and similar mistake by the Obama administration, when responsibility was given to a general, General Stanley McChrystal, who aimed at totally defeating the Taliban, rather than being content with only "degrading" them.[55] In other words, the U.S. had rebuffed an effort of traditional peacemaking, which it would have to engage in only a decade later any way, only under much more difficult circumstances.

It seems there was a psychological need, in the United States, to avenge humiliated honor on an enemy. When Karzai was about to remove this enemy without any fighting, the American side made sure that the enemy stayed. Also Karzai, on his side, had acted within the frame of honor, yet, his starting point was honor that was already satisfied, honor no longer in need of redress, since he had less reason to punish Taliban for what Al-Qaeda had done.

Ex-Taliban Abdul Salam Zaeef's verdict on the American strategy, in the documentary, is that "killing does not solve the problem, it makes it worse, fighting is not winning. The way to go is for respect, negotiation, understanding." This verdict, clearly, is the verdict of a traitor, viewed from a strong honor culture.

Only those who have understood that the world has changed from a divided into an interconnected world, know that his insight is the only insight that can bring a dignified future on a shrinking planet. In that sense, I am a radical traitor, since I wish to overcome all fault lines that divide, and only preserve those fault lines that enrich diversity, and that do so in dignifying ways.

When the best defense is a good offense, compassionate empathy can be switched off

Within the context of a strong security dilemma the need for revenge is not an individual desire, it is a systemically prescribed duty. Revenge might not be enough, though. Revenge is re-active. There is another strategy that is more pro-active, namely: *The best defense is a good offense.* Planning for offense can therefore be regarded as the most patriotic strategy. It will also be the most counterproductive strategy in a globally interconnected world since it is likely to bring back the security dilemma more than simple revenge would do. In other words, the most patriotic strategy of the past is the most destructive now.

Zainab Hawa Bangura, the Special Representative of the Secretary General the United Nations visited a community in Congo where eleven babies between the ages of six and twelve months old had been raped, and she explains:

> Yet, under the cold light of strategy and tactics, the rationale and purpose is clear. What more effective way can there be to destroy a community than to target and devastate its children? Faced with such horror, we are compelled to turn the despair in our hearts into unshakeable resolve that this will not happen to our children – a resolve that matches the ruthlessness of those who would commit such crimes with our own relentless and unwavering pursuit of

> accountability, and, ultimately, deterrence and prevention.[56]

Brain research shows that psychopathic criminals do not lack empathy; empathy is only not automatically "on," yet, it can be switched on.[57] Patriotism in the spirit of "the best defense is a good offense" may function precisely in this way: empathy is switched on for one's own people, and switched off for one's enemies. Wherever the in-group scope of justice ends, empathy is switched off. Or, more precisely, cognitive and affective empathy may still be on, so as to be able to identify the enemy's weak spots, what is switched off is compassionate empathy. Just like a romance scammer, who must split his empathy into several subparts to lure a romantic partner. Psychologist Daniel Goleman reports on his conversation with Paul Ekman, one of the first pioneering scholars who worked on emotions:

> In fact, those who fall within psychology's "Dark Triad" – narcissists, Machiavellians, and sociopaths – can actually put cognitive empathy to use in hurting people. As Ekman told me, a torturer needs this ability, if only to better calibrate his cruelty. Talented political operatives can read people's emotions to their own advantage, without necessarily caring about those people very much.[58]

In other words, the wholesale verdict that terrorists are "cold" and "without feelings" is informed by the spin of the security dilemma. Even compassionate empathy may still be "on" even when an enemy is being tortured. A torturer may feel compelled, when his own people are in dire danger, to place his feelings of compassionate empathy for his own people over and above any compassionate empathy with his enemy. Similar to a surgeon, who does not necessarily have to switch off empathy before performing painful surgery.[59] This is what the psychologists who devised "enhanced interrogation" methods for the United States may have felt.

Viewed from this perspective, it is comprehensible that around 1992, the American Psychological Association (APA) left behind their universal professional ethics and opted for the "guild ethics" of "we against them" fashioned on the security dilemma culture: "Professional ethics protect the public against abuse of professional power, expertise, and practice, and hold members accountable to values beyond self-interest. Guild ethics place members' interests above public interest, edge away from accountability, and tend to masquerade as professional ethics."[60] As mentioned earlier, James Elmer Mitchell was one of two psychologists involved in designing interrogation methods for the American secret service. He is proud of having combined patriotism with humanism.[61] Linda Hartling suggests that something akin to what law enforcement literature refers to as "noble cause corruption," "corruption committed in the name of good ends" played a role.[62] Perhaps APA leaders felt that it was their patriotic duty, in the spirit of national solidarity in the aftermath of 9/11, to loosen their existing ethical standards. This type of loyalty can also be observed in the devotion that evolves in ideological organizations and cults.[63] "Blind loyalty fuels conditions in which people will comply with harmful activity in support of a cause."[64]

Strategies for attaining security in the spirit of "the best defense is a good offense" have been widely used throughout history. Various United States administrations used them, nervous to maintain its superpower status. Wesley Kanne Clark is a retired general of the United States Army. He wrote the book *Winning Modern Wars* in 2003, where he describes a conversation that has been widely quoted and disputed since.[65] It was a conversation he had with a military officer in the Pentagon in 2001, shortly after 9/11, and it was about a plan to attack seven Middle Eastern countries within the next five years:

> As I went back through the Pentagon in November 2001, one of the senior military staff officers had time for a chat. Yes, we were still on track for going against Iraq, he said. But there was more. This was being discussed as part of a five-year campaign plan, he said, and there were a total of seven countries, beginning with Iraq, then Syria, Lebanon, Libya, Somalia, Sudan and finishing off Iran.[66]

Wesley Kanne Clark received the following explanation for the motivation for such a strategy: "I guess it's like we don't know what to do about terrorists, but we've got a good military and we can take down governments."[67] Journalist Seymour Hersh calls this kind of strategy the willing manufacturing of chaos,[68] and foreign policy analyst Stephen Zunes speaks of a "tinderbox" of terrorism that U.S. Middle East policy has created.[69]

Also patriots in Israel are faithful to securing land in this way, through offense by attrition. Terrorism or anti-Jewish hatred can even serve this aim.[70] Moshe Feiglin, Deputy Speaker of the Knesset, Knesset Member, and head of the Manhigut Yehudit (Jewish Leadership) faction of Israel's Likud party, is a faithful patriot, faithful to patriotism as defined within the security dilemma frame, when he writes:

> Gaza is part of our Land and we will remain there forever. Liberation of parts of our land forever is the only thing that justifies endangering our soldiers in battle to capture land. Subsequent to the elimination of terror from Gaza, it will become part of sovereign Israel and will be populated by Jews. This will also serve to ease the housing crisis in Israel. The coastal train line will be extended, as soon as possible, to reach the entire length of Gaza.
>
> According to polls, most of the Arabs in Gaza wish to leave. Those who were not involved in anti-Israel activity will be offered a generous international emigration package. Those who choose to remain will receive permanent resident status. After a number of years of living in Israel and becoming accustomed to it, contingent on appropriate legislation in the Knesset and the authorization of the Minister of Interior, those who personally accept upon themselves Israel's rule, substance and way of life of the Jewish State in its Land, will be offered Israeli citizenship.[71]

Noble empathy and ignoble solutions

While working as a clinical psychologist in Egypt, young Palestinian clients came to me because they were depressed. What I learned was that there is no "terrorist personality," that "compared with the general public, terrorists do not exhibit unusually high rates of clinical psychopathology, irrationality, or personality disorders," I learned that those who commit terror acts are not significant different in "self-esteem, religiosity, socioeconomic status, education, or personality traits such as introversion" from those who do not.[72]

My clients felt they should help their suffering families in Palestine, instead of studying in Cairo, preparing for a happy life.[73] Also they could be described as true patriots.

Farida, a young woman, not yet twenty years old, cried heart wrenchingly[74]:

> My father wants me to study, get married, and have a normal life. But I cannot smile and laugh and think of happy things, when my aunts and uncles, my nieces and other family members face suffering in Palestine. Their suffering is a heavy burden on me. I feel it in my body. Sometimes I cannot sleep. I feel tortured.
>
> I know Palestinians my age who do not care. They go to the discotheque and dance – they even drink alcohol. I think this is disgusting. Our people are suffering and we should stand by them. If we cannot help them directly, we should at least not mock them by living immoral lives or be heartless and forget them altogether. I feel I have no right to enjoy life as long as my people suffer.
>
> I respect my father and I try to obey him and concentrate on my studies. If it were not for him, I would go to my homeland, get married, have as many sons as possible, and educate them in the right spirit. I would be overjoyed to have a martyr as a son, a son who sacrifices his life for his people.
>
> I feel that suicide bombers are heroes, because it is hard to give your life. I want to give my life. I want to do something. I cannot just sit here in Cairo and watch my people suffer and be humiliated. I feel humiliated in their place, and feel that I humiliate them more by not helping them. I feel so powerless, so heavy; sometimes I can hardly walk.[75]

Farida's involvement was of profound sincerity, it was intense, pure, deep, and selfless. She was a highly intelligent and strong woman, with a sensitive awareness of justice; in sum, her future could only be bright. Yet, she was in danger of wasting her entire future because she was overwhelmed by the violence, neglect, thoughtlessness, and humiliation she saw her people suffer. Dreaming about sacrificing her life as the mother of sons who would give their lives to defend their people was what gave her consolation. Da'esh attracts girls now in this way, since it can offer family life in a "state" territory, girls who seek higher meaning in serving the *biopolitics* of war by producing warriors.[76]

Some of my male Palestinian clients had similar dreams, only that they wanted to give their own lives in violent resistance. It was clear that their resolve would be hardened rather than deterred by large-scale military responses to terrorism.[77] Both girls and boys were appalled by some of their friends who chose to "forget" about their people's suffering and instead "enjoy life" by feasting and drinking.

None of these young people was driven by any "will to power" or inherent "hatred" of enemies, nor were they motivated by religious fervor, nor did they mistake intifada for yet another form of fun, nor did they expect sexual gratifications, not before death and not afterwards. They were not among those young males between fifteen and thirty years of age who draw gratification from the expression of rage and therefore turn to violent acts of terror. They were only overwhelmed by despair. They suffered from too much empathy. They deeply empathized with their people's pain of humiliation – a noble, sincere, and valuable co-suffering.

As research confirms, it is indeed possible to feel humiliated on behalf of other victims, victims one identifies with, as if one were to suffer their very pain oneself.[78] This phenomenon, clearly, is magnified when media give access to the suffering of people in far-flung places.[79] Personal humiliation and intergroup humiliation interact.[80]

I thought of my clients when I heard of a letter that a young man from Marseilles wrote to his mother in 2015, just before his death as "foreign fighter" in Syria:

> When you read these words, then I have left life on this toilsome world behind me, this very troublesome world, especially since I left you. I hope you understand why I did all this, why I left everything, even though I lived in a stable situation, a wonderful family, and had a job. Why all these sacrifices? Because the community of Mohammed was humiliated. Allah has rewarded us with the reconstruction of the Caliphate. Finally, Muslims have regained their pride. A successful life is not only work, having a house, a car, a wife and children. A successful life is to worship Allah and to have his blessing.[81]

This young man, like my clients, belonged to those *caring-compelled individuals* that social psychologists Clark McCauley and Sophia Moskalenko describe, individuals, "who strongly feel the suffering of others and feel a personal responsibility to reduce or avenge this suffering." They did not belong to the group of *disconnected-disordered individuals* "with a grievance and weapons experience who are social loners and often show signs of psychological disorder."[82]

My clients were bright young people who were vulnerable to being recruited by humiliation entrepreneurs who would instrumentalize their empathy for acts of destruction. I explained to them that my personal life path had followed a similar desire to transcend personal material interests and embrace larger responsibilities. I described to them the advantages of the path of a Mahatma Gandhi or Nelson Mandela, and how they could help their people in Palestine best by creating a world that is more resilient and refrains from systemic humiliation.[83]

Our conversations took place at the American University in Cairo, not far from the Yacoubian Building that author and dentist Alaa Al-Aswany later described in his famous novel with the same title.[84] He worked in his dental clinic in Cairo a few streets away from where I spoke with my clients. When I later read his novels, also when I read the work of Mohsin Hamid from Pakistan,[85] or of Orhan Pamuk from Turkey,[86] it felt as if those authors had secretly listened in at our conversations and later written novels that would express the very same painful dilemmas and emotional journeys I discussed with my clients.[87]

When I lived in Cairo, I was familiar with many of the city's neighborhoods, among them Maadi, not knowing then that Al-Qaeda's Ayman al-Zawahiri hailed from a highly educated middle class family in Maadi. Many militants at the core of Al-Qaeda come from similar successful, professional backgrounds. Ayman al-Zawahiri, in his 2001 publication *Knights under the Prophet's Banner*, remarks that many terrorists hold values that go beyond personal material interests and personal loyalties as they "have abandoned their families, country, wealth, studies and jobs in search for jihad arenas for the sake of God.'"[88]

Inter-generational alienation

When I spoke with my clients in Cairo, it was before 1990, in other words, they were not yet affected by MTV-inspired "jihadi rap videos." Arsalan Iftikhar, a human rights lawyer and former national legal director of the Council on American-Islamic Relations, explains the new trend to go for the coolness and hype of jihad: "These are people who might not be theologically devout or even have a sound religious foundation, but they are using this new jihadi cool to justify criminal acts of terrorism."[89]

Indeed, extremism has become a subcultural trend. Processes of social bonding similar to what can be found in cults and sects are described by Suraj Lakhani, who wrote his doctoral thesis at Cardiff University on the topic of radicalization in the UK.[90] The jihadi cool epidemic could be compared with the methamphetamine epidemic that took off on the West Coast of the United States in late 2002, and now reaches Europe, still being on the rise.[91]

Jihadi cool[92] provides "street credibility,"[93] as does Al-Qaeda, and it inspires some young Muslims to see extremism as "cool."[94] Quintan Wiktorowicz has interviewed hundreds of Islamists in the United Kingdom, and his findings show that, contrary to popular belief, very religious Muslims are the most resistant to extremism.[95] Also anthropologist Scott Atran found that it is not religion but jihadi cool and solidarity among comrades that count. Most of them have no idea of religion initially, religious education is even a negative predictor for support for "jihad," and madrassas have little influence.[96] Jihadi cool is self-organized, self-motivating, self-sustaining, and it is social: friends get involved along with friends, along with those they played soccer with, this is what Atran observed.[97]

Another global Islam expert, Olivier Roy, concurs. He sees "troubled people in the jihadist ranks act out their fantasies of violence and cruelty."[98] For Roy, radical Islam is a peripheral community, a Westernized "virtual" community, rather than a pious and "actual" Muslim one. Roy sees deep inter-generational alienation and humiliation at work when young men in their twenties and thirties commit mass murder and suicide in the name of Allah.[99]

Roy's conclusions stand in contrast to the view that religion may be the main culprit. Gilles Kepel, a French political scientist and specialist on the Islamic and contemporary Arab world, for instance, highlights the dysfunctional sociology of France's suburbs or *banlieues*, in combination with the role of Islam.[100] French philosopher Abdennour Bidar diagnoses a "cancer" at the heart of Islam.[101]

Roy, on his part, cautions against rashly linking Islam with terrorism: "I find myself increasingly working with psychologists and psychoanalysts."[102] The blame for the international jihadi movement cannot be put on the legacy of colonization, or on Western foreign policy, or on exclusion and racism, and also the "culturalist" belief of a clash of civilizations and religions between Europe and the Muslim world is misleading. According to Roy, these young men are caught, not between two cultures, but between *no cultures*: They are not part of the world their fathers hail from, and not part of "real" France or England, worse, their fathers have humiliated themselves to be at the bottom of those societies. In Roy's view, this nihilistic radicalized youth revolt represents the Islamization of radicalism, and not the radicalization of Islam. Their revolt resembles that of the Baader Meinhof revolutionaries' revenge on their parents' Nazi collaboration – they just replace the bourgeois with the infidels – and they use the methods of American school shooters.

Roy observes that risk-taking behavior among young people has soared in general, and that it is accompanied by a fascination with suicide and violence: "We have to devote more attention to this dimension.... In Italy, for example, two young people just murdered one of their peer group. When apprehended, the only justification they could give for their act was that they wanted to experience what it feels like to kill. The press has called them crazy. But if the young people had screamed 'Allahu Akbar' before the deed, they would be perceived as terrorists."[103]

Crossing over *from dignity humiliation to honor revenge*

When I look at Roy's and Kepel's positions, I see validity in all of them. I see two motivational lines interlink in Kepel's and Roy's interpretations. The first line, which Kepel focuses on, is connected with the dignity humiliation of those at the bottom, those in the *banlieues* to say it simplified. This group of people might do something very dangerous, namely, *cross over* from feelings of dignity humiliation to reactions informed by the tool kit for violent revenge that honor humiliation offers. As I have explained in the Introduction, this is the most destructive form, since dignity humiliation is a more intense feeling than honor humiliation. This is why I call humiliation the *nuclear bomb of the emotions*.

The second line resonates with Roy's focus and is connected with the traditional supremacist honor culture of elites. In Japan, for instance, during its feudal past, a samurai had the right to strike with his sword and kill anyone of lower class who he thought compromised his honor. This elite culture has become "democratized" during the past decades in Western societies. The so-called self-esteem movement began with good intentions, namely, to empower the downtrodden, yet, it went too far. By now, it has created a "generation me," a generation of youths who are more confident and assertive in the market place, while they are also "more miserable than ever before."[104] In a market economy, where the customer learns that he is "king," almost every thrill attains legitimacy simply through finding a market. These youngsters do not need to cross over into honor humiliation's samurai tool kit for revenge, they are already there: it should not surprise that they create a market also for killing.

In Germany, in Hannover, around the corner of where I was born and raised, a young sixteen years old girl, Safia S., connects all worlds: She swooned for Justin Bieber and Allah at the same time, bragged about having links with Da'esh, and, on February 26, 2016, she stabbed a police officer at Hannover's train station with a kitchen knife.[105] Salafism as a way to act out protest in conflictual family relationships is now even relevant for Kindergarten staff, now being confronted with children of Salafist parents.[106]

Also humiliation is a negative predictor, says Atran, at least humiliation of oneself, since those who feel humiliated may rather become submissive. It may, however, be a different case when acts on behalf of others are at stake, for instance, when second or third generation youths in Britain sense that their parents had been humiliated.[107]

The story of Mohammed Bouyeri illustrates this intricate interplay of many factors. He is the young Dutch-Moroccan man who brutally killed Dutch film director Theo Van Gogh in 2004. This was after Van Gogh's film titled *Submission* had been aired, a film about Islam and its violence against women. Bouyeri first shot Van Gogh eight times, and then, while Van Gogh already lay on the ground, calling for mercy, Bouyeri walked up to him, calmly shot him several more times at close range, cut Van Gogh's throat and tried to decapitate him with a large knife. Then, just before fleeing, he stabbed him into his chest and attached a note to his body with a smaller knife, a note threatening Ayaan Hirsi Ali, a Somali refugee, who was a Dutch member of parliament at the time and had co-produced the film. Bouyeri had practiced decapitation with sheep before, since he saw it as an important sacred act he needed to perform. A friend reported: "Mohammed Bouyeri became virtually ecstatic when he watched horrifying snuff films."[108]

Now comes the question that terrorism expert Petter Nesser pondered together with me when we sat together in Oslo[109]: Is this young man a callous brute, no longer a human being, acting beyond comprehension? How come then that this young man once was concerned about the well-being of his social community, that he wanted to start a youth club, that he lobbied the city council of Amsterdam only to be rejected: Was this perhaps a young man who was keen to achieve something, but was repeatedly disappointed, and then "lost it"?[110]

I would label Bouyeri's case as a *cross over* case: It started out with feelings of dignity humiliation, however, he derived the response from the traditional aristocrats' tool kit of honor humiliation, now democratized through social media. As this is the most virulent and dangerous combination, this crossing over shall be expanded on in a forthcoming volume of this book project.

Bouyeri's path mirrors in many ways that of Islamist movements in general. It starts out with a perception that present-day's world affairs fall short. They fall short of their promise. An invitation was extended that turned out to be ingenuous: Human rights ideals and human rights rhetoric promise equality in dignity for all, they invite everybody to be part of one united human family where all are respected as equals. This invitation was heard and accepted by many, otherwise they would not be so disappointed. This disappointment now motivates a turn-around into a golden past of honor and glory, be it the Caliphate, or wanting to make nations "great again."

Back into a golden past of honor

Petter Nesser explained to me that when he heard Osama bin Laden and other ideologists of the movement speak, they sometimes sounded to him like peace researcher Johan Galtung laying out anti-imperialist theory. Yet, when it comes to solutions, they offer Salafist purity of thought, including its most brutal expressions, which entail not just beheadings, but even recommend the usage of more modern tools such as nuclear weapons against infidels: Even though their rhetoric is anti-globalization, they very pragmatically use globalization mechanisms, justifying it by the asymmetry of the situation and that being weak vindicates the use of all available means.[111]

We do not have to look far to see also others dream of a golden past of honor after feeling humiliated. History offers many examples. Adolf Hitler's *Third Reich* was to last for a thousand years as *Tausendjähriges Reich*, following the *First Reich*, the Holy Roman Empire that began with Charlemagne in 800 CE, and the *Second Reich*, the German Empire under the Hohenzollern dynasty (1871 – 1918).[112] Japan wanted to be great again, too, and allied with Nazi Germany. The contemporary slogan in the United States of "Making America Great Again," entails similar elements.[113]

Paul Ray and Sherry Anderson's research has been mentioned earlier.[114] It differentiates between *traditionals*, *moderns*, and *cultural creatives*, indicating that the majority of the Western population is made up of moderns, and that two main countermovements against modernity have emerged, on one side the traditionals, those who wish to turn back into an imagined past, and on the other side the cultural creatives, some of whom have turned their attention outward to become activists, while others turned it inward to gain new levels of consciousness.[115] In recent American politics, traditionals have formed a "coalition of restoration," while progressives invest into a "coalition of transformation."[116] Traditionals identify with competition in a divided world, they "dream the authoritarian dream," while progressives identify with humankind as a whole, in its diversity, and "dream the liberal dream."[117] Political activist Gilad Atzmon explains:

> The 2016 American presidential election divided America into two camps: The Americans on one side and the Identitarians on the other. The Americans are those who see themselves primarily as American patriots. They are driven by rootedness and heritage. For them, the promise to make "America great again" confirms that utopia is nostalgia and that the progressive reality is nothing short of dystopia. The Identitarians, on the other hand, are those who subscribe to progressive sectarian politics. They see themselves primarily as LGBTQ, Latino, Black, Jews, Women, and so on. Their bond with the American national or patriotic ethos is secondary and often non-existent.[118]

When we look at the countermovements, we see that experiences of humiliation inspire all of them. Cultural creatives, for instance, are inspired by dignity humiliation, by a sense that human dignity is being soiled, that the promise of equal dignity for all is being broken. For solutions, cultural creatives turn to the Paulo Freires, the Gandhis, the Mandelas. Cross over happens when people are unable to do so, unable to let dignity inform both feelings and action. Even though they start out with a sense of dignity humiliation, instead of walking the Mandela-path into the future that dignity suggests, they seek solutions in the past. They may even turn to the traditionals for solutions. This is what Mairead Maguire pointed at when she differentiated between good yearnings and wrong methods.

Incidentally, also Islam has traditionals, and they seem to split into the same two branches that also divide the cultural creatives in the West, namely, the inward- and outward-oriented branches, with the outward-oriented branch further splitting into purists and pragmatics.[119]

If we look at the global situation, then the exploitation of nature and people during the past decades has deprived many people in the Global South of their livelihoods. They face mining companies or dam builders or land grabbers or violence and war. Some may join terror groups, while others, if they have the necessary resources, may pay smugglers to help them flee and migrate to the Global North. People in the Global North, when they lose hope, may become consumers of psychoactive drugs, or, since they are lucky enough to have access to elections, they can vote, including for humiliation entrepreneurs and indignation entrepreneurs.

The solution: The moderns of our time have to wake up to their double standards and become cultural creatives.

How "bourgeois" networks work

Terrorism expert Petter Nesser describes the patterns and processes that form an effective movement. He describes the roles members play in a given network, how its members meet, who takes the initiative, how they talk to each other. Nesser differentiates between "entrepreneurs," "protégés," "misfits," and "drifters." I have observed similar processes in many other social contexts, be they future-oriented or past-oriented, constructive or destructive.[120] The entrepreneurs differ from the rest with regard to several background variables. They are more resourceful and usually older than the others. Osama bin Laden was knowledgeable, and, like him, also other terror entrepreneurs at least give the impression of being knowledgeable, particularly about religion. They are skillful speakers, charismatic personalities, and able to control their environment.

Osama bin Laden was charismatic and knowledgeable about religion, and also his foes were. On February 10, 2003, George W. Bush commented on a possible attack on Iraq: "Liberty is God's gift to every human being in the world." Osama bin Laden responded the next day: "Victory comes only from God, all we have to do is to prepare and motivate for jihad."[121] We see many such mirror images. Al-Qaeda's emphasis on fighting the *far enemy* (the United States) and the *near enemy* (repressive regimes in the Muslim world),[122] is now mirrored in the U.S. as a two-front war against the far enemy "Islamic fascism," and the near enemy, the Washington elite and its media, with the aim to restore true American capitalism.[123]

Some entrepreneurs have a higher education.[124] Nesser points at Tunisian Serhane bin Abdelmajid Fakhet, for instance, the leader of the group that committed the 2004 Madrid train bombings that killed 192 people and injured around 2,000. He had a university education, obtained a Spanish government scholarship to pursue a doctorate in economics at one of the best universities in Spain, and was employed in a real estate business where he was one of the best salesmen in the company.[125] Omar Khyam, who spearheaded a fertilizer bomb plot in the United Kingdom in 2004, was a good student at school. Djamel Beghal, a young man blessed by Osama Bin Laden, was a gifted organizer. Nesser read through Djamel Beghal's interrogation documents and got a sense of how he was looked up to and admired, how he was seen as a religious authority, how he therefore could convert many to Islam and initiate mass activities. Beghal was inspired by Salafi cleric Abu Qatada from the Four Feathers center in London and took followers to the Al-Qaeda affiliated Derunta training camp in Afghanistan. In March 2005, French authorities convicted Beghal. During his time in prison he met and mentored fellow prisoner Chérif Kouachi, one of the two brothers who committed the 2015 Charlie Hebdo shooting, as well as Amedy Coulibaly, who carried out the Fontenay-aux-Roses shooting and Porte de Vincennes siege.

Also London's Mohamed Sidique Khan, believed to be the leader responsible for the 2005 London bombings, was a resourceful person with considerable influence. On July 7, 2005, bombs were detonated on three London Underground trains and on a bus in central London, killing 52 people including the attackers and injuring over 700. Khan himself bombed the Edgware Road train, killing himself and five other people.

Nesser's observations resonate with the findings of many other analysts, all the way back to Alexis de Tocqueville and his observation that poverty causes apathy and despair, and that revolution is more likely when conditions improve.[126] Gilles Kepel's research underpins that terrorism is largely a "bourgeois" endeavor. Kepel looked at 300 militants prosecuted for the 1981 assassination of Egyptian President Anwar Sadat.[127] Historian Robert Leiken found that of 373 Islamist terrorists arrested or killed in Europe and the United States from 1993 through 2004, forty-one percent were Western nationals who were either naturalized or second-generation Europeans or converts to Islam.[128] Militant Islamism could be understood as the latest in a series of revolutionary political doctrines of the past few centuries, in line with "radical Jacobin liberalism, anarchism, communism, and fascism and other forms of radical nationalism"[129]: "Revolutions may be waged in the name of the poor and dispossessed, but they are usually made by the relatively rich."[130]

If one looks at the entrepreneurs' psychological motivations, Nesser observed, they seem to have experienced the *moral shock* that sociologist James Jasper has theorized[131]: "Especially after humiliations, revenge can become a primary goal" of social movements.[132] Moral shock can strike in many ways and in many contexts. For instance, it can strike when watching graphic film images of injustices, movies that provide the opportunity to immerse oneself into injustices and atrocities committed against those one identifies with, be these images real or used for propaganda.

Such shock experiences are soul-shattering inner upheavals of indignation, something that presupposes a strong ability to empathize. Birgit Hogefeld, a former member of the West German Red Army Faction (RAF) underpins Nesser's observation when she explains why she turned to terror: "The photo of screaming Vietnamese children after a napalm attack, 'stood out for me as a call and an obligation to act and not passively watch these crimes.'"[133] In the case of Muslims, such images may stem from Bosnia or Palestine or Iraq. One image from the infamous Abu Ghraib prison in Iraq, one that inflamed many, is on the cover of my book on humiliation and international conflict in 2006.[134]

Moral shock, however, is only the beginning. Many may simply stay there and do nothing. Political scientist Quintan Wiktorowicz has looked into the process of radicalization that follows from having a shattering experience to coming into contact, perhaps through social networks, with a culture and a system that transforms one's feelings of anger and frustration and gives them direction.[135] Once a person has reached this point, she might become a follower of a movement, or, if she shows leadership abilities, she may distinguish herself as a leader, be it as an inspirer in the spirit of the Gandhis of this world, or as a destruction entrepreneur following the Hitlers of this world.

Leadership qualities have their basis in a wide range of psychological preconditions. They may flow from an ability for wisdom, which might engender a Gandhi-like path, or, on the other pole of the spectrum, psychopathic traits can bring a Hitler to the fore. Some have explained the mass appeal of Adolf Hitler with a schizophrenic psychological structure arising out of a preponderance for "the public self": "… Hitler's development had tended from an early age toward a narcissistic fixation on a grandiose public self until not a trace remained of the private – including the emotional-self. A series of deep humiliations engendered an enormous need for compensation that escalated into a delusional relationship to his environment with all the characteristics of a paranoid schizophrenic psychosis."[136]

Entrepreneurs have a protégé, explains Petter Nesser, and a protégé is a "small version" of the entrepreneur. Both are intelligent and form the nucleus of a cell. They maintain a close relationship, they may go on leisure trips together, for instance, of which the rest of the group is not part. The entrepreneur will use the protégé to recruit others. When they are arrested, they do not waver. They will hold their ideological position. They have no regrets and will continue fighting no matter what.

A third category are the "misfits." They form the bulk of terrorist networks. They are the reason for why the impression has emerged that the core problem of terrorism is unsuccessful integration. In media coverages one reads about those misfits and how they had been subjected to racism, had been looked down on, had altogether a difficult life, which made them vulnerable to sliding into drug abuse and criminality. They are the ones who are then recruited by the entrepreneurs. For the misfits, this will be experienced as a healing process. Group psychology will work for providing them with a sense of belonging. They will enjoy being shown respect by being given tasks, important tasks, such as obtaining weapons or committing violence. When they are arrested, they will readily lay open in which way this process evolved and how they regret it. They will profess that they did not know what they got themselves into, they will explain how they were blinded and seduced by being in the presence of those holy warriors who were so fascinating and how exciting it was. They will have no strong ideologically anchoring.

The fourth category are the "drifters." Drifters will not have their own agendas, they simply follow their friends. It may be that the brother-in-law knows someone who is further connected, with whom one shares social characteristics. When they are intercepted and interrogated, they will have a propensity to distance themselves. They will admit that they ought to have realized what they became part of, yet, they closed their eyes, because they liked to think the best of their friends. They will get low prison sentences, as they were on the peri-- phery, without any strictly relevant information.

Patriots need support to become dignifiers

When I think back to Farida and her colleagues, then they displayed a depth of sincerity that indicated that they had everything needed to manifest the path of a Gandhi or Mandela. I do not know how they fared after we parted, yet, as far as I have heard, they did not choose the path of violence after our conversations. In other words, it seems that I was convincing enough with my arguments.

As mentioned above, I am a traitor. I am also an entrepreneur. I personally come from painful experiences of moral shock that were brought to me by my family background, a family that was profoundly traumatized by war and displacement. It is the shock that also Elie Wiesel felt, a shock that makes me dedicate my life to calling for "never again." However, I refuse to use protégés to recruit misfits and drifters. I refuse to build a movement based on the dominator model. I refuse using the "master suppression techniques" that social psychologist Berit Ås so well described.[137] I refuse to seduce people into becoming cannon fodder for any ideology. I refuse ideology that supposes a *Homo religiosus* or a *Homo honoris* model of human nature, where people may even commit homicide and suicide. I also refuse the *Homo economicus* model of human nature that recruits people into consumerism. I do not have protégés. I am part of a team of equals who share servant leadership and transformational leadership.[138] We congratulate misfits" with their desire for meaning and belonging. And we hail the "drifters" for their relational emphasis. We work for a world with systemic structures that enable and empower people, a world that entrusts them with the task to rise from being "useful idiots."

People like Farida are still many today, and they would need to be held by the proverbial village that it takes to raise a child. Filmmaker Robb Leech made a film about his stepbrother Richard Dart, who resembles Farida.[139] Leech documents how his stepbrother converted in 2009 to an extreme brand of Islam as expounded by Anjem Choudary, the leader of the later prohibited Islamist group

Islam4UK. The film accompanies Richard Dart until the moment he leaves for his first hajj in 2010. There are touching scenes in this documentation. For example, when Leech desperately tries to speak to the soul of his brother, yet, also the utter sincerity with which his brother sees through the dark sides of Western culture. It is tragic to follow Richard on his path into the world of honor. He is a gifted and earnest young man, and hopefully he will live long enough to grasp how destructive this path is.

Syria's President Bashar al-Assad was initially seen as a potential reformer. The international community – the global village responsible to raise its children – however, failed to guide him toward refraining from the mass crackdowns and military sieges on Arab Spring protesters in 2011, strategies that ultimately led to the Syrian Civil War.[140] Young Eric Harroun, born 1982 in Colorado, U.S.A., explains in a video how he travelled to Syria to support the Free Syrian Army in Syria, those fighting for freedom and democracy against the regime of Bashar Al-Assad.[141] "Eric was a passionate, driven man who pushed the limits of both his personal life and searching for meaning and purpose. He found it in fighting in Syria and paid dearly for it," these are the words of Robert Young Pelton, a writer and war adventurer who befriended Harroun.[142] In other words, young Eric was a true freedom fighter, as defined by Ronald Reagan in 1986: "Freedom fighters target the military forces and the organized instruments of repression keeping dictatorial regimes in power. Freedom fighters struggle to liberate their citizens from oppression and to establish a form of government that reflects the will of the people."[143] Eric's life was wasted, however, because the global village failed him and Syria. He died of an overdose. After having watched young Eric speak, you might want to watch Amer Deghayes, a 20-year-old former student from Brighton who went to Syria to fight Assad forces and you will see another earnest young man who is as sincere about his "duty to fight for victory and justice," so sincere that also he is ready to give his life.[144]

Anthropologist Scott Atran warns against the widespread assumption that "terrorists are nihilists, who simply do not care."[145] He speaks of a sense of moral virtue that can drive the desire for martyrdom – as suicide bombing is called by those who resonate with its moral virtue. It is morally virtuous to protect sacred values rather than serve the banality of here-and-now utility. Indeed, if we follow Atran, we may deduce that, just as patriots feel morally virtuous in protecting their people, so do would-be martyrs.

Research on meaning and meaning-making in life shows that it has a healing effect to align the meaning of a particular situation with a higher global meaning.[146] Even physical health and well-being improve when one succeeds in creating a sense that the world is meaningful and one's own life dignified. Commitment to a higher purpose beyond oneself helps one to come out of traumatic events – this can even include experiences of captivity or torture – with less psychopathology than if no higher meaning were assigned.[147]

Also I feel that my radical work for globally inclusive dignity gives me meaning and has healing effects. I am inspired by universal values and I am radical in my values and methods that are inspired by a Gandhi spirit rather than that of a Hitler. Sacred values are linked to emotions, explains Atran, and we are often not even aware of them until we are challenged. Also in secular contexts, sacred values reign, even though a secular person may not recognize it. She will become aware when asked to sell her children, for instance, because then she will refuse. Monetary compensation degrades sacred values into mere utility,[148] and therefore, the more monetary compensation is offered to a potential martyr's family, the less likely they will support the idea of martyrdom. When Atran asked Israel's prime minister Netanyahu about the core question he would put to Hamas, Netanyahu's question was: Would Hamas ever accept "our existence," accept "why we came here"? Palestinians had similar deeply felt and agonizing questions: On their part, they expressed their yearning for recognition and apologies for what "they" have "done to us."

At this point, we begin to see the problems that even the most well-intentioned patriots and patriotic freedom fighters face. For whose freedom should they fight? For the freedom of their in-group to keep or gain privileges, for instance? Or for freedom for all people in a world to enjoy equal dignity? And what if anarchy is the result of even the best intentions, anarchy that removes freedom from all walks of life? Political scientist and Middle East expert Shibley Telhami explains that one reason for why the Arab uprisings have not expanded beyond the early cases is that the anarchy that was the result in Syria and Libya, and the economic deprivation and insecurity in Egypt, have given rulers "a way of frightening their own public" by asking them: "Do you want to be in Aleppo and Tripoli, or Amman and Riyadh?"[149]

In September 2015, U.S. intelligence reckoned that nearly 30,000 foreign fighters from more than 100 countries had travelled to Iraq and Syria since 2011, many of them to join Da'esh.[150] In 2014, Bruce Hoffman, director of the Center for Security Studies at Georgetown University, reported: "I would say that most convincing analyses hold that there are indeed thousands of foreign fighters in Syria of whom about 2,000 are thought to be from Western countries."[151] Some of these foreign fighters are there to help more moderate forces defeat Assad, yet, the majority of foreign volunteers are ending up joining or working with extremist groups like Da'esh.[152]

In January, director of U.S. National Intelligence, James Clapper, told Congress, "We're seeing now the appearance of training complexes in Syria to train people to go back to their countries and, of course, conduct more terrorist acts." England is now describing returning militants from Syria as "the biggest security threat to the United Kingdom," more significant than the returnees from the Afghanistan and Pakistan region. It is estimated that homegrown terrorists have been responsible for seventy-eight percent of Al-Qaeda and Al-Qaeda inspired terrorist plots in the West from 2003 – 2008.[153] Since 9/11, until 2016, more than three hundred Americans have been indicted or convicted of terrorism charges.[154]

If we remember the African adage that it takes a village to raise a child, then it is the global village that fails its responsibility. The only truly constructive patriotism is patriotism for a decent global village.

Why are they so enraged?

Why are they so enraged? When I came to Egypt in 1984, I was amazed when I looked at the family photo albums: miniskirts! I lived in Egypt until 1991 and can confirm from my own experience what historian Bernard Lewis wrote in 1990, namely, that many Muslims once admired the West and emulated it, however, that this slowly gave way to "hostility and rejection": "In part this mood is due to feelings of humiliation – a growing awareness, among the heirs of an old, proud, and long dominant civilization, of having been overtaken, overborne, and overwhelmed by those whom they regarded as their inferiors."[155] In other words, as I said earlier, first, the invitation from the West was accepted. There was a "love story." Yet, love stories can turn into hatred when betrayed and then rash reactions that later may be regretted can destroy everything.[156] This is one of the messages of my 2006 book on how humiliation can create enemies: a humiliated lover's hatred can be worse than any other hatred.[157] Ibrahim Abu-Rabi was a Professor in Islamic Studies at the Department of History and Classics at the University of Alberta in Canada, a leading contemporary Muslim thinker until his premature death in 2011. He did not wish to leave the analysis of Islamism solely to Western authors and developed an eight-point analysis of why religion has gained more public prominence now than before.[158]

Why are they so enraged? British Lord Douglas Hurd formulated it for Iran, and I sense that his words are valid also for the wider Muslim world:

> Iran is an ancient country with a huge history of which it is very conscious. This is more than simply a platitude for after-dinner speeches; it is a relevant political fact. We have forgotten so much of our history and, in a way, the Iranians remember too much of theirs. They remember past glory; they remember humiliation – at our hands, Russian hands and American hands; and the coup of 1953 against Mossadegh – things which we never knew or have forgotten. Out of this comes a deep reluctance to be told by other people how they should behave.[159]

Patriotism is noble, a mixture of humble service to one's own people in avenging and preventing humiliation. Psychiatrist Vamik Volkan's theory of collective violence has been referred to earlier. He explains that if trauma experienced as humiliation is not mourned, this leads to a sense of entitlement to revenge, and, under the pressure of fear/anxiety, to collective regression and ultimately violence.[160]

Author Lawrence Wright has studied Osama bin Laden's life and background, and what motivated him.[161] Wright, in his analysis of the rhetoric of Al-Qaeda, points out that humility and humiliation are central concepts:

> Humility is a highly valued character trait in Islamic culture. When bin Laden's followers praise him, they often invoke this quality. The fact that bin Laden is from a wealthy family makes this aspect of his personality all the more appealing.
>
> Humiliation, on the other hand, is imposed from the outside. It is one of the most common words in bin Laden's vocabulary. For many Muslims who resonate with the term, their humiliation may be cultural or religious in nature – the sense of Islamic societies being overpowered by Western values, mores, and political dictates.
>
> But it is also true that a number of Muslims have been physically humiliated. Ayman al-Zawahiri, for instance, the number-two man in Al-Qaeda, the doctor always at bin Laden's elbow, was imprisoned for three years in Egypt following the Sadat assassination. Like many of his companions, he was brutally tortured.
>
> I think the particular appetite for carnage that sets Al-Qaeda apart from other terrorist organizations was born in the humiliation such men suffered in those prisons.[162]

Osama bin Laden's comment about the events of September 11 are being reported as follows: "What the United States tastes today is a very small thing compared to what we have tasted for tens of years … humiliation and contempt for more than 80 years."[163] Osama bin Laden saw Al-Qaeda actions as response to the "humiliation of his people," particularly in Palestine, as he formulated it in his *Fatwa* "Declaration of War against the Americans Occupying the Land of the Two Holy Places" in 1996 (this *Fatwa* was redistributed in 1998):

> Our youths knew that the humiliation suffered by the Muslims as a result of the occupation of their sanctities cannot be kicked and removed except by explosions and Jihad. As the poet said: "The walls of oppression and humiliation cannot be demolished except in a rain of bullets. The freeman does not surrender leadership to infidels and sinners Without shedding blood no degradation and branding can be removed from the forehead."[164]

Wright explains that bin Laden thought that he could turn the United States of America into a Divided States of America. The Soviet Union fell after their defeat in Afghanistan and bin Laden's strategy was to bring the same fate to the United States. Then Islam could take its due place as primary power in the world. It was a deep humiliation for him when American troops came to Saudi Arabia in the first Gulf war, a humiliation that was compounded by the fact that American forces included women.

Osama bin Laden was not the only one to use a language of humiliation and humiliation-for-humiliation. Also Henry Kissinger reportedly said, "They want to humiliate us and we have to humiliate them."[165] Psychohistorian Robert Jay Lifton writes:

> Indeed, at the core of superpower syndrome lies a powerful fear of vulnerability. A superpower's victimization brings on both a sense of humiliation and an angry determination to restore, or even extend, the boundaries of a superpower-dominated world. Integral to superpower syndrome are its menacing nuclear stockpiles and their world-destroying capacity. In important ways, the "war on terrorism" has represented an impulse to undo violently precisely the humiliation of 9/11.[166]

Become a bridge-builder

What we understand at the end of this chapter is that there are two kinds of counterterrorism that are diametrically opposed to each other, one informed by local patriotism and one by global patriotism. The first is embedded within the normative paradigm of ranked honor in a divided world, and the second within the normative paradigm of equal dignity for all in an interconnected world.[167] Patriotism "for us against them" contrasts patriotism "for the entire human family."

The example of honor killing is particularly useful to illustrate the normative irreconcilability that is at the heart of the clash between traditional and new paradigms: "The girl must be killed" is regarded as a sad but unavoidable outcome in the first context, while "the girl must live" is the guiding sentence in the second setting.[168] In other words, at the core of the transition from a divided world based on ranked honor toward a united world based on human rights ideals of unranking, we do not have complexity or gradual transformation. We have a stark binary "either – or," either the girl dies or lives. A human rights defender can therefore not be true to herself if she thinks that the traditional paradigm can coexist with the new one. These are not "two cultures" on a par. She cannot avoid conflict.

Present-day terrorists and counterterrorists are caught in that dilemma. Most of the time, all sides act from the vantage point of the first paradigm – where "the girl must die" – and in this way, both sides "understand each other": as a result, they simply try to out-terrorize each other.

A person tasked with countering terror who does not wish to go down that path – who wants the girl to live so to speak – will have a problem. Human rights concepts of dignified responses to terror are not necessarily understood in a world of honor. Invitations into dialogue may be interpreted and responded to as weak and dishonorable appeasement. The families I know who believe in honor killing taught me that.[169] Deeyah Khan's documentary film on the honor killing of the girl Banaz in the UK demonstrates this extremely well: The girl fled to the police after an attempt by her family to first drug her and then kill her.[170] The police brought her back to her family, spoke with the family, and left. The police believed in dialogue. What they did was hasten the killing of Banaz.

Dialogue, well-intended but wrongly approached, can work against its intentions. To work for its intentions, it needs to satisfy a number of conditions.[171] Those who wish to respond to violence and terror with strategies informed by human rights, as, for example, with dialogue, must first create acceptance for those human rights values. This is why I hope that many will read this book who are steeped in the honor code and will be inspired by my respectful explanations of the unsuitability of the honor code in an interconnected world. I hope they will be inspired to let the girl live.

So far, however, the code of honor has characterized terrorism and much of counterterrorism:

> The jihadists in Iraq strategically deploy emotional narratives to construct the myth of heroic martyrdom, demonize their intended targets, and appeal to potential recruits from around the Muslim world. These culturally astute jihadists know well the themes that resonate with the wider Muslim public, and have done an extraordinary job in harnessing three narratives to mobilize for martyrdom: humiliation of Muslims at the hands of foreigners, impotence of official Muslim governments in the face of hegemonic powers, and redemption through faithful sacrifice. This study explores how jihadists weave together these three narratives to suggest a deleterious condition that requires an immediate action, offer an explanation of the causes of this persistent condition, and present the necessary solution to overcome the problem.[172]

The problem with honor based counterterrorism is that it makes true my sincerest warnings: it no longer works in an interconnected world. In an interconnected world, the saying that it takes a village to raise a child means that the entire global community is responsible for nurturing global cohesion rather than firing up deadly terror for terror. Brian Keenan is a patriot. He was held by Shia

Muslims loyal to Hezbollah in Lebanon for four and a half years. His message after the November 2015 Paris attacks was as follows:

> What do we need to do about this? In a global dimension, we all have to take some responsibility for this. My own thoughts – after four and a half years in captivity – is that the dispossession and the anger has to be acknowledged. These people have to be offered something more than revenge or Holy War or even this perverse Islamic apocalypse.... What worries me is that as these old borders and "international zones" disappear, "security barriers" become the new borders. We've seen this in the Middle East and they are rapidly being erected across Europe. These worry me more than the term "terrorism." They create these kinds of conceptual contours – it's not just a wall, it's a wall that defines a lot of cultural beliefs and misbeliefs. We are damaging ourselves with these walls – we are damaging our ability to think, our ability to be creative.[173]

Brian Keenan is a bridge builder. Also Jo Berry, introduced earlier, has shown how fault lines can be bridged. The Provisional Irish Republican Army (IRA) member Patrick Magee killed her father in 1984. After the release of Patrick Magee in 1999, she went to meet him several times. These meetings over ten months later formed the basis for a BBC documentary film first broadcast on December 13, 2001.[174]

Brian Keenan and Jo Berry are bridge builders and global patriots of great personal courage and wisdom. In an interconnected world, these kinds of bridge builders are needed more than before. Yet, where do we find them? Who possesses the courage and wisdom needed? Perhaps minorities can help. So-called minorities often suffer from non-belonging, from being excluded from the majority's "pure" identity. I call on them to re-interpret their suffering as a privilege, as it enables them to feel with others who suffer, and at the same time strengthens their motivation to work for change. Scientist Yves Musoni is such a bridge builder. He shared this in a personal communication: "My experience working in Rwanda, being at once both, Munyarwanda Congolese Tutsi, from my father, and Rwandan Tutsi, from my mother, put me in a very special situation which made me a member of a minority as described by Amin Maalouf in his novel, *In the Name of Identity: Violence and the Need to Belong*."[175]

I hope many who have suffered trauma will read this book. This book calls on them to use their trauma to become global bridge builders. This is what I have done with my life.

Narrating the human condition in the way done in this chapter has a huge advantage: it opens space for a dignified future. The first step is to deeply understand both paradigms, the honor paradigm and the dignity paradigm, and then, in a next step, to refrain from judging representatives of either paradigm as evil. The next step is to patiently and lovingly nurture the transition from honor to dignity, without indulging in fits of indignation against the other side. We, as humankind, can refuse letting outdated cultural adaptations divide us and rather unite the world, and we can do so in dignified ways.

Chapter 14

"War for Peace" Was All We Once Knew

A Savage War of Peace is the title of a book on the Algerian war for independence from France that raged from 1954 to 1962 and saw about 1.5 million Arab Muslims perish, together with many thousands of French men and women.[1] The two brothers who committed the terror attack on the French satirical weekly newspaper *Charlie Hebdo* in Paris on January 7, 2015, Saïd and Chérif Kouachi, were of Algerian origin. Journalist Robert Fisk points out that the media coverage of this event has overlooked this important context: a history that many Frenchmen and also Algerians prefer to ignore – namely, the fact that the bloody struggle "remains the foundational quarrel of Arabs and French to this day."[2]

For the past millennia, war and peace were inseparable, they were tragically connected. *If you want peace, prepare for war*, is in a nutshell *war for peace*. The slogan *war for peace* was used in 1991 by a political leader in Montenegro, Svetozar Marović, to justify the Montenegrin assault on Dubrovnik in 1991. This slogan describes the path to peace in a mindset where peace in exchange for slavery would be too humiliating, and where power elites interpret even equality as too humiliating, equality as slavery. For them, peace therefore means "successful domination." They translate the wish "to be somebody" into "to be respected as the one on top," rather than "to be respected as one among others."[3] "Make America great again" is a slogan that encapsulates the wish to "be somebody" through remaining on top.[4]

During the past millennia, this wish for respect and recognition has created unspeakable suffering. Yet, in a divided world caught in a strong security dilemma, it is the best choice. A ruler has few alternatives but to regard staying "on top" as his main task, since, otherwise, he risks being at the bottom very fast, toppled by his own or conquered by neighboring potentates. A ruler has to keep his own people in line, always alert, in case an unexpected attack arrives from outside. Unexpected attacks from outside can best be minimized by dominating all neighbors at all times, or, at least by maintaining an advantageous power balance. Neighbors are safe neighbors as long as they show "us the reverence we deserve," and "we keep them from humiliating us." It is like the man who routinely beats his wife to remind her that she has to show him the respect and love he needs to feel he is "somebody." This struggle creates the very threats it tries to remedy.

A divided world creates the security dilemma, which, in turn, pushes for a dominator culture, where people seek the protection of strongman rulers to "manage" the security dilemma for them. This dominator culture will in turn augment the security dilemma. In short, for the past millennia, people were caught in a tragic quandary.

Alexander the Great (356 – 323 BCE[5]) can serve as an illustration for the coming into being of dominator culture. Each time I wear the iconic jewelry that I have received from the oasis Siwa in the Egyptian desert, I think of him.[6] This oasis is where Alexander the Great went to listen to the oracle. Alexander's father, the autocratic king of Macedonia, admired Athens. Proud Athenian citizens on their part, however, looked down on barbaric Macedonia and its one-man tyranny. Alexander and his father yearned to rise from this humiliation. The first rule that Alexander learned from his father was never to show weakness and always be best. His father got the best personal teacher for his son: Aristotle. Through ruthlessness, combined with intelligence, over time, father and son managed to achieve the unthinkable, namely, to conquer the Greeks. Then they even succeeded to unite the Greeks and take on their archenemy King Darius III, king of the Persian Empire. Alexander went to conquer the entire Achaemenid Empire, surrounded by a team of Greek companions who were both close friends and generals, all more or less his equals. Then came a crucial turning point, when Alexander almost lost the support of his companions. He asked them to perform the Persian custom of *proskynesis*, which is a symbolic kissing of the hand, or a prostration on the ground.[7] The Greeks, who would only bow to deities, were disgusted at Alexander's apparent attempt to deify himself by requiring them to kowtow. Alexander was so enraged at their refusal that he killed one of them, his closest friend. His friend's death shocked Alexander to the point that he retracted and stopped asking his friends to cow to him. He went back to respecting their egalitarian relationship.

Throughout history, few followed Alexander's example of retracting. It was the dominator model that became dominant, not the egalitarian relationship.[8] The Persian Empire was a long-established hierarchy, much more "civilized" in the sense of having left behind egalitarianism long ago. No one who lived in the early civilizations questioned the normalcy of hierarchy: "If egalitarianism was known, it was as a feature of some of the despised, barbarian societies that existed beyond the borders of the 'civilized' world."[9]

In the context of a strong security dilemma, during the past millennia, most people learned to bow, and they learned to draw a line where the scope of justice and sympathy for "us" would end and a different mode begin, namely, the "enemy" mode. The human potential for curiosity, people's wish to connect with the unknown and with strangers, the desire that drives modern tourism, the desire to learn about "exotic cultures," all this was strictly controlled and contained. Even nowadays, certain countries in the world regard it as a crime when people wish to leave it – North Korea comes to mind. Or, all around the world, strict visa regulations hinder the majority of the world's population to move across national borders as freely as the citizens of wealthy countries can. Only very few people can roam wherever they want on the globe, and this is also why those who flee war in Syria cannot simply take a plane to safety, as every tourist with a Western passport can. This is why they have to risk death on flimsy boats across the Mediterranean Sea.

Populations in dominator contexts are conditioned into obediently believing that authorities' reasons are "right" and have to be followed, and if authorities demonize strangers as "barbarians," or worse, this has to be embraced and not undermined. Nobel Peace Prize laureate Mairead Maguire from Northern Ireland was introduced before. She speaks of the peddling of "fearology" that fuels racism, islamophobia, hate crimes and speech, and fascism, thus crowding out tolerance for cultural diversity.[10] During the 2016 presidential race in the United States, Republican presidential candidates used that very strategy: "socialists" were the new "barbarians," as were immigrants, or Muslims, altogether those who are suspected to "hate freedom."

Freedom is regarded as hallmark of Western achievement, manifesting itself in the Western market system in an almost divine way, despite the inequality and unfreedom it engenders for those at the bottom.[11] Indeed, people from all over the world flock to the West because they "love freedom" and love the American Dream, and they are as disappointed as many Americans when they see this dream failing. The median U.S. household income in 2014 was 50,000 American dollars. If the pre-1970 productivity growth had been maintained, it would have been \$97,300 in 2014.[12] The younger generations in the United States can no longer afford their parents' dream. The 2016 presidential elections show that the "dreamers" within America are now revolting.[13] And many of my friends around the world no longer dream of travelling to America – not because they hate freedom, but because they love freedom, and freedom is not what America stands for anymore.

Fearology began in ancient times with authorities drawing on foundational fathers of religions or philosophies as underwriters of "we against them" polarizations. Later, in Europe, faith was to be placed in the kinds of experts that sociologist Michel Foucault describes.[14] Since the Cold War, specialists of the presently existing economic arrangements, originally derived from Roman legal systems (see Howard Richards analysis[15]), have taken over globally. The latter trend now creates "we at the bottom against the elites" backlashes. Some of those rebels turn back to bygone scripts, scripts of war and rebellion that prescribe violence as remedy, and this can express itself also as terrorism.

Throughout millennia, rulers have prepared followers for violence and war by using Manichaean dualism, firing up Manichaean self/other and good/evil dichotomies in people.[16] This mix is still virulent today all around the world. In its propaganda, Da'esh now takes former American President George W. Bush up on his words to Congress on September 20, 2001: "Either you are with us, or you are with the terrorists."[17] Da'esh absolutely agrees with Bush, only, from their perspective, the "terrorists" are the "American crusaders," explains Abdelasiem Hassan El Difraoui, an expert on violent Islamist internet propaganda.[18] In its online propaganda and its recruitment magazine *Dabiq*, Da'esh refers to an epic battle between invading Christians and Muslims expected in the Syrian village of Dabiq, a battle that will bring a Muslim victory and will ring in the beginning of the end of the world.[19]

In social atmospheres of such kind, people with "pure" and clear-cut identities feel at ease and are at an advantage, and therefore in power. They are those who are adverse to holding complexity, both within themselves and in the world.[20] They are those who believe that the human mind is something fixed and should stay fixed.[21] As rulers, they will have many followers, if for no other reason, then because they make life easier for them. After all, it is difficult to live with complexity; to achieve peace of mind, it is easier to depend on the concept of the divine or the expertise of "experts," it is easier to simplify the world through projecting one's own inconsistencies onto others.[22]

Adolf Hitler was such a ruler. He combined ruthlessness with seductive attraction in unprecedented ways. He drove the motto of the security dilemma to its absolute climax. As has been discussed earlier, the motto *If you want peace, prepare for war*[23] can be escalated by heeding general Carl von Clausewitz' advice that *The best defense is a good offense*. Hitler managed to top this escalation by practicing "the best defense is a good offense brought about by treachery," or even more precisely, "the best defense is a good offense by treachery, genocide, and terror attacks."

Hitler said in a speech to the press in 1938: "Circumstances have forced me, for decades, to almost exclusively talk about peace. Only by continuously emphasizing the German desire and intention for peace, was I able to win freedom for the German people, piece by piece, and to give them the armament, which will be necessary for the next step."[24] He explained that he was afraid that the German people might have believed him and developed true intentions for peace, and that he was intent on changing this misunderstanding. These are his words in 1938: "It was now necessary to gradually re-orient the German people psychologically and slowly explain to them that there are things that, if they cannot be enforced by peaceful means, must be enforced by violent means."

When he felt that Germany was prepared enough, Hitler started war by a false flag operation, so as to be able to pretend that he was merely defending his country. He manipulated the situation so that it seemed as if Poland had attacked Germany, and Germany, "peaceful Germany," had no choice but "to shoot back."[25] Terror tactics were a weapon of his way of waging war from the start. From the outset, the Wehrmacht leadership planned their air raids on Poland not as military attacks but as terrorist attacks, where no distinction was made between military and civilian targets.[26] The Polish town of Wielun, for instance, was bombed without any military reason; Hitler pretended it was done in defense. Bringing the city of Danzig (now Gdańsk) *Heim ins Reich* (home into the empire) was the first step to expanding German *Lebensraum* (literally life-space) into the east.

Yet, also Polish politicians were deeply steeped in the culture of the security dilemma. Jσzef Beck, Polish foreign minister, said in the Polish Parliament Sejm on May 5, 1939: "We in Poland do not know the concept of peace at any price. There is only one thing in the lives of men, nations and countries that is without price. That thing is honor."[27] If Hitler ever was willing to negotiate the status of Danzig, the door had closed also there.

Honor of the soldier drove also Hitler's allies. After its defeat in World War I, in the Treaty of Trianon in 1920, Hungary had lost over two thirds of its territory, mainly to Romania, but also to Czechoslovakia, Yugoslavia, and Austria. When Hitler came to power, Hungary hoped he would bring back past glory also to them. Ultimately, though, the opposite happened. Soviet military besieged Budapest for 102 days, 38,000 civilians died in the *Stalingrad on the Danube*, as the Russians called it – no city among the German allies suffered as much as Budapest. Veteran Norbert Major wonders, "Why did we fight? Even though it was sheer madness? 'Because we were soldiers! We had taken an oath! On his Highness, the Regent Horthy!' 'Only he who shoots first, survives!'"[28]

Some scholars see a change in Hitler's personality in 1919, when his writings turned from relatively apolitical to anti-Semitic.[29] In a letter in 1919, Hitler expressed his view that Jews had to be "removed."[30] One wonders, if posttraumatic stress injury[31] may have played a role. Hitler had just lived through the First World War as a soldier and had been wounded. "Many traumatized people complain about a vague sense of emptiness and boredom when they are not angry, under duress, or involved in some dangerous activity," explains trauma expert Bessel van der Kolk.[32] In other words, trauma might have driven a heightened need for stress in Hitler's life; also later, when his actions looked like those of a hazardeur, for instance, when he recklessly gambled on an easy victory over Russia.

In 1939, Hitler spoke openly of the "destruction of the Jewish race." In the celebration of the sixth anniversary of his *Machtergreifung* (seizure of power), he gave a speech to the German Reichstag, where he first bemoaned how he had been ridiculed by Jews, how they had refused to believe that he would ever be able to become the leader of Germany, how they now had to stop laughing about him, and how they had been responsible for the suffering of the German people in the past. The enthusiastic applause he received for his words shows that he could be sure that everybody in the parliament resonated with his sense of humiliation and with his conclusion: "If the international finance Jewry inside and outside Europe should succeed in plunging the world's peoples once more into a world war, then the result will not be the Bolshevization the Earth and thus the victory of Jewry, but the annihilation of the Jewish race in Europe!"[33]

Hitler was not an insane actor who took his ideas out of an intellectual vacuum. He built on the thinkers of his time, on various modern philosophers and on distinguished academics, from whom he picked what suited his mindset and worldview.[34] One of his friends said that Hitler "was not so much a distiller as a bartender of genius": "He took all the ingredients the German [tradition] offered him and mixed them through his private alchemy into a cocktail they wanted to drink."[35]

The work of Friedrich Wilhelm Nietzsche (1844 – 1900), for instance, inspired Hitler to see in democracy the mere fostering of mediocrity. Hitler was enthralled by Nietzsche's idolization of the warrior spirit. Nietzsche's view was that the creation of equality was not desirable for a culture, only the creation of stronger men was. This fired up Hitler's aspiration to breed Aryan supermen as rulers of the world: "Brutality is respectful.... Terrorism is absolutely indispensable in every case of the founding of a new power."[36] Hitler believed that the German *Volk* (people) had to be the "force within history" that Georg Wilhelm Friedrich Hegel (1770 – 1831) talked about. And this had to be done by no longer shying away from conflict. It had to be done by "coming into being" through invading Europe. From Arthur Schopenhauer (1788 – 1860) apparently he gleaned that "will" should be glorified "over reason."[37] Hitler liked also Immanuel Kant (1724 – 1804), because Kant had rejected the teachings of the Middle Ages and of Catholic dogmatic philosophy, and had deemed Judaism to be superstitious and irrational. Also the ideas of Johann Gottlieb Fichte (1762 – 1814) supported Hitler's vision of German anti-Semitic exceptionalism.

Clearly, also other cultural influences helped Hitler. Among them was the culture of the authoritarian Prussian *Obrigkeitsstaat* (authoritarian state), a culture that is still palpable today in certain segments of German society. The aforementioned Roman law tradition was the enabling backdrop for this culture. When people relate to reality as proud enforcers of strict rules and regulations that demarcate everybody's territory, they intensify the contractual thinking derived from the Roman law tradition and absolve themselves from responsibility where there is no contract. When Jewish neighbors were transported away in the middle of the night, it was outside of the role of a German citizen to take responsibility for them as fellow human beings: "What happens here, is outside of my responsibility." Thus Germans ended up standing by, rather than standing up.[38] The atmosphere in society, per design, was one of "passive-aggressive" privacy, where responsible humanitarian resistance was turned into a taboo that everyone dutifully inflicted on themselves and others.

Hitler was a particularly ruthless leader, and in my work, I have studied his personal psychological needs to punish the world.[39] He used what the security dilemma had on offer to justify and carry out his homicidal and suicidal apocalypse. His path throws into stark light that the security dilemma itself is tragic. He was in possession of so much power, not least because within the confines of a strong security dilemma more sensible and measured leaders never found enough space.

If we go further back in history, few leaders illustrate the tragedy of the security dilemma as impressively as Hannibal (247 – between 183 and 181 BCE[40]). His path shows how even the noblest of intentions and most excellent skills could turn into tragedy. History books are full of stories of strong leaders who successfully expanded the range of control of their empires, but most were lucky if they died before their successors would squander their victories and be humiliated by opponents who would turn the tables back to their advantage. Hannibal experienced all this in one lifetime. If ever humankind manages to unite, and he could come back, he would be a brilliant thinker and advisor for all of humankind. In his time, however, his brilliance led to everything between triumph, terror, and humiliation. He was an extraordinary strategist who won many important battles and was later admired even by men such as Napoléon Bonaparte. For a while, he seemed to be safely in control. He was so successful that he became a figure of terror for Rome: *Hannibal ante portas!* (Hannibal is at the gates!) was an outcry that expressed the fear and anxiety of the time, an outcry one can still hear today when danger looms. Yet, at some point, even Hannibal was defeated and had to flee into exile. He had to sell his brilliant services to other leaders as a mercenary. At the end of his life, he faced such humiliating betrayal that he took his own life with poison.[41]

Mike Ibeji is a military historian who gives a very concise description of the workings of the security dilemma and how it shapes relationships. He describes the times when Normans conquered Britain and the Battle of Hastings was fought out in 1066 CE:

> The Lord owned land, which he parceled out amongst his followers in return for service. They in turn settled the land as minor lords in their own right, surrounded by a retinue of warriors to whom they would grant gifts as rewards for good service and as tokens of their own good lordship (of which the greatest gift was land).
>
> Success in war generated more land and booty which could be passed around. If a lord wasn't successful or generous enough, his followers would desert him for a "better" lord. It was a self-perpetuating dynamic fueled by expansion and warfare in which the value of a man was determined by his warlike ability: the lord led warriors; the warrior fought for his lord; they were both serviced by non-fighting tenant farmers who owed their livelihoods to the lord; and below them came the unfree slaves.[42]

In such contexts, also religion was a matter of politics. Norway is often regarded as one of the most progressive democratic and freedom-based countries, and this is due, not least, to an exceptionally democratic and egalitarian Viking legacy. Later, when Christianity conquered their land, this legacy was pushed aside and blackened.[43] The first Viking to be associated with Christianity was King Harald Bluetooth, King of Denmark and Norway (probably born circa 935 CE), and it is unclear, whether he was forced to adopt Christianity or did it voluntarily. Ólafur Tryggvason was King of Norway from 995 to 1000 CE, and he engaged in the forcible conversion of the Norse to Christianity.[44] From today's perspective, one may say that Tryggvason was a tyrant who adopted Christianity perhaps only because it offered him *rex gratia dei*, the *divine right of kings*. This right asserts that a monarch derives the permission to rule directly from the will of God and does not have to bow to earthly authority. Tryggvason had no Christian scruples when he forced Christianity on other people by way of extortion. He took four sons of

Icelandic chieftains captive and sent their fathers an ultimatum to leave their old gods behind, or else. In Iceland, Þorgeir Ljósvetningagoði was the speaker for the Norse faction, and, it was only due to his wisdom that civil war with the Christian faction was avoided.[45] He declared that all Icelanders should take up the Christian faith in public, but that worshipping the old gods was allowed as long as it was done in private.

I learned about Icelandic wisdom in 2015 from a physics professor from Iceland, Þórarinn Stefánsson. He explained to me why the handball team of little Iceland was so successful out in the big world. What is their secret of success? "Unity in diversity," was his reply.[46] Just now, while I write this sentence, Iceland is in a state of collective elation, because their soccer team was the star of the Euro 2016 Football Tournament.[47] Like Hannibal, also Ljósvetningagoði would be a great asset were he to live now. And Þórarinn Stefánsson is worth listening to as well. They all can help humanity unite and use diversity to enrich, rather than divide.

Usually however, wisdom and moderation had little space to flourish in the context of the tragic security dilemma. Usually might was right. Pope Gregory VII (1015 – 1085) was perhaps another wise man, similar to the Icelandic elders, who fell prey to the security dilemma's brutal reality. To *go to Canossa* is an expression often used in the German language for an act of penance or submission. *The Humiliation of Canossa* refers to Henry IV, Holy Roman Emperor (1050 – 1106), a rather ruthless, cruel, and impetuous character with strong misogynist streaks.[48] In January 1077, he set off from Speyer in Germany, and walked for more than seven hundred kilometers to Canossa Castle in the north of Italy, where Pope Gregory VII resided. There, Henry "humiliated" himself on his knees (today, we would say that he humbled himself), waiting for three days and three nights before the entrance gate of the castle, while a snow blizzard raged. His aim was strategic. He wanted to obtain the revocation of a ban of excommunication the Pope had imposed on him. With his "act of humiliation," he offered Gregory a moral triumph in exchange for political advantages. As soon as he had what he needed, it became clear that Henry's humility in the face of Gregory was inauthentic, simply cloaking arrogance. Soon, Henry succeeded in destroying Gregory; he died in exile. Arrogance trumped true humility and wisdom.

Not just in Europe did Hitler-inspired ways to peace inflict humiliation and terror. China is another example. I began learning Chinese when I was nineteen, and in 1983, I traveled all over China by train, at a time when it was still officially closed to individual visitors. In 2007, we had our 9th Annual Dignity Conference in Hangzhou.[49]

The term *harmonious society* was continuously emphasized by our Chinese conference hosts and participants. They preferred this concept – as it is informed, among others, by a revival of Confucianism – over the term *social cohesion* that at the time was more frequently used in other world regions, for example, in Europe.[50] Prior to the conference, I had the privilege of being shown around in the part of Shanghai where famous Lu Xun (1881 – 1936) had lived and worked. Lu Xun (or Lu Hsun, pen name for Zhou Shuren) is being considered to be the founder of Modern Chinese literature. His name stands for humiliation, or, more precisely, for making vividly palpable, in his writings, the pain of humiliation perpetrated by feudalism. I was told that Lu Xun would love my work on humiliation, and that my 2006 book on humiliation and international conflict read as if it was written for China.[51] I was also told that it was a matter of great humiliation that names such as Shakespeare are known the world around, while the greats of China, like Lu Xun, are virtually unknown outside of China even to otherwise learned people. Lu Xun was a writer and intellectual, author of short stories, poems, essays, and literary criticism. Born in 1881 into an educated but impoverished Chinese family, he was passionate about China's liberation from foreign imperialism, passionate about abandoning those oppressive and superstitious traditions that had engendered such social and economic injustices, passionate about the plight of the poor and the peasants, altogether about problems of war, violence, and exploitation. *Call To Arms* (*Na-Han*), published in 1922, was his first collection of stories,[52] which includes his most celebrated works, such as "Diary of a Madman" (1918) and "The True Story of Ah Q," where he depicts an ignorant farm laborer who goes through a series of humiliations and finally is executed during the chaos of the revolution of 1911.[53]

Inequality was, however, not only a source of humiliation for feudal China. At the present point in history, inequality is on the rise worldwide, and elites are disconnected from the rest.[54] I have called the human rights revolution the first *continuous revolution* in history precisely to highlight that those who work for equality for dignity for all will never be able to relax their efforts as they will always face those who work for inequality.[55]

Yet, China also shows how problematic the term continuous revolution can be. Therefore, I became cautious. I began to call for a global dignity *refolution* (a term coined by Timothy Garton Ash to connote a mix of reform and revolution). By now, upon reflection, I prefer to leave behind the terminology of revolution altogether and rather speak of nurturing a *dignity movement* that brings about a dignity transition. Therefore, I also no longer think there can be something like "warriors for peace." Mao Zedong set in motion the disastrous Cultural Revolution as *perpetual revolution*, a nationwide mass terror campaign that was to challenge authority and reshape the "superstructure" of society. If we believe China specialist Lee Feignon, his motivation might have been to serve the interests of the majority,[56] yet, sadistic people, people who throve on violence, were given license to act.[57] At the time, if Mao had ordered suicide attacks, many would have enacted them.[58]

The story of Li Nanyang and her father sheds heartbreaking light on the tragic dilemmas people were drawn into. Both father and daughter were idealistic people believing in the laudable aims of the communist movement. However, at some point the father became disillusioned. As a result, he was denounced, and his daughter turned against him. It took a long time until also she began to question the revolution's wisdom, and it took many more years for them to reconcile.[59] Zheng Yi is another doubter. He was once the Red Guard leader of a rebel faction, yet, the moment came when he started having qualms. In the spring of 1989, he was active in the pro-democracy movement and was arrested. He escaped, and now he is a dissident writer living in in the United States, in Washington, D.C.

When I worked as a medical student in Bangkok in 1981, I befriended a nurse who hailed from Guangzhou. In 1983, when I was on my way to China, she asked me to privately deliver a letter to her family in Guangzhou. I met her highly educated family there, a family who had suffered immensely during the cultural revolution and still lived in trauma and fear in 1983. In highest confidentiality, I was introduced to the horrors of their experiences of utter terror and humiliation.

Yet, not only humiliation within, also humiliation from outside has been definitorial for China. The modern Chinese character is defined by the pursuit of *fuqiang*, or wealth and power, explain China experts Orville Schell and John Delury; it is the quest for the restoration of national greatness in the face of a *century of humiliation* at the hands of the Great Powers.[60] This quest drove Mao Zedong to embrace Marxism-Leninism, it drove Deng Xiaoping to go for authoritarian capitalism, and it remains the key to understanding many of China's actions today. The title of the second chapter in Schell and Delury's book is "Humiliation: Wei Yuan," describing the bitterly crushing Treaty of Nanjing in 1842. This treaty ended the Opium Wars, China's first experience with ruthless Western methods of humiliation, of which many followed. Another China expert, William Callahan, has studied the Chinese "cartography of national humiliation": "These maps do much more than celebrate the extent of Chinese sovereignty; they also mourn the loss of national territories through a cartography of national humiliation," he has reported.[61] *Never Forget National Humiliation* is the title of a book by public policy scholar Zheng Wang. He explains how past humiliation serves as a principal lens for everything that happens in and to China until the day today. In the aftermath of the NATO bombing of China's embassy in Belgrade in 1999, for instance, America's explanation that the bombing had been an accident was not accepted. All Chinese leaders believed that it was an intentional challenge to Chinese national honor.[62]

In the context of a strong security dilemma, hierarchy, love, and terror are always strongly associated. Terror is perpetrated out of love for ones superiors and their definitions of who else deserves love and who deserves hatred. Not just names such as Adolf Hitler or Mao Zedong epitomize this connection, also names like Joseph Stalin.

What connects Mao and Stalin is that they were not defeated in a war, unlike Hitler, and, perhaps as a result, they are widely venerated still today, despite the millions of people who perished due to their politics. If we look at Stalin, the exact numbers may never be known; yet, the deaths caused by Soviet terror "can hardly be lower than some fifteen million."[63] Lenin, and more so Stalin, seems to have continued the hierarchical Tsarist culture in which cruelty was "normality." They did so only with a new ideological rhetoric, a rhetoric that justified so-called purges, which simply meant terror that re-arranged hierarchy by shifting around who was up and who was down.

Historian Robert Conquest introduced the phrase *Great Terror* for the late 1930s in the Soviet Union, inspired by *la Terreur* (Reign of Terror) during the French Revolution.[64] The Soviet terror had another name as well, namely, *Yezhovshchina*, literally, the Yezhov phenomenon. Nikolai Yezhov was a Soviet secret police official who oversaw the most deadly terror period from 1936 to 1938. Victims of this terror were Communist Party and government officials, Red Army leadership, peasants, anybody who was suspected to be a "saboteur."[65]

Two books shed light on how the Yezhovshchina epoch felt for the people. One book describes this era as one of passivity, where everyone spoke in whispers, due to the paranoia, alienation, and treachery that poisoned private lives all around.[66] The other book emphasizes the eruptive force of the time and how a whole society was driven into fever, how people permanently tried to reach their limits of physical and mental exhaustion; only one month after the second big show trial had been conducted against "inner enemies," a fulminant Pushkin jubilee was held.[67]

None better than the founder of modern Russian literature, Alexander Sergeyevich Pushkin, considered by many to be the greatest Russian poet – and I studied Russian at school and would agree – illustrated the Tsarist culture of violently vying for honor that preceded this era and informed it. Pushkin had just published a touching love story when he died at the age of 37.[68] He died after a duel that he fought for the honor of his wife, the last duel of a breathtaking number of twenty-nine duels he had engaged in.

Like so many other dictators, Stalin developed an all-consuming paranoia and invented imagined threats to keep hierarchy in place. He did also not shy away from applying "capitalist" methods if they strengthened his power. Stalin admired American carmaker Henry Ford. In 1929, the Ford Motor Company signed a landmark agreement to produce cars in the Soviet Union.[69] Stalin emulated Ford in how he treated his workers, namely, by bullying, harassing, and terrorizing them.[70] The *Stakhanovite movement*, named after record-breaking worker Alexey Grigoryevich Stakhanov, aimed to demonstrate the superiority of the socialist economic system by raising standards and "squeezing out the last drop" of workers' bodies and souls. In other words, what we see at work here, is not any communist versus capitalist ideological stand-off. We see Ford and Stalin joining hands in the spirit of a shared ideology of the age-old dominator model of society. By now, a Trump-Putin affinity follows suit.

Also Red Militarism was not related to Marxist ideology as such, rather expressing the dominator approach. Dmitri Antonovich Volkogonov (1928 – 1995) was a Russian historian and colonel-general, who was head of the Soviet military's psychological warfare department. According to Volkogonov, Red Militarism as a system is likely to be found in all countries with a strong authoritarian heritage and socio-economic backwardness.[71]

Given the uninterrupted culture of oppression in Tsarist Russia and then the Soviet Union, it might be understandable why some Gulag prisoners stay loyal to the party also now after their ordeal is over, despite of all their suffering.[72] What we might not understand, however, is how it was possible that the Soviet order could ever be "sentimentalized" in the Western.[73] How come so many intellectuals in the West closed their eyes to Stalin's reign of terror? Also here, the security dilemma culture might have been at work, as it indicates that the enemy of my enemy is my friend. And if I hold grudges against my superiors, I may feel attracted by out-group leaders who dare oppose my despised superiors. What is overlooked in such cases, clearly, is that the enemy of my enemy might not be worthy of being my friend. In that way, Western sentimentalizers of the Soviet order could be said to have betrayed their own ideals: They acted within the traditional paradigm of war, failing in their own practice to transcend into a culture of global human fellowship, a fellowship that they professed to work for in their rhetoric.

If we think of Adolf Hitler, then he was the heir of a long European historical legacy. Europe experienced a "closing of mind" that lasted for one thousand years. It may have begun with the Council of Nicea in 325 CE. Roman Emperor Caesar Flavius Constantine was concerned with attaining peace and unity in the Christian Church more than he was with theology or doctrine when he nudged the three hundred bishops in the council to resolve controversial theological questions. His aim was to present the Church as a unified force to the pagans of the empire, and the resulting Nicene Creed was enforced not just by the Church, but also by the government. Internal strife in God's Church "is far more evil and dangerous than any kind of war or conflict" the emperor is reported to have said.[74] The Nicene Creed condemned the views on the nature of Jesus that Arius held, a controversial priest from Alexandria in Egypt, and it introduced strict regulations, for instance, when to celebrate Easter and how bishoprics were to operate.

Historian Charles Freeman offers a rather dark appraisal of Constantine's impact, first on the Roman world, then on Christianity, and thus on Western civilization, with repercussions still being felt to the present day.[75] Freeman argues that Constantine turned Rome from a relatively open, tolerant, and pluralistic part of the Hellenistic world into a fixed authoritarian world. The Bible, the writings of Ptolemy in astronomy, and those of Galen and Hippocrates in medicine, became the only sanctioned and sacrosanct readings. It took a thousand years before Europe, in the Renaissance, could free itself again and open up to the mindset of modern science.[76]

Also the Islamic world's golden age of openness for diverse and critical thinking was cut short at some point and disallowed to flourish further. Many orientalists blame Al-Ghazali (1058 – 1111), a Muslim theologian, jurist, philosopher, and mystic of Persian descent, and his influential book *Tahafut al-Falasifah* (*The Incoherence of Philosophers*). Al-Ghazali criticized philosophers for not being able to lay down rational explanations for metaphysical arguments, and, in a way, this "stopped critical thinking in the Islamic world."[77]

A mindset of modern science, while it has the potential to open minds, can, however, also do the opposite. Peace researcher Johan Galtung bemoans that "enlightenment came with capitalist growth against nature and the working classes," and that by now, "nature fights back, now possibly winning," while "women, young and old, nonwhites" struggle for parity.[78] Indeed, first came colonialism and empire, and with more science came also the "devil's dynamo."[79] In other words, also the Enlightenment's true potential could not yet unfold. Particularly starting from the eighteenth and nineteenth centuries, when the development of science and science-based industry accelerated, it began to impact the whole world, and increasing disastrously so.

Prior to the Industrial Revolution, spices, textiles, and luxury goods were brought to Europe from Asia. India provided England with cotton cloth and fine textiles. With science evolving, spinning and weaving machines were invented, and the trade was reversed. Cheap cotton cloth from England was now sold in India. Science provided an enormous military superiority to the industrialized nations. This superiority enabled them to appropriate, through colonization, something that was not theirs. By 1875, they dominated sixty-seven percent of the Earth's surface, and in 1914, it was eighty-five percent. They plundered their colonies for raw materials and food, and in turn sold them their own goods. Unspeakable terror and humiliation were inherent parts of this campaign. Belgian Congo was one of the worst examples. It was the private property of Leopold II and his army's men were ordered to cut off the hands of their victims to prove that they had not wasted bullets. Then there were the smallpox-infected blankets that were given to the Amerinds; naval bombardments terrorized unwilling peoples into submission; in 1854, Japan was forced to accept foreign traders; in 1856, British warships bombarded Canton in China; in 1864, European and American warships bombarded Choshu in Japan; in 1882, Alexandria was bombarded, and in 1896, Zanzibar.

Those who are awed by the achievements of science, may be tempted to believe that all of this was part of progress and that the price paid, though high, was worth it. It might be the reverse. The benefits of societies who had developed a balanced culture of unity in diversity were replaced by crude uniformity without diversity by way of might-is-right "progress." "For the Europeans and Americans of the late 19th century and early 20th century, progress was a religion, and imperialism was its crusade."[80] The world's first automatic machine gun was the Maxim gun, invented in the United States in 1884 by Hiram Maxim. Explorer and colonialist Henry Morton Stanley (1841 – 1904) commented that the machine gun would be "a valuable tool in helping civilization to overcome barbarism."[81] Industrialism spread from Britain to Belgium, Germany, and to the United States, and, though less, also to France, Italy, Russia, and Japan. A science-driven arms race ensued. When the English upgraded their old navy, also Germany wanted to have a *Platz an der Sonne* (place in the sun) as Kaiser Wilhelm II formulated it, meaning that also Germany wanted to enjoy the pleasures of a colonizer. The First World War was the result, followed by a second world war, making of the twentieth century a century of unspeakable slaughter. When I visit my parents, I face the immense trauma of this century every day.

The creation of uniformity without diversity – rather than unity in diversity – was not only a consequence of early emperor Constantine's wish to overcome discord in his empire, or later the delusion to overcome "barbarism" in the world. We see also more recent examples. Dreams were high in 1955, when the newly liberated colonies in Africa and Asia met in Bandung, Indonesia, at a conference that became constitutive for the so-called Third World.[82] In the opening speech Indonesia's President Sukarno praised unity in diversity:

> Yes, there is diversity among us. Who denies it? Small and great nations are represented here, with people professing almost every religion under the sun – Buddhism, Islam, Christianity, Confucianism, Hinduism, Jainism, Sikhism, Zoroastrianism, Shintoism, and others. Almost every political faith we encounter here – Democracy, Monarchism, Theocracy, with innumerable variants. And practically every economic doctrine has its representative in this hall – Marhaenism, Socialism, Capitalism, Communism, in all their manifold variations and combinations.
>
> But what harm is in diversity, when there is unity in desire? This Conference is not to oppose each other, it is a conference of brotherhood. It is not an Islam Conference, nor a Christian Conference, nor a Buddhist Conference. It is not a meeting of Malayans, nor one of Arabs, nor one of Indo-Aryan stock. It is not an exclusive club either, not a bloc which seeks to oppose any other bloc. Rather it is a body of enlightened, tolerant opinion which seeks to impress on the world that all men and all countries have their place under the sun – to impress on the world that it is possible to live together, meet together, speak to each other, without losing one's individual identity; and yet to contribute to the general understanding of matters of common concern, and to develop a true consciousness of the interdependence of men and nations for their well-being and survival on earth.[83]

The dream of unity in diversity was not allowed to flourish. In one country after the other, leaders were removed, with Western support,[84] driven by an American preoccupation with securing their position against the threat of the Soviet Union's expansion of communism, a preoccupation felt to be a question of life or death for America.[85] Iran's Mohammad Mossadegh was toppled in 1953 and replaced by the Shah. In 1961, Congolese independence leader Patrice Lumumba was killed and succeeded by dictator Mobutu. After the coup against Chile's Salvador Allende in 1973, Augusto Pinochet and his Chicago-educated economists began their neoliberal experiment, which was later spread by Western experts all over the developing countries. In 2006, war correspondent John Pilger interviewed Duane "Dewey" Clarridge, who ran the C.I.A. in Latin America in the 1980s. Clarridge explained that it was in the American interest, for instance, to have Salvador Allende done away with. When Pilger asked Clarridge about the rationale and ethics of overthrowing governments, Clarridge laconically replied: "Like it or lump it, we'll do what we like. So just get used to it, world."[86]

Sukarno himself was toppled about ten years after Bandung and replaced by Suharto. At least half-a-million Indonesians were slaughtered from 1965 to 1966, accused of being communists. *Time Magazine* described the suppression of the Indonesian Communist Party as "The West's best news for years in Asia."[87] Within Indonesia, the slaughter is still being hailed today as something that was "necessary," and most surviving victims still keep quiet.[88] Also the West has so far failed to acknowledge its role.[89] I regret that I did not know enough about all this in 1981, when I spent many months in Indonesia and learned about their culture and language.

If we look at the Americas, domination, humiliation, and terror have been deeply intertwined also here, not just as part of colonization, also later. The Comisión Nacional sobre la Desaparición de Personas (National Commission on the Disappearance of Persons) was created by Argentinian President Raúl Alfonsín on December 15, 1983, to investigate what had happened to the *desaparecidos* (victims of forced disappearance), and to find out more about the human rights violations of the *Dirty War*, violations perpetrated during the military dictatorship between 1976 and 1983, known as the National Reorganization Process. The commission confirmed that torture, kidnapping, and disappearances were part of the "methodology of terror" used by the military Juntas, and identified 8961 persons who were enforced disappeared. *Nunca más!* (never again!) is the title of the 1984 report.[90] Political scientist Sonia Cardenas wrote a book about human rights in Latin America, titled *A Politics of Terror and Hope*.[91]

North America was no stranger to the normality of terror either. Researchers have documented 3959 racial terror lynchings of African Americans in twelve Southern states during the period between Reconstruction and World War II, regarded as "acts of terrorism because these murders were carried out with impunity, sometimes in broad daylight, often on the courthouse lawn."[92] Many lynchings took place in the light of day, and often a town's most well-regarded white citizens were involved. Lynchings were occasions to celebrate: "Some people brought their children, dressed in their nicest clothes. And many made a day of it, inviting a photographer, then taking the photographs and using them as postcards to proudly share with friends and family."[93]

African-American author Ta-Nehisi Coates has become known recently. He focuses on the experience of the *black body*. This body is continuously in danger, both from being terrorized by fellow black men, called "crews," and from white people. He reports from his experiences as a youth, when he feared "the street":

> Crews, the young man who'd transmuted their fear into rage, were the greatest danger. The crews walked the blocks of their neighborhood, loud and rude, because it was only through their loud rudeness that they might feel any sense of security and power. They would break your jaw, stomp your face, and shoot you down to feel that power, to revel in the might of their own bodies. And their wild reveling, their astonishing acts made their names ring out. Raps were made, atrocities recounted. And so in my Baltimore, it was known that when Cherry Hill rolled through, you rolled the other way, that North and Pulaski was not an intersection but a hurricane, leaving only splinters and shards in its wake. In that fashion, the security of these neighborhoods flowed downward and became the security of the bodies living there.[94]

As a schoolboy, Coates wondered why the black heroes in the films of the civil rights movement he was shown at school were nonviolent, at a time when he was surrounded by violence, both originating from his own people and from the rest. The country he knew, "had acquired the land through murder and tamed it under slavery," and its armies "had fanned out across the world to extend their domination."[95] Coates could not fathom the discrepancy between the idolization of violence in mainstream society around him and these films emphasizing nonviolence for black people.

Coates did have good intentioned teachers who felt responsible, however, Coates became doubtful of good intentions. He finds that "what any institution, or its agents, 'intend' for you is secondary":

> I came to see the streets and the schools as arms of the same beast. One enjoyed official power of the state while the other enjoyed its implicit sanction. But fear and violence where the weaponry of both. Fail in the streets and the crews would catch you slipping and take your body. Fail in the schools and you would be suspended and sent back to those same streets, where they would take your body. And I began to see these two arms in relation – those failed in the schools justified their destruction in the streets. The society could say, "He should have stayed in the school," and then wash its hands of him.[96]

Coates suspects that the language of "intention" and "personal responsibility" only serves exoneration and the preservation of an illusionary dream: "Mistakes were made. Bodies were broken. People were enslaved. We meant well. We tried our best." Coates concludes that "good intention is a hall pass through history, a sleeping pill that ensures the Dream."[97]

Raymond Helmick, professor of conflict resolution, concurs: "Within the white population of the United States there still remains a profound lack of feeling for the humiliation suffered by our black population." Helmick adds: "It has to be understood that the problem we face today with outraged Muslims is a direct result of … the islamophobia with which we have burdened Muslims both within our own countries and abroad."[98]

Social scientist Paul Ray agrees, as also he emphasizes the role of the social context over the role of the individual. In a comment on consumer culture, Ray criticizes a continued skewed focus on the individual, among others expressed in the presently observable championing of neuroscience. He points at several hundred studies finding "that cultural differences in values and worldviews were vastly better predictors to consumer behavior, than learning of the kind mentioned in neural research, or than the kinds of variables used in conventional behaviorist or personality psychology."[99]

In other words, overly focusing on neuroscience may be misleading. Likewise, overly focusing on religion may be misleading. Throughout the past millennia, terror was regarded as a justified strategy in "war for peace," including war in the name of religion.[100] In 1683, for instance, the Ottoman Empire made a last attempt to conquer Vienna, doing so under the motto of *jihad.* This was responded to in kind by Christian powers who formed a *Holy League* to fight against the "infidels." The showdown at Vienna in September 1683 was the last conflict at Europe's borders conducted under the banner of a "holy war." After their defeat, the Ottomans were pushed back in the Balkans. The Treaty of Karlowitz signed on January 26, 1699, in modern-day Serbia, ended an era: the time of "religious wars" was over.

In the late nineteenth century, eighty percent of Muslims lived in colonies of European powers, but European dominance did not go unchallenged. When I carried out my doctoral fieldwork in Somalia in 1998, I learned a lot about the uprising of the Mahdi in Sudan. Muhammad Ahmad bin Abd Allah (1844 – 1885) was a charismatic religious leader who proclaimed himself the *Mahdi,* or messianic redeemer of the Islamic faith. He launched the *Mahdiyya* in 1881, and, until the fall of Khartoum in January 1885, he led a successful military campaign against the Turco-Egyptian government. His courage makes people in the region proud to the day today.

The Mahdi's uprising inspired German strategists in the years before World War I. Their idea was to use the military potential of Islamic resistance movements to bring Germany's colonial competitors into trouble. At the outbreak of World War I, at the insistence of Kaiser Wilhelm II, and with the help of allied Turkey, the German Reich tried to kindle a *global jihad* against British and French colonies so as to destabilize the Reich's opponents. The organizer of this "jihad made in Germany" was Max von Oppenheim (1860 – 1946), of the Oppenheim banker family in Cologne.[101] As head of the Berlin "Intelligence Bureau for the East," he was entrusted with the planning and execution of this "holy war."[102] In November 1914, the Turkish Sultan announced jihad against the Triple Entente – Great Britain, France, and Russia – and with the help of German weaponry, military operations were carried out, and assassinations, bomb attacks, and coups initiated.[103] Berlin offered training. Civilians were to be targeted with terror and sabotage. The aim was "zum wilden Aufstande zu entflammen" (to inflame wild riots).[104]

Not only did the German Kaiser instigate jihad, he also initiated terror on the high seas. He ordered a ship to stealthily sail the oceans of the world to weaken his enemies' forces through instilling fear and terror. The cruiser SMS Wolf was disguised as a normal freighter, yet, it placed mines, captured enemy freighters, plundered, and sank them.[105] The Kaiser expected the unprotected ship to never return, since it was on a suicide mission. However, after 451 days, against all expectations, only a few days after the ship had been declared lost and its crew dead, the Wolf returned to her homeport of Kiel. On February 24, 1918, it arrived with 467 prisoners of war aboard and substantial quantities of rubber, copper, zinc, brass, silk, copra, cocoa, and other plundered materials. Its surprisingly capable commander, the honorable master of this state-ordered pirate terrorism, received the highest military decorations of the German Empire.[106]

Not only the German side used terror as a tool. Neither side was innocent. In *Lawrence in Arabia: War, Deceit, Imperial Folly, and the Making of the Modern Middle East*, war correspondent Scott Anderson describes how the modern West Asia / Middle East came into being through intrigue, accidents, and failing policies during and after World War I, and how the very themes of today – jihad, oil, Zionism, colonialism – were relevant also then.[107] It might surprise his fans, but famous Lawrence of Arabia perfected guerilla tactics and in 1938 delivered to the *Encyclopædia Britannica* a "study of the science of guerrilla, or irregular, warfare," "based on the concrete experience of the Arab Revolt against the Turks 1916 – 1918."[108]

Throughout history "waves of fashion in terrorism included the European, Latin American, and Japanese 'urban terrorist' movements of the 1970s and 80s – the Baader-Meinhof Gang in Germany, Red Brigades in Italy, Montoneros in Argentina, Japanese Red Army, and so on – none of which had any political success at all. Specifically 'Islamic' terrorism really begins only in the 1990s, with the rise of radical, anachronistic forms of Sunni Islam," explains historian Gwynne Dyer.[109] Terrorism expert Peter Neumann concurs: Terrorism must be analyzed historically, each wave tends to last twenty to thirty years.[110]

Gérard Chaliand and Arnaud Blin are scholars with backgrounds and experiences that bridge cultures and continents, and as a result, they view the world from a global perspective. They edited a comprehensive book on the history of terrorism whose chapters follow terrorism's historical chronology: From the dagger-wielding Sicarii Zealots in Judea in the first century CE, to the Al-Hashshashin or Assassins in the eleventh century, to the Reign of Terror during the French Revolution, to the anarchist terrorists of the nineteenth century, Russian terrorism from 1878 to 1908, the terror of Lenin and Stalin, the wars of national liberation from colonial rule, ending with the more recent terrorism wave of 1968, and now with radical Islam.[111]

Chaliand and Blin argue that the current terrorist threat differs from previous ones only through the "democratization" of means and targets. In the past, it was sensible to aim at leaders and commit tyrannicide, while present-day mass politics with politically influential civilian populations and the availability of mass killing technologies make civilians, not leaders, preferred targets for terrorist violence. Chaliand and Blin thus disagree with Walter Laqueur's famous argument that terrorism has no historical constants and is characterized solely by its particular political and cultural environments.

Walter Laqueur was born in 1921 in Breslau, Lower Silesia, Prussia (today Wrocław, Poland), where also my mother was born, nine years after him.[112] Also he is a cosmopolitan scholar, only that in his case it was involuntary; he was forced out of his home, as he was born into a Jewish family and his parents became victims of the Holocaust. Chaliand and Blin contrast Laqueur's views in that they say that the underlying strategy of terrorism is stable over time insofar as terror as a means to intimidate audiences always uses a minimum of force, whether one examines sub-national groups, like the Irish Republican Army, or state actors, like the French government under Robespierre. What is variable are the tactics terrorists use to achieve their goals and the conditions under which they use them. Like Chaliand, Blin, and Laqueur, also I view the world from a global perspective. When I look at the situation through the lens of Max Weber's *ideal-type* approach, also I see both, global commonalities and local differences that are unique.[113]

Leader-led and leaderless jihad are intertwined, as has been laid out elsewhere in this book. Forensic psychiatrist Marc Sageman has summarized what happens: First, traumatic experiences – be they personal or learned about indirectly – spark outrage, this is then interpreted through the lens of a specific ideology that creates a sense of relief and clarity, which then can be amplified to encompass entire communities, be it online or offline.[114]

If we bring this together with what journalist Peter Bergen has to say, namely, that a new generation of English-speaking and Internet-savvy young people is now only "a mouse click away" from extremist violence, with terrorist websites having increased to more than 4,000 in 2006 from a dozen in the 1990s,[115] we understand why fear is on the rise worldwide, even in places where risks are small. For an American residing in the United States, for instance, the risk to be killed by foreign terrorists has been minute. Since September 11, 2001, it has been 5,000 times more likely to be killed by a fellow citizen armed with a gun.

Lamya Kaddor is a German citizen of Syrian ancestry, now a scholar of Islamic studies, after having worked as a teacher at a school in Dinslaken-Lohberg, which is called the "cradle of German extremism."[116] To her dismay, five of her own former students volunteered for "jihad" in Syria. She knows these young people very well and understands how they all live in very fragile life situations. She explains that they could easily have found their way into right-wing extremism, yet, since they had roots outside of Germany, Salafist extremism was the only alternative open to them.[117] Dinslaken-Lohberg is a neighborhood located in the Ruhr area of Germany, once known for its coal mines, all of which are now crumbling, leaving few opportunities for work to the region's inhabitants. According to the German Federal Crime Office, some eight hundred Germans have answered the call of recruiters and taken up arms in Syria and Iraq for Da'esh. Twenty-two violent German Salafists who are fighting in Syria hailed from Dinslaken-Lohberg alone.

By now, roughly one hundred of them are back in Germany. As a rule, those who end up in court don't talk. "But things are different with Nils D. – he's talking."[118] Nils D. claims to have been part of a special secret police unit within Da'esh, a unit with the responsibility to arrest dissidents and deserters. In some forty police interviews, he reported on torture, executions, and despotism, and how he regularly heard the prisoners' screams across the street from the jail. In short, he provided an insider's view on the gruesomeness of the paradise that is promised in propaganda videos.

Given the fact that the risk of dying in terrorist attacks is statistically so small in the West, while the fear of terrorism is so high, I join those who wonder. Some ask: What if the most significant source of terror in the world is the sovereign nation state and certain outgrowths of capitalism? John Scales Avery has been introduced earlier; he was part of a group that shared the 1995 Nobel Peace Prize for their work in organizing the Pugwash Conferences on Science and World Affairs. He writes: "Money from immensely rich corporate oligarchs buys the votes of politicians and the propaganda of the mainstream media. Numbed by the propaganda, citizens allow the politicians to vote for obscenely bloated military budgets, which further enrich the corporate oligarchs, and the circular flow continues."[119]

Industrial and colonial rivalry resulted in WWI, with its sequel WWII. Its awfulness motivated the world to become slightly more cautious, a caution, however, that was never fully followed through and that seems to dissolve ever more now. World War II was so terrible that the United Nations was set up to replace the rule of military force with a system of international law. The Nuremberg principles outlawed *crimes against peace*,[120] and Article 2 of the UN Charter requires that "All members shall refrain in their international relations from the threat or use of force against the territorial integrity or political independence of any state."[121]

What I see is that we need to urgently reinvigorate these historical moments now and refresh our memories of what they entailed. Therefore, I made an effort, in October 2015, to honor Justice Robert Jackson, the chief United States prosecutor at the Nuremberg Trials. I went to the private home in Fürth where he lived when he wrote is famous 1945 speech that lasted for several hours, a speech that deeply impressed the court and the public, and whose influence still reverberates today.[122]

Law is a mechanism for equality. Under law, the weak and the powerful are in principle equal. I often use the metaphor of traffic: As soon as there are traffic lights, small and big cars alike have to stop when it is red.[123] I resonate with John Scales Avery in lauding the United Nations for ending the era of colonialism, even if only "perhaps because of the balance of power between East and West during the Cold War."[124]

The United States had long been rather isolationist, not wanting to be drawn into European quarrels. In his farewell address on January 17, 1961, U.S. President Dwight David Eisenhower warned that the war-based economy that World War II had forced on his nation, was dangerous:

> We have been compelled to create an armaments industry of vast proportions.... This conjunction of an immense military establishment and a large arms industry is new in American experience. The total influence – economic, political, even spiritual – is felt in every city, every state house, every office in the Federal Government.... We must not fail to comprehend its grave implications. Our toil, resources and livelihood are all involved; so is the very structure of our society.... We must guard against the acquisition of unwarranted influence, whether sought or unsought, by the military-industrial complex. The potential for the disastrous rise of misplaced power exists and will persist. We must never let the weight of this combination endanger our democratic processes. We should take nothing for granted.[125]

Unfortunately, as soon as a military-industrial complex is in existence, as soon as it offers jobs and identity markers, it needs enemies to have a market. "Thus at the end of the Second World War, this vast power complex was faced with a crisis, but it was saved by the discovery of a new enemy "Communism ... now replaced by the 'War on Terror,'" writes Avery.[126] He highlights the unique position of the United States as the only large country whose economy did not lay in ruins in 1945, and how the country's economy's subsequent need for raw materials and markets drove the implementation of its roughly 1000 military bases in 150 countries and its interference in the internal affairs of many countries militarily or covertly.[127]

The memories of the awfulness of the World Wars kept the ideal of universal democracy alive until 1981. In that year, in the Summit of Cancun, American President Ronald Reagan, together with Prime Minister Margaret Thatcher of Britain, turned the clock back again.[128] America could have retreated into pre-WW II isolationism for safety, or embraced multilateralism, yet, now safety was sought in global supremacy.

When the Cold War ended with the collapse of the Soviet Union, a plan to secure the United States' eminent position in the world was outlined by the (now defunct) Project for a New American Century (PNAC), an organization created in 1997, many of whose founders became prominent members of America's Bush-Cheney administration.[129] Now known as the Foreign Policy Initiative and the Foundation for the Defense of Democracies, it became influential within the Obama-Biden administration: "Today, the U.S. government is taking actions that seem almost insane, risking a nuclear war with Russia and simultaneously alienating China."[130]

Andrew Bacevich, international relations scholar and Vietnam veteran, traces the military history of America's "permanent war" by going back to the times when American President Jimmy Carter had to concede that he had failed in convincing his Americans compatriots to let go of their sense of entitlement to limitless resources, to let go of their "conception of freedom based on expectations of more."[131] The Carter Doctrine focused instead on securing free access to oil, an argument that was still in use for the First Gulf War (1990 – 1991) led by the George H. W. Bush administration. Later, military efforts began to focus on terrorism, even though, so Bacevich, entities such as Da'esh lack significant military strength – they do not possess weapons of mass destruction, for example. Bacevich suspects that America's penchant on using military tools, by now, has cultural-psychological roots, which are regularly fired up by presidential elections. He sees it as an expression of the majority of Americans' being psychologically unprepared to let go of the ultimately self-defeating illusion of American exceptionalism and the belief that their military will bring "good into the world."[132] Bacevich recommends re-reading Reinhold Niebuhr (1892 – 1971). In 1952, when the United States had reached a peak in world power and influence, Niebuhr warned fellow Americans that "our dreams of managing history" is a source of potentially mortal danger.[133] Niebuhr was professor at the Union Theological Seminary for more than thirty years, and I think of him every year in December, as this seminary is just across the street from Teachers College of Columbia University where we have our annual Workshop on Transforming Humiliation and Violent Conflict.

The plan to secure America's place in the world seems to have been inspired by the old principle of *divide ut regnes* or *divide et impera* (divide and conquer). In the Middle East, division has now been achieved "by fanning the flames of the old sectarian conflict between Sunni Muslims and Shiite Muslims in order to overthrow unfriendly established governments and to disintegrate countries into smaller and more easily controlled parts, even though the human costs for the local populations are horrific."[134]

With what is called neocolonialism emerging, America became "great." Once great, the famous human trait of *loss aversion* kicked in and motivated those who had gained privileges to guard them.[135] Once powerful, the privileged are to be expected to create legitimacy for their own might-is-right strategies. They will find ways to manipulate the traffic lights to their advantage, so to speak. This is how the United States turned from a visionary supporter of the United Nations when they were created for the good of all humankind, into regarding the United Nations as a threat to American interests.

Philosopher Glen Martin highlights the link between "corporate imperialists" and their need to create a "stable investment climate" on one side, and on the other side their support for "brutal dictatorships in third-world countries."[136] From the corporate imperialists' point of view the current state of world affairs that involves "financial and economic warfare," is a success, not a failure. "It is only a failure from the point of view of democracy, morality, ecology, and other fundamental human values."[137] Martin characterizes the nation-state system as an inherently terrorist system and war system, for the past five centuries inherently structurally violent. Over the years, he taught me everything about the *Earth Charter*, and, in 2010, after reading my book *Gender, Humiliation, and Global Security*, he was kind enough to write me a long letter. He praised my words about love and "how love is not an emotion and not a good that descends on us from nowhere, but must become an institutionalized, culturalized, and personalized way of living on the Earth."[138] However, he closed his message by urging me to make clear in my future writing on humiliation and terrorism that the biggest source of terror in the world is the sovereign nation state and that private terrorism "is a drop in the bucket by comparison."[139]

By now, when the leaders of this world meet, they have to do so behind immense security fences. The 2010 G-20 Toronto summit for the discussion of the global financial system and the world economy, the fourth meeting of the G-20 heads of government, for instance, took place behind nearly four kilometers of two-meter high fencing surrounding the security zone at the Metro Toronto Convention Centre in Toronto, Ontario, Canada, in June 2010.

To conclude this chapter, in contexts of increasing fear, threat, risk, stress, and polarization, the human tendency to fall for biases is bound to intensify. The list of human biases that can send any situation into a downward spiral is long, ranging from *essentialization*, to *attribution error* (fundamental and ultimate), to *reactive devaluation*, or to *false polarization effect*.[140] Simplified, we tend to grant ourselves and members of our own group the benefit of the doubt, while we tend to assume the worst from members of other groups. We easily devalue positive behavior by out-group members, merely because they are out-group members. Reactive devaluation, for instance, means that any proposition for compromise that is put forward by an adversary is rejected, regardless of its usefulness, while the arguments of one's own group are regarded with sympathy, merely because they come from the own group.[141]

No wonder that humiliation entrepreneurship in the service of defending one's own personal territory and one's own in-group is on the rise by now. It is a self-centered way of dealing with the world and further intensifies the psychological biases that create precisely what is feared. All events are understood as either an appreciation for, or an attack against one's territory and identity, rather than considering that the world may also exist for other reasons than turning around "me."

The fight over the recognition or denial of the Armenian genocide may illustrate this predicament. Turkish patriots feel that their personal and national honor is being insulted by the suggestion that their country may have perpetrated a genocide. They require those suffering on the Armenian side to leave the past behind and understand that atrocities happen in all wars.[142] Those who suffer, on their part, feel doubly hurt, first through their forebears' pain, and, second, through seeing this pain being diminished and denigrated. And the world wonders. Turkey's struggle to keep a "clean reputation" creates the opposite, and it burdens the world with unresolved trauma. Turkish novelist Orhan Pamuk said this in his Nobel Lecture at the Swedish Academy in Stockholm in December 2006:

> What literature needs most to tell and investigate today are humanity's basic fears: the fear of being left outside, and the fear of counting for nothing, and the feelings of worthlessness that come with such fears; the collective humiliations, vulnerabilities, slights, grievances, sensitivities, and imagined insults, and the nationalist boasts and inflations that are their next of kin.[143]

In polarized contexts, spokespersons tend to decry the appalling behavior of others, those who perpetrate atrocities "in cold blood," implying that targeting innocent civilians is the other side's evil aim. "Look, how we are victimized by this unspeakable humiliation that cannot go unanswered, we have to stand strong and, if needed, retaliate!" is the message transmitted to the world by all sides.[144] At the same time, each side confirms that civilian casualties on the opposing side, though they may have come about by one's own actions, are unintended and unavoidable "side effects," mere collateral damage, something the opponent ought to understand and forgive. Alternatively, the fact that civilians were hit is being denied and covered up, or the civilians that were hit are re-defined as enemy combatants, or all people are declared to be combatants in a clash of civilizations.

Puzzled, imaginary onlookers from another galaxy will ask, "Don't these adversaries see that all human beings basically want to live in peace and quiet, have some reasonable quality of life and offer their children a future? Don't they see that their distorted mutual perceptions are their biggest enemy? Why don't they change their perceptions?"[145]

Chapter 15

Maintaining a Balance of Terror Is Costly

Thucydides was a historian and general who lived in Athens, Greece, circa 460 to 400 before the Common Era (BCE[1]). He has been introduced earlier in this book. Present-day political scientists and strategists speak of the *Thucydides trap* when they want to describe a situation where a new power rises and an already established powerful empire feels threatened. As a result, conflict and war can arise between the two, despite of all diplomatic efforts to avert it.[2]

Niccolo Machiavelli was an Italian Renaissance historian, politician, diplomat, philosopher, humanist, and writer. He has often been called the founder of modern political science. He lived in Florence, Italy, from 1469 to 1527 CE. He suggested that a leader (a "prince") cannot act like a private human being who is free to do good. In order to preserve the state, a leader might have to act against mercy, against faith, against humanity, against frankness, and against religion.[3]

Thomas Hobbes was the philosopher who laid the foundation of later Western political philosophy. He lived in England from 1588 to 1679. He did not have access to modern-day research and therefore committed what we call the *correspondence error* when he concluded that human nature is inherently violent, and that humans, if left to their own devices, will therefore always be in a constant state of "Warre." In his 1651 book *Leviathan*, he describes "life under conditions of anarchy" as "continual fear, and danger of violent death" where "the life of man [sic]" is "solitary, poor, nasty, brutish, and short."[4] Since this "state of nature" is such an utterly lawless state of affairs, it cannot be remedied by a social contract that is merely agreed upon by its users. In Hobbes's view only unlimited political authority, preferably absolute monarchy, is strong enough. Citizens should voluntarily bow to a strong hand.

Carl von Clausewitz was a Prussian general and military theorist who looked at the political aspects of war, and at their "moral" features (today, we would say psychological features). He was born in 1780 near Magdeburg, then Prussia, now Germany, and he died in 1831 in the very city where my mother was born, namely, Breslau, then Germany. In 1945, Breslau became part of Poland and got a new name, Wrocław. After WWII, the city was almost entirely emptied of its population – they were forcibly transported away, my mother among them – with new people moving in, populating the city.

Where do the elites we have today get their ideas from? This question is asked, for instance, by peace researcher Johan Galtung. This is his answer: "They picked Thucydides who told them that wars there will always be, then von Clausewitz who trivialized them, from Hobbes who told them that people are born violent and have to be controlled, and Machiavelli who told them that the prince has to be feared, not loved."[5]

To say it in the parlance of this book, as long as the security dilemma is strong, protecting power is the only path to survival. *War for peace* is the motto, and this means maintaining *a balance of terror*. The security dilemma acts as a selector of power-seeking people, and it amplifies power striving in people who might not be so inclined otherwise. As soon as power-seeking people have gained the upper hand in a competition for domination, they are likely to create narratives that justify why might is right, and they will institute strategies to maintain might. The fact that domination has no inbuilt endpoint will trap them in a race for ever more domination, a race that ultimately also affects their own mental health and ravages the socio- and ecospheres around them.

It is only when the security dilemma weakens, that this price no longer has to be paid. Only then can respect for equality in dignity move from an impractical ideal to a practical obligation.

At the present point in history, power seeking is still at work, only often more covertly than before. Since covert power-over strategies are much more sophisticated than overt ones, a high level of skillfulness is required to implement and maintain them. Historical sociologist Karl Polanyi spoke of the *double movement* that has been mentioned earlier in this book.[6] It is a double movement at best; at worst, it represents hypocritical double standards.

Covert strategies are also the most difficult to detect, expose, and contain for their victims. This is why an atmosphere of terror now seeps into even formerly insulated middle classes, no longer pinnable on single perpetrators, as it has become systemic and has its victims to become "believers," oblivious of the harm they do to themselves and others.[7]

Any power-over culture is harmful to its own players, be it overt or covert domination, including to the powerful dominators themselves. As alluded to earlier, to use the image of the human body, in a dominator society, elites are allowed to use their right arm to give orders, while their left arm, the one that stands for maintenance and care, is bound behind their backs. Their subordinates suffer the inverse infliction. None can use both arms; none can unfold their full potential. As long as power-over strategies are seen as legitimate, this mutilation is regarded as the price to be paid for security. This chapter focuses on describing this price.

Transcendence is being abused

Philosopher Karl Jaspers (1883 – 1969) teaches that philosophy has its origins in three sources, in awe and wonderment, in openness to doubt, and in *Grenzsituationen. Grenze* means border, limit, frontier; Grenzsituationen are fearful experiences in which familiar solutions no longer apply and a person is pushed to the limits of her being, as in near-death experiences. A lysis of the person's "superficial existence" may result, and the person may either react with denial and despair, or recover as a transformed being, with a new experience of transcendence.[8] As humans cannot avoid being exposed to crises – old age, sickness, and death, for instance, cannot be abolished – humans are thus inevitably led to such limits.

Cultural anthropologist Ernest Becker (1924 – 1974) observed that most human action aims at avoiding such lysis. For instance, we like to ignore the inevitability of death.[9] As antidote, people create a sense of worth for themselves, and many achieve this by identifying with their society's meaning systems. Societies create religious or secular cultural symbol systems, underpinned by laws, all of which provides meaning and offers transcendent immortality. Also works of art are created with the same aim.[10] Terror management theory, as part of social psychology, has already been introduced earlier, and it builds on Becker's insights.[11] From national identity to human superiority over animals, identification with country, lineage, or species, all these identifications are greater than the individual's own life.

In the context of a strong security dilemma, an experience of transcendence may lead men to agree to give their lives in war, to kill or die for the common good, writes Jaspers: "Men have, for example, risked their lives in a common struggle for a common life in the world. Solidarity was then the ultimate condition."[12] Author Ernst Jünger (1895 – 1998) brought the warrior's sense of worthiness to his readers in Germany in great intensity.[13] Being "male," for Jünger, was boldly and ruthlessly fighting on the front line, especially "man to man."[14]

Mark Twain (1835 – 1910) was prevented from publishing a short story in which he dared commit the sacrilege of criticizing what Jünger hails, namely, blind patriotic and religious fervor.[15] In his story, Twain lets young volunteers leave for battle at the beginning of the Civil War while a preacher asks God to "help them to crush the foe ... grant to them and their flag and country imperishable honor and glory." Then Twain lets a stranger enter, who points out that this prayer asks for cruelty and suffering to be brought to the world. This stranger violates the *Zeitgeist*, so to speak, he acts as a traitor, and the Zeitgeist "hits back" with its censorship.

Traitors are often seen as the worst enemies, because they threaten an established personal and cultural terror management from within. Since the security dilemma pushes for dualism rather than for complexity, an experience of transcendence may lead people to want to punish or even kill not just external enemies, but also defectors inside, those who betray their cultural worldview.

Similar dynamics may also lead young individuals into extremist action. Social psychologists and terrorism experts Clark McCauley and Sophia

Moskalenko sound like Jaspers when they describe the process of *unfreezing* that "occurs when an individual loses the everyday reassurance of relationships and routines: a parent dies, a romantic partner leaves, a job lost, a major illness strikes, or the individual moves far from home. Unfreezing is a personal crisis of disconnection, a Grenzsituation, which leaves an individual with less to lose, and into searching new directions."[16] McCauley and Moskalenko describe altogether six individual-level mechanisms that might lead a person into extremist violence: personal grievance, political grievance, slippery slope, risk and status seeking, and unfreezing.[17]

As a result of the "lysis" of unfreezing, young people move from "normality" into extremism. To use the language of the security dilemma, they move from a weaker to a stronger security dilemma framing of the world, and then they switch allegiance to the camp opposite to where they were before. They enter a world where extremism is normality, where a calcified dualistic mindset is the norm.

The downfall of the Ottoman Empire caused the entire Islamic world to *unfreeze*, one might say. Saïda Keller-Messahli could be described as a *cultural creative* within Islam. Paul Ray and Sherry Anderson's research has been mentioned before.[18] It differentiates between *traditionals*, *moderns*, and *cultural creatives*. Keller-Messahli grew up in a Muslim family in Tunisia and then came to Switzerland. She does not fight against Islam, she respects and honors this religion by advocating a progressive Islam. Her progressiveness is grounded in a deep understanding for the humiliation that inspires Islamic traditionals. We read on her website about the Ottoman Empire and how strong it initially was in its administrative and military capabilities, how it then was defeated by Western superiority, and how, in response, conservative Wahhabism arose on the Arabian Peninsula. Wahhabism saw the cause of the downfall in the peoples' neglect of the word of the Koran, and made it its mission to follow this word more closely.[19] While Keller-Messahli does not share this explanation of the downfall, she does also not use disparaging language to describe it; she uses empathic understanding as a springboard for progressive solutions. Keller-Messahli presumably will agree with calls to heed complexity, to avoid the simplification of blaming Wahhabism for terrorism,[20] yet, at the same time she also warns against its political use.[21]

Political scientist Mohammad-Mahmoud Ould Mohamedou inspires with a secular understanding of Al-Qaeda as a political rather than a religious project; he warns against dismissing Al-Qaeda as illogical and irrational and advises to engage it with arguments in a serious way.[22] We could add that also Da'esh appears to be far from irrational. In all those movements, we see what could be called moderns at work, who use very rational tools to exploit irrationality, for instance, in vulnerable adolescents. In Western countries, data analysts harvest relevant data from social platforms to use psychometrics to mobilize voters, so do Da'esh's recruiters.[23]

The significant fault line runs between traditionals and the rest, between those who look back and those who look ahead, and this is observable everywhere on the globe, irrespective of religion. In the American presidential race that unfolded while I wrote these lines at the end of 2016, the same mindset was amply played out. Many Trump supporters feel they are the only true believers, in contrast to others in the Republican Party who are just pretenders and therefore as bad as Bernie Sanders, or worse. Education expert Amra Sabic-El-Rayess offers a comparison:

> Salafis do not see Muslims as a single phalanx of religious belief and action. To Salafis, theirs is the only one true Islam; all other Muslims are pretenders. The differences between Salafis and other Muslims are clearer to Salafis than the political differences between Donald Trump and Bernie Sanders are to us.[24]

The primary fault line runs between traditionals, those who, when they lose faith in the moderns' elites, seek refuge in the mindset of a strong security dilemma, versus the cultural creatives, who attempt to transcend the security dilemma altogether. I myself grew up in a family in Europe that followed the same path after Europe's downfall after WWII, in their case the context was

Christianity. While many in my family have joined the traditionals, I have chosen to become part of the cultural creatives, thus in many ways coming closer to Muslim Keller-Messahli than to my own Christian family.

As noted before, Saïda Keller-Messahli refrains from using disparaging language to describe traditionalist deliberations; she uses empathic understanding as a foundation for progressive ways out. Traditionals, on their part, by their very rhetoric, risk stoking the security dilemma back into dangerous action:

> Eventually, Salafis fracture population. This is a tipping point in their radicalization effort. It destabilizes regions and devalues billions of dollars we invest to build socially cohesive nations. Our response to them is an engineered military attack, but that alone, without a more adept strategy to re-capture radicalized youths around the globe, only pushes these at-risk populations to societal peripheries where Salafis wait to embrace them.[25]

As psychologist Peter Coleman would express it: In conflict situations, an *interpersonal* or *intergroup attractor* promotes a *social judgment attractor*, which then reinforces the interpersonal attractor in a reciprocal mutually reinforcing feedback loop.[26] *Legitimizing myths* underpin this dynamic,[27] often entailing a *chosen trauma*.[28] Traditions are then maintained that keep the trauma alive, together with the dualism it engenders. The Orange walks, for instance, are parades held annually in Northern Ireland, Scotland, occasionally in England and throughout the Commonwealth, honoring Prince William of Orange's victory over King James II at the Battle of the Boyne in 1690. Those who attend these parades see them as vital, while Catholics, Irish Nationalists, Scottish Nationalists, and those on the political left feel that these parades as sectarian and triumphalist.

Also in Germany, with its history of a Nazi culture of *Blut und Ehre* (blood and honor), this mindset is still virulent in contemporary society.[29] This became apparent in the National Socialist Underground (NSU) scandal in 2011. Beginning in the year 2000, the right-wing extremist NSU group carried out a number of terrorist murders all over Germany, mostly on Germans who had a background from Turkey. The German police, however, failed to even consider right-wing hatred of foreigners as a motive for these murders. Ample evidence was available, but if failed to let the police search for the murderers in the right-wing milieu. Instead, the police suspected the victims' families of having caused these murders themselves, for instance, through Mafia-like affiliations, which, however, did not exist.[30] In this way, the police replicated the murderers' enemy image.

Now comes the question. What can be done? What can be done in a situation, where the mindset of a strong security dilemma is so deeply entrenched? Where a *balance of terror* provides so important a sense of sublime transcendence? It offers elites privileges and it is what is familiar. Therefore, many wish to preserve it even when the overall context no longer calls for it. This is the state of affairs in the world now: In an interconnected world, the security dilemma has a chance to attenuate, humankind could exit from the mindset of the security dilemma, yet, it does not.

In this situation, unfreezing may even be desirable, yet, in the inverse direction. This is what "democratic socialist" candidate Bernie Sanders attempted to do. Unfreezing would be the precondition for moving people's hearts and minds from a calcified dualistic mindset toward a more flexible peace-inducing mindset, toward an understanding that the appropriate expression of Jaspers' transcendence and Becker's sense of meaning and immortality is now to be found in Gandhi or Mandela and no longer in Clausewitz.

Can such unfreezing happen? Yes. It does not help, however, to simply present the arguments enumerated here to people who believe otherwise, particularly during conflict, as they will simply filter out any information that does not fit their beliefs. A *paradoxical thinking* intervention may have better chances. It means introducing information that is consistent with their beliefs, however, exaggerating it to the point that the absurdity of their stance becomes self-evident[31]: Will we become richer "on a burning planet"? No, is the warning from environmentalist Jakob von Uexküll.[32]

Also empathy can have a constructive unfreezing effect, as has been seen in the refugee crisis that unfolded in 2015 and 2016. A little boy lying dead on the beach touched hearts.[33] This is not to deny that empathy can also serve the opposite, namely, the dualistic mindset. Psychologists John "Bruce" Jessen and James Elmer Mitchell have been mentioned many times in this book. Certainly they used empathy, or at least their ability for perspective-taking, to refine their "enhanced interrogation techniques" on terrorist suspects: They put themselves into the shoes of suspects to find ever more "effective" ways to force them to offer information, and they did so driven by their empathy for their own people and their wish to protect them. Just as in the case of the German police also they fell prey to fictitious suspicions: Abu Zubaydah, a Saudi citizen, was the first prisoner to undergo "enhanced interrogation techniques," and he was tortured "for nothing," since his torturers had misjudged his access to information.[34]

To conclude this sub-section, what we learn is that a strong security dilemma is an undeniable threat in a world that is divided, a threat that cannot be wished away. When young *caring-compelled individuals* as Clark McCauley calls them, "strongly feel the suffering of others and feel a personal responsibility to reduce or avenge this suffering,"[35] then they look into the face of the tragedy of the security dilemma. They experience what Jaspers calls transcendence when they stand up to its full cruelty. They overcome selfish desires to preserve their own lives and become willing to sacrifice themselves for their own people. This is what gives the warrior script and honorable heroism such significance. It can give great satisfaction to fight in a war deemed to be just. And this motivation can be the same for young American marines[36] as for young Caliphate defenders. Part of the attraction is that such a warrior does not need to struggle with moral dilemmas. A clear white and black world of friend and enemy spares him the cumbersome experience of dissonance in complexity.[37]

Not least the present-day American gun lobby follows this script. Its supporters would never regard themselves as perpetrators. They depend on the *correspondence error* that indicates: "Because I suffer, you are an evil person. You deserve my hatred. It is not enough that I stop at prudent self-defense or waste time on empathizing with you, or on questioning my own behavior, you simply deserve that I destroy you." What is avoided is any second thought – for instance, that both may be suffering, or that both could be far from evil persons. The perpetrator may just be a poor deranged soul, for instance, yet, he will be amplified into a worthy enemy. The worthier the enemy, the more significant the opportunity for heroism.

Only in the context of a weaker security dilemma culture is it possible to think in terms of complexity and moral dilemma rather than evil/good. While Germany's perpetrator history has spawned a tacit acceptance of right-wing ideology as "normality" among the police forces, it has also inspired authors and playwrights to "train" their audiences in complexity. German television crime series such as *Tatort, Soko 110, Rosa Rot, Derrick* or *Der Kriminalist*,[38] for instance, provide descriptions of moral dilemmas and how they can nudge "good" people to behave "badly."[39] Many German crime series basically recount the famous Milgram experiment as it plays out in real life: how a context can make people who are not evil become perpetrators of evil.[40]

Peace activists often denigrate the sense of transcendence that is derivable from sacrifice in war and violence. Yet, if terrorism is to be addressed, and dignity nurtured, also peace activists themselves have to overcome the culture of indignation and denigration. The radical empathy and respect to which a previous chapter was dedicated, is required. The fact that *understanding* is different from *condoning* needs to be remembered. The wish to have arenas for heroism is a wish that remains comprehensible, notwithstanding the fact that this wish's fulfillment may be utterly misdirected. This wish can be comprehended while not condoned. As long as the world was divided, condoning it could be lifesaving; in an interconnected world, however, this is no longer the case. Now, a culture of heroism, if it is allowed to live on, risks leading to all-out collective suicide.[41] This culture, instead of being idolized or demonized, by now needs to be mourned as a grave damage that the security dilemma caused to the human psyche:

When transcendence means accepting dying and killing, this is tragic. The burden of guilt for this tragedy should not be "privatized." Its mindset should not be denigrated as the moral failure of individuals (even though, clearly this will also be the case in certain instances).[42]

What is therefore alarming is that this culture lives on even among revolutionaries who profess wanting to overcome it, including terrorists and counterterrorists. Terror, by its nature, resonates with the warrior script. The German Red Army Faction (RAF), particularly its tyrannical leader Andreas Baader, almost wallowed in the warrior script of macho maleness. He threw his weight around and terrorized and humiliated his own followers as well as his enemies in the name of liberation.[43] His entire mode of life contradicted the ideals he supposedly fought for. Terrorist expert Peter Neumann believes that Baader would have been an ideal candidate for Da'esh.[44] A slogan of the student protest movement in Germany, the *68er-Bewegung* (movement of 1968) typifies the idolization of this macho culture: "Wer zweimal mit derselben pennt, gehört schon zum Establishment" (having sex with the same woman more than twice, means that you are part of the establishment).

Peace activist and psychoanalyst Horst-Eberhard Richter (1923 – 2011) engaged in deep conversations with Birgit Hogefeld (born 1956), a former RAF member. His analysis is that RAF terrorism in Germany began as a reaction against the traumas of the parent generation. At some point, however, the movement split into peaceful reformers and violent revolutionaries. Richter tried in vain to warn them that violence would destroy the very humanity they aimed to save. Yet, the hardliners were no longer reachable. What they had done, to say it in the language of Richter's psychoanalysis, was to relinquish their superego to absolute obedience, in return for the group rewarding them with the award of a fictitious self-aggrandizement, supported by aggressive defense against their own enormous fears. Richter called it *delusional self-alienation*.[45]

Sending weapons to Nicaragua to help them create a peaceful and just country was a matter of pride for these revolutionaries. Reports were being suppressed – allegedly to "protect" the revolution – that "revolutionary commandantes," as they called themselves, sexually abused women, including Western women who came as helpers. Commandantes saw it as the duty of girls to serve them as sex objects in the name of the revolution. Naïve and idealistic women from Europe were especially willing self-humiliators.[46]

Examples of such "halfway" liberations expose the depth of the damage of the security dilemma, they expose to which degree its culture became embedded in the human psyche. As a result, even those who engage in revolution against this culture are at risk to use its very mindsets and methods in the process.

Life is being disrespected

The degradation and loss of life, including civilian life, is seen as no problem by a society steeped in the Hitler way to peace, not in times of war and not in times of peace. Examples abound. Many American pioneers, for instance, behaved like warriors. Their names became synonymous with the American dream for wealth and power as much as for unscrupulousness. Henry Ford may initially have intended to treat his workers well, yet, eventually, his factories meant life in a dictatorship, even including secret police.[47] Another of these pioneers was John D. Rockefeller, who created an oil empire, not least by driving competitors into ruin. At the same time, he would be sweeping the church on Sundays. Among the pioneers of America's entrepreneurs was also J. P. Morgan, founder of the largest stock company in the world, large enough to save the United States from bankruptcy. Also he followed the warrior script without scruples and landed in court due to questionable financial transactions. Until his death in 1913, Morgan expanded its business activities continuously like an ancient emperor, a strategy that is still popular among business corporations today.[48]

In war, not only are non-civilian lives lost. Also civilian lives are often treated as dispensable. Japan's Supreme Council for the Direction of the War (also known as the Big Six) was in power in 1945 when nuclear bombs were thrown on Japan. This council had a war faction and a peace faction.

Predictably, the war faction was not moved to surrender by the loss of life through the atomic bombs, even not after the second atomic bomb on Nagasaki that vaporized 40,000 people instantly. However, neither the peace faction was moved by loss of life.[49] It seems that it was rather the unexpected advance of Soviet troops, and the fear that they would be less sympathetic to preserving the emperor than the Americans, that motivated them to suggest ending the carnage through surrender rather than fighting on to the last man.[50] The Japanese' highest aim was to protect their core identity, the institution of the emperor, at any cost. *Hakko ichiu* is a philosophy that indicates that the emperor is at the center of the Japanese world.

Protecting it was also the motivation for Japan's militarists when they first aimed at territorial expansion. When I lived in Japan, I attempted to deeply understand this meaning system, among others, by visiting the controversial Yasukuni Shrine, built in the nineteenth century to honor those who died on behalf of the emperor.

Also the United States' prime motivations ran in similar lines. Also their aim was to secure their sphere of influence, rather than saving human lives. The second bomb on Nagasaki, for instance, may have been a signal aimed at the Soviet Union, a signal of American strength, rather than a signal aimed at Japan, or a way to save American lives.[51]

Ecocide *is being committed*

The Plundered Planet is the title of the latest report to the Club of Rome, submitted in 2013.[52] The author is the Italian physicist at the University of Florence, Ugo Bardi. He posits that the present massive exploitation of the last natural resources is a dead-end. Fracking is a sad symbol of desperation: "… it is an impotent attempt to keep going at all costs, even though you know exactly: it's a dead end."[53]

Several letters, emails, and other messages reach me each day that decry the plundering of the planet. I could fill an entire book with these messages every day. Let me mention very few recent voices. The *Chatham Report 2012* has analyzed the latest global trends of key raw materials and found how governments and other stakeholders are worsening the situation rather than bettering it, both through defensive and offensive moves, namely, by "creating new fault lines on top of existing weaknesses and uncertainties."[54] In May 2014, two teams of scientists reported that the Thwaites Glacier, a keystone holding the massive West Antarctic Ice Sheet together, is starting to collapse; in the long run, so much melting water will be released that sea levels rise by more than three meters.[55] In 2016, it became clear that perilous climate shift will happen within decades, not centuries.[56] "Among many climate scientists, gloom has set in. Things are worse than we think, but they can't really talk about it."[57]

The 2017 Doomsday clock is at two and a half minutes to midnight, back to where it was when I was born six decades ago at the height of the nuclear confrontation between Eastern and Western Bloc.[58] The 2016 Doomsday clock was still at three minutes to midnight because the diplomatic successes on Iran and in Paris in 2015 had been offset "by negative events in the nuclear and climate arenas," so that "the Doomsday Clock must remain at three minutes to midnight, the closest they've been to catastrophe since the early days of above-ground hydrogen bomb testing."[59]

"Food Is the New Oil; Land, the New Gold," is a telling title, pointing at the fact that also earlier civilizations have declined as a result of environmental overstretch – the Sumerians were brought down by rising salt levels in the soil, and the Mayans by soil erosion.[60] In our time, several such overstretches combine – the most severe soil erosion in human history,[61] with 800 million people chronically undernourished due to land degradation,[62] the depletion of aquifers, the plateauing of grain yields in the more agriculturally advanced countries, and rising temperature.

Not only food, also water is the new gold. Access to clean water and adequate sanitation is a human right. Yet, "each year 1.7 million people die as a result of poor access to water and sanitation services. Half of the world's hospital beds are occupied with people suffering from diseases related to dirty water."[63] Extractive capitalism dominates wherever we look.[64]

Stephen Purdey, international relations specialist and research affiliate of the Waterloo Institute for Complexity and Innovation at the University of Waterloo in Ontario, Canada, summarizes:

> Climate change is the biggest but only one entry in what Herman Greene calls a "parade of horribles." There's no need to list population increase, soil degradation, loss of fresh water, deforestation, ocean acidification, species extermination and so forth. The point is that humanity is rushing headlong into tremendous socio-ecological turbulence which may or may not be survivable. These are not avoidable fictions.[65]

What I observe, personally, on all continents, without exception, and despite of extremely courageous counter-initiatives, is that the exploitation of nature is being intensified in ways that are so ruthless that I wonder about the exploiters themselves and what they think of their own children. I am not afraid for myself, and I have no children, and I perfectly understand that those who live in social bubbles, particularly in bubbles of classist privilege, will be psychologically handicapped.[66] Still, to me, and to most others, it is evident that the exploiters sacrifice not just the future of some far removed generations on far removed continents, they sacrifice also their own children's future. I do know some of the wealthy of this planet personally, and I am flabbergasted to see that many of them seem to believe that protected enclaves will wait for them when the rest of the ecosphere goes down. They seem to be unaware that it is not sufficient to build gated fortress-communities or to construct one's villas on isolated luxury islands such as tiny Maui, where the number of art galleries matches New York. What is needed instead is a movement of "openhearted wealthy people" who "understand that their genuine self-interest is inextricably linked to the rest of humanity and our ability to fix the future."[67]

Yet, what awes me most is that we, as humankind, let this happen. That we are willing to gamble away our last chances for a turn-around for the illusions of a few elites. This, to me, is self-inflicted collective terror.

Arne Næss, the "father of deep ecology," was also a founding pillar of the Human Dignity and Humiliation Studies fellowship of which I am the founding president. Polly Higgins held the Arne Næss Chair at the University of Oslo in Norway for 2013 and 2014. She speaks about *leadership crime* and *ecocide law*: "When leaders fail to act or make decisions that lead to mass damage and destruction, that surely can only be called a crime."[68]

Power is being displayed too casually

Present-day readiness to disregard human life and degrade the natural environment illustrates the damage the security dilemma has inflicted on the human psyche. Another example is "too casually displayed power." Sam Engelstad was the UN's Chief of Humanitarian Affairs, and on several occasions Acting Humanitarian Coordinator in Mogadishu, Somalia, in 1994. On December 9, 1992, the United States led Operation Restore Hope in Somalia, a country ravaged by civil war, with many people dying from hunger. The goal was to calm the situation so that much needed food supplies could reach the southern part of the country. However, like the interventions that preceded it, also this one failed. In 1993, an angry crowd dragged a dead American soldier through the streets of Mogadishu.[69] In other words, the offer of help to an impoverished and ravaged country, Somalia, was responded to with acts of humiliation perpetrated against the helpers. Engelstad wrote to me (I quote with his permission):

> During my time in Somalia in 1994, humiliation was never far from the surface. Indeed, it pretty much suffused the relationship between members of the UN community and the general Somali population. In the day-to-day interaction between the Somalis and UN relief workers like ourselves, it enveloped our work like a grey cloud. Yet, the process was not well understood, and rarely intended to be malevolent.[70]

Engelstad added that, "Among the political and administrative leadership of the UN mission, however, humiliation and its consequences were far better understood and were frequently used as policy tools. Regardless of intent, it was pernicious and offensive to many of us."

Friends of Israel have shared an account of a young Israeli soldier with me where he describes how he was initiated into the casual display of power. I cannot disclose the source. His account went roughly like that:

> The first week, it was the first time for me at a checkpoint. Suddenly, the soldier on duty with me screams "stop" in Arabic. But the man in the line has not completely understood and takes one more step. The soldier screams again and the man's movements freeze in fear. My colleague decides that because the man went an extra step, he must be apprehended. I ask him: "What are you doing?" "Do not argue," he replies. "At least do not argue in front of them, because then I cannot trust you anymore. You are not reliable."
>
> After a while, a patrol leader came by and I asked him how long we should detain the man. "Listen," he said, "you can do whatever you want, whatever you feel for, if you feel there is a problem with the man, you can detain him as long as you want."
>
> I have experienced that soldiers stopped Palestinian cars, ordered the driver out and asked him to take off all four wheels, only to then confiscate the car keys. Just to humiliate. All car keys hanging from hooks on the board are keys that soldiers have confiscated from Palestinian drivers. Maybe they were out driving while it was curfew. Maybe they did something that irritated a soldier. The keys were never returned. It is not written anywhere that we should humiliate Palestinians. We learn it not in the courses either. But, still, it is part of the culture that evolves.

It was Boutros Boutros-Ghali, Secretary-General of the United Nations from 1992 to 1996, who authorized the UN intervention in Somalia in 1992 on U.S. request and under U.S. military leadership. Initially, there was worldwide support for the intervention. The *solidarist international responsibility* of state leaders was felt strongly.[71] However, this changed when images of dead American soldiers being dragged through the streets of Mogadishu threw into stark doubt whether all humans indeed belong to one family. The boundaries between "Americans" and "foreigners" became salient, together with a national or pluralist commitment. The protection of American lives and interests moved to the forefront, and during the electoral campaign for the 1996 U.S. presidential election, Boutros Ghali became the scapegoat. The "Somalia disaster" thus impacted everything, from affect, to empathy, and moral beliefs of what was considered good, appropriate, and deserving of praise, and of what a U.S. government's primary responsibility as a moral actor was supposed to be.

The difficult relationship between pluralist and solidarist commitments is built into the core of the United Nations Security Council. It places the responsibility for international peace and security into the hands of state leaders who are not elected for that purpose. They are elected for protecting the lives and promote the interests of their own populations.

When the genocidal killing began in 1994 in Rwanda, the experience in Somalia was the very stumbling block that stood in the way of help. "No other Somalia" was the warning call that obstructed U.S. and UN willingness to intervene. American President Bill Clinton later apologized to genocide survivors in Rwanda, and, by doing so, moved the balance back to the solidarist notion of moral responsibility, later being expanded into the global political commitment of the Responsibility to Protect (R2P or RtoP).[72]

However, the question remains: If interventions are to be envisioned at all, what would be a productive intervention and what an unproductive one? Is relying on military force enough? What about Sam Engelstad's insights? What about understanding the complexity of the situation and addressing the root causes? Political scientist Hussein Solomon asks this question in his book on terrorism and counterterrorism in Africa.[73] Seventy percent of the Islamists of Al-Shabaab in Somalia, for instance, hail from the Rahanweyn clan;[74] Boko Haram in Nigeria can also be seen in the light of Hausa-Fulani nationalism; the Islamists of Ansar Dine in Mali are of Tuareg origin.[75] In other words, all hail from aggrieved communities who carry experiences of humiliation. Solomon concludes that heavy-handed counterterrorism programs that rely on military and repressive tactics may only exacerbate the problem of alienation and make those who are politically and economically disenfranchised even more vulnerable to being recruited into terrorist organizations.

Necessary fear is being bypassed

Another of the damages caused by the security dilemma and the vision of peace that it pushes to the forefront is a hazardous bypassing of fear. From the use of nuclear power to the application of terror, necessary fear is denigrated as "female sissiness," which one has to be ashamed of. In many public debates about climate change, mainstream economists downplay the need for caution and predict a future with infinitely continued economic growth. Feminist theorist Julie Nelson describes how "highly gendered, sexist, and ageist attitudes" underlie this dominant advice through "highlighting the roles of binary metaphors and cultural archetypes":

> Gung-ho economic growth advocates aspire to the role of The Hero, rejecting the conservatism of The Old Wife. But in a world that is not actually as safe and predictable as they assume, the result is guidance from The Fool. Both intellectual and cultural change are necessary if the voice of The Wise Grandmother (which may come through women or men) is to – alongside The Hero – receive the attention it deserves.[76]

Psychologist Thomas Scheff has identified *bypassed shame* – shame that is not acknowledged – as the motor of violence and the source of *humiliated fury* (a term coined by psychologist Helen Block Lewis[77]).[78] In other words, The Fool, rather than turning to wisdom, gets angry when confronted with his foolishness.

Gambling with fate and trusting in providence is one way to override fear. Otto von Bismarck (1815 – 1898) is known as the "Iron Chancellor" and founder of the German Empire in 1871, and he is still regarded by many as Germany's most important statesman. Recent books and documentaries, however, paint a different picture. Not only did Bismarck design a system of contradictory alliances, worse, he also was quite an opportunists and gambler.[79] He went to duel for honor, putting his faith in providence's protection.[80] In other words, just like Adolf Hitler later, he felt that providence should guide and protect him while he gambled with fate. For author Johannes Willms, Bismarck is co-responsible for the catastrophic development of the First World War and the subsequent Nazi dictatorship.[81]

Franz Josef Strauss (1915 – 1988) from Bavaria was the German defense minister from 1956 to 1962. He played to the Bavarian culture of maleness in all his actions, and this included enthusiasm for the "ultimate nuclear weapon." Since Germany's population was tired of war, he pushed the German electricity industry to build nuclear power plants, so as to increase German expertise in this area and make nuclear weapons more acceptable.[82] The nuclear power plant in Grohnde, circa fifteen kilometers away from where I write these lines just now in the house of my parents, is operational since 1984, against the resistance of the local inhabitants. It is one of the nine nuclear power plants that are currently still operating in Germany. Residents now call for the immediate shutdown of the reactor. The reasons are growing security threats which the plant is not designed to withstand, such as potential earthquakes, technical weaknesses, and, not least, terrorist attacks.[83] Franz Josef Strauss, were he still alive, would be astonished to see how his enthusiastic push to bring nuclear power to Germany now backfires. Terrorists do not need the detour of creating an expensive military industry for themselves when they can turn their enemies' peaceful power plants into weapons directly.

Russia's radionuclides are another of myriad examples. Russia used radionuclide generators for its unmanned lighthouses in Siberia. Many of these generators, however, have since disappeared. Norway, Finland, and the United States have paid for the recovery of this contaminated material, as they fear that they might fall into the hands of terrorists and be used for "dirty bombs."[84]

Also I bypass fear to be able to do my dignity work, yet, I do not do so hazardously. If Nelson Mandela had given in to fear, he would never have achieved what he did. I do what philosopher Kwame Anthony Appiah calls for in his book on honor[85]: I work for a future where humankind, as Appiah suggests, will regard practices such as the devastation of the environment or the shredding of the social fabric as similarly dishonorable as slavery or foot binding. I bypass my fear when I stand up in the face of arguments that justify such practices. I stand up when I am confronted with suggestions that such practices represent sacred traditions, or that human nature makes them unavoidable or necessary. I stand up lovingly, because I am aware that it often is ignorance that feeds such arguments. I know only too well about *strategic ignorance* – I call it *Zweckdummheit*, meaning purposeful stupidity.[86] I meet it often, particularly when people indulge in consumerism without questioning its social and ecological "externalities."

When I suggest alternative visions of how humankind could arrange its affairs on this planet, I often encounter the same accusation of "sissiness" that also others like me face. Sometimes this denigration is thrown at me openly, sometimes it is wrapped carefully. The covert way is illustrated well in a BBC television program, where a young woman who develops urban farming in Brooklyn, New York,[87] is treated in this way.[88] A journalist, a young man, first admires her work and then says to her: "You are a charity, because you have also educational activities. But, you are also a hard-nosed business, aren't you!?" She responds: "Yes, we wish to create jobs!"[89] What we have here is somebody, a young woman, whose work is embedded in the paradigm of protecting the ecological and social fabric of this world, and then we have a young man who functions within the "male" paradigm of competition, from where maintenance for its own sake is "female" "soft-nosed." "Job creation" is the bridge that connects both; she uses this bridge and he accepts it. At the same time, both overlook the fact that also "jobs," or selling goods or services for livelihood, is part of economic arrangements that might well turn out to be infeasible if we want to create a dignified future.[90]

I deeply resonate with Catherine Odora Hoppers' mission in South Africa to introduce Indigenous Knowledge Systems into universities. She observes how cultural violence is used to legitimize acts of direct and structural violence and render them acceptable in society. This manipulation is achieved, she notes, by "changing the moral color of an act from wrong to right or to some other intermediate meaning palatable to the status quo," and "by making reality opaque, so that we do not see the violent act or fact, or that when we see it, we see it not as violent."[91]

Psychologist Arie Nadler would call what Odora Hoppers describes *safe harm*. Safe harm is a strategy to keep people who are oppressed away from making this oppression open.[92] The safe harm strategy is at the core of bullying relations.[93] Safe harm means that a perpetrator and his associates first create a power difference, then they "inform" their victims of this fact, telling them that they will "risk" harming themselves if they do not submit. No direct threats are issued, a seemingly "neutral" piece of information conceals the threat, and the sender can even assert, with good conscience, that she is merely stating facts and distributing good advice. During apartheid in South Africa, this was precisely the way social structures kept the conflict between the oppressed and oppressors conflict latent.[94]

Orwellian doublespeak is another well-used path to manipulate fear in ways so sophisticated that society as a whole can be cowed. Orwellian doublespeak hides double standards and camouflages "great evil" under "a little good."[95] Successes in attaining Millennium Development Goals, for instance, are being hailed, achievements in alleviating poverty praised.[96] Yet, one may ask: Where is the success in rescuing some from drowning in the short term, with methods that risk drowning all in the longer term? When those who allow inequality to rise hide behind successes in alleviating poverty, it means covering up a great evil with a little good. Even if global equality were to be achieved with such methods, and the rise of inequality stemmed in the short term by economic growth, planet Earth's resources would not allow for this strategy. Earth's resources cannot be plundered beyond their availability infinitely. Throwing a party is different from a long-term strategy.

This is a gigantic global conflict that is kept latent, while necessary fear is declared irrelevant.

People become helpless marionettes

In the context of a strong security dilemma, there are two kinds of "enemies," the respected ones, who are a match for males, and the vermin that must preferably be "cleaned off" by women.[97] Heinrich Himmler has, as mentioned earlier, attempted to convince his SS men to kill Jews, even though, as he made clear, he was aware that cleaning up dirt was not an honorable task for men. He defined it to be the highest form of bravery to preserve male honor while engaging in lowly female cleaning.[98] The message of the second speech that Himmler held to high ranking Nazi leaders, or Gauleiter, on October 6, 1943, in Posen, was as follows: Admittedly, killing Jews is a horribly dishonorable job, yet, as it is necessary, future generations will be thankful.[99]

In an interview, scholar and social critic Noam Chomsky reported how he was appalled by Japan's vicious crimes in Manchuria and China the 1930s.[100] Yet, later, in the early 1940s, as a young teenager, he was equally appalled by the anti-Japanese propaganda in America: "The Germans were evil, but treated with some respect: They were, after all, blond Aryan types, just like our imaginary self-image. Japanese were mere vermin, to be crushed like ants. Enough was reported about the firebombing of cities in Japan to recognize that major war crimes were underway, worse in many ways than the atom bombs."[101]

Jews and Japanese were not regarded as "real men," no real matches for honorable males, thus, they were no worthy enemies. Not just Jews and Japanese have been affected in this way, and still are. In many ways, all men are affected, because worse than failing to be a "real man" is becoming "a woman": "don't be a girl!" This is why conscientious objectors have been denigrated as sissies[102]: An objector is seen as an otherwise able man who betrays his manhood by voluntarily choosing to be "soft," "cowardly," in short, a female "sissy."

Yet, the situation may be even more complicated. Perhaps all men are "sissies" per definition, simply because fear is human. The ideal of heroic manhood is humanely unattainable – perhaps attainable only for robots. It must therefore be suspected that many males in this world suffer from their own ideal of manhood. It may well be that also a Richard "Dick" Cheney, George W. Bush, or Donald Rumsfeld were not completely convinced of their own manhood and compensated for their own doubts by way of "hyper-maleness."[103] From my years as a clinical psychologist, I know men who are afraid of being "sissies," and who are ashamed of themselves. As they shared with me, it was difficult for them to face their nagging suspicion that they may fail manhood, so they chose to rather project their self-disgust onto others. They bypassed their shame and projected it onto others, who thereafter no longer were respectable enemies but the very same unmanly creatures they feared themselves to be.[104] The claim that terrorists are cowards, even if they display considerable courage, may stem from this dynamic. After terror attacks, the routine reaction of state leaders is to "condemn" the attack and declare the perpetrators to be "cowardly" people: as if terror attacks by non-cowards would be more acceptable. How come that disgust over unmanliness can outshine due acknowledgment of enmity and crowd out sorrow over lost lives?

In this context, the belief in American exceptionalism and the turn to "enhanced interrogation techniques" may become more comprehensible. The Survival, Evasion, Resistance, and Escape program, short SERE, was established by the U.S. Air Force at the end of the Korean War (1950 – 1953) for those at high risk to be captured by the enemy. To train them for the worst-case scenario, for when they would be captured, they were subjected to mock interrogations by their own people – interrogations fashioned on those the Communist Chinese had used against American servicemen during the Korean War. The program provided training in evading capture, survival skills, and the military code of conduct: "I will never forget that I am an American, fighting for freedom, responsible for my actions, and dedicated to the principles which made my country free. I will trust in my God and in the United States of America."[105] It was in this context that "gloves off" torture of enemies became a patriotic duty. Wider societal acceptance came from fictional characters in American television series such as Jack Bauer.[106] Torture causes Jack Bauer angst, yet, "it is always the patriotic thing to do."[107] In other words, the figure of Jack Bauer taught his viewers acceptance of torture as unavoidable price to be paid for national security, obfuscating alternative paths toward that goal, and making them "helpless" to seek such alternative paths. What torture aims at is to engender a sense of helplessness in its victims. The tutoring by Jack Bauer brought an entire population into helplessness, not just the suspected terrorists who were subjected to brutal interrogation techniques.

Training in helplessness as the one provided by Jack Bauer, clearly, needs a breeding ground to become virulent. Trauma is a breeding ground, particularly transgenerational trauma that affects entire populations.[108] Trauma leads to the very tunnel vision that is at the core of the universe of honor, in contrast to a universe of dialogue in complexity. The United States of America are a relevant case. Through my clinical practice, I have met many Americans and had the opportunity to deeply understand the trauma that has been transmitted from generation to generation, and I do not speak of African-Americans. I speak of white Americans of European descent with traumatic family stories hidden behind the glorification of American bravery.[109]

In Europe, I have seen similar traumas among displaced people, my family is one of them. I have seen how displaced people become susceptible to being recruited into sects. After losing their previous anchorings, they find new homes in sects. They even accept if this new home is full of internal psychological violence.[110] Many in my family, for instance, joined the Jehovah's Witness sect. Approximately 1,000 sectarian groups exist in Germany, and they have had many recruits when millions of displaced people flooded into Germany after WWII.

Sociologist Lewis Coser speaks of "greedy institutions" or "possessive institutions."[111] These are institutions that place all-encompassing demands on their members and seek their exclusive, undivided loyalty. They do not achieve this by force; rather, they hijack people's entire personality, thereby gaining their unanimous approval and compliance.

Colonia Dignidad in Chile provides an extreme illustration. The Colonia Dignidad example also demonstrates how people in power will support each other: the regime of Chilean dictator Pinochet had his dissidents be tortured in Colonia Dignidad.[112]

Also Tom Cruise tried to forge connections in high places. Being a star and a scientologist, he had access to people in high positions and went to George Bush in 2003 to complain about the treatment Scientology suffered from in Germany. He met with Richard Armitage, then vice foreign minister, and with "Scooter" Libby, close associate of Vice-President Dick Cheney. And he spoke with Bill Clinton, asking him for support so that Scientology would get the status of a charity in the UK.[113]

The human soul is being violated

During the past millennia, as dominator cultures emerged, they caused immense psychological damage, which, in turn, triggered more violence and insecurity, and this was regarded as "normality." Humans yearn for connection, and people adapt to the relationships available to them. When there is war, the human craving to belong can only be fulfilled by paying the price of psychological self-mutilation through dividing empathy into legitimate and illegitimate empathy. If people would have a choice, they would not accept such mutilating alternatives.[114] In the context of a strong security dilemma, however, hierarchy, love, and terror are closely linked by force. Terror is perpetrated out of love, love for one's superiors who, on their part, define terror as love for "our own people." In such a context, compassionate empathy with "the enemy" transmutes into unpatriotic betrayal.

Many legal instruments were created to underpin this state-of-affairs, which, even if well-intended at the time, have detrimental effects until the day today. Ancient Mesopotamia's institutionalization of revenge, for example, may represent a legacy that continues to hamper reconciliation until today: "enshrining revenge into law led to the loss of an inner process of reconciliation and nowadays we have no tools for achieving a real inner reconciliation after harm has been done to us."[115]

Indeed even the human ability to remember can be harmed in cultures of domination/submission. Moral disengagement from the out-group makes people remember selectively those atrocities that absolve "us" and incriminate "them." As a result, the level of aggression toward out-groups rises.[116] As has been discussed earlier, beliefs have two functions: first, they are needed to understand and test reality, second, they are needed to live with ourselves and with others.[117] The result can be glaring dissonance between the two, which, when "remedied" by cognitive bias, produces artificial consonance: when the emperor has no clothes, we might not dare to even see it, let alone say it.[118] Denying that also the enemy is a fellow human being who deserves our compassion similarly damages our soul, heart, and mind. We do so because it would be too dishonorable not to.

Not only enemies were undeserving of compassion, hierarchy had to be as ruthlessly kept in its ranking order, without "undue softness," "weakness," or "female sissiness," following the Bible's saying that "the Lord disciplines the one he loves."[119] It was the duty of the "man of the house" to chastise disobedient family members; the *strict father* model of parenting was the recommended method of pedagogy, rather than the *nurturant parent* model.[120] The aim was to "break the will of the child."[121] In such a context, terms and concepts that are widely used today were unknown and unthinkable, such as *micro-aggression*,[122] or *bullying* in schools and work life,[123] or *verbal abuse* in families,[124] or the *intimate terror* of domestic violence,[125] or *PTSD*, or *trauma therapy*. In the case of honor killing, a girl who brought shame on the family by being raped, for instance, is seen as a person who deserves to die, rather than receive trauma therapy.

Many names epitomize the connection of hierarchy, security, love, and terror; Adolf Hitler, Joseph Stalin, Mao Zedong, all those who inspired followers to carry terror into the core of society. Youths enthusiastically humiliated elders in China's Cultural Revolution, youths indulged in humiliating elderly Jews in Germany, and Stalin still has enthusiastic admirers today.[126] In such contexts, terror permeated all segments of society: "nach unten treten und nach oben buckeln" is a German saying (to crawl to the bigwigs and bully the underlings). Such strategies maintain and deepen the inequality in hierarchical dominator contexts, and they aggravate the psychological damage.

Research shows that inequality in a society "damages family life by higher rates of child abuse, and increased status competition," and that there are "higher rates of bullying in schools in more unequal countries."[127] Psychologist Edward Thorndike described the *halo* and *horn* effects, or the human tendency to take one aspect of a person or thing and generalize from it.[128] In a hierarchical context, this effect is institutionalized: superior status is generalized to mean also higher inner worthiness and the right and duty to dominate, and vice versa for inferior status. Social reformer and physicist Robert Fuller calls it *rankism* when rank is essentialized.[129]

Also Sigmund Freud seems to have fallen prey to the effects of a strong security dilemma when he elevated the damage the human psyche suffers in such a context to be the norm of health. Whitewashing the *superego* and demonizing the *id* as the alleged "beast" in the human soul turns human nature upside down, writes Donald Carveth, psychotherapist and expert on social and political thought.[130] Animals are seldom as "beastly" as humans can be, and superego-driven ideologists have done incomparably more damage in the world than id-driven psychopaths. Carveth resonates with Franz Alexander and Sandor Ferenczi when he invites psychoanalysts to stop ignoring the ideologies of domination, ideologies of sexism, racism, heterosexism, classism, or childism. People internalize unconscionable superegos from unconscionable societies. Carveth sympathizes with Jean-Jacques Rousseau when he looks for the roots of morality in sympathetic identification, and, together with Pascal, he holds that "the heart has reasons reason cannot know." Psychoanalyst Donald Winnicott spoke of a *true self*, and Carveth discusses also Heidegger, Winnicott, Freud, Klein, Lacan, Mahler, and St. Paul.[131] Rationality cannot be the anchor of values, therefore replacing the superego with the rational ego is not an option for Carveth.

Also concepts such as empathy may be among the victims of the security dilemma. What is *true* empathy? What is *mature* empathy? Is it still empathy, when empathy is used to make torture more effective? In the field of brain research, we find terms such as *affective*, *compassionate*, and *cognitive* empathy.[132] Then we have *realistic* empathy,[133] *accurate* empathy,[134] and *radical* empathy.[135] We have the German phrase *Einfühlung*, which gave rise to the term of empathy in the English language. Then there is sympathy: Is it better or worse than empathy? And what about compassion?

As reported earlier, brain research shows that psychopathic criminals do not lack empathy; empathy is simply not automatically "on."[136] Which kind of empathy can be switched on and off?

The German phrase *Einfühlung* (from *ein-* or in-, and *Fühlung* or feeling) was coined in 1858 by German philosopher Rudolf Hermann Lotze as a translation of Greek *empatheia*, meaning passion, from *en-* meaning in- and *pathos* meaning feeling, together: in-feeling.[137] In 1909, psychologist Edward Titchener used the word empathy to translate the "true" meaning of the word Einfühlung.[138]

In German, it is possible to say a sentence such as "Ein Heiratsschwindler muss ein großes Einfühlungsvermögen haben" (A marriage swindler must have a great ability of "feeling" himself into the soul of his victim). This shows that in German, the phrase *Einfühlungsvermögen* does not necessarily differentiate between compassionate empathy and abusive empathy. *Einfühlungsvermögen* can include all versions of empathy, and is thus perhaps slightly more neutral than in English, where the phrase empathy seems to carry a more positive connotation. In English, based on differentiations between cognitive, affective, and motor aspects of empathy,[139] a range of phrases is used.

In foreign affairs, for instance, *realistic* empathy for the enemy is being recommended by Ralph White, a former U.S. Information Agency official, later a political scientist and psychologist at George Washington University. White explains that only through empathy can one accurately tell the story adversaries are telling themselves about "us," about themselves, and about the situation they believe they face. Realistic empathy is simply "realistic understanding" and has nothing to do with warmth or approval, with agreeing or siding with the opponent.[140] White talks about three mistakes in foreign policymaking that occur when it denies empathy: (1) not seeing an opponent's longing for peace; (2) not seeing an opponent's fear of being attacked; and (3) not seeing an opponent's understandable anger.[141]

Another alternative term is *perspective-taking*, a mere cognitive ability that also a psychopath might employ to better understand others so as to be able to manipulate them more effectively.[142]

In the English language, *sympathy* is seen by some as lesser than empathy. Offering "cheap" uncommitted sympathy is regarded as shallower than investing empathy.[143] Yet, others see sympathy as something more than empathy. White sees it in this way, namely, that sympathy adds warmth and approval to a more cognitive stepping into the others' shoes. Some also see compassion as superior to empathy, compassion as a way to protect oneself against exhaustion, for example, when healthcare workers or caregivers feel overwhelmed and burnt out by the suffering they face and feel empathy with[144]: "People would be exhausted by empathy, but compassion is limitless."[145]

Neuroscientist Tania Singer recommends training in perspective-taking and compassion for a globalizing world, so as to improve conflict resolution skills and help better understand out-groups, other cultures, and other religions.[146] Like many other scholars, also she assumes that fully developed "true" and "mature" empathy will, per definition, lead to prosocial outcomes, and that antisocial outcomes are only to be expected for people who lack the affective aspect of empathy. Singer found that empathy and compassion each activate very different neuronal structures in the brain, with empathy potentially leading to burn out, and only the practice of compassion truly contributing to well-being.[147]

If we look at terrorism, we see that also the "maturest" of empathy and the sincerest of compassion may lead to results that Tania Singer would regard as antisocial. The crucial point is the definition of prosociality, and how antisociality is believed to manifest. Indigenous practices may offer an illustration of how compassion and killing may be brought together: Animists regard animals as friends and persons, and getting to know non-human persons in nature is like getting to know another human being.[148] Many indigenous peoples, both past and present, respect animals as equal in rights to humans. Animals are hunted only for food (not for profit), and before killing them, the hunter asks permission from the animal's spirit.[149] Or, another example: A surgeon does not wish to harm the person she cuts open, the harm is meant to do good. The surgeon can be highly empathic with the patient, still she will cut the patient open. The surgeon will not have to "switch off" empathy and compassion to be able to do surgery.[150] Notwithstanding good intentions, if the methodology of this surgery is misguided, the patient may die. Still, the surgeon did apply "mature" empathy, we may assume, at least if she had no way to know about the misguidedness of her methodology. Yet another example: During the Inquisition, admittedly, some inquisitors might have found pleasure in torturing people for the sake of inflicting pain – "altruistic" evil in the name of god so to speak. However, others might have truly wished to save souls by burning bodies, to "cleanse souls from sinful bodies." Such inquisitors might have truly cared about their victims, empathically understanding that those victims lacked the "correct" faith and therefore were in need of being saved. This belief is even enshrined at the very core of the inquisitors' spirituality and their sense of "goodness," just like the surgeon would betray her Hippocratic oath if she denied her patient help.

Female genital mutilation is yet another example, as is Chinese foot-binding. All these cases show that it is not compassion or empathy that is the problem, it is the hijacking of these natural human responses by the dominator frame: "Like other human activities, when compassion and empathy are organized within an honor/dominator system, there is a mutagenic effect."[151] Honor killing has been mentioned before. It may manifest out of true compassion, believing it to be an act of love for the family, for which the daughter must be sacrificed. The mother who kills her daughter in an honor killing does not necessarily lack empathy and compassion for her daughter. Even the daughter herself might agree. Many girls, for instance, in Iraq in the aftermath of the 2003 war, have committed suicide after being raped, out of a deep understanding of the harm they represented to their families.[152] If we now come back to James Elmer Mitchell, one of the psychologists who recently helped torture terrors suspects, he may have felt the same way.[153] Also young suicide bombers may feel that such acts are the only truly compassionate acts to wake up the world, to make everybody understand the depth of their people's desperation and misery.

In the context of a strong security dilemma – "either we kill or are killed" – the rise of the dominator model of society could be seen as "collateral damage." And this damage includes "mature" empathy leading to results that many would regard as outcomes of immature empathy. Michael Hayden, former C.I.A. director acts on this insight when he warns idealistic critics of drone strikes that to keep America safe requires going to the very edge of what is possible, including drone strikes.[154] What terrorizes those living in world regions targeted by such strikes, is seen by those who resonate with Hayden as a regrettable "imperfection" of an otherwise lifesaving strategy, lifesaving for America.

Clearly, Hayden's thinking is thoroughly intelligible as long as a strong security dilemma is regarded as an unchangeably given frame. It is only from the point of view of a person who has deeply understood the historical novelty of an interconnected world that this traditional worldview can become outdated, ready to be outlawed, just as foot binding has been outlawed despite having been practiced for one thousand years. Only such a person is aware of how the traditional definition of goodness risks leading to collective suicide in the new context, and that the well-intended "surgery" applied in the past no longer is the medicine now, but the disease.[155]

Many people around the world, also those steeped in so-called Western values, do not see their responsibility for forging systemic global change for the better, for the need to intentionally shape new global frames of interconnectedness in ways that a new kind of prosociality can unfold. Many of them, and I meet them all around the world, act out of true empathy and compassion when they give to charity, for instance, while maintaining their ignorance of the wider context, and, in particular, for the fact that they are complicit in causing the very damage they wish to heal: "Another manipulation of the dominator/ capitalist/charity system – the illusion of doing good."[156] Mother Theresa, for example, surely was driven by deep empathy and compassion when she believed that suffering was a gift from God, including preventable distress caused by poverty, avoidable medical problems, or starvation.[157] Like her, many maintain an honest ignorance of the wider context and of the fact that more appropriate human interventions could very well prevent the roots of the misery they decry. Evidently, it cannot be denied that some also may engage in more intentional *strategic ignorance*.[158]

If we denounce the empathy of a person as "not mature" too quickly, in my view, we have not done enough perspective-taking training. This is an important point for terrorism studies, not least because this insight opens the door for respect. We can accord respect to the mother who kills her daughter for the honor of her family, respect for her true empathy for her family – if her motivation indeed was to save her family – and then we can proceed to the next step and explain to her that the world has changed and that this kind of "surgery" no longer is needed. Relational-cultural theory calls this approach "honoring the strategies of survival."[159] We can appreciate that this mother may feel full empathy and compassion for her daughter, but that she invests her empathy into a different worldview than we hold. From her point of view, she would betray love and care and compassion if she failed to save her family's honor, like the surgeon would betray her Hippocratic oath if not offering surgery to the patient. Or, James Elmer Mitchell might truly have wanted to save America from harm when he tortured suspected terrorists,[160] as much as suicide bombers might truly believe in the prosociality of their mission.

James Elmer Mitchell's and suicide bombers' emotions and meta-emotions are anchored within a strong security dilemma, which they regard as a fixed frame for the human condition on planet Earth. In contrast, my work is informed by the insight that the security dilemma is not fixed. I wish to contribute to attenuating it intentionally. To do so, I start by respecting Hayden and Mitchell, and all those who resonate with their views. I give them the benefit of the doubt as far as I possibly can, assuming that they indeed acted out of deep-felt empathy and compassion, and that they invested it into their definition of devotion to a noble cause. I wish to refrain from denigrating their efforts as psychologically handicapped only because they manifest a worldview that, to me, is comprehensible, albeit dangerously outdated. I respect those who wish to punish me after reading this book, be they the "warriors" of the West or non-West. I wish to respectfully explain to them why I believe that the worldview I stand for is more appropriate in an interconnected world, and why their worldview will lead to collective suicide rather than to collective salvation, even though they are deeply convinced of the opposite.[161]

In other words, stand-alone empathy or compassion training, in my view, is never sufficient. Such training would always need to be accompanied by deep reflection on what kind of worldview serves as frame for the definition of prosociality in any given case. "If empathy and compassion training was fully operational in an interconnected worldview, we would not be able to continue 'warriorism.'"[162] As mentioned above, a high degree of spontaneous empathy and compassion for the suffering of Muslims in the world can lead a young person to become a violent holy warrior. To make empathy and compassion prosocial in present-day's interconnected world, deep reflection is required on which worldview it is that can secure a dignified future for humankind, and which can not. A new kind of "medicine" may be necessary, as difficult to administer perhaps as the old, yet, no longer with the aim to heal wounds *within* the cruel context of the security dilemma, but to use global inclusiveness to altogether overcome this tragic dilemma. In the old context, allowing empathy to include the enemy carried a dire cost, the cost of facing the cruelty of the security dilemma unmitigated, as killing the enemy with empathy is more difficult than numbing empathy before killing. Only in a world free of the security dilemma can empathy become what it deserves to be, namely, loving care invested into optimal solutions, rather than into sub-optimal solutions in a sub-optimal context: "The problem of limiting one's empathy and compassion to one's in-group – this is a dominator logic. Yet, it is done as a strategy of survival. If the pressure of the security dilemma is reduced, the circle of empathy and compassion can be enlarged."[163]

Public punishment and humiliation is still being widely used today, as a tool of terror to warn the audience that they will suffer the same fate if they transgress orders. Public humiliation of people works because it can build on the fact that "not only direct experiences of humiliation trigger social pain, but also the possibility of humiliation (i.e., the threat and fear of humiliation) and being the witness of humiliation (e.g., via media)."[164] Public punishment and humiliation terrorizes not only by showing that terror is permissible, it even terrorizes people into perpetrating terror themselves to show their worthiness in this system. Da'esh uses this tool.

Just as psychological damage fuels war, in turn, war causes psychological damage. There is, for instance, the Posttraumatic stress disorder (PTSD) of veterans: "… the [U.S.] military tried to deny the ubiquity of PTSD for many years, prevalence studies made it impossible … Perhaps it is because the psychological costs of combat are paid only by relative few volunteers, who serve in faraway lands, and whose actions are condoned by law, by tradition, and by myth, that we can accept (and rationalize) the physical and psychological wounds they receive on our behalf."[165]

The security dilemma engenders a culture that inflicts psychological damage, which, in turn, deepens the security dilemma. Humiliation is a core element in this dynamic, particularly, the experience of humiliation early in life. Early in life the very development of the brain is affected.[166] New relational neuroscience shows how the human brain and physiology functions best when people are embedded in webs of caring relationships. Isolation and exclusion activate the same neural pathways as physical pain.[167] There are long-term physical and mental health benefits flowing from feeling loved, while life-long mental damages result from being neglected. While damage in otherwise healthy adults may be healed, in children, it may become structural. The brains of loved children are larger than those of neglected children, since brain cells grow and cerebral circuits develop in response to an infant's interaction with the main caregiver. Nature and nurture are entangled; the genes for brain function, including intelligence, may not even become functional if a baby is neglected during the first two years of life.[168] In cases where brains have not developed properly due to neglect in those early years of life, youths may later be incapable of responding to the incentives and punishments meant to guide society away from crime, and they may end as persistent offenders. Children who were massively beaten have a six times greater probability to turn into violent offenders than children raised lovingly and without violence.[169] Those who have suffered the powerlessness of being beaten in childhood will later be three times more likely to wish to possess a firearm so as to finally feel powerful. They will also tend to advocate tough criminal laws and the death penalty.[170]

As mentioned before, cognitive linguists George Lakoff and Mark Johnson describe the *strict father* model of parenting in contrast to the *nurturant parent* model.[171] If a society wishes to maintain its social-psychological health over several generations, what is needed are relationships that foster psychological growth, what is important is the quality of relationships, rather than quantities.[172]

A Prussian king's belligerence, for instance, may have been caused by the horrifying humiliation he suffered as a child at the hand of his father. Young Frederick II (1712 – 1786) loved the arts and at some point, he attempted to flee from his tyrannical father who wanted to make "a real man" of him. He fled with a friend, his beloved teacher, yet, they were apprehended. His father ordered the teacher to be executed in front of his son's eyes. Later, when his father died, young Frederick became king. One might have expected that he chose to be a peaceable king. But no. He became known as Friedrich der Große (Frederick the Great), not least because of his penchant for war. He attacked Silesia, the homeland of my parents, and incorporated it into Prussia. My father may have been spared much of his traumatic experiences during and after WW II had not this happened. In other words, Frederick's wounded soul acted out by attacking neighbors – psychological damage fueled the security dilemma. And this, in turn, contributed to the trauma of my family. Young Frederick was a gifted and loving young man and would surely have grown into a wise leader in a more nurturing context.

Neuroscientist James Fallon found out that seven murders had been committed within his father's family line.[173] He also found that he himself displays all the relevant neurological and genetic patterns that are present in psychopathic killers, such as loss of function in the orbital cortex, in the anterior temporal lobes, and in the strip of limbic cortices that connect the two, on top of almost all known high-risk and violence-related genes, such as the Monoamine Oxidase A (MAOA) gene. Still, Fallon became a professor and not a violent psychopath or serial killer. He believes that severe sexual, physical, or emotional abuse in early childhood triggers violence-related genes and relevant brain processes so that aggression will result. In contrast, a nurturing environment and loving family support will avoid such a path. Therefore, it is likely, he believes, that in areas of the world with never-ending experiences of violence, terrorism, and war, a penchant for violence will be transgenerationally transmitted not just via culture,[174] it will affect even people's brain processes.[175]

Research shows that humiliation is the most intense human emotion. The cognitive load of humiliation is enormous, it leads to the mobilization of more processing power and a greater consumption of mental resources than other emotions: "humiliation is a particularly intense and cognitively demanding negative emotional experience that has far-reaching consequences for individuals and groups alike."[176] Forensic clinicians, lawyers, judges, political strategists, as well as the general public, all lack insight into this fact.[177] Psychiatrist Aaron Lazare explained this in his talk at our Workshop on Transforming Humiliation and Violent Conflict at Columbia University in 2007. He made clear that one cannot expect that one's apology will immediately heal the feelings of humiliation one has caused in another. What one has to do instead, he taught us, is give the other some time: I have to repeat my apologies until healing can grow in the other's soul.[178] Overlooking this fact leads to grave misjudgments that are compounded when it is overlooked, in addition, that also being the witness of the humiliation of others can have humiliating effects. On the Israeli side, for instance, it was not enough to retreat from Gaza and expect that peace would immediately be the result, particularly not when Gazans had to witness fellow Palestinians still suffering. This is also why psychological damage that engulfs entire societies, be it outbreaks of violence in communities, or a general sense of helplessness, or a culture of submissive meekness, are all falsely regarded as human nature's and culture's norm.

Germany and Japan offer both stark illustrations of traditionally highly hierarchical societies and the systemic psychological damage they inflict. The Volkswagen emissions scandal that broke in September 2015,[179] has its roots in an authoritarian management culture in a company that inculcated the *Nibelungentreue* of everybody fearfully obeying superiors, no questions asked.[180] In Japan, it was the Olympus Corporation, a manufacturer of optics and reprography products, that built on unconditional *bushido* obedience to a degree that grown-up men behaved like fearful children: *Samurai and Idiots* is the telling title of a 2015 documentary film.[181] In October 2011, newly employed British CEO Michael Woodford was suddenly ousted, because he refused to close his eyes to the fraud that went on in the company he was head of. Instead of quietly leaving his position, however, he became one of the most highly positioned whistleblowers. In the documentary, we meet a few courageous individuals who violated the Japanese culture of collective subservience. We meet, for instance, freelance business reporter Yoshimasa Yamaguchi who was the first to publicize the scandal. We also meet Shigeo Abe, chief editor of the magazine *Facta*, who was brave enough to print Yamagushi's article. According to Abe, even today, in Japan, there are lords and servants, just as in the *Forty-Seven Ronin* legend,[182] and "Japan is a ship full of fools who sink their ship to protect their interests."[183] According to *Financial Times* commentator John Gapper, the company's directors and the head of the Audit Board engaged in *honorable fraud*, meaning that they covered up for their predecessors wrong-doing to protect them against losing face.[184] Jonathan Soble, also a journalist of *Financial Times* in Tokyo, broke the scandal internationally on October 14, 2011. He describes the culture in Japan as follows: "responsibility is so diffuse that it loses its significance. This bundle of secrets, mistakes, and faulty evaluations are given from one leader to the next and none opens it. Each holds this bundle for a while, in loyalty to their predecessors, and he can rightly say that it was not theirs."[185] Waku Miller, a native of Arizona who has resided in Japan since 1978, and a close friend of Michael Woodford, knows that "who owns Japan, and who runs it" is a complicated story.[186]

In 2005, when I lived in Osaka, the Amagasaki rail crash happened close to where I stayed. The driver of the train, young Ryūjirō Takami, was speeding to make up time he had lost before, and 107 people died, including the driver himself. He was speeding because he was afraid of punishment, as he had already committed two small mistakes a few minutes earlier when he had passed by a red light and overshot a platform. Many may say that fear of punishment is no reason to take deadly risks. However, this case reveals something else. Ten months earlier, the young man had been punished for overshooting a station platform by 100 meters.[187] On that occasion he had experienced the cruelty of humiliation that is ingrained in Japanese hierarchy. What he was afraid of having to undergo again, was *nikkin kyoiku* (literally: education on the day shift), a punishment and psychological torture program used by Japanese corporation and insidiously labeled as "retraining program." It involves being exposed to violent verbal aggressions, having to repent in extensive reports, and having to perform inferior tasks such as cleaning or weeding, often in front of colleagues.[188]

Under the Shogunate, until 1867, *kiri-sute gomen* (directly translated "authorization to cut and leave," to cut and leave the body of a victim) was the right of a samurai. A samurai could kill with his sword any lower class member who he felt had compromised his honor. Fear for life still today palpably permeates Japanese society, shining through everything from submissive politeness in everyday life, to the *hikikomori* phenomenon of young men who no longer leave their homes,[189] up to the workings of the elite establishment. The Fukushima Daiichi nuclear disaster of March 11, 2011, demonstrates how entire societies can take deadly risks. It is a self-destructive cultural code, which perilously insulates against change. Change can only come from outside such a system, through *gaijin* (foreigners), as *gaiatsu*, which means to "change through foreign force."[190] In the case of Olympus, this function was performed by a CEO from Britain. He performed the role of the witness,[191] and the role of the bystander who stands up.[192]

Also in the Volkswagen diesel scandal, change had to come from outside, in this case from American authorities.[193] Former Volkswagen CEO Winterkorn is said to have built a military management culture without which the exhaust gas scandal would not have been possible.[194]

What we learn is that if a repressive culture were to globalize, with nobody left to step in from outside, this would mean for all of humankind to collectively go down the same self-destructive path. Unfortunately, this is precisely what seems to happen at the present historical juncture.

Sociologist David Riesman and his colleagues identified three main cultural types, *tradition-directed*, *inner-directed*, and *other-directed*.[195] A tradition-directed culture follows the direction given by preceding generations, whereas inner-directed people discover their own potential within themselves. After the Industrial Revolution, the increasing ability to consume goods and afford material abundance led the new middle class to defining themselves in comparison to the way others lived, in other words, they became other-directed. This culture increasingly dominates world culture by now. On my global path, I watch the motto of "consuming goodies is good" happily globalize. A self-destructive *Nibelungentreue* to consumerism is in the process of engulfing the planet[196] in a misapplied *bushido* fashion, perpetrated by the "excellent sheep" produced by present-day educational institutions.[197] Change can only come from outside, from *gaijin*, through *gaiatsu* "change through foreign force." Unfortunately, I observe a great lack of inner-directed Gandhis and Mandelas who could step in from outside of this paradigm.

Wherever I go, I observe religion and ideology being lived in two ways that are somewhat related to Riesman's classification. Simplified said, I meet what could be called "Pharisees" (the tradition-directed and other-directed way), and "Sufis" (the inner-directed way). In saying this, I use Max Weber's "ideal type" approach, which allows for analysis and action to proceed at different levels of abstraction, as there are, clearly, huge grey areas in between.[198] I myself belong to the second group of those who are rooted organically in a larger context of meaning, similar to those indigenous people who are in deep dialogue with nature. In Christianity, mystic Meister Eckhart (circa 1260 – 1328) could be named in this context, or Rudolf Otto (1869 – 1937), who wrote about *The Holy* in all religions.[199] Religious historian Mircea Eliade spoke of *hierophany*, or the manifestation of the sacred, the sense of awe in a sacred space (from Greek *hieros*, sacred/holy, and *phainein*, to bring to light).[200] I see many indigenous peoples having a direct and holistic experience of *Gaia* as a godlike place inspiring *hierophany*, where they see all things acquiring reality, identity, and meaning through their participation in this experience.[201] In dominator contexts, the majority population, in contrast, is cut off from direct religious experience by power elites who reserve the right to *hierophany* and its interpretation for themselves.

The first group, what I call the Pharisees, are those who adhere to the letter of dogma, and in the secular version this can manifest in living in isolated in bubbles of abstract urban rules and consumerism. Unfortunately, since it is impossible to follow all rules and requirements perfectly, this orientation is prone to sow continuous frustration, invite fanatical behavior, and foreclose deep psychological and spiritual fulfillment.

I know many people who identify as Muslims, Buddhists, Hindus, or atheists, and they follow one or the other orientation to various degrees. Also Salafists can be inner-oriented mystics, while they also have "Pharisees." Their Pharisees are split into purists and pragmatics, both ultimately aiming at political impact, with purists seeking salvation in following the "right" rules *as they ought to be*, despising those who soil their "purity" by pragmatically working with the rules of the world *as they are*.[202]

Also philosopher, anthropologist, and sociologist of science Bruno Latour draws on the notion of *hierophany*. He suggests that secular left-oriented liberals might be able to bridge their divide with the religious right through taking the moral idea of *Gaia* seriously, as a space that can inspire *hierophany* in all.[203] "Gaia communities could assert that they and other conventional theistic believers are in fact worshipping the same god(s)/forces as everyone else and that this fact symbolizes our over-arching solidarity," writes Sudhir Chella Rajan from the Indian Institute of Technology Madras.[204]

I observe that other-directedness is on the increase not least through a rise in urban and suburban separation from nature. This separation leads to the kind of estrangement that, as I observe it, makes its victims more impressionable to being recruited not only into consumerism, but also into humiliation entrepreneurship· Humiliation entrepreneurship works in these cases even when the instigator is inauthentic: listeners or readers feel that they experience the very emotions that an acclaimed speaker or author ascribes to the group.[205]

Economist David Korten warns that no longer are we participants in Earth's community of life, but in a sterile, manufactured, mechanistic, regimented money driven setting of consumer society, and that this is the reason for why we accept the cultural manipulation and economic restructuring that now threatens human existence both socially and ecologically.[206] Korten explains:

> Not only are we subject to sophisticated, intentional cultural manipulation, we are subject to an economic model that disrupts the rich and complex living exchange relationships grounded in love and caring our neural circuits evolved to reward. It replaces them with impersonal financial exchanges with profit driven global corporations that value life only for its market price. I became deeply conscious of this

> displacement process and its destructive life consequences during my thirty years working in international development in Africa, Asia, and Latin America.
>
> We humans evolved to live and learn in community. Stripped of opportunities to obtain our neural rewards from the sources to which evolution wired our minds to respond, we accept the advertiser's message and buy into the false promise that the consumption of advertised products will provide us the sense of meaning and connection we seek. We get at most a brief moment of satisfaction, but we are left with the increased material clutter of things we neither need nor use – not the sense of belonging and meaning that is the source of our greatest satisfaction.
>
> Stripped of options, and bombarded with seductive promises, we keep trying and failing to get the sense of meaning and belonging we truly seek. The result is compulsive shopping, drug addiction, family breakdown, collapsing natural systems, increased incarceration rates, a refugee crisis, and most all the other societal maladies that necessitate a Great Transformation.[207]

Indeed, as Korten points out, being exposed to myriad false choices, between, say, countless different types of toothbrushes or hair shampoos, incapacitates people, keeps them from making the important choices they ought to make. The *paradox of choice*[208] causes anxiety in consumers who suffer from *choice overload*.[209] Psychologist Jean Baker Miller calls for *alternative arrangements*, to heal the terror from *false choices*.[210]

Nora Sveaass is a clinical psychologist who was a member of the UN Committee against Torture until 2013, and now she is a member of the UN Subcommittee on Prevention of Torture. When she took initiative to establish the Health and Human Rights Info platform,[211] her aim was to help highlight the connection between health and human rights, and raise awareness for why the state has the responsibility to create institutional frames that ensure that the ideal is upheld that "all human beings are born free and equal in dignity and rights." What happens at the present historical juncture could be described as a failure of the world community to create such frames at the global level.

Disdain for life, scorn for what nourishes a human being with aliveness, a "thrill of destruction," all this has even entered academia and professional life. Academic criticism is now more and more often delivered with a strain of "hatred," with "critical barbarity," giving "cruel treatment" to "experiences and ideals that non-academics treat as objects of tender concern."[212] The hermeneutics of suspicion encourage punitive attitudes and turn academia into a war zone, where scholars use theory, or simply attitude, "to burn through whatever is small, tender, and worthy of protection and cultivation."[213] The backdrop for this academic terror is an overreach of anti-liberalism, warns English professor Lisa Ruddick. She agrees that it is appropriate to accuse bourgeois liberal ideology of forgetting the influence of the market when it takes "man" as being ideally self-possessed and autonomous. Yet, anti-liberalism can go too far also and destroy aliveness itself if it altogether denies "the value of human individuality and self-boundaries."[214] Philosopher Bruno Latour adds this:

> Wars. So many wars. Wars outside and wars inside. Cultural wars, science wars, and wars against terrorism. Wars against poverty and wars against the poor. Wars against ignorance and wars out of ignorance. My question is simple: Should we be at war, too, we, the scholars, the intellectuals? Is it really our duty to add fresh ruins to fields of ruins? Is it really the task of the humanities to add deconstruction to destruction? More iconoclasm to iconoclasm?[215]

This is the context, in which now compliant professionals are being produced for the workplace, individuals who are so alienated from themselves[216] that they will not know when to call out when the emperor has no clothes.[217] Management scholar Ann Rippin reports of professional organizations,[218] where those trained in dehumanizing glossy ways of speaking and feeling, "report feeling unable to bring their whole selves to work," they feel "obliged to dismember or disaggregate themselves, having to suspend feelings, ethics, values on occasion,"[219] into "cascading workplace cultures of inauthenticity."[220]

The result is a society that throws out the positive sides of the relational dimension – such as kindness, solidarity, and a sense of worth, all of which flows from embeddedness into nurturing relations and from "engagement in mutually beneficial relations"[221] – while at the same time denying and abusing the vulnerable aspects of this dimension, namely, the need for belonging and the fact that this need can be instrumentalized for oppression. Instead, the vulnerable aspects are made to serve covert and collective manipulation of people into believing they are or should be "self-made." Advertisers are happy to inculcate the illusion of godlike selfhood in consumers. This manipulation then empties those selves, and it does so for the sake of profit maximization, for the benefit of a small elite, not for the benefit of those manipulated. The academic world could help salvage this situation. Yet, it compounds the damage when it throws out both, the positive sides of the relational dimension, plus the self's potential to be an authentically flourishing human being with a sense of worth. It throws out all aspects of the African *ubuntu* philosophy that states, "I am because of you" – it throws out all: me and you and us. This is what has motivated me and my colleagues to launch the idea of a World Dignity University.[222]

To conclude this sub-section, as this book has spelled out at length, collectivist manipulation is damaging, be it feudal or bourgeois, be it through open oppression or through the misdefinition of individualistic freedom as freedom for might to be right. Yet, this abuse is not remedied by intensifying it or by creating even more individualized zombies. What is needed instead, is interconnected individuality, an individuality that acknowledges its embeddedness into relations.[223] The proverbial village that is required to raise a child, to be effective, must anchor individual freedom in relational connectedness in equality in dignity. What I refer to as Sufis, are all those with the true self of a Winnicott or Carveth, and I would be happy to see them go out into the world and invite the Pharisees to abandon their unconscionable superegos, and instead anchor their entire being in lovingly interconnected individuality.

The nondualism of the *ubuntu* philosophy is the answer: "we are two, and we are one, and this at the same time." *Nondualism* means separation and connection; difference and connection; agreement and disagreement; one and two. It means success in achieving unity in diversity. It needs competency in nondualist thinking to grasp the value of unity in diversity and how it can become a synergistic win-win game: Unity is not the same as oppressive uniformity, and diversity is not the same as unrestricted freedom for divisiveness to take over. Unity and diversity can each grow if kept in mutual balance and magnified and celebrated simultaneously.

Gender roles are being bastardized

Not only is the human soul being damaged in the context of a dominator culture. So is the role of gender. This sub-section will be short, however, I do not wish to repeat too much here, since this topic has been mentioned earlier, and I also wrote a book on it.[224]

"I fell into the trap of performing expected gender roles, with murderous results," says Vincent Emanuele, a former U.S. Marine to Iraq, who later organized the Michigan chapter of Veterans for Peace and served on the national board of directors of Iraq Veterans Against War.[225] This is how he explains what attracted him to enlist in the U.S. military as a marine:

> I think the process was long and quite complex. First of all, I was a product of American culture which is, of course, an extremely violent culture. In other words, like many American children, I grew up playing "Army." Specifically, we would pretend-shoot our friends with plastic guns, watched countless movies that glorified warfare and played very violent video games in our spare time. In short, I was trained to be a murderer for American Empire from a very young age. I think this is a very important component to the process of indoctrinating America's youth with militaristic ideologies. No matter what, without the process of early-age cultural indoctrination, many young

Americans would be much less inclined to join the U.S. military.

For the sake of time, I'll mention a second component to this process. To me, it's quite obvious that the U.S. military provides a unique space for expressing and, more importantly, bastardizing gender roles. So, in my case, I was simply fulfilling the traditional "masculine" role of the big, tough, angry, murderous, bar-fighting, heavy drinking, womanizing asshole who cares about nothing more than superficial cultural practices and killing people. You know, the perfect American. In this context, I fell into the trap of performing expected gender roles with murderous results. There is nothing "tough" or "cool" about imprisoning, torturing or killing people. I learned this lesson quite quickly.

...

Here, I must mention military training and boot camp. Within this training routine, Marines are routinely referred to as bitches, pussies, cunts, faggots and queers. Again, the dominant culture's ideology is firmly at work during this training process. To be clear, you must implant the seeds of dehumanization in order to convince eighteen years-old kids to fly halfway around the world to murder people. Therefore, Iraqis and Afghans were referred to as hajis, sand-niggers, camel-jockeys and towel-heads during our training processes. Hence the scale, scope and horror of military training and practical application.

Furthermore, yes, even military life outside combat deployments changes people in various ways. For one, many people become very coarse, mean, thick-skinned, emotionless, so on, and so forth. Overall, you become a murderer, and a good one at that. Sure, with regards to whatever limited moral compass I possessed at the time, I think those coordinates changed dramatically. On our spare time, my fellow Marines and I would frequent strip clubs, prostitution houses, pubs and drug dealers. Is that the life of "honor, courage and commitment?" I don't think so.[226]

What Vincent Emanuele describes, among others, is sexist language not only in the military. The same has also been researched by feminists Cynthia Enloe[227] and Carol Cohn.[228] Nadine Puechguirbal has observed the continuing impact of "gender blindness" in even the most well-meaning international organizations, together with the daily challenges feminists face in protecting their integrity in peacekeeping and humanitarian work.[229]

Terrorism is being misrecognized

Richard Jackson is a scholar in critical terrorism studies.[230] Since 2012, he is the deputy director of the National Centre for Peace and Conflict Studies at the University of Otago in Dunedin, New Zealand, the very place where we had our 17th Annual Dignity Conference in 2011.[231] Germany was humiliated after WWI, and in response, it fabricated a sense of threat for itself, writes Jackson, and he wonders whether this also happens in the U.S. now. Jackson wonders why terrorism studies and peace studies have remained largely divorced from each other, despite the fact that they both study the same questions.[232] As he sees it, this separation significantly weakens the field of terrorism studies. According to him, most terrorism scholars, politicians, and the media, all overlook that it is misguided to search for causes for terrorism primarily in religion, radicalization, psychopathology, ideology, poverty, or similar explanations, while even the Pentagon's Defense Science Board is aware of the impact of U.S. military interventions overseas since the late 1990s. Indeed, Ivan Eland, director of defense policy studies at the Cato Institute, an American libertarian think tank headquartered in Washington, D.C., concludes: "The large number of terrorist attacks that occurred in retaliation for an interventionist American foreign policy implicitly demonstrates that terrorism against U.S. targets could be significantly reduced if the United States adopted a policy of military restraint overseas."[233]

In 2002, journalist Chris Hedges was part of a group of eight reporters of the *New York Times*, who were awarded the Pulitzer Prize for the paper's coverage of global terrorism in 2002. In May 2011, when Osama bin Laden was killed, his reaction was this:

> I'm not in any way naive about what al-Qaida is. It's an organization that terrifies me. I know it intimately. But I'm also intimately familiar with the collective humiliation that we have imposed on the Muslim world. The expansion of military occupation that took place throughout, in particular the Arab world, following 9/11 – and that this presence of American imperial bases, dotted, not just in Iraq and Afghanistan, but in Kuwait, Saudi Arabia, Doha – is one that has done more to engender hatred and acts of terror than anything ever orchestrated by Osama bin Laden.[234]

"The feeling of humiliation is the main source of Islamic extremism in the Middle East!" this is the view of Ehsan Shahghasemi, a Ph.D. student and member of the International Academy for Intercultural Research.[235] He elaborated his views in a follow-up personal message:

> Dear Evelin ... the topic you picked is very important in understanding why people get on airplanes and crush into buildings. In fact, in the Western mind, most say they are "crazy people." Yet, back in the Islamic World, the perceptions are different. People see how the West is advanced and they start seeing themselves as having the lower hand, particularly in military confrontations. The memories of the crusades help develop hatred as a mental framework which paves the way for proclaiming Jihad against all people of the West, including even those who have dedicated their lives to providing human relief in the most dangerous parts of the world. Also, when writing your book, please note you should know about Islam and different sects of it, particularly the Shia and the Sunni divide and the geographical, political, historical, cultural, lingual and economic contexts in which all these happen. Let me give you an example. The Shia of Afghanistan have always been a suppressed community. They have witnessed several massacres by other ethnicities during the past centuries. As a result, some of them want America to stay in Afghanistan. America oppresses the previous oppressors very well (I have traveled to Afghanistan two years ago and I survived a suicide bombing). But, at the same time they are attached to the Iranian regime which is also Shia. And, Iran is an enemy of the U.S. and sees its presence in Afghanistan as a threat. So, we see a deep divide in the Shia community in Afghanistan: Pro Iran Shia and Pro U.S. Shia. The sense of attachment to ethnicity is also very important, not for Muslims, but also for secular people. People will support for their "brothers" unconditionally. This is the way things go on!

Peace researcher Johan Galtung wrote to me in 2014 "Humiliation and terrorism sounds good, the key example of course being U.S. state terrorism, Hiroshima-Nagasaki, and recently Afghanistan, taking Pearl Harbor and 9/11 humiliation out on citizens in those cities (saving the key responsible imperial household) and on Afghanistan that had nothing to do with it (saving the half of Saudi Arabia that was behind it)."[236]

Zahid Shahab Ahmed is a peace researcher from Pakistan, who observes with sharp eyes how one man's terrorist is another man's freedom fighter, when Pakistan and India engage in cycles of humiliation over Kashmir, and how even Asian face saving and South Asian cooperation are in danger.[237]

I would like to frame the insights brought to the table by all those voices in my own language. What I see happen is that knowledge of terrorism is being subjugated to the misrecognition of reality driven by the sense of honor engendered within the culture that evolved within a strong security dilemma. What shines through is that peace studies are perceived as "dignity studies," while terror studies are "honor studies." Peace researchers urge those who study terror to do something perhaps too difficult for some of them to bring about, namely, to admit that "we" may also be guilty, and that it may not always be solely "the enemy's" religion, ideology, or insanity that inspires "their" evilness.

Peace studies also urge researchers to inquire where "their" religion and ideology comes from. Many might have forgotten that in most of the major regions of the world with high Islamic populations, forty to sixty years ago, secular leftists were the strongest political forces. This was the case, for instance, in Indonesia, the Middle East, and North Africa.[238] In the context of the Cold War, especially in the Middle East, the United States and allied states, including Saudi Arabia, supported right-wing and religious fundamentalist organizations as a counterforce to communist influence, and this included people who later founded Al-Qaeda. The Maktab al-Khidamat, or Afghan Services Bureau, for instance, was founded in 1984 by Abdullah Azzam and Osama bin Laden, with the United States as one of their main fund-raising destinations.[239] The first office in the United States was established within the Al Kifah Refugee Center in Brooklyn. The aim was to raise funds and recruit foreign mujahidin for the war against the Soviets in Afghanistan. The MAK paid the airfare for new recruits to be flown into the Afghan region for training. MAK became later the part of Al-Qaeda.

Furthermore, borders were carelessly drawn. Roberto Savio is the founder and former director-general of the international news agency *Inter Press Service*. He asks why it is that the Arab World seems to be at odds with the West even though Muslims in South Asia are more radical in terms of religious observance and views than those in the Middle East.[240] Savio offers four main reasons. First, in 1916, François Georges-Picot for France and Mark Sykes for Britain made a secret treaty to carve up the Ottoman Empire at the end of the First World War, with no consideration for ethnic and religious realities or for history.[241] Second, the colonial powers had authoritarian kings and sheiks rule these artificial countries without the participation of the people, in contrast to the process of democracy in Europe. Third, when the colonial powers left, the Arab countries had no modern political system, no modern infrastructure, and no local management, as colonial powers had not encouraged that kind of development. Fourth, in the absence of states providing education and health for their citizens, large networks of religious schools and hospitals filled this void, something that gave Muslim parties legitimacy when elections were finally permitted. Savio admits that this is a brutal compression of many decades of historical processes, yet, it is useful for understanding the anger and frustration in Middle East and why Da'esh can generate such attraction.[242]

Raymond Helmick, priest and conflict-resolution expert, draws a direct line from colonialism to Da'esh. He observes "a vast amount of denial in the West – the Christian/post-Christian West" – with respect to the origins of terrorist violence, "a refusal to recognize the uncomfortable fact that it results from a couple of centuries of colonialism":

> When the imperial banners fell from the grasp of the British and French after the Second World War, they were picked up basically by the United States,[243] whose custody of the Middle East has culminated recently in the devastation of Iraq and Afghanistan. ISIS is an effect of all this tremendous insult, understandable only as such. The fascination of ISIS with the ancient Caliphate is what has revived the Sunni-Shi'ite rivalry.[244]

It may well be that historian Gwynne Dyer is right when she says that the West gets the entire logic of terrorism backwards: "The purpose of major terrorist activities directed at the West, from the 9/11 attacks to ISIS videos, is not to 'cow' or 'intimidate' Western countries. It is to get those countries to bomb Muslim countries or, better yet, invade them."[245] Dyer believes that British Prime Minister David Cameron is naïvely playing the game of the terrorists when he says: "We will not be cowed by these sick terrorists," or when Canadian Prime Minister Stephen Harper promises, "We will not be intimidated."

What Dyer wants to say is that such rhetoric may be dangerously misinformed of the fact that the security dilemma has several layers and large depth in time: It is one thing to suddenly get the idea to attack others openly, yet, it is much more efficient to make a long-term plan and provoke the other side into attack so as to be able to appear as the morally righteous defender. Due to Western blindness to the simmering long-term sense of humiliation among those they believed to have under their control, they now underestimate the time dimension and the fact that provocation could be a strategy boiling up slowly, in a long-term fashion. Indeed, "In the Middle East, everything is connected. The North American and Northwest European habit of separating things into neatly compartmentalized topics just won't work there," writes Dan Smith, now director of the Stockholm International Peace Research Institute.[246]

Dyer continues explaining that these terrorists do not want to come to power in Canada or Britain or the U.S., but in Muslim countries, and what better way to establish revolutionary credentials and recruit local supporters than to get the West to attack first. In 2001, Osama bin Laden hoped for an American invasion of Afghanistan, and was more than successful, since he also got an U.S. invasion of Iraq. Provocation through terror still works now: The Global Terrorism Index shows that fatalities due to terrorism have risen fivefold in the thirteen years since the 9/11 attacks, despite the U.S.-led war on terror at a cost of 4.4 trillion U.S. dollars.[247] Dyer contends that terror did not rise despite of those efforts, but largely because of them: 3,361 people were killed by terrorism in 2000; 17,958 were killed in 2013. The Global Terrorism Index reports that only seven percent of terrorist organizations were eliminated by the direct application of military force, ten percent were victorious, took power, and disbanded their terrorist wings, while eighty percent dissolved by a combination of better policing and the creation of a political process that addressed the grievances of those who supported the terrorism.

As Dyer points out, it is ironic that only about five percent of the victims of the latest wave of terrorism lived in developed countries, while their deaths frequently trigger their governments to respond with ignorance and counterproductively. Dyer therefore advises that "foreigners" should keep out of the process.

If I am to add my view, then I would say that in a globally interconnected world there are no "foreigners" anymore on this planet. We are all in the same boat. And since humiliation at the hands of the West – be it meted out wittingly or unwittingly, and rightly or wrongly understood – is a significant recruiting tool for terror groups, the West is a player *inside* this conflict arena, rather than *outside*. Caring involvement would be the called-for response, rather than the traditional security dilemma inspired fight-or-flight culture, the get-involved-or-stay-away culture. All are involved, per definition, when the world is interconnected.

Also Michael Scheuer warns that only long-term global prevention can help in a situation where international affairs stoke religion and nationalism in wider populations.[248] Scheuer is a C.I.A. veteran with more than two decades of service, who ran the bin Laden station of the Counterterrorist Center from 1996 to 1999 and became known for his warnings against labeling leaders such Osama Bin Laden as pathological exceptions whose removal can solve the problem of terrorism.

What would such caring involvement and long-term global prevention involve? Would it mean, for example, to stabilize *failed states*? Why was the terminology of failed states introduced, and how it is being used? What if some see the creation of failed states as an achievement, including the terrorism that ensues? Retired general Wesley Kanne Clark was quoted earlier, and the conversation he had in the Pentagon in 2001 about a plan to go against seven Middle Eastern countries within the next five years.[249] One may say that success has been achieved. In Barack Obama's words, "in today's world, we're threatened less by evil empires and more by failing states."[250]

Failed states can indeed serve as safe havens for terrorists. "Weak government and chaos are always conducive to terrorism.... These groups do take advantage of that," reports Hans-Jakob Schindler, coordinator of a United Nations Security Council committee that monitors the Al-Qaeda sanctions list."[251] Omar Ashour is a Senior Lecturer in Security Studies and Middle East Politics at the University of Exeter, and his verdict is that Al-Qaeda in the Islamic Maghreb "exists not because of the Arab Spring but Algeria's military coup two decades ago and serious state-building failures in Algeria and northern Mali."[252]

There are doubts, however, as to whether the term *failed state* in itself is useful. Economist William Easterly suspects that the term was only introduced to facilitate the ease of superpower intervention.[253] First, the adjective *failed* insinuates that there was a successful state to start with, which might not have been the case.[254] The international legal system that is premised on state sovereignty, as well as the concept of a state itself, are historically recent inventions that do not necessarily create stability or democratic accountability.[255]

Despite the challenges of globalization, the state system might survive for some time to come, some scholars theorize, and in this context, "the populations of many failed states might benefit more from living indefinitely in a 'non-state' society than in a dysfunctional state, artificially sustained by international efforts."[256]

Terrorism may thus not only be facilitated by the presence of failed states, but also by non-failing nation states, particularly when borders had been carelessly drawn. Faith in the concept of the sovereign nation state may even detract from political responsibility to think globally. National self-interest might even hinder global solutions.

Pakistan's biggest nightmare is a strong, centralized, nationalist Afghan state – just the kind of state the foreign donor countries have been striving to create: "Such an Afghanistan, Pakistani leaders fear, will lay claim to the Pashtun areas that straddle a border that was drawn carelessly by the British and that Afghanistan has never fully accepted. They also fear that the Pashtuns might someday want a nation of their own."[257] Therefore "the Pakistani military has always distinguished between the 'good Taliban' – meaning those who fight in Afghanistan, like the Haqqanis — and the 'bad Taliban' – meaning members of the Pakistani Taliban who are at war with the Pakistani state."[258] Secretary of State Hillary Clinton and other senior administration officials visited Pakistan in October 2011 to demand that Pakistan should stop protecting the Haqqanis, "that Pakistan's spy agency either deliver the Haqqani network, a virulent part of the insurgency fighting American forces in Afghanistan, to the negotiating table, or help fight them in their stronghold in Pakistan's rugged tribal areas."[259]

The situation changed in 2015, when seven gunmen affiliated with the Tehrik-i-Taliban had conducted a terrorist attack on the Army Public School in the northwestern Pakistani city of Peshawar on December 16, 2014. The killing of children is seen as un-Islamic, even the perpetrators themselves saw it that way, and they have since felt compelled to find complicated justifications for why it was done. Since this attack happened, Pakistan's military has received free rein to do everything it considers necessary to provide security: "Thousands of soldiers were withdrawn from the eastern border with Pakistan's archenemy India and sent to fight the extremists. Military operations throughout the country were greatly expanded, and according to the armed forces, more than 2,700 militants were killed and thousands forced to flee into Afghanistan."[260]

What is the result by now? An "execution orgy," among others. The military now receives full support from a population who is grateful for more security and accepts, in return, that democratic achievements and freedoms are being curtailed. Draconian methods imposing a death penalty are practiced once more, and media freedom is restricted:

> After the school attack, the government lifted a moratorium on the death penalty imposed in 2008. Three days later, the first two prisoners who had been condemned to death were hanged, and more than 300 people have been executed since then. … The media are also expected to defer to the new power of the armed forces. "We are pressured to merely repeat the army's press releases," says a journalist in Peshawar who declined to be identified by name. "There are no reports of dead civilians and torture, merely stories about extremists who were targeted and killed, and about successes in the fight against terrorists."[261]

Kristian Berg Harpviken is the former director of the Peace Research Institute Oslo, and in 2010, he took the time to speak about the challenges to peace work as he observes them.[262] First, there is a tension between security and peace policies; in the case of Norway, for instance, NATO membership and peace policy may at times be in disharmony. Second, more work is needed to systematize a peace nation's "Hippocratic oath" of not causing harm, of not increasing danger for people in conflict. Third, others do not necessarily share Norway's political peace orientation, and this must be taken into account. To rephrase, what we learn from Harpviken is that the peace dialogue he stands for faces not just difficulties because it is not shared in traditional honor contexts, it risks also to be undermined by Western double standards. One of those double standards would be to inflict harm on others in the name of peace, or, as Harpviken formulates is, to violate the Hippocratic oath of first do no harm.

Nafeez Mosaddeq Ahmed is the director of the Institute for Policy Research and Development in London. He advises:

> We must not fall into the trap of the terrorists themselves – the inability to recognize the suffering of the Other, their wholesale demonization, the acceptance of their indiscriminate destruction as a necessary means to a "greater good." The only way forward is for people of all faith and none to stand together in rejecting the violence perpetrated in our name, whether by state or insurgent. Recognizing that the Paris atrocity is predictable blowback which is likely to worsen as we insist on narrow, reactionary militarized solutions, does not absolve the perpetrators of responsibility for their terrible crimes; but it might help us find a path to safety based on co-existence, renunciation of violence, and unity in adversity.[263]

The media carry a particular responsibility to avoid doing harm. "The Mumbai attacks were scripted and staged in a conscious effort to obtain maximum media coverage,"[264] meaning that the masterminds of the attacks turned the media into central accomplices. The media created a war story in which violence was a way of "fighting a battle," a presentation that obscured the fact that for both security forces and terrorists it was a public staging of their force.

Violence needs to be first *imagined* to be carried out, say anthropologists who study violence and conflict.[265] Representations of violence are part of the cultural repertoire of a society, and dead bodies, while they are empirical facts, are also statements in a discourse. Media workers, by selecting, framing, and editing, even during live news broadcasting, are unavoidably engaged in scripting a narrative that draws on the cultural repertoire for violence and conflict of their audiences, because otherwise those facts would not be accepted as factual.

May I end this sub-section with my warning: Terrorism is too dangerous to be used or abused in the context of honorable power play or of competition for profit, particularly so in times when one single person so inclined can cause another Chernobyl or Fukushima.[266]

All spheres of life are being colonized

The damage caused by a balance of terror as path to peace is manifold. To maintain it, society needs to maintain a high level of militarization, which, in turn, leads to the internalization of a culture of war and oppression, not just toward the "enemy" but also within one's own in-group.[267] The objectification of enemies is often already taught at an early age – a "master disconnection" is thus introduced[268] – and, as a side effect, the objectifiers themselves become less human.[269] A young man wrote about his military training experience the following: Whoever stepped out of line, or "questioned anything, considered alternatives, or attempted to think for themselves" had their "irresponsible defiance" immediately "transferred to public humiliation."[270]

"There is a clear connection between torture, ill-treatment and corrupt practices," reports the chairperson of the UN Subcommittee on the Prevention of Torture, Malcolm Evans. He presented the committee's annual report to the General Assembly's main body dealing with social, humanitarian, and cultural issues in New York in 2014.[271] Psychologist Nora Sveaass has worked for many years with survivors of trauma and forced migration and was a member of the UN Committee against Torture until 2013; now she is a member of the UN Subcommittee on Prevention of Torture. Also she sees a strong connection between mental health and human rights violations.[272]

To my observation, after forty years of global life, what is most dangerous are the ways dominator culture is maintained for its own sake, thus stoking the security dilemma back into full force where it otherwise could wane. Where the dominator culture is no longer a response to a manifest security threat, it creates its own threat through staying beyond its usefulness. I understand that it is not easy to give up familiar patterns of action that provide arenas for self-important heroism and triumphant victory, it is not easy to say goodbye to what Vamik Volkan calls chosen trauma.[273] Giving up the idea that greatness means being victorious in competition for domination, is hard. Yet, not giving it up is worse.

Presently, the existing global economic system is the strongest driver of this culture, at the same time the most concealed one, as it is underpinned by a quasi-religious belief, namely, that it is a law of nature that "the market" will be "wise."[274] I expand on this in my book on a dignity economy.[275] This belief provides triumphant victory only to a small elite, it propels quasi-religious elation to a few in Silicon Valley, it inspires masses of hopeful migrants from all around the world to follow false promises, and it provides terror entrepreneurs with ample recruits and many arenas for action. In other words, for the majority, the market does not provide wisdom; rather, it damages the health of individuals and collectives, physically and psychologically, including the global community, and it degrades our habitat, planet Earth. In other words, it leads to *sociocide*[276] and *ecocide*.[277]

As to the wisdom of the market, financial expert James Richards describes how the international monetary system has collapsed three times in the past hundred years, in 1914, 1939, and 1971, followed by periods of tumult: war, civil unrest, and significant damage to the stability of the global economy with everyday citizens as "guinea pigs."[278] Next time, he predicts, nothing less than the institution of money itself will be at risk: The fundamental problem is that money and wealth have become ever more detached; while true wealth is permanent and tangible, and has real value, money is transitory and ephemeral, and it may be worthless soon if central bankers and politicians continue on their current path.

Within today's reigning global economic frame, even the best of human traits – the desire to be generous – is narrowed down to charity, which means placing Band-Aids on wounds caused by the larger-scale context.[279] If "doing good" allows others to continue "doing bad," it is unwise. Geneviève Vaughan, the "mother" of the "mother economy" gift economy, writes that, "supposedly neutral patriarchal knowledge has validated male dominance in the fields of politics, religion, technology and economics for centuries in the West. It has given those gifts of validation to generations of tyrants everywhere."[280] Vaughan has developed the theory of a *gift economy* as an attempt to solve this problem, and she offers her work as her personal social gift to the world. What Vaughan attempts to do, so to speak, is to rescue economics and economy from the security dilemma's damaging influence.[281]

"Economic imperialism" is being committed by economists and non-economists alike, when everything is turned into "colonies of economics," be it management science, "positive" political science, psychological attribution theory, exchange theory in sociology, or location theory in geography; this is what we learn from political scientist Richard Hartwig and his mentor philosopher Paul Diesing.[282] We can add Donald Carveth's insight that even the concept of human mental health is being colonized when people internalize unconscionable superegos from unconscionable societies.[283] The *communal sharing* that Alan Page Fiske describes has been subjugated to the primacy of *market pricing*,[284] and "competent communities have been invaded and colonized by professionalized services – often with devastating results."[285] "Today the dominant narrative is that of market fundamentalism, widely known in Europe as neoliberalism," explains economist Kamran Mofid and continues: "The story it tells is that the market can resolve almost all social, economic and political problems. The less the state regulates and taxes us, the better off we will be. Public services should be privatized, public spending should be cut and business should be freed from social control. In countries such as the UK and the US, this story has shaped our norms and values for around 35 years: since Thatcher and Reagan came to power. It's rapidly colonizing the rest of the world, or as I would say: It has colonized the rest of the world."[286] Mofid's warning: "Marketization, privatization, liberalization, deregulation, self-regulation, profit-maximization, cost-minimization, highest returns to the shareholders, values-free actions and education, alternative facts, lies and deceitful thoughts, brainwashing, bribery and corruption," these are "the main ingredients of the Bastard Economics of Neoliberal Ideology."[287]

Consumerism is more in resonance with a culture of ranked honor than with equal dignity, despite of its official portrayal as being progressive. The reason is the promise that more consumption will provide a higher rank. Equal dignity can only emerge in the context of communal sharing, combined with what Fiske calls *authority ranking*, and only when that takes the form of care rather than domination.

Equal dignity can flourish only as long as quality is protected from being overly quantified. Many physicians now express unease; no longer can they tolerate being "nickeled and dimed" by insurers:

> Researchers have described two types of relationships that involve giving a benefit to someone else. In a market relationship, when you provide goods or services, you expect to receive cash or bartered goods of similar value in return. In a communal relationship, you are expected to help when there is a need, irrespective of payment. ... Caregivers should be appropriately reimbursed but should not be constantly primed by money. Success in such a model will require collegiality, cooperation, and teamwork – precisely the behaviors that are predictably eroded by a marketplace environment.[288]

Paul Diesing defines rationality in a relational fashion, describing five types of effectiveness or rationality: *technical* rationality (the efficient achievement of single goals), *economic* rationality (the efficient achievement of a plurality of goals), *social* rationality (meaning generating integrative forces in individuals and social systems), *legal* rationality (fundamental rules or rule-following), and *political* rationality (decision-making structures, such as differentiation/unification, which is the foundation of societal functioning). He would also have added *ecological* rationality had he written this after 1970. What Diesing offers, is the insight that rationality is an interrelated manifold of often conflicting outcomes of historic trends, rather than a logical system.[289]

Richard Hartwig admires Diesing for his conceptualization and points out that economic rationality has been overextended, leading to economic imperialism. Everything – from the environment to sex, or religion – is by now being conceptualized as a commodity that should be measured, priced, and treated as a morally neutral commodity. Sex can be sold and bought, despite the fact that to choose to sell and buy sexual experiences, or to reject it, is not a choice comparable with that between chocolate and vanilla ice cream. Similarly, the value and meaning of the environment is fundamentally degraded by making it a means to an end – "the master disconnection of capitalism and socialism today is the disconnection from the planet and nature."[290] What should be a source of value becomes an object of value. As a result, also the concept of freedom is degraded: "In the absence of personal or social integration, it becomes the freedom of the idle rich, a license to make choices which are trivial because they have no ultimate meaning for an individual."[291]

All segments of society are being colonized, and education is no exception. It manifests in the current trend in academia that has been described earlier, namely, the turn away from *Bildung* toward *Ausbildung* or training. The creation of "excellent sheep" is the result.[292] Education is now an "industrial sorting machine," rather than an "educational supporting experience."[293] In Germany, the corporate sector itself has developed a "master plan" for how to alter the country's educational system in their interest.[294]

Agriculture is yet another example among many where market mechanisms overrule democratic values and sound science. The present industrial model destroys soil, nutrients, water, and the dignity of people: "When we address the question of how to feed the world, we need to think relationally – linking current modes of production with our future capacities to produce, and linking farm output with the ability of all people to meet their need to have nutritious food and to live in dignity."[295]

Sociocide *is being committed*[296]

Ecocide and *sociocide* are connected, they mutually exacerbate each other and lead to the degradation of our global *socio-ecological systems*.[297] The sixth mass extinction of species is human-induced,[298] as by the end of this century flora and fauna loss is predicted to be between twenty to fifty percent of all living species on earth.[299] Between 1950 and 1990, one third of all fertile soils has been severely degraded or destroyed.[300] The rise of certain chronic diseases is being concealed.[301] New antibiotics are not being developed, not least because administering antibiotics is a rather short-term intervention and therefore not very profitable.[302]

Climate change is only one aspect of the ecological catastrophes unfolding, which will lead to even more social upheavals. Climate change will create widespread social disconnection and conflict, warns Dan Smith, now director of the Stockholm International Peace Research Institute, and former director of the Peace Research Institute Oslo and of International Alert in London:

> A demographic shift of unprecedented scale is under way. As people change habitat and ways of life, they face potential disconnection from norms that previously helped them manage relations within their communities and sustain the group's well-being. As these changes unfold, there will be some winners and more losers, with more again in between, getting by. Among the winners will be the conflict entrepreneurs, the gang leaders, the under bosses, while the foot soldiers will be recruited from among those young men who see little other (or, at least, no better) way of avoiding being losers. With most people caught in between. Unless there is dramatic change in how economies run, population growth and fast-paced urbanization will help drive continually increasing demand for natural resources across the next twenty years. This combines with rising prices to equate to growing competition for access to natural resources. There is an unmistakable risk here of big power rivalry; there also exists an international institutional framework able safely to contain exactly this kind of rivalry and reduce to negligible the risk of disputes turning violent.[303]

Social disconnections can grow from the bottom upward, or it can come from the top downward. Carol Smaldino has worked as a social work psychotherapist for over twenty-five years in the United States and in Italy, and she feels thoroughly discouraged when she observes how wealthier people increasingly care less, while poorer minorities feel ever more helpless.[304] Research is on her side, as it indeed shows that "rich people just care less."[305]

On my global journey of forty years, I have observed the thinning of the social glue in many forms and variations. I did my doctoral research in Somalia and Rwanda, on the background of Nazi Germany,[306] I have worked for many years as a clinical psychologist in Egypt, and have lived on all continents, with my most important platform being Norway. What I sense is that wherever the dominator culture has emerged, people's souls are being damaged, through "being taught that they have no choice but to bow to a maligned system."[307] I see it happen less in Somalia and Norway, and more in Germany and Rwanda, and their cultural differences can therefore illustrate the different degrees to which this process unfolds. The background for those differences may first and foremost be geopolitical location – both Norway and Somalia are located at geopolitical fringes and have no significant natural resources to offer (oil was found in Norway only recently, historically seen), while Germany and Rwanda are located in central and fertile regions. No empire has ever invested noteworthy energy into teaching Somalis and Norwegians how to bow, while populations in Germany and Rwanda have had to learn to obey over many centuries, so much so that they at some point were willing to perpetrate unspeakable atrocities on the instructions of their superiors, willing to profoundly betray and humiliate the humanity of themselves and others.

As it was largely left alone, Norway was able to emerge from a culture of proud, independent, and violent Viking warriors and adventurers throughout the past centuries, and has moved toward a culture of *likeverd* (equality in dignity), *dugnad* (communal cooperation) and global responsibility (Nansen passport). It is only now, as oil was found, that Norway no longer is a poor neighbor, and that also many Norwegians learn to bow to the seductions of global economic promises and are willing to leave their cultural heritage behind.[308] Somali culture of today resembles historical Viking culture insofar as proud warriors, when they commit violence, have as their primary motivation unrestrained pride, rather than obedience to authorities – the ravages perpetrated by the Vikings a thousand years ago could be said to have been motivated by warrior pride as much as was the quasi-genocide committed in Somalia in 1988.[309]

In Rwanda, its hierarchical culture seems to have injected a kind of social-psychological poison into society that stands in opposition to the stubborn pride of the noble warriors of Somalia, namely, excessive mistrust among subordinates. Many cultural traditions in Rwanda reflect toxic neighbor relations already long before any genocidal killings occurred, far back in history, and not just between Hutu and Tutsi, also between Hutu and Hutu and Tutsi and Tutsi. I collected many accounts of traditions of mistrust or *méfiance*. How come, for instance, that a newborn baby would be given names such as "son of hatred"?[310] Or, as an informant with a Tutsi background reported:

> There are Hutu names that illustrate that there must be quite a large amount of suspicion or *méfiance* in the Hutu population. Names may mean: "I am surrounded by hatred" (je suis dans la haine), "they will kill me" (ils me tuerions), "I am not there because they want it," or, "if they could do as they like I would not live" (je ne suis pas là grâce à eux), or "I am there only because of God."[311]

Méfiance seems to have permeated all of Rwandan society over the centuries: "The Batutsi Mwamis also manipulated a complex web of spies, and thus not only maintained their power, but developed a capacity for political intrigue and paranoia that remains to this day throughout Rwandan society."[312] In short, free and spontaneous trustful loving care and compassion, all of which is needed as social glue for a society, had been squeezed out of it. I often sense a similar social "coldness" when I come to Germany, as well as in Japan, beneath layers of rules for politeness. I grew up in Germany and lived in Japan for three years, and I have often wondered about the apparent lack of spontaneous solidarity with fellow humans, alongside a high level of submissiveness to and identification with authority (*Obrigkeitshörigkeit, Obrigkeitsdenken*). What I call the *art of humiliation* seems to have succeeded in turning populations into robot-like humans, filling them with fear and servile readiness to sell out fellow humans and shared humanity to please authorities. Hannah Arendt's notion of the banality of evil comes to mind,[313] both in connection with the Holocaust during World War II, but also with the genocide against the Tutsi in Rwanda in 1994, and, by now in the social atmosphere of world society as a whole.

One does not have to resort to extreme examples of genocide, however, less extreme instances abound. The social fabric is hollowed out wherever the security dilemma's culture sells out diversity and complexity for uniformity and for the illusion of purity. "Tissues" of a community can be damaged just as the tissues of mind and body.[314] Some manifestations of this phenomenon are tragic, for example, when heroic solidarity is punished rather than recognized and respected. The Sami people (traditionally known in English as Lapps or Laplanders), for instance, are an indigenous Finno-Ugric people in the far north of Norway, Sweden, Finland, the Kola Peninsula of Russia, and the border area between south and middle Sweden and Norway. The Sami have for centuries been the subject of discrimination and abuse by the dominant cultures surrounding them. In Norway, during World War II, Sami risked their lives to help over 3,000 desperate people who had Nazi Gestapo on their heels into safety over the border into neutral Sweden. Tragically, after the war, instead of being honored, they were demonized for their heroism – as it must be assumed, partly due to them being Sami.[315] They were falsely accused of having stolen from the people they saved, or having abandoned helpless people to die in the mountains. They were left with a deep sense of disappointment, of having been punished and betrayed by the Norwegian people and the Norwegian government for having been saviors.

Another similarly tragic story of penalized solidarity is Jovan Divjak in Sarajevo, an ethnic Serb who faced grim consequences for betraying his ethnic loyalty when he gave primacy to his love to his hometown Sarajevo and defended it against attacks from Serb forces during the Bosnian war.[316] It was a great honor for me to meet Jovan Divjak in Sarajevo in August 2016.

The impressions I got in the Nile Delta region showed me that the situation can be even more intricate. In that delta, over the past centuries, elites have wielded oppression very openly, perhaps too openly, as they did not achieve the desired docility among their subjects. Social structures in Lower Egypt (not in Upper Egypt, as it is a different case), may be as collectivistic and hierarchical as in Rwanda, Germany or Japan, yet, I found a much higher degree of resistance, of willingness to create social warmth and solidarity amongst fellow humans in defiance of authorities. Egypt had to tackle two millennia of oppression after Pharaonic greatness succumbed to Greek, Roman, Arab, French, and at last British domination. Egyptian defiance reminded me of certain aspects in "slave culture" that have carved out niches of livability for their members,[317] or of the spirit of Czech Good Soldier Schweik, a figure created by Jaroslav Hašek (1983 – 1923). The figure of Schweik epitomizes subtle resistance through humor as a disguise for obstructive subversion. Egyptian humor is similar. It gives Egyptians their reputation of being the "Czechs" of the Middle East.

Sadly, in overall terms, we live in times where the social fabric of the entire global village is being systemically thinned out, fragmented, and worn down. The samurai way of the knife is now applied also by American special operations troops, for instance, and this may contribute to "democratizing" and inspiring lone wolf acts, just as so many other tools that formerly were reserved for power elites have been democratized and are now used by whoever feels called to do so.[318] Neighbors of nuclear installations that once were designed to be peaceful, may now have to look into the skies with dread, as such installations can easily transmute into bombs, triggered even by the cutest of play-drones.

The social fabric of the global village is being thinned out and worn down also by the new form of the security dilemma, which runs its fault line between the famous "one percent" and the rest. Political analyst Naomi Klein describes the situation in ways that profoundly resonate with my global observations: "… just when we needed to gather, our public sphere was disintegrating; just when we needed to consume less, consumerism took over virtually every aspect of our lives; just when we needed to slow down and notice, we sped up; and just when we needed longer time horizons, we were able to see only the immediate present."[319] My observations resonate with all those who say that "present-day neoliberal rationality weakens the collective spirit by transforming societies and subjectivities around the notion of enterprise."[320] All this happens not only in for-profit arenas but also with nonprofit organizations. The neoliberal development paradigm restructures social formations through the instrument of external funding, and the result is that even nonprofit NGOs turn into "missionaries of the new era" of economism.[321] As current monetary systems are built on bank debt and scarcity, they are altogether incompatible with sustainability, as they produce short-term thinking, require unending economic growth, concentrate wealth in the hands of a small elite, while destroying what is often called the "social capital," or, better, "relational activity that provides for the healthy development of all people."[322]

In my beloved Egypt, I could observe at close hold how the destruction of social capital can lead to revolutions and how this is bound to end in terror. Amitai Etzioni writes: "The Western media faithfully reports every twist and turn in the evolution of the Egyptian democracy," assuming that what the Egyptian people "really" want is a secular, Western-minted democracy, while the main dynamic in Egypt is an economic one.[323] I concur. The letters I receive from my friends in Egypt lay bare the utter desperation they feel when they know that they will never be able to get married due to lack of resources, and this is only one of myriad dark shadows over their lives. Lebanese-born French author Amin Maalouf explains what happened, and this is valid not only for Lebanon or Egypt: The discourses of both, Islam and the West, have enough internal theoretical consistency to create hope, yet, in practice, both betray their own ideals.[324] The West is unfaithful to its own values, which disqualifies it in the eyes of the people it claims to acculturate into democracy. And the Arab-Muslim world no longer has the legitimacy of the family nor the patriotic legitimacy, around which it was structured historically.

It was the Egyptian avant-garde who stood up first, following Alexis de Tocqueville's observation that revolution looms not when poverty is so severe that it causes apathy and despair, but when conditions have been somewhat improving, and, in particular, when a few are benefiting and not the rest.[325] The Egyptian avant-garde had the emotional and material resources to rise up, and they toppled Hosni Mubarak.[326] They asked for dignity, and what this meant, was a decent life, with jobs. Then the Egyptian majority elected groups that sought to impose a version of Sharia on their nation, and what they wanted was, again, a decent life, with jobs. By now, strict military rule is the endgame.

The Egyptian avant-garde believed that embracing Western notions of dignity would bring jobs to the country, while the more conservative populace hoped that Islam would do the same, only to result in disappointment both of them. Neither is in a position to offer jobs and a decent life, particularly not in a global context that is exploitative and makes it an unsolvable task per definition.

Historian and Egypt expert Bjørn Utvik has studied the economic discourse of the Egyptian Islamists. He documents how their economic discourse resembles that of other radical nationalist movements in that they seek justice, development, and independence, in opposition to the injustices of the current order, and in opposition to archaic social practices and attitudes that hinder development.[327]

To my observation, no local effort for betterment, of whatever kind, can truly succeed as long as global *constitutive rules* antagonize them.[328] There is no alternative to creating trans-national and trans-local capacities, which means globally interlinking the efforts of all local "civic and ethical entrepreneurial networks that are currently in development."[329] This is why I invest my lifetime into creating a dignity movement not just locally, but globally.

We had our 27th Annual Dignity Conference in Dubrovnik, Croatia, in 2016.[330] When the Republic of Croatia became independent from Yugoslavia, first, war destroyed the country (1991 – 1995), and then destruction continued with the transition from the Yugoslavian-type communism to global market-capitalism: "... there is a widespread belief in Croatian society at large, that the pressing needs for economic and infrastructural restoration and developments following the Homeland war have made the society particularly vulnerable to exploitation by domestic and international 'snatch and grab' investors who are in league with crooked politicians."[331]

Can the media provide a counterweight, at least in the West? It seems that this is not a straightforward task either. Journalistic elites may at times be too heavily involved in the overall elite milieu to act as advocates of the public interest in critical and enlightened ways.[332] Can politicians form a counterweight? During the past decades, also the "professionalization" of politics has had its price.[333]

The result is the shattering of the social contract in general, as it was developed from the eighteenth through the twentieth centuries to mean that the laws and institutions of government should function to protect the equality, freedom, human rights, and life-possibilities of citizens. Philosopher Glen Martin points out that this contract is now being replaced with economic Darwinism: "a predatory society in which law and government operate to promote the callous exploitation of the majority by the super-wealthy few, and in which everything is commodified – from human beings to natural resources to the environment – everything is subject to merciless exploitation without regard to human welfare, the common good, or the future of our planet."[334]

The Loss of Happiness in Market Democracies is the title of a book that describes in which ways wealth does not hold its promise. Drug addiction has increased dramatically in some Western countries, particularly in the United States of America.[335] As prosperity increases in Western countries, family solidarity and community integration are being eroded, and people begin to distrust political institutions and each other. The author of this book, Robert Lane, a political scientist, urges people in the West to increase *companionship* even at the price of decreasing *income*.[336] Linda Hartling summarizes: "Lane talks about how the existing economic system leads to 'relational malnutrition.' Unfortunately, we compensate for this with consumerism."[337]

As many others, also I feel disgusted by what some call the "decadence" in the West. This decadence is a consequence of the erosion of the very *relational health* that is needed to nurture sustainable happiness. To fill in for this relational erosion, people engage in endless searches for monetary compensation that allows them to consume material goods pushed by advertisement as a substitute for healthy connection. In my book on *dignism*, I have expanded on this topic.[338]

Also sociologist Hartmut Rosa wonders why so many people in Western societies today fail to lead a "good life," even though they enjoy so much more freedoms than earlier generations. The problem, as he sees it, is the acceleration of human activity under capitalism, a regime of deadlines that causes a widespread sense of alienation.[339] Another German sociologist, Werner Seppmann, calls the current increase in violence and irrationalism *decivilization*, driven by business-styled societal systems that degrade the satisfaction of human needs into a secondary consequence of economic growth.[340] Another European writer, Ilija Trojanow, warns that those who produce nothing and consume nothing will become increasingly superfluous for the murderous logic of late capitalism.[341] He warns that also those who still believe to be the winners are deceiving themselves: also they will become victims. Nobody will be able to watch the news of the ravages of climate change and the mercilessness of neoliberal labor market policies from a safe distance in the long run.

Presently widespread beliefs that dignity can be gained through economic competition and the accumulation of possessions, coopt citizens around the world into weakening the social and ecological fabric of their communities rather than strengthening it. Georg Schramm is a German comedian who is inspired by Warren Buffet and his analysis of the war of the rich against the poor, with derivatives as weapons of mass destruction.[342] Schramm's parody starts with describing countries as junkies who are being hooked with cheap money, only for the dealers to raise the prices shortly after. Then comes the billing company and takes everything, from water, gas, and electricity to pensions, with the global collection company represented by the IMF. The "drug dealer" itself is also addicted, and, as all junkies, throws huge parties whenever drugs are secured for a few days. Billions of dollars of cheap money have been delivered to the dealer so far, and while many Americans live on ration cards, seven hundred of the richest own two-thirds of everything. Schramm asks: What can be done to remedy this situation? He suggests to look at how wars on drugs typically are being won. They are won, among others, by dismantling syndicates and drug cartels. This is what should happen also in this case. Yet, it is not. Governments are inactive because also they are customers of the dealers. Instead, the end users are left to go cold turkey whenever they rampage and attack one another.[343] Clearly, Schramm's parody entails much realism.[344]

Even remedies meant to alleviate the risks are being instrumentalized for ulterior goals, eventually increasing the risks rather than decreasing them, in that way thinning out social and ecological reserves ever more. MetLife Insurance Portfolio Manager Lawrence Oxley has written a book on how extreme climate events represent major "investing opportunities" for the stock, bond, and futures markets.[345] As long as elites are in power who are interested in maintaining their privileged status, or would-be elites try to climb up, we can expect that they will view risks through the lens of how they can serve their interests. Risks might not just be denied, neglected, or covered up, they may even be amplified to be instrumentalized.

For the average citizen, it will be ever more important to understand that the argument of "you need to support this or that political or corporate strategy, because it responds to this or that necessity or risk," may be a manipulation. The need may be very real, while the suggested solution may represent a manipulation. Since the aim of plunder is not sustainable long-term survival, the long-term result of allowing plunder to go on is suicidal for the collective. In short, as long as we, as humankind, arrange our affairs on planet Earth in ways that climate degradation improves business opportunities, humanity's survival is in danger.

History offers ample evidence for challenges and needs being real, while solutions were perilous. Adolf Hitler was able to capitalize on a problem felt by many Germans, namely, humiliated national honor combined with harsh economic conditions. His solution, however, led to mass homicide and suicide. The Cold War started out from people's legitimate desire for security. Nuclear weapons were the welcome solution: First, massive nuclear retaliation was envisioned, later "flexible retaliation" with tactical nuclear weapons,[346] and the result is that humankind has so far escaped the loss of most of life on Earth only by sheer luck.[347] Under a strong security dilemma *military* security is sought, only in an interconnected world it can *human* security be realized.

Today, the need for a *job* may traverse a similar path. More profit is made when jobs are eliminated through automatization, apart from the fact that for a functioning economy the concept of job was never essential in the first place.[348] I always wonder: People wish to have "a life,"[349] why is the concept of "job" being maintained? Why do people desperately clamber for jobs, even though this risks the annihilation of all life on Earth, this time not through one big catastrophe like nuclear weapons, but through myriad of slowly emerging catastrophes? Jobs in the military industry, for instance, contribute to war. Another social catastrophe is the rise of inequality,[350] which, in turn, has the potential to stoke religious and ideological terror and extremism, which then can link up with organized crime, all of which can be played up, or down, for ulterior goals.[351]

"De nye gigantene" (The New Giants) is the title of an article by Bent Sofus Tranøy, professor of political science in Norway, where he summarizes how the world's economy has stumbled from crisis to crisis during the past six or seven years. Growth is far lower than prior to 2008, inequality is on the rise, the financial sector is as rich, powerful, and risky as it was – not least thanks to various state subsidies – and, while some of the debt burdens have been moved onto the public balance sheets, they have not shrunk.[352]

This sad state of present affairs has not led political elites to create new thinking. It has, however, at least given space to alternative thought within the field of economy, thought that was not particularly appreciated before those crises. One example is economist Thomas Piketty.[353] In his book *Capital in the Twenty-First Century,* Piketty shows that the post-war years were a historical exception with respect to economic equality. The dominating trend throughout several hundreds of years has been that capital grows much faster than the economy in general. This has only been interrupted by capital shocks in the nineteenth century, caused by two world wars and the ending of colonies. In the course of the past thirty years, neoliberal deregulation, tax cuts, and lower economic growth, have moved us back again toward levels of inequality comparable with the eighteenth century. Andy Haldane from the Bank of England writes and speaks so creatively about these themes that *Time Magazine* has honored him as the world's most influential person in 2013.[354] Journalist Roberto Savio spells out the problems with inequality:

- inequality, with extreme wealth for a few, the middle class shrinking in rich countries, and permanent unemployment for ever more
- the rich are not paying taxes as before, because of a large number of fiscal benefits and fiscal paradises
- politics has become subservient to economic interests
- social and ecological resources are hollowed out and plundered; current consumption patterns rapidly deplete the world's non-renewable resources[355]

If political economist Karl Polanyi were still alive, he would be fascinated to see the *double movement* he described in 1944 now being driven to ever new extremes.[356] One side of the movement has faith in the blessings of a self-regulating market system, and this has spread from the Anglo-Saxon world to Central and Eastern Europe, as well as to Asia, Africa, and Latin America. The counter-movement calls for the protection of our eco- and sociospheres against these "blessings."[357]

As noted earlier, *sociocide* and terror are connected. Sherzai was thirteen years old boy when poverty made his uncle sell him to Taliban insurgents for 15,000 Pakistani rupees (170 dollars). "Then the Taliban told me to carry out a suicide attack," he reported when he later was in a juvenile correctional facility in Kabul, "They said I would be a martyr and I would go to paradise."[358]

Earlier, I have introduced Tom Koenigs, Member of the German Federal Parliament in Berlin, and Special Representative of the UN Secretary-General for Afghanistan for the United Nations Assistance Mission in Afghanistan, UNAMA. He researched the suicide attacks in Afghanistan from 2001 to 2007.[359] His report on suicide attacks in Afghanistan 2001 – 2007 would merit an entire chapter in this book:

> During 2007, UNAMA has worked to raise awareness of the impact that Afghanistan's current conflict is having on civilians and to ensure that everything possible is being done to protect them from harm. I am highlighting suicide attacks through this study because, to a greater extent than with any other form of warfare we are witnessing, the victims (around 80 percent) are civilian. Even this figure understates the problem. The immediate victims of a suicide attack are those who are killed or wounded, their families, and their friends. However, the target of such attacks is also society as a whole. Suicide attacks traumatize entire communities, undermine popular faith in institutions of the state, provoke responses that limit freedoms, and intimidate populations into a sense that hopes of peace rest only with the providers of violence. Perhaps the most tragic element of this whole phenomenon is the bomber himself (so far in Afghanistan there are no "herselfs"). To gain insights into the minds of such people, and the networks behind them, UNAMA researchers interviewed more than two dozen people arrested in failed attacks, or on suspicion of being involved. The results are detailed in Chapter VI. Some denied being suicide attackers; others did not. The overwhelming impression was that these were mere foot soldiers, some willingly involved, but several clearly duped or coerced. This impression is further borne out by recent reports of young children being recruited for suicide missions. Populations in Afghanistan, as well as across the border in Pakistan, where much (but not all) of the recruiting and training happens, clearly need to be protected from such callous exploitation. The use of children, in particular, suggests that the groups responsible for their 'recruitment' are seeing a need to employ increasing extremes of barbarity. The final chapter of this study contains recommendations. I hope these will be acted upon, and that this study in itself is not the final word on the matter, but the start of a wider exploration of what we can all do to protect Afghanistan, its neighbors, and the world, from this true problem from hell.[360]

Children are even more vulnerable to being influenced than adolescents, be it to embrace social or antisocial behavior. In Western countries, babies up to three years olds are targeted by advertisers, inspired by studies that show that children can recognize around one hundred brand logos by the age of three, and, even more importantly, that some babies "request brands as soon as they can speak."[361] These advertisers act in the spirit of retail analyst Victor Lebow, who wrote in his famous 1955 paper that Americans would have to "make consumption their way of life."[362] If they succeeded in making the buying and using of goods into a kind of ritual, and things were "consumed, burned up, worn out, replaced and discarded at an ever-increasing rate," this would not only keep the economy going, people would also find "spiritual satisfaction and ego gratification in consumption."[363]

Many readers will deem the manipulation into terrorism to be antisocial and the manipulation into consumption to be prosocial. Yet, one may argue that both manipulations are antisocial, only to different degrees and in different ways. The reason is that the pillars of our current economic arrangements may lead to destruction only somewhat slower than through terrorism, namely, through *ecocide* – remember Ugo Bardi's above-mentioned dead-end verdict – and through *sociocide*.

Chirevo Kwenda, expert on African traditional religion in South Africa, describes the failure of Lebow's enthusiastically advocated strategy.[364] Kwenda explains how social cohesion in Africa does not flow from state sovereignty, liberal democracy, the advance of modernity, or the global economy. All this is paid for by millions of African people willing to accept alienated lives. My global experience shows me that Chirevo Kwenda's observation is relevant not just for Africa, it is equally relevant even in the very heartlands of the originators of this experiment in the West. The fault line does no longer run between the West and the Non-West; people everywhere now pay the price of alienation and social exclusion, on top of ecological disintegration.

As mentioned before, together with many others, also I feel disgusted by what some call the "decadence" of the West. In my book on a dignity economy, I observe the loss of happiness and the many futile searches for compensations.[365] I feel surrounded by *fog of war*, to say it with Carl von Clausewitz, when blessings for all are promised, yet, social and ecological disintegration is what unfolds. Either those aims are being missed, or professed in bad faith. Indeed, as a psychologist, I cannot avoid concurring with Howard Richards that the social glue that traditionally was provided by the extended family cannot be expected to flow from the abstract contracts of the market.

Philosopher of social science Howard Richards summarizes: "The dynamic of capital accumulation has been a major, perhaps the major, dynamic of modern history; as has social exclusion, which is another consequence of the same normative structure."[366] Richards' conclusion, after having analyzed these issues for the past five decades, is that the problem is not a psychological one, it is not greed among certain elites, and is not the lack of regulations. Implementing more regulations will not work. Deeper change is needed. We have to go back more than two thousand years if we want to understand what is needed to rectify, namely, the ground pillars of our economic institutions.

Roman law, especially *jus gentium*, by abstracting from the empire's multicultural diversity and applying to Roman citizens and non-citizens alike, made it easier for the Roman empire to collect tribute and protect merchants.[367] An ancient Roman magistrate, the *praetor*, was tasked with settling the disputes within *jus gentium*. The modern world is built on successors of Roman law, which serves the interest of a few in the short term, while being paid for with a very high price, namely, that it is in nobody's interest in the long term.[368]

There are many ways by which Roman law principles now contribute to the shredding of our social cohesion. Here is one that has been described already in a previous chapter: "This is not my problem! This is not my responsibility!" is a cry that I hear all around the world, and it increases in tact with contemporary Roman law rules being implemented more thoroughly. People believe that there is no responsibility when there is no contract. De-solidarization is thus legitimized.

I personally feel my own humanity being terrorized, tortured, and humiliated just by watching this trend deepen everywhere around the world. In my work, I welcome all liberation struggles from whatever oppressive aspects that are connected with traditional collectivist society models, yet, their ability to create social glue should not be thrown out as well. I do see the advantages of creating larger and more abstract network of relationships, as mentioned before, I am an admirer of Paulo Freire's colleague Clodomir de Morais and his verdict that is an "artisan weakness" to not let go of control. Yet, as soon as people are dislodged from their relationships too far, unfrozen too far, as terrorism experts would say,[369] they can be sent into a rat race more effectively, which then can be made ever more brutal. By disconnecting their members, whole societies can fall prey to accepting devastating rat races. Howard Richards explains:

> It was the time when the *Gemeinschaften* of the Middle Ages were disintegrating; the time when the evils of feudalism were being superseded by the evils of capitalism; a time, one of many times, when the *dominium* of some

> meant the exclusion of many, when the consensual contract facilitated the commercial transactions of those who offered products that somebody else wanted to buy, while the dissolution of personal bonds, and their replacement by the arms-length transactions defined by the *jus gentium*, isolated those who had only labor power to sell, inspiring fear in those who succeeded in selling their labor power today but who knew they might not succeed tomorrow, and despair in those who did not succeed.[370]

Howard Richards has studied the march of Roman law to its present triumph of defining the ethics of our time and ruling the world.[371] Richards follows John Dewey's *naturalistic pragmatism*[372] and, more recently, *critical realism*.[373] He follows Charles Taylor and John Searle in that *constitutive rules* govern our bargaining society.[374] He follows Roy Bhaskar in that *generative mechanisms* produce the phenomena we can observe.[375] He follows Anthony Giddens in saying that today's post-modern condition is one of *radicalized modernity*."[376] And he follows Immanuel Wallerstein in pointing out that it is one single set of constitutive rules that defines the modern *world-system*,[377] namely, Roman law principles.[378] Richards calls for a new logic of cooperation and solidarity to become strong enough to limit the current *systemic imperative*, as Ellen Meiksins Wood calls it, running amok.[379]

The same systemic imperative has also formed the backdrop for colonialism with its massive deconstruction of indigenous cultures,[380] as much as it underpins what is now known as neoliberalism, which, as Richards suggests, should rather be called *neo-Romanism*. It also drives the so-called war on terror, in its thrust not just against people identified as extremists, but generally against traditional ways of life that resist the ethics of modernity.[381]

If mass *disconnection* is our present-day condition, and Roman law principles the root problem, then *integration* is the solution of our time to solve problems and to serve life, so suggests Richards. Earlier, Howard Richards' vision for how social structure can be aligned with their ecological context has been laid out, and the methodologies he suggests for improving it.[382] Richards recommends correcting the basic cultural structures derived from Roman law as follows: *Suum cuique* (to each his own) needs to be corrected by socially functional forms of land tenancy and socially functional forms of property in general. *Pacta sunt servanda* (agreements must be kept) needs to be enlarged by mutual beneficial reciprocity and responsibility for one another's welfare regardless of whether there is a contract. It should be acknowledged that externalities may be centralities. As Linda Hartling adds, healthy relationships are a "centrality" to survival of humankind, not an externality.[383] *Honeste vivare* (to live honestly) needs to be corrected by recognizing that our very identity is relational. *Alterum non laedere* (not hurting others by word or deed) needs to be adapted to promote an ideal of service to others, above and beyond the obligation not to harm them.

Richards suggests that these corrections will avoid reverting to the present one-size-fits-all global regime of capital accumulation, and will generate multiple ways of integrating factors of production to provide goods and services that support life.

In my work, I call for *dignism* (dignity and -ism) for future societal designs to replace the terminology of "capitalism," "socialism" or "communism" as catch words of cycles of humiliation.[384]

Wrong lessons are being drawn for the future

Does the world progress? This question elicits bruised egos and indignated counterattacks. Why is that? The problem lies with beliefs. As explained before, beliefs have two functions: first, to guide our relationship with our ecosphere, which means understanding the world and testing reality, second, to guide our relationship with our sociosphere, which means living with ourselves and with others.[385] Unfortunately, the second function often undermines the first. It can happen that we stand in the way of our own reality testing, with the highest barriers being erected by dynamics of humiliation: "It cannot be what should not be," or "I know, but I can't believe it," is the last resort for people who have linked their personal sense of worth to a certain vision of reality. Any dent on their vision is perceived as a personal violation of their honor that must be fought back. Old-fashioned traditions of dueling become astonishingly alive.[386] Even scientists fall for them, those whose identity ought to be connected with sound reality testing. When I listen to scientists speak, including very renowned scientists, anywhere in the world, I am amazed at the amount of spiteful denigration that is meted out against those who hold different opinions. The proverbial *fog of war* obscures the view on reality. I observe this dynamic unfolding more crudely in individualist Western cultures, though, where personal independence is emphasized, and more covertly in collectivist cultures that focus more on interdependence and on saving face.

Does the world progress? If we count as progress that cruelty has in many ways become less obvious, more hidden, more "refined," more "Orwellian," then the answer could be "yes."[387] The answer would be "no," however, if we consider that sugarcoating destruction does not necessarily make it less deadly. Hailing consumerism as progress, for instance, does not undo its destructiveness. In other words, lessons drawn from within the dominator culture may mislead. Today's "party of consumerism" is unsustainable, "success" achieved by way of unsustainable overuse of resources cannot last. Economic growth is not necessarily "a rising tide lifting all boats," and capital is not necessarily "trickling down to everybody." Instead, social and ecological resources may be hollowed out and plundered, with current consumption patterns rapidly depleting the world's non-renewable resources.[388] "We can no longer pretend that the creation of wealth for a few will inevitably benefit the many – too often the reverse is true," says Jeremy Hobbs, executive director of Oxfam International.[389]

Futile hopes have been generated by the Brundtland Commission and its optimistic "yes we can" moment in 1987.[390] Physicist Paul Raskin is the author of the widely known important essay in 2002 titled *Great Transition*.[391] In 2014, twelve years after the optimistic moment of 2002, he is disillusioned. Since 1987, policy and academic circles have adopted the language of sustainability, yet, at the same time, we saw "a neoliberal political-economic philosophy consolidated in centers of power, unleashing a highly unsustainable form of market-led globalization."[392] Raskin laments that the world became rich in sustainability action plans, of which he wrote a number himself, but poor in meaningful action. Science was able to illuminate the challenges, and civil action could win this or that battle, but systemic deterioration outpaced piecemeal progress. Raskin confirms my evaluation of the Rio+20 Summit 2012, in that "it could muster only a constricted vision of a greener economy, bookending a quarter century of the decline of hope."[393] Its time now, not for naïve optimism and also not for dystopian despair, but for pragmatic hope:

> The signature feature of the Planetary Phase – the enmeshment of all in the overarching proto-country, Earth – suggests an answer. The natural change agent for a Great Transition would be a vast and inclusive movement of global citizens. The world now needs citizens without borders to come together for a planetary community. ... The challenge is extraordinary, but so are the times. In transformative moments, small actions can have large consequences. The efforts of an active minority can ripple through the cultural field and release latent potential for social change.[394]

Does the world progress? Also Pablo Razeto-Barry has asked this question.[395] He is the son of Luis Razeto, a father of solidarity economics. I had the privilege of being invited into the Razeto family home and intellectual universe in 2012 in Chile through Howard Richards. Razeto and his colleagues conclude that the global ecosystem is approaching a planetary tipping point, as are local ecological systems. When forced across critical thresholds, a system can suddenly and irreversibly shift from one state to another.

A succinct summary of the many crises humankind has created for itself is given by Otto Scharmer when he points at three divides that separate us from our primary sources of life: ecological, social, and spiritual divides.[396] As to the ecological divide, humankind currently uses 1.5 planets; the social divide manifests in rising poverty, inequity, fragmentation, and polarization;

and the spiritual divide increases rates of burnout and depression in tact with the widening gap between the GDP and the actual well-being of people.[397]

Futile hopes have also been created by the important progress over the last fifty or fifty-five years in the systematic internationalization of human rights. Maria Dahle reports that a worrying development is under way already for a number of years.[398] Dahle is the director of the Human Rights House Foundation in Oslo, Norway, and she looks back on many decades of experience in the field. This is her report: Around 1980, civil society flourished. Yet, this was also the time when neoliberalism got its start. A wave of privatization followed. Ten years later, civil society faces serious restrictions. It is being choked by government-corporate alliances that use a plethora of interferences, be they legal or practical. Maria wonders: Is civil society regarded as having become too confrontational? Does it stand in the way of profit interests?[399]

In their 2017 World Report, Human Rights Watch warns that demagogues now threaten human rights, as Donald J. Trump and European populists can be seen to "foster bigotry and discrimination."[400] Economist Kamran Mofid, founder of Globalization for the Common Good, summarizes the situation after November 9, 2016, when Donald J. Trump was elected president in the United States as follows:

> Populists want to replace freedom with control, justice and equality with priority being given to "the true people," peace with polarization, caring for the earth with short-term benefits for their own nations, honesty with shameless manipulation, integrity with "power at all costs," respect with aggression.[401]

John Y. Jones is the director of the Dag Hammarskjöld Program in Oslo, Norway. Like Maria Dahle, also he has been part, for the past decades, of the Scandinavian civil society movement and its leading role in the world. Like Maria, he reports on an increased marginalization, all around the world, of all those who defend the ideal of equality in dignity. What seeps in instead is inequality – the interest of all is being replaced by the interest of a few. And this happens so slowly and parenthetically that it is difficult to notice for ordinary citizens. A seemingly harmless establishment of new institutions is be part of this process. Jones remembers that fifty years ago, former UN secretary-general Dag Hammarskjöld was prescient when he warned that the establishment of the Development Assistance Committee by the OECD would have a negative impact on the UN and the African continent.[402] (The Development Assistance Committee by the Organisation for Economic Co-operation and Development, OECD, is an international economic organization of 34 countries founded in 1961 to stimulate economic progress and world trade.)

This seeping in of inequality does not spare the very heartland and the originators of this dynamic. By the 1960s, Americans worked fewer hours than their counterparts in Europe and Japan, but by 2000, the situation had reversed, with many low-income workers now working more than one job to get by; also gender equality has stalled.[403] Philosopher Howard Richards observes that there is "a generative causal power at work pushing toward the down side, even while other generative causal powers are pushing on the up side."[404] This downward trend, since it squeezes the last drop out of people and the planet, has recently brought leaders to power who promise to turn the trend. Yet, as Howard Richards points out, neither a Donald Trump nor a Bernie Sanders have the tools to succeed.[405]

Wrong lessons have been drawn also from the seeming successes of "anti-movements." Political economist Frédéric Bastiat (1801 – 1850) is often quoted for the following words: "When plunder becomes a way of life for a group of men living together in society, they create for themselves in the course of time a legal system that authorizes it and a moral code that glorifies it."[406] He was a leader of the French laissez-faire tradition in the first half of the nineteenth century. He thought that laissez faire would serve the comfort, well-being, safety, independence, education, and dignity for all.[407] In other words, he thought that *no* law would be better than *bad* law forced upon a society by powerful men.[408] What he overlooked was that *good* law may be the solution rather than no law or bad law.[409] As mentioned earlier, also philosopher Michel Foucault, for a while, was "anti-power," believing that no power is better than bad power.[410]

Howard Richards faults post-modernist critics for leaving us with a cruel choice: either no meta-narrative or a toxic meta-narrative. He fears that the discrediting of modernity has favored the rise of fundamentalisms fatally hostile to the Enlightenment.[411] Bastiat would perhaps today vote for good law rather than no law, just as Foucault moved from anti-power to embrace good power: "And then, having carried the logic of revolt against *le pouvoir* to the extreme point where not only all social norms but logic itself became enemies, because they are inevitably accomplices of power, in the latter part of the mid-1970s, Foucault reversed engines once again. Power is good, not bad. Power is productive; without power nothing is produced, nothing is."[412]

Historian Timothy Snyder warns that wrong lessons have also been drawn from the Holocaust, both by the political left and the political right side, and I resonate with the points he makes.[413] Hitler was driven by "ecological panic" in the struggle of "races," and he was in search for *Lebensraum* (literally life-space), as it were, for instance, in the Ukraine. The mistake of the political left wing, according to Snyder, is to believe that Auschwitz was the downside of scientific thinking, while the opposite was the case. Hitler was not opposed to science per se, he only thought that any really important technology arises from the creativity of the Aryan race – like every true art – and that the concept of a universalist science was a Jewish deception. Further, focusing on Auschwitz makes it too unique and covers up wider societal responsibility and guilt for what happened. On the right side of the political spectrum, so Snyder, people think of Hitler whenever they attempt to overthrow an authoritarian regime, as was the case when the Bush administration went to war in Iraq in 2003. It has since turned out to be a rather catastrophic mistake to try to liberate a country by destroying it. Another right wing misunderstanding in the U.S. is to equate too strong a state with Nazism. The problem with the Holocaust was not too strong a state. In Austria, for instance, a strong state protected Jews until they suddenly were delivered to be killed after the take-over, not before. Hitler destroyed state structures both in Germany and other countries.

If we follow Snyder, it seems that the same mistakes are being committed now at a global level. The common good, to be protected, needs institutions, and the solution is to create beneficial state institutions, rather than removing them. This is, however, overlooked when the image of Hitler's national socialism is being invoked whenever any intervention from "above" is suggested. Most recently, the candidates for the 2016 United States presidential election have provided illustrations. Carly Fiorina, a former businesswoman and CEO, and an American Republican politician, for instance, professed that, "socialism starts when government creates a problem and then steps in to solve it."[414]

I call for *dignism* as way out.[415] Yet, what I observe with worry is that even the notion of human dignity is now being abused. Its "mission creep" has been described earlier in this book. When corporations aim to maximize profit, they promise that borrowing money to buy stuff will enhance one's dignity. Unfortunately, the opposite might happen. When global constitutive rules are too weak to protect the common good, at the end, a global dictatorship of a small elite may drive our planet and its people over the cliff. Demonizing the protection of the common good as "socialism" is doing the bidding of abusive elites. The promise of freedom and liberty hooks citizens who fail to see that it is not their liberty that will be the consequence of might-is-right freedom, but the liberty of a small elite. If the American Dream coopts the ninety-nine percent into allowing might to be right, it becomes a nightmare, ultimately also for the one percent.

As has been noted earlier, Howard Richards sympathizes with critical realism, a philosophical position that connects Enlightenment with post-modernism.[416] Enlightenment appreciates that not everything is self-referencing text, while postmodernism helps admit that the Enlightenment was not a discovery of eternal truth but a moment in the history of culture. Richards comes out in favor of *moral authority* – in favor of Emile Durkheim's thesis that every human group generates norms because the existence of social norms is a physical necessity; and he comes out in favor of Jean Piaget's thesis that human children are biologically predisposed to form groups governed by rules.[417] Richards' central category in his metaphysics is *culture-in-ecology*, meaning that humans create cultures that then can be more or less successful as adaptations to physical reality. His verdict: "We are still living in the pre-history of humanity. The history of humanity properly so-called will not begin until we are free to create institutions that solve our problems."[418]

It would be interesting to bring Howard Richards into a dialogue with anthropologists Robert Boyd and Peter Richerson and their multilevel selection theory (including its support for structural functionalism), where they see culture and social structure as a Darwinian (biological or cultural) adaptation at the group level.[419] Discourse analyst Michael Karlberg sees cultural codes being to social evolution what genetic codes are to biological evolution, as our cultural codes determine how well adapted we are to changing environments.[420] And I still have to ask Richards what he says to peace researcher Johan Galtung's concept of trilateral science,[421] to Galtung's call that consonance is needed between the *empirical*, the *foreseen*, and the *ideal* world – consonance between the world *as it is* (the data or facts positively given), the world *as it will be* (the world as predicted or theorized), and the world *as it ought to be* (values). "The world as it is can be changed, and if so the foreseen world will also be changed," and also "values may be modified," writes expert in development education Magnus Haavelsrud.[422]

Author Amin Maalouf has the last word in this chapter. His contention has been introduced earlier, namely, that the discourses of both, Islam and the West, betray their own ideals.[423] The maladjustment of the world has less to do with a *clash* of civilizations and more to do with the *depletion* of civilization. The age of ideological divisions and its debates is now followed by divisions of identity where there is no more debate. Humankind may have reached its "moral threshold of incompetence."[424]

Chapter 16

Sow the Wind and Reap the Storm

During the past millennia, all over the world, what started as liberation often ended in megalomania. Dismantling a tyrant did not mean dismantling tyranny. Revolutionaries, after succeeding to push out a tyrant, would not create a society of equal dignity for all, they would rise further, until they were the new tyrants and dominated everything and everyone in their reach. There were few exceptions.[1]

The problem with domination is that it has no inherent built-in endpoint. Domination seems useful at first, inspiring great hopes and pride, yet, later, it may turn into a terrible problem. A monster may be created that devours its creators: "Sow the wind and reap the whirlwind."[2] It is like making a deal with the devil, not counting that he's coming to collect. It means fighting smoke with fire. It means sowing dragons teeth.[3] "The spirits that I called, I cannot get rid of now," is a line from *The Sorcerer's Apprentice*, a poem by Johann Wolfgang von Goethe written in 1797.[4] There is also a saying in Arabic: "When you want everything, you lose everything."[5]

At this very moment in human history, the perhaps most powerful genies ever are out of the bottle. *Homo sapiens* means the "wise" man, the "knowledgeable" man, proud of his ability to make tools. By now, the result of such human "wisdom" is a human-made mass extinction of species on planet Earth.[6] In the future, we may expect *Homo deus* cyborgs, or genetically modified *Homo sapiens 2.0*, to take over the world, leaving all average people behind.[7] The end result may be the ultimate nightmare of "winning the battle and losing the war and the peace," the ultimate horror of "operation successful, patient dead." For humankind this would mean: operation domination successful, human species extinct and Earth scorched.

Throughout the past millennia, in a divided world, the security dilemma rewarded limitless domination – might was right, and the most ruthless dominator was victorious. It is only in today's interconnected world that this calculus changes.

Already in the past, victory was not guaranteed. Whoever welcomed dominators as saviors had to be prepared for the painful lesson that domination has no inherent endpoint and can easily devour its children. Historical examples abound. Since this is a book written in English, King Vortigern may serve as the first example. He was a fifth-century ruler among the Britons and invited the Jutes, Angles and Saxons to fight his enemies. Yet, his helpers turned out to behave like conquerors, and when the Britons tried to get rid of them, it was too late. The Britons lost their country to the Anglo-Saxons.

One of the most written-about recent incidents of "winning the war and losing the peace" is the havoc the Mujahideen wreaked after having successfully driven the Soviet Union out of Afghanistan. Journalist Patrick Martin wrote: "U.S. administrations have sought to build up the most reactionary and backward Islamic fundamentalist forces in the Middle East for many decades. Throughout the Cold War, Washington mobilized them against secular nationalist leaders viewed either as potential allies of the Soviet Union or as direct threats to the profits and property of American and European corporations."[8] By now, the wind that was sown has become a storm. Al-Qaeda and Da'esh is its name.

Many dictatorships around the world came into being in this way. What was welcomed as a rescue transmuted into a disaster. What was welcomed as a "fresh breeze," turned into a storm. In the case of Nazi-Germany's Adolf Hitler, it took only very few years from the *Ermächtigungsgesetz* (The Enabling Act) of 1933, in which the German Parliament voluntarily disempowered itself to empower Hitler so as to "save Germany," until full destruction in 1945, including the destruction of Germany itself. In my doctoral work, I took a closer look at both Germany's Adolf Hitler and Somalia's Siad Barre, trying to see what made them go for such homicidal and suicidal destruction. Both were driven by the seductive pull of continuously escalating domination, and they drove it. Both were surfers, they "surfed" on the security dilemma's culture, and by doing so, they satisfied also very personal needs, including the need to "liberate" themselves from their own sense of humiliation.

Henry Ford may serve as another and perhaps unexpected example of what may happen when an idealistic person gets power only to see his ideals crumble under the seductiveness of domination.[9] Ford was a well-meaning idealistic person and many of his insights were very laudable, also from today's point of view. For instance, the idea that investors who merely squeeze out profit rather than nurture real-life quality production, are "parasitic." Or that also workers deserve a dignified life. Ford's path, however, also shows how good intentions can turn into paranoia and tyranny when the complexities of the world combine with unintended consequences of actions. Ford went too far in trying to force everybody around him into his definition of dignity. When he faced obstacles, he thought that imposing a stronger hand was the solution. Having grown up in the old dominator world, he hoped that maximizing tactics of domination would translate into the desired success, as in the past so also in today's world.[10] He mistook skillful management of complexity as weakness. His son had this skill, yet, the father thought of it as deplorable "softness." The father, instead of self-critically examining his misguided view of strength, picked another man with a dubious biography and gave him the power to install a kind of gestapo rule amongst his workers. He also sought out scapegoats: the Jews. The price everybody ultimately paid for his misguided strategies was high, not just for the workers, who were increasingly bullied, harassed, and terrorized. It also cost Ford's only son his happiness and, ultimately, even his life. Henry Ford could not see that a different world was emerging, a world in which skills in managing complexity represent true strength, while tyranny is weakness.

It is as if Henry Ford had looked for recommendations for his power strategies in the 1578 handbook for inquisitors that spelled out the purpose of church-sanctioned terror and inquisitorial penalties: "... or punishment does not take place primarily and per se for the correction and good of the person punished, but for the public good in order that others may become terrified and weaned away from the evils they would commit."[11] Hundreds of thousands of "heretics" were tortured and murdered in God's name during the Inquisition with the very "holiest" of intentions. The blueprints for persecution originally drafted in the Middle Ages were followed also during subsequent centuries, eventually even informing the "advanced interrogation methods" recently employed at Guantanamo Bay."[12]

Christianity was not the only religion seduced into domination's push toward escalation, toward demanding ever more extreme proofs of faith and criminalizing failures to do so. Islam can serve as another example. Both the veil and fasting are not originally Muslim obligations to prove faith, this is what Sheikh Mustapha Rashid teaches, who earned his Ph.D. from Al-Azhar University in Egypt in 2013. He thus put question marks on many Muslim traditions and beliefs that others would accept as essential parts of the religion.[13] In Raqqa, the declared capital of the "Caliphate," morality police now forces women to wear the veil and black shoes only, and women are beaten "if their niqab is somehow too revealing, a veil too flimsy, or if they are caught walking on the street alone."[14]

Many revolutions have followed the pattern of overreach, even the most well-intended ones. Revolutions with the aim to improve life for common people have often succeeded in the beginning, yet, when plans for the next steps were lacking, revolutions were hijacked by power-hungry dominators. After capturing power, revolutionaries often continue to focus on fighting *against* enemies and are unprepared to begin the real work *for* creating the promised better future. The ensuing power vacuum then attracts ruthless dominators. Napoléon Bonaparte turned the French Revolution's ideal of egality into its opposite; he made himself not just king, but emperor. Vladimir Ilyich Lenin ended a promising February Revolution and turned it into an authoritarian October Revolution, only to be succeeded by Joseph Stalin, an even more ruthless leader. Saddam Hussein in Iraq,[15] and Muammar Gaddafi in Libya were overthrown in the hope that this would offer their people a better life in freedom. Yet, terror, death, and suffering at the hands of worse dominators ensued.

Life in Iraq and Syria could be happy now, if not for the futile hope that dominators can safely be instrumentalized. Since Iraq's civil strife from 2006 to 2008, politicians on all sides have used militia-fueled violence to further their political ends. Shia militias have risen in power and prominence after the Iraqi army retreated and allowed Sunni Da'esh to claim nearly a third of the country. Referring to those Shia militias as "popular mobilization," Iraqi Prime Minister Haidar al-Abadi, himself a Shia, praisingly declared that he was "proud of our society's cohesion as well as the unity of the army, police and the popular mobilization to expel IS."[16] However, this "popular mobilization," may not necessarily be the "fresh wind" serving the common good. Many fear it to be a new storm. Militia members, numbering tens of thousands, often wear military uniforms and are allegedly supported by the government but operate without any official oversight. Human rights groups have accused Shia militias of routinely abducting and killing Sunni civilians. A Sunni tribal sheikh from the Albu Ajeel village north of Tikrit, which has up to 20,000 residents, was very concerned by the re-taking of Tikrit from the so-called Islamic State: "The [Shia] militias will eliminate the entire tribe of Albu Ajeel. They won't leave a single house."[17]

On the other side of the Shia-Sunni divide, "Saudi Arabia has created a Frankenstein's monster over which it is rapidly losing control," writes journalist Patrick Cockburn in 2014, "... it may come to regret its support for the Sunni revolts in Syria and Iraq as jihadi social media begins to speak of the House of Saud as its next target."[18] Cockburn continues: "The rise of ISIS is bad news for the Shia of Iraq but it is worse news for the Sunni whose leadership has been ceded to a pathologically bloodthirsty and intolerant movement, a sort of Islamic Khmer Rouge, which has no aim but war without end." What Saudi Arabia did was adopt a dual policy, one for abroad and another for home: Outside of its borders, it encouraged extremist "jihadism" as useful tool for anti-Shia influence, while suppressing it at home, as it threatens the status quo there: "It is this dual policy that has fallen apart over the last year," warns Cockburn.[19]

Also Egypt had once played this dual strategy and sent their extremists to Afghanistan to fight communist Soviet Union, only to partake in "cleaning up the mess" later, for instance, by secretly receiving suspected terrorist in so-called renditions and subjecting them to their interrogation techniques.

When Iraqi politicians warned Western leaders that the civil war in Syria would restart conflict in Iraq, they did not listen: "I guess they just didn't believe us and were fixated on getting rid of [President Bashar al-] Assad," said an Iraqi leader.[20] Through its blindness, the West also puts at risk the Alawite and Christian minorities who support Assad for protecting them. For them, Assad's opponents are the terrorists and those who die in defending him are martyrs for the fatherland.[21]

Turkey is yet another player in this game, stoking little fires in the hope to extinguish the big fire. Turkey has the Kurds as its main nemesis and initially thought that the Da'esh militants would be of help against the Kurds – until Da'esh also turned against Turkey.[22]

The so-called dignity revolutions of the Arab Spring offer manifold illustrations of how hope, domination, and terror can connect. Allow me to look at Egypt in more depth, as I lived in Cairo from 1984 to 1991 and could get a deep sense of how uncanny the transition from savior to dictator can proceed. My beloved Tahrir Square, which I traversed almost every day during my years in Egypt, has been a core stage throughout the past decades. On January 25, 1952, it resembled a battlefield. The Egyptian people called for the withdrawal of British colonial troops from their country and demanded "freedom, bread, and social justice." On July 23 of that year, the monarchy was overthrown, and the future seemed bright. Six decades later, in February 2011, the Egyptian people chanted the very same slogans on the very same square. Only this time their anger was directed against Hosni Mubarak, who had ruled the country with an iron fist for three decades, following up on Gamal Abdel Nasser and Anwar el-Sadat in kind.[23] In 1952, a tiny elite had owned most of the land, with its inhabitants as quasi-slaves; at the end of the rule of Mubarak, once more, a small elite lived in luxury, while the masses toiled. Renowned author Alaa Al-Aswany made the disenchantment of the people more than palpable in his novels and columns that are staged in the very part of Cairo that was my home during my time in Egypt.[24]

In 1952, when the monarchy and the British were gone from Egypt, the new rulers were naïve, like so many other revolutionaries before them had been immediately after victory: they thought that this was the end of all problems, while it only was the beginning.[25] A few decades later, in 2011, once more, it began with egalitarian ideals of those youthful "dignity revolutionaries of Tahrir Square."[26] They overlooked that the majority of Egypt's population is still deeply infused with authoritarianism. They elected Mohammed Morsi as Egypt's new president. Also Morsi fell for the lure of domination, allowing the Muslim Brotherhood to monopolize the political scene. He failed to address the people's call for rights and social justice, the very issues that had inspired the uprising that had brought him to power in the first place. Instead, he quickly and unashamedly did what his predecessors had done only a bit slower and more covertly, namely, he made himself into a "pharaoh." He lasted only for one year in office before being ousted by the military on July 3, 2013. In 2014, the army was back in power, and history seems to repeat itself. In the face of such clambering for the throne of a pharaoh, Author Alaa Al-Aswany speaks of *chairophilia*, the constant pursuit of a higher position or "chair."[27]

Tunisia offers yet another illustration. As in Egypt, also in post-Arab Spring Tunisia, the moderate Islamist Ennahda (Renaissance) Movement, with Rashid Al-Ghannushi at its helm, was ill prepared for governance and thus could not survive.[28] In Tunisia, however, at least the concept of dignity survived: on June 9, 2014, Tunisia launched a Truth and Dignity Commission.[29]

If we look closer at the details of Egypt's history of liberations, we learn how saviors can transmute into destroyers and how this interlinks with present-day terror in ways that go far beyond the borders of Egypt. Let me start with the good intentions and the useful ideas: Gamal Abdel Nasser (1918 – 1970) began a land and education reform that planted useful seeds and could perhaps be re-visited now. Anwar Sadat (1918 – 1981) had the noble insight that peace is the only feasible self-preservation, rather than war, and this insight is as valuable today notwithstanding the fact that he paid for it with his life. Hosni Mubarak (born 4 May 1928) emphasized stability rather than sudden changes, and the chaos that followed his ousting made many wish he would return. Now comes the question: Where did it go wrong? All three rulers, from Nasser over Sadat to Mubarak, suffered from the infamous "Pharaoh syndrome." Aside from having good ideas, they became arrogant, pushed out rivals, and built empires for their entourages who plundered the country.

And here the terrorism we witness today all around the world has important roots. Muhammad Naguib was the first president of Egypt, and he wanted democracy. For Nasser, however, not democracy but the army was the guarantor of true revolution, and therefore, in 1952, he pushed Naguib aside. The next thing Nasser did, was waste his country's resources on amassing weapons for the army, only to lose everything in 1967 when he thought he should go to war against Israel. Then came Anwar el-Sadat. He, for his part, laid the foundation for later terrorism by letting "capitalism" create poverty-stricken neighborhoods. When Egyptians rose in a hunger revolt, Sadat called the hungry "thieves." By continuing his predecessors' policy of cruel humiliation in Egypt's prisons, Sadat produced citizens who, upon release, were filled with hatred. Back in 1965, Nasser had imprisoned Sayyed Qutb, the Muslim Brotherhood's chief ideologue, had him charged, found guilty of plotting to assassinate Nasser, and executed. Qutb was a highly complex intellectual, attracting people not least through his humility and integrity, a reason for why he inspires terror strategists to this day. When Hosni Mubarak came to power, also he went too far by trying to make his son into his successor, thus attempting to create a dynastic rule. With Mubarak, a third savior had turned into an usurper.

Egypt can serve as an illustration also for how two systems of domination can interlink and, in combination, overstretch domination. As in many other places in the world, also in Egypt, on one side there are the military institutions of the state, the traditional tools of domination that mete out terror on enemies and underlings. This has by now linked up with the corporate system that has emerged ever more forcefully in Egypt as everywhere else. In Egypt, the army has always been a hybrid military and corporate enterprise, suffused into society as a whole over decades. I was a close witness of the importance of the military clubs for weddings and other kinds of social gatherings. We see this not just in Egypt. In Myanmar, "the generals who run Burma will make sure that no one, save themselves and their friends, benefits from global markets."[30]

As has been discussed previously, in the wake of the interlinking of military and money in a globalizing world, a new fault line is being added to the traditional rifts that run between states: the new "enemy" line divides glocal elites from the rest. Also this new figuration is prone to being overstretched. In the short term, it may look like a success to dominate over rival out-group enemies or over fellow in-group members both militarily and economically. It may provide a personal and national sense of honor and bring riches to an elite. Yet, the picture may change in the longer run, in particular when the world becomes ever more interconnected and more communication tools become available. These tools enable the "losers" of this game to understand that they are losers more clearly than before, and they may raise their voices, perhaps even hit back with double force at a world that is much more vulnerable now than ever.

Egypt offers a vivid illustration. When the ferry Al Salam Boccaccio 98 sank in the Red Sea on February 3, 2006, with more than 1,400 mainly Egyptian workers returning from Saudi Arabia, more than one thousand people drowned. Mohammed Refaat El-Saeed, an Egyptian politician, scholar and writer, and general secretary of Tagammu, the National Progressive Unionist Party in Egypt, summarized how this disaster was the result of an interlink between old and new dominator systems[31]: First, rescue operations from the traditional hierarchical military system came too late, since the naval officer could not act without the orders of defense minister Marshall Mohamed Hussein Tantawi, who was asleep and the responsible officer was too afraid to wake him up. On the other side was capitalism run amok with corruption. The owner of the ferry, Mamdouh Ismail, had been involved also in its official supervision, therefore was able to cover up for how the boat had been modified and made less safe to carry more passengers and cargo. At first, the owner was acquitted, creating an uproar in the country, an uproar from people who no longer wanted to submissively accept death as the price for overstretched domination. On March 11, 2009, the initial acquittal was overturned and the owner was sentenced to seven years in prison.

Back to the trope of the righteous heroic savior who eventually leads people into demise. The security dilemma has created an arena for this trope and has in this way invited a demon that suffers from a disastrous lack of inherent limits, and this trope remains implanted in people's souls throughout the world until the day today. The 2016 presidential race in the United States illustrates the unbroken attraction of a strongman savior, in this case Donald J. Trump, on what some call his "pathway to dictatorship."[32]

Young men all around the world are infused with the idea of becoming heroes, and for them the possibility of killing and dying adds fascination. Killing and dying is seen as the royal path to truly honorable manhood by many. Thinker Paul Richards has a very particular explanation for why males may be drawn to killing and death more than females: Females have three points of contact with the *mystery of divinity* of birth, death, and giving birth, while men have only two. Killing and war could be interpreted as an attempt by males to equalize this access.[33]

Norwegian Anders Behring Breivik sees himself as a hero, a shining knight, a savior.[34] Breivik also describes himself as a co-founder of the Knights Templar network of anti-Islamists in London. On July 22, 2011, he bombed government buildings in Oslo, Norway, where eight people died. Then he began a mass shooting at a Workers' Youth League camp on the island of Utøya outside of Oslo, killing at point-blank range 69 people, mostly teenagers. The purpose of the attack, he stated, was to save Norway and Western Europe from a Muslim takeover and punish the ruling Labor Party in Norway for betraying Norway's interests. He sees himself as a holy warrior and crusader, a martyr and resistance fighter, who has sacrificed himself in a war against a "Marxist-Islamist alliance," which he fears will take over Europe if not stopped. He hopes that his actions will inspire thousands to follow in his path.

Richard the Lionheart is the name Breivik gave to one of his "mentors."[35] Both the names of Richard the Lionheart and that of Saladin have gone down in Medieval history as great military leaders and they inspire terror tactics until today. Libya's Muammar Gaddafi saw himself as the new Saladin. Saladin (1137 – 1193) was the first sultan of Egypt and Syria and the unifier of the Muslim world. In 1187, he recaptured Jerusalem for the Muslims. To regain the Holy City for the Christians, Pope Gregory VIII ordered the Third Crusade, and it was led by King of England Richard I or Richard the Lionheart (1157 – 1199), together with Emperor Frederick Barbarossa of Germany, and King Philip II of France.[36]

After his horrific deeds, Breivik was diagnosed as being mentally deranged by two psychiatrists. However, this diagnosis was later overturned.[37] "As horrific as Breivik's actions were, he cannot be dismissed as a 'madman,'" wrote journalist Max Blumenthal.[38] Blumenthal recognizes in Breivik's writings "the same themes and language as more prominent right-wing Islamophobes (or those who style themselves as 'counter-jihadists') and many conservatives in general."[39] Thomas Hegghammer is a terrorism specialist at the Norwegian Defense Research Establishment. When he read Breivik's manifesto, he found that it mirrors those of Osama bin Laden and other Al-Qaeda leaders, only with the Christian point of view replacing the Muslim one. Breivik describes the crusades, expresses a deep sense of historical grievance and calls for apocalyptic warfare to defeat the religious and cultural enemy: "It seems to be an attempt to mirror Al-Qaeda, exactly in reverse," Hegghammer explains[40]: Breivik announces a "new doctrine of civilizational war."[41]

Muammar Gaddafi, on his part, in his admiration for Saladin, ruled for four decades, courted not least by many Western leaders.[42] "CIA Helped Gaddafi Torture Libyan Dissidents," this was a news headline, after new documents were uncovered in 2011.[43] Gaddafi first wanted to unite the Arab world, but, as this failed, he turned to Africa, where he was venerated as "King of Kings." This king of kings inspired unspeakable terror. Liberian Charles Taylor, for instance, trained as a guerilla fighter in Libya, and while he was in Libya, in 1989, he formed the militia group National Patriotic Front of Liberia. In 2012, the Special Court for Sierra Leone sentenced Taylor to fifty years in prison for eleven counts, including terrorism, murder, mutilation, rape, sexual slavery, pillage, enslavement, and the use of child soldiers. He had committed the "most heinous and brutal crimes recorded in human history."[44]

The classical security dilemma was the breeding ground for the trope of the heroic savior. The arrival of the new fault line between elites and the rest now complicates and compounds the overall situation: old status and new money can augment each other or cancel each other out. Overall, however, opportunities for classical heroism diminish. As the classical security dilemma becomes less salient, its war arenas to earn glory shrink. At the same time, the new security dilemma drives most people into rather inglorious rat races with the promise that money will turn them into heroes, yet, only very few actually become heroic celebrities.

As a result, there are three security dilemmas around now: First, the classical security dilemma between states or ethnic groups, where the most successful dominator over out-groups usually also is the strongman presiding over his own in-group. Second, those in power often use divide-and-rule strategies for their in-groups, and by now, ruthless individualism in Western societies successfully pits everybody's personal territory against everybody else's territory. Third, the fact that money is not just a facilitator of exchange but a commodity that can be accumulated, creates a situation where accumulating money provides more effective weapons than the military. This, in turn, enables a global "superclass" to treat the rest of the world's population, and nature, as "enemies" waiting to be dominated and exploited. Smaller, local corporations may find themselves in a position similar to the first type of the security dilemma, or to the second.

One way to regain space for heroism in this situation is to rekindle the classical security dilemma, provoke a "clash of civilizations," or revive the Cold War fault line, or rip open old religious enmities, or create entirely new fault lines wherever simmering humiliation can be turned into open clashes of humiliation. Also the new security dilemma can be intensified by pushing societies into ever more individualistic all-against-all competition, with the promise of heroism through money. All these strategies are currently being intensified, domination is being overstretched in all arenas, often going hand in hand.

Anyone who wishes to stoke the classical security dilemma has to follow the storyline of first identifying an "enemy," and then to offer a way to heroically undo this enemy.[45] This storyline can be anything; it can even build on the crudest of innocent misunderstandings or the most wicked conspiracy theories. To illustrate the extent to which innocent misunderstandings can go, the John Frum cult may serve as an example. This cult formed on the island of Tanna, Vanuatu. After World War II, when the Americans had departed, followers of John Frum built symbolic landing strips as a kind of prayer that American airplanes would land and bring them "cargo."[46] The case of Charles Manson is a case of wicked conspiracy. It illustrates how racist imaginations can go wild. Manson quoted "the Beatles and the Bible" to tell his followers that several White Album songs including "Helter Skelter" were part of the Beatles' coded prophecy of an apocalyptic war in which racist and non-racist whites would be maneuvered into exterminating each other over the treatment of blacks.[47] Upon the war's conclusion, after black militants would kill off the few whites still around, Manson and his companions would emerge from an underground city in which they had survived in hiding. As the only remaining whites, they would rule over all blacks, who, as the vision went, were incapable of running America. Manson employed "helter skelter" as the term for this sequence of terror events.

Charles Manson did not have many followers. Already an Anders Behring Breivik has more.[48] Extremists who abuse ideologies and religions – right-wing, left-wing, and religious extremists – all define their actions within the logic of the traditional security dilemma and re-stoke it. If superpowers rekindle local wars, also the risk of world war returns. In other words, the danger currently flowing from revivals of the classical security dilemma is significant.

Similar dangers flow from the new fault line between elites and the rest. So far, millions of people all around the world have been successfully recruited into a corporate culture that glorifies competition over cooperation and crowds out solidarity. The empowerment and self-esteem movement can serve as an example. Steve Kulich, professor of intercultural communications at Shanghai International Studies University, was introduced earlier. He said at the Second International Conference on Multicultural Discourses in Hangzhou in April 2007: "First I have empowered my students. Then they became nasty people. Today, I no longer use the word 'empowerment.' I use 'entrustment.'"[49] Critical psychologist Ole Jacob Madsen confirms Kulich's observation: "The philosophy of enhancing self-esteem has been heavily criticized by psychological research, suggesting it is flawed, either making people with low self-esteem worse off,[50] or possibly creating a generation of egotistical youths with high self-esteem prone to pick on others."[51]

Madsen warns against the misuse of psychology as a legitimizing tool and describes how the idea of self-esteem is being instrumentalized for commercial interests and embraced by the general public: "Over the last decade, cosmetic surgery has become a fast growing industry in Norway. Sales of the nerve toxin Botox increased by 183 percent from a total sales volume of NOK 2.9 million in 2003, to a total sales volume of NOK 8.2 million in 2009.[52] As popular psychology literature perceives self-esteem as a deeper metaphor for the healthiness of the relationship to the self,[53] cosmetic surgery is being advertised as a deep psychological makeover, rather than merely improving a patient's physical appearance for aesthetic reasons, as this would be considered less legitimate.[54] Indeed, cosmetic surgeon Bjørn Tvedt uses this justification, saying that patients will not necessarily become happier after undergoing cosmetic surgery, "but it can help you gain self-esteem."[55] In this way, psychology is being instrumentalized to perpetrate terror on the body image, creating "fake bodies" at best, yet, at the price of manifold mental problems driven by body hatred – be it bulimia and anorexia, addiction, mass self-hatred, or senseless violence.[56]

Norway is not the only country where cosmetic surgery is on the increase. South Korea now has the highest number of surgeries performed per capita, overtaking Brazil as the plastic surgery capital of the world. "South Korean women have become so immersed in western celebrity culture that double eyelid surgery, which creates the Caucasian crease that many Asian women don't naturally have, has become as common as going to the dentist."[57] Chinese women (and men) are flocking to South Korea in hopes to attain a Caucasian look at the hands of the country's skilled surgeons.[58]

The same trend can be observed also within China, not just with respect to cosmetic surgery, also with regard to psychotherapeutic counseling. "Fake Happiness," is the title of an article that bemoans China's party state policy to preempt social unrest by creating "fake happiness" that diverts people's attention from structural forces that negatively affect their lives. Television counseling programs, for example, showcase and glorify poor or unemployed people appearing to be happy despite of their limited life circumstances.[59]

In other words, we observe how good ideas turn into destructive realities also in the case of "empowering" people. The first step, the wish to do so, is laudable, it is a kind of private version of a revolutionary liberation movement. Yet, just as large-scale revolutions have derailed before, also this one falls prey to the fact that the process of rising up from the bottom is fraught with problems and can go too far. While the initial idea is laudable, the abuse of empowerment for monetary profits or governmental irresponsibility is less laudable, and even where it succeeds, it can go too far.

This is precisely what happens now in many Western countries. Unfettered self-esteem amplifies ruthless individualism, as self-esteem depends on being better than others. The self-esteem movement has created an epidemic of narcissism and bullying in the U.S., reports Kristin Neff, scholar of human development, culture, and learning sciences.[60] Neff asks: "How can we get out of this treadmill, this constant need to feel better than others so that we can feel good about ourselves?" Her suggestion is to rather develop *self-compassion*. "Self-compassion offers the same benefits as self-esteem, but without its pitfalls," she explains, as self-compassion provides a more stable sense of self-worth and is not connected with narcissism or selfishness or self-defensive aggression.[61] Self-compassion's first component means relating to oneself kindly, acknowledging that we all are human beings, worthy of love. The second component is our shared human experience that being human means being imperfect. The third component is mindfulness. It is a mistake to believe that we need to be harsh with ourselves to avoid being self-indulgent and lazy; the opposite is true: if we are harsh with ourselves, we get depressed, and this is not the path to feeling more motivated.

The culture of needing to be "better than others" in a context of rising inequality by now seems to have eaten into the social fabric of American society from within. Scholar and social critic Noam Chomsky warns that "the Republican establishment, the mainstream corporate financial wealth, is getting to a point where it can't control the base it's mobilized."[62] He calls the Tea Party wing of the Republican Party a "radical insurgency" that can no longer be reined in, just like in Germany in the late Weimar years, when "German industrialists wanted to use the Nazis, who were a relatively small group, as a battering ram against the labor movement and the left. They thought they could control them but it turns out they were wrong. They couldn't control them. I'm not saying that will happen here, it's quite a different set of circumstances, but something similar is taking place."[63]

While I write these lines, the rise of Donald J. Trump to the presidency of the United States vindicates Chomsky's analysis. Already the first American president of the country, George Washington, warned of "pretended patriotism," the patriotism of those who thrive on division rather than unity.[64] America is not alone, of course.

Nationalism, xenophobia, right-wing and neo-nazism, all shades of populism afflict also Europe. The so-called Brexit (the exit of Great Britain from the European Union) in 2016 demonstrates the riskiness of hoping that domination entrepreneurs will remain useful servants. From a United Britain a Disunited Britain now arises, and existing fault lines are deepened rather than healed, fault lines between young and old, city and countryside, foreigners and natives. Whenever I hear that populists are hailed for being a "fresh breeze," for finally saying the truth and putting into words "what we think," I remember my father's accounts of Adolf Hitler. Hitler had a similar appeal. He was never blamed for the mistakes he made or for anything that went wrong under his watch. On the contrary. People would say, "wenn der Führer das wüsste ..." meaning, "if the Führer knew this, he would clean up this mess immediately!"

The culture of needing to be "better than others" is also eating into the participation of the United States in world society. We may assume that American President John F. Kennedy, in his inaugural address on January 20, 1961, spoke from a mindset of equal dignity for all when he promised that America does not wish to become the new tyrant after the end of colonialism. Yet, when he spoke of liberty, it seems that he did so from a mindset of honorable domination:

> Let every nation know, whether it wishes us well or ill, that we shall pay any price, bear any burden, meet any hardship, support any friend, oppose any foe to assure the survival and the success of liberty.[65]

The wish for honorable domination to preserve liberty led America down the path of overdone domination to the point of tragic absurdity. An American commander in the Vietnam War said something rather Orwellian: "In order to save the village, it became necessary to destroy it."[66] "Killing you for your own safety" is the title of an article that reminds of Orwell:

> Tyranny always treads a familiar path: first it clamors for unfettered authority to resolve some overriding problem; then it consolidates that power; next it gradually expands its vocabulary and application; finally, it turns around and uses that power to persecute everyone. Indeed, those who wield unrestrained power will inevitably abuse it. ... The cost of war is not measured solely in terms of blood and treasure. War also corrodes human morality to a point where even the most inhumane acts become perfectly acceptable.[67]

The foolishness entailed in domination let loose is summarized also by Shigeo Abe, who was introduced earlier, chief editor of the Japanese magazine *Facta*, when he says about Japan: "Japan is a ship full of fools who sink their ship to protect their interests."[68] Rowan Williams, former Archbishop of Canterbury, captures this absurdity in his 2015 Orwell Lecture at University College London: "Bureaucratic double-speak, tautology and ambiguous cliché not only dominate the language of public life from the health service to higher education, talking and writing badly also prepares the ground for military and terrorist action."[69] Peace activist Uri Avnery speaks of *absurdiocy* when he warns that there is no such thing as "international terrorism" and "to declare war on 'international terrorism' is nonsense."[70] Journalist Seymour Hersh speaks of the willing manufacturing of chaos.[71]

British historian Eric Hobsbawm (1917 – 2012) has warned that "few things are more dangerous than empires pushing their own interest in the belief they are doing humanity a favor."[72] Noam Chomsky compares the need for "U.S. credibility" with the way the Mafia maintains credibility and uses the case of Syria to reflect on the trap that this need represents.[73] Oregon author Kathy Beckwith, in her book *A Mighty Case Against War*, advises to let go of speech figures such as "Nobody wants war, but sometimes, amidst the complexities of today's world, that's our only option." Beckwith concludes that many Americans would be shocked to learn their nation's story of war and how war was "sold" and alternatives remained unconsidered.[74] Peace researcher Johan Galtung adds: "NATO does not want solutions. It uses conflicts as raw material it can process into interventions to tell the world that it is the strongest in military terms,"[75] and he continues saying that "there is a big similarity between Nazism and U imperialism: they did not know how to stop but just went on and on till they accumulated more enemies than they could manage."[76] Human Rights Watch fears that the post-9/11 shift taken by the FBI and other U.S. law enforcement agencies toward stopping terrorist plots before they occur has created a zeal that has in some cases morphed into manufacturing threats.[77] In Germany, under-cover agents intending to contain right-wing terrorism, facilitated racist murder instead.[78]

All empires seem to have eventually declined.[79] Already historian Ibn Khaldun (1332 – 1406) observed what causes empires to fall.[80] Historian Oswald Spengler (1880–1936) wrote his magnum opus on the *Decline of the West*.[81] Macro historian Arnold J. Toynbee, in his twelve-volume work of 1934 – 1961, gives several reasons for empires to fall, reasons that could all be subsumed under the heading "domination driven into extremes":

- militarism with constant warfare
- overextension – trying to control more than you can manage
- loss of legitimacy in the eyes of others
- structural economic crisis
- moral decay
- loss of intellectual and technological innovation and
- simply other powers gaining strength over time and doing things in new, creative ways[82]

Domination running amok is not the reserve of empires alone. It can be observed also in smaller countries. In Rwanda, liberation efforts ended in genocide. Whoever reads Guy Logiest's book on his participation in liberating the Hutu is touched by the joy that accompanied the "Hutu Peasant Revolution" of 1959 to 1961.[83] The genocidal killing of the former Tutsi masters that followed and culminated in the genocide of 1994, did not stem from unexplainable lust to kill, but from an inability to rise up constructively from the feelings of humiliation that motivated this liberation movement in the first place. Here is yet another case that started with enthusiasm, as a whole population felt joyfully empowered, however, then the inherent lack of limits in domination kicked in and eventually no other endpoint was found except for mass mayhem and killing. Logiest happily sowed wind and was lucky to have passed away before the storm. This makes the path of a Nelson Mandela so remarkable. He started out very similar to the Hutu in Rwanda, and when he was in power, after twenty-seven years in prison, he could have called on his black brothers and sisters to commit genocide on their former white masters. He did not do so. He did something revolutionary, something that his successors still have to understand and follow up on: he attempted to stop the paradigm of domination and tried to establish the paradigm of partnership instead.[84]

Also Benito Mussolini (1883 – 1945), known as the first fascist dictator of the twentieth century, was initially welcomed and hailed by his fellow Italians. He wanted to reinstitute the Roman Empire. Already as a child he had discovered violence as a solution for problems and later used the mindset of violence to shape the Berlin-Rome axis with another celebrated dominator, Adolf Hitler. In my interviews for my doctorate, I spoke with members of the German aristocracy, and this is what I heard: "The aristocracy thought at first, quite falsely, that they could 'domesticate' Hitler. For them he was a parvenu who hijacked their dearest theme, national sentiment, and worse, incited 'the masses,' making himself irreplaceable as their master. For those among the aristocracy who collaborated with Hitler, the need to do so was utter humiliation: they were forced to work with 'the demon,' because 'the demon' had control over the feelings of the nation. What could have been worse?"[85] With the *Ermächtigungsgesetz* (The Enabling Act) of March 24, 1933, the aristocracies' hopes to contain Hitler were sunk. The German parliament voluntarily disempowered itself to empower Chancellor Adolf Hitler to "save Germany," thus turning Hitler's government into a legal dictatorship. The parliament removed the very security valves that could hinder domination to run amok for yet another round. Hitler thrilled the masses, women were besotted with him, and young men, the "archetype of the immature young fanatic, intoxicated by a Führer-cult," proudly and self-righteously indulged in mayhem.[86]

Nazi Germany drove the cult of honor to its extremes. The book *The Nights of the Long Knives* by Hans Hellmut Kirst illustrates this in ways that enable the reader to grasp from the inside how this worked.[87] It tells the same harrowing accounts I heard also from my father and how he, a peace loving man, was almost executed for not buying into Nazi ideology. Over a span of more than ten years, I interviewed my father so as to see with his eyes his plight in Nazi Germany. Like in other families, his elder siblings were still impressed by Adolf Hitler as a savior, while the younger already saw the truth and went into resistance. The family of "Tisa" von der Schulenburg is worth reading about in this context.[88]

Adolf Hitler believed in "das Recht des Stärkeren" (might is right), the right and duty of the strongest to engage in ruthless domination. Therefore, he did not regret that the German's loyalty with him not only led to million-fold homicide, but was even suicidal, as their own country, Germany, was bombed to ashes. Hitler said on November 27, 1941, to the Danish foreign minister Scavenius and the Croat foreign minister Lorkowitsch: "I am also here ice cold. If the German people are no longer strong enough and ready to sacrifice their own blood for their existence, then they must disappear and be destroyed by another, stronger power. … I will not shed a tear for the German people."[89]

After World War II, in Germany, when the younger generation rose up against their fathers, it began with the enthusiastic creativity of "genius dilettantism." This was the term used to describe the wildly creative cultural scene in a Berlin that saw a new future dawn, a future liberated from the sins of the fathers. It was the time when Berliners lived at the very border between the two superpowers, with the expectation that they would be the first to evaporate in a nuclear cloud if the Cold War turned hot.[90] The cultural scene that arose in this context bred exultant creativity, yet, it also bred the terrorist Red Army Faction and its manipulative and self-important narcissist "hero-savior" Andreas Baader, whose vanity and ruthlessness echoed that of his declared nemesis Adolf Hitler.[91] "Genius dilettantism" went from hopeful enthusiasm to the very evil it bemoaned.

From Hitler to Gaddafi to Breivik or Baader, they all saw themselves as saviors. They all were embedded in a dominator culture that has the savior trope at its core. They all started out with a sense of enthusiasm and liberation, they were a "fresh breeze," or at least they saw themselves as such, and they all ended in terror.

Dr. Gaboose was the personal physician of late Somali dictator Siad Barre and member of his cabinet. He fled the country when he felt that he could no longer support the regime. In several long interviews in November 1998, he reflected on the dictator's personality and why he succeeded in staying on so long, from 1969 to 1991. Gaboose offered a particularly detailed view of the minute steps of escalation that characterize the journey from liberation to terror:

> I think that Siad Barre was different compared to the majority of the people. Probably that difference made him a dictator. He got some unique characteristics in his personality: vigorous – active – and charismatic. He got that ability of attracting the people around him, that energy, that atmosphere of making you secure!" … Siad Barre, I think – he was brave – I think many dictators have got this – but perhaps it is not braveness, it is madness. These people confront challenges where the normal intelligent man would say, "no, no, don't do that!" But they have got this personality to go beyond normality, beyond the common people. So you think it is brave. But I think that it was not – it was just beyond the normality of common people. Siad Barre was very intelligent. He had very little education in his life even though he was the General of the nation. When he was participating in a discussion or giving a speech – without writing, without preparing anything – the way he was articulating was just beyond imagination! Probably because of those speeches, that were so talented in the way they were articulated, he attracted many people, many Somalis. … So, he was intelligent, but more than that, he always tried to get close to the community. He was an expert in the Somali way of seeing things. Many Somalis believe that he did so many good things. Because

> he built roads, he built universities; he built so many things in the nation. But not only Siad Barre, all dictators in the first years build their nation.
> So, I think that a dictator becomes a dictator because he thinks that he has got some talents, and in these talents he sees himself above other people, above everyone. So, he believes, at the end, that he is more intelligent than others, that he sees things farther than others, that he is more sincere, that he is more, more, more ...! So, of the word "more" in every respect regarding humanity, he convinces himself. And the rest of the people become like children listening to him – not like comrades or colleagues who are discussing, giving and taking ideas from each other![92]

Prominent Somali poet Hadrawi ridiculed Barre's narcissism in a poem:

> I am the President
> I'm also the Chairman
> I'm the peoples' eyes
> their ears
> their brain
> their teacher
> their father
> I alone over this land
> Am the boss
> Who will never be unseated[93]

Dictator Siad Barre inflicted terror on the Isaaq clan, his declared enemy, on all spheres of their lives, with intellectuals being his particular nemesis. For my research, I interviewed the SORRA group (the former Hargeisa group).[94] They were a group of young Somali intellectuals who tried to rehabilitate their neglected city, a commitment Siad Barre regarded with great suspicion. He had the group imprisoned in one of the worst jails of the country in 1981, and fourteen of its members lingered in solitary confinement for eight years. They were only released on March 16, 1989, following international pressure on Barre.[95]

Siad Barre is not the only illustration of how intellectuals are targeted and education is suppressed. Another extreme example were the Khmer Rouge in Cambodia who killed the entire intellectual elite of the country, even for simply wearing glasses, as this was perceived as a sign of learnedness.

China can serve as yet another example for how the educational field can be put out of the way of dominators. The Communist Party of China "had to penetrate the university structure before it took power, and had to subvert the university once it was in power. Otherwise, it would have been impossible to transform the Chinese society and consolidate the regime."[96] In her 2015 doctoral dissertation, educational sociologist and China expert Jingyi Dong explains how this restructuring was realized in a step-by-step manner: through "political campaigns, such as the Anti-Rightist Campaign that created terror on campus, the vertical patron-client relations between the party-state and the intellectuals were fortified."[97] Dong explains that social and natural science research eventually became dominated not just by political trends, but by the leaders' personal whims, and how this contributed to the student protests in 1989. In other words, again, wind was sown, and storm was the result.

The storm shocked the elites of the country. The protests exposed how intellectuals could become influential and too dangerous to overlook. As a result, intellectuals and peasants were assigned two different roles in the economic model of the party-state: "intellectuals as a whole were subject to bribery, though they were still under strict control, while peasants were oppressed, exploited and exposed to whatever might befall them...."[98] Dong explains that during the recent process of massification, the university in China functions as the government's exploiting instrument ever more: "the intellectuals are lured to directly participate in depriving society, particularly the poor rural society."[99]

Jingyi Dong uses Pierre Bourdieu's concept of *field* to analyze the situation in China.[100] The field of power is a very special field, since it is a battlefield where holders of various forms of what Bourdieu calls *capital* struggle to exercise power over other types of capital, and particularly over their rate of exchange.[101] Many conflicts within the field of power are about seizing the economic and political resources that "enable the state to wield power over all games and over the rules that regulate them."[102] When exchange rates change, holders of capital may strive to transform the forms of capital they hold into forms that are rated as more valuable so as to maintain their position in the social space. In China, as hereditary lines are losing their currency, the educational system is a way of converting it into another form that is used in another field, namely, cultural capital.[103] Dong concludes that the rural population in China ought to wake up and understand that this path to gain and reproduce capital is treacherous. They are being lured to invest in it, but at the end, their investment will be lost, because the promise is empty. After finishing their education, some rural students even commit suicide, as they become aware that while the cost of their education has ruined their families, the promise of a well-paid job is empty and they will never be able to give anything back to their families.[104] This is *deferred elimination*, as Bourdieu called it, when people exhaust themselves for a future that ultimately is closed to them, thus eliminating themselves.[105]

It is striking to see how Dong's application of Bourdieu's analysis on China's educational system also fits the situation in other parts of the world. I observe higher education being invaded, "captured," and hollowed out in often very deceptive ways in many world regions. Literature abounds which describes dynamics in Western countries that resemble the situation in China in their basic gist.[106] What Dong reports on Chinese research universities could also be said about their Western counterparts, namely, that the academic community no longer prioritizes seeking "balanced truth," rather, "young teachers seek professional stability" within a hierarchical bureaucracy.[107] Entering the academic community remains a dream for most; their aspirations to a higher social status that would correspond to their qualifications are, however, increasingly being disappointed, even after having invested in many years of higher education. Bourdieu speaks of a "cheated generation," when an educational status no longer guarantees a corresponding social status in the labor market.[108]

The educational system is not the only societal structure that cheats its participants and terrorizes them into suicide. Also industrial agriculture terrorizes farmers into suicide, and robs the next generation of its future.[109] Frances Moore Lappé is the co-founder of Food First, the Institute for Food and Development Policy, and the Small Planet Institute. She describes capitalism as the product of an assumption of scarcity as a norm and a presumption of lack of both "goods and goodness," from energy to food to human compassion.[110] From there, she observes, we grasp the mythical "free market" as automatic and infallible force to sort out who gets what, and we "fall for the improbable notion that a market driven largely by one rule – that which brings highest return to existing wealth – will bring forth benign outcomes for all." As a result, monopoly capitalism becomes inevitable, with all its antidemocratic and human-and-nature-destroying power: "… human rights will only be fulfilled as citizens challenge the now-dominant political systems I call 'privately held governments' that make rules to favor the wealthiest."[111] Lappé suggests a solution:

> Within so-called free market economics, enterprise is driven by the central goal of bringing the highest return to existing wealth. This logic leads inexorably to the concentration of wealth and power, making hunger and ecosystem disruption inevitable. The industrial system does not and cannot meet our food needs. An alternative, relational approach – agroecology – is emerging and has already shown promising success on the ground. By dispersing power and building on farmers' own knowledge, it offers a viable path to healthy, accessible food; environmental protection; and enhanced human dignity.[112]

This chapter concludes with renowned physicist Stephen Hawking warning that humanity is at risk of self-annihilation, be it by nuclear war, global warming, or genetically-engineered viruses, and further progress in science and technology will create "new ways things can go wrong."[113]

The human inclination to behave like locusts and destroy their own substrate is evident to all who do not live in bubbles of wealth and classism that protect and blind them from being confronted with the rest of the world.[114] I see it everywhere on my global path. In my book on a dignity economy, I called on humanity to engage in dialogue on solutions[115]: How come that the wonderfully innocent human talent to make tools now ends in humankind being a species of super-predators who cause the mass extinction of other species on our planet, and ultimately their own extinction? Is this suicidal trend inherent in "communism," as Ayn Rand would be quick to conclude? Or is it inherent in "capitalism,"[116] as Marxists would say? Or in the Roman law principles that serve as foundation for both communism and capitalism, and now underpin the global *world-system*,[117] as philosopher Howard Richards has taught us? Perhaps all have in common that they were devised to be solutions to fix problems, yet, since they use domination as a tool, they create more problems?

Domination, as promising as it may seem in the beginning, as much as it may be hailed as solution at the outset, is ultimately inherently incapable of fulfilling dreams of liberation and a better life. Hope and enthusiasm all too often end in terror, either as side effect or direct result. The strategy of domination, if left to its own devices, sows wind and reaps storm. It only can be stopped by the Mandelas of this world, and only by abandoning the dominator paradigm altogether.

Wherever a dominator system is in place, it rewards the most reckless dominators. As soon as they are in power, they will develop a sense of entitlement to remain there and resist the humiliation of being reduced to equality. This may end in "sinking the ship to protect one's interests," as *Facta* chief editor Shigeo Abe formulated it.[118] At that point, change can only come from outside. Japan had its Olympus scandal, where it required *gaiatsu*, or "pressure from outside," to expose it.

What if the entire world will at some point be captured by the domination system? What if there will be no outside anymore, from where a corrective could emerge? What if the entire world becomes a ship full of fools? This is why I try, in whatever way I can, to give voice to *the periphery*. I follow peace researcher Johan Galtung in his view that new useful ideas often emerge, not in the power centers of the world, but in the periphery, in the "outside" niches.[119] And it is in those niches that I look for alternative, dignifying solutions. I therefore do everything I can to strengthen periphery-to-periphery contact, thus honoring anthropologist Clifford Geertz's interest in local-to-local connections.[120]

Also historian Ibn Khaldun was interested in the periphery, albeit his definition of periphery was different from Galtung's. Ibn Khaldun saw belligerent nomadic warriors suddenly appear from the periphery and annihilate long-standing high cultures in the blink of an eye.[121] Also historian Arnold J. Toynbee, an admirer of Khaldun, talked about belligerent "primitive barbarians" threatening from embattled border regions.[122] Galtung's periphery is where people live who are exploited by the center and are taught a culture of obedience, but from where also alternative solutions may emerge. Both Khaldun and Toynbee have theorized how empires decay from within. Toynbee, in his twelve-volume work of 1934 – 1961, lists reasons for that decay, reasons that could all be summarized as "domination driven into extremes."[123]

In 2016, we had our 27th Annual Dignity Conference in former Yugoslavia,[124] a region that can teach the world what it should better avoid. The Balkans are a formerly embattled border region between two empires, one ruled from Vienna and the other from Constantinople. Over many centuries, both empires used the region as a buffer zone and incentivized its citizens to develop a warrior-spirit in the service of defending the border. A warrior-spirit is like wind yearning to become a storm whenever an opportunity opens. Therefore, it was easy for the new world power centers of the twentieth century to fire up this spirit when the region was vulnerable. The result was all-out war and destruction for millions of people. This dynamic reminds of Somalia. The cruel Yugoslav Wars were fought from 1991 to 2001,[125] while quasi-genocide had come to Somalia in 1988.[126] In both cases, proud warriors were enthusiastic to go to war, they were not keen to make peace, and they could not be forced into peace by way of obedience, like it might have been feasible, for instance, in places like Rwanda.[127]

Through my work, I aim to encourage peripheries to think up dignified solutions for how world affairs may be shaped differently, and to invite power centers to consider joining in. Johan Galtung suggested in 1971 that power centers might themselves choose to turn away from imperialist policies, not because they are forced to, but because they see that exploitation puts world peace in danger. Or, there may be internal reasons, negative spin-off effects such as inequality or pollution, which might inspire politics of justice and care: "There are many possibilities, and they may combine into quite likely contributions towards a disruption of the system. But in general we would believe more in Periphery-generated strategies than in Center-generated ones, since the latter may easily lead to a new form of dependence on the Center."[128]

Chapter 17

How the Terror of "War for Peace" Is Still with Us

"Fear sells, fear intimidates, fear makes humans go against their best judgment," this is a formulation by Egyptian political satirist Bassem Youssef. He had to cancel his hugely popular weekly talk show *Al Bernameg* in Cairo, because he feared for his life.[1] Fear can lead to massive regression, outrage, and violence, and this can be exploited by leaders for their own advantage, says psychiatrist Vamik Volkan.[2]

Fear is also what is at the core of the security dilemma and the culture it has engendered throughout the past millennia, the culture of *If you want peace, prepare for war*. Fear drives the traditional way of keeping honorable peace: "we and our people have to stand together on top of our enemies, we have to be strong, at least appear strong, everything else would mean to shamefully succumb to humiliation."

On September 2011, for the first time since 1812, the inviolability of the American mainland was breached when the Twin Towers in New York City were attacked. This brought fear to America. It also returned, in full strength, the culture of the security dilemma. Mighty honor rhetoric returned, including its religious manifestations: "God is on Our Side" and "God Bless America" in response to "Allah's revenge."[3]

Some ask: Why did the United States magnify "many times over the initial damage caused by the terrorists?"[4] Was it a case of Cold Warriors being in search of an enemy?[5] Was it a Bush administration "bewitched" by Cold War thinking?[6] Bewitched by the "false template" of Samuel Huntington's concept of inherently incompatible "civilizations" clashing?[7] Was it American military superiority that "has irredeemably skewed the country's view of the enemy on the horizon, drawing the United States, with appalling consequences, into a gratuitous, cruel, and unwinnable conflict in the Middle East"?[8]

What about the mindset that inspires the use of terror as a weapon in an asymmetric situation? Do not war and terrorism both draw on similar mindsets, namely, on keeping one's enemies at bay, if needed crush them, while keeping one's own people in line? In all cases, it is seen as a patriotic duty, particularly that of every able-bodied man, to be willing to commit "de-individuated political murder" if called upon. Terrorism expert Alex Schmid uses the phrase *de-individuated murder* for terrorism, "to indicate that the victim matters mostly as a message generator – one victim can be easily substituted with another since the message and not the victim mainly matters to the terrorist."[9] If terrorism is de-individuated murder of civilians, is war then the individuated legitimate killing of non-civilians? Perhaps war is altogether de-individuated murder of humans, just as terrorism? Particularly modern war, which is no longer war man-to-man? World War I was the first war of straightforward horrifying de-individuated slaughter, one may say. My father was a soldier in World War II. For him, also World War II was senseless horrific de-individuated slaughter. He did not see the enemy as enemy – therefore, he was in danger of being killed by his own for being a traitor.

My father did not want to be forced to invest his feelings and his life into a narrative made up of Hitler's personal experiences of humiliation and desire for revenge. My father did not want to channel his own private feelings of frustration and humiliation into such a narrative. He did not want to follow the Nazis in their quasi-religious justifications for why specific historical events made war "necessary" to restitute national honor. My father felt that this narrative of honor was a violation of his dignity. I am happy that after this war, the narrative of war for honor could be seen as what it is, and that my father is still alive to see his resistance redeemed. My work also heals him.

But what if new occurrences of fear are so strong that the narrative of honor forces its way back into the minds of people, even those people who had almost forgotten it? If only because it is the age-old familiar response to fear? Political scientist Stephen Holmes observes that the unfamiliarity of the threat of 9/11 may have caused feelings of defenselessness to the point that they had to be repressed and replaced with a more familiar threat from the Cold War: "To repress feelings of defenselessness associated with an unfamiliar threat, the decision makers' gaze slid uncontrollably away from al Qaeda and fixated on a recognizable threat that was unquestionably susceptible to being broken into bits."[10] Holmes calls this fusion of bin Laden and Saddam Hussein a "mental alchemy, the 're-conceiving' of an impalpable enemy as a palpable enemy": the Bush administration reflexively implemented "out-of-date formulas in a radically changed security environment."[11]

All this happened in a context, where these "out-of-date formulas" had already been de-institutionalized in the United States. The Vietnam conflict had taught to "eliminate the draft, create an all-volunteer force, reduce domestic taxes, and maintain a false prosperity based on foreign borrowing," observes legal scholar Geoffrey Stone.[12] After 2001, to go back and be able to regain those "out-of-date formula" of honor and insulate them against popular "dignity resistance," solutions had to be found: Conservative lawyers re-interpreted the United States Constitution to justify the president's war-making power, to deny the legality of the Geneva Conventions, and they authored the "torture memos" for the Bush administration, writes Chalmers Johnson, professor of political science and former consultant for the C.I.A.[13]

Why is the progressives' antiwar movement in America so weak? Perhaps political scientist James Holmes is right in saying that "the humanitarian interventionism of the 1990s helped anesthetize many Americans," and that particularly the sense of guilt over having failed to stop the genocide in Rwanda was responsible?[14] After all, it were the progressives in America who had suggested a preemptive and unilateralist turn-about in American foreign policy before the Bush administration appropriated it.[15] Already psychologists Jim Sidanius and Felicia Pratto have taught that legitimizing myths can shift, and that also "liberal" legitimizing myths can justify the use of force or warfare: Massive and brutal violence was employed by Marxist and "egalitarian" revolutionary movements, from the Russian revolution to Peru's Shining Path (Sendero Luminoso), and invading Afghanistan was to liberate its women from the oppression by the Taliban.[16]

To say it in my words: Progressives saw dignity humiliation – the violation of equality in dignity for all – and wanted to remedy it with humility and dignity, while the Bush administration saw honor humiliation – the violation of supremacy – and went ahead to remedy it with "honorable" solutions. And both used their own respective legitimizing myths.

Those steeped in a mindset of honor tend to see America as the sole victim of terror. The mental frame of honor forbids the thought that some terrorists might act from a sense of honorable victimhood, and that terror might also emanate from one's own side. From an honor perspective, the phrase "one's freedom fighter is the other's terrorist" is unthinkable: "they" are terrorists and only terrorists, and "we" have freedom fighters and only freedom fighters. Conservative Americans, when facing the accusation that also the United States may have acted as a humiliator, or at least be perceived as such, will deny this angrily. They will rather accuse anyone who claims to be a victim of American humiliation of dressing up as victims to cover up for their own evilness or simply for being losers. These are indeed some of the arguments I met in reaction to my book.

The recent controversy over "No Irish Need Apply" signs in the United States offers a template. The first immigrants to America from Ireland were treated as underdogs, and the question now is: Are they portraying the truth? Were they really so badly treated as they claim? Or are they making themselves into victims?[17] Clearly, the line is seldom clear-cut: "real" and intended acts of humiliation might fail to actually elicit feelings of humiliation in targeted victims, while, on the other side, feelings of humiliation can come about through "imagined" reasons that lack any basis in reality. And between those two poles there will be many variations.

Not all historical events are automatically suitable to be used in legitimizing narratives. First, such an event needs to be interpreted. The same historical event that inspires love and veneration in one person, may arouse a sense of envy and humiliation in another. It may well be that Western power attracts hatred from envious "losers." Yet, as I wrote in my book on humiliation and international conflict in 2006, the West also attracts a huge amount admiration in the rest of the world – otherwise people would not flock to the West from all corners of the world. It is only when the promise of a better life turns out to be hollow that an expectation gap opens and a sense of humiliation might set in. All love stories carry the risk of being turned into hatred when people feel disappointed, and regrettable rash reactions may destroy all love.[18] When humiliation is felt, and it is read through the lens of dignity humiliation, the script for healing, if it wants to stay within the paradigm of dignity, ought to be the path of a Nelson Mandela or a Frantz Fanon. Also the Kennedy family worked itself out of Irish humiliation constructively, even making it all the way to American presidency. However, the script for action may also unfold in ways drastically different, namely, by "falling back" into the scripts of honor humiliation, and this may lead to hatred and terror. This is what I call *cross over*, it is what I deem to be the most destructive outflow of the dynamics of humiliation and the strongest force that hinders global solidarity. And it is a story of disappointed lovers, rather than a story of envious losers.

Concert pianist Lang Lang followed the Kennedy path. Becoming "number one" was the shared mantra of father and son in the case of concert pianist Lang Lang and his father, as much as in the case of JFK and his father, Irish businessman Joseph Patrick "Joe" Kennedy. Joe Kennedy smarted from being excluded and mistreated for being Irish, while Lang Lang's parents had their hopes destroyed by the Cultural Revolution of 1966 to 1976. Both sons succeeded; not only did they climb to the top of their fields of ambition, they also inspired much hope in others.[19]

Nelson Mandela was born in the humiliated segment of his society, yet, instead of aiming to kill his humiliators, he invested his life into creating a new society of equality in dignity. Frantz Fanon was a Martinique born Afro-Caribbean philosopher and revolutionary who initially tried to be more French than French, until he understood that he would always be "black."[20] From this insight, he set out to enlighten the world about the psychopathology of colonization.

I myself come from a displaced family and know all about these psychological dynamics from my own biography, and also I chose the path of dignity out of humiliation. Also so-called foreign fighters are often children of migrants, and both parents and children yearn for connection. The children may feel ashamed, humiliated, and furious on their own behalf, yet, perhaps even more when they see their parents failing to be respected as equals. They may choose the path of honor out of humiliation.

Personal experiences of humiliation – either experienced directly or on behalf of parents and one's own in-group – are crucial as emotional driving forces for terror. In order to become salient for action, those feelings need first to be poured into a narrative that offers a solution, be it one of love and care or one of violence and terror. Personal and historical events have to be weighed, punctuation marks set that indicate what should be seen as cause and what as effect and what the endpoint should be. This is the field of *framing* and *meta-emotion*, or how people feel about feelings.[21]

Most Da'esh leaders went through the U.S. military prison Camp Bucca that was run by the U.S. occupation forces near Omm Qasr in southeastern Iraq.[22] A coherent humiliation narrative may have emerged in that prison and been affirmed by its circumstances. Also in the West, so-called foreign fighters may radicalize out of their own private frustrations and humiliations, fired up in their own personal micro level contexts, and then affirmed by political events at macro levels. Psychologist Anthony Marsella observes: "The continued disrespect, humiliation, and vilification of Islam, implicit and explicit, in USA foreign policies and actions, especially existing counterterrorism approaches, sustain and nurture anger, resentment, and revenge."[23]

I remember a scene somewhere in the middle of Europe, twenty years ago, when a very kind, young, polite, soft-spoken, and highly educated guest scholar from Iran, a mathematician, shared with me his experience. He had idolized everything about "the West" before coming, in disregard of the mainstream consensus in his country that the West be "decadent." Yet, now he was less sure. He faced daily micro-humiliations from his European colleagues – not that they were racist or hostile to Islam, they simply were ignorant of the world and thoughtless. This was his warning: "If you, in the West, do not become more aware of how you humiliate foreigners like me, we might one day turn on you when we return to our countries and gain power." What his story illustrates is that the *contact hypothesis* may tragically fail. This hypothesis suggests that contact creates friendship – yet, unfortunately, contact can also create hateful extremism.[24] Magid and Millat are two twin brothers born in England in Zadie Smith's novel *White Teeth*, and also their story illustrates how the contact hypothesis may fail. To protect him from Western values, Magid's father sent him to grow up in Bangladesh, yet, he came back as a consummate Englishman with a white suit and Oxford English. His brother Millat, who remained in England, became a bearded fundamentalist.[25]

Through my global life, I am not confined to one perspective. I step in and out of perspectives and look at the phrase "one's freedom fighter is the other's terrorist" from all possible sides. From my meta-perspective, I see that history offers ample material for humiliation on all sides if weighed and punctuated accordingly, while terror strategies are not the solution on either side, especially as the world becomes more interconnected. I see questions always going as follows: Who started what? Was it "only collateral damage"? And what is intended?[26] Usually both sides see the other side as the one who started conflict intentionally and inflicted premeditated damage, while the damage "we" cause is legitimately re-active or unintended collateral damage. To rescue "our" moral superiority, usually each side selects the worst violations on the other side to highlight that "we are better than them, since we do not do such things."

I deeply resonate with American fear and shock on one side, just as much as I also consider author Tariq Ali's words that the "visible violence of September 11" could be seen as "a response to the invisible violence that has been inflicted on countries like Afghanistan, Pakistan, Iraq, Saudi Arabia, Egypt, Palestine and Chechnya," and that some of this, not all, "has been the direct responsibility of the United States and Russia."[27]

Leaders typically manifest scripts for what to feel and how to act that are different from the scripts their followers employ. I have discussed this with terrorism expert Petter Nesser in 2011 (see Appendix to the first part of this book project). What I see in leaders of terror movements is honor humiliation driving domination strategies, with ideology more or less serving as window dressing. Political scientist Stathis Kalyvas appears to confirm this when he says: "In short, analyzing the Islamic State as a revolutionary actor that happens to be Islamist is a much more promising avenue of interpretation than seeing it as either simply an Islamist actor or a sectarian one … we have much to learn from revisiting the action and strategy of the last generation of insurgent revolutionary actors, those of the Cold War."[28] Indeed, Da'esh, in its aggregate form, acts as a rational strategic enterprise – it weakens enemies and strengthens its own territory, in part by terrorizing people, including those it wishes to rule over.

In contrast to leaders, followers may be motivated differently. In the beginning of a revolutionary movement, true believers often give it impetus, they sacrifice their all, their inner souls, only to be pushed aside by raw power later. The trajectory from the February Revolution to the October Revolution to Joseph Stalin in the Soviet Union offers a prime example. Leon Trotsky's personal path was intricately woven into this slide from idealism to terror. As a young man, he supported the workers' union and was held in prison for that. It was in prison that he first learned about Lenin and became "radicalized." From there he rose to be the leader of the Communist troops and saved the entire Bolshevik government from demise by crushing the Kronstadt sailors. He continued his path by advocating the system of state terror that ultimately led to Stalinism. His life ended by being assassinated on the orders of Stalin himself.

Any ideological or religious belief system can attract true believers. In my clinical practice, I witnessed the horror that befalls true believers when it dawns on them that they are but puppets in a much larger power game and that their idealism is but material for others to instrumentalize. Not least true believers in the American Dream experience this disillusionment these days in the wake of the financial crises that hurt many.

Males among both leaders and followers may be prone to embrace a stronger honor culture than women, not least because it offers an arena to be "a real man." As has been laid out before, the honor culture's definition of manhood offers a sense of sublime heroism "that is lacking in the jaded, tired world of democratic liberalism," especially in the parallel worlds where Europe's immigrants mostly live.[29]

This is what anthropologist Scott Atran observes: "The challenge for democracies is to provide an alternative means of satisfying the quest for glory that motivates those who join in Isis's barbarism."[30] Atran explains: "Isis's violence is far from being nihilistic – a charge usually levelled by those who are wishfully blind to the attraction of their foes. The moral worldview of the devoted actor is dominated by what Edmund Burke referred to as 'the sublime': a need for the 'delightful terror' of a sense of power, destiny, a giving over to the ineffable and unknown."[31] Atran reports on "vacationers" for jihad, "who are going to Syria over school breaks or holidays for the thrill of adventure and a semblance of glory," and observes that beheadings turn terror into a display of triumph over and through death and destruction for Da'esh, just as the images of the collapsing Twin Towers did for Al-Qaeda.[32] There is a dark excitement here that fascinates, underpinned by the fact that the very phrase *terror* points at *tremor*, the shaking and trembling that also accompanies sexual arousal: "and so the sexual, orgasmic connotation of terrorism should not be forgotten … a lethal cocktail of excitement and fascination wrapped up in various forms of political, moral and patriotic sentiments, all in all creating a most intoxicatingly powerful archetypal whirlpool."[33] Sociologist Jack Katz studied the subjective experiences of violent criminals, and also he found that "doing stickup" represents a retaliation for everyday experiences of shame and humiliation, as the glory of domination and control reverses shameful powerlessness.[34]

Historian and Holocaust expert Thomas Kühne wrote a book about *The Pleasure of Terror*.[35] Kühne describes how the Nazi Stormtroopers (SA), from late 1929 onward, waged civil war on communists and socialists, how they unleashed brutality in dance hall battles, brawls, and knife fights, and how this brutality was committed collectively and served as social "cement," as Nazi propaganda minister Joseph Goebbels would call it. Committing moral transgressions forged bonds: "… the SA popularized the myth of revolutionizing society by violating civilian, humanitarian norms. SA men did not hide murder; they staged it."[36]

Ethologist Konrad Lorenz, in his book *On Aggression*, differentiates intragroup from intergroup aggression.[37] Among animals, groups of animals are willing to kill or be killed in defense of their community, while fighting for rank is seldom fatal. Lorenz speaks of a "communal defense response" accompanied by a *holy shiver*, a *heiliger Schauer*, a tingling of the spine when the reflex for raising hair on the back and along the outside of both arms of an animal makes the animal seem larger than it really is. Also humans may experience this shiver and mistake it for a holy experience, even though it is a pre-human vegetative activation of a fur that humans no longer have.[38] This shiver creates a sense of elation, a readiness to abandon everyday matters for "militant enthusiasm," for the sacred duty of heroically defending one's community: *Dulce et decorum est pro patria mori* (It is sweet and proper to die for one's country).[39]

This shiver may be one of the sources of the "pleasure of terror" that those who use terror tactics feel when they believe they fulfil a holy duty. "Rational considerations, criticisms, and all reasonable arguments against the behavior dictated by militant enthusiasm are silenced by a reversal of all values, making them appear not only untenable, but base and dishonorable. Men may enjoy the feeling of absolute righteousness even while they commit atrocities," explains John Scales Avery, who shared the Nobel Peace Prize for the Pugwash Conferences on Science and World Affairs in 1995.[40] Avery continues: "The communal defense mechanism can be thought of as the aspect of human emotions which makes it natural for soldiers to kill or be killed in defense of their countries. In the era before nuclear weapons made war prohibitively dangerous, such behavior was considered to be the greatest of virtues."[41] By now, the advent of nuclear weapons has "removed heroism from war."[42]

Hannah Arendt alluded to similar dynamics in her essay on violence, when she said that a community of violence will push new members to commit irreversible acts of brutality that would burn their bridges to respectable society.[43] This is also what Mark Juergensmeyer describes in his book *Terror in the Mind of God*, where he speaks about *performance violence* as a public, theatrical, symbolic statement aimed at providing a sense of empowerment, not necessarily at achieving any strategic goal.[44] Performance violence is the very point of *gonzo* productions,[45] of short low-budget videos that focus on the horror of the act itself and give only very brief explanations of the rationale of the act, explanations such as: "I'm back, Obama, and I'm back because of your arrogant foreign policy towards the Islamic State, because of your insistence on continuing your bombings."[46] Performance violence is also the point of videos of killings that highlight the act itself, as in the Sotloff and Foley videos, where the killer "beheaded his victim with a short blade and deployed the sawing motion" favored by Abu Musab al-Zarqawi, the Jordanian leader of Al-Qaeda in Iraq who was killed in a U.S. airstrike in 2006 – all these are "demonstrations of raw fanaticism, power, and unrestrained brutality."[47]

As the example of Nazi-Germany shows, the pleasure of creating blood baths is not a reserve of terrorism, it is part of the male honor and heroism script in general, also in war. In her 1908 novel, Bertha von Suttner wrote about a young man and his motivation to go to war:

> And how was it with you, yourself, youngster, the first time you went into battle ?" "Oh, enchanting, delightful!" "You need not lie, my boy; it is not the staff officer examining into your fitness for a military office, but your friend, who is questioning you." "I can only repeat, it was inspiring. Horrible? Yes, but grand! And with the consciousness that I was fulfilling man's highest duty, with god on my side, for king and country! And then: that I met death so close – dared it face to face, and it did not touch me – that filled me with a lofty sense of the peculiar glory of war, as in the old epic stories, I saw the muse of history guiding our arms to victory. A noble indignation filled me against the insolent enemy who had dared to attack a German country, and it was an intense satisfaction to gratify this hate. This desire to destroy, without being a murderer, this setting one's own life in the balance, is a singular sensation."[48]

Whoever wanted to become an SA man, Kühne explains, would have to adopt an anti-bourgeois name from the criminal underworld, like "Revolver Gob" or "Submarine." "Participating in collective violence was the entrance ticket to the group. When they met in 'storm bars' to enjoy themselves, they dwelt on war stories, and granted the most brutal comrade the greatest respect."[49] SA groups threw themselves into orgies of brutality on Jews, for instance, forcing their way into apartments, entering bedrooms and randomly shooting at couples sleeping in bed. The more important point that Kühne makes, however, is that, while sadism and hatred of Jews, and obedience or group pressure played a role – which all are established explanations of Holocaust perpetrator actions – what was at the core was "group pleasure, collective joy, the experience of togetherness and belonging."[50] "This is a gruesome example of how the need to belong can be hijacked horrifically, but also of how humans have to be abysmally broken down to participate," comments Linda Hartling.[51] Kühne explains that while some men participated enthusiastically and others refused to take part, there was a sociological mechanism that brought together collective joy and collective crime: According to an order from Heinrich Himmler, "everyone" had to carry out executions, and their readiness was being tested. To become one of "us," you had to kill at least once:

> Bruno Müller, head of Einsatzkommando 11b began a mass execution in Southern Russia in August 1941 by picking a two-year-old child and shooting it, then killing the mother. Having set the model, he asked the other officers to

follow. Everyone, he said, had to shoot at least one person.[52]

Thomas Kühne, like psychologist and Holocaust scholar Ervin Staub, points out that bullies could not have risen to alpha-male positions and taken over society without those who failed to stand up and step into their way.[53] Even those who refused to participate in fact supported the genocidal culture they rejected when they argued, "I am too weak to do this killing." In that way, they judged themselves as abnormal rather than questioning the morality of that culture.[54] "In a culture of 'tough' masculinity, of brutality and mercilessness, they represented the inbuilt 'other' of the group, thus helping to bring the hegemonic ideal into sharp focus."[55] Kühne quotes Sebastian Haffner, a biographer of Adolf Hitler, who explains that personal responsibility and consciences dissolve through the comforting "happiness of comradeship," which gives absolution if everybody does the same.[56]

The comforting happiness of comradeship formed by abuse is not a reserve of Nazi or Da'esh culture in faraway history or far away world regions. It is also part of societies otherwise proud of being different. Mina Finstad Berg is a young football fan in Norway, a country known for gender equality. Yet, Berg is dismayed at the increasingly coarse football support songs sung in Norway's football stadiums: "vi skal voldta deres horer" or "alle damer er horer" or "voldtekt er den beste sex" ("We're going to rape their whores" or "all women are whores" or "rape is the best sex").[57]

Since the traditional way of keeping peace means staying on top of enemies and keeping one's own people in line, *fourth-generation warfare* should not come as a surprise. Fourth-generation warfare means threatening another country by helping terrorists destabilize it. Indian National Security Advisor Ajit Doval, for instance, advised India to fight Pakistan with fourth-generation warfare by destabilizing Pakistan from inside with the help of violent non-state actors. Doval advised that in the case of another 2008 Mumbai type attack, "India should immediately move to help the secessionists in Balochistan."[58] The Balochistan Liberation Army has as its aim to gain greater autonomy from Pakistan and is designated as a terrorist organization by Pakistan and Britain.[59] Doval recommended this to a country, India, which was deeply traumatized by the Mumbai attacks by Pakistan-sponsored terrorists November 26–29, 2008. On the Pakistani side, clearly, Doval's ideas did not go unnoticed. Pakistani general Raza Mohammad Khan even read Doval's words publically on Pakistani television to highlight that Pakistan was in grave danger from foreign countries threatening them with terrorism.[60] Raza Mohammad Khan made public that here was a prominent foreign security adviser openly threatening to support terrorists in a neighboring country. Clearly, fourth-generation war is used on all sides.

Since the traditional way of keeping peace means staying on top of enemies and keeping one's own people in line, it is also unsurprising that even counterterrorism is being instrumentalized for such purposes. New Zealand is not the only place in the world where "terrorism act" legislation has been used against a local tribe. Māori community activist, poet and social justice advocate Keri Lawson-Te Aho wrote to me:

> Kia ora Evelin
> I am keen to write something on the recent events in New Zealand where Tūhoe, a local tribe was singled out and threatened with a new piece of legislation called the suppression of terrorism act. It has been a very destructive process for the families involved and the raids into Tūhoe territory by the police have left spiritual and psychological scars amongst the children and families involved ...
> Mauri Ora,
> Keri[61]

Not only in New Zealand, all over the world, legitimate protesters risk being branded as terrorists. The 2016 edition of the World Press Freedom Index, published by Reporters Without Borders on April 20, 2016, shows "a 'deep and disturbing' decline in media freedom" around the world, where many laws "have been adopted penalizing journalists on such spurious charges as 'insulting the president,' 'blasphemy' or 'supporting terrorism.'"[62] The response to terrorism in the United States has been called "reckless."[63]

Allow me to share my personal experiences in South America. On June 5, 2012, I gave a talk in Brasilia, the capital of Brazil, at the Committee for Human Rights and Minorities of the Chamber of Deputies, a federal legislative body and the lower house of the National Congress of Brazil. I had the privilege of being invited by Ricardo Josι Pereira Rodrigues, Senior Policy Specialist, Office of Legislative Counsel and Policy Guidance of the Chamber of Deputies.[64] I asked him about the indigenous people protesting logging in Chile who would be called "terrorists,"[65] and whether it is the case also in Brazil that legitimate protesters are vilified as terrorists. His reply was that, indeed, in the past, "when the country was under dictatorship, the subject was of major interest to those in the elite who sought to curb the actions of clandestine opposition groups."[66] He continued by saying that, however, what happens in Chile now does not happen in Brazil in the same way. Indigenous people as well as people belonging to the so called MST, the Movement of the landless, do invade big corporate farms, demonstrate, and protest, but they are not called terrorists. Even those on the right of the political spectrum decry their actions not as terrorism but as "illegal actions," and call for "police enforcement of property rights."[67] The Brazilian Constitution emphasizes that property has to have a social function, and in the past, the interpretation was that farm lands had to produce agricultural goods, rather than be used for speculative purposes, and if this rule was violated, land could be removed from its owner and used for land reform.

Recently, however, new interpretations of this law went too far for many: in some cases, land that had been owned by farmers for a hundred years was given to indigenous people, while in other cases, farmlands were given to *quilombolas*, Afro-Brazilian communities. Yet, he affirmed, "neither the quilombolas nor the Indians who protest, sometimes violently, are considered terrorists by the authorities or the media."[68]

From Brasilia, I proceeded to Recife, and from there to the Amazon, where I accompanied one of the actions of the landless movement. I got a much deeper understanding of the realities hidden behind the official story.[69] My observation is that Spanish colonial rule in South America has left behind a culture of fear, and that therefore terror has been used rather openly in the Spanish-speaking parts of South America, including the instrumentalization of terror. What I experienced in the former Portuguese colony Brazil was different, perhaps because master-underling fault lines are less clear-cut there.[70] The same conflict of interests between classical "dominators" and the rest plays out in Brazil as elsewhere, for instance, between landowners and landless – it is even starker in Brazil than elsewhere, with some *latifundia* being larger than entire countries – but it seems that methods are used in Brazil that are more sophisticated and covert than in the Spanish-speaking parts of South America.

Scandinavia is also not immune to the instrumentalization of the fear of terror. On July 24, 2014, the Norwegian Minister of Justice, together with the Norwegian Police Security Service (Norwegian: Politiets sikkerhetstjeneste, PST) and the Norwegian police, notified at a joint press conference that Norway faces a specific and time-limited terrorist threat. According to the authorities, it was not clear who or what was the alleged target for terror, but that extreme Islamists were the culprits. The Norwegian government asked people to be alert and notify the police if they saw anything suspicious. A high-level police presence was implemented all over the country, airspace blocked, museums closed, nuclear plants shut down, and border control checks increased. Five days later, the population was informed that the threat level was somewhat reduced now, but that the situation still was serious and unresolved. Swedish terrorist expert at the Swedish National Defence College, Magnus Ranstorp, criticized Norway's terror alert as untimely, and Former Danish Security director Hans-Jørgen Bonnichsen called the Norwegian police's reactions a "victory for the terrorists."[71] Ketil Lund, former Supreme Court Judge and chairman of the Norwegian Lund Commission on Government Terror Alerts, suspected that such public terror alarms (without seemingly sufficient substance), have a hidden agenda: They are meant to increase fear in the population – as fear is the political basis for surveillance, and as terror alarms increase anxiety, this helps to garner support for more surveillance.[72]

It is entirely consistent with the security dilemma culture to instrumentalize fear of terror to strengthen the dominator structure within a society. It is also consistent with this culture to believe that there can be nonviolent extremism. Terrorism expert Alex Schmid strongly counsels against cooperation with extremists and warns that there are only nonviolent radicals, and that "nonviolent extremism" is a contradiction in terms. Schmid explains that some Western security agencies and counterterrorism policymakers think of supposedly nonviolent extremists as a "firewall" – "preventing some radical youth from gliding further down the slippery slope to terrorism."[73] Schmid warns that so-called nonviolent extremist organizations reject democracy, (gender) equality, pluralism, separation of state and religion, freedom of thought and expression, man-made laws, respect for human rights and humanitarian law. Also a former extremist and member of Hizb ut-Tahrir warns:

> The central theoretical flaw in PVE [Preventing Violent Extremism, Britain's counter-radicalization strategy] is that it accepts the premise that nonviolent extremists can be made to act as bulwarks against violent extremists. Nonviolent extremists have consequently become well dug in as partners of national and local government and the police. Some of the government's chosen collaborators in "addressing grievances" of angry young Muslims are themselves at the forefront of stoking those grievances against British foreign policy; western social values; and alleged state-sanctioned "Islamophobia." PVE is thus underwriting the very Islamist ideology which spawns an illiberal, intolerant and anti-western worldview. Political and theological extremists, acting with the authority conferred by official recognition, and indoctrinating young people with an ideology of hostility to western values.[74]

Clearly, those who believe in such alliances think in terms of the friend-enemy dichotomies of the dominator world, "you are either with us or against." As Schmid warns, this belief is dangerously misguided, particularly in present-day's interconnected world.

I write these particular lines the day after the attacks on the newspaper *Charlie Hebdo* happened in Paris in January 2015. After such incidents, all news channels in the West broadcast a message that is almost ritualized and betrays that the players might be beholden to this friend-enemy dichotomy, wittingly or not: "'The enemy' wants victory by weakening our resolve, but 'we' stand tall and deny him this victory." The problem with such declarations is that in an interconnected world, victory or denying victory is an outdated choice, falling short of what is needed. Rather, what is at stake is how to make interconnectedness work. Condemning the condemnable appears as a ritual informed by an underlying mindset of war that insinuates that there is also violence that is not condemnable, that violence would be acceptable if "my side" committed it, and that the violence committed by soldiers in war is unproblematic.

The friend-enemy dichotomy might also play a role in re-stoking the Cold War. As mentioned before, the national humiliation of Russia through American arrogance has been felt deeply in Russia, as Nikolaj Sergeevič Portugalov has explained, a Russian politician who played a central role in negotiating the German reunification.[75] The election of Donald J. Trump with the help of Russia could be seen as ultimate pay-back.[76]

The friend-enemy dichotomy also means that all sides often resemble each other in violating human rights and the Geneva Conventions. Afghanistan's security apparatus, for instance, appears to be as dubious as the Taliban it is designed to fight, since it is "run by a network of strongmen, many of whom attained official authority as allies of the United States."[77]

The list of examples for how the friend-enemy dichotomy can manifest is vast, ranging from how one's own people are kept in line with an iron grip, to forcing minorities out or down, to subjecting conscience to power, or to combating foes covertly.

Marked by the horrifying experience of the Holocaust, many of those who identify as Jewish feel that it is their profound responsibility to recognize genocidal killings wherever they occur in the world. Despite of this noble wish to protect not just Jews, but all of humankind against genocidal killing, due to the *Realpolitik* of close relations between Israel and Turkey, for a long time, Israel did not confront Turkey on its denial of the Armenian genocide. Only in 2010, when the Turkish government accused Israel of "state terror" – after the Israeli raid on a Turkish aid flotilla – the American Jewish community no longer was bound to go against their own conscience.[78] Motives might have varied, but one way to describe this shift would be to say that this was a move from being bound by the friend-enemy dichotomy to being free to identify with humanity at large.

At the current point in history, in many world regions, the trend is toward strengthening the friend-enemy dichotomy rather than to identify with humanity at large. Dichotomies are made more rigid rather than dissolving them in pan-humaneness. The political culture in Turkey, for instance, is increasingly becoming threatening these days, confrontational, and defiant.[79] Examples abound. The situation at the Horn of Africa is described in an article titled, "Besieged, Abused, Ignored: Ethiopian Annihilation of the Ogaden People."[80]

And also covert applications of this mindset continue. The American war on drugs was meant as a war on radical students and blacks, if we believe writer Dan Baum. He reports that former domestic policy chief in President Nixon's administration, John Ehrlichman, told him in 1994 that the Nixon campaign of 1968, and the Nixon White House, saw the anti-war left and black people movements as their enemies and invented the war on drugs as a covert weapon against them. Since being anti-war or being black could not be made illegal, these groups were criminalized by associating hippies with marijuana and blacks with heroin: "... we could disrupt those communities. We could arrest their leaders, raid their homes, break up their meetings, and vilify them night after night on the evening news. Did we know we were lying about the drugs? Of course we did."[81]

In France, fifty percent of prison inmates are Muslims, two thirds are blacks and Arabs from disadvantaged neighborhoods, the so-called *milieu populaire*.[82] Sociologist and anthropologist Didier Fassin asks whether those groups are more criminal than the rest of society, or whether a prison machine is fed in the hope to solve socio-economic problems. Unfortunately, the outcome is disastrous, namely, the production of dangerous terrorists. Two of the three Paris terrorists of January 2015, Chérif Kouachi and Amedy Coulibaly, for instance, "met each other in prison and remained in contact since (the mid-2000s)."[83]

Economism – the new security dilemma

> *There will be no social stability or peace as long as there is hunger, poverty and inequality. Nor can we move forward if we continue to exploit our natural resources. Sustainability is a pre-condition for development.*
>
> – José Graziano da Silva, Director-General of the UN Food and Agricultural Organization[84]

> *The proposition that more investor-friendly reforms will serve the common good is treated as a given needing no proof; as if it were a joke that had already been told; as if those who did not understand the joke and did not know when to laugh, or did not know whether to laugh or cry, were not so much mistaken as left out of the conversation, deprived of voice.*
>
> – Howard Richards, 2016[85]

The classical security dilemma has a bright side, it offers protection, and a dark side, it creates the very threats against which protection is then needed. As long as weapons were less lethal, the dark side was accepted, yet, when collective suicide may be the outcome, it is no longer acceptable. The so-called free market is similar, it satisfies demand, this is the bright side, but what if it allows for demand to be created that serves only a few and ultimately is destructive to all?

"When we organize and manage the economy to maximize financial returns to money, we organize to maximize the growth of the numbers stored in financial asset accounts on computer hard drives; when we disregard the consequences for living Earth's generative systems and the social fabric of human community, this becomes a suicidal act of collective insanity," writes economist David Korten in 2016.[86]

Indeed, collective suicide may be the endgame when a system makes it possible for originators of inflammatory fake news to make a living from flooding the world with extremist frenzy, while real news makers hide behind paywalls that restrict access to their information, since otherwise they cannot be profitable.[87] Insanity put into system is when firebrand leaders come to power in a world where billions of individuals can potentially be incited to push the red button of nuclear material.[88]

The Russell-Einstein Manifesto of 1955, the founding document of the Pugwash Conferences on Science and World Affairs, ends with these words:

> Here, then, is the problem which we present to you, stark and dreadful and inescapable. Shall we put an end to the human race, or shall mankind renounce war? ... There lies before us, if we choose, continual progress in happiness, knowledge and wisdom. Shall we instead choose death because we cannot forget our quarrels? ... We appeal as human beings to human beings: Remember your humanity and forget the rest. If you can do so, there lies before you a new Paradise; if you cannot, there lies before you the threat of universal death.[89]

In 1995, the Nobel Peace Prize was awarded jointly to Pugwash Conferences on Science and World Affairs, and to its leader, Sir Joseph Rotblat. In his acceptance speech, he said:

> We have to extend our loyalty to the whole of the human race. ... A war-free world will be seen by many as Utopian. It is not Utopian. There already exist in the world large regions, for example the European Union, within which war is inconceivable. What is needed is to extend these.[90]

As mentioned earlier, economics could be said to have created a new global security dilemma, with the new fault line running between a small global superclass and the rest. And both dilemmas, the old and the new one, interact. *L'Art français de la guerre* (the French art of war) is a novel that makes palpable how the trope of killing can permeate not just war but also quotidian life, and not just the *banlieues* of French cities, but all places where proud and humiliated masculinity breeds terror.[91]

Former German defense minister Franz Josef Strauss has been introduced before. He was a man of honor and glory, enthusiastic about nuclear weapons and their potential as tactical munitions in war. He was a man of war for peace, a man steeped in the classical security dilemma. Therefore, he urged the corporate sector to construct "peaceful" nuclear power plants, to increase Germany's expertise in this field. By now, not just in Germany, these plants have become part and parcel of the new security dilemma, of the profit-maximizing paradigm, leading to dangerously failing equipment when the quality of material, personnel, and security measures is decreased to increase profit.[92]

Here is another place where both dilemmas intertwine. There is a strong convergence of environmental crime with corruption.[93] "Global environmental crime, possibly worth more than $200 billion annually, is helping finance criminal, militia and terrorist groups and threatening the security and sustainable development of many nations, notably in sub-Saharan Africa," according to a new joint United Nations-INTERPOL report.[94] Environmental crime thus bridges the classical local and the new global security dilemma. Even tourism can become part of this conundrum: During my time in Dubrovnik in 2016, with tears, its citizens exclaimed to me: "Tourism is our terrorism!"[95]

Land-grabbing is yet another case. Land has been conquered and stolen from its people by military means for ages. Now, the weapons are financial muscle and coercion. In a remote region of Ethiopia, and this is just one of many examples, a German television team found a Saudi Arabian investor group engaging in the large-scale cultivation of rice, on a huge piece of land, from which thousands of small farmers had been forced off into destitution. The manager in charge of the plant proudly exclaimed: "This is no mega project, it is a giga-project." In the future, it is possible that aid supplies to famine areas in Ethiopia will travel on the same Ethiopian road into the opposite direction of convoys of lorries with rice destined for export. When it is still on its stalk, this rice is already owned by Saudi Arabia, China, or India.[96] Locally contracted farmers working on the fields of such multinational corporations usually cannot afford to buy the very products they grow with their own hands. At the same time, affordable fresh food from the countryside no longer reaches the slums of the cities, where "fake" food sold by multinational corporations replaces "real" food and brings obesity and diabetes to the poor.[97]

What about aid supplies? Labels such as "charitable-industrial complex,"[98] or "white-savior industrial complex," expose how humanitarian considerations may simply serve as smokescreens: "If we are going to interfere in the lives of others, a little due diligence is a minimum requirement," is the desperate wish of Nigerian-American writer Teju Cole.[99] The global rich impose a coercive global order on the poor that violates their human right to subsistence, and this means that the global rich have a moral obligation to eradicate poverty, warns philosopher Thomas Pogge.[100]

Biowarfare and bioterrorism are yet another example of weaponry used in both, the classical and the new security dilemma. From a report from the Counterproliferation Center located at the Air War College in Alabama, we learn: "The recent revolution in molecular biology may have incidentally unleashed a new threat to mankind, in the form of genetically engineered pathogens, which could be used to develop many new offensive biological weapons."[101]

The revolution in molecular biology has facilitated yet another form of corporate land-grab. When farmers become dependent on genetically modified seeds, even nature is brought under the authority of corporations. "Industrial agriculture has not produced more food. It has destroyed diverse sources of food, and it has stolen food from other species to bring larger quantities of specific commodities to the market using huge quantities of fossil fuels and water and toxic chemicals in the process," this is physicist Vadana Shiva's damning verdict from India.[102]

"Barbarous corporatism" is a term that critical theologian Rudolf Siebert applies to both fascism and the ideology of liberalism, which "allows the powerful to exploit the powerless even today."[103]

The more extreme global climate degradation will become, the more investment opportunities they will represent. As mentioned before, MetLife Insurance Portfolio Manager Lawrence Oxley wrote a book on the promising investment opportunities that extreme climate events represent for the stock, bond, and futures markets.[104]

The term *economism* points at how economic activity has been deified above all else with pseudo-religious trappings, while essentially being amoral. As I observe all around the world on my global path, it has indeed become the new belief system not just in the Anglo-Saxon realm – from there, it has conquered the world.[105] The "commercialization of human feeling" spreads like a global wildfire and "manages the heart" on all continents.[106] "No religious dogma is as powerful and dangerous as the dogmas of economists who assume that we will all become richer even on a burning planet!" is the verdict from environmentalist Jakob von Uexküll.[107] Another voice, from India, says this about economism:

> Economism seems to have been erected to obscure the social, in part to hide the extraction of surplus value from the reproduction of virtally all forms of capital – cultural, economic, social, and symbolic – in Pierre Bourdieu's categorization. That is to say, most of us literally practice our ideology by feeling complacent about our own middle-class routines involving work, play, child-rearing, and leisure while focusing almost entirely on what happens to the "economy," as if it had an independent systemic pattern of its own that is entirely divorced from our own participation in the

> workings of power. But as a matter of fact, my use of the automobile, my job in a university, my membership in a church, or my mortgage payments and use of financial services such as banking or insurance are each tied to formal infrastructure that embodies exploitative relations of varying degrees toward ecosystems, cultures, and human bodies.[108]

In my book on a dignity economy, I dedicate a whole chapter to the myriad false choices that crowd out important choices.[109] "In an increasingly individualistic and consumerist society, social responsibility gets lost in the noise of markets, financial metrics, rankings, and competition," concurs Cristina Escrigas, the former executive director of, and current adviser to the Global University Network for Innovation.[110] Also German sociologist Heinz Bude agrees that *necessary* worries and fears about the state of the world at large are being channeled into small *private* worries.[111] Psychologist Anthony Marsella asks: "Why are Americans savoring the fruits of consumerism, materialism, commodification, competition when the consequences of these institutionalized values are destructive for individuals and the social fabric?"[112] Why do they not understand that the key is "Just Enough!"?

Discourse analyst Michael Karlberg points at the underlying problem, namely, in my words, the two concepts of human nature that the classical and the new security dilemma engender. The classical context stipulates that "if humans are presumed to be living out transitory lives en route to a destination of eternal salvation or damnation, and if this earthly existence is nothing more than a way of separating the saved from the damned, and if the entire process is about to reach an apocalyptic conclusion – then how does the construction of a more just and sustainable global civilization become imaginable or desirable?"[113] Equally detrimental is the new context: "if humans are presumed to be nothing more than intelligent and egoistic animals seeking to satisfy their material interests and appetites in an environment of scarce resources, with the meaning and purpose of our lives defined by success or failure in this regard – then how does the construction of a more just and sustainable global civilization become imaginable or desirable?"[114]

The new security dilemma compounds the damage from the old one, both exploiting the majority of the people on the planet except for a tiny privileged minority, and this exploitation now includes also those in the West who originally had profited from the classical security dilemma. The *moderns* have used human rights rhetoric to drive and be complicit with a project of exploitation, something that the *cultural creatives*, the human rights defenders, somehow failed to notice. As became exposed recently, it is possible that even the dignity of the Nobel Peace Prize has been abused as a stepping stone to more honor without the Nobel Committee noticing.[115]

By now, our task is to dismantle all forms of the security dilemma, the old and the new one. This will mean the loss of familiar pathways to recognition and honor for all hopeful war heroes and money heroes, a loss they might perceive as humiliating even though it represents a call for humility. It is a call for humility that suggests that it is better for humankind to survive than to continue creating life-threatening situations for the sake of providing a sense of worth through glorious domination to a few people.

To return to Titanic as an image, at times when the classical security dilemma was the only one, all people on the luxurious first floor were victors, most were beneficiaries of the military might that brought them to that floor. Then came the new security dilemma, where some became economic super-victors and created losers not just in the lower echelons of the ship, but also on the first floor. These "forgotten people" on the first floor have more power than those further down in the ship; they can elect populists who promise to bring back the old security dilemma, so that the forgotten people will be winners again over the "dangerous" people further down. While this happens, all overlook that both security dilemmas can and must be overcome if the Titanic is to stay afloat, and that any desire for win-lose victories will lead to lose-lose outcomes for everybody on Titanic. *Globalization of care* is the only solution; globalization of exploitation was a dangerous route that backfires now, risking to foreclose any chances for a globalization of care and solidarity to flourish.

Psychopathic culture

Wherever a culture of domination reigns, be it domination by way of military or financial might, dominators are sucked into leadership positions, and when they are there, they define how social and societal life ought to be lived. The result is a "creeping pathologization of society," a de-civilizing process into a culture of barbarism.[116] Cultures that allow psychopathic traits to be praised produce more psychopathy.[117]

During my time in Southeast Europe in 2016, in particular, in Sarajevo and Dubrovnik, I had the privilege of gaining deep insights into the double victimization that is the result when a war culture is first being incentivized, only to let it eat its own children later.[118] As it seems, all historically powerful neighbors of the region, from Vienna to Venice to Constantinople, have used the inhabitants of Southeast Europe as human shields between them. Even more, they gave incentives to some of them, they armed peasants, or *Wehrbauern*, to develop a warrior ethos. In this way they created a proud warrior culture, a culture that carries the inherent potential to escalate into fighting at the slightest instigation. Humiliation entrepreneurship works well in such a context. In cultures of obedience like in Rwanda, Germany, or Japan, it worked better to use arguments of duty to manipulate people into committing atrocities. In war cultures, such as Somalia, or, in this case, the Balkans, the warrior ethos waits to be instrumentalized. As a result, by now, all populations in that region are victims, victims of violence at the hand of those who first had been manipulated into a war culture and then committed the mistake of being proud of it. The following paragraph summarizes the extent and success of humiliation entrepreneurship in that region:

> The critical component of these wars – what made them escalate so quickly and so appallingly – was the single-minded, self-serving actions of a few selfish leaders who shamelessly and aggressively exploited existing resentments to advance their own interests. It wasn't until Milošević, Karadžić, Tuđman, and others expertly manipulated the people's grudges that the region fell into war. By vigorously fanning the embers of ethnic discord, polluting the airwaves with hate-filled propaganda, and carefully controlling media coverage of the escalating violence, these leaders turned what could have been a healthy political debate into a holocaust.[119]

The slogan *war for peace* was coined in 1991 by a political leader in Montenegro, Svetozar Marović, to justify the Montenegrin assault on Dubrovnik in 1991. Historian Nikola Samardžić, in his testimony at the trial of Slobodan Milošević 2002 – 2005, called the onslaught on Dubrovnik "an unjust war against Croatia, and a war in which Montenegro disgraced itself by putting itself in the service of the Yugoslav army and Slobodan Milošević."[120] Later, in 2003, Marović delivered a public apology for "all evils done by any citizen of Montenegro and Serbia to anyone in Croatia."[121]

Initially, Dubrovnik was ill-prepared for defense. Serb propaganda, however, portrayed the situation very differently, bringing back the specters of cruelty during World War II, cruelty that had been meted out by the *Ustaše*, a Croatian fascist, ultranationalist, and terrorist organization in existence from 1929 to 1945 that allied with Nazi Germany. Serb media claimed that the presence of fascist Ustaše forces and international terrorists in Dubrovnik left no choice but to attack it.[122] The specters of the victimization of Serbs once suffered at the hands of Croats were thus used to fire up the warrior spirit of heroic defense among Serbs.

On September 4, 2016, I went up on mountain Srđ just behind the city of Dubrovnik and visited Fort Imperial that was built in 1806 – 1816 during the Napoleonic Wars and now houses the exhibition called "Dubrovnik during the Homeland War, 1991 – 1995." There I saw a film from May 1991 that talked about "armed conflicts between the Croatian police and Serb terrorists." In other words, the term "terrorist" was used on all sides: international terrorists were suspected to hide inside of Dubrovnik, and those who suspected this, were called terrorists in return.

Psychologist Anthony Marsella sees mass shootings as a sign of a "trickle-down effect," not the trickling down of wealth, but of violence and pathology: We are socialized by the culture in which we live, and "this socialization can prepare us for becoming productive and responsible citizens, or demented and sociopathic persons committed to violence and destruction, driven by an ends justifies the means mentality."[123]

Indeed, we observe violence against children being universal, becoming deeply ingrained and often accepted as the norm in many societies, says a 2014 UNICEF report.[124] Over ninety per cent of all terrorist attacks between 1989 and 2014 occurred in countries where there was widespread political violence perpetrated by the state against citizens.[125] Some respond with violence to violence, others with suicide: suicide is the second leading cause of death globally in people between the ages of 15 and 29.[126]

People steeped in the mindset of a strong security dilemma will reject Marsella's insight, together with all evidence that some of their assumptions may be misguided or counterproductive in an interconnected world. "Paradigms are frequently sustained even as more and more facts cast them in doubt (so called "stubborn facts"), until the paradigm can no longer hold and the dam breaks, opening the way for a new paradigm to replace it," remarks sociologist Amitai Etzioni.[127]

Torture, for instance, does not yield useful intelligence, yet, this fact is unwelcome to some.[128] Likewise, massive incarceration does not render a more peaceful society. Punishment with institutional exclusion creates barriers to cultural citizenship and hinders a person to feel and act as a loyal member of her community.[129] The goal of punishment articulated by the European Prison Rules therefore is to "enable incarcerated individuals in the future to lead a life of social responsibility without committing criminal offenses."[130] It should be common sense that to reach this goal, relying only on incarceration does not help. Why is common sense not followed? Because there is an alternative common sense around, that of honor and domination. The result is that the proportion of persons incarcerated in the U.S. has increased by three hundred percent since 1980.[131] In The Netherlands, ten percent of convictions result in incarceration, by contrast, in America, it is seventy percent.[132]

It is also established evidence that, while handguns help individuals feel safe, they diminish safety in society at large, and it is safer for a state to guarantee its monopoly on violence with sufficient trusted police power.[133] Why is not this insight followed? Because, again, there is an alternative common sense around, the tenet of the National Rifle Association of America of "good guy with a gun stops bad guy with a gun." While this tenet has been invalidated by evidence, it is upheld by the dominator mindset.[134] Evidence also shows that taking revenge on someone, far from quelling the distress and anger that drives it, perpetuates and magnifies it, and triggers new rounds of revenge-for-revenge.[135]

Also sociologist Amitai Etzioni's message still waits to be heard when he says that it is an illusion to believe that democratization can be brought about by war.[136] War and domination can only achieve the conquering of territory and victory; the partnership paradigm cannot be established in this way.

As long as the partnership paradigm is not yet established, those used to think in the friend-enemy dichotomy seek new enemies when old enemies disappear. *How Corporate America Invented Christian America* is the title of a book that argues that during the Cold War, religion and market freedom were being linked together as a bulwark against godless socialism and to help corporate America benefit from the New Deal programs.[137] This move created a fault line that now seems to turn on its creators, writes Richard Norgaard, professor of energy and resources at the University of California at Berkeley:

> It may not be a coincidence that with the collapse of the USSR, everything the U.S. government does, other than the military, has increasingly been portrayed as socialism by the libertarian and Christian right. With the fall of an outsider, we have turned against ourselves, weakening the prospects of democratic power

> and enhancing corporate control in the supposed names of liberty and freedom.[138]

Not only do American citizens turn on themselves, also academia does. English professor Lisa Ruddick has been introduced earlier. She reports on the state of affairs in the academic world and that a culture of "intellectual sadism" now creates fear and terrorizes academics into alienating themselves from their own inner capacity to stand up. And this while standing up would be needed. For instance, standing up against idealizations of interpersonal violence, and standing up for what nourishes the aliveness of the human being.[139] To stand up for aliveness is precisely what motivates me to write this book.

During the 2016 New Year's Eve celebrations, hundreds of sexual assaults and at least five rapes were reported in the city center of Cologne in Germany, and similar incidents occurred in other cities in Germany. Young men from North Africa were identified as main perpetrators. What happened during that night resembled what I know as *taharrush gamea* (communal sexual harassment), perpetrated after the Arab Spring on Tahrir Square in Cairo, for instance. These events have exposed how damaged and damaging the gender views are that are held in traditional honor cultures. Prior to this night, this damage had been denounced primarily by far-right and anti-immigrant groups in Germany in their effort to voice concerns about cultural differences between European societies and those of North Africa and the Middle East. For them, former U.S. President George W. Bush's warning was valid that "the civilized world" needs to defend itself against evil.[140] As a result of these events, however, voices of concern now also come from people like the moderate economy professor Hans-Werner Sinn: "With the chaotic, uncontrolled immigration from backward countries, the Federal Republic of Germany faces a heap of trouble."[141]

In other words, what came to Cologne were the "psychopathic" traits of honor culture. What is usually overlooked, however, not just in Germany, is that this culture is not just coming from "outside" to them, it is manifest in the very midst of Western societies as well. The events in Cologne have at least opened eyes within Germany to their own failings in protecting women, and have inspired the sharpening of its own legal protections against sexual assaults.[142] Yet, what is allowed to continue unimpeded is the firing up of the "psychopathic" traits of honor culture for the sake of profit. I observe adolescents the world around being ever more exposed to pornography that increasingly has cruel humiliation of women as its main focus, apparently because it sells.

In the increase of brutal pornography, the classical security dilemma meets the new one. In the dominator model of society, women are seen as fair game and terrorized when they move out from under their veil into the public sphere. The security dilemma sent women into the private sphere and women who violated this arrangement were regarded as morally despicable. In such a context, both men and women believe that "shameless" women lose their moral respectability. Young men who think that such women can and should be punished and abused, are now doubly encouraged, encouraged by the new security dilemma pointing into the same direction. In the pursuit of maximizing profit, pornography has not only become more accessible than ever, it has also become more brutal. The brutalization and humiliation of women has become the core trope in present-day pornography. This trend influences society, and it is influenced by society: A UNICEF press release warns of "alarming levels of acceptance of violence against girls."[143] Half of all sexual assaults worldwide are committed against girls aged fifteen or younger.[144] As mentioned earlier, even in a progressive country like Norway, increasingly, coarse football support songs are publically sung in football stadiums. And the exposure of children and teenagers to sexual content online is highest in the Nordic countries and in some Eastern European countries.[145]

Mobile phones make it possible that already very young children are now familiar with the most callous sexual practices. Martin Daubney is the former editor of *Loaded*, a "men's lifestyle magazine." In other words, he is a man who is not given to prudishness. He resigned from his position in 2010, when he became father of a son. In his 2013 documentary film *Porn on the Brain*,[146] he asks neuroscientists, therapists and educators, and also young people themselves: Is pornography harmful to children and young people? What scientific evidence is there? The results were appalling even to him. In particular young people risk not just being traumatized but having their very brain structure detrimentally affected. The trauma can be so difficult to bear that others are harmed.[147] No longer is it the kind of pornography that was mainstream perhaps even ten years ago, reports Martin Daubney, when it included lots of fun and humor.[148] By now, pornography seems to have become part of the trend toward vitriol and cruel humiliation that can be observed in all segments of social life in all world regions. A whole generation of young people gets traumatized when already children are exposed to a "psychopathic culture" that damages their minds and souls. Daubney wonders: When young Muslims growing up in London are affected, might their reaction be to travel to help Da'esh? Has anybody asked them these questions? Or, perhaps their reaction will be to molest women in public squares?

Psychotherapist John Woods has done work with boys and confirms the harmful effects of unregulated internet pornography on boys.[149] Neuroscientist John Williams explains: "Compulsive behaviors, including watching porn to excess, overeating and gambling, are increasingly common."[150] Neuropsychiatrist Valerie Voon warns, "There are clear differences in brain activity between patients who have compulsive sexual behavior and healthy volunteers."[151] Brain activity in sex addiction mirrors that of drug addiction, and the younger the patient, the greater the level of activity in the ventral striatum in response to pornography.[152]

We can only hope (against hope) that the new president of the United States, Donald J. Trump, will not follow the path of a Franz Josef Strauss, or a Slobodan Milošević,[153] or other heroes of the *androsphere*, who revel in a "bad boy" image.[154] Earlier, I mentioned that I observe a lack of emotional-relational literacy among even the most progressive people around the world, and the rise of populism now exposes this failing to everybody's eyes. Progressives have left the emotional-relational arena wide open to the ability of populists to speak directly to the hearts and minds of invisibilized people, making them feel heard and respected. The world had hoped the U.S. would resist this trend and instead "pursue a policy of mutual respect and mutual benefit," so as to unshackle liberal democracy from being "merely a means to manipulate a gullible citizenry to tolerate the most horrible crimes of their government." The world had hoped that the U.S. would honor Benjamin Franklin's words: "Those who would give up essential Liberty, to purchase a little temporary Safety, deserve neither Liberty nor Safety."[155]

In my work, I focus on humiliation, humiliation as a violation of honor or dignity, a violation of unity in diversity. I therefore have listened deeply to the supporters of Donald Trump when I lived in New York during the election in November 2016. I got a deep sense of the humiliation that globalized corporate interests have brought to them, both under the auspices of the Republican and the Democrat "establishment." Both Bernie Sanders and Donald Trump give voice to an increasingly indignated and enraged rejection of this humiliation. They differ, however, with respect to the solutions they propose and the ways of communicating them: Sanders suggests to create a future that looks ahead, while Trump skillfully invites into the dream of a bygone past that never existed and is an illusory dream. We see "the coalition of transformation versus the coalition of restoration,"[156] or what Paul Ray calls *cultural creatives* looking into the future versus *traditionals* looking into the past,[157] both opposing the *moderns*.[158] Evidently, these dynamics are not unique to the United States; they are observable all around the world, very often without the luxury of an electoral choice, in a much more brutal life-or-death manner.

If we consider unity and diversity, then the rise of authoritarian populism is an expression of uniformity veering into division, failing to keep unity in diversity in balance. It starts with people indulging in double standards, oblivious of the fact that double standards can be more destructive to ideals than open betrayal. This is what happened with globalization. Globalization can mean many things, for instance, globalization of care. It can also mean globalization of exploitation. The problem throughout the past decades was that a globalization of exploitation occurred behind a veil of a rhetoric of care. Exploitation unfolded behind a rhetoric of freedom and rising-boats for all, and the conviction that "the market" is a thoroughly wise force. What it did, in reality, was open doors for corporate interests to be trumped through with unprecedented brutality. By now, this cover is thinning. Many of those in America and Europe who were hurt by the exploitative aspects of globalization, experienced them as oppressive uniformity imposed by dictatorial Washington, or by tyrannical Brussels. People in America and Europe are the most privileged among the victims of the globalization of exploitation, since they are in a position to vote. They are now increasingly voting for populists who turn against those other victims in the rest of the world who are even more destitute and have only their feet to respond with. The poorer are turned against the poorest. The populists promise to transport the world back into a divided world, into "freedom for us from them," instead of opting for globalization of care, which means "freedom for all."

In my work, I call for those *double* standards to be turned into a *single* standard by aligning deeds with professed ideals and work for a globalization of care.[159] It is with deep concern that I observe that it is the inverse that actually happens. With the election of Donald J. Trump in the United States, we see a "turn from a neoliberal Wilsonian globalized system of trade and alliances to a Hobbesian nation-centered system organized by thug capital (oligarchs in Russia, hedge-fund and private-equity in the greater US)."[160] The new global economic security dilemma – a global superclass pitted against the rest – is turned back into the old security dilemma of states pitted against other states.

In my work, I also call for more *dignicommunication*.[161] It was an honor for me to be asked by Paul Raskin to comment on his recent book *Earthland*.[162] In my comment, I highlight one of the "blind spots" that I observe among many of even the most enlightened progressives around the world, namely, that they neglect dignifying relationship-building work. This is what I wrote:

> As I observe it, not only the academic community lacks what might be called emotional-relational literacy. To say it in a caricature, the traditional professor/director was a man who had a female secretary who did all the relationship building work for him: she apologized to those he had insulted, and she even bought his flowers for his wife's birthday. By saying so, I do not wish to blame the professor/director or the secretary in this story, since this was "the way it was." However, in today's world, in which cooperation is essential, it becomes dangerous to maintain this habitus.[163]

Today, women and men both are taught to use the masculine script of throwing one's weight around, and the work of the "secretary" is no longer done by anyone. And this, while it is the very glue of trust that we need to nurture if we wish to overcome humiliation and create a world of care and solidarity.

If progressives want to avoid setting in motion destructive cycles of humiliation, they would need to heed, much more sincerely and deliberately than so far, research in neuroscience and psychology, for instance, on the factors that drive "we versus them" authoritarianism and how this gets toxically aligned in certain political systems, such as by now in the United States.[164] With respect to the world's population as a whole, it will be insufficient to hope that facts, ideas, or ideals by themselves will be strong enough to propel global cooperation. What is needed is a proactive, deliberate, and tangible communication effort to build credible and authentic emotional-relational bridges.

As to the second blind spot that I see among progressives – that of global governance – also this would need much more serious attention. Also Bernie Sanders' vision would have faltered, as Howard Richards explains in his piece "Turning the United States Around."[165]

This is a letter we sent to some of the participants of our 2016 Workshop on Humiliation and Violent Conflict at Teachers College of Columbia University in New York City:

> Dear participant, we have noticed your great talent of dignified and dignifying communication. As you know, in mainstream academic conferences, little attention is being paid to the quality of relationships between people. What is in the foreground is the topic, the theory, the idea, the project, the research, the thought, the possibility to get funding. Academics are not trained to approach other academics as fellow human beings, they approach them as title-bearers, or as idea-bearers, or as bearers of career or funding opportunities. They often shoot monologues at each other like bullets, without even seeking eye contact. We believe that this trend has contributed to, and is part of the incivility we see in society at large. What we would like to invite you to, is to bring your ability to be warm and inclusive, your ability to approach people with an loving curiosity and inclusivity. This talent of yours is so rare, and to us, it is more important than anything else, any topic or theme![166]

Question to you: Do you want to contribute to creating a psychopathic world? Or would you like to be part of a more meaningful world? Have you heard about the *streetlight effect*?[167] A man searches for his keys in the dark under a streetlight. Comes along another man and asks the first one whether he is sure to have lost his keys under that streetlight. No, the first man replies, but this is where the light is! This is what we do, as humankind: What is illuminated by glaring lights in mainstream society is pseudo-meaning, and if we wish to find truly fulfilling meaning, we have to get out our flashlights and look elsewhere.

Chapter 18

What Then Must We Do? Outlook into the Future …

Leo Tolstoy asked a crucial question in 1886: "What then must we do"?[1] What should citizens of cities, nations, and planet Earth do at the present point in human history?

First, we must find out where we stand: Do we, as humankind, understand how dire our situation is and how radical our responses must be? Do we understand that we do not have much time?[2]

The answer is No. Our deep culture, our collective subconscious, our unknown scripts,[3] all this supplies us with "dewy-eyed sanguinity" and stoic optimism on one side, or "world-weary cynicism"[4] on the other side, while what is needed is largely missing: a due sense of alarm. It is as if people in a burning house or on a sinking ship discuss their feelings – whether they should be depressed or not – while failing to act. And this applies to all of us, to "us the people" as much as to "the elites" or "the politicians."[5] What is needed is agency that "all cultures, classes and stations can engage with personally and immediately," explains Stephen Purdey, an international relations specialist, and he suggests that "a trenchant, potentially viral polemic that grips public attention by directly confronting our ecocidal trajectory might suit this purpose. Our existential predicament calls out for a life-or-death dialectic that can penetrate any frame of reference, cut through noise, focus the mind and spur action where nothing else will."[6]

Do we, as humankind, have the means to act? The answer is Yes. Did our ancestors see pictures of our Blue Planet from the perspective of an astronaut? Were our forebears able to see, as we do, how we humans are *one single* family living on *one tiny vulnerable* planet?[7] Did our grandparents have access to as comprehensive a knowledge base as we have about the universe and our place in it? They did not. The image of the Blue Planet is revolutionary. It anchors humankind in the universe in ways no generation before has been able to experience. For the first time, humankind can act on and manifest the fact that we are *one* family. All necessary information to do so is amply available, more than ever before. A small window of opportunity is open for humankind at the current juncture in human history, for a few years to come perhaps, an opportunity to create a decent future for our children.[8] For the first time, there is an opportunity to change both the reality and culture of domination and terror.

What are the kind of times we are living in? Modernity? Or postmodernity? If modernity has ended, has it ended in the mid- or late twentieth century? Has postmodernity started in the 1930s or 1950s or 1990s?[9] Or is continuity with the past more significant? Is postmodernist theorizing mere pseudohistory?[10] Or is there something in between? Are the times we live in only a distinctive phase of modernity, be it "late" or "high" modernity,[11] "liquid" modernity,[12] "risk" society,[13] or "network" society?[14]

I appreciate all categorizations and find merit in all of them. For instance, in postmodern critical research, I value that the "embodied, collaborative, dialogic, and improvisational aspects" of qualitative research are emphasized.[15] Also in all other categorizations, I find useful thoughts.

Here comes my conceptualization of history: We live at the cusp of a transition from the dominator way of arranging our human affairs with each other and with our planet, toward a partnership approach. The partnership approach stands for equal dignity for all, for non-domination, in solidarity.[16] The dominator approach emerged throughout the past ten millennia, or five percent of human history, in the context of the classical military security dilemma in a multi-divided world. It is now compounded by a new security dilemma, an economic one, at the global level, where corporate powers employ economic "weapons" to "conquer" world-system institutions. They can do so, not least because those institutions have weak spots that can be used as entry points.[17] As a result, the transition toward partnership is increasingly in peril, as authoritarian or neo-fascist leaders are voted in by the victims of the corporate take-over strategy wherever they have elections to go to. These authoritarian leaders capitalize on their voters' sense of humiliation[18] and direct it against scapegoats, against those who are even more desperate, those victims who have no votes except for their feet, or their terror.

Critic Fredric Jameson explains how multinational capital is now "penetrating and colonizing those pre-capitalist enclaves (nature and the unconscious) which used to offer extraterritorial and Archimedean footholds for critical effectivity."[19] The "T-treaty trinity" agreements that were being pushed through until recently, entail elements of such a corporate take-over.[20] The new American Trump administration promises to leave these treaties behind, yet, not in favor of globally inclusive and fair multilateralism but for bilateralism, with the result that "the WTO and multilateralism more generally may never recover from the setbacks."[21]

Everywhere on the globe, I experience the penetration and colonization of those pre-capitalist enclaves that Fredric Jameson refers to, even when I visit my parents in one of the richest country of the world, Germany. I am horrified that my childhood countryside paradise is now not only "silent," as Rachel Carson called it – no larks rise to the sky in the morning anymore[22] – I also have to be afraid to be poisoned, for example, when I bicycle and find the air filled with toxic substances being sprayed onto the fields. If only half of the news about glyphosate and its handling are true, then there is grave danger.[23] Sadly, what happens with glyphosate is not the exception but the norm: The common good is sold out for profits that are shielded against critical voices – shielded by way of coopting, bribing, ridiculing, or terrorizing those voices into silence – and the risks are hidden as "business secrets": In a container of Roundup, we may ask, what other toxic substances beside glyphosate are mixed in?

People always ask me: Should not the Germans who lived during Nazi times have known that millions of people were being gassed to death at an industrialized scale by their own government, and should they not have stood up? Yes, I reply, and then I add: Must not we stand up now, for example, when our living co-creatures are being brutalized at an industrialized scale?[24] How come we all fail now?

This is the diagnosis of the state of our time in a nutshell: Industrial-scale use of chemical pesticides, herbicides, and fertilizers; food production as a branch of global industry; continued reliance on fossil fuels and accelerating climate change; the transformation of fresh water into a depleting resource; and the mass extinction of other life forms. The demand for natural resources for humanity is more than fifty percent larger than what the natural systems are able to regenerate.[25]

What is the prognosis? Can we dignify our way out of our social crises? Can we technologize our way out of our ecological crises? Is our future bright, should we be enthusiastically or stoically optimistic, should we stay strong in our belief in human greatness and the human ability to remain on top of all challenges? Or are we doomed? Should we be pessimistic? Should we lament and remove hope also from those who still have hope? Should we enjoy our last days as long as it is possible? Or can we combine optimism and pessimism to be awake and look for solutions in case there may be unexpected possibilities, if ever so tiny, for a decent survival for all?[26] Perhaps there is a way for us to radically change our behavior? Perhaps we are able to fight less and consume less? I myself opt for this last choice. My work may be useless. Yet, I would not be able to sleep otherwise. "World-weary cynicism and its converse, dewy-eyed sanguinity are unhelpful; both imprison the imagination and still action."[27]

Stephen Emmott, professor of computational science at the University of Oxford, offers a pessimistic prognosis: "The problem is us… We urgently need to do – and I mean actually do – something radical to avert a global catastrophe. But I don't think we will. I think we're fucked."[28] Also the Schumacher Center's founding president, Robert Swann, concurs: "Our Earth is in crisis; our communities are in crisis. At the heart of these twin issues is an economic system that treats land, air, water, and minerals – our common inheritance – as commodities to be bought and sold on the market. An economic system distributes the income from that inheritance to a relatively few 'owners,' whose wealth increases disproportionately as a result, leading to social disruption."[29]

On the other side of the pessimism-optimism continuum, we find Silicon Valley. Spending just one week there is enough to be converted into a sect of raptured missionaries for the "sexiness" of human progress and its immitigable goodness.[30] Science writer Matt Ridley is on their side when he advocates "rational optimism," in the belief that continuing with business-as-usual will be a successful path into a dignified future, as "greed will prevail."[31]

Geographer Danny Dorling takes a middle position when he calls Stephen Emmott "the embodiment of angry pessimism."[32] Dorling's position is "practical possibilism," a middle position insofar as he also distances himself from the "rational optimism" of a Matt Ridley. Dorling's stance resonates somewhat with that of Hans Rosling, a Swedish professor of international health and development.[33]

Yet, even an optimist such as Matt Ridley has an important caveat, namely, the human propensity for hostility: "...generally speaking the more cooperative a species is within groups, the more hostility there is between groups."[34] Ridley warns that this propensity constitutes a far greater danger than climate change, the exhaustion of raw materials, or any other disaster scenario.[35]

What should we do when even an ardent optimist like Matt Ridley acknowledges that global cooperation is what is most needed and least likely to occur? Worse, humiliation research predicts that hostility will increase, not least since humiliation becomes an ever more salient factor in an interconnected world with its widening arenas for humiliation and its backlashes. When we consider that even the hardest optimist offers such a verdict, is not pessimism the only thing left on the table?

Because of all this, I advise to take humiliation into account in radically new ways. A dangerous expectation gap opens when people get into ever closer contact in a shrinking world and at the same time receive a broken promise: They hear the human rights promise of all humans belonging to one single family where all members are entitled to be respected as equals in dignity, and at the same time, this promise is broken. When respect is expected, while disrespect is experienced, a dangerous dignity gap opens and dignity humiliation raises its head as an unprecedented force.[36] In a world with too few Mandelas, with too few who can heal such gaps by inspiring dialogue for partnership, these gaps risk turning the world back into a dark past, down a familiar albeit radically counterproductive path of violent competition for domination, including the very old tool kit of honor humiliation. In this situation, feelings of humiliation can develop into the *nuclear bomb of the emotions*.[37] The Rwandan genocide, the downing of the Twin Towers, and the recent terror attacks in all parts of the world, all prove that military weapons are not needed when people driven by the desire to avenge humiliation turn everyday technology into deadly munition.[38]

After diagnosis and prognosis comes therapy. What can the therapy be? Any "therapy" in an interconnected world must give more attention to the salience of the dynamics of humiliation, more attention to its prevention and healing, and more attention to creating dignified and dignifying ways of global cooperation, so that the partnership approach can globalize. The entire third volume of this overall book project on terror, which is still to be written, aims at speaking to this topic, and this chapter will therefore only offer a brief glimpse. In short, a *dignity transition* is needed to exit from the security dilemma and to prevent and heal the *dignity dilemma* that needs our closest attention when we want a divided world to unite.

The partnership model of society, so far, has had little chance to unfold, notwithstanding the fact that rhetoric of partnership is widely used, particularly by Western military and economic "warriors," as it is popular and has traction. Partnership rhetoric is used, for instance, to invite people into the dream of freedom, while obfuscating that the game is rigged. Few have refused this invitation. Most people have become complicit even in their own domination. *Deferred elimination* is what sociologist Pierre Bourdieu calls it when people accept an invitation into exhausting themselves for a promise of a future that ultimately will be closed to them. This is a way to covertly eliminate segments of society.[39]

Even postmodernists have become complicit. Postmodernism has been described as "the spatialization of culture under the pressure of organized capitalism."[40] Also the Enlightenment seems to have brought much darkness. Philosopher and sociologist Jürgen Habermas sees the potential for liberation entailed in the Enlightenment being degraded into mass deception and a new form of enslavement.[41]

Once more: In what times do we live? Do we live in the Anthropocene? Or in the Econocene?[42] Or perhaps rather in the Capitalocene?[43] John Barry, expert of environmental policy-making, sees no "humanization of the world" happening, nor does he think that our planet has been "economized," he thinks that the Earth rather has been *capitalized*.[44] The Earth has been "rendered into commodities, monetized, and valued right from the micro-level of DNA through biotechnology to the macro-level of the entire planet..."[45] "Spaces of hope" shrink when underpaid work in poor conditions without labor rights rises, only to increase the differential that corporations profit from.[46]

While the partnership approach is being ridiculed and hindered to unfold in the face of the dominator approach, it is weakened even more when it is hailed, but with empty rhetoric. The experience of double standards, the disappointment about being invited into equal dignity only to meet indignity, creates double humiliation. When "free" market economy is hailed as the new religion that supposedly secures human rights, democracy, and the rule of law, at a time when market forces are free only in the sense of being uncontrolled, and large parts of the *demos* (the citizens of a democracy) are alienated, those who can vote may elect populists, while the less fortunate may vote with their feet and join the next migration or terror wave.[47] Frustration and anger will rise on all sides, all will feel that their sacred values are being besmirched. Some people will want to turn back to the old security dilemma, including its honor script of revenge for humiliated honor, and they will mete out terror in the name of religion, nation, race, or gender.

Present-day's superpower America, together with Europe, both are rightly proud of human rights values and ideals. Therefore they carry a particular responsibility to refrain from betraying their very own ideals by way of double standards. The ensuing humiliation will spell doom also for the rest of the world.[48]

To me, the transformation that is needed now, if humanity wishes to survive in decency,[49] is comparable in impact only with the Neolithic Revolution. The Neolithic Revolution was the first most significant turning point in human history, and we live in the midst of the second. In both cases, an entirely new situation emerged, which forced to the fore radically new adaptations. Around twelve millennia ago, we, *Homo sapiens*, had just managed to populate all continents of our planet. This is why I call it our *first round of globalization*. We adapted to the new situation of a planet filling up by learning to compete for domination. Now, in our *second round of globalization*, if we continue maximizing the first adaptation, it will spell collective suicide.[50] Pundits will "spin us to death," if we fail to develop alternative adaptations.[51]

Philosopher John Stewart Mill once coined the phrase *ramshackle states* for those states that fail to build sound institutions, and political scientist Robert Jackson described them as *quasi-states*.[52] As for now, we live in a ramshackle global village. Cities and nations face what author Robert Kaplan described as *the coming anarchy*,[53] where overpopulation, resource scarcity, crime, and disease compound cultural and ethnic identities to create a chaotic world. Physicist Paul Raskin calls it the *breakdown scenario*, where "chaos intensifies, and institutions collapse," where "a new Dark Age descends."[54]

As long as we continue with the script of competition for domination, global interconnectedness and technological advancements will help global crime and terror. Mobile phones now become weapons in war,[55] and the internet is used as a military theatre. While the role of conventional weapons and ABC weapons (atomic, biological, and chemical) diminishes, the role of D-weapons, digital weapons, increases. The threat of state-directed cyberattacks surges.[56] The intelligence organization of the United States government, the National Security Agency (NSA), is responding to this threat from the Remote Operations Center in Fort Meade in Maryland, where it prepares for future dominance in cyberspace by way of Tailored

Access Operations, using war-names such as "Hammerchant," and "Warriorpride."[57] Since April 2014, Admiral Michael Rogers is not only the director of the NSA, but also head of the Cyber Command, thus no longer simply eavesdropping on the world, but implanting digital Trojan horses throughout the digital systems of the world, so that continued domination is secured. This is achieved, for instance, through "the takeover of system controls to obtain information and technical data, including oil and gas pipelines and transport systems … and system control of power plants."[58] Documents published by *Washington Post* unveil that there is now a "black budget" for such intelligence services.[59]

Stuxnet is the name for the first digital weapon ever used, originally meant to sabotage the Iranian nuclear program. Stuxnet is a computer virus that became known in summer 2010, and was subsequently decrypted, among others, by the IT security specialist Ralph Langner and his team, in Hamburg, the very city where I began my university education in 1974.[60] Stuxnet is unique in opening Pandora's box, explains the IT expert, as nobody can be sued, because there is no proof. What it amounts to is invisible world domination. Therefore, as with ABC weapons, Langner urges, an international codex is needed also here now.[61]

Not just global crime and global terror is enabled by global technology, so is civil society. It is easier than ever to get in touch with each other. Global civil society could thus stand in the way of global crime and global terror. Yet, at the moment, the results are dim.

I see several reasons. One is the concept of maleness – the concept of what it means to be a man – and the fact that this concept is still anchored deeply in the past. Since I was born into a female body, I often feel terrorized personally, I feel my humanity and dignity violated, by the fact that the mindset of domination that emerged throughout the past millennia still characterizes world culture to the degree it does now. This culture has men as their guardians, and creates the need, for them, to neglect or denigrate the traditional female script of care and maintenance, and to even humiliate its carriers when they fail to remain "where they belong," namely, down and irrelevant. I feel terrorized by the overt and covert strategies of domination that debase equal human dignity in the name of unequal honor. I feel personally humiliated, not just by Taliban practices against women in Afghanistan, not just by rape being part of certain segments of Indian culture, to name just two so-called traditional contexts, but also by the fact that ever more brutal pornography, with its core trope of the humiliation of women, finds such willing markets, is so lucrative, and is now being implanted into the minds and hearts of young boys the world over.

Domination always begins with a promise: salvation from evil, be it salvation from hell or salvation from terror. The promise is made mainly to males: they can avoid hell and attain heaven and sexual gratification through martyrdom in military action, as in certain versions of terrorism. Or, they can attain a nice profit margin for military equipment that can terrorize terrorists into submission. Male might-is-right supremacy is hidden also in terminologies such as shareholder value or investor confidence. All this is not only humiliating here and now. In the long run, it will be destructive for all.

Might-is-right masculinity, greatness through winning over enemies, these were strategies that had a certain viability in a multi-divided world. Yet, global interconnectedness takes this option off the table.[62] "Victories" become hollow. What does victory mean when "killer drones" are "victorious" on one continent, while one single hacker on another continent can take terrible revenge? Dominators believe that crushing the enemy is the endgame; now they have to learn to think further: The new endgame is preventing the Hitlers, so as to not having to fight them later. Dominators also believe that subjugating nature is a triumph; now they have to think further: beware of the "Ozon Holes" that wait to come. Nationalism was once a future-oriented innovation. At first the old empires were dismantled, then new nation-states emerged – by the end of World War I they were a dozen – and World War II "finished the job."[63] Now the time has come to go one step further and find better ways than nationalism to satisfy the human need to belong. What is now waiting to be realized is global unity in diversity, global symbiosis and diversity.[64] To take the Titanic as metaphor again: for a long time, the walls between the cabins were the object of contention, some cabin owners conquered other cabins and then lost them again. Contemporary weapons, including the internet, now risk sinking the entire ship if such power-over strategies were continued, making them potentially suicidal.

We have entered what Paul Raskin calls the *Planetary Phase of Civilization*, where strands of interdependence weave humanity and Earth into a single community of fate on its way to *Earthland*. Raskin wonders why the pace of social evolution has quickened throughout human history, whether this acceleration is a mere coincidence or the manifestation of an underlying historical principle:

> The complexification and enlargement of society also quickens the pace of social evolution. Just as historical change moves more rapidly than biological change (and far more rapidly than geological change), so, too, is history itself accelerating. As the figure suggests, the Stone Age endured about 100,000 years; Early Civilization, roughly 10,000 years; and the Modern Era, now drawing to a close, began to stir nearly 1,000 years ago. If the Planetary Phase were to play out over 100 years, this sequence of exponentially decreasing timespans would persist.[65]

Also Paul Raskin uses the trope of a ship, when he speaks of *Earthland*, today's multi-tiered world that "overlays globalized dynamics across a mosaic of modern, pre-modern, and even remnants of Stone Age cultures":

> On board, white-knuckled passengers are awakening to their existential quandary. They tremulously inquire about location and direction, but bewildered cabin attendants can provide only disjointed information and unpersuasive reassurances. In the cockpit, the insouciant captains cast desultory glances at the flight screens or doze, awaiting instructions from perplexed navigators.[66]

Raskin crafts artful formulations to describe the passengers' psychological responses: Some discount all dangers with "sweet denial, finding distraction in passing amusements and baubles, and seeking succor in the false panaceas of free markets, religious rapture, or individual beatitude."[67] Others are despondent and confront their plight open-eyed, but, "seeing no way out," they "turn away in fatalistic despair," while most "are just trying to muddle through, keeping their heads down and hoping for the best."[68]

In the new situation of global interconnectedness, not just familiar power-over strategies become obsolete. When a new global superordinate system is in formation and "global-scale processes increasingly influence the operation and stability of subsystems," reductive partitioning into "semi-autonomous entities – states, ecosystems, cultures, territories – becomes inaccurate and misleading."[69] Also "Zombie ideologies," such as "territorial chauvinism, unbridled consumerism, and the illusion of endless growth" held dear by a "myopic and disputatious political order," need to grow into "coherent responses to systemic risks of climate change, economic instability, population displacement, and global terrorism," to name only the most emblematic.[70]

The new situation turns everybody, men and women, into "women," insofar as women always had to learn how to use indirect power, because having children made them dependent and cautious. In my book on gender and humiliation, I call on women and men to leave behind the traditional male script of winning and instead nurture the traditional female script of caring.[71] I am impressed with sociologist Nilüfer Göle and how she sees the best hope for a modern and European Islam in its Muslim women: she sees European Islam as "feminine," in contrast to the male-dominated traditional Islam.[72]

What I want to say is that all those who have learned humility during the past millennia have now something to teach the dominators. Sociologist Michèle Lamont has studied the strategies of marginalized groups all around the world and describes what they do to gain respect.[73] Our Brazilian dignity network members amaze us when they employ *jeitinho*, which means "resilience and flexibility in trying something that was denied in the first place."[74] Many indigenous peoples know how to conduct dialogue and not just control. Nature can be a good teacher of humility as well. Norway, for instance, was once a poor country, humbled by its closeness to the overwhelming forces of nature. Also my father was close to nature and humbled by it, and I have learned humility from him.

Do I aim for utopia? Yes and no. If anything, continuing with business-as-usual now is an impossible utopia. But there is also possible and necessary utopia, there are innovative visions for a better future: "In immoderate times, moderation becomes imprudent – madness in reason's mask. The business-as-usual utopianism of Market Forces ideology is an egregious case of crackpot realism," is Paul Raskin's verdict, borrowing a phrase from C. Wright Mills.[75] Again, do I aim for utopia? I resist the argument of "you are a fool if you wish for a better world!" as much as any blind Silicon valley messianic futurism. I try to protect the notion of utopia from the same distortion that the nature-versus-nurture debate has suffered at the hands of honor manipulation. I stand for radical new visions. For example, for the vision of an *empathic civilization* brought forward by social theorist and activist Jeremy Rifkin,[76] or the vision of a *decent society* by philosopher Avishai Margalit.[77]

Dialogue is the new name of the game, global dialogue, the very "peace congresses" that Alfred Nobel calls for in his testament.[78] Alfred Nobel thought of "fraternity between nations," today we need more, solidarity between all the planet's people and with our habitat. President Urho Kekkonen of Finland has been credited as the main architect of the Confidence-Building Measures that led to the establishment of the Organization for Security and Co-operation in Europe (OSCE) with the Helsinki Final Act of August 1, 1975. It contained politico-military, economic, environmental, and human rights dimensions, which served as dialogue points between the two blocs: "The simple but brilliant idea was this: We need dialogue to feel secure."[79]

Just as psychologist Jean Baker Miller calls for alternative arrangements to heal the terror flowing from false choices,[80] also sociologist Anthony Giddens warns that we overlook the true challenges of our time because attending to unnecessary problems keeps us busy:

> The threat to personal meaninglessness is ordinarily held at bay because routinized activities, in combination with basic trust, sustain ontological security. Potentially disturbing existential questions are defused by the controlled nature of day-to-day activities within internally referential systems.Mastery, in other words, substitutes for morality; to be able to control one's life circumstances, colonize the future with some degree of success and live within the parameters of internally referential systems can, in many circumstances, allow the social and natural framework of things to seem a secure grounding for life activities.[81]

Do I aim for a global Orwellian dictatorship? No. We have to be very careful to avoid it. Unprecedented alertness is what is needed. During the time I spent in Prangins, near Geneva, I often passed in front of the Castle of Coppet. This castle once belonged to Madame de Stäel (1766 – 1817), an intellectual of her time who gathered the French intelligentsia in this castle. Initially, she supported Napoléon, until she understood that he was more of a tyrant than a liberator. She wrote this in 1818:

> Far from recovering my confidence by seeing Bonaparte more frequently, he constantly intimidated me more and more. I had a confused feeling that no emotion of the heart could act upon him. He regards a human being as an action or a thing, not as a fellow-creature. He does not hate more than he loves; for him nothing exists but himself; all other creatures are ciphers. The force of his will consists in the impossibility of disturbing the calculations of his egoism; he is an able chess-player, and the human race is the opponent to whom he proposes to give checkmate. His successes depend as much on the qualities in which he is deficient as on the talents he possesses. Neither pity, nor allurement, nor religion, nor attachment to any

idea whatsoever could turn him aside from his principal direction. He is for his self-interest what the just man should be for virtue; if the end were good, his perseverance would be noble.[82]

Not only a new Napoléon, also a new Vladimir Ilyich Lenin must be prevented from hijacking the dignity movements that may wish to unfold around the world in the future. When Lenin took over in Petrograd (now Saint Petersburg), he issued the April Theses, a series of ten directives, where he denounced liberals and social revolutionaries and called for workers' councils (soviets) to assume power. Initially, the more moderate Russian intellectuals hoped that Lenin simply was out of touch with Russian reality due to his Swiss exile. They wished that he would learn, therefore they sought reconciliation with him. They failed. Moderation is per definition difficult to defend against dominators. Not least, because, very often, the true guardians of a movement's spirit are the first to be done away with when raw power takes over. Also here Russia offers many examples. The Kronstadt sailors, for instance, from their naval fortress in the Gulf of Finland not far away from Petrograd, decisively helped the Bolshevik Revolution in 1917 to succeed. Their reward, soon after, was to be destroyed. Their "crime" was that they "saw that Communism meant terror and tyranny," and that they "called for the overthrow of the Communist Government." As a result of their wish for moderation, they were "bloodily destroyed or sent into Siberian slavery by Communist troops."[83]

In 1842, the British suffered a humiliating defeat at the hands of Afghan tribesmen, it was as a result of "too casually displayed power," as Sam Engelstad would call it. Since then, the West seems to have achieved the very opposite of what it aimed for, over and over again, too. *Bitter Lake* is a 2015 BBC film by Adam Curtis that shows idealistic American engineers in Afghanistan, building dams, irrigations systems, and cities, such as the city of Lashkar Gah, as a model planned city like an American suburb.[84] In 1952, the Helmand Valley Authority was set up, modelled on the Tennessee Valley Authority created by American President Franklin Delano Roosevelt in the 1930s. This is the result now: "Hundreds of miles of canals that the Taliban now hide in were constructed by the same company that built the San Francisco Bay Bridge and Cape Canaveral."[85] Ambitious Harvard academic Walt Whitman Rostow (1916 – 2003) filled everybody with missionary enthusiasm to bring "modernity" to countries like Afghanistan, with the aim to protect them from communism and instead transform them into "proper" democratic capitalist societies like America.[86] Rostow believed that it was indeed the duty of the United States to do "good" by democratizing other nations.[87] American engineers and psychologists were driven by "modernization theory" and not yet aware that the finite nature of the global ecosystem could never sustain the globalization of practices of European and North American societies.

Rostow was not alone. These were also the times when some in the field of psychology sought salvation from what I call its "physics envy," its envy of physics for having the Newtonian machine model. In the 1960s, with a great sense of mission, "motivational psychologists set grandiose goals for themselves to transform society in a hurry, applied massive doses of inappropriate behavioral technology, and by and large failed to reach these goals," wrote psychologist David McClelland in 1978, in an attempt to rescue the mission by reining it in.[88] For Vietnam, Walt Whitman Rostow advocated "strategic hamlets," where villagers would be educated by psychologists and special cadres to become new "modern" citizens devoted to democracy. Since the Engineer was seen as the epitome of progress, a new engineering department in Kabul university was established. The King of Afghanistan, Zahir Shah, was enthused, not least since this brought him more power. Also he joined in, working to transform not just the urban elite, but all Afghans into "transitional beings." Among others, he was to abolish the burqa; he was helped by the wives of the American executives who ran the Afghan national airline: they asked Pan American Airlines to approach *Vogue Magazine* for help.[89]

Historian Arnold Toynbee visited Helmand in 1960, among others also Lashkar Gah, and he warned that this kind of engineering of modernity was doomed.[90] The very same "little America" they once built, is now a Taliban stronghold.[91] Thinkers such as Sayyid Qutb in Egypt and Mawdudi in Pakistan had similar thoughts – they all felt that what was missing was *meaning in life*, meaning that went beyond earthly engineering. Fast forward in time, to secure Saudi oil, America helped protect Wahhabism, and thus helped fill the void of meaning, with extremism. The endgame, during the past decade, descended into ever cruder polarizations and loss of complexity also among Western strategists: "We are the good ones, we stand for modernity, and whoever is against us must be Taliban and be bad."

The meaning that human beings need, is now offered by Salafists. Americans built schools and trained teachers in places likes Iraq, Pakistan, and Afghanistan, building institutions to propagate Western values, "but these buildings and institutions are hollow compared to the heart-to-heart pedagogy of the Salafi educator":

> Salafi teachers do not walk out the door when the bell rings. There is no bell and education is never-ending. The Salafi teacher is a personal ally, confidant and guide. He becomes the sole conduit of all knowledge drawn from Allah's original well of wisdom. Salafi education is the refined hunger for Islam in its earliest incarnation. To return to the greatness of Islam requires stages of self-purification, and eventually sacrifice to achieve the final restoration of the faith.[92]

What can we do now, we as humankind, as a global community, to avoid again starting something new with enthusiasm, continue with casual arrogance, and end in disaster? Earlier, historian Timothy Snyder was quoted. He warns that wrong lessons are being drawn from the Holocaust, both by the political left and the political right.[93] It is a right-wing misunderstanding in the U.S. to equate too strong a state with Nazism, while what is needed is a state that is not too strong and not too weak, a state that serves the common good, rather than particular power interests. Another misunderstanding is to equate Hitler with the dark side of progress and science. Science is needed, yet, again, a kind of science that respects life, rather than science serving particular power interests. To make science constructive, higher education would need to enable and not disable, as education expert Cristina Escrigas warns: "A society with a utilitarian, instrumentalist view of knowledge cannot be called a knowledge society. It can invent vastly profitable technologies, but it will fail to provide the conditions for all life on this planet to flourish."[94] Technological developments do have the potential to work for a better future, yet, only if technology solutions serve the common good. Triumphant promises that engineered realities will create a paradisiacal future, if modeled on Taylorism and Fordism, will turn out to be empty of meaning.[95] The ecological, social, and psychological cost for maintaining a profit-based world will be too high.[96] Norwegian Berit Ås warns: Babies cannot be produced faster, breastfeeding cannot be done faster, and all life-giving processes take their time.[97]

What then? What can be done? Why are people so willing to leave behind *communal sharing*, as anthropologist Alan Page Fiske calls the traditional way of maintaining social cohesion? Why do people allow themselves to be coopted into solipsistic "possessive" individualism and consumerism, oblivious that it risks ending in debt slavery, not just for individuals, but for entire countries?[98] How can we move out of this trap of *voluntary self-humiliation*, as I call it?

Perhaps one answer lies in connecting inward and outward orientations better? Sociologist Klaus Eder has studied the recent decline of work ethics.[99] He describes how in the United States, the Calvinist model of the Protestant ethic has shaped culture, and how its ideology has spread around the world from there. He describes how this model contains values such as "achievement for its own sake, the virtue of work over non-work, and the quest for excellence."[100] The background for this ethic was that people were unsure whether God had chosen them and they looked for evidence. By now, this search for evidence has assumed a secular cloak in the form of possessive individualism, with its clambering for "permanent proof of one's own competitiveness in the market."[101] In Europe, the German Protestant tradition of Lutheranism had a similar influence. Neither Lutheran nor

Calvinist ethics were originally intended to intrinsically motivate workers, but rather to control the work force.[102] However, there is a difference, theorizes Eder. While Calvinism validates work in a straightforward manner, a subversive force lies buried within Lutheranism: it is the genesis of an inner-worldly work ethic, or the permanent self-observation to decipher God's will.

I grew up in a Lutheran family, and I can attest to this subversiveness. During childhood and adolescence, my soul was almost torn apart between the destructive and constructive sides of this subversiveness. Eder describes the destructive side very well: In such a context, the family becomes a disciplining institution, in which its members observe themselves and each other, with work and the outer world becoming secondary to this inner struggle. "Such a person is no longer part of a collectivity that gives security and warmth but is a highly individualized self-observing and self-controlling social being."[103]

Now comes the constructive side. While Calvinism fashioned a coherent rational motivation for work, Lutheranism produced an instrumentalist work ethic in which work could also be seen as amoral when it failed to offer an adequate path to self-realization in the communion with God. Eder explains that in the Prussian work ethic, god became replaced by the state: "The Prussian functionary works as hard as the world demands and seeks self-realization by identifying, not with god, but with the state."[104] By now, the Lutheran capitalist entrepreneur has become congruent with the Calvinist entrepreneur in Germany, while the Prussian virtues of state officials represent modern German work culture as such. For Eder, the presently observable decline of the work ethic, also in Germany, may open the door for a renaissance of the Lutheran heritage, this time to legitimize self-realization outside of work.[105]

To say it short, what Eder lays out is that for Calvinism, work is the path to god, and for Lutheranism work can be a hindrance on the path to god. In its secular version, the Lutheran spirit has the potential to guide people to take notice when the outer world is no longer creating inner meaning. This can then legitimize social change to resolve this dissonance by bringing the outer world into consonance with the inner world. This is the subversiveness of the Lutheran ethic: It gives legitimacy to the voice of the child that warns that the emperor has no clothes.[106] This indeed was me, during my childhood.

What Eder conceptualizes is not a preserve of Lutheranism. It is common sense that whenever a situation turns difficult and people grow wary, they can either turn inward and give up on a dysfunctional outer world, or they can remain outward and go along with an unfit system, or, and this is my path, both orientations can complement each other. I let the inner world envision and guide action in the outer world. Earlier in this book, I referred to what I call the "Sufis" as those people who find dignity in embeddedness into life, in contrast to the "Pharisees," who cling to lifeless rules. Riesman's conceptualization of *inner*-directedness, as mentioned earlier, suggests something similar, namely, that inner-directed people can discover their own potential within themselves.[107] Classic Chinese literature differentiates between *inner* experience and *outer* circumstances which also include relationships with others; inner and outer spheres are connected through a correspondent chain of feeling, centered in the heart-mind, and mediated by *qi*, "the vital energetic source uniting both structural and functional realities of body, mind, and spirit."[108]

I am painfully aware that, if the inner world is embedded in honor, creating consonance can be disastrous. Bringing together in- and outward orientations can unleash impassioned mass movements that can perpetrate mayhem. Examples abound. The Weimarer Republic in Germany offers a sad illustration, as does the South Africa after the Boer Wars (1880 – 1902).[109] Nazi ideology was welcomed as rescue and salvation in Germany by all who were steeped in the mindset of honor, as was initially the case with apartheid in South Africa. Only too late, did people with the mindset of dignity step in. Dietrich Bonhoeffer was a Mandela for Nazi Germany. He was born in the Silesian capital of Breslau (also my mother's birth place), and on April 9, 1945, at the age of 39, he was murdered by the Nazi system for his resistance against it, in the Flossenbürg concentration camp. "Has the Bonhoeffer moment finally arrived?" is a question currently asked in the United States.[110] The Muslim world is still waiting for their Bonhoeffer, their Mandela, to lead their minds, souls, and actions to embrace dignity, rather than honor.

All around the world, I sense an atmosphere of simmering uneasiness that reminds me of the times before Nazi Germany or apartheid came into being, when solutions were yearned for but not yet established. The solutions that are being advocated now range all the way from the total destructiveness à la Nazi Germany to the dignity that Mandela attempted to manifest in South Africa. In my own case, informed by my inner resistance against a dysfunctional outer world, I attempt to give strength to a global civil society movement for the creation of a more dignified future. I try to inspire in- and outward orientations to fertilize each other, rather than have them compete with each other or destroy each other, and, further, I seek solutions within the realm of dignity rather than the realm of honor.[111] In this way, I show my respect for Bonhoeffer and Mandela.[112]

Let us think: What can citizens, cities, and nations do to prevent and heal the psychological disconnection that present-day economic arrangements produce? Why is it that not all citizens, all cities, and all nations on the planet unite to refuse partaking in dangerous races to the bottom? Why don't we all refuse to be complicit in the destructive exploitation of social and ecological resources, all of which only leads to more tragic disconnecting and myriads of humiliating consequences?

The first step toward a solution would be to deeply reflect on the widespread belief that the workings of "the market" are on a par with physical laws. I hear the following expression all around the world and describe them in my 2012 book on a dignity economy: "This is what the market requires, and we have to live with the results whatever they are."[113]

Evolutionary theory has looked at *coordination* and *motivation*, and has found that motivation thrives best when coordination is achieved in an egalitarian context rather than in an authoritarian top-down context, the reason being that collaboration in an egalitarian context creates intrinsic motivation rather than depending solely on extrinsic motivation.[114] Evolutionary theory comes to similar conclusions when it talks about *between-group selection* and *within-group selection*.[115]

Biologists David Sloan Wilson and his colleagues enumerate three misguided, though reigning "cosmologies," namely, the "holy trinity of orthodox economics"[116] of *rationality*, *greed*, and *equilibrium*, and how they play out in economic theory: (1) "natural man" as a rational, self-sufficient, egotistical individual, (2) competition among individuals supposedly leading to a well-functioning society, and (3) the assumption that there exists an ideal optimal state of nature.[117] Wilson and colleagues conclude that seen from an evolutionary perspective, it is profoundly mistaken to assume that design at the individual level, namely, the pursuit of self-interest, can straightforwardly result in design at the societal level, meaning well-functioning economies.[118] To say it with economist Christopher Barrington-Leigh: income, employment, and GDP are poor and inadequate proxies for human welfare.[119] While it is true that "selfishness beats altruism within groups," "altruistic groups beat selfish groups."[120] In an interconnected finite world, altruism is the only option, because selfish dominators' victories risk translating into all-out extinction, including that of the dominators themselves. The finiteness of planet Earth turns both missiles and bulldozers into tools for collective suicide and ecocide.

Also political scientist Robert Axelrod, who has been introduced before, and who has modeled cooperation and its evolution and complexity, found that groups in which altruism is universal will outcompete groups where all serve only their own interest, under the condition that a group of altruists always guards against attempts from non-altruists to cheat.[121] This, indeed, represents a message to all policy makers who are beholden to the "holy trinity of orthodox economics," namely, that it may not render the best results. The global community will need to be altruistic if a dignified future is to be attained; selfish dominators controlling the rest means global humiliation.

How can a misguided worldview prevail beyond its usefulness? One reason may have been the apparent success of Newtonian physics. As Newtonian physics gave rise to automation, factories, and industrialization, and, as this elicited so much admiration, its paradigm has been expanded onto all realms of the human condition. All human activity became fashioned according to the Newtonian machine and made subservient to industrialization. Forerunners of the factory were societal institutions such as the military – from Sparta's ruthless efficiency to the Prussian military machine and its discipline. Wherever certain ethics, like the Protestant work ethics as described by Max Weber, were available, this facilitated this course. Smoothly working robot-like cogwheels in a disciplined military or Newtonian machine, this was perceived as a model for health, health for the human body, for individuals, groups, and society as a whole, including world society.

One of the implementers of this path, during the nineteenth century, was economist Leon Walras (1834 – 1910), who, together with others, created a "physics of social behavior" comparable to Newtonian physics.[122] The dream was that "this would result in a system of equations that could predict human economic behavior with the same accuracy that Newton could predict the orbits of the planets."[123] No longer would it be necessary to relate theory to empirical research when theory alone were capable of predicting human economic behavior. The foundational assumption of these economics was that individuals maximize their absolute utilities.

Walras and his colleagues could not know that their dream was at odds with evolutionary theory.[124] Subsequent economists could have inquired deeper, but too few did.[125] From the point of view of contemporary science, the human body is an organic living system and its workings belong to the realm of living creatures much more than to Newtonian machines. Even physics itself has expanded, and with quantum physics having arrived on the scene, the Newtonian model is not the only one anymore. Analytical mathematical models have failed for complex physical systems, and they have failed for the study of biological or human economic systems. In sum, the overstretch of the Newtonian machine paradigm has caused immense harm. It has imposed inappropriate and ultimately deeply health-damaging strategies on the human condition. While formal analytical models and theoretical tools such as computer simulation models are useful, "they are always caricatures of the real world and must be closely related to empirical research to avoid becoming detached from reality."[126]

Why is it so difficult for these insights to be heard in the mainstream world of policy planning even today? The seeming success of Newtonian physics may indeed be one reason, a success which, furthermore, created the illusion that the security dilemma could be overcome, once-and-for-all, through one party's victorious technological domination.[127] Could it be that there are also more foundational shortcomings in Western philosophical thought? What stands behind competition-for-domination cosmologies that ultimately engender a self-destructive individualistic culture and global economic frames that undermine long-term well-being for all? *Dualism* may be the answer, a lack of understanding for *nondualism*. It has been discussed earlier in this book.

Through my work, I attempt to nurture a global coalition of *gardeners* of an egalitarian ethos that keeps dominator and free-rider strategies at bay. I refrain from following neo-conservativism in that the correct model for society should be *hunters* hunting animals in a jungle: Republican John Mica from Florida, neo-conservative American Congressional Representative, stated as a justification of the "Personal Responsibility and Work Opportunity Act" (the Welfare Reform Act) of 1996, that too much welfare for the poor classes was not good for them because, "like the animals in the zoo, they would forget how to hunt."[128] I am a gardener who attempts to keep dominators and free-riders at bay by filling the position of the dominator with a "reverse dominance hierarchy," by employing "intentional leveling mechanisms," as anthropologist Christopher Boehm would formulate it.[129]

I am inspired by economist Elinor Ostrom, who proved that it is possible, even for larger groups, to protect their commons. She received the Nobel Prize for Economics 2009 for her work on the multifaceted nature of human-ecosystem interaction and the core design principles that make it possible to successfully manage common-pool resources such as irrigation systems, forests, and fisheries.[130] I am glad that the Planetary Integrity Project is currently working on a concept for *Earth trusteeship* governance.[131] We had our 17th Annual Dignity Conference in New Zealand in 2011,[132] and we learned from our Maori friends about the Maori concept of *kaitiakitanga*, or guardianship for the environment, and are delighted that the Whanganui river now has the status of a legal personality. Or that an Indian court has now granted the Himalayan mountain ranges, glaciers, rivers, lakes, air, and forests the status of a "juristic person," who has rights equivalent to the rights of human beings.[133]

Further, I am inspired by people like Christopher Boehm, who has traced the human inclination toward domination back to primates, only to be surprised later.[134] *Homo sapiens'* closest relatives, the chimpanzees, usually develop social systems of strict dominance orders, and it is plausible that early hominids have followed this script. Boehm was surprised, however, when he tried to reconstruct the social system of our Pleistocene ancestors and did not find similar orders of dominance. What he found was that the "vast majority of indigenous societies living in bands today are characterized by a strongly egalitarian structure."[135] Boehm concluded that "egalitarianism and the rejection of strong dominance hierarchies is a basic attribute of human sociality."[136] He hypothesized that due to growing cognitive abilities, early humans may have realized that, if they themselves could not dominate, it would be best to also prevent others from doing so. As brainpower in humans increased, "strategic thinking, proto-political finessing, and coalition-seeking behavior" became feasible, which meant that wherever certain group members attempted to impose themselves on the group, the group collectively "tamed" such dominance strivings.[137]

Riane Eisler's *partnership* model of society is my favorite, and I advocate Alan Page Fiske's *communal sharing* approach to social relationships.[138] I attempt to help realize *empathic decency* in the world, worthy of a Jeremy Rifkin or Avishai Margalit.[139] I am also one of Ray and Anderson's cultural creatives. Ray and Anderson found two main countermovements against *moderns*, first, the *traditionals*, those who seek solutions in the past, and, second, the *cultural creatives*,[140] some of whom turn their attention inward to gain new levels of consciousness,[141] while others turn it outward, demonstrating for a new future in the streets. I, on my part, combine in- and outward orientations, and I seek dignity and not honor to inform them. To link back to the insights of Donald Carveth introduced earlier in this book, I find dignity being inherent in the humanness of my inner world and disallow poisonous superego voices to hijack my inner world with notions of honor.[142] I invite all groups – moderns, traditionals, and cultural creatives of both inward and outward orientations – to come together and learn from each other. Certain indigenous cultural insights from the past – that of *Living Well*, for example – wait to fully inspire future-oriented inward and outward paths.[143] *Ubuntu*'s tenet that "I am because of you" can inspire the "Sufis" of this world to go out and invite the "Pharisees" to look into their inner worlds to find the dignity of their humanness in their souls, and then join in in changing the world, so that "we can let our Pharaohs go."[144]

As mentioned before, throughout the past centuries, Norway was able to emerge from a culture of proud, independent, and violent Viking warriors and adventurers toward a culture of *likeverd* (equality in dignity), *dugnad* (communal cooperation), and global responsibility (Nansen passport). Norway manifests *liberté*, *égalité*, and *fraternité* as a lived heritage. Celebrated Norwegian writer and poet Henrik Wergeland (1808 – 1845) pointed out already in 1843 that Norway's disadvantages are also its advantages. Norway's marginal geopolitical location on this planet has protected it, as nobody "bothered" to conquer and force Norway into the kind of submission that underlings in hierarchical empires elsewhere had to endure.[145] This particular cultural heritage of Norway is the reason for why it is one of the main platforms and starting points for the global work of our Human Dignity and Humiliation Studies fellowship, and also for why we launched the idea of the World Dignity University from the University of Oslo in 2011.[146]

Norwegian philosopher Tore Frost has a particular interest in the notion of *inherent* dignity and how it came into being. It is a novel notion that seems to have appeared suddenly from nowhere and it was brought into being by the human rights declaration in 1948.[147] Frost believes that Eleanor

Roosevelt was its creator.[148] She wrote in 1948: "If the Declaration is accepted by the Assembly, it will mean that all the nations accepting it hope that the day will come when these rights are considered inherent rights belonging to every human being."[149]

Frost identifies also a Kantian justification for inherent dignity in the Article 1 of the Universal Declaration, namely, that the premise of inherent dignity lies in human freedom, and that equal rights follows from this. Frost suggests that the phrase in Article 1, if it were complete, would go as follows: "All human beings are born free in (their inherent) dignity and (therefore) they are equal in (their) human rights."[150]

The introduction of the idea of an inherent dignity is revolutionary, explicates Frost, because it places dignity inside the human being and liberates it from outside guarantors such as the authority of divinity or rationality. Equal dignity is a quality of dignity, not a quantifiable "value," and not something that can be ranked.[151] Frost warns against attempts to create definitive justifications of the inherence of dignity in human nature: On the contrary, the demand to recognize inherent dignity is a demand that needs to be without content.[152] I would like to add a question: Perhaps the situation with dignity resembles that of the impossibility of experiencing Kant's elusive *Ding an sich* (*thing in itself*), which, whether experienced or not, remains unknowable?[153]

For Frost, *love* is the foundation for human dignity: "Our emotional life, in the tension between passion and suffering, confronts us with love as the basic premise of human life in all its complexity. Love is what life is about."[154] And Frost goes even further. In his endeavor to avoid overly abstract and lifeless humanisms, he asks: Is the term respect, as in "respect for inherent dignity," sufficient? After all, respect is something humans should demonstrate to all life, not just to human life? What about "awe of (human) life"? he suggests. The word *awe* could serve as a reminder that humans are living creatures, both to be honored and to be feared. It would be awe and reverence for the human being with all its bright sides and its dark sides – after all, it is a "shaken love life" that characterizes human faring.[155] By using the word *shaken* (*rysted* in Norwegian), Frost draws on philosopher Jan Patočka, one of the original signatories and main spokespersons for the Charter 77 human rights movement in Czechoslovakia in 1977. Fellow dissident Václav Havel explains: "When Jan Patočka wrote about Charter 77, he used the term 'solidarity of the shaken.' He was thinking of those who dared to resist impersonal state power and to confront it with the only thing at their disposal, their own humanity."[156]

Social reformers Susan B. Anthony and Elizabeth Cady Stanton, as well as Rachel Carson and Dorothy Freeman, all these women gave each other courage and strength through manifesting in their relationships what I would call a deep and loving *solidarity of the shaken*.[157] This is what I have the privilege of experiencing, among others, with Linda Hartling, and I cannot imagine my life path without this depth of human connection. I recommend developing the same kind of fine, tender, and caring solidarity that we nurture between us also to every other individual, to every community, and, finally, to the global community as the only way to survive in the long term. Linda Hartling recommends to connect inherent essentialized dignity as a permanent feature of each human being in a nondualistic way with the reality of dignity that is growing through loving relationships: "we have dignity, and we develop dignity through participation in dignifying relationships."[158]

In my 2010 book on gender, humiliation, and global security, I propose that *big love* is an antidote against "big hate," and I explain that my "religion" indeed, is *love, humility, and awe for a universe too large for us to fathom*.[159] I strive to learn what I call the *literacy of love*.[160] Mahatma Gandhi spoke of *satyāgraha*. By the loving solidarity of those whose souls are shaken, so shaken that they act on their *conscience*, as Paulo Freire would call it,[161] a more compassionate society can be nurtured. Emotions can be the "engines of conversion"[162] and "a creative source of collective agency."[163]

Parents have a particular responsibility. Some Germans helped rescue Jews during the Nazi regime to escape the Holocaust. When they later looked back to understand what gave them the courage, they found that it was the memory of growing up in a family where compassion and altruism had been given priority.[164] In other words, parents have the power to create a more compassionate world by protecting and nurturing the inherent dignity of their children.

This is also the message of the Greater Good Science Center at the University of California in Berkeley. It features articles on how to achieve more compassionate marriages, schools, hospitals, workplaces, and other institutions.[165] Psychologist Dacher Keltner is the founding faculty director of the center, and he warns against assuming that selfishness, greed, and competitiveness lie at the core of human behavior. He warns against letting such assumptions guide any human affair, all the way from policy making to media portrayals of social life. What research shows, is that it is compassion that is deeply rooted in our brains, our bodies, and in the most basic ways in which we communicate.[166] Eleonore Roosevelt would be happy: indeed, dignity is *inherent*.

Can dignity and compassion find an arena to last in a world continuously traumatized by unexpected forms of violence and incessantly being pushed back into the honor paradigm? Many had hoped that the horrors of the twentieth century had ended in 1989/90.[167] Yet, instead of disappearing, war only takes on new shapes now.[168] The wars in Ukraine and the Middle East seem to be ominous continuations of the horrors of the twentieth century. Fear of major war has now returned to Europe. Political scientist Herfried Münkler traces the cultural and political evolution of violence from the wars of the twentieth century to the present day, and he calls for genuine new *geopolitical strategies* to meet the challenges of our time.

What would such genuine new geopolitical strategies have to entail? Compassion? The argument of leading politicians is usually that a strategy of compassion may be nice; yet, it is too soft in the face of hard *Realpolitik*, as the security dilemma leaves no space for softness. In my work, I argue that it is a new Realpolitik is needed, one that acknowledges that global interconnectedness makes old Realpolitik obsolete. For the first time in history, it is in the self-interest also of the powerful to create global *constitutive rules*[169] that serve the common good compassionately, and the reason is that on a burning planet not even the children of the wealthiest will survive.

Throughout history, leaders often claimed to work for the common good while concealing that they manipulate society's rules for their own advantage. In absolutist contexts, leaders may state: "These are the rules of our order that we call divine, rules which are for the common good of all people, and we expect that everybody will enthusiastically invest their self-interest into worshipping and maintaining this order, happily renouncing any other potentially possible individual choices." In contexts where "communism" informs the political system, the same declaration would go as follows: "These are the rules of Marxism-Leninism, which we call scientific, rules that are for the common good of all people, and we expect everybody to enthusiastically invest their self-interest into this common good, happily renouncing any other potentially possible individual choices." In a "capitalist" context, we would hear: "These are the rules of the free market, which we call scientific, rules that are for the common good of all people, and we expect everybody to enthusiastically invest their self-interest into the freedom of many choices, including the pseudo-freedom of false choices, happily renouncing any other potentially possible individual choices." And, following the law of domination having no endpoint, in all contexts, over time, we see destructive overreach, be it in the form of "Caesar Mania," Orwellian surveillance, or financial bubbles waiting to burst.

In an interconnected world, what should a new Realpolitik look like? *Wandel durch Annäherung* (Change through Rapprochement) is the name of a strategy that is connected with Willy Brandt, Germany's chancellor from 1969 to 1974. And it is also connected with Egon Bahr, a social democratic politician who passed away in 2015 at the age of 93, and whom I had the privilege of meeting at the Institute for Peace Research and Security Policy in Hamburg in 1993.[170] West Germany had antagonized the communist regime of East Germany head-on until these two politicians spearheaded a new *Ostpolitik* (east politics) to overcome confrontation through re-establishing talking relations. Germany was not the only originator of such a strategy. The term Ostpolitik was also used to describe Pope Paul VI's efforts toward Eastern European countries roughly at the same time, while the term *Nordpolitik* refers to similar attempts between North and South Korea since the 1980s. The encyclical letter *Laudato Si'* by the present Pope Francis in 2015 could be said to represent *Weltpolitik*, or world politics.[171]

Another requirement for a genuinely new geopolitical strategy could be to redirect all efforts that are now aimed at military solutions into making peace. Monty Marshall, director of the Center for Systemic Peace at the University of Maryland, has written widely on insecurity and how it gets diffused.[172] Global terror is the ultimate diffusion of insecurity. In my work, I highlight how the risk of diffusing insecurity increases in a globally interconnecting world, a world where old methods of domination now fail to render meek and submissive humility, and, instead, generate humiliated fury.[173]

In August 2014, Britain's former foreign secretary David Miliband acknowledged that the 2003 invasion of Iraq by the United States and the UK has led to the rise of the militant group Da'esh.[174] Reckless power play in 2003 has fostered Islamist terrorism. Sunni fear of Shia influence joined U.S.-Israeli concerns, and "by supporting Sunni militias with arms, intelligence, and money" they hoped to stem Shia influence in Iraq. Yet, this ended in fiasco, summarizes Chandra Muzaffar, president of the International Movement for a Just World.[175] Writer and peace activist Ury Avnery concurs: "For six decades my friends and I have warned our people: if we don't make peace with the nationalist Arab forces, we shall be faced with Islamic Arab forces. The Israeli-Palestinian conflict will turn into a Jewish-Muslim conflict. The national war will become a religious war."[176]

Kashmir can serve as another example of how, in a shrinking world, winning a battle risks losing the peace. Amir Rana, director of the Pak Institute for Peace Studies in Islamabad in Pakistan, posted this on September 9, 2014: "Al Qaeda sees an opportunity in India-held Kashmir, where a separatist, religio-nationalist movement has been crushed … Al Qaeda is calling radical elements towards 'pure' jihad…."[177]

Part and parcel of a new compassionate Realpolitik would also be to truly manifest R2R, the Responsibility to Protect, rather than using and abusing it erratically. "R2P is not an emergent principle of international law, as advocates claim, but an operative principle of geopolitical convenience," is a damning verdict.[178] The norm of R2P was invoked to validate the destruction of Gaddafi's Libya, yet: What about other places that might need the ethos of human solidarity? asks Richard Falk, expert on international law.[179]

Counterterrorism can be made more appropriate for the future as well. The most important step would be to overcome the mindset of masculine honor – the fear to appear weak. This fear is too widespread also in the United States: "… we have a political class that feels it must inoculate itself against allegations of weakness. Our politicians are more fearful of the politics of terrorism – of the charge that they do not take terrorism seriously – than they are of the crime itself."[180]

Sociologist Amitai Etzioni proposes a *liberal communitarian paradigm* for counterterrorism.[181] He is critical of how the concepts of the 1648 Treaty of Westphalia have become part and parcel of the beliefs, worldviews, and feelings of billions of people: "Daily news reminds one that people in very different parts of the world feel personally aggrieved, insulted, and humiliated when they hold that their nation's sovereignty has been violated, even if the troops of another nation merely crossed a minor, vague line in the shifting sands. Millions of people have shown that they are willing to die to protect the sovereignty of their nation."[182] Etzioni argues that acts of transnational terrorism need to be responded to differently than through the current normative and legal paradigms. "In the international arena, we should downplay states' right to sovereignty in favor of a paradigm that requires nation states not only to protect select common goods including the Responsibility to Protect (R2P), but also to observe a new duty, namely, not to harbor or support terrorists."[183] Paradigms of war among nations and of law enforcement are ill-suited for counterterrorism campaigns, warns Etzioni. He calls for a distinct normative and legal paradigm for dealing with transnational terrorism to be consolidated into a new future Geneva Convention.

What can we do to shoulder our very own personal responsibility? Not just Leo Tolstoy, also other historical figures, such as Henry David Thoreau, Mahatma Gandhi, and Martin Luther King can inspire us.[184] And every single citizen on this planet can inspire everyone else. During my time in Sarajevo and Dubrovnik in 2016, I asked everybody I happened to meet the following questions: What has your world region to teach the rest of the world? If we, as humanity, want to offer our children a decent future, what should we all learn from you? What must we advance and nurture and what avoid? How can we orient, for instance, our economies differently, so that economic values reflect our human values?[185] I call on every reader to ask these questions everywhere on this planet.

A young law student in Dubrovnik, nineteen years old, replied: "We need to nurture diversity. Suppressing diversity diminishes the chances for learning. To do so, we have to avoid prejudice." Another young man in Dubrovnik, twenty-six years old, shared this: "More information is needed as an antidote against manipulation. Today, it might not be as easy to manipulate young people in Serbia into hating others by the same crude propaganda as in 1991." An experienced educational activist in Sarajevo called out: "Do not teach children 'chosen trauma' in school!" A highly knowledgeable Dubrovnik woman in the middle of her life advised: "What is needed is a good economy, so that people can look into the future rather than cling to the past. And a functioning governing system would be necessary, not an inherently unstable configuration as, for instance, in Bosnia-Herzegovina." A deeply reflective female citizen of Dubrovnik who experienced the siege of Dubrovnik as a child, has hope: "There are so many bright people in the world! Cannot their combined knowledge and creativity save us all?"

John Bunzl, an advocate of "people-centered global governance," explains:

> Economic markets are, effectively, competitions which can do nothing other than place money as the highest of all values. That's what they're designed to do and that, if one thinks about it, is all they CAN do. If other values such as care, craftsmanship, meaning and fairness are to be imparted to an economy, there is really only one way that can be done and that is not through the economy itself, but through GOVERNANCE; i.e. through laws, taxes, regulations and re-distributions. These are the tools by which governments balance economic values with human values.
>
> But today we live in a global market. Even if a national government could be persuaded that appropriate increased taxes, regulations and re-distributions were a good idea, no government could actually implement them because that would increase business costs, so making the national economy uncompetitive with economies elsewhere. The result? Jobs would be lost, business and investment would go elsewhere, and the next election would be lost.
>
> Thus, a reversal of current market values can no longer be achieved on a national level but must, like climate change, financial market re-regulation, corporate taxation and much else, be dealt with on a global level. A global market, in short, requires binding governance on a global scale.[186]

In conclusion: Priority ought to be given to forming binding global governance. Only if we succeed with that, can all the other things we want – meaningful work included – become possible.[187]

This is the conclusion that John Scales Avery offers, who is part of a group that shared the 1995 Nobel Peace Prize:

> We need a new economic system, a new society, a new social contract, a new way of life. Here are the great tasks that history has given to our generation: We must achieve a steady-state economic system. We must restore democracy. We must decrease economic inequality. We must break the power of corporate greed. We must leave fossil fuels in the ground. We must stabilize and ultimately reduce the global population. We must eliminate the institution of war. And finally, we must develop a more ma-

ture ethical system to match our new technology ... It is easier to burn down a house than to build one, easier to kill a human than to raise and educate one, easier to force a species into extinction than to replace it once it is gone, easier to burn the Great Library of Alexandria than to accumulate the knowledge that once filled it, and easier to destroy a civilization in a thermonuclear war than to rebuild it from the radioactive ashes.[188]

Letter to America

Election Night Fright:
Every night on the way to bed,
Visions of apocalypse dance
through my head.
This is a man-made campaign of
pain,
Generalized terror for political
gain.

– Linda Hartling's Poem of the Day, November 7, 2016, prior to the presidential elections in the United States of America

The election of Donald J. Trump as president of the United States in November 2016 has confirmed the thrust of this book since it was begun in 2010. His election underlines one of the messages of this book, namely, that confrontational posturing, while it was once associated with courage and victory, and still is, no longer is victorious in the new context of an interconnected world. Now, it may rather create an all-out atmosphere of terror. Lone wolf warriors can no longer earn glory, even if they lead governments. In an interconnected world, courage needs to be defined in radically new ways if humankind wishes to survive as a species. Courage is now to be invested into sagacity, moderation, nuanced and complex thinking, radical respect, abstention from polarization and demonization, and unity-seeking across fault lines.

I would like to end this book with an urgent message to the United States. Whatever America does, as the presently reigning hyperpower, has immense impact on the rest of the world.[189] Whenever America betrays its ideals through hypocritical double standards and empty rhetoric, the ensuing humiliation spans the globe.[190] The U.S. carries a particular responsibility for moving away from dominator logic, away from the escalation of the security dilemma, and instead turn toward the partnership model, toward egalization, and toward unity and diversity. I know, this sounds difficult and unrealistic, and this is the best reason for why it needs to be said. This "letter to America" is intended to call on all Americans to recognize and resist when the founding principles of the U.S. – equality, liberty, democracy – are being hijacked by corporate and military interests, and destroyed through blindly instigated cycles of humiliation. Let us hear economist Kent Klitgaard:

> For a brief moment in history, a small segment of the working class, mostly white, male, and employed by large manufacturing corporations, received a share of the rising global profits of newly hegemonic US corporations. That institutional structure began to disappear amidst the deindustrialization of the 1970s. Yet some forty years later, many displaced factory workers still feel the sting of the loss of their identities and their incomes, and flocked towards a right-wing authoritarian promising to restore the old ways. The grievances are real, long-lived, and multigenerational. The transition will not be easy, as I do not see how a system in overshoot can achieve sustainability without consuming less, and few people accept less without backlash.[191]

This is the great dilemma of our time, summarizes Klitgaard: "We grow too rapidly to preserve the Holocene environment but too slowly to provide sufficient and meaningful jobs. Neither Market Forces nor piecemeal Policy Reform can possibly extricate us from this situation. We need a Great Transition.[192]

Linda Hartling had this call for me: "Evelin, America could be your case example, an example that could change the course of the world."[193] This is her diagnosis of the situation in her home country and this is her message:

> America suffers from a severe case of the dominator model that grew out of the security

> dilemma. Dominator logic has infected all aspects of American life through enterprise and business. I would love have you invite America to wake up to the dead-end and global destruction that is flowing from our businesses practices that result in false profits by destroying the environment.[194]

In my 2006 book on humiliation, I included my first "letter to America," in which I invited the people of the United States to join a globally interwoven society in the spirit of shared responsibility. I invited all Americans to take the best of their country's devotion to freedom and merge it with the best of the wisdom that the rest of the planet's cultures have accumulated, so that, together, we can create a new and better future for humankind.[195] Only in this way can America become truly great.

Eleanor Roosevelt's vision of America and the world, her notion of inherent dignity, in my view, is a vision that can and must be applied to humanity at large, in fact, it is the only vision that can secure the survival of humankind in decency on our planet. The same goes for Juliet Schor's vision of a new American dream.[196] According to what I see, the world community's survival would be in great danger if any Taliban-like culture were forced upon the world, be it from Afghanistan itself or devised by "angry white men" in the West.[197]

America and the world are at a turning point. America has everything that is needed to help move the world forward in ways that nurture the well-being of all people and the planet. Its life-enriching values and ideals, like the values of so many other countries, are all there, waiting to be fully realized in support of building a healthy interconnected world.[198] There are great dangers if America misses this opportunity. Were the United States to crumble, the power vacuum would perhaps be filled with forces similar to Da'esh, who unapologetically display the behavior and the rhetoric of a strong security dilemma culture and who do not even attempt to hide it behind human rights rhetoric. Not least very recent history has shown that worse tyrannies can emerge after regimes have fallen. I wish for America to flourish in new ways, I wish it to protect both itself and the world from an American-Made Corporate Empire that betrays its own ideals of freedom and equal dignity. To truly manifest, American values need to be liberated from being hijacked by outdated definitions, they need to be shaped in future-oriented ways.[199]

Allow me to start with gender roles. American men, as all men, will have to liberate themselves from the outdated scripts prescribing to men that to be a man, they have to engage in *Mutproben* (tests of courage) to establish their worthiness through domination. Norwegian novelist Karl Ove Knausgård bears witness of his journey, how he unlearned this script, in his magnum opus *My Struggle*.[200] Birds begin to sing when testosterone levels rise in their bodies: what if men learn to sing rather than engage in violence?[201]

The arenas for tests of courage – such as knightly war, capturing control over territory, big game hunting for status enhancement, and even heavy physical work – all have shrunk, and men themselves are the very authors of this development, through the industrialization of human activity, the invention of nuclear weapons, and the rapid extraction of finite global resources. Courage is still needed, however, urgently, yet, without *machismo*. Firefighters are still required to prove their bravery, only that macho culture now becomes obsolete. The First World War brought this new reality to its soldiers in full force for the first time, when enthusiastic warriors understood that they were mere cannon fodder to be slaughtered en masse. The head count of twenty military veterans committing suicide per day in the U.S. should tell America that no one is made for war, that machismo times are over.[202] A new courage is needed now: the courage to live in connection.

Courage is needed to acknowledge both the finiteness and interconnection of our world, and courage is needed to learn to invest solidarity and live together in post-complexity simplicity. If we do not learn "to subordinate our notions of 'rights' and 'justice' to those which can operate sustainably within the Earth's functioning ecosystem, we will become extinct."[203]

Alan Zulch is one of many who studies ecological consciousness. In his view, the inability of present-day's mainstream cultures to face limits is at the core of the problem. We engage in "narcissism, cruelty, projection, anxiety, and compulsive behavior ... we cannot get enough of what we don't really need.[204] Before long, Zulch warns, we will not have a choice: either we will consciously choose simplicity or we will perish. Zulch warns that in its Western guise, the rejection of limits and limitations is "codified into an ideology reinforced by assumptions of technological progress, endless growth economies," and that in combination, "these learned behaviors are different but no less misanthropic than other profoundly narrow-minded reactionary worldviews we are seeing blossom forth with bitterness across the globe. The end result is ecocide, too powerful for any legal framework to overcome."[205]

What Zulch advocates is *post-complexity simplicity*, or *conscious simplicity* as a survival imperative, it is not "romantic simplicity." He recommends learning from indigenous cultures and peoples, seeking their lessons in simplicity.[206] I would add indigenous lessons in solidarity.

Not only scripts for masculinity have been shaped and distorted by the security dilemma and the dominator model of society. In my book on gender, I dissect how the traditional female script can be abused and coopted in service of a dominator agenda, even when this script is not directly executed by women. When we hear that "terrorists" are to be "flushed out," minorities or infidels to be "cleansed," so as to "purify" society or spirituality, then this rhetoric draws on the traditional role description for women, namely, cleaning, washing, and scrubbing.[207] When conservative American politicians propose banning Muslim travel and policing Muslim communities, they apply the same logic.[208] The cruelty of war is "sanitized" and "whitewashed" when it is industrialized into "clean" extermination. This was true of the killing of Jews in concentration camps, it is true of killing animals in slaughterhouses, and it is true of killing terrorists through drones, all of which becomes more cruel through its "efficiency" and pseudo non-cruelty. "Segregation" was once the sanitized word for apartheid, the phrase "free market" now sanitizes exploitation. Genocide, ethnocide, sociocide, ecocide, all merge the worst aspects of the male script of heroism together with the worst of the female script of cleaning.

Under the dominator model, women had limited alternatives for action in the world. The traditional female script primarily restricted women's activities to childbearing, caregiving, and other undertakings organized to serve the traditional male script and thus the dominator system. While many of the skills associated with the traditional female script – such as upkeep and the creation of harmony – are essential to society, they were not valued as such in the dominator model.[209] Furthermore, women were taught to misrecognize these skills as all there is of female potential. Compounding this limiting predicament, cooperation and compliance with the system of domination was indispensable for women (and their children) to merely survive. In this way, women have been coopted into the continuation of dominator arrangements. Conservative leader Phyllis Schlafly, who died recently, for instance, was a significant force behind a campaign to obstruct the passage of an Equal Rights Amendment to the U.S. Constitution in the 1970s.[210] The Amendment stated: "Equality of rights under the law shall not be denied or abridged by the United States or by any State on account of sex." In her oratory, Schlafly glorified traditional roles for women that limited women's participation in society, while in her personal life, she contradicted her own message by neglecting her traditional female script duties to climb the ladder of educational and political power. Luckily, other women in the U.S., and also in other countries, have continued to liberate themselves from the limiting traditional female scripts that have kept them from developing their full potential and participation in society for much too long.

If American society can move forward without falling back on outdated scripts of masculinity and femininity, without being hijacked by modern corporate and military forms of the dominator model, then both women *and* men will be able to enjoy being liberated, free to unfold their full capabilities in all realms of life. Men will be freer to participate in the emotional sphere and caring work of family life, in short, in the private sphere, and women will be freer to participate in the public sphere. Males and females will be freer to develop new scripts of *how to be human together*.

Let me now come to the next point, terrorism. Michael Scheuer, a C.I.A. veteran with more than two decades of service, ran the Counterterrorist Center's bin Laden station from 1996 to 1999. He became known for his warnings against labeling leaders such Osama Bin Laden as pathological exceptions whose removal could solve the problem of terrorism. He warns that, even though considerable literature has been produced on various forms of social conflict and violence over the years, the sociology of terrorism is still understudied. When international conflicts, formerly the reserve of diplomats, now stoke religious and nationalistic extremism in wider populations, only long-term global prevention can help.[211] The main foci for agendas for future research that sociologist Austin Turk recommends are: the social construction of terrorism; terrorism as political violence; terrorism as communication; organizing terrorism; socializing terrorists; social control of terrorism; and theorizing terrorism.[212]

Kristian Berg Harpviken is the former director of the Peace Research Institute Oslo, and an expert on Afghanistan. His recommendation for practical solutions for a safer world is to include traditional societal structures that fit their respective locality and to connect them with non-governmental initiatives that come from outside.[213] In Afghanistan, for instance, an important traditional structure would be the *shura*, which enjoys high credibility and is deeply embedded in local cultural environments. Harpviken calls for the development of "a comprehensive concept of civil society, in addition to a critical examination of how power is distributed in synergistic relationships that span traditional-modern divides."[214]

Members of Al-Qaeda and Da'esh are warriors steeped in honor, in honor humiliation and revenge. Also many right-wing advocates around the world read from the same score. Their script risks leading the world into collective suicide, as it is an outdated score in the context of today's interconnected world. America should take seriously the idea that war does not work in the long run, even when it seems to provide short-term gains. The list of its failed social and military wars is long, from "war on terrorism," to "war on drugs," to "war on poverty," to "war on crime," or "war in Vietnam." War is an outdated response to the complex reality we are facing today. The more the world globalizes, simply launching military interventions will become an ever more unfeasible strategy:

> Unless such a radical transformation of the way life on the planet is undertaken in the decades ahead, two intertwined developments are likely to make the future inhospitable to human habitation, even if the worst catastrophes can be avoided: globalization morphing into various forms of authoritarian and oppressive political leadership intertwined with extremist movements of resistance that have no vision beyond that of striking back at the oppressors.[215]

The only hope for America – as well as for the world – is fostering a new spirit of inclusiveness, a courageous form of inclusiveness, as exemplified in words written on the Statue of Liberty: "Give me your tired, your poor, your huddled masses yearning to breathe free...." These words convey the kind of courage needed to lead the world away from the language and practices of deadly division, exclusion, terror, and war. A step in the right direction began in 2005, when U.S. policymakers in the second Bush administration sought to replace the bellicose "Global War on Terror" (GWOT) with some lower-key concept like "Struggle Against Violent Extremism" (SAVE), as terrorism expert Alex Schmid lays out.[216] Under the Obama administration, it became a "war with Al-Qaeda." The U.S. is no longer engaged in a "war on terrorism," neither is it fighting "jihadists," nor in a "global war."[217] President Obama's top homeland security and counterterrorism official "took all three terms off the table of acceptable words inside the White House," during a speech August 6, 2009, at the Center for Strategic and International Studies, a Washington think tank.[218] In 2012, the Obama administration concluded that Al-Qaeda posed no direct threat to the U.S. and scaled back the fight.

Yet, voices warn: "The common theme of frustration is that while the political will to fight a long war against a less centralized al Qaeda network wanes in America, the threat gathers overseas... 'The war is not over till the enemy says it's over,'" warns James Mattis, who served as Obama's commander of Central Command between 2010 and 2013, and is now the Secretary of Defense in the Trump administration.[219] Clearly, Mattis' warning is valid. The journey from "peace the Hitler way" to "peace the Gandhi way" cannot be made in mere rhetoric, and not by only one side. Indeed, one cannot "wish things away on a timetable."[220] Therefore, the creation of a genuinely new geopolitical strategy that cultivates a strong global culture of dignity is indispensable.

At the present juncture in history, the situation in the world feels reminiscent of the periods prior to the two World Wars. Many promising developments took place just before both WWI and WWII. Not least women became more visible in these periods and were able to contribute to society in new ways; there was a sense of and reason for optimism.[221] Yet, each time, the move toward more equality was being stopped in its tracks by brutal backlashes. Historically, whenever men felt that their honor was tarnished, they sought war. This leads to an urgent question now: What will our "angry men" do now?[222] Once more, this is a moment in history, in which we need to say to all those invested in regaining honor, especially in the United States: "Look, better change, engage in partnership at home and in the world."[223]

Let me end this letter with a little note on hidden wounds, hidden wounds of transgenerational trauma.[224] I do this not least in honor of people like American psychotherapist Carol Smaldino and organizational psychologist Peter Coleman. Carol Smaldino, in her work, highlights the *shadow*, the dark side of our souls, and since the United States is the world's present superpower, she warns, leaving its hidden wounds unhealed is dangerous for American's and all others.[225] Also Alan Zulch is aware of the treacherous traps of the shadow.[226] Psychologist Peter Coleman admonishes his American compatriots and the entire world to focus on creating healthy social and global systems rather than be enthralled or appalled by pathological strongmen: Please heal a dysfunctional and disingenuous government, he calls out, please rescue the media ethos, stop hyper-competition, and stop legitimizing violence.[227] When will journalists begin asking about unconciled trauma from past violence, is a question put also by peace researcher Johan Galtung.[228] Ruben Nelson, executive director of Foresight Canada, warns that one of the factors that feed today's cynicism and passivity "is the recognition that virtually none of our public leaders are substantial enough to peddle the hope that exists on the far side of despair":

> We must face and engage head on the official and systemic superficial optimism of our Modern cultures. This entails the courage to overcome our fear of fearfulness. Working our way through the valley of the shadow of death with heads up and eyes open, it seems to me, is a requirement. the hope that exists on the far side of despair.[229]

Some Americans may feel angry when reading this. They may not feel any need for self-reflection, and no need of acknowledging any hidden history of trauma, except for those that are "official," such as that of Pearl Harbor or 9/11. They might also feel indignant reading this book, as they believe that America has contributed to the global good in ways this book fails to address and appreciate.

Born in Europe, when I was young, I thought of Americans as "strong by nature." However, my perception changed during my time in Egypt as a psychotherapist and counselor when I discovered deeper psychological layers. Many American expatriates came to me and what we revealed, together, was that many Americans, not just African-Americans, bear transgenerational traumas in their souls that reach far back into the past and into their subconscious. Those first Europeans, those who arrived on the shores of America and fought for independence, they might have been more traumatized than heroic, with the myth of heroism being planted later, now doing a disservice to later generations, as it obfuscates the trauma that has been handed down to them. And also the civil war might not be over yet, contributing to the climate of bitter polarization in the United States now.[230]

Kathleen is a dear friend from Texas and she expressed what many of my American clients also shared with me in Cairo:

Kathleen: Americans don't really trust the UN. We don't trust anybody very much. If you think about it, the world hasn't given us much reason to trust. The American experience of the world has not been very pleasant. During the sixteenth, seventeenth, and eighteenth centuries, you used our continent as a dumping ground, a place to send your undesirables. During the twentieth century, you dragged us into two horrific world wars. The UN is a nice place to talk theory, but it's all talk. Its deliberations remind me of a college rap session. Americans have not seen any evidence that the rest of the world really wants peace. But, we've seen plenty of evidence that war and hatred is a way of life in most parts of the world.
Evelin: What kind of evidence?
Kathleen: Almost everybody who lives in the U.S. does so because there was no place else that would take them in. We are a country of exiles – people whose ancestors were not wanted anywhere else. My own great-grandparents came here because they were starving in Ireland, systematically starved to death by their British masters.
Evelin: That was a long time ago.
Kathleen: People in Bosnia fight over things that happened a thousand years ago. My family history in America goes back only one hundred years. Why should Americans have shorter memories than everyone else? Are you suggesting that we should be more forgiving, more rational, more generous, more perfect than other people? The world has given America nothing but its cast-offs, its wars, its problems. But, the world seems to expect the United States to be able to adjust immediately to its problems. ... It's a little hard for me to understand how the people of the world can feel justified doing the terrible things they have done to my countrymen and then expect us to turn around and send money, food, whatever else is needed to make things right. All Americans know that their forefathers were not wanted, not considered good enough, by the rest of the world. Sit in any social group in America and sooner or later, someone will tell a story about what happened to his grandfather before he came to the United States.[231]

Even if Kathleen's reflections and my direct experience with expatriates in Cairo provide a limited view on the mentality of Americans, it is important, I think, to note the more or less hidden *victim identity* that lies beneath their line of thinking. Historian Holger Hoock now confirms my observation that the United States has whitewashed its origins and that a shadow looms behind the myth of heroism: "I read the violent story of the American nation's not-so-immaculate conception as a cautionary tale for the modern American empire," Hoock warns.[232]

Wherever I turn on this planet, I see how a brave and heroic victim identity – whether it is conscious or not, deserved or not – can become dangerous. When an essential part of one's identity is to resist persecution and adversity from a minority perspective, then there is a problem when one has grown into a powerful majority: then one may be prone to create new images of adversaries, in this way creating new enemies, even if unwittingly.

I observe such a victim identity in many Christian groups around the world, including those far removed from any hostile discrimination. Since I was born into a Christian context, I have witnessed in my immediate social surroundings how this dynamic can unfold, in disastrous ways. Historically, early Christians were persecuted, undeniably. Yet, by now, Christians are in the majority in many parts of the world and persecution becomes less salient. When this happens, there is a problem when this identity is not healed and overcome. When a victim identity loses its foothold in reality, one way to re-invigorate it is to imagine persecution and to feed and amalgamate it with other experiences of humiliation. An even more dangerous way is to provoke persecution, which, if successful, sets in motion self-fulfilling cycles. This will be made worse by the characteristic of all brave victim identities, namely, that they make immune to criticism, since criticism only strengthens such identities. In case of unjustified criticism, such immunity may represent an asset, yet, it is a disadvantage when criticism is justified. The "blind" rejection of justified criticism will generate legitimate astonishment and resistance from the critics, and it will create misattributions that further aggravate the evil circle. The critics may fail to see the victim identity behind the outer appearance of strength and force and will attribute sheer power motives to those self-styled victims who do not listen. In that way, a brave victim identity that outlives its *raison-d'être* can create horrendous damage in the form of cycles of victimhood and aggression. I have written about the *addiction to humiliation* and its disastrous consequences in my first book.[233] Therefore, conservatives who call to make America "great again," if driven by an inner need to stand tall in the face of adversity, may risk making a great America less great.

Some may now object by saying that it is human nature, and not the outflow of trauma, to have an unquenchable psychological need for enemies, and that therefore humans will always create enemies even where there are none. I have invested my entire life to test whether it is feasible, psychologically, to live without an enemy image. My conclusion: It is not only easy to do, it is also very enjoyable. It is psychologically and practically possible, and my experience indicates this, to leave behind counterproductive retaliation and short-term *military* security measures, and instead enter into productive inclusion and long-term global *human* security. No enemy effigy is required for psychological sanity, and, from my point of view, no enemy effigy is needed to create a decent global village.

Others may feel personally humiliated when I call on them to give up their need for enemies.[234] They will cry out: "How can you want us to be left defenseless in the face of those who hate us, as we stand for liberty and democracy!" My experience from all around the world is that the American Dream is being loved, not hated. Not without reason have millions flocked to the United States in the past. The problem with love stories, however, is that they can turn sour. Promises and expectations may be too high and misunderstood, on all sides, even if nobody were to do anything wrong. When divorcees fight, they do so out of disappointed love, not out of hatred. They need counseling, rather than the tools of honorable warriorhood that only lead to ever deeper conflict and violence.

Born in Europe into a displaced family, I have become a world citizen. This means also that I profoundly feel I am a fellow American. My mission in life is to do whatever I can to contribute to healing any fault lines of "we against them" in our global family. One of the most significant problems that I see is that citizens of countries do not know what their governments do on their behalf. In Europe, refugees from Africa cause great anxiety and even hatred. Heiner Geißler is a senior German politician within the conservative Christian Democratic Union (CDU) party, in other words, he is the opposite of a left-wing firebrand. His damning verdict is that those who aggress refugees and use them as scapegoats overlook the causation of this exodus. He calls on Europeans and Americans to stop destroying the livelihoods of the people of Africa: "Corruption cannot be rewarded with arms deliveries. The exploitation of African mineral resources must be halted as well as the export of agricultural products to Africa. Africa is exploited, without the inhabitants of Africa receiving a penny."[235]

Also many of my American friends are oblivious of their country's impact on the rest of the world. Werner Weidenfeld is a German political scientist and has been a political advisor for Germany-United States relations under different chancellors for a period of twelve years. "The moment we agree with the American side," he reports, "we are best friends, we are embraced until we are afraid for our ribs because the hugs are so intense." If we disagree on minor issues, "the American government regularly asks: Where is gratitude in history! We have preserved the freedom and security of the Germans and what happens!" In case of disagreement in serious questions, however, there is no friendship lost, and arms are twisted: "then intelligence material comes on the table, material that incriminates Germany, sending the message: either you do what we want or you are hanged."[236]

Some of my fellow Americans may find solace in my words to Kathleen in 2006:

Dear Kathleen, you seek shelter in your country because the rest of the world seems so alien and hostile. You feel that you must either retreat or dominate. Looking at us as equals seems scary. We would like to apologize for every little incident that contributed to your painful isolation. And, we would like to invite you to become part of "us all." We thank you for bailing out Europe during and after the first and second world wars. We are sorry that we so often behave like ungrateful children. When you act, we accuse you of acting and when you do not act, we accuse you of non-action. You can never get it right. We apologize for our inconsistency. We apologize for our envy. It's not easy to acknowledge our powerlessness in comparison with your strength. We applaud your wish to bring a better life to the rest of the world. You have a big heart. You like to act, while the rest of us are prone to sit around wringing our hands. We admire you for this trait. There are huge problems to be solved – global terrorism, poverty, and an endangered biosphere. We need you in our midst, and in action, engaged also in long-term strengthening and prevention not just in short-term strikes. We understand that right now you are finding it hard to find safety in patience. We know that until recently you were protected by two big oceans. But please, let September 11 teach you the lesson of global interdependence, a lesson that makes helping others in humility, without humiliation, more important than ever before. Let us together evoke the spirit of the Marshall Plan and the Mandela path. We promise to try to do the same with our national identities. Please learn to love planet Earth as much as you love America. Let us help you. Put down your arms and join the global village.

This book on honor, humiliation, and terror was written, not least, to provide a response to challenges like those coming from Kathleen. Just when this book was in its final stages, Donald J. Trump was elected to lead the United States, part of a wave of authoritarianism rising around the world. This is a much more significant topic than lone wolf terrorism, because world wars may loom. In my work, I have always warned that we were lucky that the humiliation inflicted by the globalization of so-called neoliberal policies had not yet found its Hitlers. It would be misguided and dangerous to dismiss Donald Trump now as nothing more than an "insane clown."[237] The German aristocratic elite was full of highly decorated and experienced diplomats, generals, and marshals, and they looked down on Hitler as "der Gefreite" (the corporal), in other words, as a man with a ridiculously low military rank; at a maximum, Hitler was "the demon" for them. They mistakenly believed they could instrumentalize and control this negligible clown with his demonic charisma. They overlooked that he was adored like a messiah, not just by men. Many German women had used their newly-won suffrage to vote themselves back into the biopolitical role of mothers of sons-to-be-warriors. The established elites overlooked that whatever calamity Hitler caused with his policies, he himself would never be held responsible by his admirers or have his reputation tarnished. Whatever happened, for his followers, he was a victim of sabotage by envious evil traitors and adversaries: "Wenn Hitler das wüsste" was the response whenever something went wrong, meaning: "if Hitler knew this, he would remedy it."

Hitler was firmly anchored in his time's *Zeitgeist* of what George Lakoff calls the *strict father* model of parenting.[238] Fred Trump taught his son Donald the same might-is-right philosophy that inspired also Hitler: to be a winner, to be a killer, in a world with nothing but winners and losers. The son Donald is caught in a parental trap similar to that of Hitler, who was close to his mother and in fierce opposition to and competition with a ruthless dominator as a father.[239] Fred Trump had brought his killer philosophy all the way from Germany and the fact that Donald's eldest brother broke down under its weight demonstrates its unforgivable fierceness.[240] The combination of Donald Trump's Scottish and Germans heritage may indeed combine "the instincts of a puritan" with "an insatiable imagination for conquest."[241] Hitler's government became a legal dictatorship, and it ended in its destruction, rather than in a Greater Germany. Still, this never caused Hitler to doubt his path. He was satisfied all the way to the end. As reported earlier, on November 27, 1941, Hitler said to the Danish foreign minister Scavenius and the Croat foreign minister Lorkowitsch: "I am also here ice cold. If the German people are no longer strong enough ... I will not shed a tear for the German people."

In this situation, any nonchalant arrogance from intellectuals or the so-called establishment is misplaced and dangerous. Radical respect is needed, and deep understanding for the dynamics of dignity, honor, and humiliation. A new worldview and purpose waits for America, including for all Americans who share Kathleen's perspective and who feel their honor restored by Donald J. Trump's leadership. What is waiting to be accomplished is the co-creation of a *decent* global village for all people and our planet.[242] We may begin with the advice of the 34th president of the United States, Dwight David Eisenhower, that is still relevant: "do something" about the military-industrial complex.[243] There is no need to replace former "crusades against communism" with endless "wars on terror."[244] Let's remember the message of peace activist and poet William Stafford, that "the wars we haven't had saved many lives."[245] The wars we will not have will save the world. Humankind possesses an amount of knowledge today that our forebears could only dream of, and we are in the advantageous situation, if we decide so, to co-create a future for humankind that is more dignified than it was ever before. We can take the best of America's devotion to freedom and merge it with the best of the rest of the planet's cultures'

accumulated wisdom. Cooperation and reconciliation between America and the rest of the world is crucial if the global village is to enjoy peace and prosperity for all its citizens. The United Stateshas the power to facilitate or delay the development of our global society toward a culture that nurtures the rights and potentials of all its citizens. We need the people and the government of the United States, together with all others in our planetary community, as we go about creating a decent global village.

Inspiring and Thought-Provoking Questions

for in depth reflection and research

"It takes a village to raise a child," and just now the global village fails this task. This is the most significant terror the world experiences.

– Evelin Lindner in 2017

There are no great discoveries and advances as long as there is an unhappy child on earth.

– Albert Einstein[1]

We need a dignity transition to exit from the security dilemma and to prevent and heal the dignity dilemma that arises when a divided world unites.

– Evelin Lindner in 2017

YES, "disconnection is today's great threat," and connection is our best protection! "Re-humiliation" has an impressive track record of recurring when we are invisibilized. I know some people think that we share a need for recognition. I think we have a need for dignity!

– Linda Hartling,
director of Human Dignity and Humiliation Studies[2]

Resentment is like drinking poison and then hoping it will kill your enemies!

– Nelson Mandela

Wage good conflict!

– Jean Baker Miller[3]

One path is well-worn, and it's scorched; the other is not well-worn, and it's green.

– Anishinaabee (Algonquin) prophecy
as interpreted by Winona LaDuke[4]

Although it is physically possible to save the biosphere and with it the human species, it is not, as things now stand, socially possible. Society is constrained by a socially constructed reality called economic reality and the economic reality is that human needs are met by a system that either runs on profit or does not run at all.

– Howard Richards[5]

Late modern society is systematically based on immunization against social relations and leads to the repression of social relations. The inability of individuals to acknowledge social relations has become the illness of the century (the endemic disease of self-referentiality). The absence of social relations "retaliates" by causing distress and disorientation for the self, which increasingly experiences isolation, poverty (in a vital sense), and a lack of support in everyday life. To emerge out of loneliness becomes an enormous enterprise – and often a hopeless one. When we become aware of all this, social change can begin.

– Pierpaolo Donati and Margaret S. Archer[6]

"Return of dignity": Now ends a mindset, where everything has a price and only the price decides about the value. Where values are only worthwhile if they can be calculated. Where politics are an evil that stands in the way of market justice. Where the market is not only seen as more efficient – it also is given more legitimacy than democracy. Therefore pure market was pure morality. This was the wretched economism.... But those who place human dignity at the center of their deliberations recognize that no person is always a benefit optimizer, and societies are no economic aggregates.

– Jakob Augstein[7]

What we do know, we do not know in a way that serves our needs. So, we need to know in different ways, and we need to build new knowledge through new ways of knowing. The new knowledge is in the area of designing new realities, which is likely to be done by speculative and creative thinking that would be communally shared and reflected for common formulation that would be tested in a continual process of social invention.

– Betty A. Reardon,
the "mother" of peace education[8]

We need a *dignity transition* if we want to exit from the security dilemma that held the world in its cruel iron grip for the past millennia, and while we work on that, we need to prevent and heal the *dignity dilemma* that arises when a divided world unites. What do I mean when I say that?

What do we do when society is dysfunctional? What do we do when the established meanings that constitute and regulate our society's institutions are also dysfunctional?[9] What do we do when we even lack words for what should be done? Can we still envision desirable and viable futures? Do we have values for the desirable, and theory for the viable?[10] Can we bring about humankind's better future?

This is what peace psychologist Michael Britton wrote to me in 2016:

Psychopaths are not good at building long-term life structure, often succeeding brilliantly right up to the point where their lives fall apart. We can expect no less of globalization. Having wrecked up an impressive string of successes, it has brought us to the edge of collective disaster: ecological catastrophe arising from the industrialization of everything possible, massive inequality arising from the capitalization of everything possible, and suppression of cooperative problem-solving through militarization on all fronts imaginable. Predatory institutional missions set loose legions of people on tasks that have stolen the better present we could be living in, and are now stealing the better future we might have hoped for.[11]

Peter Coleman and his colleagues were mentioned earlier. They went further than previous thinkers insofar as they view systems not just as static, but as dynamic.[12] The present-day dominator model that defines the world-system could be seen as an *attractor* in their model, an attractor that is both strong and wide. An attractor is a "package" of schemata, goals, attitudes, or dispositions of dominant mental and behavioral patterns.

In Figure 2, Coleman depicts attractor A as having a weak and wide basin, and attractor B a strong and narrow basin.[13] The ball represents the current state of a system and the two valleys represent two attractors for the system. A local energy minimum is achieved when the ball rests at the bottom of the valley.

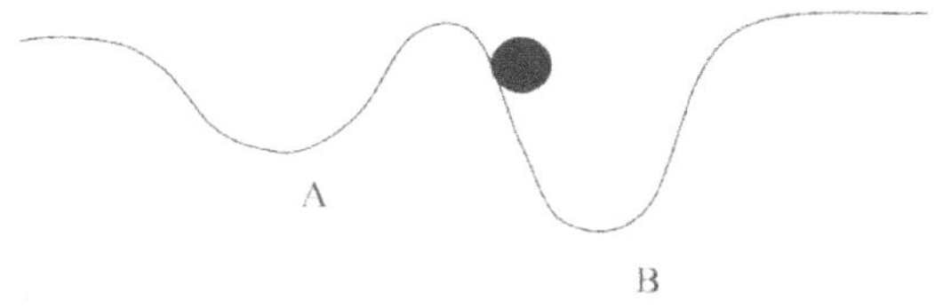

Figure 2: A dynamical system with two attractors

The width of the valley indicates the range of states that an attractor accommodates, and this may even include information and events that seem inconsistent with the attractor. The depth symbolizes the strength of resistance to change. When an attractor is strong and wide, it means that even the most wide-ranging and most striking information that contradicts it, will be assimilated in ways that reinforce it. To say it simplified, any gift of love from your enemy will be re-interpreted as poison, and even if your enemy warns you of imminent fire, you will not believe it, you will respond with what is called *reactive devaluation*.[14] In short, it is extremely difficult to move "the ball" out of a deep and wide valley into another attractor that might be waiting in latency. All this is a good description of humankind's present situation.

Peter Coleman and his colleagues developed their theory to shed more light on intractable conflicts, such as the Israeli-Palestinian conflict, and to explain how it is at all possible that seemingly absurd situations persist. A protracted malignant conflict betrays that a strong attractor with a wide basin of attraction is at work.

Now comes my question for you. Imagine, you are the peacemaker in a conflict and some of the adversaries seem very uninterested in solving the conflict. You sense that conflict is an end in itself for them, rather than a means to achieve something else. It seems that conflict is the solution for them, not the problem. What do you do in the face of a violent conflict that is prized as a chance to escape from a humiliating sense of powerlessness, for instance? Lewis Coser, a sociologist who had to flee Nazi Germany, asked questions like this. He differentiated between *realistic* and *un-realistic* conflict. An un-realistic conflict is a conflict that is an asset for its instigators, and they would not wish to have it taken from them by attempts to "solve" it.

What do you suggest should be done with such intractable conflicts? What should the world community do in the face of such intractable conflicts in their midst? Global challenges – from climate degradation to terror threats – need global cooperation to be attended to. A world torn apart by intractable conflicts is handicapped. When people are caught in cycles of humiliation, they will not cooperate. We can therefore not afford intractable conflicts and the diffusion of insecurity they cause.[15] What do you suggest?

And then, we have an even bigger conflict, a conflict that divides the entire world. The most significant intractable conflict of our time is the conflict between economic growth and planetary limits. It is fought out on one side by growth advocates who believe in human mastery over nature. They stand in opposition to others, those who warn that nature is stronger, that nature does not negotiate but simply acts, and that humble cooperation with nature is the only option: "... there is something outside society and it is nature, there is a natural reality that social reality depends on and must conform to, and when society's laws conflict with nature's laws, nature wins."[16]

In this dire situation, real science is of vital importance, while empiricist philosophies that misunderstand causal laws are treacherous.[17] Truth is not an obsolete idea; the view that truth is the correspondence of ideas with facts, *adaequatio rei et intellectus*, can be defended also today.[18] To do so, we do not have to go back to the old dualism of separating observer and observed, knower and known. We *know* because "we" are of the world: *onto-epistem-ology* is the study of practices of knowing-in-being, of "intra-actions."[19] Are you ready?

In the Introduction, I used the image of the Titanic. I call it "a ship of fools," when imminent catastrophe is overlooked because reality testing is being hampered through internal strife and enmity. The problem lies in our beliefs: we need them to understand the world and test reality, but we also need them to live with ourselves and with others.[20] The dominator model could be seen as a strong and wide attractor, which preserves everybody's sense of belonging, yet, at the price of sinking the ship.

My question to you: What can we do when worldwide ecological and social degradation, including the threat of terror, does not move the ball from an outdated and suicidal dominator world-system toward a partnership-based world-system that could offer a dignified future?

Is there a way out? Coleman says that a system with a strong attractor will resist change for a very long time. It will resist change by discounting or suppressing information or evidence outside of the basin of attraction until a great deal of such evidence has accumulated and a critical threshold of inconsistency is reached. Only at that tipping point will the system transform, and this will happen not incrementally, but in a catastrophic shift toward an attractor that is either new or was previously latent, one that provides new coherence for the perturbing information.[21]

Also philosopher Otto Neurath (1882 – 1945) used the metaphor of a ship. He explained that "we are like sailors who must rebuild their ship on the open sea, never able to dismantle it in dry-dock and to reconstruct it there out of the best materials."[22] In other words, we can no longer pretend that dry docks exist, or believe that science is something that has found a dry dock. Today, we understand that we must humbly accept and live with the fear-inducing uncertainty that our human understanding of the world is limited. There is no dry dock. What we may think of as certain will always be threatened by yet undiscovered insights and discoveries. The solution is to continuously rebuild the ship while at sea, always creating just enough structure to keep the ship afloat, but never too much rigidity that would create tipping points that cause the ship to break and sink. Stability is dynamic.

What do you answer when Leo Tolstoy asks: "What then must we do"?[23] What kinds of global futures could emerge from the turbulent changes shaping our world?[24] This is the core question asked by physicist Paul Raskin.[25] He considers three scenarios: *Conventional Worlds*, *Barbarization*, and *Great Transitions*. Conventional Worlds, or business-as-usual, is a utopian fantasy that is doomed to fail. Barbarization will be the result if the utopian fantasy is being blindly maintained and civilization descends into anarchy or tyranny. The only hope for humankind lies in bringing about a Great Transition. This means to "envision profound historical transformations in the fundamental values and organizing principles of society."[26]

Also critical theory sees three possible futures: *Future I*, the totally administered society, *Future II*, the entirely militarized society in chronic warfare, including illegal and immoral drone assassination attacks, and *Future III*, a society in which personal sovereignty and universal solidarity are reconciled. Future III represents a society of real freedom, freedom from all voluntary and involuntary enslavement, "a society, in which the religious and the secular, the sacred and the profane, revelation and enlightenment, as well as personal autonomy and universal, i.e. anamnestic, present and proleptic solidarity would be newly reconciled … a society, in which nature and spirit will no longer be commodified, but will be liberated, and will be allowed to be what they are in the process of their mutual mediation, reconciliation and liberation," in short, a society, where nature will be humanized and human beings will be naturalized.[27]

Are you a strategist? Albert Otto Hirschman is the author of several books on political economy and political ideology. In case one is dissatisfied with a situation, one can stay and seek change from within, which he terms *voice*. Or, one can leave, which he calls *exit*.[28] When an existing strategy is unsatisfactory, the voice would say: Let us do more of the same, let us do what we do, only better, let us optimize and maximize business-as-usual. Those speaking up for exit would recommend the opposite, namely, to do something completely new. I made Table 2 to illustrate the choices. Both choices can be appropriate or inappropriate, depending on the situation.

Let us take the current course of the world ship. Is it the happy course of a cruise ship, only a bit too slow, or is it the tragic course of a Titanic? Profit maximization, it seems, is a course that would better be taken off the steering wheel of our Titanic so that attempts to balance the entire system get a chance.[29] What is needed is not just less of the familiar business-as-usual strategy, but a thoroughly new course.[30]

It is different with what I call *big love*: What is needed in that case is more of the same, only better applied. Evidently, both transformations are interlinked in intricate ways. Firm love means doing something about shortsighted arrogant "heroism," firm loves rather stands for humble courage. Firm love is another word for making the effort of realistic self-evaluation, appropriate long-term preparation and implementation of the right kind of rules and institutional structures. It is not for the lazy to engage in the humble courage of truth-love or *satya*; it is not for the lazy to practice *philia*, Greek for love between friends; it is not for the lazy to nurture *agape*, Greek for gaping, as with wonder, or spiritual love for god and humankind. True heroism lies in *metta* (Pali) or *maitri*, Sanskrit for loving-kindness, friendliness, benevolence, amity, friendship, good will, sympathy, and active interest in others. It is an action plan to undo ten millennia of dominator culture and prepare for a dignified future.

	Appropriate for a situation		**Inappropriate for a situation**
More of the same	(1) When the essence of a strategy is appropriate for a given situation, its application has to be improved.		(2) It worsens the situation, if more of the same is applied where it is inappropriate.
		↖ ↘	
New approach	(3) When the essence of a strategy is inappropriate, a shift toward a qualitatively new approach is needed.		(4) It would be harmful to abandon an appropriate approach for a new and inappropriate one.

Table 2: When strategies fail

Be prepared: Whatever you think about the best course for world-society, you will be misunderstood and even vilified by the other side. For instance, if you think that a different course is needed, you will risk being misinterpreted as an enemy of what exists by those who work hard to maintain precisely that. Imagine, you are on the sinking Titanic, you see the iceberg approaching, and you call out: We must change course! You will be accused of fear-mongering, of mistrusting the fine crew who is steering the ship, and of insulting the fine engineers who built an unsinkable ship. How will you react?

What do you do when people misinterpret you? Let me share some of the misunderstandings I encounter on my global path. For instance, I regularly meet people who warn against equal dignity for all. They believe that it signifies equality, and that equality connotes that there are no differences, that all are forced to become identical copies of each other, be it that all are forced to be as poor as in North Korea, or that all are allowed to believe they deserve expensive sports cars.

Another field for misunderstandings is globalization and the fear of global dictatorship. Particularly in the United States, where freedom is often misinterpreted as the absence of human-made obstacles, the idea of creating an equal playing field through global governance is met with skepticism. What those skeptics overlook is that the absence of constraints opens space for might to become right, resulting in a vastly unequal playing field that victimizes all, particularly those at the bottom. To link back to the traffic metaphor in the Introduction, dismantling a government's traffic lights does not mean freedom. On the contrary, strongmen will set up their own lights. Just now, while I write these lines, the sense of victimhood among those who fell under the wheels of the strongmen's busses is recognized and misrecognized by presidential candidates in the United States from the left to the right side of the political spectrum.[31]

With respect to freedom, certain elements in the "T-treaty trinity,"[32] for instance, use the label of freedom, freedom for trade, to facilitate a corporate take-over that creates an uneven playing field. These treaties are now being criticized from both political poles, one inviting back into an imagined golden past, while the other invites into future-oriented solutions. President Donald J. Trump gained ground on the fear of those thrown under the bus,[33] the same strategy that authoritarians and extremists all over the world use to recruit followers of whatever ideological orientation – be it right-wing, left-wing, or religious.[34] He "picked up" those who are disappointed and hurt, and promises deliverance from dishonorable unfreedom by way of the traditional male master tool kit of honor for freedom of might to become right.

What is your position? I suspect that the problem is the security dilemma and that it has taught us all over too many millennia to accept a culture of might-is-right competition for domination. Within the classical security dilemma, whoever wishes for peace and security hopes to achieve it by way of a balance of power and military capability, and this leads to never-ending war. The newly arrived security dilemma of economics pits global and local elites against the rest with the promise of peace and well-being for all, and this leads to a limitless and disastrous exploitation of the world's social and ecological resources. While the administration of American President George W. Bush was embedded somewhat more in the classical security dilemma, incoming President Donald J. Trump appears to be more at home in the new one. Building a dominator society of military strength is the strategy in the first case, while in the second case, we meet terms such as "efficiency," "jobs," "making a living," "making money," "securing investor confidence," "wealth protection," "making deals," and "economic growth."

What if both of those manifestations of competition for domination create terror, either by design, or as side effect? What about the promise of peace and well-being? People around the world increasingly understand that many promises are empty, that those promises represent what sociologist Pierre Bourdieu calls *deferred elimination*.[35] Deferred elimination means that people are invited into exhausting themselves for a promise of a future that ultimately will be closed to them. Victims will only understand when it is too late that they have misrecognized the situation. People rightly ask now: How come that we live in a world where the recruitment and abuse of children by armed groups becomes increasingly endemic?[36] How come that the world has over forty-five million slaves, according to the 2016 study by the Global Slavery Index, including more than one million in Europe?[37]

American veterans are such victims of deferred elimination. First, they went to war, dedicated to serving their country, and then, after the Vietnam War, 60,000 veterans committed suicide, more than were killed during the war.[38] Twenty military veterans commit suicide per day in the U.S. now.[39]

Or, I had the privilege of being welcomed in South Africa in 2013,[40] and was saddened to see how long-lasting the detrimental effects of colonization and apartheid can be. Both colonization and apartheid made people ready for misrecognition. When a "successfully colonized mind" wishes to rise from oppression, great danger looms: the liberation may merely proceed from one layer of misrecognition to the next layer of misrecognition. Rising up from one layer of oppression merely to end up in the next layer of oppression is no liberation.[41] Have a look at Figure 3.

Figure 3: By Catherine Odora Hoppers, former holder of the South African Research Chair in Development Education at the University of South Africa in Pretoria/Tshwane

The crocodile's teeth symbolize the rampant destruction of social and ecological resources that is caused by present-day economic arrangements. They devour all involved, including those who believe that "bringing dialogue and peace" to local conflicts would be a good-enough solution. The supposed "need for dialogue" in local conflicts might even be a wish coming from the crocodile itself, as it would sometimes be easier to eat when every meal is bland and placid, calm and quiet, when the victims do not struggle too much. Or, the crocodile might also prefer victims who fight among each other – divide and eat. On May 29, 2013, Catherine Odora Hoppers shared this image with Howard Richards and me in Pretoria to highlight her message, namely, that we need to speak more about epistemology.[42]At the current point in human history, many layers of misrecognition must be shed, all around the world, to reach true liberation. If not, and this is my conclusion after forty years of global inquiry, a very special kind of deferred elimination may lay in waiting, namely, the elimination of humankind as a whole from its own habitat.

Are you a revolutionary? Do you wish to change the world for the better? Are you aware that you, as an idealist, may be successful in starting a revolution, however, that the betterment you may envision might have effects, or side effects, that are disastrous?

If your ideas for the future mean harking back to a golden age that never was, this is bound to fail. And even your best future-oriented ideas might end in creating yet another "Ozon hole." And even with the best of intentions, and even if you selflessly sacrifice all your energy for them, your revolution may be hijacked by power players who are not interested in your dreams at all. In short, you may end your life in bitter disappointment. What do you think, how can we all stop being victims of the *art of humiliation* and learn the *art of dignity*?[43]

Long unfinished revolutions cry out to be carried into the future in completely new ways now.[44] Napoléon Bonaparte turned the French Revolution's ideal of egality into its opposite when he crowned himself emperor. The 1917 February Revolution in Russia was carried by an enthusiastic spirit of liberation from oppression, then came

Vladimir Ilyich Lenin and turned it into an authoritarian October Revolution, only to leave the revolution to Joseph Stalin, an even more ruthless leader. Even the West was afflicted by this derailment of the revolution in Russia: Influential author Ayn Rand learned the wrong lessons from it, lessons she imported to America, which, eventually, even brought the Western economic system to its knees. Adolf Hitler is yet another example. He was initially welcomed by many as a savior, almost like a messiah. He believed in "das Recht des Stärkeren" (might is right), the right and duty of the strongest to dominate the rest. He enamored the hearts of people and abused their hopes for a better future so as to "democratically" hijack the system. Already as a child, I read the book *The Nights of the Long Knives*, which taught me how such hijacking works.[45] Also Iran's revolution in 1979 against an authoritarian rulership was originally set off by well-meaning students. Indeed, secular Iranians thought that Khomeini was only a figurehead, expecting that secular groups would take over power after the revolution.[46] Egypt's hopeful 2011 revolution has ended in military rule just now. In America, the Occupy Movement was first out in understanding that the democrats' embrace of neoliberalism was dangerous,[47] yet, its protest appeal was quickly outshone by Donald Trump.[48] Where will the Internet lead us? There we have yet another revolution that is vulnerable to being hijacked.

All around the world, many believe in might-is-right competition for domination also today, be it between races, nations, empires, or corporations. We observe this even in the smallest details. American presidential candidate Donald J. Trump, for instance, accused his rival Jeb Bush of having "no energy," in contrast to him, Trump, who describes himself as brimming with energy and as being surrounded by energetic people.[49] To illustrate what he meant by "energy," he told the story of his sons loving to kill exotic animals.[50] Also Trump himself prides himself of turning untouched nature into exclusive golf courses.[51] His energy is the energy of wanting to dominate, rather than the energy of nurturing and protecting. Economist Paul Krugman concludes: "Oligarchy, rule by the few, also tends to become rule by the monstrously self-centered. Narcisstocracy? Jerkigarchy? Anyway, it's an ugly spectacle."[52]

It is more than a spectacle. This spectacle forecloses society's most eminent task, namely, to manifest "the village that it takes to raise a child."[53] Which brings us to the topic of terrorism. The Kennedy family overcame the stigma of its Irish roots, it overcame it through ambition, culminating even in a presidency. A strong father figure, Joseph Kennedy, pushed his children not just to integrate into mainstream society, but to excel. Those who choose to become so-called foreign fighters for terror often have their father image destroyed, either that the father was absent or had humiliated the son, and it is in extremism they find solace and a new family.[54]

China-expert Jingyi Dong has been introduced before. In a personal communication on June 25, 2015, she wrote to me:

> Look at the early leaders of the Communist Party of China: Li Dazhao lost his parents before he was three years old and lost his grandparents when he was 15 years old; Chen Duxiu lost his father in childhood; Qu Qiubai's father was addicted to opium and his mother committed suicide to get rid of debt. Living in patriarchal communities, where females were marginalized, these boys lost shelter from the adult males in the family. Meanwhile, they did not get the paternal love that the community was obliged to offer. What would be the influence on their mindsets? These were unusually talented boys who would later become holders of rich academic capital and consequently participants of politics. What would they do when they grew up? Your theory can tell.

Famous Chinese writer Lu Xun (1881 – 1936), China's Shakespeare, was introduced earlier.[55] He is known for lamenting the humiliation caused by feudalism. Also he was a victim of humiliation himself after losing his father in his childhood.[56]

What can you do to nurture good parenthood throughout the global village so that it can raise its children and not lose them, and us all, to terror on people and nature? At the present juncture in human history, due to the coming-together of humanity on a shrinking planet, space opens to undo the dominator culture of the past millennia and create a future of global partnership. After millennia of domination/ submission, we can now rescue the *pristine pride* that presumably has characterized the first ninety-five percent of human history. By now, we would have to call it *equal dignity*, though, because we have lost the pristine pride that we might once have had, as it was mutilated throughout the past millennia by way of humiliation. Celebrating diversity through unity in equality in dignity is the new hoped-for future. To achieve it, parental love and care are needed. Are you ready to become a good parent for our world's children? Are you ready to save our future from drowning in terror?

How can you help children rise from humiliation without terror? So-called foreign fighters are often children who feel ashamed, humiliated, and furious when they see their parents meekly living lives at the bottom of society, lives of humiliation. A case in Rumania can illustrate what good parenthood can achieve. A young woman from Germany felt called to action when she saw extremely neglected Roma families in Rumania. She began by finding a way to nourish the children and bring them to school. This gained her the trust of the mothers. After a while, the young sons, after school, taught their fathers to become responsible members of their community, for instance, by building proper housing.[57] In other words, here were children who first learned to become critical of their parents' willingness to accept living in humiliation and then the children helped the parents to become what parents should be, namely, respected role models. This is what also foreign fighters often do at the outset; they attempt to rescue their parents' dignity by introducing into the home what they think is the "correct faith" – in the case of Islam, they may go as far as even rejecting commercial baked goods from their mothers for fear that they contain pork gelatin.[58] At this point comes our responsibility as society at large. If we say that such rules, let alone holy war, are no path to a life filled with respect, what can we offer as alternatives? Respectable jobs for the parents? In a society that is built on an economic model which systemically undermines its own promise? In a society that insinuates that a sense of personal worthiness should be derivable from a "job"? No wonder that children get disappointed when they see that their parents meekly accept their and their children's deferred elimination.

Modern humans emerged roughly 200,000 years ago on planet Earth. Since then, we have faced many challenges. Conditions of life have changed dramatically. We have survived as a species because we are adaptable. So far, our adaptation efforts were rather haphazard. To a large extent, we were puppets of our own history. Now, we find ourselves in a transitional phase similar to the one we began to traverse circa 12,000 years ago, a transition from a previous set of conditions to which we had adapted, to a radically new set of conditions. The first revolution about ten millennia ago evolved rather unsystematically, and this was inevitable, since our forebears did not yet have all the information about the world that we have today.[59] What are your ideas of how we can shape the new adaptation in constructive ways now?

Throughout the past millennia, good ideas had to "flee" to find space to flourish when they disturbed an established paradigm. When Constantinople was conquered by Ottoman Sultan Mehmed II in 1453, many Byzantine scholars fled to Europe and "seeded" the Enlightenment. Spain was intellectually impoverished when the Inquisition made its scholars leave. Anti-Semitism impoverished Germany, while the rest of the world benefited: not least present-day American universities are indebted to a strong Jewish legacy and its ongoing inspiration. What can you do so that today's good ideas are heard? In a globalizing world, there is less and less space left for people to seek refuge, people with ideas that disturb through being too innovative.

How can you contribute to intentionally co-creating a welcoming global context for good ideas? Today, we have an understanding of our planet's place in the cosmos that is much more comprehensive than that of our forebears, and we have the tools to shape our fate in purposeful ways. Today, we can sit together and reflect, we can act more deliberately and effectively than ever before in our history. Are you ready to sit with the rest of the world? The Humboldtian model of higher education of holistic *Bildung*, rather than mere *Ausbildung* (training), for instance, is still waiting to inspire the educational systems in the world.

Ours is a historically unprecedented situation that humankind is unprepared for, and many have not yet grasped its novelty. Anthropologist William Ury rightly points out that present historical times are unparalleled compared to any other period in human history: "For the first time since the origin of our species, humanity is in touch with itself."[60] Are you aware how revolutionarily new and unprecedented humankind's situation is now? Are you aware that history does not repeat itself now but is new?

I have coined the word *egalization* to match the word globalization and at the same time differentiate it from terms such as equality or equity.[61] The term egalization is short for equal dignity for all. It does not claim that everybody should become equal and that there should be no differences between people. Equal dignity can coexist with functional hierarchy as long as it regards all participants as equal in dignity; it cannot coexist, though, with a hierarchy that defines some people as lesser beings and others as higher beings. To give an example: The pilots in a plane are masters over their passengers when in the sky. Clear hierarchy and stark inequality characterize the situation. Still, the pilot team must not look down on their passengers as lesser beings.[62]

If we imagine the human world as a container with a height and a width, globalization addresses the horizontal dimension, the shrinking width. Egalization concerns the vertical dimension. Egalization is a process away from a very high container of masters at the top and underlings at the bottom, toward a flat container where all enjoy equal dignity as individuals in solidarity.

The horizontal line in the middle of Figure 4 represents the line of equal dignity in shared humility. It illustrates a worldview that resists essentializing and ranking secondary differences into differences at the core of human worthiness: the passengers in the plane may hold the "lowest" of jobs and sit in the cheapest economy class, yet, this is secondary; their essence as human beings is untouched, they are equal in dignity to the pilots. In other words, the middle line in Figure 4 does not signify that all human beings are equal, or should be equal, or ever were or will be equal, or identical, or all the same: There is no problem with people being diverse, there is no need for everybody to be the same, it is equal dignity that unites us.

Masters are invited to step down from arrogating more worth, and underlings are encouraged to rise up from humiliation, up from being held down and having lesser value ascribed to them. Masters are humbled and underlings elevated, and all are entrusted to co-create, together, a new future of equality in dignity for all, as individuals, in solidarity.

Are you part of a privileged elite who cries "foul" when asked to let go of arrogating superiority? Or are you a subordinate who believes that collectivist ranked honor is divinely ordained and that it is god's will, or your own sins of the past, that make you deserve the *karma* of being at the bottom? Or are you a depressed subordinate, cynical after hearing too much empty human rights rhetoric? Perhaps you once were an idealistic activist and now you are disappointed after having your idealism destroyed by the power structures that surround us all?[63] Or perhaps you are a revolutionary who wishes to rise up, as in old times, kill the tyrant and become the new despot? Or, are you willing to gather all of us together, as Nelson Mandela did, at the line of respect for equal dignity for all, all individuals in solidarity, as members in *one single united* human family?

No history lesson can help us now. Continuing with business-as-usual represents an impossible utopia. This have my forty years of global living taught me. Globalization – the coming together of all humankind – provides new opportunities for comparison also to people who formerly were isolated, and this turns *absolute* into *relative* deprivation for them. When coupled with the message of human rights, which deems relative deprivation to be illegitimate, all former justifications for inequality are removed, and rage and anger are free to rise.[64] In the language of dignity humiliation, it is humiliating to be shown the amenities of modern life in Western soap operas and to be invited into the family of equal human beings by human rights and freedom rhetoric, while simultaneously being deprived of those very amenities. Deprivation thus transmutes into humiliation, and humiliators may be sought out, who then become targets of revenge. This is what I call *cross over*: It starts with feelings of dignity humiliation, with all their historically unparalleled intensity, and it ends in honor humiliation's revenge strategies.

Are you working to remedy relative deprivation in the world? Do you wish for a more equal distribution of wealth for the world's population? This is a good idea. Yet, even the most equal material wealth distribution is not enough. Material wealth without respect for equal dignity can humiliate. Wealth without dignity can be felt like losing face, the face of honor and of dignity,[65] while, at the same time, providing the very means to express this disaffection. This is what early sociologist Alexis de Tocqueville has observed in 1856, when he said that the danger of revolution is greatest not when poverty is so severe that it causes apathy and despair, but when conditions have been improving, and, in particular, when a few are benefiting and not the rest.[66]

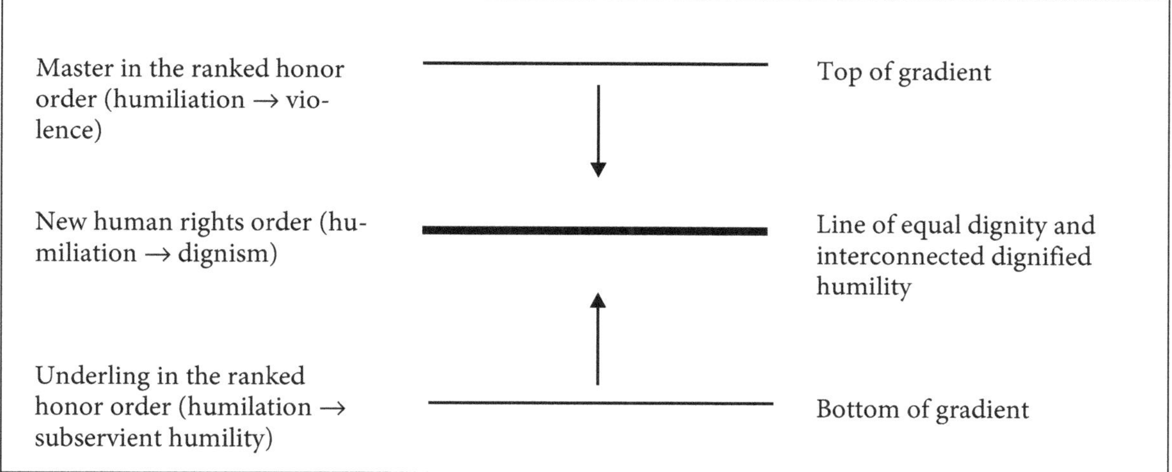

Figure 4: The historical transition to egalization

Erik Solheim was Minister of International Development in Norway, when our conversation took place in the Ministry of Foreign Affairs in Oslo, Norway, on January 10, 2011.[67] Now he is at the helm of UNEP, the United Nations' Environment Programme. Solheim recounted how a high Norwegian diplomat, an ambassador, once told him: "You must never humiliate anyone! You make enemies for life. Whatever you think about a person, never humiliating them!" What does it mean to humiliate anyone? Solheim's answer was that it varies from person to person and culture to culture, however, that the feeling is always the same, and that this is central. Solheim offered important examples of the role of humiliation and how it can be much more significant than material wealth:

> Apartheid was systemic humiliation. When Gandhi was not allowed to sit in the first class on the train, it was about humiliation, not the third class's poor conditions. He was not afraid of simple life, it was the humiliation that was at stake.
> Interestingly enough, the colonial period was perceived as humiliation at the end of the colonial era, at a point when those who had been colonized already were much better off,

> particularly in Africa (with China and India as exceptions, since they were already wealthier before).
> Tibet is another example. It would be much poorer without China. Tibet would be the poorest place in the region without China. Yet, it perceives it as humiliating to be "forced" into prosperity by China.[68]

"People can put up with poverty, but not with humiliation" is an analysis offered also for why we see a rise of deep discontent in the Western world.[69] It is a discontent which increasingly carries right-wing populists to power who exploit the growing fear, and the tunnel vision it causes, for offering simplified solutions that hazardously overlook what most needs skillful attention now: complexity.[70]

This discontent also feeds terrorism, which is yet another way to avoid complexity. Norbert Müller is a member of the board of Schura, a merger of mosque associations in Hamburg, Germany. In our conversation that took place in Hamburg, Germany, on October 22, 2010, he shared with me his views on how it was possible that highly educated young men from Hamburg set out to commit terror in New York on September 11, 2001:

> Those who came from Hamburg and participated in the 9/11 attacks in New York, were highly educated and academically successful. They did not experience social, but discursive humiliation. As academics, they had success, but as people of faith, they felt: "I can make a good career here, but only if I abrogate my heritage and my religion, for my Muslim identity is always degraded. There is a dominant culture here that is Western, and if I am living my religious identity, I experience condescension. I feel this disdain all the more, since I see myself as a successful graduate." In this way, humiliation is amplified: "I expect recognition and respect, but experience degradation": this is psychologically disparaging.[71]

Can you defend complexity when simplified solutions are presented to you? In 2016, what would you have said to those critics who wished for American President Obama to be more bellicose and deploy U.S. troops on a large scale to retake territory in Iraq or Syria?[72] What do you say to current attempts from the new American presidency to present the world as a place where "good" has to fight "evil"?

Do you have a clear conscience in life? Should you have a clear conscience? How do you conduct your life? I assume you do not harm anybody, at least not that you know of, and the politicians of this world carry the responsibility for the big decisions, not you. Still, you might be much more responsible than you think. Perhaps you close your eyes a bit too much? I continuously catch myself wanting to close my eyes.

There are many ways in which one can close one's eyes. For instance, by letting false choices crowd out important choices. Do you allow incidents of open violence, such as mass shootings or terror bombings, consume all your attention? Do you allow them to misrecognize the larger context?

We live in a world of competition for domination. Sometimes domination is openly brutal, but it is also built into our institutions as part of our "normality." Structures are background factors almost like forces of nature. The structures we live in at the current point in history fail to evoke genuine empathy with people who live far away from us, both geographically and in time, and they fail to motivate us to be the integral part of nature that we are, not its master.

Did you ever think about the fact that our entire *world-system*[73] is built on ancient Roman law principles?[74] They underlie both "communism" and "capitalism," and they cause structural violence no matter in which system. As philosopher Howard Richards has taught us, Roman law makes us believe that, if there is no contract, there is no responsibility. In other words, as soon as you have internalized Roman law principles, you may abrogate responsibility where it is needed. You may say: "This is not my responsibility! I have no written contract with coming generations! And I also have no contract with nature!" In other words, your sense of responsibility is systemically undermined.[75]

Structural violence transcends notions such as intention or guilt, because at the surface, there are no conflicts, no actors and no goals.[76] As for a way out, the focus must therefore be on the consequences, on the harm, the trauma, and the suffering. The focus must shift from guilt to responsibility. Altogether, the focus must shift away from post-hoc punishment to restorative justice,[77] to caring and thoughtful conflict transformation,[78] and, most importantly, to radical prevention. That is the main point of this book.[79]

It may therefore be within your responsibility to prevent or remove negative consequences which you have not caused and for which you feel no personal guilt. "The principle of precaution and prevention, and responsibility to prevent and forestall harmful consequences, applies irrespective of who exactly are 'to blame.'"[80] It is peace researcher Vidar Vambheim, from the periphery of this world, from the north of Norway, who calls out. Perhaps you, too, are part of the periphery, be it geographically or socially? Please speak up! Often solutions come from the periphery, not from the centers of power – alternative and dignifying solutions often remain hidden in the peripheries of power centers.[81] Please do everything to strengthen periphery-to-periphery contact, in reverence to anthropologist Clifford Geertz's interest in local-to-local connections.[82] Follow the example of Ta-Nehisi Coates, an African-American author, who now teaches the "Dreamers," as he calls those "people who believe themselves to be white," how it feels to live in a black body.[83] You are the child who has to call out when you see that the emperor has no clothes!

Perhaps Ta-Nehisi Coates has read sociologist Zygmunt Baumann, who finds hope in the most sensitive of our sense organs, our eyes and ears. When we see or hear others suffer, we hesitate to use violence, more than when we read about their suffering. Even learning about the personal experiences of others though movies, literature, art, and social and mass media can bring us closer. Also philosopher Emmanuel Lévinas finds hope in face-to-face encounters that put us in the presence of the Other and create an ethical climate of concern and responsibility that is different from that created by social structures.[84]

In other words, proximity matters. This is why I call on you to become a *global citizen of care* so that you can help create a global village that can raise its children.[85] You will enjoy being inspired by people like historian of science Andrew Pickering and his imaginative model of open-ended experimentation in the place of domination over nature and each other.[86] Or pay Vidar Vambheim a visit in Tromsø in the far north or Norway and learn from him about social network analysis, and how this analysis "can reveal violence that is inherent in social structures, rather than violence as a secondary consequence or side effect of such structures."[87] Thinking in terms of social networks can make it easier for us to see how we can have an impact in our micro environment.

Vambheim wrote about bullying and terrorism. I assume you do not participate in bullying in your direct social environment, nor do you engage in bellicose posturing on the global stage? What are you then? Are you a bystander? Bystanders usually do not consider themselves to be participants. Yet, victims often think otherwise. For them, passivity among bystanders easily feels like a signal of support for the bullies: "practically and morally bystanders are not neutral."[88] Social psychologist Ervin Staub has warned us already many years ago: The Holocaust was only possible because people stood by, rather than standing up.[89] On my part, I try to stand up, while being painfully aware that I can never stand up enough.

What can we do to stand up? Many things. Cristina Escrigas of the Global University Network for Innovation calls for five deep changes, for instance, in Higher Education: from *monoculture* to an *ecology* of knowledge, from *description* to *intervention*, from *fragmentation* to *holism*, from *individualistic* to *social* co-creation of knowledge, and from *stasis* to *dynamism*.[90]

A hierarchy of effectiveness may look like this, suggests creative thinker Wayne Visser:

- lowest impact: traditional lecturing (passing on knowledge, etc.)
- medium impact: participative instruction (lots of group work, etc.)
- higher impact: applied learning (real-life cases, work-related assignments, etc.)

- highest impact: experiential learning (disruptive contexts, out-of-comfort zone exercises, etc.)[91]

It is only the latter approach that can achieve paradigm shifts, or "Damascus-type" revelations, or "ah-ha" moments, moments that bring real change in how we see the world and how we take action. It means confronting learners with challenges. For example, if you live a privileged life, why don't you spend a week in a favela, or a tropical rainforest, or a refugee camp? Go into the prisons of this world as a global citizen of care, rather than sending people into prison as a global citizen of exploitation.

Christopher McMaster wrote a doctoral dissertation to help transform the educational system in New Zealand. He is envious of Finland that has consistently demonstrated high standards.[92] "In contrast to neoliberal educational models, in Finland there are no private schools; educational administrators are required to have been teachers; there is no standardized testing except a matriculation examination at the end of school; there is trust in teachers to choose their own methods and materials; and teaching is seen as a respected profession."[93] So, what is Finland's secret? It is this: cooperation over competition and refusing to reduce education to a market.[94] Pasi Sahlberg of the Finnish Ministry of Education and Culture is proud that "systematically focusing on teacher and leader professionalism, building trust between the society and its schools, and investing in educational equity rather than competition, choice, and other market-based reforms make Finnish schools an international model of success."[95]

Would you like to help transform the educational system? Would you like to offer, for instance, peace education programs that aim to increase empathy by "fostering more universal feelings of connection and similarity with all humankind"?[96] Would you like to offer those programs to vulnerable youths to help them regulate their emotions better and avoid being enamored by violence and terror? You will be in for a distressing disappointment. Social psychologists Baruch Nevo and Iris Brem found that peace programs that address youths of thirteen to fifteen years tend to be unsuccessful.[97] Adolescents seem to dislike peace talk, despite the fact that they are the most in need to hear it, and the most vulnerable to be recruited by terror entrepreneurs.[98] In other words, those most in need to listen, are reachable the least. Their brains are in the midst of major modifications, as most people do not reach their full brain capacity until the age twenty-five.[99] This comes in addition to general human intelligence seemingly declining since the Victorian age or even longer, particularly so since 1998, when a short period in which IQs had increased ended.[100] What can be done? What do you suggest?

Those young people, in all of their vulnerability, what do you suggest, society should do with them? The answer is: they have to be held by their social surroundings. Many youths may not be able to contain themselves, and their surroundings must shoulder this responsibility. The proverbial village must step in and hold and raise these youths. "All kids are our kids."[101] For a world free of terrorism, it is the global village who is responsible for all the world's children and youth.

Not only young people need to be held. Mutual connection is a life-giving necessity for all of us.[102] To realize this, the global community has to re-design the foundational *generative mechanisms*,[103] and *constitutive rules*[104] of our currently existing world-system, away from competition for domination toward a partnership model of society. All other interventions, as well-intentioned as they may be, will fail to cure the symptoms in the long term.

But what if the fabric of the village is systemically weakened? What if alongside the ecological resources of the planet also the social resources are squeezed thin?[105] Do you feel responsible? Or do you think that you have no contract with those youths, nor with the global village? What do you contribute to creating a global village that can hold its children? Do you sit in your cabin on the luxury floor of Titanic and think that you have no obligation to care for the rest? What do you contribute so the ship can stay afloat?[106]

Would it help if women got all power? First, also many women in power adopt the traditional script for masculinity.[107] It is not the women, but the female script of care that promises dignity in an interconnected world.[108] Much is already happening. UNESCO's Culture of Peace Programme urges the strengthening of the "female" aspect in conflict resolution efforts. The list of potential female contributions is a long one[109]: Using multi-track, "track II," and citizen-based diplomacy; installing early warning institutions; rethinking the notion of state sovereignty; setting up projects to study and understand the history of potential conflict areas, collecting this information, and making it available to decision makers; using psychology at a macro level, taking identity as a bridge; keeping communication going between warring parties; talking behind the scenes; including average people alongside the warlords in peace negotiations; developing conflict-resolution teams with less hierarchy and more creativity; setting up mediation teams; installing "truth commissions"; allowing warring parties to feel the world community's care, respect, and concern; taking opponents in a conflict out of their usual environment; taking the adversaries' personal feelings and emotions seriously; recognizing the importance of human dignity; introducing sustainable long-term approaches at the social and ecological level; progressing from spending aid money after a disaster to allocating resources to prevent it; and so on.

Yet, also "female forms of power" carry risks. Vidar Vambheim has examined the ways girls engage in bullying: it is through indirect aggression and network bullying. He warns that if this would become "a way of gaining and keeping power, also in politics and work-life, we must be able to understand its causal mechanisms, recognize its expressions, and prevent its consequences."[110]

Still, more women are needed to stand up. In the last chapter of my book on gender, I recommend women of my age, those who have had a chance to hone their capabilities, to shoulder their responsibility for the global family. Please help us heed research results that show that society may fare best with collectives of peacemaking women as main stewards of resources and containers of potential male aggressiveness.[111] Norwegian women now urge: Why is there no Department of Peace in all governments around the world, why is there only a Department of Defense?[112]

What would be the most important intervention you and me, and our societies now could envision? It would be to leave behind the dominator model and embrace the partnership model of society. It would be to leave behind all mindsets of collectivistic ranked honor and liberate each single individual from behind the mask of honor. It would mean to bestow equal dignity to every single human being and to do so in practice, not just in theory, thus fulfilling the promise that human rights ideals represent. In this way we can become responsible world citizens who, in solidarity, care for each other and our planet. In this way we can stop acting as "excellent sheep."[113]

Let me explain. On November 7, 2015, I saw the opera *Turandot*, by Giacomo Puccini.[114] This opera throws the transition from masklike honor to less masklike dignity into stark contrast. Playwright Carlo Osvaldo Goldoni (1707 – 1793) was inspired by the humanist movement and the study of philosophy. His plays promote rationality, civility, and humanism, critiquing arrogance, intolerance, and the abuse of power. He was a man of deep insights into the human psyche and used these insights to turn them, among others, against elite arrogance. In 1765, he became a tutor at the court of Versailles and a small state pension was paid to him by the Royal Civil List. This ended, though, in 1792, after the French revolution had broken out. Interestingly, the National Convention, the assembly that governed France during the most critical period of the French Revolution, voted to restore his pension, even though, sadly, only the day after his death. Still, this decision underscored Gondoli's achievement of democratizing elite culture: here was someone, who first was recognized and remunerated by the royal court and then by the people. He brought culture out from its reserve for elites and democratized it, just like the notion of humiliation was democratized at about the same time.

In 1757, in the English language, *to humiliate*, for the first time, connoted the violation of the dignity of an individual. Before 1757, only aristocrats were allowed to view humiliation as a violation. Aristocrats could go to duel to defend their honor against humiliation, while a beaten wife could not go to duel against her husband. For subordinates there was only one way to go from humiliation, namely, further down, into even meeker humility. The beaten wife had to swallow humiliation as a "lesson" to keep her from arrogance and make her "know" her lowly place. Since 1757, the *Zeitgeist* allows something new, it allows also the beaten underling to resist humiliation. Gondoli's work was thus part of the journey of the notion of human worthiness out from behind masklike collectivist ranked honor, first toward the ranked *decorum* of individuals, to finally reach the un-ranking of worthiness altogether, as enshrined in the human rights ideals. These ideals mark the final liberation of the individual from behind her mask, now being awarded equal dignity.[115]

What does it mean to liberate the individual from behind her collectivist mask of honor? During our 27th Dignity Conference in Dubrovnik in 2016, I became aware that trading communities like Venice and Dubrovnik were among the first to abolish the trade of slaves, as far back as the fifteenth century.[116] Slaves were still kept in private homes for *pro usu suo*, Latin "for one one's own use," yet, slaves could no longer be traded. It seems that ethical motives had become stronger than traders' profit motives.[117] Now, we still need to walk that path.

There are many other paths. Apology, for instance. The world is full of examples where apology and atonement is still waiting to happen, so that perpetrators, victims, and bystanders can claim or reclaim their very personal dignity. The Indonesian genocide 1965 and 1966 may serve as illustration. In this genocide, between 500,000 to one million people were killed, suspected of being Communists. This atrocity is not only not yet acknowledged, it still is being hailed, and most surviving victims cower and hide.[118] Also the West has so far failed to acknowledge their role.[119]

Are you a Nelson Mandela? This is wonderful! Yet, you alone cannot "save the world." Does that mean you can do nothing? Margaret Mead said: "Never doubt that a small group of thoughtful, committed citizens can change the world. Indeed, it is the only thing that ever has."

What should such a group do? "At present there are many good people and groups trying to do things too separately," warns Frederick Trainer, expert on sustainability and justice.[120] Many green people are working heroically to save the whale, others work hard on justice projects: "many good groups do not realize well enough that we have to think in terms of a form of satisfactory society in which we can all live well on a tiny fraction of present rich world per capita resource use."[121]

Other groups work on converting the world to dogmatic religious or ideological creeds, these are the *traditionals* that Paul Ray and Sherry Anderson described. Others are more forward-looking, they are the *cultural creatives*. Some of them believe that meditation and self-improvement is the best way, while others demonstrate in the streets.[122] Where do you stand?

As for me, I wish to build bridges between all groups and trends. Traditionals can help preserve the dignifying elements from all human cultures that ever existed, and all of us can meditate and then go out into the streets together. I resonate with Howard Richards' call: "Economics and law as we know them ought to be bracketed in parentheses, while the human family rethinks its relationships to each other and to the earth."[123]

What should we do out in the street? I have a sense that jointly envisioning new societal frames, new *generative mechanisms*,[124] new *constitutive rules*,[125] would be a good idea, and then testing them out patiently and carefully (rather than trying out something and then needing bloody revolutions to undo it). Why do I think that meditation is not enough and that societal frames need our attention? Because they have more impact than personal proclivities. Many experiments in social psychology underpin this insight. When students who played the prisoner's dilemma game were told that this was a community game, they cooperated; they cheated on each other when told that it was a Wall Street game.[126] When students tried to predict what other players would do in the next round, their predictions went wrong when they assumed that personal inclinations drove their decisions and overlooked the frames.[127] It is important to know, if we want to create a better world, that our behavior depends more on frames than on our personal inclinations.

This means that we have to frame our societies in ways that prosocial tendencies are nurtured systemically, rather than waiting for the few Mandelas to rescue us. Reciprocity theorist Alejandro Guala confirms that "the important levers for policy purposes lie outside the psychology of individuals, in the social structures that sustain and guide people's decisions in different circumstances. Less individual psychology and more social science, in a nutshell, would be my slogan for future research."[128] Even though humans are psychologically unselfish, while being biologically selfish,[129] individual prosocial tendencies cannot be taken for granted and must be systemically supported and nurtured.

How can the global village become a community village rather than a Wall Street village? Profound global systemic change is needed,[130] or what physicist Paul Raskin calls a Great Transition,[131] and this transition can only succeed with "a systemic transformation from a market-centric to a commons-centric form."[132]

Rather than engaging in war, could we simply "police" the inner affairs of our global village? Or do we have a psychological need for enemies? What do you say to politicians who, to be elected, stoke enmity and pinpoint enemies? Do you tell them that feeding on people's sense of victimhood and inferiority is dangerous? That holding on to *chosen traumas* is hazardous?[133] Do you tell them that addiction to humiliation can be suicidal?[134]

What do you say when you are asked to fight against enemies? Perhaps you could let politicians know that fighting enemies maintains want it wants to overcome, namely, enmity in the world? Let them know that there are alternative pathways. Invite them to join in with us in building trust rather than undermining it. The simple fact of *fighting against* – against something or somebody – maintains a culture of division and competition for domination. It is inherently impossible to even be a "warrior for peace." Warriorship always carries the seed of domination. *Warrior* is no longer a suitable figure of speech for the modern hero: now it is the *gardener* who is the hero.[135] I try to avoid any *anti-* and *non-* terminology, including that of nonviolence or nonkilling.[136]

Perhaps you cry out now: But bad people deserve to be called *enemies*! And enemies have to be fought! It is the globalization process itself that undermines the notion of enemy, and this proceeds even in the face of your or my resistance. The word enemy, together with related words such as *war*, *soldier*, and *victory*, does not disappear because some soft-hearted dreamers wish it. These words are losing their meaning because they no longer describe reality. When a tree dies, it bears no more fruit. Likewise, the reality that bore words such as enemy, war, and victory, is currently being undercut by globalization, whether we support this development or not.[137]

What kind of language do you use when you speak? Discourses help to construct "a social reality that is taken for granted and that advantages some participants at the expense of others."[138] Culture encodes what words mean, and discourses generate, alter, and transmit them. "Discourses include systems of categorization, metaphors, narratives, frames, and other interpretive devices that can influence cognition, perception, and action."[139] *Interpretive frames*,[140] or *normative paradigms*,"[141] are a form of *conceptual scaffolding* that we rely on to construct our understanding of the world.[142] Our attention must go to the *legitimizing myths* (Pratto) that underpin the dominant discourses that produce and reproduce power dynamics, that underpin *governmentality* (Bourdieu).[143]

Wherever and whenever the security dilemma is strong, it is an all-definitorial frame for all people in its reach. It forces the terminology of honor, enemy, revenge, war, and victory to the fore. Nobody can escape it. Now I ask you: Can this frame be changed?[144] My answer: Yes, it can. Intentionally guided globalization can bring change. At the current point in time, globalization is left to its own devices and haphazardly either attenuates or stokes enmity. We, as humankind, you, we together, can intentionally make use of globalization to attenuate the security dilemma. We can create global trust. We can create frames that make us play a global community game.

How can we do that? The highest hurdle are those people who refuse and reject this idea. It may be worth learning from martial arts. These are the five levels of the martial arts[145]:

- Lowest level: If someone comes to you with ill will and the decision to attack you, you have to subdue them with physical force. But there is no security, because they will come back with their friends and overwhelm you.
- Someone comes to you with ill will, but there is something about you that keeps them from attacking. So you have subdued them without needing to use physical force. But there is no security, because they will come back with their friends and overwhelm you.
- Someone comes to you with ill will, but there is something about you that makes them want to speak with you first. And as you are speaking, gradually, together, you find common ground. So, you have both been subdued and there is some security.
- Someone comes to you with ill will, but you know yourself so well and you are so calm, you are invisible. They do not even see you as a target. They walk past you.
- Someone comes to you with ill will. You are so filled with the wisdom of the world – Li Young Li called it the dao – that you walk through the world strewing beautiful ideas, beautiful songs. You just strew beauty, you do not know whether it is coming from you or through you into the world. The only way to achieve the fifth level is through the practice of poetry and painting.

What is appropriate *Realpolitik* for our contemporary world? Appropriate Realpolitik, as I see it, means embarking on the very visionary "idealism" that formerly was denigrated as "unrealistic." For the first time in human history, self-interest now converges with global common interest. Nobody can survive alone on the globe, let alone in opposition to others. It becomes the interest of all to join hands in cooperation among equals to solve our global social and ecological crises. Ideals of solidarity and equality in dignity and rights represent the only normative framework that is suited for an emerging globally interconnected knowledge society. The human rights ideal of equal dignity for all entails a promise that is higher than the promise of the traditional honor order, both for each individual and for society. The promise of unity in diversity is higher than that of division without unity.

Unity in diversity is the very frame within which dignity can flourish. And unity in diversity can be operationalized through the principle of *constrained pluralism*, comprising three complementary sub-principles: *irreducibility*, *subsidiarity*, and *heterogeneity*:

> Irreducibility affirms One World: the adjudication of certain issues necessarily and properly is retained at the global level of governance. Subsidiarity asserts the centrality of Many Places: the scope of irreducible global authority is sharply limited and decision-making is guided to the most local level feasible. Heterogeneity grants regions the right to pursue forms of social evolution consonant with democratically determined values and traditions, constrained only by their obligation to conform to globally mandated responsibilities.[146]

The European Union, for instance, uses the subsidiarity principle.[147] It means that local decision-making and local identities are retained to the greatest extent possible, while allowing for national, regional, and also international decision-making when needed. Subsidiarity, to succeed, requires continuous skillful calibration of the interactions between all levels, since too much centralization is as destructive as too much locally sovereign division. Also governance systems for large-scale environmental problems can only be effective through such nested layers.[148]

This is why the argument of small government versus big government is a false choice. Somalia's government is too small, while North Korea's is too big: the solution is neither *too much* nor *too little* government, but *good* governance.[149] And good governance means heeding the subsidiarity principle, and this is as valid for global governance.[150]

Maintaining unity in diversity is a balancing act that requires a high degree of cognitive sophistication, interpersonal sagacity, and dignifying communication skills. Most people think that unity in diversity is a zero-sum game and that if one wants more unity, one has to sacrifice diversity, and vice versa, and therefore they think in dualities: "cosmopolitanism versus communalism, statism versus anarchism, and top-down versus bottom-up."[151] There seems to be a very high mental hurdle that keeps many from grasping that unity in diversity is *not* a zero-sum game, on the contrary, that both unity and diversity can be increased together, and that the benefits are immeasurable. The two prongs of unity and diversity, global responsibility and regional autonomy, are both essential and complementary. Linda Hartling's mentor, pioneer in women's psychology Jean Baker Miller, speaks of *waging good conflict*, for which *zest of life* will be the reward.[152]

Are you ready to learn the skills of keeping unity in diversity in continuous balance? Cognitive scientist Bruce Schuman is convinced that if humankind is to succeed in the radical transition that is called for now, then the core challenge is to accept that there is this "foundational tension between 'Many' and 'One.'" This tension has endless implications in a form that is essentially mathematical – the term *versus* is always a signal – and they extend "across the entire range of human thinking."[153] It is not enough, however, to merely transcend dualities. We also have to embrace processual thinking: no longer clinging to fixities but moving in flux. The tension between Many and One must be balanced by all players in a never-ending process, it can never be made permanent once and for all.

The human rights revolution is part of it, since dominators will always attempt to remove the respect for equality in dignity that makes unity in diversity possible, they will always want to replace it with oppressive uniformity without unity and division instead of diversity. It is a never-ending *refolution* (a term coined by Timothy Garton Ash to connote a mix of reform and revolution). Which means that societal systems need to be created, and dignifying communication skills learned, which allow for fluid adaptations of this balance, adaptation mechanisms that make violence redundant. It means moving away from a world that clings to illusions of fixity. It means leaving behind a world where violent protests often were the only way out when failing systems refused to go.

Scandinavia can serve as an interesting historical lesson. Why is Norway the "happiest" country in the world in 2017?[154] Because they applied a *Fabian strategy*,[155] or what philosopher Karl Popper called *piecemeal social engineering*,[156] which means largely refraining from rigid dogmatisms, rather allowing ideology to unfold through being enmeshed into political processes.[157]

Are you ready? As I asked previously: Did our ancestors see pictures of our Blue Planet from the perspective of an astronaut?[158] Did our grandparents have access to the comprehensive knowledge base about the universe and our place in it that we have? For the first time, humankind can manifest the fact that we are *one single* family. Are you ready to contribute to this effort, and can you do so lovingly, despite of all the backlashes?

Are you a creative person? Creativity is sorely needed if humankind is to address its global challenges intelligently. Now is the time to create superordinate goals that can bring humanity together, goals that manifest *dignism*. It is the time to humanize globalization by merging globalization with egalization and form *globegalization*. It is time to bring *liberté*, *égalité*, *fraternité*, or *solidarité*, together into co-globegalization.[159]

Creativity can flow from our human talents and skills and how they were inspired by the diversity of human cultures throughout history. "Harvesting" our collective human wisdom from all cultures can succeed better now than ever before. Globalization can aid us. However, only if equal dignity is nurtured so as to prevent feelings of humiliation from turning benign opportunities malign. Peace psychologist Michael Britton recommends we pay attention, for instance, to the indigenous Sylix in the west of Canada: They can teach us deep listening, and they can remind us that each community has the moral responsibility to do so.[160] Incidentally, this is also the moral responsibility of the entire global village.

Why must feelings of humiliation be prevented, at least as much as is humanly possible? Why must those feelings be attended to and healed, at a minimum mitigated, even if they are utterly "irrational," and even if they are cynically stoked? Here terrorism enters. *Tikkun* editor Peter Gabel wrote in a personal message: "humiliation is the root of all evil ... it is the foundation for the very structure of the alienated self, how we develop a false outer self to protect our being against the anticipation of humiliation due to non-recognition of our essential humanity."[161] In an article titled "Humiliation Is the Root of All Terrorism," Gabel explained that "longing and vulnerability when met with non-recognition leads to humiliation, which leads to substitute imaginary visions that resolve the pain of non-recognition through prideful grandiosity, perfect unity, and dehumanization of those who dehumanized you."[162]

Gabel offers a two-pronged strategy to meet terrorist attacks. First, short-term efforts must protect public places, and do so in suitable ways. Second, and most importantly, the sympathizers who make it possible for violent actors to function need to be approached and offered an "alternative ideology":

> In today's world, some sectors of the world's population have spent decades or perhaps centuries impoverished and demeaned by the world's dominant groups. Although these dominant groups have themselves acted, often unconsciously, out of fear of the other, accumulating wealth and power to protect themselves against others and displacing that process of self-aggrandizement onto the supposedly neutral effects of a globalized economic market, they have in so doing created pockets of humiliation, in which whole communities and peoples have experienced life as discarded, unseen, uncared about, and often on the verge of starvation. This is true of whole sectors of the Middle East, where the rooted lives of whole communities of people were destroyed and demeaned by, for example the imperialist carving up of the region by Western powers following World War I, by the imposition upon them of inauthentic puppet governments, by the rise of internal dictatorships resulting from the hierarchical and alienating distortions of these earlier interventions.
> Furthermore, to the extent that members of these humiliated communities have sought escape in Western countries, they have often found themselves ghettoized and disappointed, in a sense re-humiliated refugees who were thrown into supposedly "free" societies, but where there was no plan for integrating them as fully human and for connecting them with others in a way that would have provided for them a sense of recognition, of being seen and embraced.
> Against this background of profound and diffuse non-recognition and humiliation, it is not surprising that people from these marginalized and demeaned communities would be drawn to narrative interpretations of the world that would address and explain their humiliation and offer a way out, however pathological, however much such interpretations may involve substituting for their experience of humiliation an imaginary vision of the world that can seem to restore each person's sense of recognition and value, channel the rage resulting from the long legacy of collective humiliation into purifying violence, and bring into imaginary being the "perfect" society that once existed until being destroyed and defiled by "unbelievers," by those who might prevent the vision from being realized by denying or opposing it.[163]

When terrorists engage in mass murder, Gabel warns, they seek to reverse the dehumanization that was done to them. They do so by dehumanizing their imagined oppressors, and at the same time, they seek to bring about the redemption of an imaginary world in which they will become healed, recognized, and finally included and loved as they hoped they would be from their earliest days. Gabel concludes by saying:

> We should begin to relate to these humiliated populations of the world as we always should have, with empathy and compassion and generosity and care. We should see them as our fellow human beings and offer them the recognition and affirmation and respect that they were always entitled to, but which has been systematically and often ruthlessly denied to them for decades, or even centuries, from the Crusades to World War I to the Iraq War to the present-day exploitation for our benefit of their oil reserves. In repair of disrupting, destroying

and demeaning their historical communities, we should enter into present community with them.[164]

How do we save the world, not just from terrorism, but also from the fascism that is looming larger in 2017 than just one year earlier? Howard Richards walks with us through the steps: At the basis of the cultural structure of modernity is the civil law that organizes exchange in markets, with "the juridical subject who owns property, at least property in the form of her own labor-power, and engages in buying and selling (in contracts)."[165] The result is what Mahatma Gandhi called *adharma* – the absence of *dharma*, the absence of what holds us, the absence of what maintains and keeps us. Richards calls it *individualism*, Peter Drucker, the "founder of modern management," calls it the *economic man*. The kind of society that is engendered in this way excludes many of its members per design. Richards admonishes us: We simply have to acknowledge that modernity was "badly designed." It was designed on the false assumption that "the by-products that meet needs would always be produced by a system whose deliberate product was profit."[166]

The solution is to build a society whose core goal is to work for everybody directly, rather than hoping it to be a by-product of something else. Richards: "When inclusion with dignity is the goal, it is quickly seen that there are many ways to get there, but that continuing with the status quo is not one of them." For culture to be inclusive, and in resonance with ecology, Richards recommends Bronislaw Malinowski's functional anthropology that regards cultures as more or less successful responses to physical imperatives.[167] And he advises to follow philosopher John Dewey in treating institutions as *hypotheses* rather than reifying them into *fixed givens*.[168] Social psychologist David Bargal advises to follow Kurt Lewin and his insight that social change can only happen if we accept the interdependence of theory, research, and action/practice.[169] Sociologist Andrew Pickering spoke of *open-ended experimentation*.[170]

Are you ready for open-ended experimentation? Are you ready to think in holistic and systemic terms, even in a systems-of-systems approach? When we meet complex problems, our first impulse is always to break them down into their simplest components. Yet, complex global problems cannot be addressed in this way: "The system-of-systems approach of complexity science – informed by traditional indigenous modes of thinking and visioning – provides a rigorous platform for making whole system connections and breaking disciplinary silos."[171] Complex systems researcher Stuart Alan Kauffman, for instance, speaks of "coevolution to the edge of chaos," and "the adjacent possible."[172]

Systems theorist Alexander Laszlo aims to achieve a more complete sense of the world when he speaks in terms of relationships, context, patterns, embedded systems, and processes. He uses expressions such as *glocal eco-civilization thrivability*, *deep conviviality*, *hyperconnectivity*, in short, "humanity taking on the role of curators of planetary thrivability."[173] Conviviality can be intra-personal, trans-species, or trans-generational. It can lead us to questions such as: "What would our ancestors think of our work and life here and now? What will our children's children think of our choices? How do we honor our past and create our future intentionally? How do we become active and conscious participants in the unfolding of life?" Laszlo calls on humankind to learn "to be leaders of systemic innovation in syntony with life and the life support systems of Earth."[174]

Will it be enough to think only of us, *Homo sapiens*? What about all the other sentient beings? Is humanity everything? What about leaving behind our identification with ourselves and identity with life in general? What about *lifeism* rather than humanism, humanitarian, or humanistic?[175]

New forms of leadership are needed, *selfless*, *servant*, *prosocial* leadership.[176] Wayne Visser led research on Sustainability Leadership and found "7 Habits of Highly Effective Sustainability Leaders": systemic understanding; emotional intelligence; values orientation; compelling vision; inclusive style; innovative approach; long term perspective.[177]

Have you developed such skills? I would like to invite you to join humankind in intentionally co-creating a welcoming global context for good ideas to emerge, ideas for how future-oriented adaptations may best be fashioned. Since we have a much more comprehensive understanding of our human condition than our forebears, we have all the tools needed to shape our path into the future much more purposefully than ever before. We can sit together and reflect, we can act more deliberately and effectively than we ever were able to in our entire history. We can deeply fathom how tragic the security dilemma was, and we can weaken it through an intentional globalization of care and trust. While we do so, we can keep in mind that we create a new dilemma, namely, what I call a *dignity dilemma*. Yet, the dignity dilemma can be attended to wisely, it does not have to bring back the classical security dilemma. We can dismantle all systemic humiliation and prevent cycles of humiliation from unfolding and re-stoking the security dilemma and re-fracturing our shared world. We can do so by creating global *common-unity*, a global community of mutual care, a global community that truly manifests the fact that we are *one single* family of *Homo sapiens*. We can create a global village that is capable of raising its children and honoring all life. Speaking with the image of the Titanic: We can change the course of the ship, we can change the design of the ship, and we can change how we live on the ship.

The butterfly story by evolutionary biologist Elisabet Sahtouris is inspirational. We can strive to be *imaginal cells*:

> A caterpillar can eat up to three hundred times its own weight in a day, devastating many plants in the process, continuing to eat until it's so bloated that it hangs itself up and goes to sleep, its skin hardening into a chrysalis ... Cells with the butterfly genome were held as disc-like aggregates of stem cells that biologists call "imaginal cells," hidden away inside the caterpillar' all its life, remaining undeveloped until the crisis of overeating, fatigue and breakdown allows them to develop, gradually replacing the caterpillar with a butterfly![178]

Elisabet Sahtouris suggests that the current world-system already entails many imaginal-cell humans who can emerge like butterflies and end the current crises of predation, overconsumption, and breakdown. They can help us leave behind the outdated model of our societies, namely, the well-oiled social machinery model. They can replace it with models of evolving, self-organizing and intelligent living organism.

Even though many aspects of this metaphor do not fit humankind's historical path,[179] its concluding message is in resonance with the message of this book: "If you want a butterfly world, don't step on the caterpillar, but join forces with other imaginal cells to build a better future for all!"[180]

In my first book in 2006, I suggested there are *four basic logics* at the core of the human condition:

1. The question of whether and to what extent resources are expandable (*game theory*, as developed by the discipline of philosophy),
2. The question of whether the *security dilemma* is weaker or stronger (*international relations theory*, developed by political science),
3. The question as to what extent long-term or short-term future time horizons dominate (as described in many academic disciplines, among others *cross-cultural psychology*, the famous seven-generation sustainability rule),
4. The question of how the human capacity to tighten or loosen fault lines of identification is calibrated (*social identity theory*, developed by social psychology).[181]

The most benign scenario is a combination of a weak security dilemma with an expandable pie of knowledge, where long future and past time horizons are embraced – drawing lessons from a long past time horizon for the sake of a long future time horizon – and an atmosphere of respect is nurtured. Conversely, the worst scenario brings together a short future time horizon, positioned in an environment that represents a fixed pie of resources, combined with a strong security dilemma, within which individuals or groups are exposed to humiliating assaults. Feelings of humiliation and their consequences may in that case be so strong that they override and undermine otherwise benign scenarios in a downward spiral.

This model of the human condition can help us analyze social change over long time stretches and in different world regions, as well as aid future strategy planning for governments and international organizations. It warns us that the destructive nature of the dynamics of humiliation becomes the more visible the more the other parameters veer to the benign side.[182]

Table 3 displays these four basic logics of the human condition, as there are the *pie*, the *security dilemma*, the *future time horizon*, and *social identity*.[183] The table is based on the understanding that until roughly ten thousand years ago, human communities were living in what I call the *era of pristine pride* (a). A dramatic alteration occurred when our species had completed what I call our first round of globalization and had populated all continents. In a very brief historical time span, abundant expandable pies of resources turned into fixed ones. Humanity responded with a completely new moral ethos and emotional coinage: The *era of honor* began, which legitimized the vertically ranked scale of human value and worth (b). Presently, we are participants in yet another radical turn-around, as significant as the first one ten thousand years ago, this time aspiring to the ethos and emotional coinage of an *era of equal dignity* (c). This is our second round of globalization, a journey toward a global knowledge society that treats knowledge as an expandable pie, with humankind inviting everybody into one single in-group, where the security dilemma weakens, long-term thinking becomes the norm, and practices of humiliation become delegitimized.[184]

		The future time horizon		**Social identity**	
		short	**long**	**respect**	**humiliation**
The pie	**fixed**	(b)			(b, honor humiliation)
	expandable		(a, c)	(a, c)	(c, dignity humiliation)
The security dilemma	**strong**	(b)			(b, honor humiliation)
	weak		(a, c)	(a, c)	(c, dignity humiliation)

Table 3: The human condition

YOU are needed now, YOU as an individual human being, to heal the security dilemma and the dignity dilemma and bring about a *dignity transition* to co-create what I call *globegalization*. As we live in a "terroristic"[185] apartheid world-system, where humiliation is systemic, YOU are needed to co-create a world that manifests dignity, or what I call dignity-ism, or *dignism*. Dignism, for me, describes a world where every new-born finds space and is nurtured to unfold their highest and best, embedded in a social context of loving appreciation and connection. A world, where the carrying capacity of the planet guides the ways in which everybody's basic needs are met. A world, where we are united in building trust and respecting human dignity and celebrating diversity, where we prevent unity from being perverted into oppressive uniformity, and keep diversity from sliding into hostile division.

Our global HumanDHS dignity fellowship attempts to nurture a *literacy of love*.[186] We value emotions as the "engines of conversion"[187] and as "a creative source of collective agency."[188] Mahatma Gandhi spoke of *satyāgraha*. In loving solidarity, we attempt to act on our *conscience*, as Paulo Freire calls it,[189] and help co-create a more compassionate world. I personally propose that *big love* is an antidote against "big hate," and my religion is *love, humility, and awe for a universe too large for us to fathom*.[190]

This is what you read on the Index page of our HumanDHS website:

> We are a global transdisciplinary network and collaborative community of concerned scholars, researchers, educators, practitioners, creative artists, and others. We wish to stimulate systemic change, globally and locally, to open space for dignity, mutual respect and esteem to take root and grow. Our goal is ending humiliating practices, preventing new ones from arising, and fostering healing from cycles of humiliation throughout the world. We suggest that a frame of cooperation and shared humility is necessary — not a mindset of humiliation — if we wish to build a better world, a world of equal dignity for all.

YOU are needed now, YOU as a single human being. YOU are needed to help build trust in the global village, the trust that we now need so that *Homo sapiens* can become truly *sapiens*, truly wise and knowledgeable.

Imagine, you are a young man in a little town called Arnstadt in communist East Germany in 1989.[191] You are afraid. It is to be expected that the state apparatus – the military, the police, the secret service – will soon clamp down on the people's uprising against the country's exploitative, paranoid, and cruel dictatorship· You are not a political figure, you are just an average citizen. But you can't be silent anymore. You have never owned a typewriter and never written a poem. You borrow a typewriter and you make a poem. It takes you three days. You append to it an invitation, an invitation to your fellow citizens saying that everyone should gather in the square of the city in two days' time, on September 30, 1989, at 2 pm. You type and type to make copies, on whatever paper you can find, you go to a stationery shop nearby to beg for the paper they throw away. You take the bicycle and you put your poem and your invitation up on all the walls of the city. The police removes them, but you come back and put new ones. You never get caught, not because you are clever, just out of sheer luck. September 30 comes, and you wonder: Will anybody turn up? Will anybody follow your invitation? Nobody knows that you were the one to put up those little flyers. Will people come? They come! You, single-handedly, have started the liberation of your city, you alone! You alone, in your little town, stood up against the all-powerful SED, the socialist party of East Germany![192]

This is the flyer that this lone young man, Günther Sattler, made in 1989, a flyer that helped bring down an entire regime:

"To all citizens of Arnstadt! Come on September 30, at fourteen o'clock to our peaceful rally against the arbitrarily cruel policies of the SED"

What a Life ?

what a life?
where the truth becomes a lie,
where the wrong person leads the scepter.

what a life?
where the freedom is stillborn,
where all seems already lost.

what a life?
where old men govern,
where people die at the borders.

what a life?
where the fear determines every day
where the end takes no end.

what a life?
where one no longer trusts one's neighbors,
where one no longer relies on one another.

what a life?
where you cannot be who you are,
where one so soon forgets.

what a life?
where dreams die, die,
where there is nothing more to bequeath, except shards.

what a life?
where there is everything for a few,
where the little man sees no way out.

what a life?
where love does not exist,
where one slowly freezes to death.[193]

References

See an extenced reference list at www.humiliationstudies.org/whoweare/evelin/book/05.php.

Abu-Rabi, Ibrahim M. (2007). "Modernization, democracy and human rights." In *Terrorism, democracy, the West and the Muslim world*, edited by Abdul Rashid Moten, and Noraini M. Noor, chapter 1, pp. 13–35. Singapore: Thomson Learning.

Adelman, Jeremy (2013). *Worldly philosopher: The odyssey of Albert O. Hirschman*. Princeton, NJ: Princeton University Press.

Adichie, Chimamanda Ngozi (2013). *Americanah*. New York: Knopf.

Adjerid, Abderrahmane (1992). *La hogra, ou, L'humiliation du peuple algérien*. Paris: Éditions Babylone.

Adler, Nanci Dale (1993). *Victims of Soviet terror: The story of the memorial movement*. Westport, CT: Praeger.

Adler, Nanci Dale (2004). *The Gulag survivor: Beyond the soviet system*. New Brunswick, NJ: Transaction.

Adler, Nanci Dale, Mary Chamberlain, Selma Leydesdorff, and Leyla Neyzi (Eds.) (2009). *Memories of mass repression: Narrating life stories in the aftermath of atrocity*. New Brunswick, NJ: Transaction.

Adorno, Theodor W., and Max Horkheimer (1944/2002). *Dialectic of enlightenment: Philosophical fragments*. Translated by Edmund Jephcott. Stanford, CA: Stanford University Press. German original *Philosophische Fragmente*, New York: Social Studies Association, 1944.

Adorno, Theodor W., Else Frenkel-Brunswick, Daniel J. Levinson, and R. Nevitt Sanford (1950). *The authoritarian personality*. New York: Harper and Row.

Agamben, Giorgio (1995/1998). *Homo sacer: Sovereign power and bare life*. Translated by Daniel Heller-Roazen. Stanford, CA: Stanford University Press. Italian original *Homo sacer: Il potere sovrano e la nuda vita*, Turin, Italy: Giulio Einaudi, 1995.

Agger, Inger, and Søren B. Jensen (1996). *Trauma and healing under state terrorism*. London: Zed.

Agi, Ryuhei, and Kichiro Hayashi (2007). "Construction and validation of a psychometric test for measuring analog and digital mindsets of individuals." *Journal of Intercultural Communication, SIETAR Japan, 10*, pp. 133–48.

Ahmed, Akbar S. (2013). *The thistle and the drone: How America's war on terror became a global war on tribal Islam*. Washington, DC: Brookings Institution Press.

Ahmed, Ali Jimale (1996). *Daybreak is near: Literature, clans, and the nation-state in Somalia*. Lawrenceville, NJ, and Asmara, Eritrea: Read See Press.

Ahmed, Nafeez Mosaddeq (2017). *Failing states, collapsing systems: BioPhysical triggers of political violence*. Cham, Switzerland: Springer.

Ahmed, Sara (2004). *The cultural politics of emotion*. Edinburgh: Edinburgh University Press.

Ahrens, Henning (2015). *Glantz und Gloria*. Frankfurt am Main, Germany: Fischer.

Ahrens, Steffen, and Dennis J. Snower (2014). "Envy, guilt, and the Phillips curve." *Journal of Economic Behavior and Organization, 99*, pp. 69–84.

Akerlof, George A., and Robert J. Shiller (2009). *Animal spirits: How human psychology drives the economy and why it matters for global capitalism*. Princeton, NJ: Princeton University Press.

Akerlof, George A., and Robert J. Shiller (2015). *Phishing for phools: The economics of manipulation and deception*. Princeton, NJ: Princeton University Press.

Akilu, Fatima (2015). "Hope, challenges and opportunity: Nigeria's strategy to counter violent extremism." In *Global Perspectives series*, edited by Khalid Koser, and Thomas Thorp. London: Tony Blair Faith Foundation. Supported by the initiative "Education and Security: The Challenge of Religious Diversity" at McGill University.

Al-Aswany, Alaa (2015). *Democracy is the answer: Egypt's years of revolution*. London: Gingko Library, a collection of newspaper columns written for *Al-Masry Al-Youm* between 2011 and 2014.

Al-Aswany, Alaa (2002/2004). *The Yacoubian building*. Translated by Humphrey Davies. New York: American University in Cairo Press. Egyptian original *Imārat Ya'qūbiyān*, Cairo: American University in Cairo Press, 2002.

Al-Khayyat, Sana'a (1990). *Honour and shame: Women in modern Iraq*. London: Saqi Books.

Al-Rodhan, Nayef R. F. (2008). *Emotional amoral egoism: A neurophilosophical theory of human nature and its universal security implications*. New Brunswick, NJ: Transaction.

Al-Rodhan, Nayef R. F. (2009). *Sustainable history and the dignity of man: A philosophy of history and civilizational triumph*. New Brunswick, NJ: Transaction.

Al-Rodhan, Nayef R. F. (2012). *The role of the Arab-Islamic World in the rise of the West: Implications for contemporary trans-cultural relations*. Basingstoke: Palgrave Macmillan.

Alagic, Mara, Adair Linn Nagata, and Glyn M. Rimmington (2009). "Improving intercultural communication competence: Fostering bodymindful cage painting." *Journal of Intercultural Communication, SIETAR Japan, 12*, pp. 39–55.

Alarcón, Renato D., Edward F. Foulks, and Mark Vakkur (1998). *Personality disorders and culture: Clinical and conceptual interactions*. New York: Wiley.

Albert, Mathias, Lars-Erik Cederman, and Alexander Wendt (2010). *New systems theories of world politics*. Basingstoke: Palgrave Macmillan.

Albrecht, Ulrich (1980). "Red militarism." *Journal of Peace Research, 17* (2), pp. 135–49.

Alexander, Jeffrey Charles (1995). *Fin de siècle social theory: Relativism, reduction, and the problem of reason*. New York: Verso.

Alexander, Jeffrey Charles, Dominik Bartmanski, and Bernhard Giesen (Eds.) (2012). *Iconic power: Materiality and meaning in social life*. Basingstoke: Palgrave Macmillan.

Alexander, Samuel (Ed.) (2009). *Voluntary simplicity: The poetic alternative to consumer culture*. Auckland, New Zealand: Stead and Daughters.

Alexievich, Svetlana (2013/2016). *Second-hand time*. Translated by Bela Shayevich. London: Fitzcarraldo Editions. Russian original *Время секонд хэнд*, Moscow: Vremia, 2013.

Ali, Tariq (2002). *The clash of fundamentalisms: Crusades, jihads and modernity*. London: Verso.

Alliance Development Works/Bündnis Entwicklung Hilft (BEH) (2013). *2013 World Risk Report (WRR 2013)*. Alliance Development Works/Bündnis Entwicklung Hilft (BEH).

Allport, Gordon Willard (1954). *The nature of prejudice*. Reading, MA: Addison-Wesley.

Allred, Keith G. (1999). "Anger and retaliation: Toward an understanding of impassioned conflict in organizations." In *Research on negotiations in organizations. Vol. 7*, edited by Robert J. Bies, Roy J. Lewicki, and Blair H. Sheppard, pp. 27–58. Greenwich, CT: JAI Press.

Allyn, John (1970). *The Forty-Seven Ronin story*. Rutland, VT: Tuttle.

Altemeyer, Robert Anthony (1981). *Right-wing authoritarianism*. Winnipeg, MB: University of Manitoba Press.

Altemeyer, Robert Anthony (1996). *The authoritarian specter*. Cambridge, MA: Harvard University Press.

Altemeyer, Robert Anthony (2003). "What happens when authoritarians inherit the Earth? A simulation." *Analyses of Social Issues and Public Policy, 3* (1).

Altemeyer, Robert Anthony (2009). *The authoritarians.* Winnipeg, MB: University of Manitoba, Department of Psychology.

Althoff, Gerd (2006). *Heinrich IV.* Darmstadt, Germany: Primus Verlag, Wissenschaftliche Buchgesellschaft (WBG).

Amann, Gabriele, and Rudolf Wipplinger (Eds.) (2005). *Sexueller Missbrauch: Ein Überblick zu Forschung, Beratung und Therapie. Ein Handbuch.* 3rd edition. Tübingen, Germany: dgvt-Verlag.

Amare, Azmeraw T. (2014). "Global, regional, and national age-sex specific all-cause and cause-specific mortality for 240 causes of death, 1990 – 2013: A systematic analysis for the Global Burden of Disease Study 2013." *The Lancet, 385* (9963), pp. 117–71.

Ambedkar, Bhimrao Ramji (1948). *The untouchables: Who were they and why they became untouchables?* New Delhi: Amrit Book.

Amo, Anton Wilhelm (1968). *Antonius Gvilielmus Amo Afer of Axim in Ghana: Translation of his works.* Halle, Germany: Martin Luther University Halle-Wittenberg.

Anderson, Benedict (1991). *Imagined communities.* London: Verso.

Anderson, Benedict (2006). *Imagined communities: Reflections on the origin and spread of nationalism.* Revised edition. London: Verso.

Anderson, Carol (2016). *White rage: The unspoken truth of our racial divide.* New York: Bloomsbury.

Anderson, Geraint (2008). *Cityboy: Beer and loathing in the square mile.* London: Headline.

Anderson, Harlene (2012). "Reflections on Kenneth Gergen's contributions to family therapy." *Psychological Studies, 57* (2, June, Kenneth J. Gergen and Social Constructionism), pp. 142–49.

Anderson, Scott (2013). *Lawrence in Arabia: War, deceit, imperial folly, and the making of the modern Middle East.* New York: Doubleday.

Andersson, Gavin, and Howard Richards (2013). *Unbounded organization: Embracing the societal enterprise.* Pretoria: University of South Africa Press.

Andersson, Gavin, Raff Carmen, Iván Labra, and Howard Richards (2016). "The Organization Workshop (OW): A CHAT praxis from the Global South." *Submitted for publication.*

Ando, Clifford, Paul Du Plessis, and Kaius Tuori (Eds.) (2016). *The Oxford handbook of Roman law and society*, Roman law and society. Oxford: Oxford University Press.

Angell, Marcia (2004). *The truth about the drug companies: How they deceive us and what to do about it.* New York: Random House.

Angus, Ian (2016). *Facing the anthropocene: Fossil capitalism and the crisis of the earth system.* New York: Monthly Review.

Antonovsky, Aaron (1979). *Health, stress, and coping.* San Francisco: Jossey-Bass.

Antonovsky, Aaron (1987). *Unraveling the mystery of health: How people manage stress and stay well.* San Francisco: Jossey-Bass.

Apard, Élodie (2015). "Boko Haram, le jihad en vidéo." *Politique Africaine, 138* (2), pp. 135–62.

Appiah, K. Anthony (2010). *The honor code: How moral revolutions happen.* New York: Norton.

Archer, Colin (2005). *Warfare or welfare? Disarmament for development in the 21st century. A human security approach.* Geneva: International Peace Bureau, ipb.org/i/pdf-files/Warfare_or_Welfare_Complete-versionEng.pdf.

Archer, Margaret S., Roy Bhaskar, Andrew Collier, Tony Lawson, and Alan Norrie (Eds.) (1998). *Critical realism: Essential readings.* London: Routledge.

Archer, Margaret S. (2011). "'Caritas in veritate' and social love." *International Journal of Public Theology, 5* (3), pp. 273–95.

Ardrey, Robert (1961). *African genesis: A personal investigation into the animal origins and nature of man*. New York: Atheneum Books.

Arendt, Hannah (1951). *The origins of totalitarianism*. New York: Schocken Books.

Arendt, Hannah (1961). *Between past and future: Eight exercises in political thought*. Enlarged edition. New York: Viking.

Arendt, Hannah (1963). *Eichmann in Jerusalem: A report on the banality of evil*. New York: Viking Press.

Arendt, Hannah (1970). *On violence*. London: Allen Lane.

Aristotle (1980). *The Nicomachean ethics*. Oxford: Oxford University Press.

Armelagos, George John, Alan H. Goodman, and Kenneth Jacobs (1991). "The origins of agriculture: Population growth during a period of declining health." *Population and Environment, 13* (1), pp. 9–22.

Armendariz de Aghion, Beatriz, and Jonathan Morduch (2005). *The economics of microfinance*. Cambridge, MA: Massachusetts Institute of Technology (MIT) Press.

Armstrong, Karen (2007). *Muhammad: Prophet for our time*. London: Harper Collins.

Armstrong, W. A. (1981). "The influence of demographic factors on the position of the agricultural labourer in England and Wales, c. 1750–1914." *Agricultural History Review, 29* (1), pp. 71–82.

Arrian, and Martin Hammond (2013). *Alexander the Great: The Anabasis and the Indica*. Oxford: Oxford University Press.

Arrigo, Jean Maria, and Richard V. Wagner (2007). "Psychologists and military interrogators rethink the psychology of torture." *Peace and Conflict: Journal of Peace Psychology, 13* (4), pp. 393–98.

Arum, Richard, and Josipa Roksa (2011). *Academically adrift: Limited learning on college campuses*. Chicago: University of Chicago Press.

Asal, Victor, Kathleen Deloughery, and Ryan D. King (2013). *Understanding lone-actor terrorism: A comparative analysis with violent hate crimes and group-based terrorism*. College Park, MD: A report to the Resilient Systems Division, Science and Technology Directorate, U.S. Department of Homeland Security, by the National Consortium for the Study of Terrorism and Responses to Terrorism (START), a Department of Homeland Security Science and Technology Center of Excellence Based at the University of Maryland, www.start.umd.edu/pubs/START_IUSSD_UnderstandingLoneactorTerrorism_Sept2013.pdf.

Ashcroft, Richard E. (2005). "Making sense of dignity." *Journal of Medical Ethics, 31* (11), pp. 679–82.

Ashour, Omar (2009). *The de-radicalization of jihadists: Transforming armed islamist movements*. London: Routledge.

Aslan, Reza (2005). *No god but God: The origins, evolution, and future of Islam*. New York: Random House.

Aslan, Reza (2009). *How to win a cosmic war: God, globalization, and the end of the war on terror*. New York: Random House.

Atallah, Devin G. (2017). "A community-based qualitative study of intergenerational resilience with Palestinian refugee families facing structural violence and historical trauma." *Transcultural Psychiatry, 0* (0).

Ateş, Seyran (2009). *Der Islam braucht eine sexuelle Revolution. Eine Streitschrift*. Berlin: Ullstein.

Atkinson, Anthony Barnes (2015). *Inequality: What can be done?* Cambridge, MA: Harvard University Press.

Atran, Scott (2003). "Genesis of suicide terrorism." *Science, 299* (5612, March), pp. 1534–39.

Atran, Scott (2006). "The moral logic and growth of suicide terrorism." *The Washington Quarterly, 29* (2), pp. 127–47.

Atran, Scott, Robert Axelrod, and Richard Davis (2007). "Sacred barriers to conflict resolution." *Science, 317* (5841), pp. 1039–40.

Atran, Scott (2010a). "A question of honour: Why the Taliban fight and what to do about it." *Asian Journal of Social Science, 38* (3), pp. 343–63.

Atran, Scott (2010b). *Talking to the enemy: Violent extremism, sacred values, and what it means to be human.* London: Pengin.

Atran, Scott (2010c). *Talking to the enemy: Faith, brotherhood, and the (un)making of terrorists.* New York: Ecco.

Atran, Scott, and Jeremy Ginges (2012). "Religious and sacred imperatives in human conflict." *Science, 336* (6083), pp. 855–57.

Atran, Scott (2013). "From mutualism to moral transcendence." *Behavioral and Brain Sciences, 36* (1), pp. 81–82.

Atran, Scott, Hammad Sheikh, and Angel Gomez (2014). "Devoted actors sacrifice for close comrades and sacred cause." *Proceedings of the National Academy of Sciences (PNAS) of the United States of America, 111* (50), pp. 17702–03.

Attewell, Paul, and Katherine S. Newman (2010). *Growing gaps: Educational inequality around the world.* Cary, NC: Oxford University Press.

Atuahene, Bernadette (2014). *We want what's ours: Learning from South Africa's land restitution program.* Oxford: Oxford University Press.

Atuahene, Bernadette (2016). "Dignity takings and dignity restoration: Creating a new theoretical framework for understanding involuntary property loss and the remedies required." *Law and Social Inquiry, 41* (4, Fall), pp. 796–823.

Atzmon, Gilad (2011). *The wandering who: A study of Jewish identity politics.* Winchester: Zero Books.

Auestad, Lene (Ed.) (2012). *Psychoanalysis and politics: Exclusion and the politics of representation.* London: Karnac.

Auestad, Lene (2014). *Nationalism and the body politic: Psychoanalysis and the rise of ethnocentrism and xenophobia.* London: Karnac.

Auestad, Lene (2015). *Respect, plurality and prejudice: A psychoanalytical and philosophical enquiry into the dynamics of social exclusion and discrimination.* London: Karnac.

Aust, Stefan (1985). *Der Baader Meinhof Komplex.* Hamburg, Germany: Hoffmann und Campe.

Averill, James R. (1982). *Anger and aggression: An essay on emotion.* New York: Springer.

Averill, James R. (1993). "Illusions of anger." In *Aggression and violence: Social interactionist perspectives,* edited by Richard B. Felson, and James T. Tedeschi American Psychological Association, pp. 171–92. Washington, DC: American Psychological Association.

Awan, Akil N., Andrew Hoskins, and Ben O'Loughlin (2011). *Radicalisation and media: Connectivity and terrorism in the new media ecology.* London: Routledge.

Axelrod, Robert (2006). *The evolution of cooperation.* Revised edition. New York: Basic Books.

Ayton, Andrew, and Philip Preston (2005). *The Battle of Crécy, 1346.* Woodbridge: Boydell.

Bacevich, Andrew J. (2010). *Washington rules: America's path to permanent war.* New York: Metropolitan Books.

Bacevich, Andrew J. (2016). *America's war for the greater Middle East: A military history.* New York: Random House.

Bachmann, Jan, Colleen Bell, and Caroline Holmqvist (Eds.) (2015). *War, police and assemblages of intervention.* Abingdon: Routledge.

Badgett, Mary Virginia Lee (2016). *The public professor: How to use your research to change the world.* New York: New York University Press.

Badie, Bertrand (2014). *Le temps des humiliés: Pathologie des relations internationales*. Paris: Odile Jacob.

Bagge, Sverre (2006). "The making of a missionary king: The medieval accounts of Olaf Tryggvason and the conversion of Norway." *The Journal of English and Germanic Philology, 105* (4, October), pp. 473–513.

Bailey, Thomas (2012). *Salutare animas nostras: The ideologies behind the foundation of the Templars*. Maryville, MO: Northwest Missouri State University, doctoral dissertation.

Bainham, Andrew, and International Society of Family Law (Eds.) (2006). *The International survey of family law*. Bristol: Family Law.

Bakan, Joel (2004). *The corporation: The pathological pursuit of profit and power*. Toronto: Viking Canada.

Baker, Anthony (Abdul Haqq) (2009). *Countering terrorism in the UK: A convert community perspective*. Exeter: University of Exeter, doctoral dissertation.

Baker, Anthony (Abdul Haqq) (2011). *Extremists in our midst: Confronting terror*. Basingstoke: Palgrave Macmillan.

Baldwin, James (1963). *A talk to teachers*. Delivered on October 16, 1963, as 'The Negro Child – His Self-Image'. Originally published in *The Saturday Review*, December 21, 1963, reprinted in *The Price of the Ticket, Collected Non-Fiction 1948 – 1985*, Saint Martins 1985.

Bales, Kevin (2012). *Disposable people: New slavery in the global economy*. 3rd updated edition. Berkeley: University of California Press.

Bammer, Angelika, and Ruth-Ellen Boetcher Joeres (Eds.) (2015). *The future of scholarly writing: Critical interventions*. New York: Palgrave Macmillan.

Bandura, Albert (1977). "Self-efficacy: Toward a unifying theory of behavioral change." *Psychological Review, 84* (2), pp. 191–215.

Banks, Amy, and Leigh Ann Hirschman (2016). *Wired to connect: The surprising link between brain science and strong, health relationships*. New York: TarcherPerigee.

Banks, James A., Peter Cookson, Geneva Gay, Willis D. Hawley, Jacqueline Jordan Irvine, Sonia Nieto, Janet Ward Schofield, and Walter G. Stephan (2001). "Diversity within unity: Essential principles for teaching and learning in a multicultural society." Seattle: University of Washington, Center for Multicultural Education, College of Education.

Bar-On, Daniel (1989). *The legacy of silence: Encounters with children of the Third Reich*. Cambridge, MA: Harvard University Press.

Bar-Tal, Daniel, Eran Halperin, and Joseph De Rivera (2007). "Collective emotions in conflict situations: Societal implications." *Journal of Social Issues, 63* (2), pp. 441–60.

Barad, Karen (2003). "Posthumanist performativity: Toward an understanding of how matter comes to matter." *Signs, 28* (3), pp. 801–31.

Barad, Karen (2007). *Meeting the universe halfway: Quantum physics and the entanglement of matter and meaning*. Durham: Duke University Press.

Bardi, Ugo (2013). *Der geplünderte Planet: Die Zukunft des Menschen im Zeitalter schwindender Ressourcen*. München, Germany: oekom Verlag.

Bargal, David (2011a). "Kurt Lewin's vision of organizational and social change: The interdependence of theory, research and action/practice." In *The Routledge companion of organizational change*, edited by D. M. Boje, B. Burnes, and J. Hassard, pp. 31–45. London: Routledge.

Bargal, David (2011b). "To move the world – Review of *Gender, Humiliation, and Global Security*." *Peace and Conflict: Journal of Peace Psychology, 17* (2), pp. 201–03.

Bargh, John A., and Erin L. Williams (2006). "The automaticity of social life." *Current Directions in Psychological Science, 15* (1), pp. 1–4.

Barker, Gary (2005). *Dying to be men: Youth, masculinity and social exclusion*. London: Routledge.

Barnett, Michael, and Duvall Raymond (2005). "Power in international politics." *International Organization, 59* (1), pp. 39–75.

Barney, Jay B., Judy Wicks, C. Otto Scharmer, and Kathryn Pavlovich (2015). "Exploring transcendental leadership: A conversation." *Journal of Management, Spirituality and Religion, 12* (4), pp. 290–304.

Barrett, Justin L. (2011). "Cognitive science of religion: Looking back, looking forward." *Journal for the Scientific Study of Religion, 50* (2), pp. 229–39.

Barrett, Richard, and Laila Bokhari (2009). "De-radicalisation and rehabilitation programmes targeting militant jihadists: An overview." In *Leaving terrorism behind: Individual and collective disengagement*, edited by Tore Bjørgo, and John Horgan, chapter 10, pp. 170–80. London: Routledge.

Barrington-Leigh, Christopher (2017). *Sustainability and well-being: A happy synergy*. Boston: Great Transition Initiative.

Barrington-Leigh, Christopher (2010). *Economic inequality and subjective well-being: Is inequality good for the rich?*

Barry, John (2012). *The politics of actually existing unsustainability: Human flourishing in a climate-changed, carbon-constrained world*. Oxford: Oxford University Press.

Barth, Erling, and Karl Ove Moene (2015). "Missing the link? On the political economy of Nordic egalitarianism." In *Reform capacity and macroeconomic performance in the Nordic countries*, edited by Torben M. Andersen, Michael Bergman, and Svend Erik Hougaard Jensen, chapter 3, pp. 50–68. Oxford: Oxford University Press.

Barthes, Roland (1971/1996). *Sade, Fourier, Loyola*. Translated by Richard Miller. New York: Farrar, Straus and Giroux. French original, Paris: Seuil, 1971.

Bartlett, Jamie, Jonathan Birdwell, and Michael King (2010). *The edge of violence: A radical approach to extremism*. London: Demos.

Bartlett, Steven James (2011). *Normality does not equal mental health: The need to look elsewhere for standards of good mental health*. Santa Barbara, CA: Praeger, ABC-CLIO.

Bartoschek, Sebastian (2015). *Bekanntheit von und Zustimmung zu Verschwörungstheorien – eine empirische Grundlagenarbeit*. Hannover, Germany: JMB Verlag.

Başoğlu, Metin, Susan M. Mineka, Murat Paker, Tamer Aker, Maria Livanou, and Şibel Gok (1997). "Psychological preparedness for trauma as a protective factor in survivors of torture." *Psychological Medicine, 27* (6), pp. 1421–33.

Bass, Bernard M., and Ronald E. Riggio (2006). *Transformational leadership*. 2nd edition. Mahwah, NJ: Erlbaum.

Bastiat, Frédéric (1848). "Physiologie de la spoliation." In *Sophismes économiques, 2ème Série*, chapter 1. Paris: Librarie Guillaumin.

Bastiat, Frédéric (1850). *The law*. Irvington-on-Hudson, NY: Foundation for Economic Education.

Bateman, Milford (2010). *Why doesn't microfinance work? The destructive rise of local neoliberalism*. London: Zed Books.

Bateson, Gregory (1954). *A theory of play and fantasy: Steps to an ecology of mind*. New York: Ballantine, also in *Collected Essays in Anthropology, Psychiatry, Evolution, and Epistemology*, Northvale, NJ: Jason Aronson, 1972.

Bateson, Gregory (1972). *Steps to an ecology of mind: Collected essays in anthropology, psychiatry, evolution, and epistemology*. Scranton, PA: Chandler.

Battle, Michael Jesse (1997). *Reconciliation. The ubuntu theology of Desmond Tutu*. Cleveland, OH: Pilgrim Press.

Baum, Dan (2013). *Gun guys: A road trip*. New York: Vintage Departures.

Bauman, Zygmunt (1989). *Modernity and the Holocaust*. Cambridge: Polity Press.

Bauman, Zygmunt (1992). *Intimations of postmodernity*. London: Routledge.

Bauman, Zygmunt (2000). *Liquid modernity*. Cambridge: Polity Press.

Bauman, Zygmunt (2001). "The great war of recognition." *Theory, Culture and Society, 18* (2-3), pp. 137–50.

Baumeister, Roy F., Laura Smart, and Joseph M. Boden (1996). "Relation of threatened egotism to violence and aggression: The dark side of high self-esteem." *Psychological Review, 103* (1), pp. 5–33.

Baumeister, Roy F., Jennifer D. Campbell, Joachim I. Krueger, and Kathleen D. Vohs (2003). "Does high self-esteem cause better performance, interpersonal success, happiness, or healthier lifestyles?". *Psychological Science in the Public Interest, 4* (1), pp. 1–44.

Baumeister, Roy F. (2005). "Rethinking self-esteem: Why nonprofits should stop pushing self-esteem and start endorsing self-control." *Stanford Social Innovation Review*, pp. 34–41.

Bazaara, Nyangabyaki (1992). "Land policy and evolving forms of land tenure in Masindi District, Uganda." In *Working Paper, No. 28*. Kampala, Uganda: Centre for Basic Research.

Beah, Ishmael (2007). *A long way gone: Memoirs of a boy soldier*. New York: Farrar, Straus and Giroux.

Beck, Ulrich (1986). *Risikogesellschaft: Auf dem Weg in eine andere Moderne*. Frankfurt am Main, Germany: Suhrkamp.

Becker, Ernest (1973). *The denial of death*. New York: Free Press.

Becker, Gary S. (1976). *The economic approach to human behavior*. Chicago: University of Chicago Press.

Becker, Oda (2016). *Atomstrom 2016: Sicher, sauber, alles im Griff?* Berlin: Bund für Umwelt und Naturschutz Deutschland (BUND).

Becker, Sascha O., and Ludger Wößmann (2007). "Was Weber wrong? A human capital theory of Protestant economics history." In *Munich Discussion Paper No. 2007-7*. München, Germany: University of Munich, Center for Economic Studiesm, and Ifo Institute for Economic Research.

Beckwith, Kathy (2015). *A mighty case against war: What America missed in U.S. history class and what we (all) can do now*. Lake Oswego, OR: Dignity Press.

Behrens, Kazuko Y. (2004). "A multifaceted view of the concept of amae: Reconsidering the indigenous Japanese concept of relatedness." *Human Development, 47* (1), pp. 1–27.

Beinhocker, Eric, and Nick Hanauer (2014). "Capitalism redefined: Resolving the tension between a prosperous world and a moral one." *Juncture, 21* (1), pp. 12–24.

Beinhocker, Eric D. (2006). *The origin of wealth: Evolution, complexity, and the radical remaking of economics*. Boston: Harvard Business School Press.

Belenky, Mary Field, Lynne A. Bond, and Jacqueline S. Weinstock (1997a). *A tradition that has no name: Nuturing the development of people, families, and communities*. New York: Basic Books.

Belenky, Mary Field, Blythe McVicker Clinchy, Nancy Rule Goldberger, and Jill Mattuck Tarule (Eds.) (1997b). *Women's ways of knowing: The development of self, voice, and mind*. 10th Anniversary edition. New York: Basic Books.

Bell, Daniel A. (2008). *China's new Confucianism: Politics and everyday life in a changing society*. Princeton, NJ: Princeton University Press.

Bellah, Robert Neelly (2011). *Religion in human evolution: From the Paleolithic to the Axial Age*. Cambridge, MA: Belknap.

Bellah, Robert Neelly, and Hans Joas (Eds.) (2012). *The axial age and its consequences*. Cambridge, MA: Belknap.

Bellah, Robert Neelly, and Phillip E. Hammond (2013). *Varieties of civil religion*. Eugene, OR: Wipf and Stock.

Bem, Daryl J. (1970). *Beliefs, attitudes and human affairs.* Belmont, CA: Brooks-Cole.

Benedict, Ruth (1946). *The chrysanthemum and the sword: patterns of Japanese culture.* Boston: Houghton Mifflin.

Benford, Robert D., and David A. Snow (2000). "Framing processes and social movements: An overview and assessment." *Annual Review of Sociology, 26* (1), pp. 611–39.

Benjamin, Walter (1940/1974). *On the concept of history.* Frankfurt am Main, Germany: Suhrkamp.

Bennett, Tony, and John Frow (Eds.) (2008). *The SAGE handbook of cultural analysis.* Los Angeles, CA: Sage.

Benschop, Albert (2005). *Chronicle of a political murder foretold, jihad in the Netherlands.* University of Amsterdam, Sociosite, Social Science Information System.

Benson, Peter L. (2006). *All kids are our kids: What communities must do to raise caring and responsible children and adolescents.* 2nd edition. San Francisco: Jossey-Bass.

Bentall, Richard P. (2009). *Doctoring the mind: Why psychiatric treatments fail.* London: Allan Lane.

Benton-Banai, Edward (1988). *The Mishomis book: The voice of the Ojibway.* St. Paul: Red School House, MI.

Bergen, Peter L. (2016). *United States of Jihad: Investigating America's homegrown terrorists.* New York: Crown.

Berger, John Peter (2011). *Bento's sketchbook.* New York: Pantheon.

Berger, Maurice (1996). "The mouse that never roars." In *Too Jewish? Challenging traditional identities,* edited by Norman Kleeblatt, pp. 93–107. New York: The Jewish Museum.

Berger, Peter L., and Thomas Luckmann (1966). *The social construction of reality: A treatise in the sociology of knowledge.* Garden City, NY: Doubleday.

Berger, Peter L. (1969). *A rumor of angels: Modern society and the rediscovery of the supernatural.* Garden City, NY: Doubleday.

Berkowitz, Leonard (1990). "On the formation and regulation of anger and aggression. A cognitive-neoassociationistic analysis." *The American Psychologist, 45* (4), pp. 494–503.

Berkowitz, Leonard, and Eddie Harmon-Jones (2004). "Toward an understanding of the determinants of anger." *Emotion, 4* (2), pp. 107–30.

Berlant, Lauren (2005). "The epistemology of state emotion." In *Dissent in dangerous times,* edited by Austin Sarat, pp. 46–78. Ann Arbor: University of Michigan Press.

Berlin, Isaiah (1958). *Two concepts of liberty.* Oxford: Clarendon, an Inaugural Lecture delivered before the University of Oxford on 31st October 1958.

Berlin, Isaiah (1997). *The proper study of mankind: An anthology of essays.* London: Chatto and Windus.

Bernard of Clairvaux (1977). "In praise of the new knighthood (Liber ad milites Templi: De laude novae militae)." In *The Cistercian Fathers Series: Number Nineteen, The Works of Bernard of Clairvaux: Volume Seven, Treatises III.* Kalamazoo, MI: Cistercian Publications.

Bernays, Edward Louis (1928). *Propaganda.* New York: Horace Liveright.

Berne, Eric (1972). *What do you say after you say hello? The psychology of human destiny.* New York: Bantam.

Bernstein, Basil (1971). *Class, codes and control 1: Theoretical studies towards a sociology of language.* London: Routledge and Kegan Paul.

Bernstein, Basil (1973). *Class, codes and control 2: Applied studies towards a sociology of language.* 2nd ed. edition. London: Routledge and Kegan Paul.

Bernstein, Basil (1975). *Class, codes and control 3: Towards a theory of educational transmissions.* London: Routledge and Kegan Paul.

Bernstein, Basil (1990). *Class, codes and control 4: The structuring of pedagogic discourse.* 2nd edition. London: Routledge and Kegan Paul.

Bernstein, Basil (2000). *Pedagogy, symbolic control and identity: Theory, research, critique*. Revised edition. Lanham, MD: Rowman and Littlefield.

Berry, Thomas (1999). *The great work: Our way into the future*. New York: Bell Tower.

Berry, Wendell (2009). "Inverting the economic order." *Communio: International Catholic Review, 36* (Fall), pp. 475–86.

Betanzos, Juan de, Roland Hamilton, and Dana Buchanan (1996). *Narrative of the Incas*. Austin, TX: University of Texas Press.

Beyer, Anna Cornelia (2010). *Counterterrorism and international power relations: The EU, ASEAN and hegemonic global governance*. London: I.B. Tauris.

Beyleveld, Deryck, and Roger Brownsword (2001). *Human dignity in bioethics and biolaw*. Oxford: Oxford University Press.

Bhaskar, Roy (1986). *Scientific realism and human emancipation*. London: Verso.

Bhaskar, Roy (2008). *A realist theory of science*. New introduction edition. Abingdon: Routledge.

Bially Mattern, Janice (2011). "A practice theory of emotion for international relations." In *International practices*, edited by Emanuel Adler, and Vincent Pouliot, pp. 63–86. Cambridge: Cambridge University Press.

Bidar, Abdennour (2015). *Lettre ouverte au monde musulman*. Paris: Les Liens qui Libèrent.

Billig, Michael G. (2013). *Learn to write badly: How to succeed in the social sciences*. New York: Cambridge University Press.

Bischof, Norbert (2004). *Das Kraftfeld der Mythen: Signale aus der Zeit, in der wir die Welt erschaffen haben*. 3rd edition. München, Germany: Piper.

Bischöfliches Hilfswerk MISEREOR (Ed.) (2015) *Weltgemeinwohl: Globale Entwicklung in sozialer und ökologischer Verantwortung*. Aachen, Germany: Ein interkulturelles Dialogprojekt 2012 – 2015 'Entwicklung im Dienst des Weltgemeinwohls', Zusammenfassung eines gemeinsamen Projekts des kirchlichen Entwicklungshilfswerks MISEREOR (Aachen) und des Instituts für Gesellschaftspolitik IGP München.

Bjørgo, Tore, and John Horgan (Eds.) (2009). *Leaving terrorism behind: Individual and collective disengagement*. London and New York: Routledge.

Black, Daniel P. (1997). *Dismantling black manhood: An historical and literary analysis of the legacy of slavery*. New York: Garland.

Blight, James G., and Janet M. Lang (2010). "When empathy failed: Using critical oral history to reassess the collapse of U.S.-Soviet Déétente in the Carter-Brezhnev years." *Journal of Cold War Studies, 12* (2), pp. 29–74.

Blin, Arnaud, and Gérard Chaliand (Eds.) (2007). *The history of terrorism: From antiquity to al Qaeda*. Berkeley: University of California Press.

Blok, Anton. "The Mafia of a Sicilian village, (1860-1960): An anthropological study of political middlemen." University of Amsterdam, doctoral dissertation, 1972.

Blok, Anton (1988). *The Mafia of a Sicilian village, 1860-1960: A study of violent peasant entrepreneurs*. Cambridge: Polity Press.

Blok, Anton (2001). *Honour and violence*. Oxford: Polity Press.

Blom, Philipp (2008). *The vertigo years: Change and culture in the West, 1900-1914*. London: Weidenfeld and Nicolson.

Blom, Philipp (2017). *Gefangen im Panoptikum: Reisenotizen zwischen Aufklärung und Gegenwart*. Salzburg, Austria: Residenz Verlag.

Bloom, Allan (1987). *The closing of the American mind: How higher education has failed democracy and impoverished the souls of today's students.* New York: Simon and Schuster.

Bloom, Harold (1999). *Shakespeare: The invention of the human.* London: Fourth Estate.

Boehm, Christopher (1987). *Blood revenge: The enactment and management of conflict in Montenegro and other tribal societies.* Pennsylvania: University of Pennsylvania Press.

Boehm, Christopher (1993). "Egalitarian behavior and reverse dominance hierarchy." *Current Anthropology, 34* (3), pp. 227–54.

Boehm, Christopher (1999). *Hierarchy in the forest: The evolution of egalitarian behavior.* Cambridge, MA: Harvard University Press.

Boehm, Christopher (2001). *Hierarchy in the forest: The evolution of egalitarian behavior.* Cambridge, MA: Harvard University Press.

Boehm, Christopher (2012). *Moral origins: The evolution of virtue, altruism, and shame.* New York: Basic Books.

Bohm, David (2014). *On dialogue.* London: Routledge Great Minds.

Bok, Derek Curtis (2003). *Universities in the marketplace: The commercialization of higher education.* Princeton, NJ: Princeton University Press.

Bokhari, Laila (2006). "'Paths to jihad – faces of terrorism': Interviews within radical Islamist movements in Pakistan." In *FFI rapport-2006/00935: Paths to global jihad: Radicalisation and recruitment to terror networks*, edited by Laila Bokhari, Thomas Hegghammer, Brynjar Lia, Petter Nesser, and Truls H. Tonnessen, chapter 4, pp. 30–38. Kjeller, Norway: Norwegian Defence Research Establishment. Proceedings from a Forsvarets forskningsinstitutt (FFI) seminar, Oslo, 15 March 2006.

Bokhari, Laila, Richard Barrett, John Horgan, and Tore Bjorgo (2009). "Deradicalization and rehabilitation programmes targeting religious terrorists and extremists in the Muslim world: An overview." In *Leaving terrorism behind: Individual and collective disengagement*, chapter 10, pp. 170–80. London and New York: Routledge.

Bokhari, Laila (2010). "Violence and belonging: Land, love and lethal conflict in the North-West Frontier Province of Pakistan." *Forum for Development Studies, 37* (1), pp. 137–39.

Bond, Michael Harris (1986). "Mutual stereotypes and the facilitation of interaction across cultural lines." *International Journal of Intercultural Relations, 10*, pp. 259–76.

Bond, Michael Harris (1999). "Unity in diversity: Orientations and strategies for building a harmonious multicultural society." In *Social psychology and cultural context*, edited by John Adamopoulos, and Yoshihisa Kashima, pp. 17–39. Thousand Oaks, CA: Sage.

Bond, Michael Harris, and Vivian Miu-Chi Lun (2013a). "Citizen-making: The role of national goals for socializing children." *Social Science Research, 44*, pp. 75–85.

Bond, Michael Harris, and Vivian Miu-Chi Lun (2013b). "Examining religion and well-being across cultures: The cognitive science of religion as sextant." In *Is religion natural? The Chinese challenge*, edited by Ryan Hornbeck, and Justin L. Barrett: Forthcoming.

Borchert, Wolfgang (1947). *Draußen vor der Tür. Ein Stück, das kein Theater spielen und kein Publikum sehen will.* Hamburg, Germany: Rowohlt.

Borchgrevink, Aage Storm (2012). *En norsk tragedie: Anders Behring Breivik og veiene til Utøya.* Oslo: Gyldendal.

Borchgrevink, Kaja, and Kristian Berg Harpviken (2010). "Afghanistan: Civil society between modernity and tradition." In *Civil society and peacebuilding: A critical assessment*, edited by Thania Paffenholz, chapter 11, pp. 235–57. Boulder, CO: Lynne Rienner.

Boserup, Ester (1965). *The conditions of agricultural growth: The economics of agrarian change under population pressure*. Chicago: Aldine.

Boserup, Ester (1970). *Woman's role in economic development*. London: Allen and Unwin.

Bosselmann, Klaus (2015). *Earth governance: Trusteeship of the global commons*. Cheltenham: Edward Elgar.

Bostad, Inga, and Ole Petter Ottersen (2014). "Global presence, global responsibility and the global citizen." In *Global citizen: Challenges and responsibility in an interconnected world*, edited by Aksel Braanen Sterri, chapter 1, pp. 1–3. Rotterdam, The Netherlands: Sense Publishers.

Bostock, J. Knight (1960). "The message of the 'Nibelungenlied'." *The Modern Language Review, 55* (2), pp. 200–12.

Botman, H. Russel (2000). "The OIKOS in a global economic era: A South African comment." In *Sameness and difference: Problems and potentials in South African civil society*, edited by James R. Cochrane, and Bastienne Klein, chapter X. Washington, DC: The Council for Research in Values and Philosophy.

Bourdieu, Pierre (1977). *Outline of a theory of practice*. Cambridge: Cambridge University Press.

Bourdieu, Pierre (1984a). *Distinction: A social critique of the judgement of taste*. London Routledge and Kegan Paul.

Bourdieu, Pierre (1984b). *Homo academicus*. Paris: Minuit.

Bourdieu, Pierre (1990a). *In other words: Essays towards a reflexive sociology*. Stanford, CA: Stanford University Press.

Bourdieu, Pierre (1990b). *The logic of practice*. Stanford, CA: Stanford University Press.

Bourdieu, Pierre, and Jean-Claude Passeron (1990). *Reproduction in education, society and culture*. 2nd edition. London: Sage.

Bourdieu, Pierre (1991). *Language and symbolic power*. Cambridge: Polity Press.

Bourdieu, Pierre, and Loïc J. D. Wacquant (1992). *An invitation to reflexive sociology*. Cambridge: Polity Press.

Bourdieu, Pierre (1996). *The state nobility: Elite schools in the field of power*. Cambridge: Polity Press.

Bourdieu, Pierre (1998). *La domination masculine*. Paris: Seuil.

Bouzar, Dounia (2016). "Escaping radicalism." *Scientific American Mind, 27* (3), pp. 40.

Bowles, Samuel, and Herbert Gintis (2011a). *A cooperative species: Human reciprocity and its evolution*. Princeton, NJ: Princeton University Press.

Bowles, Samuel, and Herbert Gintis (2011b). "A cooperative species." In *A cooperative species: Human reciprocity and its evolution*, chapter 1, pp. 1–7. Princeton, NJ: Princeton University Press.

Boyd, David R. (2012). *The right to a healthy environment: Revitalizing Canada's constitution*. Vancouver: University of British Columbia Press.

Boyd, Robert, and Peter J. Richerson (2009). "Culture and the evolution of human cooperation." *Philosophical Transactions of the Royal Society B: Biological Sciences, 364* (1533), pp. 3281–88.

Boyer, Pascal Robert (2001). *Religion explained: The evolutionary origins of religious thought*. New York: Basic Books.

Boyer, Pascal Robert, and James V. Wertsch (2009). *Memory in mind and culture*. Cambridge: Cambridge University Press.

Boyer, Robert (2004). *The future of economic growth: As new becomes old*. Cheltenham: Edward Elgar.

Brachman, Jarret (2008). *Global jihadism: Theory and practice*. London: Routledge.

Bradshaw, John (1990). *Homecoming: Reclaiming and championing your inner child*. New York: Bantam

Braithwaite, John (2002). *Restorative justice and responsive regulation*. Oxford: Oxford University Press.

Brandal, Nikolai, Øivind Bratberg, and Dag Einar Thorsen (2013). *The Nordic model of social democracy*. Basingstoke: Palgrave Macmillan.

Brandt, Willy, and Independent Commission On International Development Issues (1980). "Das Überleben sichern gemeinsame Interessen der Industrie- und Entwicklungsländer: Bericht der Nord-Süd-Kommission." In *North-South: A programme for survival*. Köln, Germany: Kiepenheuer und Witsch.

Brangwyn, Ben, and Rob Hopkins (2008). *Transition initiatives primer – becoming a transition town, city, district, village, community or even island*. Totnes, Devon: Transition Network.

Braudel, Fernand (1949). *La Mediterranee et le monde mediterraneen a l'epoque de Philippe II*. Paris: Armand Colin.

Braunstein, Philippe (1990). "Forêts d'Europe au Moyen-Âge." *Les Cahiers du Centre de Recherches Historiques, 6*, pp. 2–7.

Breines, Ingeborg, R. W. Connell, and Ingrid Eide (Eds.) (2000). *Males roles, masculinities and violence. A culture of peace perspective*. Paris: UNESCO.

Brendtro, Larry K., Martin Brokenleg, and Steve Van Bockern (2009). *Reclaiming youth at risk: Our hope for the future*. Revised edition. Bloomington, IN: Solution Tree.

Brinkmann, Beatriz (1999). *Itinerary of impunity: Chile 1973-1999. A challenge to dignity*. Santiago, Chile: CINTRAS.

Brinkmann, Ralf Dieter, and Kurt Hermann Stapf (2005). *Innere Kündigung: Wenn der Job zur Fassade wird*. München, Germany: C.H. Beck.

Brinkmann, Svend (2017a). *Stand firm: Resisting the self-improvement craze*. Cambridge: Polity Press.

Brinkmann, Svend (2017b). "Humanism after posthumanism: Or qualitative psychology after the 'posts'." *Qualitative Research in Psychology*, pp. 1–22.

Broushaki, Farnaz, Mark G Thomas, Vivian Link, Saioa López, Lucy van Dorp, Karola Kirsanow, Zuzana Hofmanová, *et al.* (2016). "Early Neolithic genomes from the eastern Fertile Crescent." *Science*.

Brown, Bert R. (1968). "The effects of need to maintain face on interpersonal bargaining." *Journal of Experimental Social Psychology, 4* (1), pp. 107–22.

Brown, Bert R. (1970). "Face-saving following experimentally induced embarrassment." *Journal of Experimental Social Psychology, 6* (3), pp. 255–71.

Brown, Brené (2012a). *Daring greatly: How the courage to be vulnerable transforms the way we live, love, parent, and lead*. New York: Avery.

Brown, Ellen Hodgson (2012b). *Web of debt: The shocking truth about our money system and how we can break free*. 3rd updated edition. Baton Rouge, LA: Third Millennium Press.

Brown, Rupert, and Miles Hewstone (2005). "An integrative theory of intergroup contact." In *Advances in experimental social psychology, volume 37*, edited by Mark P. Zanna, pp. 255–343. San Diego, CA: Elsevier Science.

Browning, Christopher R. (1992). *Ordinary men: Reserve Police Battalion 101 and the final solution in Poland*. New York: HarperCollins.

Bruce, Gary (2010). *The firm: The inside story of the Stasi*. Oxford: Oxford University Press.

Bruhns, Hinnerk (2014). "Der 'Soziologe' und der Krieg. Max Weber 1914-1920 – 'Dieser Krieg ist groß und wunderbar'." *Lendemains, 39* (156), pp. 60–74.

Brøgger, Jan, and Annette Halvorsen (1993). *Kulturforståelse: En nøkkel til vår internasjonale samtid*. Gjøvik, Norway: Damm.

Bråten, Stein (2013). *Roots and collapse of empathy: Human nature at its best and at its worst*. Amsterdam, The Netherlands: John Benjamins.

Buber, Martin (1923/1937). *I and Thou*. Translated by Ronald Gregor Smith. Edinburgh: Clark. German original *Ich und Du*, Leipzig: Insel Verlag, 1923.

Buckley, Brendan M., Kevin J. Anchukaitis, Daniel Penny, Roland Fletcher, Edward R. Cook, Masaki Sano, Le Canh Nam, *et al.* (2010). "Climate as a contributing factor in the demise of Angkor, Cambodia." *Proceedings of the National Academy of Sciences, 107* (15), pp. 6748–52.

Bude, Heinz (2014). *Gesellschaft der Angst*. Hamburg, Germany: Hamburger Edition, Hamburger Institut für Sozialforschung (HIS).

Bugliosi, Vincent, and Curt Gentry (1992). *Helter skelter: The shocking story of the Manson murders*. New edition. London: Arrow.

Bujo, Bénézet (2001). *Foundations of an African ethic: Beyond the universal claims of western morality*. New York: Crossroad.

Burns, Jennifer (2009). *Goddess of the market : Ayn Rand and the American right*. New York: Oxford University Press.

Burrowes, Robert J. (2011). *Why violence?* Victoria, Australia.

Bushman, Brad J., and Roy F. Baumeister (1998). "Threatened egotism, narcissism, self-esteem, and direct and displaced aggression: Does self-love or self-hate lead to violence?". *Journal of Personality and Social Psychology, 75*, pp. 219–29.

Bühler, Karl (1934/1990). *The theory of language: The representational function of language*. Translated by Donald Fraser Goodwin. Amsterdam: John Benjamin. German original *Sprachtheorie*, Jena: Fischer, 1934.

Böckler, Nils, Thorsten Seeger, Peter Sitzer, and Wilhelm Heitmeyer (Eds.) (2013). *School shootings: International research, case studies, and concepts for prevention*. New York: Springer.

Böhm, Wilhelm (Ed.) (1866). *Fürst Bismarck als Redner, vollständige Sammlung der parlamentarischen Reden Bismarcks seit 1847, sachlich und chronologisch geordnet, mit Einleitungen und Erläuterungen versehen von Wilhelm Böhm, zweiter Band: Der Ministerpräsident von Bismarck-Schönhausen 1862-1866*. Berlin, Stuttgart: Wilhelm Spemann.

Cacioppo, John T., and William Patrick (2008). *Loneliness: Human nature and the need for social connection*. New York: Norton.

Cacioppo, John T., James H. Fowler, and Nicholas A. Christakis (2009). "Alone in the crowd: The structure and spread of loneliness in a large social network." *Journal of Personality and Social Psychology, 97* (6), pp. 977.

Cacioppo, John T., Hsi Yuan Chen, and Stephanie Cacioppo (2017). "Reciprocal influences between loneliness and self-centeredness: A cross-lagged panel analysis in a population-based sample of African American, Hispanic, and Caucasian adults." *Personality and Social Psychology Bulletin*.

Cacioppo, Stephanie, John P. Capitanio, and John T. Cacioppo (2014). "Toward a neurology of loneliness." *Psychological Bulletin, 140* (6), pp. 1464–504.

Cainkar, L.ouise, and Sunaina Maira (2005). "Targeting Arab/Muslim/South Asian Americans: Criminalization and cultural citizenship." *Amerasia Journal, 31* (3), pp. 1–28.

Calcutt, Andrew (1998). *Arrested development: Pop culture and the erosion of adulthood*. London: Cassell.

Caldero, Michael A., and John P. Crank (2011). *Police ethics: The corruption of noble cause*. Third revised edition. New York: Routledge, Taylor and Francis. doi:10950009.

Calhoun, Craig (1993). "Postmodernism as pseudohistory." *Theory, Culture and Society, 10* (1), pp. 75–96.

Callahan, William A. (2009). "The cartography of national humiliation and the emergence of China's geobody." *Public Culture, 21* (1), pp. 141–73.

Callahan, William A. (2010). *China: The pessoptimist nation*. New York: Oxford University Press.

Callinicos, Alex (1989). *Against postmodernism: A marxist critique*. Cambridge: Polity Press.

Campbell, Bradley, and Jason Manning (2014). "Microaggression and moral cultures." *Comparative Sociology, 13* (6), pp. 692–726.

Camus, Albert (1951). *L'homme révolté*. Paris: Gallimard.

Canna, Sarah (Ed.) (2013). *White paper: Over a decade later ... What now? What next? A multi-layer assessment of terrorism in its current and future manifestation*. Washington, DC: Nationwide Suspicious Activity Reporting (SAR) Initiative (NSI). Proceedings from the 7th Annual Strategic Multi-layer Assessment (SMA) Conference.

Capaldo, Jeronim (2014). "The Trans-Atlantic Trade and Investment Partnership: European disintegration, unemployment and instability." In *The Global Development And Environment Institute (GDAE) working paper no. 14-03*. Medford, MA: Tufts University, The Global Development And Environment Institute (GDAE).

Caplow, Theodore (1968). *Two against one: Coalitions in triads*. Englewood Cliffs, NJ: Prentice-Hall.

Capra, Fritjof, and Ugo Mattei (2015). *The ecology of law: Toward a legal system in tune with nature and community*. Oakland, CA: Berrett-Koehler.

Cardenas, Sonia (2009). *Human rights in Latin America: A politics of terror and hope*. Philadelphia: University of Pennsylvania Press.

Carneiro, Robert Leonard (1970). "A theory of the origin of the state." *Science, 169* (3947), pp. 733–38.

Carneiro, Robert Leonard (1988). "The circumscription theory: Challenge and response." *American Behavioral Scientist, 31* (4), pp. 497–511.

Carneiro, Robert Leonard (2000). "Process vs. stages: A false dichotomy in tracing the rise of the state." In *Alternatives of Social Evolution*, edited by Nikolay Kradin, Andrey Korotayev, Dmitri Bondarenko, Victor de Munch, and Paul Wason, pp. 52–58. Vladivostok: Far Eastern Branch of the Russian Academy of Sciences.

Carneiro, Robert Leonard (2010). *The evolution of the human mind: From supernaturalism to naturalism – An anthropological perspective*. Clinton Corners, NY: Eliot Werner.

Carneiro, Robert Leonard (2012). "The circumscription theory: A clarification, amplification, and reformulation." *Social Evolution and History, 11* (2, September), pp. 5–30.

Carson, Rachel Louise (1962). *Silent spring*. Boston: Houghton Mifflin.

Carson, Richard T. (2010). "The environmental Kuznets curve: Seeking empirical regularity and theoretical structure." *The Review of Environmental Economics and Policy, 4* (1), pp. 3–23.

Carveth, Donald L. (1994). "Dark epiphany: The encounter with finitude or the discovery of the object in The body." *Psychoanalysis and Contemporary Thought, 17* (2 (Spring), pp. 215–50.

Carveth, Donald L. (2013). *The still small voice: Psychoanalytic reflections on guilt and conscience*. London: Karnac.

Castells, Manuel (1996–1998). *The information age: Economy, society and culture. Vol. 1: The rise of the network society (1996), Vol. 2: The power of identity (1997), Vol. 3: End of millennium (1998)*. Oxford: Blackwell.

Castells, Manuel, Farhad Khosrokhavar, and Alain Touraine (2014). "L'unité des grandes contestations contemporaines: Débat animé par Michel Wieviorka, à Paris, le 14 mai 2013." *Socio, 2*, pp. 139–67.

Cather, Willa Sibert (1913). *O pioneers!* Boston, New York: Houghton Mifflin Company.

Ceballos, Gerardo, Paul R. Ehrlich, Anthony D. Barnosky, Andrés García, Robert M. Pringle, and Todd M. Palmer (2015). "Accelerated modern human-induced species losses: Entering the sixth mass extinction." *Science Advances, 1* (5), pp. e1400253.

Cefaï, Daniel (2007). *Pourquoi se mobilise-t-on?* Paris: La Découverte.

Chagnon, Napoleon A. (1968). *Yanomamö: The fierce people.* New York: Holt, Rinehart and Winston.

Chagnon, Napoleon A. (2013). *Noble savages: My life among two dangerous tribes: The Yanomamö and the anthropologists.* New York: Simon and Schuster.

Chaisson, Eric J. (2001). *Cosmic evolution: The rise of complexity in nature.* Cambridge, MA: Harvard University Press.

Chakhotin, Sergei (1940). *The rape of the masses: The psychology of totalitarian political propaganda.* London: Labour Book Service.

Chaliand, Gérard, and Arnaud Blin (Eds.) (2015). *Histoire du terrorisme: De l'antiquité à Daech.* Paris: Fayard.

Chambers, Whittaker (1952). *Witness.* New York: Random House.

Chandhoke, Neera (2009). "Equality for what? Or the troublesome relation between egalitarianism and respect." In *Humiliation: Claims and context*, edited by Gopal Guru, chapter 8, pp. 140–60. New Delhi: Oxford University Press.

Chang, Ha-Joon (2010). *23 things they don't tell you about capitalism.* London: Allen Lane.

Chang, Jung, and Jon Halliday (2005). *Mao: The unknown story.* New York: Alfred A. Knopf.

Charny, Israel W. (1997). "A personality disorder of excessive power strivings." *Israel Journal of Psychiatry, 34* (1), pp. 3–17.

Charny, Israel W. (2014). "Requiem for the prevention of genocide in our time: Working toward an improbable possibility but not giving up." *Genocide Studies and Prevention: An International Journal, 7* (1), pp. Article 11.

Chase-Dunn, Christopher K., and Thomas D. Hall (1997). *Rise and demise: Comparing world-systems.* Boulder, CO: Westview Press.

Chase-Dunn, Christopher K., and Thomas D. Hall (2002). "Paradigms bridged: Institutional materialism and world-systemic evolution." In *Structure, culture, and history: Recent issues in social theory*, edited by Sing C. Chew, and J. David Knottnerus, pp. 197–216. Lanham, MD: Rowman and Littlefield, based on a paper presented at the Fourteenth World Congress of Sociology, Montreal, July 26 – August 1, 1998, wsarch.ucr.edu/archive/papers/c-d&hall/intsoc98.htm.

Chaturvedi, Vinayak (2000). *Mapping subaltern studies and the postcolonial.* London: Verso.

Chege, Michael (1996). "Africa's murderous professors." *The National Interest,* (46, Winter 1996/97), pp. 32–40.

Chomsky, Noam, and André Vltchek (2013). *On Western terrorism: From Hiroshima to drone warfare.* London: Pluto Press.

Chong, Dennis, and James N. Druckman (2007). "Framing theory." *Annual Review of Political Science, 10* (1), pp. 103–26.

Chowdhury Fink, Naureen, and Hamed El-Said (2011). *Transforming terrorists: Examining international efforts to address violent extremism.* New York: International Peace Institute (IPI).

Christopher K. Chung, M. D., and M. D. Samson J. Cho (2006). "Conceptualization of Jeong and dynamics of Hwabyung." *Psychiatry Investigation, 3* (1), pp. 46–54.

Chua, Amy (2003). *World on fire: How exporting free market democracy breeds ethnic hatred and global instability.* New York: Doubleday.

Chua, Amy (2007). *Day of empire: How hyperpowers rise to global dominance - and why they fall.* New York: Doubleday.

Chödrön, Pema (2001). *The places that scare you: A guide to fearlessness.* Boston: Shambhala.

Clark, Eric (1988). *The want makers: Inside the world of advertising.* New York: Viking.

Clark, Gregory (2014). *The son also rises: Surnames and the history of social mobility*. Princeton, NJ: Princeton University Press.

Clark, Phil (2010). *The Gacaca courts, post-genocide justice and reconciliation in Rwanda: Justice without lawyers*. Cambridge: Cambridge University Press.

Clark, Wesley K. (2003). *Winning modern wars: Iraq, terrorism, and the American empire*. New York: PublicAffairs.

Clay, Zanna, Frans B. M. de Waal, and Takeshi Furuichi (2016). "Obstacles and catalysts to peaceful coexistence in chimpanzees and bonobos." *Behaviour, 153* (9-11), pp. 1293–330.

Clinchy, Blythe McVicker, and Claire Zimmerman (1985). "Growing up intellectually: Issues for college women." In *Work in progress, No. 19*. Wellesley, MA: Stone Center Working Paper Series.

Clinchy, Blythe McVicker (1996). "Connected and separate knowing: Toward a marriage of two minds." In *Knowledge, difference, and power: Essays inspired by women's ways of knowing*, edited by Nancy Rule Goldberger, Jill Mattuck Tarule, Blythe McVicker Clinchy, and Mary Field Belenky, chapter 7, pp. 205–47. New York: Basic Books.

Clor, Harry M. (2009). *On moderation: Defending an ancient virtue in a modern world*. Waco, TX: Baylor University Press.

Coates, John M., and Joe Herbert (2008). "Endogenous steroids and financial risk-taking on a London trading floor." *Proceedings of the National Academy of Sciences (PNAS), 105* (16), pp. 6167–72.

Coates, Ta-Nehisi (2015). *Between the world and me*. New York: Spiegel and Grau.

Cochran, Molly (1999). *Normative theory in international relations: A pragmatic approach*. Cambridge: Cambridge University Press.

Cockburn, Andrew (2015). *Kill chain: The rise of the high-tech assassins*. New York: Henry Holt.

Cohen, Dov (1996). "Law, social policy, and violence: The impact of regional cultures." *Journal of Personality and Social Psychology, 70* (5), pp. 961–78.

Cohen, Dov, E. Nisbett Richard, Brian F. Bowdle, and Norbert Schwarz (1996). "Insult, aggression, and the southern culture of honor: An 'experimental ethnography'." *Journal of Personality and Social Psychology, 70* (5), pp. 945–59.

Cohen, Dov, and Richard E. Nisbett (1997). "Field experiments examining the culture of honor: The role of institutions in perpetuating norms about violence." *Personality and Social Psychology Bulletin, 23* (11), pp. 1188–99.

Cohen, Dov, and Joseph A. Vandello (1997). "Meanings of violence." *The Journal of Legal Studies, 27* (S2, June), pp. 567–84.

Cohen, Dov, Joseph A. Vandello, and Adrian Bantilla (1998). "The sacred and the social: Honor and violence in cultural context." In *Shame: Interpersonal behavior, psychopathology, and culture*, edited by Paul Gilbert, and Bernice Andrews, chapter 14, pp. 261–82. New York: Oxford University Press.

Cohen, Mark Nathan (1977). *The food crisis in prehistory: Overpopulation and the origins of agriculture*. New Haven, CT: Yale University Press.

Cohen, Mark Nathan, and Gillian Margaret Mountford Crane-Kramer (2007). *Ancient health: Skeletal indicators of agricultural and economic intensification*. Gainesville, FL: University Press of Florida.

Cohen, Mark Nathan (2009). "Introduction: Rethinking the origins of agriculture." *Current Anthropology, 50* (5), pp. 591–95.

Cohen, Stephen P., and Laila Bokhari (2011). *The future of Pakistan*. Washington, DC: Brookings Institution Press.

Cohn, Carol (1987). "Sex and death in the rational world of defense intellectuals." *Signs, 12*, pp. 687–718.

Coil, Charles R. (2009). *Primum non nocere – first do no harm: Finding common ground for human indignity.* Fayetteville: University of Arkansas, master's thesis.

Colander, David, Michael Goldberg, Armin Haas, Katarina Juselius, Alan Kirman, Thomas Lux, and Brigitte Sloth (2009). "The financial crisis and the systemic failure of the economics profession ". *A Journal of Politics and Society, 21* (2-3), pp. 249–67.

Cole, Teju (2011). *Open city.* New York: Random House.

Coleman, Peter T. (2003). "Characteristics of protracted, intractable conflict: Toward the development of a metaframework-I." *Peace and Conflict: Journal of Peace Psychology, 9* (1), pp. 1–37.

Coleman, Peter T., Robin R. Vallacher, Andrzej Nowak, and Lan Bui-Wrzosinska (2007). "Intractable conflict as an attractor: A dynamical systems approach to conflict escalation and intractability." *American Behavioral Scientist, 50* (11), pp. 1454–75.

Coleman, Peter T., Lan Bui-Wrzosinska, and Andrzej Nowak (2008). *Toward a dynamical model of power and conflict.* Chicago: Paper presented at the 21st Annual Conference of the International Association of Conflict Management, July, 2008.

Coleman, Peter T., Jennifer S. Goldman, and Katharina Kugler (2009). "Emotional intractability: Gender, anger, aggression and rumination in conflict." *International Journal of Conflict Management, 20* (2), pp. 113–31.

Coleman, Peter T. (2011). *The five percent: Finding solutions to seemingly impossible conflicts.* New York: PublicAffairs.

Collazzoni, Alberto, Cristina Capanna, Massimiliano Bustini, Paolo Stratta, Marzia Ragusa, Antonio Marino, and Alessandro Rossi (2014). "Humiliation and interpersonal sensitivity in depression." *Journal of Affective Disorders, 167,* pp. 224–27.

Collier, Paul (2013). *Exodus: Immigration and multiculturalism in the 21st century.* London: Allen Lane.

Collins, Alan (2004). "State-induced security dilemma maintaining the tragedy." *Cooperation and Conflict, 39* (1), pp. 27–44.

Collins, Chuck, Felice Yeskel, United for a Fair Economy, and Class Action (2005). *Economic apartheid in America: A primer on economic inequality and insecurity.* Revised 2nd edition. New York: New Press.

Collins, Chuck (2012). *99 to 1: How wealth inequality is wrecking the world and what we can do about iIt.* Oakland, CA: Berrett-Koehler.

Collins, Chuck (2014). *Class lives: Stories from across our economic divide.* Ithaca, NY: Cornell University Press.

Collins, Chuck (2016). *Born on third base: A one percenter makes the case for tackling inequality, bringing wealth home, and committing to the common good.* White River Junction, VT: Chelsea Green.

Collins, Patricia Hill (1990). *Black feminist thought: Knowledge, consciousness, and the politics of empowerment.* Boston: Unwin Hyman.

Collins, Robert O., and James M. Burns (2007). *A history of Sub-Saharan Africa.* Cambridge: Cambridge University Press.

Coman, Alin, Charles B. Stone, Emanuele Castano, and William Hirst (2014). "Justifying atrocities: The effect of moral-disengagement strategies on socially shared retrieval-induced forgetting." *Psychological Science.*

Comisión Nacional sobre la Desaparición de Personas (CONADEP) (1984). *Nunca más.* Buenos Aires, Argentina: Editorial Universitaria de Buenos Aires (Eudeba).

Conde, Wolney Lisboa, and Carlos Augusto Monteiro (2014). "Nutrition transition and double burden of undernutrition and excess of weight in Brazil." *The American Journal of Clinical Nutrition, 100* (6), pp. 1617S–22S.

Connell, R. W. (1996). "Teaching boys: New research on masculinity, and gender strategies for schools." *Teachers College Record, 98* (2), pp. 206–35.

Connell, R. W. (2005). *Masculinities.* 2nd edition. Cambridge: Polity Press.

Connell, R. W., and James W. Messerschmidt (2005). "Hegemonic masculinity: Rethinking the concept." *Gender and Society, 19* (6), pp. 829–59.

Connerton, Paul (1989). *How societies remember.* Cambridge: Cambridge University Press.

Connerton, Paul (2009). *How modernity forgets.* Cambridge: Cambridge University Press.

Connerton, Paul (2011). *The spirit of mourning: History, memory and the body.* Cambridge: Cambridge University Press.

Connolly, William E. (2010). *Pluralism in political analysis.* New Brunswick: AldineTransaction.

Conquest, Robert (2008). *The great terror: A reassessment.* 40th Anniversary edition. New York: Oxford University Press.

Cook, David (2010). *Jihad and martyrdom: Critical concepts in islamic studies.* London: Routledge.

Cooper, Helene (2017). *Madame president: The extraordinary journey of Ellen Johnson Sirleaf.* New York: Simon and Schuster.

Corneo, Giacomo (2014). *Bessere Welt – Hat der Kapitalismus ausgedient? Eine Reise durch alternative Wirtschaftssysteme.* Wien: Goldegg.

Corry, Stephen (2010). *Tribal peoples for tomorrow's world: A guide.* London: Survival International.

Coser, Lewis A. (1956). *The functions of social conflict.* New York: Free Press.

Coser, Lewis A. (1974). *Greedy institutions: Patterns of undivided commitment.* New York: Free Press.

Coser, Lewis A. (1977). *Masters of sociological thought: Ideas in historical and social context.* 2nd edition. New York: Harcourt Brace Jovanovich.

Cosgrove, Lisa, Sheldon Krimsky, Manisha Vijayraghavan, and Lisa Schneider (2006). "Financial ties between DSM-IV panel members and the pharmaceutical industry." *Psychotherapy and Psychosomatics, 75* (3), pp. 154–60.

Costanza, Robert, and Ida Kubiszewski (Eds.) (2014). *Creating a sustainable and desirable future: Insights from 45 global thought leaders.* Singapore: World Scientific Publishing.

Côté, James E. (2000). *Arrested adulthood: The changing nature of maturity and identity.* New York: New York University Press.

Council on Communications and Media (2011). "Children, adolescents, obesity, and the media." *Pediatrics, 128* (1), pp. 201–08.

Craigie, Emma, and Jonathan Mayo (2015). *Hitler's last day: Minute by minute.* London: Short Books.

Creed, Pamela M. (2009). *Myth, memory and militarism: The evolution of an American war narrative.* Fairfax, VA: George Mason University, doctoral dissertation, Doctor of Philosophy, digilib.gmu.edu:8080/bitstream/1920/5634/1/Creed_Pamela.pdf.

Creighton, Millie R. (1990). "Revisiting shame and guilt cultures: A forty-year pilgrimage." *Ethos, 18* (3), pp. 279–307.

Crespi, Bernard J., and Douglas Yanega (1995). "The definition of eusociality." *Behavioral Ecology, 6* (1), pp. 109–15.

Crisp, Richard J., Catriona H. Stone, and Natalie R. Hall (2006). "Recategorization and subgroup identification: predicting and preventing threats from common ingroups." *Personality and Social Psychology Bulletin, 32* (2), pp. 230–43.

Cromby, John (2012). "Beyond belief." *Journal of Health Psychology*, pp. 1–15.

Crouch, Colin (2013). *Making capitalism fit for society.* Cambridge: Polity.

Csikszentmihalyi, Milahy (1996). *Creativity: Flow and the psychology of discovery and invention.* New York: Harper Perennial.

Cullather, Nick (2002). "From new deal to new frontier in Afghanistan: Modernization in a buffer state." In *The Cold War as global conflict, Working Paper: #6*: New York University, International Center for Advanced Studies.

Curry, Susan, Edward H. Wagner, and Louis C. Grothaus (1990). "Intrinsic and extrinsic motivation for smoking cessation." *Journal of Consulting and Clinical Psycholy, 58* (3), pp. 310–16.

Cushman, Fiery, Kurt Gray, Allison Gaffey, and Wendy Berry Mendes (2012). "Simulating murder: The aversion to harmful action." *Emotion, 12* (1), pp. 2–7.

Cushman, Philip (1995). *Constructing the self, constructing America: A cultural history of psychotherapy.* Garden City, NY: Da Capo Press.

D'Antonio, Michael (2015). *Never enough: Donald Trump and the pursuit of success.* New York: Thomas Dunne.

Dahle, Maria (2008). *Human rights defenders – do they make a difference?* Oslo: Presentation given at the seminar '60th Anniversary of the Human Rights', at the Oslo Center for Peace and Human Rights, 24th November 2008.

Dahle, Maria (2011). *Introduction to Working Session 3.* Warsaw, Poland: Introduction given on 27th September 2011 at the Human Dimension Implementation Meeting 2011, organised by the Office for Democratic Institutions and Human Rights (ODIHR) of the Organization for Security and Co-operation in Europe (OSCE), 26th September–7th October 2011.

Daly, Herman E. (1991). *Steady-state economics.* Washington, DC: Island Press.

Danner, Mark (2008). "America defeated: How terrorists turned a superpower's strengths against itself." *Alternet, March 26.*

Darimont, Chris T., Caroline H. Fox, Heather M. Bryan, and Thomas E. Reimchen (2015). "The unique ecology of human predators." *Science, 349* (6250), pp. 858–60.

Daubney, Martin (2015). "The morals of the money shot." In *Values and choices in television discourse: A view from both sides of the screen*, edited by Roberta Piazza, Louann Haarman, and Anne Caborn, pp. 229–33. London: Palgrave Macmillan.

Davies, James Chowning (1969). "The J-Curve of rising and declining satisfaction as a cause of some great revolutions and a contained rebellion." In *Violence in America: Historical and comparative perspectives*, edited by Ted Robert Gurr, and Hugh Davis Graham, pp. 547–76. Washington, DC: GPO.

Davies, James Chowning (1971). *When men revolt and why: A reader in political violence and revolution.* New York: Free Press.

Davis, Wade (2009). *The wayfinders: Why ancient wisdom matters in the modern world.* Toronto: House of Anansi Press.

Dawkins, Richard (2006). *The selfish gene.* 3rd edition. Oxford: Oxford University Press.

De Atkine, Norvell B. (2004). "The Arab mind revisited." *Middle East Quarterly, 11* (3, Summer), pp. 47–55.

De Dreu, Carsten K. W., Lindred L. Greer, Gerben A. Van Kleef, Shaul Shalvi, and Michel J. J. Handgraaf (2011). "Oxytocin promotes human ethnocentrism." *Proceedings of the National Academy of Sciences, 108* (4), pp. 1262–66.

de Graaf, John, David Wann, and Thomas H. Naylor (2001). *Affluenza: The all-consuming epidemic.* San Francisco: Berrett-Koehler.

De Landa, Manuel (2002). *Intensive science and virtual philosophy.* London: Continuum.

de Ste. Croix, Geoffrey Ernest Maurice, David Harvey, Robert Parker, and Peter Thonemann (Eds.) (2004). *Athenian democratic origins and other essays.* Oxford: Oxford University Press.

de Waal, Frans B. M. (2005). *Our inner ape: A leading primatologist explains why we are who we are.* New York: Riverhead Books.

de Waal, Frans B. M. (2009). *The age of empathy: Nature's lessons for a kinder society.* New York: Harmony Books.

Decety, Jean, Chia-Yan Yang, and Yawei Cheng (2010). "Physicians down-regulate their pain empathy response: An event-related brain potential study." *NeuroImage, 50* (4), pp. 1676–82.

Deci, Edward L., and Richard M. Ryan (1985). *Intrinsic motivation and self-determination in human behavior.* New York: Plenum.

Deci, Edward L., Richard Koestner, and Richard M. Ryan (1999). "A meta-analytic review of experiments examining the effects of extrinsic rewards on intrinsic motivation." *Psychological Bulletin, 125* (6), pp. 627–68; discussion 92–700.

Deci, Edward L., and Richard M. Ryan (2002). *Handbook of self-determination research.* Rochester, NY: University of Rochester Press.

Defoe, Daniel (1715). *The family instructor: In three parts; I. Relating to fathers and children. II. To masters and servants. III. To husbands and wives.* London: printed for Eman. Matthews.

Del Re, Emanuela C., Evelin Gerda Lindner, Debidatta Aurobinda Mahapatra, Vincenzo Pace, and Valeria Fiorani Piacentini (2009). "Strategia e spontaneismo poli del nuovo terrorismo." *GNOSIS – Rivista Italiana di Intelligence, 1*, pp. 29–51.

Deleuze, Gilles (1969/1990). *The logic of sense.* Translated by Mark Lester, and Charles Stivale. New York: Columbia University Press, French original *Logique du sens*, Paris: Éditions de Minuit, 1969.

Deleuze, Gilles, and Pierre-Félix Guattari (1972/1977). *Anti-Oedipus: Capitalism and schizophrenia.* Translated by Robert Hurley, Mark Seem, and Helen R. Lane. New York: Viking Press. French original *Capitalisme et schizophrénie. L'anti-Œdipe*, Paris: Minuit, 1972.

Delkatesh, Mohamad (2011). "Humiliation: The catalyst for the Arab Revolt." *New Perspectives Quarterly, 28* (2), pp. 57–59.

Demas, Gregory E., Lance J. Kriegsfeld, Seth Blackshaw, Paul Huang, Stephen C. Gammie, Randy J. Nelson, and Solomon H. Snyder (1999). "Elimination of aggressive behavior in male mice lacking endothelial nitric oxide synthase." *The Journal of Neuroscience, 19* (RC30), pp. 1–5.

Deming, W. Edwards (1986). *Out of the crisis: Quality, productivity and competitive position.* Cambridge: Cambridge University Press.

Dennis, Clive (2006). "Humanity's worst invention: Agriculture." *The Ecologist*, pp. 22nd September. Winner of the Ecologist/Coady International Institute 2006 Essay Competition.

Dennis, Kingsley L. (2014). *Phoenix generation: A new era of connection, compassion, and consciousness.* London: Watkins Publishing.

Deresiewicz, William (2014). *Excellent sheep: The miseducation of the American elite and the way to a meaningful life.* New York: Free Press.

Déroulede, Paul (1872). *Chants du soldat.* Paris: Calmann-Lévy.

Derrida, Jacques (1982). "Différance." In *Margins of philosophy*, edited by Jacques Derrida, pp. 3–27. Chicago: Chicago University Press.

Deutsch, Morton, and Harold B. Gerard (1955). "A study of normative and informational social influences upon individual judgment." *The Journal of Abnormal and Social Psychology, 51* (3), pp. 629–36.

Deutsch, Morton (2006). "A framework for thinking about oppression and its change." *Social Justice Research, 19* (1), pp. 7–41.

Devine, Patricia G. (1989). "Stereotypes and prejudice: Their automatic and controlled components." *Journal of Personality and Social Psychology, 56* (1), pp. 5–18.

Dewey, John (1905). "The realism of pragmatism." *The Journal of Philosophy, Psychology and Scientific Methods, 2* (12), pp. 324–27.

Dewey, John (1927). *The public and its problems.* New York: Henry Holt and Company.

Dewey, John (1931). *Philosophy and civilization.* New York: G.P. Putnam.

Di Leo, Jeffrey R., Henry A. Giroux, Sophia A. McClennen, and Kenneth J. Saltman (Eds.) (2013). *Neoliberalism, education, terrorism: Contemporary dialogues.* Boulder, CO: Paradigm.

Diamond, Jared (2005). *Collapse: How societies choose to fail or succeed.* New York: Viking.

Diamond, Stephen A. (1996). *Anger, madness, and the daimonic: The psychological genesis of violence, evil, and creativity.* Albany: State University of New York Press.

Dichter, Thomas W. (2003). *Despite good intentions: Why development assistance to the third world has failed.* Boston: University of Massachusetts Press.

Dierksmeier, Claus (2015). "Human dignity and the business of business." *Human Systems Management, 34* (1), pp. 33–42.

Dierksmeier, Claus (2016). "What is 'humanistic' about humanistic management?". *Humanistic Management Journal, 1* (1), pp. 9–32.

Diesing, Paul (1962). *Reason in society: Five types of decisions and their social conditions.* Urbana: University of Illinois Press.

Đilas, Milovan (1957). *The new class: An analysis of the communist system.* London: Holt, Rinehart and Winston.

Dixon, John, Mark Levine, Steve Reicher, and Kevin Durrheim (2012). "Beyond prejudice: Are negative evaluations the problem and is getting us to like one another more the solution?". *35* (6), pp. 411–25.

Dobson, Andrew (2012). "Listening: The new democratic deficit." *Political Studies, 60* (4), pp. 843–59.

Doherty, Daniel, and Amitai Etzioni (Eds.) (2003). *Voluntary simplicity: Responding to consumer culture.* Lanham, MD: Rowman and Littlefield.

Doi, Takeo (1973/2001). *The anatomy of dependence.* Translated by John Bester. London: Kodansha International. Japanese original *"Amae" No Kôzô*, Tokyo: Kôbundô, 1973.

Doliński, Dariusz, Tomasz Grzyb, Michał Folwarczny, Patrycja Grzybała, Karolina Krzyszycha, Karolina Martynowska, and Jakub Trojanowski (2017). "Would you deliver an electric shock in 2015? Obedience in the experimental paradigm developed by Stanley Milgram in the 50 years following the original studies." *Social Psychological and Personality Science.*

Donati, Pierpaolo, and Margaret S. Archer (2015). *The relational subject.* Cambridge: Cambridge University Press.

Dong, Jingyi (2015). *A study of rural students in the higher education system in China in relation to their context.* Trondheim, Norway: Norwegian University of Science and Technology (NTNU), Department of Education and Lifelong Learning, doctoral dissertation.

Donoghue, Frank (2008). *The last professors: The corporate university and the fate of the humanities.* New York: Fordham University Press.

Doosje, Bertjan, Fathali M. Moghaddam, Arie W. Kruglanski, Arjan de Wolf, Liesbeth Mann, and Allard R. Feddes (2016). "Terrorism, radicalization and de-radicalization." *Current Opinion in Psychology, 11*, pp. 79–84.

Dorling, Danny (2013). *Population 10 billion: The coming demographic crisis and how to survive it.* London: Constable.

Dovidio, John F., Samuel L. Gaertner, and Tamar Saguy (2009). "Commonality and the complexity of 'we': Social attitudes and social change." *Personality and Social Psychology Review, 13* (1), pp. 3–20.

Dower, John W. (1999). *Embracing Defeat: Japan in the wake of World War II.* New York: Norton.

Dreyer, Edward L. (2007). *Zheng He: China and the oceans in the early Ming dynasty, 1405-1433.* New York: Pearson Longman.

Droge, Arthur J., and James D. Tabor (1992). *A noble death: Suicide and martyrdom among Jews and Christians in the ancient world.* San Francisco: HarperSanFrancisco.

Drumbl, Mark A. (2007). *Atrocity, punishment and international law.* Cambridge: Cambridge University Press.

Duckitt, John (1989). "Authoritarianism and group identification: A new view of an old construct." *Political Psychology, 10* (1), pp. 63–84.

Duckitt, John, and Kirstin Fisher (2003). "The impact of social threat on worldview and ideological attitudes." *Political Psychology, 24* (1), pp. 199–222.

Duckitt, John, Boris Bizumic, Stephen W. Krauss, and Edna Heled (2010). "A tripartite approach to right-wing authoritarianism: The authoritarianism-conservatism-traditionalism model." *Political Psychology, 31* (5), pp. 685–715.

Duffy, Regis A., and Angelus Gambatese (Eds.) (1999). *Made in God's image: The Catholic vision of human dignity.* New York: Paulist Press.

Duffy, Thomas P. (2011). "The Flexner Report — 100 years later." *The Yale Journal of Biology and Medicine, 84* (3), pp. 269–76.

Dugas, Michelle, and Arie W. Kruglanski (2014). "The quest for significance model of radicalization: Implications for the management of terrorist detainees." *Behavioral Sciences and the Law, 32* (3), pp. 423–39.

Dunlap, Riley E., Aaron M. McCright, and Jerrod H. Yarosh (2016). "The political divide on climate change: Partisan polarization widens in the U.S." *Environment: Science and Policy for Sustainable Development, 58* (5), pp. 4–23.

Durkheim, Émile (1897). *Le Suicide: Étude de sociologie.* Paris: Félix Alcan.

Durlak, Joseph A., Roger P. Weissberg, Allison B. Dymnicki, Rebecca D. Taylor, and Kriston B. Schellinger (2011). "The impact of enhancing students' social and emotional learning: A meta-analysis of school-based universal interventions." *Child Development, 82* (1, January/February), pp. 405–32.

Dusengumuremy, Jean d'Amour (2015). *No greater love: Testimonies on the life and death of Felicitas Niyitegeka.* Lake Oswergo, OR: Dignity Press.

Dweck, Carol S. (1999). *Self-theories: Their role in motivation, personality, and development.* Philadelphia: Psychology Press.

Dweck, Carol S. (2007). *Mindset – The new psychology of success: How we can learn to fulfill our potential.* New York: Random House.

Dye, Thomas R., Harmon Zeigler, late, and Louis Schubert (2015). *The irony of democracy: An uncommon introduction to American politics.* 17th edition. Boston: Wadsworth, Cengage Learning.

Eagleton, Terence Francis (1991). *Ideology: An introduction.* London: Verso.

Easterlin, Richard A., Laura Angelescu McVey, Malgorzata Switek, Onnicha Sawangfa, and Jacqueline Smith Zweig (2010). "The happiness-income paradox revisited." *Proceedings of the National Academy of Sciences (PNAS) of the United States of America, 107* (52), pp. 22463–68.

Easterly, William Russell (2013). *The tyranny of experts: Economists, dictators, and the forgotten rights of the poor.* New York: Basic Books.

Eberle, Henrik, and Hans-Joachim Neumann (2009). *War Hitler krank? Ein abschließender Befund.* Bergisch-Gladbach, Germany: Lübbe.

Eberstadt, Nicholas (2016). *Men without work: America's invisible crisis.* West Conshohocken, PA: Templeton Press.

Ebrahim, Zak (2014). *Terrorist's son: A story of choice.* New York: Simon and Schuster.

Eder, Klaus (1992). "Culture and crisis: Making sense of the crisis of the work society." In *Theory of culture*, edited by Richard Münch, and Neil J. Smelser, chapter 13, pp. 366–99. Berkeley: University of California Press.

Edkins, Jenny (2003). *Trauma and the memory of politics.* Cambridge: Cambridge University Press. doi:10.1017/CBO9780511840470.

Edmondson, Amy (1999). "Psychological safety and learning behavior in work teams." *Administrative Science Quarterly, 44* (2), pp. 350–83.

Eggers, Dave (2013). *The circle.* San Francisco: McSweeney's.

Ehrenreich, Barbara (2010). *Smile or die: How positive thinking fooled America and the world.* London: Granta.

Ehrenreich Brooks, Rosa (2005). "Failed states, or the state as failure?". *The University of Chicago Law Review, 72* (4, Fall), pp. 1159–96.

Eisenstein, Charles (2014). "Qualitative dimension of collective intelligence: Intention, wisdom, and soul." *Spanda Journal, V* (2, Collective Intelligence), pp. 65–69.

Eisler, Riane Tennenhaus (1987). *The chalice and the blade: Our history, our future.* London: Unwin Hyman.

Eisler, Riane Tennenhaus (2007). *The real wealth of nations: Creating a caring economics.* San Francisco: Berrett-Koehler.

El-Said, Hamed (2015). *New approaches to countering terrorism: Designing and evaluating counter radicalization and de-radicalization programs.* Basingstoke: Palgrave McMillan.

El-Zanaty, Fatma, Enas M. Hussein, Gihan A. Shawky, Ann A. Way, and Sunita Kishor (1996). *Egypt demographic and health survey 1995.* Calverton: National Population Council and Macro International.

Eldridge, Natalie S., Janet L. Surrey, Wendy Rosen, and Jean Baker Miller (2003). "What changes in therapy? Who changes?" In *Work in progress, No. 99.* Wellesley, MA: Stone Center Working Paper Series.

Eliade, Mircea (1949/1954). *The myth of the eternal return: Cosmos and history*. Translated by Willard R. Trask. Princeton, NJ: Princeton University Press. French original *Le mythe de l'éternel retour: Archétypes et répétition*, Paris: Gallimard, 1949.

Eliade, Mircea (1957/1959). *The sacred and the profane: The nature of religion.* New York: Harcourt. German original *Das Heilige und das Profane*, Reinbek: Rowohlt, 1957.

Elias, Damian O., Senthurran Sivalinghem, Andrew C. Mason, Maydianne C. B. Andrade, and Michael M. Kasumovic (2014). "Mate-guarding courtship behaviour: Tactics in a changing world." *Animal Behaviour, 97*, pp. 25–33.

Elias, Norbert (1939/1991). "Changes in the we-I balance." Translated by Edmund Jephcott. In *The society of individuals*, edited by Michael Schröter. Oxford: Blackwell. German original *Die Gesellschaft der Individuen*, 1939/1987.

Elias, Norbert (1939/1994). *The civilizing process (The history of manners, volume I, State formation and civilization, volume II).* Translated by Edmund Jephcott. Oxford: Blackwell. German original *Über den Prozeß der Zivilisation*, Basel, Switzerland: Verlag Haus zum Falken, 1939

Elias, Norbert (1969). *Die höfische Gesellschaft: Untersuchungen zur Soziologie des Königtums und der höfischen Aristokratie mit einer Einleitung: Soziologie und Geschichtswissenschaft.* Darmstadt, Germany: Luchterhand.

Elias, Norbert (1983/1987). *Involvement and detachment. Contributions to the sociology of knowledge.* Translated by Michael Schröter. Oxford: Basil Blackwell. German original *Engagement und Distanzierung. Arbeiten zur Wissenssoziologie I*, Frankfurt am Main: Suhrkamp, 1983.

Elias, Norbert (1985). *The loneliness of the dying.* Oxford: Blackwell.

Elias, Norbert (1996). *The Germans: Power struggles and the development of habitus in the nineteenth and twentieth centuries*. Cambridge: Polity Press.

Elias, Norbert (2000). *The civilizing process: Sociogenetic and psychogenetic investigations*. Oxford: Basil Blackwell.

Elison, Jeff, and Susan L. Harter (2007). "Humiliation: Causes, correlates, and consequences." In *The self-conscious emotions: Theory and research*, edited by Jessica L. Tracy, Richard W. Robins, and June Price Tangney, chapter 17, pp. 310–29. New York: Guilford Press.

Ellis, Bruce J., Marco Del Giudice, Thomas J. Dishion, Aurelio Jose Figueredo, Peter Gray, Vladas Griskevicius, Patricia H. Hawley, *et al.* (2012). "The evolutionary basis of risky adolescent behavior: Implications for science, policy, and practice." *Developmental Psychology, 48* (3), pp. 598–623.

Elshout, Maartje, Rob M. A. Nelissen, and Ilja van Beest (2016). "Conceptualising humiliation." *Cognition and Emotion, 0* (0), pp. 1–14.

Elster, Jon (2003). *Alchemies of the mind: Rationality and the emotions*. Cambridge: Cambridge University Press.

Elworthy, Scilla, and Gabrielle Rifkind (2005). *Hearts and minds: Human security approaches to political violence*. London: Demos.

Emmott, Stephen (2013). *Ten billion*. London: Penguin.

Engerman, Stanley L., and Eugene D. Genovese (1975). *Race and slavery in the Western hemisphere: Quantitative studies*. Princeton, NJ: Princeton University Press.

Englander, David (2013). *Poverty and Poor Law Reform in nineteenth-century Britain, 1834-1914: From Chadwick to Booth*. Florence: Taylor and Francis.

Enloe, Cynthia (1990). *Bananas, beaches and bases: Making feminist sense of international politics*. Berkeley: University of California Press.

Enloe, Cynthia (1993). *The morning after: Sexual politics at the end of the cold war*. Berkely: University of California Press.

Enloe, Cynthia (2000). *Maneuvers: The international politics of militarizing women's lives*. Berkeley: University of California Press.

Enloe, Cynthia (2004). *The curious feminist: Searching for women in a new age of empire*. Berkeley: University of California Press.

Enloe, Cynthia (2007). *Globalization and militarism: Feminists make the link*. Lanham, MD: Rowman and Littlefield.

Enmark, Kristin (2015). *Valvet, föraktet och mitt kärleksförhållande med Clark Olofsson*. Stockholm: Adlibris.

Eriksson, M., and B. Lindstrom (2005). "Validity of Antonovsky's sense of coherence scale: A systematic review." *Journal of Epidemiololgy and Community Health, 59* (6), pp. 460–66.

Escrigas, Cristina (2016). *A higher calling for higher education*. Boston: Great Transition Initiative.

Etzioni, Amitai (2013). "A liberal communitarian paradigm for counterterrorism." *Stanford Journal of International Law, 49* (2, Summer), pp. 330–70.

Evanoff, Douglas D., George G. Kaufman, and Anastasios G. Malliaris (Eds.) (2012). *New perspectives on asset price bubbles: Theory, evidence and policy*. New York: Oxford University Press.

Evans, Patricia (2010). *The verbally abusive relationship: How to recognize it and how to respond*. 3rd edition. Avon, MA: Adams.

Evans, Peter (2008). "Is an alternative globalization possible?". *Politics and Society, 36* (2, Special Issue: Between the Washington Consensus and Another World: Interrogating United States Hegemony and Alternative Visions), pp. 271–305.

Ewen, Elizabeth, and Stuart Ewen (2009). *Typecasting: On the arts and sciences of human inequality*. New York: Seven Stories Press.

Eymericus, Nicolas (1578). *Directorium Inquisitorum*. Romae: In Aedibvs Pop Rom.

Fallon, James H. (2006). "Neuroanatomical background to understanding the brain of the young psychopath." *Ohio State Journal of Criminal Law, 3* (34), pp. 341–67.

Fallon, James H. (2013). *The psychopath inside: A neuroscientist's personal journey into the dark side of the brain*. New York: Penguin.

Fanon, Frantz (1952/1967). *Black skin, white masks*. Translated by Charles Lam Markmann. New York: Grove Press. French original *Peau noire, masques blancs*, Paris: Seuil, 1952.

Fanon, Frantz (1961/1963). *The wretched of the earth*. Translated by Constance Farrington. New York: Grove Press. French original *Les damnés de la terre*, Paris: Maspero, 1961.

Farrington, David P. (1993). "Understanding and preventing bullying." *Crime and Justice, 17* (January), pp. 381–458.

Fassin, Didier (2015). *L'ombre du monde: Une anthropologie de la condition carcérale*. Paris: Seuil.

Fatemi, Sayyed Mohsen (2014). "Questioning the unquestionability of the expert's perspective in psychology." *Journal of Humanistic Psychology*, pp. 1–29.

Fattah, Khaled, and Karin M. Fierke (2009). "A clash of emotions: The politics of humiliation and political violence in the Middle East." *European Journal of International Relations, 15* (1), pp. 67–93.

Fawda, Faraj (1985). *Qabla al-Suqūt (Before downfall)*. Cairo: F. A. Fawda.

Fawda, Faraj (1988). *al-Irhāb (Terrorism)*. Cairo: Dar Misr al-Jadida lil-Nashr wal-tawzi.

Fazio, Russell H., David M. Sanbonmatsu, Martha C. Powell, and Frank R. Kardes (1986). "On the automatic activation of attitudes." *Journal of Personality and Social Psychology, 50* (2), pp. 229–38.

Fazio, Russell H. (1990). "Multiple processes by which attitudes guide behavior: The MODE model as an integrative framework." *Advances in Experimental Social Psychology, 23*, pp. 75–109.

Feather, Norman T., and Katherine Nairn (2005). "Resentment, envy, Schadenfreude, and sympathy: Effects of own and other's deserved or undeserved status." *Australian Journal of Psychology, 57* (2), pp. 87–102.

Feather, Norman T. (2008). "Effects of observer's own status on reactions to a high achiever's failure: Deservingness, resentment, schadenfreude, and sympathy." *Australian Journal of Psychology, 60* (1), pp. 31–43.

Feather, Norman T. (2015). "Analyzing relative deprivation in relation to deservingness, entitlement and resentment." *Social Justice Research, 28* (1), pp. 7–26.

Federici, Silvia (2004). *Caliban and the witch: Women, the body and primitive accumulation*. New York: Autonomedia.

Fedigan, Linda Marie (1986). "The changing role of women in models of human evolution." *Annual Review of Anthropology, 15* (1), pp. 25–66.

Feigon, Lee (2002). *Mao: A reinterpretation*. Blue Ridge Summit, PA: Ivan R. Dee.

Feldman, Marc D. (2004). *Playing sick? Untangling the web of Munchausen syndrome, Munchausen by proxy, malingering and factitious disorder*. New York: Routledge.

Feldman, Stanley (2003). "Enforcing social conformity: A theory of authoritarianism." *Political Psychology, 24* (1), pp. 41–74.

Feldman, Stanley (2013). "Comments on authoritarianism in social context: The role of threat." *International Journal of Psychology, 48* (1), pp. 55–59.

Feller, Amanda E., and Kelly K. Ryan (2012). "Definition, necessity, and Nansen: Efficacy of dialogue in peacebuilding." *Conflict Resolution Quarterly, 29* (4), pp. 351–80.

Fellman, Gordon (1998). *Rambo and the Dalai Lama: The compulsion to win and its threat to human survival.* Albany: State University of New York Press.

Fenstermacher, Laurie, and Todd Leventhal (Eds.) (2011). *Countering violent extremism: Scientific methods and strategies.* Washington, DC: Nationwide Suspicious Activity Reporting (SAR) Initiative (NSI), Topical strategic multi-layer assessment and air force research laboratory multi-disciplinary white paper in support of counter-terrorism and counter-WMD.

Fernbach, Philip M., Todd Rogers, Craig R. Fox, and Steven A. Sloman (2013). "Political extremism is supported by an illusion of understanding." *Psychological Science, XX(X)* pp. 1–8.

Ferrari, Alize J., Fiona J. Charlson, Rosana E. Norman, Scott B. Patten, Greg Freedman, Christopher J. L. Murray, Theo Vos, and Harvey A. Whiteford (2013). "Burden of depressive disorders by country, sex, age, and year: Findings from the global burden of disease study 2010." *Public Library of Science (PLoS) Medicine, 10* (11), pp. e1001547.

Festinger, Leon (1954). "A theory of social comparison processes." *Human Relations, 7* (2), pp. 117–40.

Festinger, Leon (1957). *A theory of cognitive dissonance.* Stanford, CA: Stanford University Press.

Festinger, Leon (1980). *Retrospections on social psychology.* New York: Oxford University Press.

Feuchtwang, Stephan (2011). *After the event: The transmission of grievous loss in Germany, China and Taiwan.* London: Berghahn.

Ficks, Courtney A., and Irwin D. Waldman (2014). "Candidate genes for aggression and antisocial behavior: A meta-analysis of association studies of the 5HTTLPR and MAOA-uVNTR." *Behavior Genetics, 44* (5), pp. 427–44.

Fierke, Karin M. (2004). "Whereof we can speak, thereof we must not be silent: Trauma, political solipsism and war." *Review of International Studies, 30* (4), pp. 471–91.

Figes, Orlando (2007). *The whisperers: Private life in Stalin's Russia.* New York: Picador.

Figgis, John Neville (1914). *The divine right of kings.* 2nd edition. Cambridge: Cambridge University Press.

Fine, Michelle, and Alexis Halkovic (2014). "A delicate and deliberate journey toward justice challenging privilege: Building structures of solidarity." In *The handbook of conflict resolution: Theory and practice,* edited by Morton Deutsch, Peter T. Coleman, and Eric C. Marcus, 2nd Edition edition, chapter 3, pp. 56–75. San Francisco: Jossey-Bass.

Fineman, Martha Albertson (2004). *The myth of autonomy: A theory of dependency.* New York: New Press.

Fischer-Kowalski, Marina, and Helmut Haberl (2007). *Socioecological transitions and global change: Trajectories of social metabolism and land use.* Cheltenham: Edward Elgar.

Fischer, David Hackett (1989). *Albion's seed: Four British folkways in America.* New York: Oxford University Press.

Fischer, Ernst Peter (2009). *Der kleine Darwin. Alles, was man über Evolution wissen sollte.* München, Germany: Pantheon Verlag.

Fisher-Yoshida, Beth, Kathy Dee Geller, and Steven A. Shapiro (Eds.) (2009). *Innovations in transformative learning: Space, culture and the arts.* New York: Peter Lang.

Fisher, Helen E. (2009). *Why him? Why her? Finding real love by understanding your personality type.* New York: Henry Holt.

Fisher, Roger, William Ury, and Bruce Patton (1991). *Getting to yes: Negotiating agreement without giving in.* New York: Houghton Mifflin.

Fisher, Roger, William Ury, and Bruce Patton (2011). *Getting to yes: Negotiating agreement without giving in.* 3rd revised edition. New York: Penguin.

Fisher, Ronald Aylmer (1930). *The genetical theory of natural selection.* Oxford: Clarendon Press.

Fiske, Alan Page (1991). *Structures of social life: The four elementary forms of human relations – communal sharing, authority ranking, equality matching, market pricing*. New York: Free Press.

Fiske, Alan Page (2004). "Relational models theory 2.0." In *Relational models theory: A contemporary overview*, edited by Nick Haslam, chapter 1, pp. 3–25. London: Psychology Press.

Fiske, Alan Page, and Susan T. Fiske (2007). "Social relationships in our species and cultures." In *Handbook of cultural psychology*, edited by Shinobu Kitayama, and Dov Cohen, chapter 11, pp. 283–306. New York: Guilford Press.

Flannery, Kent V., and Joyce Marcus (2003). "The origin of war: New 14C dates from ancient Mexico." *Proceedings of the National Academy of Sciences (PNAS), 100* (20), pp. 11801–05.

Folbre, Nancy (2009). *Saving State U: Why we must fix public higher education*. New York: The New Press.

Foldvary, Fred E. (2006). *The ultimate tax reform: Public revenue from land rent*. Santa Clara, CA: Santa Clara University, Civil Society Institute.

Fonagy, Peter, György Gergely, Elliot Jurist, and Mary Target (2004). *Affect regulation, mentalization, and the development of the self*. London: Karnac.

Fonagy, Peter, David Cottrell, Jeannette Phillips, Dickon Bevington, Danya Glaser, and Elizabeth Allison (2015). *What works for whom? A critical review of treatments for children and adolescents*. 2nd edition. New York: Guilford Press.

Fontan, Victoria (2001). *The dialectics of humiliation: Polarization between occupier and occupied in post-Saddam Iraq*. Human Dignity and Humiliation Studies.

Fontan, Victoria C. (2008). *Voices from post-Saddam Iraq: Living with terrorism, insurgency, and new forms of tyranny*. Westport, CT: Praeger Security International, Greenwood.

Fontan, Victoria C. (2012). *Decolonizing peace*. Lake Oswego, OR: World Dignity University Press.

Forbes, Jack D. (2008). *Columbus and other cannibals*. Revised edition. New York: Seven Stories Press.

Ford, Elizabeth (2017). *Amazing things can happen: Heartbreak and hope on the Bellevue Hospital Psychiatric Prison Ward*. New York: Regan Arts.

Forster, Edward Morgan (1910). *Howards end*. London: Edward Arnold.

Foucault, Michel (1957a). "La psychologie de 1850 à 1950." In *Histoire de la philosophie européenne, tome II: Tableau de la philosophie contemporaine*, edited by Denis Huisman, and Alfred Weber, pp. 591–606. Paris: Librairie Fischbacher, reproduit en Michel Foucault, *Dits et écrits*, Paris, Gallimard, 1994, tome I, pp. 120–137.

Foucault, Michel (1957b). "La recherche scientifique et la psychologie." In *Des chercheurs Francais s'interrogent: Orientation et organisation du travail scientifique en France*, edited by Jean Édouard Morère, pp. 173–201. Toulouse: Collection Nouvelle Recherche no. 13, reproduit en Michel Foucault, *Dits et Ēcrits*, Paris: Gallimard, 1994, tome I. pp. 137–158.

Foucault, Michel (1961). *Folie et deraison: Histoire de la folie a l'age classique*. Paris: Librairie Plon.

Foucault, Michel (1961/2006). *Madness and civilization: A history of insanity in the age of reason*. Translated by Jonathan Murphy, and Jean Khalfa. New York: Routledge. French original *Histoire de la folie à l'âge classique – Folie et déraison*, Paris: Plon, 1961.

Foucault, Michel (1966/1970). *The order of things: An archaeology of the human sciences*. New York: Pantheon Books. French original *Les mots et les choses. Une archéologie des sciences humaines,* Paris: Gallimard, 1966.

Foucault, Michel, and Gilles Deleuze (1972). "Les intellectuels et le pouvoir." *L'Arc, 49* (second trimester), pp. 3–10, reprinted in Michel Foucault, *Dits et Ēcrits*. Volume II, Paris: Gallimard, 1994.

Foucault, Michel (1975). *Surveiller et punir: Naissance de la prison*. Paris: Gallimard.

Foucault, Michel (1979). "On governmentality." *Ideology and Consciousness, 6*, pp. 5–21.

Foucault, Michel, and Colin Gordon (1980). *Power/knowledge: Selected interviews and other writings, 1972–1977.* New York: Pantheon.

Foucault, Michel (1984). "What is enlightenment? (Qu'est-ce que les lumières?)." In *The Foucault reader*, edited by Paul Rabinow, pp. 32–50. New York: Pantheon Books.

Foucault, Michel (1991). "Governmentality." In *The Foucault effect: Studies in governmentality*, edited by Graham Burchell, Colin Gordon, and Peter Miller, chapter 4, pp. 87–104. Chicago: University of Chicago Press.

Foucault, Michel (1994a). *Dits et écrits IV, 1980 - 1988.* Paris: Gallimard.

Foucault, Michel (1994b). *Dits et écrits III, 1976 - 1979.* Paris: Gallimard.

Fox, Warwick (1992). "Intellectual origins of the 'depth' theme in the philosophy of Arne Naess." *Trumpeter, 9* (2), pp. trumpeter.athabascau.ca/archives/content/v9.2/fox2.html.

Fox, Warwick (2000). *Ethics and the built environment.* London: Routledge.

Fraenkel, Carlos F. (2015). *Teaching Plato in Palestine: Philosophy in a divided world.* Princeton, NJ: Princeton University Press.

Fraenkel, Ernst (1941). *The dual state: A contribution to the theory of dictatorship.* New York: Oxford University Press.

Fraiman, Susan (2003). *Cool men and the second sex.* New York: Columbia University Press.

Frank, Jerome D. (1961). *Persuasion and healing: A comparative study of psychotherapy.* Baltimore, MD: John Hopkins University Press.

Frank, Robert H. (2011). *The Darwin economy: Liberty, competition, and the common good.* Princeton, NJ: Princeton University Press.

Frank, Robert H. (2016). *Success and luck: Good fortune and the myth of meritocracy.* Princeton, NJ: Princeton University Press.

Frank, Roberta (1984). "Viking atrocity and Skaldic verse: The Rite of the Blood-Eagle." *The English Historical Review, XCIX* (CCCXCI), pp. 332–43.

Frank, Thomas (2004). *What's the matter with Kansas? How conservatives won the heart of America.* New York: Metropolitan Books.

Frankl, Viktor Emil (1946). *Ärztliche Seelsorge. Grundlagen der Logotherapie und Existenzanalyse.* Wien: Deuticke.

Frankl, Viktor Emil (1946/1959). *Man's search for meaning: An introduction to logotherapy.* Translated by Ilse Lasch, and Gordon W. Allport. New York: Beacon Press. Earlier title *From Death-Camp to Existentialism*, 1959. German original *Ein Psycholog erlebt das Konzentrationslager*, Wien, Austria: Verlag für Jugend und Volk, 1946.

Frase, Peter (2016). *Four futures: Life after capitalism.* London: Verso.

Fraser, Nancy (2014). "Can society be commodities all the way down? Post-Polanyian reflections on capitalist crisis." *Economy and Society, 43* (4), pp. 541–58.

Frednes, Trond Einar, and Jørn Lier Horst (2015). *Badboy.* Oslo: Kagge.

Freeman, Charles P. (2003a). "Constantine and the coming of the Christian state." In *The closing of the Western mind: The rise of faith and the fall of reason*, chapter 11, pp. 154–77. New York: Knopf.

Freeman, Charles P. (2003b). *The closing of the Western mind: The rise of faith and the fall of reason.* New York: Knopf.

Freire, Paulo (1968/1970). *Pedagogy of the oppressed.* Translated by Myra Bergman Ramos. New York: Herder and Herder. Portuguese original *Pedagogia do oprimido*, 1968.

Freire, Paulo (1968/1973). *Education for critical consciousness.* Translated by Myra Bergman Ramos. New York: Seabury Press. Portuguese original *Educação e conscientização: Extencionismo rural,* Cuernavaca, México: CIDOC/Cuaderno, no. 25, 1968.

French, Jeffrey A., Kevin B. Smith, John R. Alford, Adam Guck, Andrew K. Birnie, and John R. Hibbing (2014). "Cortisol and politics: Variance in voting behavior is predicted by baseline cortisol levels." *Physiology and Behavior, 133,* pp. 61–67.

Freud, Sigmund (1939/2010). *Der Mann Moses und die monotheistische Religion: Schriften über die Religion.* Stuttgart, Germany: Philipp Reclam.

Freyd, Jennifer J., and Pamela Birrell (2013). *Blind to betrayal: Why we fool ourselves we aren't being fooled.* Hoboken, NJ: Wiley.

Freyre, Gilberto (1933). *Casa-grande e senzala: Formacao da familia brasileira sob o regimen de economia patriarchal.* Rio de Janeiro: Maria and Schmidt.

Fried, Morton H. (1967). *The evolution of political society: An essay in political anthropology.* New York: Random House.

Fried, Rebecca A. (2015). "No Irish need deny: Evidence for the historicity of NINA restrictions in advertisements and signs." *Journal of Social History.*

Frijda, Nico H. (2008). "The psychologists' point of view." In *Handbook of Emotions,* edited by Jeannette M. Haviland-Jones, Lisa F. Barrett, and Michael Lewis, pp. 68–87. New York: Guilford Press.

Fromm, Erich (1941). *Escape from freedom.* New York: Rinehart.

Fromm, Erich (1963). *War within man: A psychological enquiry into the roots of destructiveness.* Philadelphia: American Friends Service Committee.

Fromm, Erich (1973). *The anatomy of human destructiveness.* New York: Holt, Rinehart and Winston.

Fromm, Erich (1976). *To have or to be?* New York: Harper and Row.

Fromm, M. Gerard (Ed.) (2011). *Lost in transmission: Studies of trauma across generations.* London: Karnac.

Frost, Tore (2003). "Hva mener vi med respekt for menneskeverdet?" In *Samordingsrådet (SOR) rapport Nr. 3,* pp. 6–14. Oslo: Samordingsrådet (SOR).

Fry, Douglas P. (2007). *Beyond war: The human potential for peace.* Oxford: Oxford University Press.

Fry, Douglas P. (2009). "Anthropological insights for creating nonwarring social systems." *Journal of Aggression, Conflict and Peace Research, 1* (2), pp. 4–15.

Fry, Douglas P. (Ed.) (2013). *War, peace, and human nature: The convergence of evolutionary and cultural views.* New York: Oxford University Press.

Fröhling, Ulla (2012). *Unser geraubtes Leben: Die wahre Geschichte von Liebe und Hoffnung in einer grausamen Sekte.* Köln, Germany: Bastei Lübbe.

Fuchs, Eberhard, and Gabriele Flügge (2014). "Adult neuroplasticity: More than 40 years of research." *Neural Plasticity, 2014,* pp. 10.

Fuglestvedt, Ingrid (2005). "Contact and communication in Northern Europe 10 200 – 9 000 / 8 500 BP – A phenomenological approach to the connection between technology, skill and landscape." In *Pioneer settlements and colonization processes in the Barents region, Vuollerim papers in hunter-gatherer archaeology, volume 1, Vuollerim 6000 år,* edited by Helena Knutsson, pp. 79–96. Vuollerim, Sweden: Vuollerim Museum Press.

Fuglestvedt, Ingrid (2008). "How many totemic clans existed in Eastern Norway during the Late Mesolithic?" In *Facets of archeology. Essays in honour of Lotte Hedeager on her 60th birthday,* edited by Konstantinos Chilidis, Julie Lund, and Christopher Prescott, pp. 351–66. Oslo: Unipub.

Fuglestvedt, Ingrid (2010). *Why did it take so long? The pioneer condition on peninsular Scandinavia and the termination of the 'Palaeolithic way' in Europe.* Oslo: University of Oslo, Department of Archaeology, Conservation and History.

Fujiwara, Takeo, and Ichiro Kawachi (2008). "Social capital and health: A study of adult twins in the U.S.". *American Journal of Preventive Health, 35* (2), pp. 139–44.

Fulbeck, William (1602). *The second part of the Parallele, or conference of the ciuill law, the canon law, and the common law of this realme of England: Wherein the agreement and disagreement of these three lawes touching diuers matters not before conferred, is at large debated and discussed. Whereunto is annexed a table ... Handled in seauen dialogues.* London: Printed by Adam Islip for Thomas Wight.

Fuller, R. Buckminster (1981). *Critical path.* New York: St. Martin's Press.

Fuller, Robert W. (2003). *Somebodies and nobodies: Overcoming the abuse of rank.* Grabriola, BC: New Society Publishers.

Fuller, Robert W., and Pamela A. Gerloff (2008). *Dignity for all: How to create a world without rankism.* San Francisco: Berrett-Koehler.

Føllesdal, Dagfinn (1988). "Husserl on evidence and justification." In *Edmund Husserl and the phenomenological tradition: Essays in phenomenology*, edited by Robert Sokolowski, pp. 107–29. Washington, DC: Catholic University of America Press. Proceedings of a lecture series in the Fall of 1985, in Studies in Philosophy and the History of Philosophy, Vol. 18.

Føllesdal, Dagfinn, and Michael Depaul (2015). "The role of arguments in philosophy." *Journal of Philosophical Research, 40* (9999), pp. 17–23.

Gabel, Peter Joseph (2000). *The bank teller and other essays on the politics of meaning.* San Francisco: Acada.

Gadamer, Hans-Georg (1960/1989). *Truth and method.* Translated by Joel Weinsheimer, and Donald G. Marshall. London: Sheed and Ward. German original *Wahrheit und Methode: Grundzüge einer philosophischen Hermeneutik*, Tübingen, Germany: Mohr Siebeck, 1960.

Gaertner, Samuel L., and John F. Dovidio (1999). *Reducing intergroup bias: The common ingroup identity model.* Hove: Psychology Press.

Gaertner, Samuel L., John F. Dovidio, Mary C. Rust, Jason A. Nier, Brenda S. Banker, Christine M. Ward, Gary R. Mottola, and Missy Houlette (1999). "Reducing intergroup bias: Elements of intergroup cooperation." *Journal of Personality and Social Psychology, 76* (3), pp. 388–402.

Gaertner, Samuel L., John F. Dovidio, Brenda S. Banker, Missy Houlette, Kelly M. Johnson, Elizabeth A. McGlynn, and Donelson R. Forsyth (2000). "Reducing intergroup conflict: From superordinate goals to decategorization, recategorization, and mutual differentiation." *Group Dynamics: Theory, Research, and Practice, 4* (1), pp. 98–114.

Gaertner, Samuel L., Betty A. Bachman, John F. Dovidio, and Brenda S. Banker (2012). "Corporate mergers and stepfamily marriages: Identity, harmony, and commitment." In *Social identity processes in organizational contexts*, edited by Michael A. Hogg, and Deborah J. Terry, New edition, pp. 265–82. New York: Psychology Press.

Gallese, Vittorio (2003). "The roots of empathy: The shared manifold hypothesis and the neural basis of intersubjectivity." *Psychopathology, 36* (4), pp. 171–80.

Galli, Thomas (2016). *Die Schwere der Schuld: Ein Gefängnisdirektor erzählt* Berlin: Das Neue Berlin.

Galtung, Johan, Carl G. Jacobsen, Kai Frithjof Brand-Jacobsen, and Finn Tschudi (2000). *Searching for peace: The road to TRANSCEND.* London: Pluto Press in association with TRANSCEND.

Galtung, Johan Vincent (1969). "Violence, peace, and peace research." *Journal of Peace Research, 3*, pp. 167–91.

Galtung, Johan Vincent (1971). "A structural theory of imperialism." *Journal of Peace Research, 8* (2), pp. 81–117.

Galtung, Johan Vincent (1976). *Social position and social behavior: Center-periphery concepts and theories.* Oslo, Dubrovnik: University of Oslo, Inter-University Centre, Dubrovnik, Croatia.

Galtung, Johan Vincent (1977). *Methodology and ideology: Theory and methods of social research. Essays in methodology, volume 1.* Copenhagen: Christian Ejlers.

Galtung, Johan Vincent (1978). *Peace and social structure. Essays in peace research, volume 3.* Copenhagen: Christian Ejlers.

Galtung, Johan Vincent (1990). "Cultural violence." *Journal of Peace Research, 27* (3), pp. 291–305.

Galtung, Johan Vincent (1996). *Peace by peaceful means.* Oslo and London: International Peace Research Institute Oslo (PRIO) and Sage.

Galtung, Johan Vincent (2012). *Peace economics: From a killing to a living economy.* Oslo: Kolofon.

Gandhi, Arun Manilal (2003). *Legacy of love: My education on the path of nonviolence.* El Sobrante, CA: North Bay Book.

Garber, James, F. Kent Reilly, and George E. Lankford (Eds.) (2011). *Visualizing the sacred: Cosmic visions, regionalism, and the art of the Mississippian world.* Austin, TX: University of Texas Press.

Garland, Robert (2010). *Hannibal* London: Bristol Classical Press.

Gawronski, Bertram (2004). "Theory-based bias correction in dispositional inference: The fundamental attribution error is dead, long live the correspondence bias." *European Review of Social Psychology, 15* (1), pp. 183–217.

Gawronski, Bertram, and Galen V. Bodenhausen (2006). "Associative and propositional processes in evaluation: An integrative review of implicit and explicit attitude change." *Psychological Bulletin, 132* (5), pp. 692–731.

Gazzaniga, Michael S. (2011). *Who's in charge? Free will and the science of the brain.* New York: Ecco.

Gbadegesin, Segun (1991). *African philosophy: Traditional Yoruba philosophy and contemporary African realities.* New York: Peter Lang.

Geertz, Clifford (1983). *Local knowledge: Further essays in interpretive anthropology.* New York: Basic Books.

Gellately, Robert (2007). *Lenin, Stalin, and Hitler: The age of social catastrophe.* New York: Knopf.

George, Henry (1879). *Progress and poverty : An inquiry into the cause of industrial depressions and of increase of want with increase of wealth: The remedy.* New York: D. Appleton and Company.

George, Susan (2015). *Shadow sovereigns: How global corporations are seizing power.* Cambridge: Polity press.

Gepts, Paul L., Thomas R. Famula, Robert L. Bettinger, Stephen B. Brush, Ardeshir B. Damania, Patrick E. McGuire, and Calvin O. Qualset (Eds.) (2012). *Biodiversity in agriculture: Domestication, evolution, and sustainability.* New York: Cambridge University Press.

Gerbault, Pascale, Anke Liebert, Yuval Itan, Adam Powell, Mathias Currat, Joachim Burger, Dallas M. Swallow, and Mark G. Thomas (2011). "Evolution of lactase persistence: an example of human niche construction." *Philosophical Transactions of the Royal Society B: Biological Sciences, 366* (1566), pp. 863–77.

Gergen, Kenneth J., Aydan Gulrerce, Andrew Lock, and Girishwar Misra (1996). "Psychological science in cultural context." *American Psychologist, 51* (5, May), pp. 496–503.

Gergen, Kenneth J. (2010). "The acculturated brain." *Theory and Psychology, 20* (6), pp. 1–20.

Gessen, Masha (2013). *The man without a face: The unlikely rise of Vladimir Putin.* London: Granta.

Giacaman, Rita, Niveen M. E. Abu-Rmeileh, Abdullatif Husseini, Hana Sasb, and William Boyce (2007). "Humiliation: The invisible trauma of war for Palestinian youth." *Public Health, 121* (8), pp. 563–71.

Gibson, Rachel L. (2007). *Toxic baby bottles: Scientific study finds leaching chemicals in clear plastic baby bottles.* Los Angeles: Environment California Research and Policy Center.

Giddens, Anthony (1984). *The constitution of society: Outline of the theory of structuration.* Cambridge: Polity Press.

Giddens, Anthony (1990). *The consequences of modernity.* Cambridge: Polity Press.

Giddens, Anthony (1991). *Modernity and self-identity: Self and society in the late modern age.* Cambridge: Polity Press.

Gilad, Ben, and Markus Götz Junginger (2010). *Mit Business Wargaming den Markt erobern: Strategische Kriegsführung für Manager.* München, Germany: Redline Verlag.

Gilbert, Daniel T. (1998). "Speeding with Ned: A personal view of the correspondence bias." In *Attribution and social interaction: The legacy of Edward E. Jones,* edited by John M. Darley, and Joel Cooper, chapter 1, pp. 5–36. Washington, DC: American Psychological Association.

Gilbert, Daniel T. (2006). *Stumbling on happiness.* New York: Knopf.

Gilbert, Gustave M. (1947). *Nuremberg diary.* New York: Farrar, Straus.

Gill, Richardson Benedict (2000). *The great Maya droughts: Water, life, and death.* Albuquerque: University of New Mexico Press.

Gilligan, James (2000). "Punishment and violence: Is the criminal law based on one huge mistake." *Social Research, 67* (3), pp. 745–72.

Gilligan, James (2003). "Shame, guilt, and violence." *Social Research, 70* (4, Winter), pp. 1149–80.

Gilpin, Robert (1981). *War and change in world politics.* Cambridge: Cambridge University Press.

Gilpin, Robert (1988). " The theory of hegemonic war." *The Journal of Interdisciplinary History, 18* (4, Spring, The Origin and Prevention of Major Wars), pp. 591–613.

Ginges, Jeremy, Scott Atran, Douglas Medin, and Khalil Shikaki (2007). "Sacred bounds on rational resolution of violent political conflict." *Proceedings of the National Academy of Sciences (PNAS) of the United States of America, 104* (18), pp. 7357–60.

Ginges, Jeremy, and Scott Atran (2008). "Humiliation and the inertia effect: Implications for understanding violence and compromise in intractable intergroup conflicts." *Journal of Cognition and Culture, 8* (3), pp. 281–94.

Ginsberg, Benjamin (2011). *The fall of the faculty: The rise of the all-administrative university and why it matters.* Oxford: Oxford University Press.

Giroux, Henry A., and Paulo Freire (Foreword) (Eds.) (2001). *Theory and resistance in education: Towards a pedagogy for the opposition.* Westport, CT: Bergin and Garvey.

Giroux, Henry A., and Susan Searls Giroux (2004). *Take back higher education: Race, youth, and the crisis of democracy in the post-civil rights era.* New York: Palgrave Macmillan.

Giroux, Henry A. (2010). *Hearts of darkness: Torturing children in the war on terror.* Boulder, CO: Paradigm.

Giroux, Henry A. (2011). *Zombie politics and culture in the age of casino capitalism.* New York: Peter Lang.

Giroux, Henry A. (2012). *Disposable youth, racialized memories, and the culture of cruelty.* New York: Routledge.

Giroux, Henry A. (2013). *America's education deficit and the war on youth.* New York: Monthly Review Press.

Giroux, Henry A. (2014a). *Neoliberalism's war on higher education.* Chicago: Haymarket.

Giroux, Henry A. (2014b). *The violence of organized forgetting: Thinking beyond America's disimagination machine.* San Francisco: City Lights.

Gladwell, Malcolm (2000). *The tipping point: How little things can make a big difference.* Boston: Little, Brown and Company.

Gladwell, Malcolm (2005). *Blink: The power of thinking without thinking.* New York: Little, Brown and Company.

Glaser, Charles L. (1997). "The security dilemma revisited." *World Politics, 50* (1, October, Fiftieth Anniversary Special Issue), pp. 171–201.

Gleditsch, Nils Petter (2012). "Aldri for sent å være pessimist?" In *I strid for fred: Fredskontoret 1962-1972 – idealistisk fredsarbeid og bred grasrotaktivitet*, edited by Sverre Røed-Larsen, and Anne Margrete Hjort-Larsen, pp. 179–82. Oslo: Kolofon.

Glimcher, Paul W., and Ernst Fehr (Eds.) (2014). *Neuroeconomics: Decision making and the brain.* Amsterdam: Elsevier.

Gobodo-Madikizela, Pumla (2008). "Trauma, forgiveness and the witnessing dance: Making public spaces intimate." *Journal of Analytical Psychology, 53* (2), pp. 169–88.

Goetz, Rainald (2012). *Johann Holtrop: Abriss der Gesellschaft.* Berlin: Suhrkamp.

Goetzmann, William N. (2016). *Money changes everything: How finance made civilization possible.* Princeton, NJ: Princeton University Press.

Goffman, Erving (1955). "On face-work: An analysis of ritual elements of social interaction." *Psychiatry: Journal for the Study of Interpersonal Processes, 18* (3), pp. 213–31.

Goffman, Erving (1967). *Interaction ritual: Essays on face-to-face behavior.* New York: Doubleday.

Goffman, Erving (1974). *Frame analysis: An essay on the organization of experience.* New York: Harper and Row.

Goldhahn, Joakim, Ingrid Fuglestvedt, and Andrew Jones (Eds.) (2010). *Changing pictures: Rock art traditions and visions in northern Europe.* Oxford: Oxbow Books.

Goldman, Jennifer S., and Peter T. Coleman (2005a). *A theoretical understanding of how emotions fuel intractable conflict: The case of humiliation.* New York: International Center for Cooperation and Conflict Resolution, Teachers College, Columbia University.

Goldman, Jennifer S., and Peter T. Coleman (2005b). *How humiliation fuels intractable conflict: The effects of emotional roles on recall and reactions to conflictual encounters.* New York: International Center for Cooperation and Conflict Resolution, Teachers College, Columbia University.

Goldstein, Joshua S. (2001). *War and gender: How gender shapes the war systems and vice versa.* Cambridge: Cambridge University Press.

Goldstein, Joshua S. (2011). *Winning the war on war: The decline of armed conflict worldwide.* New York: Dutton/Plume.

Goldstein, Joshua S., and Jon C. Pevehouse (2016). *International relations.* 11th edition. New York: Pearson Longman.

Goldstone, Jack A., Ted Robert Gurr, and Farrokh Moshiri (1991). *Revolutions of the late twentieth century.* Boulder, CO: Westview Press.

Goldstone, Jack A., and Jay Ulfelder (2005). "How to construct stable democracies." *Washington Quarterly, 28* (1), pp. 9–20.

Goldstone, Jack A., Robert H. Bates, David L. Epstein, Ted Robert Gurr, Michael B. Lustik, Monty G. Marshall, Jay Ulfelder, and Mark Woodward (2010). "A global model for forecasting political instability." *American Journal of Political Science, 54* (1, January), pp. 190–208.

Goodale, Mark, and Sally Engle Merry (Eds.) (2007). *The practice of human rights: Tracking law between the global and the local.* Cambridge: Cambridge Univerity Press.

Goodwin, Jeff, and James M. Jasper (Eds.) (2004). *Rethinking social movements: Structure, meaning, and emotion.* Lanham, MD: Rowman and Littlefield.

Goodwin, Neva Rockefeller, Jonathan M. Harris, Julie A. Nelson, Brian Roach, and Mariano Torras (2014a). *Macroeconomics in context*. 2nd edition. Armonk, NY: Sharpe.

Goodwin, Neva Rockefeller, Jonathan M. Harris, Julie A. Nelson, Brian Roach, and Mariano Torras (2014b). *Microeconomics in context*. 3rd edition. Armonk, NY: Sharpe.

Gorbačev, Mikhail Sergeyevich (2014/2016). *The new Russia*. Cambridge: Polity. Russian original *Posle Kremlya*, Moskva: Ves mir, 2014.

Gordon, Lewis R. (2008). *An introduction to Africana philosophy*. Cambridge: Cambridge University Press.

Gore, Al (2013). *The future: Six drivers of global change*. New York: Random House.

Gornitzka, Åse, and Liv Langfeldt (Eds.) (2008). *Borderless knowledge: Understanding the 'new' internationalisation of research and higher education in Norway*. Dordrecht, The Netherlands: Springer.

Gortemaker, Heike B. (2010). *Eva Braun. Leben mit Hitler*. München, Germany: C.H. Beck.

Gorz, André (1964). *Stratégie ouvrière et néocapitalisme*. Paris: Éditions du Seuil.

Gorz, André (1967). *A strategy for labor: A radical proposal*. Boston: Beacon Press.

Gottlieb, Lynn (1995). *She who dwells within: A feminist vision of a renewed Judaism*. New York: HarperOne.

Gottman, John Mordechai, Lynn Fainsilber Katz, and Carole Hooven (1997). *Meta-emotion: How families communicate emotionally*. Mahwah, NJ: Erlbaum.

Gould, Kenneth A., Allan Schnaiberg, and Adam S. Weinberg (1996). *Local environmental struggles: Citizen activism in the treadmill of production*. Cambridge: Cambridge University Press. doi:10.1017/CBO9780511752759.

Gowdy, John, and Irmi Seidl (2004). "Economic man and selfish genes: The implications of group selection for economic valuation and policy." *The Journal of Socio-Economics, 33* (3), pp. 343–58.

Gowdy, John M., Denise E. Dollimore, David Sloan Wilson, and Ulrich Witt (2013). "Economic cosmology and the evolutionary challenge." *Journal of Economic Behavior and Organization, 90*, pp. S11–S20.

Graeber, David (2001). *Toward an anthropological theory of value: The false coin of our own dreams*. New York: Palgrave.

Graeber, David (2011). *Debt: The first 5,000 years*. New York: Melville House.

Granovetter, Mark S. (1973). "The strength of weak ties." *American Journal of Sociology, 78* (May), pp. 1360–80.

Granovetter, Mark S. (2002). "A theoretical agenda for economic sociology." In *The new economic sociology: Developments in an emerging field*, edited by Mauro Guillen, Randall Collins, Paula England, and Marshall Meyer, chapter 2, pp. 35–60. New York: Russell Sage Foundation.

Gray, John (2002). *False dawn: The delusions of global capitalism*. London: Granta Books.

Grear, Anna (2012). "Should trees have standing: 40 years on?". *Journal of Human Rights and the Environment, 3* (0), pp. 1.

Greene, Joshua David (2013). *Moral tribes: Emotion, reason, and the gap between us and them*. New York: Penguin.

Greene, Michael B. (2006). "Bullying in schools: A plea for measure of human rights." *Journal of Social Issues, 62* (1), pp. 63–79.

Greenfeld, Liah (1992). *Nationalism: Five roads to modernity*. Cambridge, MA: Harvard University Press.

Greenfeld, Liah (1996). "Nationalism and modernity." *Social Research, 63* (1), pp. 3–40.

Greenfeld, Liah (2006). *Nationalism and the mind: Essays on modern culture*. Oxford: Oneworld.

Greenleaf, Robert K. (2002). *Servant leadership: A journey into the nature of legitimate power and greatness*. 25th anniversary edition. New York: Paulist Press.

Gress, David (1985). *Peace and survival: West Germany, the Peace Movement, and European security.* Stanford, CA: Stanford University Press.

Groos, Thomas, and Nora Jehles (2015). *Der Einfluss von Armut auf die Entwicklung von Kindern: Werkstattbericht.* Bochum, Gütersloh, Germany: Ruhr-Universität Bochum, Fakultät für Sozialwissenschaft, Zentrum für interdisziplinäre Regionalforschung (ZEFIR), Arbeitspapiere wissenschaftliche Begleitforschung „Kein Kind zurücklassen!", Bertelsmann Stiftung.

Grossman, Dave (1995). *On killing: The psychological cost of learning to kill in war and society.* Boston: Little, Brown and Company.

Grossman, Henryk (2006). "The beginnings of capitalism and the new mass morality." *Journal of Classical Sociology, 6* (2), pp. 201–13.

Grothe, Mardy (2017). *Metaphors be with you: An A to Z dictionary of history's greatest metaphorical quotations.* New York: HarperCollins.

Grünewald, Stephan (2013). *Die erschöpfte Gesellschaft: Warum Deutschland neu träumen muss.* Frankfurt am Main: Campus.

Grävingholt, Jörn, Stefan Gänzle, and Sebastian Ziaja (2009). *Policy brief: Concepts of peacebuilding and state building – How compatible are they?* Bonn: German Development Institute.

Grønnerød, Cato, Pål Grøndahl, and Ulf Stridbeck (2016). "Forensic psychiatric experts under the legal microscope." *Legal and Criminological Psychology, 21* (1), pp. 15–24.

Guala, Francesco (2012). "Reciprocity: Weak or strong? What punishment experiments do (and do not) demonstrate." *Behavioral and Brain Sciences, 35* (1, February), pp. 1–15.

Guha, Ranajit, and Gayatri Chakravorty Spivak (Eds.) (1988). *Selected subaltern studies.* New York: Oxford University Press.

Gunning, Jeroen, and Richard Jackson (2011). "What's so 'religious' about 'religious terrorism'?". *Critical Studies on Terrorism, 4* (3), pp. 369–88.

Guo, Jian, Song Yongyi, and Yuan Zhou (2006). *Historical dictionary of the Chinese Cultural Revolution.* Lanham, MD: Scarecrow Press.

Gurr, Ted Robert (1970). *Why men rebel.* Princeton, NJ: Princeton University Press.

Gurr, Ted Robert (1993). "Why minorities rebel: A global analysis of communal mobilization and conflict since 1945." *International Political Science Review, 14* (2), pp. 161–201.

Gurr, Ted Robert (2000). "Ethnic warfare on the wane." *Foreign Affairs, 79* (3), pp. 52–64.

Gyekye, Kwame (2004). *Beyond cultures: Perceiving a common humanity.* Washington, DC: Council for Research in Values and Philosophy.

Göle, Nilüfer (2013). *Islam and public controversy in Europe.* Farnham: Ashgate.

Göring, Hermann (1943). "Göring's Speech of January 30, 1943." *Bulletin of International News, 20* (3, February 6), pp. 100–04.

Haavelsrud, Magnus (2015). "The academy, development, and modernity's 'other'." *International Journal of Development Education and Global Learning, 7* (2, Development Education in the Global South), pp. 46–60.

Habermas, Jürgen (1962). *Strukturwandel der Öffentlichkeit: Untersuchungen zu einer Kategorie der bürgerlichen Gesellschaft.* Neuwied, Germany: Luchterhand.

Habermas, Jürgen (1968/1972). *Knowledge and human interests.* Translated by Jeremy J. Shapiro. Boston: Beacon Press, German original *Erkenntnis und Interesse*, Frankfurt am Main, Germany: Suhrkamp, 1968.

Habermas, Jürgen (1973). *Legitimationsprobleme im Spätkapitalismus.* Frankfurt am Main, Germany: Suhrkamp.

Habermas, Jürgen (1981). *Theorie des kommunikativen Handelns (Band I: Handlungsrationalität und gesellschaftliche Rationalisierung, Band II: Zur Kritik der funktionalistischen Vernunft)*. Frankfurt am Main, Germany: Suhrkamp.

Habermas, Jürgen (1983). "Die Verschlingung von Mythos und Aufklärung – Bemerkungen zur 'Dialektik der Aufklärung' – nach einer erneuten Lektüre." In *Mythos und Moderne: Begriff und Bild einer Rekonstruktion*, edited by Karl-Heinz Bohrer. Frankfurt am Main, Germany: Suhrkamp.

Habermas, Jürgen (1985–1987). *The theory of communicative action (Volume 1: Reason and the rationalization of society, 1985, Volume 2: Lifeworld and system: A critique of functionalist reason, 1987)*. Boston: Beacon Press.

Habermas, Jürgen (1989). *The structural transformation of the public sphere: An inquiry into a category of bourgeois society*. Cambridge: Polity Press.

Habermas, Jürgen, and Peter Dews (1992). *Autonomy and solidarity: Interviews with Jürgen Habermas*. London: Verso.

Hacker, Andrew, and Claudia Dreifus (2010). *Higher education? How colleges are wasting our money and failing our kids – and what we can do about it*. New York: Times Books.

Hafez, Mohammed M. (2003). *Why Muslims rebel: Repression and resistance in the Islamic world*. Boulder, CO: Lynne Rienner.

Hafez, Mohammed M. (2007a). "Martyrdom mythology in Iraq: How jihadists frame suicide terrorism in videos and biographies." *Terrorism and Political Violence, 19* (1), pp. 95–115.

Hafez, Mohammed M. (2007b). *Suicide bombers in Iraq: The strategy and ideology of martyrdom*. Washington, DC: United States Institute of Peace Press.

Haffner, Sebastian (1978). *Anmerkungen zu Hitler*. München, Germany: Kindler.

Haffner, Sebastian (2000). *Geschichte eines Deutschen: Die Erinnerungen 1914-1933*. Stuttgart, Germany: Deutsche Verlags-Anstalt.

Haidt, Jonathan (2012). *The righteous mind: Why good people are divided by politics and religion*. London: Allen Lane.

Haldane, Andrew G. (Ed.) (2004). *Fixing financial crises in the twenty-first century*. London: Routledge.

Haldane, John Burdon Sanderson (1932). *The causes of evolution*. London: Longmans, Green and Co.

Hall, Todd H., and Andrew A. G. Ross (2015). "Affective politics after 9/11." *International Organization, 69* (04), pp. 847–79.

Hamann, Brigitte (1996). *Hitlers Wien: Lehrjahre eines Diktators*. München, Germany: Piper.

Hamdan, Gamal (2014). *Shaksiyat Misr [The character of Egypt: A study of the uniqueness of the place]*. New edition. Cairo: National Library and Archives.

Hameiri, Boaz, Roni Porat, Daniel Bar-Tal, Atara Bieler, and Eran Halperin (2014). "Paradoxical thinking as a new avenue of intervention to promote peace." *Proceedings of the National Academy of Sciences of the United States of America, 111* (30), pp. 10996–1001.

Hamid, Mohsin (2007). *The reluctant fundamentalist*. Karachi: Oxford University Press.

Hamid, Mohsin (2014). *Discontent and its civilizations: Dispatches from Lahore, New York, and London*. London: Hamish Hamilton.

Hamilton, William D. (1963). "The evolution of altruistic behavior." *The American Naturalist, 97* (896), pp. 354–56.

Hamilton, William D. (1964a). "The genetical evolution of social behaviour. II." *Journal of Theoretical Biology, 7* (1), pp. 17–52.

Hamilton, William D. (1964b). "The genetical evolution of social behaviour. I." *Journal of Theoretical Biology, 7* (1), pp. 1–16.

Hannah, Margaret (2015). *Humanising healthcare: Patterns of hope for a system under strain*. Axminster, Devon: Triarchy Press.

Hansen, David (2012). *Radical rhetoric – moderate behavior: Perceptions of Islam, shari'a, and the radical dimension in urban Pakistan*. Trondheim, Norway: Tapir.

Hansen, James (2009). *Storms of my grandchildren: The truth about the coming climate catastrophe and our last chance to save humanity*. New York: Bloomsbury.

Hansen, Lene (2000). "The little mermaid's silent security dilemma and the absence of gender in the Copenhagen school." *Millennium – Journal of International Studies, 29* (2), pp. 285–306.

Hansen, Mette Halskov, and Rune Svarverud (Eds.) (2010). *iChina: The rise of the individual in modern Chinese society*, Studies on Asian topics. Copenhagen: NIAS Press.

Harari, Yuval Noah (2014). *Sapiens: A brief history of humankind*. London: Harvill Secker. First published in Hebrew in Tel Aviv by Kinneret Zmora-Bitan Dvir.

Harari, Yuval Noah (2015/2016). *Homo deus: A brief history of tomorrow*. London: Harville Secker. Hebrew original *The History of Tomorrow*, Tel Aviv: Kinneret Zmora-Bitan Dvir.

Hardin, Garrett James (1968). "The tragedy of the commons." *Science, 162* (3859), pp. 1243–48.

Hardin, Garrett James (1998). "Extensions of 'The Tragedy of the Commons'." *Science, 280* (5364), pp. 682–83.

Hardin, Garrett James (2007). "Tragedy of the commons." In *The concise encyclopedia of economics*, 2nd edition. Indianapolis, IN: Library of Economics and Liberty.

Hardin, Russell (1995). *One for all: The logic of group conflict*. Princeton, NJ: Princeton University Press.

Hardisty, Jean V. (1999). *Mobilizing resentment: Conservative resurgence from the John Birch Society to the promise keepers*. Boston: Beacon Press.

Harner, Michael J. (1970). "Population Pressure and the Social Evolution of Agriculturalists." *Southwestern Journal of Anthropology, 26* (1), pp. 67–86.

Harré, Romano, and Paul F. Secord (1972). *The explanation of social behaviour*. Oxford: Blackwell.

Harrigan, Jane, and Hamed El-Said (2009). *Aid and power in the Arab World: World Bank and IMF policy-based lending in the Middle East and North Africa*. Basingstoke: Palgrave Macmillan. doi:10.1057/9781137001597.

Harrigan, Jane, and Hamed El-Said (2010). *Globalisation, democratisation and radicalisation in the Arab World*. Basingstoke: Palgrave Macmillan. doi:10.1057/9780230307001.

Harris, Sam, and Maajid Nawaz (2015). *Islam and the future of tolerance: A dialogue*. Cambridge: Harvard University Press.

Harrison, Paul (1999). *Elements of pantheism: A spirituality of nature and the universe*. Shaftesbury, Dorset: Element Books.

Hart, Donna, and Robert W. Sussman (2009). *Man the hunted: Primates, predators, and human evolution*. Expanded edition. Boulder, CO: Westview Press.

Harter, Susan, Sabina M. Low, and Nancy R. Whitesell (2003). "What have we learned from Columbine: The impact of the self-system on suicidal violent ideation among adolescents." *Journal of School Violence, 2* (3), pp. 3–26.

Hartling, Linda Margaret (1995). *Humiliation: Assessing the specter of derision, degradation, and debasement*. Cincinnati, OH: Union Institute Graduate School, doctoral dissertation.

Hartling, Linda Margaret (2008a). "Strengthening resilience in a risky world: It's all about relationships." *Women and Therapy, 31* (2/3/4), pp. 51–70.

Hartling, Linda Margaret (2008b). "Jean Baker Miller: Living in connection." *Feminism and Psychology, 18* (3), pp. 326–35.

Hartling, Linda Margaret, Diane Littlefield, and Jean Baker Miller (2008). *Evolving concepts in relational-cultural theory*. Wellesley, MA: Wellesley College, Jean Baker Miller Training Institute. Glossary.

Hartling, Linda Margaret, Evelin Gerda Lindner, Ulrich Josef Spalthoff, and Michael Francis Britton (2013). "Humiliation: A nuclear bomb of emotions?". *Psicología Política, 46* (Mayo), pp. 55–76.

Hartling, Linda Margaret, and Evelin Gerda Lindner (2016a). "Healing humiliation: From reaction to creative action." *Journal of Counseling and Development (JCD), 94* (4, Special Section: Relational-Cultural Theory), pp. 383–90.

Hartling, Linda Margaret, and Evelin Gerda Lindner (2016b). "Healing humiliation: From reaction to creative action." *Journal of Counseling and Development (JCD), 94, Special Section focussing on Relational Cultural Theory* (4), pp. 383–90.

Hartling, Linda Margaret, and Evelin Gerda Lindner (2017). "Can systemic humiliation be transformed into systemic dignity?" In *Power, humiliation, and violence: Understanding identity-based conflicts*, edited by Daniel Rothbart. New York: Palgrave Macmillan, forthcoming.

Hartling, Linda Margaret, and Evelin Gerda Lindner (forthcoming). "Dignity in times of crises: Awakening our need for a new social climate." In *Routledge media and humanitarian action handbook*, edited by Purnaka L. de Silva, and Robin Andersen. New York: Routledge.

Hartmann, Christian, Thomas Vordermayer, Othmar Plöckinger, Roman Töppel, Edith Raim, Pascal Trees, Angelika Reizle, Martina Seewald-Mooser, and Institut für Zeitgeschichte (Eds.) (2016). *Hitler, Mein Kampf: Eine kritische Edition*, Mein Kampf. München, Germany: Institut für Zeitgeschichte.

Hartmann, Uwe, and Martin Burkart (2007). "Erectile dysfunctions in patient-physician communication: Optimized strategies for addressing sexual issues and the benefit of using a patient questionnaire." *The Journal of Sexual Medicine, 4* (1), pp. 38–46.

Hartwig, Richard E. (1983). *Roads to reason: Transportation administration and rationality in Colombia*. Pittsburgh, PA: University of Pittsburgh Press.

Hartwig, Richard E. (2008). "Rationality, social science and Paul Diesing." *Urbana: Urban Affairs and Public Policy, IX* (Spring-Fall), pp. 1–24.

Hartzband, Pamela, and Jerome Groopman (2009). "Money and the changing culture of medicine." *New England Journal of Medicine, 360* (2), pp. 101–03.

Harvey, David (1990). *The condition of postmodernity: An enquiry into the origins of cultural change*. Oxford: Blackwell.

Harvey, David (2000). *Spaces of hope*. Edinburgh: Edingburgh University Press.

Harvey, David (2003). *The new imperialism*. Oxford: Oxford University Press.

Harvey, David (2005). *A brief history of neoliberalism*. Oxford: Oxford University Press.

Harvey, David (2011). *The enigma of capital: And the crises of capitalism*. London: Profile Books.

Harvey, David (2014). *Seventeen contradictions and the end of capitalism*. Oxford: Oxford University Press.

Hasegawa, Tsuyoshi (2005). *Racing the enemy: Stalin, Truman, and the surrender of Japan*. Cambridge, MA: Belknap.

Hatherley, Owen (2015). *The ministry of nostalgia: Consuming austerity*. London: Verso.

Haugevik, Kristin M., Julie Wilhelmsen, and Morten Skumsrud Andersen (2015). "Trusselbilder og forsvar i endring." *Internasjonal Politikk, 73* (3), pp. 340–42.

Hauser, Dorothea (1998). *Baader und Herold. Beschreibung eines Kampfes*. Frankfurt am Main, Germany: Fischer.

Hayashi, Kichiro (2003). "Current intercultural issues and challenges in Japanese business interfaces: Blending theory and practice." *Management Japan, 35*.

Hayden, Michael V. (2016). *Playing to the dge: American intelligence in the age of terror*. New York: Penguin.

Heaney, Jonathan G. (2013). "Emotions and power: A bifocal prescription to cure theoretical myopia." *Journal of Political Power, 6* (3), pp. 355–62.

Heard, Gerald (1963). *The five ages of man*. New York: Julian Press.

Heath-Kelly, Charlotte (2013). *Politics of violence: Militancy, international politics, killing in the name*. Abingdon: Routledge.

Heath-Kelly, Charlotte, Christopher Baker-Beall, and Lee Jarvis (Eds.) (2016). *Neoliberalism and terror: Critical engagements*. Abingdon: Routledge.

Heatherly, Charles L., and Heritage Foundation (1981). *Mandate for leadership: Policy management in a conservative administration*. Washington, DC: Heritage Foundation.

Hechter, Michael (1992). "The dynamics of secession." *Acta Sociologica, 35* (4), pp. 267–83.

Hedges, Chris (2002). *War is a force that gives us meaning*. New York: PublicAffairs.

Heelas, Paul (1996). *The New Age movement: The celebration of the self and the sacralization of modernity*. Oxford: Blackwell.

Heelas, Paul (2008). *Spiritualities of life: New Age romanticism and consumptive capitalism*. Malden, MA: Blackwell.

Heffermehl, Fredrik S. (2010). *The Nobel Peace Prize: What Nobel really wanted*. Santa Barbara, CA: Praeger.

Heffernan, Margaret (2011). *Wilful blindness: Why we ignore the obvious at our peril*. London: Simon and Schuster.

Heffernan, Margaret (2014). *A bigger prize: Why competition isn't everything and how we do better*. London: Simon and Schuster.

Hegel, Georg Wilhelm Friedrich (1807/1967). *The phenomenology of mind*. Translated by James Black Baillie. London: Haper and Row. German original *Phänomenologie des Geistes*, Bamberg und Würzburg: Joseph Anton Göbhardt, 1807.

Hegghammer, Thomas (2006). "Militant Islamism in Saudi Arabia: Patterns of recruitment to 'al-Qaida on the Arabian peninsula'." In *FFI rapport-2006/00935: Paths to global jihad: Radicalisation and recruitment to terror networks*, edited by Laila Bokhari, Thomas Hegghammer, Brynjar Lia, Petter Nesser, and Truls H. Tonnessen, chapter 3, pp. 22–29. Kjeller, Norway: Norwegian Defence Research Establishment. Proceedings from a Forsvarets forskningsinstitutt (FFI) seminar, Oslo, 15 March 2006.

Hegghammer, Thomas (2010/2011). "The rise of Muslim foreign fighters: Islam and the globalization of jihad." *International Security, 35* (3), pp. 53–94.

Hegghammer, Thomas, and Norwegian Defence Research Establishment (FFI) (2013). "Should I stay or should I go? Explaining variation in Western Jihadist's choice between domestic and foreign fighting." *American Political Science Review, February*, pp. 1–15.

Hegghammer, Thomas (2016). "The future of jihadism in Europe: A pessimistic view." *Perspectives on Terrorism, 10* (6).

Hegre, Håvard, and Håvard Mokleiv Nygård (2015). "Governance and conflict relapse." *Journal of Conflict Resolution, 59* (6), pp. 984–1016.

Heine, Steven J., Darrin R. Lehman, Hazel Rose Markus, and Shinobu Kitayama (1999). "Is there a universal need for positive self-regard?". *Psychological Review, 106* (4), pp. 766–94.

Heisenberg, Werner (1969/1971). *Physics and beyond: Encounters and conversations*. Translated by Arnold J. Pomerans. New York: Harper and Row. German original *Der Teil und das Ganze: Gespräche im Umkreis der Atomphysik*. München, Germany: Reinhard Piper, 1969.

Heitmeyer, Wilhelm, Joachim Müller, and Helmut Schröder (1997). *Verlockender Fundamentalismus: Türkische Jugendliche in Deutschland*. Frankfurt am Main, Germany: Suhrkamp.

Heitmeyer, Wilhelm (2010). *Deutsche Zustände, Folge 9*. Berlin: Suhrkamp.

Heitmeyer, Wilhelm, Heinz-Gerhard Haupt, Stefan Malthaner, and Andrea Kirschner (Eds.) (2011). *Control of violence: Historical and international perspectives on violence in modern societies.* New York: Springer.

Held, David (1980). *Introduction to critical theory: Horkheimer to Habermas.* Cambridge: Polity Press.

Heller, Agnes (1984). *Everyday life.* London: Routledge and Kegan Paul.

Hellestveit, Cecilie (2017). *Syria: En stor krig i en liten verden.* Oslo: Pax.

Hellesøy Harrisson, Cathrine (2016). "Hvor mye av verdens konflikter kan forklares med ydmykelse? I 40 år har psykolog Evelin Lindner forsket for å finne svaret." *Aftenposten A-Magasinet, 9. desember,* pp. 59–63.

Helliwell, John, and Christopher Barrington-Leigh (2011). "How much is social capital worth?" In *The social cure: Identity, health, and well-being,* edited by Jolanda Jetten, Catherine Haslam, and S. Alexander Haslam, pp. 55–71. Milton Park: Psychology Press.

Helman, Gerald B., and Steven R. Ratner (1992). "Saving failed states." *Foreign Policy, 89* (Winter, 1992–1993), pp. 3–20.

Helmick, Raymond G., Rodney L. Petersen, and Desmond Tutu (Foreword) (Eds.) (2001). *Forgiveness and reconciliation: Religion, public policy and conflict transformation.* Radnor, PA: Templeton Foundation Press.

Hemenway, Toby (2009). *Gaia's garden: A guide to home-scale permaculture.* 2nd edition. White River Junction, VT: Chelsea Green Publishing.

Hemmingby, Cato, and Tore Bjørgo (2016). *The dynamics of a terrorist targeting process: Anders B. Breivik and the 22 July attacks in Norway.* Basingstoke: Palgrave MacMillan.

Hendrix, Harville (2008). *Getting the love you want: A guide for couples.* 20th anniversary edition. New York: Henry Holt.

Hénin, Nicolas (2015). *Jihad Academy: Nos erreurs face â l'État islamique.* Paris: Fayard.

Henrich, Joseph, Steven J. Heine, and Ara Norenzayan (2010). "The weirdest people in the world?". *Behavior and Brain Sciences, 33* (2–3), pp. 61–83; discussion pp. 83–135.

Henrich, Natalie, and Joseph Henrich (2007). *Why humans cooperate: A cultural and evolutionary explanation.* Oxford: Oxford University Press.

Herman, Judith Lewis (2001). *Trauma and recovery.* London: Pandora.

Hermans, Erno J., Marloes J. A. G. Henckens, Marian Joëls, and Guillén Fernández (2014). "Dynamic adaptation of large-scale brain networks in response to acute stressors." *Trends in Neurosciences, 37* (6), pp. 304–14.

Herrmann, Ulrike (2013). *Der Sieg des Kapitals. Wie der Reichtum in die Welt kam. Die Geschichte von Wachstum, Geld und Krisen.* Frankfurt am Main, Germany: Westend Verlag.

Hersh, Richard H., and John Merrow (Eds.) (2005). *Declining by degrees: Higher education at risk.* New York: Palgrave Macmillan.

Herz, John H. (1950). "Idealist internationalism and the security dilemma." *World Politics, 2* (2), pp. 157–80.

Hetherington, Marc, Meri Long, and Thomas Rudolph (2016). "Revisiting the myth: New evidence of a polarized electorate." *Public Opinion Quarterly, 80* (S1), pp. 321–50.

Hetherington, Marc J., and Jonathan Daniel Weiler (2009). *Authoritarianism and polarization in American politics.* Cambridge: Cambridge University Press.

Hetherington, Marc J., and Elizabeth Suhay (2011). "Authoritarianism, threat, and Americans' support for the war on terror." *American Journal of Political Science, 55* (3), pp. 546–60.

Hewstone, Miles, Ed Cairns, Alberto Voci, Juergen Hamberger, and Ulrike Niens (2006). "Intergroup contact, forgiveness, and experience of 'the troubles' in Northern Ireland." *Journal of Social Issues, 62* (1), pp. 99–120.

Hibbing, John R., Kevin B. Smith, and John R. Alford (2014). *Predisposed: Liberals, conservatives, and the biology of political differences*. New York: Routledge.

Hickok, Gregory (2014). *The myth of mirror neurons: The real neuroscience of communication and cognition*. New York: Norton.

Higgins, Polly (2016). *Eradicating ecocide: Exposing the corporate and political practices destroying the planet and proposing the laws needed to eradicate ecocide*. 2nd edition. London: Shepheard Walwyn.

Hinde, Robert A., and Joseph Rotblat (2003). *War no more: Eliminating conflict in the nuclear age*. London: Pluto Press.

Hirschman, Albert Otto (1977). *The passions and the interests: Political arguments for capitalism before its triumph*. Princeton, NJ: Princeton University Press.

Hitchens, Christopher (2012). *No one left to lie to*. Sydney: Allen and Unwin.

Hitler, Adolf (1925–26/1999). *Mein Kampf*. Translated by Ralph Manheim. London: Pimlico. Original work published in 1925–26.

Ho, David Yau Fai (1976). "On the concept of face." *American Journal of Sociology, 81* (4), pp. 867–84.

Ho, David Yau Fai (2014). *Enlightened or mad? A psychologist glimpses into mystical magnanimity*. Lake Oswego, OR: Dignity Press.

Hobbes, Thomas (1651). *Leviathan, or, The matter, forme, and power of a common wealth, ecclesiasticall and civil*. Printed for Andrew Crooke, at the Green Dragon in St. Paul's Churchyard.

Hobsbawm, Eric J. (1962). *The age of revolution: Europe 1789–1848*. London: Weidenfeld and Nicolson.

Hobsbawm, Eric J. (1975). *The age of capital: 1848–1875*. London: Weidenfeld and Nicolson.

Hobsbawm, Eric J. (1987). *The age of empire: 1875–1914*. London: Weidenfeld and Nicolson.

Hobsbawm, Eric J. (1994). *Age of extremes: The short twentieth century 1914–1991*. London: Michael Joseph.

Hobsbawm, Eric J. (2000). *Bandits*. 2nd revised edition. London: Weidenfeld and Nicolson.

Hobson, John Atkinson (1902). *Imperialism. A study*. New York: James Pott and Co.

Hochschild, Arlie Russell (1979). "Emotion work, feeling rules, and social structure." *American Journal of Sociology, 85* (3), pp. 551–75.

Hochschild, Arlie Russell (1983). *The managed heart: Commercialization of human feeling*. Berkeley: University of California Press.

Hodgson, Geoffrey M., and Thorbjørn Knudsen (2010). *Darwin's conjecture: The search for general principles of social and economic evolution*. Chcago: University of Chicago Press.

Hoel, Dag (2014). *Armageddon halleluja! Møter med politisk kristendom*. Oslo: Spartacus.

Hoffman, Bruce (1998). *Inside terrorism*. New York: Columbia University Press.

Hoffman, David H., Danielle J. Carter, Cara R. Viglucci Lopez, Heather L. Benzmiller, Ava X. Guo, S. Yasir Latifi, and Daniel C. Craig (2015). *Report to the special committee of the board of directors of the American Psychological Association: Independent review relating to apa ethics guidelines, national security interrogations, and torture*. Chicago: Sidley Austin.

Hoffmann, Peter (1995). *Stauffenberg: A family history 1905–1944*. Cambridge: Cambridge University Press.

Hofstede, Geert (1986). "Cultural differences in teaching and learning." *International Journal of Intercultural Relations, 10* (3), pp. 301–20.

Hofstede, Geert (2001). *Culture's consequences: Comparing values, behaviors, institutions, and organizations across nations*. 2nd edition. Thousand Oaks, CA: Sage.

Holbrook, Colin, Keise Izuma, Choi Deblieck, Daniel M. T. Fessler, and Marco Iacoboni (2015). "Neuromodulation of group prejudice and religious belief." *Social Cognitive and Affective Neuroscience*.

Hollick, Malcolm (2006). *The science of oneness: A worldview for the twenty-first century.* Ropley, Hampshire: O Books.

Hollick, Malcolm, and Christine Connelly (2011). *Hope for humanity: How understanding and healing trauma could solve the planetary crisis.* Winchester: O Books.

Holmes, Stephen (2007). *The matador's cape: America's reckless response to terror.* New York: Cambridge University Press.

Holt-Lunstad, Julianne, Timothy B. Smith, and J. Bradley Layton (2010). "Social relationships and mortality risk: A meta-analytic review." *Public Library of Science (PLoS) Medicine, 7* (7), pp. e1000316.

Holtzworth-Munroe, Amy, and Jeffrey C. Meehan (2004). "Typologies of men who are maritally violent: Scientific and clinical implications." *Journal of Interpersonal Violence, 19* (12), pp. 1369–89.

Homer-Dixon, Thomas F. (2006). *The upside of down: Catastrophe, creativity, and the renewal of civilization.* Toronto: Knopf.

Honneth, Axel (1992/1995). *The struggle for recognition: The moral grammar of social conflicts.* Translated by Joel Anderson. Cambridge: Polity Press. German original *Kampf um Anerkennung*, Frankfurt am Main: Suhrkamp, 1992.

Honneth, Axel (1997). "Recognition and moral obligation." *Social Research: An International Quarterly of the Social Sciences, 64* (1, Spring, The Decent Society), pp. 16–35.

Hoock, Holger (2017). *Scars of independence: America's violent birth.* New York: Crown.

Hooper, Charlotte (2001). *Manly states: Masculinities, international relations, and gender politics.* New York: Columbia University Press.

Horgan, John (2009). *Walking away from terrorism: Accounts of disengagement from radical and extremist movements.* Abingdon-on-Thames: Routledge.

Horgan, John, and Kurt Braddock (2010). "Rehabilitating the terrorists? Challenges in assessing the effectiveness of de-radicalization programs." *Terrorism and Political Violence, 22* (2), pp. 267–91.

Horgan, John, and Kurt Braddock (2011). "Evaluating the effectiveness of de-radicalisation programs: Towards a scientific approach to terrorism risk reduction." In *Countering violent extremism: Scientific methods and strategies*, edited by Laurie Fenstermacher, and Todd Leventhal, pp. 158–63. Washington, DC: Nationwide Suspicious Activity Reporting (SAR) Initiative (NSI), Topical strategic multi-layer assessment and air force research laboratory multi-disciplinary white paper in support of counter-terrorism and counter-WMD.

Hornborg, Alf, J. R. McNeill, and Juan Martinez-Alier (Eds.) (2007). *Rethinking environmental history: World-system history and global environmental change.* Lanham, MD: Altamira Press.

Horne, Alistair (1977). *A savage war of peace: Algeria 1954–1962.* London: Macmillan.

Hornsey, Matthew J., and Michael A. Hogg (2000). "Subgroup relations: A comparison of mutual intergroup differentiation and common ingroup identity models of prejudice reduction." *Personality and Social Psychology Bulletin, 26* (2), pp. 242–56.

Horton, Richard (2004). "Rediscovering human dignity." *The Lancet, 364* (9439), pp. 1081–85.

Houellebecq, Michel (1994/1998). *Whatever.* Translated by Paul Hammond. London: Serpent's Tail, French original *Extension du domaine de la lutte*, Paris: M. Nadeau, 1994.

Houellebecq, Michel (1998/2001). *Atomised.* Translated by Frank Wynne. London: Vintage, French original *Les particules élémentaires*, Paris: Flammarion, 1998.

Houellebecq, Michel (2010/2012). *The map and the territory.* Translated by Gavin Bowd. London: Vintage, French original *La carte et le territoire*, Paris: Flammarion, 2010.

Houellebecq, Michel (2015). *Submission.* Translated by Lorin Stein. London: William Heinemann, French original *Soumission*, Paris: Flammarion, 2015.

Hsu, Francis L. K. (1948). *Under the ancestors' shadow: Chinese culture and personality*. New York: Columbia University Press.

Hsu, Francis L. K. (1953). *Americans and Chinese: Two ways of life*. New York: Henry Schuman.

Hsu, Francis L. K. (1963). *Clan, caste, and club*. New York: Van Nostrand.

Hsu, Francis L.K. (1965). "The effect of dominant kinship relationships on kin and non-kin behavior: A hypothesis." *American Anthropologist, 67* (3), pp. 638–61.

Huang, Hsuan-Ying (2014). "The emergence of the psycho-boom in contemporary urban China." In *Studies for the society for the social history of medicine: Psychiatry and Chinese history*, edited by Howard Chiang, chapter 10, pp. 183–204. London: Pickering and Chatto.

Hudson, Michael (2003). *Super imperialism: The origin and fundamentals of U.S. world dominance*. New and revised edition. London: Pluto Press.

Hudson, Michael (2012). *The bubble and beyond: Fictitious capital, debt deflation and the global crisis*. Dresden, Germany: ISLET.

Hudson, Valerie M., Bonnie Ballif-Spanvill, Mary Caprioli, and Chad F. Emmett (2012). *Sex and world peace*. New York: Columbia University Press.

Human Rights Watch (2014). *With liberty to monitor all: How large-scale US surveillance is harming journalism, law, and American democracy*. New York: Human Rights Watch and American Civil Liberties Union.

Hung, Ho-fung (2009). *China and the transformation of global capitalism*. Baltimore, MD: John Hopkins University Press.

Huntington, Samuel P. (1996). *The clash of civilizations and the remaking of world order*. New York: Simon and Schuster.

Husain, Ed (2007). *The Islamist: Why I joined radical Islam in Britain, what I saw inside and why I left*. London: Penguin Books.

Hutchinson, Emma (2016). *Affective communities in world politics*. Cambridge: Cambridge University Press.

Hutton, Patrick H., Huck Gutman, and Luther H. Martin (1988). *Technologies of the self: A seminar with Michel Foucault*. Amherst, MA: University of Massachusetts Press.

Huxley, Aldous (1932). *Brave new world*. London: Chatto and Windus.

Härtel-Petri, Roland (2014). *Crystal Meth: Wie eine Droge unser Land überschwemmt*. München, Germany: Münchner Verlagsgruppe.

Höjdestrand, Tova (2009). *Needed by nobody: Homelessness, humiliation, and humanness in post-socialist Russia*. Ithaca, NY: Cornell University Press.

Ibn Khaldun (1377/1958). *The Muqaddimah: An introduction to history, in three volumes*. Translated by Franz Rosenthal. Princeton, NJ: Princeton University Press.

Ide, Sachiko (1989). "Formal forms and discernment: Two neglected aspects of universals of linguistic politeness." *Multilingua – Journal of Cross-Cultural and Interlanguage Communication, 8* (2/3), pp. 223–48.

Iglesias, Juan (2010). *Derecho romano*. 15th edition. Barcelona, Spain: Sello Editorial.

Imhof, Lorens A., Drew Fudenberg, and Martin A. Nowak (2007). "Tit-for-tat or win-stay, lose-shift?". *Journal of theoretical biology, 247* (3), pp. 574–80.

Inglehart, Ronald, and Christian Welzel (2005). *Modernization, cultural change, and democracy: The human development sequence*. New York: Cambridge University Press.

Ingold, Tim (2000). *The perception of the environment: Essays in livelihood, dwelling and skill*. London: Routledge.

Institute for Economics and Peace (2014). *Global terrorism index 2014: Measuring and understanding the impact of terrorism*. Sydney, New York, Mexico City: Institute for Economics and Peace.

Institute for Economics and Peace (2015). *Global terrorism index 2015: Measuring and understanding the impact of terrorism*. Sydney, New York, Mexico City: Institute for Economics and Peace.

International Labour Office (ILO) (2014). *Profits and poverty: The economics of forced labour*. Geneva, Switzerland: International Labour Office (ILO), Special Action Programme to Combat Forced Labour (SAP-FL), Fundamental Principles and Rights at Work Branch (FPRW).

Internationaler Militärgerichtshof Nürnberg (1989). "Band 29: Urkunden und anderes Beweismaterial." In *Internationaler Militärgerichtshof Nürnberg (IMT): Der Nürnberger Prozess gegen die Hauptkriegsverbrecher*. München, Germany: Delphin Verlag.

Iroegbu, Patrick E. (2005). "Beginning, purpose and end of life." In *Kpim of morality ethics*, edited by Patrick E. Iroegbu, and Anthony Echekwube, pp. 440–45. Ibadan, Nigeria: Heinemann Educational Books.

Isdal, Per (2000). *Meningen med volden* Kommuneforlaget.

Ishiguro, Kazuo (2005). *Never let me go*. London: Faber and Faber.

Ismail, Tarek Z., Naureen Shah, and Andrea Prasow (2014). *Illusion of justice: Human rights abuses in US terrorism prosecutions*. New York: Human Rights Watch, The Human Rights Institute at Columbia Law School.

Ivy, Marilyn (1993). "Have you seen me? Recovering the inner child in late twentieth-century America." *Social Text*, (37), pp. 227–52.

Jabri, Vivienne (2007). *War and the transformation of global politics*. New York: Palgrave Macmillan.

Jackman, Mary (1994). *The velvet glove: Paternalism and conflict in gender, class, and race relations*. Berkeley: University of California Press, ark.cdlib.org/ark:/13030/ft958009k3.

Jackson, Richard (2010). "In defence of 'terrorism': Finding a way through a forest of misconceptions." *Behavioral Sciences of Terrorism and Political Aggression*, *3* (2), pp. 116–30.

Jackson, Richard (2011). "The failed paradigm of prevent." In *Soundings: Policy matters for Muslims in Britain*. London: Muslim Council of Britain (MCB).

Jackson, Richard, Marie Breen-Smyth, Jeroen Gunning, and Lee Jarvis (2011). *Terrorism: A critical introduction*. Basingstoke: Palgrave Macmillan.

Jackson, Robert H. (1990). *Quasi-states: Sovereignty, international relations and the third world*. Cambridge, MA: Cambridge University Press.

Jackson, Tim (2009). *Prosperity without growth: Economics for a finite planet*. London: Earthscan.

Jahoda, Gustav (2016). "On the rise and decline of 'indigenous psychology'." *Culture and Psychology*, *22* (2), pp. 169–81.

Jakobs, Hans-Jürgen (2016). *Wem gehört die Welt: Die Machtverhältnisse im globalen Kapitalismus*. München: Albrecht Knaus Verlag.

Jakobsen, Ove (2017). *Transformative ecological economics: Process philosophy, ideology and utopia*. London: Taylor and Francis.

Jameson, Fredric (1991). *Postmodernism, or, The cultural logic of late capitalism*. London: Verso.

Jameson, Fredric (1994). *The seeds of time*. New York: Columbia University Press.

Janis, Irving L., and Leon Mann (1977). *Decision making: A psychological analysis of conflict, choice, and commitment*. New York: Free Press.

Jansz, Jeroen, and Peter van Drunen (2004). *A social history of psychology*. Malden, MA: Blackwell.

Jantsch, Erich (1980). *The self-organizing universe: Scientific and human implications of the emerging paradigm of evolution*. Oxford: Pergamon Press.

Jasper, James M. (1997). *The art of moral protest: Culture, biography, and creativity in social movements.* Chicago: University of Chicago Press.

Jasper, James M. (2011). "Emotions and social movements: Twenty years of theory and research." *Annual Review of Sociology, 37* (1), pp. 285–303.

Jasper, James M. (2014). *Protest: A cultural introduction to social movements.* Cambridge: Polity.

Jasper, James M., and Jan Willem Duyvendak (2015). *Players and arenas: The interactive dynamics of protest.* Amsterdam: Amsterdam University Press.

Jaspers, Karl (1919). *Psychologie der Weltanschauungen.* Berlin: Springer.

Jaspers, Karl (1949). *Vom Ursprung und Ziel der Geschichte.* München, Germany: Piper.

Jaspers, Karl (1951). *Way to wisdom, an introduction to philosophy.* New Haven, CT: Yale University Press.

Jaynes, Julian (1976). *The origin of consciousness in the breakdown of the bicameral mind.* Boston: Houghton Mifflin.

Jeismann, Karl-Ernst (2000). "'Geschichtsbewußtsein' als zentrale Kategorie der Didaktik des Geschichtsunterrichts." In *Geschichte und Bildung*, edited by Karl-Ernst Jeismann, pp. 46–72. Paderborn: Ferdinand Schöningh.

Jemsek, Greg (2011). *Quiet horizon: Releasing ideology and embracing self-knowledge.* Bloomington: Trafford.

Jenni, Alexis (2011). *L'art français de la guerre.* Paris: Gallimard.

Jennings, Jerry L., and Christopher M. Murphy (2000). "Male-male dimensions of male-female battering: A new look at domestic violence." *Psychology of Men and Masculinity, 1* (1), pp. 21–29.

Jensen, Barbara (2012). *Reading classes: On culture and classism in America.* Ithaca, NY: Cornell University Press.

Jensen, Michael C., and William H. Meckling (1994). "The nature of man." *Journal of Applied Corporate Finance, 7* (2), pp. 4–19.

Jervis, Robert (1978). "Cooperation under the security dilemma." *World Politics, 30* (2, January), pp. 167–214.

Jervis, Robert, Richard Ned Lebow, and Janice Gross Stein (1985). *Psychology and deterrence.* Baltimore, MD: Johns Hopkins University Press.

Jervis, Robert (2006). "Understanding beliefs." *Political Psychology, 27* (5), pp. 641–63.

Job, Brian L. (Ed.) (1992). *The insecurity dilemma: National security of third world states.* Boulder, CO: Lynne Rienner.

Johnson, Chalmers Ashby (2000). *Blowback: The costs and consequences of American empire.* New York: Metropolitan Books.

Johnson, Chalmers Ashby (2004). *The sorrows of empire: Militarism, secrecy, and the end of the republic.* New York: Metropolitan Books.

Johnson, Chalmers Ashby (2006). *Nemesis: The last days of the American Republic.* New York: Metropolitan Books.

Johnson, Chalmers Ashby (2010). *Dismantling the Empire: America's last best hope.* New York: Henry Holt.

Johnson, David W., Roger T. Johnson, and Dean Tjosvold (2014). "Constructive controversy: The value of intellectual opposition." In *The handbook of conflict resolution: Theory and practice*, edited by Morton Deutsch, Peter T. Coleman, and Eric C. Marcus, 3rd edition, chapter 4, pp. 76–103. San Francisco: Jossey-Bass.

Johnson, Michael (2001). *All honourable men: The social origins of war in Lebanon.* London: Centre for Lebanese Studies and I.B. Tauris.

Johnson, Michael P. (2008). *A typology of domestic violence: Intimate terrorism, violent resistance, and situational couple violence.* Lebanon, NH: Northeastern University Press.

Johnson, Richard (2007). "Post-hegemony?". *Theory, Culture and Society, 24* (3), pp. 95–110.

Jolowicz, H. F. (1932). *Historical introduction to the study of Roman law.* Cambridge: Cambridge University Press.

Jones, Carol (2009). "State of transformation: Drag queen masculinity in two Scottish texts." *Genders, 50,* pp. Edinburgh Research Explorer.

Jones, Eric Lionel, and Societies American Council of Learned (1993). *Growth recurring: Economic change in world history.* Oxford: Clarendon Press.

Jones, Gregg (2012). *Honor in the dust: Theodore Roosevelt, war in the Philippines, and the rise and fall of America's imperial dream.* New York: New American Library.

Jones, James Edward (2006). *The post-victim ethical exemption syndrome: An outgrowth of humiliation.* New York: Paper presented at the 2006 Workshop on Humiliation and Violent Conflict, Columbia University, December 14–15, 2006.

Jones, John Y. (2008). *Careers, kings and consultants.* Human Dignity and Humiliation Studies, published also as 'Etterarbeid med mening' in *Vårt Land,* Oslo, Norway, 2008.

Jones, John Y. (2011). "Dag Hammarskjöld stood up for the UN on development." *UN Chronicle.*

Jones, Seth G., and Martin C. Libicki (2008). *How terrorist groups end: Lessons for countering Al Qai'da.* Rand Corporation.

Jordán, Javier, and Robert Wesley (2006). "The Madrid attacks: Results of investigations two years later." *Terrorism Monitor, 4* (5, March 9), pp. 1–4.

Jordan, Judith V. (2010). *The power of connection: Recent developments in relational-cultural theory.* New York: Routledge.

Jorge Fernandes Mata, Tiago (2006). *Dissent in economics: Making radical political economics and post Keynesian economics, 1960–1980.* London: London School of Economics and Political Science, doctoral dissertation.

Jost, John T., and Lee D. Ross (1999). "Fairness norms and the potential for mutual agreements involving majority and minority groups." In *Research on managing groups and teams (Vol. 2): Groups in their context,* edited by Elizabeth A. Mannix, Margaret A. Neale, and Ruth Wageman, pp. 93–114. Greenwich, CT: JAI Press.

Jost, John T., Brett W. Pelham, and Mauricio R. Carvallo (2002). "Non-conscious forms of system justification: Implicit and behavioral preferences for higher status groups." *Journal of Experimental Social Psychology, 38* (6), pp. 586–602.

Jost, John T., Mahzarin R. Banaji, and Brian A. Nosek (2004). "A decade of system justification theory: Accumulated evidence of conscious and unconscious bolstering of the status quo." *Political Psychology, 25* (6), pp. 881–919.

Jost, John T., Aaron C. Kay, and Hulda Thorisdottir (2009). *Social and psychological bases of ideology and system justification.* New York: Oxford University Press.

Joughin, Ian, Benjamin E. Smith, and Brooke Medley (2014). "Marine ice sheet collapse potentially under way for the Thwaites Glacier Basin, West Antarctica." *Science, 344* (6185), pp. 735–38.

Jozelic, Jasna (2006). *Islamisering og islams posisjon i dagens Bosnia og Hercegovina.* Bergen, Norway: Universitet i Bergen, hovedfagsoppgave i religionsvitenskap.

Juergensmeyer, Mark (2000). *Terror in the mind of god: The global rise of religious violence.* Berkeley: University of California Press.

Junger, Sebastian (2016). *Tribe: On homecoming and belonging.* New York: Twelve.

Juran, Joseph M. (1964). *Managerial breakthrough: A new concept of the manager's job.* New York: McGraw-Hill.

Jünger, Ernst (1979). *Ernst Jünger: Sämtliche Werke, 18 Bände. Band 1: Der Erste Weltkrieg*. Stuttgart, Germany: Klett-Cotta.

Jäckel, Eberhard, and Axel Kuhn (Eds.) (1980). *Hitler. Sämtliche Aufzeichnungen 1905–1924*. Stuttgart Deutsche Verlags-Anstalt.

Kaddor, Lamya (2015). *Zum Töten bereit: Warum deutsche Jugendliche in den Dschihad ziehen*. München, Germany: Piper.

Kaeuper, Richard W., and Elspeth Kennedy (Eds.) (1996). *The book of chivalry of Geoffroi de Charny: Text, context, and translation*. Philadelphia: University of Pennsylvania Press.

Kagan, Donald (1997). *Honor, interest, and nation-state*. Paper delivered at the conference 'Intangible Interests and U.S. Foreign Policy', held in 1996, published in *Commentary*, April 1997.

Kagan, Sacha (2011). *Art and sustainability: Connecting patterns for a culture of complexity*. Bielefeld, Germany: Transcript.

Kahneman, Daniel (2011). *Thinking, fast and slow*. New York: Farrar, Straus and Giroux.

Kaleck, Wolfgang, Michael Ratner, Tobias Singelnstein, and Peter Weiss (Eds.) (2007). *International prosecution of human rights crimes*. Berlin, Heidelberg: Springer.

Kaleck, Wolfgang (2016). *Unternehmen vor Gericht. Globale Kämpfe für Menschenrechte*. Berlin Wagenbach.

Kalecki, Michal (1943). "Political aspects of full employment." *Political Quarterly, 14* (4), pp. 322–30.

Kant, Immanuel (1784). "Beantwortung der Frage: Was ist Aufklärung?". *Berlinische Monatsschrift, Dezember-Heft 1784*, pp. 481–94.

Kant, Immanuel (1785). *Grundlegung zur Metaphysik der Sitten*. Riga, Latvia: Johann Friedrich Hartknock.

Kaplan, Martha (1995). *Neither cargo nor cult: Ritual politics and the colonial imagination in Fiji*. Durham, NC: Duke University Press.

Kaptelinin, Victor, and Bonnie A. Nardi (2006). *Acting with technology: Activity theory and interaction design*. Cambridge, MA: MIT Press.

Karabel, Jerome (2005). *The chosen: The hidden history of admission and exclusion at Harvard, Yale, and Princeton*. New York: Houghton Mifflin Harcourt.

Karamah – Muslim Women Lawyers for Human Rights (2008). *Zina, rape, and Islamic Law: An Islamic legal analysis of the rape laws In Pakistan – A position paper*. Washington, DC: Karamah – Muslim Women Lawyers for Human Rights.

Karatani, Kôjin (2010/2014). *The structure of world history: From modes of production to modes of exchange*. Translated by Michael K. Bourdaghs. Durham, NC: Duke University Press. Japanese original 世界史の構造, Tokyo: Iwanami, 2010.

Karatani, Kojin (2014). *The structure of world history: From modes of production to modes of exchange*. Durham, NC: Duke University Press.

Karlberg, Michael Robert (2004). *Beyond the culture of contest: From adversarialism to mutualism in an age of interdependence*. Oxford: George Ronald.

Karlberg, Michael Robert (2008). "Discourse, identity, and global citizenship." *Peace Review: A Journal of Social Justice, 20* (3), pp. 310–20.

Karlberg, Michael Robert (2012). "Reframing public discourses for peace and justice." In *Forming a culture of peace: Reframing narratives of intergroup relations, equity, and justice*, edited by Karina V. Korostelina, chapter 1, pp. 15–42. Basingstoke: Palgrave Macmillan.

Karlberg, Michael Robert (2013). *Reframing the concept of human dignity*. Paper originally presented at the conference "Reflections on Human Dignity" at the University of Maryland, April 19, 2013.

Karlberg, Michael Robert (2014). *Meaning, religion, and a Great Transition*. Boston: Great Transition Initiative.

Karsh, Efraim (2007). *Islamic imperialism: A history*. New Haven, CT: Yale University Press.

Kass, Leon (2002). *Life, liberty, and the defense of dignity: The challenge for bioethics*. San Francisco: Encounter Books.

Kasser, Tim (2017). "Living both well and sustainably: A review of the literature, with some reflections on future research, interventions, and policy." *Philosophical Transactions of the Royal Society A: Physical, Mathematical, and Engineering Sciences*, pp. forthcoming.

Katz, Jack (1988). *Seductions of crime: Moral and sensual attractions in doing evil*. New York: Basic Books.

Kauffman, Stuart A., and Sonke Johnsen (1991). "Coevolution to the edge of chaos: Coupled fitness landscapes, poised states, and coevolutionary avalanches." *Journal of Theoretical Biology, 149* (4), pp. 467–505.

Kauffman, Stuart Alan (1995). *At home in the universe: The search for the laws of self-organization and complexity*. Oxford: Oxford University Press.

Kauffman, Stuart Alan, and Arran Gare (2015). "Beyond Descartes and Newton: Recovering life and humanity." *Progress in Biophysics and Molecular Biology, 119* (3), pp. 219–44.

Kauffman, Stuart Alan (2016). *Humanity in a creative universe*. New York: Oxford University Press.

Kaufman, Alison Adcock (2010). "The 'century of humiliation,' then and now: Chinese perceptions of the international order." *Pacific Focus, 25* (1), pp. 1–33.

Kaufman, Stuart J. (2001). *Modern hatreds: The symbolic politics of ethnic war*. Ithaca, NY: Cornell University Press.

Kautsky, John H. (1982). *The politics of aristocratic empires*. Chapel Hill: University of North Carolina Press.

Keen, Sam (1986). *Faces of the enemy: Reflections of the hostile imagination*. San Francisco: Harper and Row.

Keenan, Brian (1993). *An evil cradling*. London: Vintage.

Kelly, Raymond C. (2005). "The evolution of lethal intergroup violence." *Proceedings of the National Academy of Sciences (PNAS) of the United States of America, 102* (43), pp. 15294–98.

Kelsen, Hans, and Carl Schmitt (1931/2015). *The guardian of the constitution: Hans Kelsen and Carl Schmitt on the limits of constitutional law*. Translated by Lars Vinx. Cambridge: Cambridge University Press.

Keltner, Dacher (2009). *Born to be good: The science of a meaningful life*. New York: Norton.

Keltner, Dacher, Jason Marsh, and Jeremy Adam Smith (Eds.) (2010). *The compassionate instinct: The science of human goodness*. New York: W. W. Norton.

Kemme, Stefanie, Michael Hanslmaier, and Christian Pfeiffer (2014). "Experience of parental corporal punishment in childhood and adolescence and its effect on punitiveness." *Journal of Family Violence, 29* (2), pp. 129–42.

Kendall, Diana (2007). *Sociology in our times*. Belmont, CA: Wadsworth.

Kendler, Kenneth S., John M. Hettema, Frank Butera, Charles O. Gardner, and Carol A. Prescott (2003). "Life event dimensions of loss, humiliation, entrapment, and danger in the prediction of onsets of major depression and generalized anxiety." *Archives of General Psychiatry, 60* (8), pp. 789–96.

Kennedy, Hugh (2007). *The great Arab conquests: How the spread of Islam changed the world we live in*. London: Weidenfeld and Nicolson.

Kennedy, Paul (1987). *The rise and fall of the great powers: Economic change and military conflict from 1500 to 2000*. New York: Random House.

Kepel, Gilles (1993). *Le Prophète et pharaon: Aux sources des mouvements islamistes*. Paris: Seuil.

Kepel, Gilles (2006). *Jihad: The trail of political Islam*. New edition. London: I.B. Tauris.

Kepel, Gilles (2008). *Beyond terror and martyrdom: The future of the Middle East*. Harvard: Harvard University Press.

Kepel, Gilles, and Jean Pierre Milelli (2008). *Al Qaeda in its own words*. Cambridge, MA: Belknap.

Kepel, Gilles (2015). *Terreur dans l'Hexagone: Genèse du djihad français*. Paris: Gallimard.

Kepel, Gilles (2016). *La fracture*. Paris: Coédition Gallimard / France Culture.

Kershaw, Ian (1998). *Hitler 1889–1936: Hubris*. London: Allen Lane.

Kershaw, Ian (2000). *Hitler 1936–45: Nemesis*. London: Allen Lane.

Kershaw, Ian (2011). *The end: Hitler's Germany, 1944–45*. London: Allen Lane.

Kessels, Eelco J.A.M. (Ed.) (2010). *Countering violent extremist narratives*. The Hague, The Netherlands: National Coordinator for Counter-Terrorism.

Keval, Narendra (2016). *Exploring the perversion of thinking and curiosity in racism*. London: Karnac.

Keyes, Ralph (1995). *The courage to write: How writers transcend fear*. New York: Henry Holt.

Keysers, Christian (2011). *The empathic brain: How the discovery of mirror neurons changes our understanding of human nature*. Lexington, KY: Social Brain Press.

Khalidi, Rashid (2004). *Resurrecting empire: Western footprints and America's perilous path in the Middle East*. Boston: Beacon.

Kidder, Rushworth M. (1994). *Shared values for a troubled world:: Conversations with men and women of conscience*. San Francisco: Jossey-Bass.

Kim, Kisam, and Donald Kirk (2013). *Kim Dae-jung and the quest for the Nobel: How the president of South Korea bought the peace prize and financed Kim Jong-il's nuclear program*. New York: Palgrave Macmillan. doi:10.1007/978-1-137-35309-2.

Kim, Young Yun, and Brent David Ruben (1988). "Intercultural transformation: A systems theory." In *Theories in intercultural communication*, edited by Young Yun Kim, and William B. Gudykunst, pp. 299–321. Newbury Park, CA: Sage.

Kimmel, Michael (2013). *Angry white men: American masculinity at the end of an era*. New York: Nation Books.

Kimura, Masato, and Toshihiro Minohara (Eds.) (2013). *Tumultuous decade: Empire, society and diplomacy in 1930s Japan*, Japan and global society. Toronto: University of Toronto Press.

Kindleberger, Charles P. (2013). *The world in depression 1929 – 1939*. 40th anniversary edition. Berkeley: University of California Press.

King, Martin Luther (1955). *A comparison of the conception of God in the thinking of Paul Tillich and Henry Nelson Wieman*. Boston: Boston University, doctoral dissertation.

King, Ursula (2007). "Religious education and peace: An overview and response." *British Journal of Religious Education, 29* (1), pp. 115–24.

Kingsley, Charles (1867). *The ancien regime*. Lectures at the Royal Institution.

Kingston, Christopher G., and Robert E. Wright (2010). "The deadliest of games: The institution of dueling." *Southern Economic Journal, 76* (4), pp. 1094–106.

Kinnvall, Catarina (2004). "Globalization and religious nationalism: Self, identity, and the search for ontological security." *Political Psychology, 25* (5), pp. 741–67.

Kipnis, Andrew B. (2012). *Chinese modernity and the individual psyche*. New York: Palgrave Macmillan.

Kirsch, Jonathan (2008). *The Grand Inquisitor's manual: A history of terror in the name of God*. New York: HarperCollins.

Kirschenbaum, Howard, and Valerie Land Henderson (Eds.) (1990). *Carl Rogers: Dialogues: Conversations with Martin Buber, Paul Tillich, B.F. Skinner, Gregory Bateson, Michael Polanyi, Rollo May, and others*. London: Constable.

Kirst, Hans Hellmut (1975/1976). *The nights of the long knives*. New York: Coward, McCann and Geoghegan. German original *Die Nächte der langen Messer*, Hamburg: Hoffman und Campe, 1975.

Kissinger, Henry (1957). *A world restored: Metternich, Castlereagh and the problems of peace, 1812-22*. Boston: Houghton Mifflin.

Kjos, Ingeborg (2013). *Anders Behring Breiviks manifest: En idéanalyse*. Oslo: University of Oslo, master's thesis in political science.

Klas, Gerhard (2011). *Die Mikrofinanz-Industrie: Die große Illusion oder das Geschäft mit der Armut*. Berlin: Assoziation A.

Kleinig, John (2011). "Humiliation, degradation, and moral capacity: A response to Hörnle and Kremnitzer." *Israel Law Review, 44* (1-2), pp. 169–83.

Kleinig, John, and Nicholas G. Evans (2013). "Human flourishing, human dignity, and human rights." *Law and Philosophy, 32* (5), pp. 539–64.

Klimecki, Olga M., Susanne Leiberg, Matthieu Ricard, and Tania Singer (2014). "Differential pattern of functional brain plasticity after compassion and empathy training." *Social Cognitive and Affective Neuroscience, 9* (6), pp. 873–79.

Klitgaard, Kent A. (2017). *The struggle for meaningful work*. Boston: Great Transition Initiative.

Knausgård, Karl Ove (2009–2011). *Min kamp*. Oslo: Oktober.

Knutson, Brian, G. Elliott Wimmer, Camelia M. Kuhnen, and Piotr Winkielman (2008). "Nucleus accumbens activation mediates the influence of reward cues on financial risk taking." *Neuroreport, 19* (5), pp. 509–13.

Koenigs, Michael, Liane Lee Young, Ralph Adolphs, Daniel Tranel, Fiery Cushman, Marc Hauser, and António Rosa Damásio (2007). "Damage to the prefrontal cortex increases utilitarian moral judgments." *Nature, 446* (7138, April 19), pp. 908–11.

Koenigs, Tom (2007). *Suicide Attacks in Afghanistan (2001 - 2007)*. Kabul, Afghanistan: United Nations Assistance Mission in Afghanistan.

Koestler, Arthur (1967). *The ghost in the machine*. London: Hutchinson.

Koestler, Arthur (1970). "Beyond atomism and holism – the concept of the holon." *Perspectives in Biology and Medicine, 13* (2), pp. 131–54.

Koestler, Arthur (1974). "The urge to self-destruction." In *The heel of Achilles: Essays 1968 - 1973*. London: Hutchinson. Edited version of the Sonning Prize Acceptance Address to the University of Copenhagen, April 1968, and of a paper read at the Fourteenth Nobel Symposium, Stockholm, September 1969.

Koestler, Arthur (1978). *Janus: A summing up*. London: Hutchinson.

Kogon, Eugen (1946/1950). *The theory and practice of hell: The German concentration camps and the system behind them*. New York: Farrar, Straus and Giroux. German original *Der SS-Staat: Das System der deutschen Konzentrationslager*, München, Germany: Karl Alber, 1946.

Kohn, Alfie (1990). *The brighter side of human nature: Altruism and empathy in everyday life*. New York: Basic Books.

Kohout, Barbara (2010). *Mara im Kokon: Ein Leben unter Wachtturm-Regeln*. Leipzig, Germany: Engelsdorfer Verlag.

Kohut, Heinz (1973). "Thoughts on narcissism and marcissistic rage." In *The psychoanalytic study of the child*, edited by Ruth S. Eissler. New York: Quadrangle Books.

Kolbert, Elizabeth (2006). *Field notes from a catastrophe*. London: Bloomsbury.

Kolbert, Elizabeth (2014). *The sixth extinction: An unnatural history*. New York: Henry Holt.

Kolås, Åshild (2010). "The 2008 Mumbai terror attacks: (Re-)constructing Indian (counter-)terrorism." *Critical Studies on Terrorism, 3* (1), pp. 83–98.

Kornhuber, Hans Helmut, and Lüder Deecke (1965). "Hirnpotentialänderungen bei Willkürbewegungen und passiven Bewegungen des Menschen: Bereitschaftspotential und reafferente Potentiale." *Pflüger's Archiv für die gesamte Physiologie des Menschen und der Tiere, 284* (1), pp. 1–17.

Korten, David C. (1995). *When corporations rule the world.* London: Earthscan.

Korten, David C. (2006). *The great turning: From empire to earth community.* San Francisco: Berrett-Koehler.

Koschut, Simon (2014). "Emotional (security) communities: The significance of emotion norms in inter-allied conflict management." *Review of International Studies, 40* (3), pp. 533–58.

Kraidy, Marwan M., and Patrick D. Murphy (2008). "Shifting Geertz: Toward a theory of translocalism in global communication studies." *Communication Theory, 18* (3), pp. 335–55.

Kraushaar, Wolfgang (2006). *Die RAF und der linke Terrorismus, Band 1.* Hamburg, Germany: Hamburger Edition.

Kreindler, Sara A. (2005). "A dual group processes model of individual differences in prejudice." *Personality and Social Psychology Review, 9* (2), pp. 90–107.

Kroglund, Andrew P. (2016). *Kniv, sjel og gaffel: På sporet av det sultne mennesket.* Oslo: Vega.

Krolikowski, Alanna (2008). "State personhood in ontological security theories of international relations and Chinese nationalism: A sceptical view." *The Chinese Journal of International Politics, 2* (1), pp. 109–33.

Krone-Schmalz, Gabriele (2007). *Was passiert in Russland?* München, Germany: Herbig.

Kronman, Anthony T. (2007). *Education's end: Why our colleges and universities have given up on the meaning of life.* New Haven, CT: Yale University Press.

Krueger, Alan B. (2016). *Where have all the workers gone?* Princeton, NJ: Princeton University and NBER. Paper prepared for the Boston Federal Reserve Bank's 60th Economic Conference, October 14, 2016.

Krueger, Alan B. (2017). *What makes a terrorist: Economics and the roots of terrorism.* Anniversary edition. Princeton, NJ: Princeton University Press.

Kruger, Justin, and David Dunning (1999). "Unskilled and unaware of it: How difficulties in recognizing one's own incompetence lead to inflated self-assessments." *Journal of Personality and Social Psychology, 77* (6), pp. 1121–34.

Kruse, Kevin M. (2015). *One nation under god: How corporate America invented Christian America.* New York: Basic Books.

Krüger, Jörg, Bertram Nickolay, and Sandro Gaycken (Eds.) (2013). *The secure information society: Ethical, legal and political challenges.* London: Springer London.

Krüger, Uwe (2013). *Meinungsmacht: Der Einfluss von Eliten auf Leitmedien und Alpha-Journalisten – eine kritische Netzwerkanalyse.* Köln, Germany: Herbert von Halem.

Kuan, Teresa (2015). *Love's uncertainty: The politics and ethics of child rearing in contemporary China.* Oakland, CA: University of California Press.

Kuhn, Thomas Samuel (1962). *The structure of scientific revolutions.* Chicago: University of Chicago Press.

Kundnani, Arun (2012). "Radicalisation: The journey of a concept." *Race and Class, 54* (2), pp. 3–25.

Kury, Patrick (2012). *Der überforderte Mensch: Eine Wissensgeschichte vom Stress zum Burnout.* Frankfurt am Main, Germany: Campus.

Kuźniar, Roman (2009). *Poland's foreign policy after 1989.* Leverkusen, Germany: Barbara Budrich.

Kwenda, Chirevo V. (2003). "Cultural justice: The pathway to reconciliation and social cohesion." In *What holds us together: Social cohesion in South Africa*, edited by David Chidester, Phillip Dexter, and Wilmot James, pp. 67–82. Cape Town, South Africa: Human Sciences Research Council.

Kühn, Simone, and Marcel Brass (2009). "Retrospective construction of the judgement of free choice." *Consciousness and Cognition, 18* (1), pp. 12–21.

Kühne, Thomas (2011). "The pleasure of terror: Belonging through genocide." In *Pleasure and power in Nazi Germany*, edited by Pamela E. Swett, Corey Ross, and Fabrice d'Almeida, chapter 11, pp. 234–55. Basingstoke: Palgrave Macmillan.

Lacina, Bethany, Nils Petter Gleditsch, and Bruce Russett (2006). "The declining risk of death in battle." *International Studies Quarterly, 50* (3), pp. 673–80.

Laclau, Ernesto (2005). *On populist reason*. London: Verso.

Lair, Daniel J., Katie Sullivan, and George Cheney (2005). "Marketization and the recasting of the professional self." *Management Communication Quarterly, 18* (3), pp. 307 – 43.

Lakhani, Suraj (2013). *Radicalisation as a moral career: A qualitative study of how people become terrorists in the United Kingdom*. Cardiff: Police Science Institute, School of Social Sciences, Cardiff University, doctoral dissertation.

Lakoff, George P., and Mark L. Johnson (1980). *Metaphors we live by*. Chicago: University of Chicago Press.

Lakoff, George P., and Mark L. Johnson (1999). *Philosophy in the flesh: The embodied mind and its challenge to western thought*. New York: Basic Books.

Lakoff, George P. (2002). *Moral politics: How liberals and conservatives think*. 2nd edition. Chicago: University of Chicago Press.

Lakoff, George P. (2004). *Don't think of an elephant! Know your values and frame the debate: The essential guide for progressives*. White River Junction, VT: Chelsea Green.

Lakoff, George P. (2006a). *Whose freedom? The battle over America's most important idea*. New York: Farrar, Straus and Giroux.

Lakoff, George P. (2006b). *Thinking points: Communicating our American values and vision*. New York: Farrar, Straus and Giroux.

Lakoff, George P. (2016). "Language and emotion." *Emotion Review, 8* (3), pp. 269–73.

Lambert, Robert (2008). *Salafi and Islamist Londoners: Stigmatised minority faith communities countering al-Qaida*. Presentation given at the NATO advanced research workshop 'Indigenous Terrorism: Understanding and Addressing the Root Causes of Radicalisation Among Groups with an Immigrant Heritage in Europe', Budapest, Hungary, 7–9th March, 2008.

Lambert, Robert (2011). *Countering Al-Qaeda in London: Police and Muslims in partnership*. London: C. Hurst.

Lamm, Claus, and Jasminka Majdandzic (2015). "The role of shared neural activations, mirror neurons, and morality in empathy: A critical comment." *Neuroscience Research, 90*, pp. 15–24.

Lamont, Michèle, Silva Grazielle Moraes, Jessica S. Welburn, Joshua Guetzkow, Nissim Mizrachi, Hanna Herzog, and Reis Elisa (2016). *Getting respect: Responding to stigma and discrimination in the United States, Brazil, and Israel*. Princeton, NJ: Princeton University Press.

Lane, Robert E. (2001). *The loss of happiness in market democracies*. New edition. New Haven, CT: Yale University Press.

Langer, Walter Charles (1972). *The mind of Adolf Hitler: The secret wartime report*. New York: Basic Books.

Langman, Peter (2015). *School shooters: Understanding high school, college, and adult perpetrators*. Blue Ridge Summit, PA: Rowman and Littlefield.

Langner, Ralph (2012). *Robust control system networks: How to achieve reliable control after Stuxnet*. New York: Momentum Press.

Lankford, Adam (2009). *Human killing machines: Systematic indoctrination in Iran, Nazi Germany, al Qaeda, and Abu Ghraib*. Lanham, MD: Lexington Books.

Lankford, Adam (2013). *The myth of martyrdom: What really drives suicide bombers, rampage shooters, and other self-destructive killers*. New York: Palgrave Macmillan.

Lappé, Frances Moore (2016). *Farming for a small planet: Agroecology now*. Boston: Great Transition Initiative.

Laqueur, Walter (1977). *Terrorism*. London: Weidenfeld and Nicolson.

Laqueur, Walter (2001). *A history of terrorism*. New Brunswick, NJ: Transaction.

Laqueur, Walter (2009). *Mein 20. Jahrhundert. Stationen eines politischen Lebens*. Berlin: Propyläen.

Larsen, Tord (2009). *Den globale samtalen: Om dialogens muligheter*. Oslo: Scandinavian Academic Press.

Lasch, Christopher (1991). *The culture of narcissism: American life in an age of diminishing expectations*. Revised edition. New York: Norton.

Laszlo, Alexander (2014). "Connecting the DOTS: The design of thrivable systems through the power of collective intelligence." *Systems Research and Behavioral Science, 31* (5), pp. 586–94.

Laszlo, Alexander (2015). "Living systems, seeing systems, being systems: Learning to be the system that we wish to see in the world." *Spanda Journal, I* (2, Systemic Change), pp. www.spanda.org/publications.html#journal.

Latour, Bruno (2004). "Why has critique run out of steam? From matters of fact to matters of concern." *Critical Inquiry, 30* (2, Winter), pp. 225–48.

Laverty, Anthony A., Lucia Magee, Carlos A. Monteiro, Sonia Saxena, and Christopher Millett (2015). "Sugar-sweetened and artificially sweetened beverage consumption and adiposity changes: a national longitudinal study (clinical report)." *The Lancet, 386*, pp. S49.

Lawrence, Thomas Edward (1922). *Seven pillars of wisdom*. Private edition, unabridged Oxford text.

Lawrence, Thomas Edward (1938). "Guerrilla warfare." In *Encyclopædia Britannica*. Chicago: Encyclopædia Britannica.

Lawson, Tony (2015). *Essays on the nature and state of the modern economics*. London: Routledge.

Lazare, Aaron (2004). *On apology*. New York: Oxford University Press.

Lazarsfeld, Paul F., and Robert K. Merton (1954). "Friendship as social process: A substantive and methodological analysis." In *Freedom and control in modern society*, edited by Morroe Berger, Theodore Abel, and Charles H. Page, pp. 18–66. Toronto: D. Van Nostrand.

Le Bon, Gustave (1895/1896). *The crowd: A study of the popular mind*. London: T. Fisher Unwin. French original *La psychologie des foules*, Paris: Félix Alcan, 1895.

Le Bon, Gustave (1915/1916). *Psychology of the Great War: The First World War and its origins*. Translated by E. Andrews. New York: Macmillan. French original *Enseignements psychologiques de la guerre européenne*, Paris: Ernest Flammarion, 1915.

Leach, William R. (1993). *Land of desire: From the department store to the Department of Commerce: The rise of America's commercial culture*. New York: Pantheon Books.

Leacock, Eleanor, Virginia Abernethy, Amita Bardhan, Catherine H. Berndt, Judith K. Brown, Beverly N. Chiñas, Ronald Cohen, *et al.* (1978). "Women's status in egalitarian society: Implications for social evolution." *Current Anthropology, 19* (2, June), pp. 247–75. Based on paper originally given at the annual meeting of the American Anthropological Association in November 1974.

Leakey, Richard E., and Roger Lewin (1977). *Origins: What new discoveries reveal about the emergence of our species and its possible future*. New York: E. P. Dutton.

Lebow, Richard Ned (1981). *Between peace and war: The nature of international crisis*. Baltimore, MD: Johns Hopkins University Press.

Lebow, Victor (1955). "Price competition in 1955." *Journal of Retailing, Spring*.

Lecercle, Jean-Jacques (2002). *Deleuze and language*. Basingstoke: Palgrave Macmillan. doi:10.1057/9780230599956.

Lee, Benjamin (1995). "Critical Internationalism." *Public Culture, 7* (3), pp. 559–92.

Lee, Richard B., and Irven DeVore (Eds.) (1968). *Man the hunter: The first intensive survey of a single, crucial stage of human development – man's once universal hunting way of life.* New Brunswick, NJ: AldineTransaction, collection of papers presented at the symposium 'Man the Hunter', held at the Center for Continuing Education at the University of Chicago, April 6–9, 1966.

Lee, Wayne E. (2015). "When did warfare begin? Archaeology, evolution, and the early evidence of conflict." *Quarterly Journal of Military History, 27* (2, Winter), pp. 64–71.

Leep, Matthew Coen (2010). "The affective production of others: United States policy towards the Israeli-Palestinian conflict." *Cooperation and Conflict, 45* (3), pp. 331–52.

Leidner, Bernhard, Hammad Sheikh, and Jeremy Ginges (2012). "Affective dimensions of intergroup humiliation." *Public Library of Science (PLOS) One, 7* (9), pp. e46375.

Leighton, Alexander H. (1959). *My name is legion: Foundations for a theory of man in relation to culture.* New York: Basic Books.

Leiss, William (1976). *The limits to satisfaction: An essay on the problem of needs and commodities.* Toronto: University of Toronto Press.

Leonhardt, Wolfgang (2009). *'Hannoversche Geschichten' – Berichte aus verschiedenen Stadtteilen.* Norderstedt, Germany: Books on Demand.

Leontiev, Aleksei Nikolaevich (1975/1978). *Activity, consciousness, and personality.* Translated by Marie J. Hall. Pacifica, CA: Marxist Internet Archive. Russian original *Деятельность. Сознание. Личность*, Moscow: Politisdat, 1975.

Lepper, Mark R., David Greene, and Richard E. Nisbett (1973). "Undermining children's intrinsic interest with extrinsic reward: A test of the 'overjustification' hypothesis." *Journal of Personality and Social Psychology, 28* (1, October), pp. 129–37.

Lerner, Melvin J. (1980). *The belief in a just world: A fundamental delusion.* New York: Plenum.

LeShan, Lawrence (1992). *The psychology of war: Comprehending its mystique and its madness.* Chicago: Noble Press.

Leung, Angela K. Y., and Dov Cohen (2011). "Within- and between-culture variation: Individual differences and the cultural logics of honor, face, and dignity cultures." *Journal of Personality and Social Psychology, 100* (3), pp. 507–26.

Levesque, Shannon, Michael Surace, Jacob McDonald, and Michelle Block (2011). "Air pollution and the brain: Subchronic diesel exhaust exposure causes neuroinflammation and elevates early markers of neurodegenerative disease." *Journal of Neuroinflammation, 8* (1), pp. 105–05.

Lévinas, Emmanuel (1961/1969). *Totality and infinity: An essay on exteriority.* Translated by Alphonso Lingis. Pittsburgh, PA: Duquesne University Press. French original *Totalité et infini: Essai sur l'extériorité*, The Hague, The Netherlands: Martinus Nijhoff, 1961.

Lévinas, Emmanuel (1982). *Éthique et infini – Dialogues avec Philippe Nemo.* Paris: Fayard.

Lévinas, Emmanuel (1985a). "Responsibility for the other." In *Ethics and infinity: Conversations with Philippe Nemo*, chapter 8, pp. 93–101. Pittsburgh, PA: Duquesne University Press.

Lévinas, Emmanuel (1985b). "The face." In *Ethics and infinity: Conversations with Philippe Nemo*, chapter 7. Pittsburgh, PA: Duquesne University Press.

Levine, Bruce E. (2007). *Surviving America's depression epidemic: How to find morale, energy, and community in a world gone crazy.* White River Junction, VT: Chelsea Green Publishing.

Levine, Madeline (2006). *The price of privilege: How parental pressure and material advantage are creating a generation of disconnected and unhappy kids.* New York: HaperCollins.

Levitt, Kari (2002). *Silent surrender: The multinational corporation in Canada*. Montreal, QC: McGill-Queen's University Press.

Levy, Howard S. (1992). *The lotus lovers: The complete history of the curious erotic custom of footbinding in China*. Buffalo, NY: Prometheus Books.

Lewin, Kurt (1941). "Defining the 'field at a given time'." *Psychological Review, 50* (3), pp. 292–310.

Lewin, Kurt, and Dorwin Cartwright (1951). *Field theory in social science: Selected theoretical papers*. New York: Harper and Brothers.

Lewis, Harry R. (2006). *Excellence without a soul: How a great university forgot education*. New York: Public Affairs.

Lewis, Helen Block (1971). *Shame and guilt in neurosis*. New York: International Universities Press.

Lewis, Ioan Myrddin (1998). *Peoples of the Horn of Africa: Somali, Afar and Saho*. London: Haan.

Lewis, Michael M. (1989). *Liar's poker: Rising through the wreckage on Wall Street*. New York: Norton.

Lewis, Michael M. (2010). *The big short: Inside the doomsday machine*. New York: Norton.

Lewontin, Richard (1991). *Biology as ideology: The doctrine of DNA*. New York: Harper Perennial.

Lia, Brynjar (2006). "The al-Qaida strategist Abu Mus'ab al-Suri: A profile." In *FFI rapport-2006/00935: Paths to global jihad: Radicalisation and recruitment to terror networks*, edited by Laila Bokhari, Thomas Hegghammer, Brynjar Lia, Petter Nesser, and Truls H. Tonnessen, chapter 5, pp. 39–53. Kjeller, Norway: Norwegian Defence Research Establishment. Proceedings from a Forsvarets forskningsinstitutt (FFI) seminar, Oslo, 15 March 2006.

Liberman, Varda, Steven M. Samuels, and Lee D. Ross (2004). "The name of the game: Predictive power of reputations versus situational labels in determining prisoner's dilemma game moves." *Personality and Social Psychology Bulletin, 30* (9), pp. 1175–85.

Libet, Benjamin, Curtis A. Gleason, Elwood W. Wright, and Dennis K. Pearl (1983). "Time of conscious intention to act in relation to onset of cerebral activity (readiness-potential)." *The Unconscious Initiation af a Freely Voluntary Act, 106* (3), pp. 623–42.

Lieberman, Matthew D. (2015). *Social: Why our brains are wired to connect*. Oxford: Oxford University Press.

Lietaer, Bernard A., Christian Arnsperger, Sally Goerner, and Stefan Brunnhuber (2012). *Money and sustainability: The missing link*. Axminster: Triarchy Press, a report from the Club of Rome-EU Chapter to Finance Watch and the World Business Academy.

Lifton, Robert Jay (1993). *The protean self: Human resilience in the age of fragmentation*. Chicago: University of Chicago Press.

Lifton, Robert Jay (2003). *Super power syndrome: America's apocalyptic confrontation with the world*. New York: Nations Books.

Lin, Chun, and Gregor Benton (2010). *Was Mao really a monster? The academic response to Chang and Halliday's Mao, the unknown story*. London: Routledge.

Lindlof, Thomas R., and Bryan Copeland Taylor (2011). *Qualitative communication research methods*. 3rd edition. Thousand Oaks, CA: Sage.

Lindner, Evelin Gerda (1995a). *National identity, ethics, and rational choice: Their influences on national willingness to share sovereignty*. Oslo: Project proposal developed together with The Peace Research Institute Oslo (PRIO), for the Norwegian Research Council.

Lindner, Evelin Gerda (1995b). *Identity, security, and rising Islamic fundamentalism: A study of attitudes of Muslim immigrant groups in France, Germany, and The Netherlands*. Oslo: Project proposal developed with the Peace Research Institute, Oslo (PRIO), for the European Programme Human Capital and Mobility.

Lindner, Evelin Gerda (1996). *The feeling of being humiliated: A central theme in armed conflicts. A study of the role of humiliation in Somalia, and Great Lakes Region, between the warring parties, and in relation to third intervening parties. Outline of research project.* Oslo: Doctoral project description, University of Oslo, Department of Psychology, The Norwegian Research Council, Department of Multilateral Affairs, The Royal Norwegian Ministry of Foreign Affairs. See also the French version *Le sentiment d'être humilié: Un Thème central dans des conflits armés. Une étude du rôle de humiliation en Somalie et Burundi/Rwanda, parmi les partis belligérants, et par rapport aux tiers partis intervenants.*

Lindner, Evelin Gerda (1999). "Women in the global village: Increasing demand for traditional communication patterns." In *Towards a women's agenda for a culture of peace*, edited by Ingeborg Breines, Dorota Gierycz, and Betty A. Reardon, chapter 5, pp. 89 – 98. Paris: UNESCO Publishing.

Lindner, Evelin Gerda (2000a). *The psychology of humiliation: Somalia, Rwanda / Burundi, and Hitler's Germany.* Oslo: University of Oslo, Department of Psychology, doctoral dissertation.

Lindner, Evelin Gerda (2000b). *Humiliation in the flesh. Honour is "FACE", arrogance is "NOSE UP", and humiliation is "TO BE PUT DOWN".* Oslo: University of Oslo, Department of Psychology.

Lindner, Evelin Gerda (2000c). "Were the Germans Hitler's 'willing executioners'?". *Medlemsblad for Norske leger mot atomvåpen, med bidrag fra psykologer for fred, 2*, pp. 26–29.

Lindner, Evelin Gerda (2000d). "Hitler, shame and humiliation: The intricate web of feelings among the German population towards Hitler." *Medlemsblad for Norske leger mot atomvåpen, med bidrag fra psykologer for fred, 1*, pp. 28–30.

Lindner, Evelin Gerda (2000e). "Were Hitler and Siad Barre 'Robin Hoods' who felt humiliated by their own followers? (Part I)." *Medlemsblad for Norske leger mot atomvåpen, med bidrag fra psykologer for fred, 3*, pp. 20–25.

Lindner, Evelin Gerda (2000f). *Recognition or humiliation – The psychology of intercultural communication.* Bergen, Norway: Proceedings of the ISSEI Millennium Conference Approaching a New Millennium: Lessons from the Past – Prospects for the Future, the 7th Conference of the International Society for the Study of European Ideas, Bergen, Norway, 14th–18th August, 2000.

Lindner, Evelin Gerda (2000g). *Transnational corporations and the global poor: From humiliation to dialogue.* Oslo: University of Oslo, Department of Psychology, postdoctoral research proposal.

Lindner, Evelin Gerda (2000h). *Humiliation, human rights, and global corporate responsibility.* Oslo: University of Oslo, Department of Psychology.

Lindner, Evelin Gerda (2000i). "Were ordinary Germans Hitler's 'willing executioners'? Or were they victims of humiliating seduction and abandonment? The case of Germany and Somalia." *IDEA: A Journal of Social Issues, 5* (1).

Lindner, Evelin Gerda (2001a). *The psychology of humiliation – Summary of results and what the research on humiliation added to pre-existing knowledge.* Oslo: University of Oslo, Department of Psychology. Spanish summary / versión Española, translated into Spanish by Sara Horowitz.

Lindner, Evelin Gerda (2001b). "Humiliation – Trauma that has been overlooked: An analysis based on fieldwork in Germany, Rwanda/Burundi, and Somalia." *TRAUMATOLOGYe, 7* (1), pp. Article 3 (32 pages).

Lindner, Evelin Gerda (2001c). *Moratorium on humiliation: Cultural and "human factor" dimensions underlying structural violence.* New York: Discussion paper presented at the expert group meeting on Structural Threats to Social Integration: Indicators for Conflict Prevention, Session 2: Structural Threats to Social Integrity, organized by the Social Integration Branch of the United Nations Department of Economic and Social Affairs, Division for Social Policy and Development, December 18–20, 2001, New York City.

Lindner, Evelin Gerda (2001d). *The concept of humiliation: Its universal core and culture-dependent periphery.* Oslo: University of Oslo, Department of Psychology.

Lindner, Evelin Gerda (2001e). "How research can humiliate: Critical reflections on method." *Journal for the Study of Peace and Conflict, Annual Edition 2001 – 2002*, pp. 16–36.

Lindner, Evelin Gerda (2001f). "Humiliation as the source of terrorism: A new paradigm." *Peace Research: The Canadian Journal of Peace Studies, 33* (2), pp. 59–68.

Lindner, Evelin Gerda (2001g). "Women and terrorism: The lessons of humiliation." *New Routes: A Journal for Peace Research and Action, 6, Special Issue: Targeting Women* (3), pp. 10–12.

Lindner, Evelin Gerda (2001h). *Women and terrorism: The lessons of humiliation.* Trondheim, Norway: Paper given at the Conference on Social and Community Psychology, University of Trondheim (NTNU), Department of Psychology, 9th October 2001.

Lindner, Evelin Gerda (2001i). "How research can humiliate: Critical reflections on method." *Journal for the Study of Peace and Conflict, Annual Edition 2001-2002*, pp. 16–36.

Lindner, Evelin Gerda (2001j). "Were Hitler and Siad Barre 'Robin Hoods' who felt humiliated by their own followers? (Part II)." *Medlemsblad for Norske leger mot atomvåpen, med bidrag fra psykologer for fred, 1*, pp. 20–23.

Lindner, Evelin Gerda (2001k). *Towards a theory of humiliation: Somalia, Rwanda / Burundi, and Hitler's Germany.* Oslo: University of Oslo, Department of Psychology, draft for Habilitation submitted to the University of Regensburg, Germany, Department of Psychology, October 2001.

Lindner, Evelin Gerda (2002). "Healing the cycles of humiliation: How to attend to the emotional aspects of 'unsolvable' conflicts and the use of 'humiliation entrepreneurship'." *Peace and Conflict: Journal of Peace Psychology, 8* (2), pp. 125–38.

Lindner, Evelin Gerda (2004a). *Humiliation as psychological risk factor for terrorism.* Stockholm: Lecture given at Riskkollegiet / Society of Risk Sciences, invited by Olof Söderberg, 12th October 2004.

Lindner, Evelin Gerda (2004b). "Gendercide and humiliation in honor and human-rights societies." In *Gendercide and genocide*, edited by Adam Jones, chapter 2, pp. 39–61. Nashville, TN: Vanderbilt University Press.

Lindner, Evelin Gerda, and Stefan Backe (2004). "Referat av Stefan Backe från seminariet 'Humiliation as psychological risk factor for terrorism?'." *Risknytt,* (1), pp. 2–5.

Lindner, Evelin Gerda (2005a). "Parents – The role model." *Sahil, 14* (32, April-June), pp. 9, long version, 'Parenting styles and their impact on children: Humiliation, abuse and neglect'.

Lindner, Evelin Gerda (2005b). *Globalization, human rights, terrorism, and humiliation.* New York: Lecture at the Program on Global Security and Cooperation of the Social Science Research Council (SSRC), invited by Bernice Ortega, December 6, 2005.

Lindner, Evelin Gerda (2005c). *Mature differentiation as response to terrorism and humiliation: Refrain from the language of "war" and "evil".* Lund, Sweden: The Transnational Foundation for Peace and Future Research, 22nd September 2005.

Lindner, Evelin Gerda (2006a). *"The cartoon war" of humiliation versus humiliation: What should be done?* : Human Dignity and Humiliation Studies.

Lindner, Evelin Gerda (2006b). *Is it possible to "change the world"? Some guidelines to how we can build a more decent and dignified world effectively: The case of dignifying abusers.* Human Dignity and Humiliation Studies.

Lindner, Evelin Gerda (2006c). *Making enemies: Humiliation and international conflict.* Westport, CT: Praeger Security International, Greenwood.

Lindner, Evelin Gerda (2006d). "Humiliation and reactions to Hitler's seductiveness in post-war Germany: Personal reflections." *Social Alternatives, 25* (1, Special Issue: Humiliation and History in Global Perspectives, First Quarter), pp. 6–11, edited by Bertram Wyatt-Brown, upon invitation by D. Raja Ganesan.

Lindner, Evelin Gerda, and Human Dignity and Humiliation Studies network members (2006–2017). *Appreciative nurturing.* Human Dignity and Humiliation Studies.

Lindner, Evelin Gerda (2007a). *How the human rights ideal of equal dignity separates humiliation from shame.* Human Dignity and Humiliation Studies.

Lindner, Evelin Gerda (2007b). "Avoiding humiliation – From intercultural communication to global interhuman communication." *Journal of Intercultural Communication, SIETAR Japan, 10*, pp. 21–38.

Lindner, Evelin Gerda (2007c). *How multicultural discourses can help construct new meaning.* Paper presented at the 2nd International Conference on Multicultural Discourses, 13–15th April 2007, followed by the 9th Annual Conference of Human Dignity and Humiliation Studies, Institute of Discourse and Cultural Studies, and Department of Applied Psychology, Zhejiang University, Hangzhou, China.

Lindner, Evelin Gerda (2007d). *Psychological factors in Euro-Arab relations.* Alexandria, Egypt: Lecture as part of the pilot course Young Swedish Muslim Peace Agents, 19th–27th January 2007, at the Swedish Institute, with Director Jan Henningsson, 2nd January 2007.

Lindner, Evelin Gerda (2008a). "Why there can be no conflict resolution as long as people are being humiliated." *International Review of Education, Volume 55* (May 2–3, 2009, Special Issue on Education for Reconciliation and Conflict Resolution), pp. 157–84.

Lindner, Evelin Gerda (2008b). "Beginning to understand the causes of conflicts and terrorism – and finding ways to transcend them." In *Creativity: With Pakistani children's drawings*, edited by Atle Hetland. Islamabad: Pakistan – Norway Association (PANA): An International Friendship Association in Pakistan.

Lindner, Evelin Gerda (2009a). *What Asia can contribute to world peace: The role of dignity and humiliation.* Background text for two papers: (1) "How Asia Can Contribute to World Peace Psychology: The Role of Dignity and Humiliation", in Cristina Montiel and Noraini Noor (Eds.), *The Theory and Practice of Peace Psychology in Asia*, New York, NY: Springer Science and Business Media, 2008; (2) "Peace and Dignity: More than the Absence of Humiliation – What We Can Learn From the Asia-Pacific Region", in *The Australian Centre for Peace and Conflict Studies: Occasional Papers Series*, Brisbane, Australia: University of Queensland, Australian Centre for Peace and Conflict Studies (ACPACS), after the author had spent one month (August 2007) at ACPACS and had given a lecture on *The Role of Dignity and Humiliation for Peace and Conflict Studies* on 14th August 2007.

Lindner, Evelin Gerda (2009b). *Emotion and conflict: How human rights can dignify emotion and help us wage good conflict.* Westport, CT, London: Praeger, Greenwood.

Lindner, Evelin Gerda (2009c). "Humiliation and global terrorism: How to overcome it nonviolently." In *Encyclopedia of life support systems: Nonviolent alternatives for social change*, edited by Ralph Summy, pp. 227–48. Oxford: Encyclopedia of Life Support Systems (EOLSS), developed under the auspices of UNESCO.

Lindner, Evelin Gerda (2009d). "Why there can be no conflict resolution as long as people are being humiliated." *International Review of Education, 55* (May 2–3, Special Issue on Education for Reconciliation and Conflict Resolution), pp. 157–84.

Lindner, Evelin Gerda (2009e). "Genocide, humiliation, and inferiority: An interdisciplinary perspective." In *Genocides by the oppressed: Subaltern genocide in theory and practice*, edited by Nicholas A. Robins, and Adam Jones, chapter 7, pp. 138–58. Bloomington: Indiana University Press.

Lindner, Evelin Gerda (2009f). *Peace and dignity: More than the absence of humiliation – what we can learn from the Asia-Pacific region*. Paper written for the Australian Centre for Peace and Conflict Studies (ACPACS).

Lindner, Evelin Gerda, Thomas M. Pick, Anne Speckhard, and Beatrice Jacuch (2009). "The relevance of humiliation studies for the prevention of terrorism." In *Home-grown terrorism: Understanding and addressing the root causes of radicalisation among groups with an immigrant heritage in Europe*, edited by Thomas M. Pick, Anne Speckhard, and Beatrice Jacuch, chapter Section 3, pp. 163–88. Amsterdam, The Netherlands: IOS Press, supported by the NATO Science for Peace and Security Programme, E: Human and Societal Dynamics, Vol. 60, 2009. Proceedings of the NATO advanced research workshop Indigenous Terrorism: Understanding and Addressing the Root Causes of Radicalisation Among Groups with an Immigrant Heritage in Europe, Budapest, Hungary, 7–9th March, 2008.

Lindner, Evelin Gerda (2010a). "Traumatized by humiliation in times of globalization: Transforming humiliation into constructive meaning." In *Mass trauma and emotional healing around the world: Rituals and practices for resilience, Vol. 2: Human-made disasters*, edited by Ani Kalayjian, and Dominique Eugene, chapter 20, pp. 361–82. Santa Barbara, CA: Praeger, ABC-CLIO.

Lindner, Evelin Gerda (2010b). "Disasters as a chance to implement novel solutions that highlight attention to human dignity." In *Rebuilding sustainable communities for children and their families after disasters: A global survey*, edited by Adenrele Awotona, pp. 335–58. Newcastle upon Tyne, UK: Cambridge Scholars Publishing (print), MyILibrary, www.myilibrary.com (e-book), proceedings of the international conference Rebuilding Sustainable Communities for Children and Their Families after Disasters, convened by Adenrele Awotona at the College of Public and Community Service University of Massachusetts at Boston, November 16–19, 2008.

Lindner, Evelin Gerda, and Desmond Tutu (Foreword) (2010). *Gender, humiliation, and global security: Dignifying relationships from love, sex, and parenthood to world affairs*. Santa Barbara, CA: Praeger, ABC-CLIO.

Lindner, Evelin Gerda (2011). *Terror in Norway: How can we continue from a point of utter despair? Promoting a dignity culture, not just locally, but globally*. Dunedin, New Zealand: Paper prepared for the 17th Annual Conference of Human Dignity and Humiliation Studies "Enlarging the Boundaries of Compassion", in Dunedin, New Zealand, 29th August–1st September 2011.

Lindner, Evelin Gerda (2012a). *After 22nd July: Humiliation and terrorism*. Oslo: Lecture at the University of Oslo, Centre for Gender Research / Senter for tverrfaglig kjønnsforskning, 8th February 2012.

Lindner, Evelin Gerda (2012b). *South America 2012: Reflections on a "digniventure"*. Human Dignity and Humiliation Studies.

Lindner, Evelin Gerda (2012c). *Creating a dignified world: A video message to the Brazilian people from Evelin Lindner*. Brasilia, Brasil: Comissão de Direitos Humanos e Minorias (Committee for Human Rights and Minorities), Câmara dos Deputados (Chamber of Deputies), 5th June 2012.

Lindner, Evelin Gerda (2012d). *Shame, humiliation, and humility: How human rights ideals impact their roles in the continuum of balance and the continuum of toxicity* Human Dignity and Humiliation Studies, reflections in response to Hélène Lewis questions in connection with her work on shame.

Lindner, Evelin Gerda (2012e). "Fostering global citizenship." In *The psychological components of sustainable peace*, edited by Morton Deutsch, and Peter T. Coleman, chapter 15, pp. 283–98. New York: Springer.

Lindner, Evelin Gerda (2012f). *A dignity economy: Creating an economy which serves human dignity and preserves our planet*. Lake Oswego, OR: World Dignity University Press.

Lindner, Evelin Gerda (2012g). *Humiliation and terrorism*. Oslo: Course PSYC3203, Anvendt sosialpsykologi, Universitet i Oslo / University of Oslo, Psykologisk institutt / Department of Psychology, 25th January 2012.

Lindner, Evelin Gerda (2013). *Who we are and our latest news.* Stellenbosch, South Africa: Introductory presentation, 24th April 2013, 21st Annual Conference of Human Dignity and Humiliation Studies "Search for Dignity", at the University of Stellenbosch, 24th–27th April 2013.

Lindner, Evelin Gerda, and Robert Morrell (2013). *Human dignity and humiliation studies: Transdisciplinarity in practice.* Cape Town, South Africa: Workshop on "Human Dignity and Humiliation Studies: Transdisciplinarity in Practice", convened by Robert Morrell, University of Cape Town, co-ordinator of the Programme for the Enhancement of Research Capacity (PERC), 4th July 2013.

Lindner, Evelin Gerda, and Kosheek Sewchurran (2013). *A dignity economy.* Cape Town, South Africa: Lunch time discussion to trace the connections between "A Dignity Economy", "Values Based Leadership", "Inclusive Innovation", "Business Model Innovation", and "Management and Leadership Education", convened by Kosheek Sewchurran, University of Cape Town, Graduate School of Business, Innovation Management and Information Systems, 5th July 2013.

Lindner, Evelin Gerda (2014a). "Urban dignity – global dignity: What is it? How do we achieve it? Part 1 and Part 2." *Journal of Urban Culture Research, 8 and 9, Arts and Social Outreach – Designs for Urban Dignity* (January – June, and July – December), pp. 8–22, and 8–34.

Lindner, Evelin Gerda (2014b). "Emotion and conflict: Why it is important to understand how emotions affect conflict and how conflict affects emotions." In *The handbook of conflict resolution: Theory and practice*, edited by Morton Deutsch, Peter T. Coleman, and Eric C. Marcus, chapter 12, pp. 283–309. San Francisco, CA: Jossey-Bass.

Lindner, Evelin Gerda (2014c). "Living globally: Global citizenship of dignity and care as personal practice." In *Global citizen: Challenges and responsibility in an interconnected world*, edited by Aksel Braanen Sterri, chapter 3, pp. 15–26. Rotterdam, The Netherlands: Sense Publishers.

Lindner, Evelin Gerda (2014d). *The terrorist.* Chapter for the forthcoming book *Understanding the Self of Suicidal Behaviour Among Ethnic Minorities: Who Is Killing Whom?* edited by Latha Nrugham.

Lindner, Evelin Gerda (2015a). *Reflections on the 25th Dignity Conference in Rwanda in 2015.* Human Dignity and Humiliation Studies.

Lindner, Evelin Gerda (2015b). *Tannhäuser, terrorism, revolution, and economism.* Human Dignity and Humiliation Studies.

Lindner, Evelin Gerda (2016a). *Publication list of Evelin Lindner.* Human Dignity and Humiliation Studies.

Lindner, Evelin Gerda (2016b). *The journey of humiliation and dignity, and the significance of the year 1757.* Human Dignity and Humiliation Studies.

Lindner, Evelin Gerda (2016c). "Auswirkungen von Demütigung auf Menschen und Völker." In *Gehirne zwischen Liebe und Krieg: Menschlichkeit im Zeitalter der Neurowissenschaften*, edited by Helmut Fink, and Rainer Rosenzweig, chapter 3, pp. 41–73. Münster, Germany: mentis.

Lindner, Evelin Gerda (2016d). *Reflection on Journey to Earthland: The great transition to planetary civilization.* Boston: Great Transition Initiative, Evelin Lindner on the importance of the affective and institutional dimensions of global citizenship, reflecting on Paul Raskin's book, *Journey to Earthland: The Great Transition to Planetary Civilization*, Boston: Tellus Institute, 2016.

Lindner, Evelin Gerda (2016e). *Cities at risk – From humiliation to dignity: A journey from Sarajevo to Dubrovnik, or the case of Southeast Europe.* Human Dignity and Humiliation Studies. Paper written for the 27th Annual Dignity Conference "Cities at Risk – From Humiliation to Dignity", in Dubrovnik, Croatia, 19th–23rd September 2016.

Lindner, Evelin Gerda (2017). *A global life design: Reflections and a chronological description, 2006 – 2017.* Human Dignity and Humiliation Studies.

Lindstrom, Lamont (1993). *Cargo cult: Strange stories of desire from Melanesia and beyond.* Honolulu, HI: University of Hawaii Press.

Linklater, Andrew (2005). "Dialogic politics and the civilising process." *Review of International Studies, 31* (1), pp. 141–54.

Linn, Vaddhaka (2015). *The Buddha on wall street: What's wrong with capitalism and what we can do.* Cambridge: Windhorse

Linser, Josef-Harry (2016). *Josef-Harry Linser's life story.* Human Dignity and Humiliation Studies.

Linton, Sally (1974). "Woman the gatherer: Male bias in anthropology." In *Women in perspective: A guide for cross-cultural studies*, edited by Sue-Ellen Jacobs, pp. 9-21. Urbana: University of Illinois Press.

Lipton, Michael, and Emanuel De Kadt (1988). *Agriculture-health linkages.* Geneva, Switzerland: World Health Organization.

Lira, Elizabeth (2001). "Violence, fear, and impunity: Reflections on subjective and political obstacles for peace." *Peace and Conflict: Journal of Peace Psychology, 7* (2), pp. 109–18.

Litz, Brett T., Nathan Stein, Eileen Delaney, Leslie Lebowitz, William P. Nash, Caroline Silva, and Shira Maguen (2009). "Moral injury and moral repair in war veterans: A preliminary model and intervention strategy." *Clinical Psychology Review, 29* (8), pp. 695–706.

Loewenstein, Antony (2015). *Disaster capitalism: Making a killing out of catastrophe.* London: Verso.

Lofgren, Mike (2016). *The deep state: The fall of the constitution and the rise of a shadow government.* New York: Viking.

Logiest, Guy (1982). *Mission au Rwanda. Un blanc dans la bagarre Hutu-Tutsi.* Bruxelles: Didier Hatier.

Lohmann, Georg (2014). "Ethik der radikalen Endlichkeit." *Information Philosophie, 42* (1), pp. 5–11.

Lord, Charles G., Lee D. Ross, Mark R. Lepper, and Clyde Hendrick (1979). "Biased assimilation and attitude polarization: The effects of prior theories on subsequently considered evidence." *Journal of Personality and Social Psychology, 37* (11), pp. 2098–109.

Lorenz, Konrad (1963/1966). *On aggression.* Translated by Marjorie Latzke. London: Methuen. German original *Das sogenannte Böse. Zur Naturgeschichte der Aggression*, Wien, Austria: Dr. G. Borotha-Schoeler Verlag, 1963.

Lotto, David (2016). *Terrorism: An overview.* In press.

Lowman, Rodney L. (2013). *Internationalizing multiculturalism: Expanding professional competencies in a globalized world.* Washington, DC: American Psychological Association.

Lu Xun (1981). *Call to arms (Na Han).* Beijing: Foreign Languages Press.

Lu Xun (2000a). "A madman's diary." In *Call to arms (Na Han).* Beijing: Foreign Languages Press.

Lu Xun (2000b). "The true story of Ah Q (A Q Zhengzhuan)." In *Call to arms (Na Han).* Beijing: Foreign Languages Press.

Lu Xun (2002a). *Lu Xun selected poems.* Beijing: Foreign Languages Press.

Lu Xun (2002b). *Old tales retold (Gu Shi Xin Bian).* Beijing: Foreign Languages Press.

Lu Xun (2002c). *Wandering (Pang Huang).* Beijing: Foreign Languages Press.

Lu Xun (2003). *Dawn blossoms plucked at dusk (Zhao Hua Xi Shi).* Beijing: Foreign Languages Press.

Lu Xun (2004). *Wild grass (Ye Cao).* Beijing: Foreign Languages Press.

Lugard, Frederick John Dealtry (1965). *The dual mandate in British tropical Africa.* London: Frank Cass.

Lukacs, John (1997). *The Hitler of history.* New York: Vintage.

Lunati, M. Teresa (1992). "On altruism and cooperation." *Methodus, 4* (December), pp. 69–75.

Luo, Zhitian T. (1993). "National humiliation and national assertion – The Chinese response to the twenty-one demands." *Modern Asian Studies, 27* (2), pp. 297–319.

Lurås, Helge (2015). *Hva truer Norge nå? Sikkerhetspolitiske selvbedrag etter den kalde krigen.* Oslo: Cappelen Damm.

Lutz, Catherine A., and Lila Abu-Lughod (1990). *Language and the politics of emotion*. Cambridge: Cambridge University Press.

Lüders, Michael (2015). *Wer den Wind sät. Was westliche Politik im Orient anrichtet*. München, Germany: C.H. Beck.

Lüders, Michael (2017). *Wer den Wind sät: Was westliche Politik im Orient anrichtet*. München, Germany: C.H. Beck.

Lykes, M. Brinton (2001). "Human rights violations as structural violence." In *Peace, conflict, and violence: Peace psychology for the 21st century*, edited by Daniel J. Christie, Richard V. Wagner, and Deborah Du Nann Winter, pp. 158–67. Upper Saddle River, NJ: Prentice-Hall.

Lynch, Jake (2013). *A global standard for reporting conflict*. New York: Routledge.

Lyons-Padilla, Sarah, Michele J. Gelfand, Hedieh Mirahmadi, Mehreen Farooq, and Marieke van Egmond (2015). "Belonging nowhere: Marginalization and radicalization risk among Muslim immigrants." *Behavioral Science and Policy, 1* (2), pp. 1–12.

Lyons, John O. (1978). *The invention of the self*. Carbondale: Southern Illinois University Press.

Lyons, Oren (1980). "An Iroquois perspective." In *American Indian environments: Ecological issues in native American history*, edited by Christopher T. Vecsey, Robert W. Venables, and Kai T. Erikson, pp. 171–74. Syracuse, NY: Syracuse University Press.

Lyotard, Jean-Francois (1979/1984). *The postmodern condition: A report on knowledge*. Translated by Geoffrey Bennington, and Brian Massumi. Minneapolis: University of Minnesota Press. French original *La condition postmoderne: Rapport sur le savoir*, Paris: Éditions de Minuit, 1979.

Lyotard, Jean-François (1974/1983). *Libidinal economy*. Translated by Iain Hamilton Grant. Bloomington, IN: Indiana University Press. French original *Économie Libidinale*, Paris: Minuit, 1974.

Maalouf, Amin (1998/2000). *In the name of identity: Violence and the need to belong*. Translated by Barbara Bray. New York: Arcade. French original *Les Identités Meurtrières*, Paris: Grasset, 1998.

Maalouf, Amin (2009). *Le dérèglement du monde: Quand nos civilisations s'épuisent*. Paris: Grasset.

MacDonald, Geoff, and Lauri A. Jensen-Campbell (Eds.) (2011). *Social pain: Neuropsychological and health implications of loss and exclusion*. Washington, DC: American Psychological Association.

Machiavelli, Niccolò (1532). *Il Principe*. Rome: Antonio Blado d'Asola.

MacIntyre, Alasdair, and D. R. Bell (1967). "Symposium: The idea of a social science." *Proceedings of the Aristotelian Society, 41*, pp. 95–132.

Mack, Andrew, and Zoe Nielsen (2010). *Human security report 2009/2010: The causes of peace and the shrinking costs of war*. Vancouver, BC: Human Security Report Project, Simon Fraser University.

Mackay, Hugh (1994). *Why don't people listen? Solving the communication problem*. Sydney: Pan Macmillan Australia.

Macklin, Ruth (2003). "Dignity is a useless concept." *British Medical Journal, 327* (7429, December), pp. 1419–20.

MacLure, Maggie (2015). "The 'new materialisms': A thorn in the flesh of critical qualitative inquiry?" In *Critical qualitative inquiry: foundations and futures*, edited by Gaile S. Cannella, Michelle Perez, and Penny A. Pasque. Walnut Creak, CA: Left Coast Press.

MacMurray, John (1949/1991). *Conditions of freedom*. Humanity Books. Original Toronto: Ryerson Press, 1949.

Macmurray, John (1961). *Persons in relation*. London: Faber and Faber. Fulltext at The Gifford Lectures Online.

Macpherson, Crawford Brough (1962). *The political theory of possessive individualism: Hobbes to Locke*. Oxford: Clarendon Press.

Madsen, Ole Jacob (2014a). "Psychology oblivious to psychology: Some limits on our capacity for processing psychology in society." *Theory and Psychology, 24* (5), pp. 609–29.

Madsen, Ole Jacob (2014b). *The therapeutic turn: How psychology altered western culture*. London: Routledge.

Magdoff, Fred, and John Bellamy Foster (2011). *What every environmentalist needs to know about capitalism: A citizen's guide to capitalism and the environment*. New York: Monthly Review Press.

Maine, Henry Sumner Sir (1861). *Ancient law: Its connection with the early history of society, and its relation to modern ideas*. Boston: Beacon Press.

Malcolm, Noel (1998). *Kosovo: A short history*. London: Papermac.

Malinowski, Bronislaw (1944). *A scientific theory of culture and other essays*. Chapel Hill: The University of North Carolina Press.

Malinowski, Stephan (2005). "From king to Führer: The German aristocracy and the Nazi movement." pp. S.5–28. London: German Historical Institute London.

Mallmann, Klaus-Michael, Jochen Böhler, and Matthäus Jürgen (2008). *Einsatzgruppen in Polen. Darstellung und Dokumentation*. Darmstadt, Germany: Wissenschaftliche Buchgesellschaft.

Malthus, T. R. (1798). *An essay on the principle of population, as it affects the future improvement of society. With remarks on the speculations of Mr. Godwin, M. Condorcet, and other writers*. London: printed for J. Johnson.

Managhan, Tina (2012). *Gender, agency and war: The maternalized body in US foreign policy*. Abingdon: Routledge.

Manicas, Peter T. (2006). *A realist philosophy of social science: Explanation and understanding*. Cambridge: Cambridge University Press.

Mann, Barbara Alice (2000). *Iroquoian women, the Gantowisas*. New York: Peter Lang.

Mann, Charles C. (2005). *1491: New revelations of the Americas before Columbus*. New York: Knopf.

Mann, James (2004a). *Rise of the vulcans: The history of Bush's war cabinet*. New York: Viking.

Mann, Jonathan M. (1997). "Medicine and public health, ethics and human rights." *The Hastings Center Report, 27* (3, May-June), pp. 6–13.

Mann, Michael (2004b). *Fascists*. Cambridge: Cambridge University Press.

Manning, Richard (2004). *Against the grain: How agriculture has hijacked civilization*. New York: North Point Press.

Mansel, Jürgen, and Wilhelm Heitmeyer (2009). *Precarity, segregation, and poverty in the social space*. Berlin: Deutsches Institut für Urbanistik.

Mansour, Ahmad (2015). *Generation Allah. Warum wir im Kampf gegen religiösen Extremismus umdenken müssen*. Frankfurt am Main, Germany: Fischer.

Mantel, Barbara (2014). "Assessing the threat from al Qaeda: Is the militant Islamist group still a danger to the West?". *CQ Researcher, 24* (24, June 27), pp. 555–75.

Manvell, Roger, and Heinrich Fraenkel (1962). *Goering*. New York: Simon and Schuster.

Marbach, Jan, Paul Matussek, and Peter Matussek (2007). *Affirming psychosis. The mass appeal of Adolf Hitler*. New York: Peter Lang.

Maren, Michael (1997). *The road to hell: The ravaging effects of foreign aid and international charity*. New York: Free Press.

Margalit, Avishai (1996). *The decent society*. Cambridge, MA: Harvard University Press.

Margalit, Avishai (1997). "Decent equality and freedom: A postscript." *Social Research: An International Quarterly of the Social Sciences, 64* (1, Spring, The Decent Society), pp. 147–60.

Margalit, Avishai (2002). *The ethics of memory*. Cambridge, MA: Harvard University Press.

Margolis, Howard (1982). *Selfishness, altruism, and rationality: A theory of social choice.* New York: Cambridge University Press.

Marmot, Michael (2004a). "Dignity and inequality." *The Lancet, 364* (9439), pp. 1019–21.

Marmot, Michael (2015). *The health gap: The challenge of an unequal world.* London: Bloomsbury.

Marmot, Michael G. (2004b). *The status syndrome: How social standing affects our health and longevity.* New York: Times Books.

Marquardt, Angela (2015). *Vater, Mutter, Stasi.* Köln, Germany: Kiepenheuer und Witsch.

Marsden, George M. (1994). *The soul of the American university: From protestant establishment to established nonbelief.* New York: Oxford University Press.

Marsden, Sarah V., and Alex Peter Schmid (2011). "Typologies of Terrorism and Political Violence." In *The Routledge handbook of terrorism research,* edited by Alex Peter Schmid, pp. 158–200. London, New York: Routledge.

Marsella, Anthony J., Francis L. K. Hsu, and George A. De Vos (Eds.) (1985). *Culture and self: Asian and Western perspectives.* New York: Tavistock.

Marsella, Anthony J. (2009). "Some reflections on potential abuses of psychology's knowledge and practices." *Psychological Studies, 54* (1), pp. 23–27.

Marsella, Anthony J. (2012). *Genocide: The ecology of pathways to ending lives and life.* Keaau, HI: International Academy for Intercultural Research.

Marsella, Anthony J. (2014). *Contexts of war and peace: Reflections on sources, consequences, choices.* Alpharetta, GA: Anthony Marsella.

Marsella, Anthony J. (2015). "Trends, changes, challenges in North American (Eurocentric) psychology: Rethinking assumptions, practices, and organization in socio-political contexts." *Journal for Social Action in Counseling and Psychology, 7* (1, Summer 2015), pp. 143–52.

Marshall, Graham R. (2008). "Nesting, subsidiarity, and community-based environmental governance beyond the local level." *International Journal of the Commons, 2* (1, January), pp. 75–97.

Marshall, Monty G. (1999). *Third World War: System, process, and conflict dynamics.* Lanham, MD: Rowman and Littlefield.

Marshall, Monty G. (2002). "Global terrorism: An overview and analysis." In *Occasional Paper #3.* College Park, MD: University of Maryland, Integrated Network for Societal Conflict Research (INSCR), Center for International Development and Conflict Management (CIDCM), and Center for Systemic Peace.

Marshall, Monty G., and Ted Robert Gurr (2005). *Peace and conflict 2005: A global survey of armed conflicts, self-determination movements, and democracy.* College Park, MD: Center for International Development and Conflict Management, University of Maryland.

Marshall, Monty G. (2014–2016). *Managing complexity in modern-societal systems.* Vienna, VA: Center for Systemic Peace.

Martin, Glen T. (2010). *Triumph of civilization: Democracy, nonviolence and the piloting of spaceship Earth.* Sun City, AZ: Institute for Economic Democracy Press.

Martin, Judith N., Thomas K. Nakayama, and Lisa A. Flores (2001). "A dialectical approach to intercultural communication." In *Readings in intercultural communication: Experiences and contexts,* edited by Judith N. Martin, Thomas K. Nakayama, and Lisa A. Flores, New edition, pp. 3–13. Boston: McGraw-Hill.

Martin, Mike (2014). *Intimate war: An oral history of the Helmand conflict, 1978 - 2012.* London: Hurst.

Martinez-Alier, Juan, and Inge Røpke (Eds.) (2008). *Recent developments in ecological economics.* Cheltenham: Edward Elgar.

Mason, Paul (2015). *Postcapitalism: A guide to our future.* London: Allen Lane.

Matsumoto, David Ricky (1988). "Reexamination of the universality of Face: Politeness phenomena in Japanese." *Journal of Pragmatics, 12* (4), pp. 403–26.

Matsumoto, David Ricky, Hee Seung Yoo, and Jeffery A. LeRoux (2007). "Emotion and intercultural adjustment." In *Handbook of applied linguistics, volume 7: Intercultural communication*, edited by Helga Kotthoff, and Helen Spencer-Oatley, chapter 5, pp. 77–98. Berlin: Mouton de Gruyter.

Mavor, Kenneth I., Winnifred R. Louis, and Chris G. Sibley (2010). "A bias-corrected exploratory and confirmatory factor analysis of right-wing authoritarianism: Support for a three-factor structure." *Personality and Individual Differences, 48* (1), pp. 28–33.

Max-Neef, Manfred A. (2005). "Foundations of transdisciplinarity." *Ecological Economics, 53*, pp. 5–16.

May, Rollo (1969). *Love and will.* New York: W. W. Norton.

May, Timothy Michael (2012). *The Mongol conquests in world history.* London: Reaktion Books.

Mayer, Jane (2016). *Dark money: The hidden history of the billionaires behind the rise of the radical right.* New York: Doubleday.

Mazzetti, Mark (2013). *The way of the knife: The CIA, a secret army, and war at the ends of the earth.* New York: Penguin.

McAdam, Douglas, Sidney Tarrow, and Charles Tilly (2001). *Dynamics of contention.* Cambridge: Cambridge University Press.

McCandless, Erin, and Tony Karbo (Eds.) (2011). *Peace, conflict, and development in Africa: A reader.* San Jose, Costa Rica: University for Peace.

McCarthy, Cormac (2006). *The road.* New York: Alfred A. Knopf.

McCauley, Clark, and Sophia Moskalenko (2014a). "Toward a profile of lone wolf terrorists: What moves an individual from radical opinion to radical action." *Terrorism and Political Violence, 26* (1), pp. 69–85.

McCauley, Clark, and Sophia Moskalenko (2014b). "Some things we think we've learned since 9/11: A commentary on Marc Sageman's 'The stagnation in terrorism research'." *Terrorism and Political Violence, 26* (4), pp. 601–06.

McCauley, Clark (2017). "Toward a psychology of humiliation in asymmetric conflict." *American Psychologist, 72* (3, Special Issue: Psychology of Terrorism), pp. 255–65.

McCauley, Clark, and Sophia Moskalenko (2017). "Understanding political radicalization: The two-pyramids model." *American Psychologist, 72* (3), pp. 205–16.

McCauley, Clark R., and Sophia Moskalenko (2011). *Friction: How radicalization happens to them and us.* Oxford: Oxford University Press.

McCauley, Clark R., Sophia Moskalenko, and Ben Van Son (2013). "Characteristics of lone-wolf violent offenders: A comparison of assassins and school attackers." *Perspectives on Terrorism, North America, February 7.*

McChrystal, Stanley A. (2013). *My share of the task: A memoir.* New York: Portfolio.

McClelland, David C. (1978). "Managing motivation to expand human freedom." *American Psychologist, 33* (3), pp. 201–10.

McCloskey, Deidre N. (2006–2016). *The bourgeois era (Volume 1: The bourgeois virtues: Ethics for an age of commerce, 2006, Volume 2: Bourgeois dignity: Why economics can't explain the modern world, 2010, Volume 3: Bourgeois equality: How ideas, not capital or institutions, enriched the world, 2016).* Chicago: University of Chicago Press.

McCrudden, Christopher (2013). "Reva Siegel and the role of religion in constructing the meaning of 'human dignity'." In *University of Michigan Public Law Research Working Paper No. 320.* Ann Arbor: University of Michigan.

McCullough, Michael E. (2008). *Beyond revenge: The evolution of the forgiveness instinct.* San Francisco: Jossey-Bass.

McDonald, Duff (2017). *The golden passport: Harvard business school, the limits of capitalism, and the moral failure of the MBA elite.* New York: HarperCollins.

McFadden, John (2016). *Empathizing with terrorists: An unthinkable necessity explained.* Accepted for publication in the fall of 2016 by *Tikkun.*

McGilchrist, Iain (2009). *The master and his emissary: The divided brain and the making of the Western world.* New Haven, CT: Yale University Press.

McGoey, Linsey (2012). "The logic of strategic ignorance." *The British Journal of Sociology, 63* (3), pp. 553–76.

McKinlay, Andrew, and Chris McVittie (2008). *Social psychology and discourse.* Chichester: Wiley-Blackwell.

McKnight, John (1995). *The uncaring society: Community and its counterfeits* New York: Basic Books.

McKnight, John, and Peter Block (2010). *The abundant community: Awakening the power of families and neighborhoods.* San Francisco: Berrett-Koehler.

McLuhan, Marshall (1972). *Take today: The executive as dropout.* New York: Harcourt Brace Jovanovich.

McMaster, Christopher Todd (2013). "Working the 'shady spaces': Resisting neoliberal hegemony in New Zealand education." *Policy Futures in Education, 11* (5), pp. 523–31.

McMeekin, Sean (2010). *Berlin-Baghdad Express: The Ottoman Empire and Germany's bid for World Power, 1898–1918.* Cambridge, MA: Harvard University Press.

McNamara, Robert S., and James G. Blight (2001). *Wilson's ghost: Reducing the risk of conflict, killing, and catastrophe in the 21st Century.* New York: Public Affairs.

McNeill, John Robert, and William Hardy McNeill (2003). *The human web: A bird's-eye view of world history.* New York: Norton.

McSorley, Kevin (Ed.) (2013). *War and the body: Militarisation, practice and experience.* Abingdon: Routledge.

McSorley, Kevin (2015). *War and the body: Militarisation, practice and experience.* Abingdon: Routledge.

McWhorter, John (2016). *Words on the move: Why English won't – and can't – sit still.* New York: Henry Holt.

Meadows, Donella, Jørgen Randers, and Dennis Meadows (2005). *Limits to growth: The 30-year update.* London: Earthscan.

Meadows, Donella H. (2008). *Thinking in systems: A primer.* White River Junction, VT: Chelsea Green Publishing.

Meffert, Harma, Valeria Gazzola, Johan A. den Boer, Arnold A. J. Bartels, and Christian Keysers (2013). "Reduced spontaneous but relatively normal deliberate vicarious representations in psychopathy." *Brain, 136* (8), pp. 2550–62.

Melber, Takuma (2011). "Verhört: Alliierte Studien zu Moral und Psyche japanischer Soldaten im Zweiten Weltkrieg." In *„Der Führer war wieder viel zu human, viel zu gefühlvoll": Der Zweite Weltkrieg aus der Sicht deutscher und italienischer Soldaten*, edited by Christian Gudehus, Sönke Neitzel, and Harald Welzer, chapter 414-437. Frankfurt am Main, Germany: Fischer.

Melucci, Alberto, John Keane, and Paul Mier (1989). *Nomads of the present: Social movements and individual needs in contemporary society.* Philadelphia: Temple University Press.

Melucci, Alberto (1996). *The playing self: Person and meaning in the planetary society.* Cambridge: Cambridge University Press.

Menkhaus, Ken (2003). "Bantu ethnic identities in Somalia." *Annales d'Ethiopie, 19* (1), pp. 323–39.

Merari, Ariel (2010). *Driven to death: Psychological and social aspects of suicide terrorism*. New York: Oxford University Press.

Merleau-Ponty, Maurice (1945/1962). *Phenomenology of perception*. Translated by Colin Smith. London: Routledge and Kegan Paul. French original *La phénoménologie de la perception*, Paris: Gallimard, 1945.

Merleau-Ponty, Maurice (1961/1993). "Eye and mind." Translated by Michael B. Smith. In *The Merleau-Ponty Aesthetics Reader*, edited by Galen A. Johnson, pp. 121–49. Evanston, IL: Northwestern University Press. French original *L'Œil et l'esprit*, Paris: Gallimard, 1961.

Merleau-Ponty, Maurice, and Claude Lefort (1964/1968). *The visible and the invisible: Followed by working notes*. Translated by Alphonso Lingis. Evanston, IL: Northwestern University Press. French original *Le visible et l'invisible: Suivi de notes de travail*, Paris: Gallimard.

Merryman, John Henry (1969). *The civil law tradition: An introduction to the legal systems of Western Europe and Latin America*. Stanford, CA: Stanford University Press.

Merton, Robert K. (1969). "War and the crisis of language." In *The critique of war: Contemporary philosophical explorations*, edited by Robert Ginsberg. Chicago: Henry Regnery Company.

Merz, Sibille (2012). "'Missionaries of the new era': Neoliberalism and NGOs in Palestine." *Race and Class, 54* (1), pp. 50–66.

Mesøy, Atle (2013). "Poverty and radicalisation into violent extremism: A causal link?" In *NOREF Expert Analysis, 23 January 2013*. Oslo: The Norwegian Peacebuilding Resource Centre / Norsk Ressurssenter for Fredsbygging (NOREF).

Mettan, Guy (2017). *Creating russophobia: From the great religious schism to anti-Putin hysteria*. Atlanta, GA: Clarity Press.

Metz, Thaddeus (2007). "Toward an African moral theory." *Journal of Political Philosophy, 15* (3), pp. 321–41.

Metz, Thaddeus (2010). "Human dignity, capital punishment, and an African moral theory: Toward a new philosophy of human rights." *Journal of Human Rights, 9* (1), pp. 81–99.

Metz, Thaddeus (2011). "An African theory of dignity and a relational conception of poverty." In *The humanist imperative in South Africa*, edited by John de Gruchy, pp. 233–42. Stellenbosch, South Africa: African Sun Media.

Metz, Thaddeus (2012). "African conceptions of human dignity: Vitality and community as the ground of human rights." *Human Rights Review, 13* (1), pp. 19–37.

Meyer, Christian, Christian Lohr, Detlef Gronenborn, and Kurt W. Alt (2015). "The massacre mass grave of Schöneck-Kilianstädten reveals new insights into collective violence in Early Neolithic Central Europe." *Proceedings of the National Academy of Sciences*, pp. 1–6.

Mezirow, Jack (2000). *Learning as transformation: Critical perspectives on a theory in progress*. San Francisco: Jossey-Bass.

Michalska, Kalina J., Thomas A. Zeffiro, and Jean Decety (2016). "Brain response to viewing others being harmed in children with conduct disorder symptoms." *Journal of Child Psychology and Psychiatry, and Allied Disciplines, 57* (4), pp. 510.

Midiohouan, Guy Ossito (1991). "Ahmadou Kourouma or the bitter knowledge of black humiliation." *Research in African Literatures, 22* (2), pp. 231–34.

Mielants, Eric H. (2007). *The origins of capitalism and the "rise of the West"*. Philadelphia: Temple University Press.

Mies, Maria (1986). *Patriarchy and accumulation on a world scale: Women in the international division of labour*. London: Zed Books.

Mignolo, Walter D. (2000). *Local histories/global designs: Coloniality, subaltern knowledges, and border thinking*. Princeton, NJ: Princeton University Press.

Miklian, Jason, and Niranjan Sahoo (2016). "Supporting a more inclusive and responsive urban India'." In *PRIO Policy Brief March 2016*. Oslo: Peace Research Institute Oslo (PRIO).

Milani, Abbas (2008). *Eminent Persians: The men and women who made modern Iran, 1941-1979*. Syracuse, NY: Syracuse University Press.

Milgram, Stanley (1974). *Obedience to authority*. New York: Harper and Row.

Miller, Alice (1980/2002). *For your own good: Hidden cruelty in child-rearing and the roots of violence*. Translated by Hildegard Hannum, and Hunter Hannum. 4th edition. New York: Farrar, Straus and Giroux. German original *Am Anfang war Erziehung*, Frankfurt am Main: Suhrkamp, 1980.

Miller, Alice (2006a). *The body never lies: The lingering effects of hurtful parenting*. New York: Norton.

Miller, Alice (2008a). *The drama of being a child: The search for the true self*. Revised edition. London: Virago.

Miller, Jean Baker (1976/1986). *Toward a new psychology of women*. 2nd edition. Boston: Beacon Press.

Miller, Jean Baker (1986a). "What do we mean by relationships?" In *Work in progress, No. 22*. Wellesley, MA: Stone Center Working Paper Series, Wellesley College.

Miller, Jean Baker (1986b). *Toward a new psychology of women*. 2nd edition. Boston: Beacon Press.

Miller, Jean Baker (1988). "Connections, disconnections, and violations." In *Work in progress, No. 33*. Wellesley, MA: Stone Center Working Paper Series.

Miller, Jean Baker, Irene P. Stiver, Judith V. Jordan, and Janet L. Surrey (1994). "The psychology of women: A relational approach." In *Personality and personal growth*, edited by Robert Frager, and James Fadiman, pp. 159–79. New York: Harper Collins.

Miller, Jean Baker, and Irene P. Stiver (1997). *The healing connection: How women form relationships in therapy and in life*. Boston: Beacon Press.

Miller, Jean Baker (2006b). "Forced choices, false choices." *Research and Action Report: Wellesley Centers for Women, 27* (2), pp. 16–17.

Miller, Jean Baker (2008b). "Connections, disconnections, and violations." *Feminism and Psychology, 18* (3), pp. 368–80.

Miller, Seymour M. (2013). *How to dialogue and why: S. M. Miller*. Human Dignity and Humiliation Studies.

Miller, William Ian (1993). *Humiliation: And other essays on honor, social discomfort, and violence*. Ithaca, NY: Cornell University Press.

Mills, C. Wright (1956). *The power elite*. London: Oxford University Press.

Mills, C. Wright (1958). *The causes of world war three*. New York: Simon and Schuster.

Milne, David (2008). *America's Rasputin: Walt Rostow and the Vietnam War*. New York: Hill and Wang.

Misra, Girishwar, and Anand Prakash (2012). "Kenneth J. Gergen and social constructionism." *Psychological Studies, 57* (2, June, Kenneth J. Gergen and Social Constructionism), pp. 121–25.

Mitter, Rana (2004). *A bitter revolution: China's struggle with the modern world*. New York: Oxford University Press.

Mitzen, Jennifer (2006). "Ontological security in world politics: State identity and the security dilemma." *European Journal of International Relations, 12* (3), pp. 341–70.

Modiano, Patrick (2005/2015). *Pedigree*. Translated by Mark Polizzotti. London: MacLehose. French original *Un pedigree*, Paris: Gallimard, 2005.

Moeller van den Bruck, Arthur (1923). *Das dritte Reich*. Berlin: Ring Verlag.

Moghaddam, Fathali M. (2004). "Cultural preconditions for potential terrorist groups: Terrorism and societal change." In *Understanding terrorism: Psychosocial roots, consequences, and interventions*, edited by Anthony J. Marsella, and Fathali M. Moghaddam, chapter 5, pp. 103–17. Washington, DC: American Psychological Association.

Moghaddam, Fathali M. (2009). "De-radicalisation and the staircase from terrorism." In *The faces of terrorism: multidisciplinary perspectives*, edited by David V. Canter, pp. xiv, 300 s. Chichester: Wiley-Blackwell.

Mohamedou, Mohammad-Mahmoud Ould (2011). *Understanding Al Qaeda: Changing war and global politics*. 2nd edition. London: Pluto Press.

Moïsi, Dominique (2007). "The clash of emotions: Fear, humiliation, hope and the new world order." *Foreign Affairs, 86* (8, January/February, Terrorism and Counterterrorism), pp. 8–12.

Moïsi, Dominique (2009). *The geopolitics of emotion: How cultures of fear, humiliation, and hope are reshaping the world*. New York: Doubleday.

Mokgoro, Justice Yvonne (1998). "Ubuntu and the law in South Africa." *Potchefstroom Electronic Law Journal, 1*, pp. 1–11.

Monroe, Kristen Renwick (1996). *The heart of altruism: Perceptions of a common humanity*. Princeton, NJ: Princeton University Press.

Montagu, Ashley (1989). *Growing young*. 2nd edition. Westport, CT: Bergin and Garvey.

Montaigne, Michel de (1575). *1575 essays by Michel de Montaigne*. Translated by Charles Cotton. http://philosophy.eserver.org/montaigne-essays.txt.

Montgomery, Evan Braden (2006). "Breaking out of the security dilemma: Realism, reassurance, and the problem of uncertainty." *International Security, 31* (2, Fall), pp. 7–41.

Moolman, Nico (2012). *The Boer whore*. 2nd edition. Vanderbijlpark, Gauteng, Rebublic of South Africa: Nico Moolman.

Moore, Kathleen Dean (2016). *Great tide rising: Towards clarity and moral courage in a time of planetary change*. Berkeley, CA: Counterpoint.

Morais, Clodomir Santos de (1979). *Apuntes de teoría de la organización*. Managua, Nicaragua: Programa de las Naciones Unidas para el Desarrollo (PNUD), OIT-NIC/79/010, COPERA Project.

Morais, Clodomir Santos de (1983). *Diccionario de reforma agraria: Latinoamérica*. San José, Costa Rica: EDUCA.

More, Jason W. (2014). *The Capitalocene, Part II: Abstract social nature and the limits to capital*.

More, Thomas (1516–18/2012). *The open utopia* Wivenhoe, New York, Port Watson: Minor Compositions, a complete edition, including all the letters and commendations as well as the marginal notes that were included in the first four printings of 1516–1518, translated, edited and with an introduction by Stephen Duncombe in 2012.

Morgenthau, Hans J. (1946). *Scientific man versus power politics*. Chicago: University of Chicago Press.

Morgenthau, Hans Joachim (1948). *Politics among nations: The struggle for power and peace*. New York: Alfred A. Knopf.

Morgenthau, Hans Joachim (1951). *In defense of the national interest: A critical examination of American foreign policy*. New York: Alfred A. Knopf.

Morin, Edgar (2011). *La voie: Pour l'avenir de l'humanité*. Paris: Fayard.

Morris, Albert (2009). *Civilisation hijacked: Rescuing Jesus from Christianity and the human spirit from bondage*. Bloomington: iUniverse.

Morris, Rossabi (1994). "All the Khan's horses." In *Asian topics in world history: The Mongols in world history*. New York City: Columbia University, reprinted from *Natural History*.

Morris, William (1890). *News from nowhere*. London: Published in serial form in the *Commonweal* journal beginning on 11 January 1890.

Morrison, Toni (1987). *Beloved: A novel*. New York: Alfred A. Knopf.

Moss, Michael (2013). *Salt, sugar, fat: How the food giants hooked us.* New York: Random House.

Moss, Sigrun Marie (2014). "Beyond conflict and spoilt identities: How Rwandan leaders justify a single recategorization model for post-conflict reconciliation." *Journal of Social and Political Psychology, 2* (1), pp. 435–49.

Moss, Sigrun Marie, and Johanna Ray Vollhardt (2015). "'You can't give a syringe with unity': Rwandan responses to the government's single recategorization policies." *Analyses of Social Issues and Public Policy.*

Motzfeldt Loades, Celine (2016). "Contested places and ambivalent identities: Social change and development in UNESCO enlisted Dubrovnik." *Journal of Urban Culture Research, 12* (January – June), pp. 20-37. doi: 10.14456/jucr.2016.2.

Muenster, Bettina, and David Lotto (2010). "The social psychology of humiliation and revenge: The origins of the fundamentalist mindset." In *The fundamentalist mindset: Psychological perspectives on religion, violence, and history*, edited by Charles B. Strozier, David M. Terman, and James W. Jones, pp. 71–79. New York: Oxford University Press.

Muir, William (1924). "Al-Musta'Sim, the last of the Caliphs 640–656 A.H. / 1242–1258 A.D." In *The Caliphate: Its rise, decline, and fall*, Revised edition, chapter LXXVIII, pp. 590–92. Edinburgh: John Grant.

Muller, Roland (2001). *Honor and ahame: Unlocking the door* Bloomington, IN: Xlibris

Murray, Craig (2006). *Murder in Samarkand: A British Ambassador's controversial defiance of tyranny in the war on terror.* Edinburgh: Mainstream.

Musah, Abdel-Fatau, and Kayode Fayemi (2000). *Mercenaries: An African security dilemma.* London: Pluto.

Mussel, Patrick, Andrea M. F. Reiter, Roman Osinsky, and Johnnes Hewig (2015). "State- and trait-greed, its impact on risky decision-making and underlying neural mechanisms." *Social Neuroscience, 10* (2), pp. 126–34.

Müchler, Günter (2015). *1813: Napoleon, Metternich und das weltgeschichtliche Duell von Dresden.* Darmstadt, Germany: Theiss.

Müller, Jan-Dirk (2009). *Das Nibelungenlied.* 3rd edition. Berlin: Erich Schmidt.

Müller, Jan-Werner (2003). *A dangerous mind: Carl Schmitt in post-war European thought.* New Haven, CT: Yale University Press.

Müller, Jan-Werner (2016). *What is populism?* 2. Auflage. edition. Philadelphia: University of Pennsylvania Press. German original *Was ist Populismus? Ein Essay*, Frankfurt am Main, Germany: Suhrkamp, 2016.

Münch, Richard (2011). *Akademischer Kapitalismus: Über die politische Ökonomie der Hochschulreform.* Berlin: Suhrkamp.

Münkler, Herfried (2015). *Kriegssplitter: Die Evolution der Gewalt im 20. und 21. Jahrhundert.* Berlin: Rowohlt

Nadler, Arie, and Samer Halabi (2006). "Intergroup helping as status relations: Effects of status stability, identification, and type of help on receptivity to high-status group's help." *Journal of Personality and Social Psychology, 91* (1), pp. 97–110.

Nadler, Arie (2012). "Intergroup reconciliation: Definitions, processes, and future directions." In *Oxford handbook of conflict*, edited by Linda R. Tropp, chapter 17, pp. 291–308. New York: Oxford University Press.

Nagata, Adair Linn (2006). "Transformative learning in intercultural education." *Rikkyo Intercultural Communication Review, 4*, pp. 39–60.

Nagata, Adair Linn (2007). "Bodymindfulness for skillful communication." *Rikkyo Intercultural Communication Review, 5*, pp. 61–76.

Nagel, Mechthild (2016). *Troubling justice: Towards a ludic ubuntu ethic.* Cortland, NY: Human Dignity and Humiliation Studies.

Nagel, Thomas (1986). *The view from nowhere.* New York: Oxford University Press.

Nagel, Thomas (2012). *Mind and cosmos: Why the materialist neo-Darwinian conception of nature is almost certainly false.* Oxford: Oxford University Press.

Nathanson, Donald L. (1996). "What's a script?". *Bulletin of The Tomkins Institute, 3, Spring-Summer*, pp. 1–4.

National Commission on Terrorist Attacks Upon the United States, and Thomas H. Kean (2004). *Final Report of the National Commission on Terrorist Attacks Upon the United States.* New York: Norton.

Nawaz, Maajid (2012). *Radical: My journey out of Islamist extremism.* London: WH Allen.

Nazemroaya, Mahdi Darius (2012). *The globalization of NATO.* Atlanta, GA: Clarity Press.

Neff, Kristin (2011). *Self-compassion: Stop beating yourself up and leave insecurity behind.* New York: William Morrow.

Negrao, Claudio, George A. Bonanno, Jennie G. Noll, Frank W. Putnam, and Penelope K. Trickett (2005). "Shame, humiliation, and childhood sexual abuse: Distinct contributions and emotional coherence." *Child Maltreatment, 10* (4), pp. 350–63.

Nelson, Julie A. (2010a). *Economics for humans.* Chicago: University of Chicago Press.

Nelson, Julie A. (2012). "Is dismissing the precautionary principle the manly thing to do? Gender and the economics of climate change." In *Working paper no. 12-04.* Somerville, MA: Global Development And Environment Institute at Tufts University (GDAE).

Nelson, Robert H. (2010b). *The new holy wars: Economic religion vs. environmental religion in contemporary America.* University Park: Pennsylvania State University Press.

Nesser, Petter (2006). "Jihad in Europe: Recruitment for terrorist cells in Europe." In *FFI rapport-2006/00935: Paths to global jihad: Radicalisation and recruitment to terror networks*, edited by Laila Bokhari, Thomas Hegghammer, Brynjar Lia, Petter Nesser, and Truls H. Tonnessen, chapter 2, pp. 9–21. Kjeller, Norway: Norwegian Defence Research Establishment. Proceedings from Forsvarets forskningsinstitutt (FFI) seminar, Oslo, 15 March 2006.

Nesser, Petter (2011). *Jihad in Europe: Patterns in Islamist terrorist cell formation and behaviour, 1995 – 2010.* Oslo: University of Oslo, doctoral dissertation.

Nesser, Petter (2014). *Islamist terrorism in Europe: A history.* London: Hurst.

Neubauer, Claudia, and Matthieu Calamé (2013). "Redesign progress now! The use of knowledge for a re-conceptualised human progress." In *Report higher education in the world 5: Knowledge, engagement and higher education: Contributing to social change*, chapter 56-59. Barcelona, Spain: Global University Network for Innovation (GUNI).

Neumann, Franz Leopold (1942). *Behemoth: The structure and practice of national socialism.* London: Victor Gollancz.

Neumann, Peter R. (2008a). *Joining Al-Qaeda: Jihadist recruitment in Europe.* Abingdon-on-Thames: The International Institute for Strategic Studies and Routledge.

Neumann, Peter R. (2008b). "Introduction." In *Perspectives on radicalisation and political violence*, edited by Peter R. Neumann, Jacob Stoil, and Dina Esfandiary. London: The International Centre for the Study of Radicalisation and Political Violence (ICSR), papers from the First International Conference on Radicalisation and Political Violence, London, 17–18 January 2008.

Neumann, Peter R., and Michael Lawrence Rowan Smith (2008). *The strategy of terrorism: How it works, and why it fails.* London: Routledge.

Neumann, Peter R., Jacob Stoil, and Dina Esfandiary (Eds.) (2008). *Perspectives on radicalisation and political violence*. London: The International Centre for the Study of Radicalisation and Political Violence (ICSR), papers from the First International Conference on Radicalisation and Political Violence, London, 17–18 January 2008.

Neumann, Peter R. (2009). *Old and new terrorism*. London: Polity Press.

Neumann, Peter R. (2010). *Prisons and terrorism: Radicalisation and de-radicalisation in 15 countries*. London: A policy report by the International Centre for the Study of Radicalisation and Political Violence (ICSR) in partnership with the National Consortium for the Study of Terrorism and Responses to Terrorism (START).

Neumann, Peter R. (2015). *Victims, perpetrators, assets: The narratives of Islamic State defectors*. London: The International Centre for the Study of Radicalisation and Political Violence (ICSR).

Neumann, Peter R. (2015/2016). *Radicalized: New Jihadists and the threat against the West*. Translated by Alexander Starritt. London: I.B. Tauris. German original *Die neuen Dschihadisten: ISIS, Europa und die nächste Welle des Terrorismus*, Berlin: Econ, 2015.

Neurath, Otto (1959). "Protocol sentences." In *Logical positivism*, edited by Alfred Jules Ayer, pp. 199–208. Glencoe, IL: Free Press.

Nevo, Baruch, and Iris Brem (2002). "Peace education programs and the evaluation of their effectiveness." In *Peace education: The concept, principles, and practices around the world*, edited by Gavriel Salomon, and Baruch Nevo, chapter 24, pp. 271–82. Mahwah, NJ: Erlbaum.

Newfield, Christopher (2008). *Unmaking the public university: The forty-year assault on the middle class*. Cambridge, MA: Harvard University Press.

Newman, Leonard S., Kimberley J. Duff, and Roy F. Baumeister (1997). "A new look at defensive projection: Thought suppression, accessibility, and biased person perception." *Journal of Personality and Social Psychology, 72* (5), pp. 980–1001.

Nickerson, Raymond S., and Peter Salovey (1998). "Confirmation bias: A ubiquitous phenomenon in many guises." *Review of General Psychology, 2* (2), pp. 175–220.

Nicolson, Paula (2010). *Domestic violence and psychology: A critical perspective*. London: Routledge.

Niebuhr, Reinhold (1952/2008). *The irony of American history*. Reprint edition. Chicago: University of Chicago Press, with a new introduction by Andrew J. Bacevich.

Niemi, Laura, and Liane Young (2016). "When and why we see victims as responsible: The impact of ideology on attitudes toward victims." *Personality and Social Psychology Bulletin*.

Nietzsche, Friedrich (1883–1891). *Also sprach Zarathustra: Ein Buch für Alle und Keinen*. Chemnitz: Verlag Ernst Schmeitzner.

Nietzsche, Friedrich (1883–1891/1998). *Thus spake Zarathustra: A book for all and none*. Translated by Thomas Common. Project Gutenberg. German original *Also sprach Zarathustra: Ein Buch für Alle und Keinen*, Chemnitz: Verlag Ernst Schmeitzner, 1883–1891.

Nietzsche, Friedrich (1887/2013). *On the genealogy of morals*. Translated by Michael A. Scarpitti. London: Penguin. German original *Zur Genealogie der Moral: Eine Streitschrift*, Leipzig: Verlag von C. G. Naumann, 1887.

Nikolakaki, Maria (Ed.) (2012). *Critical pedagogy in the new dark ages: Challenges and possibilities*. New York: Peter Lang. Foreword by Henry Giroux, Afterword by Ana-Maria Araújo Freire.

Nilsen, Kjell Arild, and Helge Øgrim (2015). *Kina vs. Norge: Den ukjente historien fra Maos nei til dagens krise*. Oslo: Kagge.

Ninnemann, Kristi (2015). "Hwa-Byung." In *Encyclopedia of immigrant health*, edited by Sana Loue, and Martha Sajatovic, chapter 377, pp. 862–63. New York: Springer.

Nisbett, Richard E., and Dov Cohen (1996). *Culture of honor: The psychology of violence in the south*. Boulder, CO: Westview Press.

Noma, Hiroko, and Joanna Crossman (2012). "Analogue and digital mindsets: Some implications gor intercultural communication between Western and Eastern organisations." *Asian Academy of Management Journal, 17* (1, January), pp. 115–29.

Norel, Philippe (2009). *L'histoire économique globale* Paris: Seuil.

Norgaard, Richard B. (2011). *Economism and the night sky*. The International Society for Ecological Economics.

Norgaard, Richard B. (2015). *The church of economism and its discontents*. Boston: Great Transition Initiative.

Norris, Pippa, and Ronald Inglehart (2011). *Sacred and secular: Religion and politics worldwide*. 2nd edition. Cambridge: Cambridge University Press.

Nowak, Martin A., and Roger Highfield (2011). *SuperCooperators: Altruism, evolution, and why we need each other to succeed*. New York: Simon and Schuster.

Nowak, Martin A., and Roger Highfield (2012). *Supercooperators: Beyond the survival of the fittest: Why cooperation, not competition, is the key to life*. Edinburgh: Canongate.

Nussbaum, Martha C., and Amartya Sen (1993). *The quality of life*. Oxford: Clarendon Press.

Nussbaum, Martha C. (1995). "Objectification." *Philosophy and Public Affairs, 24* (4), pp. 249–91.

Nussbaum, Martha C. (2000). *Women and human development: The capabilities approach*. Cambridge: Cambridge University Press.

Nussbaum, Martha C. (2010). *Not for profit: Why democracy needs the humanities*. Princeton, NJ: Princeton University Press.

Nussbaum, Martha C. (2013). *Political emotions: Why love matters for justice*. Cambridge, MA: Belknap.

Nussbaum, Martha Craven (1998). *Plato's Republic: The good society and the deformation of desire*. Washington: Library of Congress.

Nye, Joseph S. (2004). *Soft power: The means to success in world politics*. New York: Public Affairs.

Nyerere, Julius K. (1968). *Ujamaa: Essays on socialism*. London: Oxford University Press.

Nygård, Håvard Mokleiv. "Five essays on the political economy of regime survival." University of Oslo, Faculty of Social Sciences, Department of Political Science, doctoral dissertation, 2014.

Næss, Arne (1978). "Through Spinoza to Mahayana Buddhism or through Mahayana Buddhism to Spinoza?" In *Spinoza's philosophy of man: Proceedings of the Scandinavian Spinoza Symposium 1977*, edited by Jon Wetlesen. Oslo: University of Oslo Press.

O'Hara, Maureen (2010). "Another inconvenient truth and the developmental role for psychology in a threatened world." *Humanistic Psychologist, 38* (2), pp. 101–19.

O'Hara, Maureen, and Graham Leicester (2012). *Dancing at the edge: Competence, culture and organisation in the 21st century*. Axminster, Devon: Triarchy Press.

O'Hara, Maureen, and Andrew Lyon (2014). "Well-being and well-becoming: Reauthorizing the subject in incoherent times." In *Well-being and beyond: Broadening the public and policy discourse*, edited by Timo J. Hamalainen, and Juliet Michaelson, chapter 4. Cheltenham: Edward Elgar.

O'Mara, Shane (2015). *Why torture doesn't work: The neuroscience of interrogation*. Cambridge, MA: Harvard University Press.

O'Neill, Maggie (2007). "Re-imagining diaspora through ethno-mimesis: Humiliation, human dignity and belonging." In *Transnational lives and the media: Reimagining diaspora*, edited by Olga Guedes-Bailey, Myria Georgiou, and Ramaswami Harindranath, pp. 72–94. Basingstoke: Palgrave Macmillan.

O'Shea, Andrew, and Maeve O'Brien (Eds.) (2011). *Pedagogy, oppression and transformation in a 'post-critical' climate: The return to Freirean thinking*. London: Continuum.

Obama, Barack (2004). *Dreams from my father: A story of race and inheritance*. New York: Three Rivers Press. Originally published 1995, the 2004 edition includes a new preface by Obama and his DNC keynote address.

Oberhaus, Salvador (2007). *'Zum wilden Aufstande entflammen' – die deutsche Ägyptenpolitik 1914 bis 1918. Ein Beitrag zur Propagandageschichte des Ersten Weltkrieges*. Düsseldorf, Germany: Heinrich-Heine-Universität Düsseldorf, doctoral dissertation.

Oberschall, Anthony (2001). "From ethnic cooperation to violence and war in Yugoslavia." In *Ethnopolitical warfare: Causes, consequences, and possible solutions*, edited by D. Chirot, and Martin E. P. Seligman, pp. 119–50. Washington, DC: American Psychological Association.

Oborne, Peter (2007). *Triumph of the political class*. London: Simon and Schuster.

Odora Hoppers, Catherine Alum (Ed.) (2002). *Indigenous knowledge and the integration of knowledge systems: Towards a philosophy of articulation*. Claremont, South Africa: New Africa Books.

Odora Hoppers, Catherine Alum (2008). *Life long learning in Africa: Lessons, experiences and opportunities from cultural and cognitive justice*. Paris: Speech of Catherine Odora Hoppers, University of South Africa, Pretoria, Professor and South African Research Chair in Development Education, at the occasion of the session of the 21st century talks on the theme "Lifelong learning for all: how long to get there?" UNESCO, 29th October 2008.

Odora Hoppers, Catherine Alum, and Howard Richards (2012). *Rethinking thinking: Modernity's other and the transformation of the university*. Pretoria, South Africa: University of South Africa.

Ohnuki-Tierney, Emiko (2002). *Kamikaze, cherry blossoms, and nationalisms: The militarization of aesthetics in Japanese history*. Chicago: The University of Chicago Press.

Okuku, Juma Anthony (2006). "The Land Act (1998) and land tenure reform in Uganda." *Africa Development, 31* (1), pp. 1–26.

Oldmeadow, Julian A., and Susan T. Fiske (2012). "Contentment to resentment: Variation in stereotype content across status systems." *Analyses of Social Issues and Public Policy, 12* (1), pp. 324–39.

Oliner, Samuel P., and Pearl M. Oliner (1988). *The altruistic personality: Rescuers of Jews in Nazi Europe*. New York: Free Press.

Olson, Mancur (1982). *The rise and decline of nations: Economic growth, stagflation, and social rigidities*. New Haven: Yale University Press.

Olsson, Peter A. (2005). *Malignant pied pipers of our time: A psychological study of destructive cult leaders from Rev. Jim Jones to Osama bin Laden*. Baltimore, MD: Publish America.

Open Science Collaboration (OSC) (2015). "Estimating the reproducibility of psychological science." *Science, 349* (6251).

Opotow, Susan (1995). "Drawing the line: Social categorization, moral exclusion, and the scope of justice." In *Cooperation, conflict, and justice: Essays inspired by the work of Morton Deutsch*, edited by Barbara Benedict Bunker, and Jeffrey Z. Rubin, chapter 11, pp. 347–69. New York: Russell Sage Foundation.

Opotow, Susan (2011). "How this was possible: Interpreting the Holocaust.". *Journal of Social Issues, 67* (1), pp. 205–24.

Opp, Karl-Dieter (2009). *Theories of political protest and social movements: A multidisciplinary introduction, critique, and synthesis*. Abingdon-on-Thames: Routledge.

Oppenlander, Richard A. (2011). *Comfortably unaware – Global depletion and food responsibility... What you choose to eat*. Minneapolis, MN: Langdon Street Press.

Opperman Lewis, Hélène (2016). *Apartheid: Britain's bastard child.* Cape Town, South Africa: Reach Publishers.

Orbach, Susie (2009). *Bodies.* London: Profile.

Orentlicher, Diane F. (2016). "International norms in human rights fact-finding." In *The transformation of human rights fact-finding*, edited by Philip Alston, and Sarah Knuckey, chapter 24, pp. 501–34. New York: Oxford Scholarship Online.

Organisation for Economic Co-operation and Development (OECD) (2015). *In it together: Why less inequality benefits all.* Paris: OECD Publishing. doi:10.1787/9789264235120-en.

Orton, Michael (2011). "Flourishing lives: The capabilities approach as a framework for new thinking about employment, work and welfare in the 21st century." *Work, Employment and Society, 25* (2), pp. 352–60.

Orwell, George (1949). *Nineteen eighty-four: A novel.* London: Secker and Warburg.

Osler, Audrey (2010). *Education for cosmopolitan citizenship? A challenge for the nation-state.* Hong Kong: Centre for Citizenship Education, Hong Kong Institute of Education.

Ostrom, Elinor (1990). *Governing the commons: The evolution of institutions for collective action.* Cambridge: Cambridge University Press.

Ostrom, Elinor (2010). "Beyond markets and states: Polycentric governance of complex economic systems." *American Economic Review, 100* (3), pp. 641–72.

Ott, Michael R. (2016). "Gathering the fragments of truth, reason, hope and redemption: Walter Benjamin's critical theory of religion." *Heathwood Journal of Critical Theory, 1* (3, Reclaiming Walter Benjamin for Revolutionary Times), pp. 28–60.

Otten, Marte, and Kai J. Jonas (2013). "Humiliation as an intense emotional experience: Evidence from the electro-encephalogram." *Social Neuroscience, 9* (1), pp. 23–35.

Otto, Rudolf (1917/1923). *The idea of the holy: An inquiry into the non-rational factor in the idea of the divine and its relation to the rational.* Translated by John W. Harvey. London: Oxford University Press. German original *Das Heilige – Über das Irrationale in der Idee des Göttlichen und sein Verhältnis zum Rationalen*, Breslau: Trewendt und Granier, 1917.

Otto, Ton (2009). "What happened to cargo cults? Material religions in Melanesia and the West." *Social Analysis, 53* (1), pp. 82–102.

Outhwaite, William (1994). *Habermas: A critical introduction.* Cambridge: Polity Press.

Oxley, Lawrence J. (2012). *Extreme weather and the financial markets: Opportunities in commodities and futures.* Hoboken, NJ: Wiley.

Packard, Vance (1960). *The waste makers.* New York: David McKay.

Packard, Vance Oakley (1957). *The hidden persuaders.* New York: Random House.

Packard, Vance Oakley (1959). *The status seekers: An exploration of class behaviour in America and the hidden barriers that affect you, your community, your future.* New York: David McKay.

Packard, Vance Oakley (1972). *A nation of strangers.* New York: David McKay.

Packard, Vance Oakley (1977). *The people shapers.* Boston: Little, Brown and Company.

Packard, Vance Oakley (1983). *Our endangered children: Growing up in a changing world.* Boston: Little, Brown and Company.

Packard, Vance Oakley (1989). *The ultra rich: How much is too much?* Boston: Little, Brown and Company.

Paley, Dawn (2014). *Drug war capitalism.* Edinburgh: AK Press.

Palincsar, A. Sullivan (1998). "Social constructivist perspectives on teaching and learning." *Annual Review of Psychology, 49*, pp. 345–75.

Palmquist, Stephen R. (2015). *Comprehensive Commentary on Kant's Religion Within the Bounds of Bare Reason*. Chichester: Wiley.

Pamuk, Orhan, and Maureen Freely (2004). *Snow*. London: Faber and Faber.

Pankhurst, Reza (2013). *The inevitable Caliphate? A history of the struggle for global Islamic union, 1924 to the present*. London: Hurst.

Pantham, Thomas (2009). "Against untouchability: The discourses of Gandhi and Ambedkar." In *Humiliation: Claims and context*, edited by Gopal Guru, chapter 10, pp. 179–208. New Delhi: Oxford University Press.

Papadopoulos, Renos K. (2006). "Terrorism and panic." *Psychotherapy and Politics International, 4* (2), pp. 90–100.

Pape, Robert A. (2005). *Dying to win: The strategic logic of suicide terrorism*. New York: Random House.

Paris, Joel (2008). *Prescriptions for the mind: A critical view of contemporary psychiatry*. Oxford: Oxford University Press.

Park-Kang, Sungju (2014). *Fictional international relations*. Abingdon: Routledge.

Park, Crystal L., Susan Folkman, and Peter Salovey (1997). "Meaning in the context of stress and coping." *Review of General Psychology, 1* (2), pp. 115–44.

Park, Crystal L., and Stephen P. Hinshaw (2010). "Making sense of the meaning literature: An integrative review of meaning making and its effects on adjustment to stressful life events." *Psychological Bulletin, 136* (2), pp. 257–301.

Park, Crystal L. (2012). "Meaning, spirituality, and growth: Protective and resilience factors in health and illnes." In *Handbook of health psychology*, edited by Andrew Baum, Tracey A. Revenson, and Jerome E. Singer, 2nd edition, pp. 405–29. New York: Psycholoy Press.

Parker, Christopher S., and Matt A. Barreto (2013). *Change they can't believe in: The Tea Party and reactionary politics in America*. Princeton, NJ: Princeton University Press. doi:10.1515/9781400852314.

Parker, Rozsika (2003). "Body hatred." *British Journal of Psychotherapy, 19* (4), pp. 447–64.

Parkins, Wendy, and Geoffrey Craig (2006). *Slow living*. Oxford: Berg.

Parsons, Talcott (1951). *The social system*. London: Routledge and Kegan Paul.

Parzinger, Hermann (2015). *Die Kinder des Prometheus: Eine Geschichte der Menschheit vor Erfindung der Schrift*. 4. Aufl. (2015), 5. Aufl.(2016). edition. München, Germany: Beck.

Passer, Michael W., Ronald E. Smith, Michael L. Atkinson, John B. Mitchell, and Darwin W. Muir (2011). *Psychology: Frontiers and applications*. 4th Canadian edition. Toronto: McGraw-Hill Ryerson.

Patai, Raphael (1983). *The Arab mind*. New York: Charles Scribner.

Patrick, Stewart (2011). *Weak links: Fragile states, global threats, and international security*. Oxford: Oxford University Press.

Pavlović, Srdja (2006). "Reckoning: The 1991 siege of Dubrovnik and the consequences of the 'war for peace'." *Spaces of Identity, 5* (1, Special Issue: War Crimes).

Payne, James L. (2004). *Exploring the worldwide movement against habits of coercion, bloodshed, and mayhem*. Sandpoint, ID: Lytton.

Peccei, Aurelio (1982). "Global modelling for humanity." *Futures, 14* (2), pp. 91–94.

Penttinen, Elina (2013). *Joy and international relations: A new methodology*. Abingdon: Routledge.

Perkins, John (2004). *Confessions of an economic hit man*. San Francisco: Berrett-Koehler.

Perlin, Michael L., and Naomi Weinstein (2014). "'Friend to the martyr, a friend to the woman of shame': Thinking about the law, shame and humiliation." *Southern California Review of Law and Social Justice, September*, pp. 1–51, presented at the Workshop on Transforming Humiliation and Violent Conflict, December 6, 2013.

Pérouse de Montclos, Marc-Antoine (2015). "Boko Haram, une exception dans la mouvance djihadiste?". *Politique Étrangère, Été* (2), pp. 147–58.

Perry, Bruce D. (2007). *Maltreated children: Experience, brain development and the next generation.* New York: Norton.

Petersen, Roger D. (2002). *Understanding ethnic violence: Fear, hatred, and resentment in twentieth-century Eastern Europe.* Cambridge: Cambridge University Press.

Pettigrew, Thomas F., and Linda R. Tropp (2006). "A meta-analytic test of intergroup contact theory." *Journal of Personality and Social Psychology, 90* (5), pp. 751–83.

Pettit, Philip (1996). "Freedom as antipower." *Ethics, 106* (3), pp. 576–604.

Pettit, Philip (1997a). "Freedom with honor: A republican ideal." *Social Research: An International Quarterly of the Social Sciences, 64* (1, Spring, The Decent Society), pp. 52–76.

Pettit, Philip (1997b). *Republicanism: A theory of freedom and government.* Oxford: Clarendon Press.

Pettit, Philip (2014). *Just freedom: A moral compass for a complex world.* New York: Norton.

Phang, Sara Elise (2008). *Roman military service: Ideologies of discipline in the late Republic and early Principate.* Cambridge: Cambridge University Press.

Philip IV of France (2002). "Order to arrest the Templars (September 14, 1307)." In *The Templars*, edited by Malcolm Barber, and Keith Bate, 2nd edition, pp. 244–47. Manchester: Manchester University Press.

Phillips, Nelson, and Cynthia Hardy (2002). *Discourse analysis: Investigating processes of social construction.* Thousand Oaks, CA: Sage.

Phillips, Peter, Lew Brown, and Bridget Thornton (2006). *US electromagnetic weapons and human rights: A study of the history of US intelligence community human rights violations and continuing research in electromagnetic weapons.* Rohnert Park, CA: Sonoma State University, Project Censored, and Media Freedom Foundation.

Phillipson, Nicholas (2010). *Adam Smith: An enlightened life.* New Haven, CT: Yale University Press.

Pickering, Andrew (1995). *The mangle of practice: Time, agency, and science.* Chicago: University of Chicago Press.

Pickering, Andrew (2010). *The cybernetic brain: Sketches of another future.* Chicago: University of Chicago Press.

Pieterse, Jan Nederveen (2001). "Hybridity, so what? The anti-hybridity backlash and the riddles of recognition." *Theory, Culture and Society, 18* (2-3), pp. 219–45.

Piff, Paul K., Daniel M. Stancato, Stéphane Côté, Rodolfo Mendoza-Denton, and Dacher Keltner (2012). "Higher social class predicts increased unethical behavior." *Proceedings of the National Academy of Sciences (PNAS), 109* (11), pp. 4086–91.

Piketty, Thomas (2013/2014). *Capital in the twenty-first century.* Translated by Arthur Goldhammer. Cambridge, MA: Belknap. French original *Le capital au XXIe siècle*, Paris: Seuil, 2013.

Pingel-Schliemann, Sandra (2004). *Zersetzen: Strategie einer Diktatur.* Berlin: Robert-Havemann-Gesellschaft.

Pinker, Steven (1995). *The language instinct: The new science of language and mind.* London: Penguin.

Pinker, Steven (1997). *How the mind works.* New York: Norton.

Pinker, Steven (2002). *The blank slate: The modern denial of human nature.* London: Penguin Books.

Pinker, Steven (2011). *The better angels of our nature: Why violence has declined.* New York: Viking Adult.

Pinker, Susan (2008). *The sexual paradox: Extreme men, gifted women and the real gender gap.* Toronto: Random House Canada.

Pirson, Michael, Kenneth Goodpaster, and Claus Dierksmeier (2016). "Human dignity and business: Guest editors' introduction." *Business Ethics Quarterly, 26* (4).

Pisoiu, Daniela (2012). *Islamist radicalisation in Europe: An occupational change process.* London, New York: Routledge.

Plato (360 BCE). *The Republic: Book VI.*

Pogge, Thomas W. (2002). *World poverty and human rights: Cosmopolitan responsibilities and reforms.* Cambridge: Polity Press.

Polanyi, Karl Paul, and Joseph E. Stiglitz (Foreword) (1944/2001). *The great transformation: The political and economic origins of our time.* 2nd edition. Boston: Beacon Press, first published by Farrar and Rinehart, 1944.

Polanyi, Michael (1967). *The tacit dimension.* New York: Anchor Books.

Pollack, Robert Elliot (1999). *The missing moment: How the unconscious shapes modern science.* Boston: Houghton Mifflin.

Polman, Linda (2010). *The crisis caravan: What's wrong with humanitarian aid?* New York: Metropolitan Books.

Pope, Kenneth S., and Melba J. T. Vasquez (2007). "Ethics and critical thinking." In *Ethics in psychotherapy and counseling: A practical guide*, pp. 16–36. San Francisco: Jossey-Bass.

Pope, Kenneth S. (2011). "Are the American Psychological Association's detainee interrogation policies ethical and effective? Key claims, documents, and results." *Zeitschrift für Psychologie / Journal of Psychology, 219* (3), pp. 150–58.

Popper, Karl R. (1945). *The open society and its enemies (volume 1: The spell of Plato, volumes 2: The high tide of prophecy: Hegel, Marx, and the aftermath).* London: George Routledge and Sons.

Popper, Karl R. (1957). *The poverty of historicism.* London: Routledge and Kegan Paul.

Porpora, Douglas V. (1993). "Cultural rules and material relations." *Sociological Theory, 11* (2), pp. 212–29.

Porpora, Douglas V. (2015). *Reconstructing sociology: The critical realist approach.* Cambridge: Cambridge University Press.

Porter, Gareth (2004). *Perils of dominance: Imbalance of power and the road to war in Vietnam.* Berkeley: University of California Press.

Posen, Barry (1993). "The security dilemma and ethnic conflict." *Survival, 35* (1), pp. 27–47.

Post, Jerrold M. (2007). *The mind of the terrorist: The psychology of terrorism from the IRA to Al Qaeda.* New York: Palgrave Macmillan.

Poteete, Amy R., Marco A. Janssen, and Elinor Ostrom (2010). *Working together: Collective action, the commons, and multiple methods in practice.* Princeton, NJ: Princeton University Press.

Power, Samantha (2002). *'A problem from hell': America and the age of genocide.* New York: Basic Books.

Powers, William T. (1973). *Behavior: The control of perception.* Chicago: Aldine.

Powers, William T. (1998). *Making sense of behavior: The meaning of control.* New Canaan, CT: Benchmark.

Prashad, Vijay (2007). *The darker nations: A people's history of the third world.* New York: The New Press.

Prashad, Vijay (2012). "Dream history of the global South." *Interface: A journal for and about social movements, 4* (1, May), pp. 43–53.

Pratt, Simon Frankel (2016). "A relational view of ontological security in international relations." *International Studies Quarterly*, pp. sqw038.

Pratto, Felicia, and Andrew L. Stewart (2011). "Social dominance theory." In *The encyclopedia of peace psychology*, edited by Daniel J. Christie. Chichester: Wiley-Blackwell.

Pressman, D. Elaine (2009). *Risk assessment decision for violent political extremism.* Report by Public Safety Canada.

Price, Munro (2012). "Napoleon and Metternich in 1813: Some new and some neglected evidence." *French History, 26* (4), pp. 482–503.

Pritzker, Sonya E. (2014). *Living translation: Language and the search for resonance in U. S. Chinese Medicine.* New York: Berghahn.

Pritzker, Sonya E. (2016). "New Age with Chinese characteristics? Translating inner child emotion pedagogies in contemporary China." *Ethos, 44* (2, Special Issue: Emotion Pedagogies), pp. 150–70.

Prochaska, James O., Carlo C. DiClemente, and John C. Norcross (1992). "In search of how people change. Applications to addictive behaviors." *The American Psychologist, 47* (9), pp. 1102–14.

Publius Flavius Vegetius Renatus, and Michael D. Reeve (2004). *Epitoma rei militaris.* Oxford: Clarendon Press, written possibly in the reign of Theodosius the Great, Roman Emperor from 379–395 CE, first printed edition Utrecht, 1473.

Purdey, Stephen J. (2010). *Economic growth, the environment and international relations: The growth paradigm.* London: Routledge.

Purpura, Philip P. (2011). *Terrorism and homeland security.* Burlington: Elsevier Science.

Pushkin, Aleksandr Sergeevich (1876). *Marie: A story of Russian love.* Chicago: Jansen, McClurg.

Putnam, Robert David (1976). *The comparative study of political elites.* Englewood Cliffs, NJ: Prentice-Hall.

Putnam, Robert David (1995). "Bowling alone: America's declining social capital." *Journal of Democracy, 6,* pp. 65–78.

Putnam, Robert David (2000). *Bowling alone: The collapse and revival of American community.* New York: Simon and Schuster.

Putnam, Robert David (2007). "E pluribus unum: Diversity and community in the twenty-first century – The 2006 Johan Skytte Prize." *Scandinavian Political Studies, 30* (2, June), pp. 137–74.

Pynchon, Susan Reynolds (2005). *Resisting humiliation in schooling: Narratives and counter-narratives.* Washington, DC: University of Washington, doctoral dissertation.

Pyszczynski, Thomas A., Jeff Greenberg, and Sheldon Solomon (2003). *In the wake of 9/11: The psychology of terror.* Washington, DC: American Psychological Association.

Pyszczynski, Thomas A., Abdolhossein Abdollahi, Sheldon Solomon, Jeff Greenberg, Florette Cohen, and David Weise (2006). "Mortality salience, martyrdom, and military might: The great satan versus the axis of evil." *Personality and Social Psychology Bulletin, 32* (4), pp. 525–37.

Quataert, Donald (2000). *The Ottoman Empire, 1700-1922.* Cambridge: Cambridge University Press.

Quilligan, Michael (2013). *Understanding shadows: The corrupt use of intelligence.* Atlanta, GA: Clarity Press.

Rachman, Gideon (2017). *Easternization: Asia's rise and America's decline from Obama to Trump and beyond.* New York: Other Press.

Rancière, Jacques (2004). *The politics of aesthetics: The distribution of the sensible.* London: Continuum.

Randall, Lisa (2015). *Dark matter and the dinosaurs: The astounding interconnectedness of the universe.* New York: Ecco.

Randt, Leif (2015). *Planet Magnon.* Köln, Germany: Kiepenheuer und Witsch.

Rashid, Ahmed (2008). *Descent into chaos: How the war against Islamic extremism is being lost in Pakistan, Afghanistan and central Asia.* London: Allen Lane.

Raskin, Paul D., Tariq Banuri, Gilbert Gallopín, Pablo Gutman, Albert Hammond, Robert Kates, and Rob Swart (2002). *Great transition: The promise and lure of the times ahead.* Boston: Stockholm Environment Institute (SEI), Tellus Institute, report of the Global Scenario Group.

Raskin, Paul D. (2008). "World lines: A framework for exploring global pathways." *Ecological Economics, 65* (3), pp. 461–70.

Raskin, Paul D. (2014). *A great transition? Where we stand.* Keynote address at the biennial conference of the International Society for Ecological Economics (ISEE) in Reykjavik, Iceland, August 2014.

Raskin, Paul D. (2016). *Journey to Earthland: The great transition to planetary civilization.* Boston: Tellus Institute.

Ray, Paul H., and Sherry Ruth Anderson (2000). *The cultural creatives: How 50 million people are changing the world.* New York: Three Rivers Press.

Razeto-Barry, Pablo R., and Catalina C. Canals (2015). "Does the world progress?". *Ecological Economics*, pp. Under review.

Readings, Bill (1996). *The university in ruins.* Cambridge, MA: Harvard University Press.

Reardon, Betty A., and Asha Hans (Eds.) (2010). *The gender imperative: Human security versus state security.* New Delhi: Routledge India.

Reber, Arthur S. (1995). *The Penguin dictionary of psychology.* 2nd edition. Harmondsworth: Penguin.

Reder, Michael, Verena Risse, Katharina Hirschbrunn, and Georg Stoll (Eds.) (2015). *Global common good. Intercultural perspectives on a just and ecological transformation.* Frankfurt am Main, Germany, New York: Campus.

Redlich, Fritz (1999). *Hitler: Diagnosis of a destructive prophet.* New York: Oxford University Press.

Refsdal, Pål (2010). *Geriljareporteren.* Oslo: Versal.

Reichberg, Gregory M., Henrik Preben Syse, and Endre Begby (Eds.) (2006). *The ethics of war: Classic and contemporary readings.* Malden, MA: Blackwell Publishing.

Remy, Maurice Philip (2002). *Mythos Rommel.* München, Germany: List Verlag.

Reyna, Valerie F., and Evan A. Wilhelms (Eds.) (2015). *Neuroeconomics, judgment, and decision making*, Frontiers of cognitive psychology. New York: Psychology Press.

Ricard, Matthieu (2013/2016). *Altruism: The power of compassion to change yourself and the world.* New York: Little, Brown. French original *Playdoyer pour l'altruisme*, Paris: NiL éditions, 2013.

Rich, Bruce (1994). *Mortgaging the earth: The World Bank, environmental impoverishment, and the crisis of development.* Boston: Beacon Press.

Rich, Bruce (2013). *Foreclosing the future: The World Bank and the politics of environmental destruction.* Washington, DC: The Center for Resource Economics and Island Press.

Richards, Howard (1995). *Letters from Quebec: A philosophy of peace and justice.* San Francisco, London: International Scholars Press.

Richards, Howard (2004). *Understanding the global economy.* Revised edition. Santa Barbara, CA: Peace Education Books.

Richards, Howard, and Joanna Swanger (2006a). *Dilemmas of social democracies.* Lanham, MD: Rowman and Littlefield.

Richards, Howard, and Joanna Swanger (2006b). *The dilemmas of social democracies.* Lanham, MD: Rowman and Littlefield.

Richards, Howard, and Joanna Swanger (2008). *Manual for building cultures of peace.* New York: Springer.

Richards, Howard, and Joanna Swanger (2009). "Culture change: A practical method with a theoretical basis." In *Handbook for building cultures of peace*, edited by Joseph de Rivera, pp. 57–70. New York: Springer.

Richards, Howard (2010). *Humanizing methodologies in transformation.* Pretoria, South Africa: University of South Africa, lecture given on July 20, 2010.

Richards, Howard (2011). "Human development and the transformation of the academy." *Journal of Developing Societies, 27* (2, June), pp. 201–06.

Richards, Howard (2013). "On the genealogy of morals." In *On Foucault: Non-authoritarian authority: Philosophical contributions to building cultures of solidarity* chapter 9. Limache, Chile: howardrichards.org/peace/content/view/91/95/.

Richards, Howard, and Joanna Swanger (2013). *Gandhi and the future of economics.* Lake Oswego, OR: Dignity Press.

Richards, Howard (2014). "Unbounded organization and the unbounded university curriculum." In *University engagement and environmental sustainability*, edited by Patricia Inman, and Diana Robinson, chapter 2. Manchester: Manchester University Press.

Richards, Howard (2015). "Modernity's 'other' and the transformation of the university." *International Journal of Development Education and Global Learning, 7* (2, Development Education in the Global South), pp. 6–25.

Richards, Howard, and Gavin Andersson (2015). *Unbounded organization in community.* Lake Oswego, OR: Dignity Press.

Richards, Howard, Catherine Alum Odora Hoppers, and Evelin Gerda Lindner (2015a). *Beyond Foucault: The rise of indigenous subjugated knowledges – Dialogues with Howard Richards, Catherine Odora Hoppers, and Evelin Lindner.* Pretoria, South Africa: Inspired by the lecture series Against Foucault given by Howard Richards in Pretoria, South Africa, in 2013.

Richards, Howard, Catherine Alum Odora Hoppers, and Evelin Gerda Lindner (2015b). *Beyond Foucault: The rise of indigenous subjugated knowledges – Dialogues by Evelin Lindner, Howard Richards and Catherine Odora Hoppers.* Forthcoming. Inspired by the lecture series 'Against Foucault', given by Howard Richards in Pretoria, South Africa in 2013.

Richards, Howard (2016a). *South African elections 2016.* Limache, Chile: Chileufú – Casa de Diálogo.

Richards, Howard (2016b). *Individual and human rights.* Limache, Chile: Human Dignity and Humiliation Studies.

Richards, Howard (2016c). *The Nice terror attack: Mind at the end of its tether.* Limache, Chile: Human Dignity and Humiliation Studies.

Richards, Howard, and Gavin Andersson (2017). *Economic theory and community development.* Forthcoming.

Richerson, Peter J., Robert Boyd, and Robert L. Bettinger (1999). *The origins of agriculture as a natural experiment in cultural evolution.* Davis, CA: University of California, Center for Agricultural History.

Richerson, Peter J., and Robert Boyd (2001). "Institutional evolution in the Holocene: The rise of complex societies." In *The origin of human social institutions*, edited by Walter G. Runciman, pp. 197–204. Oxford: Oxford University Press. Proceedings of the British Academy Foundation meeting 'The Origin of Human Social Institutions', organised by Walter G. Runciman, Draft 8 22 00, April 2000.

Richerson, Peter J., Robert Boyd, and Robert L. Bettinger (2001). "Was agriculture impossible during the Pleistocene but mandatory during the Holocene? A climate change hypothesis." *American Antiquity, 66*, pp. 387–411.

Richter, Carola, and Asiem El Difraoui (Eds.) (2015). *Arabische Medien.* Konstanz, Germany: UVK Verlagsgesellschaft.

Rickards, James (2014). *The death of money: The coming collapse of the international monetary system.* New York: Portfolio.

Ricks, Thomas E. (2006). *Fiasco: The American military adventure in Iraq*. New York: Penguin Press.

Ridley, Matt (1996). *The origins of virtue: Human instincts and the evolution of cooperation*. London: Penguin.

Ridley, Matt (2010). *The rational optimist: How prosperity evolves*. New York: HarperCollins.

Rieff, David (2016). *In praise of forgetting: Historical memory and its ironies*. New Haven, CT: Yale University Press.

Riesman, David, Nathan Glazer, and Reuel Denney (1950/2001). *The lonely crowd: A study of the changing American character*. Revised edition. New Haven, CT: Yale University Press. Originally published in 1950.

Rifkin, Jeremy (2009). *The empathic civilization: The race to global consciousness in a world in crisis*. New York: Jeremy P. Tarcher.

Rifkin, Jeremy (2014). *The zero marginal cost society: The internet of things, the collaborative commons, and the eclipse of capitalism*. New York: Palgrave Macmillan.

Rignot, Eric, Jeremie Mouginot, Mathieu Morlighem, Helene Seroussi, and Bernd Scheuchl (2014). "Widespread, rapid grounding line retreat of Pine Island, Thwaites, Smith and Kohler glaciers, West Antarctica from 1992 to 2011." *Geophysical Research Letters*.

Riley, Naomi Schaefer (2011). *The faculty lounges: And other reasons why you won't get the college education you paid for*. Chicago: Ivan R. Dee.

Ringmar, Erik (2002). "The recognition game: Soviet Russia against the West." *Cooperation and Conflict, 37* (2), pp. 115–36.

Rippin, Ann (2013). "The human touch versus 'silver-handedness': The importance of the haptic in organisational life." *International Journal of Work Organisation and Emotion, 5* (4), pp. 357–68.

Risen, James (2014). *Pay any price: Greed, power, and endless war*. New York: Houghton Mifflin Harcourt.

Roach, Steven C. (2017). *Decency and difference*. forthcoming.

Robinson, William I. (2017). *Global capitalism: Reflections on a brave new world*. Boston: Great Transition Initiative.

Rock, Paul (2005). "Chronocentrism and British criminology." *The British Journal of Sociology, 56* (3), pp. 473–791.

Rockström, Johan (2015). *Bounding the planetary future: Why we need a Great Transition*. Boston: Great Transition Initiative: Toward a Transformative Vision and Practice.

Rodina, Mihaela (1999). *Blood code rules in northern Albania*. Paris: Agence France-Presse dispatch 30th June.

Rodrik, Dani (2011). *The globalization paradox: Democracy and the future of the world economy*. New York: Norton.

Roe, Paul (1999). "The intrastate security dilemma: Ethnic conflict as a 'tragedy'?". *Journal of Peace Research, 36* (2), pp. 183–202.

Roe, Paul (2005). *Ethnic violence and the societal security dilemma*. London: Routledge.

Rogers, Carl R. (1977). *Carl Rogers on personal power*. New York: Delacorte Press.

Rogers, Carl R., Harold C. Lyon, Reinhard Tausch, and Karin Lyon (2014). *On becoming an effective teacher: Person-centered teaching, psychology, philosophy, and dialogues with Carl R. Rogers and Harold Lyon*. London: Routledge.

Rogers, Everett M. (1962). *Diffusion of innovations*. New York: Free Press of Glencoe.

Rogers, Yvonne, Andrew Rutherford, and Peter A. Bibby (1992). *Models in the mind: Theory, perspective and application*. London: Academic Press.

Rolls, Edmund T. (2014). *Emotion and decision-making explained*. Oxford: Oxford University Press.

Romarheim, Anders Grindlia (2015). *War at home: Strategic narratives of the war on terrorism*. London: King's College London, School of Social Science and Public Policy, Department of War Studies, doctoral dissertation.

Ronfeldt, David F. (1996). *Tribes, institutions, markets, networks: A framework about societal evolution*. Santa Monica, CA: RAND (Research AND Development) National Security Research Division.

Roodman, David, and Jonathan Morduch (2009). "The impact of microcredit on the poor in Bangladesh: Revisiting the evidence." In *Working Paper 174*. Washington, DC: Center for Global Development.

Roosevelt, Eleanor (1948). "The promise of human rights." *Foreign Affairs, 26* (3), pp. 470–77.

Rosa, Hartmut (2005). *Beschleunigung: Die Veränderung der Zeitstrukturen in der Moderne*. Frankfurt: Suhrkamp.

Rosa, Hartmut (2010). *Alienation and acceleration: Towards a critical theory of late-modern temporality*. Malmö, Aarhus: Nordic Summer University Press.

Rosas, Alejandro (2012). "Towards a unified theory of reciprocity." *Behavioral and Brain Sciences, 35* (1), pp. 36–37.

Rose, Steven P. R., Richard Lewontin, and Leon J. Kamin (1984). *Not in our genes: Biology, ideology and human nature*. Harmondsworth: Penguin.

Rose, William (2000). "The security dilemma and ethnic conflict: Some new hypotheses." *Security Studies, 9* (4), pp. 1–51.

Rosen, Michael (2012). *Dignity: Its history and meaning*. Cambridge, MA: Harvard University Press.

Rosenberg, Morris, Carmi Schooler, Carrie Schoenbach, and Florence Rosenberg (1995). "Global self-esteem and specific self-esteem: Different concepts, different outcomes." *American Sociological Review, 60* (1), pp. 141–56.

Rosenthal, Bruce, and Donald L. Zimmerman (2012). "Hikikomori." *International Journal of Mental Health, 41* (4), pp. 82–95.

Rosenthal, Caitlin C. (2013). "From memory to mastery: Accounting for control in America, 1750–1880." *Enterprise and Society, 14* (4), pp. 732–48.

Rosenwein, Barbara H. (2006). *Emotional communities in the early Middle Ages*. Ithaca, NY: Cornell University Press.

Roskies, Adina L. (2010). "How does neuroscience affect our conception of volition?". *Annual Review of Neuroscience, 33*, pp. 109–30.

Ross, Andrew A. G. (2013). *Mixed emotions: Beyond fear and hatred in international conflict*. Chicago: University of Chicago Press. doi:10.7208/chicago/9780226077567.001.0001.

Ross, Lee D. (1995). "Reactive devaluation in negotiation and conflict resolution." In *Barriers to the negotiated resolution of conflict*, edited by Kenneth Arrow, Robert H. Mnookin, Lee D. Ross, Amos Tversky, and Robert Wilson, chapter 2, pp. 26–43. New York: Norton.

Ross, Lee D., and Andrew Ward (1996). "Naive Realism in everyday life: Implications for social conflict and misunderstanding." In *Values and knowledge*, edited by Terrance Brown, Edward S. Reed, and Elliot Turiel, chapter 6, pp. 103–35. Hillsdale, NJ: Erlbaum.

Ross, Lee D. (2012). "Reflections on biased assimilation and belief polarization." *A Journal of Politics and Society, 24* (2), pp. 233–45.

Rotering, Frank M. (2013). *The economics of needs and limits*. 2nd edition. Vancouver, BC.

Roth, Gerhard, Klaus-Jürgen Grün, and Michel Friedman (2010). *Kopf oder Bauch? Zur Biologie der Entscheidung*. Göttingen: Vandenhoeck und Ruprecht.

Roth, Wolff-Michael, Luis Radford, and Lionel LaCroix (2012). "Working with cultural-historical activity theory." *Forum: Qualitative Sozialforschung / Social Research, 13* (2), pp. Article 23.

Rothkopf, David J. (2008). *Superclass: The global power elite and the world they are making*. New York: Farrar, Straus and Giroux.

Rotter, Julian B. (1954). *Social learning and clinical psychology*. New York: Prentice-Hall.

Rousseau, Jean-Jacques (1762). *Du contrat social ou principes du droit politique*. Amsterdam, The Netherlands: Marc-Michel Rey.

Rowe, Cami (2013). *The politics of protest and US foreign policy: Performative construction of the war on terror*. Abingdon: Routledge.

Rowen Sivertsen, Barbara (2011). *Shianshenka: The rise and fall of the perfect creation*. Nesoddtangen, Norway: Birch Tree Road Publishing.

Roy, Olivier (2004). *Globalized Islam: The search for a new Ummah*. New York: Columbia University Press.

Rubin, Jeffrey Z., and Bert R. Brown (1975). *The social psychology of bargaining and negotiation*. New York: Academic Press.

Rudmin, Floyd Webster (1991). "Seventeen early peace psychologists." *Journal of Humanistic Psychology, 31* (2, Spring), pp. 12–43.

Rummel, Rudolph Joseph (1994). *Death by government*. New Brunswick, NJ: Transactions Publishers.

Ruppert, Franz (2008). *Trauma, bonding and family constellations: Understanding and healing injuries of the soul*. Frome: Green Balloon.

Rushkoff, Douglas (2009). *Life inc.: How the world became a corporation and how to take it back*. New York: Random House.

Rutkoff, Peter M. (1981). *Revanche and revision: The ligue des patriotes and the origins of the radical right in France, 1882-1900* Athens: Ohio University Press.

Ryan, Charlotte, and William A. Gamson (2006). "The art of reframing political debates." *Contexts, 5* (1), pp. 13–18.

Ryan, Christopher, and Cacilda Jethá (2010). *Sex at dawn: The prehistoric origins of modern sexuality* New York: HarperCollins.

Ryan, Stephen (1995). "Peace-building and conflict transformation." In *Ethnic conflict and international relations*, 2nd edition, pp. 129–52. Aldershot: Dartmouth Publishing.

Räpple, Eva Maria (2010). "The seductive serpent." In *Locating the past/discovering the present: Comparative perspectives on religion, culture and marginality*, edited by David Gay, and Stephen R. Reimer. Edmonton, AB: University of Alberta Press.

Rödder, Andreas (2011). *Geschichte der deutschen Wiedervereinigung*. München, Germany: C.H. Beck.

Røed-Larsen, Sverre, and Anne Margrete Hjort-Larsen (Eds.) (2012). *I strid for fred: Fredskontoret 1962-1972 – idealistisk fredsarbeid og bred grasrotaktivitet*. Oslo: Kolofon.

Røislien, Hanne Eggen, and Jo Røislien (2010). "The logic of Palestinian terrorist target choice? Examining the Israel defense forces' official statistics on Palestinian terrorist attacks 2000–2004." *Studies in Conflict and Terrorism, 33* (2), pp. 134–48.

Röpke, Andrea, and Andreas Speit (2013). *Blut und Ehre: Geschichte und Gegenwart rechter Gewalt in Deutschland*. Berlin, Germany: Ch. Links Verlag.

Sageman, Marc (2004). *Understanding terror networks*. Philadelphia: University of Pennsylvania Press.

Sageman, Marc (2008). *Leaderless jihad: Terror networks in the twenty-first century*. Philadelphia: University of Pennsylvania Press.

Sageman, Marc (2009). "Confronting Al-Qaeda: Understanding the threat in Afghanistan." *Perspectives on Terrorism, North America, 3* (4), pp. 4–25.

Sahlberg, Pasi (2011). *Finnish lessons 2.0: What can the world learn from educational change in Finland?* New York: Teachers College Press.

Sahlberg, Pasi (2015). *Finnish lessons 2.0: What can the world learn from educational change in Finland?* 2nd revised edition. New York: Teachers College Press.

Said, Edward W. (1978). *Orientalism*. New York: Pantheon Books.

Said, Edward W. (2003). *Orientalism*. London: Penguin Books.

Salecl, Renata (2004). *On anxiety: Thinking in action*. London: Routledge.

Salomon, Gavriel, and Baruch Nevo (Eds.) (2002). *Peace education: The concept, principles, and practices around the world*. Mahwah, NJ: Erlbaum.

Sanderson, Stephen K. (2007). *Evolutionism and its critics: Deconstructing and reconstructing an evolutionary interpretation of human society*. Boulder, CO: Paradigm.

Sapolsky, Robert M. (2017). *Behave: The biology of humans at our best and worst*. New York: Penguin

Sarotte, Mary Elise (2014). *The collapse: The accidental opening of the Berlin Wall*. New York: Basic books.

Sarraj, Eyad El (2002). "Suicide bombers: Dignity, despair, and the need for hope." *Journal of Palestine Studies, XXXI* (4, Summer), pp. 71–76.

Sartre, Jean-Paul (1960). *Critique de la raison dialectique*. Paris: Gallimard.

Sassen, Saskia (2014). *Expulsions: Brutality and complexity in the global economy*. Cambridge, MA: Belknap.

Satter, David (2003). *Darkness at dawn: The rise of the Russian criminal state*. New Haven, CT: Yale University Press.

Sayler, Michael (2004). *Humiliation and the poor: A study in the management of meaning*. Santa Barbara, CA: Fielding Graduate Institute, doctoral dissertation.

Scahill, Jeremy (2007). *Blackwater: The rise of the world's most powerful mercenary army*. New York: Nation Books.

Scahill, Jeremy (2013). *Dirty wars: The world is a battlefield*. New York: Nation Books.

Schacht, Robert M. (1988). "Circumscription theory: A critical review." *American Behavioral Scientist, 31* (4), pp. 438–48.

Schachter, Oscar (1983). "Human dignity as a normative concept." *The American Journal of International Law, 77* (4, October), pp. 848–54.

Scharmer, Claus Otto (2009). *Theory U: Leading from the future as it emerges: The social technology of presencing*. San Francisco: Berret-Koehler.

Scharmer, Otto, and Katrin Kaufer (2013). *Leading from the emerging future: From ego-system to eco-system economies*. San Francisco: Berrett-Koehler.

Schattschneider, Elmer Eric (1960). *The semisovereign people: A realist's view of democracy in America*. New York: Holt, Rinehart and Winston.

Schattschneider, Elmer Eric (1969). *Two hundred million Americans in search of government*. New York: Holt, Rinehart and Winston.

Scheff, Thomas J., and Suzanne M. Retzinger (1991). *Emotions and violence: Shame and rage in destructive conflicts*. Lexington, MA: Lexington Books.

Scheff, Thomas J. (1994). *Bloody revenge: Emotions, nationalism and war*. Boulder: Westview Press.

Scheff, Thomas J. (1997). *Emotions, the social bond and human reality. Part/whole analysis*. Cambridge: Cambridge University Press.

Scheff, Thomas J., and Suzanne M. Retzinger (1997). "Shame, anger and the social bond: A theory of sexual offenders and treatement." *Electronic Journal of Sociology*.

Scheff, Thomas J. (2000). "Shame and the social bond: A sociological theory." *Sociological Theory, 18* (1), pp. 84–99.

Scheff, Thomas J. (2006). "Aggression, hypermasculine emotions and relations: The silence/violence pattern." *Irish Journal of Sociology, 15* (1), pp. 24–37.

Scheff, Thomas J. (2007). *War and emotion: Hypermasculine violence as a social system.* Santa Barbara, CA.

Scheff, Thomas J. (2010). *Social-emotional origins of violence: A theory of multiple killing.* Santa Barbara, CA: University of California.

Scheff, Thomas J. (2013). "Getting unstuck: Interdisciplinarity as a new discipline." *Sociological Forum, 28* (1, March), pp. 179–85.

Scheler, Max (1912/1961). *Ressentiment.* Translated by William W. Holdheim. New York: Free Press of Glencoe. German original *Über Ressentiment und moralisches Werturteil*, Leipzig: Engelmann, 1912.

Scheler, Max (1913/1923/1954). *The nature of sympathy.* Translated by Peter Heath. London: Routledge and Kegan Paul. German originals *Wesen und Formen der Sympathie*, Bonn, Germany: F. Cohen, 1923, und *Zur Phänomenologie und Theorie der Sympathiegefühle und von Liebe und Hass*, Halle, Saale: Max Niemeyer, 1913.

Scheler, Max (1914–1916/1957). "Ordo amoris [Logic of the heart]." In *Schriften aus dem Nachlaß, Band 1: Zur Ethik und Erkenntnislehre*, edited by Maria Scheler. Bern, Switzerland: Francke Verlag.

Schell, Jonathan (2003). *The unconquerable world: Power, nonviolence, and the will of the people.* New York: Metropolitan Books.

Schell, Orville, and John Delury (2013). *Wealth and power: China's long march to the twenty first century.* Random House.

Scherer, Greg (2011). *No local: Why small scale alternatives can't change the world.* Winchester: Zeri Books.

Scheuer, Michael (2011). *Osama bin Laden.* Oxford: Oxford University Press.

Schirrmacher, Frank (2006). *Minimum: Vom Vergehen und Neuentstehen unserer Gemeinschaft.* München, Germany: Karl Blessing.

Schivelbusch, Wolfgang (2001). *Die Kultur der Niederlage.* Berlin: Alexander Fest.

Schleichert, Hubert (1999). *Wie man mit Fundamentalisten diskutiert, ohne den Verstand zu verlieren: Anleitung zum subversiven Denken.* München, Germany: C.H. Beck.

Schlosser, Eric (2013). *Command and control: Nuclear weapons, the Damascus accident, and the illusion of safety.* New York: Penguin.

Schlund-Vials, Cathy J., and Samuel Martínez (Eds.) (2017). *Interrogating the perpetrator: Violation, culpability, and human rights.* New York: Routledge.

Schlögel, Karl (2008). *Terror und Traum: Moskau 1937.* München, Germany: Carl Hanser.

Schmid, Alex Peter (Ed.) (2011). *The Routledge handbook of terrorism research.* London: Routledge.

Schmid, Alex Peter (2013). "Radicalisation, de-radicalisation, counter-radicalisation: A conceptual discussion and literature review." In *ICCT Research Paper March 2013.* The Hague, The Netherlands: The International Centre for Counter-Terrorism (ICCT).

Schmidt, Bettina E., and Ingo W. Schröder (2001). "Violent imaginaries and violent practices." In *Anthropology of violence and conflict*, edited by Bettina E. Schmidt, and Ingo W. Schröder, pp. 1–24. London: Routledge.

Schmidt, Jeff (2000). *Disciplined minds: A critical look at salaried professionals and the soul-battering system that shapes their lives.* Lanham, MD: Rowman and Littlefield.

Schmitt, Carl (1922). *Politische Theologie. Vier Kapitel zur Lehre von der Souveränität.* München, Leipzig, Germany: Duncker und Humblot.

Schmitt, Carl (1927/2007). *The concept of the political.* Translated by George D. Schwab. Expanded edition. Chicago: University of Chicago Press. German original "Der Begriff des Politischen", in *Archiv für Sozialwissenschaft und Sozialpolitik*, 1927, 58 (1), 1–33, and München, Germany: Duncker and Humblot, 1932.

Schmitt, Carl (1931). *Der Hüter der Verfassung.* Tübingen, Germany: J. C. B. Mohr.

Schmitt, Carl (1963/2004). "Theory of the partisan: Intermediate commentary on the concept of the political (1963)." *Telos*, (127, March), pp. 11–78. German original *Theorie des Partisanen: Zwischenbemerkung zum Begriff des Politischen*, Berlin: Duncker and Humblot, 1963.

Schmitz-Berning, Cornelia (2007). *Vokabular des Nationalsozialismus.* 2nd revised edition. Berlin: De Gruyter.

Schmitz, Dominic Musa (2016). *Ich war ein Salafist: Meine Zeit in der islamistischen Parallelwelt.* Berlin: Ullstein.

Schnaiberg, Allan (1980). *The environment: From surplus to scarcity.* New York: Oxford University Press.

Schneider, Kirk J. (2004). *Rediscovery of awe: Splendor, mystery and the fluid center of life.* St. Paul, MN: Paragon House.

Schneider, Kirk J. (2013). *The polarized mind: Why it's killing us and what we can do about it.* Colorado Springs, CO: University Professors Press.

Schor, Juliet (2010). *Plenitude: The new economics of true wealth.* New York: Penguin Press.

Schor, Juliet B. (1993). *The overworked American: The unexpected decline of leisure.* New York: Basic Books.

Schor, Juliet B. (1999). *The overspent American: Upscaling, downshifting and the new comsumer.* New York: Harper Perennial.

Schor, Juliet B. (2004). *Born to buy: The commercialized child and the new consumer culture.* New York: Scribner.

Schor, Juliet B., and Craig J. Thompson (2014). *Sustainable lifestyles and the quest for plenitude: Case studies of the new economy.* New Haven, CT: Yale University Press.

Schore, Allan N., and Daniela Sieff (2015). "On the same wave-length: How our emotional brain is shaped by human relationships." In *Understanding and healing emotional trauma: Conversations with pioneering clinicians and researchers*, edited by Daniela Sieff, pp. 111–36. New York: Routledge.

Schroeder, Doris (2012). "Human rights and human dignity: An appeal to separate the conjoined twins." *Ethical Theory and Moral Practice, 15* (3), pp. 323–35.

Schroeder, Doris, and Abol-Hassan Bani-Sadr (2017). *Dignity in the 21st century: Middle East and West.* Cham, Switzerland: Springer.

Schulz von Thun, Friedemann (1981). *Miteinander Reden, 1: Störungen und Klärungen.* Reinbek, Germany: Rowohlt.

Schulz von Thun, Friedemann (2007). *Miteinander reden: Fragen und Antworten.* Reinbek, Germany: Rowohlt.

Schumacher, Ernst Friedrich (1973). *Small is beautiful: A study of economics as if people mattered.* London: Blond and Briggs.

Schwartz, Barry (2004). *The paradox of choice: Why more is less.* New York: Ecco/HarperCollins.

Schwartz, Warren, Keith Baxter, and David Ryan (1984). "The duel: Can these gentlemen be acting efficiently?". *The Journal of Legal Studies, 13* (2, June), pp. 321–25.

Schwartzman, David (2016). "How much and what kind of energy does humanity need?". *Socialism and Democracy, 30* (2), pp. 97–120.

Schwarz, Hans-Peter (1997). *Konrad Adenauer: A German politician and statesman in a period of war, revolution and reconstruction: The statesman, 1952-1967.* Oxford, New York: Berghahn.

Schwarzenbach, Sibyl Ann (2009). *On civic friendship: Including women in the state*. New York: Columbia University Press.

Schweller, Randall L. (1996). "Neorealism's status-quo bias: What security dilemma?". *Security Studies, 5* (3), pp. 90–121.

Schweller, Randall L. (2011). "Rational theory for a bygone era." *Security Studies, 20* (3), pp. 460–68.

Scott, L. Plous, and G. Zimbardo Philip (2004). "How social science can reduce terrorism." *The Chronicle of Higher Education, 51* (3), pp. B.9–B10.

Scott, Niall, and Jonathan Seglow (2007). *Altruism*. Maidenhead: Open University Press.

Searle, John R. (1983). *Intentionality: An essay in the philosophy of mind*. Cambridge: Cambridge University Press.

Searle, John Rogers (1995). *The construction of social reality*. New York: Free Press.

Sebag Montefiore, Simon (2003). *Stalin: The court of the red tsar*. London: Weidenfeld and Nicolson.

Sebag Montefiore, Simon (2016). *The Romanovs 1613–1918*. London: Weidenfeld and Nicolson.

Sebald, W. G. (1992/1996). *The emigrants*. Translated by Michael Hulse. London: Harvill. German original *Die Ausgewanderten: Vier lange Erzählungen*, Frankfurt am Main, Germany: Eichborn, 1992.

Seierstad, Åsne (2013/2015). *One of us: The story of Anders Breivik and the massacre in Norway*. Translated by Sarah Death. London: Virago, Norwegian original *En Av Oss: En Fortelling Om Norge*, Oslo: Kagge, 2013.

Seierstad, Åsne (2016). *To søstre*. Oslo: Kagge forlag.

Selasi, Taiye (2013). *Ghana must go*. New York: Penguin.

Seligman, Martin E. P. (1972). "Learned helplessness." *Annual Review of Medicine, 23* (1), pp. 407–12.

Seligman, Martin E. P. (1974). "Depression and learned helplessness." In *The psychology of depression: Contemporary theory and research*, edited by Raymond J. Friedman, and Martin M. Katz, pp. 83–125. Washington, DC: V. H. Winston.

Sen, Amartya (1992). *Inequality reexamined*. Cambridge, MA: Harvard University Press.

Sen, Amartya (2001). *Development as freedom*. Oxford: Oxford University Press.

Sen, Amartya (2009). *The idea of justice*. London: Allen Lane.

Senghor, Shaka (2016). *Writing my wrongs: Life, death, and redemption in an American prison*. Detroit, MI: Drop a Gem.

Serres, Michel (1997). *The troubadour of knowledge*. Ann Arbor: University of Michigan Press.

Sewchurran, Kosheek, and Jennifer McDonogh (2015). "The phenomenon of being-in-management in executive education programmes – An integrative view." *International Journal of Development Education and Global Learning, 7* (2, Development Education in the Global South), pp. 75–88.

Shahab Ahmed, Zahid, and Khan Zeb (2016). "Direct and indirect impacts of terrorism on youth in Pakistan." *Journal of Research Society of Pakistan, 53* (1, January–June), pp. 235–49.

Shamay-Tsoory, Simone G. (2011). "The neural bases for empathy." *Neuroscientist, 17* (1), pp. 18–24.

Shane, Scott (2015). *Objective troy: A terrorist, a president, and the rise of the drone*. New York: Tim Duggan.

Shapiro, Daniel (2016). *Negotiating the nonnegotiable: How to resolve your most emotionally charged conflicts*. New York: Viking.

Shaw, Bernard (1889). *Fabian essays in socialism*. London: W. Scott.

Shaw, Martin (2000). *Theory of the global state: Globality as unfinished revolution*. Cambridge: Cambridge University Press.

Shay, Jonathan (1995). *Achilles in Vietnam: Combat trauma and the undoing of character*. New York: Simon and Schuster.

Shay, Jonathan (2002). *Odysseus in America: Combat trauma and the trials of homecoming.* New York: Scribner.

Shay, Jonathan (2011). "Casualties." *Daedalus, the Journal of the American Academy of Arts and Sciences, 140* (3), pp. 179–88.

Shay, Jonathan (2014). "Moral injury." *Psychoanalytic Psychology, 31* (2, April), pp. 182–91.

Sheets-Johnstone, Maxine (2007). *Strangers, trust, and religion: On the vulnerability of being alive.* Durham, NC: Guest lecture at Durham University, Department of Philosophy, May 2007, podcast.ic.sunysb.edu/weblog/templeton.

Shelley, Percy Bysshe (1819). *The Cenci: A tragedy, in five acts.* London: Charles and James Ollier, see *The Harvard Classics*, 1909–1914.

Sherif, Muzafer (1936). *The psychology of social norms.* Oxford: Harper.

Sherif, Muzafer (1961). *The Robbers' Cave experiment: Intergroup conflict and cooperation.* Norman: The University of Oklahoma, Institutions of Group Relations.

Sherratt, Yvonne (2013). *Hitler's philosophers.* New Haven, CT: Yale University Press.

Shiva, Vandana (2000). *Stolen harvest: The hijacking of the global food supply.* Cambridge, MN: South End Press.

Shultziner, Doron (2013). "The social-psychological origins of the Montgomery Bus Boycott: Social interaction and humiliation in the emergence of social movements." *Mobilization: An International Quarterly, 18* (2, June), pp. 117–42.

Sidanius, Jim, and Felicia Pratto (1999). *Social dominance: An intergroup theory of social hierarchy and oppression.* Cambridge: Cambridge University Press.

Siebert, Rudolf J. (2010). *Manifesto of the critical theory of society and religion: The wholly other, liberation, happiness and the rescue of the hopeless, Volumes 1-3.* Leiden, The Netherlands: Brill.

Siebert, Rudolf J., and Michael R. Ott (2016). *Walter Benjamin's critical theory of society and religion: From enslavement to freedom, happiness and redemption.* Human Dignity and Humiliation Studies.

Siegel, Reva B. (2012). "Dignity and sexuality: Claims on dignity in transnational debates over abortion and same-sex marriage." *International Journal of Constitutional Law, 10* (2), pp. 355–79.

Silke, Andrew (Ed.) (2003). *Terrorists, victims, and society: Psychological perspectives on terrorism and its consequences*, Wiley series in psychology of crime, policing, and law. Chichester: Wiley.

Simmel, Georg (1955). *Conflict: The web of group-affiliations.* Glencoe, IL: Free Press.

Singer, Tania, Ben Seymour, John P. O'Doherty, Klaas E. Stephan, Raymond J. Dolan, and Chris D. Frith (2006). "Empathic neural responses are modulated by the perceived fairness of others." *Nature, 439* (7075), pp. 466–69.

Singer, Tania, and Olga M. Klimecki (2014). "Empathy and compassion." *Current Biology, 24* (18), pp. R875–R78.

Singer, Tania, and Matthieu Ricard (Eds.) (2015). *Caring economics: Conversations on altruism and compassion, between scientists, economists, and the Dalai Lama* New York: Picador.

Singh, Neera M. (2013). "The affective labor of growing forests and the becoming of environmental subjects: Rethinking environmentality in Odisha, India." *Geoforum, 47*, pp. 189–98.

Sitter, Carmen (1995). *Die Rolle der vier Frauen im Parlamentarischen Rat: Die vergessenen Mütter des Grundgesetzes.* Münster, Germany: LIT Verlag.

Sitter, Nikolai (2017). *Terrorismens historie: Attentat og terrorbekjempelse fra Bakunin til IS.* Oslo: Dreyer.

Skidelsky, Robert, and Edward Skidelsky (2012). *How much is enough? The love of money, and the case for the good life.* London: Allen Lane.

Skjelsbæk, Inger (2013). *The political psychology of war rape: Studies from Bosnia and Herzegovina*. Abingdon: Routledge.

Skocpol, Theda, and Alexander Hertel-Fernandez (2016). *The Koch effect: The impact of a cadre-led network on American Politics*. San Juan, Puerto Rico: Paper presented at the Inequality Mini-Conference, Southern Political Science Association, January 8, 2016.

Skurdal, Ingunn, and Steinar Bryn (2012). "Dialog som verktøy i fredsbygging." In *I strid for fred: Fredskontoret 1962-1972 – idealistisk fredsarbeid og bred grasrotaktivitet*, edited by Sverre Røed-Larsen, and Anne Margrete Hjort-Larsen, pp. 175–78. Oslo: Kolofon.

Slocum, Sally (1975). "Woman the gatherer: Male bias in anthropology." In *Toward an anthropology of women*, edited by Rayna R. Reiter, pp. 36–50. New York: Monthly Review Press.

Slootman, Marieke, and Jean Tillie (2006). *Processes of radicalisation: Why some Amsterdam Muslims become radicals*. Amsterdam, The Netherlands: University of Amsterdam, Institute for Migration and Ethnic Studies.

Smedslund, Jan (1988). *Psycho-logic*. Berlin: Springer.

Smedslund, Jan (1997). "Is the 'psycho-logic' of trust universal?" In *The Language of emotions: Conceptualization, expression, and theoretical foundation*, edited by Susanne Niemeier, and René Dirven, pp. 3–13. Amsterdam, The Netherlands: John Benjamins.

Smedslund, Jan (2013). *From nonsense syllables to holding hands: Sixty years as a psychologist*. Chagrin Falls, OH: Taos Institute Publication.

Smith, Adam (1759). *The theory of moral sentiments*. London, Edinburg: Printed for A. Millar, London; and A. Kincaid and J. Bell, Edinburgh.

Smith, Adam (1776). *An inquiry into the nature and causes of the wealth of nations: In two volumes*. London: Printed for W. Strahan; and T. Cadell, in the Strand.

Smith, Anthony D. (1996). *The ethnic origins of nations*. Oxford: Basil Blackwell.

Smith, Christian (1991). *The emergence of liberation theology: Radical religion and social movement theory*. Chicago: University of Chicago Press.

Smith, Christian (2010). *What is a person? Rethinking humanity, social life, and the moral good from the person up*. Chicago: University of Chicago Press.

Smith, Dennis (1997). *The civilizing process and the care of the self: Comparing Elias and Foucault*. Bielefeld: Norbert Elias Centenary Conference, University of Bielefeld, Zentrum für interdisziplinäre Forschung, June 1997.

Smith, Dennis (1999). "'The civilizing process' and 'the history of sexuality': Comparing Norbert Elias and Michel Foucault." *Theory and Society, 28* (1), pp. 79–100.

Smith, Dennis (2001). "Organisations and humiliation: Looking beyond Elias." *Organization, 8* (3), pp. 537–60.

Smith, Eliot R., and Diane M. Mackie (2015). "Dynamics of group-based emotions: Insights from intergroup emotions theory." *Emotion Review, 7* (4), pp. 349–54.

Smith, J. W. (2005). *Economic democracy: The political struggle of the twenty-first century*. 4th edition. Suny, AZ: Institute for Economic Democracy Press.

Smith, M. Brewster, Jerome S. Bruner, and Robert W. White (1956). *Opinions and personality*. New York: Wiley.

Smith, Mark M. (1998). *Debating slavery: Economy and society in the Antebellum American South*. Cambridge: Cambridge University Press.

Smith, Wilfred Cantwell (1962). *The meaning and end of religion*. New York: Macmillan.

Smith, Zadie (2000). *White teeth*. London: Hamish Hamilton.

Smyth, Marie Breen, Jeroen Gunning, and Richard Jackson (Eds.) (2009). *Critical terrorism studies: A new research agenda*. London: Routledge.

Snow, Charles Percy (1959). *The two cultures and the scientific revolution*. Cambridge: Cambridge University Press.

Snow, David A., and Robert D. Benford (1988). "Ideology, frame resonance, and participant mobilization." In *From structure to action: Comparing social movement research across cultures*, edited by Bert Klandermans, Hanspeter Kriesi, and Sidney G. Tarrow, pp. 197–217. Greenwich, CT: JAI Press.

Snyder, Claire R. (2000). *Citizen-soldiers and manly warriors: Military service and gender in the civic republican tradition*. Lanham, MD: Rowman and Littlefield.

Snyder, Jack (1985). "Perceptions of the security dilemma in 1914." In *Psychology and deterrence*, edited by Robert Jervis, Richard Ned Lebow, and Janice Gross Stein, pp. 153–79. Baltimore, MD: Johns Hopkins University Press.

Snyder, Jack, and Robert Jervis (1999). "Civil war and the security dilemma." In *Civil wars, insecurity, and intervention*, edited by Jack Snyder, and Barbara F. Walter, pp. 15–37. New York: Columbia University Press.

Snyder, Jack, and Barbara Walters (Eds.) (1999). *The security dilemma and intervention in civil wars*. New York: Columbia University Press.

Snyder, Timothy David (2010). *Bloodlands: Europe between Hitler and Stalin*. New York: Basic Books.

Snyder, Timothy David (2015). *Black earth: The Holocaust as history and warning*. New York: Tim Duggan Books.

Snyder, Timothy David (2017). *On tyranny: Twenty lessons from the twentieth century*. New York: Tim Duggan.

Soage, Ana Belén (2007). "Faraj Fawda, or the cost of freedom of expression." *Middle East Review of International Affairs (MERIA Journal), 11* (2), pp. 26–33.

Sober, Elliott, and David Sloan Wilson (1998). *Unto others: The evolution and psychology of unselfish behavior*. Cambridge, MA: Harvard University Press.

Soeffner, Hans-Georg (1988). "Luther – Der Weg von der Kollektivität des Glaubens zu einem lutherisch-protestantischen Individualitätstypus." In *Vom Ende des Individuums zur Individualität ohne Ende*, edited by Hans-Georg Brose, and Bruno Hildenbrand, pp. 107–49. Opladen, Germany: Leske and Budrich.

Soleim, Marianne Neerland, Jens-Ivar Nergård, and Oddmund Andersen (2015). *Grenselos i grenseland: Samisk og norsk losvirksomhet i Nordre Nordland og Sør-Troms: 1940-1945*. Stamsund: Orkana akademisk.

Solomon, Hussein (2015). *Terrorism and counter-terrorism in Africa: Fighting insurgency from Al Shabaab, Ansar Dine and Boko Haram*. London: Palgrave Macmillan.

Solomon, Norman (2005). *War made easy: How presidents and pundits keep spinning us to death*. Hoboken, NJ: Wiley.

Solomon, Sheldon, Jeff Greenberg, and Thomas A. Pyszczynski (1991). "A terror management theory of social behavior: The psychological functions of self-esteem and cultural worldviews." In *Advances in experimental social psychology, Volume 24*, edited by Mark P. Zanna, pp. 93–159. Orlando, FL: Academic Press.

Solomon, Ty (2014). "The affective underpinnings of soft power." *European Journal of International Relations, 20* (3), pp. 720–41.

Solovey, Mark, and Hamilton Cravens (2012). *Cold war social science: Knowledge production, liberal democracy, and human nature*. New York: Palgrave Macmillan. doi:10.1057/9781137013224.

Soudien, Crain (2015). "Curriculum, knowledge, and the idea of South Africa." *International Journal of Development Education and Global Learning, 7* (2, Development Education in the Global South), pp. 26–45.

Sovacool, Benjamin K. (2011). *Contesting the future of nuclear power: A critical global assessment of atomic energy*. Singapore: World Scientific. doi:10.1142/7895.

Spanish National Commission for UNESCO (1986). *Seville statement on violence*. Seville, Spain: Spanish National Commission for UNESCO.

Spengler, Oswald (1918–1922/1963). *Der Untergang des Abendlandes: Umrisse einer Morphologie der Weltgeschichte*. München, Germany: C.H. Beck. Erstdruck in zwei Bänden. Erster Band: Gestalt und Wirklichkeit, Wien, Leipzig: Braumüller, 1918; in dritter Auflage München: C.H. Beck, 1919, und in einer völlig umgestalteten Ausgabe München: C.H. Beck, 1923. Zweiter Band: Welthistorische Perspektiven, München: C.H. Beck, 1922.

Spier, Fred (2010). *Big history and the future of humanity*. Chichester: Wiley-Blackwell.

Spufford, Francis, and Elizabeth Kolbert (2007). *The ends of the earth: An anthology of the finest writing on the Arctic and the Antarctic*. London: Granta Books.

Stadtwald, Kurt (1992). "Pope Alexander III's humiliation of Emperor Frederick Barbarossa as an episode in sixteenth-century German history." *Sixteenth Century Journal, 23* (4), pp. 755–68.

Stael, Germaine de, and Aurelian Craiutu (1818/2008). *Considerations on the principal events of the French Revolution*. Newly revised translation of the 1818 English edition. Indianapolis: Liberty Fund.

Stainback, Kevin, Sibyl Kleiner, and Sheryl Skaggs (2016). "Women in Power: Undoing or redoing the gendered organization?". *Gender and Society, 30* (1), pp. 109–35.

Standing, Guy (2011). *The precariat: The new dangerous class*. London: Bloomsbury Academic.

Stanley, Liz, and Sue Wise (2011). "The domestication of death: The sequestration thesis and domestic figuration." *Sociology, 45* (6), pp. 947–62.

Staub, Ervin (1989). *The roots of evil: The origins of genocide and other group violence*. Cambridge: Cambridge University Press.

Staub, Ervin (1993). "The psychology of bystanders, perpetrators, and heroic helpers." *International Journal of Intercultural Relations, 17* (3), pp. 315–41.

Staub, Ervin (2012). *Psychology and morality in genocide and violent conflict: Perpetrators, passive bystanders, and rescuers*. Washington, DC: American Psychological Association. doi:10.1037/13091-021.

Staub, Ervin (2015). *The roots of goodness and resistance to evil: Inclusive caring, moral courage, altruism born of suffering, active bystandership and heroism*. New York: Oxford University Press.

Steele, Brent J. (2007a). *Ontological security in international relations: Self-identity and the IR state*. Florence, KY: Routledge.

Steele, David (2007b). "Global society and its ancient Greek antecedents." *The European Legacy, 12* (1), pp. 1–21.

Stefánsson, Þórarinn, and Ragnheiður Karlsdóttir (2009). "Mentoring og coaching – pedagogiske hjelpe- og utviklingsperspektiver." In *Mentoring og coaching i et læringsperspektiv*, edited by Ragnvald Kvalsund, and Ragnheiður Karlsdóttir, chapter 2. Trondheim, Norway: Tapir akademisk forlag.

Steinberg, Guido (2015). *Kalifat des Schreckens. IS und die Bedrohung durch den islamistischen Terror*. München, Germany: Knaur.

Steiner, Claude M. (2003). *Emotional literacy: Intelligence with a heart*. Fawnskin, CA: Personhood Press.

Steinsland, Gro (2007). *Myth and power in the cultural transformation of the nordic countries from viking to medieval age*. Oslo: University of Oslo, Institutt for lingvistiske og nordiske studier (ILN), Centre for Advanced Study (CAS) at the Norwegian Academy of Science and Letters, lecture by Gro Steinsland, group leader at CAS 2007/2008, at the opening ceremony, September 4, 2007.

Stellmacher, Jost, and Thomas Petzel (2005). "Authoritarianism as a group phenomenon." *Political Psychology, 26* (2), pp. 245–74.

Stenner, Karen (2005). *The authoritarian dynamic*. Cambridge: Cambridge University Press.

Sterling, Peter (2016). *Why we consume: Neural design and sustainability*. Boston: Great Transition Initiative.

Stern, Klaus, and Jörg Herrmann (2007). *Andreas Baader. Das Leben eines Staatsfeindes*. München, Germany: Deutscher Taschenbuch Verlag.

Stevens, Stanley Smith (1946). "On the theory of scales of measurement." *Science 103* (2684), pp. 677–80.

Stevenson, Betsey, and Justin Wolfers (2009). *The paradox of declining female happiness*. Cambridge, MA: The National Bureau of Economic Research.

Stevenson, Bryan (2015). *Just Mercy: A story of justice and redemption*. Melbourne, Australia: Scribe Publications.

Stevenson, Paul A., and Jan Rillich (2015). "Adding up the odds – Nitric oxide signaling underlies the decision to flee and post-conflict depression of aggression." *Science Advances, 1* (2).

Steward, Dick (2000). *Duels and the roots of violence in Missouri*. Columbia: University of Missouri Press.

Stewart, Frances (2008). *Horizontal inequalities and conflict: Understanding group violence in multiethnic societies*. Basingstoke: Palgrave Macmillan.

Stiglitz, Joseph E., and Linda Bilmes (2008). *The three trillion dollar war: The true cost of the Iraq conflict*. New York: Norton.

Stiglitz, Joseph E. (2012). *The price of inequality: How today's divided society endangers our future*. New York: Norton.

Stillwell, Arlenem, Royf Baumeister, and Regane Del Priore (2008). "We're all victims here: Toward a psychology of revenge." *Basic and Applied Social Psychology, 30* (3), pp. 253–63.

Stockholm International Peace Research Institute (SIPRI) (2016). *SIPRI yearbook 2016: Armaments, disarmament and international security*. Stockholm, Sweden: Stockholm International Peace Research Institute (SIPRI).

Stone, Christopher D. (1972). "Should trees have standing? Toward legal rights for natural objects." *Southern Californa Law Review, 45*, pp. 450–501.

Stone, Geoffrey R. (2004). *Perilous times: Free speech in wartime: From the Sedition Act of 1798 to the war on terrorism*. New York: Norton.

Stone, Geoffrey R. (2007). *Top secret: When our government keeps us in the dark*. Lanham, MD: Rowman and Littlefield.

Storaker, Aslak (Ed.) (2016). *Sikkerhetspolitiske veivalg: Skjebnefellesskap med USA og NATO?* Oslo: Progressivt forlag.

Stout, Martha (2005). *Sociopath next door*. New York: Broadway Books.

Stover, Eric, and Harvey M. Weinstein (Eds.) (2004). *My neighbor, my enemy: Justice and community in the aftermath of mass atrocity*. Cambridge: Cambridge University Press.

Strack, Fritz, and Roland Deutsch (2004). "Reflective and impulsive determinants of social behavior." *Personality and Social Psychology Review, 8* (3), pp. 220–47.

Strange, Guy Le (1900). "The story of the death of the last Abbasid Caliph, from the Vatican MS. of Ibn-al-Furāt." *Journal of the Royal Asiatic Society of Great Britain and Ireland,* (April), pp. 293–300.

Strasburger, Victor C., Barbara J. Wilson, and Amy B. Jordan (2013). *Children, adolescents, and the media.* 3rd edition. Los Angeles, CA: Sage.

Strathern, Andrew, Pamela J. Stewart, and Neil L. Whitehead (Eds.) (2006). *Terror and violence: Imagination and the unimaginable.* London: Pluto Press.

Strawson, Peter Frederick (1959). *Individuals: An essay in descriptive metaphysics.* London: Methuen.

Strawson, Peter Frederick (1974). *Freedom and resentment: And other essays.* London: Methuen.

Støre, Jonas Gahr (2012). "Taming summit-mania: Ineffective communication in global dialogue." *Harvard International Review, 34* (1), pp. 12–15.

Sue, Derald Wing, Christina M. Capodilupo, Gina C. Torino, Jennifer M. Bucceri, Aisha M. B. Holder, Kevin L. Nadal, and Marta Esquilin (2007). "Racial microaggressions in everyday life: Implications for clinical practice." *American Psychologist, 62* (4), pp. 271–86.

Sugarman, Jeff, Brent Slife, and Richard T. G. Walsh (2015). "Neoliberalism and psychological ethics." *Journal of Theoretical and Philosophical Psychology, 35* (2), pp. 103–16.

Suhay, Elizabeth (2015). "Explaining group influence: The role of identity and emotion in political conformity and polarization." *Political Behavior, 37* (1), pp. 221–51.

Summy, Hilary N. (2006). *'Peace angel' of World War I: Dissent of Margaret Thorp.* Brisbane, Australia: Centre for Peace and Conflict Studies, University of Queensland.

Sundararajan, Louise (2012). *Indigenous psychology: Grounding science in culture, why and how?* : Anthropology in China.

Sundararajan, Louise (2015). *Understanding emotion in Chinese culture: Thinking through psychology.* New York: Springer.

Sundberg, Anna, and Jesper Huor (2016). *Älskade terrorist: 16 år med militanta islamister.* Stockholm: Nordstedts.

Sunstein, Cass R. (2016). *The ethics of influence: Government in the age of behavioral.* New York: Cambridge University Press.

Sussman, Robert W. (1999). "The myth of man the hunter, man the killer and the evolution of human morality." *Zygon®, 34* (3), pp. 453–71.

Suttner, Bertha von (1889). *Die Waffen nieder!* Dresden: Piersons Verlag, Band 1.

Suttner, Bertha von (1908). *'Ground arms!' – 'Die Waffen nieder': A romance of European war.* Translated by Alice Asbury Abbott. 8th edition. Chicago: A.C. McClurg.

Sveaass, Nora (2013). "Gross human rights violations and reparation under international law: Approaching rehabilitation as a form of reparation." *European Journal of Psychotraumatology, 4.*

Swidler, Leonard, and Paul Mojzes (2000). *The study of religion in an age of global dialogue.* Philadelphia: Temple University Press.

Sylvester, Christine (2013). *War as experience: Contributions from international relations and feminist analysis.* Abingdon: Routledge.

Sylvester, Christine (2015). *Masquerades of war.* Abingdon: Routledge.

Syse, Henrik Preben (2003). *Rettferdig krig? Om militærmakt, etikk og idealer.* Oslo: Aschehoug.

Syse, Henrik Preben (2009). *Måtehold i grådighetens tid.* Oslo: Cappelen Damm.

Szirtes, Tamás (2012). "Managing knowledge sharing: Case study of a consulting firm." *Society and Economy, 34* (1), pp. 139–60.

Tacey, David J. (2000). *ReEnchantment: The new Australian spirituality.* Sydney: HarperCollins.

Tacitus, Cornelius (1942). *The complete works of Tacitus: The annals; The history; The life of Cnaeus Julius Agricola; Germany and its tribes; A dialogue on oratory*. New York: The Modern library. Translated by Alfred John Church and William Jackson Brodribb from Latin. Edited and with an introduction by Moses Hadas.

Taibbi, Matt (2017). *Insane clown president: Dispatches from the 2016 circus*. New York: Spiegel and Grau.

Tainter, Joseph A. (1988). *The collapse of complex societies*. Cambridge: Cambridge University Press.

Tajfel, Henri (1970). "Experiments in intergroup discrimination." *Scientific American, 223* (5), pp. 96–102.

Tajfel, Henri, and John C. Turner (1979). "An integrative theory of intergroup conflict." In *The social psychology of intergroup relations*, edited by William G. Austin, and Stephen Worchel, chapter 3, pp. 33–48. Monterey, CA: Brooks-Cole.

Tajfel, Henri, and John C. Turner (1986). "The social identity theory of intergroup behavior." In *Psychology of intergroup relations*, edited by Stephen Worchel, and William G. Austin, pp. 204–27. Chicago: Neston-Hall.

Tanaka, Yuki, and Marilyn Young (Eds.) (2010). *Bombing civilians: A twentieth-century history*. New York: The New Press.

Tanaka, Yuki, Tim McCormack, and Gerry Simpson (Eds.) (2011). *Beyond victor's justice? The Tokyo war crimes trial revisited*. The Hague, The Netherlands: Martinus Nijhoff.

Tang, Shiping (2011). "The security dilemma and ethnic conflict: Toward a dynamic and integrative theory of ethnic conflict." *Review of International Studies, 37* (2), pp. 511–36.

Tangney, June Price (1990). "Assessing individual differences in proneness to shame and guilt: Development of the Self-Conscious Affect and Attribution Inventory." *Journal of Personality and Social Psychology, 59* (1), pp. 102–11.

Tangney, June Price, Patricia Wagner, Carey Fletcher, and Richard Gramzow (1992). "Shamed into anger? The relation of shame and guilt to anger and self-reported aggression." *Journal of Personality and Social Psychology, 62* (4), pp. 669–75.

Tangney, June Price, and Ronda L. Dearing (2002). *Shame and guilt*. New York: Guildford Press.

Tanner, Nancy Makepeace (1981). *On becoming human*. Cambridge: Cambridge University Press.

Task Force on Disorders and Terrorism (1976). *Disorders and terrorism: Report of the Task Force on Disorders and Terrorism*. Washington, DC: Law Enforcement Assistant Administration in the United States, National Advisory Committee on Criminal Justice Standards and Goals.

Taylor, Alan John Percivale (1955). *Bismarck: The man and the statesman*. London: Hamish Hamilton.

Taylor, Charles (1971). "Interpretation and the sciences of man." *Review of Metaphysics, 25* (1, September), pp. 3–51.

Taylor, Charles (1989). *Sources of the self: The making of the modern identity*. Cambridge: Cambridge University Press.

Taylor, Charles (1992). *The ethics of authenticity*. Cambridge, MA: Harvard University Press. Originally published in Canada in 1991 under the title *The Malaise of Modernity*, an extended version of the 1991 Massey Lectures.

Taylor, Charles (1993a). "To follow a rule..." In *Bourdieu: Critical perspectives*, edited by Craig Calhoun, Edward LiPuma, and Moishe Postone, chapter 3, pp. 45–60. Cambridge: Polity Press.

Taylor, Charles (1994). "The politics of recognition." In *Multiculturalism: Examining the politics of recognition*, edited by Amy Gutman, pp. 25–73. Princeton, NJ: Princeton University Press.

Taylor, Mark C. (2010). *Crisis on campus: A bold plan for reforming our colleges and universities*. New York: Alfred A. Knopf.

Taylor, Peter (1980). *Beating the terrorists? Interrogation at Omagh, Gough, and Castlereagh*. Harmondsworth: Penguin Books.

Taylor, Peter (1993b). *States of terror: Democracy and political violence*. London: BBC Books.

Taylor, Peter (1996). *The way the modern world works: World hegemony to world impasse*. Chichester: Wiley.

Taylor, Peter (1997a). *Behind the mask: The IRA and Sinn Fein*. New York: TV Books.

Taylor, Peter (1997b). *Provos: The IRA and Sinn Fein*. London: Bloomsbury.

Taylor, Peter (2000). *Loyalists*. London: Bloomsbury.

Taylor, Peter (2011). *Talking to Terrorists: A Personal Journey from the IRA to Al Qaeda*. Sydney: HarperCollins.

Taylor, Shelley E., Laura Cousino Klein, Brian P. Lewis, Tara L. Gruenewald, Regan A. R. Gurung, and John A. Updegraff (2002). "Biobehavioral responses to stress in females: Tend-and-befriend, not fight-or-flight." *Psychological Review, 109* (4), pp. 745–50.

Teichmann, Gabriele (2014). *Mehr als eine Bank: Oppenheim in Köln*. Köln, Germany: Greven.

Teilhard de Chardin, Pierre (1920–1952/1959). *The future of mankind*. Translated by Norman Denny. New York: Harper and Row. French original *L'Avenir de l'Homme*, Paris: Seuil, 1920–1952.

Tellkamp, Uwe (2008). *Der Turm: Geschichte aus einem versunkenen Land*. Frankfurt am Main, Germany: Suhrkamp.

Teo, Thomas (2015). "Critical psychology: A geography of intellectual engagement and resistance." *The American Psychologist, 70* (3, April), pp. 243–54.

Terreblanche, Sampie (2014). *Western empires: Christianity, and the inequalities between the West and the rest*. Johannesburg, South Africa: Penguin South Africa.

Terrizzi, John A., Natalie J. Shook, and W. Larry Ventis (2010). "Disgust: A predictor of social conservatism and prejudicial attitudes toward homosexuals." *Personality and Individual Differences, 49* (6), pp. 587–92.

Textor, Martin R. (1992). "Gestörte Familienstrukturen und -prozesse." In *Hilfen für Familien. Ein Handbuch für psychosoziale Berufe*, edited by Martin R. Textor, 2nd edition. Frankfurt am Main, Germany: Fischer.

Thaler, Richard, and Cass Sunstein (2008). *Nudge: Improving decisions about health, wealth and happiness*. New Haven, CT: Yale University Press.

Thandeka (1998). "The whiting of Euro-Americans: A divide and conquer strategy." *World: The Journal of the Unitarian Universalist Association, XII* (4, July/August), pp. 14–20.

The Equal Justice Initiative (EJI) (2015). *Lynching in America: Confronting the legacy of racial terror*. Montgomery, AL: The Equal Justice Initiative (EJI).

The International Panel of Eminent Personalities to Investigate the 1994 Genocide in Rwanda and the Surrounding Events (2000). *Rwanda: The preventable genocide*. Special Report, July 7, 2000, presented at the Organization of African Unity's (OAU) Summit in Lomé, Togo, July 10–12, 2000.

Ther, Philipp (2014/2016). *Europe since 1989: A history*. Princeton, NJ: Princeton University Press. German original *Die neue Ordnung auf dem alten Kontinent: Eine Geschichte des neoliberalen Europa*, Berlin: Suhrkamp, 2014.

Thesiger, Wilfred (1964). *The Marsh Arabs*. London: Longmans.

Thompson, Hunter Stockton (1970). "The Kentucky Derby is decadent and depraved." *Scanlan's Monthly, June*.

Thompson, Hunter Stockton (1979). *The great shark hunt: Strange tales from a strange time*. New York: Summit Books.

Thorndike, Edward Lee (1920). "A constant error in psychological ratings." *Journal of Applied Psychology, 4* (1, March), pp. 25–29.

Thucydides (431 BCE). *History of the Peloponnesian War*. The Internet Classics Archive.

Tiger, Lionel (1984). *Men in groups*. New York: Marion Boyars.

Tilley, James, and Sara B. Hobolt (2011). "Is the government to blame? An experimental test of how partisanship shapes perceptions of performance and responsibility." *The Journal of Politics, 73* (2), pp. 316–30.

Tillich, Paul (1954). *Love, power and justice: Ontological analyses and ethical applications*. London: Oxford University Press, given as Firth Lectures in Nottingham, England, and as Sprunt Lectures in Richmond, Virginia.

Tilly, Charles (1978). *From mobilization to revolution*. Reading, MA: Addison-Wesley.

Tilly, Charles (2004). *Social movements, 1768–2004*. Boulder, CO: Paradigm.

Tilly, Charles (2010). *Regimes and repertoires*. Chicago: University of Chicago Press.

Titchener, Edward B. (1909). *Lectures on the experimental psychology of the thought-processes*. New York: MacMillan.

Titlestad, Torgrim (2016). *Vikingtid: Motstandsrett og folkestyre*. Hafrsfjord, Norway: Saga.

Tocqueville, Alexis de (1856). *L'Ancien Régime et la Révolution*. Paris: Michel Levy.

Toffler, Alvin (1970). *Future shock*. New York: Random House.

Tolstoy, Leo (1886/1935). *What then must we do?* Translated by Aylmer Maude. Revised edition. Oxford: The World's Classics, Oxford University Press.

Tolstoy, Leo (1894). *"The kingdom of God is within you": Christianity not as a mystic religion but as a new theory of life*. New York:: Cassell.

Tomasello, Michael, Malinda Carpenter, Josep Call, Tanya Behne, and Henrike Moll (2005). "Understanding and sharing intentions: The origins of cultural cognition." *Behavioral and Brain Sciences, 28* (5), pp. 675–91.

Tomasello, Michael (2009). *Why we cooperate*. Cambridge, MA: Massachusetts Institute of Technology (MIT) Press.

Tomasello, Michael (2014). *A natural history of human thinking*. Cambridge, MA: Harvard University Press.

Tomasello, Michael (2016). *A natural history of human morality*. Harvard University Press.

Tong, Eddie M. W., Kenny W. T. Tan, Agapera A. B. Chor, Emmeline P. S. Koh, Jehanne S. Y. Lee, and Regina W. Y. Tan (2016). "Humility facilitates higher self-control." *Journal of Experimental Social Psychology, 62*, pp. 30–39.

Torres, Walter J., and Raymond M. Bergner (2010). "Humiliation: Its nature and consequences." *Journal of the American Academy of Psychiatry and the Law, 38* (2), pp. 195–204.

Totten, Samuel, William S. Parsons, and Israel W. Charny (2004). *Century of genocide: Critical essays and eyewitness accounts*. New York: Routledge.

Touraine, Alain (2000). *Can we live together? Equality and difference*. Stanford, CA: Stanford University Press.

Touraine, Alain (2003). "Equality and/or difference: Real problems, false dilemmas." *Canadian Journal of Sociology / Cahiers canadiens de sociologie, 28* (4), pp. 543–50.

Toynbee, Arnold J. (1934–1961). *A study of history, 12 volumes 1934 – 1961*. London: Oxford University Press.

Toynbee, Arnold J. (1962). *America and the world revolution: Public lectures delivered at the University of Pennsylvania, spring 1961*. London: Oxford University Press.

Trainer, Ted (2014). "The degrowth movement from the perspective of the simpler way." *Capitalism Nature Socialism*, pp. 1–18.

Trayes, Frederic George (1919). *Five months on a German raider: Being the adventures of an Englishman captured by the "Wolf"*. London: Headley.

Tremblay, Rodrigue (2010). *The code for global ethics: Ten humanist principles.* Amherst, NY: Prometheus.

Treue, Wilhelm (Ed.) (1958). *Rede Hitlers vor der deutschen Presse am 10. Nov. 1938*, Vierteljahreshefte für Zeitgeschichte, Jahrgang 6. München, Germany: Institut für Zeitgeschichte.

Trewhela, Paul (2009). *Inside Quatro: Uncovering the exile history of the ANC and SWAPO.* Auckland Park, South Africa: Jacana Media.

Trigger, Bruce G. (1993). *Early civilizations: Ancient Egypt in context.* Cairo, Egypt: American University in Cairo Press.

Tripathi, Deepak (2011). *Breeding ground: Afghanistan and the origins of Islamist terrorism.* Washington, DC: Potomac.

Tripathi, Deepak (2013a). *A journey through turbulence* Lake Oswego, OR: Dignity Press.

Tripathi, Deepak (2013b). *Imperial designs: War, humiliation and the making of history.* Washington, DC: Potomac.

Tripp, Charles (2007). *A history of Iraq.* 3rd edition. Cambridge: Cambridge University Press.

Trobisch-Lütge, Stefan (2004). *Das späte Gift.* Gießen, Germany: Psychosozial-Verlag.

Trobisch-Lütge, Stefan (2011). *Überwachte Vergangenheit – Auswirkungen politischer Verfolgung der SED-Diktatur auf die Zweite Generation.* Berlin, Germany: Freie Universität Berlin, Fachbereich Erziehungswissenschaften und Psychologie, doctoral dissertation.

Trojanow, Ilija (2013). *Der überflüssige Mensch: Unruhe bewahren.* Salzburg, Austria: Residenz Verlag.

Trotter, Wilfred (1916). *Instincts of the herd in peace and war.* London: T. Fisher Unwin.

Trow, Martin (1958). "Small businessmen, political tolerance, and support for McCarthy." *American Journal of Sociology, 64* (3, November), pp. 270–81.

Truax, Charles B., M. J. Paulson, Tien-teh Lin, and Frederick C. Thorne (1970). "Length of therapist response, accurate empathy and patient improvement." *Journal of Clinical Psychology, 26* (4), pp. 539–41.

Tuil, Karine (2016). *L'insouciance.* Paris: Gallimard.

Tunander, Ola (2009). "Democratic state vs. deep state: Approaching the dual state of the West." In *Government of the shadows: Parapolitics and criminal sovereignty*, edited by Eric Wilson, chapter 2, pp. 56–72. London: Pluto Press.

Turchin, Peter (2006). *War and peace and war: The life cycles of imperial nations.* New York: Pi Press.

Turk, Austin T. (2004). "Sociology of terrorism." *Annual Review of Sociology, 30* (1), pp. 271–86.

Turner, Adair (2012). *Economics after the crisis: Objectives and means.* Cambridge, MA: Massachusetts Institute of Technology (MIT) Press.

Turner, John C., Michael J. Hogg, Penelope J. Oakes, Stephen D. Reicher, and Margaret S. Wetherell (1987). *Rediscovering the social group: A self-categorization theory.* Oxford: Blackwell.

Twain, Mark (1904). *The war prayer.* Sacred Texts.

Twain, Mark (1916). *The mysterious stranger: A romance by Mark Twain.* Charlottesville: University of Virginia Library Electronic Text Center, recreation from Harper and Brothers, New York.

Twenge, Jean M. (2006). *Generation me: Why today's young Americans are more confident, assertive, entitled – and more miserable than ever before.* New York: Free Press.

Twenge, Jean M., and W. Keith Campbell (2009). *The narcissism epidemic: Living in the age of entitlement.* New York: Free Press.

Twenge, Jean M., W. Keith Campbell, and Brittany Gentile (2012). "Changes in pronoun use in American books and the rise of individualism, 1960 – 2008." *Journal of Cross-Cultural Psychology, 44* (3), pp. 406–15.

Twenge, Jean M., and Tim Kasser (2013). "Generational changes in materialism and work centrality, 1976 – 2007: Associations with temporal changes in societal insecurity and materialistic role modeling." *Personality and Social Psychology Bulletin, 39* (7), pp. 883–97.

Twenge, Jean M. (2014). *Generation me: Why today's young Americans are more confident, assertive, entitled – and more miserable than ever before.* Revised and updated edition. New York: Atria.

Tønnessen, Truls H. (2006). "Jihadist reactions to the Muhammad cartoons." In *FFI rapport-2006/00935: Paths to global jihad: Radicalisation and recruitment to terror networks*, edited by Laila Bokhari, Thomas Hegghammer, Brynjar Lia, Petter Nesser, and Truls H. Tønnessen, chapter 6, pp. 54–64. Kjeller, Norway: Norwegian Defence Research Establishment. Proceedings from a Forsvarets forskningsinstitutt (FFI) seminar, Oslo, 15 March 2006.

Tönnies, Ferdinand (1887/1955). *Community and association.* Translated by Charles P. Loomis. London: Routledge. German original *Gemeinschaft und Gesellschaft*, Leipzig, Berlin: Fues Verlag, 1887.

U.S. Army Human Terrain Team (HTT) AF-6 (2009). *U.S. Army Afghanistan Human Terrain Team Pashtun homosexuality report.* United States of America Army, with personal field notes by the Human Terrain Team AF-6, which was assigned to the 2nd Marine Expeditionary Battalion and co-located with British forces in Lashkar Gah, May 15, 2009.

Ullrich, Volker (2013). *Adolf Hitler: Die Jahre des Aufstiegs. Biographie.* Frankfurt am Main, Germany: Fischer.

UNEP/Wuppertal Institute Collaborating Centre on Sustainable Consumption and Production (CSCP) (2011–2012). *SPREAD sustainable lifestyles 2050.* Wuppertal. Germany: A European social platform project, project coordinator UNEP/Wuppertal Institute Collaborating Centre on Sustainable Consumption and Production (CSCP).

United Nations (2015). *The Millennium Development Goals report 2015.* New York: United Nations.

United Nations Development Programme (UNDP) (2014). *Human development report 2014: Sustaining human progress: Reducing vulnerabilities and building resilience.* New York: United Nations Development Programme (UNDP).

United Nations Population Fund (UNFPA), and United Nations Development Programme (UNDP) (2005). *The dynamics of honour killings in Turkey: Prospects for action.* New York: United Nations Population Fund (UNFPA).

United States, Congress (1973). *Energy reorganization act of 1973. Hearings, ninety-third Congress, first session, on H.R. 11510.* Washington, DC: U.S. Government.

United States Congress (1945). *To create a department of peace: Hearings before the United States House Committee on Foreign Affairs, Seventy-Ninth Congress, first session, on November 8, 1945.* Washington, DC: U.S. Government Publishing Office.

United States Department of Defense, Office of Inspector General (2014). *Joint warfighting and readiness: The army needs to improve the processes for reporting inventory losses in Afghanistan.* Washington, DC: United States Department of Defense, Office of Inspector General, DODIG-2015-009.

United States Senate Select Committee on Intelligence (2014). *Committee study of the Central Intelligence Agency's Detention and Interrogation Program.* Washington, DC: United States Senate Select Committee on Intelligence.

Updike, John (2006). *Terrorist.* New York: Alfred A. Knopf.

Ury, William (1999). *Getting to peace: Transforming conflict at home, at work, and in the world.* New York: Viking.

Ury, William (2000). *The third side: Why we fight and how we can stop.* New York: Penguin.

Ury, William (2007). *The power of a positive no: How to say no and still get to yes.* New York: Bantam.

Utvik, Bjørn Olav (2006). *The pious road to development: Islamist economics in Egypt.* London: Hurst.

Vallacher, Robin R., Peter T. Coleman, Andrzej Nowak, and Lan Biu-Wrozsinka (2010). "Rethinking intractable conflict: The perspectives of dynamical systems." *American Psychologist, 65* (4), pp. 262–78.

Vambheim, Nils Vidar (2011). "War on terror(ism) – or dialogue?". *Security Dialogues. Journal in the field of Security, Defence and Peace Studies, 3* (II), pp. 19–38.

Vambheim, Nils Vidar (2016). *Studies in conflict, violence and peace.* Trondheim, Norway: Norwegian University of Science and Technology (NTNU), Department of Education and Lifelong Learning, doctoral dissertation.

Van Boven, Leaf, Charles M. Judd, David K. Sherman, and Jeffrey Simpson (2012). "Political polarization projection: Social projection of partisan attitude extremity and attitudinal processes." *Journal of Personality and Social Psychology, 103* (1), pp. 84–100.

van der Kolk, Bessel A. (2014). *The body keeps the score: Brain, mind, and body in the healing of trauma.* New York: Viking.

Van Dijk, Teun A. (2001). "Critical discourse analysis." In *The handbook of discourse analysis*, edited by Deborah Schiffrin, Deborah Tannen, and Heidi Ehernberger Hamilton, chapter 18, pp. 352–71. Oxford: Blackwell.

Van Rythoven, Eric (2015). "Learning to feel, learning to fear? Emotions, imaginaries, and limits in the politics of securitization." *Security Dialogue, 46* (5), pp. 458–75.

Van Vuuren, Willem, and Ian Liebenberg (1994). "'Government by illusion': The legacy and its implications." In *The hidden hand, covert operations in South Africa*, edited by Anthony Minnaar, Ian Liebenberg, and Charl Schutte, pp. 25–43. Pretoria: Human Sciences Research Council.

Vance, J. D. (2016). *Hillbilly Elegy: A Memoir of a Family and Culture in Crisis.* New York: HarperCollins.

Vandello, Joseph A., and Dov Cohen (2003). "Male honor and female fidelity: Implicit cultural scripts that perpetuate domestic violence." *Journal of Personality and Social Psychology, 84* (5), pp. 997–101.

Vandello, Joseph A., Jennifer K. Bosson, Dov Cohen, Rochelle M. Burnaford, and Jonathan R. Weaver (2008). "Precarious manhood." *Journal of Personality and Social Psychology, 95* (6), pp. 1325–39.

Vaughan, Geneviève (2008). *Gift economy: The mother economy.* Paper presented to the IPRA General Conference in Leuven, Belgium, 2008, and presented to the Mother Summit in Karlsruhe, Germany, 2008.

Veldhuis, Tinka M., Ernestine H. Gordijn, Rene Veenstra, and Siegwart Lindenberg (2014). "Vicarious group-based rejection: Creating a potentially dangerous mix of humiliation, powerlessness, and anger." *Public Library of Science (PLoS) ONE, 9* (4), pp. e95421.

Verdesio, Gustavo (2005). "Latin American subaltern studies revisited: Is there life after the demise of the group?". *Dispositio, 25* (52), pp. 5–42.

Verdross, Alfred, and John D. Gorby (1979). "Fundamental human rights: The journey of an idea." *Human Rights, 8* (3, Fall), pp. 20–54.

Verdross, Alfred, and Bruno Simma (1984). *Universelles Völkerrecht: Theorie und Praxis.* 3rd completely revised edition. Berlin: Duncker und Humblot.

Verseuil, Jean (1946). *Les rois fainéants - De Dagobert à Pépin.* Paris: Critérion.

Vertigans, Stephen (2007). "Socializing terrorists in a global context." In *Terrorism, democracy, the West and the Muslim world*, edited by Abdul Rashid Moten, and Noraini M. Noor, chapter 8, pp. 157–89. Singapore: Thomson Learning.

Vetlesen, Arne Johan. *Nytt klima: Miljokrisen i samfunnskritisk lys.* Oslo: Gyldendal, 2008.

Vetlesen, Arne Johan (2015). *The denial of nature: Environmental philosophy in the era of global capitalism.* London: Routledge.

Victor, George (1998). *Hitler: The pathology of evil.* Washington, DC: Brassey's.

Villa-Vicencio, Charles, and Wilhelm Verwoerd (Eds.) (2000). *Looking back reaching forward: reflections on the Truth and Reconciliation Commission ofSouth Africa.* Cape Town, South Africa: University of Cape Town Press.

Visser, Wayne, and Polly Courtice (2011). *Sustainability leadership: Linking theory and practice.* Cambridge: University of Cambridge, Cambridge Programme for Sustainability Leadership.

Volkan, Vamik D. (1997). *Bloodlines: From ethnic pride to ethnic terrorism.* New York: Farrar, Straus and Giroux.

Volkan, Vamik D. (2001). "Transgenerational transmissions and chosen traumas: An aspect of large-group identity." *Group Analysis, 34* (1), pp. 79–97.

Volkan, Vamik D. (2004). *Blind trust: Large groups and their leaders in times of crisis and terror.* Charlottesville, VA: Pitchstone.

Volkan, Vamik D. (2006). *Killing in the name of identity: A study of bloody conflicts.* Charlottesville, VA: Pitchstone.

Volkan, Vamik D. (2013). *Enemies on the couch: A psychopolitical journey through war and peace.* Charlottesville, VA: Pitchstone.

Volkogonov, Dmitrij (1978). *Militarist character of Maoist ideology and policy.* Moscow: Military Publishing House (in Russian).

Volkogonov, Dmitrij, and Harold Shukman (1998). *The rise and fall of the Soviet empire: Political leaders from Lenin to Gorbachev.* London: HarperCollins.

von Braun, Christina (2012). *Der Preis des Geldes: Eine Kulturgeschichte.* Berlin: Aufbau Verlag.

Voon, Valerie, Thomas B. Mole, Paula Banca, Laura Porter, Laurel Morris, Simon Mitchell, Tatyana R. Lapa, *et al.* (2014). "Neural correlates of sexual cue reactivity in individuals with and without compulsive sexual behaviours." *Public Library of Science (PLoS) ONE, 9* (7), pp. e102419.

Vygotsky, Lev Semyonovich (1978). *Mind in society: The development of higher psychological processes.* Cambridge: Harvard University Press.

Wacquant, Loïc J. D. (1991). "Making class: The middle class(es) in social theory and social structure." In *Bringing class back in: Contemporary and historical perspectives*, edited by Scott G. McNall, Rhonda F. Levine, and Rick Fantasia, pp. 39–64. Boulder, CO: Westview Press.

Wadhwa, Vivek, AnnaLee Saxenian, Richard B. Freeman, and Gary Gereffi (2009). *America's loss is the world's gain: America's new immigrant entrepreneurs, part 4.* Durham, NC: Duke University.

Wagner, Michael W., Kristen D. Deppe, Carly M. Jacobs, Amanda Friesen, Kevin B. Smith, and John R. Hibbing (2015). "Beyond survey self-reports: Using physiology to tap political orientations." *International Journal of Public Opinion Research, 27* (3), pp. 303–17.

Wagner, Richard V. (2006). "Terrorism: A peace psychological analysis." *Journal of Social Issues, 62* (1), pp. 155–71.

Wainwright, David, and Michael Calnan (2002). *Work stress: The making of a modern epidemic.* Buckingham: Open University Press.

Wainwright, Tom (2016). *Narconomics: How to run a drug cartel.* New York: PublicAffairs.

Waldron, Jeremy (2012). *Dignity, rank, and rights.* New York: Oxford University Press, the Tanner Lectures on Human Values, University of California, Berkeley, April 21–23, 2009.

Walker, Julian, and Victoria Knauer (2011). "Humiliation, self-esteem, and violence." *Journal of Forensic Psychiatry and Psychology, 22* (5, Special Issue: Emotions, Emotional Regulation and Offender Treatment), pp. 724–41.

Waller, David (1996). *Rwanda: Which way now?* Oxford: Oxfam.

Waller, James (2002). *Becoming evil: How ordinary people commit genocide and mass killing.* Oxford: Oxford University Press.

Wallerstein, Immanuel Maurice (1974–1989). *The modern world-system (Volume I: Capitalist agriculture and the origins of the European world-economy in the sixteenth century, 1974, Volume II: Mercantilism and the consolidation of the European world-economy, 1600–1750, 1980, Volume III: The second great expansion of the capitalist world-economy, 1730 - 1840's, 1989).* New York: Academic Press.

Wambacq, Judith, and Christian Ciocan (2011). "Maurice Merleau-Ponty's criticism of Bergson's theory of time seen through the work of Gilles Deleuze." *Studia Phænomenologica, XI*, pp. 233–49.

Wang, Sam, and Sandra Aamodt (2011). *Welcome to your child's brain: How the mind grows from conception to college.* New York: Bloomsbury USA.

Wang, Zheng (2008). "National humiliation, history education, and the politics of historical memory: Patriotic ducation campaign in China." *International Studies Quarterly, 52* (4), pp. 783–806.

Wang, Zheng (2012). *Never forget national humiliation: Historical memory in Chinese politics and foreign relations.* New York: Columbia University Press.

Ward, Martha C., and Monica D. Edelstein (2009). *A world full of women.* Boston: Pearson.

Waring, Marilyn (1988). *If women counted: A new feminist economics.* San Francisco: Harper and Row.

Warneken, Felix, and Michael Tomasello (2008). "Extrinsic rewards undermine altruistic tendencies in 20-month-olds." *Developmental Psychology, 44* (6), pp. 1785–88.

Warner, Jeffrey (2009). *Sarajevo evolution: A tribute to survival.* Sarajevo, Bosnia: Jeff's Journalism.

Warner, Jeffrey (2014a). *Indigenous voices: Glimpses into the margins of modern development.* Chiang Mai, Thailand: Jeff's Journalism.

Warner, Jeffrey (2014b). *Dignity amidst the rubbish: Hour-by-hour with a Burmese migrant community in Thailand.* Chiang Mai, Thailand: Jeff's Journalism.

Warner, Jeffrey (2014c). *Template for the "de" of development: A case study for humankind.* Chiang Mai, Thailand: Jeff's Journalism.

Warren, Elizabeth (2017). *This fight is our fight: The battle to save America's middle class.* New York: Metropolitan Books.

Wasem, Jürgen, Hans-Dieter Nolting, Martin Albrecht, Antje Schwinger, Toon Overstijns, Marcel Mangen, and Mario Klesse (2009). *Perspektive 2020 Gesundheit als Chance: 5. Delphi-Studie zur Zukunft des Gesundheitswesens.* Berlin, Essen, Neuss, Germany: IGES Institut GmbH, Berlin, Alfried Krupp von Bohlen und Halbach Stiftungslehrstuhl für Medizin-Management, Universität Duisburg-Essen, Janssen-Cilag GmbH.

Watkins, John G., and Helen Huth Watkins (1997). *Ego states: Theory and therapy.* New York: Norton.

Watson, D. M. S., N. W. Timofeeff-Ressovsky, E. J. Salisbury, W. B. Turrill, T. J. Jenkin, R. Ruggles Gates, Ronald Aylmer Fisher, *et al.* (1936). "A discussion on the present state of the theory of natural selection." *Proceedings of the Royal Society of London. Series B, Biological Sciences (1934 - 1990), 121* (820), pp. 43–73.

Watzlawick, Paul, Janet Beavin Bavelas, and Don D. Jackson (1967). *Pragmatics of human communication: A study of interactional patterns, pathologies, and paradoxes.* New York: Norton.

Webb, Tony (2009). "On love, shame and other strong emotions." *No to Violence, 5* (1), pp. 45–73.

Webber, David, Kristen Klein, Arie Kruglanski, Ambra Brizi, and Ariel Merari (2015). "Divergent paths to martyrdom and significance among suicide attackers." *Terrorism and Political Violence*, pp. 1–23.

Weber-Guskar, Eva (2016). *Würde als Haltung. Eine philosophische Untersuchung zum Begriff der Menschenwürde*. Münster, Germany: mentis.

Weber, Max (1904-1905). "Die protestantische Ethik und der Geist des Kapitalismus." *Archiv für Sozialwissenschaften und Sozialpolitik, Band 20, 1904, Band 21, 1905* (1), pp. 1–54, 1–110.

Weber, Max (1904/1949). "Objectivity in social science and social policy." In *The methodology of social sciences*, edited by Edward Shils, and Henry Finch, pp. 49–112. Glencoe, IL: Free Press, German original 'Die „Objektivität" sozialwissenschaftlicher und sozialpolitischer Erkenntnis', in *Archiv für Sozialwissenschaft und Sozialpolitik, Band 19*, pp. 22–87, 1904.

Weber, Max (1919). *Wissenschaft als Beruf*. München, Germany: Duncker und Humblot.

Webster, David L. (2002). *The fall of the ancient Maya: Solving the mystery of the Maya collapse*. London: Thames and Hudson.

Weiner, Eugene, and Alan B. Slifka (Foreword). *The handbook of interethnic coexistence*. New York: Abraham Fund Publication, 1998.

Weininger, Elliott B. (2005). "Foundations of Bourdieu's class analysis." In *Approaches to class analysis*, edited by Erik Olin Wright, chapter 4, pp. 82–118. Cambridge: Cambridge University Press.

Weininger, Otto (1903). *Geschlecht und Charakter*. Wien, Leipzig: C. G. Braumüller.

Weiss, Harvey, and Raymond S. Bradley (2001). "What drives societal collapse?". *Science, 291* (5504), pp. 609–10.

Weisæth, Lars, and Freja Ulvestad Kärki (2014). *Fra sjokk til mestring: Norges respons på et nasjonalt traume*. Oslo: Gyldendal akademisk forlag.

Wendt, Alexander (1992). "Anarchy is what states make of it: The social construction of power politics." *International Organization, 46* (2, Spring), pp. 391–425.

Wendt, Alexander (1999). *Social theory of international politics*. Cambridge: Cambridge University Press.

Wendt, Alexander (2003). "Why a world state is inevitable." *European Journal of International Relations, 9* (4), pp. 491–542.

Wendt, Alexander, Stefano Guzzini, and Anna Leander (2006). *Constructivism and international relations: Alexander Wendt and his critics*. London: Routledge.

Wendt, Alexander (2015). *Quantum mind and social science: Unifying physical and social ontology*. Cambridge: Cambridge University Press.

Wergeland, Henrik (1843). *Henrik Wergeland, IV. Avhandlinger, opplysningsskrifter: 5te Bind 1843 – 1845*. Oslo: Dokumentasjonsprosjekt Universitetet i Bergen, Universitetet i Oslo, Universitetet i Trondheim, Universitetet i Tromsø.

West, Diana (2008). *The death of the grown-up: How America's arrested development is bringing down Western civilization*. New York: St. Martin's Press.

Wetz, Franz Josef (2014). *Die Rebellion der Selbstachtung: Gegen Demütigung*. Aschaffenburg, Germany: Alibri.

Whippman, Ruth (2016). *The pursuit of happiness: And why it's making us anxious*. London: Hutchinson.

Whitaker, Mark Douglas (2008). *Ecological revolution: The political origins of environmental degradation and environmental amelioration: Patterns, processes, outcomes; a comparative study of Japan, China, and Europe*. Madison, WI: University of Wisconsin-Madison, doctoral dissertation.

White, Jonathan R. (2014). *Terrorism and homeland security*. 8th edition. Belmont, CA: Wadsworth Cengage Learning.

White, Ralph K. (1984). *Fearful warriors: A psychological profile of U.S.-Soviet relations*. New York: Free Press.

Whitehead, Neil L., and Nasser Abufarha (2008). "Suicide, violence, and cultural conceptions of martyrdom in Palestine." *Social Research, 75* (2, Summer), pp. 395–416.

Whitehead, Stephen M. (2002). *Men and masculinities: Key themes and new directions.* Cambridge: Polity Press.

Whitson, J. A., and A. D. Galinsky (2008). "Lacking control increases illusory pattern perception." *Science, 322* (5898), pp. 115–7.

Wibye, Carl S. (2017). *Terrorens rike: Hvordan en voldelig sekt fra den arabiske ørken radikaliserte Islam.* Oslo: Gyldendal.

Wichterich, Christa (2000). *The globalized woman: Reports from a future of inequality.* London: Spinifex Press.

Wichterich, Christa (2010). *The other financial crisis: Poor women, small credits, big businesses.* Brussels: Women In Development Europe (WIDE).

Wigby, Stuart, and Tracey Chapman (2004). "Sperm competition." *Current Biology, 14* (3), pp. R100–R03.

Wijdekop, Femke (2016). *Against ecocide: Legal protection for Earth.* Boston: Great Transition Initiative.

Wijkman, Anders, and Johan Rockström (2012). *Bankrupting nature: Denying our planetary boundaries.* Abingdon-on-Thames: Routledge.

Wiktorowicz, Quintan (2004). *Islamic activism: A social movement theory approach.* Bloomington: Indiana University Press.

Wiktorowicz, Quintan (2005). *Radical Islam rising: Muslim extremism in the West.* Lanham, MD: Rowman and Littlefield.

Wilbanks, Kimberly (2008). "The female contribution to the origin of life sustaining tools." *Lethbridge Undergraduate Research Journal, 3* (1), pp. 1–8.

Wilce, James M. (2009). *Language and emotion.* Cambridge: Cambridge University Press. doi:10.1017/CBO9780511626692.

Wilce, James M., and Janina Fenigsen (2016). "Emotion pedagogies: What are they, and why do they matter?". *Ethos, 44* (2, Special Issue: Emotion Pedagogies), pp. 81–95.

Wilcox, Lauren B. (2015). *Bodies of violence: Theorizing embodied subjects in international relations.* Oxford: Oxford University Press.

Wilkerson, William S., and Jeffrey Paris (Eds.) (2001). *New critical theory: Essays on liberation.* Lanham, MD: Rowman and Littlefield.

Wilkinson, Richard G. (2005). *The impact of inequality. How to make sick societies healthier.* London: Routledge.

Wilkinson, Richard G., and Kate Pickett (2009). *The spirit level: Why more equal societies almost always do better.* London: Allen Lane.

Williams, Charles (2000). *Adenauer: The father of the new Germany.* London: Brown Little.

Williams, Raymond (1961). *The long revolution.* London: Chatto and Windus.

Willms, Johannes (2015). *Bismarck – Dämon der Deutschen: Anmerkungen zu einer Legende.* New edition. München, Germany: Deutscher Taschenbuch Verlag.

Wilshire, Bruce (1990). *The moral collapse of the university: Professionalism, purity, and alienation.* Albany: State University of New York Press.

Wilson, D. S., and E. O. Wilson (2007). "Rethinking the theoretical foundation of sociobiology." *The Quarterly Review of Biology, 82* (4), pp. 327–48.

Wilson, David Sloan (2002a). *Darwin's cathedral: Evolution, religion, and the nature of society.* Chicago: University of Chicago Press.

Wilson, David Sloan, and John M. Gowdy (2013). "Evolution as a general theoretical framework for economics and public policy." *Journal of Economic Behavior and Organization, 90*, pp. 3–10.

Wilson, David Sloan (2015). *Does altruism exist? Culture, genes, and the welfare of others.* New Haven, CT: Yale University Press.

Wilson, Edward O. (2013). *The social conquest of earth.* New York: Liveright.

Wilson, Timothy D. (2002b). *Strangers to ourselves: Discovering the adaptive unconscious.* Cambridge, MA: Harvard University Press.

Winkler, Heinrich August (2009–2015). *Geschichte des Westens (Von den Anfängen in der Antike bis zum 20. Jahrhundert, 2009, Die Zeit der Weltkriege. 1914–1945, 2011, Vom Kalten Krieg zum Mauerfall, 2014, Die Zeit der Gegenwart, 2015).* München, Germany: C.H. Beck.

Winnicott, Donald Woods (1965). "Ego distortion in terms of true and false self." In *The maturational process and the facilitating environment: Studies in the theory of emotional development*, pp. 140–52. Madison: International Universities Press.

Wintersteiner, Werner (1999). *Pädagogik des Anderen: Bausteine für eine Friedenspädagogik in der Postmoderne.* Münster, Germany: Agenda.

Wise, Tim (2015). *Under the affluence: Shaming the poor, praising the rich, and sacrificing the future of America.* San Francisco: City Lights Books.

Wiswede, Daniel, Svenja Taubner, Anna Buchheim, Thomas Münte, Michael Stasch, Manfred Cierpka, Horst Kächele, *et al.* (2014). "Tracking Functional Brain Changes in Patients with Depression under Psychodynamic Psychotherapy Using Individualized Stimuli." *Public Library of Science (PLoS) ONE, 9* (10).

Witt, Ulrich, and Georg Schwesinger (2013). "Phylogenetic footprints in organizational behavior." *Journal of Economic Behavior and Organization, 90*, pp. S33–S44.

Wixon, Vincent, and Paul Merchant (Eds.) (2014). *Sound of the ax: Aphorisms and poems by William Stafford*, Pitt Poetry Series. Pittsburgh, PA: University of Pittsburgh Press.

Wohl, Michael J. A., and Nyla R. Branscombe (2008). "Remembering historical victimization: collective guilt for current ingroup transgressions." *Journal of Personality and Social Psychology, 94* (6), pp. 988–1006.

Wohl, Michael J. A., and Jay J. Van Bavel (2011). "Is identifying with a historically victimized group good or bad for your health? Transgenerational post-traumatic stress and collective victimization." *European Journal of Social Psychology, 41* (7), pp. 818–24.

Wolf, Reinhard (2013). *Resentment in international relations.* Mainz, Germany: Paper prepared for the European Consortium for Political Research (ECPR) Workshop on Status Claims, Recognition, and Emotions in IR: Theoretical and Methodological Challenges', Mainz, March 11–16, 2013.

Woo, Choong-Wan, Leonie Koban, Ethan Kross, Martin A. Lindquist, Marie T. Banich, Luka Ruzic, Jessica R. Andrews-Hanna, and Tor D. Wager (2014). "Separate neural representations for physical pain and social rejection." *Nature Communications, 5*, pp. Article 5380.

Wood, Ellen Meiksins (2003). *Empire of capital.* London: Verso.

Wood, Ian (1994). *The Merovingian kingdoms: 450 – 751.* London: Longman.

Wood, Joanne V., W. Q. Elaine Perunovic, and John W. Lee (2009). "Positive self-statements: Power for some, peril for others." *Psychological Science, 20* (7), pp. 860–66.

Woodley, Michael A., Jan te Nijenhuis, and Raegan Murphy (2013). "Were the Victorians cleverer than us? The decline in general intelligence estimated from a meta-analysis of the slowing of simple reaction time." *Intelligence, 41* (6), pp. 843–50.

Woods, John (2003). *Boys who have abused: Psychoanalytic psychotherapy with victim / perpetrators of sexual abuse.* New York: Jessica Kingsley Publishers.

World Commission on Environment and Development, and Gro Harlem Brundtland (1987). *Our common future*. Oxford: Oxford University Press, en.wikisource.org/wiki/Brundtland_Report.

World Wildlife Fund (WWF) (2014). *Living planet report 2014: Species and spaces, people and places*. London: World Wildlife Fund (WWF), wwf.panda.org/about_our_earth/all_publications/living_planet_report/.

World Wildlife Fund (WWF), Zoological Society of London (ZSL), and Global Footprint Network (2016). *Living planet report 2016: Risk and resilience in a new era*. London: World Wildlife Fund (WWF).

Wortham, Stanton, and Kara Jackson (2012). "Relational education: Applying Gergen's work to educational research and practice." *Psychological Studies, 57* (2, June, Kenneth J. Gergen and Social Constructionism), pp. 164–71.

Wrangham, Richard W., and Dale Peterson (1996). *Demonic males: Apes and the origins of human violence*. New York: Houghton Mifflin.

Wright, Lawrence (2006). *The looming tower: Al-Qaeda and the road to 9/11*. New York: Knopf.

Wright, Lawrence (2013). *Going clear: Scientology, Hollywood, and the prison of belief*. New York: Knopf.

Wright, Philip Quincy, William M. Evan, and Morton Deutsch (Eds.) (1962). *Preventing World War III: Some proposals*. New York: Simon and Schuster.

Wu, Charlene C., Matthew D. Sacchet, and Brian Knutson (2012). "Toward an affective neuroscience account of financial risk taking." *Frontiers in Neuroscience, 6*.

Wulf, Andrea (2015). *The invention of nature. The adventures of Alexander von Humboldt – The lost hero of science*. London: John Murray.

Wyatt-Brown, Bertram (1982). *Southern honor: Ethics and behavior in the old south*. New York: Oxford University Press.

Wyatt-Brown, Bertram (2005). *The changing faces of honor in national crises: Civil War, Vietnam, Iraq, and the Southern factor*. Baltimore, MD: The Johns Hopkins History Seminar, Fall 2005.

Wyatt-Brown, Bertram (2014). *A warring nation: Honor, race, and humiliation in America and abroad*. Charlottesville: University of Virginia Press.

Wöss, Fritz (1958). *Hunde, wollt ihr ewig leben?* Hamburg, Germany, Wien, Austria: Paul Zsolnay.

Yamada, David C. (2015). "Workplace bullying and the law: U.S. legislative development 2013-15." *Employee Rights and Employment Policy Journal, 19* (1), pp. 49–59.

Yamada, David C. (2016). "Intellectual activism and the practice of public interest law." *Southern California Review of Law and Social Justice, 25* (2, June 24), pp. 127–81, Suffolk University Law School Research Paper No. 15–30.

Yang, Jie (2013). "'Fake happiness': Counseling, potentiality, and psycho-politics in China." *Ethos, 41* (3), pp. 292–312.

Yang, Jie (2015). *Unknotting the heart: Unemployment and therapeutic governance in China*. Ithaca, NY: Cornell University Press.

Yeager, David S., Adriana S. Miu, Joseph Powers, and Carol S. Dweck (2013). "Implicit theories of personality and attributions of hostile intent: A meta-analysis, an experiment, and a longitudinal intervention." *Child Development, 84* (5), pp. 1651–67.

Yiwu, Liao (2002/2008). *Corpse walker*. Translated by Wen Huang. New York: Anchor. Chinese original part of *Interviews with People from the Bottom Rung of Society*, Taipeh: Rye Field, 2002.

Yongyi, Song (2011). "Chronology of mass killings during the Chinese Cultural Revolution (1966 – 1976) " In *Online encyclopedia of mass violence*.

Yoo, John (2005). *The powers of war and peace: The constitution and foreign affairs after 9/11*. Chicago: University of Chicago Press.

Yoshikawa, Muneo Jay (1980). *The "double swing" model of Eastern-Western intercultural communication.* Honolulu: Paper prepared for the Seminar on Communication Theory from Eastern and Western Perspectives, East-West Communication Institute.

Yoshikawa, Muneo Jay (1987). "The 'double swing' model of intercultural communication between the East and West." In *Communication theory: Eastern and Western perspectives*, edited by D. Lawrence Kincaid, chapter 22, pp. 319–29. San Diego, CA: Academic Press.

Young, Richard, Stefano Orsini, and Ian Fitzpatrick (2015). *Soil degradation: A major threat to humanity.* Bristol: Sustainable Food Trust.

Zajonc, Robert B. (1980). "Feeling and thinking: Preferences need no inferences." *American Psychologist, 35* (2), pp. 151–75.

Zalasiewicz, Jan, Mark Williams, Will Steffen, and Paul Crutzen (2010). "The new world of the Anthropocene." *Environment Science and Technology, 44* (7), pp. 2228–31.

Zalewski, Marysia, and Jane Parpat (Eds.) (1998). *The 'man question' in international relations.* Boulder, CO: Westview.

Zehnpfennig, Barbara (2016). "Die Bedeutung des Kampfes in Hitlers Denken." *Totalitarianism and Democracy, 13* (1), pp. 85–106.

Zehr, Howard (2005). *Changing lenses: A new focus for crime and justice.* 3rd edition. Scottdale, PA: Herald Press.

Zihlman, Adrienne L., Alison Galloway, and Mary Ellen Morbeck (Eds.) (1997). *The evolving female: A life-history perspective.* Princeton, NJ: Princeton University Press.

Zihlman, Adrienne L. (2009). "Reflections on women in evolution: Looking back and going forward." *Voices, 9* (1, Winter), pp. 18–24.

Žižek, Slavoj (2012). *Less than nothing: Hegel and the shadow of dialectical materialism.* London: Verso.

Zubok, Vladislav (2014). "With his back against the wall: Gorbachev, Soviet demise, and German reunification." *Cold War History, 14* (4), pp. 619–45.

Zunes, Stephen (2002). *Tinderbox: US Middle East Policy and the Roots of Terrorism.* Monroe, ME: Common Courage Press.

Åhäll, Linda, and Thomas Gregory (Eds.) (2015). *Emotions, politics and war.* New York: Routledge.

Ås, Berit (2008). "De fem hersketeknikkene: Om ufarliggjøring av undertrykkernes våpen." In *Kvinner i alle land: Håndbok i frigjøring*, edited by Berit Ås, Revised edition, pp. 64–93. Oslo: Aschehoug.

NOTES

Preface

1 My warning resonates with the message of Yuval Noah Harari, 2015/2016.

2 See a summary of this Preface on www.humiliationstudies.org/whoweare/evelin/book/05.php.

3 Publius Flavius Vegetius Renatus and Reeve, 2004.

4 Schell, 2003. Solomon, 2005.

5 Margalit, 1996, 1997, 2002.

6 "Sociocide is the intended wounding-killing of a society by eliminating the prerequisites for a live, vibrant, dynamic society," writes Johan Galtung. See "Sociocide, Palestine and Israel," by Johan Galtung, TRANSCEND Media Service, October 8, 2012, www.transcend.org/tms/2012/10/sociocide-palestine-and-israel/. Johan Galtung is professor emeritus of Peace Studies and Sociology at the University of Oslo and Founder of the International Peace Research Institute Oslo (PRIO), the Galtung-Institute, and the Transcend Network. See the full note in the pdf edition of this book.

7 Higgins, 2016. See a precursor to the concept of ecocide in Christopher Stone, 1972, and for "a look back forty years later," see Anna Grear, 2012. See, furthermore, Boyd, 2012, or Angus, 2016. Consider also the sustainability principle in the Great Law of the Iroquois Confederacy and the Ley de la Madre Tierra in Bolivia. In September 2016, the International Criminal Court added environmental disasters and destruction, even land grabs, to the definition of Crimes Against Humanity, which shows that "hard" international legal instruments now follow soft law (Earth Charter) and symbolic language (ecocide, where the mens rea required cannot be demonstrated).There are voices, however, that warn that introducing a crime of ecocide in the International Criminal Court (ICC) may ultimately be undesirable, because the vehicle of an international crime overreaches and is insufficient at the same time. See Capra and Mattei, 2015. See also Ugo Mattei of the Hastings College of Law at the University of California, and his contribution to the Great Transition Network (GTN) discussion on the topic of "Against Ecocide: Legal Protection for Earth," July 5, 2016, in response to Femke Wijdekop, 2016. The ICC, due to the lack of international centralized power or independence, is just a mockery of an institution, writes Mattei. I am part in Anna Grear's network, as well as of Paul Raskin's GTN discussions. See the full note in the pdf edition of this book.

8 See, among many other relevant publications, Ahmed, 2017.

9 "Land Degradation Could Force 135 Million to Migrate in Next 30 Years," by Manipadma Jena, Inter Press Service (IPS), October 18, 2016, www.ipsnews.net/2016/10/qa-land-degradation-could-force-135-million-to-migrate-in-next-30-years/.

10 "Climate and Terrorism," by Roberto Savio, Inter Press Service (IPS), August 2, 2016, www.ipsnews.net/2016/08/climate-and-terrorism/.

11 "The Conflict Horizon 3: Only Connect," Dan Smith, Dan Smith's Blog: Analysis and Commentary on World Issues, April 25, 2014, dansmithsblog.com/2014/04/25/the-conflict-horizon-3-only-connect/. I thank Dan Smith for his support when he was the director of the Peace Research Institute Oslo (PRIO), and I devised research proposals for my doctorate, see Lindner, 1995a, Lindner, 1995b.

12 Watch Deeyah Khan: What We Don't Know About Europe's Muslim Kids, TEDxExeter, April 2016. www.ted.com/talks/deeyah_khan_what_we_don_t_know_about_europe_s_muslim_kids. It is a privilege to have Deeyah Khan as esteemed member in our Human Dignity and Humiliation Studies fellowship.

13 "The War of the Future? Picture Big Armies and Many Fronts," by Helene Cooper, The New York Times, June 10, 2016, www.nytimes.com/2016/06/11/us/the-war-of-the-future-picture-big-armies-and-many-fronts.html. I thank Linda Hartling for making me aware of this article.

14 Lindner, 2006c.

15 Lindner, 2006c, p. 48. See also The Clash of Fundamentalisms, by Ali, 2002.

16 "I Helped Create ISIS," by Vincent Emanuele, Telesur, December 18, 2015, www.telesurtv.net/english/opinion/I-Helped-Create-ISIS-20151218-0016.html. Vincent Emanuele was stationed in Iraq with the 1st Battalion, 7th Marines, 2003-2005. See also the National Intelligence Estimate (NIE) NIE 2006-02R, "Trends in Global Terrorism: Implications for the United States," April 2006, released by the Office of the Director of National Intelligence (ODNI). See, furthermore, "US Iraq War Veteran Speaks Out Before Australian Tour," an interview with Vince Emanuele, Only in America Blogspot, June 25, 2013, http://onlyinamericablogging.blogspot.com/2013/06/an-interview-with-vince-emanuele.html (originally on waca.net.au/us-iraq-war-veteran-speaks-out-before-australian-tour/). See also US Activist and Iraq War Veteran Vincent Emanuele Speaks Out, video, Information Clearing House, July 12, 2013, www.informationclearinghouse.info/article35533.htm. I thank Anthony Marsella for making me aware of Emanuele's engagement. It is a privilege to have Anthony Marsella as esteemed member in the global advisory board of our Human Dignity and Humiliation Studies fellowship.

17 Da'esh is the acronym from the Arabic name Al-Dawlah Al-Islamiyah fe Al-Iraq wa Al-Sham, for the self-proclaimed Islamic State (IS) in Iraq and Syria, or ISIL (Islamic State of Iraq and the Levant), or ISIS (the Islamic State of Iraq and Syria).

18 Abu Bakr al-Baghdadi, the leader of Da'esh survived the Camp Bucca detention center of the US Forces-Iraq. See, among others, "Jordan Executes ISIS Jihadists: Female Suicide Bomber Among Two Put to Death in Dawn Hangings in Retaliation for Terrorists Releasing Video of Pilot Being Torched to Death in Cage," by John Hall, Julian Robinson, Tom Wyke, and Steph Cockroft for MailOnline, and David Williams, Chief Reporter for the Daily Mail, February 3, 2015, www.dailymail.co.uk/news/article-2938199/Burned-alive-cage-ISIS-release-video-claiming-horrifying-murder-captured-Jordanian-pilot.html.

19 Lindner, 2012f.

20 This book was supported by a 7-months stipend from the Norwegian Non-Fiction Literature Fund in 2011.

21 Del Re, et al., 2009, Lindner, 2001f, g, h, 2004a, 2005b, c, 2008b, 2009c, 2011, 2012a, g, 2014d, 2015b, Lindner and Backe, 2004, Lindner, et al., 2009.

22 On July 22, 2011, Anders Behring Breivik bombed government buildings in Oslo, Norway, where eight people died, and then began a mass shooting at a Workers' Youth League (AUF) camp on the island of Utøya, a ca. 40 minutes car-drive outside of Oslo, killing 69 people, mostly teenagers. See an in-depth analysis of Breivik's' terrorist operation in Hemmingby and Bjørgo, 2016, an analysis of Breivik's ideas in Kjos, 2013, and an account of how he grew up in Seierstad, 2013/2015. See the full note in the pdf edition of this book.

23 In his book on the history of terrorism, Norwegian political economist Nikolai Sitter, 2017, explains how the attacks on the Norwegian government quarter and Utøya on July 22, 2011, put terrorism and counterterrorism on the agenda in Norway in an entirely new way. See the full note in the pdf edition of this book.

24 In my work, I call for the humanization of globalization, or for globegalization, a term drawn together from globalization and egalization (equal dignity for all).

25 Tellingly, my 2006 book was titled Making Enemies: Humiliation and International Conflict. Yet, long before I warned that the humiliated of this world will strike back, others had warned of the same. While I

write this book, Heinrich Geiselberger is in the process of editing a book on The Great Recession, see www.thegreatregression.eu/. Geiselberger is an editor at the leading German publisher Suhrkamp Verlag. He reminds of sociologist Ralf Dahrendorf and his twenty-year-old prediction that the 21st century will become a "century of authoritarianism." In the early nineties, Dahrendorf's work indeed inspired me to briefly become a member of the political party he supported in Germany, and be its candidate for the European Parliament in 1994 (I left the party soon after and have never joined any political party since). We were thrilled that Ralf Dahrendorf wished to participate in our Annual Dignity Conference in Berlin in 2005, and were saddened that health reasons ultimately prevented him.
In 2003, I met historian Edward Luttwak, who noted already in 1994 that it was perilous to let working people descend into such personal economic insecurity. I heard Luttwak at the Conference "Can Israel Be Secure Within Its '67 Borders?" at The Hebrew University in Jerusalem, November 16–18, 2003.
Also philosopher Richard Rorty warned of possible regressions. In the wake of Donald Trump's rise to victory, in November 2016, New Yorker editor David Remnick reminded of Rorty's 1998 book Achieving Our Country, where Rorty had predicted that Americans with less education will develop resentment at being dictated by arrogant college graduates, and that this resentment will find its outlets. See "The Political Scene," by David Remnick, New Yorker, November 28, 2016, www.newyorker.com/magazine/2016/11/28/obama-reckons-with-a-trump-presidency, and "'Something Will Crack': Supposed Prophecy of Donald Trump Goes Viral," by Edward Helmore in New York, The Guardian, November 19, 2016, www.theguardian.com/us-news/2016/nov/19/donald-trump-us-election-prediction-richard-rorty.
See also political scientist Jean Hardisty, 1999, and her book titled Mobilizing Resentment: Conservative Resurgence from the John Birch Society to the Promise Keepers. I thank Linda Hartling for having made me aware of Hardisty's work.
Norwegian historian Rune Slagstad describes how populists now challenge the modern state with its liberal democracy and the rule of law at its core. See "Carl Schmitt i Det hvite hus," by Rune Slagstad, Institutt for samfunnsforskning, Klassekampen, February 11, 2017, www.klassekampen.no/article/20170211/ARTICLE/170219981.
Slagstad warns that in the United States of America, strategists such as Richard Spencer and Stephen Bannon have now come to power, who draw on a very "dangerous mind," as Jan-Werner Müller, 2003, has expressed it, namely, Carl Schmitt (1888 – 1985), one of the twentieth century's most significant political theorists. Schmitt, 1927/2007, has inspired all sides, right-wing and left-wing, whenever they set out to leave behind compromise and consensus and return to simple dichotomies, particularly, that of friend versus enemy, which, according to Schmitt, is the very factum brutum of politics, both in form of outer and inner enemies. The Biblical admonition "Love your enemies" (Matthew 5:44) applies only in private life and not in public life, according to Schmitt. Schmitt called for "Führertum," an efficient, unified powerful state-will, not undermined by democratic control, where might – not truth – becomes right, legitimized through popular acclamation. "Souverän ist, wer über den Ausnahmezustand entscheidet," Schmitt, 1922, p. 11. See also Kelsen and Schmitt, 1931/2015, Schmitt, 1931. Schmitt admired revolutionary syndicalist Georges Sorel (1847 – 1922), who believed that the proletariat should be mobilized to fight against the other classes, until the liberating moment of the revolution would come in a final violent battle. Left-leaning thinkers such as Giorgio Agamben, Chantal Mouffe, Antonio Negri, or Slavoj Žižek have read Schmitt, but, more recently, also those of the right-wing political spectrum, not only in Poland, Hungary, and Austria, but also in the U.S.A., as, for instance, in Donald Trump's ideological surroundings. Donald Trump represents a radicalized Schmitt, says Slagstad, not only does he claim to hold the monopoly on decisions but also the "truth monopoly": the sovereign decides what is true, what is fact.
Schmitt, 1963/2004, sees the partisan (terrorist, we would say) as the last truly political actor of present times, as he does not shy away from the friend versus enemy dichotomy – the very dichotomy, from which Schmitt sees the real concept of the political emerge. The partisan/terrorist is the last truly political actor in

present-day's post-national context, because states have lost their monopoly on war, which means that non-state actors become belligerent. The primary objective of those actors is not territorial conquest, but the eradication of "decadent lifestyles," where "absolute enmity" makes civilian and military targets indistinguishable. Stephen Bannon's "clash of civilizations" narrative fits into Schmitt's thinking and is an apocalyptic mirror image of Da'esh's rhetoric.
See also Tunander, 2009, in note 98 in Chapter 1. See, furthermore, Kagan, 1997, and Fraenkel, 1941, in note 15 in the Introduction to Section Three.

26 When I began to interview people and collect material in 2010, at first, a single book in three parts was planned: Part I – The Past: Terrorism in the Context of Honor – Terror as Accepted Path to More Honor with three chapters, Chapter 1: The Security Dilemma – Too Far Apart, Chapter 2: Honor Humiliation – Pressure from Outside to Retaliate, and Chapter 3: Peace the Old Way – Keeping One's Enemies Out and One's Own People Down. Since its inception, the book project has grown into three books. The three parts of the original book project have become three volumes. This book represents the first volume.

27 Part II – The Present: Terrorism in the Context of Dignity – Terror as Unacceptable Path to More Dignity with three chapters, Chapter 4: The Dignity Dilemma – Too Close Together, Chapter 5: Dignity Humiliation – Urge from Inside to Retaliate, Chapter 6: Peace the Mandela Way – Inclusive Dialogue between Equals.

28 Part III – The Future: Toward a Terrorism-Free World with three chapters, Chapter 7: Creating a World of Unity in Diversity – Humanizing Globalization Through Egalization, Chapter 8: Walking the Gandhi and Mandela Path – Understanding, yet Not Condoning, Respecting, yet Not Appeasing, Chapter 9: Practicing the Human Dignity Way – Toward a Future of Careholdership for Global Equality in Dignity.

29 Wulf, 2015. I explain my personal global life design in more detail on the website of the Human Dignity and Humiliation Studies fellowship, www.humiliationstudies.org/whoweare/evelin.php.

30 I thank Betty Scheper for informing me of the Brownbag discussion "Global Terrorism: What the Data Says," by Aubrey Fox, executive director, Institute for Economics and Peace-USA, and moderator Jehangir Khan, director of CTITF/UNCCT, at the Counter-Terrorism Implementation Task Force (CTITF), Office of the United Nations Department of Political Affairs, December 10, 2015.

31 Intellectual activism is both a philosophy and a practice for engaging in scholarship relevant to real-world problems, writes David Yamada, 2016. It is a privilege to have David Yamada as esteemed member in the board of directors of our Human Dignity and Humiliation Studies fellowship.

32 Therapist and minister John McFadden, 2016. See the full note in the pdf edition of this book.

33 "Humiliation Is the Root of All Terrorism," by Peter Gabel, Tikkun editor at large, TruthOut, December 16, 2015, www.truth-out.org/speakout/item/34062-humiliation-is-the-root-of-all-terrorism. I thank Seymour M. (Mike) Miller and Linda Hartling for making me aware of this article. It is a privilege to have John McFadden's support for Human Dignity and Humiliation Studies.

34 See Lindner, 2006c, the section "Children, Madmen, Criminals, Enemies, or Subhumans? Which Interpretation Fits Terrorists Best?" in the book Making Enemies: Humiliation and International Conflict, pp. 96–98.

35 See for an illustration, "Responses: The Humiliation Myth: Humiliation Doesn't Explain Terrorism; the Spread of Political Islam Does. A Response to Peter Bergen and Michael Lind," by Daniel Jonah Goldhagen, Democracy: A Journal of Ideas, Spring 2007, Number 4, http://democracyjournal.org/magazine/4/the-humiliation-myth/, where Goldhagen remarks that "the 'myth of deprivation' is so manifestly inadequate that it is worth asking whether its supporters actually believe it." Also humiliation is not "the issue":

Humiliation is not the issue. An all-consuming, divinely ordained desire to impose theocratic totalitarian control is.... We should stop fixating on al Qaeda and terrorism, narrowly construed, as the overwhelming problem and recognize that the biggest danger is the Political Islamic colossus and aspiring hegemon....

"Humiliation and Terrorism: Goldhagen's Analysis," by Richard Landes, The Augean Stables, March 27, 2007, www.theaugeanstables.com/2007/03/27/humiliation-and-terrorism-goldhagens-analysis/:

In this kind of honor-shame battle, any concessions from us will fuel the triumphalism of the other side. This is, whether we like it or not, and long before Bush invaded Iraq, a fight we cannot walk away from. How we fight back still needs serious consideration. But anyone who thinks the way to deal with Arab/Muslim "humiliation" is to accommodate their demands is a dupe of demopaths and a fool.

36 "Was bedeutet es, die RAF zu verstehen? Mit RAFlern zu reden, heißt nicht, ihre Taten zu billigen. Eine Gegenrede auf Jan Philipp Reemtsma," by Horst-Eberhard Richter, Die Tageszeitung (Taz), October 27, 2004, www.taz.de/!681743/. German original translated by Lindner. I had the privilege of having the support of Jan Philip Reemtsma during my years in Hamburg 1991 – 1994, when I organized the Hamburger Ideenkette.

37 Arne Næss explained his point at length at the 2nd Annual Meeting of Human Dignity and Humiliation Studies, September 12–13, 2003, Maison des Sciences de l'Homme de l'Homme, Paris, www.humiliationstudies.org/whoweare/annualmeeting02.php. Næss described in rich detail how he would invite convicted murderers from prison into his philosophy class at Oslo University to demonstrate to his students that even murderers deserve and need to be dignified. He was adamant that only individuals who feel secure in their connection to humanity can admit to a crime, feel guilty, and show remorse. As long as people feel less than fully human, there is no reason for them to care that they have hurt others or society.

38 See, among others, the Chief of Psychiatry for Correctional Health Services in New York City, Elizabeth Ford, 2017, calling on everyone to acknowledge the humanness in all prison inmates.

39 "Children, Madmen, Criminals, Enemies, or Subhumans? Which Interpretation Fits Terrorists Best?" in Lindner, 2006c, Making Enemies: Humiliation and International Conflict, pp. 96–98.

40 The so-called public trust doctrine, which indicates that the citizens of a country own the natural resources, has been advocated in recent years as a tool to compel governments across the world to take action against climate change. See, among others, Our Children's Trust, www.ourchildrenstrust.org.

41 Philosopher of social science Howard Richards, in a personal communication on January 12, 2013:

Dear Evelin, Linda, Uli, and Michael, I am reminded of a radio newscaster named Edward R. Murrow whom my mother listened to faithfully for many years. Murrow ended every newscast citing different viewpoints on a topic and concluding, "The truth may lie somewhere in between. A view I have finally arrived at, which is expressed in Rethinking Thinking is the idea of 'speaking responsibly.' There are so many things one might say. Most of them could be regarded as true or as false or as meaningful or as meaningless in some sense or other. Whatever one might say will no doubt be understood in different ways by different hearers. It is necessary although difficult (in some senses impossible) to make a reasonable prediction concerning what the consequences of one's speech acts will be. But silence is not a responsible option. Silence also has real-world consequences that are hard to predict. The idea of "responsibility" (which is developed by Amartya Sen, 2009, in his recent book on justice) is about being responsible for the consequences of one's actions. These would include one's speech acts.

See also Amartya Sen, 2009. It is a privilege to have Howard Richards as esteemed member in the global advisory board of our Human Dignity and Humiliation Studies fellowship.

42 See, among others, Talking to the Enemy, by anthropologist Scott Atran, uploaded on November 18, 2010, https://youtu.be/6ijmBd69878, where Atran explores the evolutionary origins of religions in connection with the mindsets of extremist people in the twenty-first century. Atran calls terrorists "essential

outliers," who are holding our civilization hostage, not through what they do, but through our hysterical responses, such as the militarization of the response and the attack on civil liberties – at least in the United States, less so in Britain – responses which almost exceed what was the case during the Cold War. In the United States, Atran warns that the foreign policy is at odds with its American Dream, into which the majority of its Muslims does buy into. I thank Deeyah Khan for making me aware of this video.

43 Historian Philip Blom suggests that one need not be a writer to imagine that in fifty years, an aging authoritarian fortress Europe will face an Orthodox Russian empire, and an Islamic caliphate. See Warum es um viel mehr geht als um Obergrenzen, ttt – titel thesen temperamente, Das Erste, January 31, 2016, www.daserste.de/information/wissen-kultur/ttt/sendung/hr/sendung-vom-31012016-100.html. See the full note in the pdf edition of this book.

44 Lindner, 2006c.

45 Lindner, 2010b.

46 "Scientists Warn of Perilous Climate Shift Within Decades, Not Centuries," by Justin Gillis, New York Times, March 22, 2016, www.nytimes.com/2016/03/23/science/global-warming-sea-level-carbon-dioxide-emissions.html?_r=0. See the full note in the pdf edition of this book.

47 Schell, 2003. Solomon, 2005. None is in a better position to describe the dilemma of "winning the battle and losing the peace" than those who are used to winning battles. Six former heads of the Shin Bet, Israel's secret service agency reflected publicly on their actions and decisions in The Gatekeepers, a 2012 documentary film by director Dror Moreh. See www.thegatekeepersfilm.com/.

48 Social scientist and social activist Riane T. Eisler, 1987, developed a cultural transformation theory where she describes how otherwise widely divergent societies all around the globe employ what she has named the dominator model of society, rather than the partnership model. She describes how, from the samurai of Japan to the Aztecs of Meso-America, people lived in very similar hierarchies of domination and under a rigidly male-dominant "strongman" rule, both in the family and state. Hierarchies of domination were maintained by a high degree of institutionalized and socially accepted violence, ranging from wife- and child-beating within the family to aggressive warfare at the larger tribal or national level.
See her most recent book Eisler, 2007. Philosopher Karl Popper, 1945, spoke of irrational tribal emotions to describe the adoration of strong men and hatred of people with a different ethnicity, religion, sexual orientation, or political ideology. See the full note in the pdf edition of this book.

49 Kuhn, 1962. See also The Prince by Machiavelli, 1532, where he observes:

There is nothing more difficult to take in hand, more perilous to conduct, or more uncertain in its success, than to take the lead in the introduction of a new order to things. Because the innovation has for enemies all those who have done well under the old conditions, and lukewarm defenders in those who may do well under the new.

See also the work of the founder of the Club of Rome, Aurelio Peccei, 1982, on shifting paradigms, or "making a civilizational, or evolutionary turn." I thank Dino Karabeg for reminding me of Peccei's work.

50 Marsden and Schmid, 2011, Table 1, p. 14. See the full note in the pdf edition of this book.

51 See among others:

- "Back from the 'Caliphate': Returnee Says IS Recruiting for Terror Attacks in Germany," by Hubert Gude and Wolf Wiedmann-Schmidt, Spiegel Online International, December 16, 2015, www.spiegel.de/international/world/german-jihadist-returns-from-syria-and-gives-testimony-a-1067764.html.
- "Activating the Sleepers: Islamic State Adopts a New Strategy in Europe," by Christoph Reuter in Beirut, Spiegel Online International, March 29, 2016, www.spiegel.de/international/world/islamic-state-adopts-a-new-approach-in-europe-a-1084489.html.

52 "Next Generation Bioweapons: The Technology Of Genetic Engineering Applied To Biowarfare And Bioterrorism," by Michael J. Ainscough, Colonel, USAF, The Counterproliferation Papers, Future Warfare Series Number 14, April 2002, www.fas.org/irp/threat/cbw/nextgen.pdf, p. 11: "The recent revolution in molecular biology may have incidentally unleashed a new threat to mankind, in the form of genetically engineered pathogens, which could be used to develop many new offensive biological weapons." Source: The Federation of American Scientists (FAS), Washington, DC, www.fas.org. The FAS was founded in 1945 by scientists who worked on the Manhattan Project to develop the first atomic bombs. The USAF Counterproliferation Center is located at the Air War College, Air University, Maxwell Air Force Base, Alabama, www.au.af.mil/au/awc/awcgate/awc-cps.htm. The Counterproliferation Papers Series was established by the USAF to provide information and analysis to assist the understanding of the U.S. national security policy-makers and USAF officers to help them better prepare to counter the threat from weapons of mass destruction.

53 See for recent discussions, "Monetizing Nature: Taking Precaution on a Slippery Slope," by Barbara Unmüssig, President of the Heinrich Böll Foundation in Berlin, Germany, Great Transition Initiative, www.greattransition.org/document/monetizing-nature-taking-precaution-on-a-slippery-slope. See the full note with relevant references in the pdf edition of this book.

54 Expert on corporate sustainability management, Mark W. McElroy, Center for Sustainable Organizations, in his contribution to the Great Transition Network (GTN) discussion on the topic of "Monetizing Nature," July 22, 2014.

55 Institute for Economics and Peace, 2015. Since September 11, 2001, an American residing in the United States was five thousand times more likely to be killed by a fellow citizen armed with a gun than by a "jihadist" (Bergen, 2016), while Nigeria and Kenya have suffered much more significantly, so has eastern India, where the Maoist "Naxalite" insurgency has raged since almost 50 years.
See also a map showing the concentration and intensity (combining fatalities and injuries) of terrorist attacks that occurred worldwide in the 2014 World Map of the Global Terrorism Database (GTB) of the University of Maryland's National Consortium for the Study of Terrorism and Responses to Terrorism (START), A Center of Excellence of the U.S. Department of Homeland Security, www.start.umd.edu/gtd/images/START_GlobalTerrorismDatabase_2014TerroristAttacksConcentrationIntensityMap.jpg.

56 Institute for Economics and Peace, 2015. The Global Terrorism Index is a partnership between the Institute for Economics and Peace, and the National Consortium for the Study of Terrorism and Responses to Terrorism (START) Center at the University of Maryland. The Global Terrorism Index is a comprehensive survey of key local trends, patterns and drivers of terrorism activity in 162 countries. It draws upon START's Global Terrorism Database, which has to date codified over 140,000 terrorist incidents. See the full note in the pdf edition of this book.

57 "At Geneva Conference, Ban Calls for Global Partnership to Prevent Violent Extremism," UN News Centre, April 8, 2016, www.un.org/apps/news/story.asp?NewsID=53638#.Vw1MwHrICgx.

58 Papadopoulos, 2006.

59 The estimate of about 170 million civilians killed in the twentieth century comes from political scientist Rudolph Joseph Rummel, 1994. Around 100 million deaths can be attributed to Stalin, Mao, and Hitler. The ratio would be 340 to one, if the death from non-state groups over the same period of time is calculated at around 500,000. See the full note in the pdf edition of this book.

60 See, for instance, "In West, ISIS Finds Women Eager to Enlist," by Steven Erlanger, New York Times, October 23, 2014, www.nytimes.com/2014/10/24/world/europe/as-islamists-seek-to-fill-ranks-more-western-women-answer-their-call.html.

61 "Four Key Reasons to Understand the Irresistible Attraction of Radical Islam," by Roberto Savio, Inter Press Service (IPS), November 3, 2014, www.ipsnews.net/2014/11/opinion-the-irresistible-attraction-of-radical-islam/.

62 "The Rise of ISIS is Fueled by Iraq's Deteriorating Economic Conditions," an interview with Sabah Alnasseri, The Real News, November 3, 2014, www.informationclearinghouse.info/article40135.htm.

63 "New Freedoms in Tunisia Drive Support for ISIS," by David D. Kirkpatrick, New York Times, October 21, 2014, www.nytimes.com/2014/10/22/world/africa/new-freedoms-in-tunisia-drive-support-for-isis.html?_r=0.

64 See reports from the United Nations and Amnesty International, summarized here:

- "The Islamic State of Sexual Violence," by Aki Peritz and Tara Maller, Foreign Policy, September 16, 2014, www.foreignpolicy.com/articles/2014/09/16/the_islamic_state_of_sexual_violence_women_rape_iraq_syria.
- "Gruesome Evidence of Ethnic Cleansing in Northern Iraq as Islamic State Moves to Wipe Out Minorities," Amnesty International, September 2, 2014, www.amnesty.org/en/news/gruesome-evidence-ethnic-cleansing-northern-iraq-islamic-state-moves-wipe-out-minorities-2014-0. See the full note in the pdf edition of this book.

65 The Scottish physiologist John Scott Haldane pioneered the use of "sentinel animals," which could be caged canaries or white mice, in mining operations in the 1890s.

66 I am indebted to peace linguist Francisco Gomes de Matos for suggesting the phrase psycho-geo-historical. See the full note in the pdf edition of this book.

67 Ruben Nelson, director of Foresight Canada, in his contribution to the Great Transition Network (GTN) discussion on the topic of "A Great Transition? Where We Stand," September 17, 2014, in response to Raskin, 2014.

68 Ibid.

69 Arie Nadler wrote about radical empathy and radical reconciliation. It is a privilege to have Arie Nadler as esteemed member in the global advisory board of our Human Dignity and Humiliation Studies fellowship. Arie Nadler, 2012, p. 304:

Consistent with Arendt's terminology, I propose to label forgiveness for "radical evil" as "radical forgiveness" and the intergroup reconciliation that may follow as "radical reconciliation." ... Such an understanding was expected to culminate in empathy with the perpetrator of "radical evil," that we propose to label as "radical empathy."

Hannah Arendt, 1961, in her discussion of the moral dilemmas presented by the Jewish Holocaust, suggested an extreme category of evil, more extreme than the Kantian definition of evil. The Kantian moral imperative defines it as evil if one treats others as means to achieving some end, rather than treating them as ends in themselves. Arendt felt that radical evil goes further. The victims of Auschwitz were neither means to some end, nor an end in themselves; they were regarded as valueless and useless objects that were thus superfluous and expandable. If this is so: can radical evil ever be forgiven, and if so, under what conditions? My experience as a therapist indicates that the dehumanization of the Jews that Arendt alludes to, a dehumanization that was also meted out to others, for instance, the Tutsi in the Rwandan genocide, is not to be taken at face value (Lindner, 2009e). To my observation, people who dehumanize others, do not really believe in their claim that their victims are useless objects. They only attempt to believe it, because it would be a relief for them to be able to believe it. Truly useless objects do not merit much attention and surely no hatred. Why was so much effort invested into eradicating these particular useless objects? Because they were not truly useless. I observe something very counterintuitive at the bottom of this dynamic, namely, admiration for the power of the enemy and fear of this power. Declaring a powerful enemy to be useless is an instrument of ultimate humiliation out of overwhelming fear, based on admiration. In this sense, the victims of such treatment are means to some end, and also an end in themselves. Understanding this, to me, is radical empathy. And there can be no forgiveness, not least because the notion of forgiveness entails the illusion of closure. Something much more difficult and radical than forgiveness is needed, in my view, namely, shouldering the radical collective responsibility, of all of us together, to create the proverbial village that it takes to raise a child. This means helping those among us who cannot muster the strength to respect those they admire and fear, to do so. This book is written with this radical sense of responsibility.

70 See the journal Critical Studies on Terrorism at www.tandfonline.com/loi/rter20#.U85bp7Hzkmw. See the full note in the pdf edition of this book.

71 The Psychology of Humiliation: Somalia, Rwanda / Burundi, and Hitler's Germany was my doctoral dissertation in social psychology at the Department of Psychology of the University of Oslo, Norway (Lindner, 2000a). See more chapters and papers by Lindner in full text on www.humiliationstudies.org/whoweare/evelin02.php.

72 Making Enemies: Humiliation and International Conflict, is Lindner's first book on dignity and humiliation and how we may envision a more dignified world, and it has been characterized as a path-breaking book and been honored as "Outstanding Academic Title" for 2007 in the USA by the journal Choice. See Lindner, 2006c. For more details, see www.humiliationstudies.org/whoweare/evelin/book/01.php.
Emotion and Conflict: How Human Rights Can Dignify Emotion and Help Us Wage Good Conflict is Lindner's second book. See Lindner, 2009b. For more details, see www.humiliationstudies.org/whoweare/evelin/book/02.php.

73 Gender, Humiliation, and Global Security: Dignifying Relationships from Love, Sex, and Parenthood to World Affairs is Lindner's third book, published by Praeger. See Lindner and Desmond Tutu (Foreword), 2010. For more details, see www.humiliationstudies.org/whoweare/evelin/book/03.php.

74 A Dignity Economy: Creating an Economy that Serves Human Dignity and Preserves Our Planet is Lindner's fourth book. See Lindner, 2012f. For more details, see www.humiliationstudies.org/whoweare/evelin/book/04.php.

75 Like physicist Paul Raskin, I take a "crude-look-at-the-whole" or a CLAW, as Murray Gell-Mann would call it: "It ascends to high orbit 'above the earth' and across the centuries – 'We must rise above the earth to fully understand the world in which we live' – Socrates. From there, we can take in the contours of the whole system, the interplay of subsystems, and the slow wheels of history," writes Paul Raskin in his contribution to the Great Transition Network Initiative discussion titled "Journey to Earthland: Making the Great Transition to Planetary Civilization," November 11, 2016, in response the comments on Raskin, 2016.

76 Henrich, et al., 2010. See also Lindner, 2001e.

77 Philosopher Thomas Nagel, 2012. Social change is only possible if we accept the interdependence of theory, research and action/practice, writes David Bargal, 2011a. Read more about David Bargal in note 169 in the Inspiring and Thought-Provoking Questions at the end of Section Three.

78 Lynch, 2013.

79 Gadamer, 1960/1989. Hans-Georg Gadamer (1900 – 2002) grew up and studied classics and philosophy in the University of Breslau, where also my mother was born in 1930. I thank Hroar Klempe for reminding me of Gadamer's work in April 2016. It is a privilege to have Hroar Klempe as esteemed member in the global advisory board of our Human Dignity and Humiliation Studies fellowship.

80 Charles Eisenstein, 2014, asks, "why is it assumed without much debate that no one can have direct access to the subjective experience of another person (or non-person)? This is obvious only if we conceive and experience ourselves as fundamentally separate from each other. There are other stories of self, however. We could see ourselves, as many spiritual traditions do, not as separate beings but as 'interbeings,'

not just interdependent but interexistent." It was a privilege to have Charles Eisenstein with us in our 2012 Workshop on Transforming Humiliation and Violent Conflict at Columbia University in New York City.

81 Laszlo, 2014. I thank Dino Karabeg for introducing us to Alexander Laszlo and thank him also for accepting to become a member in our Human Dignity and Humiliation Studies fellowship.

82 The notion of living translation is a methodological and theoretical framework originally developed by Pritzker, 2014, to understand the translation of Chinese medicine into practice in the United States. It means that ideologies of language, emotion, and personhood mediate embodied interactions, within which the meaning and implications of specific semiotic and linguistic registers are made and remade.

83 I thank philosopher Dagfinn Kåre Føllesdal for his support in formulating initial questions in 1996. I had the privilege of participating in his Ethics Programme of the Norwegian Research Council 1995 – 1996. Dagfinn Føllesdal's publications span many decades, see, among others, Føllesdal, 1988, Føllesdal and Depaul, 2015. See Dagfinn Føllesdal's reflections on humiliation and how I should approach the study of this phenomenon in the pdf edition of this book.

84 I am acutely aware that many of my readers may be disappointed with me as much as Daniel Goldhagen was when he read Peter Bergen and Michael Lind's account of terrorism. I resonate with Richard Landes' reaction to Goldhagen's thoughts in "Humiliation and Terrorism: Goldhagen's Analysis," by Richard Landes, The Augean Stables, March 27, 2007, www.theaugeanstables.com/2007/03/27/humiliation-and-terrorism-goldhagens-analysis/. See more in note 35 in this Preface.

85 In his book A Global Standard for Reporting Conflict, director of the University of Sydney's Centre for Peace and Conflict Studies, Jake Lynch, 2013, constructs an argument identifying what constitutes good journalism. See the full note in the pdf edition of this book.

86 It was a privilege to sit with Barnett Pearce on June 11, 2003, in the cafeteria of Teachers College at Columbia University, have lunch and intense conversations, years before his much too early passing, and to have him as esteemed member in the global advisory board of our Human Dignity and Humiliation Studies fellowship. See www.cmminstitute.net/about/about-cmm. See the full note in the pdf edition of this book.

87 "Life on Earth Is Dying," by Robert J. Burrowes, Human Wrongs Watch, December 6, 2016, https://human-wrongs-watch.net/2016/12/07/life-on-earth-is-dying/: "On the day that you read this article, 200 species of life on Earth (plants, birds, animals, fish, amphibians, insects, reptiles) will cease to exist. Tomorrow, another 200 species will vanish forever." For background reflections, see also Talking to the Enemy, by anthropologist Scott Atran, see note 42 in this Preface.

88 Sociologist Aaron Antonovsky researched how people manage stressful situations and stay well. See, among others, Antonovsky, 1979, 1987, Eriksson and Lindstrom, 2005.

89 Pinker, 2011.

90 See for the network's publications www.humiliationstudies.org/publications/publications.php, and for the author's www.humiliationstudies.org/whoweare/evelin02.php.

91 Escrigas, 2016.

92 "Nature's Solutions: The IUCN Perspective," interview with Julia Marton-Lefèvre, director general of the International Union for the Conservation of Nature, Great Transition Initiative, September 2014, http://greattransition.org/publication/nature-s-solutions-the-iucn-perspective.

93 Max-Neef, 2005, Abstract. I thank Catherine Odora Hoppers for reminding me of Max-Neef's article, in an invitation she kindly sent to me on August 9, 2014, to "Healing and Citizenship Education as the First Principles in the Philosophy of Higher Education," 7th South African Research Chairs Initiative (SARChI) Retreat, November 22–24, 2014, convened by the DST/NRF South African Research Chair in Development Education, funded by the Department of Science and Technology (DST), managed by the National Research Foundation (NRF), and hosted by the University of South Africa (UNISA). Catherine Odora Hoppers holds

a South African Research Chair in Development Education at the University of South Africa. It is a privilege to have her and her brother George as esteemed members in the global advisory board of our Human Dignity and Humiliation Studies fellowship.

94 Ruben Nelson, director of Foresight Canada, in his contribution to the Great Transition Network (GTN) discussion on the topic of "A Great Transition? Where We Stand," September 17, 2014, in response to Raskin, 2014.

95 Neumann, 2008b. See also Neumann, 2008a, 2009, 2010, Neumann and Smith, 2008, Neumann, et al., 2008. The International Centre for the Study of Radicalisation (ICSR), http://icsr.info/.

96 Rock, 2005.

97 Schmid, 2013, p. 56.

98 "When Nothing Is Cool," by Lisa Ruddick, Criticism, The Point, 2015, http://thepointmag.com/2015/criticism/when-nothing-is-cool, an abridged version of an article in Bammer and Boetcher Joeres, 2015. See also Jameson, 1991, Latour, 2004, and Jones, 2009. Ruddick asks why academia has not been able "to shift away from norms that make ruthlessness look like sophistication," and writes:

Some years ago Eve Kosofsky Sedgwick touched on this complex in her well-known essay on paranoid reading, where she identified a strain of "hatred" in criticism. Also salient is a more recent piece in which Bruno Latour has described how scholars slip from "critique" into "critical barbarity," giving "cruel treatment" to experiences and ideals that non-academics treat as objects of tender concern. Rita Felski's current work on the state of criticism has reenergized the conversation on the punitive attitudes encouraged by the hermeneutics of suspicion. And Susan Fraiman's powerful analysis of the "cool male" intellectual style favored in academia is concerned with many of the same patterns I consider here.

I thank Michael Britton for making me aware of this article. I thank Michael Britton for making me aware of this article. It is a privilege to have Michael Britton on the board of directors of our Human Dignity and Humiliation Studies fellowship.

99 Lindner, 2001i.

100 Arendt, 1963.

101 In Lindner and Desmond Tutu (Foreword), 2010, Gender, Humiliation, and Global Security, I highlight the notion of what I call big love.

102 "The Scourge of Illiteracy and the Authoritarian Nightmare," by Henry A. Giroux, Hamilton Spectator, April 25, 2016, www.thespec.com/opinion-story/6513400-the-scourge-of-illiteracy-and-the-authoritarian-nightmare/.

103 I resonate with Georg Lohmann, 2014, and his position that, in contrast to theories, which show meaning in a logical way, images and metaphors can make meaning palpable in an interpretative way, for instance, the meaning of the notion of a "good life." See the original in German in Lohmann, 2014, p. 11. Like Amitai Etzioni, I am not a legal scholar, and I am also not an expert in counterterrorism. I focus on the generalist perspective that I have developed throughout the course of my lifetime. See Etzioni, 2013, p. 334. See the full note in the pdf edition of this book.

104 I very much resonate with indigenous psychologist Louise Sundararajan when she uses the image of painting. She suggests that emotions have to be described with a "gentle paint brush, rather than to nail discreet emotions down, if there is such a thing, with codified labels and categorizations," Sundararajan, 2015, p. 75. See also the description of critical and post-structural inquiry given in "Thinking Critically About Critical Thinking: Whose Thinking, Whose Benefits?" by Hank Stam, professor of psychology at University of Calgary, for the Day in Qualitative Psychology, the opening meeting of the Special Interest Group (SIG) in Critical and Poststructural Psychology at the International Congress of Qualitative Inquiry,

University of Illinois at Urbana-Champaign, Wednesday, May 17, 2017, http://icqi.org/pre-congress-days/a-day-in-qualitative-psychology/. See also the description of the purpose and history of the Coalition for Critical Qualitative Inquiry (CCQI) Special Interest Group (SIG), http://icqi.org/pre-congress-days/critical-qualitative-inquiry/. See the full note in the pdf edition of this book.

105 Derrida, 1982.

106 I had the privilege of meeting Kichiro Hayashi, professor emeritus of Aoyama Gakuin University, Tokyo, at the 20th Annual Conference of SIETAR Japan, June 25–26, 2005, at Rikkyo University in Tokyo. I thank Adair Linn Nagata for inviting me to that conference. The title of Hayashi's contribution was "Management by dialogue (not by objective)!" He explained that it can create immense creativity to bring together people with very different styles and ask them NOT to compromise. When mutual contradictory and equally compelling stances clash, this can lead to new insights. Analogue high-context communication and value as in Japan tends to lead to organic organizations, while digital low-context communication and value leads to mechanistic organizations like in the West. Analogue and digital perception and communication, according to Hayashi, are zero-order beliefs or mental models (akin to related concepts, such as life-worlds, scripts, Husserl's concept of horizon, or Bachnik's of tacit meaning). A Japanese manager will always need more information because he wants to understand a situation like a holistic painting; he will, however, not be aware why he always asks for more information. See Agi and Hayashi, 2007, Hayashi, 2003. See also Noma and Crossman, 2012.

107 Dewey, 1931, p. 220.

108 The Norwegian philosopher Arne Næss developed the notion of the "depth of intention," the "depth of questioning" or "deepness of answers." Greater depth means continuing to ask questions at the point at which others stop asking. Næss writes "our depth of intention improves only slowly over years of study. There is an abyss of depth in everything fundamental," Næss, 1978, p. 143. Warwick Fox, in his paper "Intellectual Origins of the 'Depth' Theme in the Philosophy of Arne Næss," explains: "The extent to which a person discriminates along a chain of precizations (and, therefore, in a particular direction of interpretation) is a measure of their depth of intention, that is, the depth to which that person can claim to have understood the intended meaning of the expression," Fox, 2000, p. 5. See also Fox, 1992. Arne Næss was a pillar of the Foundational Conference of Human Dignity and Humiliation Studies at the Maison des Sciences de l'Homme de l'Homme in Paris in September 12–13, 2003, www.humiliationstudies.org/whoweare/annualmeeting/02.php. Arne Næss was a highly esteemed member in the global advisory board of the Human Dignity and Humiliation Studies fellowship.

109 Maggie MacLure, 2015, p. 8. See also Bruno Latour, 2004, and the full note in the pdf edition of this book.

110 See Belenky, et al., 1997a, Belenky, et al., 1997b, Clinchy, 1996. In connected knowing "one attempts to enter another person's frame of reference to discover the premises for the person's point of view," explain Clinchy and Zimmerman, 1985. See also Lindner and Desmond Tutu (Foreword), 2010.

111 Listening into voice is an expression coined by Linda Hartling and explained as follows in a personal communication on June 4, 2009:

The expression "listening into voice" draws our attention to the fact that human communication is a bi-directional experience. It is a phrase that encourages us to attune to the fundamental relational nature of speaking. It reminds us to look beyond the individualist myth that speaking is a one-way experience in which the speaker is solely responsible for communicating effectively. Speaking is interactive. It is a two-way experience in which both (or all) people participating in the relationship can chose to listen and engage in a way that will help others to effectively express and clarify their ideas.

112 Human Dignity and Humiliation Studies (HumanDHS), www.humiliationstudies.org.

113 Billig, 2013. See the full note in the pdf edition of this book.

114 The Neuroscience of Compassion, by Tania Singer, presentation given at the 2015 annual meeting of the World Economic Forum, with the theme "new global context," held in Davos, January, 21–24, 2015, published on March 9, 2015, https://youtu.be/n-hKS4rucTY, see also www.weforum.org. I thank Linda Hartling for making me aware of this video. In this presentation, Tania Singer explains that her aim is to improve global cooperation and to see how we can become better global citizens. Singer regards the training of perspective-taking as crucially important in a globalizing world, as it would improve conflict resolution skills and help to better understand out-groups, other cultures, and other religions. She and her colleagues define three different "modules" of compassion, which represent three different neurological networks, see also Klimecki, et al., 2014:

- Presence: attention and interoceptive awareness
- Affect: emotion/contagion, care/compassion/gratitude, prosocial motivation, dealing with difficult emotions, empathy (as different from compassion)
- Cognitive perspective-taking/mindreading: meta-cognition, perspective-taking on others, perspective-taking on others, mentalizing, theory of mind (the ability to attribute mental states, such as beliefs, intents, desires, pretending, knowledge, to oneself and others, and to understand that the mental states of others may be different to mine)

For Singer, empathy is a precursor to compassion, which can lead to antisocial behavior, for example, when healthcare workers or caregivers feel overwhelmed and burnt out by the suffering they face. Therefore, she advises to transform empathy into compassion, as compassion as a warm and caring emotion does not involve being invaded by the other persons' feelings.

The results of the trainings that Singer et al. have carried out show that the stable preferences that economists see as foundational (you are either altruistic or egoistic) are not as stable. Preferences can change, even at the level of the neurological networks. No longer can the neo-classicistic image of the Homo economicus be taken for granted. Singer works with Dennis Snower on caring economics and suggests that while the typical utility functions in economic theory is consumption, which, if emphasized, leads to selfish behavior, emphasizing care leads to prosocial behavior (see, among others, Ahrens and Snower, 2014).

Singer et al. differentiate seven motivation systems, based on psychological and biological knowledge, which if activated, influence decisions:

- Achievement is the motivation to be best
- Anger leads to aggressive behavior
- Consumption leads to selfish behavior
- Power leads to competitive behavior
- Fear and threat lead to defensive behavior
- Affiliation means that one wishes to belong to an in-group, which, of course, can turn out to be antisocial if it is built on out-group enmity
- Care leads to prosocial behavior

For policy making, if we wish for global cooperation, Singer recommends to use her results to create a context that activates the care motivation.

115 Holbrook, et al., 2015. This research shows that the experience of threat increases ideological responses. Innovative experiments using transcranial magnetic stimulation, a method to incapacitate specific regions of the brain temporarily, appear to show that both belief in God and prejudice towards immigrants can be reduced by directing magnetic energy into the brain, in this case, the posterior medial frontal cortex, a part of the brain associated with detecting problems and triggering responses. See also "Research that Is Simply Beyond Belief," by Alistair Keely, University of York, October 14, 2015, www.york.ac.uk/news-and-events/news/2015/research/psychologist-brian-magnetic/. See the full note in the pdf edition of this book.

116 The formulation "waging good conflict" was coined by Jean Baker Miller, 1976/1986.

117 Psychologist Carol Dweck, 1999, found that the challenges of life can be approached with an ego-oriented performance orientation or a task-oriented learning-mastery orientation, or as Linda Hartling would express it, a fixed mindset versus a growth mindset. Those with an ego orientation entertain an implicit entity theory of intelligence, they regard intelligence as fixed and try to look smart and avoid mistakes. Others think that intelligence is malleable, they adhere to an incremental theory of intelligence, and have an intrinsic motivation to achieve mastery in a task, desire to learn new things, even if they might get confused, make mistakes, and not look smart. Students with mastery goals are basically more successful. See also Dweck, 2007.

Psychologist David Yeager, et al., 2013, examined how holding a fixed mindset versus a growth mindset can influence interpretations of other people's hostile intent. In a meta-analytic study of eight independent samples that included 1,128 students, Yeager and his colleagues found that a fixed mindset predicted hostile attributions equally for males and females, and for students from communities with higher and lower levels of violence. "In a following study, Yeager found that by experimentally changing implicit theories to a more incremental growth mindset substantially reduced attributions of hostile intent in both urban and suburban schools. In a final study, Yeager found that a short-term intervention (two class sessions) could result in more benign intent attributions over an eight-month school year," in Hartling and Lindner, forthcoming.

118 Even after having been kidnapped in Syria, journalist Nicolas Hénin, 2015, calls for radical respect. See the full note in the pdf edition of this book.

119 Alex P. Schmid, 2013, p. 1:

The popularity of the concept of "radicalization" stands in no direct relationship to its actual explanatory power regarding the root causes of terrorism. It was brought into the academic discussion after the bomb attacks in Madrid and London in 2004 and 2005 by European policymakers who coined the term "violent radicalization." It has become a political shibboleth despite its lack of precision.

See also The Routledge Handbook of Terrorism Research that Alex Schmid edited, Schmid, 2011. See, furthermore, Hansen, 2012, who found that the radical rhetoric among people in Pakistan, was not accompanied by a desire for extremist action. David Hansen holds a Ph.D. in South Asian Studies from the University of Oslo in Norway, and foresees that the terror threat from the Taliban will get people to acknowledge that the Taliban's version of Islam is not theirs.

120 "Religious Fundamentalism-Extremism-Violence," by Johan Galtung, TRANSCEND Media Service, February 8, 2016, www.transcend.org/tms/2016/02/religious-fundamentalism-extremism-violence/.

121 See the influence of botanist Joseph Banks (1743 – 1820), who took part in Captain James Cook's first voyage (1768 – 1771). He was a major supporter of the internationalist nature of science, science for its own sake, in contrast to science being subjugated to the competition for profit.

122 See Foucault, 1957a, and Foucault, 1957b. I thank Howard Richards for reminding us of this part of Foucault's work in Lecture Two of Beyond Foucault: The Rise of Indigenous Subjugated Knowledges, by Howard Richards in Pretoria, South Africa, May 4, 2013, http://youtu.be/IcilckWWE1Y. See for more Richards, et al., 2015a. It is a privilege to have Howard Richards, Catherine Odora Hoppers, and her brother George as esteemed members in the global advisory board of our Human Dignity and Humiliation Studies fellowship.

123 Lecture Two of Beyond Foucault: The Rise of Indigenous Subjugated Knowledges, by Howard Richards in Pretoria, South Africa, May 4, 2013, http://youtu.be/IcilckWWE1Y.

124 "Failure to Replicate: Crisis or Chrysalis for Psychological Science?" by Lisa M. Osbeck, submitted to the APA Annual Convention in Denver, August 4–7, 2016, with a Cross-Divisional symposium devoted to the replication crisis in psychology. See Open Science Collaboration (OSC), 2015. See the full note in the pdf edition of this book.

125 Psychologists Jansz and Drunen, 2004, emphasize "that the positivist view," far from being a correct reflection of the history of psychology, is first and foremost an article of faith, since psychology has contributed to oppression as much as to social progress. See also Lindner, 2001e. See the full note with relevant references in the pdf edition of this book.

126 Open Science Collaboration (OSC), 2015.

127 See, for example, Lindner, 2001e. See also Lindner and Desmond Tutu (Foreword), 2010.

128 See for the conferences of Human Dignity and Humiliation Studies, www.humiliationstudies.org/whoweare/annualmeetings.php.

129 Robert Elliot Pollack, Ph.D., is a biology professor at the Department of Biological Sciences, and director of the Center for the Study of Science and Religion at Columbia University. See the full note in the pdf edition of this book.

130 Robert Pollack, 1999, explains how the human brain continually filters the present through memories and emotions of the past. It takes the brain a second to process perceptions, and, therefore, what we think is the present actually happened a second ago. In addition, painful memories are being repressed. See also Lindner, 2009b. See the full note in the pdf edition of this book.

131 Ibid.

132 "For Thanksgiving: What We Have to Do With 'Twelve Years a Slave,' the Movie," by Carol Smaldino, Huffington Post, November 26, 2013, www.huffingtonpost.com/carol-smaldino/for-thanksgiving-what-we-_b_4344576.html. Carol Smaldino is an esteemed member in our Human Dignity and Humiliation Studies fellowship. See the full note in the pdf edition of this book.

133 Cristina Escrigas, 2016, describes this trend most cogently.

134 Journalist James Risen, 2014. See also "In the Darkness of Dick Cheney," by Mark Danner, The New York Review of Books, March 6, 2014, www.nybooks.com/articles/archives/2014/mar/06/darkness-dick-cheney/, where Danner reviews The World According to Dick Cheney, a film directed by R. J. Cutler and Greg Finton, In My Time: A Personal and Political Memoir, by Dick Cheney, with Liz Cheney, and Heart: An American Medical Odyssey, by Dick Cheney and Jonathan Reiner, MD, with Liz Cheney. Danner explains: "At close range Cheney, still in his early thirties, had seen the secret organs of executive power, notably the CIA, exposed to the light, humiliated, leashed. If it was true that 'after 9/11, the gloves came off,' Cheney, as a young and unlikely power in the Nixon and Ford White Houses, had had a front-row seat to observe the methods by which Congress first put those gloves on." See the full note with relevant references in the pdf edition of this book.

135 "Instead of Bombing IS (Part B)," by Jan Øberg, Transnational Foundation for Peace and Future Research (TFF) PressInfo # 281, October 7, 2014, http://blog.transnational.org/2014/10/tff-pressinfo-282-instead-of-bombing-isis-concrete-proposals-part-b/. It is a privilege to have Jan Øberg as esteemed member in the global advisory board of the Human Dignity and Humiliation Studies fellowship. See also Stiglitz and Bilmes, 2008, and "Post-9/11 Wars Have Cost Nearly $5 Trillion (and Counting): Report," by Nadia Prupis, Common Dreams, September 13, 2016, www.commondreams.org/news/2016/09/13/post-911-wars-have-cost-nearly-5-trillion-and-counting-report.

136 I forego full-time employment, for instance, as a professor at a national university, as this would lock me into a national interest context. This book is being supported by the independent Non-Fiction Writers and Translators Organisation in Norway by a seven-months stipend given in 2011.

137 Find my personal reflections, written down on October 16, 2013, in the full note in the pdf edition of this book.

138 Find the full quote from a letter I wrote to Linda Hartling on October 24, 2013, in the full note in the pdf edition of this book.

139 See reflections on excluded knowledges in the dialogue that Howard Richards, Catherine Odora Hoppers, and Lindner conducted after Richards' Lecture Two of Beyond Foucault: The Rise of Indigenous Subjugated Knowledges, given in Pretoria, South Africa, May 4, 2013, http://youtu.be/IcilckWWE1Y, and http://youtu.be/emYEFqqTOoE. See for more Richards, et al., 2015a. It is a privilege to have Howard Richards, Catherine Odora Hoppers, and her brother George as esteemed members in the global advisory board of our Human Dignity and Humiliation Studies fellowship.

140 Ross, 1995. It was a privilege to have Lee Ross as my doctoral advisor, and later as esteemed member of the first hour in the global advisory board of our Human Dignity and Humiliation Studies fellowship.

141 Schmid, 2013, p. iv. See the full note in the pdf edition of this book.

142 "The Poisoned Poor" was the title of a panel discussion in 2015 at the United Nations in New York. See the full note in the pdf edition of this book.

143 Schmid, 2013, p. 50.

144 Neumann, 2010.

145 Schmid, 2013, p. 39.

146 Freire, 1968/1970, 1968/1973, and Morais, 1979, 1983. See Andersson and Richards, 2013, Chapter IV, p. 15, of the unpublished manuscript:

De Morais, in contradistinction to Freire, sets forward not two but three levels of awareness. He adds to Freire's two, which are: the naïve level and the critical level. The third is the organizational level of awareness. At the naïve level a person is aware of problems but is unable to understand their cause (and so may blame God or the Fates). The critically conscious person is able to identify the factors responsible for problems, and their inter-relationship. Organizational awareness is reached when the person has the ability to act together with others to address a problem or attain particular results. Organizational awareness manifests what de Morais calls a "methodological rationality."

147 Fanon, 1952/1967, 1961/1963.

148 See also Slavoj Žižek, 2012. See the full note in the pdf edition of this book.

149 Space Exploration – A Powerful Symbol of Global Cooperation, Jim Zimmerman, NASA, interviewed by Susan T. Coleman, The Peacebuilding Podcast, December 13, 2016, http://us11.campaign-archive1.com/?u=e5c2110f5cc4fe346c79bf3d1&id=06298a46ca&e=e7c4dd8362. I thank Judit Révész for making me aware of this interview.

150 See http://thebulletin.org/timeline. See also the William J. Perry Project (www.wjperryproject.org) that was created by the former U.S. secretary of defense to work toward a world in which nuclear weapons are never used again.

151 Becker, 2016.

152 Researchers Jennifer Doudna and Emmanuelle Charpentier independently explored the CRISPR/Cas system in bacteria to learn how bacteria create their immune defenses. The U.S. Intelligence director James Clapper warns that this new technology can be used as a biological weapon of mass destruction: "Statement for the Record: Worldwide Threat Assessment of the US Intelligence Community, Senate Armed Services Committee," by James R. Clapper, director of National Intelligence February 9, 2016, www.dni.gov/files/documents/SASC_Unclassified_2016_ATA_SFR_FINAL.pdf. See the full note in the pdf edition of this book.

153 See the Geneva Conference on Preventing Violent Extremism – The Way Forward, April 7–8, 2016, Palais des Nations, Geneva, Switzerland, www.un.org/counterterrorism/ctitf/en/geneva-conference-preventing-violent-extremism, and its "Plan of Action to Prevent Violent Extremism," Seventieth session, Agenda items 16 and 117, Culture of peace, The United Nations Global Counter-Terrorism Strategy, Report

of the Secretary-General, www.un.org/en/ga/search/view_doc.asp?symbol=A/70/674&referer=/english/&Lang=E.

154 Ury, 1999, p. xvii. I thank William Ury for his support since I first met him in 1999. I had the privilege of participating in the launch of the Coexistence Initiative in Belfast in 1999.

155 "Gorgeous Glimpses of Calamity," by Michael Benson, New York Times, August 16, 2013, www.nytimes.com/2013/08/18/opinion/sunday/gorgeous-glimpses-of-calamity.html?_r=0. Michael Benson is a photographer and filmmaker. See the full note in the pdf edition of this book.

156 Lindner, 2012f.

157 "The Degrowth Alternative," by Giorgos Kallis, The Great Transition Initiative, www.greattransition.org/publication/the-degrowth-alternative. See also note 295 in the Introduction, and note 114 in the Inspiring Questions to Section Two.

158 Bauman, 2000.

159 "The Charitable-Industrial Complex," by Peter Buffett, son of investor Warren Buffett, New York Times, July 26, 2013, www.nytimes.com/2013/07/27/opinion/the-Charitable-industrial-complex.html?hpw&_r=0. See also "The White-Savior Industrial Complex," by Teju Cole, The Atlantic, March 21, 2012, www.theatlantic.com/international/archive/2012/03/the-white-savior-industrial-complex/254843/. See, furthermore, Fontan, 2012, and Lindner, 2010b. For the topic of conservation, see "A Challenge to Conservationists: Can We Protect Natural Habitats Without Abusing the People Who Live in Them?," by Mac Chapin, World Watch Magazine, November/December 2004, Volume 17, Number 6, www.worldwatch.org/epublish/1/102. See the full note in the pdf edition of this book.

160 Michael Britton in a personal communication on June 16, 2013.

161 Bhaskar, 2008.

162 Taylor, 1971, 1993a, Searle, 1995. Searle speaks of "institutional facts," for instance, with respect to property rights and contract rights, see Manicas, 2006. See, furthermore, Porpora, 1993, Donati and Archer, 2015, and Richards, 2004. I thank Howard Richards for including me into his life-long journey of reflecting on social change.

163 Wallerstein, 1974–1989. See also Harvey, 2005. Howard Richards in a personal communication on October 23, 2016: "According to Immanuel Wallerstein the global economy is the one and only object of study of the social sciences today; everything else is caught up in a web of causes and effects where the structure of the global economy is the principal cause." See also Lindner, 2012f. Others use a slightly different terminology, for instance, Johan Galtung, 1976, when he speaks of actor, system, and structure, where the actors may be persons, districts, nations or regions, and a system is a certain sector of social life, such as work, education, economic transactions, family life, while a structure ties several systems together, meaning that actors interact with each other in more than one context: a society is a structure that is self-sufficient and can survive even if cut off from the rest. See the full note in the pdf edition of this book.

164 "The Rational Optimist," review by Samuel Brittan, The Financial Times, June 12, 2010, www.ft.com/intl/cms/s/2/b2cbb506-74de-11df-aed7-00144feabdc0.html#axzz3Cq4fyzJ8.

165 Lindner, 2014c, 2017. I follow sociologist Alain Touraine, when he asks how a transnational economy can be reconciled with the reality of introverted communities. His explanation is that a few social rules of mutual tolerance and respect for personal freedom are not sufficient and that deeper bonds must and can be forged. Touraine argues that people can and should create a personal life-project and construct an active self or "subject," with the ultimate aim to form meaningful social and political institutions. See Touraine, 2000, and Touraine, 2003.
In his work, Alain Touraine focuses on social and political conflict. I would have liked to attend the debate moderated by Michel Wieviorka in Paris in 2014, see Castells, et al., 2014. It is a privilege for me to be

associated with the Maison des Sciences de l'Homme in Paris since 2001, initially through social psychologist Serge Moscovici. The first two conferences of Human Dignity and Humiliation Studies were inspired and hosted by Hinnerk Bruhns, and supported by Michel Wieviorka, at the Maison des Sciences in 2003 and 2004, see www.humiliationstudies.org/whoweare/annualmeetings.php. It is a privilege to have Hinnerk Bruhns and other renowned colleagues from France as esteemed members in the global advisory board of our Human Dignity and Humiliation Studies fellowship.

166 Inga Bostad, professor and director of the Norwegian Centre for Human Rights coined the term Dignihome on June 2, 2014, in her introduction to Lindner's talk "Dignity, Humiliation, and Terrorism: How to Think Globally." At first, we called our initiative Dialogue Homes, then came Inga Bostad's Dignihomes, and now we sometimes also use the term Dignilogue Homes. See www.humiliationstudies.org/whoweare/whoweare.php. Philosopher Inga Bostad is a disciple of Arne Næss and a highly esteemed member in the global advisory board of the Human Dignity and Humiliation Studies fellowship. She hosted the launch of the World Dignity University initiative on June 24, 2011, in her capacity as Vice-Rector of the University of Oslo. It is a privilege to have Inga Bostad as esteemed member in the global advisory board of our Human Dignity and Humiliation Studies fellowship.

167 Forster, 1910.

168 Bernard Werber, science fiction writer, in L'Encyclopédie du savoir relatif et absolu or Livre secret des fourmis. English: The Encyclopedia of Absolute and Relative Knowledge.

Acknowledgments

1 For my global life path see www.humiliationstudies.org/whoweare/evelin.php. See also Lindner, 2016a, 2017.

Introduction

See additional material at www.humiliationstudies.org/whoweare/evelin/book/05.php.

1 Berlin, 1997, p. 129: "The pattern, and it alone, brings into being and causes to pass away and confers purpose, that is to say, value and meaning, on all there is. To understand is to perceive patterns. … To make intelligible is to reveal the basic pattern."

2 Ury, 1999, p. xvii.

3 Allen White, Senior Fellow of the Tellus Institute for a Great Transition, see www.tellus.org/about/people#, in his contribution to the Great Transition Network (GTN) discussion on the topic of "Common Wealth Trusts: Structures of Transition," July 13, 2015.

4 Maalouf, 2009. I thank Mai-Bente Bonnevie for making me aware of this book. It is a privilege to have Mai-Bente Bonnevie, as well as her partner Fredrik Heffermehl, as esteemed members in the global advisory board of our Human Dignity and Humiliation Studies fellowship. See Heffermehl, 2010.
See a summary of the book on CDurable.info, http://cdurable.info/Amin-Maalouf-Le-dereglement-du-monde,1660.html. Translated from French by Lindner:

> The central thesis of this long essay could be summarized as follows: the maladjustment of the world has less to do with a "clash of civilizations" and more with the simultaneous depletion of civilization. Humankind has reached its "moral threshold of incompetence." The age of ideological divisions and

its debates is now followed by divisions of identity, where there is no more debate. Islam and the West: both discourses have their theoretical consistency, but each, in practice, betrays its own ideals. The West is unfaithful to its own values, which disqualifies it in the eyes of the people it claims to acculturate to democracy. The Arab-Muslim world no longer has neither the legitimacy of the family nor the patriotic legitimacy around which it was historically structured. Living in humiliation and regressive nostalgia for its "Golden Age," the era of Islamism succeeding the era of nationalism, it is condemned to a headlong rush into radicalism. These "symmetrical maladjustments" are only one element of a broader global derangement that requires humanity to come together to deal with the emergencies, like climatic degradation which threatens all peoples. And if prehistory of humanity ended before our eyes, opening in the great convulsions, a new chapter of human history begins?

See the French original in the full note in the pdf edition of this book.

5 The ship of fools is an allegory, originating from Plato, 360 BCE.

6 "When the End of Human Civilization Is Your Day Job," by John H. Richardson, Esquire, July 7, 2015, www.esquire.com/news-politics/a36228/ballad-of-the-sad-climatologists-0815/.

7 "Tactical Nuclear Weapons in Europe," by John Scales Avery and the Danish Pugwash Group, TRANSCEND Media Service, March 23, 2015, www.transcend.org/tms/2015/03/tactical-nuclear-weapons-in-europe/.

8 "Anwohner wollen Stilllegung von Grohnde erzwingen – Atomkraftgegner drohen mit Klage," by Peter Mlodoch, Weser Kurier, March 26, 2015, www.weser-kurier.de/region_artikel,-Atomkraftgegner-drohen-mit-Klage-_arid,1088361.html. On January 31, 2015, regional groups met in Hannover to prepare for the 4th anniversary of the Fukushima disaster and for subsequent activities. Also in Hannover, on March 14, 2015, under the motto "Fukushima warns! – Decommission the AKW Grohnde," the Regional Conference Grohnde presented lectures and held discussion sessions covering the current situation in Fukushima, an inventory of nuclear waste, and informed about the legal action against the nuclear Grohnde. See "Regionalkonferenz Grohnde: Fukushima-Aktion am 14. März in Hannover," http://ag-schacht-konrad.de/index.php?option=com_content&task=view&id=1495&Itemid=280.

9 It is important to note that a global citizens movement, or global civil society, does not mean NGOs that are funded by interests that stand against the creation of global dignity for all. See Robinson, 2017. Anthropologist David Harvey, scholar of critical geography, speaks of "co-revolution," "co-evolution," "subversion," "the movement," the "Party of Indignation," or a "slow movement across the spheres." See the full note in the pdf edition of this book.

10 Publius Flavius Vegetius Renatus and Reeve, 2004.

11 Lindner and Desmond Tutu (Foreword), 2010.

12 Active SETI, also known as messaging to extraterrestrial intelligence (METI), consists of sending signals into space in the hope that they will be picked up by an alien intelligence. Stephen Hawking made a documentary series for the Discovery Channel, and he advises, "If aliens visit us, the outcome would be much as when Columbus landed in America, which didn't turn out well for the Native Americans," see "Stephen Hawking Takes a Hard Line on Aliens," by Leo Hickman, The Guardian, April 26, 2010, www.theguardian.com/commentisfree/2010/apr/26/stephen-hawking-issues-warning-on-aliens.

13 Ruben Nelson in his contribution to the Great Transition Network Initiative discussion titled "Journey to Earthland: Making the Great Transition to Planetary Civilization," October 5, 2016, in response to Raskin, 2016. See the full note in the pdf edition of this book.

14 John Fullerton, now a new member of the Club of Rome, in his contribution to the Great Transition Network Initiative discussion titled "Journey to Earthland: Making the Great Transition to Planetary Civilization," October 31, 2016, in response to Raskin, 2016. See the full note in the pdf edition of this book.

15 Toffler, 1970. I thank Qin Shao for reminding me of Toffler's book Future Shock. It is a privilege to have Qin Shao as esteemed member in the global advisory board of our Human Dignity and Humiliation Studies fellowship.

16 "The Call of the Nation," by Uri Avnery, Human Wrongs Watch, December 10, 2016, https://human-wrongs-watch.net/2016/12/13/the-call-of-the-nation/.

17 Lindner, 2006c.

18 Ury, 1999, p. 108. It is a privilege to have William Ury as esteemed member in the global advisory board of our Human Dignity and Humiliation Studies fellowship.

19 In my work, I apply the ideal-type approach as described by sociologist Max Weber, 1904/1949. See also Coser, 1977, p. 224. See the full note in the pdf edition of this book.

20 Clearly, there is a connection between equality and equal dignity – the connection is entailed in the human rights stipulation that equal chances and enabling environments for all are necessary to protect human dignity.

21 Discourse analyst Michael Karlberg, 2013, explains that, indeed, such a new social order would not be without hierarchy. Hierarchy is, however, no longer a structure of dominance or an outcome of power-seeking behavior: "Organic hierarchy provides the organization, coordination, and efficiency by which the diverse potentialities of autonomous individuals can be realized and their energies can be applied in productive ways that promote the common good."

22 Fuller and Gerloff, 2008. It is a privilege to have Robert Fuller as esteemed members in the global advisory board of the Human Dignity and Humiliation Studies fellowship.

23 I had the privilege of participating in the launch of the Coexistence Initiative in Belfast in 1999, and was impressed by the various ways coexistence can be conceptualized and criticized. See also Weiner and (Foreword), 1998.

24 Neoliberaler Kahlschlag – Butterwegge: Grundeinkommen wäre Ende des Sozialstaats, 3sat, October 13, 2016, www.3sat.de/page/?source=/makro/magazin/doks/189268/index.html.

25 Hartling and Lindner, 2017.

26 Francisco Gomes de Matos in a personal communication on June 29, 2010.

27 Schell, 2003.

28 Lindner and Desmond Tutu (Foreword), 2010. See a review by social psychologist and Kurt Lewin expert David Bargal, 2011b. Read more about David Bargal in note 169 in the Inspiring and Thought-Provoking Questions at the end of Section Three.

29 See Desmond Tutu in Lindner and Desmond Tutu (Foreword), 2010, p. vii. See also an interview with Sharon Davis titled Moment of Truth, ABC Radio National "Background Briefing," May 4, 1997, www.abc.net.au/rn/talks/bbing/stories/s10597.htm.

30 It is a privilege to have Michael Britton as on the board of directors of Human Dignity and Humiliation Studies.

31 Arendt, 1961.

32 See Arie Nadler, 2012, p. 304. See more in note 69 in the Preface.

33 Lindner, 2009e.

34 In 2005, U.S. policymakers in the second Bush administration sought to replace the bellicose "Global War on Terror" (GWOT) with lower-key concepts like "Struggle Against Violent Extremism" (SAVE), explains Alex Schmid, 2013, p. 10. Under the Obama administration it became a "war with al Qaeda." See the full note in the pdf edition of this book.

35 In many publications, the question is being asked why states and international relations organizations participate in the "global war on terrorism." See, among many, Beyer, 2010.

36 Berlin, 1997, p. 129: "The pattern, and it alone, brings into being and causes to pass away and confers purpose, that is to say, value and meaning, on all there is. To understand is to perceive patterns. … To make intelligible is to reveal the basic pattern."

37 See, among others, Staub, 1989, 1993, 2012, 2015.

38 Eisler, 1987. See note 48 in the Preface.

39 Ibid.

40 Since I wrote the book A Dignity Economy, the topic of inequality has become ever more pressing and widely discussed. See Lindner, 2012f. Already when I wrote my book, everybody told me about Richard Wilkinson's and Kate Pickett's work. See, among others, Wilkinson, 2005, and Wilkinson and Pickett, 2009. See also https://youtu.be/zYDzA9hKCNQ. See, furthermore, the Equality Trust at www.equalitytrust.org.uk. Since then, more authors have become household names, such as Stiglitz, 2012, Thomas Piketty, 2013/2014, Atkinson, 2015, or Frank, 2016. See also a publication by the Organisation for Economic Co-operation and Development (OECD), 2015, for why all benefit from more equality. See also the full note 1 of Chapter 11 in the pdf edition of this book.

41 See Howard Richards' observation that amid all the ups and downs there is "a generative causal power at work pushing toward the down side, even while other generative causal powers are pushing on the up side," see "Individual and Human Rights," by Howard Richards, Chileufú, October 20, 2016, http://chileufu.cl/individual-and-human-rights/.

42 See, among many other relevant publications, Ahmed, 2017. See the full note in the pdf edition of this book.

43 Der Publizist Sebastian Haffner (1907 – 1999) im "Sonntagsgespräch" mit Guido Knopp, Zweites Deutsches Fernsehen, December 20, 1987, www.zdf.de/ZDFzeit/Mein-Kampf-mit-Hitler-26139114.html. See also Haffner, 1978. See the full note in the pdf edition of this book.

44 Human security, rather than national security, means "freedom from fear" and "freedom from want" for human beings, rather than the security of states. See "Human Security in Theory and Practice: An Overview of the Human Security Concept and the United Nations Trust Fund for Human Security, United Nations Human Security Unit, www.un.org/humansecurity/sites/www.un.org.humansecurity/files/human_security_in_theory_and_practice_english.pdf. See also Archer, 2005, Elworthy and Rifkind, 2005, Mack and Nielsen, 2010, Reardon and Hans, 2010. See, furthermore, the Human Security Report Project by the Human Security Research Group, www.hsrgroup.org/human-security-reports/human-security-report.aspx.

45 See note 149 in the Preface.

46 This is known to be a Chinese Proverb. See the full note in the pdf edition of this book.

47 See the work on relational-cultural theory conducted at the Jean Baker Miller Training Institute (www.jbmti.org), at Wellesley Centers for Women, Wellesley College (www.wcwonline.org). Linda Hartling is the former Associate Director of the JBMTI, and now the director of Human Dignity and Humiliation Studies. See her doctoral dissertation on humiliation, Hartling, 1995, and recent work, for instance, Hartling and Lindner, 2016a, 2017.
Psychiatrist Robert J. Waldinger became known for a TED talk that went viral: What Makes a Good Life? Lessons from the Longest Study on Happiness, December 2015, www.ted.com/talks/robert_waldinger_what_makes_a_good_life_lessons_from_the_longest_study_on_happiness. He talks about his findings from a 75-year-long Harvard study on adult happiness. This study rendered three main lessons about relationships: The first lesson is that social connections are beneficial for

health, while health declines when loneliness and isolation prevail. Isolated people live shorter lives than people who are not lonely. Unfortunately, Waldinger notes, at any given time, more than one in five Americans will report that they are lonely. The second lesson is that it is not the quantity of one's close relationship that counts, but the quality. Only warm relationships are protective. Getting a divorce may promote health more than living in a high-conflict marriage, for example. The third lesson is that good relationships protect both body and brain. People in unsafe relationships experience earlier memory decline. I thank Linda Hartling for making me aware of Waldinger's TED talk. See also Schwarzenbach, 2009, on Civic Friendship. It is a privilege to have Sibyl Schwarzenberg as esteemed member in the global advisory board of our Human Dignity and Humiliation Studies fellowship.

48 Correspondent inference theory indicates that we infer that other people's actions correspond to their underlying personality and disposition. Some psychologists have used the terms correspondence bias and fundamental attribution error interchangeably. See, among others, Gilbert, 1998. Others theorize that they are independent phenomena, with the correspondence bias resulting from a much wider range of processes. See, among others, Gawronski, 2004, Gawronski and Bodenhausen, 2006. See also note 93 in Chapter 1.

49 "Make Russia Great Again? Aleppo and a Plea from Another World," by Juan Francisco Lobo, openDemocracy, December 24, 2016, www.opendemocracy.net/juan-francisco-lobo/make-russia-great-again-aleppo-and-plea-from-another-world.

50 In my work, I apply the ideal-type approach as described by sociologist Max Weber, 1904/1949. See also Coser, 1977, p. 224. See the full note in the pdf edition of this book.

51 Lindner, 2006c.

52 Lindner and Desmond Tutu (Foreword), 2010, pp. 84–88. Honor killings have been reported in many parts of the world, including Bangladesh, Britain, Brazil, Ecuador, Egypt, India, Israel, Italy, Jordan, Pakistan, Morocco, Sweden, Turkey, and Uganda. There is a vast amount of literature addressing honor killing. See, for instance, a summary and evaluation of qualitative research about honor killings, United Nations Population Fund (UNFPA) and United Nations Development Programme (UNDP), 2005. Many prefer to use the term femicide rather than honor killing, since the main focus is on killing women. The issue of femicide is much larger, see, among others, "Female Infanticide Worldwide: The Case for Action by the UN Human Rights Council," by the Asian Centre for Human Rights (ACHR), New Delhi, June 2016, www.stopfemaleinfanticide.org/files/Femalefoeticideworldwide.pdf.

53 Lindner, 2016b.

54 Derrida, 1982.

55 Karlberg, 2013, p. 1.

56 Bateson, 1954, is often credited for the initial concept of an interpretive frame. He pointed out that discrete communicative acts are rendered meaningful within larger interpretive frames. Building on these insights, Goffman, 1974, conceptualized frames as cognitive schemata or mental frameworks that shape our perceptions, interpretations, and representations of reality; mentally organize our experience; and provide normative guides for our actions. Following this work by Bateson and Goffman, the concept of frames and framing has been conceptualized with different nuances across the social and psychological sciences. See the full note in the pdf edition of this book.

57 The Psychology of Humiliation: Somalia, Rwanda / Burundi, and Hitler's Germany was my doctoral dissertation in social psychology at the Department of Psychology of the University of Oslo, Norway. See Lindner, 2000a. See more chapters and papers by Lindner in full text on www.humiliationstudies.org/whoweare/evelin02.php.

58 Making Enemies: Humiliation and International Conflict is Lindner's first book on dignity and humiliation and how we may envision a more dignified world, and it has been characterized as a path-

breaking book and been honored as "Outstanding Academic Title" for 2007 in the USA by the journal Choice. See Lindner, 2006c. It came out in 2006 in Praeger, with a Foreword by the father of the field of conflict resolution, Morton Deutsch. The book discusses dignity and humiliation and how we may envision a more dignified world. It first lays out a theory of the mental and social dynamics humiliation and proposes the need for "egalization" (the undoing of humiliation) for a healthy global society. It then presents chapters on the role of misunderstandings in fostering feelings of humiliation; the role of humiliation in international conflict; and the relationship of humiliation to terrorism and torture. It concludes with a discussion of how to defuse feelings of humiliation and create a dignified world. See more details on www.humiliationstudies.org/whoweare/evelin/book/01.php.
Emotion and Conflict: How Human Rights Can Dignify Emotion and Help Us Wage Good Conflict is Lindner's second book. See Lindner, 2009b. It is about dignity and how realizing its promise can help improve the human condition at all levels – from micro to meso to macro levels. The book came out in Praeger in 2009, with a Foreword by the father of the field of conflict resolution, Morton Deutsch. It uses a broad historical lens that captures all of human history, from its hunter-gatherer origins to the promise of a globally united knowledge society in the future. It emphasizes the need to recognize and leave behind malign cultural, social, and psychological effects of the past. The book calls upon the world community, academics and lay people alike, to own up to the opportunities offered by increasing global interdependence. See www.humiliationstudies.org/whoweare/evelin/book/02.php.

59 Gender, Humiliation, and Global Security: Dignifying Relationships from Love, Sex, and Parenthood to World Affairs is Lindner's third book, published by Praeger. See Lindner and Desmond Tutu (Foreword), 2010. Archbishop Desmond Tutu kindly contributed with a Foreword (asked for a prepublication endorsement, he kindly offered to contribute with a Foreword). The book rounds off with an Afterword by Linda Hartling, director of Human Dignity and Humiliation Studies, in honor of Jean Baker Miller and Don Klein. For more details, see www.humiliationstudies.org/whoweare/evelin/book/03.php.
The book was "highly recommended" by Choice (in July 2010). See the full note in the pdf edition of this book.

60 A Dignity Economy: Creating an Economy that Serves Human Dignity and Preserves Our Planet is Lindner's fourth book. See Lindner, 2012f. It is the first publication of Dignity Press, published in its imprint World Dignity University Press, with a Foreword by Linda Hartling, director of Human Dignity and Humiliation Studies, and Ulrich Spalthoff, director of Dignity Press. See more on www.dignitypress.org/wdu-press-books/dignity-economy. See brief endorsements on www.humiliationstudies.org/whoweare/evelin/book/04.php#endorsement.

61 Bateson, 1954. See also Chong and Druckman, 2007.

62 Goffman, 1974.

63 Snow and Benford, 1988, p. 213. See also Ryan and Gamson, 2006, p.14: "Like a picture frame, an issue frame marks off some part of the world. Like a building frame, it holds things together. It provides coherence to an array of symbols, images, and arguments, linking them through an underlying organizing idea that suggests what is essential – what consequences and values are at stake. We do not see the frame directly, but infer its presence by its characteristic expressions and language. Each frame gives the advantage to certain ways of talking and thinking, while it places others 'out of the picture.'"

64 Bhaskar, 2008.

65 See note 162 in the Preface.

66 See note 163 in the Preface.

67 Richards and Andersson, 2017, Introduction.

68 Stephan Feuchtwang in a personal communication on November 14, 2002.

69 Anthony Marsella speaks of fractionation, hegemonic globalization, and recommends Lifeism, in "Addressing Fractionation: Principles for Arbitrating the 'Common Good,'" Anthony J. Marsella, TRANSCEND Media Service, May 1, 2017, www.transcend.org/tms/2017/05/addressing-fractionation-principles-for-arbitrating-the-common-good/.

70 "Trump Marks the End of a Cycle," by Roberto Savio, Inter Press Service (IPS), February 21, 2017, www.ipsnews.net/2017/02/trump-marks-the-end-of-a-cycle/.

71 Carson, 1962. See also American Experience: Rachel Carson, documentary film directed by Michelle Ferrari, Public Broadcasting Service (PBS), 2017, www.pbs.org/video/2365935530/, www.pbs.org/wgbh/americanexperience/films/rachel-carson/. I thank Linda Hartling for sharing this wonderful film with me. Our relationship can be described just like the one between Rachel Carson and Dorothy Freeman. Earlier, Linda Hartling showed me Not for Ourselves Alone: The Story of Elizabeth Cady Stanton & Susan B. Anthony, documentary film by Ken Burns, 1999, National Public Radio (NPR) and WETA, www.pbs.org/stantonanthony/.

72 Linda Hartling, in a personal communication on April 12, 2017.

73 "UN Chief Issues Warning on the Rise of Fascism," by Peter Walker, Independent, December 9, 2016, www.independent.co.uk/news/world/politics/united-nations-chilling-warning-rise-fascism-human-rights-prince-zeid-a7464861.html. See also "Warning Against Rising Intolerance, UN Remembers Holocaust and Condemns Anti-Semitism," United Nations News Centre, www.un.org/apps/news/story.asp?NewsID=56058#.WI3BB_KOWgy. See, furthermore, "Trump Marks the End of a Cycle," by Roberto Savio, Inter Press Service (IPS), February 21, 2017, www.ipsnews.net/2017/02/trump-marks-the-end-of-a-cycle/. See also Marine le Pen – Frontfrau der europäischen Rechten, documentary film by Michael Welch, Janine Bechthold, Tina Roth, and Olga Sviridenko, Das Erste, April 10, 2017, www.daserste.de/information/reportage-dokumentation/dokus/sendung/marine-le-pen-106.html.

74 I thank Linda Hartling for sharing her impressions of meeting Gandhi's grandson Arun M. Gandhi at the "Messages of Peace" Conference, September 20, 2009, at Marylhurst University in Oregon, USA. Gandhi described the crucial lessons he learned from his grandfather about the lifelong practice of nonviolent action. He also offered a rare glimpse into how the women in his grandfather's life shaped the development of nonviolent principles and practices. Gandhi, 2003, p. 91: "You cannot change people's hearts by law," Grandfather said. "You can only change hearts by love." See also arungandhi.org.

75 See note 83 in the Preface.

76 Lindner, 1996, 2000a.

77 Hartling, 1995.

78 Schmid, 2013, p. 31.

79 There were a few books and movies during my youth, which highlighted the theme of Nazi Germany just after the war, books I read – for instance, Borchert, 1947 – and movies I saw hundreds of times when I was young. They influenced me deeply, and I am infinitely thankful to the film makers for their nuanced way of making the Nazi era palpable for those born later. My father, being a teacher, was able to bring a film projector and film rolls to our house during vacations. I saw films such as In jenen Tagen (In Those Days, 1947, Helmut Käutner), Ein Tag – Bericht aus einem deutschen Konzentrationslager 1939 (A Day – Report from a German Concentration Camp in 1939, 1965, Egon Monk), Der Schlaf der Gerechten (The Sleep of the Just, 1962, Rolf Hädrich), Die Brücke (The Bridge, 1959, Bernhard Wicki), Wir Wunderkinder (We Wunderkinder, 1958, Kurt Hoffmann), Hunde, wollte ihr ewig leben, based on the novel with the same title by Fritz Wöss, 1958 (Stalingrad: Dogs, Do You Want to Live Forever?, 1959, Frank Wisbar). All films make the moral dilemmas and grotesqueness of the Nazi era palpable, but also show how humanness at times could shine through. The first film, In jenen Tagen, for example, addresses issues of collective guilt during

the Nazi era, highlighting certain people's private resistance while they publically accepted the Nazi repression. Most movies are no longer shown, except for a few. Repetitions of Die Brücke, for instance, are still being shown regularly on German television.

80 "Lieber tot als Sklav": "... wer weiße Fahnen hißt und sich kampflos ergibt, ist des Todes," Leonhardt, 2009, p. 80.

81 Lindner, 2006c, pp. 25–26.

82 Sustainable development expert Gwendolyn Hallsmith in her contribution to the Great Transition Network (GTN) discussion on the topic of "Monetizing Nature," July 31, 2014. See the full note in the pdf edition of this book.

83 See note 40 in the Introduction.

84 Lindner, 2014c.

85 Bourdieu uses the term field for spheres such as economy, politics, arts, journalism, bureaucracy, science, and education. The position of agents in a field depends on the volume of economic, cultural, or political capital that they possess, but also on how different forms of capital are distributed, see Bourdieu and Wacquant, 1992, p. 108, or Bourdieu, 1996, p. 278. I commend Jingyi Dong for having applied Bourdieu's conceptualization on China, and thank her for having taught me much about Bourdieu's theory. See Dong, 2015.

86 Bruce Fisher in his contribution to the Great Transition Network Initiative discussion titled "The Struggle for Meaningful Work," January 18, 2017, in response to Klitgaard, 2017.

87 Berger, 2011, p. 77, quoted by Arancha García del Soto, from MUNDUBAT, a Basque NGO from Bilbao, and also the Global Leader for Peace at Haverford College in Pennsylvania, U.S.A, when she was a panelist at the Conference "Human Rights and Humanitarianism: Contradictory or Co-Dependent?" Columbia University Morningside Campus International Affairs Building, October 30, 2013. See also note 415 in this Introduction.

88 In German, there is the word Schicksalsgemeinschaft or a "community of shared destiny."

89 Peace psychologist Anthony Marsella made a list of the "characteristic ethos of popular American culture": Consumerism, materialism, commodification, inequality, violence and power, individual self-interest, celebrity identification and pre-occupation, competition, financial greed, rapid and continuous change, hedonism, and transgressive ideology. See "Popular American (USA) Culture: A Dysfunctional and Destructive Life Context," by Anthony J. Marsella, TRANSCEND Media Service, November 11, 2013, www.transcend.org/tms/2013/11/popular-american-usa-culture-a-dysfunctional-and-destructive-life-context/. It is a privilege to have Anthony Marsella as esteemed member in the global advisory board of our Human Dignity and Humiliation Studies fellowship.

90 See, among others, Lane, 2001. Depression is the second most common cause of disability worldwide after back pain, according to a review of research, see Ferrari, et al., 2013. See also Lane, 2001. See, furthermore, "What if Sociologists Had as Much Influence as Economists?" by Neil Irwin, New York Times, March 17, 2017, www.nytimes.com/2017/03/17/upshot/what-if-sociologists-had-as-much-influence-as-economists.html. I thank Linda Hartling for making me aware of this article. According to the World Health Organisation (WHO, www.who.int), major depression (i.e. severe depressed mood that is episodic in nature and recurs in 75–80 percent of cases) is now the leading cause of disability worldwide with a lifetime prevalence of 17 percent in the Western world, thus ranking fourth among the ten leading causes of global disease burden. In addition, the WHO states that depression is the most common mental disorder leading to suicide and they project that, at its present rate of growth, depression will be the second leading contributor to global disease burden by 2020. See also "A Plea to Address Global Youth Depression," by economist Kamran Mofid, Globalization for the Common Good Initiative (GCGI), February 10, 2015,

www.gcgi.info/index.php/kamran-s-blog/665-a-plea-to-address-global-youth-depression. It is a privilege to have Kamran Mofid as esteemed member in the global advisory board of the Human Dignity and Humiliation Studies fellowship.
The following story of "The Depressed Baker" was shared by psychologist Jan Smedslund, 2013, pp. 134–135:

She was a 65 year old woman who had been committed to the emergency ward by her son because she just sat in a chair all day long and did nothing. She talked willingly, and told me that she was a recent widow, that she had in the course of the last year lost her three (and only) best friends, and also her job in a bakery that she had loved. Her children lived in another city. She had a small apartment, but saw no other people. She had never had any particular interests, except her work, and caring for her husband and children. She had tried some of the obvious possibilities, such as finding a new job, travelling, etc., to no avail. After some sessions, our conversations came to a stop. My final response was to state that, since there appeared to be nothing more to say, and since I understood that she had a good reason to feel depressed, we could just be silent together. After a while, she asked if she could hold my hand. Then we just sat there for some time. The next day I heard that she had volunteered to bake a birthday cake for a fellow patient, and then she gradually expanded her volunteer work in the hospital kitchen. After some weeks she left the hospital apparently restituted to her normal functioning.

See the full note in the pdf edition of this book.

91 Sociologist Émile Durkheim, 1897, in his book on suicide, developed the concept of anomie, understood as absence of norms, or too rigid norms, leading to apathy and detachment. Novelist Michel Houellebecq captures the many aspects and experiences of anomie in his work, see, among others, Houellebecq, 1994/1998, 1998/2001, 2015.

92 See the work on loneliness by John Cacioppo and colleagues. Perceived social isolation has increased in industrialized countries, and in the U.S., loneliness now affects over forty percent of older adults. "The development of effective interventions for loneliness is still needed," so Cacioppo, et al., 2014, p. 1497. Loneliness not only has numerous negative health effects, it also leads to self-centeredness, see Cacioppo, et al., 2017. See also Cacioppo, et al., 2009, Cacioppo and Patrick, 2008.
See, furthermore, "The Swedish Theory of Love: Why Swedes Are So Lonely," by John-David Ritz, Vice, November 10, 2015, www.vice.com/en_se/read/the-swedish-theory-of-love-or-why-we-swedes-are-so-lonely-234. I thank Guri Lorentzen Østbye for making me aware of the film and the article.

93 I resonate with indigenous psychologist Louise Sundararajan, 2015, and her suggestion that we ought to replace the binary theories of collectivism and individualism with a more nuanced explanatory framework. Sundararajan differentiates between group-based collectivism and relational collectivism. Conformity to hierarchy, authority, social norms, and adaptation to social pressure characterizes group-based collectivism, whereas communal connections, other-directedness, and genuine care for others is the hallmark of relational collectivism.

94 The Emperor's New Clothes is a short tale by Danish author Hans Christian Andersen (Danish: Kejserens nye Klæder). The Emperor parades before his subjects in his new clothes, which he believes are clothes that are invisible to those who are unfit for their positions, stupid, or incompetent. No one is courageous enough to speak out and say that there are no clothes at all. Only a child cries out, "But he isn't wearing anything at all!"

95 Perhaps my childhood experience of roaming freely on a farm gave me the experiences necessary to develop a particular level of spatial seeing and thinking. See the full note in the pdf edition of this book.

96 Karen Barad, 2003, p. 819: "Discourse is not what is said; it is that which constrains and enables what can be said. Discursive practices define what counts as meaningful statements. Statements are not the mere utterances of the originating consciousness of a unified subject; rather, statements and subjects emerge from

a field of possibilities. This field of possibilities is not static or singular but rather is a dynamic and contingent multiplicity." Karen Barad earned her doctorate in theoretical physics, building on insights from Niels Bohr, and is known for her theory of agential realism, where she follows Niels Bohr in questioning the dualisms of object/subject, knower/known, nature/culture, and word/world. Karen Barad asks: Does scientific knowledge represent an independently existing reality accurately? Does language accurately represent its referent? Does a given political representative, legal counsel, or piece of legislation accurately represent the interests of the people allegedly represented? (Barad, 2003, p. 804). See the full note with relevant references in the pdf edition of this book.

97 Physicist Michio Kaku has impressed me when he used the metaphor of a shallow pond for the idea of hyperspace: for fish in a shallow pond, the universe is two-dimensional; the fish cannot imagine what we know, those who look down from a bridge and can go forward, backward, left, and right, like the fish, but, in addition, also up and down. I have always felt to be the person on the bridge looking down on me, the fish. See Michio Kaku: The Flash Gordon of Physics, uploaded on May 31, 2011, https://youtu.be/jYiiiE2fwmc, http://bigthink.com.

98 Latour, 2004.

99 When I did my doctoral research in Somalia and Rwanda in 1998 and 1999, I grew increasingly uneasy with the idea that doing science means being an "expert" who "looks down" on "samples" of people to "study them." I wrote an article on how research can humiliate (Lindner, 2001i), where I reflected on the notion of equality in dignity and how it means the dismantling of social systems of ranked honor, and how also science ought to follow and dismantle hierarchy. When I wrote my article in 2001, I was not aware of the ongoing ontological material turn in philosophy and science, also called new materialism, new empiricism, posthuman studies, actor network theory, affect theory, material feminism, or process philosophy, see Professor of Education Maggie MacLure, 2015, p. 3. MacLure introduces the reader to many of the theorists who have mobilized this turn, such as Karen Barad, 2007, who talks about material-discursive assemblage, or Gilles Deleuze, 1969/1990, who speaks of assemblage, or, as Jean-Jacques Lecercle, 2002, explains, a logic of unholy mixtures, she introduces to Andrew Pickering, 1995, who uses the term mangle, or to Manuel De Landa, 2002, who speaks of manifold. See the full note with relevant references in the pdf edition of this book.

100 "Inverted refrigerator," quoted in Vambheim, 2016, p. 87, as a term coined by social anthropologist Thomas Hylland Eriksen.

101 I thank Peter Coleman and Beth Fisher-Yoshida for making me aware of the book Tribe by Sebastian Junger, 2016, where Junger describes the significance of the sense of belonging, for instance, the intimate bonds of platoon life that combat veterans experience. Junger suggests that the loss of closeness that comes at the end of deployment may explain the high rates of post-traumatic stress disorder suffered by military veterans. This was also what I had learned in Sarajevo and Dubrovnik during the time I lived there in 2016, when people I met would talk about the solidarity they experienced during the siege and how they miss this today. In 2017, Sebastian Junger and Nick Quested came out with the documentary film Hell on Earth: The Fall Of Syria And The Rise of ISIS, where they explain how Da'esh could rise not least because democracy was seen as a greater threat by the ruling government in Syria. See http://channel.nationalgeographic.com/hell-on-earth/. It is a privilege to have Beth Fisher-Yoshida and Peter Coleman as esteemed members in our Human Dignity and Humiliation Studies fellowship, together with Ardian Adžanela and other friends in Sarajevo and Dubrovnik.

102 Schöne neue Welt: "Die Welt wird auf den Kopf gestellt," documentary film on Silicon Valley by Claus Kleber, Zweites Deutsches Fernsehen, 2016, www.zdf.de/schoene-neue-welt/schoene-neue-welt-43773220.html. See also, "Silicon Valley and the Search for Happiness," by Kamran Mofid, Globalization for the Common Good Initiative (GCGI), May 19, 2017, http://gcgi.info/index.php/blog/858-silicon-valley-and-the-search-for-happiness. See the full note in the pdf edition of this book.

103 Beverly Crawford, research director at the Center for German and European Studies at Berkeley, gave an excellent introduction to international relations and gender at the Sommerakademie Friedens- und Konfliktforschung in Loccum, Germany, July 20–25, 1997. See the full note with relevant references in the pdf edition of this book.

104 Lee Badgett, 2016 describes the problems an "activist scholar" faces.

105 See Belenky, et al., 1997a, Belenky, et al., 1997b, Clinchy, 1996. In connected knowing "one attempts to enter another person's frame of reference to discover the premises for the person's point of view," Clinchy and Zimmerman, 1985. See also Lindner and Desmond Tutu (Foreword), 2010.

106 See Marmot, 2004b. See also "Status and Stress," by Moises Velasquez-Manoff, New York Times, July 27, 2013, http://opinionator.blogs.nytimes.com/2013/07/27/status-and-stress/?src=me&ref=general&_r=0. This article is part of The Great Divide, a series on inequality – the haves, the have-nots and everyone in between – in the United States and around the world, and its implications for economics, politics, society and culture. The series moderator is Joseph E. Stiglitz, a Nobel laureate in economics, a Columbia professor and a former chairman of the Council of Economic Advisers and chief economist for the World Bank. I thank Linda Hartling for making me aware of this article.

107 Paul Street in "The Plutocracy Grinds On," July 25, 2013, www.paulstreet.org/?p=987. See the full note in the pdf edition of this book.

108 Hitchens, 2012, pp. 17–18.

109 Jeismann, 2000.

110 Matsumoto, et al., 2007, p. 92: "With Emotion Regulation (ER), "people voyage through life; without it, they vindicate their lives." It is a privilege to have David Matsumoto as esteemed member in the global advisory board of our Human Dignity and Humiliation Studies fellowship.

111 Sheets-Johnstone, 2007. For Lévinas the "space of love" is the space of ambivalence(s), the space of otherness(es). To be ethical, one must be willing to enter this space. Communication is more than the exchange of information, it is the very vulnerability of myself that I bring.

112 Groos and Jehles, 2015, discuss the impact of poverty on children's development. See the full note in the pdf edition of this book.

113 Galtung explained this point at the Higher Education for Peace Conference in Tromsø, Norway, May 4–6, 2000; see www.peace.uit.no.

114 See Cristina Escrigas, 2016. See the full note in the pdf edition of this book.

115 "Changing the Political Climate: A Transitional Imperative," by Richard Falk, Great Transition Initiative, September 2014, http://greattransition.org/publication/changing-the-political-climate-a-transitional-imperative. See the full note in the pdf edition of this book.

116 Smedslund, 2013, p. 118. It was a great privilege to have Jan Smedslund as advisor for my doctoral research, supporting my advisor Reidar Ommundsen, and later as head of my doctoral committee at the University of Oslo in 2001. He was the first one who made me think of dignity humiliation being different from honor humiliation. Later, both became highly esteemed members in the global advisory board of our Human Dignity and Humiliation Studies fellowship. I wish to thank both for decades of crucial support.

117 Smedslund, 2013.

118 Smedslund, 1988, 1997.

119 Lindner, 2001d.

120 See Ruben Nelson, strategic futures thinker, http://foresightcanada.com/ruben-nelson-biography/. He draws on the scholarship of historians of religion (see, for instance, Wilfred Smith, 1962, on the reification of religion), humanistic psychologists (such as Rollo May, 1969), sociologists of knowledge (such as Peter L.

Berger and Luckmann, 1966), philosophers of personhood (such as John Macmurray, 1961) and appliers of complexity theory (such as Thomas Homer-Dixon, 2006).

121 Evelin Lindner's Invitation to Join the World Dignity University Initiative, a video where Lindner is being interviewed by Ragnhild Nilsen about her vision of the World Dignity University. This dialogue took place at the University in Oslo in Norway on February 8, 2011. See https://youtu.be/A8voZQ0t6bU. See the full note in the pdf edition of this book.

122 See more in Lindner, 2016b.

123 "Respekt for menneskets verdighet – en hovedfaktor i alle forsoningsprosesser," lecture by philosopher Tore Frost, representative of the prize committee, during the award ceremony of the Blanche Majors Reconciliation Prize 2012 being awarded to HRH Crown Prince Haakon, Peace House in Risør, Norway, June 13, 2012, www.aktive-fredsreiser.no/forsoningspris/2012/hovedtale_respekt_menneskeverd.htm. Translated and summarized from the Norwegian original by Lindner. See the full note in the pdf edition of this book.

124 Macklin, 2003, Abstract.

125 "The Stupidity of Dignity," by Steven Pinker, The New Republic, May 27, 2008, https://newrepublic.com/article/64674/the-stupidity-dignity. I thank Linda Hartling for making me aware of Pinker's article.

126 Linda Hartling in a personal communication on August 29, 2016.

127 See note 84 in the Preface. See also Lindner, 2006c, on Somali warlord Osman Ato, p. 85. See the full note in the pdf edition of this book.

128 My book titled Making Enemies: Humiliation and International Conflict, came out in 2006 in Praeger with the term humiliation hesitantly accepted in the title. See Lindner, 2006c. Other publishers had not wished this term to be part of the title of a book altogether. The only book that had been published before, at least to my awareness, with the phrase humiliation in the title, was William Ian Miller, 1993, and his book on Humiliation: And Other Essays on Honor, Social Discomfort, and Violence. My book was subsequently honored as "Outstanding Academic Title" by the journal Choice for 2007 in the USA.

129 A few examples of many are Prime Minister of India Narendra Modi, President of the Philippines Rodrigo "Rody" Roa Duterte, also known as Digong, or Prime Minister of Hungary Viktor Mihály Orbán. Also novelists make this trend palpable through their work, such as Henning Ahrens, 2015, who shows how it affects, for instance, rural areas in Germany.

130 "The End of a Cycle?" by Roberto Savio, Inter Press Service (IPS), December 6, 2016, www.ipsnews.net/2016/12/italian-politics-the-end-of-a-cycle/.

131 Lutz and Abu-Lughod, 1990, Foucault, 1991, Rancière, 2004. See also Fierke, 2004 and Barnett and Raymond, 2005.

132 Hartling and Lindner, 2016a. See also Lindner, 2016b.

133 See, among others, Sarraj, 2002, Sayler, 2004, Giacaman, et al., 2007, Elison and Harter, 2007, Walker and Knauer, 2011.

134 Leidner, et al., 2012.

135 Kendler, et al., 2003.

136 Otten and Jonas, 2013, p. 33.

137 See for research on inertia, for instance, Leidner, et al., 2012. According to anthropologist Scott Atran, humiliation is a negative predictor for terrorism, since those who feel humiliated become submissive. However, it is different to act on behalf of others' exposure to humiliation, such as the second or third generation of Muslims in Britain who believe that their parents were humiliated. See, among others, Ginges

and Atran, 2008.
See for an illustration, "Wave of Indigenous Suicides Leaves Canadian Town Appealing for Help," by Liam Stack, New York Times, March 18, 2016, www.nytimes.com/2016/03/19/world/americas/canada-youth-suicide.html. I thank Linda Hartling for making me aware of this article.

138 Galtung, 1969.

139 "Wave of Indigenous Suicides Leaves Canadian Town Appealing for Help," by Liam Stack, New York Times, March 18, 2016, www.nytimes.com/2016/03/19/world/americas/canada-youth-suicide.html. Linda Hartling commented in a personal communication on March 21, 2016: "Canada's indigenous populations demonstrate the deleterious effect of continuous humiliation: they are driven into waves of suicide as an outflow of "cumulative humiliation," of a lingering trauma of colonialism and prejudice, of 'cultural genocide.'"

140 Lewis, 1971.

141 Freire, 1968/1970, 1968/1973, and Morais, 1979, 1983.

142 Lindner, 2016b.

143 Ibid.

144 See, for instance, political scientist Simon Koschut's overview over publications relevant for the "emotional turn" in international relations theory: Åhäll and Gregory, 2015; Bially Mattern, 2011; Edkins, 2003; Fattah and Fierke, 2009; Hall and Ross, 2015; Hutchinson, 2016; Koschut, 2014; Leep, 2010; Ross, 2013; Solomon, 2014; Van Rythoven, 2015; Wilcox, 2015. The narrative of humiliation in the Middle East, for instance, shows the intertextuality of emotions, and that "emotions have a history," Fattah and Fierke, 2009, p. 70.
See also an interview that Alexandros Koutsoukis conducted with Steven C. Roach on November 2, 2016, as part of a series of interviews under the motto "Resurrecting IR Theory," where Roach discusses affective values in international relations, the value of resilience, and how to theorize emotional actions, www.e-ir.info/2016/11/02/interview-steven-c-roach/.
Recent literature on war and conflict deals with aspects of emotion and discourse analysis in social constructivist terms. See, for instance, the book series War, Politics and Experience edited by Christine Sylvester, 2013, 2015. See a description of this series on www.routledge.com/War-Politics-and-Experience/book-series/WPE. See a selection of relevant publications in Managhan, 2012, Heath-Kelly, 2013, McSorley, 2013, McSorley, 2015, Rowe, 2013, Park-Kang, 2014, Bachmann, et al., 2015, Schlund-Vials and Martínez, 2017. See, especially, Inger Skjelsbæk, 2013. See also Elina Penttinen, 2013, on how "the mechanistic-deterministic worldview derived from the Newtonian model has influenced the epistemology and methodology of IR (i.e., the idea that the world is constituted of independent fragments), and seeks ways to develop a new methodology for IR by drawing on the potential of a non-fragmented worldview."
See the full note in the pdf edition of this book.

145 Lindner, 2009b, pp. 18–20. One among myriad ways of describing emotions is to say that they are "socially recognized, structured episodes of affectively valenced response, such as joy or fear … a sub-category of patterned affective reactions," in contrast to "affective dynamics" that are "the range of ways embodied mental processes and the felt dimensions of human experience influence thought and behavior," Hall and Ross, 2015, p. 848.
Indigenous psychologists, however, are critical of Western approaches, see, for instance, Louise Sundararajan, 2015, p. 200: "In contrast to the Western notion of emotion as a disruptive force to be regulated by reason and cognition... the Chinese consider the human capacity for responding to impact affectively as a positive quality to be enhanced through expanding consciousness. Consciousness expands not by reason or cognition but by mind-to-mind transactions."

146 Elster, 2003. I appreciated learning from Jon Elster in our meeting in Paris on November 26, 2003.

147 See relational-cultural theory and cultural-historical activity theory. Linda Hartling builds on relational-cultural theory, as developed by her mentor Jean Baker Miller and colleagues, see, among others, Hartling, et al., 2008. Linda Hartling is the former Associate Director of the Jean Baker Miller Training Institute, and it is an immense privilege to have her now as the director of Human Dignity and Humiliation Studies. Relational-cultural theory (CRP) evolved from the work of Jean Baker Miller, M.D., pioneer in women's psychology. It assumes that humans have a natural drive toward relationships, and it applies a growth-in-connection model of human growth and development to organizational settings. See Miller, 1976/1986, and for an overview, among others, Hartling, et al., 2008, and Jordan, 2010.

148 Cultural-historical activity theory builds on the work by Lev Vygotsky, 1978, and Aleksei Leontiev, 1975/1978. Its philosophical premise is that human physical and mental activity is integrally connected to large-scale cultural and historical processes and vice versa. It studies the culturally and historically situated, materially, and socially mediated process by which humans purposefully transform natural and social reality, including themselves. Community is seen to be central to all forms of learning, communicating, and acting, which means that community is central to the process of learning-by-doing, of making tools of all kinds, of communicating, and of making meaning and acting. The term cultural-historical activity theory (CHAT) was coined by Michael Cole and used by Yrjö Engeström for the various lines of work that had been inspired by Vygotsky. See for recent publications, for instance, Kaptelinin and Nardi, 2006, Roth, et al., 2012. See also Richards and Andersson, 2015. I am indebted to Howard Richards and Gavin Andersson for bringing me to South Africa in 2013, and to the Organization Workshop (OW), a CHAT-based organizational learning method developed by Gavin Andersson, et al., 2016, as summarized in this Abstract:

Cultural-Historical Activity Theory (CHAT), is a theoretical framework which traces its roots to activity theory approaches first developed in Russian Psychology (by Vygotsky and Leontiev, in particular). The Organization Workshop (OW) is a CHAT-based organizational learning method with its roots, unusually, in the global South. Among the many scholarly applications of CHAT-related approaches of the last two decades, the OW stands out – together with the Finnish Change Laboratory (CL) and the French Clinique de l'Activité/Activity Clinic (AC) – as a field praxis-oriented laboratory method specifically geared to the world of work. OW is a large-group capacitation method. Organization is not taught. Participants achieve organization. It was initiated in the 1960s by the Brazilian lawyer, sociologist, and political activist Clodomir Santos de Morais, who discovered, in his own experience, that a large group facing common challenges, given freedom of organization, access to a common resource pool and appropriate support from facilitators, could learn to organize itself. From Brazil, the "laboratorios organizacionales" spread out in the seventies to most of Latin America where they were applied at times on a national scale. The method was transferred in the eighties to English-speaking southern Africa where most of the theoretical work exploring its CHAT roots originated. Recently this eminently southern CHAT-based laboratory method has started to find applications in the North.

It is a privilege to have Howard Richards and Gavin Andersson as esteemed members in our Human Dignity and Humiliation Studies fellowship.

149 Donati and Archer, 2015, go far beyond the "plural subject" of analytical philosophers and speak of the "relational subject." They treat "the relation" between people as real and regard relational "goods" and "evils" as having causal effects upon agents and their subsequent actions. See also Jervis, 2006. See the full note in the pdf edition of this book.

150 Wilson and Gowdy, 2013.

151 New York Times economics columnist Robert Frank, 2011, argues that competition alone will not solve present-day problems, and that Charles Darwin's understanding of competition describes economic reality more accurately than Adam Smith's. Frank shows that economic competition, far from creating a perfect world, tends to encourage behaviors that are harmful to the group and to individuals. See also Corneo, 2014,

and Mammon: Per Anhalter durch das Geldsystem, film by Philipp Enders, https://absolutmedien.de/film/4047/MAMMON+-+PER+ANHALTER+DURCH+DAS+GELDSYSTEM.

152 Lindner, 2007b, Lindner and Desmond Tutu (Foreword), 2010, p. 136. See also "Tribalism, Nationalism and Fascism," by John Scales Avery, Human Wrongs Watch, January 5, 2017, https://human-wrongs-watch.net/2017/01/06/tribalism-nationalism-and-fascism/.

153 The journal Psychological Studies published a special issue titled "Kenneth J. Gergen and Social Constructionism." Misra and Prakash, 2012, highlight, on p. 123, that "in seeing human activities as culturally bound, we can envision alternative futures, especially with the understanding of phenomena like neural plasticity." In the same issue of the journal, Anderson, 2012, speaks of therapy as "relational recovery," highlighting that knowledge is not an individual cognitive construction but a communal one, that language is not representational but a dynamic social process, and that a person is not a bounded self but a "multi-being." Wortham and Jackson, 2012, argue that education should enhance relationships rather than an individual's mind, since individuals are woven into contextualized knowledge. See the full note in the pdf edition of this book.

154 See note 73 in this Introduction.

155 Linser, 2016. It was a great privilege to be part of Jo Linser's family, and to have Nimrod Sheinman as esteemed member in our Human Dignity and Humiliation Studies fellowship.

156 Vance, 2016. See also note 25 in the Preface.

157 "Anticipating India," by Shekhar Gupta, The Indian Express, April 26, 2014, http://indianexpress.com/article/opinion/columns/anticipating-india, quoted in Miklian and Sahoo, 2016.

158 Rechtsextremismus: Wie Neonazis das Dorf Jamel erobert haben, by Silke Hasselmann, Deutschland Radio, August 18, 2015, www.deutschlandradiokultur.de/rechtsextremismus-wie-neonazis-das-dorf-jamel-erobert-haben.1001.de.html?dram:article_id=328595. Mecklenburg-Vorpommern (known as Mecklenburg-West Pomerania in English) is a thinly populated marginal federated state in northern Germany that offers opportunities to militant extremists.

159 Da'esh is the acronym from the Arabic name Al-Dawlah Al-Islamiyah fe Al-Iraq wa Al-Sham, for the self-proclaimed Islamic State (IS) in Iraq and Syria, or ISIL (Islamic State of Iraq and the Levant), or ISIS (the Islamic State of Iraq and Syria).

160 "The Lure Of The Syrian War: The Foreign Fighters' Bosnian Contingent," by Vlado Azinović and Muhamed Jusić, Atlantic Initiative, 2015, http://atlanticinitiative.org/images/THE_LURE_OF_THE_SYRIAN_WAR_THE_FOREIGN_FIGHTERS_BOSNIAN_CONTINGENT/The_Lure_of_the_Syrian_War_-_The_Foreign_Fighters_Bosnian_Contingent.pdf, Introduction.

161 Hitler, 1925–26/1999, p. 167.

162 See for a recent publication Maartje Elshout, et al., 2016. In her research, the prototype structure identified the fear of being humiliated in the future as "afraid of repetition" or "preventing repetition." While it first only seemed a peripheral feature, in the recall study, it became the most central feature of all, Maartje Elshout in a personal communication on February 7, 2017. See also Hartling and Lindner, 2016a, 2017.

163 Lindner, 2000a.

164 "Liechtenstein's Populists Gain Ground," by Sara Stefanini, Politico, February 5, 2017, www.politico.eu/article/liechtensteins-populists-gain-ground/.

165 Ashcroft, 2005, p. 679. I thank Charles Coil, 2009, for making me aware of Ashcroft's article.

166 Macklin, 2003.

167 Beyleveld and Brownsword, 2001.

168 This position is inspired by the writings on development and freedom of Amartya Sen, 1992, and Martha Nussbaum, 2000. Ashcroft also points at more recent articles in The Lancet, such as Marmot, 2004a, or Horton, 2004.

169 Ashcroft describes this position as mainstream in European bioethics and theological writing on bioethical topics, as exemplified by Leon Kass, 2002.

170 Karlberg, 2013. See also Chong and Druckman, 2007. See the full note in the pdf edition of this book.

171 Lakoff and Johnson, 1999. See also Lindner, 2005a. See the work by political scientist Stanley Feldman, for instance, Feldman, 2003. Read more in "The Rise of American Authoritarianism," by Amanda Taub, Vox, March 1, 2016, www.vox.com/2016/3/1/11127424/trump-authoritarianism#change. See also note 24 in the Introduction to Section One.
In the early 1990s, political scientist Stanley Feldman did innovative research. Feldman, a professor at SUNY Stony Brook, believed authoritarianism could be an important factor in American politics in ways that had nothing to do with fascism, but that it could only reliably be measured by unlinking it from specific political preferences. For Feldman, authoritarianism was a personality profile rather than a political preference, and in his questionnaires he therefore asks about parenting goals. He developed the definitive measurement of authoritarianism by asking four simple questions that appear to focus on parenting but are in fact designed to reveal how highly the respondent values hierarchy, order, and conformity over other values. This were his questions: Please tell me which one you think is more important for a child to have:
- independence or respect for elders?
- obedience or self-reliance?
- to be considerate or to be well-behaved?
- curiosity or good manners?

172 Karlberg, 2013.

173 Karlberg, 2013, p. 7.

174 Karlberg, 2013, points at a number of authors, such as Bowles and Gintis, 2011b, Henrich and Henrich, 2007, Henrich, et al., 2010, de Waal, 2009, Keltner, 2009, Tomasello, 2009, Scott and Seglow, 2007, Margolis, 1982, Sober and Wilson, 1998, Fellman, 1998, Monroe, 1996, Lunati, 1992, Lewontin, 1991, Kohn, 1990, Rose, et al., 1984, Spanish National Commission for UNESCO, 1986, Axelrod, 2006, Leakey and Lewin, 1977, Becker, 1976.

175 Karlberg, 2008. Karlberg also points at Monroe, 1996, Kohn, 1990.

176 Karlberg, 2013.

177 Mann, 1997, p. 12. See also Charles R. Coil, 2009.

178 See Richards, 2016b. And see Tillich, 1954, and King, 1955.

179 Howard Richards, Research Professor of Philosophy, Earlham College. It is a privilege to have Howard Richards as esteemed member in the global advisory board of our Human Dignity and Humiliation Studies fellowship.

180 Richards, 2016b.

181 It was a great privilege to have Don Klein as founding member of the Human Dignity and Humiliation Studies fellowship and member of its board of director until his passing in 2007. We always hold his memory dear.

182 Lindner and Desmond Tutu (Foreword), 2010. During my adolescence, I survived its traumatic experiences through reading Viktor Frankl, 1946/1959, Erich Fromm, 1976, and others. See also Rollo May,

1969. I resonate with the field of affect theology and their focus on the heart of faith, tracking how human emotions become religious feelings. See http://revthandeka.org/affect-theology-thandeka.html.

183 Wergeland, 1843, p. 23. See the original Norwegian quote in the full note in the pdf edition of this book. I thank Bernt Hagtvet and Nikolai Brandal for making me aware of this quote. It is a privilege to have Bernt Hagtvet as esteemed member in the global advisory board of our Human Dignity and Humiliation Studies fellowship.

184 Nagata, 2007.

185 See note 165 in the Preface.

186 Coleman, et al., 2007, Coleman, 2011, Coleman, et al., 2008, Vallacher, et al., 2010. See for more, "Project on Dynamical Systems, Peace, Conflict and Social Change," by Peter Coleman, http://ac4.ei.columbia.edu/ac4-supported-initiatives/dynamical-systems-theory-at-columbia-university-v2/. See also Coleman, et al., 2009, Goldman and Coleman, 2005b, a. Peter Coleman is Professor of Psychology and Education Director at the Morton Deutsch International Center for Cooperation and Conflict Resolution (MD-ICCCR). He and his colleagues use a dynamical systems approach to conceptualize the intransigence entailed in intractable conflict. The Human Dignity and Humiliation Studies fellowship is honored to have Morton Deutsch and Peter Coleman, together with Claudia Cohen, Beth Fisher-Yoshida, Andrea Bartoli, and many others of their colleagues, as esteemed members of the first hour in our global advisory board.

187 "Dignity's Due: Why Are Philosophers Invoking the Notion of Human Dignity to Revitalize Theories of Political Ethics?," by Samuel Moyn, The Nation, November 4, 2013, www.thenation.com/article/176662/dignitys-due#, review of Waldron, 2012. I thank Volker Berghahn for making me aware of these publications.

188 "Freedom vs. Dignity: A Sustainable History Thesis for the Arab Spring," by Nayef R.F. Al-Rodhan, Georgetown Journal of International Affairs, November 7, 2013, http://journal.georgetown.edu/freedom-vs-dignity-a-sustainable-history-thesis-for-the-arab-spring-by-nayef-al-rodhan/. Nayef R.F. Al-Rodhan is a Senior Member of St. Antony's College at Oxford University, Oxford, United Kingdom, Senior Fellow and Centre director of the Centre for the Geopolitics of Globalization and Transnational Security at the Geneva Centre for Security Policy, Geneva, Switzerland. He is the author of, among others, Al-Rodhan, 2009, 2012.

189 Ibid.

190 "Dignity Deficit Fuels Uprisings in the Middle East," by Nayef Al-Rodhan, Yale Global, September 10, 2013, yaleglobal.yale.edu/content/dignity-deficit-fuels-uprisings-middle-east.

191 Ibid.

192 "Fractured Lands: How the Arab World Came Apart," by Scott Anderson, New York Times, August 11, 2016, www.nytimes.com/interactive/2016/08/11/magazine/isis-middle-east-arab-spring-fractured-lands.html.

193 Tim Weiskel in his contribution to the Great Transition Network (GTN) discussion on the topic of "A Higher Calling for Higher Education," June 1, 2016, in response to Escrigas, 2016.

194 Lindner, 2009b, Lindner and Desmond Tutu (Foreword), 2010. See a review by social psychologist and Kurt Lewin expert David Bargal, 2011b. Read more about David Bargal in note 169 in the Inspiring and Thought-Provoking Questions at the end of Section Three.

195 Kenneth Gergen, 2010, p. 5, noted that the brain may be thought of "as an instrument for achieving culturally constructed ends." See the full note in the pdf edition of this book.

196 Snow, 1959.

197 Foucault, 1979, 1991, Foucault and Gordon, 1980. See also Lutz and Abu-Lughod, 1990, Rancière, 2004, Fierke, 2004 or Barnett and Raymond, 2005. See more in note 47 in Chapter 1.

198 Habermas, 1968/1972, p. 4. See also Fatemi, 2014.

199 "'Die andere Ansicht' – Niedergang oder Sieg des Rechtsstaats?," by Thomas Fischer, Zeit Online, August 25, 2015, www.zeit.de/gesellschaft/zeitgeschehen/2015-08/abweichende-meinung-rechtskultur-fischer-im-recht/komplettansicht. Thomas Fischer is a federal judge in Karlsruhe.

200 McCauley and Moskalenko, 2014b.

201 Billig, 2013.

202 See "The Ties That Bind Captive to Captor," by Frank M. Ochberg, Los Angeles Times, April 8, 2005, http://articles.latimes.com/2005/apr/08/opinion/oe-ochberg8. Frank M. Ochberg is co-founder of the National Center for Critical Incident Analysis and former associate director of the National Institute of Mental Health. See the book that one of the hostages, Kristin Enmark, 2015, wrote more than four decades after the event. Read about an interview with her: "Hun er opphavet til begrepet stockholmsyndromet," by Odvin Aune, NRK, September 18, 2015, www.nrk.no/kultur/hun-er-opphavet-til-begrepet-stockholmsyndromet-1.12561167. See the full note in the pdf edition of this book. See also Lindner, 2009b, p. 133.

203 Sherratt, 2013.

204 Chege, 1996.

205 Kevin Clements, in a personal communication on August 21, 2007.

206 See the Inside Job transcript, September 2010, www.sonyclassics.com/awards-information/insidejob_screenplay.pdf.

207 Western-liberal political philosophy regards the forms of dignity that can be legally respected and protected by a state as the right to self-determination, autonomy, and agency, see Rosen, 2012. The concept of dignity-as-autonomy is consistent with the social contest frame of dignity, see Karlberg, 2013: "When human nature is conceived largely in terms of self-interested motives playing out within competitive social arenas, then the autonomy of individuals and groups to pursue their own interests, within a set of rules that apply equally to all, takes on paramount importance."

208 Schachter, 1983, p. 849. See also Charles R. Coil, 2009.

209 See Lindner, 2016b, Also Rosen, 2012, p. 11, explains that dignity "originated as a concept that denoted high social status and the honors and respectful treatment that are due to someone who occupied that position." See also Karlberg, 2013. Michael Karlberg speaks of the social command frame of dignity, in contrast to the social contest frame and the social body frame. See the full note in the pdf edition of this book.

210 Schleichert, 1999, p. 17. See the full note in the pdf edition of this book.

211 See, for instance, John MacMurray, 1949/1991, Isaiah Berlin, 1958.
See also Whose Freedom, by George Lakoff, 2006a, where he addresses freedom, "this most beloved of American political ideas": "Since September 11, 2001, the Bush administration has relentlessly invoked the word 'freedom.' Al-Qaeda attacked us because 'they hate our freedom.' The U.S. can strike preemptively because 'freedom is on the march.' Social security should be privatized in order to protect individual freedoms. The 2005 presidential inaugural speech was a kind of crescendo: the words 'freedom,' 'free,' and 'liberty,' were used forty-nine times in President Bush's twenty-minute speech."
See also "Bastard Economics of Greedy Neoliberalism and the Killings of the Innocents in London Tower," by Kamran Mofid, Globalization for the Common Good Initiative (GCGI), June 16, 2017, http://gcgi.info/index.php/archive/867-bastard-economics-of-greedy-neoliberalism-and-the-killings-of-the-innocents-in-london-tower:

For years successive governments have built what they call a bonfire of regulations. They have argued that "red tape" impedes our freedom and damages productivity. Britain, they have assured us, would be a better place with fewer forms to fill in, fewer inspections and less enforcement. But what they call red tape often consists of essential public protections that defend our lives, our futures and the rest of the living world. The freedom they celebrate is highly selective: in many cases it means the freedom of the rich to exploit the poor, of corporations to exploit their workers, landlords to exploit their tenants and industry of all kinds to use the planet as its dustbin. As RH Tawney remarked, "Freedom for the pike is death for the minnows."

See, furthermore, "China Convinces G20 Nations with 'Fair' Communique," by Jorge Valero in Hangzhou, EurActiv, September 6, 2016, www.euractiv.com/section/global-europe/news/china-convinces-g20-nations-with-fair-communique/. See the full note in the pdf edition of this book.

212 "The Future of the United States of America," by Howard Richards, TRANSCEND Media Service, January 2, 2017, www.transcend.org/tms/2017/01/the-future-of-the-united-states-of-america/.

213 Since solidarity is a moral obligation rather than a law, a relationship rather than a status, social concord rather than a contract, and communal rather than individual, fraternité is the most delicate part to be integrated into the motto. Fraternity was defined in the Declaration of the Rights and Duties of Man and the Citizen of 1795 (Déclaration des droits et des devoirs de l'homme et du citoyen de 1795) as such: "Do not do to others what you would not wish to be done to you; always do the good to others you wish to receive" (Ne faites pas à autrui ce que vous ne voudriez pas qu'on vous fît; faites constamment aux autres le bien que vous voudriez en recevoir).

214 Lindner, 2012f, Chapter 8. Robert K. Greenleaf (1904 – 1990) was the founder of the modern Servant leadership movement and the Greenleaf Center for Servant Leadership. See the 25th anniversary edition of Greenleaf, 2002.

215 See note 212 above.

216 Lindner, 2000b; Lakoff and Johnson, 1980, 1999. See also the work of phenomenological philosopher Maurice Merleau-Ponty (1908 – 1961), who emphasized the body as the primary site of knowing the world, strongly influenced by Edmund Husserl and Martin Heidegger. See Merleau-Ponty, 1945/1962, 1961/1993, Merleau-Ponty and Lefort, 1964/1968.

217 Wetz, 2014. I thank Carsten Frerk for making me aware of this book. See the full note in the pdf edition of this book.

218 Karlberg, 2013.

219 Weber-Guskar, 2016.

220 Schroeder and Bani-Sadr, 2017, Chapter 4: Middle East and West: Can Common Ground Be Found? Abstract, p. 89. I thank Sultan Somjee for sharing this manuscript with me.

221 Schroeder, 2012, Abstract: "In conclusion, proponents of universal human rights will fare better with alternative frameworks to justify human rights rather than relying on the concept of dignity."

222 Schroeder and Bani-Sadr, 2017, Chapter 4: Middle East and West: Can Common Ground Be Found? Abstract, p. 89.

223 In my work, I apply the ideal-type approach as described by sociologist Max Weber, 1904/1949. See also Coser, 1977, p. 224. See the full note in the pdf edition of this book.

224 Lindner, 2006c.

225 Etzioni, 2013, p. 333.

226 Gottman, et al., 1997, Wilce, 2009.

227 Crespi and Yanega, 1995. Several different levels of sociality are differentiated, such as presociality (solitary but social), subsociality, parasocial (including communal, quasisocial, and semisocial), and

eusocial. The term eusocial includes organisms (originally, only invertebrates) with the following features: 1. Reproductive division of labor (with or without sterile castes), 2. Overlapping generations, 3. Cooperative care of young.

228 Wilson, 2013. See also "Interview with Edward O. Wilson: The Origin of Morals," by Philip Bethge and Johann Grolle, Spiegel Online International, February 26, 2013, www.spiegel.de/international/spiegel/spiegel-interview-with-edward-wilson-on-the-formation-of-morals-a-884767.html. See, furthermore, Edward O. Wilson on the Human Condition, FORA.tv., April 20, 2012, http://fora.tv/2012/04/20/Edward_O_Wilson_The_Social_Conquest_of_Earth.

229 Honneth, 1992/1995, Honneth, 1997.

230 Bauman, 2001.

231 Chandhoke, 2009.

232 Scheler, 1912/1961.

233 Scheler, 1913/1923/1954.

234 Taylor, 1994.

235 Taylor, 1992.

236 Greenfeld, 1992, 1996, 2006. See also Hechter, 1992. See more in Lindner, 2009f.

237 See Heine, et al., 1999.

238 Wendt, 2003, pp. 510–511. See also Ringmar, 2002. I am thankful for having had the chance to communicate with Alexander Wendt, for the first time in 2005.

239 Political scientist Reinhard Wolf, 2013, draws on Frijda, 2008, p. 73, when he speaks of ressentiment as emotional attitude, or a persistent affective disposition, which creates biases toward perceived offenders. Wolf focuses particularly on hierarchical social settings, where a resenting person or group feels that others enjoy undeserved power and/or prestige. Wolf draws on Feather, 2008, Feather and Nairn, 2005, Oldmeadow and Fiske, 2012, and Petersen, 2002. While resentful feelings are more difficult to detect than open anger, indirect evidence for the experience can be found, in particular, in discourse. The reason is that the desire to bring someone down from a weak position can only be achieved through the help of allies. Those allies, however, must first be mobilized, they have to be convinced, grievances must be explained, and the "offenders'" status delegitimized. See also Koschut, 2014, or Petersen, 2002. Wolf advises researchers who wish to detect this phenomenon to watch out for accusations of supposedly unfair status shifts, for the invocation of normative principles that call for rectifying "unfair" policies, for justifications for retributive measures, for insinuations which tarnish the social or moral status of the "wrongdoers," for signs of Schadenfreude when the other experiences setbacks, and, at last, the presence of revenge fantasies. See also more recent work by Feather, 2015. See the full note in the pdf edition of this book.

240 Philosopher Howard Richards lives in Chile, and works often in South Africa. I had the privilege of joining him in both places. See Lindner, 2012b, Richards, et al., 2015a.

241 "An Interview with Dr. Nora Sveaass: Why Torture Is Wrong," by Nilantha Ilangamuwa, CounterPunch, October 11–13, 2013, www.counterpunch.org/2013/10/11/why-torture-is-wrong/. Nora Sveaass is an internationally renowned psychologist who became a member of the Committee against Torture in the United Nations (UNCAT). Sveaass is currently an associate professor at the Department of Psychology in the University of Oslo, Norway. It is a privilege for me to be included in her teaching program.
See also the work of Beatriz Brinkmann, 1999. I thank Wolfgang Kaleck for making me aware of Brinkmann's work. Brinkmann's experience in prison in Chile is described in "Belagerungszustand in Chile: Wer ist ein Terrorist?" by Freimut Duve, Die Zeit, October 31, 1986, http://pdf.zeit.de/1986/45/wer-ist-ein-terrorist.pdf. Brinkmann is working with the International Rehabilitation Council for Torture Victims

(CINTRAS), in Chile, a center for mental health and human rights, that works to alleviate the physical and emotional suffering of persons affected by torture or other forms of political repression. See www.irct.org. I thank Freimut Duve for his support for the Global Responsibility Festival "Hamburger Ideenkette" that I organized in Hamburg, Germany, in 1993, see www.humiliationstudies.org/whoweare/evelin/03.php.

242 Health and Human Rights Info, www.hhri.org/about/.

243 The International Center for Transitional Justice (ICTJ) is an international nonprofit organization specializing in the field of transitional justice with www.ictj.org. I thank also Wolfgang Kaleck for making me aware of this organization.

244 I thank Wolfgang Kaleck, et al., 2007, for explaining to me, during our meeting in Berlin on May 17, 2011, that there is no standard model for dealing with the past, but that a number of precedents have been established through the work of special rapporteurs and experts of the United Nations on the issues of impunity, reparations, and best practices in transitional justice. The principles against impunity were initially formulated by Louis Joinet in 1997 and later revised by Diane F. Orentlicher in 2005. Louis Joinet was a longtime UN expert and one of the main architects behind the Convention against Enforced Disappearances, and Diane Orentlicher is professor of international law and co-director of the Center for Human Rights and Humanitarian Law at Washington College of Law. The "Joinet/Orentlicher" principles are based on the precepts of state responsibility and the inherent right of redress for individual victims of grave human rights violations. See the reports submitted by Theo Van Boven (E/CN.4/Sub.2/1993/8), Louis Joinet (E7CN.4/Sub.2/1997/20/Rev.1), Diane Orentlicher (E/CN.4/2005/102/Add.1), and Cherif Bassiouni (E/CN.4/2000/62), and also Orentlicher, 2016.

245 Margalit, 1996, 1997, 2002.

246 See, among others, Kleinig, 2011, Kleinig and Evans, 2013.

247 See Pettit, 1996, 1997a, 2014.

248 Fuller and Gerloff, 2008. It is a privilege to have Robert Fuller as esteemed member in the global advisory board of the Human Dignity and Humiliation Studies fellowship.

249 "Features: A Matter of Pride: Why We Can't Buy Off the Next Osama bin Laden," by Peter Bergen and Michael Lind, Democracy: A Journal of Ideas, Winter 2007, Number 3, http://democracyjournal.org/magazine/3/a-matter-of-pride/. See for a recent publication, Bergen, 2016. See, furthermore, "The Future by Al Gore – Review," by John Gray, The Guardian, January 31, 2013, www.theguardian.com/books/2013/jan/31/the-future-al-gore-review. See Gore, 2013. See, furthermore, Pratto and Stewart, 2011, or Jost, et al., 2009. Compare also Tocqueville, 1856.

250 Pape, 2005.

251 Moïsi, 2007, p. 8. I thank Selina Köhr for making me aware of this commentary by Dominque Moïsi. See also Moïsi, 2009.

252 See note 35 in the Preface.

253 Lindner, 2001f.

254 Huntington, 1996.

255 Lindner, 2006c, p. 172. See also Moïsi, 2007.

256 Lindner, 2002, p. 127.

257 Adapted from Lindner, 2006c, pp. 171–72.

258 "Critical thinking #3: An Interview with the Literary Critic Dwight Garner," by David Wolf, Prospect, October 15, 2013, www.prospectmagazine.co.uk/art-books/interview-with-dwight-garner/#.UnY2lBCmYnP.

259 Schmid, 2013, p. 59. Kessels, 2010.

260 Keyes, 1995. I thank Linda Hartling for making me aware of this book and sharing her notes.

261 See reflections on excluded knowledges in the dialogue that Howard Richards, Catherine Odora Hoppers, and Lindner conducted after his Lecture Two of Beyond Foucault: The Rise of Indigenous Subjugated Knowledges, given in Pretoria, South Africa, May 4, 2013, http://youtu.be/IcilckWWE1Y, and http://youtu.be/emYEFqqTOoE. See for more Richards, et al., 2015a. It is a privilege to have Howard Richards, Catherine Odora Hoppers, and her brother George as esteemed members in the global advisory board of our Human Dignity and Humiliation Studies fellowship.

262 Escrigas, 2016, pp. 7–8: "Today, education is focused on maximizing the content of the curriculum, some of which will soon become obsolete. To address the rapid evolution of knowledge, the prevailing educational paradigm needs to shift from a focus on knowing to one on being... .We must find ways for specialization to coexist with education for global citizenship."

263 "What Orwell Can Teach Us About the Language of Terror and War," by Rowan Williams, The Guardian, December 12, 2015, www.theguardian.com/books/2015/dec/12/words-on-war-a-summons-to-writers-orwell-lecture. I thank Ken Pope and Linda Hartling for making me aware of this article. Merton, 1969, wrote an essay on "War and the Crisis of Language," in which he develops an Orwellian polemic against the corruption of writing and how the speech of military strategists and of politicians is characterized "by a narcissistic finality."

264 In 2017, the scientists in charge of the Doomsday Clock set the clock at just two and a half minutes from the apocalypse, considering that the Earth is now closer to oblivion than it has ever been since 1953, at the height of the nuclear confrontation between the U.S.A. and the Soviet Union. See http://thebulletin.org/timeline. See also the William J. Perry Project (www.wjperryproject.org) that was created by the former U.S. secretary of defense to work toward a world in which nuclear weapons are never used again.

265 "Scientists Warn of Perilous Climate Shift Within Decades, Not Centuries." See more in note 46 in the Preface. See also the first book by climate scientist James Hansen, 2009.

266 "The Conflict Horizon 3: Only Connect," Dan Smith, Dan Smith's Blog: Analysis and Commentary on World Issues, April 25, 2014, dansmithsblog.com/2014/04/25/the-conflict-horizon-3-only-connect/. See the full note in the pdf edition of this book.

267 Schirrmacher, 2006. I thank Axel Rojzcyk for making me aware of this book.

268 "The Torah of Nonviolence: An Interview with Rabbi Lynn Gottlieb," by Emma Varvaloucas, Tricycle, Fall 2012, www.tricycle.com/web-exclusive/torah-nonviolence. Lynn Gottlieb is one of the first ten women to become a rabbi and the first woman ordained as a rabbi in the Jewish Renewal Movement, Rabbi Lynn is a committed peace activist who grounds her life in nonviolence. I thank Nimrod Sheinman for making me aware of this article. See also Gottlieb, 1995. It is a privilege to have Nimrod Sheinman as esteemed member in our Human Dignity and Humiliation Studies fellowship. I will never forget how he and his family welcomed me to spend many days, in November 2003, with his father-in-law, Joseph-Harry Linser, a Holocaust survivor, to chronicle his horrifying experiences. See his life story in Linser, 2016.

269 In The Public and its Problems, philosopher John Dewey, 1927, defends democracy against journalist Walter Lippmann's argument that the "bewildered herd" can never become "omnicompetent citizens" and therefore needs experts. Yet, also these experts, as outsiders, would be incapable of effective action. John Dewey (1859 – 1952) agreed with the assertion of Lippmann (1889 – 1974) that the modern world was becoming too complex for citizens to grasp all its aspects, but Dewey, unlike Lippmann, believed that the public (a composite of many "publics" within society) could form a "Great Community" that could become educated about issues, come to judgments and arrive at solutions to societal problems.

270 Douglas Schuler in his contribution to the Great Transition Network (GTN) discussion on the topic of "A Higher Calling for Higher Education," June 2, 2016, in response to Escrigas, 2016. See

www.publicsphereproject.org/sites/default/files/enablers.pdf. See the full note in the pdf edition of this book.

271 Papadopoulos, 2006, pp. 98–99.

272 Claudia Neubauer, Fondation Charles Léopold Mayer (FPH), in her contribution to the Great Transition Network (GTN) discussion on the topic of "A Higher Calling for Higher Education," May 25, 2016, in response to Escrigas, 2016. See also Neubauer and Calamé, 2013. See, furthermore, Fellman, 1998. John Amos Comenius (1592 – 1670) speaks of gardens. He is a Czech philosopher, pedagogue and theologian, considered to be the "father of modern education." Philosopher Henning Vierck has even created a Comenius garden in one of the most socially vulnerable parts of Berlin, see Der Comeniusgarten in Berlin, ttt – titel thesen temperatmente, Das Erste, July 24, 2016, www.daserste.de/information/wissen-kultur/ttt/sendung/comeniusgarten-berlin-neukoelln-100.html. See the full note in the pdf edition of this book.

273 "The Election, Lao Tzu, a Cup of Water," by Ursula Kröber Le Guin, Book View Café, November 21, 2016, http://bookviewcafe.com/blog/2016/11/21/the-election-lao-tzu-a-cup-of-water/. I thank Linda Hartling of making me aware of her fellow Portland citizen Ursula Le Guin and her work.

274 Ibid.

275 This paragraph is adapted from Lindner, et al., 2009.

276 Lindner, 2014d. See also Lindner, 2001f, Lindner, 2001g, Lindner, 2001h, Lindner, 2004a, Lindner and Backe, 2004, Lindner, 2005b, Lindner, 2005c, Lindner, 2008b, Lindner, 2009c, Lindner, et al., 2009, Lindner, 2011, Lindner, 2012a, Lindner, 2012g, Lindner, 2014d. See also Del Re, et al., 2009.

277 Lindner, 2016b.

278 Lindner, 2006c.

279 Rosa, 2005, 2010. Hartmut Rosa is a professor of Sociology at the Friedrich Schiller University of Jena in Germany, and the head of the Max-Weber center of advanced cultural and social studies of the University of Erfurt. See also Why Are We Stuck Behind the Social Acceleration? TED talk by Hartmut Rosa, March 11, 2015, https://youtu.be/7uG9OFGId3A. How to have a good life in light of rapid social acceleration? Rosa reflects on how to overcome the feeling of mute and silent world. Rosa's argument is that modern societies are subjected to too close-meshed time regimes that regulate, coordinate, and control them outside of any ethical concepts.

280 Parkins and Craig, 2006. See also the 2016 Stanford University's 125th Commencement Address by historical documentary filmmaker Ken Burns, June 12, 2016, http://news.stanford.edu/2016/06/12/prepared-text-2016-stanford-commencement-address-ken-burns/. I thank Linda Hartling for making me aware of this address.

281 See note 83 in the Preface.

282 See a summary composed in 2011 of Volume I: The Past: Terrorism in the Name of Honor – Terror as Accepted Path to Honor/Domination (the headings have changed slightly since):

Volume I, Section 1: The Security Dilemma – Too Far Apart

The first sections of this book invite the reader into understanding the landscape within which tactics of terror are inscribed. For this analysis, phenomena such as circumscription, which is a term used in anthropology, and the security dilemma, a term used in political science, are central. This conceptualization not only helps understanding in general by opening space for novel and constructive interpretations of present-day reality, but, most importantly, it opens space to manifest rejection in respectful ways.

Volume I, Section 2: Honor Humiliation – Outside Pressure to Kill

Honor is the term used in this book to denote the cultural script of the duty to kill one's enemies, to go to duel-like combat when one's status is threatened by equal peers or enemies, and for inferiors to remain in their due lowly place. This script still informs cultures in many parts of the world today. Terrorism often draws on this cultural script. It is therefore crucial to understand its inner logic. This section looks at the intricate and often hideous ways in which the ranking of human worth into supposedly higher beings who deserve more, and lesser beings who deserve less, was enforced throughout long stretches of human history in most world regions.

Terrorism is inscribed into the conundrum of overtly enforced and covertly achieved rankings, as they both stand in opposition to the ideal of equality in dignity. If I have learned to obey, and furthermore learned to identify with my masters definitions of the world, I am a useful tool in the hands of terror entrepreneurs, be they engaged in terror or war on terror.

Volume I, Section 3: Peace à la Hitler – Keeping One's Enemies Out and One's Own People Down

The security dilemma is a tragic dilemma that keeps all players in a permanent state of terror. Leaders live in unrelenting fear of neighboring rulers – alliances can always very quickly morph into enmity – and subalterns are kept in fear of their superiors and their enemies.

This section explains how peace is defined and enforced in cultures shaped by a strong security dilemma. Peace, in such a context, is regarded as the calm and quiet that reigns when power arrangements are stable, both vertically (with respect to out-groups), and horizontally (with respect to a ruler's in-group subordinates). Such stability is typically achieved through recipes of Realpolitik, i.e. pragmatic carrots-and-sticks negotiations that aim at creating allegiances by threatening with violence or by offering material and/or status rewards.

This concept of Realpolitik is the most influential road map, until today, both nationally, but, more importantly, internationally. Tribal honor in Pakistan is imbued with it, as is the Southern honor in the United States that historian Bertram Wyatt-Brown describes in his book with the same title. Honor often plays a strong role at the level of powerful international elites dealing with each other. It is strong in foreign policy matters, in armed services and diplomatic staffs, more so than among the lower echelons of the average citizen. A passion to retain a state's "honorable" preeminence, as Donald Kagan proposes, applies in today's world no less than it did earlier, even where "national honor" is partly concealed by human rights rhetoric and no longer invoked as openly as in the past.

283 See a summary composed in 2011 of Volume II: The Present: Terrorism in the Name of Dignity – Terror as Unacceptable Path to More Dignity (the headings have changed slightly since):

Volume II, Section 1: The Dignity Dilemma – Too Close Together

Anthropologists call the coming-together of humankind that characterizes our times the ingathering of the tribes of the Earth: "For the first time since the origin of our species, humanity is in touch with itself."

The security dilemma is characterized by two binary opposites, namely, inside versus outside, and up versus down. Ingathering, or the shrinking of the world through globalization, affects both dualities. The result is that dignity and humiliation acquire hitherto unknown salience. This is of crucial relevance for understanding motives behind and strategies for tactics of terror, both with respect to terror and to war on terror, and their evaluations.

This section describes how in an increasingly globalizing and interdependent world, which is at the same time exposed to human rights ideals, no longer is it the fear entailed in the security dilemma but the wounds from failing respect for equality in dignity and rights which play a key role. Metaemotions, or how people feel about feelings, change profoundly: no longer is humiliation regarded as prosocial if perpetrated on underlings, but as antisocial in all cases. Might is no longer automatically accepted as right.

Volume II, Section 2: Dignity Humiliation – Inner Urge to Kill

Please read the following account and reflect whether it causes gut feelings of revulsion in you, or the joy they produced just a few hundred years ago. Sir James George Frazer (1854 – 1941), professor of social anthropology at Liverpool University, wrote about historic practices:

In the midsummer fires formerly kindled on the Place de Grève at Paris it was the custom to burn a basket, barrel, or sack full of live cats, which was hung from a tall mast in the midst of the bonfire; sometimes a fox was burned. The people collected the embers and ashes of the fire and took them home, believing that they brought good luck. The French kings often witnessed these spectacles and even lit the bonfire with their own hands. In 1648 Louis the Fourteenth, crowned with a wreath of roses and carrying a bunch of roses in his hand, kindled the fire, danced at it and partook of the banquet afterwards in the town hall.

This section highlights the deep change in the scope of human sensibilities that began a few hundred years ago. The idea of interpersonal forgiveness, with its accompanying ideas of apology, remorse, and a change of heart on the part of the wrongdoer, did not exist in ancient Greece and Rome, nor was it fully present in the Hebrew Bible or in the New Testament. This is what, for instance, philologist David Konstan shows in his work. Interpersonal forgiveness is a creation of the eighteenth and nineteenth centuries. Forgiveness had formerly been God's sole prerogative. Divine forgiveness had first to be secularized to shape the backbone of what is today known as interpersonal forgiveness.

The concept of humiliation provides another illustration. The earliest recorded use of to humiliate meaning to mortify or to lower or to depress the dignity or self-respect of someone does not occur until 1757. In other words, the English language, the connotations of the verbs to humiliate and to humble parted around two hundred fifty years ago, going into opposite directions. Until that time, the verb to humiliate did not signify the violation of dignity. To humiliate meant merely to lower or to humble (to remind underlings of their due place), and this was widely regarded as a prosocial activity.

Volume II, Section 3: Peace à la Mandela – Inclusive Dialogue Between Equals

Human rights ideals represent a normative u-turn – no longer is the subjugation of the socio- and ecosphere by small dominator elites regarded as God-given. The new ideal is respect, mutuality, and balance. It is dialogue among partners considering each other as equals in dignity and rights, and it is respect for the planet's ecosphere.

A person who is set to commit terrorist acts to redress humiliated honor, will not be open to the same arguments of dissuasion as a person who is motivated by humiliated dignity. Empathy and dialogue in an atmosphere of mutual understanding and respect may be unacceptable as redress of matters of honor but rather be understood as weakness and cowardice.

A person whose urge to inflict terror flows from humiliated dignity, in contrast, may be much more open to such arguments. Through having connected to the emotions that surround the concept of dignity, she is "primed" to respond positively to empathy, dialogue, mutual understanding, respect, and individual dissent and responsibility. This priming must be recognized and responded to wisely if the threat of terrorism is to be reduced.

This section explains that responding wisely means acknowledging that dignity humiliation can only be healed through truly empathic dialogue and through true integrity of understanding and respect. The depth of the pain that flows from dignity humiliation must be acknowledged. Dignity humiliation cannot be redressed through the rhetoric of Realpolitik, nor through narrow rational choice approaches to negotiation, nor through bribing or threatening with "lessons" of shock and awe – all those strategies are informed by the calculus of domination and submission of ranked honor. And it can certainly not be mended by professing human rights ideals while betraying them with double standards.

284 See a summary composed in 2011 of Volume III: The Future: Toward a Terror-Free World (the headings have changed slightly since):

Volume III, Section 1: Creating a World of Unity in Diversity – Humanizing Globalization Through Egalization

The global village is one village, not two, not three, and not several villages. This fact is the most important paradigm-shifting force in the imagery and reality of one interconnected world. The reason is that it weakens the security dilemma. This dilemma is so tragic that it can lead to war even when nobody desires it and the involved players are ever so peaceable otherwise. The weakening of the security dilemma is an unprecedented historic window of opportunity as it has never presented itself to humankind ever before. It opens space not only to unite globally, but also to replace power-over strategies with mutuality that is embedded in equality in dignity. Coercive hierarchies can now transmute into creative networks of unity in diversity. No longer must the human family be fragmented and ranked, but can be united and equal. Tactics of terror are no longer necessary and can be unlearned. This section urges that this window of opportunity must be grasped proactively if it is not to be lost.

Volume III, Section 2: Practicing the Gandhi and Mandela Way – Understanding but Not Condoning, Respecting but Not Appeasing

In an honor context, offering dialogue risks appearing "weak," while showing readiness to defend oneself with violence signals "I am strong." As long as all actors adhere to such a code, there is no contradiction; raw might is victorious and all agree with the outcome even if it hurts.

This section shows how the situation grows complicated and far more hurtful when two different sets of ground rules clash. In a context, in which people judge coercive domination to be an unethical and immoral violation of dignity codes, introducing the old code of honor produces violations of the new code, and vice versa. This can severely deepen wounds on all sides, rather than healing them.

Responding with scripts of dignity to terror that is scripted by honor, or vice versa, will fail. Strategies of dignity will cause violations of honor, and vice versa. Strategies of dignity can only succeed, if the human rights ideals and values of equality in dignity are first explained and advocated.

Volume III, Section 3: Practicing the Human Dignity Way – Careholdership for Global Equality in Dignity

This section is future-oriented and provocative. It discusses controversial and challenging visions for the future from the perspective of Human Dignity and Humiliation Studies.

The most significant historical process of present times is that an emerging globally connected knowledge society opens space to liberate ideals, metaphysical concepts, cultural and psychological scripts, feelings, and emotions from being instrumentalized to serve the security dilemma. This process opens space, for example, for Martin Buber's concept of loving I-Thou relationships characterized by mutual respect for equal dignity to replace the old concept of love and hatred as commodified tools to survive the security dilemma. This process also opens space to recover the prosocial aspects of shame in fundamentally new ways, the notion of "prosociality" no longer being equated with docile subservience of underlings, but with relationships of mutuality between equals.

This section maps out how tactics of terror can be healed and prevented in a united world characterized by the human rights ideals of equality in dignity for all. Since tactics of terror are part and parcel of a fragmented world of inequality in honor, no other transition is comprehensive enough to decrease terror than the transition to unity in diversity as manifestation of unity in equal dignity. Such a large-scale changeover cannot be brought about by one person or one nation, and it seems therefore like a far-fetched strategy for decreasing tactics of terror. Still, it is the single most important focus every citizen must hold, at every moment and in every single detail of life. And this is valid also for all who are concerned about terror. This section presents a variety of possible interventions at macro, meso and micro levels.

285 Lindner, 2006c, p. 52.

286 "Keynote Dialogue: In conversation with William Ury, Co-Author, Getting to Yes, USA, Geraldine McAteer and Jackie Redpath from Northern Ireland together with speakers from Bosnia, Israel, and South Africa," at the launching of the Co-existence Initiative of the State of the World Forum in Belfast, Northern Ireland, in May 2–9, 1999.

287 Waller, 2002.

288 Morgenthau, 1946.

289 Nietzsche, 1887/2013.

290 See Craig Murray #NoWar2016, World Beyond War, September 26, 2016, https://youtu.be/COjqnowC1JA, where he uses the example of Sierra Leone. When I was in Sierra Leone in 1976, I learned about the Hut Tax War of 1898, a violent local resistance against a severe tax on huts imposed by British colonial forces. Murray draws a line from this war to the cruelties perpetrated later in the region, and how those atrocities were used as pretext to renew the colonization of resources through Western power players. See also Murray, 2006. Like Murray, also I have been confronted with the argument that "shooting them" is the only way to deal with people who use terror tactics, rather than dissecting historical cycles of humiliation. See the full note in the pdf edition of this book.

291 Ridley, 1996.

292 Chagnon, 1968, and see for a more recent publication, Chagnon, 2013.

293 Pinker, 2002. His first two popular books are Pinker, 1995, 1997.

294 Lakoff, 2006a. See note 211 in this Introduction.

295 See the Eurobarometer 79.3, 2013, showing the results to the question: "Please tell me if you tend to trust or tend not to trust: Political Parties, the National Government, the National Parliament," http://ec.europa.eu/public_opinion/archives/eb/eb79/eb79_first_en.pdf. In 2013, trust in national parliament stood in Central and Eastern Europe at 17 percent, in Southern Europe at 19 percent, in Western Europe at 39 percent, and in Northern Europe at 63 percent. Trust in national government in 2013 stood in Central and Eastern Europe at 22 percent, in Southern Europe at 19 percent, in Western Europe at 37 percent, and in Northern Europe at 48 percent. Trust had gone down since it was measured in 2008 for all national institutions in all countries.

296 See also "Why the P2P and Commons Movement Must Act Trans-Locally and Trans-Nationally," by Michel Bauwens, P2P Foundation, June 12, 2016, https://blog.p2pfoundation.net/p2p-commons-movement-must-act-trans-locally-trans-nationally/2016/06/16. I thank Uli Spalthoff for making me aware of this article. Bauwens recommends Karatani, 2014. Like Alan Page Fiske, 1991, in Structures of Social Life, also Karatini recognizes four basic modes of social life, and these modes exist at all times and in all places. As to levels of measurement, psychologist Stanley Smith Stevens, 1946, developed the best known classification with four levels, or scales of measurement: nominal, ordinal, interval, and ratio. See also note 114 in the Inspiring Questions to Section Two.

297 See, among others, Kautsky, 1982.

298 Lindner, 2016b. See also Brendtro, et al., 2009, for saying "you no longer belong to our group" amounts to the ultimate form of punishment of social death. I thank Mechthild Nagel, for making me aware of Brendtro's work. See also the work of ethologist Konrad Lorenz, 1963/1966, who, in his book On Aggression, describes intergroup aggression as being different from intragroup aggression. Among animals, fights for rank are seldom fatal, while, by contrast, groups of animals might fight to the death among each other, willing to kill or be killed in defense of their community.

299 Karlberg, 2013. Discourse analyst Michael Karlberg describes three contrasting deep interpretive frames within which the concept of human dignity can be understood: the social command frame, the social command frame of dignity, in contrast to the social contest frame and the social body frame. He points out that these frames sometimes co-exist in contradictory or fragmented ways. Also George Lakoff, 2006b, explains that people employ interpretive frames in unconscious ways that are not always consistent or coherent, and that can change over time. See the full note in the pdf edition of this book.

300 Carol Anderson, 2016, speaks of "white rage, the unspoken truth of our racial divide."

301 The third of the five axioms of communication by Gregory Bateson, 1972, drawn on by Watzlawick, et al., 1967, refers to the sender and the receiver of information structuring the communication flow differently, each seeing their own behavior as a reaction to the other's behavior.
When I was a psychology student in Hamburg, Germany (1974 – 1978), one of my professors was Friedemann Schulz von Thun, 1981, who built his four-sides model of communication on Watzlawick's insights and on the three sides of the Organon model by Karl Bühler, 1934/1990. The four sides of communication begin with the "matter layer" pertaining to data and facts, second, there is the layer of self-revealing or self-disclosure of the speaker – intended or not – pertaining to motives, values, or emotions, third, there is the "relationship layer" as it is intended or understood, and, fourth, the "appeal layer" points at what the speaker is aiming at. Every layer can be misunderstood separately.

302 Schulz von Thun, 1981, p. 62.

303 See note 238 in this Introduction.

304 Keval, 2016.

305 Keval, 2016, book description.

306 See note 73 in this Introduction.

307 Keval, 2016, book description.

308 Robert Muller (1923 – 2010), former UN Under-Secretary General, stood for the vision of the United Nation that I highly appreciate. He is widely quoted as having said that we ought "to see the world with global eyes, to love the world with a global heart, to understand the world with a global mind, and to merge with the world with a global spirit." James Paul served for nearly nineteen years as executive director of the New York-based Global Policy Forum tracking the politics of the United Nations, and he explains that, in theory, "the Secretary General fills these posts independently, drawing on the best candidates worldwide. The Charter mandates independence of UN staff from government interference." The problem is that this does not necessarily happen in practice: "Even the most effective incumbents serving in these P5-controlled posts symbolize a system of disregard for the Charter, disrespect for the opinions of other nations, and contempt for the very idea of neutrality of the international civil service," see "UN Not Serving the Global Good: Big Powers Set to Grab High Level Un Posts," by Thalif Deen, Inter Press Service (IPS), October 18, 2016, www.ipsnews.net/2016/10/big-powers-set-to-grab-high-level-un-posts/.

309 Sadly, the UN Interagency Framework Team for Preventive Action (FT) that Gay Rosenblum-Kumar had developed over more than twenty years was dismantled in 2014. I thank her for inviting me to share my work with her colleagues nearly every year during my annual stays in New York. For the first time this was at a brown bag lunch titled "Humiliation, Conflict Management, and Policy Making" at the Governance and Public Administration Branch of the Department of Economic and Social Affairs at the United Nations, on December 15, 2004. It is a privilege to have Gay Rosenblum-Kumar as esteemed member in the global advisory board of our Human Dignity and Humiliation Studies fellowship.

310 Lindner, 2016b.

311 See, among others, Lindner, 2001e, Lindner, 2014c, or Lindner, 2017.

312 Lindner, 2012b.

313 See for a list of past and future conferences www.humiliationstudies.org/whoweare/annualmeetings.php. See where we stand in 2015 at www.humiliationstudies.org/whoweare/whoweare.php#status.

314 It is a privilege to have Paul Stokes, College Lecturer in the Department of Sociology at the National University of Ireland in Dublin, as esteemed member in the global advisory board of our Human Dignity and Humiliation Studies fellowship.

315 Project 1: Refugees and Humiliation: How Dignity is Degraded When You Are a Refugee, or a Displaced or Stateless Person, www.humiliationstudies.org/research/projects.php#unu. This project was envisioned in 2005 as a large research project with 21 research teams of young scholars and their academic advisors, prepared by Evelin Lindner and Paul Stokes, invited by Ramesh Thakur and to be conducted in cooperation with the United Nations University (UNU), Tokyo, Japan. Article 1 of the Universal Declaration of Human Rights of 1948 states that "all human beings are born free and equal in dignity and rights." In this research project we asked: What happens when rights and dignity are violated? What are the long-term effects? What is, for example, the long-term effect on people who are born, live and die as refugees, in refugee camps? What are the inter-generational effects? How are second and third generation refugees affected? Due to lack of finances, this project could not be realized.
Project 2: Terrorism and Humiliation: Why People Choose Terrorism, www.humiliationstudies.org/research/projects.php#unu. This project was envisioned in 2005 as a large research project with 9 research teams of young scholars and their academic advisors, prepared by Evelin Lindner and Paul Stokes, invited by Ramesh Thakur and to be conducted in cooperation with the United Nations University (UNU), Tokyo, Japan. The question guiding this project was: Why do people choose terrorism? This question merited deeper probing. The project aimed at shedding more light on the choices made by people who choose terrorism, so as to help prevent terrorism more efficiently. Due to lack of finances, this project could, however, not be realized.

316 It is a privilege to have Zahid Shahab Ahmed as esteemed member in our Human Dignity and Humiliation Studies fellowship. In 2016, Zahid Shahab Ahmed joined the Alfred Deakin Institute for Citizenship and Globalization of Deakin University in Australia as a postdoctoral fellow. See, for instance, Shahab Ahmed and Zeb, 2016. See also Krueger, 2017. And see an endorsement of the argument that terrorism does not follow from poverty, but from lack of freedom, in "The Roots of Terrorism," by Sultan Mehmood, Dawn, March 3, 2016, www.dawn.com/news/796177/the-roots-of-terrorism:

A cursory analysis of the START Global Terrorism Database reveals that over the past decade, Pakistan has had the highest number of terrorism-related deaths in the world. In fact, the death toll exceeds the combined terrorism-related deaths for both Europe and North America. Hence, an understanding of terrorism, its dynamics, its causes, the reasons for its escalation and de-escalation is of utmost importance to Pakistan. … To understand what causes terrorism, one need not ask how much of a population is illiterate or in abject poverty. Rather one should ask who holds strong enough political views to impose them through terrorism. It is not that most terrorists have nothing to live for. Far from it, they are the high-ability and educated political people who so vehemently believe in a cause that they are willing to die for it. The solution to terrorism is not more growth but more freedom.

317 Lindner, 2011.

318 See also Romarheim, 2015, or Grønnerød, et al., 2016, or Mesøy, 2013.

319 It is a privilege to have Kristian Berg Harpviken, former director of the Peace Research Institute Oslo (PRIO), and many of its present and former members, as esteemed members in the global advisory board of our Human Dignity and Humiliation Studies fellowship.

320 Hegghammer, 2016. See the full note in the pdf edition of this book.

321 Lindner, 2001c. I thank Monty G. Marshall for his immense support since 2001. Monty Marshall contributed to the expert meeting with his talk on Structural Indicators Measurement and Application to session # 4, Indicators of Social System Vulnerability and Resilience to Violent Conflict. It is a privilege to have Monty Marshall as esteemed member in the global advisory board of our Human Dignity and Humiliation Studies fellowship since its inception. See, among others, Marshall, 1999, 2002, 2014–2016. See for the work of Ted Gurr, among many others, Goldstone, et al., 2010, Gurr, 1970. I thank Monty Marshall for bringing Jack Goldstone to our 2008 Annual Conference of Human Dignity and Humiliation Studies, as

part of the Wergeland Year for Human Dignity, in Oslo, Norway, June 23 – July 1, 2008, www.humiliationstudies.org/whoweare/annualmeeting/11.php. It is a privilege to have also Jack Goldstone as esteemed member in the global advisory board of our Human Dignity and Humiliation Studies fellowship.

322 It is a privilege to have Clark McCauley as esteemed member in the global advisory board of our Human Dignity and Humiliation Studies fellowship. See his most recent publication in McCauley, 2017, and McCauley and Moskalenko, 2017. See a list over our workshops at www.humiliationstudies.org/whoweare/annualmeetings.php. See also the work of psychologist Arie Kruglanski, among others, Doosje, et al., 2016, Dugas and Kruglanski, 2014. It is a privilege to have Arie Kruglanski as esteemed member in the global advisory board of our Human Dignity and Humiliation Studies fellowship.

323 Schmid, 2013.

324 See Lambert, 2008, and Lindner, et al., 2009. See also Lambert, 2011.

325 Lindner, 2012b.

326 Lindner, 2014a.

327 Lindner, 2013, Lindner and Morrell, 2013, Lindner and Sewchurran, 2013, Richards, et al., 2015a, Lindner, 2015a.

328 Lindner, 2016a.

329 Erik Solheim was Minister of International Development when our conversation on humiliation and terrorism took place in the Ministry of Foreign Affairs in Oslo, Norway, on January 10, 2011. Solheim's reflections are summarized and translated from Norwegian by Lindner. See the full note in the pdf edition of this book.

330 Psychologists Jim Sidanius and Felicia Pratto speak of legitimizing myths, or compelling cultural ideologies that are taken as self-apparently true in society and that disguise the use of force and discrimination and make it acceptable. See Sidanius and Pratto, 1999. See an overview in "Power Inequities," by Máire A. Dugan, Beyond Intractability, February 2004, www.beyondintractability.org/essay/power-inequities. See also Pratto and Stewart, 2011, where they describe how legitimizing myths change over time. Read more in Chapter 2, and See the full note in the pdf edition of this book.

331 See Volkan, 1997, 2004, 2006, 2013.

332 See more on the notion of misrecognition in Lindner, 2009b, Chapter 5 and 8 of the book Emotion and Conflict, pp. 129–137. Concepts such as méconnaissance (misrecognition) and naturalization were used by Roland Barthes, Pierre Bourdieu, and Michel Foucault (among others). They address how power structures use the concealed nature of habitus to manipulate not just overtly but covertly and stealthily, making it much more difficult to rid oneself of these manipulations.

333 See note 184 in this Introduction.

334 For instance, Tocqueville, 1856. See also "The Future by Al Gore – Review," by John Gray, The Guardian, January 31, 2013, www.theguardian.com/books/2013/jan/31/the-future-al-gore-review. See Gore, 2013. See, furthermore, Pratto and Stewart, 2011, or Jost, et al., 2009. See, furthermore, note 249 in this Introduction.

335 Lerner, 1980.

336 Galtung, 1996, p. 199.

337 Kuhn, 1962.

338 Ibid.

339 Jervis, 2006.

340 Carveth, 2013.

341 See note 201 in this Introduction.

342 See Arie Nadler, 2012, p. 304. See more in note 69 in the Preface.

343 Suttner, 1889. See also Heffermehl, 2010.

344 See note 146 in the Preface.

345 Fanon, 1952/1967, 1961/1963.

346 See also Slavoj Žižek, 2012, and his message that an emancipatory project needs to resist any smooth reconciliation and dare to look into the face of all that is lacking.

347 The work of neuroscientists such as Jean Decety shows that desensitization to own or other people's pain may be beneficial, for example, in physicians, but can also lead to an overall blunting of emotional sensitivity. See Decety, et al., 2010. Children with conduct disorder and callousness exhibited dampened hemodynamic response to viewing others being harmed in the insula, a region which plays a key role in empathy and emotional awareness. See Michalska, et al., 2016. See also van der Kolk, 2014. I thank Linda Hartling for reminding me of van Kolk's book.

348 van der Kolk, 2014. I thank Linda Hartling for reminding me of this book.

349 Staub, 1989, 1993, 2012, 2015.

350 Mimi Stokes-Katzenbach, Sustainable Creatives (www.dramaticsustainability.com), in her contribution to the Great Transition Network (GTN) discussion on the topic of "Monetizing Nature," July 31, 2014.

351 Lars Weisæth and Kärki, 2014. See the full note in the pdf edition of this book.

352 Silke, 2003.

353 McCauley, 2017, p. 263. McCauley refers to the 9/11 attack, and my suggestion in Lindner, 2006c, pp. 98 –100, that it was humiliating for a superpower like America to be so grievously injured and insulted by an enemy that did not even have the status of being a state. See also Scott and Philip, 2004.

354 "Education in the Context of 'Divided' Memories – How can a 'Pedagogy of Conflict Elaboration' Contribute?" by Monique Eckmann, School for Social Work at the University of Applied Sciences, Western Switzerland, Geneva, The European Wergeland Centre (EWC), August 2013, www.theewc.org/uploads/content/statement_MEckmann_final_2.pdf. See also Edmondson, 1999, p. 354, and "New Research Reveals Surprising Truths about Why Some Work Groups Thrive and Others Falter," by Charles Duhigg, New York Times, February 25, 2016, www.nytimes.com/2016/02/28/magazine/what-google-learned-from-its-quest-to-build-the-perfect-team.html. I thank Linda Hartling for making me aware of this article.

355 "Education in the Context of 'Divided' Memories – How can a 'Pedagogy of Conflict Elaboration' Contribute?" by Monique Eckmann, August 2013, www.theewc.org/uploads/content/statement_MEckmann_final_2.pdf.

356 Hudson, et al., 2012.

357 "Human Rights Violation," UNiTE to End Violence against Women campaign, http://endviolence.un.org/situation.shtml.

358 The estimate of about 170 million civilians killed in the twentieth century comes from political scientist Rudolph Joseph Rummel, 1994. Around 100 million deaths can be attributed to Stalin, Mao, and Hitler. The ratio would be 340 to one, if the death from non-state groups over the same period of time could be calculated at around 500,000.

359 "Good Morning, Beautiful Business," Judy Wicks, Twenty-Fourth Annual E. F. Schumacher Lecture, Stockbridge, MA, E. F. Schumacher Society (now New Economics Institute), October 2004, http://centerforneweconomics.org/publications/lectures/wicks/judy/good-morning-beautiful-business?utm_source=Schumacher+Center+eNewsletter&utm_campaign=1959b415a9-Wicks+eNews&utm_medium=email. See also Barney, et al., 2015. I learned very much in the Thirtieth Annual E. F. Schumacher Lectures on November 20, 2010, the Thirty-First Annual E. F. Schumacher Lectures on November 5, 2011, and the Thirty-Fourth Annual E. F. Schumacher Lectures on November 15, 2014, all in New York City. See the full note in the pdf edition of this book.

360 "How a Danish Town Helped Young Muslims Turn Away from ISIS," by Hanna Rosin, National Public Radio (NPR), July 15, 2016, www.npr.org/sections/health-shots/2016/07/15/485900076/how-a-danish-town-helped-young-muslims-turn-away-from-isis?utm_campaign=storyshare&utm. I thank Deb Reich for making me aware of this article.

361 "'Always Agitated. Always Mad': Omar Mateen, According to Those Who Knew Him," by Dan Barry, Serge F. Kovaleski, Alan Blinder And Mujib Mashal, New York Times, June 18, 2016, www.nytimes.com/2016/06/19/us/omar-mateen-gunman-orlando-shooting.html.

362 Hartling and Lindner, 2017, quoting from "Overcompensation Nation: It's Time to Admit that Toxic Masculinity Drives Gun Violence: Our National Attachment to Dominance Models of Manhood Is a Major Reason Why We Have So Much Violence," Amanda Marcotte, Salon, June 13, 2016, www.salon.com/2016/06/13/overcompensation_nation_its_time_to_admit_that_toxic_masculinity_drives_gun_violence/, and "Troubled. Quiet. Macho. Angry. The Volatile Life of the Orlando Shooter," by Kevin Sullivan and William Wan, Washington Post, June 17, 2016, www.washingtonpost.com/national/troubled-quiet-macho-angry-the-volatile-life-of-omar-mateen/2016/06/17/15229250-34a6-11e6-8758-d58e76e11b12_story.html.

363 Taylor, et al., 2002. This may have an evolutionary background. While men were killed, women were often captured alive when communities were invaded and conquered. They may have adapted to this situation by developing a specific reaction to stress.

364 "Put up your dukes," means "get ready to fight," with "dukes" standing for fists.

365 Johnson, et al., 2014. See also Fraenkel, 2015.

366 Johnson, et al., 2014.

367 See, among others, Rogers, 1977, Kirschenbaum and Henderson, 1990, Rogers, et al., 2014. Reinhard Tausch, a student of Carl Rogers, was my professor when I studied psychology and specialized as clinical psychologist at the University of Hamburg, Germany, 1974 – 1978.

368 See Belenky, et al., 1997a, Belenky, et al., 1997b, Clinchy, 1996. In connected knowing "one attempts to enter another person's frame of reference to discover the premises for the person's point of view," explain Clinchy and Zimmerman, 1985. See also Lindner and Desmond Tutu (Foreword), 2010.

369 Clinchy and Zimmerman, 1985.

370 Belenky, et al., 1997b.

371 Heller, 1984. See also social psychologist, feminist, and politician Berit Ås, 2008. See more in notes 66 and 67 in Chapter 7.

372 See, among others, Habermas, 1962, 1981, 1985–1987, 1989.

373 On November 16, 2011, writer and peace scholar Janet Gerson took me to Zuccotti Park and The Atrium in New York City, where most of the Occupy Wall Street activities took place. I thank Janet for sharing with me her insights into the Occupy movement, her doctoral research, and I thank her for reminding me of the significance of the notion of grappling. See www.humiliationstudies.org/whoweare/evelinpics11.php.#OWS.

374 As to the concept of nudging, see, among others, Thaler and Sunstein, 2008, or Sunstein, 2016. For reflections on Conditions of Freedom, see, for instance, John MacMurray, 1949/1991, and on resistance to manipulation, see, among others, Thomas Teo, 2015. I thank Louise Sundararajan for making me aware of Teo's work.

375 Deutsch, 2006.

376 Dobson, 2012.

377 Linda Hartling in a personal communication on June 4, 2009.

378 Miller, 2013.

379 Buber, 1923/1937.

380 Nussbaum and Sen, 1993. See also, among others, Orton, 2011.

381 Freire, 1968/1973, O'Shea and O'Brien, 2011.

382 Bohm, 2014.

383 Scharmer, 2009.

384 Swidler and Mojzes, 2000.

385 Inga Bostad, Vice-Rector of the University in Oslo, Norway, sent a personal message after the 22/7 terror attacks in Oslo and Utøya. In this message, she encouraged and urged everybody to engage in dialogue. Her message was recorded on August 26, 2011, by Lasse Moer, see http://youtu.be/hbOBj_UJt2Y. See also Bostad and Ottersen, 2014. See also note 166 in the Preface.

386 See classic publications by McNeill and McNeill, 2003, or Chaisson, 2001. See also Spier, 2010, Harari, 2014, 2015/2016. See, furthermore, the 2016 Stanford University's 125th Commencement Address by historical documentary filmmaker Ken Burns, June 12, 2016, http://news.stanford.edu/2016/06/12/prepared-text-2016-stanford-commencement-address-ken-burns/. I thank Linda Hartling for making me aware of his address.

387 Arendt, 1963. See also Vita Activa - The Spirit of Hannah Arendt, documentary film by Ada Ushpiz, 2016, https://zeitgeistfilms.com/film/vitaactivathespiritofhannaharendt.

388 Lindner, 2015a.

389 Diamond, 2005, Chapter 10: Malthus in Africa: Rwanda's Genocide, pp. 326–327. I thank Yves Musoni for making me aware of this quote. It is a privilege to have Yves Musoni as esteemed member in our Human Dignity and Humiliation Studies fellowship.

390 Sustainability is yet another term that has been hijacked by economism throughout the past years. Within the international legal system, "a resource economics definition of sustainability encourages development, while granting dispensation to public choice that sacrifices human and environmental integrity for instrumental economic objectives" writes philosopher John Martin Gillroy in his contribution to the Great Transition Network (GTN) discussion on the topic of "Sustainability and Well-Being: A Happy Synergy," March 3, 2017, in response to Barrington-Leigh, 2017.

391 Lindner and Desmond Tutu (Foreword), 2010.

392 Listening into-voice is explained by Linda Hartling as in a personal communication on June 4, 2009. See note 111 in the Preface.

393 Edmondson, 1999, p. 354. See also "New Research Reveals Surprising Truths about Why Some Work Groups Thrive and Others Falter," by Charles Duhigg, New York Times, February 25, 2016, www.nytimes.com/2016/02/28/magazine/what-google-learned-from-its-quest-to-build-the-perfect-team.html. I thank Linda Hartling for making me aware of this article.

394 Schmid, 2013, p. 55.

395 Fernbach, et al., 2013, p. 945. I thank Linda Hartling for making me aware of this article.

396 Kruger and Dunning, 1999.

397 Nickerson and Salovey, 1998.

398 Lord, et al., 1979, Ross, 2012.

399 Lazarsfeld and Merton, 1954.

400 Van Boven, et al., 2012.

401 "The U.S. Media's Problems Are Much Bigger than Fake News and Filter Bubbles," by Bharat N. Anand, Harvard Business Review, January 05, 2017, https://hbr.org/2017/01/the-u-s-medias-problems-are-much-bigger-than-fake-news-and-filter-bubbles?curator=MediaREDEF:

Three forces combine to create the media coverage of political campaigns we observe today: connected media, which spreads messages faster than traditional media; fixed costs and advertising-reliant business models in traditional media, which amplify sensational messages; and viewers' news consumption patterns, which leads to people sorting across media outlets based on their beliefs and makes messages they already agree with far more effective. Each reinforces the others. Without these enabling factors, even the best marketing campaign would go nowhere, and fake news or leaked information from cyberattacks would have little effect.

I thank Seymour M. (Mike) Miller for making Linda and me aware of this article. See the full note in the pdf edition of this book.

402 "Farewell, America," by Neal Gabler, Moyers, November 10, 2016, http://billmoyers.com/story/farewell-america/#.WFS69xeyis0.facebook, written after November 8, 2016, when Donald Trump was voted in to lead the United States. Gabler writes that no matter how the rest of the world looked at America on November 7, 2016, this will now change. See the full note in the pdf edition of this book.

403 Schmid, 2013, p. 55.

404 Horgan and Braddock, 2010, p. 280: "At the very least, it might be more appropriate to collectively refer to these programs as 'risk reduction' initiatives – regardless of the operational differences, resources, and expected outcomes (let alone terminology), attempting to reduce re-engagement in terrorism is the one unambiguous common thread between these initiatives." See also Horgan, 2009, Bjørgo and Horgan, 2009, Bokhari, et al., 2009, Horgan and Braddock, 2011, Canna, 2013.

405 Schmid, 2013, p. 53.

406 Fenstermacher and Leventhal, 2011, Executive Summary, p. 10.

407 Schmid, 2013, p. 56. See another quote from Schmid, 2013, p. 53, in the full Pdf version of this book.

408 McCauley and Moskalenko, 2011, pp. 95–148, and pp. 149–192. See for his most recent publication on that topic McCauley, 2017. It is a privilege to have Clark McCauley as esteemed member in the global advisory board of our Human Dignity and Humiliation Studies fellowship.

409 "First Report of the Working Group on Radicalisation and Extremism that Lead to Terrorism," by the United Nations Counter-Terrorism Implementation Task Force (CTITF), 2008, www.un.org/en/terrorism/pdfs/radicalization.pdf.

410 Elaine Pressman, 2009, Table 7, p. 24, quoted in Schmid, 2013, p. 47. See more in the pdf edition of this book.

411 Schmid, 2013, pp. 41–42. See also Bjørgo and Horgan, 2009, and Horgan and Braddock, 2011. As to the last point, Schmid writes, p. 49: "Perhaps most important is to prevent teaming up with foreign and domestic partners in the fight against terrorism who lack credibility and legitimacy in the eyes of those who are in need of de-radicalization, the radical milieu, the wider constituency which the terrorists try to appeal to, and other relevant domestic and foreign audiences."

412 Schmid, 2013, p. 50.

413 Schmid, 2013, p. 55.

414 The United Nations Global Counter-Terrorism Strategy, Resolution 60/288, adopted by the General Assembly on September 8, 2006, www.un.org/ga/search/view_doc.asp?symbol=A/RES/60/288.

415 Schmid, 2013, pp. 58–59. See also "The Revised Academic Consensus Definition of Terrorism" at www.terrorismanalysts.com/pt/index.php/pot/article/view/schmid-terrorism-definition/html, and "Interview with Professor Alex Schmid about Defining Terrorism," by Edwin Bakker, Leiden University, September 9, 2014, https://youtu.be/eRLvBooAm8o.

416 "Human Rights and Humanitarianism: Contradictory or Co-Dependent?" conference at Columbia University's School of International and Public Affairs, October 30, 2012. See also the Speaking Out Case Studies website (www.speakingout.msf.org) with a series of studies from Médecins Sans Frontières that openly examine and analyze the organization's actions and decision-making process during humanitarian emergencies that have motivated it to speak out. See the full note in the pdf edition of this book. See also note 87 in this Introduction.

417 "Cross Roads or Cross Purposes? Tensions Between Military and Humanitarian Providers," by Solomon Major, The Strategic Studies Institute (the U.S. Army's Institute for Geostrategic and National Security Research and Analysis), 2012, http://strategicstudiesinstitute.army.mil/pubs/parameters/Articles/2012summer/Major.pdf, p. 86.

418 Jost and Ross, 1999.

419 See Lindner, 2006c, Chapter 7: Humiliation Addiction, in the book Making Enemies: Humiliation and International Conflict. See also the conceptualization of the post victim ethical exemption syndrome as an outgrowth of humiliation, by James Edward Jones, 2006. See, furthermore, Lewis Coser, 1956, and his differentiation of realistic and un-realistic conflict. First and foremost, conflict simply presupposes a relationship and social interaction. Not all hostile impulses lead to social conflict, and not every conflict is accompanied by aggressiveness. Realistic conflicts are those that arise from frustration of specific demands and are pursued toward the attainment of specific results. Other pathways than conflict are taken if available. Realistic conflict is thus a means, unlike non-realistic conflict, which is an end in itself. It is fed by one antagonist's need to release tension. The main point is the release of aggressiveness, and the target of hostility can easily change. Clearly, realistic conflicts can also be accompanied by distorted sentiments. Conflict may be motivated by both, realistic conflict issues and parties' affective investment in the conflict. See a summary of Coser, 1956, by the University of Colorado's Conflict Research Consortium Staff, at www.colorado.edu/conflict/peace/example/coser.htm.

420 BCE stands for "Before the Common Era," and is equivalent to BC, which means "Before Christ."

421 Aristotle, 1980.

422 Kidder, 1994.

423 Norway has emerged from the current economic crisis relatively unscathed, not least due to its artful moderation. Philosopher Henrik Syse, 2009, has advised Norwegian banks and explains his view on moderation. Syse refers to the work of Clor, 2009. I am immensely thankful for his support since we first met in Dagfinn Føllesdal's Ethics Programme of the Norwegian Research Council in 1995. It is a privilege to have Henrik Syse as esteemed member in the global advisory board of our Human Dignity and Humiliation Studies fellowship since its inception. See for another Norwegian voice calling for moderation, for example, Vetlesen, 2008.

424 Miller, 1976/1986.

425 Francisco Gomes de Matos is a pillar of Human Dignity and Humiliation Studies from their inception, and a founding member of our World Dignity University initiative.

Section One

See additional material at www.humiliationstudies.org/whoweare/ evelin/book/05.php.

1 BCE stands for "Before the Common Era," and is equivalent to BC, which means "Before Christ."

2 Publius Flavius Vegetius Renatus and Reeve, 2004.

3 "Nicht durch Reden und Majoritätsbeschlüsse werden die großen Fragen der Zeit entschieden – das ist der große Fehler von 1848 und 1849 gewesen – sondern durch Eisen und Blut." Otto von Bismarck was a conservative Prussian statesman who dominated German and European affairs from the 1860s until 1890. This quote is taken from his speech to the Budget Commission of the Prussian Diet on September 30, 1862, published in Böhm, 1866, p. 12.

4 "The Soldier's Faith," by Oliver Wendell Holmes, leading US intellectual and Supreme Court associated jurist, addressing the Harvard 1895 graduating class, http://people.virginia.edu/~mmd5f/holmesfa.htm.

5 "Understanding Hitler's Anti-Semitism," by Edward Delman, The Atlantic, September 9, 2015, www.theatlantic.com/international/archive/2015/09/hitler-holocaust-antisemitism-timothy-snyder/404260/. See also Snyder, 2010, 2015, 2017. See the full note in the pdf edition of this book.

6 The slogan "The War for Peace" was coined in 1991 by Svetozar Marović, when he was the vice president of the ruling Democratic Party of Socialists (DPS) in Montenegro, to justify the Montenegrin reservists' assault on Dubrovnik and Konavle in 1991. Later Marović became the president of Serbia and Montenegro (until June 2006, when Montenegro declared its independence). Historian Nikola Samardžić, in his testimony at the trial of Slobodan Milošević 2002–2005, pointed out that the onslaught on Dubrovnik "was an unjust war against Croatia, and a war in which Montenegro disgraced itself by putting itself in the service of the Yugoslav army and Slobodan Milošević," see Pavlović, 2006. On September 10, 2003, Marović delivered a public apology for "all evils done by any citizen of Montenegro and Serbia to anyone in Croatia," see "Marović i Mesić razmenili izvinjenja građanima Hrvatske i SCG," B92, September 9, 2003, www.b92.net/info/vesti/index.php?yyyy=2003&mm=09&dd=10&nav_id=119131.

7 Stover and Weinstein, 2004.

8 "Fear Thy Neighbor as Thyself: Antinomies of Tolerant Reason" was the title of the lecture that philosopher Slavoj Žižek held at the Institute for Human Sciences at Boston University on November 26, 2007, where he addressed perception, identity, and the "other." See www.egs.edu/faculty/slavoj-zizek/videos/fear-thy-neighbor-as-thyself/.

Introduction to Section One

1 Altemeyer, 1981. See the archive of the original Global Change Game Website, http://web.archive.org/web/20020805124207/www.mts.net/~gcg/index.html.

2 Altemeyer, 1996, Altemeyer, 2003.

3 See for a discussion of layers of complexity, for instance, Lindner, 2001d. And see my explanations of the Weberian ideal-type approach.

4 See, among others, Niemi and Young, 2016. I thank Linda Hartling for making me aware of this research. "Caring" and "fairness" are called "individualizing values" in this article, versus "loyalty-binding values." I concur with Linda Hartling to call them "connectedness-compassion values" versus "loyalty-binding values." See also "Who Blames the Victim?" by Laura Niemi and Liane Young, New York Times, June 24, 2016, www.nytimes.com/2016/06/26/opinion/sunday/who-blames-the-victim.html.

5 I appreciate this article: "Why the P2P and Commons Movement Must Act Trans-Locally and Trans-Nationally," by Michel Bauwens, P2P Foundation, June 12, 2016, https://blog.p2pfoundation.net/p2p-commons-movement-must-act-trans-locally-trans-nationally/2016/06/16. See more in note 295 in the Introduction, and note 114 in the Inspiring Questions to Section Two.
See also Ann Mische, professor at the Kroc Institute for International Peace Studies, and her contribution to the Great Transition Network Initiative discussion titled "Journey to Earthland: Making the Great Transition to Planetary Civilization," November 2, 2016, in response to Raskin, 2016. Like me, she observes "a troubling anti-institutionalism in some sectors of the counter-hegemonic left," or "a certain tendency in some critical-emancipatory approaches to dismiss the reform of governance institutions as simply the development of 'new forms of governmentality'" aimed a social disciplining and (self-)control." Mische admits that there is certainly truth to this, but "some institutional arrangements are better than others, in terms of inclusion, accountability, conflict resolution and effective and fairly distributed service provision," and "these differences in governance structures matter for both local and global futures." See the full note in the pdf edition of this book.

6 Admiration for Nelson Mandela's path, clearly, stands in contrast to the revulsion at the brutal concentration camps that his fellow brothers had implemented. See Trewhela, 2009.

7 See, among others, Bourdieu, 1977, or Bourdieu, 1991. See also Bernstein, 1971, 1973, 1975, 1990, 2000. I thank Vidar Vambheim for reminding me of Bernstein's work and that Bernstein introduced the concept of framing to describe how control of mental frames is used to regulate thinking and behavior in educational contexts. Bernstein describes framing as a mental process and a technique to exclude certain aspects of reality from entering the communication.

8 When Kamran Mofid changed from an "economist as usual" into "an economist for the common good," he was criticized and told if he could not remain a "good" economist, then, he should consider becoming a priest or a social worker. See his blog "Thank You Archbishops for Speaking Truth to Power," by economist Kamran Mofid, Globalization for the Common Good Initiative (GCGI), February 1, 2015, www.gcgi.info/index.php/kamran-s-blog/660-thank-you-archbishops-for-speaking-truth-to-power. It is a privilege to have Kamran Mofid as esteemed member in the global advisory board of the Human Dignity and Humiliation Studies fellowship.

9 Coates, 2015, p. 146. See also Midiohouan, 1991.

10 The first paragraph of Article 1 of the Universal Declaration of Human Rights (UDHR), adopted by the United Nations General Assembly on December 10, 1948, www.un.org/en/documents/udhr/.

11 See also my planned book on human nature.

12 See note 278 in the Introduction.

13 Neuroendocrinologist Robert Sapolsky, 2017, wrote about the context-dependency of behavior. Social psychologist, psychoanalyst, sociologist, and humanistic philosopher Erich Fromm, 1963, wrote an essay titled War within Man: A Psychological Enquiry into the Roots of Destructiveness, followed by commentaries by Jerome Frank, Paul Tillich, Hans Morgenthau, Roy Menninger, Pitirim Sorokin, and Thomas Merton. Fromm's essay first discusses whether human nature is good or evil. Fromm describes two basic personality types, the biophile and necrophile. The necrophile is a perverted personality attracted to death, while the biophile is an optimistic personality attracted to life. Sigmund Freud developed a similar concept, that of the life instinct Eros and the death instinct Thanatos. Yet, like me, Fromm hypothesizes that these are not innate personality traits but that the necrophile is a secondary potentiality, when the primary, life-favoring potentialities cannot develop, either due to being hindered or failing. When a child is born into a social context of love, security, justice, and freedom, it will be able to unfold the biophilic personality. The last part of the essay warns that the necrophilous attraction to death, war, and destruction is intensified through being mechanized in modern industrial society.

14 Pettit, 1997b, 2014.

15 Eisler, 1987. See note 48 in the Preface.

16 Fuller, 2003, Fuller and Gerloff, 2008.

17 "The Foreign Policy Essay: The Prisms Through Which Americans View the Middle East," by Shibley Telhami and Katayoun Kishi, Lawfare: Hard National Security Choices, February 1, 2015, www.lawfareblog.com/2015/02/the-foreign-policy-essay-the-prisms-through-which-americans-view-the-middle-east/. Shibley Telhami is the Anwar Sadat Professor for Peace and Development of the University of Maryland and a non-resident senior fellow at the Brookings Institution. It is a privilege to have Shibley Telhami as esteemed member in the global advisory board of the Human Dignity and Humiliation Studies fellowship. Katayoun Kishi is a Ph.D. candidate in the department of government and politics at the University of Maryland. They found that two clusters of prisms, or worldviews, or core identities are explanatory, namely, human rights versus on the right. See the full note in the pdf edition of this book.

18 See note 170 in the Introduction, and note 24 in the Introduction to Section One.

19 Bond and Lun, 2013a, p. 83. I had the privilege of meeting cross-cultural psychologist Michael Harris from Hong Kong, when he taught at a Sommerakademie Friedens- und Konfliktforschung, July 11–16, 1999, in Clemenswerth, Germany. Michael Bond is an esteemed member from the first moment in the global advisory board of the Human Dignity and Humiliation Studies fellowship. See for an explanation of the dimensions found Bond and Lun, 2013a, p. 79. See the full note in the pdf edition of this book.

20 In my work, I apply the ideal-type approach as described by sociologist Max Weber, 1904/1949. See also Coser, 1977, p. 224. See the full note in the pdf edition of this book.

21 Adolf Hitler's words, on November 27, 1941, to the Danish foreign minister Scavenius and the Croat foreign minister Lorkowitsch were: "I am also here ice cold. If the German people are no longer strong enough and ready to sacrifice their own blood for their existence, then they must disappear and be destroyed by another, stronger power ... I will not shed a tear for the German people," translated by Lindner from the German original, Haffner, 1978, p. 139.

22 National Commission on Terrorist Attacks Upon the United States and Kean, 2004, p. 39. See the full note in the pdf edition of this book. I thank psychology professor Hroar Klempe for reminding me on January 24, 2015. He followed the 9/11 attacks' live coverage on CNN and observed how it was first interpreted as an accident, and then, half an hour later, became a case of terror. It is a privilege to have Hroar Klempe as esteemed member in the global advisory board of our Human Dignity and Humiliation Studies fellowship.

23 The Norwegian original of this sentence is as follows: "Hvis en person kan lage så mye hat, hvor mye kjærlighet kan vi da ikke lage sammen." This was said by Helle Gannestad, a member of AUF of Møre og Romsdal in a CNN interview (AUF is the Workers' Youth League, Norway's largest political youth organization and affiliated with the Norwegian Labour Party), who survived the attack by Anders Behring Breivik, who shot dead 69 participants of a Workers' Youth League (AUF) summer camp on the island of Utøya. Gannestad's utterance spread and even became a Facebook page. See "Kjærlighetsbudskapet sprer seg i alle kanaler," VG, July 24, 2011, www.vg.no/nyheter/innenriks/terrorangrepet-22-juli-politikk-og-samfunn/kjaerlighetsbudskapet-sprer-seg-i-alle-kanaler/a/10080708/. See the full note in the pdf edition of this book. Norwegian Prime Minister Jens Stoltenberg took this sentence up and said on July 22, 2011: "Om én mann kan vise så mye hat, tenk hvor mye kjærlighet vi alle kan vise sammen." CNN was involved in broadcasting both 9/11 and the Norwegian reaction to terror ten years later. Both sentences were uttered by individuals and became historical markers, thus underlining the role and responsibility of individuals and how they can trigger the attitude that follows.

24 Sociologist and philosopher Theodor Adorno is known for having shed light on authoritarianism. Three core components were originally listed by Adorno, et al., 1950, p. 148:

• authoritarian submission (submissive, uncritical attitude toward idealized moral authorities of the in-group)
• authoritarian aggression (a general aggressiveness, directed against various persons, which is perceived to be sanctioned by the established authorities)
• conventionalism (adherence to conventional, middle-class values).

See also Altemeyer, 1981, 1996, 2003, 2009, and the archive of Altemeyer's original Global Change Game Website, http://web.archive.org/web/20020805124207/www.mts.net/~gcg/index.html. See Stenner, 2005, for more recent work on authoritarianism, as being latent until activated by a perception of threat (social threat theory), or Hetherington and Weiler, 2009, on authoritarian views being expressed under threat. See Suhay, 2015, for the insight that, while an increase in threat does trigger political behavior, physical threats such as terrorism may lead non-authoritarians to behave like authoritarians, while more abstract social threats, such as the erosion of social norms or demographic changes, does not have that effect. See for a readable summary, "The Rise of American Authoritarianism," by Amanda Taub, Vox, March 1, 2016, www.vox.com/2016/3/1/11127424/trump-authoritarianism#change, where Jonathan Haidt speaks of a button being pushed that says: "In case of moral threat, lock down the borders, kick out those who are different, and punish those who are morally deviant." The article goes on to describe the five policies that authoritarians generally and Donald Trump voters specifically were likely to support:
• Using military force over diplomacy against countries that threaten the United States
• Changing the Constitution to bar citizenship for children of illegal immigrants
• Imposing extra airport checks on passengers who appear to be of Middle Eastern descent in order to curb terrorism
• Requiring all citizens to carry a national ID card at all times to show to a police officer on request, to curb terrorism
• Allowing the federal government to scan all phone calls for calls to any number linked to terrorism.

I thank William M. Lafferty for making me aware of this article.

See also "The Best Predictor of Trump Support Isn't Income, Education, or Age. It's Authoritarianism," by Matthew MacWilliams, Vox, February 23, 2016, www.vox.com/2016/2/23/11099644/trump-support-authoritarianism.

In his 2016 campaign to become president of the United States, Donald Trump skillfully targeted the fears related to terrorism and immigration among authoritarians, focusing less on topics such as abortion or small government, thus following the path to success scripted in Hetherington and Suhay, 2011.

See, furthermore, Hardisty, 1999, or "Donald Trump's Presidential Run Began in an Effort to Gain Stature," by Maggie Haberman and Alexander Burns, March 12, 2016, New York Times, www.nytimes.com/2016/03/13/us/politics/donald-trump-campaign.html?smprod=nytcore-ipad&smid=nytcore-ipad-share. I thank Linda Hartling for making me aware of this article, and of Hardisty's work already many years ago.

See also an article highlighting that supporters of Donald Trump are average middle class, "Dangerous Idiots: How the Liberal Media Elite Failed Working-Class Americans," by Sarah Smarsh, The Guardian, October 13, 2016, www.theguardian.com/media/2016/oct/13/liberal-media-bias-working-class-americans.

Interestingly, views on parenting styles are the strongest predictors of authoritarianism; see the work on parenting styles by Feldman, 2003, 2013, or Hetherington and Weiler, 2009, and compare it with the work by Lakoff and Johnson, 1999. Read more about Feldman's approach in note 170 in the Introduction. See also Lindner, 2005a. The rise of ideals of equal dignity create alternatives that were not present in the past, when, for instance, spanking was universally accepted as proper pedagogy, and erodes boundaries that once were fixed. It seems that authoritarians have stronger gag reflexes than liberals and react with strong disgust, among others, for homosexual orientations. See Terrizzi, et al., 2010. After 9/11, "the disgusting terrorist" was constructed using the performativity of disgust, see, for instance, Sara Ahmed, 2004. Ideologies are being experienced and embodied, they are not simply ideas or concepts, see Wilce, 2009.

Listen to The United States of Anxiety, Episode 7: This Is Your Brain on Politics, WNYC (nonprofit, noncommercial, public radio stations located in New York City), November 3, 2016, www.wnyc.org/story/united-states-of-anxiety-podcast-episode-7. In this WNYC broadcast the field of biopolitics is being explored, the biology of political differences, see, among others, French, et al., 2014, Hibbing, et al., 2014, Wagner, et al., 2015. Biological information systems seem to be at play to form differences between conservative and liberals. Conservatives respond differently to fear than liberals and lock onto negative images more, while liberals seek novelty, new and pleasurable stimuli. In short: conservatives are scared, liberals are creative. The journalists collaborated with researchers for a pilot study that showed that those higher on the stress hormone cortisol voted less, while the cortisol baseline for Trump voters was twice as high as compared to Hillary Clinton voters.
See the full note with relevant references in the pdf edition of this book.

25 Duckitt, et al., 2010, p. 687. The traditional view was that RWA is a personality dimension, however, "new approaches have begun to suggest that RWA might be better conceptualized as social attitudes and values. A second issue, which arises partly out of this personality versus social attitude issue, is that of whether RWA is a unidimensional or multidimensional construct," John Duckitt, et al., 2010, pp. 686–687. "Right-Wing Authoritarianism (RWA) has been conceptualized and measured as a unidimensional personality construct comprising the covariation of the three traits of authoritarian submission, authoritarian aggression, and conventionalism," John Duckitt, et al., 2010, Abstract. However, so the authors continue, "new approaches have criticized this conceptualization and instead viewed these three 'traits' as three distinct, though related, social attitude dimensions." See for more, among others, Duckitt and Fisher, 2003, or Mavor, et al., 2010. See also Duckitt, 1989, Feldman, 2003, Kreindler, 2005, Stellmacher and Petzel, 2005, Stenner, 2005. Duckitt and Fisher, 2003. See the full note in the pdf edition of this book.

Chapter 1

1 "The Worst Mistake in the History of the Human Race," by Jared Diamond, Discover Magazine, May 1987, pp. 64–66, www.ditext.com/diamond/mistake.html: "Archaeologists studying the rise of farming have reconstructed a crucial stage at which we made the worst mistake in human history. Forced to choose between limiting population or trying to increase food production, we chose the latter and ended up with starvation, warfare, and tyranny." See also Manning, 2004, Hemenway, 2009, or Harari, 2014, who also share the view that the agricultural revolution was history's "biggest fraud." See, furthermore, "Is Sustainable Agriculture an Oxymoron?" Toby Hemenway, Permaculture Activist, Number 60, May, 2006, www.patternliteracy.com/203-is-sustainable-agriculture-an-oxymoron.

2 See, among others, Ryan and Jethá, 2010, and "The New York Times Misleads on Monogamy: Why Do Even the Best Journalists Mislead Readers About Human Sexual Evolution?" by Christopher Ryan, Psychology Today, September 16, 2013, www.psychologytoday.com/blog/sex-dawn/201309/the-new-york-times-misleads-monogamy.

3 Dennis, 2006. See also Kroglund, 2016.

4 Gepts, et al., 2012.

5 See the website of agricultural machinery manufacturer Claas, www.norway.claas.com/fascination-claas/history/product-history/combine-harvesters/dominator-mega.

6 Charles Franklin Kettering (1876 – 1958) was an American inventor, engineer, businessman, and the holder of many patents. Two of his ideas contributed to large-scale damage of the environment; the first was leaded gasoline, and the second was the invention of the Freon refrigerant for refrigeration and air conditioning systems. The CFCs in Freon are implicated in the depletion of the ozone layer, as human-

made halocarbon refrigerants, solvents, propellants, and foam-blowing agents (CFCs, HCFCs, freons, halons) are the source of photodissociation in the stratosphere.

7 See note 6 in the Preface, and the full note in the pdf edition of this book.

8 Higgins, 2016. See note 7 in the Preface.

9 Wijdekop, 2016. The strategy is "to add ecocide to the Rome Statute of the International Criminal Court (ICC) as the fifth crime against peace (along with genocide, crimes of aggression, crimes against humanity, and war crimes), and to have ecocide law introduced in the national jurisdictions of the member states of the ICC."

10 See also "Uttarakhand HC Declares Air, Glaciers, Forests, Springs, Waterfalls Etc. As Legal Persons," LiveLaw News Network, April 1, 2017, www.livelaw.in/uttarakhand-hc-declares-air-glaciers-forests-springs-waterfalls-etc-legal-persons/. We thank Anna Grear for making us aware of these news.

11 Linda Sheehan, Executive Director of the Earth Law Center in Redwood City, CA, in her contribution to the Great Transition Network (GTN) discussion on the topic of "Against Ecocide: Legal Protection for Earth," July 31, 2016, in response to Femke Wijdekop, 2016. See the full note in the pdf edition of this book.

12 I use quotation marks to highlight that I do not mean these nouns to mean rigidly separate entities. In my view, commonalities and processual approaches would characterize the phenomena in question more appropriately.

13 See Anderson, 2006, for imagined communities.

14 See, for the correspondence bias, among others, Gilbert, 1998, and Gawronski, 2004, Gawronski and Bodenhausen, 2006.

15 Margalit, 1996, 1997, 2002.

16 See note 163 in the Preface.

17 William Ury: The Walk from "No" to "Yes," TEDxMidwest, 2010, www.ted.com/talks/william_ury.html. See his foundational books, Fisher, et al., 2011, Ury, 2000, 2007. William Ury helped found the Abraham Path project, a long-distance walking trail across the Middle East which connects the sites visited by the patriarch Abraham as recorded in ancient religious texts and traditions. It is a privilege to have William Ury as esteemed member in the global advisory board of the Human Dignity and Humiliation Studies fellowship.

18 Robert Leonard Carneiro, in a personal meeting at the American Museum of Natural History in New York City, November 6, 2013. It is a privilege to have Robert Carneiro as esteemed member in the global advisory board of the Human Dignity and Humiliation Studies fellowship.

19 See also Witt and Schwesinger, 2013. Groups that grow larger and want to fission and migrate into a separate territory need unoccupied land.

20 Rowen Sivertsen, 2011. It is a privilege to have Barbara Rowen Sivertsen as esteemed member in the Human Dignity and Humiliation Studies fellowship.

21 See an interesting recent overview over the "big questions" related to the origin of the Universe, our galaxy, our Solar System, and life, along with the process by which scientists explore new concepts, in Randall, 2015.

22 The Higgs boson was discovered in July 2012 in the Large Hadron Collider in Switzerland, and its mass is 126 giga-electron-volts. See a very accessible description in "New Physics Complications Lend Support to Multiverse Hypothesis," by Natalie Wolchover, Quanta Magazine, May 24, 2013, www.simonsfoundation.org/quanta/20130524-is-nature-unnatural/.

23 "New Physics Complications Lend Support to Multiverse Hypothesis," by Natalie Wolchover, Quanta Magazine, May 24, 2013, www.simonsfoundation.org/quanta/20130524-is-nature-unnatural/.

24 Heisenberg, 1969/1971. See also episode 6, Werner Heisenberg: Der Teil und das Ganze, produced by BR-alpha, ARD-alpha, by Eva Maria Steimle, www.br.de/mediathek/video/sendungen/werner-heisenberg/teil-und-das-ganze100.html#filterEntireBroadcast=false&moreMoreCount=0&tab=bcastInfo&jump=tab. See the full note in the pdf edition of this book. See also Alexander Wendt's work, for instance, Wendt, 2015. I am thankful for having had the chance to communicate with Alexander Wendt, for the first time in 2005.

25 See Kolbert, 2014, for an accessible description of how the present-day atmosphere evolved.

26 See, among others, Montagu, 1989.

27 "Oldest Homo Sapiens Fossil Claim Rewrites Our Species' History," by Ewen Callaway, Nature, June 7, 2017, www.nature.com/news/oldest-homo-sapiens-fossil-claim-rewrites-our-species-history-1.22114. Remains from Morocco dated to 315,000 years ago push back our species' origins by 100,000 years — and suggest we didn't evolve only in East Africa.

28 The Holocene is the current geological epoch which started approximately 11,700 years ago, when the glaciers began to retreat, and the Neolithic Revolution unfolded. Some also call it the Anthropocene, because it is the epoch, when human activities started to have a significant global impact on Earth's ecosystems, see, for instance Zalasiewicz, et al., 2010. The reasons for and circumstances of the rise of agriculture are hotly discussed, see, among many others, Richerson, et al., 1999, Richerson, et al., 2001, Richerson and Boyd, 2001, Boyd and Richerson, 2009. See also recent findings that farming in the Fertile Crescent did not begin in a single population, but rather was tried out all over the Fertile Crescent, a region in the Middle East including modern-day Iraq, Jordan, Syria, Israel, Palestine, southeastern Turkey and western Iran. The descendants of the early farmers from the Zagros Mountains on the border between Iraq and Iran probably migrated east, taking their farming techniques to that part of the world, while those from the Turkey region migrated north into Europe and introduced farming there. See the work of the palaeogenetics team around Joachim Burger, Broushaki, et al., 2016. I thank Linda Hartling for making me aware of these new findings.

29 In the case of territorial circumscription, it is landscape that stands "in the way," while social circumscription means that other people "stand in the way." Circumscription theory has been developed by anthropologist and curator of the American Museum of Natural History in New York City, Robert Leonard Carneiro. See, among others, Carneiro, 1970, 1988, 2000, 2010, 2012. See, furthermore, Sanderson, 2007, and Schacht, 1988. It is a privilege to have Robert Carneiro as esteemed member in the global advisory board of our Human Dignity and Humiliation Studies fellowship.

30 Lindner, 2006c, p. 12.

31 See, for instance, The Limits to Growth, a 1972 book about the computer simulation of exponential economic and population growth with finite resource supplies, updated in Meadows, et al., 2005.

32 John Bellamy Foster wrote about cleric and scholar Thomas Robert Malthus in his contribution to the Great Transition Network (GTN) discussion on the topic "Marxism and Ecology: Common Fonts of a Great Transition," October 9, 2015: "His treatment of the population-food problem was directed at justifying class hierarchy and poverty. It had nothing to do with an ecological perspective, which, as Eric Ross has shown, only came to be associated with his thought with the rise of neo-Malthusianism in the 1940s, and even then lacked any scholarly basis."

33 Malthus, 1798.

34 Tim Jackson of the Centre for Environmental Strategy at the Faculty of Engineering and Physical Sciences, University of Surrey in the UK, in his contribution to the Great Transition Network (GTN) discussion on the topic "Marxism and Ecology: Common Fonts of a Great Transition," October 1, 2015. See also Jackson, 2009.

35 "The Next Genocide," by Timothy Snyder, New York Times, September 12, 2015, www.nytimes.com/2015/09/13/opinion/sunday/the-next-genocide.html?_r=0. See also Snyder, 2010, 2015, 2017.

36 See, among others, Carneiro, 1970, 1988, 2000, 2010, 2012. See, furthermore, Sanderson, 2007, or Schacht, 1988. It is a privilege to have Robert Carneiro as esteemed member in the global advisory board of our Human Dignity and Humiliation Studies fellowship.

37 Chase-Dunn and Hall, 2002, and Chase-Dunn and Hall, 1997.

38 See a "A philosophical interpretation of ubuntu" in Metz, 2012. I thank Francisco Gomes de Matos for making me aware of Thaddeus Metz' work. Philosopher Thaddeus Metz is a humanities research professor at the University of Johannesburg. Desmond Tutu used ubuntu as foundation for his Truth Commissions in South Africa, see Battle, 1997. I am profoundly grateful to Archbishop Desmond Tutu for contributing with the Foreword to the book Gender, Humiliation, and Global Security. See Lindner and Desmond Tutu (Foreword), 2010. See also note 162 and 163 in Chapter 5.

39 Ingrid Fuglestvedt in a personal communication on October 17, 2011. See note 2 in this Chapter 1.

40 See Catherine Odora Hoppers and her brother George in conversation on June 7, 2013, at www.humiliationstudies.org/whoweare/videos.php# SARChI. It is a privilege to have Catherine Odora Hoppers and her brother George as esteemed members in the global advisory board of the Human Dignity and Humiliation Studies fellowship.

41 Richards, 2016a. Nyerere, 1968.

42 Bazaara, 1992, p. 8, quoted in Okuku, 2006.

43 See, among others, Armstrong, 1981.

44 Grossman, 2006.

45 Mielants, 2007.

46 Foucault, 1961/2006.

47 "Against Foucault: Early Foucault, Part Four," video lecture by Howard Richards, Pretoria, South Africa, May 8, 2013, taped by Justine Richards, http://youtu.be/pwDiTMUpJ_Q. See the text also on www.humiliationstudies.org/documents/Richards04EarlyFoucaultPartFour8May2013.pdf. Richards, et al., 2015a, is the book that resulted from these lectures and dialogues. It is a privilege to have Howard Richards as esteemed member in the global advisory board of the Human Dignity and Humiliation Studies fellowship. See also note 196 in the Introduction.

48 Foucault, 1961, p. 90.

49 Inspired by Howard Richards' presentation "Against Foucault: Early Foucault, Part Four," Catherine Odora Hoppers and Evelin Lindner engaged in a dialogue with Howard Richards. See note 47 above. It is a privilege to have Catherine Odora Hoppers and Howard Richards as esteemed members in the global advisory board of the Human Dignity and Humiliation Studies fellowship.

50 "Human Dignity and Humiliation Studies: Transdisciplinarity in Practice," talk given by Evelin Lindner at the Programme for the Enhancement of Research Capacity (PERC) Workshop, University of Cape Town, South Africa, convened by PERC coordinator Robert Morrell. July 4, 2013.

51 "The Very Survival of Africa's Indigenous Peoples 'Seriously Threatened,'" by Baher Kamal, Inter Press Service (IPS), May 3, 2017, www.ipsnews.net/2017/05/the-very-survival-of-africas-indigenous-peoples-seriously-threatened/.

52 Lindner, 2012b. See also the Thirty-First Annual E. F. Schumacher Lectures on November 5, 2011, in New York City (www.neweconomicsinstitute.org), where I learned from the panel "Voices of Today's Youth: Occupy Wall Street and Youth for a New Economy" that Harvard University owns ten percent of the

endowments of U.S. universities and that they have bought land in Africa the size of France. See, furthermore, "US Universities in Africa 'Land Grab,'" by John Vidal and Claire Provost, The Guardian, June 8, 2011, www.theguardian.com/world/2011/jun/08/us-universities-africa-land-grab. The authors report that institutions including Harvard and Vanderbilt use hedge funds to buy land in deals that may force local farmers off their land.

Then watch the documentary film Our Man in Sudan, by Shuchan Tan, Al Jazeera, May 30, 2013, www.aljazeera.com/programmes/witness/2013/05/201352814223449553l.html.

See also Machtfaktor Erde. Beutezüge im Klimawandel, a documentary film by Angela Andersen und Claus Kleber, Zweites Deutsches Fernsehen, http://machtfaktorerde.zdf.de/#home. In a remote region of Ethiopia, the ZDF team finds a Saudi Arabian investor group which has seized land for the cultivation of rice and has evicted thousands of small farmers. "No mega-project, a giga-project," is how the responsible manager describes this project. See the full note in the pdf edition of this book.

53 See, among others, Harvey, 2003, Federici, 2004.

54 Canadian economist Rodrigue Tremblay discusses the "T-treaty trinity," the Trans-Pacific Partnership (TPP), Trade in Services Agreement (TiSA), and the Transatlantic Trade and Investment Partnership (TTIP). See "Barack Obama's Meager Legacy of Incomplete Accomplishments and of Provoked Wars: What Happened? by Rodrigue Tremblay, May 30, 2016, www.thecodeforglobalethics.com/pb/wp_0b5e796a/wp_0b5e796a.html#LEGACY:

Such agreements, negotiated in near complete secrecy, pursue geopolitical objectives. They are an attempt to build a worldwide economic and financial order that supersedes national states and they represent also an effort to protect the corporate and banking elites – the establishment 1 percent – against national governments. In the case of the TTIP, its geopolitical objective is to prevent European countries from developing comprehensive trade agreements with Russia. In the case of TPP, the objective is to isolate China. In the eyes of Washington D.C. neocon planners, they are part of ongoing economic warfare.

See also Tremblay, 2010. It is a privilege to have Rodrigue Tremblay as esteemed member in the global advisory board of our Human Dignity and Humiliation Studies fellowship. See also "Lessons from the Demise of the TPP," by Jomo Kwame Sundaram and Anis Chowdhury, Inter Press Service (IPS), January 5, 2017, www.ipsnews.net/2017/01/lessons-from-the-demise-of-the-tpp/.

55 Robinson, 2017.

56 Robinson, 2017: "This corporate-driven globalization has brought a vast new round of global enclosures as hundreds of millions of people have been uprooted and converted into surplus humanity."

57 Robinson, 2017.

58 See note 12 in the Introduction.

59 Betanzos, et al., 1996.

60 Witt and Schwesinger, 2013. Groups that grow larger and want to fission and migrate into a separate territory need unoccupied land.

61 Ury, 1999.

62 Intensification means domesticating plants and animals, and developing agricultural systems. See, among others, Boserup, 1965, Cohen, 1977, 2009, Richerson, et al., 1999, Richerson, et al., 2001, Richerson and Boyd, 2001, Boyd and Richerson, 2009. See also Ury, 1999.

I thank Merle Lefkoff for reminding me of the work of economist Ester Boserup, 1970, who studied economic and agricultural development and suggested that men have an advantage in farming over women as soon as plough agriculture is practiced, since, unlike the hoe or digging stick, the plough requires more upper body strength, grip strength, and burst of power. Recent research supports her suggestion that traditional plough-use is positively correlated with attitudes of gender inequality, see "Women and the

Plough," by Alberto Alesina, Paola Giuliano, and Nathan Nunn, VoxEU.org, policy portal of the Centre for Economic Policy Research (CEPR), July 2, 2011, http://voxeu.org/article/modern-gender-roles-and-ancient-farming.

63 Lindner, 2000a. Farmers who plant crops are bound to be more sedentary than, for example, livestock farmers. The latter become more mobile when the size of their flock increases, but this is not to be confused with the mobility of foragers. There is no direct transition from foraging to mobile livestock farming, except for in Africa, explains, for example, Parzinger, 2015.

64 See Suhay, 2015. See more in note 24 in the Introduction to Section One.

65 "Why Steven Pinker, Like Jared Diamond, Is Wrong," by Stephen Corry, Truthout, June 11, 2013, http://truth-out.org/opinion/item/16880-the-case-of-the-brutal-savage-poirot-or-clouseau-or-why-steven-pinker-like-jared-diamond-is-wrong. See also Corry, 2010.

66 The controversies surrounding anthropologist Napoléon Chagnon, 2013, may serve as an illustration of the heated debate about human nature. I thank Robert Carneiro for sharing with me his deep insights into this debate.

67 There is a large amount of literature on ontological security that infers emotions onto states by ascribing "personhood" to states and assuming that states can act out of fear, shame, or anxiety. See, among others, Mitzen, 2006, Steele, 2007a, Krolikowski, 2008, or Pratt, 2016. Ontological security is a mental state that steers clear of existential fear by avoiding dissonance and creating a cocoon of continuity and certainty. Sociologist Anthony Giddens, 1991, links ontological security to a meaningful life of positive and stable emotions, insulated from chaos and anxiety. Sociologist Norbert Elias, 1985, and his work on death is related. See also Stanley and Wise, 2011. Relevant is also terror management theory, as proposed by Jeff Greenberg, Sheldon Solomon, and Tom Pyszczynski. See the first complete formal statement of terror management theory including epistemological assumptions and proposal for an experimental existential psychology in Solomon, et al., 1991, and more recent publications related to the events of September 11, 2001, Pyszczynski, et al., 2003. I had the privilege of being invited, together with Tom Pyszczynski, one of the fathers of terror management theory, to the NATO Advanced Research Workshop "Indigenous Terrorism: Understanding and Addressing the Root Causes of Radicalisation among Groups with an Immigrant Heritage in Europe," in Budapest, Hungary, in March 7–9, 2008, see Lindner, et al., 2009, in the proceedings.

68 See Herz, 1950. Under the conditions of the security dilemma, the Hobbesian fear of surprise attacks from outside one's nation's borders reigns. Barry Posen and Russell Hardin discuss the emotional aspects of the security dilemma and how they play out between ethnic groups as much as between states, see Posen, 1993, and Hardin, 1995, or Rose, 2000. See also Collins, 2004, Hansen, 2000, Jervis, 1978, Job, 1992, Musah and Fayemi, 2000, Posen, 1993, Snyder, 1985, Snyder and Walters, 1999, or Schweller, 2011. See for the critical turn in international relations theory, the notion of positive security and the so-called Copenhagen School, for example, Roe, 1999, 2005. I appreciate political scientist Jack S. Levy's 2016 course "Theories of War And Peace" at Rutgers University, http://home.uchicago.edu/~mjreese/CurrentStudents/LevyPS522.pdf. He recommends, among others, Glaser, 1997, Montgomery, 2006, Schweller, 1996, Snyder and Jervis, 1999, Tang, 2011.

See also an interview that Alexandros Koutsoukis conducted with Steven C. Roach on November 2, 2016, as part of a series of interviews under the motto "Resurrecting IR Theory," where Roach discusses affective values in international relations, the value of resilience, and how to theorize emotional actions, www.e-ir.info/2016/11/02/interview-steven-c-roach/. Roach acknowledges the influence of Alexander Wendt, 2015, and his quantum mind approach to IR, which reaches beyond the materialist problems of social inquiry, including the mind-body duality/problem. Wendt seeks to unify quantum theory and social ontology, thus mapping the imaginary contours of a global human consciousness (note also Lindner's communication with Wendt in 2005). Roach also acknowledges Andrew Linklater, 2005, and his work on dialogical ethics, the ethics of harm in world politics, and the moral possibilities of producing dialogue across states. Furthermore, he points at Sara Ahmed, 2004, and her book The Cultural Politics of Emotion, where she describes how emotions can "stick," how they can structure social relations by attaching themselves to values and anchor judgments and beliefs relating to justice, peace, cooperation, resilience, or tolerance. Roach also draws on Gilles Deleuze and Félix Guattari's texts on the micropolitics of desire and sees affects as social and relational phenomena that resonate with unconscious feelings, and that it may take several decades for affects to become norms. He follows Guattari and Deleuze and Guattari, 1972/1977, in seeing the body of being capable of producing "assemblages" with other bodies to form collective identities: "Our feelings challenge authority unconsciously. They 'circulate' within and through these assemblages or functional structures." Lyotard, 1974/1983, offers a related perspective on the micropolitics of desire. Roach, 2017, is working on a book on decency and diversity, where he touches upon the volatile politics of the International Criminal Court, global terrorism, and human rights abuses. Inspired by the writings of William Connolly, 2010, on pluralism, Roach explores the moral possibility of cultural pluralism in world politics and asks which role decency can play for global pressures on cultural movements. He is critical of idealist assumptions of fixed absolute points in our moral understanding of a good society, such as presented, for instance, in Political Emotions by Martha Nussbaum, 2013, where she emphasizes love, and how love needs to transcend one's circumstances.

69 Ralph K. White, a former U.S. Information Agency official, later a political scientist and psychologist at George Washington University, was the foremost advocate of what he called realistic empathy in foreign affairs. White contends that only through empathy can one accurately tell the story adversaries are telling themselves about "us," about themselves, or about the situation they believe they face. See also James Blight and Lang, 2010, pp. 38–39. I thank John McFadden for making me aware of this work. White makes a clear distinction between empathy and sympathy. See the full of quote of White, 1984, pp. 160–16, in the full note in the pdf edition of this book. White identified three critical mistakes in foreign policymaking that prevent empathy from occurring: (1) not seeing an opponent's longing for peace; (2) not seeing an opponent's fear of being attacked; and (3) not seeing an opponent's understandable anger, see White, 1984, pp. 162–163. See also the work of psychotherapist Charles Truax, et al., 1970, on accurate empathy. I thank John McFadden also here for making me aware of this work. See the full note in the pdf edition of this book.

70 Lindner, 2017.

71 2009 Annual Conference of Human Dignity and Humiliation Studies, "World Peace Through Humiliation-Free Global Human Interactions," in Honolulu, Hawai'i, August 20–22, 2009, www.humiliationstudies.org/whoweare/annualmeeting/13.php.

72 "Japan Broke U.S. Code Before Pearl Harbor, Researcher Finds," by Valerie Reitman, Los Angeles Times, December 7, 2001, http://articles.latimes.com/2001/dec/07/news/mn-12562.

73 Ibid.

74 "Historian Seeks to Clear Embassy of Pearl Harbor 'Sneak Attack' Infamy," by Tai Kawabata, Japan Times, December 9, 2014, www.japantimes.co.jp/news/2014/12/09/national/history/historian-seeks-to-clear-embassy-of-pearl-harbor-sneak-attack-infamy/#.VIg4Ho0cR9A. See also Seconds From Disaster: Pearl Harbor, documentary film series 4, 2011, featuring scholar Toshihiro Minohara, http://natgeotv.com/uk/seconds-from-disaster, and https://youtu.be/7bok8TLtz40. Seconds from Disaster is an American documentary television series that first began broadcasting in 2004 on the National Geographic Channel. See also Kimura and Minohara, 2013.

75 McNamara and Blight, 2001.

76 Translated from German by Lindner from Suttner, 1889, pp. 110.

77 Lindner, 2006c, p. 12.

78 Bauman, 1992, wrote on p. x–xi: "… the world of nature … had to be beheaded and deprived of autonomous will and power of resistance. … The world was an object of willed action: a raw material in the work guided and given form by human designs. … Left to itself, the world had no meaning. It was solely the human design that injected it with a sense of purpose. So the earth became a repository of ores and other 'natural resources,' wood turned into timber and water – depending on circumstances – into an energy source, waterway or the solvent of waste."

79 Lindner, 2006c, p. 13.

80 "How to Protect Nuclear Plants from Terrorists," by Allison Macfarlane, Phys.org, April 14, 2016, http://phys.org/news/2016-04-nuclear-fromterrorists.html.

81 Summy, 2006.

82 "As a Vote on Entering World War I Approached, the Only Woman in Congress Faced an Agonizing Choice," by Will Englund, The Washington Post, April 6, 2017, www.washingtonpost.com/news/retropolis/wp/2017/04/06/as-a-vote-on-entering-world-war-i-approached-the-u-s-entry-into-world-war-i-the-only-woman-in-congress-faced-an-agonizing-choice/?utm_term=.61e64f4e05cb. See the full note in the pdf edition of this book.

83 Røed-Larsen and Hjort-Larsen, 2012. I thank Linda Hartling for making me aware of this article.

84 See note 143 in the Introduction.

85 "Stanford Expert Describes How the U.S. And China Can Manage Their Relationship and Avoid Conflict," by Clifton B. Parker, Stanford Report, August 20, 2014, http://news.stanford.edu/news/2014/august/us-china-relations-082014.html. See also, "Thucydides Trap," by Karl Eikenberry, American Review, August 4, 2014, http://americanreviewmag.com/stories/Thucydides-Trap. See, furthermore, Syse, 2003.

86 Kelly, 2005.

87 Thucydides, 431 BCE, Chapter I.

88 "The Neuroscience Guide to Negotiations With Iran," by Nicholas Wright and Karim Sadjadpour, The Atlantic, January 14, 2014, www.theatlantic.com/international/archive/2014/01/the-neuroscience-guide-to-negotiations-with-iran/282963/. I thank Karmit Zysman for making me aware of this article.

89 The leaders of Egypt (Hosni Mubarak), the Palestinian Authority (Yasser Arafat), Libya (Muammar Gaddafi), Syria (Bashar al-Assad), Iran (Mohamed Khatami) and Pakistan (Pervez Musharraf), strongly denounced the 9/11 attacks on the Twin Towers immediately, later also Iraq's president Saddam Hussein.

90 "2002 State of the Union Address – President George W. Bush," January 29, 2002, http://georgewbush-whitehouse.archives.gov/news/releases/2002/01/print/20020129-11.html.

91 The Joint Comprehensive Plan of Action, is an international agreement on the nuclear program of Iran reached in Vienna on July 14, 2015, between Iran, the P5+1 (the five permanent members of the United Nations Security Council – China, France, Russia, United Kingdom, United States – plus Germany), and the European Union.

92 Publius Flavius Vegetius Renatus and Reeve, 2004.

93 See, among others, Gilbert, 1998. Social psychology describes different types of attribution biases. Just to name a few, when assessing other people's behavior, we tend to commit the correspondence bias and fundamental attribution error, as well as the ultimate attribution error vis-á-vis out-groups, and then commit the actor-observer bias when we look at ourselves. Social psychologist Morton Deutsch, "father" of the field of conflict resolution, has written about the attribution error very early. Social psychologist Lee Ross is one of those whose name is crucially connected with research on the fundamental attribution error, which, according to him, is no less than the conceptual bedrock for the field of social psychology.

Correspondent inference theory indicates that we infer that other people's actions correspond to their underlying personality and disposition. Some psychologists have used the terms correspondence bias and fundamental attribution error interchangeably. See, among others, Gilbert, 1998. Others theorize that they are independent phenomena, with the correspondence bias resulting from a much wider range of processes. See, among others, Gawronski, 2004, Gawronski and Bodenhausen, 2006.

94 Translated from German by Alice Asbury Abbott, Suttner, 1908, pp. 177. German original in Suttner, 1889, pp. 108–109. See the German original in the full note in the pdf edition of this book.

95 Hobbes, 1651.

96 Carl Schmitt, 1922, p. 11: "Souverän ist, wer über den Ausnahmezustand entscheidet."

97 Hans Joachim Morgenthau, when he was director of the Center for the Study of American Foreign Policy at the University of Chicago from 1950 – 1968, see, among others, Morgenthau, 1948, 1951.

98 Tunander, 2009. I thank Kimberly Eriksen for having drawn my attention to this chapter. See Tunander's conclusion summarized in the full note in the pdf edition of this book. See also note 15 in the Introduction to Section Three.

99 See also Rashid, 2008.

100 A listed presentation of these thoughts may look as follows:
(1) No war, (2) unavoidable war in defense, and (3) war as livelihood through raiding or "bellum se ipsum alet"):
• Belligerent raiding culture of tribal peoples (2, circumscription causes terror)
• Agriculture (2, terrorists can be raiders who need to be stopped, or freedom fighters who need to find and learn non-violent pathways to undo domination)
• Raiding (3, raiding is a culture of terror that must be stopped)
• Pre-12,000 years and trade (no war, 1, raiders are terrorists who need to be stopped).

101 Kelly, 2005.

102 Flannery and Marcus, 2003.

103 See note 12 in the Introduction.

104 Sedentary populations cannot flee as easily as nomad populations. And even their armies were often fashioned on rather rigid models. In contrast, many nomadic armies had an overall command structure that was more flexible. For instance, while Mongol civil, social, and military structure was built on obedience and firm discipline, leaders on each level were free to execute their orders in the way they considered best. In the case of the Mongols, particularly hardy steeds allowed for a particularly superior degree of mobility, as their horses provided both transport and food. See Morris, 1994. Mongol warriors could survive by only drinking from their mare's blood and their milk, since they could digest milk, unlike, for instance, their Chinese foes. In societies with milk-producing animals and pastoralism, the ability to digest fresh milk through adulthood, which is genetically coded for by LCT variants, provides a nutritional advantage. See Gerbault, et al., 2011. See for a recent publication on the Mongol conquests in the context of world history, May, 2012. See also "Why Nomads Win: What Ibn Khaldun Would Say About Afghanistan," by Gerard Russell, Huffington Post, April 11, 2010, www.huffingtonpost.com/gerard-russell/why-nomads-win-what-ibn-k_b_447878.html.

105 "Why Nelson Mandela Was on a Terrorism Watch List in 2008," by Caitlin Dewey, Washington Post, December 7, 2013, www.washingtonpost.com/news/the-fix/wp/2013/12/07/why-nelson-mandela-was-on-a-terrorism-watch-list-in-2008/.

106 "Chinese Fans Angered After Lady Gaga Meets with Dalai Lama," Australian Broadcasting Corporation, www.abc.net.au/news/2016-06-28/chinese-fans-angered-as-lady-gaga-meets-dalai-lama/7549044.

107 See, among others, Reichberg, et al., 2006, or Syse, 2003.

108 Scheff, 2010.

109 Scheff, 1994.

110 Elias, 1983/1987.

111 "The World's First Multinational," by Nick Robins, New Statesman, December 13, 2004, www.newstatesman.com/politics/politics/2014/04/worlds-first-multinational.

112 "Whose Side is God, god, g_d On?," by Anthony J. Marsella, TRANSCEND Media Service, January 7, 2013, www.transcend.org/tms/2013/01/whose-side-is-god-god-g_d-on/.

113 See note 372 in the Introduction.

114 Dreyer, 2007. Zheng He presented gifts of gold, silver, porcelain, and silk, and received novelties such as ostriches, zebras, camels, and ivory.

115 Charles Mann, 2005, wrote a well-written book that offers a broad overview.

116 Lindner, 2009a. See also "Curriculum Reviewer Barry Spurr Mocks 'Abos, Mussies, Women, Chinky-Poos,'" New Matilda, October 16, 2014, https://newmatilda.com/2014/10/16/curriculum-reviewer-barry-spurr-mocks-abos-mussies-women-chinky-poos/. Professor of English, Barry Spurr, referred to Aboriginal Australians as "human rubbish tips."

117 "'Country Belonging to Me': Land and Labour on Aboriginal Missions and Protectorate Stations, 1830–1850," by Jessie Mitchell, Eras Journal, Edition Six – November 2004, www.arts.monash.edu.au/publications/eras/edition-6/mitchellarticle.php.

118 Thieves by Law (Ganavim Ba Hok), documentary film by Alexander Gentelev, 2010, charts the rise of Russian organized crime in the wake of the fall of the Soviet Union. In the film, several noted crime figures are being interviewed, a number of which are currently wanted by Interpol. See the film with English subtitles Real Russian Mafia, published on October 28, 2012, https://youtu.be/imNE5CEjZW4. According to Satter, 2003, p. 46: "what drove the process was not the determination to create a system based on universal values but rather the will to introduce a system of private ownership, which, in the absence of law, opened the way for the criminal pursuit of money and power."

119 "UN Senior Officials Urge Countries to Boost Their Efforts to Combat Human Trafficking," United Nations News Centre, April 3, 2012, www.un.org/apps/news/story.asp?NewsID=41696#.VSEgx-HICOY: "At any given time across the globe, some 2.4 million people are victims of human trafficking, a crime that generates $32 billion annually, rivalling the profits reaped by the illicit trade in arms and drugs. Every year, thousands of people fall into the hands of traffickers, in their own countries and abroad, with women comprise two thirds of trafficking victims."

120 Theodor De Bry was the first to prepare detailed copper plate engravings of travels to the Americas that exhibited any accuracy of detail or scope, see http://bancroft.berkeley.edu/Exhibits/nativeamericans/lg13.html.

121 Lindner, 2012b.

122 Nilsen and Øgrim, 2015. See also "Norwegian Authors: Norway Should not Apologize to China in China," by Maria Andreasdottir, Scandasia, September 9, 2015, http://scandasia.com/norwegian-authors-norway-should-not-indulge-china/.

123 Lindner, 2006c, pp. 103–104.

124 Eisler, 1987. See note 48 in the Preface.

125 Sociologist and philosopher Georg Simmel (1858 – 1918) taught that within groups, conflicts are tests of leadership and solidarity, and between groups, they create boundaries and gaps, see Simmel, 1955. See also Caplow, 1968. I thank Vidar Vambheim for reminding me of this literature.

126 Michael Tomasello, 2016, a developmental and comparative psychologist, describes two key evolutionary steps, shaping two kinds of "we," one human-to-human, and the other in-group versus out-group. Prior to the Neolithic revolution, humans foraged together and shared the resources as equally deserving partners, based on shared senses of trust, respect, and responsibility. This changed when distinct cultural groups emerged and morals became legitimate only for those who were part of "us." Contemporary humans possess therefore two kinds of morals, one based on direct face-to-face encounters with other individuals, and another one that is based on one's in-group's prescription of loyalty, conformity, and cultural identity, connected with certain moral rules of right and wrong.

127 Lindner and Desmond Tutu (Foreword), 2010.

128 Lindner and Desmond Tutu (Foreword), 2010, p. 48.

129 Taylor, et al., 2002.

130 See evidence in the massacre mass grave of Schöneck-Kilianstädten that reveals new insights into collective violence in Early Neolithic Central Europe, Meyer, et al., 2015.

131 See the section "How the 'art of domination' was perfected in systems of ranked honor" in Lindner, 2009b, Chapter 5: How History and Culture Can Humiliate, in the book Emotion and Conflict, pp. 60–64.

132 Pratto and Stewart, 2011, Sidanius and Pratto, 1999. See an overview in "Power Inequities," by Máire A. Dugan, Beyond Intractability, February 2004, www.beyondintractability.org/essay/power-inequities. Read more in Chapter 2, and see also note 329 in the Introduction.

133 Jost, et al., 2004, Jost, et al., 2009, Jost, et al., 2002, Jost and Ross, 1999.

134 See note 184 in the Introduction.

135 Lindner, 2012f. See also Lakoff, 2006a. See the full note in the pdf edition of this book.

136 Ambedkar, 1948. Ambedkar argued that the "broken" tribes of ancient India had suffered oppression partly because of their allegiance to Buddhism, and partly because of their beef-eating.

137 Lindner, 2000a, pp. 253–264.

138 Anthropologist and Somalia-expert Ioan Lewis, 1998, p. 52: "… the Somali themselves... and various writers... consider these outcaste peoples to be the remnants of previous populations indigenous to Somaliland whom the Hamites conquered." I met with Ioan Lewis at his home in London and learned from him on May 31, 1999, together with Dennis Smith.

139 Lewis, 1998, p. 51: "They hunt with bow and arrow poisoned with an alkaloidal extract (wabayo) obtained from a species of euphorbia."

140 This informant referred to the Madiban, which is the name of one of those minorities, but they are not the only ones to incite fear. Lewis, 1998, p, 53: "The Yibir are despised by all Somali, who never speak to them if they can avoid doing so, and are feared for their skill in witchcraft. Whenever a son is born to a noble Somali the first Yibir who approaches the family has the right to a gift, samanyo." My low caste interlocutors offered me their views in January 1999 in Nairobi:

Somalis are killers; we minorities are not killers. We Midgan made a secret poison for hunting, a secret that we never revealed, because we knew that they [the Somalis] would start killing people if they knew how to make this poison. … We are skilled professionals, we are the forerunners of modern scientists, we know how to work [as opposed to "free" nomads who somehow just wait for their animals to eat by themselves], and we renounce violence; altogether, we represent the seeds of modern civilization within Somali society... We are low castes, but in our hearts we feel superior and think that we deserve higher respect and recognition. … But they will learn. Until recently a young Somali man would brag about his father and say: "My father has killed ninety-nine men!" Today increasingly more people would ask: "Why do you sit with this person??? He has killed people, he is a criminal!"

141 Jingyi Dong, 2015, p. 87:

Two events in the 1950s could serve as milestones in the process: First, the system began an "institution and discipline adjustment" (yuanxi tiaozheng 院系调整) in 1952, which gradually phased out some of the former national universities, all the private or church funded universities and terminated some liberal arts disciplines such as law, political science and sociology (Haibo Wang, 2006). The new system was mainly composed of technology and engineering colleges that were oriented towards economic development. Second, the Anti-rightist Campaign in 1957 marginalized academic authorities and expelled a great number of the top teachers and students from the campus (S. Ding 1993, 2007). Intellectuals not only lost the freedom to research and teach, but faced the potential threat of arrest without recourse to the law (Y. Gao, 2007). These two events are important indicators: The former meant the reconstruction of the university by government ordinance; the latter meant the implementation, aided with the reshaped structure, of more severe state policies that were often manifested in the form of political campaigns.

142 Kuan, 2015, p. 98–99.

143 "SA finally African, all thanks to Zuma," by Prince Mashele, Sowetan, May 9, 2016, www.sowetanlive.co.za/news/2016/05/09/sa-finally-african-all-thanks-to-zuma. Prince Mashele is the executive director of the Centre for Politics and Research and co-author of The Fall of the ANC. We thank Hélène Opperman Lewis for making us aware of this article.

144 Martin, 2010, p. 166.

145 Robinson, 2017.

146 Martin, 2010, p. 166. Glen T. Martin is the President of the World Constitution and Parliament Association (www.worldparliament-gov.org), President of the Institute on World Problems (www.earth-constitution.org), and professor of philosophy at Radford University (www.radford.edu/gmartin). It is a privilege to have Glen Martin as esteemed member in the global advisory board of our Human Dignity and Humiliation Studies fellowship.

147 Martin, 2010, p. 166. Smith, 2005.

148 Seligman, 1974.

149 United States Senate Select Committee on Intelligence, 2014.

150 Black, 1997. I thank also Michelle Fine for sharing with me her experiences with her African-American students in New York City on November 20, 2004.

151 In a meeting in New York City on December 14, 2014, Gay Rosenblum-Kumar kindly shared with me the stories that are being told in her family, stories of the Shtetl where women would call on their men in despair: "Why do you not defend us?"
In his blog "Schlemiel in Theory," Menachem Matthew Feuer discusses how Jewish males typically were ridiculed in the media, as if their emasculation reflected their real nature and was not forced upon them (the so-called correspondence error), see http://schlemielintheory.com/. See also Berger, 1996. It is a privilege to have Gay Rosenblum-Kumar as esteemed member in the global advisory board of our Human Dignity and Humiliation Studies fellowship.

152 I thank Michelle Fine for explaining to me, in New York City in 2002, her experiences with her African-American students. See also Fine and Halkovic, 2014. We were very privileged to have Michelle Fine in our very first workshop on humiliation and violent conflict, at Columbia University, convened by Morton Deutsch, in 2003.

153 Robert J. Burrowes has a lifetime commitment to understanding and ending human violence. He has done extensive research since 1966 in an effort to understand why human beings are violent and has been a nonviolent activist since 1981. He is the author of Why Violence?, Burrowes, 2011. See also http://robertjburrowes.wordpress.com, http://thepeoplesnonviolencecharter.wordpress.com (Charter),

http://tinyurl.com/flametree (Flame Tree Project), and http://anitamckone.wordpress.com (Songs of Nonviolence).

154 "Thousands Hold Vigil As UC Santa Barbara Reacts to Shootings," by Valerie Strauss, The Washington Post, May 25, 2014, www.washingtonpost.com/blogs/answer-sheet/wp/2014/05/25/thousands-hold-vigil-as-uc-santa-barbara-reacts-to-shootings.

155 "Inside the 'Manosphere' that Inspired Santa Barbara Shooter Elliot Rodger," by Caitlin Dewey, Washington Post, May 27, 2014, www.washingtonpost.com/news/the-intersect/wp/2014/05/27/inside-the-manosphere-that-inspired-santa-barbara-shooter-elliot-rodger/.

156 Kimmel, 2013. It is a privilege to have Michael Kimmel as esteemed member in the global advisory board of our Human Dignity and Humiliation Studies fellowship. See also "What Is the Manosphere?" by "Dalrock," Dalrock blog, May 15, 2013, http://dalrock.wordpress.com/2013/05/15/what-is-the-manosphere/.
See, furthermore:
• "The Sexodus, Part 1: The Men Giving Up On Women And Checking Out Of Society," by Milo Yiannopoulos, Breitbart, December 4, 2014, www.breitbart.com/Breitbart-London/2014/12/04/The-Sexodus-Part-1-The-Men-Giving-Up-On-Women-And-Checking-Out-Of-Society, and
• "The Sexodus, Part 2: Dishonest Feminist Panics Leave Male Sexuality In Crisis," by Milo Yiannopoulos, Breitbart, December 9, 2014, www.breitbart.com/Breitbart-London/2014/12/09/The-Sexodus-Part-2-Dishonest-Feminist-Panics-Leave-Male-Sexuality-In-Crisis. I thank Camilla Hsiung for making me aware of this article.
Read in Lindner and Desmond Tutu (Foreword), 2010, Gender, Humiliation, and Global Security, about my reflections after many years of psychotherapeutic work and social psychological inquiry, p. 38:

> Throughout my almost four decades of experience as a counselor, psychotherapist, and social psychologist, I have noticed a dynamic in families that seems to be duplicated in what is called the manosphere. When children grow up, parents ought to protect them. It is not easy, however, even for the best intentioned parent, to offer protection without being oppressive or at least appearing to be oppressive. Children might at times accuse their parents of undue domination, rightly or wrongly, and some parents might respond with accusing their children of ingratitude. In traditional family settings, when a mother has built her identity on protecting children, she might lose her anchoring when they grow up, and she might be particularly prone to feeling disrespected by her children. Committing the correspondence error, she might even infer that her children intentionally hold her in contempt, while they in reality only wish to become independent adults. I observe some men reacting in similar ways, in their relationships with their children, however, also with respect to women. By committing the correspondence bias, they accuse women of intending to hurt men, while the women simply wish to emancipate themselves, and might do so at times as unsteadily and tentatively as adolescents. "Under the laws of the Twelve Tables or lex duodecim tabularum – the ancient foundation of Roman law – the head of the family, pater familias, had vitae necisque potestas, or the 'power of life and death,' over his children and his slaves, often also over his wife. He had the power to kill or sell into slavery those he had 'under his hand' or sub manu (emancipation is the deliverance out of the hand of pater familias)."

157 "The Shootings Are Not Senseless," by Jim Dowd, The Gloucester Clam, October 4, 2015, http://gloucesterclam.com//?s=shootings. I thank Nora Femenia for making me aware of this blog and for her support for Human Dignity and Humiliation Studies.

158 "'Cultural Marxism': A Uniting Theory for Rightwingers Who Love to Play the Victim," by Jason Wilson, The Guardian, January 19, 2015, www.theguardian.com/commentisfree/2015/jan/19/cultural-marxism-a-uniting-theory-for-rightwingers-who-love-to-play-the-victim. See the full note in the pdf edition of this book.

159 Asal, et al., 2013: Overall, locations where lone-actor terrorism occurs tend to share more demographic similarities with the locations of violent hate crime offending than with the locations of group-based terrorism.

160 "Saving Passengers of the Good Ship 'Titan … Earth,'" by Robert J. Burrowes, Human Wrongs Watch, April 8, 2015, http://human-wrongs-watch.net/2015/04/08/saving-passengers-of-the-good-ship-titan-earth/.

161 Lyons, 1980. Consider the sustainability principle in The Great Law of the Iroquois Confederacy and the Ley de la Madre Tierra in Bolivia. In Lindner, 2012f, A Dignity Economy, I refer to the work of Elinor Ostrom, who received the Nobel Prize for Economics 2009. She is considered one of the leading scholars in the study of common pool resources. Her work emphasizes the multifaceted nature of human-ecosystem interaction and argues against any singular "panacea" for individual social-ecological system problems. See, among others, Poteete, et al., 2010.

162 Gaertner and Dovidio, 1999, Gaertner, et al., 1999.

163 In 2009, we held our annual HumanDHS conference in Hawai'i, and Linda Hartling, Rick Slaven, and Evelin Lindner met with Princess Lehuanani, member of the original royal Hawai'ian family, on Maui on August 29, 2009. In 2011, we held our annual HumanDHS conference in New Zealand, and Carmen Hetaraka, of Maori background, participated. See www.humiliationstudies.org/whoweare/annualmeetings.php. It is a privilege to have Carmen Hetaraka and Michelle Brenner, who brought Carmen to us, as esteemed members in our Human Dignity and Humiliation Studies fellowship.

164 Hardin, 1968, 1998, 2007.

165 Hardin, 2007.

166 Braunstein, 1990.

167 Trow, 1958.

168 "Martin Trow, Leading Scholar in Higher Education Studies, Dies at 80," by Sarah Yang, Media Relations, March 2, 2007, http://berkeley.edu/news/media/releases/2007/03/02_trow.shtml.

169 See, among others, Heitmeyer, 2010, Heitmeyer, et al., 2011, Mansel and Heitmeyer, 2009.

170 Wainwright and Calnan, 2002.

171 See notes 90, 91, and 92 in the Introduction.

172 "Terrorism: Ultimate Weapon of the Global Elite," by Robert J. Burrowes, TRANSCEND Media Service, February 16, 2015, www.transcend.org/tms/2015/02/terrorism-ultimate-weapon-of-the-global-elite/.

173 Robinson, 2017.

Chapter 2

1 "Is Critique Secular? The Renouncers," by Robert N. Bellah, Social Science Research Council Blog "The Immanent Frame," August 11, 2008, http://blogs.ssrc.org/tif/2008/08/11/the-renouncers/. The Immanent Frame was founded in October 2007 in conjunction with the U.S. Social Science Research Council's program on Religion and the Public Sphere. It publishes interdisciplinary perspectives on religion, secularism, and the public sphere. See also Bellah, 2011, Bellah and Joas, 2012, and Bellah and Hammond, 2013, where Bellah expresses the hope that American civil religion can make an essential contribution to a "global order of civility and justice."

2 Christopher Boehm, 1993, 1999, 2012. See also Witt and Schwesinger, 2013, p. S38. See the full note in the pdf edition of this book.

3 Mark D. Whitaker, 2008, studied Environmental Sociology at the University of Wisconsin-Madison, USA. In his 2008 doctoral dissertation, he argues that environmental movements are not a novel feature of world politics, but a durable feature of a degradative political economy. He has analyzed China, Japan, and Europe over 2,500 years and shows how religio-ecological movements arose against state-led environmental degradation: "As a result, origins of our large scale humanocentric "axial religions" are connected to anti-systemic environmental movements. Many major religious movements of the past were "environmentalist" by being health, ecological, and economic movements, rolled into one. Since ecological revolutions are endemic to a degradation-based political economy, they continue today." I thank Michael Bauwens for making me aware of Whitaker's research.

4 Stadtwald, 1992. Islam-critical political scientist and author Hamed Abdel-Samad sees in Luther a parallel to the Salafist movement insofar as they advocate a return to the letters of original religious texts. See Warum Luther feiern? – Zweifel an einem deutschen Mythos; Über die Gründe der Spiritualität – Wozu glauben?; Helfen oder schaden Religionen? – Eine Gegenwartsdiagnose Aspekte, Zweites Deutsches Fernsehen, April 7, 2017, with theologian Margot Käßmann, Friedrich C. Delius, Hamed Abdel-Samad, and singer Adel Tawil, moderated by Katty Salié and Jo Schück. See the full note in the pdf edition of this book.

5 Habermas, 1973.

6 Bellah, 2011, p. 573.

7 BCE stands for "Before the Common Era," and is equivalent to BC, which means "Before Christ."

8 Jaspers, 1949. See also Bellah, 2011. The list of names is long: Confucius and Laozi in China, Buddha's teachings in India, Israel's biblical prophets, Zoroaster in Iran, in Greece the epic poems Iliad and Odyssey, the natural philosophers (such as Thales, Anaximander, and Anaximenes), and Socrates, Plato, and Aristotle.

9 The egalitarian message is still difficult to bring forward today. See also note 2 in Chapter 1.

10 Witt and Schwesinger, 2013, p. S38: dominators used "draconian, public punishment of insurgents to deter and suppress" egalitarian sentiments." See also the work of historian of religion Wilfred Smith, 1962, on the reification of religion.

11 Religious Factors in the Diplomacy of Violent Conflicts, by Raymond G. Helmick, Conference on "International Politics, Diplomacy and Religion," European University Institute, Florence, Italy, May 5, 2015. Priest of the New England Jesuit Province, Raymond Helmick has worked with conflict since 1972, and it is a privilege to have him as esteemed member in the global advisory board of our Human Dignity and Humiliation Studies fellowship.

12 Ibid.

13 Freud, 1939/2010.

14 Wilson, 2002a.

15 Sidanius and Pratto, 1999. See also Pratto and Stewart, 2011. See an overview in "Power Inequities," by Máire A. Dugan, Beyond Intractability, February 2004, www.beyondintractability.org/essay/power-inequities. See also note 329 in the Introduction.

16 Kaufman, 2001, p. 212.

17 Bischof, 2004. In their research on extremism, Bischof and his colleagues found that the father played no role in psychological motivation, only the mother. In his conceptualization, Bischof relates the mother figure in a child's development with Tiamat, a primordial goddess of Mesopotamian religion, and with Marduk, who stands for a child's healthy development in building stable boundaries of the self (Ich-

Grenzen), while he sees two ways of failing, namely, the way of Anu and Kingu. Bischof connects leftist extremists with Anu and a failed revolt against the mother. As a result, they see everything that is foreign as desirable and "good," generating a preference for concepts such as multiculturalism. Leftist extremists would see the father as too weak. They would profess: "When I look in the mirror, I see my mother, and I wish to throw up." In contrast, Bischof associates right-wing extremists with Tiamat's son Kingu, who wishes to fight for his mother, yet, also he without success. Bischof points at Adolf Hitler and his idolization of his mother. Blood and Soil (German: Blut und Boden) is their ideology. For them, the mother did not deserve the father. See the full note in the pdf edition of this book.

18 Morris, 2009. Morris argues that worship of an ancient mythical god has produced distorted political and social systems, which is now the foundation of present-day values and worldviews among general populations in a world controlled by a few small powerful groups in the area of religion, politics, and commerce, who use fear and greed to gain wealth and power for their particular limited group, rather than for the common good. We read about the author's background on www.civilisationhijacked.com/#!bio/c1ktj. See the full note in the pdf edition of this book.

19 Steinsland, 2007. See the research group on "The Power of the Ruler and the Ideology of Rulership in Nordic Culture 800–1200," at the Centre for Advanced Study, 2007/2008, www.cas.uio.no/research/0708rulership/index.php. Because Christianity arrived relatively late in the North, the transition of ideologies in this region is well documented. Steinsland analyzes, for example, the eddaic poem Skirnismål and its depiction of the so-called myth of the sacred marriage (the Greek technical term is hieros gamos), or the erotic alliance between a god and a giant woman, which rendered the ruler special and gave him and his lineage a unique position with regard to other people. With Christianity, a related, medieval ideology of rulership was imported, namely, the depiction of the king as an image of the Heavenly God. See also Lindner, 2009b, p. 63.

20 Pratto and Stewart, 2011.

21 See Volkan, 1997, 2004, 2006, 2013.

22 Volkan, 2004.

23 Vallacher, et al., 2010, 269.

24 Jost, et al., 2004, Jost, et al., 2009, Jost, et al., 2002, Jost and Ross, 1999.

25 Jost, et al., 2004.

26 Pratto and Stewart, 2011, Sidanius and Pratto, 1999. See an overview in "Power Inequities," by Máire A. Dugan, Beyond Intractability, February 2004, www.beyondintractability.org/essay/power-inequities. See also note 329 in the Introduction.

27 Jost, et al., 2004, Jost, et al., 2009, Jost, et al., 2002, Jost and Ross, 1999.

28 See note 186 in the Introduction.

29 Norgaard, 2015.

30 Kendall, 2007, p. 569. See also Weber, 1904-1905.

31 Smith, 1759. I thank Howard Richards for his summary. The phrase "invisible hand" appears only once in Smith's book on the wealth of nations and this moreover in a different context. It seems that it was taken out of its context later, and suffered a fate similar of Darwin's "survival of the fittest." See a concise and accessible presentation in Capitalism, a documentary series in six episodes, by documentary filmmaker Ilan Ziv, www.tamouzmedia.com/in-production.htm.

32 Acres of Diamonds, was delivered by Russell Conwell over 5000 times at various times and places from 1900 to 1925. See audio and text on www.americanrhetoric.com/speeches/rconwellacresofdiamonds.htm. His view of poverty was in resonance with defenders of the Indian caste system:

> Some men say, "Don't you sympathize with the poor people?" of course I do, or else I would not have been lecturing these years. I won't give in but what I sympathize with the poor, but the number of poor who are to be with is very small. To sympathize with a man whom God has punished for his sins, thus to help him when God would still continue a just punishment, is to do wrong, no doubt about it, and we do that more than we help those who are deserving. While we should sympathize with God's poor-that is, those who cannot help themselves – let us remember that is not a poor person in the United States who was not made poor by his own shortcomings, or by the shortcomings of someone else. It is all wrong to be poor, anyhow. Let us give in to that argument and pass that to one side.

See also "Trump's Success Shows Many Americans Believe only in America," by Giles Fraser, The Guardian, March 3, 2016, www.theguardian.com/commentisfree/belief/2016/mar/03/donald-trump-success-shows-many-americans-believe-only-in-america:

> When the Pilgrim Fathers got in their little boats and sailed to the new world, they took with them a narrative that had begun to build in England, that the protestant English were actually the chosen people. America, then, was to be the new Israel. The pilgrims had landed safe on Cannan's side, the promised land. The original 13 colonies in North America "were nothing other than a regeneration of the twelve tribes of Israel" as one American newspaper put it in 1864.
>
> In other words, America became its own church and eventually its own god. Which is why the only real atheism in America is to call into question the American dream – a dream often indistinguishable from capitalism and the celebration of winners. This is the god Trump worships. He is its great high priest. And this is why evangelicals vote for him. But the God of Jesus Christ it is not. The death of God comes in many diverse and peculiar forms. In America, it is the flag and not the cross that takes pride of place in the sanctuary.

33 Figgis, 1914.

34 Jameson, 1994. Quoted in McMaster, 2013. See also Harvey, 2005, or the case of China taken up in Hansen and Svarverud, 2010, describing how globalization and neoliberalism create new hybrid cultural, political, and economic practices on top of prevailing Confucian ethics and communist practices.

35 "A Short History of Neo-liberalism: Twenty Years of Elite Economics and Emerging Opportunities for Structural Change," by Susan George, Conference on Economic Sovereignty in a Globalising World, Bangkok, Thailand, March 24–26, 1999, www.globalexchange.org/resources/econ101/neoliberalismhist. Quoted in McMaster, 2013. See also George, 2015.

36 Hirschman, 1977. See also Adelman, 2013, and "Understanding Society – Innovative Thinking About a Global World: Hirschman on the Passions" by Daniel Little, May 14, 2013, http://understandingsociety.blogspot.no/2013/05/hirschman-on-passions.html.

37 Social mobility has been found to be extremely slow, across countries and eras, see, for example, Clark, 2014.

38 Witt and Schwesinger, 2013, p. S39.

39 Witt and Schwesinger, 2013, p. S40.

40 Droge and Tabor, 1992, p. 136.

41 Whitehead and Abufarha, 2008. See also Strathern, et al., 2006.

42 Whitehead and Abufarha, 2008, p. 395.

43 Mona Eltahawy explained her views on January 30, 2015, at "World Woman," an event organized by Deeyah Khan and Fuuse at Riksscenen in Oslo, Norway, January 30–31, 2015, http://fuuse.net/world-woman/about/.

44 Aslan, 2005, 2009.

45 "What I Want to Be Thankful for on Thanksgiving: An Ode to Edward Snowden," by Carol Smaldino, Huffington Post, www.huffingtonpost.com/carol-smaldino/what-i-want-to-be-thankfu_b_6216182.html. It is a privilege to have Carol Smaldino as esteemed member in our Human Dignity and Humiliation Studies fellowship.

46 "Religious Fundamentalism-Extremism-Violence," by Johan Galtung, TRANSCEND Media Service, February 8, 2016, www.transcend.org/tms/2016/02/religious-fundamentalism-extremism-violence/.

47 Ibid.

48 Karlberg, 2013, p. 7. See the full note in the pdf edition of this book.

49 Walter Benjamin to Ludwig Strauss in his letter of November 21, 1912, quoted in Ott, 2016.

50 See, among others, Cohen, 2009, Cohen and Crane-Kramer, 2007, or Armelagos, et al., 1991, Lipton and De Kadt, 1988.

51 Manning, 2004.

52 Warner, 2014a. See also Warner, 2009, 2014b, c.

53 Consider the sustainability principle in The Great Law of the Iroquois Confederacy and the Ley de la Madre Tierra in Bolivia.

54 See the work of Alexander Wendt, 2015, as one example among many. I am thankful for having had the chance to communicate with Alexander Wendt, for the first time in 2005.

55 Bruce Schuman in his contribution to the Great Transition Network (GTN) discussion on the topic of "Meaning, Religion, and a Great Transition," November 12, 2014, in response to Karlberg, 2014.

56 Heard, 1963.

57 Hollick, 2006, Hollick and Connelly, 2011. I thank Sigurd Støren for making me aware of this work. Sigurd Støren, Malcolm Hollick, and Christine Connelly are esteemed members in the global advisory board of our Human Dignity and Humiliation Studies fellowship.

58 See the list of the Laureates of the Planetary Consciousness Award 1996 – 2004 on www.clubofbudapest.org/laureats-planet-consc.php.

59 Karlberg, 2014. See also Karlberg, 2004, 2008, 2012.

60 Paul Nieuwenhuis, Cardiff Business School, in his contribution to the Great Transition Network (GTN) discussion on the topic of "Against Ecocide: Legal Protection for Earth," July 19, 2016, in response to Femke Wijdekop, 2016.

Chapter 3

1 Miller, 1976/1986, p. 72. I thank Linda Hartling for recommending this quote as an introduction into this chapter.

2 I am working on a book on what we call "human nature," where I will discuss the topics of this section in more depth.

3 See, among others, Barrington-Leigh, 2017, Helliwell and Barrington-Leigh, 2011. Already in the early 1970s, economist Richard Easterlin, et al., 2010, discovered a paradox, namely, that while happiness was strongly correlated with income within each country and varied widely across countries, a country did not necessarily become any happier on average when it became richer.

4 Barrington-Leigh, 2017, and Barrington-Leigh, 2010: "The main finding is that in countries where subjective well-being depends more strongly on one's rank in the income distribution, people are less happy across the entire income distribution."

5 Fuchs and Flügge, 2014, Abstract. I thank Linda Hartling for making me aware of this article. See the full note in the pdf edition of this book.

6 Fuglestvedt, 2010, Goldhahn, et al., 2010. See also note 2 in Chapter 1.

7 Nowak and Highfield, 2012.

8 Social psychologist Morton Deutsch was the director emeritus of the Morton Deutsch International Center for Cooperation and Conflict Resolution (MD-ICCCR) at Teachers College, Columbia University, in New York City. He is one of the founders of the study of cooperation, and emphasizes the advantages of cooperation, for instance cooperation's superiority to competition. It was a privilege to have Morton Deutsch as esteemed member in the board of directors of our Human Dignity and Humiliation Studies fellowship. He was the honorary convener of our annual Workshop on Transforming Humiliation and Violent Conflict, hosted by the Morton Deutsch International Center for Cooperation and Conflict Resolution (MD-ICCCR), as part of the Advanced Consortium on Cooperation, Conflict, and Complexity (AC4), Columbia University, New York City. Morton Deutsch passed away on March 13, 2017, 97 years old, and we will honor his legacy by continuing with this workshop series. See www.humiliationstudies.org/whoweare/annualmeetings.php.

9 Tomasello, 2014, Tomasello, et al., 2005. Michael Tomasello found two core dimensions: reading intentions, and socially interacting with others.

10 Crespi and Yanega, 1995. Several different levels of sociality are differentiated including presociality (solitary but social), subsociality, parasocial (including communal, quasisocial, and semisocial), and eusocial. The term eusocial originally includes organisms (originally, only invertebrates) with the following features: 1. Reproductive division of labor (with or without sterile castes), 2. Overlapping generations, 3. Cooperative care of young.

11 Wilson, 2013. See also "Interview with Edward O. Wilson: The Origin of Morals," by Philip Bethge and Johann Grolle, Spiegel Online International, February 26, 2013, www.spiegel.de/international/spiegel/spiegel-interview-with-edward-wilson-on-the-formation-of-morals-a-884767.html.
See, furthermore, Edward O. Wilson on the Human Condition, FORA.tv., April 20, 2012, http://fora.tv/2012/04/20/Edward_O_Wilson_The_Social_Conquest_of_Earth.

12 Wilson and Wilson, 2007, https://pdfs.semanticscholar.org/7694/67447fc718c5c0069391958c77df93af7882.pdf, p. 27. See David Sloan Wilson, 2015, for why both between-group selection and within-group selection may be important, rather than only the latter. See also Wilson's science blog, beginning with "Truth and Reconciliation for Group Selection I: Why It Is Needed," October 23, 2009, http://scienceblogs.com/evolution/2009/10/23/truth-and-reconciliation-for-g/. It was a privilege to meet David Sloan Wilson in March 2016 in Oslo, Norway, and to learn from him in the context of "Kontrapunkt," an event organized by Nina Witoszek, Alida Boye, and Helge Iberg.

13 Lindner, 2000a.

14 "A Failed State that Is Succeeding in Parts," The Economist, August 29, 1999, www.economist.com/node/234829.

15 Ibid.

16 Ibn Khaldun, 1377/1958, is a historiographer, historian, and a forerunner of the contemporary disciplines of sociology and demography, who addressed themes such as politics, urban life, economics, and

knowledge. I studied him when I lived and worked as a clinical psychologist in Cairo, Egypt, from 1984–1991. I saw him describe the very contrast between sedentary life and nomadic life that was very apparent for me while living in Cairo. Ibn Khaldun described how desert warriors lose power when they conquer a city. Ibn Khaldun's central concept was that of aṣabiyyah, or "social cohesion," or "group solidarity," arising in tribes and other small kinship groups, sometimes intensified by religious ideology, therefore also identifiable as "tribalism." I observed the workings of clan cohesion later first hand during my doctoral research in Somaliland in 1998. According to Ibn Khaldun, this cohesion has two sides: while it helps groups to accumulate power, it also contains within itself psychological, sociological, economic, and political seeds of the group's downfall, when a new group arrives with more vigorous cohesion. See also, "Why Nomads Win: What Ibn Khaldun Would Say About Afghanistan," by Gerard Russell, Afghanistan and Middle East specialist, Huffington Post, April 11, 2010, www.huffingtonpost.com/gerard-russell/why-nomads-win-what-ibn-k_b_447878.html.

17 Witt and Schwesinger, 2013. See also Deci and Ryan, 1985, for the argument that an egalitarian group structure creates a prosocial attitude, and motivates group members to identify with the group and to attend to an assigned task, particularly when the task is based on a consensus. In this way, an intrinsic work motivation is created.

18 Witt and Schwesinger, 2013.

19 See more in Lindner, 2016e.

20 The Late Pleistocene is a geochronological age of the Pleistocene Epoch beginning 127.000/126.000 years ago and ending 11.784 (± 69) years ago. The age represents the end of the Pleistocene epoch and is followed by the Holocene epoch.

21 See, for instance, Fuglestvedt, 2005, and Fuglestvedt, 2008. BCE stands for "Before the Common Era," and is equivalent to BC, which means "Before Christ."

22 See a readable popular presentation in "Neanderthals Were People, Too," by Jon Mooallem, New York Times, January 11, 2017, www.nytimes.com/2017/01/11/magazine/neanderthals-were-people-too.html. I thank Linda Hartling for making me aware of this article. I am proud of having 2.8 percent DNA from Neanderthals!

23 Witt and Schwesinger, 2013.

24 Jaynes, 1976. I thank Finn Tschudi for making me aware of this book.

25 McGilchrist, 2009. I thank Howard Richards for making me aware of this book.

26 Kornhuber and Deecke, 1965, Libet, et al., 1983, Kühn and Brass, 2009.

27 The potential implications of this research for free will, highly relevant for conflict studies, have been discussed at great length in the literature, see, for instance, Roskies, 2010, or Gazzaniga, 2011.

28 Devine, 1989, Fazio, 1990. See the full note in the pdf edition of this book.

29 See also Lindner, 2009b, Chapter 2: How Emotions Affect Conflict, in the book Emotion and Conflict.

30 Passer, et al., 2011. I thank Nils Vidar Vambheim for reminding me of the work of Michael Passer and his colleagues. Karen Barad earned her doctorate in theoretical physics, building on insights from Niels Bohr, and is known for her theory of agential realism, and she writes, in Barad, 2003, p. 810: "Indeed, there is a host of material-discursive forces – including ones that get labeled 'social,' 'cultural,' 'psychic,' 'economic,' 'natural,' 'physical,' 'biological,' 'geopolitical,' and 'geological' – that may be important to particular (entangled) processes of materialization."

31 Berkowitz, 1990.

32 Berkowitz and Harmon-Jones, 2004. Leonard Berkowitz sadly passed away on the very day that I write these lines, in January 2016, almost ninety years old.

33 Milgram, 1974. A replication of the Milgram experiments in 2017 showed that even today, people are still willing to harm others in pursuit of obeying authority, see Doliński, et al., 2017.
See also Curiosity: How Evil are You? Authority and Obedience: The Milgram Experiment, by Eli Roth, 2011, reproducing results similar to the original Milgram experiment, though the highest-voltage punishment used was 165 volts, rather than 450 volts, https://curiosity.com/playlists/authority-and-obedience-the-milgram-experiment-BOON2XVU/?utm_source=dsc&utm_medium=rdr&utm_campaign=rdrwork.
See also a book by Steven Bartlett, 2011, where he seeks to understand, among others, the psychology of people who possess what the author has called "moral intelligence," which allow a person to resist when asked to participate in abusive behavior. It is a privilege to have Steven Bartlett as esteemed member in the global advisory board of our Human Dignity and Humiliation Studies fellowship.

34 60 Minutes: What the Last Nuremberg Prosecutor Alive Wants the World to Know, CBS-TV News, May 7, 2017, www.cbsnews.com/news/what-the-last-nuremberg-prosecutor-alive-wants-the-world-to-know/. At 97, Ben Ferencz is the last Nuremberg prosecutor alive and he has a far-reaching message for today's world. I thank Libby and Len Traubman for reminding me of this quote.

35 Bauman, 1989.

36 Isdal, 2000. Per Isdal is a psychotherapist working with violent men. . I thank Nils Vidar Vambheim for reminding me of Isdal's work.

37 A young Palestinian man told me that he felt triumph when he was beaten and humiliated by the military – he was almost killed – because this was proof that he resisted oppression (personal communication, 2004). He would have felt unbearable shame and guilt had he accepted humiliation and not stood up to it, he said. There is a Somali proverb: "A man deserves to be killed, not humiliated."
See also Hartling, et al., 2013, where we discuss studies of Palestinians living in Gaza and the West Bank. Ginges and Atran, 2008, found that humiliation leads to an "inertia effect" (p. 281), which suppresses violent action, a finding supported by research carried out by Leidner, et al., 2012, indicating that humiliation is accompanied by feelings of powerlessness and a decreased likeliness to engage in violence. In their study of over 7000 twins, also Kendler, et al., 2003, described depressogenic effect of humiliation. Elison and Harter, 2007, noted a history of depression and signs of depression in the school shooters they studied.
In conclusion, as it seems, under certain conditions, humiliation inhibits violent action, at least in the short term, yet, the chronic and cumulative effect of humiliation may lead to violence in the long term. While scholars continue to investigate how humiliation may have the power to change individuals into ticking time bombs, so Harter et al., 2003, and Torres and Bergner, 2010, we must also explore what happens when political leaders, terrorist leaders, or entire nations "lit the fuse of humiliation," Fattah, 2013.

38 Hewstone, et al., 2006, Passer, et al., 2011.

39 Sherif, 1961.

40 Tajfel, 1970.

41 Galtung, 1978.

42 Ryan, 1995.

43 Hermans, et al., 2014. I learned from Guillén Fernández on October 10, 2015, at the Symposium "Gehirne zwischen Liebe und Krieg – Menschlichkeit in Zeiten der Neurowissenschaften," Fürth, Germany, October 9–11, 2015, www.turmdersinne.de/de/symposium/symposium-2015/programm. Fernández' research shows the influence of a wide range of factors, from neurotransmitters such as noradrenaline that initiate the stress reaction to corticosteroids restoring homeostasis by normalizing/desensitizing brain processing in the aftermath of stress. To gain a stable psychic balance, everything from experience and feedback, to genetic protection, to food and neurotransmitters such as corticosteroids and serotonin can help, while persistence of noradrenaline, together with genetic risk, childhood trauma, and stress can lead to

an enduring imbalance that may be associated with PTSD, social phobia, specific phobia, and generalized anxiety disorder. See the full note with relevant references in the pdf edition of this book.

44 Holbrook, et al., 2015. See more in note 115 in the Preface.

45 See, among others, Gilbert, 1998.

46 Ibid.

47 Koenigs, et al., 2007.

48 The sadistic personality disorder appeared in an appendix of the revised third edition of the APA's Diagnostic and Statistical Manual of Mental Disorders (DSM-III-R), but the later versions of the DSM (DSM-IV, DSM-IV-TR and DSM-5) do not include it. Yet, the term is used in common language and is grappled with in professional circles. Israel W. Charny proposes to include "A Personality Disorder of Excessive Power Strivings" in the Diagnostic and Statistical Manual of Mental Disorders IV (DSM-IV), see Charny, 1997, see also Charny, 2014. See the full note with relevant references in the pdf edition of this book.

49 Roth, et al., 2010, Wiswede, et al., 2014. I was able to learn from Gerhard Roth on October 11, 2015, at the Symposium "Gehirne zwischen Liebe und Krieg – Menschlichkeit in Zeiten der Neurowissenschaften," Fürth, Germany, October 9–11, 2015, www.turmdersinne.de/de/symposium/symposium-2015/programm.

50 Fonagy, et al., 2015, Fonagy, et al., 2004. I was able to learn from Svenja Taubner, who works with Peter Fonagy, on October 10, 2015, at the Symposium "Gehirne zwischen Liebe und Krieg – Menschlichkeit in Zeiten der Neurowissenschaften," Fürth, Germany, October 9–11, 2015, www.turmdersinne.de/de/symposium/symposium-2015/programm. Mentalization is being defined as the ability of a person to envision mental states in her own self and in others. The "alien self" arises when caregivers fail to adequately have their infant's "mind in mind." Clinical psychologist John Auerbach suggests to use the term "alien identity" rather than "alien self," see his review of Fonagy's Affect Regulation, Mentalization, and the Development of the Self, Winter 2005, pp. 35–38, www.apadivisions.org/division-39/publications/reviews/affect.aspx.

51 Koestler, 1974.

52 See, among others, Fisher, 1930, Haldane, 1932, Watson, et al., 1936, or Hamilton, 1963, 1964b, a. For more recent explanations, see, among others, "Richard Dawkins, Edward O. Wilson, and the Consensus of the Many," by David Sloan Wilson, January 1, 2015, https://evolution-institute.org/article/richard-dawkins-edward-o-wilson-and-the-consensus-of-the-many/. See also "Human Nature: An Evolutionary Paradox," by John Scales Avery, Human Wrongs Watch, August 15, 2016, https://human-wrongs-watch.net/2016/08/17/human-nature-an-evolutionary-paradox/.

53 "Human Nature: An Evolutionary Paradox," by John Scales Avery, Human Wrongs Watch, August 15, 2016, https://human-wrongs-watch.net/2016/08/17/human-nature-an-evolutionary-paradox/.

54 See, among others Ardrey, 1961, Lee and DeVore, 1968, or Tiger, 1984. See also note 2 in Chapter 1.

55 See, for instance, Zihlman, 2009, or Wilbanks, 2008. Sally Linton, 1974, was possibly the first to write a feminist reaction to Man the Hunter in her 1974 chapter "Woman the Gatherer." Baskets and slings may have been the first tools invented, tools for carrying infants and gathered food. Early hominin groups were rather centered around the mother-infant relationship than the mate relationship, see Slocum, 1975, Leacock, et al., 1978, Tanner, 1981, Fedigan, 1986, Zihlman, et al., 1997, Sussman, 1999, Hart and Sussman, 2009, Ward and Edelstein, 2009.

56 Parzinger, 2015.

57 "The Worst Mistake in the History of the Human Race," by Jared Diamond, Discover Magazine, May 1987, pp. 64–66, www.ditext.com/diamond/mistake.html.

58 Witt and Schwesinger, 2013.

59 Boserup, 1965; Cohen, 1977.

60 Bowles and Gintis, 2011a).

61 Cohen, 2009, Cohen and Crane-Kramer, 2007, or Armelagos, et al., 1991, Lipton and De Kadt, 1988.

62 See an overview in Witt and Schwesinger, 2013. The emergence of hierarchically stratified society began with the figure of the locum tenens (Latin for "one holding a place"), then, with the delegation of power governorship and fiefdom emerged, eventually giving rise to feudal state systems. See early work by Fried, 1967, Harner, 1970, or Jones and American Council of Learned, 1993.

63 Heller, 1984.

64 See for a discussion of terror, panic, and polarization Renos Papadopoulos, 2006, who draws on his expertise in the Greek roots of notions such as terror and panic, and combines it with his Jungian orientation.

65 Holbrook, et al., 2015. See more in note 115 in the Preface.

66 Whitson and Galinsky, 2008.

67 Bartoschek, 2015.

68 Bartoschek, 2015.

69 Twain, 1916, Chapter 9.

70 Translated from German by Alice Asbury Abbott, Suttner, 1908, pp. 171–172. The last paragraph is translated by Lindner. See the German original in Suttner, 1889, pp. 105–106, and in the full note in the pdf edition of this book.

71 Military psychology addresses this topic. See, for example, Grossman, 1995. See also Cushman, et al., 2012. I thank Ulrich Spalthoff for making me aware of this research.

72 "Suicide Rate Spikes Among Young Veterans," by Leo Shane III, Stars and Stripes, January 9, 2014, www.stripes.com/report-suicide-rate-spikes-among-young-veterans-1.261283. Researchers found that the risk of suicide for veterans is 21 percent higher when compared to civilian adults. From 2001 to 2014, as the civilian suicide rate rose about 23.3 percent, the rate of suicide among veterans jumped more than 32 percent. See the "VA Suicide Prevention Program Facts about Veteran Suicide," U.S. Department of Veterans Affairs, July 2016, www.va.gov/opa/publications/factsheets/Suicide_Prevention_FactSheet_New_VA_Stats_070616_1400.pdf.

73 I admire veteran Drew Pham's analysis of his need to kill as a path to gaining respect, see "The Long March Ahead: A Veteran's Place in Resistance," by Drew Pham, November 22, 2016, www.wrath-bearingtree.com/2016/11/the-long-march-ahead-a-veterans-place-in-resistance/. It is a great privilege for me to know Drew Pham personally, in his capacity of working at the Morton Deutsch International Center for Cooperation and Conflict Resolution (MD-ICCCR) at Teachers College, Columbia University, New York City.

74 Lee, 2015.

75 See note 156 in Chapter 1.

76 "Women Are Incapable of Love, Period," comment 9518 by "fgsfdf," to the question "Are the vast majority of women truly incapable of experiencing reciprocal love and attraction?" Dalrock blog, June 8, 2011, http://dalrock.wordpress.com/2011/06/08/are-the-vast-majority-of-women-truly-incapable-of-experiencing-recriprocal-love-and-attraction/#comment-9518. The author of the Dalrock blog identifies himself as follows: "I'm a happily married man living with my sexy wife and our two wonderful kids in the Dallas/Fort Worth area. I'm very interested in how the post-feminist world impacts myself and my family, and am using this blog to explore these kinds of issues."

77 "Why Invest in Women?" The United States Agency for International Development (USAID), http://50.usaid.gov/infographic-why-invest-in-women/. See also "An Economy for the 99 Per Cent," Oxfam International Briefing Paper, January 16, 2017, www.oxfam.org/sites/www.oxfam.org/files/file_attachments/bp-economy-for-99-percent-160117-en.pdf. See, furthermore, "Inequality (II): "It Will Take 170 Years for Women to Be Paid as Men Are," by Baher Kamal, Inter Press Service (IPS), January 17, 2017, www.ipsnews.net/2017/01/inequality-ii-it-will-take-170-years-for-women-to-be-paid-as-men-are/.

78 Darimont, et al., 2015.

79 Global wildlife populations have fallen by 58 percent since 1970, and if the trend continues the decline could reach two-thirds among vertebrates by 2020, according to World Wildlife Fund (WWF), et al., 2016. See also Ceballos, et al., 2015, Kolbert, 2006, Spufford and Kolbert, 2007, and Kolbert, 2014.
See, furthermore, Davis, 2009, and The Wayfinders, the 2009 Massey Lecture by Wade Davis, Convocation Hall, Toronto, uploaded November 20, 2011, on https://youtu.be/KfbGdoTQKuM. See also philosopher Alan Wilson Watts (1915 – 1973), and his Alan Watts: A Conversation with Myself in four parts, beginning with https://youtu.be/8aufuwMiKmE.

80 See a statistical overview over foreign fighters in Iraq and Syria, updated on January 29, 2015, on www.rferl.org/contentinfographics/infographics/26584940.html.

81 Wang and Aamodt, 2011.

82 Carveth, 2013. I thank Michael Britton for making me aware of this book. Also Maria Montessori followed a similar line in her educational theory, when she called on instructors to "give priority to the inner teacher who animated" the child. The trope of the wisdom of the inner teacher that sits at our hearts is also to be found, for instance, in Tibetan Buddhists. Psychoanalyst Susie Orbach, 2009, observed that parental and societal pressure leads to a false self in the sense of a skewed self, where certain aspects of the self are overemphasized, at the expense of others, making the person distrust herself, thus an inner splitting of mind and body leading to a falsified sense of one's own body.
Sociologist David Riesman, et al., 1950/2001, may have had similar dynamics in mind when he identified three main cultural types: tradition-directed, inner-directed, and other-directed. The tradition-directed and other-directed types may tend to Carveth's category of "unconscionable superego," while the inner-directed person may have access to sympathetic identification.

83 Carveth, 2013, see the book description at www.karnacbooks.com/product/the-still-small-voice-psychoanalytic-reflections-on-guilt-and-conscience/33543/. See the full note in the pdf edition of this book.

84 Inner child therapy was developed by John Bradshaw, 1990, and others, loosely building on both Freudian and Jungian psychoanalysis. Recovery work invites into emotionally charged "regression" for an active "reparenting" process to heal from being "stuck at various earlier developmental stages" when one's "necessary narcissistic needs were not lovingly met," Ivy, 1993, p. 236.

85 See for a discussion of the significance of rationality versus emotions my reflections on emotion and conflict in Lindner, 2009b, 2014b.

86 "Word of the Year 2016 Is...," Oxford Dictionaries, https://en.oxforddictionaries.com/word-of-the-year/word-of-the-year-2016.

87 Sundararajan, 2015, p. 168. See also Pritzker, 2016. See the network of indigenous psychologists that Louise Sundararajan gathers, of which I am a member. See also Sundararajan, 2012. See a scathing critic of the journey of the field of indigenous psychology by Gustav Jahoda, 2016. Jahoda's article has elicited efforts to rebut his negative evaluation, see, among others, Marsella, 2009, and more on www.indigenouspsych.org/Discussion/forum/Archives/PDF/Jahoda%20on%20IP%20and%20rebuttals.pdf. See the full note in the pdf edition of this book.

88 Bell, 2008.

89 Hsuan-Ying Huang, 2014, explains that private for-profit companies offer expensive two to seven days psychological counseling courses promising that participants will learn to master the methods of self-adjustment, "by which you can enhance your quality of life, increase your working efficiency, educate your children more successfully and better handle your family relationships," Huang, 2014, p. 195. It is part of a multibillion dollar industry of the self in China that feeds on a frantic search for greater health and happiness through individual self-cultivation.

90 Kipnis, 2012, p. 7.

91 Yang, 2015, p. 6.

92 Kuan, 2015, p. 98–99.

93 Buber, 1923/1937.

94 Miller, 2008a. "True self" and "false self" are concepts introduced into psychoanalysis in 1960 by Donald Winnicott, 1965.

95 Dower, 1999, p. 157.

96 Ibid.

97 Grothe, 2017, p. 212. I thank Linda Hartling for making me aware of this quote.

98 Lindner and Desmond Tutu (Foreword), 2010.

99 See note 117 in the Preface.

100 Dweck, 2007, or Yeager, et al., 2013.

101 "Islamic State 'Demolishes' Ancient Hatra Site in Iraq," BBC News, March 7, 2015, www.bbc.com/news/world-middle-east-31779484.

102 "Who You Really Are: DNA Ancestry Tests May Be Marketed as the Key to Your Genetic Fate, but the Truth Is That a Myriad of Environmental Factors Influence the Way Your DNA Is Expressed and Inherited," by Robert Pollack and Patricia Williams, Columbia University, www.columbia.edu/cu/biology/faculty-data/robert-pollack/resources/2014%20GeneWatch.pdf. See also "Interplay Between Social Experiences and the Genome: Epigenetic Consequences for Behavior," by Frances A. Champagne, Department of Psychology, Columbia University, New York, USA, http://champagnelab.psych.columbia.edu/docs/Adv%20Genetics%202012.pdf.

103 Lindner, 2009b, Lindner, 2014b, Lindner and Desmond Tutu (Foreword), 2010.

104 Huntington, 1996.

105 "UN Security Council Seats Taken by Arms Exporters," by Lyndal Rowlands, Inter Press Service (IPS), November 28, 2016, www.ipsnews.net/2016/11/un-security-council-seats-taken-by-arms-exporters/.

106 Neuro-warfare would include electromagnetic warfare (electric field, magnetic field, microwaves), acoustic warfare (infrasound, ultrasound), and light warfare (ultraviolent, flashing, strobe), see Marsella, 2012. See also, among others, Phillips, et al., 2006: "This research explores the current capabilities of the US military to use electromagnetic (EMF) devices to harass, intimidate, and kill individuals and the continuing possibilities of violations of human rights by the testing and deployment of these weapons. To establish historical precedent in the US for such acts, we document long-term human rights and freedom of thought violations by US military/intelligence organizations. Additionally, we explore contemporary evidence of on-going government research in EMF weapons technologies and examine the potentialities of continuing human rights abuses."

107 Lindner, 2006c, p. 48.

108 Pritzker, 2016, p. 167.

109 Pieterse, 2001, Abstract. I thank Jan for the very enriching meeting we had in Paris on September 23, 2002.

110 Pieterse, 2001, Abstract.

111 Anthony Marsella, in a personal communication on January 25, 2014. Anthony Marsella is a past president of Psychologists for Social Responsibility, emeritus professor of psychology at the University of Hawaii, and past director of the World Health Organization Psychiatric Research Center in Honolulu. He is known nationally and internationally as a pioneer figure in the study of culture and psychopathology who challenged the ethnocentrism and racial biases of many assumptions, theories, and practices in psychology and psychiatry. In more recent years, he has been writing and lecturing on peace and social justice. He has published 15 edited books, and more than 250 articles, chapters, book reviews, and popular pieces. It is a privilege to have Anthony Marsella as esteemed member in the global advisory board of our Human Dignity and Humiliation Studies fellowship.

112 Leighton, 1959.

113 Mark Granovetter did research on whether people find jobs through strong or weak social ties. Granovetter builds on Tönnies' differentiation of Gemeinschaft versus Gesellschaft, see Tönnies, 1887/1955, and Granovetter, 1973, 2002.

114 According to Francis Hsu, different relationships are privileged in different societies: In China, the dominant dyad is father-son, in India mother-son, in Africa siblings. In Japan it is father-son, with mother-son as subdominant dyad, in America husband-wife. See Hsu, 1948, 1953, 1963, Hsu, 1965, Marsella, et al., 1985. I thank Jacqueline Howell Wasilewski for being the first to make me aware of Hsu's concept of dominant dyads.

115 Marsella, 2012.

116 Lee, 1995.

117 See note 87 in this Chapter 3.

118 Gergen, et al., 1996.

119 Nagel, 1986.

120 Taylor in Lowman, 2013, pp. 52–53.

121 Lindner, 2007b.

122 Gergen, et al., 1996, quoted in Marsella, 2015. Marsella warns that North American psychology is wrongly driven by a commitment to the following:

1. Individuality – The individual is the focus of behavior. Determinants of behavior reside in the individual's brain/mind, and interventions must be at this level rather than the broader societal context.
2. Reductionism – Small, tangible units of study that yield well to controlled experimentation are favored.
3. Experiment-based Empiricism – An emphasis on experiments with controls and experiment group comparisons and uses of ANOVA analyses that often account for 5–10 percent of the variance, and this is considered "science." Lab studies are often favored over field studies.
4. Scientism – The belief that methods of the physical sciences can be applied similarly to social and behavioral phenomena, which results in spurious methods and conclusions that are inappropriate to the subject under study or that avoid studying certain subjects.
5. Quantification/Measurement – "If something exists, it can be measured, said Edward Thorndike. Unless something under study can be quantified, it is not acceptable for study. This, of course, leads to "operationalism" as the standard for assessing concepts.
6. Materialism – Favors variables for study that have a tangible existence rather than higher order

constructs – I can see it and touch it under a microscope.
7. Male Dominance – Years of male dominance favors particular topics, methods, and populations for study – remember "involutional melancholia," the psychiatric disease of middle-aged women, or the labeling of transgender as an illness. While this is changing, we must be alert to its legacy.
8. "Objectivity" – Assumption that we can identify and understand immutable aspects of reality in a detached way, unbiased by human senses and knowledge.
9. Nomothetic Laws – Search for generalized principles and "laws" that apply to widespread and diverse situations and populations because of an identification and admiration for the physical sciences.
10. Rationality – Presumes a linear, cause-effect, logical, material understanding of phenomena and prizes this approach in offering and accepting arguments and data generation.

123 Lindner, 2009d.

124 See note 13 in the Introduction to Section One.

125 Lindner, 2000a.

Chapter 4

1 Verseuil, 1946.

2 Nye, 2004.

3 See note 331 in the Introduction.

4 Eagleton, 1991, p. 111. Theorist and politician Antonio Gramsci uses the phrase hegemony for when a ruling class manipulates society to the point that elite views become the reigning Weltanschauung. While authoritarian rule is openly dominating, cultural hegemony works through cooption.

5 See note 201 in the Introduction.

6 Carveth, 2013.

7 Galtung, 1996, p. 199.

8 Roman law was introduced for this purpose. See Richards, 2013, as well as Iglesias, 2010, Richards, 1995, 2010, Richards and Swanger, 2006b, and Chapter 4 in Odora Hoppers and Richards, 2012. I thank Howard Richards for making me aware of the analysis of the sociological background of Roman law by Ferdinand Tönnies, 1887/1955. See also Jolowicz, 1932, and Merryman, 1969. See, furthermore, the work of Norbert Elias, 1939/1994, 1969. Howard Richards in a personal Communication on October 15, 2016:

My point about Roman law is that it deliberately abstracted from primary groups and local culture in order to create a Law of Nations suitable for organizing their vast empire and commerce within it on the basis of a few simple rules applicable to everybody. Now their civil law has become the frame for the global economy.

See for a recent overview over Roman law and society, Ando, et al., 2016. Roman law (Latin: ius romanum) has its origins in ancient Rome, including the Roman military jurisdiction and the legal developments spanning a thousand years of jurisprudence, from the Twelve Tables or lex duodecim tabularum (circa 449 BCE) to the Corpus Juris Civilis (529 CE) by the Byzantine Emperor Justinian I. It got renewed attention in the early Middle Ages. English and North American common law, among others, is strongly influenced by Roman law, actively using a Latin legal glossary, for example stare decisis, culpa in contrahendo, pacta sunt servanda. See more in note 368 in Chapter 15.

9 The contact hypothesis, or the hope that contact will foster friendship, was proposed by Gordon Allport, 1954, suggesting that relations between groups can be improved through positive intergroup contact.

However, this hypothesis proved not to work in all cases, only under certain conditions, namely, the following four: equal status, cooperation, common goals, institutional support. The hypothesis is valid at the aggregate level, though, as shown by a meta-analysis by Pettigrew and Tropp, 2006. Intergroup contact can also have "ironic" effects: "… there is mounting evidence that nurturing bonds of affection between the advantaged and the disadvantaged sometimes entrenches rather than disrupts wider patterns of discrimination. Notably, prejudice reduction interventions may have ironic effects on the political attitudes of the historically disadvantaged, decreasing their perceptions of injustice and willingness to engage in collective action to transform social inequalities," Dixon, et al., 2012, Abstract. I thank Sigrun Marie Moss for making me aware of this research on the "ironic" effects of intergroup contact.

10 See for social identity theory Tajfel and Turner, 1979, and for self-categorization theory Turner, et al., 1987.

11 Kinnvall, 2004, p. 756. I thank Sigrun Marie Moss for making me aware of Kinnvall's work.

12 "I Know Why Poor Whites Chant Trump, Trump, Trump," by Jonna Ivin, STIR, April 1, 2016, www.stirjournal.com/2016/04/01/i-know-why-poor-whites-chant-trump-trump-trump/. See also Thandeka, 1998.

13 Fanon, 1952/1967. See also Midiohouan, 1991.

14 Bourdieu and Passeron, 1990, p. 159.

15 Thandeka, 1998.

16 See Müller, 2016, for a discussion of how populists pit "ordinary people," "decent people," and "real people" against those who are neither ordinary nor decent, nor even real.

17 Lindner, 2000a.

18 Lindner, 2000i, or Lindner, 2000d, e, c, 2001j, or Lindner, 2001k, 2006d.

19 If one searches for personal experiences of humiliation in the private life of Adolf Hitler, one of the most widely mentioned relevant experiences is that Hitler was rejected by the prestigious Vienna Academy of Fine Arts in 1907. Many other hypotheses have been considered, for example, that he suffered from the humiliation of having a micropenis. See Craigie and Mayo, 2015. Hitler was born, not in Germany, but in Austria, to a strong sense of humiliation among the Germans in Austria that their "fatherland," namely, Germany, shamefully neglected them. Others, such as Marbach, et al., 2007, have suggested that Hitler simply suffered from psychosis. See also Langer, 1972, or Fromm, 1973. Fritz Redlich, 1999, however, rejected such an interpretation.
Or did Hitler project his wish to save his mother from his father onto world politics? Psychotherapist George Victor, 1998, in searching for sources for Hitler's antisemitism, suggested that his self-loathing and especially his hatred of Jews had their origin in the abuse that he suffered as a child at the hands of his father, who, as Hitler may have believed, had descended from Jews.
I personally find it interesting to consider the extreme contrast Hitler was exposed to in his relationship with his mother and his father. Indeed, it has been confirmed that Hitler had a brutal father and that his mother overprotected him. She had lost four of her six children, only Adolf and his sister Paula survived. He more than adored his mother. When she died, her personal physician Dr. Bloch reported that he had never seen anybody grieve as much as her son Adolf, see Kershaw, 1998, 2000. If his father had, or was thought of having, a Jewish background, and his father abused Adolf, combined with the fact that his mother idolized him and vice versa, also given the strong sense that Germany shamefully neglected them, Hitler's mission could indeed have been to save his mother (Germans in Austria) from the abuse of his father (Germany + Jews). This would illuminate the astonishing fact that Hitler seemed satisfied with the German people perishing if they failed his expectations. Hitler reportedly said on November 27, 1941, to the Danish foreign minister Scavenius and the Croat foreign minister Lorkowitsch: "I am also here ice cold. If the German people are no longer strong enough and ready to sacrifice their own blood for their existence, then they

must disappear and be destroyed by another, stronger power. … I will not shed a tear for the German people," translated by Lindner from the German original, Haffner, 1978, p. 139.
See also Hitler privat – Das Leben des Diktators, documentary film by Michael Kloft, 2010, which attempts to come closer to the personality of Adolf Hitler. This documentary asks: Who was Hitler privately, beyond him being a symbol of violence and inhumanity, fanatical racism and perverted nationalism, war and genocide, the incarnation of evil, a monster of history?
Psychiatrist Renato D. Alarcón and his colleagues observe that Hitler's henchmen were tried at Nuremberg by victors who incinerated hundreds of thousands of civilians in Dresden, Tokyo, Nagasaki, and Hiroshima, and, to defeat Hitler, had cooperated with Josef Stalin, whose crimes had begun a decade earlier than Hitler's and, unlike Hitler's concentration camps, had long been well-known in the West. Alarcón, et al., 1998, ask the crucial question (excerpt from a draft, www.vakkur.com/hx/hit_len_stal.html):

So was Hitler suffering from a true personality disorder or was he simply the epitome of the evil of which his society of origin, including those who fought him, is capable? Or is the entire concept of personality disorder simply a medicalization of many behaviors and attitudes that most cultures traditionally label as evil?

Hitler privat – Das Leben des Diktators, www.zdf.de/dokumentation/zdfinfo-doku/hitler-privat-das-leben-des-diktators-100.html, or www.fernsehserien.de/hitler-privat/episodenguide/0/22470:
- Part 1: Der Künstler. See also Hamann, 1996, and Gortemaker, 2010.
- Part 2: Der Soldat.
- Part 3: Der "Führer."
- Part 4: Der Kriegsherr.

20 "Did WHCD [White House Correspondents' Dinner] Humiliation Drive Trump to Run for President?" by Mark Joyella, Adweek, September 22, 2016, http://adweek.it/2dnOeyF. I thank Linda Hartling for making me aware of this article. See also President Obama Roasts Donald Trump at White House Correspondents' Dinner! Video uploaded on April 30, 2011, at https://youtu.be/k8TwRmX6zs4. See the full note in the pdf edition of this book.

21 "Trump: World Won't Laugh Any More," BBC News, www.bbc.com/news/av/world-us-canada-40128556/trump-world-won-t-laugh-any-more: "In explaining why he is pulling out of the Paris climate deal, President Trump says the world will no longer take advantage of the US." I thank Rigmor Johnsen for making me aware of the attention this part of Trump's argument received in the media outside of the U.S.

22 Farrington, 1993. I thank Vidar Vambheim for making me aware of Farrington's work, see Vambheim, 2016.

23 See, among many other relevant publications, Sebag Montefiore, 2003, 2016.

24 Vambheim, 2016, p. 14.

25 Schattschneider, 1960, p. 36, see also Schattschneider, 1969. Neumann, 1942, Mills, 1956. See also Putnam, 1976.

26 Neumann, 1942. See also Mills, 1956, Dye, et al., 2015.

27 Fraenkel, 1941.

28 Tunander, 2009, p. 56. I thank Kimberly Eriksen for making me aware of Tunander's work. See also note 15 in the Introduction to Section Three.

29 See note 331 in the Introduction.

30 Pierre Bourdieu gave much thought to honor,connecting it to the concept of méconnaissance (misrecognition). He describes honor as a game of challenge and counterchallenge. Bourdieu, 1977, pp. 11–12:

• to challenge a person is to accord him a certain dignity, for it connotes a recognition of equality
• to challenge a person incapable of responding is to dishonor oneself only a challenge coming from an equal deserves to be taken up.

31 See more in the section "How the 'art of domination' was perfected in systems of ranked honor" in Lindner, 2009b, Chapter 5: How History and Culture Can Humiliate, in the book Emotion and Conflict, pp. 60–64.

32 This was what influential author Ayn Rand decried. I have studied Ayn Rand, who came to America from Russia, and, in her interviews, praises the 1917 February Revolution in Russia and the spirit of liberation from oppression that carried it. See, for instance, the Ayn Rand biography by Jennifer Burns, 2009. I thank Linda Hartling for sharing documentary material about Ayn Rand with me. See, among others, Love and Power, the first in a BBC2 documentary series by Adam Curtis, May 23, 2011, www.bbc.co.uk/programmes/b011k45f. It explores the idea that humans have been colonized by the machines they have built. "The New Age of Ayn Rand: How She Won over Trump and Silicon Valley," by Jonathan Freedland, The Guardian, April 10, 2017, www.theguardian.com/books/2017/apr/10/new-age-ayn-rand-conquered-trump-white-house-silicon-valley?CMP=Share_iOSApp_Other. I thank Linda Hartling for making me aware of this article. See, furthermore, a review of the series "All Watched Over by Machines of Loving Grace," by Sam Wollaston, The Guardian, May 23, 2011, www.guardian.co.uk/tv-and-radio/2011/may/23/review-machines-of-loving-grace. Read more in Chapter 4: When Scarcity and Environmental Degradation Become Systemic, in Lindner, 2012f, A Dignity Economy, pp. 57–58:

> Then came the October Revolution, which hijacked the process and coopted people back into oppression. It did so, among other methods, by abusing the argument of altruism and asking people to offer themselves to the state. This is why Ayn Rand came to reject altruism and highlight the virtue of uninhibited self-interest. And her philosophy became "mainstream" due to her influence on some of the most powerful shapers of frames for human endeavor on the globe, including people like Alan Greenspan. Clearly, Ayn Rand was a highly intelligent woman. When she speaks, she seems to replay her resistance to a painfully oppressive mother, something that might have made her somewhat defensive, hard, even arrogant, and opposed to and disdainful not just of oppression, but also of warmth and solidarity. Her arrogance may have been misperceived as mastery by her followers. When "mainstreamed," this misperception might have helped lend legitimacy to coldness throughout society.

33 The phrase "possessive individualism" was the best-known contribution to political philosophy by Crawford Brough Macpherson, 1962 (1911 – 1987). The theory of "possessive individualism" describes an individual who conceives of herself as the sole proprietor of his or her skills and owes nothing to society. See also Lakoff, 2006a, asking Whose Freedom? See more in note 211 in the Introduction.

34 See note 40 in the Introduction.

35 Robinson, 2017. See also Rothkopf, 2008, or Jakobs, 2016.

36 See note 196 in the Introduction.

37 Easterly, 2013, recommended in "Communitarian Observations: The Moon, Facebook, and Iraq," by Amitai Etzioni, Institute for Communitarian Policy Studies, July 30, 2014.

38 Moss, 2013, recommended in "Communitarian Observations: The Moon, Facebook, and Iraq," by Amitai Etzioni, Institute for Communitarian Policy Studies, July 30, 2014, where he refers to his article "Facebook's Experiment: Trivial Pursuit," by Amitai Etzioni, Huffington Post, July 8, 2014, www.huffingtonpost.com/amitai-etzioni/facebooks-experiment-triv_b_5567519.html.

39 "Spirit and Place" is an essay by David Tacey based on Chapter 4: Spirit and Place, in David Tacey, 2000. It is republished in "Food for the Journey," E News, Number 84, April 30, 2015. We read there about contemplation:

> Aboriginal spirituality, then, is a spirituality of deep seeing, deep listening, bush receptivity. Miriam-Rose Ungunmerr describes this, using a word from Ngangikurungkurr language, as dadirri, and says this "is something like what you [white people] call 'contemplation.'" The celebrant has to conjure up the right mood, perform a kind of trick on the separate self, so that it will not create a barrier between the celebrant and the spirit of the land. This kind of receptive spirituality is very hard for us Westerners to achieve, because we come from a "conquering" consciousness which forever strives to impose our own mental and psychological life upon the reality of the world. Aboriginal spirituality does not impose a metaphysical machinery upon the landscape; it sees through the landscape to the mythic forms and spirits behind it.

I thank Hilarie Roseman for sharing this essay with me, and for her ongoing support for Human Dignity and Humiliation Studies. See also philosopher Alan Wilson Watts (1915 – 1973), and his Alan Watts: A Conversation with Myself in four parts, beginning with https://youtu.be/8aufuwMiKmE. See the full note in the pdf edition of this book.

40 Polanyi and Joseph E. Stiglitz (Foreword), 1944/2001.

41 Grossman, 2006. Mielants, 2007.

42 Becker and Wößmann, 2007. The centuries-old Judaic rule that male Jews had to read the Torah in the synagogue, and to teach it to their sons, may account for Jewish economic prosperity as merchants,and, similarly, Protestant regions economic progressiveness relative to Catholic regions may stem from higher literacy in Protestant regions, encouraged by Martin Luther's emphasis on everyone reading the Gospel.

43 McCloskey, 2006–2016.

44 Fiske, 2004. See also note 295 in the Introduction, and note 114 in the Inspiring Questions to Section Two.

45 Scheler, 1914–1916/1957. Scheler states that the human being, before she can be an ens cogitans (a "thinking being") or an ens volens (a "volitional being"), is an ens amans, a loving being.

46 Ferdinand Tönnies (1855 – 1936) was a major contributor to sociological theory and field studies. Tönnies is best known for his distinction between two types of social groups – Gemeinschaft and Gesellschaft (Tönnies, 1887/1955). He explains that community is based on family life, rests on harmony, and is developed and ennobled by folkways, morals, and religion, with morality being an expression of religious beliefs and forces, intertwined with family spirit and folkways.

47 Szirtes, 2012, p. 139.

48 Sundararajan, 2012.

49 Graeber, 2011.

50 In a recent article, social philosopher Nancy Fraser, 2014, explores the strengths and weaknesses of the classic 1944 book The Great Transformation by Karl Polanyi and Joseph E. Stiglitz (Foreword), 1944/2001, where he traced the roots of capitalist crisis to efforts to create "self-regulating markets" in land, labor and money. Fraser, 2014, Abstract:

> The effect was to turn those three fundamental bases of social life into "fictitious commodities." The inevitable result, Polanyi claimed, was to despoil nature, rupture communities and destroy livelihoods. This diagnosis has strong echoes in the twenty-first century: witness the burgeoning markets in carbon emissions and biotechnology in child-care, schooling and the care of the old and in financial derivatives. In this situation, Polanyi's idea of fictitious commodification affords a promising basis for an integrated structural analysis that connects three dimensions of the present crisis: the ecological, the social and the financial.

I thank Mai-Bente Bonnevie for reminding me of Fraser's work in this context!

51 "How the Internet Is Transforming from a Tool of Liberation to One of Oppression," by Astra Taylor, Huffington Post, June 5, 2014, www.huffingtonpost.com/astra-taylor/internet-oppression-liberation_b_5449838.html.

52 Sugarman, et al., 2015, p. 113. Sundararajan quotes Sugarman as saying that when rationality of the economic order prevails over that of democracy, we have neoliberalism, or, as Solovey and Cravens, 2012, would say, we have capitalistic democracy.

53 Standing, 2011. I thank David Calderoni in São Paulo for introducing me to Guy Standing's work in 2012. It is a privilege to have David Calderoni as esteemed member in the global advisory board of the Human Dignity and Humiliation Studies fellowship.

54 Yogi Hendlin in his contribution to the Great Transition Network Initiative discussion titled "The Struggle for Meaningful Work," January 17, 2017, in response to Klitgaard, 2017. Agamben, 1995/1998.

55 Richards, 2016a. See also historian Philipp Ther, 2014/2016, p. x, and his summary of the main pillars of neoliberal ideology: "Blind belief in the market as an adjudicator in almost all human affairs, irrational reliance on the rationality of market participants, disdain for the state as expressed in the myth of 'big government,' and the uniform application of the economic recipes of the Washington Consensus." See also "Is Europe Disintegrating?" by Timothy Garton Ash, The New York Review of Books, January 19, 2017, www.nybooks.com/articles/2017/01/19/is-europe-disintegrating/. I thank Elenor Richter-Lyonette for making me aware of this article.

56 Piketty, 2013/2014.

57 See, among others, Barth and Moene, 2015. See also Lerner, 1980.

58 See, among others, Wilkinson, 2005, and Wilkinson and Pickett, 2009. See also Jakobsen, 2017.

59 Lindner, 2009b, p. 85.

60 "The Mission Creep of Dignity: Dignity Has Less to Do with Autonomy or Independence Than with Intrinsic Worth and the Ability to Flourish," by Mark Regnerus, MercatorNet, January 20, 2015, www.mercatornet.com/articles/view/the_mission_creep_of_dignity. I thank Hilarie Roseman for making me aware of this article.

61 Dignity 2.0 might have started earlier than Regnerus suggests, already in 1948, when political rights first were emphasized. Western-liberal political philosophy sees the forms of dignity that can be legally respected and protected by a state as the right to self-determination, autonomy, and agency (Rosen, 2012).

62 Smith, 2010.

63 Archer, 2011. See also Rosen, 2012.

64 See also Duffy and Gambatese, 1999.

65 See also McCrudden, 2013, and his analysis of Siegel, 2012, where she discusses the use of dignity terminology by the Catholic Church in relation to abortion and same-sex marriage, where she differentiates "dignity as autonomy," from "dignity as equality," and "dignity as life." McCruden rejects any monolithic representation of Catholic thought and highlights that there "is an intense discussion currently occurring within the community of Catholic theologians and within communities of Catholics more generally about human rights, the role of women, and gay rights, with a wide variety of different viewpoints being expressed and debated."

I also thank Francisco Gomes de Matos for sending me "Human Dignity is the Right of All," by Fr. Shay Cullen, The People's Recovery Empowerment and Development Assistance (PREDA) Foundation, November 4, 2016, www.preda.org/fr-shays-articles/human-dignity-is-the-right-of-all/.

66 Smith, 1991.

67 See the work of international law expert Alfred Verdross (1890–1980), who, in his legal philosophy, drew on the common good purpose of the state laid out by Augustine of Hippo and Thomas Aquinas, see, among others Verdross and Gorby, 1979, Verdross and Simma, 1984.

68 Bischöfliches Hilfswerk MISEREOR, 2015, and Reder, et al., 2015.

69 Karlberg, 2013. The concept of dignity-as-autonomy is consistent with the social contest frame of dignity: "When human nature is conceived largely in terms of self-interested motives playing out within competitive social arenas, then the autonomy of individuals and groups to pursue their own interests, within a set of rules that apply equally to all, takes on paramount importance."

70 "How Everyone Can Win," Bahá'í World News Service, Bahá'í International Community, May 10, 2005, http://news.bahai.org/story/370.

71 Karlberg, 2013, p. 12.

72 Ibid.

73 Ray and Anderson, 2000. Social scientists Paul H. Ray and Sherry Ruth Anderson, through their surveys, identified three main cultural trends. First, the moderns, the cultural movement that started about 500 years ago and that endorses the "realist" worldview of either big business, big government, or big media, or past socialist, communist, or fascist movements. Then, the first countermovement against the moderns are the traditionals, the religious right and rural populations. The most recent countermovement are the cultural creatives, who value strong ecological sustainability for the planet, support women's issues, personal growth, authenticity, and are wary of big business. The cultural creatives movement is currently flowing together from two branches that both started out around 1960 and initially antagonized each other, namely, the consciousness movement, an inward-oriented movement, focusing on the inner state of the psyche, and the social movement, an outward-oriented movement, focusing on action for peace in the streets.
When Ray and Anderson published their work in 2000, in the United States, traditionals comprised about 24 to 26 percent of the adult population (approximately 48 million people), moderns about 47 to 49 percent (approximately 95 million), and cultural creatives are about 26 to 28 percent (approximately 50 million). In the European Union, the cultural creatives were about 30 to 35 percent of the adult population. I thank Steve Halls for giving me Ray and Anderson's book in Osaka, Japan, in 2004, when he was leaving his post as director of International Environmental Technology Centre (IETC) in Osaka and cleared his desk.

74 Taylor, 1989, Heelas, 1996, 2008, Wilce, 2009. This trend is now being introduced from the West, for instance, to China, see Pritzker, 2016, p. 152: "Inner child workshops in China can be said to function in much the same way. Indeed, salons geared towards the inner child in this Beijing center consist of adaptations of exercises developed by a European psychologist who leads longer inner child workshops, variably focused on 'transforming emotions,' 'transforming beliefs,' and 'meeting true self,' when he is in town." "Emotion pedagogies" are taught, which means teaching the self "as a reflexive object to be cultivated and improved through voluntary effort under expert guidance," Wilce and Fenigsen, 2016, p. 89.

75 "The Torture Colony," by Bruce Falconer, The American Scholar, Essays – Autumn 2008, September 1, 2008, https://theamericanscholar.org/the-torture-colony/. In a remote part of Chile, an German evangelist cult leader built a utopia community whose members helped the Pinochet regime torture and kill dissidents. When I was in Chile in 2012, due to time pressure, I failed realizing my plan to visit this community to attempt getting a sense of how such indignity was possible under the banner of dignity. See also Fröhling, 2012.

76 Kirk Schneider, 2004, writes in the Introduction to his book on the "rediscovery of awe": "The starting point of consciousness is awe. We humans first experience the world (cosmos) as overwhelming. From the moment we are aware, we are aware of our meagerness. From the moment we reflect on the world, we sense how hopeless, helpless, and vulnerable we are. And yet, close on the heels of this shuddering despair is a riveting sense of possibility."

77 "Gandhi's Strategy for Success – Use More than One Strategy," by Mark Engler and Paul Engler, Waging Nonviolence, March 17, 2017, http://wagingnonviolence.org/feature/gandhi-strategy-success/. I thank Linda Hartling for making me aware of this article.

78 Kant, 1784.

79 Adorno and Horkheimer, 1944/2002, p. 1. See a concise summary of Adorno's work in the Stanford Encyclopedia of Philosophy, first published May 5, 2003, with substantive revision October 10, 2011, http://plato.stanford.edu/entries/adorno/.

80 Adorno and Horkheimer, 1944/2002, p. 1.

81 Dialectic of Enlightenment by Adorno and Horkheimer, 1944/2002, German original Dialektik der Aufklärung: Philosophische Fragmente, 1944/1947; Madness and Civilization by Foucault, 1961/2006, French original Histoire de la folie à l'âge classique – Folie et déraison, 1961; and "What is Enlightenment?" by Foucault, 1984.

82 Held, 1980.

83 Habermas, 1983.

84 Dialektik der Aufklärung is a collection of essays by Max Horkheimer und Theodor Adorno that is regarded as one of the fundamental works on the critical theory of the Frankfurt School, first published in 1944. See the English translation, Dialectic of Enlightenment, Adorno and Horkheimer, 1944/2002.

85 Habermas and Dews, 1992, p. 187, as quoted in Outhwaite, 1994.

86 Habermas, 1983.

87 See, among others, Wilkerson and Paris, 2001. First-generational critical theorists of the Frankfurt School where followed by a second generation, such as Jürgen Habermas. Third generation critical theories incorporate postmodernism, poststructuralism, social constructionism, and neopragmatism. While the sociology of culture regards factors outside of culture as independent variable, such as economical and political interests, impacting on culture, cultural sociology sees ideas and symbolic processes as independent impacts on social institutions, on politics, and on culture itself, see Alexander, 1995, or for a recent publication, Alexander, et al., 2012. Culture is no longer identified with a single concept, but include both social sciences and humanities, see Bennett and Frow, 2008.

88 Collins, 1990.

89 Lindner, 2006c, p. 25.

90 Bauman, 1992, wrote on p. x–xi: "… the world of nature … had to be beheaded and deprived of autonomous will and power of resistance. … The world was an object of willed action: a raw material in the work guided and given form by human designs. … Left to itself, the world had no meaning. It was solely the human design that injected it with a sense of purpose. So the earth became a repository of ores and other 'natural resources,' wood turned into timber and water – depending on circumstances – into an energy source, waterway or the solvent of waste."

91 Lindner, 2006c, p. 25.

92 Raskin, et al., 2002. See also Raskin, 2008, and Brangwyn and Hopkins, 2008.

93 BCE stands for "Before the Common Era," and is equivalent to BC, which means "Before Christ."

94 Paul Raskin, in "When Hope and History Can Rhyme," a personal communication to the Great Transition Initiative (GTI) Announcements List, December 30, 2011.

95 See note 196 in the Introduction.

96 See, among others, Tripathi, 2011, 2013b, a. It is a privilege to have Deepak Tripathi as esteemed member in the global advisory board of the Human Dignity and Humiliation Studies fellowship.

97 Tripathi, 2013b, p. 80.

98 Ibid.

99 Said, 1978.

100 Tripathi, 2013b, p. 80, Said, 2003, p. 206.

101 Stephen James Purdey in his contribution to the Great Transition Network (GTN) discussion on the topic of "Economics for a Full World," May 15, 2015. See also Purdey, 2010, and http://stephenpurdey.com/.

102 Kurt Grimm in his contribution to the Great Transition Network (GTN) discussion on the topic of "Meaning, Religion, and a Great Transition," November 24, 2014, in response to Karlberg, 2014.

103 Lindner, 2008a.

104 "2013 Nobel Prize in Economics: An Opportunity Missed," by economist Kamran Mofid, Globalization for the Common Good Initiative (GCGI), October 16, 2013, www.gcgi.info/blog/475-2013-nobel-prize-in-economics-an-opportunity-missed: "Greed, selfishness, individualism and short-termism were conflated with freedom and democracy and elevated to the status of moral philosophy. The fatal flaws of this ideology have fueled the reckless risk-taking, greed and arrogance that led to Wall Street's downfall and the loss of confidence in financial/banking sectors the world over." It is a privilege to have Kamran Mofid as esteemed member in the global advisory board of the Human Dignity and Humiliation Studies fellowship.

105 Broken Treaties: An Oral History Tracing Oregon's Native Population, documentary film by Eric Cain and John Rosman, OPB, March 20, 2017, www.opb.org/artsandlife/series/brokentreaties/oregon-tribes-oral-history-broken-treaties/. I thank Linda Hartling for showing me this documentary.

106 Dunlap, et al., 2016. I thank Linda Hartling for making me aware of Dunlap's work.

107 "The Year of Microterrorism," by Fareed Zakaria, Time, December 15, 2010, http://content.time.com/time/specials/packages/article/0,28804,2036683_2037181_2037470,00.html.

108 "Terror on the Cheap: Financing Lone Actor and Small Cell Attacks," by Tom Keatinge, director of the Centre for Financial Crime and Security Studies (RUSI), RUSI Analysis, August 17, 2015, www.rusi.org/go.php?structureID=commentary&ref=C55D1C7FA31DB6#.Vdmz4JfICOY.

109 "Why Drones Work: The Case for Washington's Weapon of Choice," by Daniel Byman, Foreign Affairs, July/August 2013, www.foreignaffairs.com/articles/somalia/2013-06-11/why-drones-work.

110 "Terror from Above: Will ISIS Launch a Mass Drone Attack on a Stadium?" by Clive Irving, The Daily Beast, February 24, 2016, www.thedailybeast.com/articles/2016/02/24/will-isis-launch-a-mass-drone-attack-on-a-stadium.html.

Chapter 5

1 BCE stands for "Before the Common Era," and is equivalent to BC, which means "Before Christ."

2 Hafez, 2007a, Lankford, 2013.

3 See note 262 in the Introduction.

4 Porter, 2004.

5 Forbes, 2008, p. xvi.

6 Howard Richards in his upcoming book Economic Theory and Community Development.

7 Ibid.

8 Stille Reserven, 2016 film by Valentin Hitz., www.stillereserven.at/.

9 Plato (circa 428 – 348 BCE) recommended justice, wisdom, courage, and moderation (or sophrosyne, a sense of limit, moral sanity, self-control, and moderation guided by true self-knowledge). Faith, hope, and love were added later, together constituting the seven cardinal virtues. Aristotle highlighted phronesis (Latin prudentia), or "practical wisdom." Norway is a place where moderation is still being highlighted today: philosopher Henrik Syse, 2009, has advised Norwegian banks on moderation. It is a privilege to have Henrik Syse as esteemed member in the global advisory board of our Human Dignity and Humiliation Studies fellowship.

10 When I was a psychology student in Hamburg, Germany (1974 – 1978), one of my professors was Friedemann Schulz von Thun, 2007, who has developed his thoughts on values by building on Aristotle, philosopher Nicolai Hartmann (1926), and psychologist Paul Helwig (1936).

11 Willms, 2015.

12 Taylor, 1955.

13 Schivelbusch, 2001.

14 Göring, 1943.

15 Allyn, 1970.

16 "Tredje verden-prosjektets død skaper et monster: Sekter uten grenser" (The Third World Project's Death Creates a Monster: Sects Without Borders), by Yohan Shanmugaratnam, Klassekampen, July 3, 2014, p. 2. Shanmugaratnam refers to Prashad, 2007. I thank Gerdelin Bodvin for making me aware of this article. It is a privilege to have Gerdelin Bodvin as esteemed member in our Human Dignity and Humiliation Studies fellowship.

17 Prashad, 2007.

18 See note 418 in the Introduction.

19 "Terrorism: Ultimate Weapon of the Global Elite," by Robert J. Burrowes, TRANSCEND Media Service, February 16, 2015, www.transcend.org/tms/2015/02/terrorism-ultimate-weapon-of-the-global-elite/.

20 "Why Elites Love Drones," by Robert J. Burrowes, Human Wrongs Watch, May 25, 2015, http://human-wrongs-watch.net/2015/05/25/why-elites-love-drones/. See also Cockburn, 2015.

21 Lindner, 2012b.

22 "Rio+20 Ends in Failure, Corporate Capture," posted by Pratap Chatterjee, CorpWatch Blog, June 27, 2012, www.corpwatch.org/article.php?list=class&type=104&class=21.

23 "Social Forum Calls for Fight Against Corruption, to Defend the Amazon," by Milagros Salazar, Inter Press Service (IPS), May 3, 2017, www.ipsnews.net/2017/05/social-forum-calls-for-fight-against-corruption-to-defend-the-amazon/.

24 Femke Wijdekop, in her reply to the Great Transition Network (GTN) discussion on the topic of "Against Ecocide: Legal Protection for Earth," August 5, 2016. Wijdekop, 2016, formed the basis for this discussion. See also the project "Defending Environmental Defenders," a collaborative project of IUCN Netherlands, Friends of the Earth and Global Witness, www.iucn.nl/en/recent/dutch-postcode-lottery-helps-improve-safety-of-environmental-defenders.

25 Ibid. The Ecological Law and Governance Association (ELGA), a new global network of scholars, practitioners and students of environmental law, has been officially launched in Siena, Italy, October 13-15, 2017. See www.elga.world/.

26 The name "dry hair" comes from the observation that the hair of Africans is so tightly coiled that it does not get wet when bathing in the river.

27 See http://planetsave.com/2011/05/29/outrag-grows-over-new-brazilian-rain-forest-law/.

28 See “Agrarian Reform in Brazil,” Food and Agriculture Organization of the United Nations (FAO), 2000, first published on www.fao.org/righttofood/KC/downloads/vl/docs/AH264.pdf, now available at www.fian.org/fileadmin/media/publications/Agrarian-Reform-in-Brazil-2000.pdf.

29 Daniel Baron and Manoela Souza worked closely with art educator Maria do Espírito Santo da Silva, who was killed together with José Claudio Ribeiro in rural New Ipixuna, www.humiliationstudies.org/documents/BaronCohenArtEducatorMariaSilva.pdf.

30 On the April 27, 2013, Evelin Lindner wrote to Daniel Baron from the 2013 Human Dignity and Humiliation Studies conference “In Search for Dignity,” in Stellenbosch, South Africa, April 24–27, 2013, where Dan spoke via Skype from the Amazon in Brazil:

Dear Dan, We still are deeply touched by your account of the dramatic events in Cabelo Seco, including the violence experienced by a young artist-leader from the Latinhas de Quintal (Backyard Drums). “We” includes the participants of the 2013 conference “In Search for Dignity,” held April 24–27, 2013, in Stellenbosch, South Africa.

Please receive our message of solidarity with the young Afro-Indigenous musicians of the band “Backward Drums.” Their decision not to participate in the centenary celebrations funded by the multinational mining company Vale, presently threatening the Amazon, is a bold protest and gives us hope that more and more people will resist against further destruction of our world’s most rich and vulnerable ecosystems.

At our conference we acknowledge and applaud the brave fight of these young people. We like to confirm our solidarity to them.

Signed: Participants of the 2013 Human Dignity and Humiliation Studies conference “In Search for Dignity.”

31 “Chile Must Stop Using Anti-Terrorism Law against Mapuche Indigenous Group – UN expert,” United Nations News Centre, July 13, 2013, www.un.org/apps/news/story.asp?NewsID=45538#.U-zr2GOTKNw.

32 “UN Experts Urge Ethiopia to Halt Violent Crackdown,” ECADF Ethiopian News, January 21, 2016, http://ecadforum.com/2016/01/21/un-experts-urge-ethiopia-to-halt-violent-crackdown/.

See also “UN Experts Urge Ethiopia to Stop Using Anti-terrorism Legislation to Curb Human Rights,” The Office of the United Nations High Commissioner for Human Rights (OHCHR), September 18, 2014, www.ohchr.org/en/NewsEvents/Pages/DisplayNews.aspx?NewsID=15056&LangID=E.

The protesters oppose the Government’s “Addis Ababa Integrated Development Master Plan” to expand the capital’s municipal boundaries, which would lead to deforestation, to mass evictions, and the seizure of agricultural land in the Oromia region. Many Oromos fear that the Tigray and Amhara intend to uproot them from their fertile lands under the pretense of development.

33 See note 40 in the Introduction.

34 Sarotte, 2014.

35 Die sieben Irrtümer der Deutschen Einheit: Glücksfall oder Milliardengrab? ZDF-History, Zweites Deutsches Fernsehen, September 19, 2010, www.zdf.de/zdf-history/die-sieben-irrtuemer-der-deutschen-einheit-5443030.html. In this documentary film Nikolaj Sergeevič Portugalov very calmly explains how the national humiliation of Russia through American arrogance is almost intolerable to him. American foreign minister James Baker and German chancellor Helmut Kohl had promised to refrain from moving NATO’s borders closer to Russia, and they broke that promise. See the full note in the pdf edition of this book.

36 Sarotte, 2014. Promises were given, for example, by United States Secretary of State James Baker.

37 Zubok, 2014.

38 “NATO Agrees Russian Deterrent but Avoids Cold War Footing,” by Robin Emmott and Phil Stewart, Brussels, Reuters, February 10, 2016, www.reuters.com/article/us-nato-russia-idUSKCN0VJ1J5.

39 See the warnings of the German diplomate Wolfgang Ischinger: "The risk that warlike hostilities arise, is now greater than in the last 25 years" (Die Gefahr, dass sich kriegerische Kampfhandlungen ergeben, ist heute größer als in den letzten 25 Jahren), in Panorama, Das Erste, June 23, 2016, http://daserste.ndr.de/panorama/Ischinger-2-fuer-panode,panorama6390.html. See the full note in the pdf edition of this book.
See also Haugevik, et al., 2015. See, furthermore, "NATO Mission Creep in Eastern Europe Fomenting Cold War II," by Robert Bridge, RT (originally Russia Today), February 10, 2016, www.rt.com/op-edge/332059-nato-mission-creep-eastern-europe/. See also "How NATO Is Becoming a Threat to Europe," by Harry Blain, Open Democracy, January 27, 2017, www.opendemocracy.net/can-europe-make-it/harry-blain/how-nato-is-becoming-threat-to-europe.

40 "The Cool War," by David Rothkopf, Foreign Policy, February 20, 2013, http://foreignpolicy.com/2013/02/20/the-cool-war/.

41 Rödder, 2011. See also Geheimakte Einigung, ZDF History, Zweites Deutsches Fernsehen, September 27, 2015, www.zdf.de/zdf-history/zdf-history-5989332.html, https://youtu.be/3YYcraBgNIg. See the full note in the pdf edition of this book.

42 Krone-Schmalz, 2007.

43 "Solve the Ukraine Crisis Now," by Jonathan Power, Transnational Foundation for Peace and Future Research (TFF) PressInfo # 298, December 30, 2014, http://blog.transnational.org/2014/12/a-way-out-of-the-ukrainian-imbroglio/.

44 "As Germany Marks Fall of the Berlin Wall, Gorbachev Warns of New Cold War," Philip Oltermann in Berlin, The Guardian, November 9, 2014, www.theguardian.com/world/2014/nov/08/gorbachev-cold-war-threat-berlin-wall-25th-anniversary. See also Gorbačev, 2014/2016.

45 "Nobel Peace Winners Fear 'New, More Dangerous Cold War,'" by AFP, The Times of Israel, www.timesofisrael.com/nobel-peace-winners-fear-new-more-dangerous-cold-war/#ixzz3Lug5Sq00. See, furthermore, "New Nuclear Arms Race Underway," by Mark Blackwood and Paul Mitchell, World Socialist Web Site, December 6, 2014, www.wsws.org/en/articles/2014/12/06/nucl-d06.html.

46 "Much Stronger Than During the First Cold War. Why Is NATO so Irrational?" by Jan Øberg, Transnational Foundation for Peace and Future Research (TFF) PressInfo # 381, June 29, 2016, http://blog.transnational.org/2016/06/tff-pressinfo-381-much-stronger-than-during-the-first-cold-war-why-is-nato-so-irrational/.

47 "Cold War Warnings 1998 – 2014," by Jan Øberg, Transnational Foundation for Peace and Future Research (TFF), August 11, 2014, http://blog.transnational.org/2014/08/tff-pressinfo-cold-war-warnings-1998-2014/.

48 "How Did Western Europe Cope with a Much Stronger Soviet Union and Warsaw Pact?" by Jan Øberg, Transnational Foundation for Peace and Future Research (TFF) Press Info # 385, TFF Series "The New Cold War" # 6, August 29, 2016, http://blog.transnational.org/2016/08/tff-pressinfo-385/.

49 Quoted in "Trump and the Deep State," by John Scales Avery, Human Wrongs Watch, February 19, 2017, https://human-wrongs-watch.net/2017/02/20/trump-and-the-deep-state/, referring to Lofgren, 2016. See also "Gefährliche Propaganda," by Christoph Schult and Klaus Wiegrefe, Der Spiegel, 30/16, July 23, 2016, pp. 42-43, https://magazin.spiegel.de/SP/2016/30/145947650/?utm_source=spon&utm_campaign=centerpage: A network around NATO Commander Philip Breedlove tried to push for weapons supplies to Ukraine from the West with dubious information.

50 Journalist Guy Mettan, 2017, describes the historical, religious, ideological, and geopolitical roots of the antipathy toward Russia in various European nations over thirteen centuries since Charlemagne competed with Byzantium for the title of heir to the Roman Empire.

51 "Brisbane: A Show of Western Weakness," by Jan Øberg, Transnational Foundation for Peace and Future Research (TFF) Press Info, www.icontact-archive.com/uY4CWN-9Ks3n5LBkjUdhzbfhttz5G3iI?w=4.

52 "Truth to Power," by Noam Chomsky and David Mcneill, Japan Times, February 22, 2014, www.japantimes.co.jp/news/2014/02/22/world/noam-chomsky-truth-to-power/.

53 "The Coming War on China," by John Pilger, Transcend Media Services, December 5, 2016, www.transcend.org/tms/2016/12/the-coming-war-on-china/. See also The Coming War on China, documentary film by John Pilger, 2017, http://johnpilger.com/videos/trailer-the-coming-war-on-china.

54 Gefährliche Verbindungen: Donald Trump und seine Geschäftspartner, documentary film by Johannes Hano und Alexander Sarovic, Zweites Deutsches Fernsehen, May 24, 2017, www.heute.de/zdfzoom-dokumentation-gefaehrliche-verbindungen-trump-und-seine-geschaeftspartner-47232790.html. See the full note in the pdf edition of this book.

55 "Global Tide of Nuclear Abolition Has Ebbed Causing Tensions Among Nations, Ban Warns," United Nations News Centre, April 28, 2015, www.un.org/apps/news/story.asp?NewsID=50720#.VWLjtkbICOZ.

56 Bailey, 2012, p. 6.

57 Ibid.

58 See note 8 in Chapter 4. See also note 368 in Chapter 15.

59 The project "Digitisation historical heritage (Sachsenspiegel online)" is a joint project of the Herzog August Bibliothek Wolfenbüttel and the University of Applied Sciences Braunschweig / Wolfenbüttel. See www.hab.de/en/home/research/projects/sachsenspiegel-online.html.

60 "A Special Relationship: The United States Is Teaming Up with Al Qaeda, Again," by Andrew Cockburn, Harper's Magazine, Letter from Washington, January 2016 issue, https://harpers.org/archive/2016/01/a-special-relationship/1/. The Egyptian preacher Abu Hamza, now serving a life sentence on terrorism charges, visited Saudi Arabia in 1986, and later recalled the constant public injunctions to join the jihad: "You have to go, you have to join, leave your schools, leave your family." The whole Afghanistan enterprise, he explained, "was meant to actually divert people from the problems in their own country." It was "like a pressure-cooker vent. If you keep [the cooker] all sealed up, it will blow up in your face, so you have to design a vent, and this Afghan jihad was the vent." See also Cockburn, 2015.

61 Bitter Lake, BBC documentary film by Adam Curtis, 2015, https://youtu.be/VRbq63r7rys. I thank Drew Pham for making me aware of this film. See also Martin, 2014.

62 "Enormous Sense of Hopelessness and Anger," by Noam Chomsky and Melissa Parker, Smashing Interviews Magazine, January 21, 2016, http://smashinginterviews.com/interviews/newsmakers/noam-chomsky-interview-enormous-sense-of-hopelessness-and-anger-reflected-in-appeal-of-trump-and-sanders.

63 "The War Has Reached Damascus, But For Now It Is Not A Warzone," by Robert Fisk, The Independent, April 12, 2013,. www.independent.co.uk/voices/comment/robert-fisk-the-war-has-reached-damascus-but-for-now-it-is-not-a-warzone-8569212.html.

64 See note 60 above.

65 During my time as a psychotherapist in Cairo, Egypt, from 1984 to 1991, I had the privilege of having many American clients, who were so generous to open up to me and give me deep insights into the transgenerational historical traumas that inflict many families in the United States. Not only slavery was a historical trauma, also people who came from Europe to America carry deep traumas.

66 See a review of Stephen Holmes, 2007, in "A Guide for the Perplexed: Intellectual Fallacies of the War on Terror," by Chalmers Johnson, TomDispatch.com, October 22, 2007, www.alternet.org/story/65838/bush%27s_response_to_9_11_was_deadlier_than_the_attacks_themselves. I thank Anthony Marsella for making me aware of this essay. Chalmers Ashby Johnson (1931 – 2010) was an American author and professor emeritus of the University of California, San Diego, who had served in the Korean War, and was a consultant for the C.I.A. from 1967 to 1973. He is the author of the Blowback Trilogy: Blowback (Johnson, 2000), The Sorrows of Empire (Johnson, 2004), and Nemesis: The Last Days of the American *Republic* (Johnson, 2006). See also, Johnson, 2010. Stephen Holmes builds his argument, among others, on James Mann, 2004a, who describes the Bush administration's Cold War thinking.

67 "Enormous Sense of Hopelessness and Anger," by Noam Chomsky and Melissa Parker, Smashing Interviews Magazine, January 21, 2016, http://smashinginterviews.com/interviews/newsmakers/noam-chomsky-interview-enormous-sense-of-hopelessness-and-anger-reflected-in-appeal-of-trump-and-sanders.

68 See the documentary film TERRA X: Imperium – Der letzte Kampf der Ritter, Geburtsstunde einer neuen Elite, Zweites Deutsches Fernsehen, July 10, 2011, www.zdf.de/terra-x/imperium-der-letzte-kampf-der-ritter-geburtsstunde-einer-neuen-elite-5366426.html for a succinct overview. See the full note in the pdf edition of this book.

69 Bailey, 2012.

70 "Child Immigrant Turned Rotterdam Mayor Aids Refugees," by Jo Biddle, Agence France Press (AFP), October 20, 2015, news.yahoo.com/child-immigrant-turned-rotterdam-mayor-aids-refugees-063943009.html. I thank PL de Silva for making me aware of this article. As the son of a Sunni Muslim imam, Rotterdam mayor Ahmed Aboutaleb, Holland's first Muslim immigrant mayor, tackles what he sees as a deep lack of knowledge and misconceptions about Islam: "Jihadist is the completely wrong word. I am a jihadist. I'm doing the right thing for the city the entire day. I'm a jihadist. … There are 68 definitions of jihad, if you remove a spike from the street or a piece of glass ... to prevent a bicycle being harmed by the spike, you are a jihadist."

71 Bernard of Clairvaux, 1977, Chapter 1. The date of the Liber de laude is uncertain; it must have been written between 1120, when the Templars were founded, and 1136, when Hugh of Payens, the first Master of the Templars, died, to whom it was addressed.

72 King Philip IV of France, 2002, in his "Order to Arrest the Templars" of September 14, 1307.

73 "Mass Migration, EU, European Nationalisms," by Johan Galtung, Transcend Media Service, 12 May 2016, www.transcend.org/tms/2016/05/mass-migration-eu-european-nationalisms/.

74 IS, also known as the Islamic State of Iraq and the Levant (ISIL) and the Islamic State of Iraq and Syria (ISIS). I resonate with those who use "Da'esh" – the Arabic acronym for the Islamic State in Iraq and Levant – to avoid the word "Islamic" when referring to the militants, see the open letter by Muslim scholars and religious authorities to Abu Bakr al-Baghdadi, the leader of IS in Iraq, pointing out in theological terms why his group's actions are un-Islamic, www.lettertobaghdadi.com. See also "IS: Neither Islamic Nor State, But Is It a Caliphate?" by Mamoon Alabbasi, Middle East Eye, July 24, 2015, www.middleeasteye.net/in-depth/features/neither-islamic-nor-state-it-caliphate-2004595104.

75 Bostock, 1960, p. 212.

76 Bostock, 1960, p. 203.

77 Bostock, 1960, p. 202.

78 Bostock, 1960, p. 212.

79 Ibid.

80 Göring, 1943.

81 Lindner, 2006c, p. 51.

82 Rockström, 2015. See also Wijkman and Rockström, 2012. Johan Rockström is professor in environmental science at Stockholm University and executive director of Stockholm Resilience Centre. His research has focused on global water resources and strategies to build resilience in water scarce regions of the world. Since 2010, he has played a leading role in developing the Planetary Boundaries framework. He served as co-chair of the Future Earth transition team and is the vice-chair of the science advisory board of the Potsdam Institute for Climate Impact research (PIK).
The first Planetary Boundaries analysis was published in 2009 after a two-year research and consultation exchange among global change scientists. The analysis suggested that humanity had transgressed three of the nine planetary boundaries: biodiversity loss, climate change, and nitrogen loading. The researchers focused on nine planetary boundary processes and systems that are needed to sustain a Holocene-like state of the planet. For seven of them they proposed quantitative boundaries, whereof three had relatively robust scientific support (climate change, stratospheric ozone depletion, and ocean acidification), while four carried large uncertainties (land use change, freshwater use, rate of loss of biodiversity, and interference with nitrogen and phosphorous cycles). For the other two (aerosol loading and chemical pollution), information was too limited to permit the determination of quantified boundaries.
A new round of PB research was conducted and the update published in January 2015. The new analysis treats climate change and biosphere integrity as "core boundaries," which means high-order manifestations of how breaching the other boundaries by can disrupt the Earth system. The new analysis concludes that four out of nine boundaries have already been transgressed. Two are in the high risk zone (biosphere integrity and interference with the nitrogen and phosphorous cycles), and two others are in the danger zone (climate change and land use change).
The original nine PBs remain relevant, but the revised analysis includes several improvements: to include the release of radioactive materials and nanomaterials, chemical pollution has been renamed "introduction of novel entities." The biodiversity boundary is now referred to as "biosphere integrity" and it now has two dimensions: genetic diversity (as before) and functional diversity, which means using the "biosphere intactness index," a measure of species abundance. The land use change boundary no longer simply uses the proxy of maximum cropland, but considers now minima for rainforests, temperate forests, and boreal forest cover. The nitrogen boundary now also includes human-induced reactive nitrogen from modern cultivation. The phosphorous boundary is now defined in two ways, first for oceans, as originally, and the other for freshwater systems. The uncertainty range for the climate change boundary has been narrowed to 350 to 450 ppm CO2 (from 350 to 550 ppm CO2).

83 Sustainable development expert Gwendolyn Hallsmith, in her contribution to the Great Transition Network (GTN) discussion on the topic of "Monetizing Nature," July 31, 2014.

84 Neuroscientist Peter Sterling in his contribution to the Great Transition Network (GTN) discussion on the topic "Marxism and Ecology: Common Fonts of a Great Transition," September 18, 2015. See also Sterling, 2016. Remember also Leiss, 1976.

85 Rockström, 2015. See also Wijkman and Rockström, 2012. See note 82 in this Chapter 5.

86 Richard Heinberg in his contribution to the Great Transition Network (GTN) discussion on the topic of "Bounding the Planetary Future: Why We Need a GT," March 20, 2015.

87 Global wildlife populations have fallen by 58 percent since 1970, and if the trend continues the decline could reach two-thirds among vertebrates by 2020, according to World Wildlife Fund (WWF), et al., 2016. See more in note 79 in Chapter 3.

88 World Wildlife Fund (WWF), 2014. See more in note 79 in Chapter 3.

89 Ted Trainer in his contribution to the Great Transition Network (GTN) discussion on the topic "The Degrowth Alternative," January 26, 2015:

> Our enormous (and probably insoluble) problem is to get them to shift to what I term The Simpler Way. We will make little or no progress while the supermarket shelves remain well-stocked. Our chances will begin to improve when the crunches start impacting in rich countries, the multi-faceted "peaks" in oil, energy, materials supply, the accelerating ecological impacts, the financial turmoil, and the social breakdown fueled by the inequality and deprivation neo-liberal doctrine inevitably inflicts. Our task is to work hard during the short window of opportunity we have to get local alternative communities up and running as best we can, so that when people start to realize that the consumer-capitalist system will not provide for them they can see around them at least indicators of the kind of alternative they need to help build in their towns and suburbs.

See also Alexander, 2009, Doherty and Etzioni, 2003, Trainer, 2014. Ted (F.E.) Trainer is an Australian academic, and an advocate of economic de-growth, simple living, and "conserver" lifestyles. Trainer is on the faculty of the Simplicity Institute, Office of Environmental Programmes, Melbourne University, Australia, see http://simplicityinstitute.org/ted-trainer. He works with the Simpler Way project, which has primarily been about trying to show that the required alternative ways would be easily, cheaply, and quickly built if people wanted to do that. See www.socialsciences.arts.unsw.edu.au/tsw/TheAltSoc.lng.html for a detailed sketch. Trainer shows that the "decoupling claim" is not feasible. It claims that economic growth can be separated from demand for materials and energy, thus enabling these to be kept down to sustainable levels. Trainer presents evidence from about thirty studies, which all indicate that little or no decoupling is taking pace, let alone on the scale that ecomodernists assume is possible. See "Decoupling: The Issue, and Collected Evidence," July 8, 2016, http://thesimplerway.info/DECOUPLING.htm, "But Can't Technical Advance Solve the Problems?," April 9, 2016, http://thesimplerway.info/TECHFIX.htm, "The Extreme Implausibility of Ecomodernism," March 16, 2016, http://thesimplerway.info/ECOMODERNISMcrit.htm. See also "History Has Knocked Very Loudly on Our Door. Will We Answer?" World Future Forum 2016 – Opening Speech by Jakob von Uexküll, March 15, 2016, www.worldfuturecouncil.org/2016/03/15/world-future-forum-2016-opening-speech-jakob-von-Uexküll/.

See, furthermore, "Consume More, Conserve More: Sorry, But We Just Can't Do Both," by George Monbiot, The Guardian, November 24, 2015, www.theguardian.com/commentisfree/2015/nov/24/consume-conserve-economic-growth-sustainability.

90 Neuroscientist Peter Sterling in his contribution to the Great Transition Network (GTN) discussion on the topic "Marxism and Ecology: Common Fonts of a Great Transition," September 18, 2015.

91 United Nations Development Programme (UNDP), 2014.

92 Ibid.

93 See a description of Naseer Memon's background on the website of the Center for Peace and Civil Society (CPCS) at www.cpcs.org.pk/aboutus/resourcepersons.php.

94 "Human insecurity: A recent UNDP report paints a grim picture of human development in the country," by Naseer Memon, The News on Sunday (Pakistan), November 2, 2014, http://tns.thenews.com.pk/undp-report-and-human-insecurity/#.VF-AUsn4phU.

95 Dong, 2015, Chapter 4, from pp. 84–111.

96 Bourdieu defines the field of power as a "… field of forces structurally determined by the state of the relations of power among forms of power, or different forms of capital... [In this field, the] objective is no longer the accumulation of or even the monopoly on a particular form of capital... but rather the determination of the relative value and magnitude of the different forms of power that can be wielded in the different fields," Bourdieu, 1996, pp. 264–265.

97 See, among others, the book by Deresiewicz, 2014, Excellent Sheep, see www.billderesiewicz.com/books/excellent-sheep:

Excellent Sheep takes a sharp look at the high-pressure conveyor belt that begins with parents and counselors who demand perfect grades and culminates in the skewed applications Deresiewicz saw firsthand as a member of Yale's admissions committee. As schools shift focus from the humanities to "practical" subjects like economics and computer science, students are losing the ability to think in innovative ways. Deresiewicz explains how college should be a time for self-discovery, when students can establish their own values and measures of success, so they can forge their own path. He addresses parents, students, educators, and anyone who's interested in the direction of American society, featuring quotes from real students and graduates he has corresponded with over the years, candidly exposing where the system is broken and clearly presenting solutions.

See also Bloom, 1987, Wilshire, 1990, Putnam, 1995, Readings, 1996, Schmidt, 2000, Giroux and Paulo Freire (Foreword), 2001, Bok, 2003, Giroux and Giroux, 2004, Hersh and Merrow, 2005, Karabel, 2005, Levine, 2006, Lewis, 2006, Kronman, 2007, Donoghue, 2008, Newfield, 2008, Gornitzka and Langfeldt, 2008, Folbre, 2009, Nussbaum, 2010, Taylor, 2010, Osler, 2010, Hacker and Dreifus, 2010, Richards, 2011, Riley, 2011, Arum and Roksa, 2011, Ginsberg, 2011, Jensen, 2012, Giroux, 2014a, or Frank, 2016. See, furthermore, "Schooling Ourselves in an Unequal America," by Rebecca Strauss, New York Times, June 16, 2013, http://opinionator.blogs.nytimes.com/2013/06/16/schooling-ourselves-in-an-unequal-america/?src=me&ref=general.

As to the UK, see "Coalition of Thinkers Vow to Fight Marketisation of Universities," by Shiv Malik, The Guardian, November 8, 2012, www.guardian.co.uk/education/2012/nov/08/coalition-thinkers-fight-marketisation-universities, where we read that the purpose of university is being "grossly distorted by the attempt to create a market in higher education." See also "Why I am Not a Professor OR the Decline and Fall of the British University," by Mark Tarver, 2007, www.lambdassociates.org/blog/decline.htm.

For Germany, see Münch, 2011. See also how the corporate sector in Germany has developed a "master plan" for how to change the educational system, in "Die Hochschule der Zukunft: Das Leitbild der Wirtschaft," by Dieter Hundt, Präsident, Bundesvereinigung der Deutschen Arbeitgeberverbände e. V. (BDA), and Hans-Peter Keitel, Präsident, Bundesverband der Deutschen Industrie e. V. (BDI), Berlin, February 2010, www.arbeitgeber.de/www%5Carbeitgeber.nsf/res/Hochschule_der_Zukunft.pdf/$file/Hochschule_der_Zukunft.pdf. I thank Ines Balta for making me aware of this publication.

98 Sean Cannady in his contribution to the Great Transition Network (GTN) discussion on the topic of "A Higher Calling for Higher Education," May 2, 2016, in response to Escrigas, 2016.

99 Ibid.

100 Sean Cannady, in his contribution to the Great Transition Network (GTN) discussion on the topic of "A Higher Calling for Higher Education," May 2, 2016, in response to Escrigas, 2016. See the full note in the pdf edition of this book.

101 "The Great Divide: College, the Great Unleveler," by Suzanne Mettler, New York Times, March 1, 2014, http://opinionator.blogs.nytimes.com/2014/03/01/college-the-great-unleveler/?_php=true&_type=blogs&src=me&ref=general&_r=0.

102 2014 Annual Conference of Human Dignity and Humiliation Studies, "Returning Dignity," in Chiang Mai, Thailand, March 8–12, 2014, www.humiliationstudies.org/whoweare/annualmeeting/23.php.

103 See the videos that we made to document the important hours of learning at www.humiliationstudies.org/whoweare/videos.php#thailand.

104 The Lazy School's First Student Peter Dering, video recorded by Evelin Lindner on March 14, 2014, in at the Pgak' Nyau (Karen) village Ban Nong Thao, on our post-conference Excursion, March 13–14, 2014. See the high density version edited by Mark Petz, http://youtu.be/ek4lGpSQgpk.

105 Sahlberg, 2011. See also "Finland Education Success," https://youtu.be/qRJ1hgN7uAU. I thank Adair Linn Nagata for making me aware of this link. It is a privilege to have Adair Linn Nagata as esteemed member in the global advisory board of our Human Dignity and Humiliation Studies fellowship.

106 Alexander Laszlo in his contribution to the Great Transition Network Initiative discussion titled "The Struggle for Meaningful Work," January 28, 2017, in response to Klitgaard, 2017. I thank Dino Karabeg for connecting me with Alexander Laszlo.

107 See note 8 in Chapter 3.

108 Turchin, 2006. I thank Lene Auestad for making me aware of Turcin's work. See Auestad, 2012. See also Auestad, 2014, 2015.

109 See also Lee, 2015.

110 See, for instance, Heffernan, 2011, and Heffernan, 2014. I thank Brian Ward for making us aware of Heffernan's work. See the full note in the pdf edition of this book.

111 Raskin, 2014, 2016, Raskin, et al., 2002.

112 Christoph Bals from Germanwatch in his contribution to the Great Transition Network (GTN) discussion on the topic of "Meaning, Religion, and a Great Transition," December 1, 2014, in response to Karlberg, 2014.

113 Gilad and Junginger, 2010. The German title of this book is Strategische Kriegsführung für Manager, English: Strategic Warfare for Managers. See also www.clausewitz.org. Also for sociologist Weber, war was a kind of natural phenomenon of political history, a form of unavoidable "eternal struggle of nations" (ewiges Ringen der Nationen) comparable to economic competition, only that economic war is conducted with "peaceful ammunition" (friedliche Kampfmittel), see Bruhns, 2014, p. 63. See more in note 75 in Chapter 11.

114 The Corporation, documentary film by law professor Joel Bakan, directed by Mark Achbar and Jennifer Abbott, 2003, see www.bibliotecapleyades.net/sociopolitica/sociopol_globalelite08.htm. See also Bakan, 2004, The Corporation: The Pathological Pursuit of Profit and Power. I thank ecological economist, environmental scientist and futurist Richard Sanders for making me aware of this work.

115 John B. Fullerton, founder and president of the Capital Institute, in his contribution to the Great Transition Network (GTN) discussion on the topic of "The Church of Economism and Its Discontents," on November 30, 2015, in response to Norgaard, 2015. See the full note in the pdf edition of this book.

116 Berry, 2009, p. 476.

117 The Great Divide: Inequality Is Not Inevitable," by Joseph E. Stiglitz, New York Times, June 27, 2014, http://opinionator.blogs.nytimes.com/2014/06/27/inequality-is-not-inevitable/. I thank Linda Hartling for making me aware of this article.

118 Buffett: "There Are Lots of Loose Nukes Around the World," interview with Lou Dobbs, CNN, May 25, 2005, http://edition.cnn.com/2005/US/05/10/buffett/index.html.
See also "In Class Warfare, Guess Which Class Is Winning," by Ben Stein, New York Times, November 26, 2006, www.nytimes.com/2006/11/26/business/yourmoney/26every.html?_r=0, with a similar quote: "There's class warfare, all right, but it's my class, the rich class, that's making war, and we're winning." See, furthermore, "Socialism? The Rich Are Winning the US Class War: Facts Show Rich Getting Richer, Everyone Else Poorer," by Bill Quigley, CommonDreams.org, October 25, 2010, www.commondreams.org/views/2010/10/25/socialism-rich-are-winning-us-class-war-facts-show-rich-getting-richer-everyone. Bill Quigley is associate director of the Center for Constitutional Rights and a law professor at Loyola University New Orleans:

> The rich talk about the rise of socialism to divert attention from the fact that they are devouring the basics of the poor and everyone else. Many of those crying socialism the loudest are doing it to enrich

or empower themselves. They are right about one thing – there is a class war going on in the US. The rich are winning their class war, and it is time for everyone else to fight back for economic justice.

Nick Hanauer is another among the extremely wealthy, who believes that the super-rich need to wake up and realize that life in fortress-like ghettos is not worth living, see Beinhocker and Hanauer, 2014. Hanauer foresees pitchforks coming for his "fellow .01 percenters" just as during the French Revolution in the eighteenth century, if the super-rich do not address the issue of increasing wealth inequality: "The Pitchforks Are Coming … For Us Plutocrats," by Nick Hanauer, Politico Magazine, July/August 2014, www.politico.com/magazine/story/2014/06/the-pitchforks-are-coming-for-us-plutocrats-108014. In Germany, a group of wealthy individuals calls for higher taxes for the wealthy. Retired physician Dieter Lehmkuhl, for example, says that it is time the wealthy came to the aid of their country. Lehmkuhl "reckons that if the 2.2 million Germans who have personal fortunes of more than €500,000 ($750,000) paid a tax of five percent this year and next, it would provide the state with €100 billion," in "Wealthy Germans Launch Petition For Higher Taxes," The Local, October 22, 2009, www.thelocal.de/money/20091022-22755.html.

119 Buffett: Debt Politics like "Nuclear" Bomb, CNN, October, 4, 2013, http://money.cnn.com/video/news/2013/10/04/n-warren-buffett-charlie-munger-debt-ceiling.fortune: "Billionaire Warren Buffett says fighting over the debt ceiling 'ought to be banned as a weapon' like 'nuclear bombs, too horrible to use.' His partner Charlie Munger says Buffett 'understated how awful it is' calling the practice 'deeply immoral.'"

120 See note 46 in Chapter 4.

121 Durkheim, 1897.

122 Weber, 1919.

123 "Ein 'stahlhartes Gehäuse' ist kein 'Iron Cage': Über Forscher, die kein Deutsch können," by Dirk Kaesler, Literaturkritik, Number 1, January 2012, Glosse, www.literaturkritik.de/public/rezension.php?rez_id=16239. See the German text in the full note in the pdf edition of this book.

124 Sassen, 2014.

125 See note 50 in Chapter 4.

126 Hartling, 2008a.

127 Heatherly and Heritage Foundation, 1981.

128 Raskin, 2016, p. 49.

129 "Mrs. Thatcher: The First Two Years," by Ronald Butt, The Sunday Times, May 3, 1981, www.margaretthatcher.org/document/104475.

130 Twenge, 2014, Deresiewicz, 2014.

131 "Unless It Changes, Capitalism Will Starve Humanity by 2050," by Drew Hansen, Forbes, February 9, 2016, www.forbes.com/sites/drewhansen/2016/02/09/unless-it-changes-capitalism-will-starve-humanity-by-2050/#20716d4f4a36.

132 "History Has Knocked Very Loudly on Our Door. Will We Answer?" World Future Forum 2016 – Opening Speech by Jakob von Uexküll, March 15, 2016, www.worldfuturecouncil.org/2016/03/15/world-future-forum-2016-opening-speech-jakob-von-Uexküll/. Uexküll offers the WFC Global Policy Action Plan (GPACT) as a new manual for responsible leadership, a new consensus, which may become known as the Hamburg consensus. Even the UN SDG strategy suffers from dangerous religious dogma, says Uexküll, as it will take 207 years to eliminate poverty with the proposed strategy, and the global economy would have to grow 175 times of its present size" – an obvious impossibility.

133 "Washington Rules Change, Again," by Jomo Kwame Sundaram, Inter Press Service (IPS), February 16, 2017, www.ipsnews.net/2017/02/washington-rules-change-again/. Jomo Kwame Sundaram, a former economics professor, was United Nations Assistant Secretary-General for Economic Development, and received the Wassily Leontief Prize for Advancing the Frontiers of Economic Thought in 2007.

134 "4 Questions for Fathali M. Moghaddam," by Sara Martin, APA Monitor on Psychology, April 2017, pp. 25-26, www.apamonitor-digital.org/apamonitor/201704?pg=40#pg40. I thank Louise Sundararajan for making me aware of this article.

135 "Why Authoritarians Attack the Arts," by Eve L. Ewing, New York Times, April 6, 2017, www.nytimes.com/2017/04/06/opinion/why-authoritarians-attack-the-arts.html?action=click&pgtype=Homepage%C2%AEion=CColumn&module=MostEmailed&version=Full&src=me&WT.nav=MostEmailed. I thank Linda Hartling for making me aware of this article.

136 See, among others, Carroll, 2001. See also "'Je suis français, je suis juif, je suis musulman. Je suis Charlie': On the trail of Convivencia," by Raja Sakrani, Käte Hamburger Kolleg "Recht als Kultur," January 2015, www.recht-als-kultur.de/de/aktuelles/diskurs/. I thank Hinnerk Bruhns for making me aware of this article. It is a privilege for me to be associated with the Maison des Sciences de l'Homme in Paris since 2001, first through social psychologist Serge Moscovici. The first two conferences of Human Dignity and Humiliation Studies were inspired and hosted by Hinnerk Bruhns, and supported by Michel Wieviorka, at the Maison des Sciences in 2003 and 2004, see www.humiliationstudies.org/whoweare/annualmeetings.php. It is a privilege to have Hinnerk Bruhns and other renowned colleagues from France as esteemed members in the global advisory board of our Human Dignity and Humiliation Studies fellowship.

137 Tripathi, 2013b.

138 In Chapter 7: Iraq Under Occupation and Dictatorship, Tripathi, 2013b, p. 95, quotes Karsh, 2007, p. 90:

The terrified [Abbasid] caliph, Mu'tasim, accompanied by his sons, ministers and other members of his coterie, produced himself to Hulagu. He was forced to disclose his treasures and was ridiculed for having failed to put them to good use in the city's defense. Ten days later the hapless suzerain was taken to a neighboring village and executed, apparently by being rolled in a carpet and trampled to death by horses, as the Mongols would not shed royal blood by the sword. Meanwhile, Baghdad was thoroughly ravaged and plundered, with most of its inhabitants brutally slaughtered.

See also Tripp, 2007.

139 BCE stands for "Before the Common Era," and is equivalent to BC, which means "Before Christ."

140 Ex-chief editor of the German magazine Der Spiegel, Stefan Aust, and Frank Gensthaler, explain in their 2014 documentary film Bedingt abwehrbereit: Die Geschichte hinter der "Spiegel"-Affäre (Limited Defense Capability: The Story Behind the Spiegel-Scandal) the rearmament of Americans and Russians during the Cold War of the sixties, using sovereign archival material and comments of witnesses, see more on http://programm.ard.de/TV/daserste/bedingt-abwehrbereit/eid_2810612072468149.

141 "Beeindruckend aktuell," by Daland Segler, Frankfurter Rundschau, May 8, 2014, www.fr-online.de/tv-kritik/tv-kritik---bedingt-abwehrbereit--beeindruckend-aktuell,1473344,27061446.html: "Wer sich vor Augen führt, dass Bundeswehr und US-Armee bereit waren, Deutschland dem Erdboden gleich zu machen, wird seine Überzeugung, Wahn sei ein Wesensmerkmal des Militärs, nie mehr ändern."

142 Original German text translated by Lindner. Helmut Schmidt in the documentary film Bedingt abwehrbereit: Die Geschichte hinter der "Spiegel"-Affäre: "Die sovjetischen Generale wussten, wer immer anfängt, es wird ein atomarer Weltkrieg. Davor hatten sie Schiss, mit Recht!"

143 "Mass Shooters, Firearms, and Social Strains: A Global Analysis of an Exceptionally American Problem," by Adam Lankford, paper presented at the American Sociological Association's 110th Annual Meeting in Chicago on August 23, 2015.

144 "Al Qaeda Without Bin Laden: How Terrorists Cope With their Leader's Death," Brynjar Lia, ForeignAffairs.com and CNN.com, May 11, 2011, www.foreignaffairs.com/articles/67846/brynjar-lia/al-qaeda-without-bin-laden. See also other publications by Brynjar Lia and co-authors, Bokhari, 2006, Hegghammer, 2006, Lia, 2006, Nesser, 2006, Tønnessen, 2006.

145 Jones and Libicki, 2008. I thank Nils Vidar Vambheim for making me aware of this monograph. See Vambheim, 2016, p. 114.

146 Jones and Libicki, 2008, report that in forty percent of overall cases of terrorist groups, violence ends when leaders are eliminated due to efficient intelligence, local informers, and local police investigation.

147 "What Orwell Can Teach Us About the Language of Terror and War," by Rowan Williams, The Guardian, December 12, 2015, www.theguardian.com/books/2015/dec/12/words-on-war-a-summons-to-writers-orwell-lecture. I thank Ken Pope and Linda Hartling for making me aware of this article.

148 See Tajfel and Turner, 1986, for a review of social identity theory.

149 Serres, 1997.

150 "The Case for Contamination," by Kwame Anthony Appiah, New York Times Magazine, January 1, 2006, www.nytimes.com/2006/01/01/magazine/the-case-for-contamination.html?_r=0.

151 Lévinas, 1961/1969, 1982, 1985b, a.

152 Wintersteiner, 1999.

153 "Winning the War of Ideas," by Robert R. Reilly, The Claremont Institute, Volume VII, Number 3 – Summer 2007, www.claremont.org/crb/article/winning-the-war-of-ideas/. The Claremont Institute is an American conservative think tank based in Claremont, California. I thank Nils Vidar Vambheim for making me aware of this monograph. See Vambheim, 2016, p. 117.

154 Jackson, 2011, quoted in Lakhani, 2013, p. 2.

155 Schmid, 2013, p. 8. Schmid describes the concept of radicalism as entailing two main elements, reflecting thought/attitude on one side, and action/behavior on the other side:

> 1. Advocating sweeping political change, based on a conviction that the status quo is unacceptable while at the same time a fundamentally different alternative appears to be available to the radical;
> 2. The means advocated to bring about the system-transforming radical solution for government and society can be non-violent and democratic (through persuasion and reform) or violent and non-democratic (through coercion and revolution).
> Radicals then are not per se violent and while they might share certain characteristics (e.g. alienation from the state, anger over a country's foreign policy, feelings of discrimination) with (violent) extremists, there are also important differences (such as regarding the willingness to engage in critical thinking).38 It does not follow that a radical attitude must result in violent behavior – a finding well established by decades of research.

156 Schmid, 2013, p. 7:

> "Radical" was, at least in the second half of nineteenth century England, "almost as respectable as 'liberal.'" In fact, the term was used at times to describe a wing of the Liberal Party. Many of the radicals, like the suffragettes in the late nineteenth and early twentieth century were mostly non-violent activists. Their demonstrative public direct actions in support of women being allowed to vote were often illegal but not illegitimate, certainly not by today's standards. In fact, some of the nineteenth century radical demands have become mainstream entitlements today. In other words, the content of the concept "radical" has changed quite dramatically in little more than a century: while in the nineteenth century, 'radical' referred primarily to liberal, anti-clerical, pro-democratic, progressive political positions, contemporary use – as in "radical Islamism" – tends to point in the opposite direction: embracing an anti-liberal, fundamentalist, anti-democratic and regressive agenda.

157 Schmid, 2013, p. 10.

158 Schmid, 2013, p. 8. See also Moghaddam, 2009, p. 280.

159 Schmid, 2013, p. 4:

> Causes for radicalization that can lead to terrorism ought to be sought not just on the micro level but also on meso and macro levels:
> 1. Micro level, i.e. the individual level, involving e.g. identity problems, failed integration, feelings of alienation, marginalization, discrimination, relative deprivation, humiliation (direct or by proxy), stigmatization and rejection, often combined with moral outrage and feelings of (vicarious) revenge;
> 2. Meso level, i.e. the wider radical milieu – the supportive or even complicit social surround – which serves as a rallying point and is the 'missing link' with the terrorists' broader constituency or reference group that is aggrieved and suffering injustices which, in turn, can radicalize parts of a youth cohort and lead to the formation of terrorist organizations;
> 3. Macro level, i.e. role of government and society at home and abroad, the radicalization of public opinion and party politics, tense majority – minority relationships, especially when it comes to foreign diasporas, and the role of lacking socio-economic opportunities for whole sectors of society which leads.

160 Howard Richards reported this conclusion from his historical readings in 2013 in Pretoria, South Africa, during his lectures "Against Foucault," in Pretoria, South Africa, developed further for publication, see Richards, et al., 2015a.

161 Kwenda, 2003.

162 Odora Hoppers, 2008.

163 See also the work by Margaret Archer, 2011, and Mark Regnerus. See, for instance, "The Mission Creep of Dignity: Dignity Has Less to Do with Autonomy or Independence Than with Intrinsic Worth and the Ability to Flourish," by Mark Regnerus, MercatorNet, January 20, 2015, www.mercatornet.com/articles/view/the_mission_creep_of_dignity. I thank Hilarie Roseman for making me aware of this article.

164 Metz, 2010, 2011, 2012. Metz summarizes anthropological and sociological findings from a variety sources, including, Fortes and Evans-Pritchard (1940), Forde (1954), Abraham (1962), Carlston (1968), Mbiti (1990), Gyekye (1996) and Wiredu (2008). See also note 38 in Chapter 1. I thank Francisco Gomes de Matos for making us aware of Metz' work.

165 Botman, 2000; see also Bujo, 2001, p. 88. Quoted in Metz, 2012.

166 Metz, 2012.

167 Metz, 2007.

168 Metz, 2012.

169 Gbadegesin, 1991, p. 65.

170 Mokgoro, 1998, p. 3.

171 Gyekye, 2004, p. 16.

172 Iroegbu, 2005, p. 442.

173 Mimi Stokes-Katzenbach, Sustainable Creatives (www.dramaticsustainability.com), in her contribution to the Great Transition Network (GNT) discussion on the topic of "Monetizing Nature," July 31, 2014. Mimi Stokes-Katzenbach has a focus on Sustainability as an Art. See also Kagan, 2011. See, furthermore, the work of Gilbert, 2006.

174 Ibid.

175 Richard Heinberg, educator and senior fellow at the Post Carbon Institute, in his contribution to the Great Transition Network (GTN) discussion on the topic of "Bounding the Planetary Future: Why We Need a Great Transition (GT), March 3, 2015.

176 See among many other publications, for instance, Webster, 2002. See also Olson, 1982, Tainter, 1988, or Diamond, 2005. Particular emphasis to climate change as reason for demise is given by Weiss and Bradley, 2001, and Gill, 2000.

177 Climate change as reason for demise is emphasized by Buckley, et al., 2010. I had the privilege of spending time in Siem Reap and Angkor in 2014, see www.humiliationstudies.org/whoweare/videos.php#angkor.

178 See note 50 in Chapter 4.

179 The Trans-Pacific Partnership (TPP), Trade in Services Agreement (TiSA), and the Transatlantic Trade and Investment Partnership (TTIP). See also note 54 in Chapter 1.

180 In Hidden Persuaders, social critic Vance Packard, 1957, explains the sophisticated creation of needs by the advertising industry. In The Status Seekers, Packard, 1959, describes Americans' struggle to climb the ladder within the society's social stratification. In Waste Makers, Packard, 1960, criticizes planned obsolescence, illustrating Karl Marx's saying, "The production of too many useless things results in too many useless people." In A Nation of Strangers, Packard, 1972, chronicles the wearing down of communal structure through frequent geographical transfers of corporate executives. In The People Shapers, Packard, 1977, highlights how human behavior is manipulated by the use of psychological and biological testing. In Our Endangered Children, Packard, 1983, warns of the dangers with American preoccupation with money, power, status, and sex. In The Ultra Rich: How Much Is Too Much? Packard, 1989, examines the lives of thirty American multimillionaires and their debaucheries.
With regard to Hidden Persuaders, also the work of Allan Schnaiberg is still relevant, who described three theories of consumption: 1) the Pure Consumption Model, suggesting consumer sovereignty, the neoclassical model; 2) the Distorted Consumption Model, where corporations create needs and demand; 3) the Structured Consumption Model, where government infrastructure shapes our consumption patterns. See, for instance, Schnaiberg, 1980, or Gould, et al., 1996.
I thank Sheldon Krimsky for reminding me of the work of Packard and Schnaiberg, in his contribution to the Great Transition Network (GTN) discussion on the topic of "Why We Consume: Neural Design and Sustainability," January 29, 2016.
See also the work of psychologist Martin Textor, 1992, working in Germany, and warning, since many years, that the social fabric of society is being worn down.

181 John Barry in his contribution to the Great Transition Network (GTN) discussion on the topic of "Economics for a Full World," May 18, 2015:

> Indeed, and taking inspiration from authors such as Daly and other contemporary "heterodox political economists" such as Tim Jackson, Molly Scott-Cato, Juliet Schor, Peter Victor and Giorgos Kallis (as well as older thinkers like Nicholas Georgescu-Roegen, Ivan Illich, Karl Polanyi and E.F. Schumacher), my own suggestion for moving beyond undifferentiated economic growth as a permanent feature of the economy rests on the following three criterion or tests for any economic policy or strategy:
>
> 1. does it increase or decrease carbon intensity, resource use, and pollution?
> 2. does it increase or decrease socio-economic inequalities?
> 3. does it increase or decrease qualitative measures of human flourishing? See Barry, 2012.
>
> And this is why Daly's essay and others point out the neoclassical economic growth "emperor has no clothes" are an invitation for economics to return to its roots in "political economy" and integrate political, democratic as well as ethical and normative dimensions within how we think about and

design policies and institutions for the creation and sustaining of the human metabolism with nature that is the human economy.

A significant issue at the heart of our problems is measurement and the use and dominance of GDP. After all, what gets measured gets done. Apart from the well-known problems of GDP as a measure of social welfare (not differentiating "goods" from "bads" primary amongst them), GDP since its creation in the mid war and post-war period has enabled thinking about the economy to become separated from the "real fundamentals" of the human economy, namely, the natural world. As GDP is just a monetary figure (after all, it measures the monetary value of exchanges in a given year), one could be seduced into thinking that as monetary measures can grow infinitely ("angelic" in Daly's or "noumenal" in the older language of Immanuel Kant), economic growth can equally infinitely grow beyond the biophysical limits of the planet. But, given that money is a claim on resources/goods, unless we can eat inflation, and unless we simply view monetary increases in the value of economic activity as the object of economic growth, this monetized conception of GDP is a form of double think. It presents the phenomenal (in Kantian terms) or "throughput / resources / energy / pollution" (in Daly's) as noumenal.

182 John Barry in his contribution to the Great Transition Network (GTN) discussion on the topic of "Economics for a Full World," May 18, 2015.

183 Barry, 2012.

184 Howard Richards in his contribution to the Great Transition Network (GTN) discussion on the topic of "Economics for a Full World," May 26, 2015.

185 In 1975, the Law Enforcement Assistant Administration in the United States formed the National Advisory Committee on Criminal Justice Standards and Goals. One of the five volumes that the committee wrote was on Disorders and Terrorism, Task Force on Disorders and Terrorism, 1976. The Task Force classified terrorism into six categories.

186 See note 118 in this Chapter 5.

187 In 1975, the Law Enforcement Assistant Administration in the United States formed the National Advisory Committee on Criminal Justice Standards and Goals. One of the five volumes that the committee wrote was on Disorders and Terrorism, Task Force on Disorders and Terrorism, 1976. The Task Force classified terrorism into six categories.

188 See note 6 in the Introduction to Section One.

189 In 1975, the Law Enforcement Assistant Administration in the United States formed the National Advisory Committee on Criminal Justice Standards and Goals. One of the five volumes that the committee wrote was on Disorders and Terrorism, Task Force on Disorders and Terrorism, 1976. The Task Force classified terrorism into six categories.

190 See, among others, the work of the Vienna group on material flow analysis and the long durée of civilizational metabolic transitions, Fischer-Kowalski and Haberl, 2007. Or the group in Barcelona on ecological distribution conflicts at the frontiers of an expanding global metabolism, Hornborg, et al., 2007, Martinez-Alier and Røpke, 2008.

191 Purpura, 2011.

192 See, among others, Nicolson, 2010, and Holtzworth-Munroe and Meehan, 2004.

193 See, among others, Raskin, et al., 2002. See also Ruben Nelson, director of Foresight Canada, in a personal communication on the Great Transition Network list in a discussion on the topic of "Marxism and Ecology: Common Fonts of a Great Transition," September 3, 2015, on the comparison between the Great Transformation we need today and the earlier transformations in the form of human civilization – from nomadic-tribal to settled communities and from settled communities to Modern/Industrial. He writes:

On the one hand, the earlier transitions were long (over at least a millennia), unconscious (in the sense of not deliberately intended and planned), regional in scope, and optional (those who chose the then known way of living were not penalized by death). On the other hand, we today appear to face a Great Transition that is short (by any historical standard), must be consciously intentional, must be scale to global and is not optional (death is the alternative).

194 See, among others, Fry, 2007, 2009, 2013.

195 Lindner, 2007b.

196 Nussbaum, 1998, Sen, 2001.

197 See note 6 in the Introduction to Section One.

198 John Fullerton, now a new member of the Club of Rome, in his contribution to the Great Transition Network Initiative discussion titled "Journey to Earthland: Making the Great Transition to Planetary Civilization," October 31, 2016, in response to Raskin, 2016:

> I particularly liked Paul's near dismissal of the "Conventional Worlds" scenarios – both Market Forces and Policy Reform variations, what Paul calls "the false god of moderation that invites us to passively drift down the garden path to barbarization." Of course, this is precisely the path we (collectively) are on, with all the well-meaning focus on "green growth," internalizing "externalities" (an oxymoron), calls for greater market transparency with Environmental, Social, and Governance (ESG) metrics (our idolatry of markets and their ability to guide us is a deadly confusion of means and ends), Divest/Invest campaigns, quantifying in monetary terms ecosystem services offered by vital and priceless ecosystem function, circular economy manufacturing processes, impact investing, carbon demand-side reduction targets, more progressive taxation regimes, and on and on. ALL are essential incremental change, part of any ultimate solution. All are important work. But mostly what they accomplish is the extension of our runway, not systemic change, because they do not involve a fundamental change in the way we think. They could lull us into false confidence that we are on the right track. Collectively, they are the result of our intellectually lazy or simply ignorant preference to worship what Paul calls the "false god of moderation," or simply represent the only way we can have our voices heard. We must see this for what it is, our ongoing 500-year-old Modern Era (and thus deeply ingrained literally into our DNA) reductionist mindset of treating symptoms like carbon emissions rather than seeking and then addressing root causes, holistically understood.

199 Raskin, 2016, Raskin, et al., 2002.

200 It is important to note that a global citizens movement, or global civil society, does not mean NGOs that are funded by interests that stand against the creation of global dignity for all. Anthropologist David Harvey, scholar of critical geography, for instance, speaks of "co-revolution," "co-evolution," "subversion," "the movement," the "Party of Indignation," or a "slow movement across the spheres." In his book The Enigma of Capital, Harvey, 2011, introduces seven "activity spheres" – such as technologies and organizational forms; social relations; institutional and administrative arrangements; production and labour processes; relations to nature; human reproduction; and mental conceptions of the world – and describes how capital "revolves through" these spheres "in search of profit": "Perhaps we should just define the movement, our movement, as anti-capitalist or call ourselves the Party of Indignation, ready to fight and defeat the Party of Wall Street and its acolytes and apologists everywhere, and leave it at that," Harvey, 2011, p. 260.

201 Michael Bauwens, in his contribution to the Great Transition Network Initiative discussion titled "Journey to Earthland: Making the Great Transition to Planetary Civilization," October 31, 2016, in response to Raskin, 2016. Bauwens points at macro-historian Kojin Karatani, 2010/2014, as one voice among others providing maps of civilizational transitions. Karatani suggests that a key element of such transitions is a reconfiguration of modes of exchange, and that a future civilization will have to return to

both the commons and reciprocity mechanisms as key drivers for the exchange of human value and natural resources. For the past years, Bauwens has also built on Alan Page Fiske, 1991, and his Structures of Social Life, and on David Ronfeldt, 1996, and his TIMN framework (Tribes, Institutions, Markets, and Networks). Bauwens writes:

> Karatani takes a multi-modal approach. This means he recognizes and shows that at least four modes of exchange have existed throughout history and throughout all regions of the world, but what matters is their internal configuration, and especially, what is the dominant mode of exchange in any given system, which acts as an "attractor" for the others. Karatani starts with describing the dominance of pooling in early nomadic societies based on kinship bands, the dominance of reciprocity and the gift economy in tribal federations; the dominance of state and rank-based redistribution ("Authority Ranking") in pre-capitalist class formations and finally, the dominance of the capitalist market. This means that civilisational transitions, marked by the evolution of one dominant exchange system to another, are regular occurrences in world history, and they are quite systematically described in Karatani's remarkable synthesis. On the European continent, the two last of such transitions were the 10th transition of the post-Roman plunder economy into the feudal land-based economy, brilliantly described in Robert Moore's First European Revolution, and the 15th century start of the transition to a market-based economy.

202 "The Worst Mistake in the History of the Human Race," by Jared Diamond, Discover Magazine, May 1987, pp. 64–66, www.ditext.com/diamond/mistake.html.

203 Author Charles Eisenstein in a personal communication on July 26, 2014. The ideas of consensus decision-making, participatory democracy, and prefiguraritve politics was current in the Occupy movement.

204 Huntington, 1996.

205 Lindner, 2006c, p. 48.

206 Lindner, 2006c.

207 The missing equipment accounts for around $419.5 million in losses, according to a report, which was issued in late October 2014, and marked "for official use only," see United States Department of Defense, 2014.

208 See note 74 in this Chapter 5.

209 "Letter from Iraq: What We Left Behind: An Increasingly Authoritarian Leader, a Return of Sectarian Violence, and a Nation Worried for Its Future," by Dexter Filkins, New Yorker, April 28, 2014, www.newyorker.com/magazine/2014/04/28/what-we-left-behind: "American diplomats in Iraq sent a rare dissenting cable to Washington, complaining that the U.S., with its combination of support and indifference, was encouraging Maliki's authoritarian tendencies. 'We thought we were creating a dictator' …"

210 Lindner, 2000a.

211 Lindner, 2006c, p. 48.

212 Greenfeld, 1992, 1996, 2006. See also Hechter, 1992. See more in Lindner, 2009f.

213 "Erdogan: Sick, Collapsing Europe Will Pay for Humiliating Turkey," by Selwyn Duke, Observer, April 14, 20/17, http://observer.com/2017/04/recep-tayyip-erdogan-europe-will-pay-for-humiliating-turkey/.

214 "Why Turkish Germans Are So Attached to Recep Erdogan," by Serdar Somuncu, Spiegel Online International, April 22, 2016, www.spiegel.de/international/world/why-turkish-germans-are-so-attached-to-recep-erdogan-a-1088732.html.

215 Lindner, 2000a, and Lindner, 2000f. See also Smith, 1996, or Greenfeld, 1996. See an illustration of my point in "Arab Women on the Move: Trends - Countertrends," by Raouf Ebeid, Political Islam Online, November 1, 2009, http://politicalislam.org/Articles/PI%20570%20Arab%20Women%20on%20the%20Move%20-%20Trends%20-%20Countertrends.pdf.

216 Richards, 2016c.

217 Paul Nieuwenhuis, Cardiff Business School, in his contribution to the Great Transition Network (GTN) discussion on the topic of "Against Ecocide: Legal Protection for Earth," July 19, 2016, in response to Femke Wijdekop, 2016.

Inspiring and Thought-Provoking Questions to Section One

1 Publius Flavius Vegetius Renatus and Reeve, 2004.

2 "The World is Over-Armed and Peace Is Under-Funded," by Ban Ki-moon, United Nations Office for Disarmament Affairs (UNODA), August 30, 2012, www.un.org/disarmament/update/20120830/. I thank Ingeborg Breines for making me aware of this quote. It is a privilege to have Ingeborg Breines as esteemed member in the global advisory board of our Human Dignity and Humiliation Studies fellowship.
See also the Yearbook by the Stockholm International Peace Research Institute (SIPRI), 2016, which confirms the evaluation of the previous year, namely, that the relatively positive trend of the past ten years toward less violence and a more effective conflict management, seems broken.
See "World Military Spending: Increases in the USA and Europe, Decreases in Oil-Exporting Countries," Stockholm International Peace Research Institute (SIPRI), April 24, 2017, www.sipri.org/media/press-release/2017/world-military-spending-increases-usa-and-europe.

3 The Joint Comprehensive Plan of Action, is an international agreement on the nuclear program of Iran reached in Vienna on July 14, 2015, between Iran, the P5+1 (the five permanent members of the United Nations Security Council – China, France, Russia, United Kingdom, United States – plus Germany), and the European Union.

4 "Truth to Power," by Noam Chomsky and David Mcneill, Japan Times, February 22, 2014, www.japantimes.co.jp/news/2014/02/22/world/noam-chomsky-truth-to-power/.

5 International Peace Bureau, Geneva, Switzerland, 2016, www.ipb2016.berlin/congress/. I thank the Bureau's former co-president, Ingeborg Breines for having included me into her work as far back as 1995, when she was the Director of Women and a Culture of Peace at UNESCO, and Special Adviser to the Director-General on Women, Gender and Development. It is a privilege to have Ingeborg Breines as esteemed member in the global advisory board of our Human Dignity and Humiliation Studies fellowship since its inception.

6 "Disarm! For a Climate of Peace: Creating an Action Agenda," The International Peace Bureau (IPB)World Congress 2016 on Military and Social Spending, Berlin, September 30, 2016, www.ipb2016.berlin/.

7 International Peace Bureau, Geneva, Switzerland, 2016, www.ipb2016.berlin/congress/.

8 See also Storaker, 2016, and Ingeborg Breines' contribution.

9 "Hva er en feministisk utenrikspolitikk, temahefte forklart," by Elisabeth Kristiansen, Fred og frihet, Number 1, 2016, WILPF Norge – Internasjonal kvinneliga for fred og frihet, www.ikff.no/wp-content/uploads/2012/05/Fred-og-frihet-nr-1-2016.pdf, pp. 12–14. I thank Trine Eklund for making me aware of the renewed focus in Scandinavia on establishing a fredsdepartement in Scandinavia. It is a

privilege to have Trine Eklund as esteemed member in the global advisory board of the Human Dignity and Humiliation Studies fellowship.

10 As for the United States of America, the idea of a Department of Peace was introduced already for America's first government in the 1700s by Benjamin Rush. See also hearings before the United States House Committee on Foreign Affairs, United States Congress, 1945. More recently, congressman Dennis Kucinich has kept the idea alive in his political campaigns. For an overview over early peace psychologists, see Rudmin, 1991. It is a privilege to have Floyd Rudmin as esteemed member in the global advisory board of the Human Dignity and Humiliation Studies fellowship.

11 "Commas to Prevent Misunderstanding," www.ucalgary.ca/uofc/eduweb/grammar/course/punctuation/3_4j.htm.

12 See the third of the five axioms of communication by Gregory Bateson, 1972, drawn on by Watzlawick, et al., 1967: The sender and the receiver of information structure the communication flow differently, each seeing their own behavior as a reaction to the other's behavior.
When I was a psychology student in Hamburg, Germany (1974 – 1978), one of my professors was Friedemann Schulz von Thun, 1981, who built his four-sides model of communication on Watzlawick's insights and on the three sides of the Organon model by Karl Bühler, 1934/1990. The four sides of communication begin with the "matter layer" pertaining to data and facts, second, there is the layer of self-revealing or self-disclosure of the speaker – intended or not – pertaining to motives, values, or emotions, third, there is the "relationship layer" as it is intended or understood, and, fourth, the "appeal layer" points at what the speaker is aiming at. Every layer can be misunderstood separately. For example, a wife may have prepared a meal and eats it with her husband, when he says: "There is something green in the soup." On the matter layer he points at something being green, on the self-revealing layer he discloses that he does not know what it is, on the relationship layer he indicates that she certainly knows what it is, and on the appeal layer he asks her to let him know what it is. His wife may understand, on the matter layer, that there is something green, and might infer, at the self-revealing layer, that this makes her husband feel uncomfortable. On the relationship layer she may hear him saying that, in his eyes, she is a bad cook, and, on the appeal layer, that she should leave the green out next time. Ultimately, the wife may reply, irritated: "My God, if you do not like it here, you can eat somewhere else!," Schulz von Thun, 1981, p. 62.

13 Social anthropologist Paul Connerton, 1989, pp. 2–3: "Concerning memory as such, we may note that our experience of the present largely depends upon our knowledge of the past. We experience our present world in a context which is causally connected with past events and objects, and hence with reference to events and objects which we are not experiencing when we are experiencing the present … our experiences of the present largely depend upon our knowledge of the past, and that our images of the past commonly serve to legitimate a present social order." See also Connerton, 2009, 2011. I thank Jasna Jozelic, 2006, for reminding me of Connerton's work.

14 Connerton, 1989, p. 17: "The production of more or less informally told narrative histories turns out to be a basic activity for characterization of human actions. It is a feature off all communal memory."

15 Anderson, 1991.

16 Connerton, 1989, p. 15.

17 Raskin, 2016, in resonance with books such as More, 1516–18/2012, Morris, 1890, Fuller, 1981, Berry, 1999, Korten, 2006, Morin, 2011. Also writers such as Peter Frase, 2016, make typologies of possible future – in his case it is communism, rentism, socialism, or exterminism – using two intersecting spectrums, one ranging from inequality to hierarchy and the other from scarcity to abundance. Frase resonates with Walter Benjamin, 1940/1974, and his warning that, as history is controlled by the victors, we are moving backwards into the future, a move that is illusionary. He is joined in these warnings by many others, among them journalists such as Owen Hatherley, 2015, who writes on architecture, politics, and culture.

18 The noosphere, sometimes written as noösphere, is the sphere of human thought, from the Greek νοῦς, nous, or mind, and σφαῖρα, sphaira, or sphere, in lexical analogy to atmosphere and biosphere. Presumably, it was introduced by mineralogist and geochemist Vladimir Ivanovich Vernadsky (1863 – 1945), and developed further by Jesuit priest-theologian and a distinguished geologist-paleontologist, Pierre Teilhard de Chardin (1881 – 1955) and philosopher Édouard Le Roy (1870 – 1954). Teilhard de Chardin, 1920–1952/1959, taught that humanity, through collective cooperation, can achieve the noosphere, where people refrain from thinking only of themselves, and instead contribute to a universal heightening of consciousness. See "The Cosmic Plenum: Teilhard's Gnosis: Cosmogenesis," by Beatrix Murrell, Stoa del Sol, San Diego, CA, www.bizint.com/stoa_del_sol/plenum/plenum_2.html.

19 Adapted from Lindner, 2006c, pp. 43–44, italics and quotation marks simplified.

20 Snyder, 2000.

21 Keen, 1986.

22 See the Theater Review: "Ulysses as an American Slave," by Charles Isherwood, New York Times, October 28, 2014, www.nytimes.com/2014/10/29/theater/father-comes-home-from-the-wars-by-suzan-lori-parks-at-the-public-theater.html?_r=0.

23 Lakoff, 2006a. See more in note 211 in the Introduction.

24 "Human Security in Theory and Practice: An Overview of the Human Security Concept and the United Nations Trust Fund for Human Security, United Nations Human Security Unit, www.un.org/humansecurity/sites/www.un.org.humansecurity/files/human_security_in_theory_and_practice_english.pdf. I am proud of my connection with the Boutros-Boutros Ghali family through Katrina Vrebalovich, daughter of Britt Boutros-Boutros-Ghali.

25 The Bibliotheca Alexandrina (English: Library of Alexandria) is a major library and cultural center located on the shore of the Mediterranean Sea in the Egyptian city of Alexandria, commemorating the Library of Alexandria that was lost in antiquity. See www.bibalex.org. Ambassador Aly Maher El Sayed is an advisor and official spokesman. I had the privilege of meeting him in Alexandria in 2007. I was invited to give a lecture as part of the pilot course "Young Swedish Muslim Peace Agents," at the Swedish Institute in Alexandria, Egypt, by its director Jan Henningsson, January 19–27, 2007. See Lindner, 2007d. It is a privilege to have also Jan Henningsson as esteemed member in the global advisory board of our Human Dignity and Humiliation Studies fellowship.

26 Ambassador Aly Maher El Sayed in a personal communication on January 28, 2014. It was a privilege to have Ambassador Aly Maher El Sayed as esteemed member in the global advisory board of our Human Dignity and Humiliation Studies fellowship. We will always honor is memory.

Appendix to Section One

1 Lindner, 2012b.

2 Lindner, 2014a.

3 Lindner, 2013, Lindner and Morrell, 2013, Lindner and Sewchurran, 2013, Richards, et al., 2015a, Lindner, 2015a.

4 Lindner, 2016a.

5 Erik Solheim was Minister of International Development when our conversation on humiliation and terrorism took place in the Ministry of Foreign Affairs in Oslo, Norway, on January 10, 2011. I have summarized and translated our conversation from Norwegian. See the full summary in the full note in the pdf edition of this book.

6 Abid Raja is a Norwegian lawyer and politician for the Liberal Party (Venstre). He was born in Oslo into a family of Pakistani descent in 1975. In 2010, he was awarded the Fritt Ord Honorary Award of Freedom of Speech. I have summarized and translated our conversation from Norwegian. See the full summary in the full note in the pdf edition of this book. Among others, Abid Raja called out: "And those who have the most expertise, where are they? Where is the Institute of Criminology, for instance? People read newspapers and the "temperature" of fear in society rises. Researchers would have the influence to lower the temperature of the debate, bringing new concepts and de-stigmatize a large group. … Social democratic moral relativism causes scientists to be too afraid! They suffer from an inferiority complex! They need to shoulder their responsibility!"

7 Sageman, 2008.

8 Here Aase alluded to the failure of the self-esteem movement, see psychologists Twenge and Campbell, 2009, and their book with the telling title The Narcissism Epidemic: Living in the Age of Entitlement. Psychoanalyst Heinz Kohut has worked on narcissistic injury, see Kohut, 1973, p. 380. See note 10 in Chapter 8.

9 Nesser, 2006, 2011, 2014, Tønnessen, 2006. See also a qualitative study of biographies of extremists, recommended to me by the security police in Hamburg: Die Sicht der Anderen: Eine qualitative Studie zu Biographien von Extremisten und Terroristen, by Saskia Lützinger, 2010, https://haskala.de/wp-content/uploads/2010/09/band40_die_sicht_der_anderen.pdf.

10 See also Chowdhury Fink and El-Said, 2011, p. 28.

11 Schmid, 2013, p. 49.

12 Temarapport: Hvilken bakgrunn har personer som frekventerer ekstreme islamistiske miljøer i Norge før de blir radikalisert? ekstern rapport, Politiets sikkerhetstjeneste (Norwegian Police Security Service, PTS), Oslo, Norway, September 12, 2016, www.pst.no/media/82236/2016_09_08_radikaliseringsprosjektets-rapport_ugradert.pdf.

13 Saïda Keller-Messahli expressed this view in the magazine PARDONNEZ-MOI, in TV5Monde, August 6, 2016.

14 Kepel, 2015. See also Kepel, 2006, 2008, 2016, Kepel and Milelli, 2008.

15 See, for instance, Bokhari, 2006, Hegghammer, 2006, Lia, 2006, Nesser, 2006, Tønnessen, 2006.

16 Bokhari, 2006. See also Bokhari, 2010, Cohen and Bokhari, 2011.

17 Petter Nesser is a senior researcher with the Terrorism Research Group at the Norwegian Defence Research Establishment (FFI). See Nesser, 2006, 2011, 2014, Tønnessen, 2006. I have summarized and translated our conversation from Norwegian. See the full summary in the full note in the pdf edition of this book. Nesser refers to, among others, Utvik, 2006, and Benschop, 2005.

18 Tore Bjørgo is professor at the University of Oslo and Director at "Center for Research on Extremism: Right-Wing Extremism, Hate Crime and Political Violence" (CREX). He is also adjunct professor at the Norwegian Police University College (PHS), where he has been professor of police science (since 2004) and research director (2005-2007). I was introduced to him in 1995 by J.'Bayo Adekanye, researcher at the Peace Research Institute Oslo (PRIO). It was a privilege to speak with him in his office in Oslo on February 13, 2012. I have summarized and translated our conversation from Norwegian. See the full summary in the full note in the pdf edition of this book.

19 Benjamin Hermansen (1985 – 2001) was a Norwegian-born Ghanaian boy whose father was born in Ghana, his mother was Norwegian. He was stabbed to death at Holmlia in Oslo, Norway, on January 26, 2001, by people from the Neo-Nazi group Boot Boys. Joe Erling Jahr (born 1981) and Ole Nicolai Kvisler (born 1979) were convicted of the murder and sentenced to 16 and 15 years in prison respectively, later this was increased to 18 and 17 years. A third defendant, a young woman, was convicted on a lesser charge.

20 "Aussie 'Jihadist' Andrew Ibrahim Wenham in Norway Mosque Battle," by Sally Neighbour, The Australian, November 04, 2010, www.theaustralian.com.au/national-affairs/aussie-jihadist-andrew-ibrahim-wenham-in-norway-mosque-battle/story-fn59niix-1225947543380.

21 Hamed El-Said is professor and chair of International Business and Political Economy at the Manchester Metropolitan University, UK, and has published extensively on the Middle East and North Africa and undertook a secondment to the UN Interregional Crime and Justice Research Institute (UNICRI), where he worked as an Associate Expert on Radicalisation and Extremism. In 2008, he led the research team of the United Nations Counter-Terrorism Implementation Task Force's Working Group on Addressing Radicalisation and Extremism that Lead to Terrorism. His works include El-Said, 2015, Chowdhury Fink and El-Said, 2011, Harrigan and El-Said, 2010, Harrigan and El-Said, 2009. See more on http://hamedelsaid.co.uk.

22 Second Chance in Saudi Arabia – Saudi's Rehab, documentary film by Francis Mead, United Nations Television, 2011, as part of a series of films made for the UN looking at how and why people leave terror groups. See http://vimeo.com/23135636. We thank Ariel Lublin for making me aware of this film by her partner Francis Mead and bringing him to our 2009 Workshop on Humiliation and Violent Conflict, Columbia University, New York, December 10-11, 2009. It is a privilege to their support for the work of Human Dignity and Humiliation Studies.

23 Dr. Hameed Khalil i. Al-Shaygi, http://faculty.ksu.edu.sa/alshaijy/Pages/cve.aspx.

24 See Lindner, 2006c, the section "Children, madmen, criminals, enemies, or subhumans? Which interpretation fits terrorists best?" in Chapter 5: Humiliation and Conflict, in the book Making Enemies: Humiliation and International Conflict, pp. 96–98.

25 Koenigs, 2007. For those who wish to acquire a feel for the pathways of radicalization, Koenigs recommends Updike, 2006.

26 Koenigs, 2007, p. 2.

27 Koenigs, 2007, p. 15: "Al-Qaeda deliberately timed Massoud's assassination to precede the attacks in the United States. Anticipating a US military response, Al-Qaeda assassinated Mullah Omar's arch foe in order both to secure Osama bin Laden's relations with his Taliban protectors, and to eliminate the United States' most obvious partner in any retaliation that they might carry out on Afghan soil."

28 Norbert Müller is on the board of Schura Hamburg (SCHURA – Rat der islamischen Gemeinschaften in Hamburg e.V.), a merger of mosque associations in Hamburg, Germany. The conversation on humiliation and terrorism with Norbert Müller took place in Hamburg on October 22, 2010. I have summarized and translated our conversation from German. See the full summary in the full note in the pdf edition of this book.

29 Wolfgang Kaleck is a civil rights attorney and the general secretary for the European Center for Constitutional and Human Rights. I had the privilege of learning from him in Berlin on May 17, 2011. See, among other publications, Kaleck, et al., 2007, and Kaleck, 2016. I have summarized and translated our conversation from German. See the full summary in the full note in the pdf edition of this book. Kaleck recommends looking at the International Center for Transitional Justice (http://ictj.org/) with their motto "Justice, Truth, Dignity." This is their vision: "We strive for societies to regain humanity in the wake of mass atrocity. For societies in which impunity is rejected, dignity of victims is upheld, and trust is restored; where truth is the basis of history. We believe that this is an ethical, legal, and political imperative and the cornerstone of lasting peace." See also note 241 and 244 in the Introduction.

30 Aurangzaib Khan, journalist in North Pakistan, in a personal communication on May 3, 2011. I thank Ikhlaq Hussein for having introduced me to Aurangzaib Khan. It is a privilege to have Judit Révész and later also her husband Ikhlaq Hussein as core pillars of our Human Dignity and Humiliation Studies fellowship since its very inception.

31 "Pakistan's Swat Valley: 'The Land of The Terrorists,'" by Nick Schifrin, ABC News, January 26, 2008, http://abcnews.go.com/International/story?id=6731636.

32 I thank Shahid Kamal and his wife for receiving me most graciously in their home in Berlin. It is a privilege to have Shahid Kamal as esteemed member in the global advisory board of our Human Dignity and Humiliation Studies fellowship.

33 Lindner, 2000a. It is a privilege to have Gary Page Jones as esteemed member in the global advisory board of our Human Dignity and Humiliation Studies fellowship.

34 See for discussions, among others, Lindner, 2001e, or Lindner, 2015a.

35 Rogers, 1962.

36 Prochaska, et al., 1992.

37 Bandura, 1977.

38 "Theories of Behavior Change," Communication for governance and accountability program (Commgap), a global program at the World Bank, Washington, DC, http://siteresources.worldbank.org/EXTGOVACC/Resources/BehaviorChangeweb.pdf.

39 "Participatory Action-Research in Post-Conflict Situations: The Example of the War-Torn Societies Project," by Agneta M. Johannsen, Berghof Handbook for Conflict Transformation, March 30, 2001, www.berghof-foundation.org/fileadmin/redaktion/Publications/Handbook/Articles/johannsen_hb.pdf. It is a privilege to be able to benefit from the insights of Norbert Ropers and his colleagues of the Berghof Foundation since 1994.

40 I thank Matt Bryden for sharing his immense knowledge, experience, and insights with me. It is a privilege to have Matt Bryden as esteemed member in the global advisory board of our Human Dignity and Humiliation Studies fellowship. See for the War-torn Societies Project (1994–1998), www.unrisd.org/unrisd/website/projects.nsf/(httpProjects)/0ABD701FB4400BA880256B64003D053B?OpenDocument:

> The War-torn Societies Project aimed to assist the international community and national and local actors to better understand and respond to the complex challenge of rebuilding war-torn societies in post-conflict situations. It encouraged main external and internal actors in these societies to collectively analyze the complex interactions between peace-keeping, relief, rehabilitation and development activities, and between local, national and external actors. Participatory action-research was used as a tool to jointly define policies that could lead to a better integration of different forms of international assistance – humanitarian, economic, political, military – and to a better alignment of such assistance with local and national efforts.
>
> The project was a joint activity of UNRISD and the Programme for Strategic and International Security Studies (PSIS) of the Graduate Institute of International Studies in Geneva. It worked at the country level with Country Project Groups made up of representatives of main internal and external actors, and at the central level with a group of experienced policy makers and operational actors who constitute the project's stakeholders. The project also worked in close collaboration with national and international research organizations which pursue similar objectives, and operated within the wider network of organizations concerned with post-conflict and peace-building issues.
>
> The project is no longer affiliated with UNRISD.

41 O'Neill, 2007. Maggie O'Neill is based in Criminology and Social Policy at Loughborough University, UK, and it is a privilege to have her as esteemed member in the global advisory board of our Human Dignity and Humiliation Studies fellowship.

42 "Brighton Bombing 25 Years on: Making Friends with My Father's Killer," by Chris Hall, The Guardian, October 10, 2009, www.theguardian.com/lifeandstyle/2009/oct/10/brighton-bomb-conservative-anniversary. I am very grateful to Jo Berry for sharing her deep-felt experiences with me.

43 It is a privilege to have Jo Berry as esteemed member in the global advisory board of our Human Dignity and Humiliation Studies fellowship. We had our Skype meeting on May 5, 2011, and met again at the Cardozo Law School's Journal of Conflict Resolution Annual Symposium titled "Negotiating the Extremes: Impossible Political Dialogues in the 21st Century," in New York City on November 5, 2012.

44 See also Brown, 2012a.

45 See note 37 in the Preface.

46 Daniel Bar-On, 1989, interviewed children of Nazi criminals and wrote the book titled Legacy of Silence: Encounters with Children of the Third Reich. It was a privilege to have Dan Bar-On as esteemed member in the global advisory board of the Human Dignity and Humiliation Studies fellowship, and we hold his memory dear.

47 It is a privilege to have Annette Engler as one of the "Nurturers of Dignity" in our Human Dignity and Humiliation Studies fellowship.

48 Ford, 2017.

Section Two

See additional material at www.humiliationstudies.org/whoweare/ evelin/book/05.php.

1 Camus, 1951.

2 "A Question of Honour," by Suzanne Goldenberg, The Guardian, May 27, 1999, www.theguardian.com/world/1999/may/27/gender.uk1.

3" Humiliation Is the Root of All Terrorism," by Tikkun editor at large Peter Gabel, TruthOut, December 16, 2015, www.truth-out.org/speakout/item/34062-humiliation-is-the-root-of-all-terrorism. I thank Seymour M. (Mike) Miller and Linda Hartling for making me aware of this article.

4 "The Humiliation Factor," by Thomas Friedman, New York Times, November 9, Section 4, p. 11, 2003, www.nytimes.com/2003/11/09/opinion/the-humiliation-factor.html. See also "Connect the Dots," by Thomas L. Friedman, New York Times, September 25, 2003, www.nytimes.com/2003/09/25/opinion/connect-the-dots.html:

Sure, poverty doesn't cause terrorism – no one is killing for a raise. But poverty is great for the terrorism business because poverty creates humiliation and stifled aspirations and forces many people to leave their traditional farms to join the alienated urban poor in the cities–all conditions that spawn terrorists.

5 A young man in France, of Arab background talks to anthropologist Scott Atran, one of the few experts who spoke directly with Al-Qaeda fighters. In "The Arena: What drives Westerners to fight for ISIL?" Al Jazeera, September 11, 2015, www.aljazeera.com/programmes/upfront/2015/09/arena-drives-westerners-fight-isil-150911150353299.html. I thank Sultan Somjee for making me aware of this interview. It is a privilege to have Sultan Somjee as esteemed member in the global advisory board of the Human Dignity and Humiliation Studies fellowship.

6 Faisal Shahzad, the suspect in the failed car bombing in New York's Times Square, Pakistani-born naturalized U.S. citizen, was frustrated with the state of the Muslim world and sought a way to "fight back." CNN obtained two e-mails, he sent to a large group of recipients in February 2006. Read the full e-mail at

http://i2.cdn.turner.com/cnn/2010/images/05/17/shahzad.pdf. See "E-Mails Paint Times Square Suspect As Frustrated Muslim," by Susan Candiotti, CNN, May 18, 2010, http://edition.cnn.com/2010/CRIME/05/17/times.square.suspect.emails/.

7 "When Generosity Hurts: Bill Gates, Public School Teachers and the Politics of Humiliation," by Henry A. Giroux, TruthOut, October 5, 2010, http://truth-out.org/archive/component/k2/item/92120:when-generosity-hurts-bill-gates-public-school-teachers-and-the-politics-of-humiliation. I thank Brian Ward for having made us aware of this article. See for Giroux's other publications, among others: Di Leo, et al., 2013, Giroux, 2010, 2011, 2012, 2013, 2014a, b, Nikolakaki, 2012. It is a privilege to have Brian Ward as esteemed member in our Human Dignity and Humiliation Studies fellowship. I very much thank him and his family for hosting me during our 2011 Annual Conference of Human Dignity and Humiliation Studies, "Enlarging the Boundaries of Compassion," in Dunedin, New Zealand, August 29 – September 1, 2011, www.humiliationstudies.org/whoweare/annualmeeting/17.php

Introduction to Section Two

1 Banaz: A Love Story, documentary film directed and produced by Deeyah Khan, 2012, https://youtu.be/VepuyvhHYdM. The film chronicles the life and death of Banaz Mahmod, a young British Kurdish woman killed in 2006 in South London on the orders of her family in a so-called honor killing. It is a privilege to have Deeyah Khan as esteemed member in our Human Dignity and Humiliation Studies fellowship.

2 Ahmad Manour Vis-à-vis, Talk with Frank A. Meyer, 3sat, February 1, 2016, www.3sat.de/mediathek/?mode=play&obj=56762. See the full note in the pdf edition of this book. See also Mansour, 2015. See also Lindner, 2000f.

3 Hafez, 2007a, pp. 111–112. See also Hafez, 2003, 2007b. See, furthermore, Garber, et al., 2011, Lankford, 2009, 2013.

4 Translated from German by Alice Asbury Abbott, Suttner, 1908, pp. 34–36. German original in Suttner, 1889, pp. 12–13. See the German original in the full note in the pdf edition of this book.

5 Fromm, 1941.

6 Terror management theory was originally proposed by Jeff Greenberg, Sheldon Solomon, and Tom Pyszczynski. See the first complete formal statement of terror management theory including epistemological assumptions and proposal for an experimental existential psychology in Solomon, et al., 1991, and more recent publications related to the events of September 11, 2001, Pyszczynski, et al., 2003.

7 Cultural anthropologist Ernest Becker, 1973, wrote about this in his book The Denial of Death.

8 See note 67 in Chapter 1.

9 Pyszczynski, et al., 2006.

10 Moghaddam, 2004, p. 112.

11 Shay, 1995, 2002, 2014. See also Herman, 2001. Listen to Shay's talk at the Narrative Medicine VA Workshop, Columbia University Medical Center, March 9, 2012, "Dr. Jonathan Shay – "Moral Injury," published on April 27, 2012, https://youtu.be/XBkCg6_ISpQ. I thank Mark Singer for reminding me of Jonathan Shay's work.

12 Jonathan Shay in his talk at the Narrative Medicine VA Workshop, Columbia University Medical Center, March 9, 2012, "Dr. Jonathan Shay – "Moral Injury," published on April 27, 2012, https://youtu.be/XBkCg6_ISpQ.

13 See note 72 in Chapter 3.

14 Shay, 2011, p. 181.

15 "The Salem Award for Human Rights and Social Justice: Dr. Jonathan Shay: Advocating for Veterans," http://salemaward.org/jonathan-shay-97.html.

16 Litz, et al., 2009.

17 Shay, 2014.

18 Ibid.

19 James Edward Jones, 2006, paper presented at the 2006 Workshop on Humiliation and Violent Conflict, Columbia University, New York, December 14–15, 2006: "Persons affected by the PVEE syndrome often defend, minimize and/or rationalize the most outrageous attitudes held and acts carried out by themselves or members of their particular group. When you talk to such people, you will quickly find that the reason that they take such a usually untenable position is because 'their people' either are or have been victimized by one or more other groups. This is the golden rule turned on its head: 'Do bad unto others because they (or someone else) did something bad to you.' It is a deceptively simple and somewhat pervasive point of view..." It is a privilege to have James Edward Jones as esteemed member in the global advisory board of our Human Dignity and Humiliation Studies fellowship.

20 Lindner, 2006c.

21 See note 119 in the Preface.

22 John Horgan at the START conference at the University of Maryland, College Park, September 1, 2011, quoted in Schmid, 2013, p. 17.

23 Schmid, 2013, p. 37. See also Kundnani, 2012.

24 McCauley and Moskalenko, 2011. It is a privilege to have McCauley as esteemed member in the global advisory board of the Human Dignity and Humiliation Studies fellowship.

25 Kundnani, 2012, p. 20, Schmid, 2013, p. 4.

26 Schmid, 2013, footnote 10. See also Awan, et al., 2011, p. 1.

27 Lindner, 2006c.

28 See Lindner and Desmond Tutu (Foreword), 2010.

29 Leo Tolstoy (1828 – 1910), in Tolstoy, 1894.

30 Ury, 1999, p. 108. It is a privilege to have William Ury as esteemed member in the global advisory board of our Human Dignity and Humiliation Studies fellowship.

31 Homo sapiens might have appeared even earlier, as far back as 300,000 years ago. See "Oldest Homo Sapiens Fossil Claim Rewrites Our Species' History," by Ewen Callaway, Nature, June 7, 2017, www.nature.com/news/oldest-homo-sapiens-fossil-claim-rewrites-our-species-history-1.22114. Remains from Morocco dated to 315,000 years ago push back our species' origins by 100,000 years — and suggest we didn't evolve only in East Africa.

32 Pettit, 1997b.

33 Eisler, 1987. See note 48 in the Preface.

34 In his cultural dimensions theory, Hofstede, 2001, describes national cultures along six dimensions: power distance, individualism, uncertainty avoidance, masculinity, long term orientation, and indulgence versus restraint. I resonate with Anthony Marsella who warns that Hofstede's dimensions are Western constructions and do not capture the dimensions of indigenous peoples: "The oppositional dimensions are often a continuum," Anthony Marsella, in a personal communication to Louise Sundararajan's indigenous psychology group on February 11, 2017. I also appreciate Michael Harris Bond's cautionary words: "As for

teaching and learning, I have always appreciated Hofstede's attempt to apply his initial four dimensions to the instructional dynamic that he wrote in 1986 for the International Journal of Intercultural Relations. No data beyond his wide personal experience, but lots of testable hypotheses on offer. As for whether the "Western" approach of dimensionalizing [rating along a scale the degree of an operationalized construct] makes sense or whether it defeats any attempt to scientize indigenous constructs, I would be eager to hear what the alternative approach might be if we are doing social science...." Michael Harris Bond, in a personal communication to Louise Sundararajan's indigenous psychology group on February 15, 2017. See Bond, 1986, Hofstede, 1986. It is a privilege to have Anthony Marsella and Michael Harris Bond as esteemed members in the global advisory board of the Human Dignity and Humiliation Studies fellowship from its inception.

35 Hafez, 2007a, pp. 111–112. See also Hafez, 2003, 2007b.

Chapter 6

1 Translated from German by Alice Asbury Abbott, Suttner, 1908, p. 118. German original, Suttner, 1889, p. 68. See the German original in the full note in the pdf edition of this book.

2 Translated from German by Alice Asbury Abbott, Suttner, 1908, pp. 254–255. German original, Suttner, 1889, pp. 153. See the German original in the full note in the pdf edition of this book.

3 German original: On September 23, 1916, Max Weber wrote in a letter to Hans Schnitger, uncle of Marianne Weber: "Der Tod für das Vaterland ist der einzige, bei dem der Mensch sicher ist, für ein irdisches Gut zu sterben, welches Dessen wert ist. ... Der Krieg ist 'die dunkle Erhabenheit dieser größten aller Prüfungen'," quoted in Bruhns, 2014, p. 61, translated from German by Lindner.

4 Bruhns, 2014.

5 Bruhns, 2014, p. 63. See also Gilad and Junginger, 2010, or www.clausewitz.org.

6 Kissinger, 1957. See also "Ich, Sohn des Glücks," by Michael Stürmer, Die Welt, October 29, 2005, www.welt.de/print-welt/article174042/Ich-Sohn-des-Gluecks.html. See also Neues vom Wiener Kongress, documentary film by Roswitha und Ronald P. Vaughan, 2014, http://tv.orf.at/orf3/stories/2674402/.

7 See, among others, Kissinger, 1957, Price, 2012, Müchler, 2015.

8 Déroulede, 1872, quoted in Rutkoff, 1981, p. l61. I thank Thomas Scheff for making me aware of this work.

9 This treaty included the now infamous war-guilt clause imposing complete responsibility for the war on the Germans and demanding that they "make complete reparation for all ... loss and damage" caused: "The Allied and Associated Governments affirm and Germany accepts the responsibility of Germany and her allies for causing all the loss and damage to which the Allied and Associated Governments and their nationals have been subjected as a consequence of the war imposed upon them by the aggression of Germany and her allies," Versailles Treaty 1919, part VIII, section I, article 231. See also Haffner, 1978, and Elias, 1996, or Mann, 2004b.

10 See note 35 in the Preface.

11 "Humiliation and Terrorism: Goldhagen's Analysis," by Richard Landes, The Augean Stables, March 27, 2007, www.theaugeanstables.com/2007/03/27/humiliation-and-terrorism-goldhagens-analysis/.

12 Ibid.

13 On January 25, 1932, Adolf Hitler wrote an open letter to Heinrich Brüning (1885 – 1970), a German Center Party politician and academic, who served as Chancellor of Germany during the Weimar Republic

from 1930 to 1932. The letter was published in Völkischer Beobachter, Number 29, January 29, 1932: "Die unerbittliche Handhabung aber dieses Vertrages, die, wie Sie meinen, in den ersten fünf Jahren jeden deutschen Wiederaufbau zerstörte, wäre ganz unmöglich gewesen, wenn nicht gewisse 'deutsche' Parteien zu jeder Erpressung, Schmach und Schande ihre Zustimmung gegeben hätten."

14 Historian Ian Kershaw, 2011, describes how the German refusal to surrender and to accept defeat would eventually lead to the deaths of millions.

15 Galtung, 1996, p. 210–211. See also "Carriers of Cosmology," by Johan Galtung, Princeton University, Center of International Studies, November 1986, www.transcend.org/galtung/papers/Carriers%20of%20Cosmology.pdf.

16 Kaufman, 2001, p. 212.

17 Lindner, 2000a, Lindner, 2006c, Lindner and Desmond Tutu (Foreword), 2010, quoted in Vambheim, 2016, p. 20. Peace researcher Vidar Vambheim draws on the notion of memes, introduced by evolutionary biologist Richard Dawkins, 2006, analogous to genes, to characterize cultural codes. Memes are seen as cultural replicators that survive, reproduce and proliferate in a meme pool. It is a privilege to have Nils Vidar Vambheim as esteemed member in the global advisory board of the Human Dignity and Humiliation Studies fellowship.

18 Galtung, 1996, Galtung, et al., 2000. See also Galtung's description of the Dichotomy-Manicheism-Armageddon (DMT) syndrome at "Cultural Peace: Some Characteristics," by Johan Galtung, Transcend articles, October 12, 2003, www.transcend.org/files/article121.html. See also "Expert Colloquy – Dialogue Serving Intercultural and Inter-Religious Communication – Strasbourg," Council of Europe, October 7–9, 2002, interview with Johan Galtung, www.coe.int/T/E/Com/Files/Events/2002-10-Intercultural-Dialogue/Interview_galtung.asp. See, furthermore, LeShan, 1992.

19 Vambheim, 2016, p. 20. Peace researcher Vambheim describes Galtung's work on civilization and violence as an "impressionistic" approach to the problem, see Galtung, 1996, pp. 197–274. Vambheim also points at Alice Miller's insights of how direct and indirect violence in childhood may spawn the projection of evil mental content onto others and violence later in adulthood, resulting in atrocities like mass-murder in war, see Miller, 1980/2002, Miller, 2006a.

20 Jihad: A Story of the Others, documentary film by Deeyah Khan, 2015, http://fuuse.net/jihad-a-story-of-the-others/. See also "Popstjernen som slo tilbake," by Hanne Skartveit, VG, September 19, 2015, www.vg.no/nyheter/meninger/islam-debatten/popstjernen-som-slo-tilbake/a/23527457/. See the full note in the pdf edition of this book. See the debate after the Norwegian premiere of the film on August 25, 2015, on https://youtu.be/AfyweFfQA-w.
See also Ein Sommer im Dschihad, documentary film by Panorama, Norddeutscher Rundfunk, July 28, 2015, www.daserste.de, https://youtu.be/7eDbRhP5Ky4. Ebrahim B. is a young man from Wolfsburg in Germany and he is the first German Da'esh-returnee who talks openly in front of a camera. He now distances himself from Da'esh. He explains, translated from the German original by Lindner:

> "When you go there, you're dead," says Ebrahim B. "I want to explain," says Ebrahim B., "not only in my city, not just in Germany and not only in Lower Saxony, not only in Europe, but worldwide, I wish that the truth becomes known." The truth about what he has experienced, the truth about the IS, the terror of the 'Islamic State.' Ebrahim B. has seen it. He was in Syria and Iraq and has voluntarily reported as suicide bomber according to the German Federal Attorney General. He is one of about 700 Germans who have joined the IS so far. But at some point it has probably done "click" for him, and has turned around.

See the German original in the full note in the pdf edition of this book.

21 Read about the psychology of terrorism in Post, 2007, and on its history in Blin and Chaliand, 2007, White, 2014, and on research on terrorism in Schmid, 2011.

22 See, among others, the work done by Ted Gurr, 1970, 1993, 2000.

23 See, among others, Stewart, 2008. Stewart explains the difference between relative deprivation and horizontal inequalities (HI), in "Horizontal Inequalities As a Cause of Conflict: A Review of CRISE Findings," by Frances Stewart, Centre for Research on Inequality, Human Security and Ethnicity, http://r4d.dfid.gov.uk/pdf/outputs/inequality/crise-overview-1.pdf: "... the HI hypothesis differs from relative deprivation in its view that the relatively rich, as well as the relatively poor, may initiate conflict. In Burundi, for example, the Tutsi have attacked the poorer Hutu; and the relatively rich area of Biafra initiated the Nigerian Civil War of the late 1960s. Such incidents seem to be motivated by fear that an existing situation is not sustainable without force and that the relative prosperity of the group is, or may be, subject to attack."

24 Kennedy, 2007. See also Khalidi, 2004.

25 "Defending Islamofascism: It's a Valid Term. Here's Why," by Christopher Hitchens, Slate, October 22, 2007, www.slate.com/articles/news_and_politics/fighting_words/2007/10/defending_islamofascism.html.

26 Holmes, 2007, p. 63.

27 Nietzsche, 1887/2013.

28 Holmes, 2007, p. 64.

29 Thomas Scheff, in a personal communication, in Oslo, Norway, on October, 23, 2002. Lower classes adopted dueling as an expression of equality in the United States by the Jacksonian Era, see Steward, 2000.

30 Gottman, et al., 1997.Wilce, 2009.

31 Etzioni, 2013.

32 Singer, et al., 2006, in their research on empathic neural responses shows that "empathy-related responses were significantly reduced in males when observing an unfair person receiving pain." Abstract: "This effect was accompanied by increased activation in reward-related areas, correlated with an expressed desire for revenge. We conclude that in men (at least) empathic responses are shaped by valuation of other people's social behavior, such that they empathize with fair opponents while favoring the physical punishment of unfair opponents, a finding that echoes recent evidence for altruistic punishment."

33 Lindner, 2000a.

34 Volkan, 2004. See also Volkan, 1997.

35 See note 138 in Chapter 1.

36 "Neighbour Quarrels Hit New Extreme," by Nina Berglund, News in English, April 11, 2014, www.newsinenglish.no/2014/04/11/neighbour-quarrels-hit-new-extreme/. See also Lindner, 2011, or Lindner, 2014c.

37 Matsumoto, 1988, and Ide, 1989. It is a privilege to have David Matsumoto as esteemed member in the global advisory board of our Human Dignity and Humiliation Studies fellowship.

38 Ho, 1976. It is a privilege to have David Yau Fai Ho as esteemed member in the global advisory board of our Human Dignity and Humiliation Studies fellowship. See also his book published by our Dignity Press, Ho, 2014.

39 Victoria Fontan at the 2003 Annual Conference of Human Dignity and Humiliation Studies, September 12–13, 2003, at the Maison des Sciences de l'Homme de l'Homme, in Paris; see www.humiliationstudies.org/whoweare/annualmeeting02.php. She discusses sharaf, ihtiram, and ird also in Chapter 1 in Fontan, 2008. See also Johnson, 2001. Victoria Fontan hosted the 2006 Annual Conference of Human Dignity and Humiliation Studies, September 6–9, 2006, at the United Nations-mandated University for Peace in San José, Costa Rica; see www.humiliationstudies.org/whoweare/annualmeeting07.php. It is a

privilege to have Victoria Fontan as esteemed member in the global advisory board of our Human Dignity and Humiliation Studies fellowship.

40 Sociologist Wilhelm Heitmeyer defines three dimensions in which recognition can be attained, dimensions that follow a similar path of differentiation as that described by Victoria Fontan in Iraq, formulating them, however, in a Western context: the sociostructural dimension of material goods can generate opportunities for positional recognition, the institutional dimension of fairness and justice can offer opportunities for moral recognition, while the personal dimension can provide opportunities for emotional recognition. See, among others, Heitmeyer, et al., 2011.

41 "The Effects of Humiliation on The Economic, Socio-Cultural Rights and Access to Justice of Muslim Women in Mindanao," by Imelda Deinla, Jessica Los Baños, contribution to Terrorism and Humiliation: Why People Choose Terrorism, envisioned as a large research project in 2005, prepared by Evelin Lindner and Paul Stokes, invited by Ramesh Thakur, United Nations University (UNU), Tokyo, with nine research teams of young scholars and their academic advisors. Due to lack of finances, this project could not be realized.
I would like to thank Lourdes Quisumbing and Patricia Licuanan for their insights at the UNESCO expert meeting "Towards a Women's Agenda for a Culture of Peace," April 25–18, 1995, invited by Ingeborg Breines and supported by Betty Reardon. See also Lindner, 1999. It is a privilege to have Ingeborg Breines and Lourdes Quisumbing as esteemed members in the global advisory board of our Human Dignity and Humiliation Studies fellowship. I also thank Betty Reardon for her untiring support for our dignity work.

42 Schwartz, et al., 1984, Kingston and Wright, 2010, Appiah, 2010.

43 Alexander Hamilton, whose portrait appears on ten dollar notes, died in a duel in 1804, and Andrew Jackson, who adorns the 20 dollar bill, was seriously wounded in two duels.

44 Steward, 2000.

45 Steward, 2000.

46 Kagan, 1997. See also Hooper, 2001.

47 Goffman, 1955, Goffman, 1967.

48 Social psychologist Bert R. Brown, 1968, carried out experiments which showed that "when bargainers have been made to look foolish and weak before a salient audience, they are likely to retaliate against whoever caused their humiliation. Moreover, retaliation will be chosen despite the knowledge that doing so may require the sacrifice of all or large portions of the available outcomes," Brown, 1968, p. 119.

49 Lévinas, 1961/1969, 1982, 1985b, a.

50 "Albania's Young Blood Feud 'Hostages,'" BBC News, news.bbc.co.uk/go/pr/fr/-/2/hi/europe/7727658.stm, November 11, 2008. See other evidence relating to blood feuds in Boehm, 1987, Malcolm, 1998, or Rodina, 1999.

51 Benedict, 1946. See also Tangney, 1990, Tangney and Dearing, 2002, Tangney, et al., 1992.

52 Doi, 1973/2001.

53 Lindner, 2007b. See also Creighton, 1990, or Behrens, 2004.

54 Scholars who analyzed slavery note that sometimes a very special accommodation-resistance dialectic of obeying but not necessarily complying evolved, which allowed slaves to carve out a degree of autonomous and very distinctive culture, which eschewed the values embraced by the master class. See, for instance, Engerman and Genovese, 1975, and Smith, 1998.

55 Dower, 1999, p. 157.

56 See, among others, Patai, 1983, De Atkine, 2004. Raphael Patai's book on the Arab Mind allegedly inspired US military officials responsible for the torture and abuse of prisoners at Abu Ghraib that "Arabs

are particularly vulnerable to sexual humiliation." See "The Gray Zone: How a secret Pentagon program came to Abu Ghraib," by Seymour M. Hersh, New Yorker, Annals of National Security May 24, 2004, www.newyorker.com/magazine/2004/05/24/the-gray-zone.

57 Roland Muller, 2001, uses the Bible to introduce honor, shame, and fear-based cultures:
• guilt-innocence: mostly in the Western world.
• shame-honour: mostly in non-Western areas, such as Asia, South America and the Middle East.
• fear-power: mostly associated with Africa, and parts of South America and Asia.
See "Fear, Shame and Guilt," by Mark Naylor, Cross Cultural Impact for the 21st Century, Articles on cross-cultural issues, Bible translation etc., August 1, 2010, http://impact.nbseminary.com/89-fear-shame-and-guilt/: "... believers who seek to communicate the significance of the cross of Christ across cultural barriers will need to be aware of the cultural values and perspectives of the people they are addressing in order to discover appropriate metaphors that reveal the gospel message in a way that speaks to their felt needs. In this article, I use Roland Muller's three cultural dichotomies as a model towards analyzing cultures for the purpose of discovering an explanation of the atonement that will connect with the hearers."

58 In my work, I apply the ideal-type approach as described by sociologist Max Weber, 1904/1949. See also Coser, 1977, p. 224. See the full note in the pdf edition of this book.

59 See, among others, the work of social anthropologist and historian Anton Blok, 1972, Blok, 2001. See also "Lunch with the FT: Elisabetta Tripodi," by John Lloyd, Financial Times, January 10, 2014, https://next.ft.com/content/d41e19ce-785e-11e3-a148-00144feabdc0.
See, furthermore, Die Frauen der Mafia (Women of Ndrangheta), documentary film by Barbara Conforti, Zweites Deutsches Fernsehen, 2016, www.zdf.de/ZDFmediathek/beitrag/video/2646728/Die-Frauen-der-Mafia?bc=svp;sv0#/beitrag/video/2646728/Die-Frauen-der-Mafia, uploaded onto many YouTube channels, among others, on https://youtu.be/XDc2DHlRQ6g. See the full note in the pdf edition of this book.

60 This theory has been rejected by the Antimafia Commission "Commissione parlamentare di inchiesta sul fenomeno della criminalità organizzata mafiosa o similar," www.camera.it/_bicamerali/nochiosco.asp?pagina=/_bicamerali/leg15/antimafia/home.htm.

61 "Terror on Trial: First Hand Report on the Hofstadgroep Trial," by Emerson Vermaat, Militant Islam Monitor, December 12, 2005, www.militantislammonitor.org/article/id/1400, italics in original. I thank Petter Nesser for recommending this article to me. A young woman, Malika Shabi, wanted to testify at the Hofstadgroup trial. But then she and members of her family began to receive serious threats. A letter addressed to her arrived in the mailbox of her parents, who hated Nouredine el Fatmi and his friends. The letter ordered Shabi to change or withdraw her statement to the police. "It is not allowed for Muslims to collaborate with unbelievers, especially if it is directed against Muslims," the letter said. "Don't you fear the curse of Allah? May Allah lead you or break your back." Shabi, now only 17 years old, and her family were terrified. Although she denied it, it was a clear death threat. In court, Shabi did not want to look at the other defendants, keeping silent all the time and refusing even to answer introductory questions by the judge such as: "Is your name Malika Shabi?"

62 Hobsbawm, 2000. See also Anton Blok, http://noblebandits.asu.edu/Bio/Blok.html.

63 See an analysis of the intricacies, by Blok, 1988, with a Foreword by Charles Tilly.

64 Miller, 1993, p. 175, italics in original.

65 Miller, 1993, p. 177.

66 Lindner, 2016b.

67 Miller, 1993, endnote 3 of Chapter 5.

68 Miller, 1993, p. 177, see Elias, 1939/1994.

69 Translated by Lindner.

70 Fulbeck, 1602, p. 20, see http://babel.hathitrust.org/cgi/pt?id=osu.32437121569947;view=1up;seq=67.

71 Lindner, 2000a.

72 See note 138 in Chapter 1.

73 Sahih Muslim. Kitab al-Hajj: Hadith 159, http://sunnah.com/muslim/15/159.

74 Armstrong, 2007.

75 Scheff, 2000.

76 Emotions "are the very means by which the power game is played," Heaney, 2013, p. 358, and there are "feeling rules," which govern how to feel in different social contexts, Hochschild, 1979.
See also the work of Robert Burrowes, 2011. He writes about socialization within the dominator context in "Most Attitudes and Beliefs are Outcomes of Fear," by Robert Burrowes, Human Wrongs Watch, http://human-wrongs-watch.net/2015/07/08/most-attitudes-and-beliefs-are-outcomes-of-fear/.

77 Bourdieu, 1977.

78 Bourdieu, 1977, pp. 11–12.

79 Hebrews 12:6, revised English version. Epistle to the Hebrews, or Letter to the Hebrews, is a text of the New Testament.

80 Steward, 2000.

81 Frank, 1984. The blood eagle was a method of execution for "worthy" enemies that is sometimes mentioned in poetry and the Norse sagas, believed to have been perpetrated on King Ælla of Northumbria, Halfdan son of King Haraldr Hárfagri of Norway, King Maelgualai of Munster, and possibly Archbishop Ælfheah of Canterbury. It was performed by cutting the skin of the victim by the spine, breaking the ribs so they resembled blood-stained wings, and pulling the lungs out through the wounds in the victim's back. Salt was sprinkled in the wounds

82 Caliph Al-Musta'sim, Abbasid ruler of Baghdad, died in 1258 at the hands of Mongol Hulagu Khan, see Strange, 1900. Some accounts claim that he died by being rolled up in a rug and trampled to death by horses – rather than being beheaded – due to the belief that spilling royal blood would bring bad luck. See also Muir, 1924.

83 The Asante (Ashanti) Empire was an African Empire located in present day Ghana, Togo, and Ivory Coast, in the latter part of the 1600s, see Collins and Burns, 2007. Practitioners of sorcery and witchcraft received death not by decapitation, for their blood was not to be shed.

84 The master-slave dialectic is a famous passage by Georg Wilhelm Friedrich Hegel, 1807/1967, in his Phenomenology of Spirit/Mind (Geist in German means both, "spirit" and "mind"). Herrschaft und Knechtschaft in German can also be translated into lordship and bondage.

85 Lira, 2001, Lykes, 2001.

86 White, 1984.

87 Oberschall, 2001.

88 Wagner, 2006.

89 See also Tønnessen, 2006, or Lindner, 2006a.

90 "How Liberian Women Delivered Africa's First Female President," by Helene Cooper, New York Times, March 5, 2017, www.nytimes.com/2017/03/05/world/africa/liberia-president-ellen-johnson-sirleaf-women-voters.html. In her book on the rise of President Ellen Johnson Sirleaf of Liberia, Helene Cooper, 2017, tells the story of Liberian women waking up to the fact that their vote could liberate their country from the unimaginable brutality and all-out destructiveness of the male supremacy in their country.

91 Lindner, 2000a.

92 See, among others, "Khat in the Horn of Africa: A Scourge or Blessing?" by James Jeffrey, Inter Press Service (IPS), March 12, 2017, www.ipsnews.net/2017/03/khat-in-the-horn-of-africa-a-scourge-or-blessing/.

93 "Seven Scary Facts About Widening Gender Gap," by IPS World Desk, Inter Press Service (IPS), March 3, 2017, www.ipsnews.net/2017/03/seven-scaring-facts-about-widening-gender-gap/, reporting that "women still carry out between two to 10 times more unpaid care work than men": "Women across the globe are facing new threats, which risk dismantling decades of hard-won rights and derailing the effort to end extreme poverty, an international confederation of civil society organisations has revealed ahead of International Women's Day on March 8, 2017."

94 See a study by Alan Krueger, 2016, former chairman of the President's Council of Economic Advisers, of the opioid epidemic in America, where roughly 7 million men, nearly half of all prime working-age male labor-force dropouts, currently take pain medication on a daily basis. According to American Time Use Surveys by the Bureau of Labor Statistics (www.bls.gov/tus/) the majority of these prime-age un-working men do not contribute to civil society work either: "Their routine, instead, typically centers on watching – watching TV, DVDs, Internet, hand-held devices, etc. – and indeed watching for an average of 2,000 hours a year, as if it were a full-time job." See "Our Miserable 21st Century," by Nicholas N. Eberstadt, Commentary Magazine, February 15, 2017, www.commentarymagazine.com/articles/our-miserable-21st-century/. See also Eberstadt, 2016: "Some of these gnawing problems are by no means new: A number of them (such as family breakdown) can be traced back at least to the 1960s, while others are arguably as old as modernity itself (anomie and isolation in big anonymous communities, secularization and the decline of faith). But a number have roared down upon us by surprise since the turn of the century – and others have redoubled with fearsome new intensity since roughly the year 2000."

95 As the phrase "status zero," or "Status Zer0," has negative connotation, it became replaced by "NEET," or "neet," meaning a young person who is "Not in Education, Employment, or Training." See, among others, Attewell and Newman, 2010.

96 "America's 'Quiet Catastrophe': Millions of Idle Men," by George F. Will, Washington Post, October 5, 2016, www.washingtonpost.com/opinions/americas-quiet-catastrophe-millions-of-idle-men/2016/10/05/cd01b750-8a57-11e6-bff0-d53f592f176e_story.html.

97 "Fundamentalism and Populism Pose Deepening Threat to Women Human Rights Defenders, UN Experts Warn," United Nations News Centre, November 25, 2016, www.un.org/apps/news/story.asp?NewsID=55645#.WDniRH2OWgx

98 I saw Guilleme Tell at the Metropolitan Opera in New York City, see the program on www.metopera.org/metoperafiles/season/2016-17/operas/guillaume_tell/programs/102916%20Tell.pdf.

99 The libretto of Guillaume Tell by Gioachino Rossini in English: www.murashev.com/opera/Guillaume_Tell_libretto_English_Act_2. See the French original at http://opera.stanford.edu/Rossini/GuillaumeTell/acte2.html: "Mathilde: 'Dans celle qui t'aime, Oui, c'est l'honneur même Qui dicte sa loi.' Arnold: 'Dans celle que j'aime, Oui, c'est l'honneur même Qui dicte sa loi.'"

100 Lindner, 2016b.

101 Composer Giacomo Puccini (1858 – 1924) based his opera Turandot on Friedrich Schiller's 1801 adaptation of an earlier text by Carlo Gozzi, with the original story going back to twelfth-century Persian poet Nizami.

102 Göle, 2013, book description: "Göle sees the best hope for a modern and European Islam in the Muslim women who--in contrast to the men--demonstrate their commitment to their heritage by wearing head scarfs while participating in modern Western life. In manifesting their professional and public experience in their own communities, they become the agents of change and modernism. Göle thus sees European Islam as "feminine," in contrast to the male-dominated traditional Islam."

103 Lindner and Desmond Tutu (Foreword), 2010.

104 I saw Aida at the Metropolitan Opera in New York City several times, among others, on November 5, 2016. See the program on www.metopera.org/metoperafiles/season/2016-17/operas/aida/programs/110516 Aida.pdf.

105 According to Helen Fisher, 2009, "explorers" express dopamine and tend to be risk-taking, curious, creative, impulsive, optimistic and energetic, while "builders" express the serotonin system and tend to be cautious but not fearful, calm, traditional, community-oriented, persistent and loyal. "Directors" express the testosterone system and tend to be analytical, decisive, tough-minded, debate-oriented, possibly aggressive, while "negotiators," both men or women, express the estrogen system and tend to be broadminded imaginative, compassionate, intuitive, verbal, nurturing, altruistic and idealistic.

106 Lindner and Desmond Tutu (Foreword), 2010. According to primatologist Frans de Waal, bonobos "make love, not war," in contrast to chimpanzees, who "use violence to get sex, while bonobos use sex to avoid violence." Bonobos, previously known as "pygmy chimpanzees," are among the most sexual of all living animals. Sexual activity connects not just males and females, more importantly, females build coalitions among themselves, which enable them to contain male supremacy and aggressiveness. The fundamental difference between Homo sapiens' two closest relatives, bonobos and chimpanzees, is "that one resolves sexual issues with power, while the other resolves power issues with sex," de Waal, 2005, p. 19. De Waal suggests that bonobo females are able to contain males because bonobos live in ecological niches that offer more resources, while female chimpanzees tend to be alone when they come across males. See Clay, et al., 2016. I highly appreciated meeting Frans de Waal, and listening to his talk Empathy and Emotional Communication: Primate Origins, in Freie Universität Berlin, April 11, 2011. See also note 2 in Chapter 1.

107 Howard Richards in Lecture Twelve of Beyond Foucault: The Rise of Indigenous Subjugated Knowledges, given in Pretoria, South Africa, May 26, 2013, http://youtu.be/voUdwSZPAR0. See for more Richards, et al., 2015a. It is a privilege to have Howard Richards as esteemed member in the global advisory board of our Human Dignity and Humiliation Studies fellowship.

108 "Hanzai rosire no chishiki" (I.e savoie comme crime), interview with Shugi Terayama, translated by Ryoji Nakamura from Japanese into French, Jyôkyô, April 1976, pp. 43–50, reprinted in Foucault, 1994b, pp. 79–86, p. 85. Translated from French by Lindner. See the French original in the full note in the pdf edition of this book. See also Richards, et al., 2015a.

109 "Technologies of the Self" (Les techniques de soi), University of Vermont, October 1982, translated by F. Durant-Bogaert, in Hutton, et al., 1988, pp. 16–49, translated into French and reprinted in Foucault, 1994a, pp. 783–813, p. 785. See also Richards, et al., 2015a.

110 "L'éthique du souci de soi comme pratique de la liberté," interview with H. Becker, R. Fornet-Betancourt, A. Gomez-Müller, January 20, 1984, Concordia. Revista Internacional de Filosofía, Number 6, July-December 1984, pp. 99–116. Translated and reprinted in Foucault, 1994a, pp. 708–729, p. 727. Translated by Howard Richards and Evelin Lindner from the French original. See the French original in the full note in the pdf edition of this book. See also Richards, et al., 2015a.

111 Weininger, 1903. In Weininger's last diary entries he wrote: "Der Haß gegen die Frau ist nichts anderes als der Haß gegen die eigene, noch nicht überwundene Sexualität." Or, "The hatred of women is none other than the hatred of one's own, not yet overcome sexuality." In other words, in the spirit of the correspondence bias, amorality is attributed by Weininger to women without considering that they may only appear to him to be "anti-moral" due to the systemic pressures they had to adapt to for centuries. Weininger's own sexuality (together with his Jewish background) falls thus prey to a sad misattribution unnecessarily, one may conclude.

112 Nietzsche, 1883–1891, www.gutenberg.org/cache/epub/7205/pg7205.txt: "Alles am Weibe ist ein Räthsel, und Alles am Weibe hat Eine Lösung: sie heisst Schwangerschaft. Der Mann ist für das Weib ein

Mittel: der Zweck ist immer das Kind. Aber was ist das Weib für den Mann? Zweierlei will der ächte Mann: Gefahr und Spiel. Desshalb will er das Weib, als das gefährlichste Spielzeug. Der Mann soll zum Kriege erzogen werden und das Weib zur Erholung des Kriegers: alles Andre ist Thorheit. ... "Du gehst zu Frauen? Vergiss die Peitsche nicht!" – Also sprach Zarathustra."

113 "Negative Religious Views of Women," compiled by Eva Maria Räpple, professor of philosophy and religious studies at College of DuPage, Glen Ellyn IL, www.cod.edu/PEOPLE/FACULTY/raepple/Religion%20Global/Negative%20Religious%20Views%20of%20 Women.htm:

- Hinduism: It is the nature of women to seduce men in this (world); for that reason, the wise are never unguarded in the (company of) females. For women are able to lead astray in (this) world not only a fool, but even a learned man, and (to make) him a slave of desire and anger. (When creating them) Manu allotted women (a love of their) bed (of their) seat and (their) ornaments, impure desires, wrath, dishonesty, malice, and bad conduct. See Laws of Manu, translator G. Buhler. Sacred books of the East, volume 25. Oxford: Clarendon Press, 1886, 2:213, p. 69; 9:14, p. 330.
- Theravada Buddhism: "How are we to conduct ourselves, Lord, with regard to womankind?" "As not seeing them, Ananda." "But if we should see them, what should we do?" "No talking, Ananda." "But if they should speak to us, Lord, what are we to do?" "Keep wide awake, Ananda." See Maha Parinnibana Suttana, 5:9, Digha Nikaya 2:141, in Rhys Davids, Dialogues of the Buddha, Volume 2, p. 154.
- Mahayana Buddhism: You should know that when men have close relationships with women, they have close relationships with evil ways.... Fools lust for women like dogs in heat... Women can ruin the precepts of purity. They can also ignore honor and virtue. Causing one to go to hell, they prevent rebirth in heaven. Why should a wise delight in them? See the Speech of the Buddha to King Udayana, from the Mahratnakuta, quote in Paul, Women in Buddhism, pp. 30, 31, 41–42.
- Christianity: Do you not all know that each of you (Women) is also an Eve? ...You are the Devil/s gateway, you are the unsealer of the forbidden tree, you are the first deserter of the divine law, you are the one who persuaded him who the devil was too weak to weak to attack. How easily you destroyed man, the image of God! Because of the death which you brought upon us, even the Son of God had to die. See Tertullian, Church Father, in De Cultu Feminarum 1:1, quote in D. Bailey, The Man Woman Relation.
- Islam: Men are the maintainers of women because Allah has made some of them to excel others and because they spend out of their property; the good women are therefore obedient, guarding the unseen as Allah has guarded; and (as to) those on whose part you fear desertion, admonish them, and leave them alone in the sleeping-places and beat them; then if they obey you, do not seek a way against them; surely Allah is High, Great. See the Koran, translator M. H. Shakir; Electronic Text Center, University of Virginia (10/19/01), http://etext.virginia.edu/koran.html, 4:34.

See also Räpple, 2010.

114 Translated from German by Lindner, see the original German text in Bruhns, 2014, p. 68. See the German original in the full note in the pdf edition of this book.

115 "Where Are the Women? How the UN is Falling Short on Gender and Conflict," by Louise Bosetti and Hannah Cooper, United Nations University, Centre for Policy Research, November 17, 2015, http://cpr.unu.edu/where-are-the-women-how-the-un-is-falling-short-on-gender-and-conflict.html. See also "Preventing Conflict, Transforming Justice, Securing the Peace: Global Study on UNSC Resolution 1325," by Radhika Coomaraswamy, UN Women, http://wps.unwomen.org/~/media/files/un%20women/wps/highlights/unw-global-study-1325-2015.pdf.

116 "Women's Progress Uneven, Facing Backlash – UN Rights Chief," by the IPS World Desk, Inter Press Service (IPS), www.ipsnews.net/2017/03/womens-progress-uneven-facing-backlash-un-rights-chief/.

117 See note 156 in Chapter 1.

118 Rush: NFL Wearing Pink For Breast Cancer Proves There's A National Assault On Masculinity. Limbaugh: "The Chickification Of Everything Is Taking Place... Feelings Are Triumphing Over Common Sense," in the October 24 edition of Premiere Radio Networks' The Rush Limbaugh Show, 2013, http://mediamatters.org/video/2013/10/24/rush-nfl-wearing-pink-for-breast-cancer-proves/196580.

119 "Violence Against Women: Positive Peace," by Johan Galtung, TRANSCEND Media Service, March 27, 2017, www.transcend.org/tms/2017/03/violence-against-women-positive-peace/.

120 Lindner and Desmond Tutu (Foreword), 2010, Goldstein, 2001.

121 Hartmann and Burkart, 2007.

122 See also Islamist im Staatsauftrag, documentary film, 2015, Zweites Deutsches Fernsehen, www.zdf.de/zdfinfo/islamist-im-staatsauftrag-40414950.html. This documentary features Irfan Peci, once one of the main Salafist propagandists in Germany, before he was imprisoned and persuaded to become one of the main informants of the intelligence agency. See the full note in the pdf edition of this book.

123 Ein Sommer im Dschihad, documentary film by Panorama, Norddeutscher Rundfunk, July 28, 2015, www.daserste.de, https://youtu.be/7eDbRhP5Ky4. See the full note in the pdf edition of this book.

124 Bourdieu, 1998.

125 Lindner, 2004b.

126 Phang, 2008. For Greek, Persian, or Roman troops, for instance, if a town refused to surrender through negotiations and had to be taken by force, mass rape, not only of women, was often felt to be a rightful punishment.

127 "Stop Rape Before India Becomes a Replica of the Middle Ages," by Stephen Gill, January 11, 2013, http://journalismandwomen.blogspot.no/2013/01/stop-rape-before-india-becomes-replica.html. See also www.stephengill.ca; stephengillcriticism.info.

128 "Denis Mukwege: It Is Time We All Acknowledged Rape as War Weapon Destroys Humanity," by Ludovica Iaccino, International Business Times, February 11, 2016, www.ibtimes.co.uk/denis-mukwege-it-time-we-all-acknowledged-rape-war-weapon-destroys-humanity-1542629. See, furthermore, "Sexual Violence in Conflict 'Legitimate Threat' to Peace and Security – Un Deputy Chief," United Nations News Centre, May 15, 2017, www.un.org/apps/news/story.asp?NewsID=56758#.WRuz2OvygkI.

129 Taylor, et al., 2002.

130 Tacitus, 1942. Senator and a historian of the Roman Empire Publius (or Gaius) Cornelius Tacitus circa 56 – after 117 CE) wrote two major works, the Annals and the Histories, that span the history of the Roman Empire from the death of Augustus in CE 14 to the years of the First Jewish–Roman War in CE 70.

131 I have also frequently heard, for instance, in Somalia, that female circumcision began with the pharaohs of Egypt, as early as the Third Dynasty (3000 – 2800 BCE), that a princess forced this practice on her potential rival females to protect her position with the pharaoh by making it more difficult for him to access those rivals. The term "pharaonic circumcision" is used throughout the Middle East and it describes a full infibulation which means the total removal of the external genitalia, and suturing to a tiny hole which allows for urination, but must then be cut open for sex. See also I min mors navn, documentary film by Hilde Merete Haug, featuring Farhia Luul Makerow, NRK, 2017, www.nrk.no/presse/programomtaler/i-min-mors-navn-1.13333391. See, furthermore, The Dream of Knowledge, a documentary film by Gerd Inger Polden, NRK, 1999, which documents how the discontinuation of the practice of female genital cutting in a number of Senegalese villages is being achieved not as a result of applying pressure or punishment, but voluntarily. See the full note in the pdf edition of this book. It is a privilege to have Gerd Inger Polden as esteemed member in the global advisory board of our Human Dignity and Humiliation Studies fellowship.

132 For mate guarding and sperm competition, see, among others, Wigby and Chapman, 2004, or Elias, et al., 2014.

133 Seyran Ateş, 2009, is a German lawyer and Muslim feminist born in Istanbul, Turkey, of Kurdish descent. She received death threats for her work in Germany, and had to go into hiding for certain periods.

134 Lindner, 2000a, p. 149.

135 Lindner and Desmond Tutu (Foreword), 2010, pp. 84–88. See more in note 52 in the Introduction.

136 See Lindner and Desmond Tutu (Foreword), 2010, Gender, Humiliation, and Global Security, p. 79:

> "Indeed, for a woman, being alone with an unrelated man is expected to risk leading to unfaithfulness almost by design. Zina, in Islam, means extramarital and premarital sex, for which Islamic law prescribes harsh punishments. In the Islamic state of Mauritania, for instance, rape is not defined in the country's law. Victims of rape remain silent, because, for a woman to allege she has been raped is to run the risk of imprisonment for zina. She will be accused of having provoked the situation and having tempted the man into sex. If she gets pregnant, this will be taken as proof that she consented, because it is regarded to be biologically impossible to become pregnant through rape. Although their legality is disputed, punishments for zina are still practiced. The documentary film Women on the Frontline provides an impressive account of this practice."

See also Karamah – Muslim Women Lawyers for Human Rights, 2008.

137 Fontan, 2001, p. 7. See also Al-Khayyat, 1990.

138 "Saudi Blood Money Ruling Angers Activists," Al Jazeera, February 4, 2013, www.aljazeera.com/news/middleeast/2013/02/201323223618362435.html.

139 See, among others, Gilbert, 1998.

140 See note 19 in the Introduction to Section Two.

141 First step: her body represents his honor. Second step: if her body is severed, his honor is severed. Third step: the correspondence bias makes him believe that she is the source of this violation, therefore she must have intended it. Fourth step: punishing her. Fifth step: punishing her beyond all limits, in the spirit of Jimmy Jones' ethical exemption syndrome.

142 "State Department: Sexual Abuse of Boys on the Rise in Afghanistan," by Melanie Hunter, CNS News, March 19, 2014, http://cnsnews.com/news/article/melanie-hunter/state-department-sexual-abuse-boys-rise-afghanistan. See also U.S. Army Human Terrain Team (HTT) AF-6, 2009, and Afghanistan 2013 Human Rights Report, U.S. Department of State, Bureau of Democracy, Human Rights, and Labor, Washington, DC, www.state.gov/documents/organization/220598.pdf.

143 Afghanistan 2013 Human Rights Report, U.S. Department of State, Bureau of Democracy, Human Rights, and Labor, Washington, DC, www.state.gov/documents/organization/220598.pdf, p. 44.

144 "Bacha Bazi: An Afghan Tragedy," by Chris Mondloch, Foreign Policy Magazine, October 28, 2013, http://southasia.foreignpolicy.com/posts/2013/10/28/an_afghan_tragedy_why_rampant_pedophilia_is_a_hurdle_to_peace.

145 Human Terrain Team (HTT) AF-6: Research Update and Findings, Pashtun Sexuality, U.S. Army, with personal field notes by Human Terrain Team AF-6, which was assigned to the 2nd Marine Expeditionary Battalion and co-located with British forces in Lashkar Gah, dated May 15, 2009, https://info.publicintelligence.net/HTT-PashtunSexuality.pdf, p. 4.

146 Ibid., p. 13.

147 The Malala Fund, www.malala.org.

148 Lindner and Desmond Tutu (Foreword), 2010, p. 32.

149 "The ISIS Crackdown on Women, by Women," by Kathy Gilsinan, The Atlantic, July 25, 2014, www.theatlantic.com/international/archive/2014/07/the-women-of-isis/375047/.

150 Deeyah Khan's witness account is illustrative, see "Deeyah Khan: Solidarity Doesn't Cost Anything," published on October 31, 2014, on YouTube (unlisted), where Deeyah Khan, born in Norway to immigrant parents from Afghanistan and Pakistan, shares how she was targeted by members of her own immigrant community in Norway and then also in the UK, as a young musician. And she explains her motivation for telling the story of Banaz, a young girl, who was killed, see her documentary film Banaz: A Love Story, 2012, at https://youtu.be/VepuyvhHYdM.

151 "Online Harassment of Women Isn't Just a Gamer Problem," by Noah Berlatsky, Pacific Standard: The Science of Society, September 15, 2014, www.psmag.com/navigation/books-and-culture/online-harassment-women-isnt-just-gamer-problem-90518/. See also "'Legitimate Rape' Rarely Leads to Pregnancy, Claims US Senate Candidate," by Matt Williams, The Guardian, August 19, 2012, www.theguardian.com/world/2012/aug/19/republican-todd-akin-rape-pregnancy. Republican U.S. Senate candidate Representative Todd Akin of Missouri stated that pregnancy rarely occurs as a result of what he called "legitimate rape."

152 Rune Øygard (born 1959) represented the Norwegian Labour Party, and served as Mayor of Vågå from 1995 to 2012. On December 17, 2012, he was found guilty of child sexual abuse, including sexual intercourse with a 13-year old girl, and sentenced to 4 years imprisonment.

153 El-Zanaty, et al., 1996. See the graphical presentation of the statistical results of women accepting beatings also at www.unfpa.org/swp/2005/english/ch7/index.htm#fig5. See, furthermore, "Violence Against Women in Egypt," a report prepared for the Committee on the Elimination of Discrimination against Women, 24th session, January 15–February 2, 2001, by Carin Benninger-Budel, www.omct.org/pdf/VAW/EgyptEng2001.pdf. See also "Social Statistics in Egypt," presented by Bothaina El Deeb at the Expert Group Meeting on Setting the Scope of Social Statistics, convened by the United Nations Statistics Division, in collaboration with the Siena Group on Social Statistics, May 6–9, 2003, unstats.un.org/unsd/Demographic/meetings/egm/Socialstat_0503/docs/no_32.pdf.

154 "UN Sounds Alarm to End 'Global Pandemic' of Violence Against Women," UN News Centre, November 25, 2014, www.un.org/apps/news/story.asp?NewsID=49443#.VHaVQ8l5VhW.

155 "Jimmy Carter Addresses Issues of Human Rights," by Annie Schugart, The Crimson, November 20, 2014, www.thecrimson.com/article/2014/11/20/carter-discusses-human-rights/.

156 Lindner, 2012f, p. 192.

157 Anderson, 2008.

158 "Berkshire Hathaway's Annual Report to Shareholders" in 2002, www.berkshirehathaway.com/2002ar/2002ar.pdf.

159 "Re-define," keynote speech by Sony Kapoor, May 14, 2009, Deutscher Gewerkschaftsbund (DGB)-Kapitalismuskongress, Berlin, Germany, May 14–15, 2009. Sony Kapoor is a former investment banker and derivatives trader in India, the UK, and the United States. See his witness accounts in various media. Re-Define is a non-partisan, international think tank, of which Kapoor is the managing director, see http://re-define.org.
See also Lindner and Desmond Tutu (Foreword), 2010, p. 56. See, furthermore, Anderson, 2008, and "Share Traders More Reckless Than Psychopaths, Study Shows," Spiegel Online International, September 26, 2011, www.spiegel.de/international/Zeitgeist/0,1518,788462,00.html.

160 Martin Husamuddin Mayer is an ethnologist and Islamic scholar from Germany, who, through long journeys through North and West Africa converted to the Muslim faith. He has worked among others as a pastor for the Muslims in the youth detention center in Wiesbaden.

161 "Vom deutschen Jugendknast in den Heiligen Krieg: Als Versager und Krimineller hinein, als Fundamentalist wieder raus: Deutsche Gefängnisse bieten einen Nährboden für religiösen Radikalismus," by Marina Kormbaki, Hannoversche Allgemeine, September 24, 2014, www.haz.de/Nachrichten/Politik/Deutschland-Welt/Terrorismus-Vom-deutschen-Jugendknast-in-den-Heiligen-Krieg: "Strafgefangene sind die ideale Klientel für religiös-extremistische Rekrutierer, weil sie die Hemmschwelle zur Gewalt schon überschritten haben."

162 Ibid. See the full note in the pdf edition of this book.

163 Violence Prevention Networks, Berlin, Germany, www.violence-prevention-network.de/home.

164 "Extremisten sind antireligiös," Thomas Mücke, interviewed by Stefanie Reulmann, heute.de, September 19, 2014, www.heute.de/interview-mit-thomas-muecke-vom-violence-prevention-network-ueber-die-zunehmende-radikalisierung-muslimischer-jugendlicher-35059684.html. See the original German text in the full note in the pdf edition of this book.

165 In German: "prekäre Anerkennungsverhältnisse," see also Mansel and Heitmeyer, 2009.

166 Heitmeyer, et al., 1997. See also Kaddor, 2015, who dissects the motives of the about 550 German "foreign fighters," the youngest of them thirteen years old, who have left Germany until 2015, mainly to join Da'esh.

167 Mansour, 2015.

168 Gary Barker has carried out research on engaging men and boys in the Balkans, Brazil, South Asia, Sub-Saharan Africa, Central America, the Caribbean and the US, including in post-conflict settings. He holds a doctorate in child and adolescent development and a master's degree in public policy. He has been awarded an Ashoka Fellowship and a fellowship from the Open Society Institute for his work. Read more of his biographical background in the full note in the pdf edition of this book.

169 Barker, 2005.

170 Juergensmeyer, 2000, p. ix. See also Vambheim, 2011.

171 "Gender, Class, and Terrorism," by Michael Kimmel, XY (a website focused on men, masculinities, and gender politics), July 10, 2009, www.xyonline.net/content/gender-class-and-terrorism. It is a privilege to have Michael Kimmel as esteemed member in the global advisory board of the Human Dignity and Humiliation Studies fellowship.

172 See note 18 in this Chapter 6.

173 "Jihad Masculinity," by Deeyah Khan, Huffington Post, July 10, 2015, www.huffingtonpost.co.uk/deeyah-khan/jihad-deeyah-khan_b_7770578.html?utm_hp_ref=uk. It is a privilege to have Deeyah Khan as esteemed member in our Human Dignity and Humiliation Studies fellowship.

174 Refsdal, 2010.

175 Urix spesial: Dugma – knappen til paradise, Aktualitetsmagasin fra NRKs utenriksredaksjon (Actuality Magazine from NRK's foreign editorial), NRK2, March 16, 2016, https://tv.nrk.no/program/NNFA53031616/urix-spesial-dugma-knappen-til-paradiset. Translated from Norwegian by Lindner. See it in the full note in the pdf edition of this book.

176 "The Science Behind ISIL's Savagery," by Ian Robertson, The Telegraph, September 14, 2014, www.telegraph.co.uk/comment/11041338/The-science-behind-Isils-savagery.html. Ian Robertson is professor of psychology at Trinity College Dublin, and was the founding director of Trinity College Institute of Neuroscience.

177 De Dreu, et al., 2011.

178 De Dreu, et al., 2011.

179 Fraiman, 2003.

180 Fraiman, 2003, xi, xii.

181 Jones, 2009. See also "When Nothing Is Cool," in note 98 in the Preface.

182 Lindner, 2016b.

183 See Krueger, 2017. And see an endorsement of the argument that terrorism does not follow from poverty, but from lack of freedom, in "The Roots of Terrorism," by Sultan Mehmood, Dawn, March 3, 2016, www.dawn.com/news/796177/the-roots-of-terrorism. See more in note 316 in the Introduction.

184 "Overcompensation Nation: It's Time to Admit that Toxic Masculinity Drives Gun Violence," by Amanda Marcotte, Salon, June 13, 2016, www.salon.com/2016/06/13/overcompensation_nation_its_time_to_admit_that_toxic_masculinity_drives_gun_violence/. I thank Linda Hartling for making me aware of this article.

185 Lee, 2015.

186 Lindner, 2000a.

187 Ahmed, 2013.

188 See also "Terror: The Hidden Source," by Malise Ruthven, The New York Reviews of Books, October 24, 2013, www.nybooks.com/articles/archives/2013/oct/24/terror-hidden-source/.

189 See also de Ste. Croix, et al., 2004.

190 Donald J. Trump twittered from his account @realDonaldTrump: "The concept of global warming was created by and for the Chinese in order to make U.S. manufacturing non-competitive." See https://twitter.com/realdonaldtrump/status/265895292191248385?lang=en.

191 Jean-Paul Sartre, 1960, in his book Critique of Dialectical Reason, develops a philosophy of revolution in terms of the wills of subjective consciousness. See also Discussion 8 in Richards, et al., 2015a.

192 Watching the 2002 film Die SS, by Christian Deick and Annette von der Heyde, makes palpable the depth of dedication and feeling of empowerment that the SS mustered to elicit in some of its members, who were proud of being important fighters, rather than mere cannon fodder: "Wir waren Hitleristen! Meine Ehre heißt Treue!" See www.new-video.de/film-guido-knopp-ss/.

193 See also Petersen, 2002.

194 See, among others, Berlant, 2005, or Laclau, 2005.

195 Zehnpfennig, 2016, Abstract. See also Forschungsobjekt "Mein Kampf," talk by Barbara Zehnpfennig, Bayrischer Rundfunk, December 12, 2016, www.br.de/fernsehen/ard-alpha/sendungen/logos/forschungsprojekt-mein-kampf-100.html. See, furthermore, the new commented edition of Hitler's Mein Kampf, Hartmann, et al., 2016. See the full note in the pdf edition of this book.

196 "Demütigung ohne Scham, als Rächer! 'Morden im Rampenlicht'," by Martin Altmeyer, Spiegel Online, 31/2016, July 30, 2016, www.spiegel.de/spiegel/inszenierung-von-groessenwahn-essay-von-martin-altmeyer-a-1105637.html: Was treibt Amokläufer, und woher kommt der Hass der Islamisten? Psychoanalytiker Martin Altmeyer über die öffentliche Inszenierung von Allmacht und Größenwahn.

197 "A Guide for the Perplexed: Intellectual Fallacies of the War on Terror," by Chalmers Johnson, TomDispatch.com, October 22, 2007, www.alternet.org/story/65838/bush%27s_response_to_9_11_was_deadlier_than_the_attacks_themselves, a review of Stephen Holmes (2007). See more in note 66 in Chapter 5.

198 Peace psychologist Daniel J. Christie, in a personal communication to peace linguist Francisco Gomes de Matos, December 28, 2012. Both are esteemed members in the global advisory board of the Human Dignity and Humiliation Studies fellowship.

199 The email was sent out by Former U.S. Ambassador to the United Nations, John Bolton, on March 12, 2014. See the full note in the pdf edition of this book. I highly respect the depth of his conviction. See also Chapter 13.

200 The concept of locus of control was developed by Julian B. Rotter in 1954, see Rotter, 1954.

201 One example among many is described in "The New and Ancient Story: Reflections on Damanhur (Part 1)," by Charles Eisenstein, Charles' Main Website, August 2, 2015, www.thenewandancientstory.net/home/reflections-on-damanhur-part-1.

202 The tradition of painfully twisted deformed feet began late in the Tang Dynasty (618 – 906) and flourished until it was finally outlawed in the 1911 Revolution of Sun Yat-Sen. It began as a luxury among the rich but soon spread throughout society. For an entire millennium, millions of young Chinese women paid with a painful life to serve the honor of their husbands. The women were reduced to the status of dependent and helpless toys through this practice, while their husbands gained honorable status by imitating their elite. Howard Levy, 1992, describes the torturous details of feet bones being repeatedly broken, their growth stunted, to fit into the desired lotus shape.

203 Christopher K. Chung and Samson J. Cho, 2006.

204 Ninnemann, 2015.

205 "That Other School Shooting," by Jay Caspian Kang, New York Times, March 28, 2013, www.nytimes.com/2013/03/31/magazine/should-it-matter-that-the-shooter-at-oikos-university-was-korean.html?pagewanted=all&_r=0. See also "Korean Rage: Stereotype or Real Issue?" by Winston Chung MD, April 10, 2012, http://blog.sfgate.com/wchung/2012/04/10/korean-rage-stereotype-or-real-issue/.

206 "Examining Anger in 'Culture-Bound' Syndromes," by Sandra L. Somers, Psychiatric Times, January 01, 1998, www.psychiatrictimes.com/cultural-psychiatry/examining-anger-culture-bound-syndromes.

207 Lindner, 2009b, pp. 26–27.

208 The (MAOA) gene (also called "warrior gene") is located on the X chromosome. A meta-study shows that both the serotonin transporter gene (5HTTLPR) and the 30 base pair variable number of tandem repeats of the monoamine oxidase A gene (MAOA-uVNTR) were significantly associated with antisocial behavior, see Ficks and Waldman, 2014.

209 Demas, et al., 1999, Stevenson and Rillich, 2015.

210 For the link between masculinity and violence, see, for example, Breines, et al., 2000, Connell, 1996, Connell, 2005, Goldstein, 2001, Whitehead, 2002, Wrangham and Peterson, 1996, Zalewski and Parpat, 1998. Connell and Messerschmidt, 2005 have recently refined their presentation of the nature of gender hierarchy, the geography of masculine configurations, the process of social embodiment, and the dynamics of masculinities. See also "Reducing Men's Violence: The Personal Meets the Political," by Michael S. Kimmel, paper presented at the expert group meeting "Male Roles and Masculinities in the Perspective of a Culture of Peace," Oslo, Norway, September 24–28, 1997. It was a great privilege for me to be invited by Ingeborg Breines to this the expert group meeting and meet in person eminent scholars such as Michael Kimmel and Robert W., later Raewyn Connell. It is a privilege to have many scholars working in this field as esteemed members in our Human Dignity and Humiliation Studies fellowship.

211 Harter, et al., 2003, p. 312. Harter, et al., 2003, investigated 12 high-profile school shooters, all of whom described having experienced profound humiliation; they had been ridiculed, taunted, teased, harassed, and bullied by peers, spurned by someone they had been romantically interested in, put down publically by a teacher or school administrator. I thank Clark McCauley, 2017, for making me aware of this study.

212 Langman, 2015. On July 22, 2016, a teenage shooter killed nine people and injured 27 in a mass shooting in Munich, Germany. He was impressed by Norwegian mass shooter Anders Behring Breivik. Langman's book was found at his home, which he seemed to have studied in preparation for his deed, see "Munich

Shooting," by Amber Jamieson, The Guardian, July 23, 2016, www.theguardian.com/world/2016/jul/23/munich-shooter-why-kids-kill-book-psychologist-peter-langman.

213 "Die Auswirkungen von Armut, Hunger und psycho-sozialer Not auf die pränatale und frühkindliche Gehirnentwicklung," by Peter Boppel, 2008, http://amnesty-heilberufe.de/wp-content/uploads/n2008-boppel.armut_gehirn.pdf. See the summary: "The results of hunger and psychological stress for the brain of the child are presented, as they are described in literature, which can influence the mother and the growing child prenatally as well as in early childhood. It shows that the worst damage takes place within the phase of growth and combination of dendrites, which is the time between descent and the third/fourth year of life. These damages can be very drastic and even irreversible in some cases. It is discussed, whether malnutrition and psychological stress can rather lead to depressive disorder zones in female bodies while in male bodies they could rather lead to borderline disorder zones. For men, these could display an evolutive process of adaption to warrior personalities in conflict areas, while women are handicapped in their development, and, at the same time, social sorrow and misery are perpetuated."

214 See for a vivid introduction the BBC documentary film Ancient Worlds, part 3, "The Greek Thing," www.bbc.co.uk/programmes/b00w8pwp. I thank Lasse Moer for making me aware of this documentary.

215 Furor Teutonicus (Teutonic fury) is a Latin phrase generally attributed to the Roman poet Marcus Annaeus Lucanus, see Diamond, 1996.

216 Male culture, often characterized by pride of the "rational" male mind, ironically, tufts its honorable male courage on what could safely be called "irrational" abandon of this very mind. I discuss this inconsistency in my book Emotion and Conflict.

217 See Lindner, 2006c, Chapter 7: The Humiliation Addiction, in the book Making Enemies: Humiliation and International Conflict.

218 "How We Learned to Kill," by Timothy Kudo, New York Times, February 27, 2015, www.nytimes.com/2015/03/01/opinion/sunday/how-we-learned-to-kill.html. I thank Linda Hartling for making me aware of this article. See also Grossman, 1995.

219 United States Senate Select Committee on Intelligence, 2014.

220 In Seligman's original experiments, dogs "learned helplessness." See "Architects of C.I.A. Interrogation Drew on Psychology to Induce 'Helplessness,'" by Benedict Carey, New York Times, December 10, 2014, www.nytimes.com/2014/12/11/health/architects-of-cia-interrogation-drew-on-psychology-to-induce-helplessness.html?_r=0: "Nearly a half-century later, a pair of military psychologists became convinced that the theory provided a basis for brutal interrogation techniques, including waterboarding, that were supposed to eliminate detainees' 'sense of control and predictability' and induce 'a desired level of helplessness,' the Senate report said." See also Seligman, 1974. See also Hoffman, et al., 2015.

221 "The Psychologists Who Taught the C.I.A. How to Torture (and Charged $180 Million)," by Katherine Eban, Vanity Fair, December 10, 2014, www.vanityfair.com/online/daily/2014/12/psychologists-cia-torture-report: "The psychologists had previously been Air Force trainers in a program called SERE (Survival Evasion Resistance Escape), which subjected military members to mock interrogations mimicking those 'used against American servicemen during the Korean war to produce false confessions.'"

222 "Psychologist Defends Harsh CIA Interrogations," by Ken Dilanian, Huffington Post, December 25, 2014, www.huffingtonpost.com/2014/12/10/psychologist-james-mitchell-cia-torture_n_6302526.html.

223 "Two Psychologists' Role in CIA Torture Program Comes into Focus," by Joseph Tanfani and W.J. Hennigan, Los Angeles Times, December 14, 2014, www.latimes.com/world/afghanistan-pakistan/la-fg-torture-psychologists-20141214-story.html#page=1:

"In the "Salt Pit," a then-secret CIA prison in Afghanistan, John "Bruce" Jessen watched carefully in late 2002 as five agency officers rushed into a darkened cell and grabbed an Afghan detainee named Gul Rahman. "It was thoroughly planned and rehearsed," Jessen later explained, according to a CIA investigator's report. "They dragged him outside, cut off his clothes and secured him with Mylar tape," before beating him and forcing him to run wearing a hood. When he fell, they dragged him down dirt passageways, leaving abrasions up and down his body. Jessen added a critique. "After something like this is done, interrogators should speak to the prisoner to give [him] something to think about," he told the investigator. On Nov. 20, 2002, Rahman was found dead in his unheated cell. He was naked from the waist down and had been chained to a concrete floor. An autopsy concluded that he probably froze to death...On April 15, 2002, they [Jessen and Mitchell] were at a secret CIA prison in Thailand supervising an interrogation of the CIA's first Al Qaeda prisoner, Abu Zubaydah, who had been captured in Pakistan. The early interrogation was relatively benign. Zubaydah, who was recovering from gunshot wounds, was put in an all-white room with bright lights. Guards wore all black uniforms, including gloves, ski masks and goggles, and communicated only by hand signals. Loud rock music was played to "enhance his sense of hopelessness."

224 "New Poll Finds Majority of Americans Think Torture Was Justified After 9/11 Attacks," by Adam Goldman and Peyton Craighill, The Washington Post, December 16, 2014, www.washingtonpost.com/world/national-security/new-poll-finds-majority-of-americans-believe-torture-justified-after-911-attacks/2014/12/16/f6ee1208-847c-11e4-9534-f79a23c40e6c_story.html.

225 "How U.S. Torture Left Legacy of Damaged Minds," by Matt Appuzzo, Sheri Fink, and James Risen, New York Times, October 9, 2016, www.nytimes.com/2016/10/09/world/cia-torture-guantanamo-bay.html: Beatings, sleep deprivation, menacing and other brutal tactics have led to persistent mental health problems among detainees held in secret C.I.A. prisons and at Guantánamo. I thank Linda Hartling for making us aware of this article. See also the Guantánamo Testimonials Project, the Center for the Study of Human Rights in the Americas (CSHRA), with Chief investigator Professor Almerindo Ojedo, http://humanrights.ucdavis.edu/projects/the-guantanamo-testimonials-project/index. I thank Francisco Gomes de Matos for making me aware of this project.
See, furthermore, "Washington Buries the CIA Torture Report," by Patrick Martin, World Socialist Web Site, January 8, 2015, www.wsws.org/en/articles/2015/01/08/pers-j08.html: "Far from being shamed or humiliated by the detailed exposure of their criminality, those most implicated in the establishment and operation of the torture chambers have brazenly defended their conduct. … From former Vice President Dick Cheney to ex-CIA directors George Tenet, Michael Hayden and Porter Goss, to the operational head of the interrogation program, Jose Rodriguez, they have displayed a well-justified confidence that the Obama administration will protect them from any consequences."

226 O'Mara, 2015.

227 "C.I.A. First Planned Jails Abiding by U.S. Standards," by Matt Apuzzo and James Risen, New York Times, December 10, 2014, www.nytimes.com/2014/12/11/us/politics/cia-first-planned-jails-abiding-by-us-standards-.html. I thank Linda Hartling for making me aware of this article.

228 Altemeyer, 1996.

229 Altemeyer, 1996.

230 See note 221 in this Chapter 6.

231 See Megyn Kelly on Exclusive Interview with Dr. James Mitchell, Fox News, December 16, 2014, http://video.foxnews.com/v/3946118068001/megyn-kelly-on-exclusive-interview-with-dr-james-mitchell/?#sp=show-clips. Mitchell describes his fear, as he feels suddenly turned into a scapegoat. He describes his patriotism, for he has done everything because he wanted to protect America. He rejects the torture report with the argument that he was not asked. And he is a "mild torturer," who found some

conditions overdone, for example, the Ministry of Justice's waterboarding. The requirements said that every twenty seconds water must be poured over the prisoner's head under a cloth. Then the tortured could breathe once, then followed the next twenty seconds. This then goes on for twenty minutes or so. Mitchell, originally a psychologist who has done "research" on such techniques, and in the secret hideouts of the CIA applied them so frequently that no longer remembers the details, according to an interview. He now prides itself on the show to have relaxed rules: at twenty second intervals, the patient suffocates, Mitchell said, so he changed it to ten second intervals. So in a session there were ten seconds of water, then a deep breath, ten seconds of water, plus he found after careful consideration, twice twenty seconds, and only once forty seconds. Only with Sheikh Mohammed, whom Mitchell called evil and arrogant, nothing worked. He had the talent, said Mitchell, during waterboarding, to absorb the water over the nose and spit it out directly from the mouth.

232 "Scars of Bangladesh Independence War 40 Years On," by Shahzeb Jillani, South Asia Editor, BBC World Service, December 13, 2011, www.bbc.co.uk/news/world-asia-16111843.

233 Ibid.

234 Ibid.

235 The 2001 Indian Parliament attack in New Delhi on December 13, 2001, was carried out by the Lashkar-e-Taiba (Let) and Jaish-e-Mohammed (JeM) terrorist groups. Though formally banned as terrorist organization by Pakistan, experts believe that Pakistan's main intelligence agency, the Inter-Services Intelligence (ISI), continues to give LeT help and protection.

236 "Pervez Musharraf's Mixed Legacy," by Chris Morris, BBC News, Islamabad, August 18, 2008, http://news.bbc.co.uk/2/hi/south_asia/7567592.stm.

237 Shahab Ahmed and Zeb, 2016. It is a privilege to have Zahid Shahab as esteemed member in our Human Dignity and Humiliation Studies fellowship.

238 In 2016, Zahid Shahab Ahmed has joined the Alfred Deakin Institute for Citizenship and Globalization of Deakin University in Australia as a postdoctoral fellow. See, for instance, Shahab Ahmed and Zeb, 2016. See also Krueger, 2017. And see an endorsement of the argument that terrorism does not follow from poverty, but from lack of freedom, in "The Roots of Terrorism," by Sultan Mehmood, Dawn, March 3, 2016, www.dawn.com/news/796177/the-roots-of-terrorism. See more in note 316 in the Introduction.

239 Petter Nesser is a senior researcher with the Terrorism Research Group at the Norwegian Defence Research Establishment (FFI). I thank him for sharing his very deep, nuanced, and differentiated insights in a thoroughly informative conversation in Oslo on June 17, 2011. It was very enriching for me to also share with him my experiences with young clients during my years as psychological counselor in Cairo, Egypt, from 1984 to 1991. I have summarized and translated our conversation from Norwegian. See also Nesser, 2006, 2011, 2014, Tønnessen, 2006. See more in the Appendix to Section One.

240 "The Five Found Guilty Yesterday: Portrait of an Extremist Cell," The Guardian, May 1, 2007, www.theguardian.com/uk/2007/may/01/politics.terrorism.

241 Allyn, 1970.

242 Göring, 1943.

243 Lindner, 2000a.

244 Holmes, 2007, p. 82. See a review of this book in "A Guide for the Perplexed: Intellectual Fallacies of the War on Terror," by Chalmers Johnson, Asia Times Online, October 22, 2007, www.atimes.com/atimes/Middle_East/IJ24Ak01.html. See more in note 66 in Chapter 5.

245 Kaeuper and Kennedy, 1996.

246 Ayton and Preston, 2005.

247 I had the privilege of supporting Jan Brøgger with the interviews he carried out in Egypt for his book on culture, Brøgger and Halvorsen, 1993. See, among others of Foda's (or Fawda's) publications, Fawda, 1985, or Fawda, 1988. See also Soage, 2007.

248 Hamdan, 2014. See also "Inventing the Geography of Egyptian Nationalism (Watanīya): A Review of Gamal Hamdan's The Personality of Egypt and his Personal History," by Eiji Nagasawa, www2.econ.hit-u.ac.jp/~areastd/mediterranean/mw/pdf/18/16.pdf.

249 "Inventing the Geography of Egyptian Nationalism (Watanīya): A Review of Gamal Hamdan's The Personality of Egypt and his Personal History," by Eiji Nagasawa, www2.econ.hit-u.ac.jp/~areastd/mediterranean/mw/pdf/18/16.pdf.

250 "Awrāq Jamāl Hamdān" (Gamal Hamdan's Papers), Al-Musawwar, April 15, 1994, quoted in "Inventing the Geography of Egyptian Nationalism (Watanīya): A Review of Gamal Hamdan's The Personality of Egypt and his Personal History," by Eiji Nagasawa, www2.econ.hit-u.ac.jp/~areastd/mediterranean/mw/pdf/18/16.pdf.

251 Reza Pankhurst belongs to Hizb ut Tahrir, an organization founded in the 1950s to campaign for the restoration of the caliphate, while confirming to be opposed to terrorist violence, see "LSE Tutor Says He Is Victim of McCarthyite Witch-Hunt over Hizb ut-Tahrir membership," by Owen Bowcott, The Guardian, January 17, 2010, www.theguardian.com/uk/2010/jan/17/reza-pankhurst-mccarthyite-witchhunt.

252 Pankhurst, 2013.

253 Schmid, 2013, p. 54.

254 Ibid.

255 Ibid.

256 Ibid.

257 See note 118 in Chapter 5.

258 "Fighting for Next Generation, Kids File Climate Suit Against US Government," by Deirdre Fulton, Common Dreams, August 13, 2015, www.commondreams.org/news/2015/08/13/fighting-next-generation-kids-file-climate-suit-against-us-government. I thank Michael Britton for making me aware of this article. See also the first book by climate scientist James Hansen, 2009, and "Scientists Warn of Perilous Climate Shift Within Decades, Not Centuries." See more in note 46 in the Preface.

259 Historian Eric Hobsbawm, 1994, as quoted on the New Humanist blog, October 1, 2012, http://blog.newhumanist.org.uk/2012/10/eric-hobsbawm-1917-2012.html. Eric Hobsbawm was an honorary associate of the Rationalist Association and a friend to New Humanist. He contributed the quoted passage to a feature marking the 10th anniversary of 9/11.

260 I thank sociologist Dennis Smith for coining the words conquest/relegation/reinforcement/inclusion humiliation. See Smith, 2001. It is a privilege to have Dennis Smith as esteemed member in the global advisory board of our Human Dignity and Humiliation Studies fellowship, since its inception, being among the major initial nurturers of this idea even prior to its further manifestation.

261 Bourdieu, 1991, p. 51.

262 Lindner, 2001b.

263 Hellestveit, 2017.

264 I thank my friends in Crimea for their deep sharing in 2016, and honor their wish not to expose their names.

265 Marshall, 2002, pp. 2–3. It is a privilege to have Monty Marshall as esteemed member in the global advisory board of our Human Dignity and Humiliation Studies fellowship.

266 Marshall, 2002, pp. 2–3.

267 Hoffman, 1998, p. 43.

268 Wolfgang Kaleck is a civil rights attorney and the general secretary for the European Center for Constitutional and Human Rights. I had the privilege of learning from him in Berlin on May 17, 2011. See, among other publications, Kaleck, et al., 2007, and Kaleck, 2016. Kaleck's reflections are summarized and translated from German by Lindner. See more in the Appendix to Section One.

Chapter 7

1 Lindner and Desmond Tutu (Foreword), 2010.

2 Lindner and Desmond Tutu (Foreword), 2010, p. 52.

3 Syrische Flüchtlinge: Kein Asyl für Kriegsdienstverweigerer, by Arnd Henze, Das Erste, May 10, 217, www.tagesschau.de/inland/asyl-muenster-urteil-101.html: "Belehrung über 'soldatische Pflicht': Der Soldat muss die menschliche Regung der Furcht überwinden. (...) Furcht vor persönlicher Gefahr entschuldigt eine Tat nicht, wenn die soldatische Pflicht verlangt, die Gefahr zu bestehen."

4 Remy, 2002. See also Mythos Rommel, documentary film in three parts by Maurice Philip Remy, Das Erste, 2002, Der Krieger; Der Verlierer; Der Verschwörer, June 2005, https://web.archive.org/web/20031005133534/. See the full note in the pdf edition of this book.

5 Mythos Rommel, 2002 documentary film.

6 Ibid.

7 Mythos Rommel, 2002 documentary film. See a summary in German by Lindner in the full note in the pdf edition of this book.

8 Hoffmann, 1995.

9 Verräterkinder – Die Töchter und Söhne des Widerstands, documentary film by Christian Weisenborn, Das Erste, 2014, see the trailer at https://youtu.be/vmsQNMeShbI, and see also www.ardmediathek.de/tv/Dokumentationen-und-Reportagen/Verr%C3%A4terkinder/hr-fernsehen/Video?bcastId=26131780&documentId=35557026. In 1942, Weisenborn's parents (Günther and Margarete Weisenborn) were sentenced as members of the Rote Kapelle and escaped execution only by sheer luck. See https://de.wikipedia.org/wiki/Verr%C3%A4terkind. See the full note in the pdf edition of this book.

10 Matthias Erzberger sagte im Salongwagen zu einem Franzosen. "Wir werden hier nicht wie Feinde behandelt, sondern wie Abschaum." Der Franzose: "Das seid Ihr auch für mich!" See Gewaltfrieden: Die Legende vom Dolchstoß und der Vertrag von Versailles, documentary film by Bernd Fischerauer, 2010, part 1: https://youtu.be/A_6WBSL6xKc, part 2: https://youtu.be/T9owJ1wp2KA.

11 Malinowski, 2005.

12 Gilbert, 1947, Manvell and Fraenkel, 1962.

13 The exhibition "Verbrechen der Wehrmacht" created heated protests; see www.verbrechen-der-wehrmacht.de/docs/home_e.htm.

14 Internationaler Militärgerichtshof Nürnberg, 1989.

15 Posen speech, October 4, 1943, Internationaler Militärgerichtshof Nürnberg, 1989, p. 145. See the full note in the pdf edition of this book.

16 Translated from German by Lindner, see the original German text in Bruhns, 2014, p. 65: "Die Probe darauf, ob wir ein großes Kulturvolk sind, haben wir abgelegt: Menschen, die inmitten einer raffinierten Kultur leben, die dann trotzdem draußen dem Grausen des Krieges gewachsen sind (was für einen Senegal-Neger keine Leistung ist!), und die dann trotzdem so zurückkommen, so grundanständig, wie die große Mehrzahl unserer Leute, – das ist echtes Menschentum."

17 "When History Humiliates Former Enemies," by Jennifer Lind, CNN, http://edition.cnn.com/2014/01/03/opinion/lind-japan-war-memories/.

18 Terror in Mumbai, documentary film by Dan Reed for England's Channel 4 Dispatches, 2009, www.quicksilvermedia.tv/productions/production/terror-in-mumbai. Reed's reflections on his own reading of the transcripts are quoted in Kolås, 2010, p. 86.

19 Kolås, 2010, p. 85.

20 Kolås, 2010, p. 96.

21 "Proposed new Indian anti-terror laws would violate human rights," Amnesty International, December 23, 2008, www.amnesty.org/en/latest/news/2008/12/proposed-new-indian-anti-terror-laws-would-violate-human-rights-20081223/.

22 A series of coordinated terrorist attacks occurred in Paris and its northern suburb, Saint-Denis, on the evening of 13 November 2015. In the weeks leading up to the Paris attacks, Da'esh and its branches had claimed responsibility for the downing of Metrojet Flight 9268 on October 31 and the suicide bombings in Beirut on November 12, 2015

23 "Beirut, Also the Site of Deadly Attacks, Feels Forgotten," by Anne Barnard, New York Times, November 15, 2015, www.nytimes.com/2015/11/16/world/middleeast/beirut-lebanon-attacks-paris.html.

24 The suicide bombing on Sultan Ahmet Square on January 12, 2016, killed 10 people, all of them German citizens.

25 "In Outcry Over Siege, Two Indias Emerge," by Emily Wax, Washington Post, December 8, 2008, www.washingtonpost.com/wp-dyn/content/article/2008/12/08/AR2008120803685.html?sid=ST2008120900105/.

26 See Böckler, et al., 2013, and "A Study of Active Shooter Incidents in the United States Between 2000 and 2013, Unclassified," by the U.S. Department of Justice, Federal Bureau of Investigation, Washington Navy Yard, Washington, DC, September 16, 2013, www.fbi.gov/about-us/office-of-partner-engagement/active-shooter-incidents/a-study-of-active-shooter-incidents-in-the-u.s.-2000-2013. See, furthermore, "New FBI Report Casts Doubt on NRA's 'Good Guy Stops Bad Guy' Nonsense," by Mike Weisser, Huffington Post, September 29, 2014, www.huffingtonpost.com/mike-weisser/fbi-report-active-shooters_b_5900748.html: "More than half (56 percent) were terminated by the shooter who either took his or her own life, simply stopped shooting or fled the scene. Another 26 percent ended in the traditional Hollywood-like fashion with the shooter and law enforcement personnel exchanging gunfire and in nearly all of those situations the shooter ended up either wounded or dead. In 13 percent of the shooting situations, the shooter was successfully disarmed and restrained by unarmed civilians, and in 3 percent of the incidents the shooter was confronted by armed civilians, of whom four were on-duty security guards and one person was just your average 'good guy' who happened to be carrying a gun."

27 "Forget the Sex and Violence; Shame Is the Ratings Leader" by Alessandra Stanley, New York Times, November 20, 2002, www.nytimes.com/2002/11/20/arts/television/20BACH.html?pagewanted=all. I thank Carol Smaldino for reminding me of this article.

28 "Is Virtual Reality Show Addiction a Gateway Drug to the Election of Donald Trump?" by Carol Smaldino, Huffington Post, June, 28, 2016, www.huffingtonpost.com/carol-smaldino/is-virtual-reality-show-a_b_10682194.html.

29 Lindner, 2009e, pp. 138–139.

30 Lindner, 2009e, pp. 268–269.

31 Lindner, 2000i.

32 "Marsh Arab Rebellion: Grievance, Mafias and Militias in Iraq," by Juan Cole, Fourth Wadie Jwaideh Memorial Lecture, Department of Near Eastern Languages and Cultures, Indiana University, Bloomington, 2008, www-personal.umich.edu/~jrcole/iraq/iraqtribes4.pdf.
"The 'Garden of Eden' Becomes a UNESCO World Heritage Site," by J. Weston Phippen, The Atlantic, July 18, 2016, www.theatlantic.com/news/archive/2016/07/unesco-iraq-marsh/491801/.

33 "The Iraqi Campaign against the Marsh Arabs: Ecocide as Genocide," by Joseph W. Dellapenna, Jurist: The Legal Education Network, January 31, 2003, http://jurist.law.pitt.edu/forum/forumnew92.php. See also Thesiger, 1964.

34 Lindner, 2006c, p. 67.

35 Hendrix, 2008.

36 "The Lessons of Anwar al-Awlaki," by Scott Shane, New York Times, August 27, 2015, www.nytimes.com/2015/08/30/magazine/the-lessons-of-anwar-al-awlaki.html?_r=0. I thank Linda Hartling for making me aware of this article. See also Arrigo and Wagner, 2007, or Shane, 2015.

37 Saif Allah (pseudonym), "jihadi" analyst on the Risalat al-Umma forum in 2005; McCauley and Moskalenko, 2011, p. 157, Schmid, 2013, p. 3.

38 Lindner, 2006c, p. 32, Hartling, et al., 2013.

39 Seligman, 1972.

40 See note 221 in Chapter 6.

41 See note 220 in Chapter 6.

42 See note 223 in Chapter 6.

43 Lex Duodecim Tabularum, more informally simply Duodecim Tabulae. See an international survey over contemporary family law in Bainham and International Society of Family Law, 2006.

44 The Dalit Mushar (a rat-eating caste) in Bihar, or the so-called minorities in Somalia, are just two very concrete extreme contemporary examples of many, both during history and in present times.

45 "Why Is There peace?," by Steven Pinker, Greater Good Magazine, April 2009, http://greatergood.berkeley.edu/article/item/why_is_there_peace.

46 The argument of cost is relevant even nowadays. In 2009, New Mexico has outlawed executions as the 15th State in the United States. The director of the ACLU Capital Punishment Project, John Holdridge, explains that economic reasoning stood behind the ban, citing "the exorbitant cost to the taxpayers of maintaining the death penalty." This quote is to be found widely on the Internet, see, among others, at news.yahoo.com/s/afp/20090326/ts_alt_afp/usexecutionjustice.

47 Wood, 1994

48 Quataert, 2000.

49 In the classic tripartite representation, Jesus is presented as the one who judges, the one who blesses, and the one who teaches.

50 "Mann mit dem Schwert? Das Relief an der Marktkirche sorgt bei Betrachtern für Fragezeichen," Maike Schaper, Dewezet, October 17, 2014, p. 22. See the full note in the pdf edition of this book.

51 "Recovering the Doctrine of the Vengeance of God," by Thomas Dalton, January 9, 2015, www.daltonthomas.org/blog/2015/1/7/recovering-the-doctrine-of-the-vengeance-of-god.

52 Special Latin America Issue of the Peace and Conflict Monitor: Violence in Latin America and the Caribbean, April 01, 2012, see www.internationalpeaceandconflict.org/forum/topic/show?id=780588%3ATopic%3A723987&xgs=1&xg_source=msg_share_topic#.VfQ2SJfICOb. This special collection of articles was compiled for the Peace and Conflict Monitor of the United Nations mandated University for Peace (UPEACE) in Costa Rica, highlighting the problem of violence in Latin America and the Caribbean (LAC).

53 Cardenas, 2009, p. 59. See also Paley, 2014.

54 "'War on Terror' Has Indigenous People in Its Sights," by Gustavo González, Inter Press Service (IPS), June 6, 2005, www.ipsnews.net/2005/06/latin-america-war-on-terror-has-indigenous-people-in-its-sights/.

55 Cardenas, 2009, p. 60.

56 Ibid.

57 Ibid.

58 Cardenas, 2009, p. 62.

59 In the documentary film Porn On The Brain, aired on Channel 4 on September 30, 2013, presenter Martin Daubney, journalist and father of a boy of four, asks neuroscientists, therapists and educators, and also young people: Is pornography really harmful to children and young people? What scientific evidence is there? The results are that particularly young people risk not just being traumatized but having their very brain structure affected. The trauma can then be so difficult to bear that others are being hurt. Channel 4 is a British public-service television broadcaster. See also Daubney, 2015, Abstract:

> Martin Daubney is an award-winning journalist and broadcaster. He was the longest-ever serving editor of the men's magazine Loaded. However, when he became a father, he found himself reassessing his attitude to lads' magazines and pornography. The journey led to his involvement in the Channel 4 documentary Porn on the Brain, where he investigated how teenagers' pornography habits have changed, and the effect that modern pornography — its content and accessibility — is having on their brains.

See, furthermore, "Experiment that convinced me online porn is the most pernicious threat facing children today," by Martin Daubney, Daily Mail Online, September 25, 2013, www.dailymail.co.uk/femail/article-2432591/Porn-pernicious-threat-facing-children-today-By-ex-lads-mag-editor-MARTIN-DAUBNEY.html. See, furthermore, Nur Porno im Kopf, 3sat, October 16, 2014, www.3sat.de/page/?source=/wissenschaftsdoku/sendungen/178675/index.html. See the full note in the pdf edition of this book.

60 "Teen Girls Gang-Raped and Hanged from a Tree – Police," by Nita Bhalla, Reuters, May 29, 2014, http://in.reuters.com/article/2014/05/29/uk-india-killings-idINKBN0E91AI20140529.

61 Lindner, 2000i.

62 Bruce, 2010.

63 ZDF-History: Operation "Zersetzung" – Der geheime Terror der Stasi, Zweites Deutsches Fernsehen, http://history.zdf.de/ZDF/zdfportal/programdata/c5479add-a5dd-35ff-99cf-ca2843da6ec4/20189842?generateCanonicalUrl=true, see also https://youtu.be/vHJAfWtyeOo. Translated by Lindner from the German original, See the full note in the pdf edition of this book. See also Pingel-Schliemann, 2004, and Trobisch-Lütge, 2004, 2011.

64 McLuhan, 1972, p. 92.

65 Berit Ås, in a personal conversation in her home in Asker, Norway, May 31, 2014. See also Ås, 2008. See the video on Male Master Suppression Techniques that we created on May 31, 2014, in the home of Berit Ås

at http://youtu.be/mRASpPcI8hk. Berit Ås explains how she started out with five master suppression techniques and later extended them.

66 Berit Ås is professor of social science, the first female party leader in Norway (Democratic Socialists, AIK), a peace activist and feminist. See more in note 371 in the Introduction.

67 "Neighbour Quarrels Hit New Extreme," by Nina Berglund, News in English, April 11, 2014, www.newsinenglish.no/2014/04/11/neighbour-quarrels-hit-new-extreme/.

68 Leidner, et al., 2012.

69 See, among others, Sarraj, 2002, Sayler, 2004, Giacaman, et al., 2007, Elison and Harter, 2007, Walker and Knauer, 2011.

70 See for research on inertia, for instance, Leidner, et al., 2012. According to anthropologist Scott Atran, humiliation is a negative predictor for terrorism, since those who feel humiliated become submissive. However, it is a different case to act on behalf of others' exposure to humiliation, such as the second or third generation of Muslims in Britain who believe that their parents were humiliated. See, among others, Ginges and Atran, 2008.
Canada's indigenous populations demonstrate the deleterious effect of continuous humiliation. See note 139 in the Introduction.

71 Galtung, 1969.

72 See note 139 in the Introduction.

73 Lewis, 1971.

74 See, among others, Sarraj, 2002, Sayler, 2004, Giacaman, et al., 2007, Elison and Harter, 2007, Walker and Knauer, 2011.

75 Ahmed, personal communication, 2004. I heard Ahmed's account many times also from other people, in many variations. They all tell me that living in perpetual despair forces one into experiences one would have thought to be impossible before. See Lindner, 2009f, p. 36, also Lindner, 2007a, or Lindner, 2012d.

76 Accounts like this led me to doubt that humiliation and shame are always connected: feelings of humiliation can occur without shame. Torturers inflict humiliation to create deep shame, however, as I have learned from torture victims, they can succeed in insulating themselves from such onslaughts or they may even feel humiliation as a triumph.

77 "Demütigung ohne Scham, als Rächer! 'Morden im Rampenlicht'," by Martin Altmeyer, Spiegel Online, 31/2016, July 30, 2016, www.spiegel.de/spiegel/inszenierung-von-groessenwahn-essay-von-martin-altmeyer-a-1105637.html: Was treibt Amokläufer, und woher kommt der Hass der Islamisten? Psychoanalytiker Martin Altmeyer über die öffentliche Inszenierung von Allmacht und Größenwahn.

78 I had several conversations with members of security police in different countries. Trond Hugubakken is communications director at Politiets sikkerhetstjeneste, PST (the Norwegian Police Security Service is the police security agency of Norway, comparable to the British MI5 Security Service), and Josefine Aase was a senior advisor, when our conversation took place in the Oslo headquarters on February 4, 2011. See more in the Appendix to Section One.

79 David Cook is a historian at Rice University, Texas, U.S.A., who studies Muslim apocalypticism, see, among others, Cook, 2010. According to Muslim apocalypticism, the battles preceding the Day of Judgment will take place in modern Syria, with a final showdown in the year 1500 of the Islamic Hijra calendar, or A.D. 2076. See also Utvik, 2006, and how the Muslim Brotherhood was inspired by Nazi Germany. Clearly, there are differences between terrorist organizations such as Al-Qaeda and the path of Adolf Hitler. Hitler was without power at first, however, he was able to get into a position of power: "Al-Qaeda will never be in such a position," explained Petter Nesser, senior researcher with the Terrorism Research Group at the Norwegian Defence Research Establishment (FFI), during our thoroughly informative conversation in Oslo

on June 17, 2011. It was very enriching for me to also share with him my experiences with young clients during my years as psychological counselor in Cairo, Egypt, from 1984 to 1991. I have summarized and translated our conversation from Norwegian. See also Nesser, 2006, 2011, 2014, Tønnessen, 2006.

80 Badie, 2014. I thank Yves Musoni and Rigmor Johnsen for making me aware of this book. See also "L'Occident face à la revanche des humiliés," by Yidir Plantade, Le Monde, April 2, 2014, www.lemonde.fr/idees/article/2014/04/02/l-occident-face-a-la-revanche-des-humilies_4394400_3232.html.

81 I am extremely appreciative of the meeting with Bertrand Badie on December 15, 2015, and his generosity in including me into his thinking. I have summarized and translated his words from French. It is a privilege to have Bertrand Badie as esteemed member in the global advisory board of the Human Dignity and Humiliation Studies fellowship.

82 James Madison (1751 – 1836), Father of the U.S. Constitution, 4th American President, in a letter to Thomas Jefferson, May 13, 1798. I thank Rodrigue Tremblay for making me aware of this quote.

83 Miller, 1988, p. 5. See also Miller, 2008b, and Hartling, 2008b.

84 Galtung, 1996, p. 199.

85 Elias, 1939/1994. See also Elias, 2000. With respect to gender, see also Smith, 1997, 1999.

86 "Trump's Political Lesson: Humiliate, or Be Humiliated," by Alex Shephard and Laura Reston, New Republic, December 6, 2016, https://newrepublic.com/article/139176/trumps-political-lesson-humiliate-humiliated.

87 See also Lindner and Desmond Tutu (Foreword), 2010, Gender, Humiliation, and Global Security.

88 Audun Bjørlo Lysbakken and Kristian Norheim on Dagsnytt Atten (Daily News Eighteen), NRK, August 13, 2014. Audun Bjørlo Lysbakken is the leader of the Socialist Left Party (SV). Kristian Norheim is a member of the conservative Progress Party (FrP) and its expert on international relations. See the full note in the pdf edition of this book.

89 On Dagsnytt Atten (Daily News Eighteen), NRK, September 14, 2015. See the full note in the pdf edition of this book.

90 Helge Lurås is the founder and director of the Centre for International and Strategic Analysis (SISA). He has experience from the Norwegian Institute of International Affairs (NUPI), Norwegian Armed Forces, NATO, the UN and from private sector consultancy, www.strategiskanalyse.no/index.php/en/employee-detail?contact_id=3. See, among others, Lurås, 2015.

91 Håvard Mokleiv Nygård is a senior research at the Peace Research Institute Oslo (PRIO). See, among others, his work on the "conflict trap," where low levels of development lead to conflict and conflict leads to yet lower levels of development, see Hegre and Nygård, 2015, Nygård, 2014. See, furthermore, Collier, 2013, or "States of Fragility 2015: Meeting Post-2015 Ambitions," Organisation for Economic Co-operation and Development (OECD), March 26, 2015, www.oecd.org/dac/governance-peace/publications/documentuploads/SOF2015.pdf. Please note that the Editorial of this report is co-signed by Erik Solheim, a supporter of the World Dignity University Initiative (see https://youtu.be/XfzrteRAyzM?list=ULXfzrteRAyzM). See an introduction to the report on www.oecd.org/dac/states-of-fragility-2015-9789264227699-en.htm.

92 "'Is ethnicity the root cause of conflict in Africa?' 'Does ethnicity kill?' Why do some multi-ethnic states disintegrate into civil war and others, despite ethnic pluralism, have not faced wars and armed conflicts? Are all conflicts not in some ways about identity or the contesting of identities?" these are questions asked, for instance, in McCandless and Karbo, 2011.
Note also the Centre for Research on Inequality, Human Security and Ethnicity (CRISE), whose primary objective is to understand why some multi-ethnic countries are peaceful while others experience violent conflict. See "Horizontal Inequalities As a Cause of Conflict: A Review of CRISE Findings," by Frances

Stewart, Centre for Research on Inequality, Human Security and Ethnicity, 2010, http://r4d.dfid.gov.uk/pdf/outputs/inequality/crise-overview-1.pdf. See more in note 23 in Chapter 6.

93 Anthony Marsella, in a personal communication on June 26, 2013. See also "Lifeism: Beyond Humanity," Anthony J. Marsella, TRANSCEND Media Service, March 17, 2014, www.transcend.org/tms/2014/03/lifeism-beyond-humanity/.

94 In their book on trauma and healing under state terrorism, Agger and Jensen, 1996, differentiates four categories of mechanisms of psychological warfare: direct repression, indirect repression, social marginalization and individual marginalization. Each of these methods tends to diminish human dignity, cultural dignity and personal sense of worth.

95 Jackman, 1994. I thank Arie Nadler for reminding me of Jackman's work.

96 Foucault, 1975, p. 166–175. See also Lecture 13 of Richards, et al., 2015a.

97 Foucault, 1975, p. 175–183. See also Lecture 13 of Richards, et al., 2015a.

98 Foucault, 1975, p. 217–227. See also Lecture 13 of Richards, et al., 2015b, a.

99 Foucault, 1975, p. 215. See also Lecture 13 of Richards, et al., 2015a.

100 "Stir Crazy," by Clifford Geertz, book review of Discipline and Punish, New York Review of Books, January 26, 1975, www.nybooks.com/articles/archives/1978/jan/26/stir-crazy/.

101 See Richards, 1995, Richards, 2004, Richards and Swanger, 2006b, Richards and Swanger, 2013, Odora Hoppers and Richards, 2012. Richards recommends also Searle, 1995, Harré and Secord, 1972, Taylor, 1971, MacIntyre and Bell, 1967, and other works by the same authors. I would assume that Richards has also read George, 1879, on public revenue from land rent, an idea that obtained its greatest popularity in the U.S. in the late 1800s, see also Foldvary, 2006. It is a privilege to have Howard Richards, Catherine Odora Hoppers, and her brother George as esteemed members in the global advisory board of our Human Dignity and Humiliation Studies fellowship.

102 Maine, 1861.

103 See note 8 in Chapter 4. See also note 368 in Chapter 15.

104 See note 163 in the Preface.

105 Richards and Andersson, 2017, Introduction.

106 After the commons were enclosed in England, starting during the sixteenth century, what sociologist Eric Mielants, 2007, calls "terroristic" laws were introduced that criminalized idleness, thus pushing people into early capitalist manufacturing.

107 East Germany, formally the German Democratic Republic or GDR (German: Deutsche Demokratische Republik or DDR), was a state within the Eastern Bloc during the Cold War period.

108 Günther Jauch, Sunday evening political television talk show on Das Erste. See the full note in the pdf edition of this book.

109 Lewis, 1989. See also The Colbert Report, October 28, 2014, http://thecolbertreport.cc.com/videos/c7wjzg/michael-lewis.

110 "Let's Get This Class War Started," by Chris Hedges, Truthdig, October 20, 2013, www.truthdig.com/report/item/lets_get_this_class_war_started_20131020.

111 Cather, 1913.

112 Lane, 2001. See also notes 90, 91, and 92 in the Introduction.

113 "How the Pursuit of Happiness Has Made Us Nervous Wrecks," by Ruth Whippman, Wharton School of the University of Pennsylvania, December 8, 2016, http://knowledge.wharton.upenn.edu/article/how-the-

pursuit-of-happiness-has-made-us-nervous-wrecks/. I thank Ulrich Spalthoff and Linda Hartling for making me aware of Whippman, 2016.

114 "Leader's Edge," interview with Charles Handy by Stephen Bernhut, Ivey Business Journal, March/April 2004, Reprint # 9B04TB06, pp. 1–7, www.iveybusinessjournal.com, p. 4: "Here we are, we're supposed to be great, prosperous and successful countries and people are unhappy, not because they're badly treated, not because they're badly managed, but because they're actually not using their lives in the way that I think is fully productive. And I call this a sort of 'corporate sin.'"

115 Deming, 1986.

116 This information has already found its way into the public eye, see, for instance, "On the happy trail," by Mark Honigsbaum, The Guardian, April 4, 2004, www.guardian.co.uk/society/2004/apr/04/mentalhealth.observermagazine.

117 Holt-Lunstad, et al., 2010. I had the privilege of learning from Roman Wittig about his work on the role of friendship for chimpanzees, on October 10, 2015, at the Symposium "Gehirne zwischen Liebe und Krieg – Menschlichkeit in Zeiten der Neurowissenschaften," Fürth, Germany, October 9–11, 2015, www.turmdersinne.de/de/symposium/symposium-2015/programm.

118 Dierksmeier, 2015, Dierksmeier, 2016. I thank Heidetraut von Weltzien Høivik for keeping me in the loop of publications in the field of business ethics. It is a privilege to have thank Heidetraut von Weltzien Høivik as esteemed member in the global advisory board of the Human Dignity and Humiliation Studies fellowship.

119 Marmot, 2015. I thank Linda Hartling for suggesting to replace Marmot's term of "degree of control" with the term "sense of influence."

120 Grünewald, 2013.

121 "Clinical Depression Costs Economy up to 22 Billion Euros Each Year," New Report from Allianz Deutschland AG und RWI, www.allianz.com/en/press/news/studies/news_2011-04-13.html. See also notes 90, 91, and 92 in the Introduction.

122 "Innere Kündigung: Statisten am Schreibtisch, 17. Mai 2010, Süddeutsche Zeitung, www.sueddeutsche.de/karriere/innere-kuendigung-statisten-am-schreibtisch-1.375928-2. See the full note in the pdf edition of this book.

123 Brinkmann and Stapf, 2005. See also "Innere Kündigung," www.innerekuendigung.de/.

124 "Fra målstyrt mistillit til kvalitetsorientert samarbeid og ledelse," by Johan Nygaard, Helsetjenesten aksjonen, June 2, 2015, http://helsetjenesteaksjonen.no/V01/wp-content/uploads/2015/06/%C3%85PENT-BREV.02.06.2015.pdf.

125 "The End of Performance Management (As We Know It)," by Bjarte Bogsnes – Vice President – Performance Management Development at Statoil, June 12, 2012, www.managementexchange.com/hack/end-performance-management-we-know-it.

126 Mennoniten – Alleine im Paradies? documentary film by Mercedes Ibaibarriaga, 3sat, April 10, 2013, www.3sat.de/programm/?d=20130410, see also https://youtu.be/eLB7VT9ITJ8. The documentary film "Mennonites" presents the faith community in Bolivia. See the full note in the pdf edition of this book.

127 Mennoniten – Alleine im Paradies?, documentary film by Mercedes Ibaibarriaga, 3sat, April 10, 2013, www.3sat.de/programm/?d=20130410, see also https://youtu.be/eLB7VT9ITJ8. See the full note in the pdf edition of this book.

128 See note 97 in Chapter 5.

129 Linda Hartling, in a personal communication on September 8, 2015.

130 For the Thirty-First Annual E. F. Schumacher Lectures on November 5, 2011, in New York City, see www.neweconomicsinstitute.org. Juliet Schor was one of the speakers, in addition to speakers such as Gar Alperovitz, and "Voices of Today's Youth: Occupy Wall Street and Youth for a New Economy," a panel comprised of Occupy Wall Street participants and other student activists.

131 See also McDonald, 2017. I thank Linda Hartling for sharing her notes of this book with me. See, furthermore, "How Economics Became a Science: A Forgotten Episode in the Discipline's History Reveals How Diversity Was Killed in Economics," by Giorgos Kallis, Adbuster, April 2, 2014, www.adbusters.org/magazine/112/battle-soul-economics.html, where environmental scientist Giorgos Kallis asks: "The economic crisis has supposedly started a soul-searching process in the economics profession. Five years into the crisis and economists still offer more of the same in response. 'Create new.' 'Cut red-tape.' 'Liberalize finance in the rest of the world.' Why do economists keep getting it so wrong? Innovation feeds on diversity, but diversity is scarce in economics." Kallis points at a Ph.D. thesis written by Jorge Fernandes Mata, 2006, on how radical economists were purged from US campuses following the student movement against the war in Vietnam. Kallis explains the story in his contribution to the Great Transition Network (GTN) discussion on the topic of "The Church of Economism and Its Discontents," on November 3, 2015, in response to Norgaard, 2015: "This is an incredible story of faculty battles with documented intervention and harassment from the FBI. And it included the purge of today famous, then deemed too radical, economists like Sam Bowles or Herbert Gintis from Harvard leading, directly or indirectly, to the departure of even more moderate progressives, such as Leontief, Galbraith, or Hirschmann. This ideological purge of alternative voices from economics departments was part and parcel of the neo-liberal transformation of Reagan and Thatcher that followed, and it explains why the belief system of economism is so entrenched today and so hard to change. We know today (and this is no conspiracy, but well documented academic knowledge) that neo-liberalism did not just happen; it was partly planned by think-tanks, economic and political interests. Controlling academia, and especially the powerful field of economics, was part of the project." See the full note in the pdf edition of this book.

132 Juliet Schor is the Co-founder of the Center for a New American Dream, www.newdream.org, and author of several books, see Schor, 2010, Schor, 1993, 1999, 2004, Schor and Thompson, 2014. An animation provides a vision of what a post-consumer society could look like, with people working fewer hours and pursuing re-skilling, homesteading, and small-scale enterprises that can help reduce the overall size and impact of the consumer economy, see www.julietschor.org/2011/08/video-new-dream-mini-views-visualizing-a-plenitude-economy/.

133 "Harvard Students Demand Alternative Economics," by Dan DiMaggio, Dollars and Sense Magazine, July/August 2003 issue, www.dollarsandsense.org/archives/2003/0703dimaggio.html.

134 "An Innovative Approach to Terror Propaganda Through Social Media," by Joe Charlaff, Homeland Security Today (HSToday), August 3, 2015, www.hstoday.us/briefings/daily-news-analysis/single-article/an-innovative-approach-to-terror-propaganda-through-social-media/75326fa89080f75ddfb4a7ec72ee7b9e.html.

135 Quilligan, 2013.

136 "The CIA and the Media: How Americas Most Powerful News Media Worked Hand in Glove with the Central Intelligence Agency and Why the Church Committee Covered It Up," by Carl Bernstein, October 20, 1977, www.carlbernstein.com/magazine_cia_and_media.php.

137 "Google Is Not What It Seems," by Julian Assange, Newsweek, October 24, 2014, www.newsweek.com/assange-google-not-what-it-seems-279447.

138 Pantham, 2009, p. 184.

139 Pantham, 2009, p. 185.

140 Acres of Diamonds, by Russell Herman Conwell, first given in 1913, see www.americanrhetoric.com/speeches/rconwellacresofdiamonds.htm. See also note 32 in Chapter 2.

141 See, among others, Goldstone, et al., 2010, Goldstone, et al., 1991, Gurr, 1970, Marshall and Gurr, 2005. See also the related concept of horizontal inequalities, see, for instance, the work by international development expert Frances Stewart, 2008. Stewart explains the difference between relative deprivation and horizontal inequalities (HI) in "Horizontal Inequalities As a Cause of Conflict: A Review of CRISE Findings," by Frances Stewart, Centre for Research on Inequality, Human Security and Ethnicity, http://r4d.dfid.gov.uk/pdf/outputs/inequality/crise-overview-1.pdf. See more in note 23 in Chapter 6.

142 Goldstone and Ulfelder, 2005, p. 9. Jack Goldstone is an esteemed member in the global advisory board of our Human Dignity and Humiliation Studies fellowship, together with Monty Marshall, who brought Jack to us. See also Goldstone, et al., 2010.

143 See Krueger, 2017. And see an endorsement of the argument that terrorism does not follow from poverty, but from lack of freedom, in "The Roots of Terrorism," by Sultan Mehmood, Dawn, March 3, 2016, www.dawn.com/news/796177/the-roots-of-terrorism. See more in note 316 in the Introduction.

144 Goldstone and Ulfelder, 2005, pp. 19–20.

145 Goldstone and Ulfelder, 2005, p. 20.

146 Lindner, 2012f, p. 136.

Chapter 8

1 "The Money Exchange Dealers of Kabul: A Study of the Hawala System in 2003 Afghanistan," by Samuel Munzele Maimbo, World Bank working paper series, Number 13, http://documents.worldbank.org/curated/en/2003/08/2613565/money-exchange-dealers-kabul-study-hawala-system-afghanistan.

2 Tong, et al., 2016. I thank Linda Hartling for making me aware of this study.

3 See Lindner, 2016b. Around 1750, for the first time, travelers began to insert themselves as subjects with a personal perspective into their travel reports, I thank Barnett Pearce for making me aware of Lyons, 1978. I thank Jon Elster for making me aware that the "birth of the self" began much earlier, with Michel de Montaigne, 1575, in his Essays. See, furthermore, Bloom, 1999, on Shakespeare and "the invention of the human," or the Baudelairean flâneur, or the emigrant of W. G. Sebald, 1992/1996, or, more recently, Cole, 2011. It was a privilege to have Barnett Pearce as esteemed member in the global advisory board of our Human Dignity and Humiliation Studies fellowship until his passing, and we will always honor his spirit.

4 Kingsley, 1867, p. 1, www.pagebypagebooks.com/Charles_Kingsley/The_Ancien_Regime/Lecture_I_Caste_p1.html.

5 "Vatican Admits Galileo Was Right," New Scientist, November 7, 1992, www.newscientist.com/article/mg13618460-600-vatican-admits-galileo-was-right/.

6 International relations specialist and research affiliate of the Waterloo Institute for Complexity and Innovation at the University of Waterloo in Ontario, Canada, Stephen Purdey, in his contribution to the Great Transition Network Initiative discussion titled "Journey to Earthland: Making the Great Transition to Planetary Civilization," October 24, 2016, in response to Raskin, 2016.

7 Siebert and Ott, 2016, p. 6.

8 See, among others, the work of historian of science, Ernst Peter Fischer, 2009.

9 Lindner, 2016b.

10 See a few examples for relevant literature, for instance, Lasch, 1991, Putnam, 2000, Baumeister, et al., 1996, Bushman and Baumeister, 1998, Baumeister, et al., 2003, Baumeister, 2005, Levine, 2007, Twenge and Campbell, 2009, Wood, et al., 2009, Ehrenreich, 2010, Twenge, et al., 2012, Twenge and Kasser, 2013, Twenge, 2014. See also how Howard Richards includes Foucault, 1961/2006, and Frank, 1961, in his chapter in Richards, 2013.
See "Column: This Is What Happens When You Take Ayn Rand Seriously," by Denise Cummins, Public Broadcasting Service (PBS), February 16, 2016, www.pbs.org/newshour/making-sense/column-this-is-what-happens-when-you-take-ayn-rand-seriously/. Cummins presents two case studies that show the disastrous consequences of following Ayn Rand's philosophy, namely, the company Sears, and the country Honduras. I thank Linda Hartling for making me aware of this article. See also note 32 in Chapter 4. Also psychoanalyst Heinz Kohut has worked on narcissistic injury, see Kohut, 1973, p. 380: "One sees the need for revenge, for righting a wrong, for undoing the hurt by whatever means, and a deeply anchored, unrelenting compulsion in the pursuit of all these aims which gives no rest to those who have suffered a narcissistic injury – these are features which are characteristic for the phenomenon of narcissistic rage in all its forms and which sets it apart from other kinds of aggression."

11 Galtung, 1969.

12 Christoph Bals from Germanwatch in his contribution to the Great Transition Network (GTN) discussion on the topic of "Meaning, Religion, and a Great Transition," December 1, 2014, in response to Karlberg, 2014.

13 Quoted by Christoph Bals from Germanwatch in his contribution to the Great Transition Network (GTN) discussion on the topic of "Meaning, Religion, and a Great Transition," December 1, 2014, in response to Karlberg, 2014. See the full note in the pdf edition of this book.

14 It is a privilege to have Catherine Odora Hoppers and her brother George as esteemed members in the global advisory board of the Human Dignity and Humiliation Studies fellowship, together with Howard Richards.

15 Odora Hoppers and Richards, 2012. See a review in Cultural and Pedagogical Inquiry, 2014, 6 (1, Special Issue), pp. 67–69, https://ejournals.library.ualberta.ca/index.php/cpi/article/download/22935/17082.

16 "Indigenous Knowledge Systems: An Invisible Resource in Literacy Education," by Catherine Odora Hoppers. SGI Quarterly: A Buddhist Forum for Peace, Culture and Education, January 2003, www.sgiquarterly.org/feature2003Jan-4.html. See also Odora Hoppers and Richards, 2012,Richards, et al., 2015a. See, furthermore, Richards, 2015, Haavelsrud, 2015, Sewchurran and McDonogh, 2015, and Soudien, 2015, in the International Journal of Development Education and Global Learning, Volume 7, Number 2, 2015, edited by Odora Hoppers. Soudien recommends drawing on the concept of the transaction in John Dewey for a new approach to knowing while Haavelsrud uses Odora Hoppers' term of transformation by enlargement for the academy, by scientific methodologies inspired by forms of transdisciplinarity, praxis, and trilateral science as described by Johan Galtung, 1977, see Haavelsrud, 2015, pp. 54–55:

> Central to his concept of trilateral science is the relationship between three worlds. The world as it is (the data or facts positively given), the world as it will be (the world as predicted or theorized) and the world as it ought to be (values). He argues that all three can be changed and adapted to each other through scientific work implying that the gaps and differences between the three worlds (the empirical, the foreseen, and the ideal) are reduced through transformations in all three. The three worlds may become more similar with the contribution of this kind of transformative scientific knowledge production. So science aims at consonance among the three. The world as it is can be changed, and if so the foreseen world will also be changed. Values may be modified.

17 See, among others, Boyer, 2001, Boyer and Wertsch, 2009. The recurrent properties of religious concepts and norms in different cultures are "parasitic upon standard cognitive systems that evolved outside of

religion, such as agency-detection, moral intuition, coalitional psychology and contagion-avoidance," http://artsci.wustl.edu/~pboyer/PBoyerHomeSite/index.html.

18 Barrett, 2011, p. 230. I thank cross-cultural psychologist Michael Harris Bond for making me aware of Barrett's work. See Bond's involvement in the project Is Religion Natural? The Chinese Challenge, http://thethrivecenter.org/research/is-religion-natural-the-chinese-challenge/. See more in note 19 in the Introduction to Section One.

19 In the year 2001, I wrote an article titled "The Concept of Humiliation: Its Universal Core and Culture-Dependent Periphery," Lindner, 2001d, see the Abstract: "This article argues that the concept of humiliation may be deconstructed into seven layers, including a) a core that expresses the universal idea of 'putting down,' b) a middle layer that contains two opposed orientations towards 'putting down,' treating it as, respectively, legitimate and routine, or illegitimate and traumatizing, and c) a periphery whose distinctive layers include one pertaining to cultural differences between groups and another four peripheral layers that relate to differences in individual personalities and variations in patterns of individual experience of humiliation."

20 2015 Annual Conference of Human Dignity and Humiliation Studies, "Toward A Life of Dignity for All," in Kigali, Rwanda, June 2–5, 2015, www.humiliationstudies.org/whoweare/annualmeeting/25.php. I had the privilege of living in a Catholic convent in Kigali, see photos on www.humiliationstudies.org/whoweare/evelin/pics15.php.

21 "For Rwandans, the Pope's Apology Must be Unbearable," by Martin Kimani, The Guardian, March 29, 2010, www.theguardian.com/commentisfree/belief/2010/mar/29/pope-catholics-rwanda-genocide-church.

22 Dusengumuremy, 2015.

23 Elias, 1939/1994. See also Elias, 2000. With respect to gender, see also Smith, 1997, 1999.

24 See Smith, 2001.

25 McCullough, 2008.

26 Webb, 2009, p. 16.

27 See note 8 in Chapter 4. See also note 368 in Chapter 15.

28 Gress, 1985.

29 Müller, 2009.

30 "Secession Divides Texas Republicans," by Chris Cillizza, The Washington Post, April 23, 2009, http://voices.washingtonpost.com/thefix/republican-party/secession-divides-texas-republ.html?wprss=thefix.

31 The Act of Killing (2012) and The Look of Silence (2014), are documentary films by Joshua Oppenheimer. The Act of Killing is a portrait of the perpetrators of the 1965 Indonesian genocide, in which perhaps a million people suspected of being Communists were killed. In The Look of Silence the focus is on the murder of a single victim, Ramli Rukun. In 2014, after a screening of The Act of Killing for US Congress members, Oppenheimer called on the U.S. to acknowledge its role in the killings.

32 "Joshua Oppenheimer Won't Go Back to Indonesia," interview by Adam Shatz, New York Times, July 9, 2015, www.nytimes.com/2015/07/12/magazine/joshua-oppenheimer-wont-go-back-to-indonesia.html?_r=1. Oppenheimer states that the West shares considerable responsibility for the mass killings in Indonesia. Particular the United States "provided the special radio system so the Army could coordinate the killings over the vast archipelago."

33 In 1991, Shaka Senghor, 2016, shot and killed a man. He was, he says, "a drug dealer with a quick temper and a semi-automatic pistol." He spent nineteen years in jail, seven of which in solitary confinement. His message is that people are indeed redeemable. See his memoir published in 2016, and his TED talk Why

Your Worst Deeds Don't Define You, 2014, www.ted.com/talks/shaka_senghor_why_your_worst_deeds_don_t_define_you?language=en.
See also Thomas Galli, 2016, a German prison governor, who calls in question the usefulness of the concept of the current prison system. Its purpose was to replace historical practices of cruel corporal punishment with making criminals fit to return into society. However, argues Galli, far from being helped, this aim is even undermined by the current prison system. Those who enter prison, rather than being made fit for freedom in society at large, are integrated into a community of fellow prison inmates who might even be more bent toward crime and violence than they are.
See, furthermore, the work of psychiatrist James Gilligan. Unable to tolerate disrespect, violent criminals chose to become enraged and violent rather than feel humiliated. The remedy is not to fight back at them, but to help them build a more constructive substance for their sense of worth. Acquiring a college education, for instance, provides such substance. See, among others, Gilligan, 2000, or Gilligan, 2003.
See, furthermore, Cainkar and Maira, 2005. See also the sub-section "Children, madmen, criminals, enemies, or subhumans? Which interpretation fits terrorists best?" in Lindner, 2006c, Chapter 5: Humiliation and Conflict, in my book Making Enemies: Humiliation and International Conflict, pp. 96–98.

34 Barrett and Bokhari, 2009.

35 "How a Danish Town Helped Young Muslims Turn Away from ISIS," by Hanna Rosin, National Public Radio (NPR), July 15, 2016, www.npr.org/sections/health-shots/2016/07/15/485900076/how-a-danish-town-helped-young-muslims-turn-away-from-isis?utm_campaign=storyshare&utm. I thank Deb Reich for making me aware of this article.

36 Algeria: The Terrorist Who Came Home, documentary film by Francis Mead, United Nations Television, 2010, www.unmultimedia.org/tv/21stcentury/2010/10/quitting-terrorism-in-algeria.html. See the script here: www.un.org/webcast/pdfs/21century46.pdf. We thank Ariel Lublin for making me aware of this film by her partner Francis Mead and bringing him to our 2009 Workshop on Humiliation and Violent Conflict, Columbia University, New York, December 10-11, 2009. It is a privilege to their support for the work of Human Dignity and Humiliation Studies.

37 See note 22 and 23 in the Appendix to Section One.

38 The script of Algeria: The Terrorist Who Came Home, www.un.org/webcast/pdfs/21century46.pdf. See also Barrett and Bokhari, 2009.

39 Ibid.

40 "Saudi Initiatives in Countering Terrorism: ICPVTR Visit to Saudi Arabia," International Centre for Political Violence and Terrorism Research (ICPVTR), S. Rajaratnam School of International Studies (RSIS), Nanyang Technological University (NTU) Singapore, February 6–14, 2010, www.rsis.edu.sg/wp-content/uploads/2015/04/Report-Saudi-Initiatives-in-Countering-Terrorism.pdf.

41 Read more about Hamed El-Said in note 21 in the Appendix to Section One.

42 Ebrahim, 2014. I thank Annette Anderson-Engler for making me aware of this young man's work. It is a privilege to have Annette Engler as one of the "Nurturers of Dignity" in our Human Dignity and Humiliation Studies fellowship.

43 Sundberg and Huor, 2016. See also Anna Sundberg var gift med en global terrorist: – Det tok to uker å radikalisere meg, Anna Sundberg interviewed by Fredrik Skavlan, NRK, March 4, 2016, www.side2.no/aktuelt/anna-sundberg-sluttet-seg-til-jihad-som-ung---det-tok-to-uker-a-radikalisere-meg/3423199527.html. See the full note in the pdf edition of this book.

44 "An Internal Struggle: Al Qaeda's Syrian Affiliate Is Grappling with Its Identity," by Charles Lister, Brookings Institute, May 31, 2015, www.brookings.edu/blogs/markaz/posts/2015/05/31-syria-isis-lister.

45 Schmitz, 2016.

46 "How Do You Deradicalise Returning Isis Fighters?" by Jon Henley, The Guardian, November 12, 2014, www.theguardian.com/world/2014/nov/12/deradicalise-isis-fighters-jihadists-denmark-syria.

47 "Denmark De-Radicalization Program Aims to Reintegrate, Not Condemn," by Kelly Cobiella, NBC News, www.nbcnews.com/storyline/isis-terror/denmark-de-radicalization-n355346.

48 See note 81 in Chapter 13.

49 Hénin, 2015. It is interesting that the German translation of this book highlights its critical view on the role of the West in the very title: Der IS und die Fehler des Westens: Warum wir den Terror militärisch nicht besiegen können (Zürich, Switzerland: orell füssli), while the English translation does not do so: Jihad Academy: The Rise of Islamic State (New Delhi: Bloomsbury).

Chapter 9

1 See note 201 in the Introduction.

2 Kristin Enmark, 2015. See more in note 202 in the Introduction.

3 The term méconnaissance was first introduced by psychologist Henri Wallon (1879 – 1962).

4 Kant, 1784.

5 Kuhn, 1962.

6 Negating a frame activates that frame, as explained, among others, by Lakoff, 2002, 2004, 2016. Listen also to On The Media: Normalize This! How Talking About Trump Makes Him Normal in Your Brain, Brooke Glastone speaks with George Lakoff, WNYC-FM New York Public Radio, December 2, 2016, www.wnyc.org/story/george-lakoff/: "According to George Lakoff, a cognitive linguist and author of Don't Think Of An Elephant! Know Your Values and Frame the Debate, the very fundamentals of journalism should be redefined in order to stave off normalizing Trump. Lakoff and Brooke discuss the unconscious effects that Trump's language, image, and name have on the brain."
Listen also to On The Media: Normalize This! Masha Gessen on the "Impulse to Normalize," Brooke Glastone speaks with Masha Gessen, WNYC-FM New York Public Radio, December 2, 2016, www.wnyc.org/story/masha-gessen-impulse-normalize/. Gessen calls on the media to focus on the gap between facts and the truth and to bridge the gap between reporting the facts and telling the truth. See also Gessen, 2013. Listen, furthermore, to On The Media: Normalize This! Left Language, Right Language, Brooke Glastone speaks with John McWhorter, WNYC-FM New York Public Radio, December 2, 2016, www.wnyc.org/story/left-language-right-language/, and see McWhorter, 2016, to reflect on ways to avoid obscuring the truth.
Psychotherapy uses the fact that negation activates what is negated in the form of paradox intervention, see Watzlawick, et al., 1967, and paradox intention, see Viktor Frankl, 1946.

7 ee note 163 in the Preface.

8 Bhaskar, 2008.

9 See note 162 in the Preface.

10 See note 60 in Chapter 5.

11 "Obama Weighing Talks With Putin on Syrian Crisis," by Peter Baker and Andrew E. Kramer, New York Times, September 15, 2015, www.nytimes.com/2015/09/16/world/middleeast/white-house-split-on-opening-talks-with-putin.html?_r=0.

12 Translated from German by Alice Asbury Abbott, Suttner, 1908, pp. 119–120. German original in Suttner, 1889, p. 69. See the German original in the full note in the pdf edition of this book.

13 Ohnuki-Tierney, 2002.

14 See also Melber, 2011.

15 See Sergei Stepanovich Chakhotin, 1940, as one of the first thinkers to describe the effect of propaganda on the psychology of masses and warning against the techniques used by the Nazi Party.

16 "'Für seinen unermüdlichen Kampf': Die Verleihung der Ehrenbürgerwürde an Adolf Hitler durch die Stadt Hameln," by Bernhard Gelderblom, Dewezet, April 18, 2017, www.dewezet.de/hintergrund/hintergrund-seite_artikel,-die-verleihung-der-ehrenbuergerwuerde-an-adolf-hitler-durch-die-stadt-hameln-_arid,2365469.html, p. 16, German original of the honorary citizen letter that was presented to Adolf Hitler by the city of Hamelin on the Bückeberg on his birthday on April 20, 1933. German original translated by Lindner: "The city of Hamelin has on April 20, 1933, presented the Reich Chancellor Adolf Hitler, the creator of the Third Reich, the leader of the German people united in national socialism, in gratitude for his tireless struggle and as a special expression of the national socialist attitude of its citizenry, with the honorary citizenship of Hamelin. The entire citizenry pledges loyal allegiance for all time." See the German original in the full note in the pdf edition of this book.

17 In 1976, I did a school psychology internship on the training ship Kariba of the German Africa Lines, DAL, during its journey from Europe along the coast of West Africa: from Senegal to Sierra Leone, to Ivory Coast, Ghana, Togo, Benin, and finally to Cameroon.

18 Beah, 2007.

19 "In an IS Training Camp, Children Told: Behead the Doll," by Zeina Karam and Bram Janssen, Associated Press, July 19, 2015, http://bigstory.ap.org/article/fcc0fe9b92bb49[2]5bc0f3bd401cc13/training-camp-children-told-behead-doll.

20 "We Can Defeat ISIS," by Amitai Etzioni, Huffington Post, August 4, 2015, www.huffingtonpost.com/amitai-etzioni/we-can-defeat-isis_b_7933364.html.

21 "Facts About Child Soldiers," Human Rights Watch, December 3, 2008, www.hrw.org/news/2008/12/03/facts-about-child-soldiers.

22 Wang and Aamodt, 2011.

23 "We Should Have Listened to the Broken Teenagers, BBC News, May 16, 2017, www.bbc.com/news/magazine-39924586. I thank Rigmor Johnsen for making me aware of this article.

24 Kindesmissbrauch – Und kein Ende, by Gert Scobel, 3sat, September 17, 2015, www.3sat.de/page/?source=/scobel/182692/index.html. See the full note in the pdf edition of this book. See also Amann and Wipplinger, 2005.

25 Generation Jihad, documentary film in three episodes by Peter Taylor, 2010, http://thewatchseries.to/serie/generation_jihad: "Peter Taylor has worked for a year investigating who these young Muslim extremists are and how they become radicalized and tracked their networks around the world. He clarifies how teenagers were recruited via the internet and finds out why some of Britain's young extremists are prepared to support violence against their fellow citizens." See also Taylor, 2011. See, furthermore, Taylor, 1980, 1993b, 1996, 1997a, b, 2000.

26 Bourdieu and Wacquant, 1992, p. 24.

27 Die Sprache von Al-Qaida (The language of Al-Qaeda), documentary film by Abdelasiem Hassan El Difraoui and Mark Johnston, Arte/WDR, 2008, see, among others, https://youtu.be/zj5v5hb5cOE. This documentary gives the floor to a number of terrorism experts, from Brynjar Lia to Tom Quiggin to Brian Fishman, and Jarret Brachman, 2008. See also "Life Term for Terror Ringleader," by Isabel Teotonio, The Star, January 19, 2010, www.thestar.com/news/crime/2010/01/19/life_term_for_terror_ringleader.html: "The architect of an Al Qaeda-inspired terror plot to cripple Canada's economy and unleash mass carnage

by blowing up buildings in downtown Toronto has been sentenced to life in prison." See the full note in the pdf edition of this book.

28 Neumann, 2015. See also "ISIS Defectors Reveal Disillusionment," by Kimiko de Freytas-Tamura, New York Times, September 20, 2015, www.nytimes.com/2015/09/21/world/europe/isis-defectors-reveal-disillusionment.html?_r=0. See also Husain, 2007, or Baker, 2009.

29 "Report on the Investigation of the Peasant Movement in Hunan," by Mao Zedong, March 1927, http://afe.easia.columbia.edu/ps/china/mao_peasant.pdf. See also Mitter, 2004.

30 Dong, 2015, p. 75.

31 Dong, 2015.

32 Bourdieu and Passeron, 1990.

33 Galtung, 1990, p. 294.

34 Ibid.

35 Dong, 2015, p. 73, where Dong quotes Galtung, 1969, p. 170.

36 Dong, 2015, p. 80. Dong refers to the following source: Fangyi Huang, 2012. 黄方毅忆父文集：黄炎培与毛泽东周期率对话 (In Memory of My Father: A Conversation between Huang Yanpei and Mao on " Historical Periodicity"). Beijing: People' s Publishing House.

37 Dong, 2015, p. 73.

38 Dong, 2015, p. 74.

39 Fred Magdoff in his contribution to the Great Transition Network (GTN) discussion on the topic of "Marxism and Ecology: Common Fonts of a Great Transition," September 12, 2015. Magdoff is professor emeritus of plant and soil science at the University of Vermont and a longtime commentator on political-economic topics. See also Magdoff and Foster, 2011.

40 See Lindner, 2009b, Chapter 8: How We Can Reinvent Our Contexts, in the book Emotion and Conflict, pp. 129–137.

41 Cromby, 2012.

42 Gottman, et al., 1997.

43 Deci and Ryan, 2002.

44 Becker, 1973, pp. X-Y, quoted in Bond and Lun, 2013b, p. 8.

45 Bond and Lun, 2013b, p. 8.

46 Lewin, 1941, Lewin and Cartwright, 1951.

47 Bourdieu, 1977.

48 Foucault, 1966/1970.

49 Foucault, 1979, 1991, Foucault and Gordon, 1980.

50 Bourdieu, 1977, p. 17. Many other thinkers use the term habitus as well, among them sociologist Norbert Elias, for whom a particular habitus is a psychic structure that is embedded in the broader social relationships of what we experience as "civilization," see Elias, 1939/1994.

51 Anderson, 2006.

52 Giddens, 1984.

53 "Truth and Reconciliation for Group Selection," blog by David Sloan Wilson, http://evolution.binghamton.edu/dswilson/wp-content/uploads/2010/01/Truth-and-Reconciliation.pdf. It was a privilege to meet David Sloan Wilson in March 2016 in Oslo, Norway, and to learn from him in the context of "Kontrapunkt," an event organized by Nina Witoszek, Alida Boye, and Helge Iberg.

54 Linda Hartling builds on relational-cultural theory. See more in note 147 in the Introduction.

55 Cultural-historical activity theory builds on the work by Lev Vygotsky, 1978, and Aleksei Leontiev, 1975/1978. See more in note 148 in the Introduction.

56 See, for example, Janis and Mann, 1977, Jervis, et al., 1985, Lebow, 1981.

57 Kuhn, 1962.

58 Strawson, 1959. See also his thoughts on resentment, Strawson, 1974.

59 Etzioni, 2013, p. 333.

60 Searle, 1983.

61 Polanyi, 1967.

62 Bem, 1970.

63 Mackay, 1994.

64 Rogers, et al., 1992.

65 Zajonc, 1980.

66 Lakoff, 2006b, p. 25. See also www.rockridgeinstitute.org.

67 Lakoff, 2006a, p. 12. See more in note 211 in the Introduction.

68 Bernstein, 1975, 1990, pp. 16, 36–39. See also Bernstein, 2000. Basil Bernstein (1924 – 2000) was a linguist and researcher at the Institute of Education, University of London. I thank Vidar Vambheim for making me aware of Bernstein's work.

69 Galtung, 1996, p. 210–211.

70 Nathanson, 1996. Donald L. Nathanson, MD, is the founding executive director emeritus of the Tomkins Institute.

71 Berne, 1972.

72 Bargh and Williams, 2006.

73 Gladwell, 2005.

74 Strack and Deutsch, 2004.

75 Fazio, et al., 1986, Devine, 1989.

76 The "associative-propositional evaluation" model (APE) describes how implicit and explicit attitude change is guided by a distinction between associative and propositional processes, see Gawronski and Bodenhausen, 2006.

77 Geertz, 1983, p. 75.

78 Berger and Luckmann, 1966.

79 Parsons integrates not only sociological concepts, but also psychological, economic, political, and religious or philosophical components, see Parsons, 1951.

80 American television comedian Stephen Colbert is said to have coined the word "truthiness." See "Truthiness or Trustiness?" by Benjamin Zimmer, Language Log, October 26, 2005, http://itre.cis.upenn.edu/~myl/languagelog/archives/002586.html.

81 Palincsar, 1998.

82 Berger, 1969, quoted in Bond and Lun, 2013b. See Bond's involvement in the project Is Religion Natural? The Chinese Challenge, http://thethrivecenter.org/research/is-religion-natural-the-chinese-challenge/. It is a privilege to have Michael Harris Bond as esteemed member in the global advisory board of the Human Dignity and Humiliation Studies fellowship.

83 Stephan Feuchtwang in a personal communication on November 14, 2002. See also Feuchtwang, 2011.

84 Lindner, 2006c, p. 60.

85 Stephan Feuchtwang in a personal communication on November 14, 2002.

86 Clive Stafford Smith in The Secret War on Terror, documentary film by Peter Taylor, 2011, http://docuwiki.net/index.php?title=The_Secret_War_on_Terror.

87 Lindner, 2012f.

88 Miller, 2006b. See her first, seminal book, Miller, 1976/1986.

89 Coleman, 2003, p. 17. The Human Dignity and Humiliation Studies fellowship is honored to have Morton Deutsch and Peter Coleman, together with Claudia Cohen, Beth Fisher-Yoshida, Andrea Bartoli, and many others of their colleagues, as esteemed members of the first hour in our global advisory board. See also Holbrook, et al., 2015. See more in note 115 in the Preface.

90 See, for example, Fisher, et al., 1991. We learn there that we need to focus on interest and not on position to attain an optimal outcome. If two people fight over an orange, for example, sharing it equally would solve the conflict, however, not optimally. The optimal solution would be to ask more detailed questions and consider, for example, that one person wishes to use the skin of the orange for a cake while the other wants to extract the juice from the fruit meat. As a result, the outcome would be that both have 100 percent of their interest served, not just 50 percent of their initial positions. Not that such a positive outfall can be guaranteed – sometimes a situation simply does not entail the potential for win-win solutions – but by not searching for such potential win-win solutions, those solutions are overlooked and untapped.

91 Moore, 2016, p. 212. I thank Linda Hartling for making me aware of this book.

92 Weininger, 2005.

93 Bourdieu, 1990b, p. 135.

94 Wacquant, 1991, Bourdieu, 1991.

95 Elliott Weininger refers to Bourdieu, 1984b, 1990a, 1991, and writes:

> The upshot of Bourdieu's approach is that the endless debate between proponents of nominalist and realist views of class is shown to be misguided. The opposition between these views must not be understood as an epistemological alternative that confronts the class analyst. To the contrary, nominalism and realism amount to what might be described as distinct moments of the social process. … Social actors, it must be insisted, are distributed across an objective structure of positions which conditions the probability that any particular set of individuals will share the same lifestyle, the same collective name, or an organizational membership.

96 Richards and Swanger, 2009.

97 See Richards, 1995, Richards, 2004, Richards and Swanger, 2006b, Odora Hoppers and Richards, 2012, Richards and Swanger, 2013. Richards builds on, among others, Searle, 1995, Harré and Secord, 1972, Taylor, 1971, MacIntyre and Bell, 1967, and other works by the same authors. It is a privilege to have Howard Richards, Catherine Odora Hoppers, and her brother George as esteemed members in the global advisory board of our Human Dignity and Humiliation Studies fellowship.

98 Critical realism is being associated with names such as Roy Bhaskar, Rom Harré, Margaret Archer, Heikki Patomaki, and others. See for an overview over critical realism, Archer, et al., 1998. See also the book description of Porpora, 2015:

> Critical realism is a philosophy of science that positions itself against the major alternative philosophies underlying contemporary sociology. … Douglas V. Porpora argues that sociology currently operates with deficient accounts of truth, culture, structure, agency, and causality that are all better served by a critical realist perspective. This approach argues against the alternative sociological

perspectives, in particular the dominant positivism which privileges statistical techniques and experimental design over ethnographic and historical approaches. However, the book also compares critical realism favourably with a range of other approaches, including poststructuralism, pragmatism, interpretivism, practice theory, and relational sociology.

99 Richards and Swanger, 2009.

100 Richards and Andersson, 2017, Introduction.

101 Đilas, 1957.

102 Herman Daly in his contribution to the Great Transition Network (GTN) discussion on the topic of "Marxism and Ecology: Common Fonts of a Great Transition," September 14, 2015.

103 Vambheim, 2016, p. 90.

104 See the letter on www.jumbomail.me/en/Downloads.aspx?sid=645A457974395655476744464B3342347436653838673D3D. See also "Pardon Plea by Adolf Eichmann, Nazi War Criminal, Is Made Public," by Isabel Kershner, New York Times, January 27, 2016, www.nytimes.com/2016/01/28/world/middleeast/israel-adolf-eichmann-holocaust.html?_r=0.

105 Paul Nieuwenhuis, Cardiff Business School, in his contribution to the Great Transition Network (GTN) discussion on the topic of "Against Ecocide: Legal Protection for Earth," July 19, 2016, in response to Femke Wijdekop, 2016.

Chapter 10

1 See note 334 in the Introduction.

2 "Suicide Is Now the Biggest Killer of Teenage Girls Worldwide. Here's Why," by Nisha Lilia Diu, The Telegraph, May 25, 2015, www.telegraph.co.uk/women/womens-health/11549954/Teen-girls-Suicide-kills-more-young-women-than-anything.-Heres-why.html#comment-2045825875. Vikram Patel was the founding director of the Centre for Global Mental Health at the London School of Hygiene and Tropical Medicine and now spends much of the year in Delhi, where he works for the Public Health Foundation of India.

3 Erik Solheim was Minister of International Development when the interview took place in the Ministry of Foreign Affairs in Oslo, Norway, on January 10, 2011. Read more in the Appendix to Section One.

4 Le Bon, 1895/1896. Edward Louis Bernays, 1928, the nephew of Sigmund Freud, combined Freud's psychoanalytical concepts with the work of Gustave Le Bon on crowd psychology, and with Wilfred Trotter, 1916, and his ideas on the instincts of the "herd." See also Clark, 1988. Bernays was among the first to influence the market, for instance, the market of cigarettes, by luring women into smoking by manipulating images of women smokers as torches of freedom. I thank Diane Summer for being the first to make me aware of this manipulation, in 2007, in Brisbane, Australia.

5 Riesman, et al., 1950/2001.

6 A sense of deprivation or inequality, both in relation to others or in relation to expectations, can drive social movements. When expectations have outgrown actual material situations, the "J-curve" model developed by James Chowning Davies, 1969, is thought to be appropriate to explain political revolutions. See also Gurr, 1970, Davies, 1971.

7 Benford and Snow, 2000, Snow and Benford, 1988.

8 In Theories of Political Protest and Social Movements, sociologist Karl-Dieter Opp, 2009, presents his version of rational choice theory, where he includes a number of cultural concepts and shows that several other approaches rely on rational-choice assumptions without being aware of it, or making it explicit.

9 See note 165 in the Preface.

10 The motivation for movement participation is seen as a form of post-material politics and newly created identities, particularly those from the "new middle class." See the work of Ronald Inglehart, for instance, the Inglehart–Welzel Cultural Map – World Values Survey wave 6 (2010 – 2014) on www.worldvaluessurvey.org/images/Cultural_map_WVS6_2015.jpg, explained on www.worldvaluessurvey.org/WVSContents.jsp. Note also Inglehart and Welzel, 2005, and Norris and Inglehart, 2011.

11 Sociologist and philosopher Jürgen Habermas advocates public deliberation and hopes that in the future, a deliberative democracy can evolve, based on equal rights and obligations of citizens, see, among others, Habermas, 1962, 1981, 1985–1987, 1989. See also Alberto Melucci, et al., 1989, and Melucci, 1996.

12 The work of sociologist and political scientist Charles Tilly (1929 – 2008) spanned several decades, see McAdam, et al., 2001, Tilly, 1978. Tilly distinguishes between three kinds of claims for social movements: Identity claims declare that "we" constitute a unified force, such as "we, the Cherokees," standing claims assert ties to other political actors, for example excluded minorities, while program claims support or oppose actual or proposed actions. See Tilly, 2004. Tilly argues that regimes shape contentious repertoires by determining zones of prescribed, tolerated, and forbidden repertoires, by constituting potential claimants and potential objects of claims, and by producing issues, events, and governmental actions around which social movements rise and fall. See Tilly, 2010.

13 Jasper, 2011, p. 290. See also Shultziner, 2013. Jasper, 1997, sees four dimensions play distinct roles in social protest movements, namely, resources, strategy, biography, and culture. See also Cefaï, 2007.

14 Jasper, 1997, p. 106.

15 "Elie Wiesel's Acceptance Speech," on the occasion of the award of the Nobel Peace Prize in Oslo, December 10, 1986, www.nobelprize.org/nobel_prizes/peace/laureates/1986/wiesel-acceptance_en.html. I thank Linda Hartling for alerting when Elie Wiesel had passed away on July 2, 2016, and pointing out his important words on humiliation.

16 See Sherif, 1936, Festinger, 1954, 1957, 1980, Deutsch and Gerard, 1955.

17 Kim and Ruben, 1988.

18 Hayashi, 2003.

19 See, for example, Mezirow, 2000. See also Fisher-Yoshida, et al., 2009. Beth Fisher-Yoshida is the academic director of a Master of Science in Negotiation and Conflict Resolution at the School of Continuing Education at Columbia University, ce.columbia.edu/Negotiation-and-Conflict-Resolution/Beth-Fisher-Yoshida-Biography?context=974. It is a privilege to have her as esteemed member in the global advisory board of our Human Dignity and Humiliation Studies network, together with Adair Linn Nagata, and also Barnett Pearce (whom we so tragically lost much too early). See also Alagic, et al., 2009, Nagata, 2006, 2007.

20 Lindner, 2009b, pp. 130–137.

21 In a series of experiments in a lab at the University of Pennsylvania, dogs were given a series of mild shocks and learned that they could do nothing to stop them. Later, the shocks were repeated, yet, this time, only a small barrier hindered the dogs to avoid them: they simply had to leap over this small barrier. Yet, they sat in their boxes passively whining. They had given up trying. In the words of the scientists, they had "learned helplessness." See Seligman, 1974.

22 Jervis, 2006.

23 Carveth, 2013.

24 See note 331 in the Introduction.

25 The term méconnaissance was first introduced by psychologist Henri Wallon (1879 – 1962).

26 Kant, 1784.

27 I sense that the security dilemma's most recent cultural product, Western individualism, has usurped the English translation. Maturity is an individualistic concept, and it has something to do with growing up. My point is that this Unmündigkeit is not an individual psychological problem, nor general human forgetfulness. It is the result of large-scale social pressure and it would be a category mistake to seek solutions at the wrong level of analysis and action.

28 Adorno, et al., 1950.

29 Miller, 1980/2002.

30 See note 170 in the Introduction, and note 24 in the Introduction to Section One.

31 "Why Trump?" by George Lakoff, Huffington Post, March 3, 2016, www.huffingtonpost.com/george-lakoff/why-trump_1_b_9372450.html. I thank Michael Britton for making me aware of this article.

32 Festinger, 1954, 1957, 1980.

33 Adler, 1993, 2004, Adler, et al., 2009. I had the privilege of being introduced to Nanci Dale Adler's research in 2008, through her talk "The Communist Within: Narratives of Loyalty to the Party Before, During, and After the Gulag," at the Center for Studies of Holocaust and Religious Minorities in Norway, October 1, 2008. See also Höjdestrand, 2009. Adler builds her interpretation on the work on cognitive dissonance by Leon Festinger, 1954, 1957.

34 Miller and Stiver, 1997.

35 Eldridge, et al., 2003, p. 2.

36 "Why Trump?" by George Lakoff, Huffington Post, March 3, 2016, www.huffingtonpost.com/george-lakoff/why-trump_1_b_9372450.html. I thank Michael Britton for making me aware of this article.

37 Van Dijk, 2001.

38 Phillips and Hardy, 2002, p. 15. See also Karlberg, 2013.

39 Galtung, 1996, p. 199.

40 Guha and Spivak, 1988.

41 See, among others, Chaturvedi, 2000, Mignolo, 2000, Verdesio, 2005. I thank Magnus Haavelsrud for making me aware of the latter publications. See also Haavelsrud, 2015.

42 Habermas, 1985–1987.

43 Collins, 1990.

44 See note 201 in this Introduction.

45 Reber, 1995.

46 Kuhn, 1962.

47 Etzioni, 2013, p. 334.

48 Kaufman, 2001, p. 212.

49 Volkan, 2004.

50 See Volkan, 1997, 2004, 2006, 2013.

51 Read more in Chapter 2, and see also note 329 in the Introduction.

52 Sidanius and Pratto, 1999, p. 44.

53 Jost, et al., 2004, Jost, et al., 2009, Jost, et al., 2002, Jost and Ross, 1999.

54 Jost, et al., 2004, Abstract. See also What's the Matter with Kansas? How Conservatives Won the Heart of America, by Thomas Frank, 2004, where the author asks why working class populations voted against their best economic interests: they tended to vote conservative despite Conservatives not being equitable when it came to the rights of working class people. See the full note in the pdf edition of this book.

55 Read more in Chapter 2, and see also note 329 in the Introduction.

56 Jost, et al., 2004, Jost, et al., 2009, Jost, et al., 2002, Jost and Ross, 1999.

57 See note 184 in the Introduction.

58 Such as Kuhn, Sidanius, Pratto, and Jost.

59 Lerner, 1980.

60 See, for example, Janis and Mann, 1977, Jervis, et al., 1985, or Lebow, 1981.

61 "Mental Health Awareness Month in a Climate of Denial," by Carol Smaldino, Huffington Post, May 11, 2016, www.huffingtonpost.com/carol-smaldino/mental-health-awareness-m_b_9895080.html.

62 Ibid.

63 Ibid.

64 See note 19 in the Introduction to Section Two.

65 "Why an Assassinated Psychologist – Ignored by US Psychologists – Is Being Honored," by Bruce E Levine, Truthout, November 16, 2014, www.truth-out.org/opinion/item/27244-why-an-assassinated-psychologist-ignored-by-us-psychologists-is-being-honored. I thank Salman Türken for making me aware of this article.

66 "Psychiatric Views on the 2014 News," by Steven Moffic, Psychiatric Times, December 30, 2014, www.psychiatrictimes.com/blogs/couch-crisis/psychiatric-views-2014-news. See also "The Senate Report on the C.I.A.'s Torture and Lies," Editorial Board, New York Times, December 9, 2014, www.nytimes.com/2014/12/10/opinion/the-senate-report-on-the-cias-torture-and-lies.html. Accessed December 30, 2014.

67 See note 87 in Chapter 3.

68 Dong, 2015.

69 Koenigs, 2007. For those, who wish to acquire a feel for the pathways of radicalization, Koenigs recommends Updike, 2006.

70 Koenigs, 2007, p. 2.

71 Koenigs, 2007, p. 15: "Al-Qaeda deliberately timed Massoud's assassination to precede the attacks in the United States. Anticipating a US military response, Al-Qaeda assassinated Mullah Omar's arch foe in order both to secure Osama bin Laden's relations with his Taliban protectors, and to eliminate the United States' most obvious partner in any retaliation that they might carry out on Afghan soil." See also the Appendix to Section One.

72 See note 25 in Chapter 9.

73 Arendt, 1963.

74 Van Vuuren and Liebenberg, 1994. I thank Zuzana Luckay for making me aware of these authors. It is a privilege to have Zuzana Luckay in our Human Dignity and Humiliation Studies fellowship.

75 Le Bon, 1895/1896.

76 Trotter, 1916. See also Clark, 1988.

77 Bernays, 1928.

78 Translated from German by Alice Asbury Abbott, Suttner, 1908, pp. 96–97.

79 Translated from German by Alice Asbury Abbott, Suttner, 1908, pp. 96–97. German original in Suttner, 1889, pp. 52–53. See the German original in the full note in the pdf edition of this book.

80 "Bitter Memories of War on the Way to Jail," by Chris Hedges, Truthdig, December 20, 2010, www.truthdig.com/report/item/bitter_memories_of_war_on_the_way_to_jail_20101220.

81 Ibid.

Chapter 11

1 See the full note in the pdf edition of this book. See also note 40 in the Introduction.

2 See note 68 in Chapter 1.

3 See also Robinson, 2017.

4 Left-leaning American political analyst and historian Thomas Frank confirmed in a BBC news hour that his views on globalized capitalism are very similar to those voiced, for instance, by Stephen Bannon. Listen to What Does Steve Bannon Think? BBC Newshour Extra with Frances Sellers, senior writer at The Washington Post, Christopher Caldwell, from the right leaning Weekly Standard, and Thomas Frank, February 3, 2017, www.bbc.co.uk/programmes/p04qx7vv.

5 Heath-Kelly, et al., 2016, write about terrorism and neoliberalism as connected in multiple, complex, and often camouflaged ways.

6 Wise, 2015. I thank John Bilorusky for making me aware of this book. See also "Barack Obama's Meager Legacy of Incomplete Accomplishments and of Provoked Wars: What Happened? by Rodrigue Tremblay in note 54 in Chapter 1.

7 See, for example, Lair, et al., 2005.

8 McGoey, 2012. See also "What Will Future Generations Condemn Us For?" by Kwame Anthony Appiah, Washington Post, September 26, 2010, www.washingtonpost.com/wp-dyn/content/article/2010/09/24/AR2010092404113.html.

9 Matt Taibbi about the U.S. Securities and Exchange Commission (SEC), which, to him, appeared "somehow worse than corrupt – it's hard to find the right language, but 'aggressively clueless,'" quoted in Elizabeth Warren, 2017, p. 87. I thank Linda Hartling for sharing her notes on Warren's book with me.

10 Mark McElroy in his contribution to the Great Transition Network (GTN) discussion on the topic of "Against Ecocide: Legal Protection for Earth," August 2, 2016, in response to Femke Wijdekop, 2016.

11 Ibid.

12 Guy Dauncey contribution to the Great Transition Network (GTN) discussion on the topic of "Sustainability and Well-Being: A Happy Synergy," March 2, 2017, in response to Barrington-Leigh, 2017. Guy Dauncey currently works on his next book, titled The Economics of Kindness: The End of Capitalism and the Birth of a New Cooperative Economy.

13 See, among others, Paley, 2014.

14 Kogon, 1946/1950, p. 19. See also Siebert and Ott, 2016.

15 Siebert and Ott, 2016, p. 2. Leo Löwenthal, a first generation member of Max Horkheimer's Institute for Social Research, stated that Benjamin's work ought to be heard as an "alarm clock that in each minute rings for sixty seconds" "to awaken people out of their soporific and hopeless enchantment and melancholic conformity to the catastrophic, life-threatening danger from the very same system that was further

unfolding in the 19th fin de siècle European society due to the developing crises of the capitalist social production system that manifested itself in the horror of World War I, the Great Depression and the rise of fascism," Ott, 2016, p. 5.

16 Wainwright, 2016. Wainwright points out that societies have the choice between a drug business controlled by the state, or by organized crime, and that the state would be the preferable actor. See also Paley, 2014.

17 Watch, for instance, Wie korrupt ist Deutschland?, a documentary film by Steffen Mayer and Chris Humbs, Zweites Deutsches Fernsehen, 2016, www.zdf.de/zdfzeit/korruption-42796414.html. The analysis that the investigators of the documentary conclude with, is that corruption in Germany is widespread and structurally ingrained. It is not just a matter of money being exchanged, it is also that the quality of materials used, for instance in building projects, is being thinned out and diminished. At the end, only the visible facade of a project looks intact, while the substance is precarious. The Volkswagen emissions scandal of 2015 shows how the thinning out of quality turns into fraud. See the full note in the pdf edition of this book.

18 "FKI Asks Assembly to Revise Anti-Corruption Law," by Kim Yoo-chul, Korea Times, July 29, 2016, www.koreatimes.co.kr/www/news/tech/2016/07/133_210689.html.

19 The German military, for instance, is creating a new cyberwar section with 13 500 employees: "Ursula von der Leyen: Bundeswehr rüstet gegen Attacken aus dem Internet," Die Zeit, 26. April 2016, www.zeit.de/politik/deutschland/2016-04/ursula-von-der-leyen-bundeswehr-aufruestung-cyberkrieg-angriffe-internet.

20 Lawson, 2015. I thank Howard Richards for making me aware of this book.

21 "The Future of the United States of America," by Howard Richards, TRANSCEND Media Service, January 2, 2017, www.transcend.org/tms/2017/01/the-future-of-the-united-states-of-america/: "Consequences of the basic social structure: 1A. There is a chronic insufficiency of inducement to invest. It is not only the case that the bread and butter of the people, their employment and their dignity, depend on the confidence of investors. It is also the case that investor confidence perpetually flags, lags, and threatens to collapse. … 2A. There is a chronic insufficiency of effective demand. This is no small matter because profits depend on sales, while investment, and therefore output and employment, depend on expectations of profit."

22 Harvey, 1990. I thank Howard Richards for making me aware of this book.

23 See note 21 above.

24 "Corruption Perceptions Index 2016," Transparency International (TI), Berlin, January 25, 2017, http://files.transparency.org/content/download/2089/13368/file/2016_CPIReport_EN.pdf. José Ugaz, chair of TI: "In too many countries, people are deprived of their most basic needs and go to bed hungry every night because of corruption, while the powerful and corrupt enjoy lavish lifestyles with impunity."

25 "Steve Bannon: 'We're Going to War in the South China Sea ... No Doubt,'" by Benjamin Haas, The Guardian, February 2, 2017, www.theguardian.com/us-news/2017/feb/02/steve-bannon-donald-trump-war-south-china-sea-no-doubt.

26 Lindner, 2014c.

27 See, among others, Pérouse de Montclos, 2015, or Apard, 2015. Watch also Boko Haram: The Origins of Evil, documentary film by Xavier Muntz, 2016, www.javafilms.fr/spip.php?article2103.

28 Mohammed Yusuf founded Boko Haram in 2002, and following its July 2009 uprising, he was captured by the Nigerian military who handed him over to the Nigerian police force, who then summarily executed him in public view.

29 Lüders, 2015.

30 Peter Lundberg, UN Deputy Humanitarian Coordinator Nigeria, see "Nigeria's humanitarian crisis 'can no longer be ignored,' UN says, launching $1 billion appeal," United Nations News Centre, December 2, 2016, www.un.org/apps/news/story.asp?NewsID=55702#.WERbjX2OWgx.

31 Akilu, 2015.

32 "Brexit: The Key Lessons – Now is the Time for Hope to Build on the Ruins," by economist Kamran Mofid, Globalization for the Common Good Initiative (GCGI), June 29, 2016, www.gcgi.info/index.php/blog/799-brexit-the-key-lessons-now-is-the-time-for-hope-to-build-on-the-ruins. It is a privilege to have Kamran Mofid as esteemed member in the global advisory board of our Human Dignity and Humiliation Studies fellowship.

33 See note 91 and 92 in the Introduction.

34 See, for instance, the "Conclusions of the Council of the European Union and the Member States Meeting Within the Council on Enhancing the Criminal Justice Response to Radicalisation Leading to Terrorism and Violent Extremism," by the Council of the European Union, Press release 845/15 Justice Home Affairs, November 20, 2015, www.consilium.europa.eu/en/meetings/jha/2015/11/20/.
See also Generation Dschihad, documentary film by Albrecht Knechtel, Norddeutscher Rundfunk, 2016, www.arte.tv/guide/de/060207-000-A/generation-dschihad. See also Steinberg, 2015. See the full note in the pdf edition of this book.

35 Ellis, et al., 2012.

36 Graeber, 2001.

37 On June 5, 2008, more than one thousand representatives from indigenous communities across the Americas gathered in Lima, Peru, and agreed on a new social system, called Living Well. See, among others, www.villageearth.org/pages/Projects/Peru/perublog/2008/06/living-well-development-alternative.html#. See also the Journal of Indigenous Wellbeing, http://journalindigenouswellbeing.com. Consider also the sustainability principle in The Great Law of the Iroquois Confederacy and the Ley de la Madre Tierra in Bolivia.

38 Schumacher, 1973, p. 4.

39 After the commons were enclosed in England, starting during the sixteenth century, what sociologist Eric Mielants, 2007, calls "terroristic" laws were introduced that criminalized idleness, thus pushing people into early capitalist manufacturing.

40 See note 163 in the Preface.

41 Chris Barrington-Leigh on the Great Transition Network Initiative discussion titled "Sustainability and Well-Being: A Happy Synergy," April 17, 2017, in response to the list members' comments to Barrington-Leigh, 2017.

42 See note 35 in the Preface.

43 Hardin, 1998. Elinor Ostrom received the Nobel Prize for Economics 2009. She is considered one of the leading scholars in the study of common pool resources. Her work emphasizes the multifaceted nature of human–ecosystem interaction and argues against any singular "panacea" for individual social-ecological system problems. See, for example, Poteete, et al., 2010.

44 Rousseau, 1762.

45 Chris Barrington-Leigh on the Great Transition Network Initiative discussion titled "Sustainability and Well-Being: A Happy Synergy," April 17, 2017, in response to the list members' comments to Barrington-Leigh, 2017.

46 John Atkinson Hobson, 1902, explained what he saw, namely, that imperial expansion is driven by a search for new markets and investment opportunities overseas. His book gained Hobson an international

reputation, and influenced people such as Vladimir Lenin and Leon Trotsky, as well as The Origins of Totalitarianism by Hannah Arendt, 1951. See also the Military-Industrial Complex Speech by Dwight D. Eisenhower, 34th President of the United States, on January 17, 1961, Public Papers of the Presidents, Dwight D. Eisenhower, 1960, pp. 1035–1040,
http://coursesa.matrix.msu.edu/~hst306/documents/indust.html, see also https://youtu.be/8y06NSBBRtY. In this farewell speech Eisenhower warns of the military industrial complex.
See, furthermore, "Why Is the Military-Industrial Complex Sometimes Called 'The Devil's Dynamo'?" by John Scales Avery, TRANSCEND Media Service, June 30, 2014, www.transcend.org/tms/2014/06/the-devils-dynamo/, where Avery describes how the military-industrial complex involves a circular flow of money, like the electrical current in a dynamo, driving a diabolical machine. It started with unequal distribution that neither the rich nor the poor could buy back the total output of their society:

> The incomes of the poor were insufficient, and rich were too few in number. The rich had finite needs, and tended to reinvest their money. As Hobson pointed out, reinvestment in new factories only made the situation worse by increasing output. Hobson had been sent as a reporter by the Manchester Guardian to cover the Second Boer War. His experiences had convinced him that colonial wars have an economic motive. Such wars are fought, he believed, to facilitate investment of the excess money of the rich in African or Asian plantations and mines, and to make possible the overseas sale of excess manufactured goods. Hobson believed imperialism to be immoral, since it entails suffering both among colonial peoples and among the poor of the industrial nations. The cure that he recommended was a more equal distribution of incomes in the manufacturing countries.

In his farewell address (January 17, 1961) US President Dwight D. Eisenhower warned of the dangers of the war-based economy that World War II had forced his nation to build:

> "We have been compelled to create an armaments industry of vast proportions," Eisenhower said, "...Now this conjunction of an immense military establishment and a large arms industry is new in American experience. The total influence – economic, political, even spiritual – is felt in every city, every state house, every office in the federal government. ...We must not fail to comprehend its grave implications. Our toil, resources and livelihood are all involved; so is the very structure of our society. ... We must stand guard against the acquisition of unwarranted influence, whether sought or unsought, by the military-industrial complex. The potential for the disastrous rise of misplaced power exists and will persist. We must never let the weight of this combination endanger our democratic processes. We should take nothing for granted.

Military-Industrial Complex Speech by Dwight D. Eisenhower, 34th President of the United States, on January 17, 1961, Public Papers of the Presidents, Dwight D. Eisenhower, 1960, pp. 1035–1040, http://coursesa.matrix.msu.edu/~hst306/documents/indust.html, see also https://youtu.be/8y06NSBBRtY. See more in note 127 in Chapter 14, and in note 199 in Chapter 18.

47 Korten 2006, private communication to Riane Eisler, cited in Eisler, 2007, p. 16. Economist Richard T. Carson, 2010, explains that economists have "lost a decade or more" on believing in the false promise of the wealth-pollution argument. They erroneously assumed that increases in wealth will automatically translate into improved environmental conditions. See also note 48 in the Preface.

48 See note 6 in the Preface, and the full note in the pdf edition of this book.

49 Higgins, 2016. See note 7 in the Preface.

50 Oppenlander, 2011. See also Cowspiracy: The Sustainability Secret, a 2015 environmental documentary film following filmmaker Kip Andersen as he shows that animal agriculture is the leading cause of deforestation, water consumption and pollution, is responsible for more greenhouse gases than the transportation industry, and is a primary driver of rainforest destruction, species extinction, habitat loss,

topsoil erosion, ocean "dead zones," and virtually every other environmental ill. See www.cowspiracy.com, https://youtu.be/S-XP79o8gqQ.

51 Expert on corporate sustainability management, Mark W. McElroy, Center for Sustainable Organizations, in his contribution to the Great Transition Network (GTN) discussion on the topic of "Monetizing Nature," July 22, 2014.

52 See for recent discussions, "Monetizing Nature: Taking Precaution on a Slippery Slope," by Barbara Unmüssig, President of the Heinrich Böll Foundation in Berlin, Germany, www.greattransition.org/document/monetizing-nature-taking-precaution-on-a-slippery-slope. See also Costanza and Kubiszewski, 2014, or Rotering, 2013. See also Lindner, 2012f, A Dignity Economy.

53 Richard Sanders, founder of Quest 2025 (www.quest2025.net), in his contribution to the Great Transition Network (GTN) discussion on the topic of "Monetizing Nature," July 25, 2014.

54 "The Free-Trade Regime: Oligarchy in Action," by Moritz Laurer, originally published by Foreign Policy in Focus, May 13, 2014, www.resilience.org/stories/2014-05-13/the-free-trade-regime-oligarchy-in-action. See, furthermore, "Neoliberalism: Oversold?" by Jonathan D. Ostry, Prakash Loungani, and Davide Furceri, The International Monetary Fund (IMF), Finance and Development, June 2016, Volume 53, Number 2, www.imf.org/external/pubs/ft/fandd/2016/06/pdf/ostry.pdf.

55 See, for instance, "Wir haben euch gewarnt," Präsident Idriss Déby Itno interviewed by Susanne Koelbl, Der Spiegel 42/2016, October 15, 2016, p. 86.

56 "'Corporate Trojan Horse': Obama Pushes Secretive TPP Trade Pact, Would Rewrite Swath of U.S. Laws," with Lori Wallach, director of Public Citizen's Global Trade Watch, Democracy Now, as guest, October 04, 2013, www.democracynow.org/2013/10/4/a_corporate_trojan_horse_obama_pushes: "The agreement has 29 chapters, and only five of them have to do with trade. The other 24 chapters either handcuff our domestic governments, limiting food safety, environmental standards, financial regulation, energy and climate policy, or establishing new powers for corporations." See also note 54 in Chapter 1.

57 Geld regiert die Welt: Die Macht der Finanzkonzerne – Reportage, documentary film by Tilman Achtnich and Hanspeter Michel, Das Erste, 2014, http://programm.ard.de/TV/daserste/die-story-im-ersten--geld-regiert-die-welt/eid_2810611333298235. See the full note in the pdf edition of this book.

58 Alliance Development Works/Bündnis Entwicklung Hilft (BEH), 2013.

59 "Hungary Says Donald Trump Inspired Its Latest Policy to Detain All Asylum Seeker," by Aamna Mohdin, Quartz, February 07, 2017, https://qz.com/904689/hungary-says-donald-trump-inspired-its-latest-policy-to-detain-all-migrants/.

60 Rodrik, 2011.

61 Mann, 2000.

62 Terreblanche, 2014. I thank Michael Britton for reminding me Terreblanche's work.

63 "Just Peace in Past and Present Context: Climate Change as Threat to Peace and Future," talk given by Raymond G. Helmick, S.J., at the University of Iceland, May 3, 2014, in preparation of a conference of the World Council of Churches on the Just Peace theme to be held in Iceland in 2015. See the quote in the full note in the pdf edition of this book. See also Bacevich, 2010, George, 2015.

64 "Refugee Crisis: Brought to You by Western Imperialism," by André Vltchek, Human Wrongs Watch, September 20, 2015, http://human-wrongs-watch.net/2015/09/21/refugee-crisis-brought-to-you-by-western-imperialism/.

65 "What if Sociologists Had as Much Influence as Economists?" by Neil Irwin, New York Times, March 17, 2017, www.nytimes.com/2017/03/17/upshot/what-if-sociologists-had-as-much-influence-as-economists.html. I thank Linda Hartling for making me aware of this article.

66 Maureen O'Hara in a personal communication to Louise Sundararajan's Indigenous Psychology Network list on December 6, 2013. Maureen O'Hara, 2010, uses the term psychosphere to refer to the holistic, "interconnected, interpenetrated mutually influential system of narratives, symbols, images, representations, languages, metaphors, patterns of life, values, epistemologies, cognitive habits, rituals, religions, power relationships, sports, forms of commerce, governance, metaphysics, art, and technologies" that delineates the psychological context of individual and group life. O'Hara concludes that in her view, Malcolm Gladwell, Daniel Kahneman, and Martin Seligman in the U.S., and Lord Richard Layard in the United Kingdom "represent a new round of scientism and self-colonialization in the West. Their non-reflexive 'econothink' brilliantly serves the interests of corporatization and the interests of the established power elites who wish to decontextualize wellbeing from the economic and political circumstances." See also O'Hara and Leicester, 2012, O'Hara and Lyon, 2014.

67 Anthony Marsella in his response to Maureen O'Hara on Louise Sundararajan's Indigenous Psychology Network list on January 14, 2014.

68 See Lindner, 2009b, Chapter 8: How We Can Reinvent Our Contexts, in the book Emotion and Conflict.

69 Educator and consultant David Hutchins, DH International Quality College, in a personal communication on June 14, 2013. Hutchins was responsible for the inspiration and organization of the event "The Japanese Approach to Product Quality," held at the Institute of Directors in 1979, which Kaoru Ishikawa attended for his only visit to Europe.

70 Juran, 1964.

71 Philosopher John Gray reviews Moral Tribes by Joshua Greene, 2013, in The Guardian, January 17, 2014, www.theguardian.com/books/2014/jan/17/moral-tribes-joshua-greene-review. See also Gray, 2002.

72 Lerner, 1980. See also Lindner, 2014c.

73 "Islam and the West: Roads toward Peace," by Johan Galtung, TRANSCEND Media Service, September 14, 2015, www.transcend.org/tms/2015/09/islam-and-the-west-roads-toward-peace/.

74 See, for example, Lair, et al., 2005.

75 Strategische Kriegsführung für Manager (Strategic Warfare for Managers) is the title of a "guide" book for managers by Gilad and Junginger, 2010. See also note 113 in Chapter 5. Also for sociologist Max Weber war was a kind of natural phenomenon of political history, a form of unavoidable "eternal struggle of nations" (ewiges Ringen der Nationen), comparable to economic competition, only that economic war is conducted with "peaceful ammunition" (friedliche Kampfmittel), see Bruhns, 2014, p. 63.
The result is a quasi-military business culture. The Aldi concern in Germany, for instance, is organized like a military campaign; its founders, the brothers Karl and Theodor Albrecht, learned military logistics in WWII. Another result is that managers are expected to hide all vulnerabilities, to distance themselves from their very own humanity. They learn to appear to be in control even if their life falls apart. The choice is between total control or suicide. On January 26, 2014, the former Deutsche Bank manager William Broeksmit hanged himself in his apartment in London. On the same day, Tata Motors CEO Karl Slym jumped from the twenty-second floor of a luxury hotel in Bangkok. In August 2013, the financial director of Zurich Insurance, Pierre Wauthier, hanged himself in his home in Switzerland. One month earlier, Carsten Schloter, head of the Swisscom telecommunications company, was found dead at home. The former Siemens financial director and former showcase manager Heinz-Joachim Neubürger took his own life on February 5, 2015. His daughters spoke at his funeral to the managers who had gathered and asked them to change their culture. See "Siemens: Tod eines Managers," by Kerstin Bund, Die Zeit, June 18, 2015, www.zeit.de/2015/23/siemens-heinz-joachim-neubuerger-selbstmord/komplettansicht.

76 "Immer mehr Menschen kaufen eine Waffe," by Martin Schneider, Süddeutsche Zeitung, December 6, 2015, www.sueddeutsche.de/bayern/boom-immer-mehr-menschen-kaufen-eine-waffe-1.2769959.

77 Lindner and Desmond Tutu (Foreword), 2010, p. 140: "Psychologist and journalist Susan Pinker, 2008, points out that women – unlike men – tend to prefer people-oriented careers, or, more precisely, careers oriented toward living organism (not things). Pinker created uproar and was attacked for betraying the feminist cause. Indeed, if the feminist struggle's success is framed within the paradigm of traditional male life designs, her reflections do undermine the feminist struggle. However, Pinker's story may also reflect success: women are in the process of not only rising to visibility in a male public sphere, but of redesigning the world to make it more sustainable for all."

78 Stevenson and Wolfers, 2009.

79 See, among others, Bentall, 2009, Cushman, 1995, and Pope and Vasquez, 2007. I thank Linda Hartling for these links.

80 Fujiwara and Kawachi, 2008. I thank Linda Hartling for making me aware of this seminal study.

81 "The Rise of Chronic Noncommunicable Diseases: an Impending Disaster," Margaret Chan, director-general of the World Health Organization, April 27, 2011, www.who.int/dg/speeches/2011/global_forum_ncd_20110427/en/.

82 See, for instance, Angell, 2004. See also videos.med.wisc.edu/videos/940. For a historical perspective on how medicine evolved in the United States and from there informed many other parts of the world, see, among others, Duffy, 2011. I thank Inge Lindseth for making me aware of this article.

83 Gibson, 2007.

84 "Child Food Adverts 'Misleading," BBC News, December 14, 2008, news.bbc.co.uk/go/pr/fr/-/2/hi/health/7779438.stm.

85 "This Is How Much Celebrities Get Paid To Endorse Soda And Unhealthy Food," by Allison Aubrey, National Public Radio (NPR), June 7, 2016, www.npr.org/sections/thesalt/2016/06/07/481123646/this-is-how-much-celebrities-get-paid-to-endorse-soda-and-unhealthy-food. I thank Linda Hartling for making me aware of this article.

86 See, among others, "Psychiatrists Revise the Book of Human Troubles," by Benedict Carey, New York Times, December 18, 2008, www.nytimes.com/2008/12/18/health/18psych.html. See also Cosgrove, et al., 2006, or Paris, 2008. I thank Eugenia Tsao for the last two references.

87 Eugenia Tsao in a personal communication on July 3, 2009.

88 Wasem, et al., 2009.

89 See Dr. Aryeh Shander on RBC Transfusions 1, where Aryeh Shander, MD, FCCM, FCCP, and clinical professor of anesthesiology, medicine and surgery at the Mount Sinai School of Medicine, speaks at the Patient Safety Science and Technology Summit on January 14, 2013, https://youtu.be/7SpOWDUXq7M.

90 Böses Blut – Kehrtwende in der Intensivmedizin, documentary film by Ulrike Gehring, Südwestrundfunk, 2014, www.daserste.de/information/reportage-dokumentation/dokus/videos/boeses-blut-kehrtwende-in-der-intensivmedizin-100.html. See the full note in the pdf edition of this book.

91 Hannah, 2015.

92 People are living longer throughout the world, partly due to lower rates of cardiovascular disease deaths in high-income countries and child deaths in low-income countries, while disparities remain among regions. See Amare, 2014.

93 "Inequality and Democracy," by Roberto Savio, Other News, May 17, 2014, www.other-news.info/2014/05/inequality-and-democracy/:

> Is economic growth "a rising tide lifting all boats," and is "capital trickling down to everybody"? The United Nations claims that extreme poverty worldwide has been halved. The number of people living on less than 1.25 dollars a day fell from 47 percent in 1990 to 22 percent in 2010. There are still

1.2 billion people living in extreme poverty, but a new middle-class is emerging worldwide, even if the success in the numbers is due basically to Brazil, China and India. So, the argument from the defenders of the present economic model is "if there are a few super rich, why do we ignore the enormous progress that has created 1 billion new middle-class citizens?"
The neoliberal period unleashed by the Washington Consensus made financial capitalism doing better than productive capitalism.
Problems:
• Inequality, with extreme wealth for a few, the middle class shrinking in rich countries, and permanent unemployment for ever more
• the rich are not paying taxes as before, because of a large number of fiscal benefits and fiscal paradises
• politics has become subservient to economic interests
• social and ecological resources are hollowed out and plundered. Current consumption patterns rapidly deplete the world's non-renewable resources, according to a new UNEP report released on June 7, 2014 ("176 percent Rise in Metal Prices, 260 percent Rise in Energy Prices Marks Era of Soaring Costs as Resources Decline," by United Nations Environment Programme-hosted International Resource Panel (IRP), June 6, 2014, www.unep.org/newscentre/Default.aspx?DocumentID=2791&ArticleID=10885&l=en).

See also note 177 in this Chapter 11.

94 "The Cost of Inequality: How Wealth and Income Extremes Hurt Us All," Oxfam, January 18, 2013, www.oxfam.org/sites/www.oxfam.org/files/cost-of-inequality-oxfam-mb180113.pdf.

95 "Annual Income of Richest 100 People Enough to End Global Poverty Four Times Over," Oxfam, January 19, 2013, www.oxfam.org/en/pressroom/pressrelease/2013-01-19/annual-income-richest-100-people-enough-end-global-poverty-four-times.

96 See www.oxfam.org/en/pressroom/pressrelease/2013-01-19/annual-income-richest-100-people-enough-end-global-poverty-four-times.

97 See, among many others, Colander, et al., 2009, or Lewis, 2010.

98 Stiglitz, 2012. See also Wilkinson and Pickett, 2009, Piketty, 2013/2014, Atkinson, 2015, or Frank, 2016. See also a publication by the Organisation for Economic Co-operation and Development (OECD), 2015, for why all benefit from more equality. See, furthermore, Herrmann, 2013, in Wie solidarisch ist Deutschland? – Warum Arme arm bleiben und die Reichen reicher werden, documentary film by Eva Schötteldreier, Westdeutscher Rundfunk Köln, 2016, www.daserste.de/information/reportage-dokumentation/dokus/wie-solidarisch-ist-deutschland-100.html. See the full note in the pdf edition of this book.

99 See Lindner, 2012f. The list of relevant references would be extremely long. Here are only a few references in the place of many, ranging from Crouch, 2013, to Rifkin, 2014, or Mason, 2015. See also "Yet Another Nobel Prize in Economics: An Affront to Humanity and Truth," by economist Kamran Mofid, Globalization for the Common Good Initiative (GCGI), October 12, 2015, http://gcgi.info/index.php/kamran-s-blog/735-yet-another-nobel-prize-in-economics-an-affront-to-humanity-and-truth. See also Der Banker: Master of the Universe, a documentary film by Marc Bauder, 2013, https://youtu.be/NaRb5wRYnW4.

100 "Democracy v. Concentrated Wealth: In Search of a Louis D. Brandeis Quote," by Peter Scott Campbell, The Green Bag 2D, Spring 2013, pp. 251–256, http://greenbag.org/v16n3/v16n3_articles_campbell.pdf.

101 "Working for the Few: Political Capture and Economic Inequality," Oxfam Briefing Paper, January 20, 2014, www.oxfam.org/sites/www.oxfam.org/files/bp-working-for-few-political-capture-economic-inequality-200114-en.pdf.

102 Ibid.

103 See, among others, Akerlof and Shiller, 2009, Evanoff, et al., 2012, Glimcher and Fehr, 2014, Rolls, 2014, Reyna and Wilhelms, 2015. Wu, et al., 2012, write:

> More recently, although traditional economic theorists have endorsed the rationally grounded "Efficient Markets Hypothesis" (Samuelson, 1965; Fama, 1970), unpredicted and rapid rises and crashes of the market valuation of technology and housing sectors have raised new questions about investor rationality. Critics of the Efficient Markets Hypothesis have contended that investors consistently exhibit irrational tendencies including overconfidence (Barber and Odean, 2001; Gervais and Odean, 2001), loss aversion (Kahneman and Tversky, 1979; Shefrin and Statman, 1985; Odean, 1998), herding (Huberman and Regev, 2001), psychological accounting (Tversky and Kahneman, 1981), miscalculation of probabilities (Lichtenstein et al., 1981), and regret (Bell, 1982; Clarke et al., 1994). These "irrational" biases have been attributed to psychological factors with emotional overtones – including fear, greed, and other affective reactions to price fluctuations and shocks to wealth. In an attempt to explain individual and market anomalies, an expanding field of research has begun to examine links between emotion and "irrational" decision-making (Loewenstein, 2000).

104 Knutson, et al., 2008: "Viewing erotic pictures for 15 heterosexual men increased their financial risk taking, partially mediated by increases in nucleus accumbens (NAcc) activation." See also Wu, et al., 2012.

105 Inside Job transcript, September 2010, www.sonyclassics.com/awards-information/insidejob_screenplay.pdf.

106 A Cambridge University study found a direct link between the amount of money traders make and testosterone levels. See Coates and Herbert, 2008.

107 Mussel, et al., 2015, Abstract: "… greed may explain risky and reckless behavior in diverse settings, such as investment banking, and may account for phenomena such as stock market."

108 David Schwartzman, 2016, explained that not just peace with each other, but also peace with the planet depends on dismantling the military-industrial complex (the "MIC"); see his contribution to the Great Transition Network Initiative discussion titled "Journey to Earthland: Making the Great Transition to Planetary Civilization," October 25, 2016, in response to Raskin, 2016:

> "The MIC is responsible for a colossal waste of energy and material resources that should be going to meet the needs of humans and ecosystems around the world. Nearly $2 trillion is spent annually on global military expenditures, with the US spending about half the total amount. Furthermore, the nuclear industry is integrated into the MIC, and the threat of nuclear attack is a long-standing instrument of imperial policy. The possibility of a nuclear war continues, with nuclear weapons now being possessed by nine nations. Fulfilling Eisenhower's 1961 warning, the MIC plays the dominant role in setting the domestic/foreign policy agenda of the big powers, in particular the US. But most relevant to the threat of catastrophic climate change is the role of the Pentagon as the 'global oil-protection service' of the MIC. The U.S.'s imperial agenda actively blocks the global cooperation and equity required for a successful prevention program on climate change. This is the critical obstacle posed by the MIC, not the sizable, but widely exaggerated greenhouse gas emissions of the Pentagon itself. We should recognize that critical contradictions within capital regarding energy policy exist, and a Global Green New Deal (GGND) strategy must capture the 'solar' faction of capital into a multi-class alliance to force demilitarization and termination of the perpetual war dynamic."

See the Military-Industrial Complex Speech by Dwight D. Eisenhower, 34th President of the United States, on January 17, 1961, Public Papers of the Presidents, Dwight D. Eisenhower, 1960, pp. 1035–1040, http://coursesa.matrix.msu.edu/~hst306/documents/indust.html, see also https://youtu.be/8y06NSBBRtY. In this farewell speech Eisenhower warns of the military industrial complex. See more in note 46 in Chapter 11, in note 127 in this Chapter 14, and in note 199 in Chapter 18.

109 See a first-hand account in "Juno Dawson: Can We Stop Twitter Trolls Making Money out of Hate?" by Juno Dawson, Glamour, August 3, 2016, www.glamourmagazine.co.uk/features/living-travel/2016/08/juno-dawson-on-online-trolls.

110 "Gefährden Meinungsroboter die Demokratie?" by Adrian Lobe, Spektrum der Wissenschaft, October 14, 2016, www.spektrum.de/news/gefaehrden-meinungsroboter-die-demokratie/1426157. An Internet bot is a software application that runs automated tasks (scripts) over the Internet.

111 Miller, 2006b.

112 Eisler, 2007. See also note 48 in the Preface.

113 Smith, 1776.

114 Sustainable development expert Gwendolyn Hallsmith, in her contribution to the Great Transition Network (GTN) discussion on the topic of "Monetizing Nature," July 31, 2014.

115 Loewenstein, 2015.

116 "It Is Profitable to Let the World Go to Hell," by Jo Confino, The Guardian, January 19, 2015, www.theguardian.com/sustainable-business/2015/jan/19/davos-climate-action-democracy-failure-jorgen-randers, an article in the Davos 2015 series that covers news and views from the World Economic Forum meeting in January 2015 at Davos-Klosters, Switzerland.

117 von Braun, 2012. See also Norgaard, 2015.

118 See also 85 Jahre Weltwirtschaftskrise 1929, documentary film by Peter Beringer, 3sat, 2014, www.3sat.de/page/?source=/dokumentationen/178822/index.html. See the full note in the pdf edition of this book.

119 The Confederated Tribes of Grand Ronde in Oregon, USA, www.grandronde.org/ikanum/index.html, see under "Traditional Lifeways," and "Traditional Land Management."

120 See note 8 in Chapter 4. See also note 368 in Chapter 15.

121 Anthropologist Alan Page Fiske describes basic relational models. Fiske found that people, most of the time and in all cultures, use just four elementary and universal forms or models for organizing most aspects of sociality. These models are: (1) communal sharing, CS, (2) authority ranking, AR, (3) equality matching, EM, and (4) market pricing, MP. See Fiske, 1991, Fiske and Fiske, 2007, and an introduction on www.sscnet.ucla.edu/anthro/faculty/fiske/relmodov.htm.

122 Lindner and Desmond Tutu (Foreword), 2010.

123 See Buber, 1923/1937.

124 See note 10 in Chapter 8.

125 Richards, 2010.

126 See, among others, Dewey, 1905.

127 See note 98 in Chapter 9.

128 See note 162 in the Preface.

129 Bhaskar, 2008.

130 Giddens, 1990. I was very impressed when listening to Giddens talking at the 1984 World Congress of the International Sociological Organization that took place in Bielefeld, Germany, and attracted 3,678 participants. I am still thankful to Inge Wonneberger-Reichert for sending me to this congress. Radicalized modernity grew out of industrial modernity with its focus on order, calculability, science, and instrumental rationality, as well as social control by institutions. Radicalized modernity lays bare its negative after-effects: consumerism and individualism breaking down the family and other socializing institutions, time-space

distanciation leading to social contact becoming impersonal, and mutual trust diminishing. See also Zygmunt Bauman, 2000, and his notion of a liquid modern world.

131 Richards, 2013.

132 See note 163 in the Preface.

133 Wood, 2003.

134 Mies, 1986.

135 Howard Richards refers to Vivienne Jabri, 2007, director of the Centre for International Relations and Senior Lecturer in International Relations in the Department of War Studies, King's College London.

136 Richards, 2013.

137 Polanyi and Joseph E. Stiglitz (Foreword), 1944/2001.

138 Morais, 1979.

139 Granovetter, 1973.

140 Tönnies, 1887/1955.

141 Schirrmacher, 2006. I thank Axel Rojzcyk for making me aware of this book. Linda Hartling commented on August 14, 2016: "People in America primarily remember the Donner Party incident as cannibalism, rather than as example of survival through family cohesion."

142 McCauley, et al., 2013.

143 Richards, 2013.

144 Howard Richards and Catherine Odora Hoppers have been referred to previously in this book, and their insistence that more regulatory rules are not enough, what is needed are new constitutive rules. It was an important moment for me to hear political economist Gar Alperovitz in the Thirty-First Annual E. F. Schumacher Lectures on November 5, 2011, in New York City (www.neweconomicsinstitute.org), when he explained how he had lost faith, after decades of working for reform, after decades of hoping that the format of cooperatives, for instance, would provide the hoped-for break-through. He now calls for much more comprehensive and far-reaching new orientations. These are, clearly, only three of a myriad similar voices. See also my 2012 book on A Dignity Economy. Ted Trainer, of the limits to growth movement in Australia, sees capitalism as "the problem and no reforms within it or version of it can enable a sustainable and just world," in "A Critique of No Local, the Book Arguing that Localism Can't Save the Planet," by Ted Trainer, September 1, 2016, shared in a personal communication, where he critiques Greg Scherer, 2011. Trainer explains in this text how neither a myopic localist approach is feasible, nor is the leftist globalist idea that "the class in control of the industrial affluence and growth system" should be replaced so that a new central power could "redirect the system to more just outcomes." The latter is not feasible, Trainer argues, because we have entered the era of limits.

145 Richards and Swanger, 2006b.

146 Capitalism, a documentary series in six episodes, by documentary filmmaker Ilan Ziv, www.tamouzmedia.com/in-production.htm. See my summary and overview over this documentary film in the full note in the pdf edition of this book. For Ayn Rand, see also note 32 in Chapter 4. A global selection of experts is given the floor in this documentary, such as Nicholas Phillipson, 2010, and Robert and Edward Skidelsky and Skidelsky, 2012, from Britain, together with Ha-Joon Chang, 2010, who has a background from Korea, then Robert Boyer, 2004, and Philippe Norel, 2009, from France, Anton Wilhelm Amo, 1968, from Ghana, and Lewis Gordon, 2008, working on Africana Studies. Yuval Noah Harari, 2014, is from Israel, Kari Levitt, 2002, from Canada. Voices from the United States are Elizabeth and Stuart Ewen and Ewen, 2009, Michael Hudson, 2012, David Graeber, 2011, David Harvey, 2014, Noam Chomsky and Vltchek, 2013, as well as Eric Mielants, 2007, together with Ho-fung Hung, 2009, working on China. The

film demonstrates, among others, to what extent "capitalism" is a social construction rather than a scientific necessity, as can be seen by the present-day rejection of slavery, for instance, or the rejection of child labor. It was once regarded as a "good" rather than an "evil," when children had work that earned their keep. See Defoe, 1715. The film includes important voices from Asia, for instance, Ha-Joon Chang, 2010, who criticizes the glorification of self-interest, as promoted, for instance, by Paul Ryan, Republican Party nominee for Vice President of the United States in the 2012 election. Ryan professes having learned from Ayn Rand, and defends democratic capitalism, individualism, and freedom, as the moral foundations of America. Economist Ho-Fung Hung, 2009, based in the U.S.A., working on China, makes the point that capitalism was created by imperialism, with gunboats. At the beginning of the free market stood the Opium Wars (1839 – 1842, and 1856 – 1860). In Hung's view, the globalization of the past twenty to thirty years resembles this pattern. In the fourth episode of the documentary film, Vandana Shiva is given the floor in the documentary to describe the painful consequences of the now reigning commodity fetishism: 260,000 farmers have committed suicide in India; they were caught in a debt trap due to seeds having been turned into a commodity. Biotechnology patent lawyer Kevin Noonan concludes: life has become a product. And this happens increasingly so. Prior to this trend taking over, vaccines such as the polio vaccine were still not being patented, and Dr. Salk explained why: "can you patent the sun? The patent belongs to humankind!" David Harvey concludes that the biggest fetish, of course, is money, and the credit system, the insatiability for return on notional capital. The documentary ends with the question: Why has capitalism not yet collapsed? Tristram Hunt explains: capitalism has not yet collapsed because governments have been forced to bail out the so-called free market. The bailouts after 2008 represent inverted Darwinism, where the unfittest wins: Bankrottokratie, die victory of bankrupt banks.

147 Mielants, 2007.

148 The Poor Law Amendment Act was an important piece of social legislation in 1834. Its principles and the workhouse system dominated attitudes to welfare provision for the next eighty years. The Royal Commission on the Poor Laws and Relief of Distress 1905 – 1909, was a body set up by the British Parliament in order to investigate how the Poor Law system should be changed, and it produced two conflicting reports, the Majority Report that confirmed the established Zeitgeist, and the Minority Report that opposed it in saying that society should not expect the poor to be responsible for their affliction alone. David Englander, 2013, explores the changing ideas on poverty over this period and assesses current debates on Victorian attitudes to the poor.

149 Graeber, 2011, p. 334. See also Graeber, 2001.

150 Smith, 1759. I thank Howard Richards for his concise summary.

151 See the concise and accessible presentation in Capitalism, a documentary series in six episodes, by documentary filmmaker Ilan Ziv, www.tamouzmedia.com/in-production.htm.

152 Acres of Diamonds, by Russell Herman Conwell, first given in 1913, see www.americanrhetoric.com/speeches/rconwellacresofdiamonds.htm. See also note 32 in Chapter 2.

153 International Labour Office (ILO), 2014. Kevin B. Bales is a co-founder and previously president of Free the Slaves. See, among others, Bales, 2012. See also documentaries on specific areas:

- The Dark Side of Chocolate, documentary film by Miki Mistrati and U. Roberto Romano, Bastard Film and TV, 2010, https://youtu.be/7Vfbv6hNeng. The film shows the exploitation and slave trading of African children to harvest chocolate, still occurring nearly ten years after the cocoa industry pledged to end it.
- Blood in the Mobile, documentary film by Frank Piasecki Poulsen, 2010, https://youtu.be/wQhlLuBwOtE. The film addresses the issue of conflict minerals such as Coltan by examining illegal cassiterite mining in the North-Kivu province in eastern DR Congo, in particular, in Bisie.

154 I thank Linda Hartling for sharing documentary material about Ayn Rand with me. See more in note 32 in Chapter 4.

155 "Financial Crisis 'Like a Tsunami,' "BBC News, October 10, 2008, news.bbc.co.uk/go/pr/fr/-/2/hi/business/7687101.stm.

156 Harvey, 2014.

157 Indeed, the United Nations Economic Commission for Africa explains in 2014 that illicit financial flows are a major drain on Africa's resources for development. See "Tracking Africa's Stolen Billions," The United Nations Economic Commission for Africa (UNECA), October 14, 2014, www.uneca.org/stories/tracking-africa%E2%80%99s-stolen-billions: "International coordination is needed to slow the flow of stolen assets.... The use of anonymous trust companies shields individuals responsible for illicit capital flows from attention or prosecution. Added to this, weak corporate governance codes have created space for transnational corporations to operate with a degree of impunity, Charles Abugre Akelyira, a Ghanaian economist and the African regional director of the United Nations' Millennium Campaign, says: 'This laxity of corporate governance was largely created in the 1980s, 1990s structural adjustment programmes. They date back to this period where, under the weight of indebtedness, the international financial institutions basically pushed these governments to dismantle strong corporate governance regimes in the name of encouraging private sector investments and expanding the market,' he says. 'In that sense, governments or the elites that run the state also found a way to arrange these corporate governance structures around their petty personal advantages.'" This is the final report: Illicit Financial Flows: Report of the High Level Panel on Illicit Financial Flows from Africa, commissioned by the AU/ECA Conference of Ministers of Finance, Planning and Economic Development, Addis Abeba: United Nations Economic Commission for Africa (UNECA), February 26, 2015, www.uneca.org/sites/default/files/PublicationFiles/iff_main_report_26feb_en.pdf.

158 Leach, 1993.

159 The Century of the Self, British television documentary series by filmmaker Adam Curtis, 2002, www.imdb.com/title/tt0432232/.

160 "The New Age of Ayn Rand: How She Won over Trump and Silicon Valley," by Jonathan Freedland, The Guardian, April 10, 2017, www.theguardian.com/books/2017/apr/10/new-age-ayn-rand-conquered-trump-white-house-silicon-valley?CMP=Share_iOSApp_Other. I thank Linda Hartling for making me aware of this article. See more in note 32 in Chapter 4.

161 Ibid. See also the Ayn Rand biography by Jennifer Burns, 2009.

162 See also de Graaf, et al., 2001.

163 Robert F. Kennedy Speeches, Remarks at the University of Kansas, March 18, 1968, www.jfklibrary.org/Research/Research-Aids/Ready-Reference/RFK-Speeches/Remarks-of-Robert-F-Kennedy-at-the-University-of-Kansas-March-18-1968.aspx. I thank Sandra Waddock for making me aware of this quote, in her reply to Great Transition Network Discussion "The Degrowth Alternative," January 7, 2015.

164 "Eurokrise: Die Troika: Macht ohne Kontrolle," by Harald Schumann, Der Tagesspiegel, February 24, 2015, www.tagesspiegel.de/politik/eurokrise-die-troika-macht-ohne-kontrolle/11406286.html.

165 "End 'Gross Indignity,' Greek FM Varoufakis Tells Germany," BBC News, 5 February 2015, www.bbc.com/news/world-europe-31147112. I thank Linda Hartling for making me aware of this article.

166 "We Need an Alternative to Trump's Nationalism. It Isn't the Status Quo," by Yanis Varoufakis, The Guardian, January 22, 2017, www.theguardian.com/commentisfree/2017/jan/22/trumps-nationalism-response-not-globalization. I thank Rigmor Johnsen for making me aware of this article.

167 "End 'Gross Indignity,' Greek FM Varoufakis Tells Germany," BBC News, 5 February 2015, www.bbc.com/news/world-europe-31147112. I thank Linda Hartling for making me aware of this article.

168 Takis Ioannides, in a personal communication on April 13, 2014. Takis Ioannides is an esteemed member in our Human Dignity and Humiliation Studies fellowship.

169 Takis Ioannides, in a personal communication on October 20, 2014.

170 Atuahene, 2016, p. 796:

> Involuntary property loss is ubiquitous. During conquest and colonialism, European powers robbed native peoples of their lands; wars and civil conflicts have undermined and rearranged ownership rights; communist regimes have upended existing ownership rights in attempts to usher in a more egalitarian property distribution; and most constitutional democracies sanction the forced taking of property as long as the state pays just compensation and it is for a public purpose. In some of these examples, state or nonstate actors have taken property from an individual or a group and material compensation is an appropriate remedy. In other instances, however, the property confiscation resulted in the dehumanization or infantilization of the dispossessed, and so providing material compensation is not enough because they lost more than their property – they were also deprived of their dignity. In We Want What's Ours: Learning from South Africa's Land Restitution Program (Atuahene, 2014), I labeled this dual harm a "dignity taking" and argued that the appropriate remedy is something more than mere compensation for things taken (reparations). What is instead required, I argue, is "dignity restoration," which addresses deprivations of both property and dignity by providing material compensation to dispossessed populations through processes that affirm their humanity and establish their agency.

Bernadette Atuahene is a Professor of Law at Chicago-Kent College of Law, Illinois Institute of Technology. We thank Michael Perlin for making us aware of this article. It is a privilege to have Michael Perlin as esteemed member in the global advisory board of the Human Dignity and Humiliation Studies fellowship.

171 Fiske, 2004.

172 Lindner, 2015a. See the 2015 Annual Conference of Human Dignity and Humiliation Studies, "Toward A Life of Dignity for All," in Kigali, Rwanda, June 2–5, 2015, www.humiliationstudies.org/whoweare/annualmeeting/25.php.

173 Caught in Micro Debt, documentary film shown on Norwegian state television November 30, 2010. See also Brennpunkt: Fanget i mikrogjeld, www.nrk.no/nett-tv/klipp/688333/. See, furthermore, Bateman, and www.odi.org.uk/events/documents/2447-presentation-m-bateman.pdf. See, furthermore, Roodman and Morduch, 2009, Armendariz de Aghion and Morduch, 2005, Dichter, 2003, as well as Wichterich, 2000, 2010. Wichterich starts her 2011 paper as follows:

> India is in the midst of a financial crisis that shows striking similarities to the US subprime crisis, both in its origins and the rescue strategies used. Just as the cheap mortgage granted to low-income households in the USA, the microcredits given to poor women in rural areas worked out as financialization of everyday live and integration of the women into the global financial market with its return-based logic. This jeopardized the social processes and the very objectives at the heart of the initial nonprofit microfinance model. The growth of this sector led to an over-supply of microcredits in villages and in turn to the over-indebtedness of women, the collapse of repayments and a capital shortage of the microfinance institutions. What seems at first sight to be a specifically Indian crisis results in fact from the market rationale of growth, overheating, and crisis.

174 2015 Annual Conference of Human Dignity and Humiliation Studies, "Toward A Life of Dignity for All," in Kigali, Rwanda, June 2–5, 2015, www.humiliationstudies.org/whoweare/annualmeeting/25.php.

175 See howardrichards.org, Richards and Swanger, 2006b, Richards, 2011. See also:
• "Constructing a New Global Dispensation Beyond Economics," by Howard Richards, keynote talk at an international conference on "Democracy, Human Rights and Social Justice in a New Global Dispensation – Challenges and Transformations," University of South Africa, Pretoria, February 1–3, 2010,

howardrichards.org/pacem/index.php?option=com_content&task=view&id=137&Itemid=163.
• "Humanizing Methodologies in Transformation," by Howard Richards, lecture at the University of South Africa, Pretoria, July 20, 2010.
• "An Ethical Alternative to the Philosophy of Friedrich von Hayek," by Howard Richards, presentation to the Rethinking Economics group, Santiago de Chile, January 20, 2011.

176 Lindner, 2006c, p. 176.

177 Stephen Purdey in his contribution to the Great Transition Initiative (GTN) discussion on the topic "Economics for a Full World." May 15, 2015:

> Instead of trying to transition to a steady-state economy, government leaders worldwide are still fixated on the pursuit of economic growth as a top policy priority. If a "major change in philosophical vision and ethical practice" is required to defeat this fixation, then we'll first need a good understanding of its power to persuade. Here are two examples, one political and one ethical, of this power. First, economic growth is politically expedient. Growth, as John Kenneth Galbraith once called it, is the ultimate social lubricant. It draws support and approbation from all sectors of society – rich and poor, employers and employees, public and private sectors alike, because they all stand to gain. The "rising tide lifts all boats" mantra is universally appealing and therefore politically compelling. It is also, of course, a utopian economic model which hints at an abrogation of governmental responsibility, even as it helps us understand the lure of growth.

See also note 93 in this Chapter 11.

178 "How Do We Make the Economy Work for the Poor?" by Howard Richards, http://unboundedorganization.org/wp-content/uploads/2015/09/Chapter-Two-cwp-September-10.pdf, Chapter 2 in Economic Theory and Community Development, http://unboundedorganization.org/related-material/.

179 Polanyi and Joseph E. Stiglitz (Foreword), 1944/2001.

180 Kahneman, 2011.

181 Lindner, 2006c, pp. 46–47.

182 Gray, 2002. See also Gray's review of Moral Tribes by Joshua Greene, 2013, in The Guardian, January 17, 2014, www.theguardian.com/books/2014/jan/17/moral-tribes-joshua-greene-review, where Gray writes:

> If you think some version of Darwinism provides the best available account of humankind's place in the world (as I do) you will accept that morality has evolved along with the human animal. That doesn't mean morality can be understood using Green's fashionable mix of game theory and sociobiology. How human beings think and feel about morality is integral to what it means to them, but Greene tends to displace these culturally accreted understandings by clever-sounding theoretical notions – including ideas borrowed from the prevailing versions of market economics.
> When he defends utilitarianism as a universal "meta-morality" that can regulate "trade-offs" among tribal moralities, it's no accident that he describes this super-morality as a common currency. This is an author who assures the reader that "participation in modern market economies, far from turning us into selfish bean counters, has expanded the scope of human kindness." For Greene and thinkers like him, market exchange seems to be a model for moral life.

See also Gray, 2002.

183 Capaldo, 2014.

184 Neuroscientist Peter Sterling, 2016, begins his essay with this paragraph:

> Exponential economic growth is rapidly destabilizing the biosphere. Among the many factors that stimulate such growth is the human tendency to consume goods and services far beyond what is required to meet basic needs. We have to grasp what drives this tendency in order to manage it. The

brain's core circuits were long believed to stimulate us to seek pleasure – greedily and selfishly – while higher cortical circuits try to rein us in. Neuroscience now shows that the core circuits serve not pleasure per se, but efficient learning. When we obtain a reward that our frontal cortex values highly, the core circuit delivers a chemical pulse that we experience as satisfaction – so we repeat the behavior. Satisfaction is brief and diminishes as a particular reward becomes predictable. This circuit design works well for pre-industrial societies in which rewards are varied and unpredictable. But capitalism shrinks the diversity of possible rewards, leaving the remainder less satisfying, and making stronger doses, i.e., more consumption, necessary. The path toward sustainability must, therefore, include re-expanding the diversity of satisfactions.

I thank Paul Raskin for having invited the Great Transition Network list into a discussion of Sterling's essay.

185 Linn, 2015. I thank Linda Hartling for making me aware of this book.

186 "James Risen Prepared to 'Pay Any Price' to Report on War on Terror Amid Crackdown on Whistleblowers," interview with Amy Goodman and Michael Hayden, Democracy Now, October 14, 2014, www.democracynow.org/2014/10/14/james_risen_prepared_to_pay_any. See Risen, 2014. See also "A Not Very Private Feud Over Terrorism," by Marc Sageman, New York Times, June 8, 2008, www.nytimes.com/2008/06/08/weekinreview/08sciolino.html?_r=4&scp=1&sq=marc+sageman&st=nyt&oref=slogin&oref=slogin&: "... the huge counterterrorism machine, which costs the United States billions of dollars and has created armies of independent security consultants and counterterrorism experts in the last seven years."

187 "Seven Years Since the Wall Street Crash," by Nick Beams, Human Wrongs Watch, September 15, 2015, http://human-wrongs-watch.net/2015/09/15/seven-years-since-the-wall-street-crash/.

188 "Authoritarianism, Class Warfare and the Advance of Neoliberal Austerity Policies," by Henry A. Giroux, Truthout, January 5, 2015, http://truth-out.org/news/item/28338-the-shadow-of-fascism-and-the-poison-of-neoliberal-austerity-policies.

189 "The Rise of ISIS is Fueled by Iraq's Deteriorating Economic Conditions," The Real News, November 3, 2014, https://youtu.be/OocGnXBG5BM. I thank Anthony Marsella for making me aware of this video.

190 See note 46 in this Chapter 11.

191 "Illegal Trade in Wildlife and Timber Products Finances Criminal and Militia Groups, Threatening Security and Sustainable Development." United Nations Environmental Programme (UNEP), June 24, 2014, www.unep.org/newscentre/default.aspx?DocumentID=2791&ArticleID=10906&l=en.

192 "Legalisiert den Handel mit Drogen," by Tobias Käufer, Hannoversche Allgemeine, September 15, 2015, www.haz.de/Sonntag/Gastkommentar/drogenhandel-legalisieren. Translated from German by Lindner, see the original German quote in in the full note in the pdf edition of this book. See also Paley, 2014.

193 Wood, 2003.

194 Richards and Andersson, 2017, Introduction.

195 Adresseavisen (a regional newspaper in Trondheim, Norway), January 26, 2015, http://adressa.alda.no/bestillpluss?1&aviskode=ADR&artRefId=10578437&targetUrl=http%253A%252F%252Fwww.adressa.no%252F%253Fservice%253DpaywallRedirect%2526articleUrl%253Dhttp%253A%252F%252Fwww.adressa.no%252Fpluss%252Fnyheter%252Farticle10578437.ece: "Dagens samfunn har klare totalitære trekk: Kontroll- og målesamfunnet har klare totalitære trekk, mener førsteamanuensis Tord Larsen." See also Larsen, 2009. Read also about sociologist Hartmut Rosa, 2005, 2010, in note 278 in the Introduction.

196 See note 8 in Chapter 4. See also note 368 in Chapter 15.

197 Howard Richards, in a personal communication reflecting on Norman Kurland's work, January 12, 2013:

I do not think it is responsible to be simply "in favor of private property" or "against private property" or to say "Marx was right" or "Marx was wrong." I do not think the words "capitalism" or "socialism" in most of the ways they are commonly understood can name something one can be simply "for" or "against." (In the end, however, I come out being "for" both socialism and capitalism, properly defined, i.e. defined as I think it best to define them. I am working on these paradoxes in an essay I am working on in Spanish tentatively titled "How to Achieve Socialism without Socialism." They are also somewhat explained in my talk at University of Cape Town, where I explain also why the debate has to go back to indigenous practices of community and transcend modern western categories.) ...

I met Adler when I was working for Robert Hutchins (I worked for him in 1960 – 1965) and I had the impression that he shared Hutchins' view which is also that of Aristotle and is part of the social teachings of the Catholic Church and of most churches that property is in principle common (given by God or Nature) to everyone, while the separation of property into "mine" and "thine" is a practical arrangement due to the fact that holding property in common is often impractical. As St. Thomas says we who own property have legal dominion, but the duty to use the property to serve others. In Gandhi s view we should regard ourselves as "trustees" of our property. ... This is sometimes called in secular terms the view that property rights serve social functions.

On the other hand Hutchins and traditional ethics generally are quite aware of the desirable function of property in establishing respect for persons and the integrity and freedom of human personalities. This does not need to lead to denying the social functions of property and the need to revise property institutions in the light of their social functions.

I agree with Norm that when Marx wrote that Communism consists of abolishing private property Marx was recommending something neither practical nor desirable. I do not want to underestimate the tragedy and human suffering that have resulted from that impractical and undesirable idea. But this does not imply that we have nothing to learn from Marx. Nor does it imply that we should underestimate the tragedy and human suffering that have resulted from imposing unenlightened ideas about private property by violence, torture, lies and all the rest –the latter being closer to home for one who writes from Chile.

I also think that unrestricted property rights (full respect for the dominium of Roman law) make it impossible to achieve social inclusion. As far as I can tell without taking time for more study, the Kelso idea is not really unrestricted property rights because it involves redistribution so that everybody has access to property. This would raise the issue how to make redistribution practical, how to carry it out without shutting down the dynamics that make the economy work (given that it does not in any case work very well)....

198 I thank Linda Hartling for emphasizing the centrality of human relationships.

Inspiring and Thought-Provoking Questions to Section Two

1 Jihad: A Story of the Others, documentary film by Deeyah Khan, 2015, http://fuuse.net/jihad-a-story-of-the-others/. See more in note 20 in Chapter 6.

2 United States, 1973, p. 248.

3 See note 19 in the Introduction to Section Two.

4 The International Panel of Eminent Personalities to Investigate the 1994 Genocide in Rwanda and the Surrounding Events, 2000, Chapter 16, paragraph 4.

5 Jihad: A Story of the Others, documentary film by Deeyah Khan, 2015, http://fuuse.net/jihad-a-story-of-the-others/. See more in note 20 in Chapter 6.

6 The "godfather of the British jihadi movement," Abu Muntasir, recruited dozens of young men to fight in foreign wars. Starting at minute 35:00 of the film, he sobs: "I rather live as slaves and have my kids go to school... I don't want this false... what is this: honor! I am happy to be a coward!" He regrets "opening the way for people to join terror groups such as Islamic State and al-Qaida," writes Tracy McVeigh in "'Recruiter' of UK Jihadis: I Regret Opening the Way to Isis," The Guardian, June 13, 2015, www.theguardian.com/world/2015/jun/13/godfather-of-british-jihadists-admits-we-opened-to-way-to-join-isis.

7 Harris and Nawaz, 2015, Nawaz, 2012. See also his TED talk Maajid Nawaz: A Global Culture to Fight Extremism, July 14, 2011, https://youtu.be/EZwxKPv1CwA. I thank Deeyah Khan for making me aware of Nawaz's work.

8 Read more about Jo Berry in the Appendix to Section One.

9 Brown, 2012a.

10 "For Thanksgiving: What We Have to Do With 'Twelve Years a Slave,' the Movie," by Carol Smaldino, Huffington Post, November 26, 2013, www.huffingtonpost.com/carol-smaldino/for-thanksgiving-what-we-_b_4344576.html. Carol Smaldino is an esteemed member in our Human Dignity and Humiliation Studies fellowship.

11 "Mental Health Awareness Month in a Climate of Denial," by Carol Smaldino, Huffington Post, May 11, 2016, www.huffingtonpost.com/carol-smaldino/mental-health-awareness-m_b_9895080.html.

12 "When the End of Human Civilization Is Your Day Job," by John H. Richardson, Esquire, July 7, 2015, www.esquire.com/news-politics/a36228/ballad-of-the-sad-climatologists-0815/.

13 See, for instance, Miller, 1976/1986, 2008b.

14 See note 10 in Chapter 8.

15 Steve Kulich, at the Second International Conference on Multicultural Discourses in Hangzhou, China, April 13–15, 2007. See also Lindner, 2007a.

16 The Space between Self-Esteem and Self Compassion, by Kristin Neff, TEDxCentennialParkWomen, February 6, 2013, https://youtu.be/IvtZBUSplr4. I thank Linda Hartling for making me aware of this talk. See also Neff, 2011.

17 Ibid. See also note 10 in Chapter 8.

18 See note 10 in Chapter 8.

19 See note 32 in Chapter 4.

20 Lindner, 2012f, pp. 57–58.

21 "The End of Identity Liberalism," by Mark Lilla, New York Times, November 18, 2016, www.nytimes.com/2016/11/20/opinion/sunday/the-end-of-identity-liberalism.html.

22 "Donald Trump's Election a Rejection of Identity Politics," by Paul Kelly, The Australian, January 28, 2017, www.theaustralian.com.au/.../donald-trumps-election-a-rejection-of-identity-politics/.../147b11c08b64702d3f9be1821416cb72.

23 "The End of Identity Liberalism," by Mark Lilla, New York Times, November 18, 2016, www.nytimes.com/2016/11/20/opinion/sunday/the-end-of-identity-liberalism.html.

24 Campbell and Manning, 2014.

25 Twenge, 2014.

26 "The Coddling of the American Mind," by Greg Lukianoff, and Jonathan Haidt, The Atlantic, September 2015, www.theatlantic.com/magazine/archive/2015/09/the-coddling-of-the-american-mind/399356/.

27 "The Righteous Mind," by Jonathan Haidt, September 7, 2015, http://righteousmind.com/where-microaggressions-really-come-from/. See also Haidt, 2012. See also note 273 in the Introduction.

28 Margalit, 2002.

29 See note 19 in the Introduction to Section Two.

30 See Lindner, 2006c, Chapter 7: The Humiliation Addiction, in my book Making Enemies: Humiliation and International Conflict.

31 "The End of Identity Liberalism," by Mark Lilla, New York Times, November 18, 2016, www.nytimes.com/2016/11/20/opinion/sunday/the-end-of-identity-liberalism.html.

32 "Call for Action to Curb Attacks on Environmental Campaigners," IRIN – Humanitarian news and analysis (a service of the UN Office for the Coordination of Humanitarian Affairs), August 22, 2014, www.irinnews.org/report/100518/call-for-action-to-curb-attacks-on-environmental-campaigners.

33 Ibid.

34 ZDF-History: Operation "Zersetzung" – Der geheime Terror der Stasi, Zweites Deutsches Fernsehen, http://history.zdf.de/ZDF/zdfportal/programdata/c5479add-a5dd-35ff-99cf-ca2843da6ec4/20189842?generateCanonicalUrl=true, see also https://youtu.be/vHJAfWtyeOo. See also Pingel-Schliemann, 2004, and Trobisch-Lütge, 2004, 2011. See the full note in the pdf edition of this book.

35 "When Generosity Hurts: Bill Gates, Public School Teachers and the Politics of Humiliation," by Henry A. Giroux, TruthOut, October 5, 2010, http://truth-out.org/archive/component/k2/item/92120:when-generosity-hurts-bill-gates-public-school-teachers-and-the-politics-of-humiliation. I thank Brian Ward for having made us aware of this article.

36 Ibid. See some of Giroux's publications: Di Leo, et al., 2013, Giroux, 2010, 2011, 2012, 2013, 2014a, b, Nikolakaki, 2012.

37 See note 54 in Chapter 1.

38 "Unsere schönen neuen Kleider. Gegen die marktkonforme Demokratie – für demokratiekonforme Märkte," Dresdner Rede 2012, Ingo Schulze, February 26, 2012, www.nachdenkseiten.de/upload/pdf/SchulzeDresden.pdf. See also "Thesen gegen die Ausplünderung der Gesellschaft: 'Kapitalismus braucht keine Demokratie'," Ingo Schulze, Süddeutsche Zeitung, January 12, 2012, www.sueddeutsche.de/kultur/thesen-gegen-die-auspluenderung-der-gesellschaft-kapitalismus-braucht-keine-demokratie-1.1255949.

39 Howard Richards in a personal communication on February 25, 2013.

40 See note 2 in the Preface.

41 See, for example, www.brainyquote.com/quotes/quotes/m/mayeramsch170274.html.

42 See also "How Obama Could Beat the Debt Ceiling and Go Out a Hero," by Ellen Brown, CounterPunch, October 28, 2015, www.counterpunch.org/2015/10/28/how-obama-could-beat-the-debt-ceiling-and-go-out-a-hero/. See also Goetzmann, 2016.

43 "Democracy v. Concentrated Wealth: In Search of a Louis D. Brandeis Quote," by Peter Scott Campbell, The Green Bag 2D, Spring 2013, pp. 251–256, http://greenbag.org/v16n3/v16n3_articles_campbell.pdf.

44 Etzioni, 2013, p. 334.

45 Paul Raskin in his contribution to the Great Transition Network Initiative discussion titled "Journey to Earthland: Making the Great Transition to Planetary Civilization," November 11, 2016, in his response to the comments on Raskin, 2016: "In other words, fixating on 'the Anthropocene' confuses cause and effect: the enlargement of the human project (the Planetary Phase) is the cause, and the enlargement of human impacts (the Anthropocene) is the effect. The inversion dehistoricizes the source of the problem as a diffuse 'humanity' (rather than a particular social formation), and thereby depoliticizes the response ('we have met

the enemy, and he is us'). The 'Planetary Phase,' besides having an evocative ring, carries a comprehensive understanding of the challenge, and urges a comprehensive movement for addressing it."

46 Norgaard, 2015.

47 More, 2014.

48 "Anthropocene Is the Wrong Word," by Kathleen Dean Moore, Earth Island Journal, Spring 2013, www.earthisland.org/journal/index.php/eij/article/anthropocene_is_the_wrong_word/.

49 The Holocene is a geological epoch that began approximately 11,700 years BCE and continues to the present. The new term Anthropocene is used informally for the latest part of modern history and of significant human impact since the epoch of the Neolithic Revolution around 12,000 years Before Present.

50 Rockström, 2015. See also Wijkman and Rockström, 2012. See more in note 82 in Chapter 5.

51 On classism, have a look at Barbara Jensen, 2012.

52 Freyd and Birrell, 2013. I thank Linda Hartling for making me aware of this book.

53 How poverty is being exploited, how poor people and countries are being duped by globally active corporations, has been widely described. See, among others, Klas, 2011, on the "illusion" of microfinance. See for the abuse of the fact that convenience food made in Europe is a status symbol in the Global South, Das Geschäft mit der Armut: Wie Lebensmittelkonzerne neue Märkte erobern, documentary film by Joachim Walther, 3sat, 2016, www.3sat.de/programm/?viewlong=viewlong&d=20170412&dayID=ClnDaN12&cx=123. See the full note in the pdf edition of this book. Nutrition is also the theme of the work of Carlos Monteiro at the School of Public Health at the University of São Paulo in Brazil, see Conde and Monteiro, 2014, Laverty, et al., 2015. Giftiger Treibstoff für Afrika, is a documentary film by Isabelle Ducret und Marie-Laure Widmer Baggiolini, 3sat, 2017, www.3sat.de/mediathek/?mode=play&obj=65870. In Europe, strict quality standards apply for fuels. Swiss companies sell fuels which do not comply with these regulations to Africa.

54 Gorz, 1964, 1967. See also "A Feminism Where 'Lean In' Means Leaning On Others," by Gary Gutting and Nancy Fraser, The Stone (The Stone is a forum for contemporary philosophers and other thinkers on issues both timely and timeless), October 15, 2015, http://opinionator.blogs.nytimes.com/2015/10/15/a-feminism-where-leaning-in-means-leaning-on-others/. I thank Linda Hartling for making me aware of this interview.

55 Rockström, 2015.

56 Ibid.

57 Ibid.

58 Daly, 1991.

59 I first began to learn about the significance of the notion of unity in diversity in 1994, when cross-cultural psychologist Michael Harris Bond from Hong Kong taught at the Sommerakademie Friedens- und Konfliktforschung, July 11–16, 1999, in Clemenswerth, Germany. See Bond, 1999. See more in note 19 in the Introduction to Section One.

60 See Yoshikawa, 1980, 1987.

61 Martin, et al., 2001.

62 Hartling and Lindner, 2017, quoting "Killings and Racial Tensions Commingle with Divided and Divisive Politics," by Dan Balz, Washington Post, July 8, 2016, www.washingtonpost.com/politics/killings-and-racial-tensions-commingle-with-divided-and-divisive-politics/2016/07/08/5a422e08-451e-11e6-88d0-6adee48be8bc_story.html?utm_term=.8f5203cf84a3.

63 Hartling and Lindner, 2017, quoting Putnam, 2007.

64 Banks, et al., 2001, p. 13.

65 See note 165 in the Preface.

66 See also Lindner, 2007b.

67 See, among others, “Missing: Political Creativity,” by Johan Galtung, TRANSCEND Media Service, May 15, 2017, www.transcend.org/tms/2017/05/missing-political-creativity/.

68 See note 37 in Chapter 11.

69 Catherine Alum Odora Hoppers edited the International Journal of Development Education and Global Learning, Volume 7, Number 2, “Development Education in the Global South,” 2015, http://ingentaconnect.com/content/ioep/ijdegl/2015/00000007/00000002/art00002. It is a privilege to have not only Catherine Odora Hoppers and her brother George, but also other authors in this issue as esteemed members in the global advisory board of our Human Dignity and Humiliation Studies fellowship, namely, Richards, 2015, Haavelsrud, 2015, and Sewchurran and McDonogh, 2015. Crain Soudien, 2015, recommends drawing on the concept of the transaction in John Dewey for a new approach to knowing, while Haavelsrud uses Odora Hoppers' term of transformation by enlargement for the academy, by scientific methodologies inspired by forms of transdisciplinarity, praxis, and trilateral science as described by Johan Galtung, 1977, see Haavelsrud, 2015, pp. 54–55:

> The concept of trilateral science describes the relationship between three worlds, the empirical, the foreseen, and the ideal world, or, in other words, the world as it is (the data or facts positively given), the world as it will be (the world as predicted or theorized) and the world as it ought to be (values). The gaps and differences between the three worlds can be reduced by transformations in all three. The aim of science should be to achieve greater consonance among the three: “The world as it is can be changed, and if so the foreseen world will also be changed. Values may be modified.”

See also Odora Hoppers, 2002, and her article “Indigenous Knowledge Systems: An Invisible Resource in Literacy Education,” The Soka Gakkai International (SGI) Quarterly: A Buddhist Forum for Peace, Culture and Education, January 2003, www.sgiquarterly.org/feature2003Jan-4.html.
See also Odora Hoppers and Richards, 2012, Richards, et al., 2015a.

70 Kjell Skyllstad in a personal communication on December 15, 2014.

71 Battle, 1997.

72 For essayist Arthur Koestler's theory of holons and holarchies, see Koestler, 1967, 1970, 1978. I thank John Bunzl for reminding me of Koestler's work. It is a privilege to have John Bunzl's support.

73 Braithwaite, 2002. It is a privilege to have John Braithwaite as esteemed member in the global advisory board of our Human Dignity and Humiliation Studies fellowship.

74 Powers, 1973, 1998.

75 I had the privilege of listening to Phil Clark and Joanna Quinn during the “International Symposium on Restorative Justice, Reconciliation and Peacebuilding,” at the New York University School of Law, November 11–12, 2011, www.iilj.org/RJRP/about.asp. They introduced me to the work of Sally Engle Merry and Mark A. Drumbl, see Goodale and Merry, 2007, and Drumbl, 2007. I learned that British colonizers set up a “relationships commission” as far back as 1898. Lord Lugard wrote about the “dual mandate” in Africa, see Lugard, 1965. See also Clark, 2010.

76 See, for instance, europa.eu/scadplus/glossary/subsidiarity_en.htm.

77 Marshall, 2008.

78 Gaertner, et al., 2012.

79 See, among others, Hornsey and Hogg, 2000, Brown and Hewstone, 2005, Crisp, et al., 2006, Dovidio, et al., 2009. I thank Sigrun Marie Moss for reminding me of the more recent developments in this field. See Moss, 2014, Moss and Vollhardt, 2015.

80 Gaertner, et al., 2000.

81 Moss, 2014, Moss and Vollhardt, 2015.

82 Lindner, 2012e.

83 Elias, 1939/1991, pp. 226–227.

84 Patrick Modiano, 2005/2015, grappled with questions of identity and roots in all his novels.

85 Nigerian author Chimamanda Ngozi Adichie, 2013, felt "black" for the first time when she came to the Unites States of America. Gilad Atzmon, 2011, writes about the wound of Jewish identities.

86 Selasi, 2013.

87 World Passport, https://en.wikipedia.org/wiki/World_Passport. It has been a great privilege to have Garry Davis in our conference in Honolulu in 2009, and in our workshop in New York the year before he passed away. His support for our dignity work has been deeply appreciated.

88 Lifton, 1993.

89 Matsumoto, et al., 2007, p. 92: "With Emotion Regulation (ER), 'people voyage through life; without it, they vindicate their lives.'" It is a privilege to have David Matsumoto as esteemed member in the global advisory board of our Human Dignity and Humiliation Studies fellowship.

90 See, among many others, Csikszentmihalyi, 1996.

91 In a way, my position is more radical than that of Klitgaard, 2017.

92 As to "personal branding," see Lair, et al., 2005. I discussed this topic in January 29, 2007, in Harrania, near Cairo, Egypt, with Sophie Wissa-Wassef, who makes a point of protecting her artists' creativity by not disclosing to them whether their art sells or not. See www.humiliationstudies.org/intervention/art.php#ramseswissawassef or www.wissa-wassef-arts.com/intro.htm. See also Rushkoff, 2009. I thank Keith Grennan for this reference.

93 Pleasantville is a film written, produced, and directed by Gary Ross in 1998. See also The Clonus Horror (1979) or The Island (2005). Remember also the 1999 film The Matrix. See, furthermore, the work of novelists such as Aldous Huxley, 1932, or Kazuo Ishiguro, 2005, Michel Houellebecq, 2010/2012, Dave Eggers, 2013, or Leif Randt, 2015, as well as Uwe Tellkamp, 2008, who asks whether it is possible to guard one's dignity in the face of attempts to brainwash entire populations, as happened in East Germany before it collapsed in 1989.

94 Rosenthal, 2013. See also Pirson, et al., 2016. I thank Heidi von Weltzien Høivik and Bjørn Ekelund, both esteemed members in our Human Dignity and Humiliation Studies fellowship, for connecting me with Michael Pirson. See also "The Messy Link Between Slave Owners and Modern Management, by Katie Johnston, Harvard Business School Working Knowledge, January 16, 2013, http://hbswk.hbs.edu/item/the-messy-link-between-slave-owners-and-modern-management.

95 "Don't Blame Corbyn for the Sins of Blair, Brown and New Labour," by Ken Loach, The Guardian, February 28, 2017, www.theguardian.com/commentisfree/2017/feb/28/dont-blame-corbyn-sins-blair-brown-new-labour.

96 Jensen and Meckling, 1994, p. 10: "Like it or not, individuals are willing to sacrifice a little of almost anything we care to name, even reputation or morality, for a sufficiently large quantity of other desired things; and these things do not have to be money or even material goods."

97 Tom Bowerman, Director of PolicyInteractive Research, policyinteractive.org, February 1, 2017: "The top five ordering of priorities for workplace choice from highest to lowest are: 1) doing a job I can be proud

of; 2) enjoying work, having fun; 3) being with people I respect; 4) earning a good salary; and 5) learning new things, having new experiences."

98 Lindner, 2012f. See also Klitgaard, 2017, or Richards and Andersson, 2017.

99 Scholar Vandana Shiva received the Right Livelihood Award in 1993.

100 Read about "the economics of manipulation and deception" in Akerlof and Shiller, 2015.

101 Kant, 1785, chapter 1, see the German original on http://gutenberg.spiegel.de/buch/grundlegung-zur-methaphysik-der-sitten-3510/1: "Im Reiche der Zwecke hat alles entweder einen Preis, oder eine Würde. Was einen Preis hat, an dessen Stelle kann auch etwas anderes als Äquivalent gesetzt werden; was dagegen über allen Preis erhaben ist, mithin kein Äquivalent verstattet, das hat eine Würde."

102 Singh, 2013. See also Kasser, 2017. Kasser discusses suggestions that engaging in pro-ecological behaviors (PEBs, such as recycling, eating locally, political activism) increases people's measures of subjective well-being (SWB, such as happiness, life satisfaction, and hedonic balance), and vice versa. In other words, pro-ecological behavior might make happy, or happy people might engage in pro-ecological behavior. Other variables may be prioritizing intrinsic values over extrinsic values such as money or status, or mindfulness, or a choice to lead a more simple lifestyle. Tim Kasser writes in his contribution to the Great Transition Network Initiative discussion titled "Sustainability and Well-Being: A Happy Synergy," March 12, 2017, in response to Barrington-Leigh, 2017:

> a) prioritizing intrinsic values (for personal growth and relationships) over extrinsic values (for money, image and status); b) how mindful one is (i.e., how focused a person is on accepting and attending to one's momentary experiences); and c) whether one has made a choice to work less and lead a more voluntarily simple lifestyle. Each of these three variables has been empirically associated with BOTH greater SWB and more engagement in PEBs, suggesting each could potentially explain the documented positive correlation.

103 I deeply resonate with Mimi Stokes-Katzenbach, who writes the following in her contribution to the Great Transition Network (GTN) discussion on the topic of "Sustainability and Well-Being: A Happy Synergy," April 1, 2017, in response to Barrington-Leigh, 2017: "If Positive Psychology is to make a useful contribution to transcending our common tragic fate, and is to help bring us through our global emergency in planetary thrivability, it must, first, develop a definition of happiness that includes our present, and tragic, environmental reality, and the inherent nature-human interdependency; second, also develop a definition of happiness that does not include these same ecological factors, i.e., answer my question, What kind of happiness is individual well-being in a tragic ecological reality?" Consider also well-being-oriented indicators that go beyond subjective happiness:

- Amartya Sen and Martha Nussbaum's "Capability Approach" measures items such as inequality, education, health, or environmental sustainability, rather than measuring the outcome, namely, happiness. See www.iep.utm.edu/sen-cap.
- Amartya Sen was involved in developing the OECD's Better Life Index, which builds on the work of the Commission on Measurement of Economic Performance and Social Progress (or the Stiglitz-Sen-Fitoussi Commission) and asks people to rank their nation on eleven indicators: housing (conditions and spending), income (household income and financial wealth), jobs (earnings, job security, unemployment), community (quality of social support network), education, environmental quality, governance (involvement in democracy), health, life satisfaction (happiness), safety, and work-life balance. See www.oecdbetterlifeindex.org/#/11111111111.
- The Redefining Progress's Genuine Progress Indicator (GPI) looks at health care, safety, a clean environment, and other indicators of wellbeing, starting with personal consumption data, then measuring income distribution; housework, volunteering, and higher education; crime; resource depletion; pollution; long-term environmental damage; changes in leisure time; defensive expenditures; lifespan of consumer

durables and public infrastructure; and dependence on foreign assets. See www.rprogress.org/sustainability_indicators/genuine_progress_indicator.htm.
• Bhutan's Gross National Happiness Indicator includes non-economic aspects of wellbeing and sustainability. The index consists of 33 measures and has the four pillars of good governance, sustainable socio-economic development, cultural preservation, and environmental conservation classified into nine domains: psychological wellbeing, health, education, time use, cultural diversity and resilience, good governance, community vitality, ecological diversity and resilience, and living standards. See www.grossnationalhappiness.com.
I thank Carroll School Scholar of Corporate Responsibility and Professor of Management Sandra Waddock, for her contribution to the Great Transition Network (GTN) discussion on the topic of "Sustainability and Well-Being: A Happy Synergy," April 1, 2017, in response to Barrington-Leigh, 2017.

104 The Happy Planet Index (HPI) is an index of human well-being and environmental impact that was introduced by the British think-tank New Economics Foundation (NEF) in July 2006. See http://happyplanetindex.org/.

105 See, for instance, the "Terrorist Exclusion List," by the U.S. Department of State Under Secretary for Civilian Security, Democracy, and Human Rights, Bureau of Counter-terrorism, Office of the Coordinator for Counter-terrorism, December 29, 2004, www.state.gov/j/ct/rls/other/des/123086.htm.

106 Recent research in the U.S. has shed light on the influence of elite anti-tax advocacy groups hijacking the conservative agenda, even though their interests are not necessarily aligned with other conservative interests such as business interests, or the interests of angry, culturally fearful conservative populists. The most significant elite anti-tax advocacy organization seems to be the US nationwide, multipurpose political federation called Americans for Prosperity (AFP), as part of "weaponized" conservative philanthropy. See Theda Skocpol and Hertel-Fernandez, 2016, as well as Jane Mayer, 2016, and her book on Dark Money. I thank Glyn Rimmington for making me aware of book by Mayer. See also "Who Owns the GOP?" by Theda Skocpol, Dissent, February 3, 2016, and their referral to Parker and Barreto, 2013, see www.dissentmagazine.org/online_articles/jane-mayer-dark-money-review-koch-brothers-gop:

> Research by political scientist Christopher Parker at the University of Washington reinforces our conclusion that ordinary Tea Party activists and sympathizers are worried about sociocultural changes in the United States, angry and fearful about immigration, freaked out by the presence in the White House of a black liberal with a Muslim middle name, and fiercely opposed to what they view as out of control "welfare spending" on the poor, minorities, and young people. Many Tea Partiers benefit from Social Security, Medicare, and military veterans' programs, and do not want them to be cut or privatized. About half of Tea Party activists or sympathizers are also Christian conservatives intensely concerned with banning abortion and repealing gay marriage. … Ideas and passions may be similar across time, but, according to our research, angry, culturally fearful conservative populists not controlled from above are a major force in the early twenty-first-century United States.

When I try to look at the situation through the lens of dignity and humiliation, then people who until now felt dejected and shameful seem to be increasingly willing to develop a burning sense of victimhood they did not deserve, of sense of humiliation strong enough to cry out for action (I have studied this dynamic in depth in Nazi Germany). Politicians such as Bernie Sanders attempt to identify factual root causes, while populists first bundle and instigate anger and then channel it toward scapegoats, those they mistake for humiliators, wittingly or unwittingly giving cover to the actual humiliators. Organizations such as the AFP could be described as Trojan Horses that cannibalize and dominate their hosts by way of what I call "the art of humiliation."

107 "The Birth of Philanthrocapitalism: The Leading New Philanthropists See Themselves As Social Investors," The Economist, February 23, 2006, www.economist.com/node/5517656. Listen to Weekend Edition Sunday: 2016 Philanthropy Trends: Americans Donate Record $373 Billion, NPR's Ailsa Chang

speaks with Chuck Collins of the Institute for Policy Studies, WNYC-FM New York Public Radio, December 4, 2016, www.wnyc.org/story/534ecfa141812e2b6d9d869e/, where Collins explains that it is not GoFundMe or Crowdrise but megadonors who are behind the current rise in charitable giving. Megadonors increase the risk that recipients morph their mission according to the donors' wishes, and megadonors withdraw funds from the tax revenue that is needed to maintain the infrastructure. Collins uses Yale University as an example for an island of fancy buildings in a dilapidated context. See also Collins, 2012, 2014, 2016, Collins, et al., 2005.

108 In Lindner, 2006c, in the section "Love, Help, and Humiliation," in the book Making Enemies: Humiliation and International Conflict, I write on page 79 that cases of misunderstandings that have humiliating effects are difficult to deal with. "Cases of help and love that are "misunderstood" as humiliation are even more difficult. We find benevolent helpers on one side, no evil perpetrators at all, yet help and love sometimes cause deep feelings of humiliation in the recipients. Only one participant identifies this event as humiliation, the other labels it as help or love. The following vignette may illustrate the case of help and humiliation": "I have cancer. I have no money for medicine. You come to help me. You bring me chocolate. You feel good. I appreciate your good intentions. However, don't you see that I need medicine? Don't you see that you serve your own interests more than mine by bringing me chocolate? You have proved to yourself and your friends that you are a helpful human being.
But what about me? You buy yourself a good conscience and I pay the price. I feel painfully humiliated by your blindness and ignorance. I am bitter. I understand you do not know better. You are naïve and well-intentioned, but to me, you seem either stupid or evil. A little more effort to understand my situation would really help! And by the way, how much money did you earn with these pesticides that caused my cancer?" See also Lindner, 2010b. See, furthermore, Nadler and Halabi, 2006, or Rosen, 1983.

109 "When Restless Billionaires Trip on Their Toys," by Andrew Ross Sorkin, January 11, 2016, New York Times, www.nytimes.com/2016/01/12/business/dealbook/billionaires-who-trip-on-their-toys.html.

110 See the Eurobarometer 79.3, 2013, showing the results to the question: "Please tell me if you tend to trust or tend not to trust: Political Parties, the National Government, the National Parliament," http://ec.europa.eu/public_opinion/archives/eb/eb79/eb79_first_en.pdf. In 2013, trust in national parliament stood in Central and Eastern Europe at 17 percent, in Southern Europe at 19 percent, in Western Europe at 39 percent, and in Northern Europe at 63 percent. Trust in national government in 2013 stood in Central and Eastern Europe at 22 percent, in Southern Europe at 19 percent, in Western Europe at 37 percent, and in Northern Europe at 48 percent. Trust had gone down since it was measured in 2008 for all national institutions in all countries.

111 See note 295 in the Introduction, and note 114 in the Inspiring Questions to Section Two.

112 Bhaskar, 2008.

113 See note 162 in the Preface.

114 See also "Why the P2P and Commons Movement Must Act Trans-Locally and Trans-Nationally," by Michel Bauwens, P2P Foundation, June 12, 2016, https://blog.p2pfoundation.net/p2p-commons-movement-must-act-trans-locally-trans-nationally/2016/06/16. Bauwens recommends Karatani, 2014, who does not see capitalism as a mere mode of production, with state and nation as mere epiphenomena of capital, but as a triarchy combining Capital-State-Nation. Bauwens also reminds us of The Great Transformation by Karl Polanyi and Joseph E. Stiglitz (Foreword), 1944/2001, a history of the emergence and perpetuation of capitalism from the late eighteenth century to the 1940s, in which Polanyi sees a double movement at play, namely, between the market forces or the "Smithian" capitalism of the nineteenth century on one side, and society on the other side, or the nation, to speak with Karatani, who forces the market back into a more "social" order. For example, the Fordist period inspired a labor movement to force a re-alignment of society around the welfare state, with the backlash starting in the eighties, when these

social protections were "deregulated" again in favor of the 1 percent, with the result that workers are impoverished again in favor of the oligarchic elites. In other words, the nation, or what remains of community and reciprocity dynamics, revolts and mobilizes, and, if successful, it forces the state to discipline capital. Bauwens observes what also I observe all around the world, namely, that after the systemic crisis of 2008 this uprising fails, even though a Polanyian backlash can be found nearly everywhere on the globe: Both Donald Trump and Bernie Sanders in the 2016 U.S. electoral cycle "represent the Polanyian double movement, and are reacting against the effects of neoliberalism and its destruction of the U.S. middle class," writes Bauwens. Trump speaks for the white middle class and workers and wishes to bring the back a better past, while Sanders represents those who suffer from precarity and envision a different future. The problem, however, is that this time the Polanyian double movement is hindered by capital having developed a transnational logic and capacity. Financial neoliberalism has globalized and fundamentally weakened the capacity of the nation-state to discipline its activities:

> Faced with an all-powerful transnational capitalism, the various nation-state systems have proven pretty powerless to effect any change. Dare to challenge the status quo and paralyzing capital flight is going to destroy your country! This is one of the explanations of the deep distrust that people are feeling towards the current political system, which simply fails to deliver towards any majoritarian social demand.
>
> Look at how the moderately radical Syriza movement in Greece was put under a European protectorate and had to abandon Greek sovereignty; or look at how the more antagonistically-oriented Venezuelan government is crumbling, along with other progressive governments in Latin America.
>
> So, while the electorate may vote for parties that promise to change the status quo and eventually bring to power movements like Podemos, a Labour Party under the leadership of Corbyn, or a Democratic Party strongly influenced by the Sanders movement, their capacities for change will be severely restricted.

The solution that Bauwens sees, resonates with my global observations, namely, that there is no alternative to creating transnational and translocal capacities, which means globally interlinking the efforts of all the local "civic and ethical entrepreneurial networks that are currently in development." This is why I invest my life time into creating a dignity movement not just locally, but globally.

Section Three

See additional material at www.humiliationstudies.org/whoweare/ evelin/book/05.php.

1 Le Bon, 1915/1916, p. 391. This 1999 edition of the book has a new introduction by Martha Hanna and a new Foreword by Irving Louis Horowitz. The book was originally published in London by T. Fisher Unwin, in 1916.

2 The Wehrmacht Oath of Loyalty to Adolf Hitler, August 2, 1934.

3 Preface, Shelley, 1819, www.bartleby.com/18/4/1003.html.

4 Baldwin, 1963.

5 "Mysterious Connections that Link Us Together," Azar Nafisi, National Public Radio (NPR), July 18, 2005, www.npr.org/templates/story/story.php?storyId=4753976. I thank Libby and Len Traubman for making us aware of this quote, and for their ongoing support for Human Dignity and Humiliation Studies.

Introduction to Section Three

1 Wright, et al., 1962.

2 A recent book by Eric Schlosser, 2013, is based on previously classified material that the author discovered through the Freedom of Information Act in the U.S.A. There are many other examples of "glitches," among others, the 1979 NORAD Computer Glitch. Read more on www.history.com/news/history-lists/5-cold-war-close-calls. See the full note in the pdf edition of this book. The panic subsided after NORAD consulted its satellite data and realized the nuclear warning was little more than a false alarm. Upon further inspection, they discovered that a technician had accidentally run a training program simulating a Soviet attack on the United States. The incident sent shock waves through the international community – Soviet leader Leonid Brezhnev even wrote President Jimmy Carter a letter noting the "tremendous danger" caused by the error – but it was not the last time a computer issue led to a nuclear scare. Computer chip failures would later lead to three more false alarms at NORAD in the following year.

3 Stanislav Petrov was only recently acknowledged and widely recognized for his actions in averting a potential nuclear war in 1983. Among others, he was awarded the Dresden Preis 2013 in Germany.

4 See in this context also Lindner, 2012f, A Dignity Economy.

5 "When Generosity Hurts: Bill Gates, Public School Teachers and the Politics of Humiliation," by Henry A. Giroux, TruthOut, October 5, 2010, http://truth-out.org/archive/component/k2/item/92120:when-generosity-hurts-bill-gates-public-school-teachers-and-the-politics-of-humiliation. I thank Brian Ward for having made us aware of this article. See for some of Giroux's publications, Di Leo, et al., 2013, Giroux, 2010, 2011, 2012, 2013, 2014a, b, Nikolakaki, 2012.

6 "The Good News About Nuclear Destruction," by Shane Connor, WND (formerly WorldNetDaily), August 24, 2006, www.wnd.com/2006/08/37591/. Shane Connor is a consultant and developer of civil defense solutions to government, military, private organizations, and individual families.

7 This is the topic of Lindner, 2006c, Making Enemies: Humiliation and International Conflict.

8 Quoted from http://dirtywars.org/the-book, Scahill, 2013. See also Scahill, 2007, in an interview in the German newspaper: "Drohnenkrieg der USA: ‚Jeder Tote wird zum Terroristen erklärt," Daniel Haufler interviews Jeremy Scahill, Frankfurter Rundschau, October 25, 2013, www.fr-online.de/politik/drohnenkrieg-der-usa--jeder-tote-wird-zum-terroristen-erklaert-,1472596,24783178.html: "Obama als Ankläger, Richter, Jury und Henker: Die USA führen ihre Kriege mit Drohnen und Propaganda. Ein Verstoß gegen das Völkerrecht, sagt Enthüllungsjournalist Jeremy Scahill."

9 Hobbes, 1651.

10 Lindner and Desmond Tutu (Foreword), 2010, p. 53.

11 Wyatt-Brown, 1982. See also Wyatt-Brown, 2014. See also Cohen, 1996, Cohen and Nisbett, 1997, Cohen, et al., 1996, Cohen and Vandello, 1997, Cohen, et al., 1998, Leung and Cohen, 2011, Nisbett and Cohen, 1996, Vandello, et al., 2008, Vandello and Cohen, 2003.

12 "Looking for a Fight: A New History of the Philippine-American War," by Candice Millard, New York Times, February 17, 2012, www.nytimes.com/2012/02/19/books/review/a-new-history-of-the-philippine-american-war.html?pagewanted=all&_r=0. Jones, 2012.

13 Jones, 2012, p. 24.

14 Jones, 2012, p. 10.

15 Kagan, 1997. See also political scientist Ernst Fraenkel, 1941, who refers to sociologist Emil Lederer, who argues that the "power state" or "Machtstaat" is distinct from the "regular" legal state or Rechtsstaat, which "has its historical origins in the European aristocratic elite, which still played an important role within

European society after the triumph of democracy. This elite acted behind the scene in the 1920s, but considered it necessary to intervene in support of the Nazi Party in the 1930s to prevent a possible socialist takeover," see Tunander, 2009, p. 56.

16 "Enormous Sense of Hopelessness and Anger," by Noam Chomsky and Melissa Parker, Smashing Interviews Magazine, January 21, 2016, http://smashinginterviews.com/interviews/newsmakers/noam-chomsky-interview-enormous-sense-of-hopelessness-and-anger-reflected-in-appeal-of-trump-and-sanders.

17 See a discussion in Lindner, 2009b, Chapter 8: How We Can Reinvent Our Contexts, in the book Emotion and Conflict.

18 "The Commission on Security and Cooperation in Europe: Political Pluralism in the OSCE Mediterranean Partners? Testimony by Shibley Telhami," July 9, 2014, www.sadat.umd.edu/pub/TelhamiTestimony2.pdf. Shibley Telhami is the Anwar Sadat Professor for Peace and Development at the University of Maryland. It is a privilege to have Shibley Telhami as esteemed member in the global advisory board of our Human Dignity and Humiliation Studies fellowship.

19 "Unter falschen Vorzeichen," by Manfred Ertel, Der Spiegel 39/2013, September 21, 2013, www.spiegel.de/spiegel/print/d-113750825.html, p. 103: "Ich merkte immer mehr, wie ich manipuliert wurde. Sie hörten mir nicht zu, wollten keinen Dialog, sie hatten nur ein Ziel: ihre Meinung zu verteidigen und durchzusetzen."

20 "A War to End All Innocence: The Enduring Impact of World War I," by A. O. Scott, New York Times, June 20, 2014, www.nytimes.com/2014/06/22/arts/the-enduring-impact-of-world-war-i.html?_r=0.

21 "Bassem Youssef: Fear Has No Future," Deutsche Welle, June 30, 2014, www.dw.de/bassem-youssef-fear-has-no-future/a-17747272. Bassem Youssef spoke at the World Conference Center in Bonn in Germany on the occasion of the 2014 Deutsche Welle Global Media Forum.

22 Identity and the Prism of Perspective, Shibley Telhami at TEDxUMD, July 5, 2014, https://youtu.be/ywFn-G8DXk4. This is the description text: "'Why is Barack Obama black?' This is the question Shibley Telhami starts with to understand the roots of identity. He concludes that identity affirms itself when under attack." It is a privilege to have Shibley Telhami as esteemed member in the global advisory board of our Human Dignity and Humiliation Studies fellowship.

23 See in this context also Lindner, 2012f, A Dignity Economy.

24 Kalecki, 1943: "Under a laissez-faire system the level of employment depends to a great extent on the so-called state of confidence. If this deteriorates, private investment declines, which results in a fall of output and employment (both directly and through the secondary effect of the fall in incomes upon consumption and investment). This gives the capitalists a powerful indirect control over government policy: everything which may shake the state of confidence must be carefully avoided because it would cause an economic crisis."

25 Howard Richards in a personal communication on February 9, 2014. See also Richards and Swanger, 2006b, 2008. Richards is a philosopher of social science and scholar of peace and global studies.

Chapter 12

1 See, among others, the work of Alexander Wendt, 1992, 1999, social constructivist scholar in the field of international relations. I communicated with Alexander Wendt for the first time in 2005.

2 Schmitt, 1927/2007. See also "Carl Schmitt i Det hvite hus," by Rune Slagstad, Institutt for samfunnsforskning, Klassekampen, February 11, 2017, www.klassekampen.no/article/20170211/ARTICLE/170219981. Norwegian historian Rune Slagstad

describes how populists now challenge, at its core, the modern state with its liberal democracy and the rule of law. See more in note 25 in the Preface. See also Tunander, 2009, in note 98 in Chapter 1. See, furthermore, Kagan, 1997, and Fraenkel, 1941, in note 15 in the Introduction to Section Three.

3 Schmitt, 1927/2007.

4 Schmitt, 1963/2004.

5 "Carl Schmitt i Det hvite hus," by Rune Slagstad, Institutt for samfunnsforskning, Klassekampen, February 11, 2017, www.klassekampen.no/article/20170211/ARTICLE/170219981. See more in note 25 in the Preface. See also Tunander, 2009, in note 98 in Chapter 1. See, furthermore, Kagan, 1997, and Fraenkel, 1941, in note 15 in the Introduction to Section Three.

6 rinkmann, 2017b.

7 Wendt, 1992. See his later work Albert, et al., 2010, Wendt, 1999, 2003, 2015, Wendt, et al., 2006.

8 "The 'Hero Syndrome,'" by Sergeant Ben D. Cross, Arkansas State Police, School of Law Enforcement Supervision Session XLIII, November 1, 2014, www.cji.edu/site/assets/files/1921/the_hero_syndrome.pdf.

9 Feldman, 2004.

10 Axelrod, 2006.

11 Imhof, et al., 2007. See also Nowak and Highfield, 2011.

12 See, among others, Axelrod, 2006, Liberman, et al., 2004, Imhof, et al., 2007, Nowak and Highfield, 2011. See also Bernstein, 1971, 1973, 1975, 1990, 2000. See more in note 7 in the Introduction to Section One. See also Chong and Druckman, 2007.

13 Liberman, et al., 2004, Abstract. See the full note in the pdf edition of this book.

14 Guala, 2012, Abstract.

15 Snow and Benford, 1988, p. 213. See also Ryan and Gamson, 2006, p.14: "Like a picture frame, an issue frame marks off some part of the world. Like a building frame, it holds things together. It provides coherence to an array of symbols, images, and arguments, linking them through an underlying organizing idea that suggests what is essential – what consequences and values are at stake. We do not see the frame directly, but infer its presence by its characteristic expressions and language. Each frame gives the advantage to certain ways of talking and thinking, while it places others 'out of the picture-'"

16 McKinlay and McVittie, 2008.

17 Lindner and Desmond Tutu (Foreword), 2010.

18 Taylor, et al., 2002.

19 "Journey through Terror," by Peter Taylor, BBC News, April 15, 2008, http://news.bbc.co.uk/2/hi/uk_news/magazine/7347154.stm.

20 Harald Jäger was born in 1943 and is a former East German Stasi lieutenant colonel who, on November 9, 1989, disobeyed orders and opened up the Bornholmer Straße border crossing, thus being the first to open the Berlin Wall. His final graduation thesis as a diplomated law expert in 1981 was titled Die Bildung der Spezialistentruppen "Sicherheit und Terrorabwehr" in den Grenzzollämtern der Zollverwaltung der DDR als Voraussetzung zur zielgerichteten und differenzierten Einbeziehung der Angehörigen der Zollverwaltung der DDR in das System der Terrorabwehr an den Grenzübergangsstellen der DDR.

21 Côté, 2000.

22 West, 2008.

23 See note 73 in Chapter 4.

24 Jihad: A Story of the Others, documentary film by Deeyah Khan, 2015, http://fuuse.net/jihad-a-story-of-the-others/. See more in note 20 in Chapter 6.

25 Calcutt, 1998.

26 Lindner, 2006b.

27 Ibid.

28 Jasper, 1997.

29 Galtung, 1971, 1976.

30 Vambheim, 2011.

31 Vambheim, 2011, p. 15.

32 "Wir lieben den Tod," by Adel S. Elias, Der Spiegel 43/1997, October 20, 1997, www.spiegel.de/spiegel/print/d-8805772.html, pp. 204–209. See the full note in the pdf edition of this book.

33 See note 18 in Chapter 6.

34 Juergensmeyer, 2000, pp. 184–195.

35 Vambheim, 2011, p. 15.

36 Ibid.

37 Galtung, et al., 2000.

38 See the Inglehart–Welzel Cultural Map – World Values Survey wave 6 (2010 – 2014) on www.worldvaluessurvey.org/images/Cultural_map_WVS6_2015.jpg, and explained on www.worldvaluessurvey.org/WVSContents.jsp. Note also Inglehart and Welzel, 2005, and Norris and Inglehart, 2011.

39 See note 6 in the Introduction to Section One.

40 "What Americans Really Think About Muslims and Islam," by Shibley Telhami, Brookings Institution Press, December 9, 2015, www.brookings.edu/blogs/markaz/posts/2015/12/09-what-americans-think-of-muslims-and-islam-telhami#.Vmhur0cUDt8.twitter. Telhami finds that the views of two important American constituencies on Middle East policy, Evangelicals and American Jews, are particularly contrasting:

Among those identifying themselves as Jewish Americans (5 percent of the sample), only 20 percent say that Islamic and Western religious and cultural tradition are incompatible. This contrasts with 55 percent of Evangelical Christians. While 43 percent of Jewish Americans have favorable views of Islam (which is slightly higher than the national total of 37 percent), only 18 percent of Evangelicals feel the same. And 55 percent of Jewish Americans express favorable views of Muslims, in contrast to only 38 percent of Evangelicals.

It is a privilege to have Shibley Telhami as esteemed member in the global advisory board of our Human Dignity and Humiliation Studies fellowship.

41 Asal, et al., 2013.

42 "Defining Christian Zionism," by Donald Wagner, www.christianzionism.org/articlesN.asp#Wagner02. Reverend Dr. Donald Wagner, an ordained Presbyterian minister, is associate professor of Religion and Middle Eastern Studies, and executive director of the Center for Middle Eastern Studies at North Park University. He served from 1980 to 1989 as national director of the Palestine Human Rights Campaign. He is the author of Anxious for Armageddon (1995), and Dying in the Land of Promise: Palestine and Palestinian Christianity from Pentecost to 2000 (revised edition, 2003). I thank Sam Bahour for making me aware of this text. See also Hoel, 2014.

43 Ibid.

44 "How to (Almost) Eliminate the Partisan Divide on the Middle East," by Shibley Telhami, The Washington Post, December 14, 2015, www.washingtonpost.com/news/monkey-cage/wp/2015/12/14/how-

to-almost-eliminate-the-partisan-divide-on-the-middle-east/. It is a privilege to have Shibley Telhami as esteemed member in the global advisory board of our Human Dignity and Humiliation Studies fellowship. He explains that, overall, 13 percent of Americans identify as Evangelical and 11 percent as non-Evangelical Born-Again Christians, with Evangelicals being overwhelmingly white, while non-Evangelical Born-Again Christians include 20 percent African Americans and 10 percent Hispanics.

45 See also Juergensmeyer, 2000.

46 Summary of the violence and disruption statistics of 2015, gathered by the United States National Abortion Federation (NAF), http://5aa1b2xfmfh2e2mk03kk8rsx.wpengine.netdna-cdn.com/wp-content/uploads/2015-NAF-Violence-Disruption-Stats.pdf.

47 "2 Abortion Foes Behind Planned Parenthood Videos Are Indicted," by Manny Fernandez, New York Times, January 25, 2016, www.nytimes.com/2016/01/26/us/2-abortion-foes-behind-planned-parenthood-videos-are-indicted.html.

48 See note 46 above.

49 "Expert Colloquy – Dialogue Serving Intercultural and Inter-Religious Communication – Strasbourg," Council of Europe, October 7–9, 2002, interview with Johan Galtung, www.coe.int/T/E/Com/Files/Events/2002-10-Intercultural-Dialogue/Interview_galtung.asp. See also Galtung, 1996, Galtung, et al., 2000. See, furthermore, the description of the Dichotomy-Manicheism-Armageddon (DMT) syndrome in "Cultural Peace: Some Characteristics," by Johan Galtung, Transcend articles, October 12, 2003, www.transcend.org/files/article121.html. See also LeShan, 1992.

50 "Ted Cruz's Campaign Is Fueled by a Dominionist Vision for America," commentary by John Fea, Washington Post, February 4, 2016, www.washingtonpost.com/national/religion/ted-cruzs-campaign-is-fueled-by-a-dominionist-vision-for-america-commentary/2016/02/04/86373158-cb6a-11e5-b9ab-26591104bb19_story.html?utm_term=.bc4329410da8.

51 "Mecca Makeover: How the Hajj Has Become Big Business for Saudi Arabia," by Riazat Butt in Mecca, The Guardian, November 14, 2010, www.theguardian.com/world/2010/nov/14/mecca-hajj-saudi-arabia.

52 "The Architects of the War on Islam," by Maniza Naqvi, 3 Quarks Daily, August 6, 2012, www.3quarksdaily.com/3quarksdaily/2012/08/the-architects-of-the-war-on-islam.html#comments. I thank Judit Révész for making me aware of this article. Maniza Naqvi was born in Lahore Pakistan in 1960, and now works at the World Bank in Washington DC, U.S.A, also working in the areas of peace, poverty alleviation, demobilization of militaries and building good governance at community levels in post conflict countries, see www.sawnet.org/books/authors.php?Naqvi+Maniza.

53 Abu-Rabi, 2007, p. 33.

54 "Expert Colloquy – Dialogue Serving Intercultural and Inter-Religious Communication – Strasbourg," Council of Europe, October 7–9, 2002, interview with Johan Galtung, www.coe.int/T/E/Com/Files/Events/2002-10-Intercultural-Dialogue/Interview_galtung.asp.

55 See Lindner, 2006c, the section "Apologies from the world! What the world can do for America," in Chapter 5: Humiliation and Conflict, in the book Making Enemies: Humiliation and International Conflict, pp. 102–105.

56 Acres of Diamonds, was delivered by Russell Conwell over 5000 times at various times and places from 1900–1925, see audio and text on www.americanrhetoric.com/speeches/rconwellacresofdiamonds.htm. His view of poverty was somewhat in resonance with defenders of the Indian caste system. See more in note 32 in Chapter 2.

57 Jones, 2006.

58 See, for instance, philosopher Alan Wilson Watts (1915 – 1973), and his Alan Watts: A Conversation with Myself in four parts, beginning with https://youtu.be/8aufuwMiKmE.

59 Father Athanase Seromba, who led the Nyange parish massacre and was sentenced to fifteen years in jail, was asked by one of the refugees: "'Father, can't you pray for us?' Seromba replied: 'Is the God of the Tutsi still alive?' Later, he would order a bulldozer to push down the church walls on those inside and then urge militias to invade the building and finish off the survivors," in "For Rwandans, the Pope's Apology Must Be Unbearable," by Martin Kimani, The Guardian, March 29, 2010, www.theguardian.com/commentisfree/belief/2010/mar/29/pope-catholics-rwanda-genocide-church.

60 Lindner and Desmond Tutu (Foreword), 2010.

61 Kaufman, 2001.

62 Rashid, 2008. See also Tunander, 2009, and the discussion of Morgenthau earlier in this book.

63 Vambheim, 2011, p. 15.

64 Lindner, 2006c, p. 76.

65 "Former Nuclear Blast Sites in Russia's Murmansk Region to Become a National Park," by Alexey Pavlov, translated by Maria Kaminskaya, Bellona, January 23, 2011, http://bellona.org/news/future-energy-system/2011-01-former-nuclear-blast-sites-in-russias-murmansk-region-to-become-a-national-park.

66 Vambheim, 2016. I had the privilege of being one of Vambheim's opponents when he defended his doctorate, and it is a privilege to have him on the global advisory board of our Human Dignity and Humiliation Studies fellowship.

67 Vambheim, 2011, p. 18, italics in original.

68 Chödrön, 2001. I thank Linda Hartling for making me aware of the work of Prema Chödrön.

69 Chödrön, 2001, Chapter 17: Bodhisattva Activity. See the full note in the pdf edition of this book.

70 Chödrön, 2001, Chapter 13: Meeting the Enemy. See the full note in the pdf edition of this book.

71 Dignicommunication – a term coined by Evelin Lindner on November 2, 2014. See more on www.humiliationstudies.org/whoweare/whoweare.php#digniwords.

72 Habitat III took place in Quito, Ecuador, October 17–20, 2016, as the major United Nations Conference on Housing and Sustainable Urban Development. Presidents, ministers, and other representatives from 170 countries, 200 mayors and delegations from 500 cities, met to discuss and adopt the New Urban Agenda, a global strategy for 21st century sustainable urbanism. After this conference, many questions remain unanswered: How will cities be able to fully implement the provisions of the recently concluded Paris agreement on the environment and carry the costs involved? What about standing up against the increasing malpractice of grabbing and transforming public space to serve commercial interests? What about the urban-rural divide? Activists are concerned over the reduction of the Habitat Agenda to a solely urban focus and call to "give adequate priority to the continuity – indeed, the symbiosis – between rural and urban areas," see "A Needed Cornerstone for Habitat III: The Right to the City," by Isabel Pascual, Citiscope, February 15, 2016, http://citiscope.org/habitatIII/commentary/2016/02/needed-cornerstone-habitat-iii-right-city. I thank Kjell Skyllstad for making me aware of this publication. See also "Governments and Social Movements Disagree on Future of Cities," by Emilio Godoy, Inter Press Service (IPS), October 25, 2016, www.ipsnews.net/2016/10/governments-and-social-movements-disagree-on-future-of-cities/.

73 See note 295 in the Introduction, and note 114 in the Inspiring Questions to Section Two.

74 See note 162 in the Preface.

75 Richards and Andersson, 2017. See also, "The Grim State of South Africa One Year after Nelson Mandela," by Andrew Kenny, The Spectator, December 6, 2014, www.spectator.co.uk/2014/12/beyond-the-rainbow/#.

76 See my discussion of the globalization process and its consequences in Lindner, 2006c, pp. 44–45: "Conservatives around the world may insist, for example, that bad people deserve to be called enemy. This

word, and related words such as war, soldier, and victory, will not disappear because some soft-hearted dreamers wish it. These words are losing their meaning because they no longer describe reality. When a tree dies, it bears no more fruit. Likewise, the reality that bore words such as enemy, war, and victory is currently dying, through globalization, whether we support this development or not."

77 Kury, 2012.

78 See, among many other publications, Schwarz, 1997, Williams, 2000.

79 Publius Flavius Vegetius Renatus and Reeve, 2004.

80 See, among others, Lindner, 2012f, A Dignity Economy, where I spell out the opportunities for change.

Chapter 13

1 Hardisty, 1999, p. 6: "… a strong commitment to individual rights and freedoms for everyone, even my political enemies, has helped me in the study of the right. It helps to block my urge to demonize the rightist who demonize feminists and lesbians…." I thank Linda Hartling for having made me aware of Hardisty's research already many years ago. See also an article highlighting that supporters of Donald Trump are not the caricatures journalists depict, but middle class: "Dangerous Idiots: How the Liberal Media Elite Failed Working-Class Americans," by Sarah Smarsh, The Guardian, October 13, 2016, www.theguardian.com/media/2016/oct/13/liberal-media-bias-working-class-americans. See also "President Obama Admits His Biggest Mistake: Arrogance," by Chris Cillizza, The Washington Post, November 17, 2015, www.washingtonpost.com/news/the-fix/wp/2015/11/17/president-obamas-biggest-mistake-in-office-thinking-you-can-separate-politics-from-policy/?utm_term=.a92c265fc1ff.

2 See note 24 in the Introduction to Section One.

3 "Remembering Ireland's 1916 Easter Rising," by Mairead Maguire, Nobel Peace Laureate, TRANSCEND Media Service, April 11, 2016, www.transcend.org/tms/2016/04/remembering-irelands-1916-easter-rising/.

4 For instance, "corruption committed in the name of good ends," Caldero and Crank, 2011, p. 2. I thank Linda Hartling for making me aware of this book. See also Hartling and Lindner, 2017.

5 Wambacq and Ciocan, 2011, p. 233. See Nietzsche, 1883–1891/1998, in Zarathustra: X. WAR AND WARRIORS: "By our best enemies we do not want to be spared, nor by those either whom we love from the very heart... My brethren in war! I love you from the very heart. I am, and was ever, your counterpart. And I am also your best enemy."

6 I thank Carol Smaldino for making me aware of the book by Ryan Stevenson, 2015, where he describes the experience of "brokenness," just as all of us are broken from the experience of being human.

7 Read on Friederike Nadig on www.bpb.de/geschichte/deutsche-geschichte/grundgesetz-und-parlamentarischer-rat/39112/friederike-nadig-spd. Article 4, paragraph 3 of the Constitution of Germany (The Basic Law for the Federal Republic of Germany, German: Grundgesetz für die Bundesrepublik Deutschland) says: „Niemand darf gegen sein Gewissen zum Kriegsdienst mit der Waffe gezwungen werden" (No one may be compelled against his conscience to render military service under arms). Friederike Nadig (1897 – 1970), member of the Social Democratic Party of Germany, pushed for equal rights for men and women, particularly, for equal pay and equal rights of illegitimate and legitimate children. In addition, she was one of the most active proponents of the right to conscientious objection. The Federal Republic of Germany was the first country in the world to include to right of conscientious objection into its constitution. See also Sitter, 1995.

8 Soldaten und Verweigerer: "Wir waren die Ersten!" documentary film by Carsten Günther, Das Erste, 2011. See the full note in the pdf edition of this book.

9 See note 3 in Chapter 7.

10 I appreciate the approach of Dan Baum, 2013, who provides the reader with a deeper understanding of the reasons for why people love weapons. I thank Michael Greene for making me aware of this book. It is a privilege to have Michael Greene as esteemed member in the global advisory board of our Human Dignity and Humiliation Studies fellowship.

11 "President Obama Admits His Biggest Mistake: Arrogance," by Chris Cillizza, The Washington Post, November 17, 2015, www.washingtonpost.com/news/the-fix/wp/2015/11/17/president-obamas-biggest-mistake-in-office-thinking-you-can-separate-politics-from-policy/?utm_term=.a92c265fc1ff.

12 See, among others, Obama, 2004, and Fanon, 1952/1967, 1961/1963.

13 "Obama Regrets His Attack on 'Stupid' Police for 'Racist' Arrest of Harvard Scholar," by Mail Foreign Service, Daily Mail, July 25, 2009, www.dailymail.co.uk/news/article-1201199/Obama-regrets-attack-stupid-police-racist-arrest-Harvard-scholar.html. See Obama: I Don't Know All The Facts But The Police Acted Stupid!, Fox News, posted on YouTube on July 23, 2009, https://youtu.be/qYUrY2GtBfc.

14 "But I tell you, love your enemies, bless those who curse you, do good to those who hate you, and pray for those who mistreat you and persecute you," this sentence is quoted from the King James Version of the Bible, and it appears in the 44th verse of the fifth chapter of the Gospel of Matthew in the New Testament of the Bible as part of the Sermon on the Mount.

15 Marquardt, 2015.

16 John Bolton in a personal communication to his supporters on March 12, 2014.

17 Michelle Fine and Halkovic, 2014, p. 58: "Opotow, 2011, in extending Deutsch's theorizing, has demonstrated that these distinct justice frameworks have profound consequences for influencing a nation's, community's, or person's scope of justice, arguing that justice principles of deserving are extended only to those who are considered to be a part of one's own moral community. Thus, the narrower one's sense of community is, the narrower is one's scope of justice." See also Opotow, 1995. I thank Morton Deutsch for having introduced me to Michelle Fine and Susan Opotow in 2002, and for the great privilege of being able to learn from all since then.

18 Hoffman, et al., 2015.

19 "Inverted refrigerator," quoted in Vambheim, 2016, p. 87, as a term coined by social anthropologist Thomas Hylland Eriksen.

20 "The Coalition of Transformation vs. the Coalition of Restoration," by Ronald Brownstein, The Atlantic, November 21, 2012, www.theatlantic.com/politics/archive/2012/11/the-coalition-of-transformation-vs-the-coalition-of-restoration/265512/.

21 On the evening of November 13, 2015, a series of coordinated terrorist attacks occurred in Paris, France. 130 people were killed. The so-called Islamic State claimed responsibility for the attacks.

22 Pamela Geller, in a communication to her list subscribers, November 16, 2015.

23 Wyatt-Brown, 1982. See also Wyatt-Brown, 2014, and Cohen, 1996, Cohen and Nisbett, 1997, Cohen, et al., 1996, Cohen and Vandello, 1997, Cohen, et al., 1998, Leung and Cohen, 2011, Nisbett and Cohen, 1996, Vandello, et al., 2008, Vandello and Cohen, 2003.

24 Wyatt-Brown, 2005, p. 2.

25 Nisbett and Cohen, 1996.

26 Fischer, 1989, p. 843.

27 See note 23 above.

28 "Donald Trump: The Best US President for Global Peace with His 'Coherent' Foreign Policy," by Leo Semashko, supported by several signatories, December 3, 2016, Peace for Harmony, http://peacefromharmony.org/?cat=en_c&key=685. The authors quote Martin Luther King Jr. saying "We must shift the arms race into a peace race," and then continue: "This shift was began by Donald Trump, making America great again, saving it from the ruins and inspiring peace globalization instead of war globalization."

29 The authors of the above quoted text on the Peace for Harmony site refer to Donald J. Trump's Foreign Policy Speech, April 27, 2016, www.donaldjtrump.com/press-releases/donald-j.-trump-foreign-policy-speech.

30 "The Messy Truth," by Team Van Jones, November 06, 2016, www.vanjones.net/the_messy_truth_trailer: "In America today, the establishment is on the ropes, the rebels are on the rise, and now the people are ready to talk. People aren't just talking, they're screaming at the top of their lungs. But we can't seem to listen. In the midst of all the inflammation and toxicity of the election season, we've all lost the ability to step into someone else's shoes and see each other as human beings. We don't all have to agree, but we can learn a lot from each other. At a certain point people might surprise themselves and say something they hadn't already thought or heard." According to Jones, Donald Trump as a leader is "much worse" than many people are ready to accept, but many of his voters – except those Jones calls "bigots" – are "much better," namely, those who found some of Donald Trump's remarks "disgusting but not disqualifying." See his interview with Trevor Noah on The Daily Show, December 5, 2016, www.cc.com/full-episodes/np0e6l/the-daily-show-with-trevor-noah-december-5--2016---van-jones-season-22-ep-22032.

31 The Danger of a Single Story, TED talk by Chimamanda Ngozi Adichie, October 7, 2009, https://youtu.be/D9Ihs241zeg: "Our lives, our cultures, are composed of many overlapping stories. Novelist Chimamanda Adichie tells the story of how she found her authentic cultural voice – and warns that if we hear only a single story about another person or country, we risk a critical misunderstanding." I thank Drew Pham for making me aware of this talk.

32 "This Is What 'Whitelash' Looks Like," by John Blake, CNN, November 20, 2016, http://edition.cnn.com/2016/11/11/us/obama-trump-white-backlash/. See also Anderson, 2016.

33 Jost and Ross, 1999.

34 "What Does Alternative for Germany (AfD) Want?" BBC News Service, September 5, 2016, www.bbc.com/news/world-europe-37274201.

35 Trond Einar Frednes and Horst, 2015, describe the "laws" of gang culture in great detail, and how "normality" entails cruelty as expected tool, rather than cruelty necessarily flowing from the perpetrator's disturbed psychology (even though this might be the case in addition).

36 Maalouf, 1998/2000. I thank Yves Musoni for reminding me of this book.

37 Jennings and Murphy, 2000, Abstract:

The field of domestic violence has concentrated its theories, research, and treatment methods on the male–female dimensions of the problem. However, male–male issues also play a crucial role. The authors explain how traditional male socialization and rigid sex role stereotyping can have emotional and behavioral consequences that are displaced onto male–female relationships. In particular, "humiliation" is a potent and pervasive social mechanism that dominates male psychology, causing multiple problems in male self-esteem and interpersonal relations. Humiliation is the social form of shame and is deeply rooted in the same-sex relations of childhood groups, rituals of passage, and problematic relationships with father figures.

I thank Linda Hartling for making me aware of this article.

38 "On the Frontline in Syria: The Danish Gangster who Turned Jihadi," by Nagieb Khaja, The Guardian, July 7, 2014, www.theguardian.com/world/2014/jul/07/european-jihadi-danish-gangster-frontline-syria.

39 Psychiatrist and sociologist Marc Sageman describes a less religious third wave of Al-Qaeda inspired terrorism, following two waves that were more religious. Some individuals involved in terrorism now seem to "discover" religion mere weeks before getting active. See Sageman, 2004, 2008, 2009, and "A Not Very Private Feud Over Terrorism," by Mark Sageman, New York Times, June 8, 2008, www.nytimes.com/2008/06/08/weekinreview/08sciolino.html?_r=4&scp=1&sq=marc+sageman&st=nyt&oref=slogin&oref=slogin&. See also Gunning and Jackson, 2011, and Lakhani, 2013.

40 "Criminal Pasts, Terrorist Futures: European Jihadists and the New Crime-Terror Nexus," by Rajan Basra, Peter R. Neumann, and Claudia Brunner, International Centre for the Study of Radicalisation (ICSR), King's College, London, http://icsr.info/wp-content/uploads/2016/10/ICSR-Report-Criminal-Pasts-Terrorist-Futures-European-Jihadists-and-the-New-Crime-Terror-Nexus.pdf. See also Neumann, 2015/2016.

41 "How Muslims Compare With Other Religious Americans In Intensity of Religious Identity, Not Unlike Evangelicals," by Robert Ruby and Greg Smith, Pew Forum on Religion and Public Life, Muslim, July 6, 2007, www.pewresearch.org/2007/07/06/how-muslims-compare-with-other-religious-americans/. See also "The World's Muslims: Religion, Politics and Society," by James Bell, Pew Research Center's Forum on Religion and Public Life, Polling and Analysis, April 30, 2013, www.pewforum.org/files/2013/04/worlds-muslims-religion-politics-society-full-report.pdf.

42 Ibid.

43 See note 42 in Chapter 12.

44 See note 44 in Chapter 12.

45 "West Bank Rabbi Dov Lior: Jewish law permits destruction of Gaza." News Brief of The Global Jewish News Source (JTA), July 24, 2014, www.jta.org/2014/07/24/news-opinion/israel-middle-east/west-bank-rabbi-dov-lior-jewish-law-permits-destruction-of-gaza.

46 "Krigeren med de ni liv," by Cato Guhnfeldto, Aftenposten. November 5, 2012, p. 4: "Det er klart man tok gale avgjørelser også innen motstandsbevegelsen. Men man må huske på at det var krig. Det hendte vi måtte drepe uten å være sikker på at vedkommende var angiver. Men avgjørelsene var riktige der og da."

47 "The World's Muslims: Religion, Politics and Society," in note 41 in this Chapter 13.

48 Afghanistan: The Price of Revenge, documentary film by Alberto Marquardt, Al Jazeera, May 31, 2013, www.aljazeera.com/programmes/specialseries/2013/05/2013531103439130667.html.

49 McCauley, 2017. Also Negrao, et al., 2005, suggest that the experience of humiliation is a combination of anger and shame. Feeling outraged and thinking of revenge is part of the syndrome of anger, while feeling confused, deficient, small, and sullied is part of the syndrome of shame, explains Clark McCauley, 2017, and suggests (p. 260) that:

1. the emotional experience of humiliation is a combination of anger and shame;
2. the anger is in response to the perpetrator's enforced, unjust lowering of the victim; and
3. the shame is in response to the victim's failure to resist or retaliate.

McCauley, 2017, p. 260, also refers to sociologist Jack Katz, 1988, who studied the subjective experiences of violent criminals. At the root of their behavior, Katz found shame, anger, and humiliation. "Doing stickup" represented a retaliation for everyday experiences of shame and humiliation, the glory of domination and control reversed shameful powerlessness. It is a privilege to have Clark McCauley as esteemed member in the global advisory board of our Human Dignity and Humiliation Studies fellowship.

50 "Political and Social Psychologists Weigh In," by Tori DeAngelis, APA Monitor, September 2011, Volume 42, Number 8, www.apa.org/monitor/2011/09/bin-laden.aspx.

51 "Humiliation in Asymmetric Conflict," by Clark McCauley, contribution to the 2008 Workshop on Humiliation and Violent Conflict, Columbia University, New York, December 11–12, 2008, www.humiliationstudies.org/documents/McCauleyNY08meeting.pdf.

52 Afghanistan: The Price of Revenge, documentary film by Alberto Marquardt, Al Jazeera, May 31, 2013, www.aljazeera.com/programmes/specialseries/2013/05/201353110343913O667.html.

53 For an exploration of the notion of honor of the Taliban, see, among others, Atran, 2010a. In April 2017, the Taliban carried out their most deadly attack on a military installation in nearly five years: "Taliban Kills More Than 140 Afghan Soldiers in Suicide Assault," by Bill Roggio, Long War Journal, April 22, 2017, www.longwarjournal.org/archives/2017/04/taliban-kills-more-than-100-afghan-soldiers-in-suicide-assault.php.

54 "Rumsfeld Rejects Plan To Allow Mullah Omar 'To Live in Dignity': Taliban Fighters Agree to Surrender Kandahar," by Brian Knowlton, New York Times, December 7, 2001, www.nytimes.com/2001/12/07/news/07iht-attack_ed3__7.html.

55 McChrystal, 2013. See also "McChrystal details tension between Pentagon and Obama White House," by Matt Williams in New York, The Guardian, January 6, 2013, www.theguardian.com/world/2013/jan/06/stanley-mcchrystal-pentagon-obama-white-house.

56 Security Council Open Debate on Sexual Violence in Council, April 17, 2013, Security Council Chamber Statement, by Zainab Hawa Bangura, the Special Representative of the Secretary General the United Nations, www.peacewomen.org/assets/file/SecurityCouncilMonitor/Debates/SexualViolence/April2013/srsg_svic_2013.pdf.

57 Meffert, et al., 2013. See also Watkins and Watkins, 1997. I thank Michael Britton for making me aware of the work done by the Watkins.

58 "Compassion: Hot to Help: When Can Empathy Move Us to Action?," by Daniel Goleman, March 1, 2008, Greater Good in Action, http://greatergood.berkeley.edu/article/item/hot_to_help.

59 During my time in medicine, I did surgery, and therefore I know that it is not necessary to switch off empathy to be able to carry out surgery.

60 See Hoffman, et al., 2015, and "The Hoffman Report and the American Psychological Association: Meeting the Challenge of Change," by Kenneth S. Pope, September 15, 2015, http://kspope.com/kpope/Hoffman.php. I thank Linda Hartling for keeping me informed about the path that APA is taking. See, furthermore, "The Code not Taken: The Path from Guild Ethics to Torture and our Continuing Choices," by Kenneth S. Pope, Canadian Psychological Association John C. Service Member of the Year Award Address, 2016, http://kspope.com/PsychologyEthics.php, Abstract:

Psychology's controversial role in torture in settings like Abu Ghraib, Bagram, and Guantánamo fractured a comforting façade and raised questions about how we can best serve the profession. The controversy confronts us with choices about what our profession is, what it means, what it does – who we are, what we mean, what we do. It asks whether our lives and organizations reflect professional ethics or guild ethics. Professional ethics protect the public against abuse of professional power, expertise, and practice, and hold members accountable to values beyond self-interest. Guild ethics place members' interests above public interest, edge away from accountability, and tend to masquerade as professional ethics. Psychology's path to involvement in torture began before 9/11 and the 'war on terror' with a move from professional ethics to guild ethics. In sharp contrast to its previous codes, APA's 1992 ethics code reflected guild ethics, as did the subsequent 2002 code (APA, 2002). Guild ethics are reflected in the questionable nature of APA's, 2006, 2007a, 2008a, and 2015 policies on interrogation and torture. This article examines tactics used to maintain the façade of professional ethics despite over a decade of publicized reports – in newspapers, professional journals, books, reports published by human rights organizations, and other widely available sources – of documentary evidence of psychology's organizational involvement in what came to be called "enhanced interrogations." It asks if we use versions of these tactics in our individual lives. If a credible identity, integrity, and professional ethics are not reflected in our individual lives, it is unlikely they will thrive in our profession and organizations.

61 See note 231 in Chapter 6.

62 Hartling and Lindner, 2017, quoting Caldero and Crank, 2011, p. 2.

63 Hartling and Lindner, 2017, quoting Jemsek, 2011.

64 Hartling and Lindner, 2017, quoting Olsson, 2005.

65 Clark, 2003.

66 Clark, 2003, p. 130.

67 General Wesley Clark: Wars Were Planned – Seven Countries In Five Years, uploaded on YouTube on September 11, 2011, https://youtu.be/9RC1Mepk_Sw: "He said, 'I guess it's like we don't know what to do about terrorists, but we've got a good military and we can take down governments.' And he said, 'I guess if the only tool you have is a hammer, every problem has to look like a nail.' … And he said, 'This is a memo that describes how we're going to take out seven countries in five years, starting with Iraq, and then Syria, Lebanon, Libya, Somalia, Sudan and, finishing off, Iran.'"

68 "The Redirection: Is the Administration's New Policy Benefitting Our Enemies in the War on Terrorism?" by Seymour M. Hersh, New Yorker, Annals of National Security, March 5, 2007, www.newyorker.com/magazine/2007/03/05/the-redirection. See also "Barack Obama's Meager Legacy of Incomplete Accomplishments and of Provoked Wars: What Happened?" by Rodrigue Tremblay, May 30, 2016, www.thecodeforglobalethics.com/pb/wp_0b5e796a/wp_0b5e796a.html#LEGACY. See more by Canadian economist Rodrigue Tremblay, 2010. It is a privilege to have Rodrigue Tremblay as esteemed member in the global advisory board of our Human Dignity and Humiliation Studies fellowship.

69 Zunes, 2002.

70 "Echoes from the Warsaw Ghetto in Gaza," an Interview with Cecilie Surasky by Christiana Voniati, Countercurrents, June 19, 2010, www.countercurrents.org/voniati190610.htm.

71 "Op-Ed: My Outline for a Solution in Gaza," by Moshe Feiglin, Arutz Sheva, July 15, 2014, www.israelnationalnews.com/Articles/Article.aspx/15326#.U8tjALHCfZc.

72 Scott and Philip, 2004. See a research bibliography and links on terrorism at www.socialpsychology.org/peace.htm#terrorism. I thank Francisco Gomes de Matos for discussing this point with me.

73 Studies by Ariel Merari and others have found that Palestinian suicide bombers often have at least one relative or close friend who was killed or injured by the other side. See for recent publications, Merari, 2010, Webber, et al., 2015.

74 Lindner, 2006c, pp. 113–114.

75 Farida's predicament resonates with what Toni Morrison, 1987, describes in her novel Beloved, where she describes the killing of a baby so as to protect it from the fate of slavery. I thank Morton Deutsch for making me aware of this novel.

76 According to Michel Foucault, 1975, when war is seen as imminent, biopolitique is on the table: The male body is imaged as the soldier's body and the female body as the reproductive body of preferably male offspring. Lindner and Desmond Tutu (Foreword), 2010, p. 49: "In this fashion, during the past millennia, everything became subordinate to preparedness for defense against invaders, with only the methods of enforcing this subordination varying. Sparta, for instance, wanted its women to put their wombs at the service of the larger community, encouraging them to bear sons even for Spartans who were not their

husbands. In most other cultures, women's wombs were the exclusive assets of their husbands. Nationalist discourses before and during World War II, in Japan, as well as in Germany, followed the same strategy, and also the Soviet government adopted a similar practice." See also Åsne Seierstad, 2016, writing about to young sisters, of Somali origin, who left Norway to travel to Syria. I have fond memories of my visit to Åsne and her family in their home in Oslo on September 22, 2010.

77 Silke, 2003.

78 The experiences of others can be experienced as if they are one's own experiences. If other people suffer humiliation, this can be felt as own injury. Research on social identification and empathy is relevant. Research on mirror neurons has been hailed by some as explanation, however, this has been rejected as irrelevant hype by others. In September 2012, the first "Mirror Neurons: New Frontiers Summit" took place in Erice, Sicily, Italy. An overview is given in "What's So Special about Mirror Neurons?" by Ben Thomas, Scientific American, November 6, 2012, http://blogs.scientificamerican.com/guest-blog/2012/11/06/whats-so-special-about-mirror-neurons/. Christian Keysers was a leading investigator in Parma in the research group that made the original discoveries of mirror neurons from 2000 to 2004, see his recent book Keysers, 2011. See also Bråten, 2013. See for a very critical appraisal, Hickok, 2014.
In my work, I describe the pathways of personal experiences of humiliation and how they can be channeled into narratives of humiliation at the group level. This can be achieved through top-down propaganda and recruitment – such as, for instance, in Nazi-Germany, Rwanda, or in movements instigating terror and hatred – or through bottom-up mechanisms that exist, for instance, in clan-based societies such as Somalia. See Lindner, 2000a, for my doctoral dissertation.

79 See also Lindner, et al., 2009.

80 Is personal grievance qualitatively different from group grievance? Veldhuis, et al., 2014, found similar ratings of humiliation after experiencing personal rejection in a computer game and rejection that also included in-group members. In contrast, Smith and Mackie, 2015, suggest that personal and intergroup emotions may be qualitatively distinct. McCauley and Moskalenko, 2011, identify two separate mechanisms that can move individuals to terrorist action for personal grievance and group grievance, mechanisms that often work together. See also McCauley, 2017.

81 See two documentaries made in France:
• La chambre vide, documentary film by Jasna Krajinovic, Arte France, 2015, www.arte.tv/guide/fr/058864-000-A/la-chambre-vide#details-description. See the full note in the pdf edition of this book.
• Djihad, les contre-feux, documentary film by Laetitia Moreau, Arte France, 2015, www.arte.tv/guide/fr/060819-000-A/djihad-les-contre-feux?autoplay=1#details-description. In this film, a mother in Marseilles is presented who lost her young son in Syria.

This is the letter he wrote to her before his death translated by Lindner from the French original:

When you read these words, then I have left life on this toilsome world behind me, this very troublesome world, especially since I left you. I hope you understand why I did all this, why I left everything, even though I lived in a stable situation, a wonderful family, and had a job. Why all these sacrifices? Because the community of Mohammed was humiliated. Allah has rewarded us with the reconstruction of the Caliphate. Finally, Muslims have regained their pride. A successful life is not only work, having a house, a car, a wife and children. A successful life is to worship Allah and to have his blessing.

See the French original in the full note in the pdf edition of this book. See also the work by French anthropologist Dounia Bouzar, 2016, and how she dissects how vulnerable teenagers are recruited into a desire to sacrifice themselves in "holy war" by way of professionally organized integration methodologies that are also know from sects in general.

82 McCauley and Moskalenko, 2014a.

83 Devin Atallah, 2017, has studied Palestinian refugee families who face structural violence and historical trauma, and explains resilience in terms of three interrelated themes: (a) Muqawama/resistance to military siege and occupation; (b) Awda/return to cultural roots despite historical and ongoing settler colonialism; and (c) Sumoud/perseverance through daily adversities and accumulation of trauma.

84 Al-Aswany, 2002/2004, Al-Aswany, 2015.

85 Hamid, 2007, 2014. I thank Kristian Berg Harpviken, former director of the Peace Research Institute Oslo (PRIO), for reminding me of this author in 2010.

86 Pamuk and Freely, 2004.

87 See also Røislien and Røislien, 2010, for a discussion "the logic of Palestinian terrorist target choice." I thank Kristian Berg Harpviken, former director of the Peace Research Institute Oslo (PRIO), for making me aware of this article.

88 Quoted in Vertigans, 2007, p. 167. See extracts of Ayman Al-Zawahiri's Knights under the Prophet's Banner, 2001, at www.fas.org/irp/world/para/ayman_bk.html.

89 "Jihadi Cool: Terrorist Recruiters' Latest Weapon," by Dina Temple-Raston, National Public Radio (NPR), March 26, 2010, www.npr.org/templates/story/story.php?storyId=125186382.

90 Lakhani, 2013.

91 Breaking Bad is a crime drama television series by Vince Gilligan, originally aired on the AMC network (entertainment company headquartered in New York City) for five seasons, from January 20, 2008, to September 29, 2013. It is the story of Walter White (Bryan Cranston), a high school chemistry teacher diagnosed with terminal lung cancer. To secure his family's financial future before he dies, he, and a former student, turn to producing and selling crystallized methamphetamine.
The methamphetamine epidemic took off on the West Coast of the United States in late 2002. See "Unnecessary Epidemic," by Steve Suo, The Oregonian, October 03, 2004, www.oregonlive.com/special/oregonian/meth/stories/index.ssf?1003_unnecessary_epidemic.html.
Now this epidemic reaches Europe, see Härtel-Petri, 2014. The statistics are alarming, as ever younger individuals, especially young girls, increasingly use the drug. Crystal meth was originally used recreationally, but now it reaches an ever wider range of customers, wider than that of cannabis or heroin. In 2016, it is "conquering" Berlin, see "Horror-Droge auf dem Vormarsch Crystal Meth erobert Berlin," Berliner Kurier, March 27, 2003, www.berliner-kurier.de/berlin/polizei-und-justiz/horror-droge-auf-dem-vormarsch-crystal-meth-erobert-berlin-23789654.
Some users and dealers profess that they were inspired by the film Breaking Bad. See Crystal Meth: Die Horror-Droge, documentary film by Christian P. Stracke, Zweites Deutsches Fernsehen, 2016, www.zdf.de/ZDFmediathek/beitrag/video/2312448/Crystal-Meth-Die-Horror-Droge#/beitrag/video/2312448/Crystal-Meth-Die-Horror-Droge, see also, among others, https://youtu.be/bDpnF0UqaO8. See the full note in the pdf edition of this book.

92 Sageman, 2008, "Jihadi Cool: Terrorist Recruiters' Latest Weapon," by Dina Temple-Raston, National Public Radio (NPR), March 26, 2010, www.npr.org/templates/story/story.php?storyId=125186382.

93 Husain, 2007, Baker, 2009, 2011.

94 Bartlett, et al., 2010, Slootman and Tillie, 2006, Pisoiu, 2012.

95 "New Terrorism Adviser Takes A 'Broad Tent' Approach," by Dina Temple-Raston, National Public Radio (NPR), January 24, 2011, www.npr.org/2011/01/24/133125267/new-terrorism-adviser-takes-a-broad-tent-approach. See also Wiktorowicz, 2004.

96 See note 42 in the Preface.

97 Atran, et al., 2014

98 "Radicalisation Is Not the Result of Failed Integration," Interview with French extremism researcher Olivier Roy, by Michaela Wiegel, Quantara.de, March 29, 2016, https://en.qantara.de/content/interview-with-french-extremism-researcher-olivier-roy-radicalisation-is-not-the-result-of. Gilles Kepel has recently criticized Olivier Roy for his views. See "'That Ignoramus': 2 French Scholars of Radical Islam Turn Bitter Rivals," by Adam Nossiter, The New York Times, July 12, 2016, www.nytimes.com/2016/07/13/world/europe/france-radical-islam.html. See also Roy, 2004.

99 Roy, 2004. See also "ISIL Is Really a Revolt by Young Muslims Against their Parents' Generation," by Emma-Kate Symons, Quartz, December 3, 2015, https://qz.com/562128/isil-is-a-revolt-by-young-disaffected-muslims-against-their-parents-generation/. See, furthermore, "Terrorism Has Come About in Assimilationist France and Also in Multicultural Britain. Why Is That?" by Kenan Malik, The Guardian, November 15, 2016, www.theguardian.com/commentisfree/2015/nov/15/multiculturalism-assimilation-britain-france.

100 Kepel, 2015. See also Kepel, 2006, 2008, Kepel and Milelli, 2008. See also Tuil, 2016 .

101 See Bidar, 2015. See also "Open Letter to the Muslim World," by Abdennour Bidar, Reset DOC, January 14, 2015, www.resetdoc.org/story/00000022484. French original: "Lettre ouverte au monde musulman," by Abdennour Bidar, Huffington Post, January 9, 2015, www.huffpostmaghreb.com/abdennour-bidar/lettre-ouverte-au-monde-m_1_b_6443610.html.

102 See note 98 above.

103 Ibid.

104 Twenge, 2006. See for more examples of relevant literature, for instance, Lasch, 1991, Putnam, 2000, Baumeister, et al., 1996, Bushman and Baumeister, 1998, Baumeister, et al., 2003, Baumeister, 2005, Twenge and Campbell, 2009, Wood, et al., 2009, Ehrenreich, 2010, Twenge, et al., 2012, Twenge and Kasser, 2013, or Levine, 2007.

105 "From Hanover to IS: The Case of Safia S.," by Sabrina Pabst, Deutsche Welle, October 19, 2016, www.dw.com/en/from-hanover-to-is-the-case-of-safia-s/a-36094144.

106 beRATen e.V. – Beratungsstelle zur Prävention neo-salafistischer Radikalisierung, Hannover, www.beraten-niedersachsen.de/.

107 Ginges and Atran, 2008. Canada's indigenous populations are even driven into waves of suicide by suicides as an outflow of "cumulative humiliation" (Linda Hartling). See more in note 139 in the Introduction.

108 "Terror on Trial: First Hand Report on the Hofstadgroep Trial," by Emerson Vermaat, Militant Islam Monitor, December 12, 2005, www.militantislammonitor.org/article/id/1400. I thank Petter Nesser for recommending this article to me.

109 Petter Nesser is a senior researcher with the Terrorism Research Group at the Norwegian Defence Research Establishment (FFI). See more in the Appendix to Section One.

110 I thank Petter Nesser for recommending to me, as the best description, the book by Albert Benschop, 2005, Chronicle of a Political Murder.

111 See note 109 above.

112 Schmitz-Berning, 2007. The phrase Third Reich was originally coined by the German thinker Arthur Moeller van den Moeller van den Bruck, 1923, in his book Das Dritte Reich. He distinguished two separate periods, the First Reich The Age of the Father, the Holy Roman Empire that began with Charlemagne in 800 CE, the Second Reich, The Age of the Son, the German Empire under the Hohenzollern dynasty (1871 – 1918), the Third Reich, The Age of the Holy Ghost, after the interval of the Weimar Republic (1918 – 1933). Although van den Bruck did not join the Nazi Party, the phrase Third Reich was nevertheless adopted by the Nazis for the totalitarian state they wanted to set up once in power. Many Germans saw in Hitler a

German Messiah; the way he conducted the Nuremberg Rallies, just before the Autumn Equinox highlighted this impression. In 1939, the German press, however, was no longer to use the phrase. The official terms were then "German Reich," "Greater German Reich," or "National Socialist Germany."

113 It was first used by Ronald Reagan during his 1980 presidential campaign.

114 See note 73 in Chapter 4.

115 Taylor, 1989, Heelas, 1996, 2008, Wilce, 2009. This trend is now being introduced from the West to other world regions. There is a "psycho-boom" (xinli re), for instance, in China, see Huang, 2014, using translations of Pema Chödrön, Ken Wilber, and Eckhart Tolle. Sonya Pritzker, 2016: "Inner child workshops in China can be said to function in much the same way. Indeed, salons geared towards the inner child in this Beijing center consist of adaptations of exercises developed by a European psychologist who leads longer inner child workshops, variably focused on 'transforming emotions,' 'transforming beliefs,' and 'meeting true self,' when he is in town."

116 "The Coalition of Transformation vs. the Coalition of Restoration," by Ronald Brownstein, The Atlantic, November 21, 2012, www.theatlantic.com/politics/archive/2012/11/the-coalition-of-transformation-vs-the-coalition-of-restoration/265512/.

117 Liberaler Traum – autoritärer Traum? Philipp Blom über Demokratie und was sie gefährdet, by Judith Heitkamp, Bayerischer Rundfunk, October 19, 2016, www.br.de/radio/bayern2/kultur/kulturwelt/blom-gespraech-100.html. See also a recent publication by historian Philip Blom, 2017. See the full note in the pdf edition of this book.

118 "On Trump's Victory," by Gilad Atzmon, November 10, 2016, www.gilad.co.uk/writings/2016/11/10/on-trumps-victory. I thank Hans-Joachim Dietze for making me aware of this quote. See also Atzmon, 2011.

119 Petter Nesser is senior researcher with the Terrorism Research Group at the Norwegian Defence Research Establishment (FFI). Read more about him in the Appendix to Section One. See Nesser, 2006, 2011, 2014, Tønnessen, 2006. Here are some of my notes of our conversation in Oslo on June 17, 2011, which I summarized and translated from Norwegian:

The Salafi movement is diverse, comprising everything from introverted mystics to groups that are political in thinking and action. Al Qaeda rhetoric may be against politics, but they do want political change. The groups that Nesser studies are very much opposed to the Muslim Brotherhood because they look at them as impure, since they compromise themselves for politics. Original Saudi Arabian Salafist thought combines now with ideologies of violent struggle from the Egypt of the sixties and seventies and the so-called Afghan Arabs.

120 Read more about Petter Nesser in the Appendix to Section One.

121 "Islam Right Now," by Johan Galtung, TRANSCEND Media Service, September 5, 2016, www.transcend.org/tms/2016/09/islam-right-now/:

George Bush on February 10, 2003, on a possible attack on Iraq: "Liberty is God's gift to every human being in the world," in Washington Post, 10 Feb 2003. Osama bin Laden on February 11, 2003: "victory comes only from God, all we have to do is to prepare and motivate for jihad," Audio message conveyed by jorgenj@peace.uit.no.

Galtung recommends "The Salafiscape in the Wake of the Arab Spring," by Abbas Aroua, www.cordoue.ch.

122 "ISIS vs. Al Qaeda: Jihadism's Global Civil War," by Daniel L. Byman, and Jennifer R. Williams, Brookings, February 24, 2015, www.brookings.edu/articles/isis-vs-al-qaeda-jihadisms-global-civil-war/.

123 "Carl Schmitt i Det hvite hus," by Rune Slagstad, Institutt for samfunnsforskning, Klassekampen, February 11, 2017, www.klassekampen.no/article/20170211/ARTICLE/170219981. See more in note 25 in

the Preface. See also Tunander, 2009, in note 98 in Chapter 1. See, furthermore, Kagan, 1997, and Fraenkel, 1941, in note 15 in the Introduction to Section Three.

124 See note 249 in the Introduction.

125 Jordán and Wesley, 2006 .

126 Tocqueville, 1856. See also "The Future by Al Gore – Review," by John Gray, The Guardian, January 31, 2013, www.theguardian.com/books/2013/jan/31/the-future-al-gore-review. See also Gore, 2013. See, furthermore, note 249 in the Introduction.

127 Kepel, 1993.

128 "Europe's Angry Muslims," by Robert S. Leiken, Foreign Affairs, July/August 2005, www.foreignaffairs.com/articles/europe/2005-07-01/europes-angry-muslims.

129 "Features: A Matter of Pride: Why We Can't Buy Off the Next Osama bin Laden," by Peter Bergen and Michael Lind, Democracy: A Journal of Ideas, Winter 2007, Number 3, http://democracyjournal.org/magazine/3/a-matter-of-pride/.

130 Ibid.

131 Goodwin and Jasper, 2004, Jasper, 1997, 2011, 2014, Jasper and Duyvendak, 2015.

132 Jasper, 2011, p. 290. See also Shultziner, 2013. Jasper, 1997, sees four dimensions play distinct roles in social protest movements, namely, resources, strategy, biography, and culture. See also Cefaï, 2007.

133 "Teroristen: Letzte Chance," Stefan Berg and Michael Sontheimer, Der Spiegel, February 13, 2010, www.spiegel.de/spiegel/print/d-69065794.html. German original translated by Lindner: "'Das Foto von schreienden vietnamesischen Kindern nach einem Napalm-Angriff,' so Hogefeld später, 'war für mich eine einzige Aufforderung und Verpflichtung, zu handeln und den Verbrechen nicht zuzuschauen.'"

134 Lindner, 2006c, Making Enemies: Humiliation and International Conflict.

135 Wiktorowicz, 2004, 2005.

136 The mass appeal of Adolf Hitler, for instance, has been explained with a schizophrenic structure that arose out of a preponderance of the public self. See Marbach, et al., 2007.

137 Ås, 2008. See more in notes 65 and 66 in Chapter 7.

138 Bass and Riggio, 2006. I thank Avi Shahaf of reminding me of Bass' Transformational Leadership Theory. Transformational leaders hold positive expectations of their colleagues and care about their personal growth. Transformational leadership is said to have occurred when engagement in a group results in leaders and followers raising one another to increased levels of motivation and morality. Four components "I's" describe transformational leadership:

- Idealized Influence (II): a transformational leader "walks the talk," and is admired for this.
- Inspirational Motivation (IM): a transformational leader inspire and motivate others.
- Individualized Consideration (IC): a transformational leader is genuinely concerned with the personal growth of their colleagues.
- Intellectual Stimulation (IS): a transformational leader challenges others to attain their highest goals.

139 My Brother the Islamist, documentary film produced and directed by filmmaker Robb Leech, 2011, www.mybrothertheislamist.com/, see also www.bbc.com/news/entertainment-arts-23969422.

140 In 2017, Sebastian Junger and Nick Quested came out with the documentary film Hell on Earth: The Fall Of Syria And The Rise of ISIS, where they explain how Da'esh could rise not least because democracy was seen as a greater threat by the ruling government in Syria. If the world community had intervened early on, subsequent carnage could perhaps have been avoided or minimized. See http://channel.nationalgeographic.com/hell-on-earth/. See also Sebastian Junger, 2016, and more in note 101 in the Introduction.

141 The American Jihadist: Eric Harroun in His Own Words, April 12, 2014, https://youtu.be/97ndpOAlD50. Harroun was found dead, of an accidental overdose, in his home on April 8, 2014. I thank Deeyah Khan of finding this video in the context of her research for her documentary Jihad: A Story of the Others. See also Husain, 2007.

142 "US Army Vet Eric Harroun, Who Fought in Syria, Died at Home," by James Gordon Meek, ABC News, April 10, 2014, http://abcnews.go.com/Blotter/eric-harroun-us-army-vet-fought-syria-died/story?id=23273218.

143 "Radio Address to the Nation on Terrorism," by Ronald Reagan, May 31, 1986, online by Gerhard Peters and John T. Woolley, The American Presidency Project, www.presidency.ucsb.edu/ws/?pid=37376.

144 The Rise of British Jihadists in Syria, published June 26, 2014, https://youtu.be/fxDuENvxw_o. I thank Deeyah Khan of finding this video in the context of her research for her next documentary. See also https://news.vice.com/video/british-jihadists-in-syria.

145 See Atran, 2003, 2006, 2010c, b, 2013, Atran, et al., 2007, Atran and Ginges, 2012, Atran, et al., 2014, Ginges, et al., 2007. See note 42 in the Preface.

146 See Park, et al., 1997, Park and Hinshaw, 2010, Park, 2012. Crystal Park locates her research within health psychology. See also early work on cognitive dissonance by social psychologist Leon Festinger, 1957, 1980.

147 Başoğlu, et al., 1997.

148 See, among others, Deci, et al., 1999, p. 658: "… tangible rewards tend to have a substantially negative effect on intrinsic motivation. … Even when tangible rewards are offered as indicators of good performance, they typically decrease intrinsic motivation for interesting activities." Already in 1973, psychologists Mark R. Lepper and David Greene tested the over-justification hypothesis, see Lepper, et al., 1973. Extrinsic motivation can undermine intrinsic motivation, see, for instance Curry, et al., 1990. Helping behavior in children seems to be intrinsically motivated and is diminished when extrinsic incentives are offered. See Warneken and Tomasello, 2008, Abstract: "The current study investigated the influence of rewards on very young children's helping behavior. After 20-month-old infants received a material reward during a treatment phase, they subsequently were less likely to engage in further helping during a test phase as compared with infants who had previously received social praise or no reward at all. This so-called over-justification effect suggests that even the earliest helping behaviors of young children are intrinsically motivated and that socialization practices involving extrinsic rewards can undermine this tendency."

149 "The Commission on Security and Cooperation in Europe: Political Pluralism in the OSCE Mediterranean Partners? Testimony by Shibley Telhami," July 9, 2014, www.sadat.umd.edu/pub/TelhamiTestimony2.pdf. Shibley Telhami is the Anwar Sadat Professor for Peace and Development at the University of Maryland, and it is a privilege to have him as esteemed member in the global advisory board of our Human Dignity and Humiliation Studies fellowship.

150 Final Report of the Task Force on Combating Terrorist and Foreign Fighter Travel, Washington DC, The U.S. House of Representatives Homeland Security Committee, September 2015, https://homeland.house.gov/wp-content/uploads/2015/09/TaskForceFinalReport.pdf. In March 2015, the U.S. House of Representatives Homeland Security Committee launched a bipartisan Task Force on Combating Terrorist and Foreign Fighter Travel. Eight Members of Congress were charged with examining the threat to the United States from "foreign fighters" – individuals who leave home, travel abroad to terrorist safe havens, and join or assist violent extremist groups. The Task Force assessed domestic and overseas efforts to obstruct terrorist travel, as well as security gaps. It was released on September 29, 2015. The document maintains that "despite concerted efforts to stem the flow, we have largely failed to stop Americans from traveling overseas to join jihadists."

See also Al-Qaida, the Islamic State, and the Future of the Global Jihadi Movement: A Conversation with

Ambassador Tina Kaidanow, The Brookings Institution, Washington, DC, September 16, 2015, www.brookings.edu/~/media/events/2015/09/16-global-jihad/20150916_alqaeda_isis_jihad_transcript.pdf.

151 "Are Thousands of Westerners and Americans Fighting with Extremists in Iraq and Syria?" by Steve Contorno, researched by Steve Contorno, edited by Angie Drobnic Holan, PolitiFact (a project of the Tampa Bay Times), June 18, 2014, www.politifact.com/truth-o-meter/statements/2014/jun/18/mike-rogers/are-thousands-westerners-and-americans-fighting-ex/. See also an accessible overview in Mantel, 2014.

152 Ibid.

153 Sageman, 2004, 2008, 2009.

154 Bergen, 2016.

155 "The Roots of Muslim Rage," by Bernard Lewis, The Atlantic, September 1990, www.theatlantic.com/magazine/archive/1990/09/the-roots-of-muslim-rage/4643/2/. I thank Deepak Tripathi for making me aware of this article. It is a privilege to have him as esteemed member in the global advisory board of our Human Dignity and Humiliation Studies fellowship. See also Tripathi, 2013b, and his book published in Dignity Press, Tripathi, 2013a.

156 Lindner, 2006c, p. 68.

157 Lindner, 2006c.

158 Abu-Rabi, 2007, p. 34–35, Conclusion. See the full note in the pdf edition of this book.

159 Lord Douglas Hurd of Westwell (Conservative) on February 9, 2006, during three hours of deliberations on Iran policy at the House of Lords, where several members discussed their country's history of intervention in Iranian affairs. See "Glory and Humiliation: Iran, Britain and that Coup, The House of Lords Reviews Bitter British-Iranian History," by Arash Norouzi, The Mossadegh Project, February 12, 2006, www.mohammadmossadegh.com/news/house-of-lords/. I thank Deepak Tripathi for making me aware of this article. It is a privilege to have him as esteemed member in the global advisory board of our Human Dignity and Humiliation Studies fellowship. See also Tripathi, 2013b, and his book published in Dignity Press, Tripathi, 2013a.

160 Volkan, 2004. See also Volkan, 1997.

161 See, for instance, Wright, 2006. See also Creed, 2009.

162 "My Trip to Al Qaeda: Six Questions for Lawrence Wright," by Scott Horton, Harper's Magazine, September 6, 2010, http://harpers.org/blog/2010/09/my-trip-to-al-qaeda-six-questions-for-lawrence-wright/.

163 In Lifton, 2003, p.105.

164 See "Osama Bin Laden's Jihad," and text of Fatwahs and Declaration of War, www.mideastweb.org/osamabinladen1.htm. I thank Tony Webb for making me aware of this website.

165 See Danner, 2008, p. 3.

166 "American Apocalypse: How 'Superpower Syndrome' Is Ravaging the World," by Robert Jay Lifton, The Nation, December 4, 2003, www.thenation.com/article/american-apocalypse. See also Lifton, 2003. I thank Linda Hartling for making me aware of this quote. See also the work by David Lotto, such as in Muenster and Lotto, 2010, and Lotto, 2016.

167 For more on normative paradigms, see Etzioni, 2013.

168 Lindner and Desmond Tutu (Foreword), 2010, pp. 84–88. See more in note 52 in the Introduction.

169 Lindner and Desmond Tutu (Foreword), 2010, p. 86:

I believe it is important that people in the West, including those who are otherwise far removed from the world of honor, learn to better understand it. At a minimum, in an increasingly interconnected world, it is unwise to stay uninformed about the larger world. Honor killings may not touch them, but global extremism may – and much terrorism is fed by the same honor code. To help those who wish to break free from this code – for instance, the girl who asks for protection against honor killing or the girl who wishes to flee from being forced into marriage – people in the West must know more about their predicament. One of the problems is that well-intentioned people who are removed from the frontline may be unaware of how unforgiving the world of honor can be, or they may choose to overlook its harshness, particularly when motivated by the desire to respect other cultures, and/or daunted by the enormity of its potential for cruelty, and/or intimidated by their incapability to respect cruelty. One unfortunate result may be that they are in danger of letting down the victims. And, last but not least, if the culture of honor is to be invited into a culture of human rights, rather than uninformed laissez-faire or stereotyped rejection, we need to be able to apply respectful and informed rejection to concepts that violate human dignity.

Officials from the United Kingdom High Commission in Islamabad, who rescue forced marriage victims who are British citizens in a frontline job, know all about the cruel choice that these girls face: remaining in a forced marriage, or fleeing and losing their family forever. Within the United Kingdom, Crown Prosecution Service lawyer Nazir Afzal travels the country to warn against the danger that British authorities may be tempted to bridge the gap between those two moral worlds through mediation when approached by a girl who fears for her life and seeks help. Attempts of mediation run the risk to humiliate the immigrant family to the degree that killing is hastened rather than avoided. Also Jasvinder Sanghera knows everything about this predicament. She is an activist and advocate for women's rights and cofounder and director of Karma Nirvana. Having been a victim of forced marriage herself, she has emerged from it more resourceful.

170 Banaz: A Love Story, documentary film directed and produced by Deeyah Khan, 2012, https://youtu.be/VepuyvhHYdM. The film chronicles the life and death of Banaz Mahmod, a young British Kurdish woman killed in 2006 in South London on the orders of her family in a so-called honor killing.

171 Norwegian politician Jonas Gahr Støre, 2012, warned that much of so-called dialogue in international meetings is rather useless. Steinar Bryn is affiliated with the Nansen Academy since 1989 as the head of Nansen Dialogue Network in Norway, and he explains what needs to be taken care of to make dialogue useful. See Skurdal and Bryn, 2012, or Feller and Ryan, 2012.

172 Hafez, 2007a, Abstract.

173 "Robert Fisk: 'We Remain Blindfolded About Isis' Says the Man Who Should Know," by Robert Fisk, The Independent, November 15, 2015, www.independent.co.uk/voices/robert-fisk-we-remain-blindfolded-about-isis-says-the-man-who-should-know-a6735426.html. See also Keenan, 1993.

174 "Brighton Bombing 25 Years on: Making Friends with My Father's Killer," by Chris Hall, The Guardian, October 10, 2009, www.theguardian.com/lifeandstyle/2009/oct/10/brighton-bomb-conservative-anniversary. Read more about Jo Berry in the Appendix to Section One. It is a privilege to have Jo Berry as esteemed member in the global advisory board of our Human Dignity and Humiliation Studies fellowship.

175 Yves Musoni in a personal communication on December 25, 2011. I thank Yves Musoni for reminding me of Maalouf, 1998/2000. It is a privilege to have Yves Musoni as esteemed member in our Human Dignity and Humiliation Studies fellowship.

Chapter 14

1 Horne, 1977. See also Adjerid, 1992.

2 "Charlie Hebdo: Paris Attack Brothers' Campaign of Terror Can Be Traced Back to Algeria in 1954: Algeria is the Post-Colonial Wound that Still Bleeds in France," by Robert Fisk, The Independent, January 9, 2015, www.independent.co.uk/voices/comment/charlie-hebdo-paris-attack-brothers-campaign-of-terror-can-be-traced-back-to-algeria-in-1954-9969184.html. I thank Margunn Bjørnholt for making me aware of this article.
See also Salafistes, documentary film by Lemine Ould Mohamed Salem and François Margolin, 2016, www.allocine.fr/film/fichefilm_gen_cfilm=244500.html. See more in note 42 in Chapter 15.

3 Taylor, 1994, p. 25: "A number of strands in contemporary politics turn on the need, sometimes the demand, for recognition. The need, it can be argued, is one of the driving forces behind nationalist movements in politics." See also Fuller, 2003.

4 It was first used by Ronald Reagan during his 1980 presidential campaign.

5 BCE stands for "Before the Common Era," and is equivalent to BC, which means "Before Christ."

6 See www.humiliationstudies.org/whoweare/evelin/pics16.php#siwa. When I lived and worked in Cairo, Egypt, from 1984 to 1991, I received the necklace you see on the photo as a gift, together with a large bracelet and ring. It came from the oasis Siwa, the very oasis where Alexander the Great once listened to the oracle, two thousand years ago. Siwa is a very remote oasis in the desert west of the Nile Delta, a very rare salt oasis with a unique age-old culture. The necklace, of solid heavy silver, was part of a family's heritage, for centuries, always worn by the girl that was ready to get married next. But now money had arrived in the oasis. As happens all around the world, invaluable riches are given away for pennies and replaced by valueless plastic. When I received this necklace, I wanted to give it back to Siwa immediately, I want to tell its people there that they should never sell out their cultural heritage. But, I was told, if I did so, the necklace would simply be sold again, and I should rather wear it to tell the story. Today, only two of those necklaces are known to exist, mine, and one single one in the museum of Siwa.

7 Arrian and Hammond, 2013.

8 Eisler, 1987. See note 48 in the Preface.

9 Trigger, 1993, p. 52.

10 "Violence Is a Preventable Disease," by Mairead Maguire, Inter Press Service (IPS), February 9, 2016, www.ipsnews.net/2016/02/violence-is-a-preventable-disease/. See also "On World Day, UN Agencies Urge Countering Threats to Cultural Diversity," United Nations News Centre, May 21, 2017, www.un.org/apps/news/story.asp?NewsID=56804#.WSGEbsklGqA.

11 Norgaard, 2015.

12 "Is Robust American Growth a Thing of the Past?" by Edward Luce, Financial Times, February 19, 2016, www.ft.com/intl/cms/s/2/80c3164e-d644-11e5-8887-98e7feb46f27.html.

13 "History Has Knocked Very Loudly on Our Door. Will We Answer?" World Future Forum 2016 – Opening Speech by Jakob von Uexküll. See note 132 in Chapter 5. As to the term "dreamers," see also Coates, 2015. I thank Peter Coleman for giving me Coates's book as a gift!

14 Foucault, 1979, 1991, Foucault and Gordon, 1980.

15 Richards, 2013.

16 LeShan, 1992. See also note 18 in Chapter 6.

17 "Address to a Joint Session of Congress and the American People," by George W. Bush, The White House, United States Capitol, Washington, DC, http://georgewbush-whitehouse.archives.gov/news/releases/2001/09/20010920-8.html.

18 Asiem El Difraoui in "Gestohlene Symbolik, Propaganda, Terror: Das Online-Magazin "Dabiq" – und der Widerstand, ttt – titel thesen temperatmente, Das Erste, January 7, 2016, www.daserste.de/information/wissen-kultur/ttt/sendung/islamischer-staat-magazin-dabiq-100.html. See also Richter and El Difraoui, 2015. See the full note in the pdf edition of this book.

19 Dabiq is a town in northern Syria, the site of the battle of Marj Dabiq in 1516, in which the Ottoman Empire defeated the Mameluke Sultanate of Egypt. According to Islamic eschatology, Dabiq is one of two possible locations for an epic battle between invading Christians and Muslims. It will bring a Muslim victory and the beginning of the end of the world. Da'esh has named their online propaganda and recruitment magazine Dabiq, first published in July 2014 in English and other languages. See copies reproduced at the Clarion Project's website, www.clarionproject.org/news/islamic-state-isis-isil-propaganda-magazine-dabiq#.

20 See the work by Monty Marshall, 2014–2016, on complexity. His foundational premises are, he wrote in a personal message on February 5, 2016, "that social identity groups are the universal organizing units of a peaceful social order which are self-actuating, self-organizing, self-regulating, and self-correcting." It is a privilege to have Monty Marshall as esteemed member in the global advisory board of our Human Dignity and Humiliation Studies fellowship since its inception.

21 See note 117 in the Preface.

22 Newman, et al., 1997, have found evidence for the hypothesis of defensive projection, whereby people's own hostile and threatening personality traits are projected onto others and serve to justify the subject's aggressive behavior towards them. I thank Nils Vidar Vambheim for drawing my attention to this research.

23 Publius Flavius Vegetius Renatus and Reeve, 2004.

24 Translated by Lindner from Hitler's speech to the German press on November 10, 1938, www.zum.de/psm/ns/hitler13_aussen.php, as quoted in Treue, 1958, p. 175ff. See the German original in the full note in the pdf edition of this book.

25 Adolf Hitler: Reichstagsrede mit Kriegserklärung an Polen, Berlin, Deutscher Reichstag in der Kroll-Oper, September 1, 1939, www.nationalsozialismus.de/dokumente/adolf-hitler-reichstagsrede-mit-kriegserklaerung-an-polen-vom-01-09-1939-volltext/.

26 Mallmann, et al., 2008.

27 Kuźniar, 2009.

28 In Hitlers Verbündete (3/3): Rumänien und Ungarn, film by Peter Prestel and Rudolf Sporrer, www.phoenix.de/hitlers_verbuendete/285540.htm, translated from German by Lindner. Veteran Norbert Major says: "Warum haben wir gekämpft? Obwohl es Wahnsinn war? "Weil wir Soldaten waren! Wir hatten einen Eid geleistet! Auf seine Durchlaucht, den Reichsverweser Horthy!" Nur wer zuerst schiesst, überlebt!"

29 Lukacs, 1997.

30 Adolf Hitler in a letter on September 16, 1919, in Jäckel and Kuhn, 1980, p. 88, see also www.lpb-bw.de/publikationen/pogrom/pogrom4.htm. See the German original in the full note in the pdf edition of this book.

31 Shay, 2011, p. 181.

32 van der Kolk, 2014, p. 31. I thank Linda Hartling for reminding me of this book.

33 Adolf Hitler in a public declaration to the German Reichstag in Berlin on January 30, 1939, translated by Lindner from Kurt Bauer, Lehrveranstaltung "Schlüsseltexte und –dokumente zur Geschichte des Nationalsozialismus," Universität Wien, Institut für Zeitgeschichte, Wintersemester 2008/09, www.kurt-

bauer-geschichte.at/PDF_Lehrveranstaltung%202008_2009/20_Hitlerrede_1939-01-30.pdf, pp. 14–15. See the German original in the full note in the pdf edition of this book.

34 Sherratt, 2013.

35 Sherratt, 2013, p. 25.

36 Sherratt, 2013, p. 26.

37 Sherratt, 2013, p. 21.

38 Staub, 1989, 1993, 2012, 2015.

39 Lindner, 2000d, a, e, i, c, 2001j, 2006d.

40 BCE stands for "Before the Common Era," and is equivalent to BC, which means "Before Christ."

41 Garland, 2010 .

42 "English and Norman Society," by Mike Ibeji, BBC, February 17, 2011, www.bbc.co.uk/history/british/normans/society_01.shtml.

43 Historian Torgrim Titlestad, 2016, explains that it is no coincidence that Norway is often regarded as one of the most progressive democratic and freedom-based countries. Viking sagas show how widespread democratic thinking was in Norse communities and how the Norse thing system and the individual's legal status are the source of Norway's modern democratic system. Viking sagas show that plunder and conquest were not the main characteristic of Viking times, but rather struggles for freedom, people resisting authoritarian rulers, and insistence on freedom of religion.

44 Bagge, 2006.

45 "Þorgeir Ljósvetningagoði – The Conversion to Christianity in 1000 AD," Saga Museum, Reykjavik, Iceland, www.sagamuseum.is/overview/thorgeir-ljosvetningagodhi.

46 Stefánsson and Karlsdóttir, 2009. Þórarinn Stefánsson (Eagle of Thor) is the husband of Ragnheidur Karlsdottir, whom I met on January 23, 2015, in connection with the doctoral defense of Jingyi Dong, in which I served as opponent. I am profoundly thankful to him for sharing his life story and insights with me. Stefansson is a physicist, and he started out with studying electrons and ions and how they move. Yet, since the topic of fusion never took off, and solid state became en vogue, he turned to looking at how students learn. For instance, the most challenging task is to learn something that changes slowly: you can teach a child the clock if you move it quickly, not when you let it go at its speed. Stefansson began to understand the importance of practice, and that students need to test their theoretical knowledge in practice. In the case of physics, this would mean a laboratory. Yet, he met resistance among this fellow physicists, who had a preference for theory, not least because they were proud of their students being brighter than others, believing that listening to lectures was all they needed.

When he studied learning theories, Stefansson found a few, each of them not excellent, but, taken together, useful: On one side, there is what is going on "in the head," and we can look at Piaget and how he used Darwin as analogy, or zoology, since he was originally a zoologist; we can look at Vygotsky who took Marx as analogy or the development of societies; and we can look at information theory. And on the other side, there is "behavior." Most scholars make the mistake of specializing only in one.

47 "How did Iceland become Europe's giant-slayers?" by Simon Usborne, The Guardian, June 28, 2016, www.theguardian.com/football/shortcuts/2016/jun/28/iceland-europes-giant-slayers-unbeaten-run-euro-2016-france-quarter-finals-success.

48 Althoff, 2006.

49 2007 Annual Conference of Human Dignity and Humiliation Studies, in Hangzhou, China, April 13–16, 2007, www.humiliationstudies.org/whoweare/annualmeeting/09.php. See also Lindner, 2007c.

50 See, for example, www.chinacsr.com/en/2007/10/11/1744-china-plans-harmonious-society-measurement-standard, and ec.europa.eu/employment_social/social_inclusion/jrep_en.htm.

51 Lindner, 2006c.

52 Lu Xun, 1981.

53 Lu Xun, 2000a, b. See also Lu Xun, 2002a, b, c, 2003, 2004. I thank Jingyi Dong for her personal communication on June 25, 2015, where she shared her views on the role of Lu Xun with me. She took an image by Catherine Hoppers as starting point, an image that depicts a white and a black man fighting, oblivious of the fact that they stand in the mouth of a crocodile that will eat both. This image aims to visualize that a global economic system will eat all, and that it would be preferable to focus attention on the crocodile rather than on infighting. See this image in the Inspiring and Thought-Provoking Questions to Section Three and more images and photos on www.humiliationstudies.org/whoweare/evelin/pics13.php. See Dong's message in the full note in the pdf edition of this book.

54 See note 40 in the Introduction. In China, the novelist Liao Yiwu could perhaps be called the new Lu Xun. Yiwu, 2002/2008, has interviewed people for whom the "new" China – the China of economic growth and globalization – is no more beneficial than the old. Like Yiwu, also Belarusian Svetlana Alexievich, 2013/2016, describes the horrors of our time by recording the testimonies of witnesses.

55 Lindner, 2000h.

56 Feigon, 2002, p. 140. Feignon's views on Mao Zedong are criticized as being too forgiving, as opposed to Chang and Halliday, 2005, who might have been too polemically negative of Mao Zedong, see Lin and Benton, 2010.

57 Chang and Halliday, 2005, has been criticized as being too polemically negative of Mao Zedong, see Lin and Benton, 2010.

58 Guo, et al., 2006, Yongyi, 2011. Song Yongyi, a librarian at California State University, Los Angeles, leads a coalition of scholars, who published the Chinese Cultural Revolution Database, with 40,000 entries, including unpublished speeches, documents, and other information, www.chineseupress.com/chinesepress/promotion/cultural-revolution-cd-new2006/e_revolution.htm, see also http://prchistory.org/remembrance/. Song was jailed for five years during the Cultural Revolution. See also "Rediscovering History in China," a project by Ian Johnson, www.ian-johnson.com/index.php?page=china-rediscovering-the-past-and-the-present.

59 Morning Sun, a two-hour documentary film by Carma Hinton, Geremie Barmé, and Richard Gordon, 2003, attempts "to create an inner history" of the Great Proletarian Cultural Revolution (circa 1964 – 1976), www.morningsun.org/about/index.html. Morning Sun is a presentation of the Independent Television Service (ITVS) and the Center for Asian American Media (formerly NAATA), with the participation of Arte and the BBC: "Li Rui and his daughter Li Nanyang. Li Rui, the Communist Party veteran who drew international attention for his recent call for political reform at the 16th Party Congress, was at one time Mao's secretary. As an idealistic youth, he traveled to the Communist base at Yan'an in the late 1930s, and he first suffered revolutionary persecution there during the early 1940s. As one of Mao's secretaries, he briefly had access to the inner circle of China's ruling elite in the 1950s, but his criticisms of the Great Leap Forward led to his denunciation and exile. His daughter, Li Nanyang, was discriminated against in school because of her father's downfall. A sincere believer in the ideals of the revolution, Li Nanyang rejected her father as an enemy of the Party; it was many years before the two could reconcile."

60 Schell and Delury, 2013. I thank Linda Hartling for making me aware of this book. Orville Schell was educated at Harvard University and the University of California, Berkeley and is the author of numerous books and articles on China. The former dean of the Graduate School of Journalism at Berkeley, he is presently the Arthur Ross Director of the Center on U.S.-China Relations at the Asia Society in New York

City. John Delury received his Ph.D. in modern Chinese history at Yale University, where he wrote his dissertation on the Ming-Qing Confucian scholar Gu Yanwu. He taught at Brown, Columbia, and Peking University, and was associate director of Asia Society's Center on U.S.-China Relations. He is currently an assistant professor of East Asian studies at Yonsei University in Seoul. See also Kaufman, 2010, Luo, 1993.

61 Callahan, 2009, p. 141. See also Wang, 2008. William Callahan is the director of the Asian Studies in Europe and China project, director of the Centre for Contemporary Chinese Studies, and Senior Lecturer in International Politics at the Department of Politics at the University of Durham in the United Kingdom. It is a privilege to have William Callahan as esteemed member in the global advisory board of our Human Dignity and Humiliation Studies fellowship. Callahan reports of a collection of explicit photographs and descriptions of rape and sexual abuse stemming from Japanese wartime atrocities, which depict women "in negative ways as the violated national bodies that challenge national honor – and demand nationalist revenge," Callahan, 2010, p. 179.

62 Wang, 2012. I thank Selina Köhr for making me aware of this book. See also Wang, 2008. Zheng Wang is a Public Policy Scholar at the Kissinger Institute on China and the United States of the Woodrow Wilson International Center for Scholars. See also "Never Forget National Humiliation," by Gideon Rachman, Financial Times, August 27, 2012, www.ft.com/intl/cms/s/2/634a39ec-e888-11e1-8ffc-00144feab49a.html#axzz2VpjEJcjw.

63 Conquest, 2008, Front matter.

64 Conquest, 2008, Gellately, 2007.

65 Figes, 2007.

66 Ibid.

67 Schlögel, 2008.

68 Pushkin, 1876, Marie: A Story of Russian Love. This novel allows a deeper understanding of Russia during the reign of Catherine the Great, with honor being at the core of its love romances as well as of its murders and conquests.

69 "May 31, 1929: Ford Signs Agreement with Soviet Union," This Day in History, www.history.com/this-day-in-history/ford-signs-agreement-with-soviet-union.

70 American Experience: Henry Ford, documentary film as part of the collection The Titans, 2013, www.pbs.org/wgbh/americanexperience/films/henryford/.

71 Volkogonov, 1978, in Albrecht, 1980, p. 139: "According to Volkogonov, Red Militarism is not related to Marxist ideology as such; it is to be found in countries characterized by socio-economic backwardness, is likely to be found in countries with a strong authoritarian heritage, and is related to nationalism, which spills over into hegemonism and chauvinism. Manifestations of Red Militarism are to be sought in the composition of party leadership and the relative share of military activities in the economy. The combination of these elements is considered to provide for an excessive, self-sustaining development; Red Militarism 'makes use of all elements of the state structure to build up the military potential with the aim of attaining expansionist and hegemonic aims.'" See also Volkogonov and Shukman, 1998.

72 Adler, 1993, 2004, Adler, et al., 2009.

73 Conquest, 2008.

74 Vita Constantini (Life of Constantine the Great), a panegyric written in Greek in honor of Constantine the Great by Eusebius of Caeserea in the fourth century CE, never completed due to the death of Eusebius in 339, Chapter XII: Constantine's Address to the Council concerning Peace, www.documentacatholicaomnia.eu/03d/0265-0339,_Eusebius_Caesariensis,_Vita_Constantini_%5BSchaff%5D,_EN.pdf.

75 Freeman, 2003a.

76 Freeman, 2003b. I thank Lasse Moer for making me aware of this book.

77 "Did al-Ghazali Kill the Science in Islam?" by Nuh Aydin, Fountain Magazine, Perspectives, Issue 87 / May – June 2012, www.fountainmagazine.com/Issue/detail/did-al-ghazali-kill-the-science-in-islam-may-june-2012. I thank Lasse Moer for making me aware of this article.

78 "Religious Fundamentalism-Extremism-Violence," by Johan Galtung, TRANSCEND Media Service, February 8, 2016, www.transcend.org/tms/2016/02/religious-fundamentalism-extremism-violence/.

79 "Why Is the Military-Industrial Complex Sometimes Called 'The Devil's Dynamo'?" by John Scales Avery, TRANSCEND Media Service, June 30, 2014, www.transcend.org/tms/2014/06/the-devils-dynamo/. See more in note 46 in Chapter 11, in note 127 in this Chapter 14, and in note 199 in Chapter 18.

80 Ibid.

81 Ibid.

82 The Bandung Conference was the first large-scale Asian–African or Afro–Asian conference, of twenty-nine Asian and African states, most newly independent, which took place on April 18–24, 1955, in Bandung, Indonesia. Nearly one-quarter of the Earth's land surface and a total population of 1.5 billion people was represented.

83 "Speech by President Sukarno of Indonesia at the Opening of the Conference," Bandung, Indonesia, April 18, 1955, "The World and Japan" Database Project, Database of Japanese Politics and International Relations, Institute for Advanced Studies on Asia, University of Tokyo, source: The Ministry of Foreign Affairs Republic of Indonesia, www.ioc.u-tokyo.ac.jp/~worldjpn/documents/texts/docs/19550418.S1E.html.

84 "Tredje verden-prosjektets død skaper et monster: Sekter uten grenser" (The Third World Project's Death Creates a Monster: Sects Without Borders), by Yohan Shanmugaratnam, Klassekampen, July 3, 2014.

85 "Telegram to the Secretary of State, Department of State," by George K. Kennan, National Security Archive, 1946, http://nsarchive.gwu.edu/coldwar/documents/episode-1/kennan.htm.

86 "In an Age of 'Realists' and Vigilantes, there is Cause for Optimism," by John Pilger, September 19, 2013, http://johnpilger.com/articles/in-an-age-of-realists-and-vigilantes-there-is-cause-for-optimism.

87 Totten, et al., 2004, p. 245.

88 See note 31 in Chapter 8.

89 See note 32 in Chapter 8.

90 Comisión Nacional sobre la Desaparición de Personas (CONADEP), 1984.

91 Cardenas, 2009.

92 The Equal Justice Initiative (EJI), 2015. See also "Facing the Past: Lynching and American Civic Memory," by Karen Murphy, Facing Today, February 19, 2015, http://facingtoday.facinghistory.org/facing-the-past-lynching-and-american-civic-memory/. See photographs and postcards of lynching in America at http://withoutsanctuary.org/.

93 "Facing the Past: Lynching and American Civic Memory." See note 92 above.

94 Coates, 2015, pp. 22–23. I thank Peter Coleman for giving me this book as a present in November 2015. It is a privilege to have Peter Coleman as esteemed member in the global advisory board of our Human Dignity and Humiliation Studies fellowship.

95 Coates, 2015, p. 32.

96 Ibid.

97 Ibid.

98 Raymond G. Helmick, Senior Associate of the Preventive Diplomacy Program and professor of conflict resolution at the Department of Theology, Boston College, U.S.A., wrote in a personal communication on December 4, 2014:

> Great public concerns that are directly results of humiliation and failure to recognize the dignity of people. Both the Islamic State crisis, that so occupies international worry this year, and the eruption of anger over the Ferguson and now also New York killings of unarmed black Americans fall into that class.
> The ways people speak of responding to these crises are so lacking in respect for those who are expressing their frustrations in this way are further provocations to more of the same indignation. Much of our American political system is crying out for more and more military involvement in a battle with ISIS. It has to be understood that the problem we face today with outraged Muslims is a direct result of what we were told, from the deck of an aircraft carrier, was "Mission Accomplished" eleven years ago. The accomplishment of that mission is manifest only now in this present surge of violence from people who have been profoundly insulted by the Americans' and the West's assumption of superiority to them and all their aspirations in the wars in Iraq (both wars: 1990–1991 and since 2003) and Afghanistan and the resulting islamophobia with which we have burdened Muslims both within our own countries and abroad. Within the white population of the United States there still remains a profound lack of feeling for the humiliation suffered by our black population.

It is a privilege to have Raymond Helmick as esteemed member in the global advisory board of our Human Dignity and Humiliation Studies fellowship.

99 Paul H. Ray, in his contribution to the Great Transition Network (GTN) discussion on the topic "Why We Consume: Neural Design and Sustainability," January 14, 2016. See the full quote in the pdf edition of this book. See also Ray and Anderson, 2000.

100 See the five episodes of Der heilige Krieg (The Holy War): Das Schwert des Propheten; Kreuzzug nach Jerusalem; Die Türken vor Wien; Dschihad für den Kaiser; Terror für den Glauben, www.fernsehserien.de/der-heilige-krieg/episodenguide.

101 Teichmann, 2014.

102 Read also Anderson, 2013, on Curt Prüfer, who worked under the supervision of Max von Oppenheim. Von Oppenheim instructed Prüfer on strategies of sabotage against the British rule in Egypt.

103 McMeekin, 2010.

104 Oberhaus, 2007.

105 SMS Wolf (formerly the Hansa freighter Wachtfels) was an armed merchant raider of the Imperial German Navy in World War I.

106 The prisoners reported that they were treated honorably on board, see, among others, Frederic George Trayes, 1919, who later wrote about his experiences. The crew of the ship was less satisfied, as they suffered greatly under the ill treatment from the arrogance of their own officers, who acted according to the hierarchical military system of the time and upheld status differences in a situation that called for solidarity, since all were exposed to the same dangers. The reality of "we will all swim or sink together" did not translate into lessening elite arrogance.

107 Anderson, 2013.

108 Lawrence, 1938. See also his autobiography, Lawrence, 1922.

109 "IS Want Western Countries to Invade: What's The Purpose of "Global" Terrorism?" by Gwynne Dyer, Information Clearing House, November 30, 2014, www.informationclearinghouse.info/article40350.htm.

110 Neumann, 2015/2016.

111 Blin and Chaliand, 2007, Chaliand and Blin, 2015.

112 Laqueur, 1977, 2001, 2009.

113 In my work, I apply the ideal-type approach as described by sociologist Max Weber, 1904/1949. See also Coser, 1977, p. 224. See the full note in the pdf edition of this book.

114 Sageman, 2008.

115 Bergen, 2016.

116 "Die deutsche Wiege der Extremisten," by Stefan Kreitewolf, Das Handelsblatt, March 1, 2015, www.handelsblatt.com/politik/deutschland/salafisten-in-dinslaken-die-deutsche-wiege-der-extremisten/11417998.html.

117 Bedrohen Salafisten Deutschland? Südwestrundfunk, January 11, 2016, www.planet-wissen.de/videoplanetwissenbedrohensalafistendeutschland100.html. See also Kaddor, 2015. See the full note in the pdf edition of this book.

118 "'IS' Secret Police – The Trial of Nils D.," by Matthias von Hein, Deutsche Welle, January 19, 2016, www.dw.com/en/is-secret-police-the-trial-of-nils-d/a-18990262.

119 "Why Is the Military-Industrial Complex Sometimes Called 'The Devil's Dynamo'?" by John Scales Avery, TRANSCEND Media Service, June 30, 2014, www.transcend.org/tms/2014/06/the-devils-dynamo/. See more in note 46 in Chapter 11, in note 127 in this Chapter 14, and in note 199 in Chapter 18.

120 "Crimes against peace: (i) Planning, preparation, initiation or waging of war of aggression or a war in violation of international treaties, agreements or assurances; (ii) Participation in a common plan or conspiracy for the accomplishment of any of the acts mentioned under (i)." See Principle VI in Principles of International Law recognized in the Charter of the Nürnberg Tribunal and in the Judgment of the Tribunal, with commentaries 1950, http://legal.un.org/ilc/texts/instruments/english/commentaries/7_1_1950.pdf.

121 Charter of the United Nations, Chapter I: Purposes and Principles, www.un.org/en/sections/un-charter/chapter-i/.

122 Opening Statement before the International Military Tribunal by Justice Robert H. Jackson, Chief of Counsel for the United States, to the International Military Tribunal in the Palace of Justice at Nuremberg, Germany, November 21, 1945, www.roberthjackson.org/collection/speeches/as-nuremberg-prosecutor-945-1946/.

123 Lindner, 2006c, p. 25ff.

124 "Why Is the Military-Industrial Complex Sometimes Called 'The Devil's Dynamo'?" by John Scales Avery, TRANSCEND Media Service, June 30, 2014, www.transcend.org/tms/2014/06/the-devils-dynamo/. See more in note 46 in Chapter 11, in note 127 in this Chapter 14, and in note 199 in Chapter 18.

125 Military-Industrial Complex Speech by Dwight D. Eisenhower, 34th President of the United States, on January 17, 1961, Public Papers of the Presidents, Dwight D. Eisenhower, 1960, pp. 1035–1040, http://coursesa.matrix.msu.edu/~hst306/documents/indust.html, see also https://youtu.be/8y06NSBBRtY. In this farewell speech Eisenhower warns of the military industrial complex. See more in note 46 in Chapter 11.

126 "Why Is the Military-Industrial Complex Sometimes Called 'The Devil's Dynamo'?" by John Scales Avery, TRANSCEND Media Service, June 30, 2014, www.transcend.org/tms/2014/06/the-devils-dynamo/. See more in note 46 in Chapter 11, in note 199 in Chapter 18, and in the next note.

127 Ibid.: "Since World War II, the United States has interfered either militarily or covertly in the internal affairs of very many countries. These include China, 1945–49; Italy, 1947–48; Greece, 1947–49; Philippines, 1946–53; South Korea, 1945–53; Albania, 1949–53; Germany, 1950s; Iran, 1953; Guatemala, 1953–1990s; Middle East, 1956–58; Indonesia, 1957–58; British Guiana/Guyana, 1953–64; Vietnam, 1950–73; Cambodia,

1955–73; The Congo/Zaire, 1960–65; Brazil, 1961–64; Dominican Republic, 1963–66; Cuba, 1959–present; Indonesia, 1965; Chile, 1964–73; Greece, 1964–74; East Timor, 1975–present; Nicaragua, 1978–89; Grenada, 1979–84; Libya, 1981–89; Panama, 1989; Iraq, 1990–present; Afghanistan 1979–92; El Salvador, 1980–92; Haiti, 1987–94; Yugoslavia, 1999;'and Afghanistan, 2001–present." See also "How Many Muslim Countries Has the U.S. Bombed Or Occupied Since 1980?" by Glenn Greenwald, The Intercept, November 11, 2014, https://firstlook.org/theintercept/2014/11/06/many-countries-islamic-world-u-s-bombed-occupied-since-1980/.

128 See, for instance, "International Is Out and National Is Again Back," by Roberto Savio, Inter Press Service (IPS), July 13, 2016, www.ipsnews.net/2016/07/international-is-out-and-national-is-again-back/. See also historian VijayPrashad, 2012, who describes how the Brandt Report was ridiculed, for instance, by Ronald Reagan: "Reagan mocked the proceedings, particularly those 'who mistake compassion for development, and claim massive transfers of wealth somehow, miraculously, will produce new well-being.' The North-South dialogue effectively ended." The Brandt Report was written by the Independent Commission, first chaired by then German Chancellor Willy Brandt in 1980, to review international development issues and it illuminated the drastic differences in the economic development for the North and South hemispheres of the world. See Brandt and Independent Commission On International Development Issues, 1980.

129 Similar strategic thoughts were already developed in the "Wolfowitz Doctrine" (unofficial name) of 1992, which flowed into the foreign policy principles of Amirian President George W. Bush.

130 "Why Is the Military-Industrial Complex Sometimes Called 'The Devil's Dynamo'?" by John Scales Avery, TRANSCEND Media Service, June 30, 2014, www.transcend.org/tms/2014/06/the-devils-dynamo/. See more in note 46 in Chapter 11, in note 127 in this Chapter 14, and in note 199 in Chapter 18. See also "The Blundering Obama Administration and its Apparent Incoherent Foreign Policy," by Rodrigue Tremblay July 11, 2014, www.thenewamericanempire.com/tremblay=1160.htm.

131 "Scholar and Retired Army Officer Andrew Bacevich on the U.S. War for the Greater Middle East," Andrew J. Bacevich with Stephen Kinzer, Boston Review, April 4, 2016, http://bostonreview.net/us/andrew-j-bacevich-interviewed-stephen-kinzer-war-greater-middle-east. See his most recent book, Bacevich, 2016.

132 How We Got Into a Permanent War? Andrew Bacevich in the Brian Lehrer Show, WNYC-FM New York Public Radio, November 23, 2016, www.wnyc.org/story/how-we-got-permanent-war/. See also, "Ending Endless War: A Pragmatic Military Strategy," by Andrew J. Bacevich, Foreign Affairs, September/October 2016, www.foreignaffairs.com/articles/united-states/2016-08-03/ending-endless-war.

133 Niebuhr, 1952/2008.

134 "The Blundering Obama Administration and its Apparent Incoherent Foreign Policy," by Rodrigue Tremblay July 11, 2014, www.thenewamericanempire.com/tremblay=1160.htm. It is a privilege to have Rodrigue Tremblay as esteemed member in the global advisory board of our Human Dignity and Humiliation Studies fellowship.

135 Jost and Ross, 1999.

136 Martin, 2010, p. 166. Glen T. Martin is the President of the World Constitution and Parliament Association (www.worldparliament-gov.org), President of the Institute on World Problems (www.earth-constitution.org), and professor of philosophy at Radford University (www.radford.edu/gmartin). It is a privilege to have Glen Martin as esteemed member in the global advisory board of our Human Dignity and Humiliation Studies fellowship.

137 Martin, 2010, p. 166.

138 Glen Martin in a personal communication on January 28, 2010. The Earth Charter provides a template for global analysis and action. The mission of the Earth Charter Initiative is to promote the transition to

sustainable ways of living and a global society founded on a shared ethical framework that includes respect and care for the community of life, ecological integrity, universal human rights, respect for diversity, economic justice, democracy, and a culture of peace. See www.earthcharter.org.

139 Martin points at section 8.3 titled: "The Sovereign Nation-State as Inherently Terrorist" in Martin, 2010.

140 "My collateral damage is your evil intention! Bias can humiliate," in Lindner, 2006c, Chapter 5 of the book Making Enemies: Humiliation and International Conflict, pp. 70–71. The list of irrational biases and interference effects is long, from the halo effect, the "Florida effect," framing effects, anchoring effects, the confirmation bias, outcome bias, hindsight bias, availability bias, the focusing illusion, and so on, see, for instance, Kahneman, 2011, or Wilson, 2002b, or Ross and Ward, 1996.

141 Ross, 1995.

142 Discussions about these topics took place in the context of the 2010 Annual Conference of the Human Dignity and Humiliation Studies, "Peace at Home, Peace in the World," in Istanbul, Turkey, April 28–30, 2010, www.humiliationstudies.org/whoweare/annualmeeting/15.php.

143 Orhan Pamuk held his Nobel Lecture on December 7, 2006, at the Swedish Academy, Stockholm. See www.nobelprize.org/nobel_prizes/literature/laureates/2006/pamuk-lecture.html. I thank Rigmor Johnson for sending me this quote. The lecture was titled "Babamın Bavulu" (My Father's Suitcase) and was given in Turkish. In the lecture he allegorically spoke of relations between Eastern and Western civilizations using the theme of his relationship with his father (translation by Maureen Freely):

What literature needs most to tell and investigate today are humanity's basic fears: the fear of being left outside, and the fear of counting for nothing, and the feelings of worthlessness that come with such fears; the collective humiliations, vulnerabilities, slights, grievances, sensitivities, and imagined insults, and the nationalist boasts and inflations that are their next of kin... Whenever I am confronted by such sentiments, and by the irrational, overstated language in which they are usually expressed, I know they touch on a darkness inside me. We have often witnessed peoples, societies and nations outside the Western world–and I can identify with them easily–succumbing to fears that sometimes lead them to commit stupidities, all because of their fears of humiliation and their sensitivities. I also know that in the West–a world with which I can identify with the same ease–nations and peoples taking an excessive pride in their wealth, and in their having brought us the Renaissance, the Enlightenment, and Modernism, have, from time to time, succumbed to a self-satisfaction that is almost as stupid.

144 Lindner, 2006c, p. 71.

145 Ibid.

Chapter 15

1 BCE stands for "Before the Common Era," and is equivalent to BC, which means "Before Christ."

2 "Stanford Expert Describes How the U.S. And China Can Manage Their Relationship and Avoid Conflict," by Clifton B. Parker, Stanford Report, August 20, 2014, http://news.stanford.edu/news/2014/august/us-china-relations-082014.html. See also "Thucydides Trap," by Karl Eikenberry, American Review, August 4, 2014, http://americanreviewmag.com/stories/Thucydides-Trap. See, furthermore, Syse, 2003.

3 Machiavelli, 1532.

4 Hobbes, 1651.

5 "Police Mediation: An Idea Whose Time Has Come," by Johan Galtung, TRANSCEND Media Service, January 25, 2016, www.transcend.org/tms/2016/01/police-mediation-an-idea-whose-time-has-come/.

6 Polanyi and Joseph E. Stiglitz (Foreword), 1944/2001.

7 Sassen, 2014.

8 Jaspers, 1919.

9 Becker, 1973.

10 Giuseppe Verdi's Messa da Requiem may serve as an example. It had its first performance at the San Marco church in Milan, Italy, on May 22, 1874. It deeply moves its listeners, still today, and the reason is that it was written to honor a much missed person. On May 22, 1873, Alessandro Manzoni died, the great romantic poet of Italy. Verdi was so cast down by grief that he could not attend the funeral. Manzoni had, like Verdi, worked for the unification of Italy, for humanity and justice. Verdi's Requiem Mass, however, was not only written for Manzoni, it revolves around the idea of humanity and its rebellion against death in general, it laments life's impermanence altogether.
In commemoration of the destruction of the city of Dresden on February 13, 1945, a Requiem is traditionally performed in Dresden. It was Rudolf Kempe, who, in 1951, founded this tradition with Verdi's Requiem. Also in 2005 Verdi's Requiem Mass was on the program.

11 The theory was originally proposed by Jeff Greenberg, Sheldon Solomon, and Tom Pyszczynski. See more in note 6 in the Introduction

12 Jaspers, 1951, p. 20.

13 Jünger, 1979.

14 Jünger, 1979, p. 85. See also Hedges, 2002.

15 Twain, 1904.

16 McCauley, et al., 2013. It is a privilege to have Clark McCauley as esteemed member in the global advisory board of our Human Dignity and Humiliation Studies fellowship.

17 McCauley and Moskalenko, 2014a, McCauley, et al., 2013.

18 See note 73 in Chapter 4.

19 Reformbewegungen, www.forum-islam.ch/de/reformbewegungen/index.php. Summarized and translated from the German original by Lindner. See the German original in the full note in the pdf edition of this book.

20 "Don't Blame 'Wahhabism' for Terrorism," by Mohammed Alyahya, New York Times, October 19, 2016, www.nytimes.com/2016/10/20/opinion/dont-blame-wahhabism-for-terrorism.html?_r=0.

21 For former Norwegian ambassador Carl Schiøtz Wibye, 2017, Wahhabism is not to a religion, rather a sect built on extreme fantasies of a desperate desert preacher in the 1700s, later globalized through Saudi Arabia's revenues from oil, ultimately leading to Taliban, Al-Qaeda, and Da'esh. In his view, the most dangerous aspect is the practice of takfir, or excommunication, declaring another self-professed Muslim a kafir or unbeliever.

22 Mohamedou, 2011.

23 "The Data That Turned the World Upside Down," by Hannes Grassegger and Mikael Krogerus, Motherboard, January 28 2017, https://motherboard.vice.com/en_us/article/how-our-likes-helped-trump-win.

24 "Who Gets Radicalized? What I Learned From My Interviews With Extremist Disciples," by Amra Sabic-El-Rayess, Huffington Post, June 19, 2016, www.huffingtonpost.com/entry/who-gets-radicalized-what-i-learned-from-my-interviews_us_5765fddce4b0ed0729a1c5c3.

25 Ibid.

26 See note 184 in the Introduction.

27 Psychologists Jim Sidanius and Felicia Pratto speak of legitimizing myths, or compelling cultural ideologies that are taken as self-apparently true in society and that disguise the use of force and discrimination and make it acceptable. See Sidanius and Pratto, 1999. See an overview in "Power Inequities," by Máire A. Dugan, Beyond Intractability, February 2004, www.beyondintractability.org/essay/power-inequities. See also Pratto and Stewart, 2011, where they describe how legitimizing myths change over time. Read more in Chapter 2, and see also note 329 in the Introduction.

28 For the notion of chosen trauma, see Volkan, 1997, 2004, 2006, 2013.

29 Expert journalists for right-wing extremism Röpke and Speit, 2013, cover text: "The racially motivated crimes of Nationalsozialistischer Untergrund (NSU) with probably ten murders and several bomb attacks reveal a new dimension of right-wing violence in Germany. But this is not an isolated case. Since 1949, right-wing extremists have repeatedly formed terrorist groups that operated with a similar pattern: small clandestine cells, robberies for the procurement of money and weapons, attacks against immigrants, political opponents and societal institutions. A look behind the scenes reveals that the perpetrators of yesterday and today are not isolated and that the danger this poses was underestimated by the authorities for decades."

30 The Nationalsozialistischer Untergrund (National Socialist Underground, or NSU) was a far-right German terrorist group uncovered in November 2011, after having committed murder and bank robberies throughout the country since 2000. The Attorney General of Germany called the NSU a "right-wing extremist group," who has the purpose to "kill out of xenophobic and anti-state sentiments all citizens of foreign origin," see the "Haftbefehl gegen die Brandstifterin von Zwickau wegen mutmaßlicher Mitgliedschaft in der terroristischen Vereinigung 'Nationalsozialistischer Untergrund (NSU)'," by Harald Range, Attorney General of Germany, November 12, 2011, www.generalbundesanwalt.de/de/showpress.php?themenid=13&newsid=419.
See also Der Kuaför aus der Keupstrasse, documentary film by Andreas Maus, 2015, https://youtu.be/R8PnnuOUlwc. The film tells the story of the nail bomb attack in front of a Turkish hairdresser in Cologne, Keupstraße, on June 9, 2004. It focuses on the consequences for the victims and their families, who, for years, were treated as the main suspects. The film reconstructs the police investigation on the basis of interrogation protocols. It is clear that for the police the victims were the perpetrators, because they excluded the possibility that the crime had a xenophobic motive. Only years later, the attack was associated with the so-called Nazi underground (NSU). The film shows how the bombings, but perhaps even more the subsequent suspicions, have profoundly shaken lives in the Mülheim district. The case of Cologne was mirrored in the other cities in Germany, where the NSU murdered and the victims were suspected. The film opens the discussion on the question of structural xenophobia in Germany in a new way, namely, from the perspective of those affected.

31 Hameiri, et al., 2014, Abstract. See the full note in the pdf edition of this book.

32 See note 132 in Chapter 5.

33 "Shocking Images of Drowned Syrian Boy Show Tragic Plight of Refugees," by Helena Smith in Athens, The Guardian, September 2, 2015, www.theguardian.com/world/2015/sep/02/shocking-image-of-drowned-syrian-boy-shows-tragic-plight-of-refugees.

34 Abu Zubaydah cooperated already before torture was used, and he was not part of the inner leadership circle of Al-Qaeda, see, among others, "ICRC Report on the Treatment of Fourteen 'High Value Detainees' in CIA Custody," by the International Committee of the Red Cross, New York Review of Books, February 2007, www.nybooks.com/media/doc/2010/04/22/icrc-report.pdf, pp. 28–31. See also note 223 in Chapter 6.

35 McCauley and Moskalenko, 2014a.

36 See note 73 in Chapter 3.

37 Festinger, 1954, 1957, 1980.

38 See, among others, Der Kriminalist: Schein und Sein Season 2, Episode 7, January 18, 2008, www.imdb.com/title/tt1158829/.

39 German crime TV series are very different from those authored, for instance, by Agatha Christie and her focus on the intellectual challenge in exposing a cold-blooded perpetrator who is usually driven by greed. They are also different to many American series that play on "good versus evil," with the courage required on the good side to overcome evil being celebrated with huge explosions and dangerous stunts.

40 Milgram, 1974.

41 Solomon, 2005.

42 Respecting, understanding, while not condoning, this is also the rationale behind Salafistes, a documentary film by Lemine Ould Mohamed Salem and François Margolin, 2016, www.allocine.fr/film/fichefilm_gen_cfilm=244500.html. This documentary film goes to Mauritania, Tunisia, Algeria, and the Sharia zone in northern Mali between 2012 and 2015. Preachers of holy war, such as imams, sheikhs, and chairmen of sharia courts explain what they consider to be a righteous Islam. They explain why a thief's hand should be cut off, and why they are at war with the West. France was in uproar about the film and some argued that it ought to be forbidden, because it provided too much of a propaganda stage for extremist Islamists.

43 Aust, 1985, Hauser, 1998, Kraushaar, 2006, Stern and Herrmann, 2007.

44 "Die Behörden tappen im Dunkeln," Peter Neumann interviewed by Britta Sandberg, Der Spiegel 42/2016, October 15, 2016, pp. 22–23.

45 "Was bedeutet es, die RAF zu verstehen? Mit RAFlern zu reden, heißt nicht, ihre Taten zu billigen. Eine Gegenrede auf Jan Philipp Reemtsma," by Horst-Eberhard Richter, Die Tageszeitung (Taz), October 27, 2004, www.taz.de/!681743/. German original translated by Lindner: "Dessen absoluten Gehorsam bestimmte, psychoanalytisch formuliert, eine totale Übereignung des persönlichen Überichs. Dafür belohnte ihn die Gruppe mit der Verleihung einer fiktiven Selbstüberhöhung, abgestützt durch aggressive Abwehr enormer Ängste." See also note 36 in the Preface.

46 "Nicaragua: Die Sex-Affären der Commandantes! Totgeschwiegen! Weil das sonst dem Gegner helfen könnte!," Der Spiegel 31/1998, July 27, 1998, pp. 128–132.

47 American Experience: Henry Ford, documentary film as part of the collection The Titans, 2013, www.pbs.org/wgbh/americanexperience/films/henryford/.

48 Gilad and Junginger, 2010. See also Korten, 1995.

49 See, among others, historian Yuki Tanaka's work, Tanaka, et al., 2011, Tanaka and Young, 2010.

50 Hasegawa, 2005.

51 See Seconds From Disaster: Nagasaki: The Forgotten Bomb, documentary film series 6, 2013, featuring historian Tsuyoshi Hasegawa, http://natgeotv.com/uk/seconds-from-disaster/, https://youtu.be/lRosq6Q_yZE. Seconds from Disaster is an American documentary television series that first began broadcasting in 2004 on the National Geographic Channel. This episode is an analysis of the controversial claim that the second atomic bomb attack on Nagasaki was essential to bringing a swift end to World War II. See also Kimura and Minohara, 2013. See my summary of the film in the full note in the pdf edition of this book.

52 Bardi, 2013.

53 Professor in physical chemistry at the University of Florence, Italy, Ugo Bardi in "Der geplünderte Planet" – der Club of Rome und die globale Ressourcen-Krise, ttt – titel thesen temperamente, Das Erste, June 16, 2013, www.daserste.de/information/wissen-kultur/ttt/sendung/hr/sendung_vom_16062013-

114.html. Translated by Lindner from the German original: “Es ist keine Lösung des Energieproblems, es ist ein ohnmächtiger Versuch, um jeden Preis weiterzumachen, obwohl man genau weiß: Es ist Dead End.” See the full note in the pdf edition of this book.

54 “A Chatham House Report: Executive Summary,” December 2012, www.chathamhouse.org/sites/default/files/public/Research/Energy,%20Environment%20and%20Development/1212r_resourcesfutures.pdf. Chatham House (The Royal Institute of International Affairs) in London promotes the rigorous study of international questions and is independent of government and other vested interests. It is precluded by its Charter from having an institutional view. The opinions expressed in this publication are the responsibility of the authors. I thank Dan Smith, director of International Alert, for discussing this report in his blog “Resources – the Coming Crunch and Some Things That Could Be Done About It,” on Dan Smith’s Blog: Analysis and Commentary on World Issues, January 7, 2013, dansmithsblog.com/2013/01/07/resources-the-coming-crunch-and-some-things-that-could-be-done-about-it/.

55 See Joughin, et al., 2014, and Rignot, et al., 2014.

56 “Scientists Warn of Perilous Climate Shift Within Decades, Not Centuries,” See more in note 46 in the Preface. See also the first book by climate scientist James Hansen, 2009.

57 “When the End of Human Civilization Is Your Day Job,” by John H. Richardson, Esquire, July 7, 2015, www.esquire.com/news-politics/a36228/ballad-of-the-sad-climatologists-0815/.

58 See note 262 in the Introduction.

59 “It Is Still 3 Minutes to Midnight: 2016 Doomsday Clock Statement,” edited by John Mecklin, Bulletin of the Atomic Scientists, January 21, 2016, http://thebulletin.org/sites/default/files/2016%20doomsday%20clock%20statement%20-%20final[5].pdf. See note 262 in the Introduction.

60 “Food Is the New Oil; Land, the New Gold,” by Lester R. Brown, president of the Earth Policy Institute, Human Wrongs Watch, February 7, 2013, human-wrongs-watch.net/2013/02/09/20442/.

61 “Spotlighting Humanity’s ‘Silent Ally,’ UN launches 2015 International Year of Soils,” United Nations News Centre, December 5, 2014, www.un.org/apps/news/story.asp?NewsID=49520#.VJSJGf8At. FAO director-general José Graziano da Silva. He warns: “Unfortunately, 33 percent of our global soil resources are under degradation and human pressures on soils are reaching critical limits, reducing and sometimes eliminating essential soil functions.”

62 “On Day to Combat Desertification, UN calls for action to restore land resources,” United Nations News Centre, June 17, 2016, www.un.org/apps/news/story.asp?NewsID=54255#.V2V_qaLICgy. See also “Land Degradation Could Force 135 Million to Migrate in Next 30 Years,” by Manipadma Jena, Inter Press Service (IPS), October 18 2016, www.ipsnews.net/2016/10/qa-land-degradation-could-force-135-million-to-migrate-in-next-30-years/.

63 FIVAS is working to map out and spread information on issues affecting water in the global south. They aim to influence national and international policies to maintain the rights of individuals and to protect the environment. Bearing forth the voice of affected groups is central to our work towards Norwegian authorities, Norwegian companies and in international networks. www.fivas.org/ENGLISH.aspx.

64 See, among others, Capra and Mattei, 2015, or Angus, 2016.

65 Stephen Purdey, international relations specialist and research affiliate of the Waterloo Institute for Complexity and Innovation at the University of Waterloo in Ontario, Canada, in his contribution to the Great Transition Network Initiative discussion titled “Journey to Earthland: Making the Great Transition to Planetary Civilization,” October 24, 2016, in response to Raskin, 2016. Herman Greene is the President of the Center for Ecozoic Societies, www.ecozoicsocieties.org.

66 I therefore planned for a postdoctoral research project where I would contact TNC boards to find out more, see Lindner, 2000g. See also Collins, 2016. For classism, have a look at Barbara Jensen, 2012.

67 Collins, 2016, p. 4. I thank Linda Hartling for making me aware of Collins' book.

68 Polly Higgins, in a personal message, October 3, 2013. See also Higgins, 2016. See note 7 in the Preface.

69 "U.S Soldier Dragged through Mogadishu," by Alex Selwyn-Holmes, Iconic Photos, March 10, 2010, https://iconicphotos.wordpress.com/2010/03/10/u-s-marine-dragged-through-mogadishu/.

70 Sam Engelstad in a personal communication on September 28, 1999, quoted with his permission. See also Lindner, 2001a.

71 See, among others, Cochran, 1999. In social and political philosophy, cosmopolitanism regards all human beings as one single moral community, while pluralists see the nation-state as the relevant community unit.

72 "Text of President Clinton's address to genocide survivors at the airport in Kigali, Rwanda, as provided by the White House," CBSNews, March 25, 1998, www.cbsnews.com/news/text-of-clintons-rwanda-speech/.

73 Solomon, 2015.

74 Read more about the Rahanweyn in Ken Menkhaus, 2003. It was an enriching experience for me to meet Ken Menkhaus and his wife in Nairobi, Kenya, and learn from them, on December 19, 1998.

75 Solomon, 2015.

76 Nelson, 2012, Abstract. See also Goodwin, et al., 2014b, Nelson, 2010a.

77 Lewis, 1971.

78 Scheff and Retzinger, 1991, Scheff, 1994, Scheff, 1997, Scheff, 2000, Scheff, 2006, Scheff, 2007, Scheff, 2013, Scheff and Retzinger, 1997.

79 "Der 'Eiserne Kanzler': Demontage einer Kultfigur," by Sven Felix Kellerhoff, Die Welt, October 7, 2012, www.welt.de/welt_print/article921164/Der-Eiserne-Kanzler-Demontage-einer-Kultfigur.html.
See also the film: Historische Ereignisse: Vor 150 Jahren: Bismarck – Kanzler und Dämon, part 1: Vom Landjunker zum Reichsgründer, and part 2: Regierungsgewalt und Machtverlust, documentary film by Christoph Weinert, 2012,
www.phoenix.de/content/phoenix/die_sendungen/diskussionen/historische_ereignisse/527387?datum=2012-10-07.

80 "Das Duell: Wie ein Unnaer den Lauf der deutschen Geschichte beeinflusste," by Klaus Seifert, Lokalkompass.de, January 20, 2012, www.lokalkompass.de/unna/kultur/das-duell-d127400.html.

81 Willms, 2015.

82 Akte D, part 1: Das Versagen der Nachkriegsjustiz, part 2: Das Kriegserbe der Bahn, part 3: Die Macht der Stromkonzerne, Das Erste, 2014, www1.wdr.de/fernsehen/dokumentation_reportage/wdr-dok/sendungen/das-versagen-der-nachkriegsjustiz-100.html. See the full note in the pdf edition of this book.

83 See note 8 in the Introduction.

84 "Sibirien: Suche nach verschollenen Atombatterien," Der Spiegel, 41/2013, October 7, 2013, p. 132, and www.spiegel.de/spiegel/print/d-115560291.html.

85 Appiah, 2010.

86 McGoey, 2012. See also "What Will Future Generations Condemn Us For?" by Kwame Anthony Appiah, Washington Post, September 26, 2010, www.washingtonpost.com/wp-dyn/content/article/2010/09/24/AR2010092404113.html.

87 Brooklyn Grange, www.brooklyngrangefarm.com.

88 Horizons – Innovative Ways to Feed an Ever Expanding Urban Population, BBC World News, April 28 and 29, 2012, www.modernghana.com/news/388493/1/horizons-innovative-ways-to-feed-an-ever-expanding.html. BBC World News' Horizons speaks to pioneers in the USA and The Netherlands about innovative ways to feed an ever expanding urban population.

89 Ibid.

90 Richards and Swanger, 2006b, Lindner, 2012f.

91 Lecture 15 in Richards, et al., 2015a.

92 Salomon and Nevo, 2002, discussed in Vambheim, 2016, p. 9.

93 Salomon and Nevo, 2002, quoted in Vambheim, 2016, p. 9.

94 Galtung, 1996.

95 Orwell, 1949.

96 United Nations, 2015. The number of people living on less than $1.25 a day has been reduced from 1.9 billion in 1990 to 836 million in 2015, although the target of halving the proportion of people suffering from hunger was narrowly missed.

97 See also Lindner and Desmond Tutu (Foreword), 2010.

98 Lindner and Desmond Tutu (Foreword), 2010.

99 Internationaler Militärgerichtshof Nürnberg, 1989.

100 "Truth to Power," by Noam Chomsky, and David Mcneill, Japan Times, February 22, 2014, www.japantimes.co.jp/news/2014/02/22/world/noam-chomsky-truth-to-power/.

101 Ibid.

102 Soldaten und Verweigerer: "Wir waren die Ersten!" documentary film by Carsten Günther, Das Erste, 2011. See the full note in the pdf edition of this book.

103 Historian Henrik Eberle and Hans-Joachim Neumann, a professor emeritus of medicine at Berlin's Charité University Hospital, recently attempted to discover whether Hitler was ill and this could serve as an explanation for the monstrosity of his decisions. See Eberle and Neumann, 2009. Adolf Hitler took an early version of "Viagra" before he spent time with Eva Braun. No evidence was found that Hitler had syphilis, which he had identified as a "Jewish Disease" and raged against in his autobiography Mein Kampf. The records, made by medical officer Dr. Josef Steiner Brin when Hitler was briefly jailed for a failed coup in 1923, said that he had "right-sided cryptorchidism" but was otherwise "healthy" and "strong" (cryptorchidism is caused by a testicle not descending into the scrotum during puberty), see Ullrich, 2013. In other words, he might have doubted his own "manhood."

104 Lindner and Desmond Tutu (Foreword), 2010.

105 "Training Code of Conduct, Survival, Evasion, Resistance, and Escape (SERE)," Army Regulation 350–30, Training, https://fas.org/irp/doddir/army/ar350-30.pdf. SERE was a program established by the U.S. Air Force at the end of the Korean War (1950 – 1953) for those at high risk to be captured by the enemy. The program provided U.S. military personnel, U.S. Department of Defense civilians, and private military contractors with training in evading capture, survival skills, and the military code of conduct.

106 Jack Bauer is a character in the Fox television series 24, who, among others, worked as a member of the Counter Terrorist Unit (CTU) based in Los Angeles, and during Season 7 working with the FBI in Washington, DC

107 "Whatever It Takes: The Politics of the Man Behind '24,'" by Jane Mayer, New Yorker, February 19, 2007, www.newyorker.com/magazine/2007/02/19/whatever-it-takes. See the Torture Made in USA, documentary film by Marie-Monique Robin, 2009. And see Pope, 2011.

108 See Vamik Volkan, 2001, for the transgenerational transmissions and chosen traumas, or the work of Michael Wohl, who speaks of a multigenerational picture of the dynamics of trauma. See Wohl and Branscombe, 2008, Wohl and Van Bavel, 2011. Franz Ruppert, 2008, works with multigenerational trauma and family constellations. See also Gobodo - Madikizela, 2008, or Fromm, 2011.
See, furthermore, Hélène Opperman Lewis, 2016, who convened our 2013 Annual Dignity Conference in South Africa, and who sheds light on the impact of the Boer Wars. It is a privilege to have Hélène Lewis as esteemed members in our Human Dignity and Humiliation Studies fellowship. I so much thank her for giving me The Boer Whore by Nico Moolman, 2012, to read.
Steve Olweean, President of the International Humanistic Psychology Association, explains: "Every society and culture has its traditional victim story, if we look back far enough. It emerges in our folklore, our arts, our monuments, our historic icons of group identity and belonging, and at times our justification and readiness for retribution, particularly toward descendants of past perpetrators, or simply those who remind us of them," http://cbiworld.org/home/conferences/tt/:

> Transgenerational Trauma is seen as an underlying and complex global syndrome that divides, polarizes, and perpetuates enemy images, has been a central basis for past conflict and wars, and is a potent fuel for the eruption of violence in the present and future. Understanding it's dynamics and implications, and developing ways to effectively prevent and treat it, are essential to healing and reconciliation within and between communities, establishing compassionate local and global relations, and achieving sustainable peace.

109 See the section "Apologies from the world! What the world can do for America," in Lindner, 2006c, Chapter 5: Humiliation and Conflict, in the book Making Enemies: Humiliation and International Conflict, pp. 102–105.

110 Kohout, 2010.

111 Coser, 1974. See also Lewis Coser, 1956,.

112 See note 75 in Chapter 4.

113 Wright, 2013. The 2015 documentary film Going Clear: Scientology and the Prison of Belief directed by Alex Gibney and produced by Home Box Office (HBO), is based on Wright's book. It was released, also internationally, despite a sustained campaign by Scientology to block its release.

114 I thank Linda Hartling for reminding me of Jean Baker Miller's conceptualization of strategies of disconnection: a.k.a. strategies of survival as "ways for staying out of connection because the only relationships that had been available were in some fundamental way disconnecting and violating... There was good reason to develop these strategies," Miller, et al., 1994, p. 3. Miller and Stiver, 1997, p. 105: "Methods people develop to stay out of relationship in order to prevent wounding or violation. These begin as the form through which psychological problems are expressed, but can become the main problem. They evolve out of a person's attempt to find some way to make or preserve connection, in."

115 Beyond Revenge, documentary film, Pressenza Berlin, 2016, www.pressenza.com/2016/10/beyond-revenge-documentary-film-freely-available-online/, and https://youtu.be/JLZ9fU6Ljgs. The film traces mechanisms of revenge back to the first big states of Mesopotamia, where this mechanism was institutionalized in the form of law and punishment and executed by state authorities. The message the film conveys is that enshrining revenge into law had detrimental consequences insofar as it "led to the loss of an inner process of reconciliation" and that therefore, "nowadays we have no tools for achieving a real inner reconciliation after harm has been done to us. We yearn for punishment even though it cannot heal the inner damage that has happened to us." The documentary gives the floor to people who share their very

personal process of reconciling with violence, sometimes after decades of suffering from resentment, fear, and bitterness. They describe a sense of liberation, a gain in energy and happiness through reconciliation that goes far beyond mere forgiveness. Luz Jahnen, co-producer and author of the study that was the basis for the documentary, reports that the film has elicited "gratitude," for that this topic was presented in such a way that viewers could confront their own experiences more clearly.

116 Coman, et al., 2014. I thank Linda Hartling for making me aware of this research.

117 Jervis, 2006, p. 641. Jervis suggests going back fifty years, revisiting the typology introduced by M. Brewster Smith, et al., 1956.

118 "Will Trump Ever Be Blamed?" by Olga Khazan, The Atlantic, April 4, 2017, www.theatlantic.com/science/archive/2017/04/will-trump-ever-take-the-blame/521769/. I thank Linda Hartling for making me aware of this article. "Beliefs are like possessions," and what is being intensified through dynamics of humiliation is "trait polarization," according to Hetherington, et al., 2016, as well as "selective evaluation," and "selective attribution," see Tilley and Hobolt, 2011.
In Nazi-Germany, the following outcry was widely heard when something went wrong: "Wenn das der Führer wüßte!" (If only Hitler knew about this!). In other words, even the worst disaster was not attributed to Adolf Hitler. Whatever happened, he would save them, this was their conviction; if only he knew, if only he were in a position to intervene, he would certainly do so. He himself judged the situation along the following lines: At the very end, when Germany was already utterly destroyed, he concluded that the Germans themselves had failed him, that they had not been strong enough in their Opferbereitschaft (willingness to give their all), and therefore deserved to go down. In short: his plan was good, his intentions were good, but he was failed and undermined by the very people he wanted to lift into greatness. Until the very last moment, people believed in him, in the Endsieg (final victory), and even in the face of disaster people there were still enough "believers" around to shoot fellow Germans who no longer wanted to "give everything to the last man." While Italy abandoned Benito Mussolini much earlier, a majority of Germans stayed strong in their belief in Hitler.

119 Hebrews 12:6, The Bible, New International Version (NIV), www.biblegateway.com/passage/?search=Hebrews+12:6.

120 Lakoff and Johnson, 1999. See also Lindner, 2005a.

121 Miller, 2006a.

122 Sue, et al., 2007.

123 See, among others, Greene, 2006, and Yamada, 2015. It is a privilege to have Michael Greene and David Yamada as esteemed members in the global advisory board of our Human Dignity and Humiliation Studies fellowship.

124 Sue, et al., 2007, Evans, 2010. I thank Ines Balta for making me aware of Patricia Evans' work.

125 Johnson, 2008.

126 Adler, 1993, 2004, Adler, et al., 2009.

127 See note 40 in the Introduction, and see the full note 1 of Chapter 11 in the pdf edition of this book.

128 Thorndike, 1920.

129 Fuller, 2003, Fuller and Gerloff, 2008.

130 Carveth, 2013. I thank Michael Britton for making me aware of Carveth's work. It is a privilege to have Michael Britton as member on the board of directors of our Human Dignity and Humiliation Studies fellowship.

131 Carveth, 1994.

132 Meffert, et al., 2013. See also Watkins and Watkins, 1997. I thank Michael Britton for making me aware of the work done by the Watkins.

133 See note 69 in Chapter 1.

134 See the work of psychotherapist Charles Truax, et al., 1970, on accurate empathy. I thank John McFadden also here for making me aware of this work.

135 Arie Nadler wrote about radical empathy and radical reconciliation. See more in note 69 in the Preface.

136 Meffert, et al., 2013.

137 Online Etymology Dictionary, www.etymonline.com/index.php?search=empathy&searchmode=none.

138 Titchener, 1909, Gallese, 2003, Bråten, 2013.

139 Shamay-Tsoory, 2011.

140 See note 69 in Chapter 1.

141 White, 1984, pp. 162–163.

142 Lamm and Majdandzic, 2015. See also Shamay-Tsoory, 2011. See, furthermore, "Compassion: Hot to Help: When Can Empathy Move Us to Action?," by Daniel Goleman, March 1, 2008, Greater Good in Action, http://greatergood.berkeley.edu/article/item/hot_to_help. Goleman reports: "In fact, those who fall within psychology's 'Dark Triad' – narcissists, Machiavellians, and sociopaths – can actually put cognitive empathy to use in hurting people. As Ekman told me, a torturer needs this ability, if only to better calibrate his cruelty. Talented political operatives can read people's emotions to their own advantage, without necessarily caring about those people very much."

143 The Power of Empathy, by Brené Brown, http://tinyurl.com/z9wc5x9, or https://youtu.be/jz1g1SpD9Zo. I thank Floyd Webster Rudmin for making me aware of this talk. It is a privilege to have him as esteemed member in the global advisory board of our Human Dignity and Humiliation Studies fellowship. See also Brown, 2012a.

144 See note 114 in the Preface.

145 Linda Hartling, summarized Tania Singer's research results in a personal communication on September 3, 2016, as concluding that "empathy is not enough":

> To feel with others is not enough, indeed, it can lead to "empathy fatigue," which has been called "compassion fatigue" in mental health circles. Singer suggests that compassion is empathy + the judgment/wisdom of thought available through frontal lobes. Jean Baker Miller might describe this as "feeling-thought" based on an assumption of human connection as healthy.

146 See note 114 in the Preface.

147 Singer and Klimecki, 2014, contrast empathic distress and compassion as follows:
• Empathic distress: self-related emotion, negative feelings, e.g., stress, poor health, burnout, withdrawal and non-social behavior.
• Compassion: other-related emotion, positive feelings, e.g., love, good health, approach and prosocial motivation.

148 Ingold, 2000. I thank Ingrid Fuglestvedt for reminding me of this reference.

149 Harrison, 1999.

150 During my time in medicine, I did surgery, and therefore I know that it is not necessary to switch off empathy to be able to carry out surgery.

151 Linda Hartling in a personal communication on September 3, 2016.

152 Fontan, 2008. See also Fontan, 2012. It is a privilege to have Victoria Fontan as esteemed member in the global advisory board of our Human Dignity and Humiliation Studies fellowship.

153 See note 231 in Chapter 6.

154 Hayden, 2016. See also "Playing to the Edge" To Fight Terrorism, Michael Hayden interviewed by Trevor Noah, The Daily Show, February 25, 2016, www.cc.com/video-clips/evluqc/the-daily-show-with-trevor-noah-michael-hayden----playing-to-the-edge--to-fight-terrorism. See, furthermore, "To Keep America Safe, Embrace Drone Warfare," by Michael Hayden, New York Times, February 19, 2016, www.nytimes.com/2016/02/21/opinion/sunday/drone-warfare-precise-effective-imperfect.html.

155 I thank Kirk Schneider, 2013, author of The Polarized Mind, past president of the Society for Humanistic Psychology of the APA (2015 – 2016) and vice-president of the Existential-Humanistic Institute, for contacting me and making me aware of his work.

156 Linda Hartling in a personal communication on September 3, 2016.

157 "I Don't Think She Deserved The Nobel," Anirudh Bhattacharyya interviews Genevieve Chenard, Outlook, March 18, 2013, www.outlookindia.com/magazine/story/i-dont-think-she-deserved-the-nobel/284270.

158 McGoey, 2012. See also "What Will Future Generations Condemn Us For?" by Kwame Anthony Appiah, Washington Post, September 26, 2010, www.washingtonpost.com/wp-dyn/content/article/2010/09/24/AR2010092404113.html.

159 Linda Hartling in a personal communication on September 3, 2016.

160 See note 231 in Chapter 6.

161 Solomon, 2005.

162 Linda Hartling, in a personal communication on September 3, 2016.

163 Ibid.

164 Hartling and Lindner, 2016b. See also MacDonald and Jensen-Campbell, 2011.

165 "PTSD: The Futile Search for the 'Quick Fix,'" by Kali Tal, Scientific American, February 26, 2013, http://blogs.scientificamerican.com/guest-blog/2013/02/26/ptsd-the-futile-search-for-the-quick-fix/?WT_mc_id=SA_CAT_MB_201302274900. I thank Rigmor Johnsen for making me aware of this article.

166 Pynchon, 2005, Perry, 2007. See also "Orphans' Lonely Beginnings Reveal How Parents Shape A Child's Brain," by Jon Hamilton, National Public Radio (NPR), February 24, 2014, www.npr.org/sections/health-shots/2014/02/20/280237833/orphans-lonely-beginnings-reveal-how-parents-shape-a-childs-brain.

167 Woo, et al., 2014.

168 See, among others, Schore and Sieff, 2015.

169 Kemme, et al., 2014. See also Von Menschen und Waffen, a documentary film by Thomas Lauterbach, Südwestrundfunk, 2013, www.swr.de/junger-dokumentarfilm/junger-dokumentarfilm-menschen-waffen/-/id=100850/did=12168610/nid=100850/1a9bw85/. This film was made after the Winnenden school shooting on March 11, 2009, at a secondary school in Winnenden, Baden-Württemberg, in southwestern Germany, resulting in sixteen deaths, including the suicide of the perpetrator, a seventeen years old young man, who had graduated from the school one year earlier. See the full note in the pdf edition of this book.

170 "Wandel der Kindererziehung in Deutschland: Mehr Liebe, weniger Hiebe," by Christian Pfeiffer, Süddeutsche Zeitung, January 15, 2012, www.sueddeutsche.de/politik/wandel-der-kindererziehung-in-deutschland-mehr-liebe-weniger-hiebe-1.1258028:

Danach werden mit Gegenständen oder sonst massiv geschlagene Kinder später sechsmal häufiger zu Mehrfach-Gewalttätern als gewaltfrei und liebevoll erzogene. Dreimal so oft geraten sie in kriminelle oder rechtsextreme Jugendcliquen. Sie konsumieren fünfmal häufiger regelmäßig Cannabis und schwänzen viermal häufiger für mindestens zehn Tage im Jahr die Schule. Eine weitere Befragung zeigt die Folgen bei Erwachsenen. Wer in der Kindheit die Ohnmacht des Geschlagenen erlitten hat, möchte später dreimal häufiger eine scharfe Schusswaffe besitzen und sich so endlich mächtig fühlen. Außerdem befürwortet er tendenziell ein hartes Strafrecht sowie die Todesstrafe.

171 Lakoff and Johnson, 1999. See also Lindner, 2005a.

172 Banks and Hirschman, 2016. I thank Linda Hartling for making me aware of this book. See also Hartling, 2008a, Lieberman, 2015, or Miller, 1986a.

173 Fallon, 2013.

174 See note 108 in this Chapter 15.

175 Fallon, 2013. See also Fallon, 2006.

176 Otten and Jonas, 2013, p. 33.

177 Perlin and Weinstein, 2014, Collazzoni, et al., 2014, Torres and Bergner, 2010. I thank Leonard Morgenbesser for making me aware of the latter article.

178 For the 2007 Workshop on Transforming Humiliation and Violent Conflict at Columbia University see /www.humiliationstudies.org/whoweare/annualmeeting/10.php. See also Lazare, 2004. It was a privilege to have Aaron Lazare as esteemed member in the global advisory board of our Human Dignity and Humiliation Studies fellowship, and we honor his spirit since he passed away in 2015.

179 "Volkswagen: The Scandal Explained," by Russell Hotten, BBC News, December 10, 2015, www.bbc.com/news/business-34324772. German automaker Volkswagen Group was found to have intentionally programmed turbocharged direct injection (TDI) diesel engines in about eleven million cars worldwide, and in 500,000 in the United States, during model years 2009 through 2015, to activate certain emissions controls only during laboratory emissions testing. The programming caused the vehicles' nitrogen oxide (NOx) output to meet US standards during regulatory testing, but emit up to 40 times more NOx in real-world driving.

180 "Fear and Respect: VW's Culture under Winterkorn," by Andreas Cremer and Tom Bergin, Reuters, October 10, 2015, www.reuters.com/article/us-volkswagen-emissions-culture-idUSKCN0S40MT20151010.

181 Samurai and Idiots: The Olympus Affair (BBC title: 1.7 Billion Dollar Fraud: Full Exposure), documentary film by Hyoe Yamamoto, 2015, Vesuvius, Point du Jour, in cooperation with BBC, Arte, ZDF, SVT, DR, www.pointdujour-international.com/catalogueFiche.php?idFiche=38282&PHPSESSID=55a81bc6a21f799774889fced7d4899c. See also www.bbc.co.uk/programmes/b054f7qp.

182 A band of ronin (leaderless samurai) avenged the death of their master.

183 See for a deep analysis also "Japan Right Now – And the USA," by Johan Galtung, TRANSCEND Media Service, Number 432, June 13, 2016, www.transcend.org/tms/2016/06/japan-right-now-and-the-usa/.

184 "Olympus's Deceit Was Dishonourable," by John Gapper, Financial Times, November 9, 2011, www.ft.com/cms/s/0/60ba6782-0abd-11e1-b9f6-00144feabdc0.html.

185 "More Than a Clash of the Cultures at Olympus," by Jonathan Soble, Financial Times, October 14, 2011, http://search.ft.com/search?queryText=More+than+a+clash+of+the+cultures+at+Olympus.

186 "Who Owns Japan? And Who Runs It?" British Chamber of Commerce in Japan, July 11, 2012, www.bccjapan.com/events/2012/7/who-owns-japan-and-who-runs-it/.

187 "JR, Train Driver Faulted in Final Report on Crash," The Japan Times, Kyodo News, June 29, 2007, www.japantimes.co.jp/news/2007/06/29/news/jr-train-driver-faulted-in-final-report-on-crash/#.VtKmruaOWgw.

188 I thank my dear friend Tohru Tada for explaining me more in a personal communication on October 9, 2013. He wrote that everything is hearsay, because the Japan Railways Group conceals the practice of nikkin kyouiku. It appears, however, that not all train personnel who make mistakes are forced into nikkin

kyouiku, but that this "re-education" is particularly being used as harassment for people disliked by the leadership (e.g. those who belong to certain trade unions). Japanese websites on this practice give examples of nikkin kyouiku, such as having to write long self-critical reflections or meaningless reports that have nothing to do with the mistakes one had committed, to weed a field, to clean up toilets, and so forth. This is often conducted in front of other workers.

189 Rosenthal and Zimmerman, 2012.

190 I thank Tohru Tada, Tina Ottman, and Lisa Rogers for kindly explaining everything to me in personal communications in January 2016.

191 Ury, 1999.

192 Staub, 1989, 1993, 2012, 2015.

193 On September 18, 2015, the United States Environmental Protection Agency (EPA) issued a notice of violation of the Clean Air Act to German automaker Volkswagen Group.

194 "Führungskultur bei VW soll Abgas-Skandal ermöglicht haben," Die Zeit, October 29, 2015, www.zeit.de/wirtschaft/2015-10/volkswagen-aufsichtsrat-stephan-weil-kritikkultur.

195 Riesman, et al., 1950/2001.

196 Norgaard, 2015.

197 See note 97 in Chapter 5.

198 In my work, I apply the ideal-type approach as described by sociologist Max Weber, 1904/1949. See also Coser, 1977, p. 224. See the full note in the pdf edition of this book.

199 Otto, 1917/1923. See also Palmquist, 2015. I thank Mark Singer for making me aware of Stephen Palmquist's work on philosopher Emmanuel Kant. It is a privilege to have Kant expert Mark Singer as esteemed member in our Human Dignity and Humiliation Studies fellowship. From my point of view, Palmquist rightly points out that religious Schwärmerei as Kant calls it, is not correctly translated with "fanaticism" nor "enthusiasm." However, also Palmquist's suggestion of "delirium" does not resonate with me. The best term for me, since it also encapsulates Kant's disdain for this phenomenon, would be "puppy love." I personally feel the same sentiment that Kant feels: I reject religion that expresses itself in any form of "puppy love," while I do not reject "critical mysticism."

200 In his book The Sacred and the Profane, Eliade, 1957/1959, partially builds on Otto's The Idea of the Holy, showing how religion emerges from the experience of the sacred.

201 Eliade, 1949/1954.

202 See note 119 in Chapter 13.

203 "Facing Gaia: A New Enquiry Into Natural Religion," the Gifford Lectures by Bruno Latour, University of Edinburgh, 2013, www.giffordlectures.org/lectures/facing-gaia-new-enquiry-natural-religion.

204 Sudhir Chella Rajan in his contribution to the Great Transition Network Initiative discussion titled "Journey to Earthland: Making the Great Transition to Planetary Civilization," September 26, 2016, in response to Raskin, 2016.

205 Intergroup emotions theory has provided strong evidence for the affective impact of texts which address identity groups, see, among others, Smith and Mackie, 2015.

206 David Korten, in his contribution to the Great Transition Network (GTN) discussion on the topic "Why We Consume: Neural Design and Sustainability," January 24, 2016, responding to Sterling, 2016.

207 Ibid.

208 Schwartz, 2004. See also Choice, a RSA animate, where Renata Salecl explores the paralyzing anxiety and dissatisfaction that surround limitless choice. Does the freedom to be the architects of our own lives actually

hinder rather than help us? Does our preoccupation with choosing and consuming actually obstruct social change? See https://youtu.be/1bqMY82xzWo, and the RSA's free public events program www.thersa.org/events. See also Salecl, 2004.

209 See also Chapter 8: When False Choices Crowd Out Important Choices, in Lindner, 2012f, A Dignity Economy.

210 Miller, 2006b. See her first, seminal book, Miller, 1976/1986, 1986b.

211 Read about the International Society for Health and Human Rights on www.hhri.org/about/.

212 Jones, 2009. See also Latour, 2004, and "When Nothing Is Cool," in note 98 in the Preface.

213 "When Nothing Is Cool," see note 212 above.

214 Ibid.

215 Latour, 2004, p. 225.

216 Carveth, 2013. See also Carveth, 1994, for his discussion of Heidegger, Winnicott, Freud, Klein, Lacan, Mahler, and St. Paul with respect to what Winnicott, 1965, would call "true self."

217 See note 212 above.

218 Rippin, 2013.

219 See note 212 above.

220 Linda Hartling in a personal communication on September 3, 2016.

221 Ibid.

222 World Dignity University initiative, www.worlddignityuniversity.org/joo/.

223 The model of emotion described by cultural theorist Sara Ahmed, 2004, indicates that emotions are not "in" either the individual or the social, but "produce the very surfaces and boundaries that allow the individual and the social to be delineated as if they are objects," Ahmed, 2004, p. 10.

224 Lindner and Desmond Tutu (Foreword), 2010.

225 "US Iraq War Veteran Speaks Out Before Australian Tour." See more in note 16 in the Preface.

226 Ibid.

227 See, among others, Enloe, 1990, 1993, 2000, 2004, 2007.

228 Cohn, 1987.

229 "Inside UN Peacekeeping: Policy Changes that Work for Women," with Nadine Puechguirbal, Senior Gender Advisor, UN Department of Peacekeeping Operations, and Cynthia Enloe, research professor, International Development, Community and Environment Department, Clark University, talk at the Consortium on Gender, Security and Human Rights at UMass Boston, October 4, 2012. I thank Muna Killingback for making me aware of this event. It is a privilege to have Muna Killingback as member in our Human Dignity and Humiliation Studies fellowship. In the invitation to the event, the speakers were introduced as follows: "Puechguirbal, drawing on over a decade of experience working inside UN peacekeeping missions – and Enloe, reflecting on her experience of trying to forge feminist questions about militarized politics – will candidly discuss the continuing impact of "gender blindness" on even well-meaning international organizations, as well as the daily challenges feminists face in keeping their integrity in peacekeeping and humanitarian work."

230 Gunning and Jackson, 2011, Jackson, 2010, Jackson, et al., 2011, Smyth, et al., 2009. See also http://richardjacksonterrorismblog.wordpress.com/. I thank Birgit Brock-Utne for introducing me to Jackson's work.

231 2011 Annual Conference of Human Dignity and Humiliation Studies, "Enlarging the Boundaries of Compassion," in Dunedin, New Zealand, August 29 – September 1, 2011, www.humiliationstudies.org/whoweare/annualmeeting/17.php.

232 "The Subjugated Knowledge of Terrorism," by Richard Jackson, January 3, 2012, richardjacksonterrorismblog. See his talk titled Unknown Knowns: The Subjugated Knowledge of Terrorism at a conference "A Decade of Terrorism and Counter-Terrorism since 9/11: Taking Stock and New Directions in Research and Policy," University of Strathclyde, Glasgow, UK, at https://vimeo.com/29262905.

233 "Does U.S. Intervention Overseas Breed Terrorism? The Historical Record," by Ivan Eland, Cato Institute Foreign Policy Briefing, Number 50, December 17, 1998, http://object.cato.org/sites/cato.org/files/pubs/pdf/fpb50.pdf.

234 "Chris Hedges Speaks on Osama bin Laden's Death," by Chris Hedges, Truthdig, May 2, 2011, www.truthdig.com/report/item/chris_hedges_speaks_on_osama_bin_ladens_death_20110502/.

235 Ehsan Shahghasemi in a personal communication on February 12, 2014. Ehsan Shahghasemi is a Ph.D. Candidate at the Department of Communication of the University of Tehran.

236 Johan Galtung, in a private communication with Lindner, January 27, 2014, published here with his permission.

237 "Can SAARC Survive India and Pakistan's Squabbles? A key international body is being swamped by rivalry," by Zahid Shahab Ahmed, National Interest, September 1, 2016, http://nationalinterest.org/feature/can-saarc-survive-india-pakistans-squabbles-17556?page=show. It is a privilege to have Zahid Shahab Ahmed as esteemed member in our Human Dignity and Humiliation Studies fellowship. See the full note in the pdf edition of this book.

238 "Some Myths about Muslims," by Nivedita Menon, TRANSCEND Media Service, June 30, 2014, www.transcend.org/tms/2014/06/some-myths-about-muslims/. Examples are the Indonesian Communist Party, the Nasserite and Ba'athist regimes in Egypt, Syria and Iraq, or the Iranian government of Mohammed Mossadegh.

239 "Monograph on Terrorist Financing – Staff Report to the National Commission on Terrorist Attacks Upon the United States" by John Roth, Douglas Greenburg, and Serena Wille, 2004, www.9-11commission.gov/staff_statements/911_TerrFin_Monograph.pdf.

240 "The Paris Killings – A Fatal Trap for Europe," by Roberto Savio, Inter Press Service (IPS), January 12, 2015, www.ipsnews.net/2015/01/opinion-the-paris-killings-a-fatal-trap-for-europe/: "A Pew Research Center on the Muslim world inform us that it is in South Asia that Muslims are more radical in terms of observance and views. In that region, those in favor of severe corporal punishment for criminals are 81 percent, compared with 57 percent in the Middle East and North Africa, while those in favor of executing those who leave Islam are 76 percent in South Asia, compared with 56 percent in the Middle East."

241 Ibid.: "Thus the Arab countries of today were born as the result of a division by France and Britain. A few of those countries, like Egypt, had an historical identity, but countries like Iraq, Arabia Saudi, Jordan, or even the Arab Emirates, lacked even that. It is worth remembering that the Kurdish issue of 30 million people divided among four countries was created by European powers."

242 Ibid.

243 Khalidi, 2004.

244 See note 11 in Chapter 2.

245 "IS want Western Countries to Invade: What's The Purpose of "Global" Terrorism?" by Gwynne Dyer, Information Clearing House, November 30, 2014, www.informationclearinghouse.info/article40350.htm.

246 "The US-Iranian-Syrian Diplomatic Dance," by Dan Smith, Dan Smith's Blog: Analysis and Commentary on World Issues, October 9, 2013, dansmithsblog.com/2013/10/09/the-us-iranian-syrian-diplomatic-dance/.

247 Institute for Economics and Peace, 2014.

248 See, among others, Scheuer, 2011.

249 General Wesley Clark: Wars Were Planned – Seven Countries In Five Years. See more in note 67 in Chapter 13.

250 "Remarks of President Barack Obama – State of the Union Address As Delivered," The White House, Office of the Press Secretary, January 13, 2016, www.whitehouse.gov/the-press-office/2016/01/12/remarks-president-barack-obama-%E2%80%93-prepared-delivery-state-union-address.

251 "Jihadists Deepen Collaboration in North Africa," by Carlotta Gall, New York Times, January 1, 2016, www.nytimes.com/2016/01/02/world/africa/jihadists-deepen-collaboration-in-north-africa.html?smid=tw-share&_r=3.

252 "The Algerian Tragedy," by Omar Ashour, Project Syndicate, January 25, 2013, www.project-syndicate.org/commentary/the-origins-of-algeria-s-hostage-crisis-by-omar-ashour?barrier=true. See also Ashour, 2009. There are voices, however, who suspect that more sinister intentions may have been behind the "Arab Spring" uprisings and the chaos in the Middle East in general, namely, that it rather was a chaos stoked from outside. See "Barack Obama's Meager Legacy of Incomplete Accomplishments and of Provoked Wars: What Happened?" by Rodrigue Tremblay, May 30, 2016, www.thecodeforglobalethics.com/pb/wp_0b5e796a/wp_0b5e796a.html#LEGACY. See more by Canadian economist Rodrigue Tremblay, 2010. See also "The Redirection: Is the Administration's New Policy Benefitting Our Enemies in the War on Terrorism?" by Seymour M. Hersh, New Yorker, Annals of National Security, March 5, 2007, www.newyorker.com/magazine/2007/03/05/the-redirection.

253 "Top 5 Reasons Why 'Failed State' Is a Failed Concept," by William Easterly and Laura Freschi, Aid Watch, January 13, 2010, http://aidwatchers.com/2010/01/top-5-reasons-why-%E2%80%9Cfailed-state%E2%80%9D-is-a-failed-concept/: "One can only speculate about the political motives for inventing an incoherent concept like 'state failure.' It gave Western states (most notably the US superpower) much more flexibility to intervene where they wanted to (for other reasons): you don't have to respect state sovereignty if there is no state. After the end of the Cold War, there was less hesitation to intervene because of the disappearance of the threat of Soviet retaliation. 'State failure' was even more useful as justification for the US to operate with a free hand internationally in the 'War on Terror' after 9/11." The term "failed state" came to prominence with the publication of Helman and Ratner, 1992. See also "Failed States Are a Western Myth," by Elliot Ross, The Guardian, June 28, 2013, www.theguardian.com/commentisfree/2013/jun/28/failed-states-western-myth-us-interests.

254 "Think Again: Failed States," by James Traub, Foreign Policy, June 20, 2011, http://foreignpolicy.com/2011/06/20/think-again-failed-states/. See also Patrick, 2011.

255 Ehrenreich Brooks, 2005..

256 Ibid.

257 "For Pakistan, Deep Ties to Militant Network May Trump U.S. Pressure," by Pir Zubair Shah and Carlotta Gall, New York Times, October 31, 2011, www.nytimes.com/2011/11/01/world/asia/haqqani-militants-act-like-pakistans-protected-partners.html?hp.

258 Ibid.

259 Ibid.

260 "'Execution Orgy': Pakistan Learns from a Brutal Terrorist Attack," by Hasnain Kazim, Spiegel Online International, December 14, 2015, www.spiegel.de/international/world/pakistan-security-improves-in-wake-of-deadly-school-attack-a-1067740.html.

261 Ibid.

262 Kristian Berg Harpviken spoke at the conference "Konfliktløsning, fredskultur og flerkulturell forståelse," at the Nordland Akademi for Kunst og Vitenskap, Melbu, Vesterålen, Norway, July 5–8, 2010, www.nordland-akademi.no. It is a privilege to have Kristian Berg Harpviken as esteemed member in the global advisory board of our Human Dignity and Humiliation Studies fellowship.

263 "Blowback in Paris," by Nafeez Ahmed, Middle East Eye, January 8, 2015, www.middleeasteye.net/columns/blowback-paris-1534074535. Nafeez Mosaddeq Ahmed is director of the Institute for Policy Research and Development in London, http://iprd.org.uk.

264 Kolås, 2010, Abstract. I thank Kristian Berg Harpviken for making me aware of this article.

265 Schmidt and Schröder, 2001, pp. 8–9.

266 Sovacool, 2011.

267 "Coming Home to Roost: American Militarism, War Culture, and Police Brutality," by Colin Jenkins, The Hampton Institute, February 27, 2014, www.hamptoninstitution.org/coming-home-to-roost.html. Jenkins describes the summer of 1994, when he participated in a U.S. Army Basic Training in Columbia, South Carolina, 19 years old. The following words of U.S. Army General George Patton were loudly disseminated from the loudspeakers: "Americans love to fight, traditionally. All real Americans love the sting and clash of battle … you are here because you are real men and all real men like to fight!... Americans love a winner! Americans will not tolerate a loser! Americans despise cowards! Americans play to win all of the time. I wouldn't give a hoot in hell for a man who lost and laughed. That's why Americans have never lost nor will ever lose a war; for the very idea of losing is hateful to an American!"

268 Linda Hartling in a personal communication on September 3, 2016.

269 According to philosopher Martha Nussbaum, 1995, a person may be objectified if they are treated:
- as a tool for another's purposes (instrumentality)
- as if lacking in agency or self-determination (denial of autonomy, inertness)
- as if owned by another (ownership)
- as if interchangeable (fungibility)
- as if permissible to damage or destroy (violability)
- as if there is no need for concern for their feelings and experiences (denial of subjectivity).

270 See note 267 above.

271 "Briefing General Assembly, UN rights expert urges dual fight against torture, corruption," United Nations News Centre, October 21, 2014, www.un.org/apps/news/story.asp?NewsID=49136#.VEjhSxY08ud.

272 Nora Sveaass took initiative to establish Health and Human Rights Info (www.hhri.org), to make professional experiences and resources more easily accessible to health professionals working with people exposed to human rights abuses, armed conflict, forced migration and other human rights violations. See also Sveaass, 2013.

273 For the notion of chosen trauma, see Volkan, 1997, 2004, 2006, 2013.

274 Norgaard, 2015. See also Lindner, 2012f.

275 See Chapter 8 of Lindner, 2012f, A Dignity Economy.

276 See note 6 in the Preface, and the full note in the pdf edition of this book.

277 Higgins, 2016. See note 7 in the Preface.

278 Rickards, 2014.

279 Lindner, 2012f.

280 Vaughan, 2008. It is a privilege to have Geneviève Vaughan as esteemed member in the global advisory board of our Human Dignity and Humiliation Studies fellowship.
See also Goodwin, et al., 2014a. Leading feminist theorists Julie A. Nelson and Neva Goodwin suggest that a feminist perspective is essential for understanding issues such as financial crisis, climate change, and behavioral economics. See, for instance, Goodwin, et al., 2014a, Nelson, 2010a. I had the privilege of meeting Neva Goodwin at the Thirtieth Annual E. F. Schumacher Lectures "Voices of a New Economics," in New York City on November 20, 2010.

281 Lindner, 2012f.

282 Diesing, 1962. See also Hartwig, 1983, and Hartwig, 2008. I thank Morton Deutsch and Eric Marcus for making me aware of Diesing's work.

283 Carveth, 2013.

284 Sundararajan, 2012.

285 "Overwhelmed by these social services, the spirit of community falters: families collapse, schools fail, violence spreads, and medical systems spiral out of control. Instead of more or better services, the basis for resolving many of America's social problems is the community capacity of the local citizens," McKnight, 1995, book description. I thank Howard Richards for making me aware of this book by John McKnight, and that by McKnight and Block, 2010. The Community Development Program at the Institute for Policy Research at Northwestern University in Evanston, Illinois, has established the Asset-Based Community Development Institute based on three decades of research and community work by John P. Kretzmann and John L. McKnight.

286 "People's Tragedy: Neoliberal Legacy of Thatcher and Reagan," by Kamran Mofid, Globalization for the Common Good Initiative (GCGI), October 15, 2014, http://www.gcgi.info/index.php/blog/627-people-s-tragedy-neoliberal-legacy-of-thatcher-and-reagan. It is a privilege to have Kamran Mofid as esteemed member in the global advisory board of our Human Dignity and Humiliation Studies fellowship.

287 "Economics, Globalisation and the Common Good: A Lecture at London School of Economics," by Kamran Mofid, Globalization for the Common Good Initiative (GCGI), May 12, 2015, http://www.gcgi.info/index.php/news/694-economics-globalisation-and-the-common-good-a-lecture-at-londonschool-of-economics.

288 Hartzband and Groopman, 2009, p. 103. I thank Linda Hartling for making me aware of this article.

289 Diesing, 1962. See also Hartwig, 1983, and Hartwig, 2008. I thank Morton Deutsch and Eric Marcus for making me aware of Diesing's work.

290 Linda Hartling in a personal communication on September 3, 2016.

291 Hartwig, 2008, p. 4.

292 "Die Hochschule der Zukunft: Das Leitbild der Wirtschaft." See more in note 97 in Chapter 5.

293 Linda Hartling, in a personal communication on September 8, 2015.

294 "Die Hochschule der Zukunft: Das Leitbild der Wirtschaft." See more in note 97 in Chapter 5.

295 Lappé, 2016.

296 See note 6 in the Preface, and the full note in the pdf edition of this book.

297 Ecology and Society is a leading journal for the discussion of nature-society interactions, for which the term social-ecological and similar expressions have become mainstream terminology.

298 Global wildlife populations have fallen by 58 percent since 1970, and if the trend continues the decline could reach two-thirds among vertebrates by 2020, according to World Wildlife Fund (WWF), et al., 2016. See more in note 79 in Chapter 3.

299 World Wildlife Fund (WWF), et al., 2016.

300 Young, et al., 2015.

301 Das Gift im Kuhstall – Sterbende Tiere, kranke Menschen, documentary film, Westdeutscher Rundfunk Köln, 2013, www.ardmediathek.de/wdr-fernsehen/die-story?documentId=17138936, and https://youtu.be/c4uUx507ZZU. See the full note in the pdf edition of this book.

302 Antibiotika ohne Wirkung? documentary film by Antje Büll, Norddeutscher Rundfunk, February 10, 2014, www.ndr.de/ratgeber/gesundheit/infektion_immunsystem/antibiotika283.html, and https://youtu.be/D_7rsOQ2VSI. See the full note in the pdf edition of this book.

303 "The Conflict Horizon 3: Only Connect," Dan Smith, Dan Smith's Blog: Analysis and Commentary on World Issues, April 25, 2014, dansmithsblog.com/2014/04/25/the-conflict-horizon-3-only-connect/.

304 Carol Smaldino, in a personal communication on April 21, 2013. Carol Smaldino is an esteemed member in our Human Dignity and Humiliation Studies fellowship.

305 "Rich People Just Care Less," by Daniel Goleman, New York Times, October 5, 2013, opinionator.blogs.nytimes.com/2013/10/05/rich-people-just-care-less/?_r=1&. See also Piff, et al., 2012.

306 Lindner, 2000a.

307 Linda Hartling in a personal communication on September 3, 2016.

308 Lindner, 2014c.

309 These atrocities committed are being labelled quasi genocide, since the victims, the members of the Isaaq clan, were not systematically exterminated, in contrast to Rwanda, for instance, where even "half-blood" were potential targets for extermination. Also, until the end of the genocide, there were Isaaq ministers in the government, something that would have been unthinkable in Rwanda. See the report by a United Nations employee who does not wish to be named, December 1998, Hargeisa, in Lindner, 2000a, p. 58.

310 Lindner, 2000a, p. 173.

311 Lindner, 2010a, pp. 22–23.

312 Waller, 1996, p. 4.

313 Arendt, 1963.

314 See Bar-Tal, et al., 2007, for a discussion of the societal implications of collective emotions, for example, in conflict situations.

315 Soleim, et al., 2015. See also "Risikerte livene sine – ble fratatt all ære," by Stig Brøndbo, February 19, 2015, https://uit.no/nyheter/artikkel?p_document_id=406292.

316 Sarajevo My Love, a film by Eylem Kaftan, published on June 12, 2013, https://youtu.be/nmuqWmALnjo. The film portrays Jovan Divjak, an ethnic Serb who defended Sarajevo against attack from Serb forces during the Bosnian war. I thank Ardian Adžanela for making us aware of this film and for introducing me to Jovan Divjak on August 7, 2016. See the video we created, Jovan Divjak Reflects on Human Dignity, https://youtu.be/3-oQecU8hLs.

317 Scholars who analyzed slavery note that sometimes a very special accommodation-resistance dialectic of obeying but not necessarily complying evolved, which allowed slaves to carve out a degree of autonomous and very distinctive culture, which eschewed the values embraced by the master class. See, for instance, Engerman and Genovese, 1975, and Smith, 1998.

318 Mazzetti, 2013. See the full note in the pdf edition of this book.

319 "The Change Within: The Obstacles We Face Are Not Just External," by Naomi Klein, The Nation, May 12, 2014, www.thenation.com/article/179460/change-within-obstacles-we-face-are-not-just-external#. I thank Rigmor Johnsen for making me aware of this article.

320 Merz, 2012.

321 Ibid.

322 Linda Hartling in a personal communication on September 3, 2016: "I don't like the term social capital ... because it comes from the frame of economics." See furthermore, Dennis Meadows' Foreword to Bernard Lietaer, et al., 2012. See also Goetzmann, 2016.

323 "It's the Egyptian Economy, Stupid," by Amitai Etzioni, National Interest, January 24, 2013, http://nationalinterest.org/commentary/its-the-egyptian-economy-stupid-7984.

324 Maalouf, 2009. See more in note 4 in the Introduction.

325 Tocqueville, 1856. See also "The Future by Al Gore – Review," by John Gray, The Guardian, January 31, 2013, www.theguardian.com/books/2013/jan/31/the-future-al-gore-review. See Gore, 2013.

326 There are voices, however, who suspect that more sinister intentions may have been behind the "Arab Spring" uprisings and the chaos in the Middle East in general, namely, that it rather was a chaos stoked from outside. See "Barack Obama's Meager Legacy of Incomplete Accomplishments and of Provoked Wars: What Happened?" by Rodrigue Tremblay, May 30, 2016, www.thecodeforglobalethics.com/pb/wp_0b5e796a/wp_0b5e796a.html#LEGACY. See more by Canadian economist Rodrigue Tremblay, 2010. See also "The Redirection: Is the Administration's New Policy Benefitting Our Enemies in the War on Terrorism?" by Seymour M. Hersh, New Yorker, Annals of National Security, March 5, 2007, www.newyorker.com/magazine/2007/03/05/the-redirection.

327 Utvik, 2006. I thank Petter Nesser for making me aware of Utvik's work.

328 See note 162 in the Preface.

329 See note 295 in the Introduction, and note 114 in the Inspiring Questions to Section Two.

330 2016 Annual Conference of Human Dignity and Humiliation Studies, "Enlarging the Boundaries of Compassion," in Dubrovnik, Croatia, September 19 – 23, 2016, www.humiliationstudies.org/whoweare/annualmeeting/27.php

331 Motzfeldt Loades, 2016, p. 34.

332 Krüger, 2013.

333 "How Spin Doctors Destroyed Our Democracy – and What We Can Do to Repair It," by Andreas Whittam Smith, The Independent, July 13, 2016, www.independent.co.uk/voices/broken-democracy-spin-doctors-destroyed-uk-politics-theresa-may-repair-it-a7135146.html. Andreas Whittam Smith is The Independent's founding editor, and in this article, he explains how the professionalization of politics has turned the business of Westminster into a brand, with dangerous consequences. I thank Kamran Mofid for making me aware of this article. See also Oborne, 2007.

334 "The Moral Collapse of U.S. and Global Society – and the Necessary Conditions for Rebirth," by Glen T. Martin, OpEdNews, April 29, 2014, www.opednews.com/articles/The-Moral-Collapse-of-U-S-by-Dr-Glen-T-Martin-Democracy_Earth_Morality-Morals_Values-140429-270.html. I thank Ernesto Kahan for making us aware of this article. It is a privilege to have Ernesto Kahan and Glen Martin as esteemed members in the global advisory board of our Human Dignity and Humiliation Studies fellowship.

335 "World Drug Report 2016," by the United Nations Office on Drugs and Crime (UNODC), www.unodc.org/doc/wdr2016/WORLD_DRUG_REPORT_2016_web.pdf. Heroin use and related overdose deaths have increased sharply over the last two years in some countries in North America and Western and

Central Europe, with new psychoactive substances remaining a serious concern: "heroin continues to be the drug that kills the most people and this resurgence must be addressed urgently."

336 Lane, 2001.

337 Linda Hartling in a personal communication on September 3, 2016.

338 Lindner, 2012f.

339 See note 278 in the Introduction.

340 "Schleichende Pathologisierung der Gesellschaft," Werner Seppmann über die Zunahme von Gewalt und Irrationalismus in der Gesellschaft, interviewed von Reinhard Jellen, Teil 2, heise online, November 23, 2011, www.heise.de/tp/artikel/35/35916/1.html. Translated from German by Lindner: "Daily competition is made absolute by people, made subjective and personal, and accepted as natural and without alternative, if not even declared to be part of the realm of freedom. In that way, people practice and internalize the very exclusion that is shown to them by the institutions." See the German original in the full note in the pdf edition of this book.

341 Trojanow, 2013. Translated from the German original by Lindner: "An essay on human dignity in late capitalism. Those who produce nothing and consume nothing are superfluous, according to the murderous logic of late capitalism. Overpopulation is the biggest problem of our planet, this is the opinion of international elites. But if humanity is to be reduced, then who is going to disappear, asks Trojanov in his humanist polemic against the superfluity of humans. In his penetrating analysis, he runs the gamut from the ravages of climate change on the mercilessness of neoliberal labor market policies to the mass media apocalypses that we, the apparent winner, follow with enthusiasm. But we deceive ourselves: It is also about us. Everything is at stake." See the German original in the full note in the pdf edition of this book.

342 "Warren Buffet on Derivatives," www.fintools.com/docs/Warren%20Buffet%20on%20Derivatives.pdf, edited excerpts from the Berkshire Hathaway annual report for 2002.

343 Neues aus der Anstalt, with Urban Priol, Erwin Pelzig, Georg Schramm, Jochen Malmsheimer, Volker Pispers, and Max Uthoff, Zweites Deutsches Fernsehen, October 1, 2013, www.zdf.de/ZDFmediathek/#/beitrag/video/1997428/Neues-aus-der-Anstalt-vom-1-Oktober. Summary in German by Lindner in the full note in the pdf edition of this book.

344 Rich, 1994, 2013, Brown, 2012b. Even if only ten percent of what John Perkins, 2004, has to say is true, it is profoundly worrying. See also an interview by Mike McCormick of Talking Stick TV in Seattle, at https://youtu.be/yTbdnNgqfs8.

345 Oxley, 2012.

346 See note 82 in this Chapter 15.

347 A book by Eric Schlosser, 2013, is based on previously classified material that the author discovered through the Freedom of Information Act in the U.S.A. See more in note 2 in the Introduction to Section Three.

348 R. Buckminster Fuller said in "The New York Magazine Environmental Teach-In" by Elizabeth Barlow, New York Magazine, March 30, 1970, see books.google.de/books?id=cccDAAAAMBAJ&printsec=frontcover&redir_esc=y#v=onepage&q&f=false, p. 30: "We should do away with the absolutely specious notion that everybody has to earn a living. It is a fact today that one in ten thousand of us can make a technological breakthrough capable of supporting all the rest. The youth of today are absolutely right in recognizing this nonsense of earning a living. We keep inventing jobs because of this false idea that everybody has to be employed at some kind of drudgery because, according to Malthusian Darwinian theory he must justify his right to exist. So we have inspectors of inspectors and people making instruments for inspectors to inspect inspectors. The true business of

people should be to go back to school and think about whatever it was they were thinking about before somebody came along and told them they had to earn a living."

349 Tom Bowerman, Director of PolicyInteractive Research, policyinteractive.org, February 1, 2017: "The top five ordering of priorities for workplace choice from highest to lowest are: 1) doing a job I can be proud of; 2) enjoying work, having fun; 3) being with people I respect; 4) earning a good salary; and 5) learning new things, having new experiences."

350 See note 40 in the Introduction.

351 Journalist Janne Teller made a good case for macro-economic pressures leading people to look for scapegoats, in Culture Magazine Aspekte, in Zweites Deutsches Fernsehen, May 9, 2014, www.zdf.de/aspekte/kultur-im-zdf-aspekte-themen-am-9.-mai-2014-mit-mando-diao-janne-teller-katty-salie-bibiana-beglau-rechtsruck-in-ungarn-33026630.html. See the full note in the pdf edition of this book. See also "Partners in Crime? The EU, Its Strategic Partners and International Organised Crime," Fride: A European Think Tank for Global Action (FRIDE ceased its think tank activities on December 31, 2015, for economic reasons), www.fride.org/descarga/WP5_EU_Strategic_partners_and_international_organised_crime.pdf, page 7: "Increasingly, terrorist groups resort to criminal activities to fund their campaigns, when they have not traded political aims for economic gain." In March 2016, The National Consortium for the Study of Terrorism and Responses to Terrorism – better known as START – launched an online course on "The Terror-Crime Nexus and Chemical, Biological, Radiological and Nuclear (CBRN) Threats." START is a university-based research and education center comprised of an international network of scholars committed to the scientific study of the causes and human consequences of terrorism in the United States and around the world, www.start.umd.edu/news/start-launches-online-course-terror-crime-nexus-and-cbrn.

352 "De nye gigantene," by Bent Sofus Tranøy, Klassekampen, July 5, 2014, www.klassekampen.no/article/20140705/PLUSS/140709933, p. 3.

353 Piketty, 2013/2014.

354 Haldane, 2004. Another author is Adair Turner, 2012, working with Institute of New Economic Thinking (INET), a think tank financed by the hedge fund billionaire George Soros.

355 "Inequality and Democracy," by Roberto Savio, Other News, May 17, 2014, www.other-news.info/2014/05/inequality-and-democracy/. See notes 93 and 177 in Chapter 11.

356 Polanyi and Joseph E. Stiglitz (Foreword), 1944/2001.

357 See note 295 in the Introduction, and note 114 in the Inspiring Questions to Section Two.

358 "My Uncle sold Me for 170 Dollars to Be a Suicide Bomber," by Subel Bhandari and Hares Kakar, Deutsche Presse-Agentur, November 30, 2011, found on www.rawa.org/temp/runews/2011/11/30/my-uncle-sold-me-for-170-dollars-to-be-a-suicide-bomber.html. News from the Revolutionary Association of the Women of Afghanistan (RAWA).

359 Koenigs, 2007. For those who wish to acquire a feel for the pathways of radicalization, Koenigs recommends Updike, 2006.

360 Koenigs, 2007, p. 3–4.

361 "The Next Great American Consumer: Infants to 3-Year-Olds: They're a New Demographic Marketers are Hell-Bent on Reaching," by Brian Braiker, Adweek, September 26, 2011, www.adweek.com/news/advertising-branding/next-great-american-consumer-135207. According to Victor C. Strasburger, professor of pediatrics at the University of New Mexico School of Medicine, children under the age of seven are "psychologically defenseless" against advertising. "We've created a perfect storm for childhood obesity – media, advertising, and inactivity," said Strasburger as lead author of a policy statement

published June 27, 2011, by the American Academy of Pediatrics (AAP) Council on Communications and Media. "American society couldn't do a worse job at the moment of keeping children fit and healthy – too much TV, too many food ads, not enough exercise, and not enough sleep," he said, quoted from aap.org/advocacy/releases/june2711studies.htm, referring to the Council on Communications and Media, 2011. See also Strasburger, et al., 2013.

In Sweden, all advertisements aimed at children under the age of twelve have been banned. In the U.S., business is trying to prevent regulation on advertising to children, see "Will Food Industry's New Marketing Guidelines Satisfy the Feds?," by Katy Bachman, Adweek, July 15, 2011, www.adweek.com/news/advertising-branding/will-food-industrys-new-marketing-guidelines-satisfy-feds-133437.

It seems that the language of "values" and "ecology" has been applied to the market in particularly blunt ways in the U.S., see the self-representation of the Right Media Exchange, the Platform for Premium Digital Advertising, www.rightmediablog.com (discontinued by Yahoo in 2015). See the full note in the pdf edition of this book.

362 Lebow, 1955.

363 Ibid.

364 6th Julius Nyerere Annual Lecture on Lifelong Learning "Engaging Critically with Tradition, Culture, and Patriarchy through Lifelong Learning: What would Julius Nyerere say?" By Catherine A. Odora Hoppers, University of the Western Cape, September 3, 2009.

365 Lindner, 2012f.

366 In Richards, 2013. See also Richards, 1995, and Richards, 1995, Richards and Swanger, 2006b, a.

367 See note 8 in Chapter 4, and note 368 further down.

368 "The Future of the United States of America," by Howard Richards, TRANSCEND Media Service, January 2, 2017, www.transcend.org/tms/2017/01/the-future-of-the-united-states-of-america/:

Already in the second century after Christ the Romans needed a Great Simplification. Like the British in the nineteenth century, the Romans in the second century found that they could not trade or govern in a vast diverse empire without imposing some simplicity on it. Roman law, and especially the jus gentium that applied alike to Roman citizens and to non-citizens, was a Great Simplification, and by the same token it was an eclipse of community. The empire was an overwhelming military force interested in collecting tribute and in protecting merchants, but not interested in how its component ethnic groups gave meaning to their lives and exchanged matter and energy with the physical environment. The law abstracted from the empire's multicultural diversity with its wealth of languages, spiritual and material practices, moral codes, kinship and marriage obligations, patterns of mutual obligations, ceremonies, rituals, and stories. Simplifying for the sake of commerce and for the sake of public administration, it classified certain rules as "natural." The word "natural" meant "the same everywhere." In practice, "everywhere" meant "wherever Rome rules."

Fast forwarding past the Middle Ages, a millennium and a half later, in the sixteenth to eighteenth centuries, the successor states of the Roman Empire were constructing the cultural and social structures of modernity. For their Great Simplification, they "received" the ideal of rule of law that antiquity had bequeathed them, but only to encounter another obstacle to modernization. Living in a Europe (formerly known as "Christendom") dotted with great cathedrals, the modernizers had to achieve a certain distance from God. God had then and still has today the inconvenient trait of telling people what to do. ("Islam" means "submission" or "submission of desires to the will of God.") It was impossible to build a social and cultural structure around market exchange while God was constantly butting in commanding people to feed the hungry, give drink to the thirsty, clothe the naked, bury the dead, shelter the traveler, comfort the sick, and ransom the captive (the traditional Seven Works of Mercy, roughly following Matthew 25: 31-46).

Enlightenment minds like Jean-Jacques Rousseau rose to the occasion by substituting "Nature" for "God" (comparing the Spiritual Exercises of Saint Ignatius and Emile by Rousseau will show that wherever Ignatius wrote "God" Rousseau wrote "Nature"). What Nature commanded was first and foremost what Roman law said was natural, which was in turn first and foremost the constitutive rules of markets. Although the idea that Nature had decreed laissez faire economics framed by a social contract guaranteeing pre-existing natural rights, encountered much opposition in France and in England with their long and complex intellectual traditions, it encountered little opposition in the new United States of America. As has been outlined above, once such ideas and their corresponding institutions are in place it becomes inevitable, or nearly so, that the physical welfare of the people will come to depend on an always precarious confidence of investors. It was not the 1% who created the double whammy to serve their own interests, and it was not created during Ronald Reagan's presidency in the 1980s. The double whammy was created by history; its roots go back at least to an eclipse of community in the second century; and it does not serve anybody's interests.

369 McCauley, et al., 2013.

370 Richards, 2013.

371 See note 8 in Chapter 4. See also note 368 in Chapter 15.

372 See, among others, Dewey, 1905.

373 See note 98 in Chapter 9.

374 See note 162 in the Preface.

375 Bhaskar, 2008.

376 Giddens, 1990. See more in note 130 in Chapter 11.

377 See note 163 in the Preface.

378 Richards, 2013.

379 Wood, 2003.

380 Mies, 1986.

381 Howard Richards refers to Vivienne Jabri, 2007, director of the Centre for International Relations and Senior Lecturer in International Relations in the Department of War Studies, King's College London.

382 See, among others, Richards, 1995, Richards, 2004, Richards and Swanger, 2006b, and also Bhaskar, 1986. The phrase "social structure" is a contested concept, and in resonance with Douglas Porpora, 2015, Howard Richards defines social structure as "material relations among social positions and social constructs." See "The Future of the United States of America," in Howard Richards, TRANSCEND Media Service, January 2, 2017, www.transcend.org/tms/2017/01/the-future-of-the-united-states-of-america/, and Porpora, 1993: "Although the social relations (like the relation of buyer to seller, or the relation of employer to employee), the social positions (like the position of owner), and the social constructs (like contracts) are constituted by cultural rules, the social structure thus constituted is material."

383 I thank Linda Hartling for emphasizing the centrality of human relationships.

384 Lindner, 2012f.

385 Jervis, 2006.

386 Lindner and Desmond Tutu (Foreword), 2010.

387 Peace researcher Nils Petter Gleditsch, 2012, for instance, calls for more recognition for what the peace movement has achieved. He refers to pioneers of the peace movement such as Sonja Lid, co-founder of the first peace office (fredskontor) in Norway in 1962, when Cold War nuclear bomb testing endangered the health of people. He refers to Joshua Goldstein, 2011, to James Payne, 2004, or Steven Pinker, 2011, see also

Lacina, et al., 2006. It is a great privilege for me to know both Sonja Lid and Nils Petter Gleditsch. I admire their work infinitely, see an overview over the work of the peace offices in Røed-Larsen and Hjort-Larsen, 2012.

388 "Inequality and Democracy," by Roberto Savio, Other News, May 17, 2014, www.other-news.info/2014/05/inequality-and-democracy/. See notes 93 and 177 in Chapter 11.

389 See www.oxfam.org/en/pressroom/pressrelease/2013-01-19/annual-income-richest-100-people-enough-end-global-poverty-four-times.

390 World Commission on Environment and Development and Brundtland, 1987.

391 Raskin, et al., 2002. See also Raskin, 2008, and Brangwyn and Hopkins, .

392 Raskin, 2014, p. 4. Sustainability, unfortunately, is yet another term that has been hijacked by economism throughout the past years. Within the international legal system, "a resource economics definition of sustainability encourages development, while granting dispensation to public choice that sacrifices human and environmental integrity for instrumental economic objectives" writes philosopher John Martin Gillroy in his contribution to the Great Transition Network (GTN) discussion on the topic of "Sustainability and Well-Being: A Happy Synergy," March 3, 2017, in response to Barrington-Leigh, 2017.

393 Raskin, 2014, p. 4.

394 Raskin, 2014, p. 7.

395 Razeto-Barry and Canals, 2015.

396 "10 Insights on the Ego-2-Eco Economy Revolution," by Otto Scharmer, September 10, 2013, www.blog.ottoscharmer.com/?p=557. Otto Scharmer is a Senior Lecturer at MIT and founding chair of the Presencing Institute. See also Scharmer and Kaufer, 2013. I thank Lynn King, Chinese American global leadership coach, trainer, and consultant, for talking to me about Otto Scharmer's work. It is a privilege to have Lynn King as esteemed members in the global advisory board of our Human Dignity and Humiliation Studies fellowship.

397 See note 171 in Chapter 1.

398 "The Mythology of Freedom and Democracy," by Dhananjayan Sriskandarajah, Inter Press Service (IPS), November 7, 2016, www.ipsnews.net/2016/11/the-mythology-of-freedom-and-democracy/. Women who step up to defend human rights are facing worsening obstacles amid a global trend of fundamentalism and populism, a group of United Nations experts has warned, see "Fundamentalism and Populism Pose Deepening Threat to Women Human Rights Defenders, UN Experts Warn," United Nations News Centre, November 25, 2016, www.un.org/apps/news/story.asp?NewsID=55645#.WDniRH2OWgx.

399 Maria Dahle, at the occasion of the United Nations' 60-years Jubilee in 2008 in Oslo, and the OSCE conference in 2011 in Warsaw. Maria Dahle shared her insights with me in person in Oslo on February 13, 2013. The Office for Democratic Institutions and Human Rights (ODIHR) is the principal institution of the Organization for Security and Cooperation in Europe (OSCE). ODIHR organizes an annual meeting in Warsaw to review the implementation of a broad range of OSCE human dimension commitments, including in the areas of human rights and fundamental freedoms, elections, the promotion of tolerance, use of the death penalty, and the rights of national minorities. The Human Dimension Implementation Meeting (HDIM) lasts 10 working days and is attended by representatives of OSCE participating States, NGOs, and international organizations and institutions. See Dahle, 2011. See also Dahle, 2008.

400 "World Report 2017: Demagogues Threaten Human Rights: Trump, European Populists Foster Bigotry, Discrimination," Human Rights Watch, January 12, 2017, www.hrw.org/news/2017/01/12/world-report-2017-demagogues-threaten-human-rights.

401 "The New Brexit and Trumpian World Order: Will They Engulf Europe and the Rest of the World?" by Kamran Mofid, Globalization for the Common Good Initiative (GCGI), November 12, 2016,

www.gcgi.info/index.php/blog/830-will-brexit-trump-style-revolt-engulf-europe-and-the-rest-of-the-world#.WCeGvatiQKc.gmail.

402 Jones, 2011. See also Jones, 2008.

403 "Why Gender Equality Stalled," by Stephanie Coontz, New York Times, February 16, 2013, www.nytimes.com/2013/02/17/opinion/sunday/why-gender-equality-stalled.html?pagewanted=all&_r=0. See real median household income in the United States, according to the Census Bureau's annual figures, https://fred.stlouisfed.org/series/MEHOINUSA672N.

404 "Individual and Human Rights," by Howard Richards, by Chileufú, October 20, 2016, http://chileufu.cl/individual-and-human-rights/.

405 "Turning the United States Around," by Howard Richards, Chileufú, http://chileufu.cl/turning-the-united-states-around/.

406 Bastiat, 1848, French original: "Lorsque la Spoliation est devenue le moyen d'existence d'une agglomération d'hommes unis entre eux par le lien social, ils se font bientôt une loi qui la sanctionne, une morale qui la glorifie."

407 Bastiat, 1848, French original: "Je parle à quiconque tient la Richesse pour quelque chose. – Entendons par ce mot, non l'opulence de quelques-uns, mais l'aisance, le bien-être, la sécurité, l'indépendance, l'instruction, la dignité de tous."

408 Bastiat, 1850.

409 Bastiat's reflections remind of the thinking that Ayn Rand later brought to the United States later; see my analysis in Chapter 4 of Lindner, 2012f. See also note 32 in Chapter 4.

410 "Against Foucault: Middle Foucault, Part Twelve," video lecture by Howard Richards, Pretoria, South Africa, May 26, 2013, taped by Justine Richards, youtu.be/voUdwSZPAR0. See also the book that resulted from these lectures and dialogues, Richards, et al., 2015a. In this lecture, Richards analyzed the middle period of Foucault's thinking (1970 – 1976): "Even before Foucault cast power in the role of general enemy, power had been groomed for the role because it had played a somewhat similar role in the past. Whatever else 'power' ('le pouvoir') denoted, power was the entity that had re-established itself by putting down the revolts in France in 1848, in 1870, and in 1940. (Foucault and Deleuze, 1972, p. 308) It tended to be the word that named whatever put down popular revolts anywhere; so that if the revolt was successful one said the people won; if the revolt failed one said power won."

411 Richards, 2014: "So we have a problem: Nothing authorizes us to believe that humanity today is so different from humanity in the past that today we can get our act together and work in concert to solve our problems without sharing a metanarrative that tells us who we are and what our role is in the great scheme of things. But liberal economics is a toxic brew. It shreds community more than it builds it. It smothers diversity and imposes the crudest and most violent forms of cognitive injustice. Its growth imperative and its systematic demand to create conditions for capital accumulation and ever more capital accumulation are killing the biosphere very rapidly, so rapidly that if we think in a perspective of geological time the end of life on this planet is the equivalent of only a few seconds away. Sometimes we seem to face a cruel choice: either no metanarrative or a toxic metanarrative. Either civil wars between mutually incompatible ethnic fundamentalisms which in principle can share no common ground, or else a secular state imposing certain death by liberal economics on one and all. ... My second simple question is: 'Where are we going?' The beginning of a simple answer is: 'We are going to a green future.' The simple reason why we are going to a green future is that we cannot possibly go to any other future. Failing to maintain the delicate equilibriums of the biosphere is not an option. Human cultures whose constitutive rules and basic norms are incompatible with the laws of physics, the laws of chemistry, and the facts of biology are not sustainable."

412 "Against Foucault: Middle Foucault, Part Twelve," video lecture by Howard Richards, Pretoria, South Africa, May 26, 2013, taped by Justine Richards, youtu.be/voUdwSZPAR0. See also the book that resulted from these lectures and dialogues, Richards, et al., 2015a. In this lecture, Richards analyzed the middle period of Foucault's thinking (1970 – 1976).

413 "Ein katastrophaler Fehler": SPIEGEL-Gespräch Der amerikanische Historiker Timothy Snyder über die Vorbedingungen des Holocaust – und die gefährlichen Folgen unbedachter Nahostpolitik, Der Spiegel 44/2015, November 24, 2015, pp. 140–143. See the original German text, pp. 140–141, in the full note in the pdf edition of this book. See also Snyder, 2010, 2015, 2017.

414 "Carly Fiorina: 'This Is How Socialism Starts,'" by Greg Richter, NewsMax, November 10, 2015, www.newsmax.com/Headline/carly-fiorina-dodd-frank-how-socialism/2015/11/10/id/701604/.

415 Dignity-ism or dignism, see, among others, Lindner, 2012f: A world where every newborn finds space and is nurtured to unfold their highest and best, embedded in a social context of loving appreciation and connection. A world, where the carrying capacity of the planet guides the ways in which everybody's basic needs are met, a world, where we are united in respecting human dignity and celebrating diversity, where we prevent unity from being perverted into oppressive uniformity, and keep diversity from sliding into hostile division.

416 See note 98 in Chapter 9.

417 "Against Foucault: Early Foucault, Part Three," video lecture by Howard Richards, Pretoria, South Africa, May 6, 2013, taped by Justine Richards, http://youtu.be/OD001HfydoY. See also the book that resulted from these lectures and dialogues, Richards, et al., 2015a.

418 Inspired by Howard Richards' lecture "Against Foucault: Early Foucault, Part Ten," Catherine Odora Hoppers and Evelin Lindner engaged in a dialogue with Howard Richards, Pretoria, South Africa, May 22, 2013, taped by Justine Richards, https://youtu.be/wZoikaoun7E. See also the book that resulted from these lectures and dialogues, Richards, et al., 2015a. See the full note in the pdf edition of this book.

419 Boyd and Richerson, 2009.

420 Karlberg, 2004, p. 2.

421 Galtung, 1977, pp. 59–65.

422 Haavelsrud, 2015, pp. 54–55.

423 Maalouf, 2009. See more in note 4 in the Introduction.

424 Maalouf, 2009.

Chapter 16

1 George Washington (1732 – 1799) was the first President of the United States, and he stepped down, even though he could have stayed on in power. In his Farewell Address of 1796, he warns future generations of the political dangers to avoid for the original values of the country to prevail. Among others, he warns against the "impostures of pretended patriotism" of people who thrive on division rather than unity. See the Address at http://avalon.law.yale.edu/18th_century/washing.asp.

2 The Bible, English Standard Version, Hosea 8:7: "For they sow the wind, and they shall reap the whirlwind." See also Lüders, 2015. See a book about Western interventions in Iran, Iraq, and Syria, by correspondent Michael Lüders, 2017, with the same title.

3 "To sow dragon's teeth," is a metaphor that refers to actions that lead to conflict. In Greek mythology, it is part of the classical legends of Cadmus and Jason. According to legend, dragon's teeth grow into fully armed warriors after being sown.

4 Translated by Lindner from "Die ich rief, die Geister, werd' ich nun nicht los," in Der Zauberlehrling.

5 This proverb was shared by Adil Abd al-Mahdi, a former Iraqi vice-president, see "Letter from Iraq: What We Left Behind: An Increasingly Authoritarian Leader, a Return of Sectarian Violence, and a Nation Worried for Its Future," by Dexter Filkins, New Yorker, April 28, 2014, www.newyorker.com/magazine/2014/04/28/what-we-left-behind.

6 See note 79 in Chapter 3.

7 Harari, 2015/2016, and "Homo Sapiens 2.0? We Need a Species-Wide Conversation About the Future of Human Genetic Enhancement," by Jamie Metzl, TechCrunch, May 1, 2016, https://techcrunch.com/2016/05/01/homo-sapiens-2-0-we-need-a-species-wide-conversation-about-the-future-of-human-genetic-enhancement/.

8 "ISIS Atrocities and US Imperialism," by Patrick Martin, World Socialist Web Site (WSWS), September 4, 2014, www.wsws.org/en/articles/2014/09/04/pers-s04.html.

9 American Experience: Henry Ford, documentary film as part of the collection The Titans, WGBH Educational Foundation, 2012, www.pbs.org/wgbh/americanexperience/films/henryford/.

10 "The Neurochemistry of Power: Implications for Political Change," by Nayef Al-Rodhan, Politics in Spires, University of Cambridge, February 27, 2014, http://politicsinspires.org/neurochemistry-power-implications-political-change/. Nayef Al-Rodhan is a philosopher, neuroscientist, and geostrategist. He is a senior member of St. Antony's College at Oxford University, Oxford, United Kingdom, Senior Fellow and director of the Centre for the Geopolitics of Globalization and Transnational Security at the Geneva Centre for Security Policy, Geneva, Switzerland. See his work in Al-Rodhan, 2008, 2009.

11 Eymericus, 1578. Latin original: "...quoniam punitio non refertur primo & per se in correctionem & bonum eius qui punitur, sed in bonum publicum ut alij terreantur, & a malis committendis avocentur."

12 Kirsch, 2008.

13 "The Sheikh Who Lifted the Veil: Talking to Sheikh Mustapha Rashid," by Myra Abdallah, Now, June 26, 2014, https://now.mmedia.me/lb/en/interviews/553382-the-sheikh-who-lifted-the-veil. I thank Vidal Ruse for making me aware of this article.

14 "Telling the Truth About ISIS and Raqqa," by David Remnick, New Yorker, November 22, 2016, www.newyorker.com/news/news-desk/telling-the-truth-about-isis-and-raqqa.

15 "How to Win a War and Lose the Peace," by Paddy Ashdown, The Telegraph, October 15, 2006, www.telegraph.co.uk/news/uknews/1531454/How-to-win-a-war-and-lose-the-peace.html.

16 "The Problem with Iraq's Offensive against the Islamic State," IRIN – Humanitarian news and analysis (a service of the UN Office for the Coordination of Humanitarian Affairs), March 2, 2015, www.irinnews.org/report/101183/the-problem-with-iraq-s-offensive-against-the-islamic-state.

17 Ibid.

18 "Iraq Crisis: How Saudi Arabia Helped Isis Take over the North of the Country," by Patrick Cockburn, The Independent, July 13, 2014, www.independent.co.uk/voices/comment/iraq-crisis-how-saudi-arabia-helped-isis-take-over-the-north-of-the-country-9602312.html.

19 Ibid.

20 Ibid.

21 "Syria Archbishop Calls on West to Back President Bashar al-Assad in War Against Islamist Rebels," by Colin Freeman, The Telegraph, October 13, 2015,

www.telegraph.co.uk/news/worldnews/middleeast/syria/11929694/Syria-archbishop-calls-on-West-to-back-President-Bashar-al-Assad-in-war-against-Islamist-rebels.html.

22 "Die Türkei ist das Drehkreuz des globalen Dschihad," by Banu Güven and Claus Christian Malzahn, Die Welt, September 9, 2014, www.welt.de/politik/ausland/article132246350/Die-Tuerkei-ist-das-Drehkreuz-des-globalen-Dschihad.html. See also Türkei – Drehkreuz des Terrors? documentary film by Halil Gülbeyaz, Norddeutscher Rundfunk, 2016, www.arte.tv/guide/de/065356-000-A/tuerkei-drehkreuz-des-terrors. See the full note in the pdf edition of this book. During the 2010 Annual Conference of Human Dignity and Humiliation Studies, "Peace at Home, Peace in the World," in Istanbul, Turkey, April 28–30, 2010, we were able to gain deep insight into the psychological depth of this situation, see also www.humiliationstudies.org/whoweare/annualmeeting/15.php.

23 Les pharaons de l'Egypte moderne / Pharao im heutigen Ägypten, documentary film by Jihan El Tahri, Arte France 2015, part 1: Gamal Abdel Nasser, http://tinyurl.com/z5k5rrf, part 2: Anwar el-Sadat, http://tinyurl.com/gn58p53, part 3: Husni Mubarak, http://tinyurl.com/gndcoq3. See the full note in the pdf edition of this book.

24 Al-Aswany, 2002/2004, Al-Aswany, 2015, column written for Al-Masry Al-Youm, January 20, 2014.

25 See note 23 above.

26 See, for instance, Delkatesh, 2011. There are voices, however, who suspect that more sinister intentions may have been behind the "Arab Spring" uprisings and the chaos in the Middle East in general, namely, that it rather was a chaos stoked from outside. See more in note 326 in Chapter 15.

27 Al-Aswany, 2015, column written for Al-Masry Al-Youm, January 20, 2014.

28 Ennahdha – Une histoire tunisienne / Ennahdha – Tunesien im Wandel, by Christophe Cotteret, Arte France / Belgium, 2011, http://tinyurl.com/hnuehnp. See the full note in the pdf edition of this book.

29 On June 9, 2014, Tunisia launched a Truth and Dignity Commission (TDC) to establish the truth about human rights violations, thus joining more than forty other countries that have instituted truth commissions in the aftermath of massive human rights abuses, https://youtu.be/rLGa3EuEZQo.

30 "Think Again: Failed States," by James Traub, Foreign Policy, June 20, 2011, http://foreignpolicy.com/2011/06/20/think-again-failed-states/. See also Guns, Briefcases, and Inequality: The Neglected War in Kachin State + Prospects for Peace and National Reconciliation in Burma/Myanmar, presentation by Alex Moodie from the Burma Partnership, who spoke about the looting of Burma and how the new way of conquering is military-connected business "investment," on March 9, 2014, at the 2014 Annual Conference of Human Dignity and Humiliation Studies, "Returning Dignity," in Chiang Mai, Thailand, March 8–12, 2014, www.humiliationstudies.org/whoweare/annualmeeting/23.php.

31 Les pharaons de l'Egypte moderne / Pharao im heutigen Ägypten, documentary film by Jihan El Tahri, Arte France 2015, part 3: Husni Mubarak, http://tinyurl.com/gndcoq3. See the full note in the pdf edition of this book.

32 "Pathway to Dictatorship: How Donald Trump Would Reshape America," by Thomas Homer-Dixon, co-authored with Jack Goldstone, Toronto Globe and Mail, October 17, 2016, www.homerdixon.com/2016/10/18/how-donald-trump-would-reshape-america/. It is a privilege to have Jack Goldstone as esteemed member in the global advisory board of our Human Dignity and Humiliation Studies fellowship.

33 Paul Richards, in his September 2006 talks.

34 For an English text, see, among many others, "Anders Behring Breivik Attacks Inspired by Serbian Nationalists, Court Hears," The Guardian, April 18, 2012, www.theguardian.com/world/2012/apr/18/anders-behring-breivik-serb-nationalists. See, furthermore, among innumerable publications in Norway, Borchgrevink, 2012.

35 See Anders Behring Breivik's Complete Manifesto "2083 – A European Declaration of Independence: De Laude Novae Militiae, Pauperes commilitones Christi Templique Solomonici," by Andrew Berwick (anglicized pseudonym of Anders Breivik), July 22, 2011, 1515 pages, as he posted it online at https://publicintelligence.net/anders-behring-breiviks-complete-manifesto-2083-a-european-declaration-of-independence/. See a complete list of comments Anders Behring Breivik has left at Document.no at www.document.no/anders-behring-breivik/, July 23, 2011. What is being called "right-wing" extremism expresses itself in two main branches in Norway, with a smaller branch focusing on race, which would include anti-Semitism, and a larger branch, to which also Breivik belonged, focusing on culture and nation. See an in-depth analysis of Breivik's' terrorist operation in Hemmingby and Bjørgo, 2016, and an analysis of Breivik's ideas in Kjos, 2013, and an account of how he grew up in Seierstad, 2013/2015. See more in note 22 in the Preface.

36 See also Stadtwald, 1992.

37 See also Grønnerød, et al., 2016.

38 "Max Blumenthal: Anders Behring Breivik, a Perfect Product of the Axis of Islamophobia," July 23, 2011, http://maxblumenthal.com/2011/07/anders-behring-breivik-a-perfect-product-of-the-axis-of-islamophobia/. See more in note 35 above.

39 Max Blumenthal: Anders Behring Breivik, a Perfect Product of the Axis of Islamophobia," July 23, 2011, http://maxblumenthal.com/2011/07/anders-behring-breivik-a-perfect-product-of-the-axis-of-islamophobia/. See more in note 35 above.

40 "Oslo Suspect Wrote of Fear of Islam and Plan for War," by Steven Erlanger, and Scott Shane, New York Times, July 23, 2011, www.nytimes.com/2011/07/24/world/europe/24oslo.html?_r=1&nl=todaysheadlines&emc=tha2. See more work by Hegghammer, 2010/2011, and Hegghammer and Norwegian Defence Research Establishment (FFI), 2013.

41 "The Rise of the Macro-Nationalists," by Thomas Hegghammer, New York Times, July 30, 2011, www.nytimes.com/2011/07/31/opinion/sunday/the-rise-of-the-macro-nationalists.html?_r=0.

42 See a new sociopolitical documentary film, Mad Dog: Gaddafi's Secret World, hosted by Christopher Olgiati, published by BBC, broadcasted as part of BBC Storyville series in 2014, www.bbc.co.uk/programmes/b03tj0n0.

43 "CIA Helped Gaddafi Torture Libyan Dissidents, Documents Show," by Joseph Fitsanakis, Intelnews.org, September 5, 2011, http://intelnews.org/2011/09/05/01-812/.

44 "Charles Taylor Conviction Upheld on Appeal: Judges Confirm 50-Year Prison Sentence for Liberian Ex-President," by Matthew Rhodes, International Justice, ICC, Institute for War and Peace Reporting (IWPR), ACR Issue 363, September 27, 2013, http://iwpr.net/report-news/charles-taylor-conviction-upheld-appeal. See also Charles Taylor Sentence, by The Human Rights Channel on YouTube, https://youtu.be/1OBj_Bx1njI?list=PL7826159DABA873FF.

45 "The Long Shadows of History," by Johan Galtung, TRANSCEND Media Service, September 15, 2014, www.transcend.org/tms/2014/09/the-long-shadows-of-history/.

46 There is a recent trend in Melanesian religious and political movements to discard the term cargo cult as being analytically and ethically inadequate, see, among others, Kaplan, 1995, Lindstrom, 1993. Others argue that the term remains useful, not least to understand the central moral and existential crisis flowing from the pressure on the traditional exchange system and notions of personhood and fairness that underlies cargo cults, and as "a vantage point for a culture-critical approach to Western society, as it challenges the sharp distinction between religious and economic values that makes it difficult to understand contemporary moral paradoxes," Otto, 2009, Abstract.

47 See Bugliosi and Gentry, 1992. See also The Trial of Charles Manson, by Douglas O. Linder, University of Missouri-Kansas City School of Law, 2008, http://law2.umkc.edu/faculty/projects/ftrials/manson/manson.html. Read the testimony of prosecution witness Paul Watkins about the meaning of Helter Skelter at "Testimony of Paul Watkins in the Charles Manson Trial," http://law2.umkc.edu/faculty/projects/ftrials/manson/mansontestimony-w.html, and read about "The Influence of the Beatles on Charles Manson," http://law2.umkc.edu/faculty/projects/ftrials/manson/mansonbeatles.html.

48 Researcher Lars Gule has personally discussed with Breivik on the Internet: "Forsker: – Breivik har 12–15.000 meningsfeller i Norge," Tim Peters, Eva-Therese Grøttum, Dennis Ravndal, Jarle Grivi Brenna, VG, June 1, 2012, www.vg.no/nyheter/innenriks/terrorangrepet-22-juli-rettssaken/forsker-breivik-har-12-15-000-meningsfeller-i-norge/a/10054092/. See the full note in the pdf edition of this book. See also Breivik's Ideas "Shared by Many," BBC Radio, July 25, 2011, http://news.bbc.co.uk/today/hi/today/newsid_9547000/9547585.stm. See more in note 35 above.

49 Steve Kulich at the Second International Conference on Multicultural Discourses in Hangzhou, April 13–15, 2007. See also Lindner, 2007c.

50 Wood, et al., 2009.

51 Baumeister, et al., 1996, in Madsen, 2014a, p. 612.

52 Madsen, 2014a, p. 621. See also "Botox-salget til himmels" (Sales of Botox rocketing), by Bodil Sundbye, VG, 2010, March 22, 2010, http://minmote.no/index.php/2010/03/botox-salget-til-himmels/. See the full note in the pdf edition of this book.

53 Madsen, 2014b, Rosenberg, et al., 1995.

54 Madsen, 2014a, pp. 621–622.

55 "Trening vs kirurgi" (Working out Versus Surgery), by Silje K. Førsund, Kvinner og Klær, July 16, 2010, pp. 11–18, p. 18. See also "How 'Empowerment' Became Something for Women to Buy," by Jia Tolentino, New York Times, April 12, 2016, www.nytimes.com/2016/04/17/magazine/how-empowerment-became-something-for-women-to-buy.html. I thank Linda Hartling for making me aware of this article.

56 Parker, 2003.

57 "South Korean Girls' Obsession with Double Eyelid Surgery as They Strive to Look Like 'Pretty Western Celebrities,'" by Daily Mail Reporter, Daily Mail, October 24, 2012, www.dailymail.co.uk/femail/article-2222481/South-Korean-girls-obsession-double-eyelid-surgery-strive-look-like-pretty-western-celebrities.html

58 "Images of 20 Chinese Women Before and After Plastic Surgery Draw Eyes Online," by Katie Nelson, Shanghaiist, November 10, 2014, http://shanghaiist.com/2014/11/10/20-women-before-after-plastic-surgery.php.

59 Yang, 2013.

60 The Space between Self-Esteem and Self Compassion, by Kristin Neff, TEDxCentennialParkWomen, February 6, 2013, https://youtu.be/IvtZBUSplr4. I thank Linda Hartling for making me aware of this talk. See also Neff, 2011. See, furthermore, among others, Lasch, 1991, Lasch, 1991, Putnam, 2000, Bushman and Baumeister, 1998, Baumeister, et al., 2003, Baumeister, 2005, Levine, 2007, Twenge and Campbell, 2009, Wood, et al., 2009, Ehrenreich, 2010, Twenge, et al., 2012, Twenge and Kasser, 2013, Twenge, 2014. See also how Howard Richards includes Foucault, 1961/2006, and Frank, 1961, in his chapter in Richards, 2013.

61 The Space between Self-Esteem and Self Compassion, by Kristin Neff, TEDxCentennialParkWomen, February 6, 2013, https://youtu.be/IvtZBUSplr4.

62 "On Shutdown, Waning US Influence, Syrian Showdown," Noam Chomsky interviewed by Harrison Samphir, Truthout, October 9, 2013, http://truth-out.org/news/item/19287-in-conversation-with-noam-chomsky-on-us-politics-global-affairs-and-capitalist-reform. In this interview, Noam Chomsky offers his perspective on the U.S. government shutdown, the Syrian civil war, capitalist reform in South America and more in a Truthout interview.

63 Ibid.

64 George Washington (1732 – 1799) was the first President of the United States, and he stepped down, even though he could have stayed on in power. In his Farewell Address of 1796, he warns future generations of the political dangers to be avoided for the original values of the country to prevail. See the Address at http://avalon.law.yale.edu/18th_century/washing.asp.

65 American president John F. Kennedy, in his inaugural address on January 20, 1961, www.jfklibrary.org/Asset-Viewer/BqXIEM9F4024ntFl7SVAjA.aspx.

66 "What Orwell Can Teach Us About the Language of Terror and War," by Rowan Williams, The Guardian, December 12, 2015, www.theguardian.com/books/2015/dec/12/words-on-war-a-summons-to-writers-orwell-lecture. This is an edited extract of the 2015 Orwell lecture with the full version available at theorwellprize.co.uk/the-orwell-lecture-2015/. I thank Ken Pope and Linda Hartling for making me aware of this article.

67 "The Orwellian Paradigm: Killing You, for Your Own Safety," by Faisal Moghul, Anti War, April 13, 2013, http://original.antiwar.com/faisal-moghul/2013/04/12/the-orwellian-paradigm/.

68 Shigeo Abe in Samurai and Idiots: The Olympus Affair. See more in note 181 in Chapter 15.

69 See note 66 above

70 "The Reign of Absurdiocy," by Uri Avnery, Human Wrongs Watch, November 30, 2015, http://human-wrongs-watch.net/2015/11/30/the-reign-of-absurdiocy/. Avnery explains how terrorism is a weapon, a method of operation, to frighten the victims into surrendering to the will of the terrorist, often used by oppressed peoples, for instance, the French Resistance to the Nazis in World War II.

71 "The Redirection: Is the Administration's New Policy Benefitting Our Enemies in the War on Terrorism?" by Seymour M. Hersh. See more in note 326 in Chapter 15.

72 "America's Imperial Delusion: The US Drive for World Domination Has No Historical Precedent," by Eric Hobsbawm, The Guardian, June 14, 2003, www.theguardian.com/world/2003/jun/14/usa.comment.

73 "On Shutdown, Waning US Influence, Syrian Showdown," Noam Chomsky interviewed by Harrison Samphir, Truthout, October 9, 2013, http://truth-out.org/news/item/19287-in-conversation-with-noam-chomsky-on-us-politics-global-affairs-and-capitalist-reform.

74 Beckwith, 2015. Kathy Beckwith summarized her research and her reasons for hopefulness in this way (personal message on April 21, 2016): "Once people learn why we've gone to war, and what alternatives we ignored, they'll question claims made today. They'll see the patterns of how war is sold. The truth is there are alternatives that offer more security and uphold justice far better, for a lot less cost and destruction, and there's no reason in the world we can't use them instead of war. I didn't start out with that book title; it came from what I discovered." It is a privilege to have Kathy Beckwith's book A Mighty Case Against War in our Dignity Press, www.dignitypress.org.

75 Johan Galtung in his endorsement of a book on NATO by sociologist and geopolitical analyst Mahdi Darius Nazemroaya, 2012: "A very timely book. Yes, US-led NATO is globalizing, like the US-led finance economy. No doubt also for it to protect the latter, the 'free market.' It is a classical case of overstretch to help save the crumbling US Empire and Western influence in general, by countries most of whom are bankrupt by their own economic mismanagement. All their interventions share two characteristics. The conflicts could have been solved with a little patience and creativity, but NATO does not want solutions. It

uses conflicts as raw material it can process into interventions to tell the world that it is the strongest in military terms. And, with the help of the mainstream media, it sees Hitler everywhere, in a Milosevic, a bin Laden, a Hussein, a Qaddafi, in Assad, insensitive to the enormous differences between all these cases. I hope this book will be read by very, very many who can turn this morbid fascination with violence into constructive conflict resolution." I thank Anthony Marsella for making me aware of this book.

76 "Interview with Johan Galtung: The Pioneering International Peace Research Association He Founded in 1964," by Antonio C. S. Rosa, TRANSCEND Media Service, on the occasion of the IPRA 2014 – 50th Anniversary Conference, July 28, 2014, www.transcend.org/tms/2014/07/interview-with-johan-galtung-the-pioneering-international-peace-research-association-he-founded-in-1964/.

77 Ismail, et al., 2014, quoted from "Government Agents 'Directly Involved' in Most High-Profile US Terror Plots," by Spencer Ackerman, Guardian UK, July 21, 2014, http://readersupportednews.org/news-section2/318-66/24903-government-agents-directly-involved-in-most-high-profile-us-terror-plots. I thank Anthony Marsella for making me aware of this book.

78 "Vom Bundesamt für Verfassungsschutz betreutes Morden?" Presserklärung der Nebenklage NSU-Prozess, Prozessbericht aus Sicht der Nebenklage im Prozess gegen Verantwortliche des "Nationalsozialistischen Untergrund," 7. April, 2016, www.nsu-nebenklage.de/blog/2016/04/07/07-04-2016-presserklaerung/.

79 International relations have been theorized widely, and I am privileged to have received the advice of Joshua Goldstein and Pevehouse, 2016, at important moments. Economic historian Charles Kindleberger, 2013, is often regarded as the father of hegemonic stability theory. Political economist Robert Gilpin, 1981, 1988, argues that history has seen subsequent international orders that all have in common that they are created by hegemonic states as a result of war. The prevailing order is always shaped to serve the dominant major powers' interests. The system will therefore necessarily be challenged by rising powers. The most dangerous moment in world politics occurs when the weakened main power no longer stands ready to enforce the rules of the established order. This breeds uncertainty, insecurity and risk behavior, claims Gilpin. He agrees with Paul Kennedy, 1987, and his analyses of "imperial overstretch" being one of the reasons that hegemons fall. Gilpin adds that all hegemons inevitably fall because it is difficult to stay as hegemon.

80 See note 79 above.

81 Spengler, 1918–1922/1963.

82 Toynbee, 1934–1961.

83 Logiest, 1982.

84 See Desmond Tutu's Foreword in Lindner and Desmond Tutu (Foreword), 2010.

85 Lindner, 2000a, pp. 245–246. See Lindner's conversation with members of the former German aristocracy, among others, on August 3, 1999, in Eitorf-Merten, Germany: "Hitler wurde als der 'Dämon', das Böse schlechthin, angesehen."

86 "Der Orden unter dem Totenkopf: 16. Fortsetzung Die Waffen-SS im Krieg," by Heinz Höhne, Der Spiegel 5/1967, January 30, 1967, www.spiegel.de/spiegel/print/d-45549385.html: "… Urtyp des unreifen, vom Hitler-Kult trunkenen Jungfanatikers Ultra-Nazi …"

87 Kirst, 1975/1976. I thank my father for making me aware of this book. He received it as a gift from his students when he was a teacher shortly after it had been published. His students demanded that he read passages of this book aloud to them, so that they would be able to grasp what had befallen Germany before they had been born.

88 Tisa von der Schulenburg, www.tisa-von-der-schulenburg.de/. See also "High-Born Prussians Who Defied Their Origin," by Michael Kimmelman, New York Times, July 15, 2009, www.nytimes.com/2009/07/16/arts/design/16abroad.html?_r=0.

89 Translated by Lindner from the German original, Haffner, 1978, p. 139.

90 Punk auf der Insel – Wilde Jahre West-Berlin, documentary film by Margarete Kreuzer, rbb, 2015, www.rbb-online.de/doku/k-l/wilde-jahre-west-berlin.html. See the full note in the pdf edition of this book.

91 Aust, 1985, Hauser, 1998, Kraushaar, 2006, Stern and Herrmann, 2007.

92 Lindner, 2000a, pp. 329–330. See also Lindner, 2000e, 2001j.

93 In Ahmed, 1996, p. 103.

94 Hargeisa is the capital of the North. Members of the Hargeisa group founded the SORRA group (Somali Relief and Rehabilitation Association) in 1990. See parts of my conversation with the group in Hargeisa, Somaliland, on December 1, 1998, in the video documentation Somaliland: The SORRA group and "The alphabet through the wall," as part of the doctoral research The Psychology of Humiliation: Somalia, Rwanda / Burundi, and Hitler's Germany. See links to the videos on www.humiliationstudies.org/whoeware/videos.php.

95 Lindner, 2000a, p. 58.

96 练乙铮 "学术自由几钱斤? (How Much Money Is Academic Freedom Worth?), by Yizheng Lian, Hong Kong Economic Journal, September 2, 2011, http://blog.yahoo.com/_2EWF3ONIDZEGUFEZDQTPJOTBHI/articles/420217. Quoted in Dong, 2015, p. 97. Lian was a consultant on CCCPC policy in Hong Kong from 1998, and was removed from office by the Hong Kong government in 2004.

97 Dong, 2015, p. 98.

98 Dong, 2015, p. 99.

99 Dong, 2015, p. 99.

100 Bourdieu uses the term field. See more in note 85 in the Introduction.

101 Dong, 2015, p. 33, Bourdieu and Wacquant, 1992, pp. 114–115.

102 Dong, 2015, p. 33, Bourdieu and Wacquant, 1992, pp. 99–100.

103 Dong, 2015, p. 36, Bourdieu and Wacquant, 1992, pp. 219, 276–278.

104 Dong, 2015, p. 148.

105 Bourdieu and Passeron, 1990, p. 159.

106 See note 97 in Chapter 5.

107 张俊超 大学青年教师发展现状及应对策略 (Current Development and Strategies of Young University Teachers), by Junchao Zhang, Beijing: CSSPW, 2009, quoted in Dong, 2015, p. 89.

108 Bourdieu, 1984a.

109 Lappé, 2016: "The seed market, for example, has moved from a competitive arena of small, family-owned firms to an oligopoly in which just three companies – Monsanto, DuPont, and Syngenta – control over half of the global proprietary seed market. Worldwide, from 1996 to 2008, a handful of corporations absorbed more than two hundred smaller independent companies, driving the price of seeds and other inputs higher to the point where their costs for poor farmers in southern India now make up almost half of production costs. And the cost in real terms per acre for users of bio-engineered crops dominated by one corporation, Monsanto, tripled between 1996 and 2013."

110 Frances Moore Lappé in her response on April 22, 2016, to the Great Transition Network (GTN) discussion on the topic "Farming for a Small Planet: Agroecology Now," based on Lappé, 2016.

111 Ibid.

112 Lappé, 2016.

113 "Hawking: Humans at Risk of Lethal 'Own Goal,'" by David Shukman, BBC News Services, January 19, 2016, www.bbc.com/news/science-environment-35344664.

114 On classism, have a look at Barbara Jensen, 2012.

115 Lindner, 2012f.

116 Tim Jackson, Centre for Environmental Strategy, at the Faculty of Engineering and Physical Sciences, University of Surrey in the UK, in his contribution to the Great Transition Network (GTN) discussion on the topic "Marxism and Ecology: Common Fonts of a Great Transition," October 1, 2015:

> The question of whether there is an inherent growth imperative in contemporary society is of course an extremely important one. A number of ecological economists have argued not only that there is such an imperative, but that it flows inevitably from some rather basic features of capitalism, such as the creation of money as credit and the charging of interest on debt. If this were shown to be the case, it would certainly seem to rule capitalism out of any sustainable form of post-growth or steady-state economy. But as my colleague Peter Victor and I have recently argued, this does not in fact seem to be the case. Our recent paper to Ecological Economics illustrates a quasi-stationary economy which is entirely consistent with the existence of credit creation and a money system based on interest-bearing debt.
>
> A more credible candidate for a growth imperative lies in the relentless pursuit of labor productivity. At the very least, a continual reduction in the labor required to produce a given level of economic output leads through simple arithmetic to a stark choice between growth and unemployment. There are answers to this dilemma, for instance, by reducing working hours, by structural shifts towards low productivity sectors, and by redistributing the ownership of capital assets.

See also Jackson, 2009.

117 See note 163 in the Preface.

118 Shigeo Abe in Samurai and Idiots: The Olympus Affair. See more in note 181 in Chapter 15.

119 Galtung, 1971, 1976. In Lindner, 2016e, I discuss Ibn Khaldun and Arnold Toynbee and how they speak of the periphery versus the center, as does also peace researcher Johan Galtung. However, there is a difference. While Toynbee focuses on the embattled border region and the "hardened" culture it can give rise to, Galtung speaks of the exploited periphery where a culture of obedience is being engendered, but, where also alternative solutions may emerge.

120 Kraidy and Murphy, 2008: "Galtung's theory sees the global as a sine qua non intermediary between various locals. In contrast, Geertz's translocal orientation reflects a web-like network with sensitivity to periphery-to-periphery contact."

121 Ibn Khaldun, 1377/1958, is a historiographer, historian, and a forerunner of the contemporary disciplines of sociology and demography, who addressed themes such as politics, urban life, economics, and knowledge. I studied him when I lived and worked as a clinical psychologist in Cairo, Egypt, from 1984–1991. See more in note 16 in Chapter 3.

122 See also "The Settlers' Prussia," by Uri Avnery, Human Wrongs Watch, October 17, 2015, http://human-wrongs-watch.net/2015/10/18/the-settlers-prussia/ and original at http://zope.gush-shalom.org/home/en/channels/avnery/1445000540/.

123 Toynbee, 1934–1961.

124 2016 Annual Conference of Human Dignity and Humiliation Studies, "Cities as Risk – From Humiliation to Dignity," in Dubrovnik, Croatia, September 19–23, 2016, www.humiliationstudies.org/whoweare/annualmeeting/27.php. See also Lindner, 2016e.

125 Former Yugoslavia is the territory that was up to 25 June 1991 known as The Socialist Federal Republic of Yugoslavia (SFRY). Six republics made up the federation: Bosnia and Herzegovina, Croatia, Macedonia, Montenegro, Serbia (including the regions of Kosovo and Vojvodina) and Slovenia.

126 These atrocities committed are being labelled "quasi genocide," since the victims, the members of the Isaaq clan, were not systematically exterminated, in contrast to Rwanda, for instance, where even "half-blood" were potential targets for extermination. Also, until the end of the genocide, there were Isaaq ministers in the government, something that would have been unthinkable in Rwanda. See the report by a United Nations employee who does not wish to be named, December 1998, Hargeisa, in Lindner, 2000a, p. 58.

127 Lindner, 2016e.

128 Galtung, 1971, p. 109.

Chapter 17

1 "Bassem Youssef: Fear Has No Future," Deutsche Welle, June 30, 2014, www.dw.de/bassem-youssef-fear-has-no-future/a-17747272.

2 See, among others, Volkan, 2004.

3 Ali, 2002.

4 "A Guide for the Perplexed: Intellectual Fallacies of the War on Terror," by Chalmers Johnson, see note 4 above. See more in note 66 in Chapter 5.

5 "Why Is the Military-Industrial Complex Sometimes Called 'The Devil's Dynamo'?" by John Scales Avery, TRANSCEND Media Service, June 30, 2014, www.transcend.org/tms/2014/06/the-devils-dynamo/. See more in note 46 in Chapter 11, in note 127 in Chapter 14, and in note 199 in Chapter 18.

6 See note 4 above.

7 Huntington, 1996.

8 Holmes, 2007, p. 72. Chalmers Johnson, in his review of Holmes book, recommends Ricks, 2006, to understand how the 2003–2011 Iraq war was lost. See the review here: "A Guide for the Perplexed: Intellectual Fallacies of the War on Terror," by Chalmers Johnson, TomDispatch.com, October 22, 2007, www.alternet.org/story/65838/bush%27s_response_to_9_11_was_deadlier_than_the_attacks_themselves.

9 Schmid, 2013, p. 15.

10 Holmes, 2007, p. 312.

11 Holmes, 2007, p. 106, Mann, 2004a.

12 Stone, 2004, see also Stone, 2007.

13 "A Guide for the Perplexed: Intellectual Fallacies of the War on Terror," by Chalmers Johnson, see note 4 above. John Yoo, 2005, is a prominent member of the Federalist Society, an association of conservative Republican lawyers. See also Quilligan, 2013.

14 "A Guide for the Perplexed: Intellectual Fallacies of the War on Terror," by Chalmers Johnson, see note 4 above. See also Power, 2002.

15 Power, 2002.

16 Pratto and Stewart, 2011.

17 Fried, 2015.

18 Lindner, 2006c, p. 67.

19 "Pianist Lang Lang: An Avante Garde Pianist," by Na Young Kwon, International Examiner, October 21, 2009, www.iexaminer.org/2009/10/avante-garde-pianist/.

20 Fanon, 1952/1967. See also Midiohouan, 1991.

21 Gottman, et al., 1997.

22 "The Mysterious Link Between the US Military Prison Camp Bucca and ISIS Leaders," by Mohammed Mahmoud Mortada, Al-Akhbar, September 13, 2014, http://english.al-akhbar.com/node/21519.

23 "The Paradoxical Consequences of USA Counter-Terrorism Programs: Jihadist Terrorist Perceived Motives and Successes," by Anthony J. Marsella, TRANSCEND Media Service, October 20, 2014, www.transcend.org/tms/2014/10/the-paradoxical-consequences-of-usa-counter-terrorism-programs/.

24 See note 9 in Chapter 4.

25 Smith, 2000.

26 Allred, 1999, Averill, 1982, 1993.

27 Ali, 2002.

28 "The Logic of Violence in the Islamic State's War," by Stathis N. Kalyvas, Washington Post, July 7, 2014, www.washingtonpost.com/blogs/monkey-cage/wp/2014/07/07/the-logic-of-violence-in-islamic-states-war/.

29 "Jihad's Fatal Attraction: The Challenge for Democracies Is to Provide an Alternative Means of Satisfying the Quest for Glory that Motivates those who Join in Isis's Barbarism," by Scott Atran, The Guardian, September 4, 2014, www.theguardian.com/commentisfree/2014/sep/04/jihad-fatal-attraction-challenge-democracies-isis-barbarism. I thank Deeyah Khan for making me aware of this article.

30 Ibid.

31 Ibid.

32 Ibid.

33 Papadopoulos, 2006, pp. 92 and 95.

34 Katz, 1988. I thank McCauley, 2017, for making me aware of Katz's research. It is a privilege to have Clark McCauley as esteemed member in the global advisory board of our Human Dignity and Humiliation Studies fellowship.

35 Kühne, 2011. It is a privilege to have Thomas Kühne as esteemed member in the global advisory board of our Human Dignity and Humiliation Studies fellowship.

36 Kühne, 2011, p. 239.

37 Lorenz, 1963/1966. It should not be forgotten, however, that Konrad Lorenz' "cathartic" model of instincts and of aggression is now widely believed to be incorrect. Human aggression is not a nervous energy that has to be dissipated in some way, be it harmlessly through some substitutes for aggression, or, if not, then through actual fighting.

38 A number of physiological reactions create the "hero face" posturing of a chimpanzee as well as of a Homo sapiens. These reactions range from a raised head, stuck-out chin, slightly raised and inward rotated arms, and a stiffened body through tighter striated musculature. The aim is to appear more threatening, even if only by bluff, since raised hair produces no more than a pretense of strength. A cat humps its back, also here making the animal appear bigger and thus more dangerous than it really is.

39 BCE stands for "Before the Common Era," and is equivalent to BC, which means "Before Christ."

40 "Human Nature: An Evolutionary Paradox," by John Scales Avery, Human Wrongs Watch, August 15, 2016, https://human-wrongs-watch.net/2016/08/17/human-nature-an-evolutionary-paradox/.

41 Ibid.

42 Ibid. See also Hinde and Rotblat, 2003.

43 Arendt, 1970.

44 Juergensmeyer, 2000.

45 The word gonzo seems to first have been used in 1970 in connection with an article by Hunter S. Thompson, "The Kentucky Derby Is Decadent and Depraved," Thompson, 1970, who later popularized gonzo journalism as a style of journalism that is written without claims of objectivity, often including the reporter as part of the story via a first-person narrative. See also Thompson, 1979.

46 "The Pornography of Jihadism," by Simon Cottee, The Atlantic, September 12, 2014, www.theatlantic.com/international/archive/2014/09/isis-jihadist-propaganda-videos-porn/380117/2/. I thank Deeyah Khan for making me aware of this article.

47 Ibid.

48 Translated from German by Alice Asbury Abbott, Suttner, 1908, pp. 142. German original, Suttner, 1889, p. 84. See the German original in the full note in the pdf edition of this book.

49 Kühne, 2011, p. 239.

50 Kühne, 2011, p. 237.

51 Linda Hartling in a personal communication on September 4, 2016.

52 Kühne, 2011, p. 241.

53 Staub, 1989, 1993, 2012, 2015.

54 Browning, 1992.

55 Kühne, 2011, p. 242.

56 Haffner, 2000.

57 "Med hilsen fra en tribunehore," by Mina Finstad Berg, Maddam.no, September 9, 2014, http://maddam.no/2014/09/med-hilsen-fra-en-tribunehore/.

58 NSA Ajit Doval Sir Speech at SASTRA University, published on November 26, 2014, https://youtu.be/v4RaCJrT51w.

59 "Proscribed Terror Groups or Organisations," Counter-Terrorism Policy Paper by the Home Office of the Government of the United Kingdom, July 12, 2013, last updated November 2, 2015, www.gov.uk/government/publications/proscribed-terror-groups-or-organisations--2.

60 Defence and Diplomacy: Terrorists Targeting Schools, hosted by Sultan Mehmood Hali, Pakistan Television Corporation (PTV), published on February 4, 2016, https://youtu.be/z1YAZMWsdu0, with guests Lt. Gen Raza Muhammad Khan, Former President National Defence University of Islamabad, and Atle Hetland, a Norwegian Social Scientist: "Having been beaten back by the Military Operation Zarb-e-Azb, the terrorists have started targeting educational institutions. Their rationale appears to be reach soft targets and also deny the future generations of Pakistan education, which they badly need." The two guests "examine the problem from a military and social angle." It is a privilege to have Atle Hetland as esteemed member in our Human Dignity and Humiliation Studies fellowship.

61 Keri Lawson-Te Aho in a personal communication on January 18, 2014.

62 "A 'Deep and Disturbing' Decline in Media Freedom," World Press Freedom Index, Reporters Without Borders (RSF), April 20, 2016, https://rsf.org/en/deep-and-disturbing-decline-media-freedom. See also

"Right to Information Dead on Arrival at UN," by Thalif Deen, Inter Press Service (IPS), January 19, 2017, www.ipsnews.net/2017/01/right-to-information-dead-on-arrival-at-un/.

63 Holmes, 2007. See a review of this book in "A Guide for the Perplexed: Intellectual Fallacies of the War on Terror," by Chalmers Johnson, see note 4 in this Chapter 17.

64 Lindner, 2012c. I thank Francisco Gomes de Matos for being my guardian in Brazil and introducing me to a number of important people and organizations.

65 "UN Expert Urges Chile to Stop Using Anti-Terrorism Legislation and to Adopt National Strategy to Address the Mapuche Question," The Office of the United Nations High Commissioner for Human Rights (OHCHR), July 30, 2013, www.ohchr.org/EN/NewsEvents/Pages/DisplayNews.aspx?NewsID=13599&LangID=E: "The United Nations Special Rapporteur on human rights and counter-terrorism, Ben Emmerson, today urged Chilean authorities to refrain from applying anti-terrorism legislation in connection with the Mapuche indigenous peoples' land protests. At the end of his first official visit to Chile, the expert also called on the Government to place the Mapuche question as one of the top priorities of the national political dialogue."

66 Ricardo Josı Pereira Rodrigues in a personal communication on July 12, 2012.

67 Ibid.

68 Ibid.

69 Lindner, 2012b.

70 Gilberto Freyre (1900–1987) was the "father" of lusotropicalism. I thank Clara Becker for making me aware of Freyre's work, and also the work of Sérgio Buarque de Holanda. Gilberto de Mello Freyre was a Brazilian sociologist, anthropologist, historian, writer, painter and congressman. His best-known work is Casa-Grande e Senzala (literally, The Plantation Big House and the Slave Quarters, Freyre, 1933, but translated into English as Masters and the Slaves). The book is considered a classic of modern cultural anthropology. It depicts life on traditional plantations and the miscegenation (racial mixing crossbreeding, interbreeding) that emerged in this context. Freyre's argument is that miscegenation had a positive influence in Brazil rather than representing a weakness. This was a new point of view, paving the way for Afro-Brazilian art and literature to be highly regarded rather than denigrated, and to Brazil becoming proud of their very unique Brazilian culture. According to Freyre's analysis, the Portuguese tendency to miscegenation among colonized peoples provided the background for this development. Even though Freyre never used the phrase "racial democracy" in his published works, his argument was that Brazil, even though far from being a paradise of racial harmony, still was a place of much greater social cohesion than other, comparable world regions.

71 "Swedish Expert Slams Norway Terror Alert," The Local, July 28, 2014, www.thelocal.se/20140728/sweden-slams-norways-terror-alert-tactics. See also Human Rights Watch, 2014, With Liberty to Monitor All: How Large-Scale US Surveillance Is Harming Journalism, Law, and American Democracy.

72 "Strategi for økt overvåking: Tidligere høyesterettsdommer og leder for Lundkommisjonen om offentlige terroralarmer" (Strategy for Increased Surveillance: Former Supreme Court Judge and Chairman of the Lund Commission on Government Terror Alerts), by Emilie Ekeberg og Lars Thorvaldsen, Klassekampen, August 1, 2014, www.klassekampen.no/article/20140801/ARTICLE/140809998. Translated by Lindner from the original Norwegian text. See the Norwegian original in the full note in the pdf edition of this book.

73 Schmid, 2013, pp. 10.

74 Schmid, 2013, p. 11, quoting from Countering Radicalisation in America: Lessons from Europe, Special Report Number 262, by Lorenzo Vidino, United States Institute of Peace, Washington, DC, November 2010, see www.usip.org/events/countering-radicalization-lessons-europe.

75 Die sieben Irrtümer der Deutschen Einheit: Glücksfall oder Milliardengrab? ZDF-History, Zweites Deutsches Fernsehen, September 19, 2010, www.zdf.de/zdf-history/die-sieben-irrtuemer-der-deutschen-einheit-5443030.html. See more in note 35 in Chapter 5.

76 See note 54 in Chapter 5.

77 "Afghanistan's U.S.-Funded Torturers and Murderers," by John Sifton, Asia advocacy director, Human Rights Watch, published in Foreign Policy, March 6, 2015, www.hrw.org/news/2015/03/06/afghanistan-s-us-funded-torturers-and-murderers, who subtitles: "The United States continues to fund and support a network of abusive Afghan strongmen in the name of security. It's time to stop": "Human Rights Watch (HRW) has documented systematic, gross human rights violations by some of these forces that has included numerous cases of torture, extrajudicial executions of civilians, and forced disappearance of detainees. The findings raise concerns about Afghan government and U.S. efforts to arm, train, vet, and hold accountable the country's security apparatus – run by a network of strongmen, many of whom attained official authority as allies of the United States in the fight against the Taliban."

78 "American Jewish Community Ends Support of Turkish Interests on Hill," by Eli Lake, The Washington Times, June 8, 2010, www.washingtontimes.com/news/2010/jun/8/jewish-community-ends-support-turkey-capitol-hill/?page=all.

79 "Turkey's Doctrine of Pre-emptive Authoritarianism," by Mustafa Akyol, Al-Monitor, April 10, 2014, www.al-monitor.com/pulse/originals/2014/04/authoritarian-turkey-preemptive-erdogan.html#.

80 "Besieged, Abused, Ignored: Ethiopian Annihilation of the Ogaden People," by Graham Peebles, CounterPunch, February 8–10, 2013, www.counterpunch.org/2013/02/08/ethiopian-annihilation-of-the-ogaden-people/.

81 "Legalize It All: How to Win the War on Drugs," by Dan Baum, Harper's Magazine, April 2016, http://harpers.org/archive/2016/04/legalize-it-all/. See also "Report: Aide Says Nixon's War on Drugs Targeted Blacks, Hippies," by Tom LoBianco, CNN, March 24, 2016, http://edition.cnn.com/2016/03/23/politics/john-ehrlichman-richard-nixon-drug-war-blacks-hippie/. I thank Michael Britton for making me aware of these articles.
For another example, see "Israel Mows the Lawn," by Mouin Rabbani, London Review of Books, Volume 36 (15), July 31, 2014, www.lrb.co.uk/v36/n15/mouin-rabbani/israel-mows-the-lawn. On page 8, we read that in 2004, a year before Israel's unilateral disengagement from the Gaza Strip, Dov Weissglass, advisor to Ariel Sharon, explained the initiative's purpose to an interviewer from Haaretz: "The significance of the disengagement plan is the freezing of the peace process … And when you freeze that process, you prevent the establishment of a Palestinian state, and you prevent a discussion on the refugees, the borders and Jerusalem. Effectively, this whole package called the Palestinian state, with all that it entails, has been removed indefinitely from our agenda. And all this with … a [US] presidential blessing and the ratification of both houses of Congress … The disengagement is actually formaldehyde. It supplies the amount of formaldehyde that is necessary so there will not be a political process with the Palestinians."

82 Fassin, 2015. I thank Hinnerk Bruhns for making me aware of the work of sociologist and anthropologist Didier Fassin.

83 "'Je suis français, je suis juif, je suis musulman. Je suis Charlie': On the trail of Convivencia," by Raja Sakrani, Käte Hamburger Kolleg "Recht als Kultur," January 2015, www.recht-als-kultur.de/de/aktuelles/diskurs/.

84 "Latin America and the Caribbean Can Make Hunger History – UN Agricultural Agency," United Nations News Centre, January 25, 2017, www.un.org/apps/news/story.asp?NewsID=56043#.WI3BWvKOWgx.

85 Richards, 2016a. See also historian Philipp Ther, 2014/2016, p. x, and his summary of the main pillars of neoliberal ideology in note 55 in Chapter 4.

86 David Korten in his contribution to the Great Transition Network Initiative discussion titled "Journey to Earthland: Making the Great Transition to Planetary Civilization," September 21, 2016, in response to Raskin, 2016.

87 "The U.S. Media's Problems Are Much Bigger than Fake News and Filter Bubbles," by Bharat N. Anand. See note 401 in the Introduction.

88 "Have Twitter Bots Infiltrated the 2016 Election?" by Andrew McGill, The Atlantic, June 2, 2016, www.theatlantic.com/politics/archive/2016/06/have-twitter-bots-infiltrated-the-2016-election/484964/. See also Hellesøy Harrisson, 2016.

89 "Interview with John Scales Avery, One of the Greatest Living Intellectuals on Earth," by Binu Mathew, Human Wrongs Watch, March 15, 2017, https://human-wrongs-watch.net/2017/03/23/interview-with-john-scales-avery-one-of-the-greatest-living-intellectuals-on-earth/.

90 Ibid.

91 Jenni, 2011.

92 Akte D, part 1. See note 82 in Chapter 15.

93 "UN Report Reveals Convergence of Environmental Crime with Corruption, Raft of Other Illegal Activities," United Nations News Centre, December 9, 2016, www.un.org/apps/news/story.asp?NewsID=55763#.WFAr5H2OWgx.

94 "Illegal Trade in Wildlife, Timber Products Funding Criminals, Armed Groups – Joint UN Report," United Nations News Centre, June 24, 2014, www.un.org/apps/news/story.asp?NewsID=48122#.U80hg7Hzkmy.

95 Lindner, 2016e. The environmental cost of turbo-tourism is one of several aspects that inspire the outcry "tourism is terrorism." Hrvoje Carić, of the Institute for Tourism in Zagreb, Croatia, has calculated in 2015 that one-year income from cruise ships was 52.8 million Euros, while the cost of environmental damage was as high as 390 million Euros. In other words, the direct cost of pollution for the Croatian part of the Adriatic exceeds the financial benefits for the Croatian economy seven times, not even counting indirect damage.

96 See the end of part 1.2 of Der erschöpfte Planet – Machtfaktor Erde, documentary film by Angela Andersen and Claus Kleber, Zweites Deutsches Fernsehen, 2011, part 1.1: http://youtu.be/58FbrvB94Qs, part 1.2: http://youtu.be/ZAMD7CrUbHk, part 1.3: http://youtu.be/YifhqsGKB0M, part 2.1: http://youtu.be/5JW8qw1-9f4, part 2.2: http://youtu.be/QE3YHYCbIMM, part 2.3: http://youtu.be/CUIkRM_lrlI. See the full note in the pdf edition of this book.

97 Das Geschäft mit der Armut: Wie Lebensmittelkonzerne neue Märkte erobern, documentary film by Joachim Walther. See note 53 in the Inspiring and Thought-Provoking Questions to Section Two.

98 "The Charitable-Industrial Complex," by Peter Buffett, son of investor Warren Buffett, New York Times, July 26, 2013, www.nytimes.com/2013/07/27/opinion/the-charitable-industrial-complex.html?hpw&_r=0. See also Fontan, 2012, and Lindner, 2010b.

99 Teju Cole has been credited with coining the term White-Savior Industrial Complex. See note 159 in the Preface.

100 Pogge, 2002. It has been a great privilege for me to learn from Thomas Pogge, starting more than twenty years ago, when he was part of the Ethics Programme of the Norwegian Research Council, led by Dagfinn

Føllesdal. Earlier, we studied at Hamburg University at the same time, without meeting then. Altruism and compassion can and must go together, see, for instance, Singer and Ricard, 2015, or Ricard, 2013/2016. Note the effective altruism movement that goes beyond traditional altruism or classical charity. Journalist Linda Polman, 2010, is highly critical to donating to any charity, particularly those funded and beholden to national interests, except for one, namely, Médecins Sans Frontières (MSF), also known as Doctors Without Borders.

101 "Next Generation Bioweapons: The Technology Of Genetic Engineering Applied To Biowarfare And Bioterrorism," by Michael J. Ainscough, Colonel, USAF, The Counterproliferation Papers, Future Warfare Series Number 14, April 2002, www.fas.org/irp/threat/cbw/nextgen.pdf, p. 11. See note 52 in the Preface.

102 Shiva, 2000, p. 12.

103 Siebert, 2010, p. 812, quoted in "Individual and Collective Misfortune: Possibilities of Transcendence," by Reimon Bachika, Human Dignity and Humiliation Studies, 2016, www.humiliationstudies.org/publications/publications.php.

104 Oxley, 2012.

105 Lindner, 2016b. See also Norgaard, 2011, 2015, Nelson, 2010b or a new journal of Implicit Religion, a journal of the Centre for the Study of Implicit Religion and Contemporary Spirituality at Middlesex University, UK, http://socrel.oxfordjournals.org/content/61/2/local/advertising.pdf.

106 Hochschild, 1983.

107 "History Has Knocked Very Loudly on Our Door. Will We Answer?" World Future Forum 2016 – Opening Speech by Jakob von Uexküll, World Future Forum 2016 – Opening Speech by Jakob von Uexküll. See note 132 in Chapter 5.

108 Sudhir Chella Rajan, expert on climate and migration, in his contribution to the Great Transition Network (GTN) discussion on the topic of "The Church of Economism and Its Discontents," on November 21, 2015, in response to Norgaard, 2015.

109 See Chapter 8 of Lindner, 2012f, A Dignity Economy.

110 Escrigas, 2016. Cristina Escrigas is the former executive director of, and current adviser to, the Global University Network for Innovation (GUNi), an organization created by UNESCO, the United Nations University, and the Technical University of Catalonia (UPC). She was previously director of the UNESCO Chair in Higher Education Management, developing strategies for universities in Spain and Latin America. She has conducted numerous research projects and organized international conferences on emerging issues in higher education.

111 Bude, 2014

112 "The 'Just Enough' Policy: Behavioral Control of Collective Protest through Minimum Reward," by Antony J. Marsella, TRANSCEND Media Service, June 22, 2014, www.transcend.org/tms/2014/06/the-just-enough-policy-behavioral-control-of-collective-protest-through-minimum-reward/. See the full note in the pdf edition of this book.

113 Karlberg, 2014: "… if humans are presumed to be nothing more than intelligent and egoistic animals seeking to satisfy their material interests and appetites in an environment of scarce resources, with the meaning and purpose of our lives defined by success or failure in this regard – then how does the construction of a more just and sustainable global civilization become imaginable or desirable? And what would motivate the struggle and sacrifice required to bring it about? Likewise, if humans are presumed to be living out transitory lives en route to a destination of eternal salvation or damnation, and if this earthly existence is nothing more than a way of separating the saved from the damned, and if the entire process is about to reach an apocalyptic conclusion – then how does the construction of a more just and sustainable

global civilization become imaginable or desirable? And what would motivate the struggle and sacrifice required to bring it about?"

114 Karlberg, 2014. See note 113 above.

115 Kim and Kirk, 2013.

116 "Schleichende Pathologisierung der Gesellschaft," Reinhard Jellen interviewt Werner Seppmann über die Zunahme von Gewalt und Irrationalismus in der Gesellschaft, Telepolis, November 23,.2011, www.heise.de/tp/artikel/35/35916/1.html.

117 Stout, 2005. I thank Michael Britton for making me aware of Martha Stout's work.

118 We had our 2016 Annual Dignity Conference in Dubrovnik, Croatia, where I lived throughout September 2016. Prior to that, I spent the month of August 2016 in Sarajevo. I deeply thank the family of Ardian Adžanela for wonderfully welcoming me in their midst in Sarajevo. See the article I wrote during these months, Lindner, 2016e.

119 "Understanding Yugoslavia," by Cameron Hewitt, Rick Steve's Europe, www.ricksteves.com/watch-read-listen/read/understanding-yugoslavia.

120 Pavlović, 2006.

121 "Marović i Mesić razmenili izvinjenja građanima Hrvatske i SCG," B92, September 9, 2003, www.b92.net/info/vesti/index.php?yyyy=2003&mm=09&dd=10&nav_id=119131.

122 "Reckoning: The 1991 Siege of Dubrovnik and the Consequences of the 'War for Peace,'" by Srdja Pavlovic, www.yorku.ca/soi/_Vol_5_1/_HTML/Pavlovic.html.

123 Marsella, 2014. Marsella sees the causes of the mass acts of violence both specific to the people, forces, and circumstances of each instance, but also as residing in larger and enduring sets of forces and events that exists at different levels of our lives, and that interact and cascade off one another in an ever amplified and self-defeating cycle of individual and societal deviancy.
Marsella enumerates the roots of violent shooting and bombing events:
• formative causes (e.g., genetics, temperament, early life experiences, characterological dispositions, social structural circumstances, race, poverty),
• precipative causes (e.g., bullying, rejection, humiliation, perceived abuses by government),
• exacerbative causes (e.g., membership in violence groups, gun availability and accessibility), and
• maintenance causes (e.g., membership in a broader culture and/or milieu that justifies violence, sanctions it, and legitimates as a way to resolve individual and social inequities). See more in the full note in the pdf edition of this book.

124 "Evidence on Rampant Violence Against Children 'Compels Us to Act' – UNICEF Report," United Nations News Centre, September 4, 2014, www.un.org/apps/news/story.asp?NewsID=48639#.VAsGi2Pitru.

125 Institute for Economics and Peace, 2015. See note 55 and 56 in the Preface.

126 "'Now Is the Time to Act,' UN Urges on Release of First Global Report on Suicide Prevention," United Nations News Centre, September 4, 2014, www.un.org/apps/news/story.asp?NewsID=48637#.VAsGYmPitrt: "More than 800,000 people commit suicide every year – around one person every 40 seconds."

127 Etzioni, 2013, p. 334:

> Thomas Kuhn pointed out that even scientific paradigms resist change, even though the essence of the scientific methodology is openness to new evidence. Paradigms are frequently sustained even as more and more facts cast them in doubt (so called "stubborn facts"), until the paradigm can no longer hold and the dam breaks, opening the way for a new paradigm to replace it. The reason for such persistence is that to form a normative paradigm (and a symbiotic legal code) requires great effort and investment.

> Decades of moral dialogue, consensus building, legislation, court cases, and public education slowly build such a paradigm. Millions of people come to believe in it, weave it into their worldview and political preferences, and even intertwine it with their personal identities. Hence the strain of dissonance between the paradigm and reality may be high before one can expect a paradigm to break down and it be replaced with a new one. This Article suggests that, when possible, a more gradual transition is to be preferred, and seeks to contribute toward that end.

See also Mental Health Awareness Month in a Climate of Denial," by Carol Smaldino, Huffington Post, May 11, 2016, www.huffingtonpost.com/carol-smaldino/mental-health-awareness-m_b_9895080.html.

128 "James Mitchell: 'I'm Just a Guy Who Got Asked to Do Something for His Country,'" by Jason Leopold, The Guardian, April 18, 2014, www.theguardian.com/world/2014/apr/18/james-mitchell-cia-torture-interview. I thank Linda Hartling for making me aware of this article.

129 Cainkar and Maira, 2005. See also Galli, 2016.

130 "Recommendation Rec(2006)2 of the Committee of Ministers to member states on the European Prison Rules," Council of Europe, Strasbourg, France, January 11, 2006, http://legislationline.org/documents/action/popup/id/8028.

131 "Collateral Costs: Incarceration's Effect on Economic mobility," Pew Charitable Trusts, 2010, www.pewtrusts.org/~/media/legacy/uploadedfiles/pcs_assets/2010/CollateralCosts1 pdf.pdf.

132 "Sentencing and Corrections Practices in Germany and the Netherlands: Implications for the United States," by Ram Subramanian and Alison Shames, Vera Institute of Justice, New York, October 2013, www.vera.org/sites/default/files/resources/downloads/european-american-prison-report-v3.pdf.

133 Traditionally, the police force in Northern European countries has enjoyed considerable trust, however, throughout the past decades, the trend to shrink the public sector has weakened the local capabilities of the police force even in countries such as Norway. See, for instance, "Befolkningen fortjener mer politi," by Ingelin Killengren, director of the Norwegian police force, 2008, www.politi.no/vedlegg/lokale_vedlegg/politidirektoratet/Vedlegg_251.pdf.

134 "New FBI Report Casts Doubt on NRA's 'Good Guy Stops Bad Guy' Nonsense," by Mike Weisser. See also Böckler, et al., 2013, and "A Study of Active Shooter Incidents in the United States Between 2000 and 2013, Unclassified," by the U.S. Department of Justice, Federal Bureau of Investigation, Washington Navy Yard, Washington, DC. See more in note 26 in Chapter 7.

135 Stillwell, et al., 2008.

136 "We Can Defeat ISIS," by Amitai Etzioni, Huffington Post, August 4, 2015, www.huffingtonpost.com/amitai-etzioni/we-can-defeat-isis_b_7933364.html.

137 Kruse, 2015, quoted by Richard Norgaard in his reply to the contributions to the Great Transition Network (GTN) discussion on December 8, 2015, on his essay The Church of Economism and Its Discontents, Norgaard, 2015.

138 Richard B. Norgaard, professor of energy and resources at the University of California at Berkeley, USA, in his reply to the contributions to the Great Transition Network (GTN) discussion on December 8, 2015, on his essay The Church of Economism and Its Discontents, Norgaard, 2015.

139 See note 181 in Chapter 6.

140 "2002 State of the Union Address," by President George W. Bush, January 29, 2002, http://georgewbush-whitehouse.archives.gov/news/releases/2002/01/print/20020129-11.html.

141 "Warum geschlossene Grenzen auch Freiheit bedeuten," by Hans-Werner Sinn, Die Zeit, February 1, 2016, www.welt.de/wirtschaft/article151713703/Warum-geschlossene-Grenzen-auch-Freiheit-bedeuten.html.

142 "Sexualstrafrecht: 'Nein ist Nein' als Grundtenor," by Nico Fried, Süddeutsche Zeitung, Mai 1, 2016, www.sueddeutsche.de/politik/sexualstrafrecht-nein-ist-nein-als-grundtenor-1.2975249.

143 "Nearly One in Four Adolescent Girls Experience Physical Violence: Alarming Levels of Acceptance of Violence Against Girls," UNICEF, October 10, 2014, www.unicef.org/media/media_76221.html.

144 "Stand Up for and Invest in Teenage Girls, UN Says on World Population Day," United Nations News Centre, July 11, 2016, www.un.org/apps/news/story.asp?NewsID=54427#.V4aYUKLICgx.

145 "EU Kids Online: National Perspectives," by Leslie Haddon, Sonia Livingstone, and the EU Kids Online network, October 2012, www.lse.ac.uk/media@lse/research/EUKidsOnline/EU%20Kids%20III/Reports/PerspectivesReport.pdf.

146 See note 59 in Chapter 7.

147 Woods, 2003.

148 "Experiment That Convinced Me Online Porn Is the Most Pernicious Threat Facing Children Today," by Martin Daubney. See note 59 in Chapter 7.

149 Woods, 2003. John Woods is a member of the British Psychotherapy Foundation and the Institute of Group Analysis, a consultant psychotherapist at the Portman Clinic, and works with adults and children who have shown harmful sexual behavior. He has written books and articles on various clinical topics, dramatic monologues, and full length plays dealing with psychotherapeutic engagement with trauma and abuse.

150 "Brain Activity in Sex Addiction Mirrors that of Drug Addiction," by Nick Olejniczak, Research, University of Cambridge, July 11, 2014, www.cam.ac.uk/research/news/brain-activity-in-sex-addiction-mirrors-that-of-drug-addiction. Dr. John Williams is the Head of Neuroscience and Mental Health at the Wellcome Trust, and he warns: "Compulsive behaviors, including watching porn to excess, over-eating and gambling, are increasingly common. This study takes us a step further to finding out why we carry on repeating behaviors that we know are potentially damaging to us. Whether we are tackling sex addiction, substance abuse or eating disorders, knowing how best, and when, to intervene in order to break the cycle is an important goal of this research."

151 Voon, et al., 2014.

152 "Brain Activity in Sex Addiction Mirrors that of Drug Addiction," by Nick Olejniczak: "The researchers also asked the participants to rate the level of sexual desire that they felt whilst watching the videos, and how much they liked the videos. Drug addicts are thought to be driven to seek their drug because they want – rather than enjoy – it. This abnormal process is known as incentive motivation, a compelling theory in addiction disorders. ... Dr Voon and colleagues also found a correlation between brain activity and age – the younger the patient, the greater the level of activity in the ventral striatum in response to pornography. Importantly, this association was strongest in individuals with compulsive sexual behavior. The frontal control regions of the brain – essentially, the "brakes" on our compulsivity – continue to develop into the mid-twenties and this imbalance may account for greater impulsivity and risk taking behaviors in younger people."

153 See note 73 in Chapter 3.

154 Rainald Goetz, 2012, wrote a novel about an egomaniacal manager's rise and fall, similar to the true trajectory of Thomas Middelhoff, a highflying German corporate manager, who, even after being sentenced to three years in prison in 2014, still proudly displays a "bad boy" image.

155 "The Tyranny of Democracy," by Paul Larudee, TRANSCEND Media Service, November 21, 2016, www.transcend.org/tms/2016/11/the-tyranny-of-democracy/.

156 "The Coalition of Transformation vs. the Coalition of Restoration," by Ronald Brownstein, The Atlantic, November 21, 2012.

157 Philosopher Walter Benjamin, 1940/1974, warned that, as history is controlled by the victors, we are moving backwards into the future, a move that is illusionary. He is joined in these warnings by many others, among them journalists such as Owen Hatherley, 2015, who writes on architecture, politics, and culture.

158 Ray and Anderson, 2000.

159 Lindner, 2014c. See also lawyer Amy Chua, 2003, and her discussion of how exporting market democracy may breed ethnic hatred and global instability. See sociologist Peter Evans, 2008, for the potential of counter-hegemonic globalization movements to challenge the contemporary view of globalization as neoliberal globalization.

160 Bruce Fisher in his contribution to the Great Transition Network Initiative discussion titled "The Struggle for Meaningful Work," January 18, 2017, in response to Klitgaard, 2017.

161 Lindner and Human Dignity and Humiliation Studies network members, 2006–2017.

162 Raskin, 2016, Lindner, 2016d.

163 Lindner, 2016d.

164 Hetherington and Weiler, 2009.

165 "Turning the United States Around," by Howard Richards, Chileufú, http://chileufu.cl/turning-the-united-states-around/.

166 2016 Workshop on Transforming Humiliation and Violent Conflict at Columbia University in New York City, December 8–9, 2016. See also Lindner and Human Dignity and Humiliation Studies network members, 2006–2017.

167 "Why Scientific Studies Are So Often Wrong: The Streetlight Effect," by David H. Freedman, Discover Magazine, December 10, 2010, http://discovermagazine.com/2010/jul-aug/29-why-scientific-studies-often-wrong-streetlight-effect.

Chapter 18

1 Tolstoy, 1886/1935.

2 The situation is so urgent that it is time for disaster ethics (Katastrophenethik), explains Thomas Metzinger, professor for theoretical philosophy at the University of Mainz, in Die Kraft des Guten: Warum das egoistische Gen nur die halbe Wahrheit ist, by Gert Scobel, 3sat, April 13, 2017, www.3sat.de/page/?source=/scobel/188236/index.html. See the full note in the pdf edition of this book.

3 "Evolving Democracy," by Johan Galtung, TRANSCEND Media Service, February 13, 2017, www.transcend.org/tms/2017/02/evolving-democracy/.

4 Raskin, 2016, pp. 110–111.

5 Nina Jensen is a Norwegian marine biologist and secretary general of World Wildlife Fund Norway, and she is the sister of the Norwegian Minister of Finance, Siv Jensen. Nina Jensen explains the inadequacy of climate and environmental policies around the world as follows: Politicians "obviously have not enough knowledge and expertise about how bad the situation actually is, how tremendous the effects of climate change and loss of biodiversity will be and to what extent also economic assets will be at stake. Had politicians really understood these relationships, they would act on a whole different scale." See "Føling for fjæra: Danse med ulver, dykke med haier, Portrettet av Nina Jensen" Klassekampen, February 11, 2017, p. 38–40. What makes her testimony particularly interesting is that even she, clearly, is not able to adequately alert her very own sister, a politician and finance minister.

6 Stephen Purdey, international relations specialist and research affiliate at the Waterloo Institute for Complexity and Innovation, University of Waterloo, Ontario, Canada, in his contribution to the Great Transition Network Initiative discussion titled "Journey to Earthland: Making the Great Transition to Planetary Civilization," September 21, 2016, in response to Raskin, 2016.

7 Space Exploration – A Powerful Symbol of Global Cooperation, Jim Zimmerman, NASA. See note 149 in the Preface.

8 Read more about the so-called public trust doctrine in note 40 in the Preface.

9 Lyotard, 1979/1984.

10 Callinicos, 1989, Calhoun, 1993.

11 Giddens, 1990, Giddens, 1991.

12 Bauman, 2000.

13 Beck, 1986.

14 Castells, 1996–1998.

15 Lindlof and Taylor, 2011.

16 Pettit, 1997b.

17 See note 163 in the Preface.

18 "Keynes' Limitations and Trump's Disasters, by Howard Richards, Chileufú, November 2016, http://chileufu.cl/keynes-limitations-and-trumps-disasters/: "The rust belt workers of America were not only impoverished by free trade, runaway industries, weakened unions and porous borders, but also humiliated. They were cast in the role of the uneducated, the xenophobic, the prejudiced, the homophobes, the sexists and the racists. The new world order sells free trade as a humanitarian ideal not only by packaging it as impeccable rationality which only the stupid fail to understand, but also by packaging it as love for neighbor on a global scale that only the hardhearted fail to appreciate. The flipside is that American workers are cast in the role of the stupid and the hateful. The losers become the deplorables..."

19 Jameson, 1991, Chapter 1, section VI, www.marxists.org/reference/subject/philosophy/works/us/jameson.htm.

20 See note 54 in Chapter 1.

21 "Lessons from the Demise of the TPP," by Jomo Kwame Sundaram and Anis Chowdhury, Inter Press Service (IPS), January 5, 2017, www.ipsnews.net/2017/01/lessons-from-the-demise-of-the-tpp/.

22 Carson, 1962. See more in note 71 in the Introduction.

23 Gift im Acker – Glyphosat, die unterschätzte Gefahr? documentary film by Volker Barth, Westdeutscher Rundfunk Köln, 2015, www.ardmediathek.de/radio/die-story/Gift-im-Acker-Glyphosat-die-untersch%C3%A4/WDR-Fernsehen/Video?bcastId=7486242&documentId=31418678, and https://youtu.be/tWZspPPB85U.
See other documentaries in notes 301 and 302 in Chapter 15:

- Das Gift im Kuhstall – Sterbende Tiere, kranke Menschen
- Antibiotika ohne Wirkung?

24 "Agricultural Revolution in Germany: We Want It and We Can Do It," by Dirk Zimmermann, Greenpeace, January 25, 2017, www.greenpeace.org/international/en/news/Blogs/makingwaves/ariculture-revolution-germany-berlin/blog/58577/.

25 World Wildlife Fund (WWF), 2014. See more in note 79 in Chapter 3.

26 Linda Hartling in a personal communication on September 4, 2016: "Awake is William Stafford's answer to the question, are you an optimist or a pessimist. He said he is just awake."

27 Raskin, 2016, pp. 110–111.

28 Emmott, 2013.

29 “War and Peace, Climate Change and Citizen Responses,” communication from the Schumacher Center for a New Economics, September 9, 2014, http://us5.campaign-archive2.com/?u=69d509d113032e3126c4543ce&id=3df2710e&e=5017fb4435.

30 Schöne neue Welt: “Die Welt wird auf den Kopf gestellt,” documentary film on Silicon Valley by Claus Kleber, Zweites Deutsches Fernsehen, 2016, www.zdf.de/schoene-neue-welt/schoene-neue-welt-43773220.html. See the full note in the pdf edition of this book.

31 “Crowded Planet,” review by Clive Cookson, The Financial Times, July 12, 2013, www.ft.com/cms/s/2/a7e5ba20-e7e4-11e2-9aad-00144feabdc0.html#axzz3Cq4fyzJ8. See Ridley, 2010.

32 Danny Dorling, 2013, professor of geography at the University of Sheffield.

33 Hans Rosling and Steven Pinker have been criticized of having a positivity bias, also called Pollyannaism, which means remembering pleasant items more accurately than unpleasant ones. The 1913 novel Pollyanna by Eleanor H. Porter describes a girl who tries to find something to be glad about in every situation. See also “A Confused Statistician,” by Anne H. Ehrlich and Paul R. Ehrlich, Millennium Alliance for Humanity and Biosphere, November 12, 2013, http://mahb.stanford.edu/blog/a-confused-statistician.

34 Ridley, 2010, p. 88.

35 “The Rational Optimist,” review by Samuel Brittan, The Financial Times, June 12, 2010, www.ft.com/intl/cms/s/2/b2cbb506-74de-11df-aed7-00144feabdc0.html#axzz3Cq4fyzJ8.

36 Lindner, 2007a.

37 Lindner, 2002, p. 127.

38 See also lawyer Amy Chua, 2003, and her discussion of how exporting free market democracy may breed ethnic hatred and global instability.

39 Bourdieu and Passeron, 1990, p. 159.

40 Jameson, 1991. See also “When Nothing Is Cool,” in note 98 in the Preface.

41 Habermas and Dews, 1992, p. 187, as quoted in Outhwaite, 1994.

42 Norgaard, 2015.

43 More, 2014.

44 John Barry, in his contribution to the Great Transition Network (GTN) discussion on the topic of “The Church of Economism and Its Discontents,” on November 9, 2015, in response to Norgaard, 2015.

45 Ibid.

46 Harvey, 2000.

47 Social psychologist Jonathan Haidt, 2012, in his book The Righteous Mind, identifies mass immigration as trigger for authoritarian responses. Psychologist Svend Brinkmann, 2017a, sees unbridled individualism electing collectivist responses. Foreign affairs commentator Gideon Rachman, 2017, in his book Easternization, explains that it was economic globalization that brought a protectionist response to the fore. “In essence, the populist surge is an illiberal democratic response to decades of undemocratic liberal policies,” writes political scientist Cas Mudde in “Europe's Populist Surge: A Long Time in the Making,” by Cas Mudde, Foreign Affairs, November/December 2016, www.foreignaffairs.com/articles/europe/2016-10-17/europe-s-populist-surge.

48 “Schöne, verdammte Norm: Gerade Frankreich und die USA sollten nicht dem Rechtspopulismus verfallen,” essay by Dirk Kurbjuweit, Spiegel Online, December 12, 2015, pp. 92–93,

https://magazin.spiegel.de/SP/2015/51/140390039/?utm_source=spon&utm_campaign=centerpage. See also Winkler, 2009–2015.

49 Margalit, 1996, 1997, 2002.

50 Solomon, 2005.

51 Solomon, 2005. See also Galtung, 2012.

52 Jackson, 1990.

53 "The Coming Anarchy," by Robert D. Kaplan, The Atlantic, February 1994, www.theatlantic.com/magazine/archive/1994/02/the-coming-anarchy/304670/, pp. 44–76.

54 Raskin, 2016, p. 27. See also the 1979 dystopian film Mad Max by George Miller, or novelist Cormac McCarthy, 2006, describing a father and his young son's journey across post-apocalyptic America some years after an extinction event when the land is covered with ash and devoid of life. Sociologist Peter Frase, 2016, sees "exterminism" as one of four possible futures: communism, rentism, socialism, and exterminism. Frase arrives at this categorization by using two intersecting spectrums, one ranging from inequality to hierarchy and the other from scarcity to abundance. Frase reminds us of Walter Benjamin, 1940/1974, and his warnings that we are moving backwards into the future, a move that is illusionary. He is joined in these warnings by many others, among them journalists such as Owen Hatherley, 2015, who writes on architecture, politics, and culture.

55 "Mobiles now Become Weapons As Tactics Change In Syria's New Phoney War," by Robert Fisk, The Interdependent, April 12, 2013, www.independent.co.uk/news/world/middle-east/mobiles-become-weapons-as-tactics-change-in-syrias-new-phoney-war-8570465.html.

56 Schlachtfeld Internet – Wenn das Netz zur Waffe wird, a co-production of Norddeutscher Rundfunk, the US broadcaster WGBH and the Austrian Servus TV, by Svea Eckert und Alexandra Ringling and James Bamford, see http://youtu.be/-dGdRwsWaEc. See for media coverage in Germany, for instance, "'Schlachtfeld Internet': Das schwarze Budget der NSA," von René Martens, Die Zeit, January 12, 2015, www.zeit.de/kultur/film/2015-01/schlachtfeld-internet-snowden-ard. See the full note in the pdf edition of this book.

57 "Kontrollierte Eskalation," Der Spiegel 4/2015, January 17, 2015, p. 29, and "The Digital Arms Race: NSA Preps America for Future Battle," by Jacob Appelbaum, Aaron Gibson, Claudio Guarnieri, Andy Müller-Maguhn, Laura Poitras, Marcel Rosenbach, Leif Ryge, Hilmar Schmundt, and Michael Sontheimer, Spiegel Online International, January 17, 2015, www.spiegel.de/international/world/new-snowden-docs-indicate-scope-of-nsa-preparations-for-cyber-battle-a-1013409.html. See also www.spiegel.de/fotostrecke/photo-gallery-controlled-escalation-fotostrecke-122938.

58 See also Krüger, et al., 2013.

59 "'Black budget' Summary Details U.S. Spy Network's Successes, Failures and Objectives," by Barton Gellman and Greg Miller, The Washington Post, August 29, 2013, www.washingtonpost.com/world/national-security/black-budget-summary-details-us-spy-networks-successes-failures-and-objectives/2013/08/29/7e57bb78-10ab-11e3-8cdd-bcdc09410972_story.html?hpid=z1.

60 Langner, 2012.

61 Langner, 2012.

62 Schell, 2003.

63 "The Call of the Nation," by Uri Avnery, Human Wrongs Watch, December 10, 2016, https://human-wrongs-watch.net/2016/12/13/the-call-of-the-nation/: "The human mind changes much slower than material circumstances. It limps at least three or four generations behind, clinging to outdated ideas and

ideals, while political, economic and military realities race ahead. Modern nationalism arose only some two or three centuries ago. It is a comparatively recent invention. Some believe that it was created by the French revolution. A notable historian argued that it was created by the Spanish settlers in South America, who wanted to get rid of Spanish imperialism and constitute themselves as independent nations. Be that as it may, nationalism quickly became the dominant force in the world. By the end of World War I, it had broken up the old empires and created a dozen new nation-states. World War II finished the job. The nation state stands on two legs: the material and the spiritual. The material need to create larger markets and defend them against other large markets was obvious. The spiritual need of belonging to a human group was less so."

64 "Evolving Democracy," by Johan Galtung, TRANSCEND Media Service, February 13, 2017, www.transcend.org/tms/2017/02/evolving-democracy/.

65 Raskin, 2016, p. 11.

66 Raskin, 2016, p. 2.

67 Ibid.

68 Ibid.

69 Raskin, 2016, p. 13.

70 Raskin, 2016, p. 21.

71 Lindner and Desmond Tutu (Foreword), 2010.

72 Göle, 2013.

73 Lamont, et al., 2016.

74 Gabriela Saab in a personal communication on January 14, 2017: "The word for this resilience and flexibility in trying something that was denied in the first place is jeitinho (little flair, little way, little knack). It is a way of life in Brazil (for good and bad, that is important!). It means we would always (always!) try again and hope someone is going to be nice to us and help. Never get disappointed before trying once more! And the magic is that it usually works!" It is a privilege to have Gabriela Saab as esteemed member in the core leadership group of our Human Dignity and Humiliation Studies fellowship.

75 Raskin, 2016, p. 45. Mills, 1958.

76 Rifkin, 2009.

77 Margalit, 1996, 1997, 2002.

78 "Full Text of Alfred Nobel's Will," www.nobelprize.org/alfred_nobel/will/will-full.html.

79 "How Did Western Europe Cope with a Much Stronger Soviet Union and Warsaw Pact?" by Jan Øberg, Transnational Foundation for Peace and Future Research (TFF) Press Info # 385, TFF Series "The New Cold War" # 6, August 29, 2016, http://blog.transnational.org/2016/08/tff-pressinfo-385/.

80 Miller, 2006b. See her first, seminal book, Miller, 1976/1986. See also note 208 in Chapter 15.

81 Giddens, 1991, p. 202. I thank Dino Karabeg for reminding me of this quote.

82 Stael and Craiutu, 1818/2008, p. 407.

83 Chambers, 1952, pp. 469–460.

84 Bitter Lake, BBC documentary film by Adam Curtis, 2015, https://youtu.be/VRbq63r7rys. I thank Drew Pham for making me aware of this film.

85 "Kabul: City Number One – Part 3," by Adam Curtis, BBC Blogs, October 13, 2009, www.bbc.co.uk/blogs/adamcurtis/entries/302443a3-c143-3a71-8046-10ba64464fe6. Rostow laid out his theory in a book he called "The Stages of Economic Growth: A Non-Communist Manifesto."

86 "Kabul: City Number One – Part 3," by Adam Curtis, BBC Blogs, October 13, 2009, www.bbc.co.uk/blogs/adamcurtis/entries/302443a3-c143-3a71-8046-10ba64464fe6: "Walt Whitman Rostow … said that if you put the right technologies in place and educated key elites then the countries would inevitably develop into advanced capitalist societies. They would go through a series of logical stages (there were five) until you got what he modestly called 'Rostovian Lift-off.' Rostow laid out his theory in a book he called The Stages of Economic Growth: A Non-Communist Manifesto."

87 Milne, 2008.

88 McClelland, 1978, addressed entrepreneurial development and training in achievement thinking and behavior for small business owners in India, Tunisia, Iran, Poland, Malawi and the US.

89 "Kabul: City Number One – Part 3," by Adam Curtis, BBC Blogs, October 13, 2009, www.bbc.co.uk/blogs/adamcurtis/entries/302443a3-c143-3a71-8046-10ba64464fe6.

90 Toynbee, 1962, Cullather, 2002.

91 See also Martin, 2014.

92 "Who Gets Radicalized? What I Learned From My Interviews With Extremist Disciples," by Amra Sabic-El-Rayess, Huffington Post, June 19, 2016, www.huffingtonpost.com/entry/who-gets-radicalized-what-i-learned-from-my-interviews_us_5765fddce4b0ed0729a1c5c3.

93 "Ein katastrophaler Fehler": SPIEGEL-Gespräch Der amerikanische Historiker Timothy Snyder über die Vorbedingungen des Holocaust – und die gefährlichen Folgen unbedachter Nahostpolitik, Der Spiegel 44/2015, November 24, 2015, pp. 140–143. See the original German text, pp. 140–141, in the full note in the pdf edition of this book. See also Snyder, 2010, 2015, 2017.

94 Escrigas, 2016. See more in note 110 in Chapter 17.

95 Ted (F.E.) Trainer is an Australian academic, and an advocate of economic de-growth, simple living, and "conserver" lifestyles. He shows that the "decoupling claim" is not feasible. It claims that economic growth can be separated from demand for materials and energy, thus enabling these to be kept down to sustainable levels. See more in note 89 in Chapter 5.

96 Many are impressed by the truly impressive promises waiting in technological progress, yet, many hope that the question of "promises for whom?" will solve itself. Albert Hammond is a social entrepreneur who holds degrees engineering and applied mathematics, and he summarizes those promises in his contribution to the Great Transition Network Initiative discussion titled "The Degrowth Alternative," February 1, 2015. See the quote in the full note in the pdf edition of this book.

97 Berit Ås, in a personal conversation in her home in Asker, Norway, May 31, 2014. See more in notes 65 and 66 in Chapter 7.

98 See note 33 in Chapter 4.

99 Eder, 1992.

100 Eder, 1992, p. 378.

101 Ibid.

102 Sociologist Hans-Georg Soeffner, 1988.

103 Eder, 1992, p. 378.

104 Eder, 1992, p. 379.

105 Ibid.

106 Melba Padilla Maggay is a social anthropologist and president of the Institute for Studies in Asian Church and Culture. See her article "Church-State Tensions on Human Rights," by Melba Padilla Maggay, Philippine Daily Inquirer, August 12, 2016, http://opinion.inquirer.net/96433/church-state-tensions-on-

human-rights. Melba Maggay calls on the church of the Philippines to stand up against the "campaign against drugs and the rising body count of those killed on mere suspicion of being drug users and pushers." She warns that the separation of church and state should not be driven to amoral extremes: "Luther's doctrine of the 'two swords' can be applied only to the institutional aspects of state-church relationship, but not to individuals' moral choices, nor to the church's prophetic role as conscience if society." I thank George Patterson for making me aware of this article.

107 Riesman, et al., 1950/2001.

108 Pritzker, 2014, p. 40. See also Sundararajan, 2015.

109 I very much thank Hélène Lewis for giving me the book by Nico Moolman, 2012.

110 "Has the Bonhoeffer Moment Finally Arrived?" by Stephen R. Haynes, Huffington Post, November 28, 2016, www.huffingtonpost.com/stephen-r-haynes/has-the-bonhoeffer-moment_b_13275278.html. Stephen Haynes teaches courses on the Holocaust and Dietrich Bonhoeffer.

111 Historian George Marsden, 1994, in The Soul of the American University: From Protestant Establishment to Established Nonbelief, explains how in the U.S., most universities were originally founded with a mainly Protestant orientation, while earlier in Europe the Catholic origin of universities was dominant. Subsequently, universities bridged sectarian religious divides by becoming more secular or "liberal," guided by Enlightenment philosophy. Today many Western universities are ahistoric in their secularity, almost denying their Christian origins.

112 "Von Demütigung zu Terror und Krieg: Erniedrigung kann zu Gewalt führen, kann sie auch zu Liebe führen?" talk given by Evelin Lindner on October 11, 2015, at the 2015 Symposium "Gehirne zwischen Liebe und Krieg – Menschlichkeit in Zeiten der Neurowissenschaften," organized by gemeinnützige Turm der Sinne / Tower of the Senses GmbH, Nürnberg, Germany, www.auditorium-netzwerk.de/Neuerscheinungen-2015/Oktober-2015/Lindner-Evelin-Von-Demuetigung-zu-Terror-und-Krieg::31734.html. See also Lindner, 2016c.

113 Lindner, 2012f.

114 Witt and Schwesinger, 2013. See also Deci and Ryan, 1985, for the argument that an egalitarian group structure creates a prosocial attitude, and motivates group members to identify with the group and to attend to an assigned task, particularly when the task is based on a consensus. In this way, an intrinsic work motivation is created.

115 See, among others, David Sloan Wilson, 2015, for why both between-group selection and within-group selection may be important, rather than only the latter. See more in note 12 in Chapter 3.

116 Colander, et al., 2009.

117 Gowdy, et al., 2013, Abstract: "The intellectual histories of economics and evolutionary biology are closely intertwined because both subjects deal with living, complex, evolving systems. Because the subject matter is similar, contemporary evolutionary thought has much to offer to economics. In recent decades theoretical biology has progressed faster than economics in understanding phenomena like hierarchical processes, cooperative behavior, and selection processes in evolutionary change."

118 Wilson and Gowdy, 2013, p. S8. See also Gowdy and Seidl, 2004.

119 Barrington-Leigh, 2017.

120 Wilson and Wilson, 2007, https://pdfs.semanticscholar.org/7694/67447fc718c5c0069391958c77df93af7882.pdf, p. 27.

121 Axelrod, 2006.

122 Beinhocker, 2006.

123 Wilson and Gowdy, 2013, p. S6.

124 Wilson and Gowdy, 2013.

125 Frank, 2011.

126 Wilson and Gowdy, 2013, p. S6. See also Hodgson and Knudsen, 2010.

127 See Elina Penttinen, 2013, on how "the mechanistic-deterministic worldview derived from the Newtonian model has influenced the epistemology and methodology of IR (i.e., the idea that the world is constituted of independent fragments), and seeks ways to develop a new methodology for IR by drawing on the potential of a non-fragmented worldview." See the full note in the pdf edition of this book. See also note 143 in the Introduction.

128 Siebert and Ott, 2016, p. 33.

129 Boehm, 2001. Witt and Schwesinger, 2013, explain in footnote 4:

> In a survey analyzing 48 small primordial societies, partly organized as egalitarian hunter–gatherers, partly as chiefdoms, Boehm (1993) reports regular intentional sanctions placed on leaders who overstepped their prerogatives or on individuals trying to usurp the group such as public opinion and open discussion in councils, criticism and ridicule, and open disobedience. In more severe cases, the egalitarian alliance also ostracized the leader and terminated his leadership. In some cases, the African !Kung, the Australian aborigines, and the south American Yaruro even executed former leaders or "extremely aggressive men." Bingham (1999) has speculated that the threat of being injured by stone-throwing – a technique that must at some time have been invented in human phylogeny – may have been instrumental in guaranteeing a balance of power within the early groups.

130 Ostrom, 1990, 2010.

131 The Planetary Integrity Project: Creating a Safe Operating Space in Law and Governance, 2016, http://planetaryboundariesinitiative.org/wp-content/uploads/2016/10/PIP-Report-Sept-2016.pdf.

132 2011 Annual Conference of Human Dignity and Humiliation Studies, "Enlarging the Boundaries of Compassion," in Dunedin, New Zealand, August 29 – September 1, 2011, www.humiliationstudies.org/whoweare/annualmeeting/17.php.

133 The Next Step: Earth Trusteeship, by Klaus Bosselmann, at the Fifth Interactive Dialogue of the United Nations General Assembly on Harmony with Nature, United Nations Headquarters, NewYork, April 21, 2017. Klaus Bosselmann is Professor of Law and Director of the New Zealand Centre for Environmental Law at the University of Auckland, and Chair of the IUCN World Commission on Environmental Law Ethics Specialist Group. See also Bosselmann, 2015.

134 Christopher Boehm, 1993, 1999, 2012.

135 Witt and Schwesinger, 2013, p. S36. See also note 2 in Chapter 1.

136 Witt and Schwesinger, 2013, p. S36.

137 Ibid.

138 Eisler, 1987, Fiske, 1991.

139 Rifkin, 2009. Margalit, 1996, 1997, 2002.

140 See note 73 in Chapter 4.

141 See note 115 in Chapter 13.

142 Carveth, 2013. I thank Michael Britton for making me aware of this book. Also Maria Montessori thought in a similar line in her educational theory, when she called on instructors to "give priority to the inner teacher who animated" the child. The trope of the wisdom of the inner teacher that sits at our hearts is also to be found, for instance, in Tibetan Buddhists.

143 See note 37 in Chapter 11.

144 Linda Hartling in a personal communication on September 4, 2016.

145 Wergeland, 1843, p. 23. See the original Norwegian quote in the full note in the pdf edition of this book. I thank Bernt Hagtvet and Nikolai Brandal for making me aware of this quote. It is a privilege to have Bernt Hagtvet as esteemed member in the global advisory board of our Human Dignity and Humiliation Studies fellowship.

146 Lindner, 2014c.

147 Frost, 2003, p. 11.

148 "Fra Roosevelt til Brundtland," foredrag under prisutdelingen av Tore Frost, Fangenes testament pris 2011 tildeles filosof Tore Lindholm, Fredshuset i Risør, 25. juni 2011, www.aktive-fredsreiser.no/fredsdager/2011/fangenes_testamente_2011.htm. See the original Norwegian text in the full note in the pdf edition of this book. It was a great honor and immense joy for me to receive the 2009 Prisoner's Testament" Peace Award (Fangenes testament pris), www.aktive-fredsreiser.no/fredsdagen/2009/takketale_evelin_lindner.htm.

149 Roosevelt, 1948.

150 "Respekt for menneskets verdighet – en hovedfaktor i alle forsoningsprosesser," tale under prisutdelingen av filosof Tore Frost, representant for priskomitéen, Blanche Majors Forsoningspris 2012 tildeles HKH Kronprins Haakon, Fredshuset i Risør, 13. juni 2012, www.aktive-fredsreiser.no/forsoningspris/2012/hovedtale_respekt_menneskeverd.htm. Translated from the Norwegian original by Lindner: "Alle mennesker er født frie i (deres iboende) verdighet og (er derfor) like i (deres) menneskerettigheter."

151 "Respekt for menneskets verdighet – en hovedfaktor i alle forsoningsprosesser," tale under prisutdelingen av filosof Tore Frost, representant for priskomitéen, Blanche Majors Forsoningspris 2012 tildeles HKH Kronprins Haakon, Fredshuset i Risør, 13. juni 2012, www.aktive-fredsreiser.no/forsoningspris/2012/hovedtale_respekt_menneskeverd.htm. Translated and summarized from the Norwegian original by Lindner. See the original Norwegian quote in the full note in the pdf edition of this book.

152 "Respekt for menneskets verdighet – en hovedfaktor i alle forsoningsprosesser," tale under prisutdelingen av filosof Tore Frost, representant for priskomitéen, Blanche Majors Forsoningspris 2012 tildeles HKH Kronprins Haakon, Fredshuset i Risør, 13. juni 2012, www.aktive-fredsreiser.no/forsoningspris/2012/hovedtale_respekt_menneskeverd.htm. Translated and summarized from the Norwegian original by Lindner: "Det er også klokt ikke å forsøke seg på defintive begrunnelser av denne karakter. Kravet om anerkjennelse av menneskets iboende verdighet er et postulat uten innhold."

153 See note 199 in Chapter 15.

154 "Respekt for menneskets verdighet – en hovedfaktor i alle forsoningsprosesser," tale under prisutdelingen av filosof Tore Frost, representant for priskomitéen, Blanche Majors Forsoningspris 2012 tildeles HKH Kronprins Haakon, Fredshuset i Risør, 13. juni 2012, www.aktive-fredsreiser.no/forsoningspris/2012/hovedtale_respekt_menneskeverd.htm. Translated from the Norwegian original by Lindner: "Vårt følelsesliv, i spennet mellom lidenskap og lidelse, konfronterer oss med kjærligheten som selve grunnpremisset for menneskelivet i hele dets kompleksitet. Kjærligheten er hva livet dreier seg om."

155 "Respekt for menneskets verdighet – en hovedfaktor i alle forsoningsprosesser," tale under prisutdelingen av filosof Tore Frost, representant for priskomitéen, Blanche Majors Forsoningspris 2012 tildeles HKH Kronprins Haakon, Fredshuset i Risør, 13. juni 2012, www.aktive-fredsreiser.no/forsoningspris/2012/hovedtale_respekt_menneskeverd.htm. Translated and summarized

from the Norwegian original by Lindner. See the original Norwegian quote in the full note in the pdf edition of this book.

156 "Politics and Conscience," speech by Václav Havel, 1984, www.vaclavhavel.cz/showtrans.php?cat=clanky&val=73_aj_clanky.html&typ=HTM: "In an author's note, Havel writes, 'This speech was written for the University of Toulouse, where I would have delivered it on receiving an honorary doctorate, had I attended.' Havel, of course, had no passport and could not travel abroad. At the ceremony at the University of Toulouse-Le Mirail on May 14, 1984, he was represented by the English playwright Tom Stoppard. The essay first appeared in Prague in a saynizdat collection called The Natural World as Politicol Problem: Essays on Modern Man (Prague: Edice Expedice, Volume 188, 1984). The first English translation, by Erazim Kohák and Roger Scruton, appeared in the Salisbury Review, Number 2 (January 1985). This is the translation used here."

157 See the documentary film American Experience: Rachel Carson. See more in note 71 in the Introduction. See also Carson, 1962.

158 Linda Hartling in a personal communication on September 4, 2016.

159 Lindner and Desmond Tutu (Foreword), 2010. See a review by social psychologist and Kurt Lewin expert David Bargal, 2011b. Read more about David Bargal in note 169 in the Inspiring and Thought-Provoking Questions at the end of Section Three.

160 Emotional Literacy is a book by Claude M. Steiner, 2003, a psychotherapist who has written extensively about transactional analysis (TA). I thank Janet Gerson of reminding me of Steiner's work.

161 Freire, 1968/1973.

162 Rosenwein, 2006, pp. 19;197–202.

163 Ross, 2013, pp. 9, 45–46.

164 Oliner and Oliner, 1988.

165 The Greater Good Science Center at the University of California, Berkeley, CA, http://greatergood.berkeley.edu/about.

166 Keltner, et al., 2010, p. 15. I thank Linda Hartling for making me aware of this particular book edited by Dacher Keltner.

167 See also the idea of a "long sixteenth century" (circa 1450 – 1640), by historian Fernand Braudel, 1949, or the "long nineteenth century" (1789 – 1914), by historian Eric Hobsbawm, in Hobsbawm, 1962, 1975, 1987.

168 Münkler, 2015.

169 See note 162 in the Preface.

170 Wandel durch Annäherung, presentation by Egon Bahr, July 15, 1963, at the Evangelical Academy in Tutzing, Germany, German original: www.fes.de/archiv/adsd_neu/inhalt/stichwort/tutzinger_rede.pdf; English translation: "Change through Rapprochement," http://germanhistorydocs.ghi-dc.org/sub_document.cfm?document_id=81.

171 Encyclical Letter Laudato Si' of the Holy Father Francis on Care For Our Common Home, May 23, 2015, http://w2.vatican.va/content/francesco/en/encyclicals/documents/papa-francesco_20150524_enciclica-laudato-si.html.

172 Marshall, 1999. It is a privilege to have Monty Marshall as esteemed member in the global advisory board of our Human Dignity and Humiliation Studies fellowship since its inception.

173 "Humiliated fury" is a term coined by psychologist Helen Block Lewis in Lewis, 1971. I thank Thomas Scheff for making me aware of Lewis's work. See for some of his work, Scheff and Retzinger, 1991, Scheff, 1994, Scheff, 1997, Scheff, 2000, Scheff, 2006, Scheff, 2007, Scheff, 2013, Scheff and Retzinger, 1997.

174 "Obama Warns of Long Campaign as Iraq Strikes Continue against Isis," by Martin Chulov in Irbil, Mark Townsend in London, Jon Swaine in New York, The Observer, August 10, 2014, www.theguardian.com/world/2014/aug/09/obama-isis-northern-iraq-kurds-long-term-airdrops. See also David Miliband in an exclusive interview: "David Miliband: 'I Want Ed to Succeed. I'm Sure He Feels the Same About Me,'" by Jon Swaine in New York, The Observer, August 9, 2014, www.theguardian.com/politics/2014/aug/09/david-miliband-interview-new-york.

175 "The Truth about the IS," by Chandra Muzaffar, TRANSCEND Media Service, September 2014, www.transcend.org/tms/2014/09/the-truth-about-the-is/.

176 "God Wills It!" by Ury Avnery, Uri Avnery's Column, September 6, 2014, www.avnery-news.co.il/english/. Ury Avnery is a journalist, writer, peace activist, a former member of the Israeli parliament Knesset, and the founder of Gush Shalom.

177 Amir Rana, director of the Pak Institute for Peace Studies (http://san-pips.com), September 9, 2014, https://plus.google.com/u/0/114138804998079535274/posts?cfem=1.

178 "Egypt: Polarisation and Genocide," by Richard Falk, Global Justice in the 21st Century, August 24, 2013, https://richardfalk.wordpress.com/2013/08/24/1295/. Richard Falk is Albert G. Milbank Professor Emeritus of International Law at Princeton University and visiting distinguished professor in Global and International Studies at the University of California, Santa Barbara. He is also the United Nations Special Rapporteur on Palestinian human rights.

179 "Egypt: Polarisation and Genocide," by Richard Falk, Global Justice in the 21st Century, August 24, 2013, https://richardfalk.wordpress.com/2013/08/24/1295/. Falk is dismayed at the brutality with which the Muslim Brotherhood in Egypt is being crushed after its deposal in the military coup of 2013, and how little protest this brutality elicits. He writes: "Think of it: the group that had prevailed in a series of free elections throughout the nation is scapegoated overnight into 'terrorists' that must be crushed." He concludes:

> These Egyptian developments also raise awkward questions about whether there exist outer limits to the politics of self-determination, which has authenticated many national movements against European colonialism and oppressive rule. Egypt is in the throes of what might be called a process of Satanic self-determination, and there is no prospect of humanitarian intervention even if the motivation were present, which it isn't. Who would even have the temerity to invoke the norm of Responsibility to Protect (R2P), so pompously relied upon to validate the destruction of Gaddafi's Libya, in the dire circumstances of the Muslim Brotherhood? R2P is not an emergent principle of international law, as advocates claim, but an operative principle of geopolitical convenience.
>
> The ethos of human solidarity means that none of us dedicated to human rights, to the accountability of leaders for crimes against humanity, and to the quest for humane governance should abandon Egypt in this tragic hour of need. At the same time, we need to admit that there is no politics of human solidarity capable of backing up the ethos even in the face of genocidal tremors.

180 "Governments Can Reduce Our Dignity to that of Tagged Animals," by Edward Snowden, The Guardian, May 3, 2016, www.theguardian.com/us-news/2016/may/03/edward-snowden-assassination-complex-governments-tagged-animals-drone-warfare-whistleblower. In his Foreword in The Assassination Complex, a new book about drone warfare, Snowden explains why leaking information about wrongdoing is a vital act of resistance. I thank Ulrich Spalthoff for making me aware of this article. It is a privilege to have Ulrich Spalthoff as member on the board of directors of our Human Dignity and Humiliation Studies fellowship, and director of Dignity Press.

181 Etzioni, 2013.

182 Etzioni, 2013, p. 335: "Daily news reminds one that people in very different parts of the world feel personally aggrieved, insulted, and humiliated when they hold that their nation's sovereignty has been violated, even if the troops of another nation merely crossed a minor, vague line in the shifting sands.

Millions of people have shown that they are willing to die to protect the sovereignty of their nation, an indication of the depth of their commitment to this precept. The same complex of normative ideas is also tied to the strongly held precepts of self-determination that played a key role in the dismantling of colonial empires and the rise of independent nation states. The right of state sovereignty is trumpeted by the governments and citizens of both autocracies and democracies – all of whom readily decry foreign intervention into their affairs on nationalist grounds. The liberal international order as a normative paradigm, which is centered on the respect for sovereignty, is ensconced in a slew of international laws and institutions, such as the International Criminal Court (ICC) and most notably in the Charter of the United Nations (UN)."

183 Etzioni, 2013, Abstract.

184 "Individual Responsibility," by John Scales Avery, Human Wrongs Watch, January 20, 2017, https://human-wrongs-watch.net/2017/01/20/individual-responsibility/.

185 Lindner, 2016e.

186 John Bunzl in his contribution to the Great Transition Network Initiative discussion titled "The Struggle for Meaningful Work," January 19, 2017, in response to Klitgaard, 2017.

187 See, for instance, "Ecuador Revives Campaign for UN Tax Body," by Thalif Deen, Inter Press Service (IPS), January 27, 2017, www.ipsnews.net/2017/01/ecuador-revives-campaign-for-un-tax-body/.

188 "Interview with John Scales Avery, One of the Greatest Living Intellectuals on Earth," by Binu Mathew, Human Wrongs Watch, March 15, 2017, https://human-wrongs-watch.net/2017/03/23/interview-with-john-scales-avery-one-of-the-greatest-living-intellectuals-on-earth/.

189 See Amy Chua, 2007, on hyperpower, Michael Hudson, 2003, on super imperialism, or Richard Johnson, 2007, on how the concept of hegemony remains useful. Watch also the interview "The Moment of Empire" that Harry Kreisler conducted with Amy Chua on November 21, 2007, as part of the "Conversations with History" at the Institute of International Studies, University of California, Berkeley. See www.youtube.com/watch?v=QenLlFx4cCQ. In this interview, Chua explains the advantages of the "inclusivity of tolerance": The best and brightest will never be in one ethnicity; tolerance is a necessary, even though not sufficient element to become or remain a hyperpower (an empire that dominates the world). What Chua found in her research was that hyperpowers, throughout history, to maximize power, made use of diversity rather than suppressing it, and they did so through inclusive tolerance. See more in the full note in the pdf edition of this book. Chua warns that too much tolerance, however, too much diversity, is as subversive as too much intolerance. In the case of too much tolerance, unity – or what Chua calls "glue" – lacks. America was the first democratic hyperpower. According to a study, foreign-born entrepreneurs stood behind one in four U.S. technology startups over the past decade. See also Wadhwa, et al., 2009. When military domination is no longer feasible, the question arises as to how to create the "glue" of good-will and loyalty. Persians and Mongols used military power, Rome granted citizenship also to non-Romans, however, the United States, if it wishes to preserve power, can do neither. Chua explains the advantages of building "glue" through immigration (incorporating the best and brightest from all around the world) and outsourcing (creating links of loyalty in other parts of the world). Chua predicts that China, since it is an ethnically defined society, will never become a hyperpower, even if the United States were to fall. To summarize Chua's arguments, she speaks up for unity in diversity, and warns against letting unity in diversity veer toward uniformity and division.
The advantages of inclusivity, one may argue, however, are not valid for hyperpowers only. The global community is a case, at the highest global scale. There are also less grand scale cases, and as present-day example Indonesia may serve. Mohammad Yazid, staff writer at the Jakarta Post, explains that the lesson for Indonesia is that "the majority needs to promote tolerance, mutual respect, protection and empathy for ethnic, religious and political minorities." See "From Jakarta to Kosovo – What's the Big Attraction?" by

Mohammad Yazid, Jakarta Post, June 5, 2007, www.thejakartapost.com/news/2007/06/05/jakarta-kosovo-what039s-big-attraction.html.

190 "Schöne, verdammte Norm: Gerade Frankreich und die USA sollten nicht dem Rechtspopulismus verfallen," essay by Dirk Kurbjuweit, Spiegel Online, December 12, 2015, pp. 92–93, https://magazin.spiegel.de/SP/2015/51/140390039/?utm_source=spon&utm_campaign=centerpage. See also Winkler, 2009–2015.

191 Kent Klitgaard, 2017, in his response to comments on the Great Transition Network Initiative discussion titled "The Struggle for Meaningful Work," on February 16, 2017.

192 Ibid.

193 Linda Hartling in a personal communication on September 6, 2016.

194 Linda Hartling in a personal communication on September 4, 2016.

195 Lindner, 2006c, Chapter 5.

196 Juliet B. Schor is the Co-founder of the Center for a New American Dream, www.newdream.org.

197 Kimmel, 2013.

198 2016 Stanford University's 125th Commencement Address by Ken Burns, June 12, 2016, http://news.stanford.edu/2016/06/12/prepared-text-2016-stanford-commencement-address-ken-burns/. Ken Burns, historical documentary filmmaker, and I thank Linda Hartling for making me aware of his address.

199 "Why Is the Military-Industrial Complex Sometimes Called 'The Devil's Dynamo'?" by John Scales Avery, TRANSCEND Media Service, June 30, 2014, www.transcend.org/tms/2014/06/the-devils-dynamo/: "Why Is the Military-Industrial Complex Sometimes Called "The Devil's Dynamo"?" by John Scales Avery, TRANSCEND Media Service, June 30, 2014, www.transcend.org/tms/2014/06/the-devils-dynamo/: "When the Cold War ended with the collapse of the Soviet Union, a Washington-based think tank called 'Project for a New American Century' maintained that a strategic moment had arrived: The United States was now the sole superpower, and it ought to use military force to dominate and reshape the rest of the world. … The Nuremberg principles, which were used in the trial of Nazi leaders after World War II, explicitly outlawed 'Crimes against peace: (i) Planning, preparation, initiation or waging of war of aggression or a war in violation of international treaties, agreements or assurances; (ii) Participation in a common plan or conspiracy for the accomplishment of any of the acts mentioned under (i).'" See more in note 46 in Chapter 11, and in note 127 in Chapter 14.

200 Knausgård, 2009–2011.

201 "Testosterone In Male Songbirds May Enhance Desire To Sing But Not Song Quality," Johns Hopkins University, December 18, 2013, http://releases.jhu.edu/2013/12/18/testosterone-in-male-songbirds-may-enhance-desire-to-sing-but-not-song-quality/. I thank Linda Hartling for making me aware of the connection between testosterone and birdsong.

202 See note 72 in Chapter 3.

203 Tim Weiskel, Cambridge Climate Research Associate, in his contribution to the Great Transition Network (GTN) discussion on the topic of "Against Ecocide: Legal Protection for Earth," August 1, 2016, in response to Femke Wijdekop, 2016: "The fundamental problem (as the Odum brothers pointed out decades ago) is that humans maximize for net return while nature maximizes for gross return. As a species, we operate at fundamental cross-purposes with the governing 'laws' of Earth's ecosystem. If we do not learn that, AND learn to subordinate our notions of 'rights' and 'justice' to those which can operate sustainably within the Earth's functioning ecosystem, we will become extinct."

204 Alan Zulch, in his contribution to the Great Transition Network (GTN) discussion on the topic of "Against Ecocide: Legal Protection for Earth," August 1, 2016, in response to Femke Wijdekop, 2016. Alan Zulch is a program officer with the Kalliopeia Foundation, with a master's degree in transpersonal psychology and bachelor's in conservation and resources from U.C. Berkeley. He previously worked with the Global Oneness Project and the Global MindShift Foundation following twelve years in the corporate world managing web, call centre and telecommunications teams. See http://ourworld.unu.edu/en/contributors/alan-zulch.

205 Alan Zulch, ibid.

206 Alan Zulch explains (ibid.) that simplification will occur because in a dissipative structure such as the Earth, entropy can only be mitigated through simplicity: "We are on a finite planet, facing predicaments that Bill Rees well describes. Before long, simplifying won't be a lifestyle choice or political stance, but a condition. As ecologist Jacopo Simonetta has pointed out, we're not facing an energy crisis, we're in an entropy crisis. We have insufficient capacity to dissipate entropy in our increasingly complex closed system. And this isn't just physical entropy, but, fascinatingly, cultural, too, as Simonetta points out (www.cassandralegacy.blogspot.com/2016/03/the-other-side-of-global-crisis-entropy.html)." Zulch thinks that the human failure to understand or manage entropy is related to "our culture's inability to face limits, death, endings, closure, the shadow. Rather than face such realities directly, we moderns too often marginalize, banish, and deny them." In resonance with Carol Smaldino, Zulch reminds that, "as true for all shadow material, what we refuse to face consciously re-emerges from the underworld in distorted fashion, in the form of narcissism, cruelty, projection, anxiety, and compulsive behavior (Think consumption habits: 'You can never get enough of what you don't really need.')."

207 See Lindner and Desmond Tutu (Foreword), 2010.

208 Sarah Lyons-Padilla, et al., 2015, see a summary in "I've Studied Radicalization – and Islamophobia Often Plants the Seed," by Sarah Lyons-Padilla, The Guardian, June 13, 2016, www.theguardian.com/commentisfree/2016/jun/13/radicalisation-islamophobia-orlando-shooting-florida-muslims-trump. I thank Rigmor Johnsen for making me aware of this Guardian article, and am glad to have her as esteemed member in our Human Dignity and Humiliation Studies fellowship. Sarah Lyons-Padilla builds on research done by Arie Kruglanski, see, among others, Doosje, et al., 2016, Dugas and Kruglanski, 2014. It is a privilege to have also Arie Kruglanski as esteemed member in the global advisory board of our Human Dignity and Humiliation Studies fellowship.

209 Fineman, 2004, Waring, 1988.

210 "Phyllis Schlafly, 'First Lady' of a Political March to the Right, Dies at 92," by Douglas Martin, September 5, 2016, New York Times, www.nytimes.com/2016/09/06/obituaries/phyllis-schlafly-conservative-leader-and-foe-of-era-dies-at-92.html. I thank Linda Hartling for making me aware of Phyllis Schlafly and her life mission.

211 See, among others, Scheuer, 2011.

212 Turk, 2004, Abstract: "The sociology of terrorism has been understudied, even though considerable literatures on various forms of social conflict and violence have been produced over the years. The aim here is to note what has been learned about the social origins and dynamics of terrorism in order to suggest agendas for future research. Arguably the main foci of sociological studies of terrorism should be (a) the social construction of terrorism, (b) terrorism as political violence, (c) terrorism as communication, (d) organizing terrorism, (e) socializing terrorists, (f) social control of terrorism, and (g) theorizing terrorism. For each issue, I provide a brief summary of current knowledge, with bibliographic leads to more detailed information, as well as identify research issues." I thank Kristian Berg Harpviken, for making me aware of this article.

213 Borchgrevink and Harpviken, 2010. It is a privilege to have Kristian Berg Harpviken as esteemed member in the global advisory board of our Human Dignity and Humiliation Studies fellowship.

214 Borchgrevink and Harpviken, 2010, p. 254.

215 "Why Foreign Military Intervention Usually Fails in the 21st Century," by Richard Falk, Transnational Foundation for Peace and Future Research (TFF), December 3, 2014, http://blog.transnational.org/2014/12/why-foreign-military-intervention-usually-fails-in-the-21st-century/.

216 Schmid, 2013, p. 10.

217 "White House: 'War on Terrorism' Is Over," by The Washington Times, August 6, 2009, www.washingtontimes.com/news/2009/aug/06/white-house-war-terrorism-over/?feat=home_headlines. See also, "Obama Administration Says Goodbye to 'War on Terror,'" by Oliver Burkeman in Washington, The Guardian, March 25, 2009, www.theguardian.com/world/2009/mar/25/obama-war-terror-overseas-contingency-operations: "US defence department seems to confirm use of the bureaucratic phrase 'overseas contingency operations.'"

218 Ibid.

219 "'Over My Dead Body': Spies Fight Obama Push to Downsize Terror War," by Eli Lake, The Daily Beast, May 21, 2014, www.thedailybeast.com/articles/2014/05/21/over-my-dead-body-spies-fight-obama-push-to-downsize-terror-war.html.

220 Ibid.

221 Historian Philipp Blom, 2008, draws together such diverse examples as the industrialization with its assembly line method and minimum wage, quantum physics and the discovery of radioactivity, advances in aviation and shipbuilding, the emergence of new views on the human psyche, such as in psychoanalysis, the staging of new music, such as by Igor Stravinsky, or women's rights, and Futurism.

222 Kimmel, 2013.

223 "2014 No Good. May All Good Forces Unite in 2015!" by Johan Galtung, Transcend Media Service, December 31, 2014, www.transcend.org/tms/2014/12/2014-no-good-2015-any-better/. Galtung lists 15 current areas that are openly or latently conflictual. See the full note in the pdf edition of this book.

224 See note 108 in Chapter 15.

225 See Carol Smaldino's deep reflections published in Huffington Post. For three recent postings, consider:
- "Mental Health Awareness Month in a Climate of Denial," by Carol Smaldino, Huffington Post, May 11, 2016, www.huffingtonpost.com/carol-smaldino/mental-health-awareness-m_b_9895080.html.
- "Psychological Policy For Presidents: The Deplorable Dilemma," by Carol Smaldino, Huffington Post, September 17, 2016, www.huffingtonpost.com/carol-smaldino/psychological-policy-for-_b_12059406.html.
- "Life after Hate with Ex-White Supremacist Christian Picciolini," Carol Smaldino, Huffington Post, May 10, 2017, www.huffingtonpost.com/entry/5913779ae4b04e66b8c3ad99.

It is a privilege to have Carol Smaldino as esteemed member in the global advisory board of our Human Dignity and Humiliation Studies fellowship.

226 Alan Zulch. See note 206 in this Chapter 18.

227 "Don't Blame Trump: Heal Thyself, America," by Peter T. Coleman, Huffington Post, July 24, 2016, www.huffingtonpost.com/entry/dont-blame-trump-heal-thyself-america_us_5794d247e4b0e002a3138ef1.

228 "21 September 2016: 10 Pointers," by Johan Galtung, TRANSCEND Media Service, September 26, 2016, www.transcend.org/tms/2016/09/21-september-2016-10-pointers/. And see "The State of the World–By Journalism," by Johan Galtung, TRANSCEND Media Service, September 23, 2016, www.transcend.org/tms/2016/09/the-state-of-the-world-by-journalism/.

229 Ruben Nelson in his contribution to the Great Transition Network Initiative discussion titled "Journey to Earthland: Making the Great Transition to Planetary Civilization," September 14, 2016, in response to Raskin, 2016.

230 See, among others, Rieff, 2016, or Wyatt-Brown, 1982. See also Wyatt-Brown, 2014.

231 Lindner, 2006c, pp. 103–104.

232 "A Conversation with Holger Hoock," May 9, 2017, http://holgerhoock.com/wp-content/uploads/2017/02/A-Conversation-with-Holger-Hoock.pdf. Hoock, 2017. I thank Linda Hartling for making me aware of this book

233 See Lindner, 2006c, Chapter 7: The Humiliation Addiction, in my book Making Enemies: Humiliation and International Conflict.

234 Wyatt-Brown, 1982. See also Wyatt-Brown, 2014, and Cohen, 1996, Cohen and Nisbett, 1997, Cohen, et al., 1996, Cohen and Vandello, 1997, Cohen, et al., 1998, Leung and Cohen, 2011, Nisbett and Cohen, 1996, Vandello, et al., 2008, Vandello and Cohen, 2003.

235 "Interview zum Mittelmeer-Drama: CDU-Veteran Geißler zur Flüchtlingspolitik: 'Scharfmacherische faule Ausrede'," with Martina Fietz, Focus, April 21, 2015, www.focus.de/politik/deutschland/interview-zum-mittelmeer-drama-cdu-veteran-geissler-zur-fluechtlingspolitik-scharfmacherische-faule-ausrede_id_4626161.html. Translated from German by Evelin Lindner.

236 Wie die USA von Deutschland aus den Kampf gegen den Terror führen, ARD Fernsehdiskussion Beckmann, Das Erste, November 28, 2013, published on November 29, 2013, on https://youtu.be/AaKB79tWhDU. Translated from German by Evelin Lindner. See the German original in the full note in the pdf edition of this book. See also "US Threatens to Penalize Allies on UN Voting," by Thalif Deen, Inter Press Service (IPS), February 7, 2017, www.ipsnews.net/2017/02/us-threatens-to-penalize-allies-on-un-voting/.

237 Taibbi, 2017.

238 "Why Trump?" by George Lakoff, Huffington Post, March 3, 2016, www.huffingtonpost.com/george-lakoff/why-trump_1_b_9372450.html. I thank Michael Britton for making me aware of this article.

239 D'Antonio, 2015. Donald Trump's mother hailed from the Isle of Lewis, the largest island of the Outer Hebrides, off Scotland's northwest coast. Its culture of humble collaborative egalitarianism represents an extreme contrast to Donald Trump's approach. See "Donald Trump's Mother Was an Immigrant – From a Remote Rugged Island in Scotland," by Carol Zall, Public Radio International (PRI), October 29, 2016, www.pri.org/stories/2016-10-29/donald-trumps-mother-was-immigrant-remote-rugged-island-scotland.

240 Fred Jr. died an alcoholic, 42 years old, in 1981.

241 Trump's mixture of Scottish and German background has been labeled, by novelist Joseph Conrad, as "possibly the worst heritage you could have, because Scots-Germans have, as he said, the instincts of a puritan, combined with an insatiable imagination for conquest." See "Donald Trump's Mother Was an Immigrant – From a Remote Rugged Island in Scotland," by Carol Zall, Public Radio International (PRI), October 29, 2016, www.pri.org/stories/2016-10-29/donald-trumps-mother-was-immigrant-remote-rugged-island-scotland.

242 Margalit, 1996, 1997, 2002.

243 Military-Industrial Complex Speech by Dwight D. Eisenhower, 34th President of the United States, on January 17, 1961, Public Papers of the Presidents, Dwight D. Eisenhower, 1960, pp. 1035–1040, http://coursesa.matrix.msu.edu/~hst306/documents/indust.html, see also https://youtu.be/8y06NSBBRtY. See more in note 46 in Chapter 11.

244 "Why Is the Military-Industrial Complex Sometimes Called 'The Devil's Dynamo'?" by John Scales Avery, TRANSCEND Media Service, June 30, 2014, www.transcend.org/tms/2014/06/the-devils-dynamo/: "Since World War II, the United States has interfered either militarily or covertly in the internal affairs of very many countries." See more in note 46 in Chapter 11, in note 127 in Chapter 14, and in note 199 in this Chapter 18.

245 Wixon and Merchant, 2014, p. 2. I thank Linda Hartling for sharing this quote with me.

Inspiring and Thought-Provoking Questions to Section Three

1 Albert Einstein (1879 – 1955), German original: "Es gibt keine großen Entdeckungen und Fortschritte, solange es noch ein unglückliches Kind auf Erden gibt." Kinderhilfe für Siebenbürgen is a contemporary project inspired by Einstein's saying. Jenny Rasche, a young woman from Germany, felt called to action when she saw extremely neglected Roma families in Rumania. She began by finding a way to nourish the children and bring them to school. This gained her the trust of the mothers. After a while, the young sons, after school, taught their fathers to become responsible members of their community, for instance, by building proper housing. See www.roma-kinderhilfe.de/index.php/de/.

2 Linda Hartling in a personal communication on December 18, 2015, in favor of Tikkun editor Peter Gabel's usage of the term re-humiliation, and of Joyce Fletcher's term of being invisibilized. Fletcher, like Hartling, uses the work of Jean Baker Miller to apply a growth-in-connection model of human growth and development to organizational settings.

3 Jean Baker Miller coined the phrase waging good conflict, a term that was central for my book Emotion and Conflict (2009). Waging good conflict means refraining from the domination techniques that were employed by leaders in the past.

4 "Stopping the Snake: Indigenous Protesters Shut Down Construction of Dakota Access Pipeline," Amy Goodman with Winona LaDuke, Joye Braun, Ajamu Baraka, Democracy Now, August 18, 2016, www.democracynow.org/2016/8/18/stopping_the_snake_indigenous_protesters_shut. Winona LaDuke is a Native American activist and executive director of the group Honor the Earth. She lives and works on the White Earth Reservation in northern Minnesota. She was the Green Party vice-presidential nominee in 1996 and 2000. Winona LaDuke:

> ...the system is crumbling all around us. And at the end of the fossil fuel era, it's time to move towards an elegant transition. But in the final thrashings of the fossil fuel era, what you have is a lot of extreme behavior going on. You have extreme extraction. You have, you know, tar sands mining. You have blowing-up, you know, oil rigs. And you have endless, endless contamination. And at the same time, you have climate change happening. You know, in our teachings, we talk about this as the time when you've got to make a choice between two paths as a country. One path is well-worn, and it's scorched; the other is not well-worn, and it's green.

See for more the Seven Fires Prophecy and Benton-Banai, 1988. The prophecy is interpreted in different ways by LaDuke and Benton-Banai. I thank Winona LaDuke's assistant Nicolette Stagle for helping me understand.

See also "Seven Fires Prophecy of the Anishnabe People and the Process of Reconciliation," with Grandfather William Commanda, Keeper of the Seven Fires Wampum Belt of the Anishnabe (Algonquin) Peoples, often called "The Gandhi of the Indian World," www.oneprayer.org/Seven_Fires_Prophecy.html:

> We believe that the road towards blind materialism, the choice for the majority of humanity and especially the Light Skinned or European/American, created an environment where Nature and Natural People have suffered immensely. In the end, it can only lead to our collective destruction. Our

way is above all a Spiritual Path. We are not, nor have we ever, been slaves to the material path. Our strength lies in our native ability to go beyond all that happened to our people in the past 508 years. The joining together of the material knowledge of the West with the spiritual wisdom and values of the Indigenous Peoples of this land is a path of healing and survival for all humanity.

5 Richards and Andersson, 2017, Chapter 1: South Africa Now as Threat and as Promise.

6 Donati and Archer, 2015, p. 14. I thank Linda Hartling for making me aware of this quote. The Swedish Theory of Love is a 2016 Swedish documentary film directed by Erik Gandini, where sociologist Zygmunt Bauman explains that independence strips people from the ability of socializing. I thank Guri Lorentzen Østbye for making me aware of this film.

7 "Im Zweifel links: Wiederkehr der Würde," by Jakob Augstein, Der Spiegel 13/2017, March 25, 2017, p. 10, https://magazin.spiegel.de/SP/2017/13/150231519/?utm_source=spon&utm_campaign=centerpage. German original translated by Lindner: "Now ends a mindset, where everything has a price and only the price decides about the value. Where values are only worthwhile if they can be calculated. Where politics are an evil that stands in the way of market justice. Where the market is not only seen as more efficient – it also is given more legitimacy than democracy. Therefore pure market was pure morality. This was the wretched economism…. But those who place human dignity at the center of their deliberations recognize that no person is always a benefit optimizer, and societies are no economic aggregates." See the German original in the full note in the pdf edition of this book.

8 Betty A. Reardon in a personal communication on July 6, 2010, in Melbu, Vesterålen, Norway. I am deeply thankful to Betty Reardon for her untiring support for our dignity work since we first met in 1995. It was a great privilege to meet her for the first time at the UNESCO expert meeting "Towards a Women's Agenda for a Culture of Peace," April 25–18, 1995, invited by Ingeborg Breines. I had the privilege of having a chapter in her edited book, see Lindner, 1999. See for one of her recent publications, Reardon and Hans, 2010.

9 Barthes, 1971/1996. I thank Howard Richards for reminding me of this book by Roland Barthes.

10 "Bringing In the Future: An Essay on Time," by Johan Galtung, TRANSCEND Media Service, November 21, 2016, www.transcend.org/tms/2016/11/bringing-in-the-future-an-essay-on-time/.

11 "Toward a Post-Predatory World," by Michael Britton, 2016, unpublished essay.

12 See note 184 in the Introduction.

13 Vallacher, et al., 2010, p. 256.

14 Ross, 1995. It was a privilege to have Lee Ross as my doctoral advisor, and later as esteemed member of the first hour in the global advisory board of our Human Dignity and Humiliation Studies fellowship.

15 Marshall, 1999. See also Dan Shapiro, 2016, on How to Resolve Your Most Emotionally Charged Conflicts. It is a privilege to have Monty Marshall and Dan Shapiro as esteemed members in the global advisory board of our Human Dignity and Humiliation Studies fellowship since its inception.

16 Richards and Andersson, 2017, Introduction.

17 Bhaskar, 2008. See Richards and Andersson, 2017, Introduction.

18 Searle, 1995, Chapter 9. See Richards and Andersson, 2017, Introduction.

19 Barad, 2003, p. 829. Physicist Niels Bohr speaks of intra-actions and that one must reject the presumed inherent separability of observer and observed, knower and known.

20 Jervis, 2006, p. 641. Jervis suggests going back fifty years, revisiting the typology introduced by M. Brewster Smith, et al., 1956.

21 See on tipping points, among others, Gladwell, 2000.

22 Neurath, 1959, p. 201.

23 Tolstoy, 1886/1935.

24 See for the projection of four possible sustainable lifestyles for 2050, UNEP/Wuppertal Institute Collaborating Centre on Sustainable Consumption and Production (CSCP), 2011–2012.

25 Raskin, et al., 2002, p. 14.

26 Raskin, et al., 2002, p. 15.

27 Siebert and Ott, 2016, p. 12.

28 Hirschman, 1977. See also Adelman, 2013, and "Understanding Society – Innovative Thinking About a Global World: Hirschman on the Passions" by Daniel Little, May 14, 2013, http://understandingsociety.blogspot.no/2013/05/hirschman-on-passions.html.

29 "More of the Same: World Bank Doing Business Report Continues to Mislead," by Anis Chowdhury and Jomo Kwame Sundaram, Inter Press Service (IPS), December 15, 2016, www.ipsnews.net/2016/12/more-of-the-same-world-bank-doing-business-report-continues-to-mislead.

30 See note 144 in Chapter 11.

31 "Tapping the Victim Syndrome!" Voters as Victims Fuel Trump's Appeal," by Anthony J. Marsella, TRANSCEND Media Service, June 13, 2016, www.transcend.org/tms/2016/06/tapping-the-victim-syndrome-voters-as-victims-fuel-trumps-appeal/.

32 See note 54 in Chapter 1.

33 "Fear of Terrorism Lifts Donald Trump in New York Times/CBS Poll," by Jonathan Martin and Dalia Sussman, New York Times, December 10, 2015, www.nytimes.com/2015/12/11/us/politics/fear-of-terrorism-lifts-donald-trump-in-new-york-times-cbs-poll.html?_r=0.

34 Germany is only one among many examples, where the strategy of "picking up" disaffected youths is being practiced. Andrea Müller, expert for right-wing extremism, Jugendbildungsstätte Bremen, LidiceHaus, Bremen, Germany, observes this strategy since many years.

35 Bourdieu and Passeron, 1990.

36 "Impunity Leads Perpetrators to Continue Child Rights Violations in DR Congo – UN Report," United Nations News Centre, www.un.org/apps/news/story.asp?NewsID=48316#.U84t7bHzkmy.

37 "The Global Slavery Index 2016 Report," Global Slavery Index (www.globalslaveryindex.org), http://assets.globalslaveryindex.org/downloads/Global+Slavery+Index+2016.pdf.

38 Der Vietnamkrieg: Gesichter einer Tragödie / La sale guerre (The Vietnam War – Faces of a Tragedy), French/German documentary film by Christel Fomm, Westdeutscher Rundfunk Köln, 2015, see also https://youtu.be/6_LVr_IUtKE. See also "Vietnamkrieg – Gesichter einer Tragödie" Krieg im Spiegel der Medien," by Daland Segler, Frankfurter Rundschau, April 14, 2015, www.fr-online.de/tv-kritik/-vietnamkrieg---gesichter-einer-tragoedie--krieg-im-spiegel-der-medien,1473344,30425514.html. See the full note in the pdf edition of this book.

39 See note 72 in Chapter 3.

40 We had the 2013 Annual Conference of Human Dignity and Humiliation Studies, "Search for Dignity," in Stellenbosch, South Africa, April 24–28, 2013, www.humiliationstudies.org/whoweare/annualmeeting/21.php. I was privileged to live in different parts of South Africa subsequent to our conference and become profoundly enriched by the people I met.

41 History offers many examples. From social servitude only to fall into economic and political dependency, this was the fate of the peasantry of Sicily when it arose from feudalism, see Blok, 1988.

42 See more images and photos on www.humiliationstudies.org/whoweare/evelin/pics13.php. I thank Jingyi Dong for her personal communication on June 25, 2015, where she shared her views on the role of Lu Xun

with me. She took an image by Catherine Hoppers as starting point, an image that depicts a white and a black man fighting, oblivious of the fact that they stand in the mouth of a crocodile that will eat both. This image aims to visualize that a global economic system will eat all, and that it would be preferable to focus attention on the crocodile rather than on infighting. See Dong's message in the full note in the pdf edition of this book. See also Lu Xun, 2000a, b. See also Lu Xun, 2002a, b, c, 2003, 2004.

43 Watch Square Idée, a series on Arte, http://sites.arte.tv/square/fr/square-idee-square-0. See, for instance:
• Comment va la démocratie ? (How is democracy doing?), May 10, 2015, with Francis Fukuyama and Geoffroy de Lagasnerie, who speaks about "l'art de la révolte" (the art of revolt), http://info.arte.tv/fr/comment-va-la-democratie, or https://youtu.be/OrAabVskKLM.
• Meeting Snowden: Avec Birgitta Jonsdottir, Larry Lessig et Edward Snowden, May 29, 2017, http://sites.arte.tv/square/fr/meeting-snowden-square, or https://youtu.be/giHR8NHYyUM.
See the full note in the pdf edition of this book.

44 Raymond Williams, 1961, academic, novelist, and critic, wrote in The Long Revolution, p. 10: "It seems to me that we are living through a long revolution, which our best descriptions only part interpret. It is a genuine revolution, transforming men and institutions; continually and variously opposed by explicit reaction and by pressure of habitual forms and ideas. Yet it is a difficult revolution to define, and its uneven action is taking place over so long a period that it is almost impossible not to get lost in its exceptionally complicated process." I thank Tony Webb for making me aware of Williams' discussion. The Levellers were members of a political movement during the English Civil Wars which emphasized popular sovereignty, extended suffrage, equality before the law, and religious tolerance, all of which were expressed in the manifesto "Agreement of the People" (issued between 1647 and 1649). The trope of the "unfinished revolution" has been taken up by many authors, among them Shaw, 2000, Steele, 2007b. See also the unfinished revolution of Douglas Engelbart, to which Dino Karabeg introduced me, as well as reminding me of the work of Erich Jantsch, 1980, or Donella Meadows, 2008.

45 Kirst, 1975/1976. I thank my father for making me aware of this book. He received it as a gift from his students when he was a teacher shortly after it had been published. His students demanded that he read passages of this book aloud to them, so that they would be able to grasp what had befallen Germany before they had been born.

46 Milani, 2008.

47 "It Was the Democrats' Embrace of Neoliberalism That Won It for Trump," by Naomi Klein, The Guardian, November 9, 2016, www.theguardian.com/commentisfree/2016/nov/09/rise-of-the-davos-class-sealed-americas-fate.

48 Recent research in the U.S. has shed light on the influence of elite anti-tax advocacy groups hijacking the conservative agenda, even though their interests are not necessarily aligned with other conservative interests such as business interests, or the interests of angry, culturally fearful conservative populists. The most significant elite anti-tax advocacy organization seems to be the US nationwide, multipurpose political federation called Americans for Prosperity (AFP), as part of "weaponized" conservative philanthropy. See Theda Skocpol and Hertel-Fernandez, 2016, as well as Jane Mayer, 2016, and her book on Dark Money. I thank Glyn Rimmington for making me aware of book by Mayer. See also "Who Owns the GOP?" by Theda Skocpol, Dissent, February 3, 2016, www.dissentmagazine.org/online_articles/jane-mayer-dark-money-review-koch-brothers-gop. When I try to look at the situation through the lens of dignity and humiliation, then people who until now felt dejected and shameful seem to be increasingly willing to develop a burning sense of victimhood they did not deserve, of sense of humiliation strong enough to cry out for action (I have studied this dynamic in depth in Nazi Germany). Politicians such as Bernie Sanders attempt to identify factual root causes, while populists first bundle and instigate anger and then channel it toward scapegoats, those they mistake for humiliators, wittingly or unwittingly giving cover to the actual humiliators.

Organizations such as the AFP could be described as Trojan Horses that cannibalize and dominate their hosts by way of what I call "the art of humiliation."

49 "Donald Trump on Jeb Bush Attack: He's a 'Very Low-Energy Kind of Guy,' 'Had to Do Something,'" by David Sherfinski, The Washington Times, September 2, 2015, www.washingtontimes.com/news/2015/sep/2/donald-trump-jeb-bush-attack-hes-very-low-energy-k/.

50 "Donald Trump: Your Sons Love for Hunting African Animals Has Nothing to Do With the Second Amendment," by Tanya Young Williams, Huffington Post, October 20, 2015, www.huffingtonpost.com/tanya-young-williams/donald-trump-your-sons-lo_b_8333534.html. I thank Linda Hartling for making me aware of this article.

51 A Dangerous Game, 2014, U.S. feature film, www.adangerousgamemovie.com/. I thank Linda Hartling for making me aware of this film.

52 "Privilege, Pathology and Power," by Paul Krugman, New York Times, January 1, 2016, www.nytimes.com/2016/01/01/opinion/privilege-pathology-and-power.html. I thank Linda Hartling for making me aware of this article.

53 See note 34 above.

54 "Stories from ISIS Recruits: Drugs, Money and Preying on Youth," by Chaker Khazaal, Huffington Post, March 1, 2016, www.huffingtonpost.com/chaker-khazaal/stories-from-isis-recruit_b_9349974.html. Lebanese social worker Maya Yamout reports: "In fact, many of those I interviewed had the absent-father syndrome. They missed their father figure, so ISIS and other terrorist organizations send someone like a Sheikh to pretend they're there for them. Next thing you know, they are in Syria or Iraq fighting." Nancy and Maya Yamout conducted interviews with thirty-five suspected terrorists being jailed in Lebanon for their master's program at the Modern University for Business and Science in Beirut, Lebanon, and found out that all interviewed terrorists had their father image destroyed, either the father was absent or had humiliated the son. They conducted interviews with thirty-five suspected terrorists being jailed in Lebanon.

55 Lindner, 2006c.

56 Lu Xun, 2000a, b. See also Lu Xun, 2002a, b, c, 2003, 2004. I thank Jingyi Dong for her personal communication on June 25, 2015, where she shared her views on the role of Lu Xun with me. She explained: "The communist movement in China started from the university campus, then penetrated into the army, then to rural society, and ultimately Mao established a field with a unique structure. My ultimate ambition is to trace this trajectory by the light of your theory. I would like to highlight the difference between you and Lu Xun: Lu Xun asked a question, and you have the key to the question!" See also note 53 in Chapter 14.

57 Jenny Rasche, a young woman from Germany was inspired by Albert Einstein's saying: "Es gibt keine großen Entdeckungen und Fortschritte, solange es noch ein unglückliches Kind auf Erden gibt" (There are no great discoveries and advances as long as there is an unhappy child on earth). She founded the project Kinderhilfe für Siebenbürgen. See www.roma-kinderhilfe.de/index.php/de/.

58 See for more details, for instance, Preventing Terrorism and Countering Violent Extremism and Radicalization that Lead to Terrorism: A Community-Policing Approach, www.osce.org/secretariat/116516, EXIT-Deutschland: www.exit-deutschland.de, SAVE – Sisters Against Violent Extremism: www.women-without-borders.org/save/, Aufklärungsnetzwerk gegen Radikalisierung (RAN): http://ec.europa.eu/dgs/home-affairs/what-we-do/networks/radicalisation_awareness_network/index_en.htm.

59 With respect to humankind having all the knowledge, see, as one example, David Schwartzman, 2016, and his calculations of "how much and what kind of energy" humanity needs. The so-called public trust doctrine, which indicates that the citizens of a country own the natural resources, has been advocated in

recent years as a tool to compel governments across the world to take action against climate change, see, among others, Our Children's Trust, www.ourchildrenstrust.org.

60 Ury, 1999, p. xvii.

61 Clearly, there is a connection between equality and equal dignity – the connection is entailed in the human rights stipulation that equal chances and enabling environments for all are necessary to protect human dignity.

62 Discourse analyst Michael Karlberg, 2013, explains that, indeed, such a new social order would not be without hierarchy. See more in note 21 in the Introduction.

63 See, for instance, Michael Maren, 1997, and his book on a humanitarian worker's "road to hell." This book was being read by almost all humanitarian aid workers I met in Africa in 1998 and 1999, when I carried out my doctoral research, and all resonated with its sad message. We thank Anton Verwey, formerly UNHCR, for sharing his path with us in our 27th Dignity Conference in Croatia in 2016, www.humiliationstudies.org/whoweare/annualmeeting/27.php. While many idealists try to solve problems for people on the ground, those in power positions, including in humanitarian organizations, are often beholden to the power hierarchy they are part of, lest they will lose their position, including their privileges.

64 Lindner, 2006c, p. 43.

65 See, among others, Brown, 1970, Rubin and Brown, 1975.

66 Tocqueville, 1856. See also "The Future by Al Gore – Review," by John Gray, The Guardian, January 31, 2013, www.theguardian.com/books/2013/jan/31/the-future-al-gore-review. See also Gore, 2013.

67 Until being appointed minister, Erik Solheim was as a diplomat and a participant in the Norwegian delegation that worked to resolve the Sri Lankan Civil War before the outbreak of Eelam War IV. On May 3, 2016, United Nations Secretary-General Ban Ki-moon announced that Solheim takes over the post of executive director of UNEP, the United Nations' Environment Programme, in June 2016. Read more about Erik Solheim in the Appendix to Section One.

68 Erik Solheim was Minister of International Development in Norway, when the interview took place in the Ministry of Foreign Affairs in Oslo, Norway, on January 10, 2011. Solheim's reflections are summarized and translated from Norwegian by Lindner. It is a privilege to have the support of Erik Solheim for the World Dignity University initiative, see humiliationstudies.org/education/education.php.

69 "A Painful Lesson From Brexit: Why DiEM25 needs a simpler message," by Brian Eno and Yanis Varoufakis, DiEM25, July 4, 2016, https://diem25.org/a-painful-lesson-from-brexit-why-diem25-needs-a-simpler-message/. Yanis Varoufakis is a Greek economist, academic and politician, who served as the Greek Minister of Finance from January to July 2015. I thank Rigmor Johnsen for making me aware of this article and for her support to Human Dignity and Humiliation Studies.

70 See for a discussion of terror, panic, and polarization Renos Papadopoulos, 2006, who draws on his expertise in the Greek roots of notions such as terror and panic, and combines it with his Jungian orientation.

71 Norbert Müller is on the board of Schura Hamburg (SCHURA – Rat der islamischen Gemeinschaften in Hamburg e.V.), a merger of mosque associations in Hamburg, Germany. The interview with Norbert Müller took place in Hamburg on October 22, 2010. Müller's reflections are summarized and translated from German by Lindner. Müller sees two groups being radicalized, apart from the highly educated group, there is a second group: "Then there are the outsiders with criminal backgrounds, petty criminals who were once in jail, young men who then discover religion for themselves and find a holding point there. This is a new-islamization, a re-conversion, just like there are born-again Christians and Muslims, where religion is used as identity reinforcement." See more in the Appendix to Section One.

72 "Press Conference by President Obama," Antalya, Turkey, Kaya Palazzo Resort, White House, November 16, 2015, www.whitehouse.gov/the-press-office/2015/11/16/press-conference-president-obama-antalya-turkey.

73 See note 163 in the Preface.

74 Richards, 2013, Wallerstein, 1974–1989. See also Harvey, 2005.

75 See note 180 in Chapter 5.

76 Galtung, 1996, p. 76–77.

77 See, among others, Zehr, 2005, Braithwaite, 2002, or Villa-Vicencio and Verwoerd, 2000. It is a privilege to have Howard Zehr, John Braithwaite, and Charles Villa-Vicencio as esteemed members in the global advisory board of our Human Dignity and Humiliation Studies fellowship.

78 See, among others, Helmick, et al., 2001. It is a privilege to have Raymond Helmick as esteemed member in the global advisory board of our Human Dignity and Humiliation Studies fellowship, together with several contributors to this book, such as Andrea Bartoli, Ervin Staub and Laurie Anne Pearlman, Donna Hicks, or Olga Botcharova.

79 See a diagram of how to broaden the focus of peacebuilding to include also the pre-conflict situation in Grävingholt, et al., 2009, p. 5.

80 Vambheim, 2016, p. 16.

81 Galtung, 1971, Galtung, 1976. In Lindner, 2016e, I discuss Ibn Khaldun and Arnold Toynbee and how they speak of the periphery versus the center, as does also peace researcher Johan Galtung. See more in note 119 in Chapter 16.

82 Kraidy and Murphy, 2008. See note 120 in Chapter 16.

83 Coates, 2015, p. 146. See also Midiohouan, 1991.

84 Lévinas, 1961/1969, 1982, 1985b, a.

85 Lindner, 2014c.

86 Pickering, 2010.

87 Vambheim, 2016, p. 24, italics in original.

88 Vambheim, 2016, p. 51.

89 Staub, 1989, 1993, 2012, 2015.

90 Escrigas, 2016.

91 Wayne Visser, Kaleidoscope Futures, in his contribution to the Great Transition Network (GTN) discussion on the topic of "A Higher Calling for Higher Education," May 24, 2016, in response to Escrigas, 2016.

92 McMaster, 2013. Finland has demonstrated high standards even on Organisation for Economic Co-operation and Development measurements like the Programme for International Student Assessment.

93 McMaster, 2013, p. 524.

94 Sahlberg, 2015.

95 Ibid.

96 Vambheim, 2016, p. 145. According to a survey of middle and high school students in the United States, less than one third indicated that their school provided a caring, encouraging environment, and less than half reported that they had competencies such as empathy, conflict resolution and decision-making skills, see Benson, 2006. See also Durlak, et al., 2011, and an Annotated Bibliography over Social and Emotional Learning Research at www.edutopia.org/sel-research-annotated-bibliography. See also CASEL:

Collaborative for Academic, Social, and Emotional Learning (www.casel.org), of which psychologist and science journalist Daniel Goleman is a co-founder.

97 Nevo and Brem, 2002. I thank Nils Vidar Vambheim for making me aware of this publication.

98 Particularly displaced youths are vulnerable, see "Displaced Youth: Selling Souls to Sex and Drugs," by Rose Delaney, Inter Press Service (IPS), July 15 2016, www.ipsnews.net/2016/07/displaced-youth-selling-souls-to-sex-and-drugs/. See also "UNHCR's Engagement with Displaced Youth: A Global Review," by Rosalind Evans and Claudia Lo Forte, with Dr. Erika McAslan, United Nations High Commissioner for Refugees, Policy Development and Evaluation Service (PDES), March 2013, www.unhcr.org/513f37bb9.pdf.

99 Wang and Aamodt, 2011.

100 See an accessible summary of the IQ variation over time in the human population and some of the explanations in "People Getting Dumber? Human Intelligence Has Declined Since Victorian Era, Research Suggests," by Macrina Cooper-White, Associate Science Editor, The Huffington Post, May 22, 2013, www.huffingtonpost.com/2013/05/22/people-getting-dumber-human-intelligence-victoria-era_n_3293846.html. See also Woodley, et al., 2013, or Levesque, et al., 2011.

101 Benson, 2006.

102 See note 146 in the Introduction for relational-cultural theory and cultural-historical activity theory.

103 Bhaskar, 2008.

104 See note 162 in the Preface.

105 See, among many, King, 2007, and Vetlesen, 2015.

106 See Ugo Mattei, Hastings College of Law at the University of California, and his contribution to the Great Transition Network (GTN) discussion on the topic of "Against Ecocide: Legal Protection for Earth," July 5, 2016, in response to Femke Wijdekop, 2016. The ICC, because of the lack of international centralized power or independence, is just a mockery of an institution, writes Mattei. See more in note 7 in the Preface and See the full note in the pdf edition of this book.

107 Stainback, et al., 2016.

108 "Why a Feminist Foreign Policy Is Needed More than Ever," by Margot Wallström, Minister for Foreign Affairs of Sweden, Inter Press Service (IPS), March 7, 2017, www.ipsnews.net/2017/03/why-a-feminist-foreign-policy-is-needed-more-than-ever/: "The world is torn by conflicts that are perhaps more complex and more difficult to solve than ever before. Almost half of all conflicts reoccur within five years. Over 1.5 billion people live in fragile states and conflict zones. In order to respond to these global challenges, we need to connect the dots and see what drives peace. We need to change our policies from reactive to proactive, focusing on preventing rather than responding."

109 Lindner, 2006c, p. 156, adapted from Lindner, 1999.

110 Vambheim, 2016, p. 94.

111 Lindner and Desmond Tutu (Foreword), 2010. According to primatologist Frans de Waal, bonobos "make love, not war," in contrast to chimpanzees, who "use violence to get sex, while bonobos use sex to avoid violence." See more in note 106 in Chapter 6 and see also note 2 in Chapter 1.

112 "Hva er en feministisk utenrikspolitikk, temahefte forklart," by Elisabeth Kristiansen, Fred og frihet, Number 1, 2016, WILPF Norge – Internasjonal kvinneliga for fred og frihet, www.ikff.no/wp-content/uploads/2012/05/Fred-og-frihet-nr-1-2016.pdf, pp. 12–14. I thank Trine Eklund for making me aware of the renewed focus in Scandinavia on establishing a fredsdepartement in Scandinavia. It is a privilege to have Trine Eklund as esteemed member in the global advisory board of the Human Dignity and Humiliation Studies fellowship.

113 Deresiewicz, 2014.

114 Lindner, 2016b, pp. 11–12.

115 Lindner, 2016b.

116 During our 27th Dignity Conference in Dubrovnik in 2016, I became aware that trading communities like Venice and Dubrovnik interestingly where among the first to abolish the trade of slaves, even though slaves were still kept in private homes, and it was allowed to keep them pro usu suo, Latin for one's own use. It seems that Christian motives were stronger than the profit motive. See "Dubrovnik Republic Abolished Slavery before Many World Powers Did," Welcome Dubrovnik: Dobro Došli u Dubrovnik, Number 28, 2016, pp. 32–33, www.tzdubrovnik.hr/user_files/made/welcome/w28web.pdf. See the full note in the pdf edition of this book.

117 "Dubrovnik Republic Abolished Slavery before Many World Powers Did," Welcome Dubrovnik: Dobro Došli u Dubrovnik, Number 28, 2016, pp. 32–33, www.tzdubrovnik.hr/user_files/made/welcome/w28web.pdf, p. 33.

118 The Act of Killing (2012) and The Look of Silence (2014), are documentary films by Joshua Oppenheimer. See more in note 31 in Chapter 8.

119 "Joshua Oppenheimer Won't Go Back to Indonesia," interview by Adam Shatz. See more in note 32 in Chapter 8.

120 Ted Trainer, in a personal communication on January 17, 2015, in response to my message following his contribution to the Great Transition Network (GTN) Discussion on the topic "The Degrowth Alternative," January 15, 2015. Ted (F.E.) Trainer is an Australian academic, and an advocate of economic de-growth, simple living, and "conserver" lifestyles. Read more in note 89 in Chapter 5. See also Trainer, 2014.

121 Ted Trainer, in a personal communication on January 17, 2015, in response to my message following his contribution to the Great Transition Network (GTN) Discussion on the topic "The Degrowth Alternative," January 14, 2015:

Many green people are working heroically to save the whale for instance, but not realizing that their ultimate goals cannot be achieved unless we scrap the present global economic system, and much of the culture of consumerism. Meanwhile many on the red-left are working hard on justice etc. projects but not clearly aware that resource limits rule out any vision of a good society in which all live affluently. I think we will see a coming together as conditions worsen, so that we all go on focusing on our particular interests but see ourselves as part of a coalition that realizes that consumer-capitalism has to be replaced. Above all my perspective is that many good groups do not realize well enough that we have to think in terms of a form of satisfactory society in which we can all live well on a tiny fraction of present rich world per capita resource use.

122 See note 73 in Chapter 4.

123 "Keynes' Limitations and Trump's Disasters, by Howard Richards, Chileufú, November 2016, http://chileufu.cl/keynes-limitations-and-trumps-disasters/.

124 Bhaskar, 2008.

125 See note 162 in the Preface.

126 See, among others, Axelrod, 2006, Liberman, et al., 2004, Imhof, et al., 2007, Nowak and Highfield, 2011. See also Bernstein, 1971, 1973, 1975, 1990, 2000. I thank Vidar Vambheim for reminding me of Bernstein's work and that Bernstein introduced the concept of framing to describe how control of mental frames is used to regulate thinking and behavior in educational contexts. Bernstein describes framing as a mental process and a technique to exclude certain aspects of reality from entering the communication. See also Chong and Druckman, 2007.

127 Liberman, et al., 2004, Abstract. See the full note in the pdf edition of this book.

128 Guala, 2012b, p. 51, where Gualas reminds of the work of Putnam, 2000, that shows the strong link between the weak reciprocity manifested in continuous participation in the activities of the local community, and more general prosocial attitudes such as altruism. Guala concludes: "The capacity to cultivate long-term relationships is correlated with people's willingness to cooperate outside the small circle of friends and family, and it is subject to medium-term cycles of growth and decay."

129 Rosas, 2012, p. 37. Philosopher and experimental economist Francesco Guala's target article was Guala, 2012a, and his response to the comments, Guala, 2012b, p. 51: "No reciprocity theorist today would claim that prosocial emotions (including anger at injustice, or punitive drives generally) are unreal. Similarly, no one would seriously argue that human behavior is always calculative or strategic. Apart from psychopaths we are all (psychologically) prosocial, altruistic people. Rosas puts it nicely, saying that humans are psychologically unselfish, but biologically selfish creatures."

130 John Fullerton, now a new member of the Club of Rome, in his contribution to the Great Transition Network Initiative discussion titled "Journey to Earthland: Making the Great Transition to Planetary Civilization," October 31, 2016, in response to Raskin, 2016:

I particularly liked Paul's near dismissal of the "Conventional Worlds" scenarios – both Market Forces and Policy Reform variations, what Paul calls "the false god of moderation that invites us to passively drift down the garden path to barbarization." Of course, this is precisely the path we (collectively) are on, with all the well-meaning focus on "green growth," internalizing "externalities" (an oxymoron), calls for greater market transparency with Environmental, Social, and Governance (ESG) metrics (our idolatry of markets and their ability to guide us is a deadly confusion of means and ends), Divest/Invest campaigns, quantifying in monetary terms ecosystem services offered by vital and priceless ecosystem function, circular economy manufacturing processes, impact investing, carbon demand-side reduction targets, more progressive taxation regimes, and on and on. ALL are essential incremental change, part of any ultimate solution. All are important work. But mostly what they accomplish is the extension of our runway, not systemic change, because they do not involve a fundamental change in the way we think. They could lull us into false confidence that we are on the right track. Collectively, they are the result of our intellectually lazy or simply ignorant preference to worship what Paul calls the "false god of moderation," or simply represent the only way we can have our voices heard. We must see this for what it is, our ongoing 500-year-old Modern Era (and thus deeply ingrained literally into our DNA) reductionist mindset of treating symptoms like carbon emissions rather than seeking and then addressing root causes, holistically understood.

131 Raskin, 2016, Raskin, et al., 2002.

132 See note 201 in Chapter 5.

133 Volkan, 2004.

134 See note 418 in the Introduction.

135 See note 270 in the Introduction.

136 Perhaps such terminologies are necessary at the beginning of awareness movements, yet, I believe, they ought to be avoided at later stages, since they draw too much attention to what they want to avoid. See more in note 6 in Chapter 9.

137 Lindner, 2006c, p. 45.

138 Phillips and Hardy, 2002, p. 15.

139 The field of Michael Karlberg is the study of discourse as a social force. See Karlberg, 2013, Conclusion. See the full note in the pdf edition of this book.

140 Bateson, 1954, is often credited for the initial concept of an interpretive frame. He pointed out that discrete communicative acts are rendered meaningful within larger interpretive frames. Building on these insights, Goffman, 1974, conceptualized frames as cognitive schemata or mental frameworks that shape our

perceptions, interpretations, and representations of reality; mentally organize our experience; and provide normative guides for our actions. Following this work by Bateson and Goffman, the concept of frames and framing has been conceptualized with different nuances across the social and psychological sciences. See the full note in the pdf edition of this book.

141 Etzioni, 2013.

142 Snow and Benford, 1988, p. 213.

143 Van Dijk, 2001.

144 Chong and Druckman, 2007.

145 The story of the Five Levels of Martial Arts, was told by Li Young Li at the symposium "Snowdrift Dialogues" in February 2014, and re-told by Kim Stafford, the son of the Oregon pacifist, poet, and activist William Stafford in the Peace Poet William Stafford Centennial Celebration Talk by Kim Stafford (son), taped by the Tualatin Valley Community TV on February 13, 2014, and published on 18 February 18, 2014, https://youtu.be/pmOds9pF8cg, see also www.ci.oswego.or.us/loreads. In this talk, William Stafford's son Kim discusses his father's daily writing practice, and how this led to a life of compassion and witness. Kim is an essayist and poet who has taught writing at Lewis and Clark College and other colleges and workshops locally and abroad for over 30 years. I thank Linda for telling us about Kim Stafford's talk.

146 Raskin, 2016, p. 84.

147 See, for instance, europa.eu/scadplus/glossary/subsidiarity_en.htm.

148 Marshall, 2008.

149 See note 10 in Chapter 8.

150 See note 295 in the Introduction, and note 114 in the Inspiring Questions to Section Two.

151 Raskin, 2016, p. 84.

152 Miller, 1986a.

153 Bruce Schuman in his contribution to the Great Transition Network Initiative discussion titled "Journey to Earthland: Making the Great Transition to Planetary Civilization," September 24, 2016, in response to Raskin, 2016.

154 World Happiness Report 2017, http://worldhappiness.report/ed/2017/: "Norway has jumped from 4th place in 2016 to 1st place this year, followed by Denmark, Iceland and Switzerland in a tightly packed bunch." See the full note in the pdf edition of this book.

155 Shaw, 1889.

156 Popper, 1957.

157 Brandal, et al., 2013.

158 Space Exploration – A Powerful Symbol of Global Cooperation, Jim Zimmerman, NASA, interviewed by Susan T. Coleman, The Peacebuilding Podcast, December 13, 2016, http://us11.campaign-archive1.com/?u=e5c2110f5cc4fe346c79bf3d1&id=06298a46ca&e=e7c4dd8362. I thank Judit Révész for making me aware of this interview.

159 Lindner and Desmond Tutu (Foreword), 2010.

160 Jeannette Armstrong holds the Canada Research Chair in Okanagan Indigenous Knowledge and Philosophy at the University of British Columbia. She works with "Unveiling Syilx Okanagan Traditional Knowledge," see www.chairs-chaires.gc.ca/chairholders-titulaires/profile-eng.aspx?profileId=3020.

161 Tikkun editor at large Peter Gabel in a personal communication on December 1, 2010:

Dear Evelin and Linda, Thank you for this good letter and for creating such an important field as Humiliation Studies. In my book The Bank Teller and Other Essays on the Politics of Meaning (Gabel,

2000) and in my as yet unpublished The Desire for Mutual Recognition, I argue in effect that humiliation is the root of all evil and show how it is the foundation for the very structure of the alienated self, how we develop a false outer self to protect our being against the anticipation of humiliation due to non-recognition of our essential humanity. It sounds like the two of you and your group have been creating exactly the kind of organization needed to bring this kind of awareness to a larger audience, and perhaps to help change this continuing intergenerational replication of fear of the other, rage, and social separation.

162 "Humiliation Is the Root of All Terrorism," by Tikkun editor at large Peter Gabel, TruthOut, December 16, 2015, www.truth-out.org/speakout/item/34062-humiliation-is-the-root-of-all-terrorism. I thank Seymour M. (Mike) Miller and Linda Hartling for making me aware of this article.

163 Ibid.

164 Ibid.

165 How to Save the World from Fascism, And Meet Human Needs in Harmony with Nature," by Howard Richards, April 14, 2017, Chileufú, http://chileufu.cl/.

166 Ibid.

167 Malinowski, 1944.

168 How to Save the World from Fascism, And Meet Human Needs in Harmony with Nature," by Howard Richards, April 14, 2017, Chileufú, http://chileufu.cl/.

169 Social change is only possible if we accept the interdependence of theory, research and action/practice, writes David Bargal, 2011a. See more in note 77 in the Preface.

170 Pickering, 2010.

171 Merle Lefkoff in a personal communication on December 18, 2015. See also the Center for Emergent Diplomacy (ECOS), www.emergentdiplomacy.org. It is a privilege to have Merle Lefkoff as esteemed member in the global advisory board of our Human Dignity and Humiliation Studies fellowship.

172 Merle Lefkoff lives in the Santa Fe region, where theoretical biologist, and complex systems researcher Stuart Alan Kauffman was faculty in residence at the Santa Fe Institute dedicated to the study of complex systems from 1986 to 1997. We thank her for reminding us of the paper "Coevolution to the Edge of Chaos," by Kauffman and Johnsen, 1991, and of the classic At Home in the Universe by Kauffman, 1995. For his thoughts on "The Adjacent Possible," see the Edge Foundation, November 9, 2003, www.edge.org/conversation/the-adjacent-possible. See also his recent work in Kauffman, 2016, Kauffman and Gare, 2015. Merle Lefkoff shared her insights at the 27th Dignity Conference in Dubrovnik, Croatia, on 21st September 2016, where she facilitated a Dignilogue titled "Indigenous Knowledge and the New Science of Complex Adaptive Systems," see https://youtu.be/ZmVxqHnSo40.

173 Laszlo, 2014. I thank Dino Karabeg for connecting me with Alexander Laszlo.

174 Laszlo, 2015. See also Dennis, 2014.

175 Anthony Marsella, in a personal communication on June 26, 2013. See also "Lifeism: Beyond Humanity," Anthony J. Marsella, TRANSCEND Media Service, March 17, 2014, www.transcend.org/tms/2014/03/lifeism-beyond-humanity/.

176 Witt and Schwesinger, 2013, p. S37: "It is not sufficient for leadership to rely solely on authority conferred to them. Instead, leadership must be based on personal capabilities and skills that allow the leaders at their level of responsibility to exert pro-social dominance … and promote group interests, negotiate compromises where group interests and organizational goals are in conflict, and seek consensus regarding task assignments."

177 See Visser and Courtice, 2011, or "The 7 Habits of Effective Sustainability Leaders" by Wayne Visser, www.waynevisser.com/articles/7-habits-sustainability-leaders.

178 The butterfly story by evolutionary biologist Elisabet Sahtouris, www.sahtouris.com/noflash.php?ref=5_3,0.

179 The butterfly metaphor gives the impression as if the path of humankind is pre-programmed and rather free of human intent and agency.

180 The butterfly story by evolutionary biologist Elisabet Sahtouris, www.sahtouris.com/noflash.php?ref=5_3,0.

181 Lindner, 2006c, p. 45.

182 Also from Lindner, 2000a, p. 439.

183 Adapted from Lindner, 2000a, p. 439. See also Lindner, 2006c, p. 48.

184 Lindner, 2006c, p. 47.

185 After the commons were enclosed in England, starting during the sixteenth century, what sociologist Eric Mielants, 2007, calls "terroristic" laws were introduced that criminalized idleness, thus pushing people into early capitalist manufacturing.

186 Emotional Literacy is a book by Claude M. Steiner, 2003, a psychotherapist who has written extensively about transactional analysis (TA). I thank Janet Gerson of reminding me of Steiner's work.

187 Rosenwein, 2006, pp. 19;197–202.

188 Ross, 2013, pp. 9, 45–46.

189 Freire, 1968/1973.

190 Lindner and Desmond Tutu (Foreword), 2010.

191 See "Was für ein Leben," Blog Arnscht, Arnstadt, Geschichte, Leute, September 30, 2009, https://blog-arnscht.de/2009/09/was-fur-ein-leben/. I thank Christoph Rosenau for making me aware of Günther Sattler and his flyer for freedom. Without Christoph Rosenau's and his family's support since 1978, my dignity work would not be possible.

192 SED is the acronym Sozialistische Einheitspartei Deutschlands.

193 Translated by Lindner from the German original: "An alle Bürger von Arnstadt! Kommt alle am 30. September um 14 Uhr zur friedlichen Kundgebung gegen die willkürliche Politik der SED," Flugblatt von Günther Sattler, www.ddr89.de/ddr89/texte/aufruf14.html:

WAS FÜR EIN LEBEN ?

was für ein leben?
wo die wahrheit zur lüge wird,
wo der falsche das zepter führt.

was für ein leben?
wo die freiheit tot geboren,
wo schon scheint alles verloren.

was für ein leben?
wo alte männer regieren,
wo noch menschen an grenzen krepieren.

was für ein leben?
wo die angst den alltag bestimmt,
wo das ende kein ende nimmt.

was für ein leben?
wo man seinen nachbarn nicht mehr traut,
wo man nicht mehr aufeinander baut.

was für ein leben?
wo man nicht sein kann, der man ist,
wo man so schnell vergißt.

was für ein leben?
wo träume sterben, sterben,
wo es nichts mehr gibt zum vererben, außer scherben.

was für ein leben?
wo es für wenige alles gibt,
wo der kleine keinen ausweg sieht.

was für ein leben?
wo liebe nicht existiert,
wo man langsam erfriert.

Index

More Dignity Press books

Available at www.dignitypress.org or major booksellers

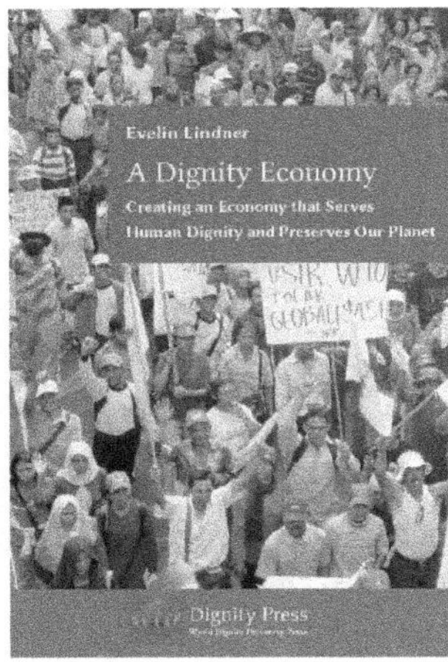

Evelin Lindner

A Dignity Economy

460 pages, 28.00 US-$

ISBN 978-1-937570-03-3

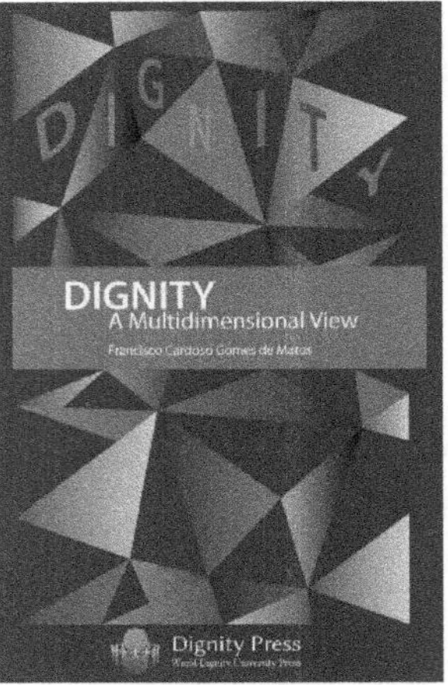

Francisco C. Gomes de Matos

Dignity Multidimensional

144 pages, hardcover, 16.00 US-$

ISBN 978-1-937570-37-8

Victoria Fontan

Decolonizing Peace

220 pages, softcover, 16.00 US-$

ISBN 978-1-937570-15-6

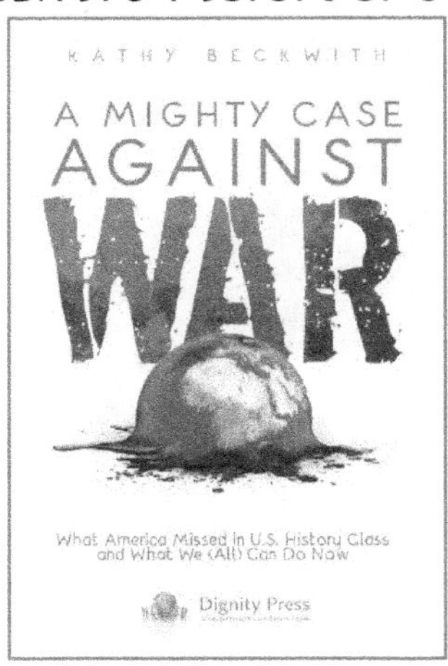

Kathy Beckwith

A Mighty Case Against War

vii + 293 pages, softcover, 15.00 US-$

ISBN 978-1-937570-68-2

More Dignity Press books

Available at www.dignitypress.org or major booksellers

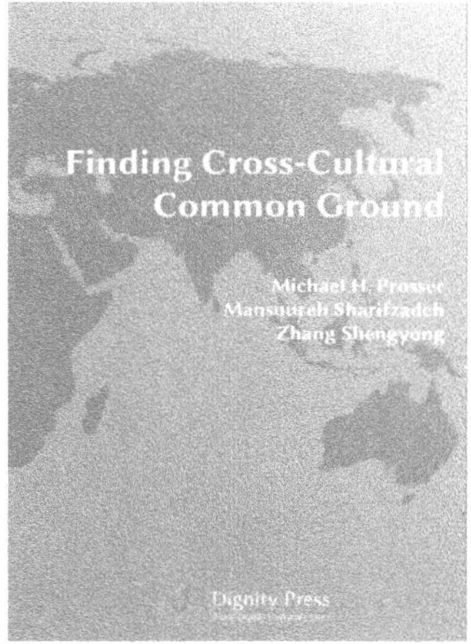

Michael H. Prosser

Finding Cross-Cultural Common Ground

511 pages, 22.00 US-$

ISBN 978-1-937570-25-5

Hilary Roseman

Generating Forgiveness

432 pages, softcover, 20.00 US-$

ISBN 978-1-937570-48-4

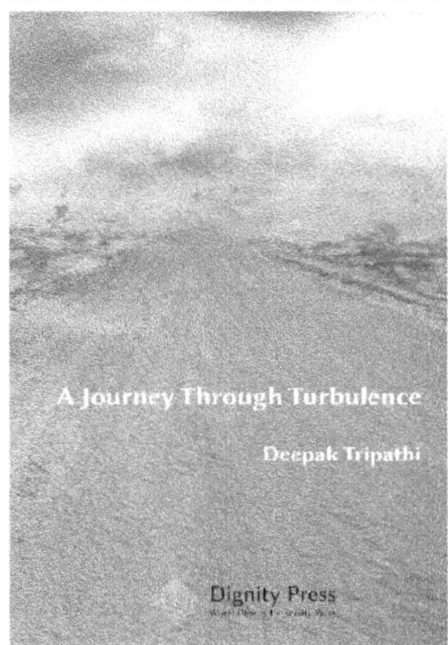

Deepak Tripathi

A Journey Through Turbulence

255 pages, softcover, 18.00 US-$

ISBN 978-1-937570-32-3

Gavin Andersson, Howard Richards

Unbounded Organizing in Community

104 pages, softcover, 9.80 US-$

ISBN 978-1-937570-60-6

www.ingramcontent.com/pod-product-compliance
Lightning Source LLC
Chambersburg PA
CBHW081424270326
41932CB00019B/3092

* 9 7 8 1 9 3 7 5 7 0 9 7 2 *